Fifth Edition

Human Motivation

Robert E. Franken
University of Calgary

WADSWORTH

™

THOMSON LEARNING

Australia • Canada • Mexico • Singapore • Spain • United Kingdom • United States

WADSWORTH

THOMSON LEARNING

Sponsoring Editor: *Vicki Knight*

Editorial Assistant: *Dan Moneypenny*

Marketing: *Joanne Terhaar*

Assistant Editor: *Jennifer Wilkinson*

Project Editor: *Kim Svetich-Will*

Production: *Forbes Mill Press*

Manuscript Editor: *Robin Gold*

Permissions Editor: *May Kay Polsemen*

Interior Design: *Roy R. Neuhaus*

Cover Design: *Vernon T. Boes*

Cover Photo: *Mark Cosslett*

Print Buyer: *Nancy Panziera*

Compositor: *TBH Typecast, Inc.*

Printing and Binding: *R.R. Donnelley & Sons, Crawfordsville*

For more information about this or any other Brooks/Cole product, contact:
WADSWORTH/THOMSON LEARNING
10 Davis Drive
Belmont, CA 94002-3098 USA
www.wadsworth.com
1-800-423-0563 (Thomson Learning Academic Resource Center)

Printed in the United States of America
10   9   8   7   6   5   4   3   2   1

Library of Congress Cataloging-in-Publication Data

Franken, Robert E.,
      Human motivation / Robert E. Franken. — 5th ed.
          p.   cm.
      Includes bibliographical references and index.
      ISBN 0-534-55530-6
      1. Motivation (Psychology).   I. Title.

BF503.F7   2002
153.8—dc21

                                              2001046471

Brief Contents

Contents

Part Two   Analyzing Some Basic Motivational Systems

Chapter Three

Hunger and Eating   56

Part Three   Emotions and Motivation

Part Four   Growth Motivation and Self-Regulation

Chapter Twelve

From Curiosity to Creativity   333

Chapter Thirteen

Need for Control, Mastery, and Self-Esteem   359

Preface

For centuries, scholars from diverse backgrounds and disciplines have speculated about what motivates humans. Explanations have ranged from those that suggest that human behavior is totally determined—such as by our genetic structure—to those that suggest that humans have complete control over their destiny because they have a will. These diverse explanations were not subjected to any scientific scrutiny until the beginning of the twentieth century. As a result, we now have a much clearer understanding of what motivates humans. It turns out that we are not born to play out predetermined roles in this universe, nor do we have complete freedom to do what we want. We are limited by our biology, but, interestingly, we are also limited by our failure to dream because thoughts do make a difference. Sometimes by making small changes we alter the course of our own behavior and, at least to some degree, alter the course of behavior of others. One implication of this is that we can change the course of history—a controversial but exciting idea.

This book is divided into four parts. In Part I, we examine the major issues and organizing principles that delineate the topic of motivation. Chapter 1 starts with a discussion of the major issues and ends with a brief overview of the major theories that have been proposed to account for motivated behavior. I argue, based on empirical research, that the best way to understand motivation is to analyze various motivation systems through their primary components: biological, learned, and cognitive. In Chapter 2, we examine in detail what it means to take a components approach and what it means when we say that a behavior has a biological basis, a learned basis, or a cognitive basis. Even though it is possible to break behavior down into its various components, the behavior we observe in the end is something much more than its separate components. What we observe is something that can be compared to a piece of music that comes from a number of talented musicians—each playing his or her part but perfectly attuned to what the other musicians are playing. Although we don't fully understand in many, or perhaps most, cases how these components work together, we are at least realizing that there are many players. This book will examine some of the players and, thus, will help us to begin to understand the roots of our behavior, the first step in changing our behavior.

In Part 2, we analyze several basic motivational systems from a components perspective. In Chapter 3, we examine not only why people eat but also why some people are inclined to become overweight. We look at the fascinating and perplexing question of why people who become overweight find it so difficult to shed those excess pounds. In Chapter 4, we examine the whole issue of sexual behavior: Why is it that some people are promiscuous and others ore not? Why do some people stay in love but others do not? Why are some people attracted to members of the same sex but others are attracted to members of the opposite sex? In Chapter 5, we analyze peak performance. The ability to attain peak performance is often difficult because peak performance requires that we simultaneously attain an optimal state of arousal, focus our attention on the task at hand, and rid our mind of thoughts that might undermine our performance. In Chapter 6, we look at the links between alertness, ability to process information, quality of sleep, and the tendency to dream. We will look at such questions as why our ability to process information is often impaired when we don't get enough sleep or the right kind of sleep, or don't dream. In Chapter 7, we look at the question of drug use, drug abuse and addiction. Drug use seems, at least on the surface, to be maladaptive, so we examine what it is about our biology, the environment, and the way we think that leads individuals to take drugs. In Chapter

8, we examine aggression and coercive behavior. It has been suggested that one of the things that has helped us to survive as a species is our aggressive nature. How do we reconcile this with the observation that human aggression is one of society's major problems?

In Part 3, we examine the role that emotions plays in motivation. Although emotions were commonly treated in the past as distinct from motivation, the current view is that emotions play an integral role in motivation. They can both sustain and undermine goal-directed behavior, for example. That means if we are to attain the goals we have set for ourselves, we need to ensure that our emotions are contingent with our goals; otherwise, we will find it impossible to reach our goals.

In this section on emotions, we begin with a discussion of stress. Psychologists have done a great deal of work on stress and have shown that the management of stress is perhaps one of the most important things that we need to address if we want to live happy and successful lives. Research on this topic is abundant and the implications are clear. Stress not only tends to undermine goal-directed behavior, it also tends to undermine our health. Although health is not the main focus of this book, we will see that motivation and health are intimately linked.

In addition to stress, we need to learn to manage a number of other goal-incongruent emotions. In Chapter 10, we examine fear and anxiety, which have been shown, over and over, to undermine goals-directed behavior. Fear and anxiety often paralyze people into inaction. We also examine pessimism and depression. It has been shown repeatedly that people who adopt a pessimistic attitude often become depressed and that when people are depressed, their motivation virtually stops. Recent work on guilt and shame indicate again that these emotions are highly debilitating and also undermine goal-directed behavior.

The main goal-congruent emotions are happiness, hope, optimism, attachment, belongingness, and empathy. When people are happy, hopeful, or optimistic, they are inclined to work hard toward their goals. In Chapter 11, we review research that shows being happy, hopeful, or optimistic helps us to persist in pursuing our goals. One main antecedent of achievement and success, it has been found, is a willingness to per-

sist. In the course of examining goal-directed behavior, researchers have found that people who tend to succeed in achieving their goals are characterized by such qualities as relatedness. Although some people adopt the view that they do not need other people, research indicates that people who accept and develop their social skills tend to be more successful than those who do not. In addition, people with developed social skills tend to be physically and psychologically healthier. In this chapter, we will also examine the motivation for risk-taking behavior. Risk-taking behavior is a sign of positive health and adjustment, whereas its absence is a sign of neuroticism.

In Part 4, I talk about growth motivation and self-regulation. The idea that organisms are motivated toward development and growth has captured the imagination of many motivation theorists. As more and more research is being done, it is becoming increasing clear to many theorists that humans have an innate disposition to realize their potential.

If the motivation for growth is innate in humans (and perhaps in animals to some degree), then why do people not all grow at the same rate? Why do some people succeed whereas others do not? Why do some people have big dreams but others do not? The answer is starting to emerge. Not all people are equipped to the same degree with the ability to do at least two things: to manage and to set goals. The new focus in motivation is that people need to learn how to manage their emotions (such as the emotion of self-doubt), and they need to learn how to set appropriate goals. The exciting thing is that people can be taught these skills. This new focus for motivation has been dubbed the self-regulation of motivation.

In Chapter 12, we examine the early work on growth motivation that came out of the research on curiosity and exploratory behavior. This early work on curiosity and exploratory behavior led theorists to suggest that organisms are characterized by a tendency toward growth. People are innately motivated to find out all they can about the world in which they live. We will also examine creativity and attempt to show that creativity develops from the motivation to discover all that life has to offer. Certain people called sensation seekers appear to be born with stronger curiosity and exploratory drives. As a result of these strong drives, they tend, among other things, to be more creative and more unconventional. In Chapter 13, we review research showing that humans are motivated to become competent—something that has its roots in the need to control. People develop a sense of self-esteem and self-worth from their sense of competency and achievements.

Finally, in Chapter 14, we review a portion of the research on self-regulation of behavior. We examine, among other things, the principles of goal setting, the principles for managing one's emotions, and the principles for fine tuning one's goal-directed behavior. In this chapter, we look at the research pertaining to the way people can learn to manage their thinking so that they can become fully functional and fully self-actualized. We also discuss how a person can develop a fully differentiated self-concept. From a fully developed and differentiated self-concept we set difficult goals and entertain the idea that there are possible selves. In the final analysis, in developing a highly differentiated self-concept people come to achieve their true potential.

Although this book was written mainly for psychology majors, I have kept in mind that motivation is interesting to just about everyone. Over the years I have had students from business, counseling, education, engineering, nursing, physical education, and social work who took my course because they felt that knowing something about human motivation would help them in their chosen professions. Other students in such fields as art, history, and philosophy have said they simply want to know something about their own personal motivations. Because motivation courses often attract a diverse population, I have tried to make the book easily understood by readers with little background in psychology, yet challenging to those who are familiar with the subject.

Many people have contributed directly or indirectly to the preparation of this book. Students in the various motivation classes that I teach have given me the inspiration and the feedback that helped shape the organization and the content. Discussions with colleagues and graduate students have helped sharpen my thinking. To all those people, I say thank you.

I thank the reviewers who gave me many wonderful suggestions. Had I incorporated all their wonderful ideas and suggestions, this book would have been twice its present length. They are Brad Brubaker, Indiana State University; Robert Gehring, University of Southern Indiana; Donna Hardy, California State University, Northridge; Carol C. Hayes, Delta State University; Lynda Honour, California State University, Northridge; J. C. Malone, University of Tennessee; Ralph Noble, Rensselaer Polytechnic Institute; Ian Payton, Bethune Cookman College; Chryslyn E. Randell, Metropolitan State College of Denver; Jeff Swartwood, State University of New York, Cortland; and Leland Swenson, Loyola Marymount University.

I want to thank my editor, Vicki Knight, for her help and support throughout this project. Also thanks to all the people at Wadsworth in the production phase who did the figures, the layout, the cover, the permissions, the copyediting, and proofing. Their efforts are greatly appreciated.

Finally, I thank my wife, Helen, who has given me so much love and support.

Robert E. Franken

To Helen
Ryan and Tara
Renee and Cam
Madison

Chapter One

Themes in the Study of Motivation

- *What causes behavior?*
- *Do all behaviors represent an attempt to adapt? What about drug use?*
- *Why do some people persist while others give up?*

- *Why are some people more motivated than others?*
- *Do humans have instincts?*
- *How much of our behavior is learned?*
- *Do humans have a will?*

Chris looks at his watch. It is 8 A.M. Outside the window, the sky is clear and the sun is shining; it looks like it's going to be a great day. Suddenly, his thoughts turn to mountain climbing. He imagines himself executing a difficult move, while his friend looks on in admiration. This brief fantasy gives him a warm and satisfied feeling. As he heads toward the bathroom, he notices the pile of books on his desk, and the warm feeling fades. The philosophy paper he was assigned isn't falling into place, and he isn't sure what he should do. A feeling of tenseness begins to take hold. While he brushes his teeth, his thoughts turn back to climbing. If there is one thing Chris really likes, it's climbing. He has an idea: Why not go climbing for a few hours? It would help clear his head and help get his thoughts together. Then he could finish the paper later. Impressed by that logic, Chris picks up the phone and begins dialing his friend. The warm feeling begins to return.

We are constantly faced with choices. Should we do what our heart tells us, or what our head tells us? Should we think about our future, or should we enjoy life now? Chris decided to follow his feelings, but another person might think, "If I work hard on my paper I might be able to take some time off tomorrow to do some climbing." Still another person might reason, "If I do well in my classes, I can do some climbing in the summer."

These choices can have significant consequences. For example, research shows that the ability to delay short-term gratification is an important element of achievement and success. One study found that children who were better able to delay immediate gratification at the age of 4 were more academically competent and had greater ability to deal with stress when they reached adolescence (Shoda, Mischel, & Peake, 1990). The ability to delay immediate gratification seems to be linked to some underlying personality qualities that have a genetic basis. One such quality is impulsivity. People who are high in impulsivity tend to engage in activities that have an immediate short-term appeal (Zuckerman, 1994). Accordingly, they are likely to have difficulty in delaying short-term gratification. Likewise, there is evidence that some people are attracted to novelty; anything new or different tends to capture their attention. Like impulsivity, this tendency

appears to be inherited. For example, even at 3 days old, children have been found to differ in their interest in novelty, and this difference can be linked to an enzyme that they have inherited (Sostek, Sostek, Murphy, Martin, & Born, 1981). The bottom line is that the ability to delay gratification involves something more than self-control.

The environments in which we have been raised also seem to shape our ability to delay gratification. In particular, environments that show there is a benefit to delaying gratification tend to produce children who are better at doing so (e.g., Bandura & Mischel, 1965). It makes sense that children who understand the advantage of delaying gratification in return for a later reward would tend to include that behavior in their repertoire.

What role does willpower play in this process? A growing body of research indicates that people can actively learn to take control of their lives by learning how to self-regulate (Metcalfe & Mischel, 1999). As we will see in the last chapter, self-regulation involves altering patterns of thinking. It starts with learning to self-monitor, a process that can help us to correct faulty thinking. Let's take another look at Chris. He told himself that climbing for a few hours would help clear his head, so that he could finish his paper later. Do we really believe that Chris is only going for a few hours? Is he really going to come right home afterwards, or will he and his friend celebrate their climb with a few beers? When he comes home, how likely is he to start on his paper? What about the effects of alcohol on his ability to think?

If Chris is trained to monitor his thinking carefully and to reflect on the likely outcome of his decisions, he can probably learn to delay gratification, at least to some degree. Because of his impulsive nature, he might never have as much self-control as others do; nevertheless, he should be able to gain a great deal more control. Practical Application 1-1 summarizes the hot/cool theory of delay of gratification. According to this theory, delay of gratification involves learning to create plans (narratives) to deal with the temptations we face. This theory illustrates how it is possible to integrate biological, learned, and cognitive ideas and, in many ways, is a prototype for how we will view motivated behavior in this book.

Plan of This Chapter

We will begin by considering some of the themes that are central to the thinking of motivational theorists and then briefly survey some of the major theories proposed by motivational psychologists over the years. It will be easier to understand current theoretical explanations of behavior if we understand some concerns of past theorists.

➡Theories represent an attempt to make sense of a certain body of facts. It is every theorist's goal to account for the greatest number of facts with the fewest possible concepts. Thus, as we will see, most theorists attempt to organize facts around a few central constructs. The theories reviewed in this chapter were successful, at least for a period of time, because they were able to explain an existing body of facts. However, research is always producing new facts. When theories lose their power to explain the available data, they need to be modified or perhaps abandoned. Some of the theories that we will discuss have lost their explanatory power, but they have provided an important legacy of psychological constructs. If we understand the classic theories, we will better understand why current theories have taken their present form.

What Causes Behavior?

Motivation theorists start with the assumption that, for every behavior, there is a cause. Their goal is to identify those causes. Motivation theorists tend to be eclectic; they draw on findings and principles from different disciplines. In the past, books about motivation were written from a single disciplinary perspective. Theorists might attempt to explain behavior solely from an analysis of biological mechanisms, for example. That tradition died because it was not possible to explain all behaviors through a single underlying mechanism or system. To understand biological structures, for example, we must understand the role of the environment. Without certain forms of environmental input, many structures fail to mature (Plomin & DeFries, 1998).

Motivation theorists want to know what instigates behavior. Although it is important to show that behaviors change as a result of certain interventions—for instance, therapy or the administration of rewards—motivation theorists want to get to the root cause: What causes action? They want to know what role biology, learning, and cognition play.

In the 1960s and 1970s, when learning theorists were able to show that a wide variety of behaviors could be increased, decreased, or changed by administering rewards, many psychologists and laypeople came to believe that most—if not all—human behavior can be explained on the basis of learning principles. Only after it was demonstrated that there are pervasive constraints on what we can and cannot learn did psychologists begin to moderate their extravagant claims about the role of learning in our lives. Finally, with the demonstration by cognitive psychologists that thinking causes behavior and does not merely accompany it, the argument that all behavior could be explained by the principles of learning was put to rest. Learning is central to understanding action but is not the only cause.

Approach and Avoidant Causes

Psychologists distinguish between approach causes and avoidant causes (Higgins, 1997). In approach behavior, people do things because of something they want, desire, or need. This is often conceptualized in terms of a specific goal object; they may, for example, want to eat a sandwich because they are hungry. Sometimes the want, desire, or need does not immediately give rise to a specific goal object. If we want independence, for example, we cannot visualize a single object; we may think of a variety of things—for example, having our own room, having a car, or having money.

In avoidant behavior, people do things to avoid something. Once again, that can often be defined in terms of a specific goal object. Fear of insects or snakes falls in this category. Anxiety, by contrast, may not immediately elicit a specific goal object. People who are anxious are often unable to specify the source; they simply experience a generalized sense of dread.

Avoidant causes tend to be very compelling; that is, not only are they aversive or noxious but they are also difficult—or impossible—to ignore. People who are afraid of insects or snakes, for example, feel a strong and immediate need to distance themselves from those goal objects. Because people are often unable to specify the source of their anxiety, they attempt to deal with it by finding a safe place. For example, a person who experiences anxiety at a party, without knowing its exact source, might decide to leave. It seems that the reason avoidant causes are so compelling is that they often involve threats to our survival. From a biological perspective, two primary goals are to survive and reproduce. If anything poses a threat to our survival, we need to deal with it immediately.

Even avoidant causes that do not threaten our survival tend to evoke the same reaction. Some theorists (e.g., LeDoux, 1996) have suggested that humans and animals are designed (or have evolved) to err on the side of being cautious because it is better to treat something as a threat and survive than to take the risk that it is not and die.

Not all people are equally anxious; some are more anxious from birth (Watson & Clark, 1984). As a result, they are more likely to engage in avoidant behaviors. Even thinking of certain activities is enough to make them anxious. They may avoid eating certain foods because they fear they will get sick; they might avoid traveling for fear of injury; or they might avoid meeting new people in the hope of avoiding conflicts of opinion. In contrast, extraverts and sensation seekers spend more time in approach behaviors. They see the world as a source of opportunities and excitement. They might go to new restaurants to savor different foods; they might talk to strangers in cafes to see how other people think; or they might take risks, such as

Practical Application 1-1

A Hot/Cool Theory of Delay of Gratification

Many writers have talked about the failure of willpower but only recently has there been a comprehensive theoretical model to account for this failure. According to the hot/cool model, two underlying systems control behavior (Metcalfe & Mischel, 1999). The hot emotional system is designed for quick emotional responding to unconditional or conditional triggers. This system tells us to go when we think of doing something that we like such as mountain climbing or spending time with friends. It is a system that is based on feeling and is largely under stimulus control. That is, this system is readily activated should we encounter a stimulus that promises us a reward. The cool system is designed for complex representation and thought. It is devoid of emotion, however, it can represent emotions and weave them into an ongoing narrative that takes into account such things as strategies for reaching goals. This system develops later in life and needs to be strengthened through practice. The two systems can be summarized as follows:

Hot System	*Cool System*
"Go"	"Know"
Simple	Complex
Reflexive	Reflective
Fast	Slow
Develops early	Develops late
Accentuated by Stress	Attenuated by Stress
Stimulus control	Self-control

One of the main features of this model concerns the role of learning in developing the cool system. One basic assumption is that as a result of using the cool system on a repeated basis, it will become the main system that dominates behavior. The theory acknowledges that we often fail in our attempts to exert willpower. In short, we often yield to temptation. What we need to do to avoid temptation is to design more elaborate cognitions (metacognitions) that will allow us to delay gratification in the face of a strong stimulus.

Take the example of Chris. One can see from this example that Chris could run into trouble. Although he was able to create a plan that seemed to make sense, it hang gliding or traveling the world (Zuckerman, 1994).

Basic Themes of Contemporary Motivation Theories

As a preliminary overview of contemporary motivation theories, let's look at some fundamental concepts that have guided the thinking and research of motivation theorists.

Behavior Represents an Attempt to Adapt

A central theme of contemporary motivation theory is that all behavior represents an attempt to adapt to the environment. Operating on that underlying assumption, motivation theorists then ask about the origin of that adaptive behavior: What mechanisms or principles will allow us to explain it? Scientists often determine whether they understand the cause of an event by asking themselves if they can predict the conditions under which it will occur. Over the years, psychologists have developed a very sophisticated methodology to help them identify causes.

Evolutionary psychology is a relative new discipline that has its roots in Darwinian theory. Throughout this book, we will discuss some of the ideas that have come from the evolutionary perspective, which gives us a glimpse of why certain brain systems and behaviors likely evolved in the first place. By asking the question, "what problems faced our ancestors," we get some idea about why certain adaptations took place rather than others. Within this context, we can

potentially has at least one serious flaw. Among other things, he reasoned in the abstract that when it came time to go home after climbing to finish his paper he would have the capacity to do so. The question is, will he? One thing that is essential when creating such narratives, as Chris created, is to recognize and plan for the power of stimulus control. A great deal of research has shown that when the stimulus is hidden from view it is much easier to delay gratification, but when the stimulus is present it is very hard to delay gratification (Metcalfe and Mischel, 1999). What this means is that we need to learn to distance ourselves from the temptation, both mentally and physically. Sometimes it is as simple as distracting oneself. Is Chris going to be able to resist having a few beers with friends? Won't he be overwhelmed by the situation or past habits? Without a clear plan for dealing with this problem, there is good reason to expect Chris will fail. You might think of some examples in your own life that illustrate this point and perhaps how you have learned to overcome them.

What the model suggests is that there are two systems working in concert. What allows the hot to take charge, according to this theory, is faulty thinking (failure to have or develop contingency plans), for example. Some 30 years ago I had trouble quitting smoking except for short periods of time. It wasn't until I identified all the conditions that triggered me to relapse that I finally could successfully quit. For each situation, I had a plan to deal with that specific situation.

One core idea in the hot/cool model is that we need to learn how to create plans (narratives) that will allow us to prevail in the midst of temptation. Then we develop this thing that we call willpower.

One final point. According to the theory, stress tends to shift control to the hot system. In other words, when we are stressed we are more likely to give in to temptation. For that reason it is recommended that people do not try to implement a behavior, such as quitting smoking, until stress is low, otherwise, they are less likely to succeed. You might think of some examples from your own life when the presence of stress played a central role in your yielding to temptation.

better appreciate why we are what we are and why we do what we do.

The Importance of Determining What Arouses and Energizes Behavior

Humans interact with their environment in two basic ways: They need to master the environment, on the one hand, while looking out for their survival, on the other (e.g., White, 1959). In addressing these needs, humans often experience a conflict: Do they put their survival needs first, or do they put their mastery needs first? Research suggests that survival needs will take precedence: If I am in the middle of learning something new and my survival needs are threatened, I will abandon learning in favor of survival.

Research suggests that I have no choice in this matter. My nervous system is designed to ensure that I attend to survival needs. When I am threatened, the part of the brain that deals with survival takes over and runs my behavior. Sensory input into the brain simultaneously travels along two distinct routes: One route takes the message to the part of the brain that deals with threats; the other route takes the message to the part of the brain that deals with rational analysis. The part of the brain that deals with survival gets the message first, and that is presumably why my initial reaction is often emotional (LeDoux, 1992). Because the system that analyzes threats is very crude, it can be wrong. When the rational brain analyzes the situation more carefully, it may decide that my survival is not being threatened and try to shut down the emotional system. For example, if someone criticizes a paper I have written, my nervous system may react as though that person has physically attacked me. Instead of reacting in a rational way (calm, cool, and collected, like Mr. Spock of *Star Trek*), I respond with an insult. At one level of awareness, I might know that this behavior is inappropriate, but I find it impossible to control myself. Psychologists have discovered that our nervous system often reacts as though our survival is being threatened in our daily lives.

By knowing what events in the environment arouse survival circuitry in the brain, we can better understand why people react as they do. The activation of brain circuitry and the energization of behavior are

closely linked. Once activated, the neural circuitry related to survival often remains active until the arrival of feedback that the threat is no longer present. Knowing how to shut down this circuitry, therefore, is critical. We all know people who have carried anger about some event for years. Research shows that such anger not only gets in the way of new learning but also has negative health implications (LeDoux, 1996). Obviously, for the motivation theorist, understanding what arouses and energizes a behavior is fundamental.

Understanding What Governs the Direction of Behavior

Without direction, we would not be able to survive. Getting food, for example, demands that we engage in goal-directed behavior. We must focus our attention on one alternative rather than another, and we must sustain that focus until our hunger needs are met. Need theory suggested that needs are what give direction to behavior (e.g., Murray, 1938). According to this explanation, when a need is aroused, we are more or less automatically pushed in the right direction. Research has shown that this explanation is inadequate. Both past learning and how we think about things (our cognitions) also play an important role. For example, some people eat to entertain themselves or to escape as well as for nourishment; others become restrained eaters because they want to be thin. According to current thinking, needs are conceptualized as dispositions; that is, they might give the impetus and even some of the direction for certain behaviors, but by themselves they do not fully explain why people do what they do.

Goal theory suggests that goals give rise to actions (Locke & Latham, 1990). According to this theory, goals create a tension, individuals move toward the goal to reduce that tension. Thus, both the direction and the energy for behavior are the result of the goals. Where do these goals come from? They might have their origins in our biology, our learning, or our thinking; typically, however, the goal that ultimately motivates us is a blend of all three. Though the need for energy might create the biological drive we call hunger, what we decide to eat (our goal object) is shaped by our past habits and our thinking. Although our initial impulse might be to eat a hamburger (an old habit), we might decide instead to have a plate of pasta because we have become concerned about the amount of fat in our diet (a new cognition or a new way of thinking).

Understanding Persistence

The motivational psychologist's interest in persistence, more than anything else, distinguishes motivation from other branches of psychology. For example, persistence is one of the main predictors of success (e.g., Seligman, 1990); it is often much more important than academic intelligence. Traditional reward theory suggests that we are inclined to repeat behaviors that make us feel good (positive reinforcement) and discontinue behaviors that make us feel bad (negative reinforcement). Withdrawal of rewards is normally sufficient to produce the extinction of a learned response. According to traditional reward theory, events that make us feel bad (aversive or noxious stimuli) will be avoided. We might assume, therefore, that experiencing adversity and failure would cause an individual to give up. Interestingly, some give up, but others persist.

Over the years, numerous theories have been advanced to account for persistence of behavior in the face of no reward, adversity, and failure. One early explanation suggested that frustration cues that arise when we are not rewarded after we reach a goal actually become conditioned to the approach response (Amsel, 1962). According to this explanation, negative feelings come to act as a signal that reward is forthcoming. This idea is analogous to the old maxim of aerobics instructors: "No pain, no gain." Although this turned out to be a very powerful explanation, it was based on the idea that behavior must be rewarded intermittently. What about persistence when there are no rewards? A more cognitive explanation suggests that persistence grows out of intrinsic motivation (e.g., Deci & Ryan, 1991). According to intrinsic theories of motivation, people come to believe that engaging in a certain behavior will result in a certain outcome. Many intrinsic motivation theories propose that the reward comes from mastering or developing competence; that is, while the carrot at the end of the path provides the direction for behavior, the process of mastering or developing competence provides the immediate reward that sustains the goal-directed behavior.

One difficulty with such theories is they cannot fully explain why people persist when they seemingly are making no progress toward a goal. According to intrinsic motivation theories, progress toward the goal rewards or provides the motivation for behavior. Why, then, do individuals persist when they are making no discernible progress? It has been suggested that people who persist under these conditions have developed optimism or hope; that is, they have learned to dismiss or manage adversity and failure (Seligman, 1990; Snyder et al., 1991). We will be considering optimism and hope in a later chapter.

Beyond its theoretical interest, understanding the nature and origins of persistence is also important from an applied perspective. To succeed, people need to learn how to persist in the face of failure and adversity.

Understanding the Role of Feelings

Motivation theorists have always been interested in how people feel. As we'll see, most motivation theories have addressed the issue of how much positive or negative *affect* is associated with a particular event. A central assumption of affect theories is that people approach things to experience positive affect and avoid things to guard against experiencing negative affect.

The distinction between approach and avoidant motivation, which we discussed earlier, is based on the idea that feelings are an important determinant of behavior. Current research indicates that feelings are often caused by chemical reactions in our body or brain (e.g., Zuckerman, 1994). In other words, they are real and not imagined. Some theorists have suggested that we should monitor our feelings so we can guide our actions because our feelings are more closely linked to our survival than is rational thought (LeDoux, 1992). Buck (1999) has suggested that affects are voices of our genes. They tell us how we are adapting to and interacting with our environment. Others have argued that feelings represent a more primitive part of the brain at work and therefore it is not worth the time or effort to listen to it. According to this perspective, our feeling brain hasn't caught up with the computer age, and therefore we need to learn to ignore our feelings.

Whether listening to our feelings is going to increase our chances of survival or make us more happy is not clear. What I think is clear is that negative feelings can and often do undermine goal-directed behavior while positive feelings can and often do sustain goal-directed behavior. That is why motivation theorists today are interested in understanding feelings.

Accounting for Individual Differences

Evolutionary psychologists and others are interested only in general principles of behavior, whereas motivation theorists are interested in why individuals behave the way they do. Evolutionary psychologists, for example, argue that the ultimate motivation for sexual behavior is an underlying biological inclination to ensure that our genes survive in future generations. The immediate pleasure or reward that we get from sexual behavior is merely a mechanism in service of that goal. They further argue that, to ensure that their genes survive in future generations, males use one strategy and females use another. According to an evolutionary analysis, for example, males are programmed to be more promiscuous than females (Buss, 1994). Even though that principle might help explain certain gender differences, it does not explain individual differences within each gender. When we look at individual male and female behavior we can see many males who are not promiscuous and many females who are. Why are there differences within genders? According to motivation theorists, other forces modify certain underlying biological tendencies. Both learned and cognitive factors can modify, at least to some degree, the way individuals behave. The challenge is to understand how, when, and why learning can exert such a powerful role over our underlying biology. In Chapter 4, we will talk about the fact that humans are inclined to form long-term bonds and that this tendency needs to be incorporated into any theory that attempts to explain human sexual behavior. We are more than just individuals who look after ourselves. We are social beings who form relationships and create culture, some of the many things that give us happiness.

The Question of Self-Regulating Behavior

Like clinical psychologists, motivation theorists believe that it is possible to help people regulate their behavior. Clinical psychologists tend to focus on how to make people more normal, whereas motivational psychologists are more concerned with what makes people exceptional: How did this person become president of a company or a country? How did this individual become a rock star? How did this person muster the energy and skills to climb the highest mountain in the world?

Motivation theorists are fascinated with discovering why someone of average talent unexpectedly succeeds or why someone of exceptional talent unexpectedly fails. For the motivational theorist, the answer can be found in motivational principles. If the underlying reasons can be identified, then people can be taught how to alter the course of their lives. Higgins (1997), for example, has talked about the need to understand the role of self-focus in helping humans to achieve goals (approach motivation) and to keep themselves safe and out of harms way (avoidant motivation). In the last chapter of this book, we will look at the work of motivation theorists who believe that, at least to some degree, humans can learn to self-regulate their behavior and thereby control their lives.

Do Humans Have a Will?

One of the most controversial ideas in all of psychology is that humans have a will (volition). The idea of will implies that people can create their own destiny. It has been suggested, for example, that people can create new possible selves, and then construct paths that will enable them to become one of those possible selves (e.g., Markus & Nurius, 1986). In other words, humans can dream (fantasize) about possible selves—about achieving some goal, becoming a different person, or doing something they have never done before. Next, they can adopt one of these possible selves as their goal, and then, by coupling such a goal with knowledge of how to achieve goals, can make their dreams a reality. Such theories suggest that people are not mere products of biology or the environment in which they live. Instead of being passive individuals reacting to the forces about them, individuals can actively construct a world in which they see themselves succeeding and achieving. In Chapter 14, we will examine the research that allows us to entertain the possibility of rising above the forces that strive to control us.

The concept of volition suggests that there are few—if any—limits on what we can do and what we can become. Most psychologists believe that we are limited by our biology, our ability to learn, and our ability to think and solve problems. To change, we need to work within those limitations. For example, although individuals can often learn to play the piano with some proficiency, they might not have the underlying talent to become concert pianists. Similarly, although individuals can learn to do certain arithmetic calculations with some speed, they will never be able to compete with computers.

Most psychologists hold to a more limited view of volition that has come to be called *self-regulation of behavior*. According to the concept of self-regulation, we can learn to do things that will enable us to make certain changes in our lives: for example, to better focus our attention, to set goals, to generate paths to goals, and to avoid negative thinking. In short, we can learn to maximize skills and abilities that we already possess or we learn to develop new skills through careful thought and practice.

Theories of Motivation: A Historical Survey

Over the years, many different motivation theories have been advanced. Each of these theories has grown out of a somewhat different focus or concern. Although the theories that I will discuss are very different in many respects, they all have grown out of a similar concern, to account for the arousal, direction, and persistence of behavior. Those three words are what define the focus of motivation. Other disciplines in psychology are also concerned about arousal, direction, and persistence of behavior, but these three are at the core of any motivational analysis.

In this chapter, I will identify some of the major issues and concerns that have shaped the development of motivation as we know it today. At least six major lines of inquiry can be identified, each of which developed from attempts to conceptualize motivation from a somewhat different perspective: (1) instinct theories, (2) need/personality theories, (3) drive/learning theories, (4) growth and mastery motivation theories, (5) humanistic theories, and (6) cognitive theories.

I should warn the reader that my presentation of the various theories is very brief. Many of the theories I present were modified and, therefore, had greater explanatory scope than I suggest in my discussion. My goal here is to identify the key concepts that gave rise to each of these theories.

Instinct Theories

The idea of instinct can be traced to such early writers as Thomas Aquinas (ca. 1225–1274). To explain why animals tended to behave adaptively, he suggested that they were equipped with instincts that provided the energy, direction, and persistence of behavior. Instincts were conceptualized as "purposive activities implanted in the animal by nature or the creator for the guidance of the creature in the attainment of ends useful to it in its own preservation or the preservation of the species, and the avoidance of the contrary" (Wilm, 1925, p. 40). We would use different language today, but the underlying idea remains essentially the same.

Aquinas believed that animals had instincts, but he did not accept that humans had instincts. He argued that humans had a dual nature—physical and nonphysical, or body and mind (intellect)—but that the physical side of humans was governed by different laws than those governing animals. The reason for this distinction came from the idea that humans were a special creation of God. Among other things, they were equipped with a soul and rational thought and, consequently, could be held responsible for their actions. The problem with instincts, as initially conceptualized, was that instincts, rather than the soul or rational thought, were believed to cause behavior. Consequently, Aquinas offered two distinct theories of motivation: one for animals and one for humans.

Many early scientists grappled with the profound similarity between animal and human motivation. Superficially, it appeared that humans and animals operated by the same laws. At the same time, there seemed to be profound differences. René Descartes (1596–1650) provided an explanation that reconciled these two views: The behavior of the body, below the level of willed action, could be explained mechanically (instincts), but behaviors that had to do with such things as moral conduct were under the control of the will. Descartes argued that the body and the mind (will, soul) interacted, and he suggested that the site of the interaction was the pineal gland. Certain physical acts, such as sexual behavior, were under the control of the mind and not simply the product of some mechanical mechanism.

This dualistic conception appealed to both the scientists and the Catholic Church. According to Descartes' explanation, humans could be held responsible for their moral actions, a position that was consistent with the church's idea of special creation. The Catholic Church, apparently feeling threatened by the view that human motivation could perhaps be explained by instincts, had forbidden scientists from pursuing this question. Having accepted Descartes' view, the authorities relaxed that ban.

Descartes' position raised an issue with which psychologists have grappled ever since: Exactly how do the biological and cognitive sides of a person interact? Is it true that our cognitive side has ultimate control? Are there times when the cognitive side loses control? In criminal proceedings, for example, the question of insanity (whether a person understands his or her actions were wrong) has very important implications. Similarly, a finding of medical abnormalities (such as a brain tumor) can dramatically alter the question of whether a person can be held responsible for his or her actions.

Charles Darwin

Evolutionary Theory

Although Descartes suggested that humans share some of the instincts observed in animals, he maintained that we, unlike animals, could control those instincts. Evolutionary theory aroused the wrath of the Catholic Church by suggesting that human motivation was caused by the same processes that give rise to animal behavior.

Charles Darwin argued that the physical features of animals and humans and their behavior were caused by their biological structure. He further argued that the underlying biological structure of all species was constantly undergoing change as a result of environmental pressures. This idea, of course, challenged the idea of special creation. He suggested that the mechanism or principle that caused this change was *natural selection*. According to natural selection, members of a species with physical or behavioral attributes that allowed them to better deal with environmental

pressures would survive and reproduce; as a result, they would pass along this biological structure to their offspring. In contrast, members of the species that could not survive would not reproduce and their biological structure would, over time, be lost. For example, if certain members of a species could escape their predators because their coloration and patterning allowed them to blend into their environment, they would survive. As a result, their biological characteristics would also survive. However, if the environment changed and their coloration and patterning no longer protected them from predators, they would die before they reproduced and their biological characteristics would be lost.

Gregor Mendel (1822–1884), a contemporary of Charles Darwin (1809–1882), advanced the idea of genetics. Although Darwin did not know about Mendel's theories, Darwin's ideas can be explained by genetic theory. According to genetic theory, new genes emerge through a process called mutation. Thus, over time, a species can evolve; it can become more intelligent or more aggressive. Obviously, according to genetic theory, change would take time.

Note that Darwin's contribution was not the discovery of evolution, as people often think; it had already been well documented that selective breeding could be used to produce animals with certain physical characteristics. Darwin's contribution was the suggestion that natural selection is the mechanism by which evolution occurs.

Darwin's work prompted a radical reexamination of the causes and origins of human motivation. Darwin argued that what he had observed in animals also held true for humans; the principles governing humans and animals were the same (Darwin, 1872). Further, evolutionary concepts implied that the route to understanding human behavior lay through observation of humans in relation to their environment. Previously, human behavior had been thought to be largely independent of environmental and biological influences. What governed behavior, it was thought, was the rational mind, which was cultivated, in the growing child, through education and the positive influence of parents and other adults.

Instincts and Motivation

Under Darwin's influence, biologists began to look at motivation in terms of instincts. In the early theories of instinct, behaviors were regarded as predetermined or fixed by our biological structure. Instincts were thought to account not only for the arousal of behavior but for the direction and persistence of behavior as well.

Psychologists were also greatly affected by Darwin's ideas. Early psychologists such as William McDougall (1871–1938) attempted to explain behavior through a limited number of instincts. That attempt ultimately failed, but psychologists have continued to pursue the study of biology. Originally called physiological psychology, this discipline came to be known as the neurosciences when research began to focus on the structure of the brain and nervous system. More recently, the emergence of evolutionary psychology has marked a return to the study of the biological side of behavior from an evolutionary perspective.

Sigmund Freud

Over the years, both biologists and psychologists have come to recognize that beyond inherited factors, learning and cognition also play an important role in behavior. Because the concept of instincts is often understood to imply that the causes of behavior are innate, psychologists tend to avoid this term today. Instead, they speak of genetics or simply biology.

Freud's Instinct Theory

Sigmund Freud (1856–1939) viewed the biological side of humans as providing the energy, or impulse, for behavior (Freud, 1900/1953, 1911/1949, 1915/1934, 1915/1949, 1923/1947). He posited a group of instincts, each with its own source of energy and its appropriate goal object. Although each instinct was hypothesized to have its own source of energy, Freud suggested that they all drew their energy from a general source called *libido.* Unlike the biologists who saw instincts as providing not only the energy but also the direction for behavior, Freud viewed instincts as an energy source, with the direction of behavior subject to some of the principles of learning and cognition. The process was assumed to work as follows. When the energy associated with one of the instincts built up, it would become a source of tension for the person. To reduce the tension, the person would be inclined to seek out the appropriate goal object. Freud suggested that instincts give rise to representations of the goal object. He suggested, however, that humans could, and often did, substitute goal objects that could partially drain off the goal energy. For example, certain artistic endeavors (dancing, painting, music) might be used to symbolically replace the real goal object. The problem, as Freud conceptualized it, is that, in the course of development, certain goal objects have been associated with punishment, and therefore, rather than approach the goal object, the person will tend to avoid it. For example, a child who has been taught that sex is dirty or bad may be inclined to avoid sex as an adult; a child taught that it is bad to show anger could inhibit the natural tendency to express aggression.

Two things can happen when goal objects have been blocked. First, the person can learn to make alternative plans for attaining those goal objects; this process leads to the development of the ego. Second, if the ego has not fully developed or the prohibitions associated with the goal object are excessively rigid or strong, the person may redirect the energy along routes that will reduce the tension but do not lead to the appropriate goal object. For example, a person with a strong sex urge could redirect the energy by reading about sex; a person who feels anger toward her boss might redirect that anger through aggression toward her husband and children. Although redirecting energy in this way might, for a time, reduce the tension associated with the instinct, Freud argued that such methods would never be satisfactory because every instinct has an appropriate goal object. The tension would continue to surface from time to time in the form of neurotic anxiety. Neurotic people, according to Freud, constantly fear that their instincts will get out of control. Freud's goal as a therapist was to help people discover why they had redirected the energy for their instincts—in short, why they felt guilt or fear whenever they considered satisfying their instincts. Freud

believed that the instincts were not bad and that the only way to achieve a happy life was to satisfy them. He argued that many young children learn inappropriate ways of dealing with their instincts or learn that the gratification of certain instincts is inherently bad. He believed that people could get rid of the guilt and fear associated with instincts if they gained insight into the conditions surrounding the acquisition of these feelings. Such feelings were often learned very early in life, so it was necessary, Freud argued, for the analyst to help patients rediscover their childhoods.

Although Freud believed that insight into the origins of a problem—in other words, a new cognition—was sufficient to alter the course of behavior, many therapists have concluded that this is often not so. Wolpe (1969), for example, has argued that extensive relearning is often necessary.

Summary and Comment

Biologists have used the word *instinct* to refer to the belief that there is an innate or biological basis for adaptive behavior. Biologists initially conceptualized instincts as behaviors that emerged from hardwiring in the brain that were triggered by some event in the environment. Migration of birds, for example, was thought to be an unlearned behavior that was triggered by some environmental event such as time of year, the absence of an adequate food supply, or some other yet undetermined event. According to biologists, behaviors such as migration evolved to ensure the survival of the species.

More recently, biologists have acknowledged that learning often plays an important role in modifying a fixed action pattern or some underlying genetic disposition. A continuing question for biologists is to what degree learning plays a role in the execution of an adaptive response such as migration. Does availability of food along the migration route, for example, modify the migration pattern?

Although the concept of instinct has remained a useful concept for biologists, psychologists have largely abandoned it. The reason it has remained a viable concept for biologists but not for psychologists grew out of their different theoretical objectives. Psychologists have always been interested in creating a broad theory of human behavior that can both explain and predict behavior. One underlying principle of theory construction is to use the fewest number of constructs as possible—the law of parsimony. The problem with adopting the concept of instinct as a major conceptual tool is that it became necessary to invent more and more instincts to explain all the behaviors observed in humans. More important perhaps, the concept of instinct was not very useful for predicting new behaviors. Because it referred to a specific behavior that occurred in a specific context, identifying one instinct did not help in predicting what an animal might do in a different context. In contrast to psychologists, biologists have not been particularly interested in a comprehensive theory that could be applied to all animals. The theoretical model that has mainly driven biology is evolutionary theory. The study of migration in birds, for example, is a way of understanding how survival of the fittest occurred and of determining how much is genetic and how much is learned. For biologists, having large numbers of instincts is consistent with evolutionary theory. Each species would evolve a unique way to adapting and thus surviving.

Motivated by the desire to achieve parsimony, McDougall subsumed all the various instincts under a few broad headings. But he did something more. He linked each of those broad classes of instincts to a corresponding emotion and suggested that the emotions gave rise to instincts. Biologists saw no need to postulate the existence of some underlying emotion or motivation. Instincts evolved through evolutionary process. For them, instincts and emotions were more or less synonymous, both simply the result of hardwiring that had a genetic basis. By introducing a motivational construct that was more primary than instinct, McDougall shifted the focus of understanding behavior to motivational constructs. In short, the term *instinct* lost its usefulness. Instincts were no different from any other behavior.

Psychologists have, for the most part, abandoned the concept of instincts but not evolutionary theory. A recent extension or elaboration of evolutionary theory postulates that animals and humans are motivated by the desire to ensure their genes survive in future generations; this idea has stimulated a wide range of theories and studies. According to this most recent version of evolutionary theory, the reason animals and humans do what they do is not to ensure their own survival but, rather, the survival of their genes in future genera-

tions (e.g., Buss, 1994). Thus, the reason animals and humans engage in sexual behavior, for example, is ultimately linked to the need or desire to produce offspring that will carry their genes. The pleasure that we may receive is merely a mechanism that has evolved to ensure we will engage in sexual behavior and thereby reproduce.

The important thing to keep in mind is that the word *instinct* has come to mean different things not only for different disciplines but also for the same disciplines at different times in history. Biologists tend to see instincts as behavioral patterns that grow out of hardwiring in the brain, whereas psychologists have come to think of instincts more as a source of motivation. Perhaps it was for this reason psychologists abandoned the word *instinct* and came instead to use such words as *needs, drives,* or *urges.*

Need Theories

According to the learning theorist, individual differences are the result of learning. But how do such differences arise? Is our destiny as individuals simply the result of being in the right place at the right time? Surely, the orderliness of the universe is due to something more than the whims of reinforcement. Consider siblings who grow up to be very different. How can that be if they have been exposed in the family to similar types of reinforcement and similar information?

An obvious way to deal with individual differences is to argue that we are born with them. Need theory grew out of the idea that the energy, direction, and persistence of behavior are due to the existence of needs. Abandoning the unworkable idea that there must be an instinct for each different behavior, need theorists suggested that we are born with a limited set of needs that can be modified through learning.

Murray's Need Theory

Henry Murray (1893–1988) (1938) proposed that humans can be characterized by a limited set of needs (Table 1-1). He explained individual differences in terms of differences in the strength of the individual's needs, in striking contrast to the view that individual differences are due mainly to learning.

Murray was not particularly concerned with whether needs were innate or learned; he accepted the

Table 1-1.   Murray's list of basic human needs.

Human Need	Description
Abasement	To surrender. To seek and enjoy injury, blame, criticism, punishment. Self-depreciation. Masochism.
Achievement	To overcome obstacles and attain a high standard. To rival and surpass others. To strive and to master.
Affiliation	To form friendships and associations. To greet, join, and live with others. To cooperate and converse sociably with others.
Aggression	To assault or injure another. To fight. To oppose forcefully. To belittle, harm, blame, accuse, or depreciate another. To revenge an injury.
Autonomy	To resist influence or coercion. To defy conventions. To be independent and free to act according to impulse.
Counteraction	To master or make up for a failure by renewed effort. To overcome a weakness. To maintain honor, pride, and self-respect.
Defendance	To defend oneself against blame, criticism, belittlement. To offer explanations and excuses. To resist probing.
Deference	To admire and willingly follow a superior allied other. To cooperate with a leader. To praise, honor, or eulogize.
Dominance	To influence or control others. To persuade, prohibit, dictate, command. To restrain. To organize the behavior of a group.
Exhibition	To attract attention to one's person. To make an impression. To excite, amuse, stir, amaze, intrigue, shock, or thrill others.
Harm avoidance	To avoid pain, physical injury, illness, and death. To escape from a dangerous situation, to take precautionary measures.
Infravoidance	To avoid failure, shame, humiliation, ridicule. To refrain from action because of the fear of failure.
Nurturance	To nourish, aid, or protect a helpless other. To express sympathy. To take care of a child. To feed, help, support, comfort, nurse, heal.
Order	To arrange, organize, put away objects. To be tidy and clean. To be scrupulously precise.
Play	To relax, amuse oneself, seek diversion and entertainment. To have fun, to play games. To laugh, joke, and be merry. To act for fun without further purpose.
Rejection	To snub, ignore, or exclude another. To remain aloof and indifferent. To be discriminating.
Sentience	To seek and enjoy sensuous impressions.
Sex	To form and further an erotic relationship. To engage in sexual activity.
Succorance	To seek aid, protection, or sympathy. To cry for help. To plead for mercy. To adhere to an affectionate, nurturing parent. To be dependent, to have support.
Understanding	To analyze experience, to abstract, to discriminate among concepts, to define relations, to synthesize ideas.

Source: From *Explorations in Personality,* by Henry A Murray. Copyright © 1938, renewed 1966 by Henry A. Murray. Used by permission of Oxford University Press, Inc.

idea that they could be acquired. His aim was to see if all human behavior could be explained by a limited number of needs.

As we see, Table 1-1 lists psychological needs, rather than more physical needs such as the need for food or water. Murray spent much of his life attempt-ing to measure these needs. He invented the Thematic Apperception Test, a projective test in which people were presented with a picture and asked to tell a story about it. These stories were then systematically ana-lyzed to determine the degree to which they reflected the needs that Murray had proposed.

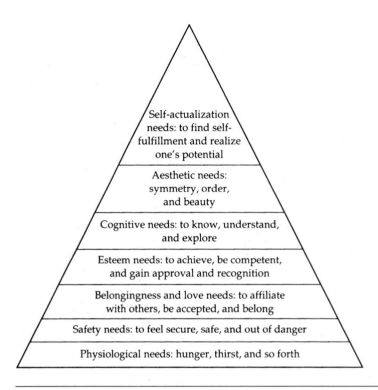

Figure 1-1. Maslow's hierarchy of needs. The needs are arranged in the form of a pyramid, with the most basic or primary needs at the bottom (Maslow, 1943, 1970).

Currently, the main proponent of need theory is David McClelland, who has worked for more than 40 years to validate the need for achievement and, to a lesser extent, the need for affiliation and the need for power. His work shows that the need to achieve plays a fundamental role in behavior. We will return to this topic in Chapter 13.

Maslow's Need Hierarchy

Abraham Maslow (1908–1970) is perhaps one of the best-known need theorists. He argued that the basic physiological needs are associated with deficiency, and the higher-order needs with growth. This is consistent with the distinction between avoidant and approach motivation. In Maslow's view, needs can be grouped in categories, which are arranged in a hierarchical fashion, with the more basic or primary needs at the bottom (Figure 1-1). Only when the needs at the most basic level are satisfied does the next set of needs become relevant; people will be concerned about safety needs only when their physiological needs (for food, water, and warmth) have been met. Likewise, before they ad-

dress their belongingness and love needs, their need to feel secure, safe, and out of danger must be met. As we see in Figure 1-1, people are ultimately motivated by the need for self-actualization, but only after their other needs have been met. We'll return to Maslow's ideas later in this chapter.

Strengthening and Acquiring Needs

Many early psychologists came to believe that although humans were born with a certain set of basic needs, these needs could be strengthened through rewards. They conceptualized needs that we are born with as dispositions to action and that through the process of rewarding these dispositions they could be strengthened and made into stable and strong needs. Thus, by coupling the concept of need and reward, it became possible to incorporate the idea that the environment is important in shaping human motivation, an idea that was warmly received by psychologists who believed that learning plays an important role in the development of needs.

Some psychologists suggested that some needs were perhaps caused mainly by environmental influences. David McClelland's (1985) work on the achievement motive is based on this proposition. He argued, among other things, that children rewarded for achievement would grow up to have a strong achievement motive. In his research, McClelland was able to show that certain parenting styles were more likely to produce a strong need to achieve compared with other parenting styles, evidence consistent with the idea that rewards do play an important role in creating and strengthening needs.

The Factor Analytic Tradition

As research in need theory continued, the number of supposed needs steadily grew. Because one basic scientific principle is to explain phenomena based on the fewest possible concepts, the proliferation of needs concerned motivation theorists. They began to wonder whether this wide range of needs grew out of a smaller set of underlying needs or dispositions. This question was addressed by factor analysis, a statistical procedure that establishes whether different people group a certain set of items in the same way. If different people group things in a similar way, it might be because they are operating out of similar psychological structures. Using factor analysis, Raymond Cattell (1905–1998) proposed a 16-factor model (1971). That was followed by Hans Eysenck's (1916–1997) three-factor model (1991). More recently, Costra and McCrae (1992) have suggested a five-factor model. One reason that different numbers of factors emerged in these studies is that the researchers began with different sets of items. The items that are used in factor analyses normally come from existing personality tests. To measure a certain personality trait, researchers design items that will measure this trait at different points along a theoretical continuum that goes from high to low. One reason different numbers of factors emerge in these studies is that researchers initially select different items for inclusion in the test they give to participants.

According to Costra and McCrae (1992), five basic factors underlie all personality measures:

1. *Extraversion* (also called positive emotionality), characterized by gregarious, assertive, and excitement-seeking tendencies.

2. *Neuroticism* (also called negative emotionality), characterized by anxiety, angry hostility, depression, and self-consciousness.

3. *Agreeableness*, characterized by warmth, compassion, and sympathy versus critical, distrustful, and skeptical attitudes.

4. *Conscientiousness*, characterized by productivity, ethical behavior, and responsibility versus self-indulgence and inability to delay gratification.

5. *Openness to experience* (also called intellect), characterized by having a wide range of experiences, valuing intellectual matters, and being aesthetically reactive (versus being gender stereotyped, holding conservative values, and being uncomfortable with complexities).

By assuming there can be a wide range of interactions between these five factors, this model can account for both the complexity and diversity of behavior. There is also considerable evidence that each factor can be linked to particular biological systems. In short, these five factors tend to reflect underlying biological dispositions.

However, theorists still do not agree about how many factors are necessary to adequately describe behavior. Recently, Benet and Waller (1995) suggested that seven factors are needed to ensure cross-cultural generality using a Spanish population. There is also disagreement about how to define or name these factors. As we see from the description of the five factors, a certain degree of complexity must be reintroduced to define these factors so that they are meaningful to nonspecialists. Nonetheless, the principle that human behavior can be described based on a common underlying set of dispositions has now been widely accepted.

Summary

The measurement of needs has occupied psychologists for some time. The idea that needs give rise to action is no longer accepted in psychology. The present position is that needs give rise to dispositions. Whether these dispositions lead to action depend on circumstances such as past rewards and how we think about the world. Factor analysis has provided psychologists with a more empirical way to establish the underlying psychological structure of human motivation. Currently, research suggests that all of human behavior can be explained in terms of 5 to 7 basic needs or dispositions and that each of these needs or dispositions can be linked to biological systems.

Maslow argued that the basic physiological needs are related to deficiency and the higher-order needs to growth. This distinction is consistent with the idea that human action is caused by both avoidant and approach needs. Maslow also contended that needs are arranged hierarchically. This is consistent with the idea that deficiency needs are more compelling than growth needs.

Learning Theories

Watson's School of Behaviorism

Learning theories grew out of the belief that behavior could be better explained by principles of learning than by instinct. John B. Watson (1878–1952), who later founded the school of behaviorism, concluded that there were only three innate emotional reactions—fear, rage, and love—from which all other emotions were learned or derived (Watson & Morgan, 1917). One of the most compelling arguments that learning, rather than instinct, is the basis of behavior is that people raised in different cultures behave quite differently. The existence of cultural differences suggests that behavioral patterns are shaped by the environment (for example, by modeling) and are not hardwired (Boring, 1950). Although early learning theorists such as Watson did not completely abandon the idea that biology plays a role in behavior, their aim was to show that behavior can be largely explained by the principles of classical conditioning or instrumental learning (sometimes called reward learning).

Hull's Drive Theory

One of the most influential learning theorists was Clark Hull (1884–1952). Central to Hull's theory was the idea that the wide variations in human behavior can be explained by the principles of learning. According to Hull, the activation of a drive leads to random behavior. In the course of that behavior, the organism accidentally performs a response that reduces a drive. When that happens, the behavior leading to drive re-

duction is strengthened. Over time, with repeated reduction of that drive, a habit is formed. For example, if a hungry dog discovers, while in that deprived state, that knocking over a garbage can leads to food, the dog will develop a habit of knocking over garbage cans. Thus, unlike Freud, who suggested that instincts give rise to representations of goal objects, Hull suggested that the goal object is discovered in the course of random behavior.

According to Hull, the reduction of a drive produces reinforcement. In his theory, drives activate habits. Hull suggested a multiplicative relationship between drives and habits:

Behavior = Drives × Habits

According to this formulation, when a habit is weak, it takes a strong drive (such as hunger) to produce behavior (such as knocking over garbage cans). However, if the habit is highly developed, then a weak drive can activate it. Thus, his theory can explain why even a well-fed dog will knock over garbage cans and eat garbage. In Hull's theory, drives provide the energy for behavior; without drives, there would be no behavior.

For a time, Hull's theory was widely accepted by psychologists. It took from instinct theories the basic idea that behavior is caused by drives, but it was also able to account for individual differences. One of Hull's important contributions was his explanation of how weak drive states can activate a strong habit and thus produce action. We are creatures of habit; Hull was able to tell us why.

Skinner's Reinforcement Theory

In the 1960s and 1970s, B. F. Skinner's theory came to replace drive theory. Skinner (1904–1990) suggested that it was not necessary for a drive to be reduced for learning to occur. A number of experiments during that era showed that animals and humans would learn a behavior even if no biological drive were reduced. For example, rats learned to press a bar to drink a nonnutritive substance such as a saccharin solution. According to Hull, the rats could not learn this behavior without reinforcement, and reinforcement can only occur if a biological drive is being reduced. In other studies, male rats maintained a high level of sexual interest

B. F. Skinner

and activity even if prevented from ejaculating during intercourse. If sexual behavior is for purposes of reproduction, then ejaculation would be essential for reinforcement to occur; by Hull's theory, the rats should lose interest in sexual activity.

Skinner's theory represented a major shift away from the biological basis of behavior. According to Skinner, behavior is under the control of external rewards. Positive rewards increase the probability of a behavior, and negative rewards decrease its probability.

Skinner described himself as an empiricist. He said he did not believe in constructing theories; he was only interested in talking about observable behavior. He deliberately used such phrases as "increasing the probability of a response" to emphasize that he was talking about observables. For him, words like "strengthen" were mentalistic constructs that could not

be observed. Even though the main construct in his theory was reward, he was not particularly interested in whether it made people feel good or bad.

Skinner was able to demonstrate that persistence is often greater if an organism is only rewarded some of the time, rather than each time it makes a desired response (partial reinforcement). While other psychologists constructed theories to explain why partial reinforcement leads to persistence (Amsel, 1962), Skinner was content to show that different types of partial reinforcement contingencies (what he called *schedules of reinforcement*) produce different forms of persistence. In this way, he demonstrated that such things as persistence could be explained without reference to biology.

Although Skinner claimed he did not have a theory, others have argued that he did. The essence of his theory is that it is possible to radically change behavior. In his two books *Walden II* (Skinner, 1948) and *Beyond Freedom and Dignity* (Skinner, 1971), Skinner describes how people can be happy and how emotions such as aggression can be eliminated by the principles of reinforcement. The theme of *Beyond Freedom and Dignity* (Skinner, 1971) is that we can create a perfect state by arranging reward contingencies in a certain way. To do that, we need to give up certain ideas, such as the need for dignity and freedom; and to surrender control to a benevolent superstate.

Research stimulated by Skinner's ideas has shown that it is possible to radically alter behavior through the systematic application of rewards. This line of research, called *behavior modification*, showed that it is often possible to alter widely diverse behaviors associated with, for example, drug use, eating patterns, family relationships, delinquency, and the acquisition of skills.

According to Skinnerian thinking, the energy, the direction, and the persistence of behavior are due to reinforcement contingencies; it is not necessary to postulate anything more. Psychologists have since demonstrated that rewards are only part of the story. Nonetheless, Skinner's legacy was to demonstrate that behavior is often under the control of rewards and can be altered simply by altering reward contingencies.

Social Learning Theories

According to Skinner's theory, rewards are external. Social learning theorists challenged that view by demonstrating that people can also learn by modeling the behavior of another person. They went on to suggest that we can acquire a new behavior simply by observing that it produces some desired outcome for another person. This argument explains why people will engage in a behavior for which they have never personally received a reward. Thus, two main features that distinguish social learning theory from the theories of Hull and Skinner are (1) the tendency to view behavior as occurring independently of environmental contingencies and (2) the assumption that organisms can acquire experiences (habits) in the absence of direct experience or reward.

Social learning theorists were not concerned, for the most part, with determining how such behaviors were functional or instrumental for the individual's survival. They were intent on showing that much, if not all, human behavior comes from information that humans process about the environment. For example, numerous studies have addressed the question of vicarious motivators (Bandura, 1986). These studies demonstrated that by observing others, individuals can often determine ahead of time what actions will bring pain (punishment) and what actions will bring satisfaction (reinforcement). Moreover, individuals can learn not only to avoid making certain mistakes but also to design an optimal course of action for achieving desired ends.

Social learning theorists were able to explain a wide range of behaviors that had no immediate survival value. At the height of social learning theory, it was popular to say that, for example, aggression was nothing more than imitative behavior caused by watching aggression and violence on television. In that case, one way to get rid of aggression would be to eliminate aggression and violence from television. As it turns out, it's not that simple. Individuals seem to be born with different dispositions toward aggression. Nonetheless, television does contribute indirectly to aggression. (We'll return to this topic in Chapter 8.)

According to social learning theory, information can account for the source (energy), the direction, and the persistence of behavior. Like Skinnerians, social learning theorists did not view the underlying biology as important. Although they relied mainly on principles of learning to explain behavior, they did introduce rudimentary cognitive concepts (Berkowitz, 1990). In particular, they suggested that people develop expectations. As the result of watching aggression, for exam-

ple, individuals develop ideas about what aggressive behaviors would be appropriate in certain situations. Such expectations can be thought of as if/then learning: "If this situation arises, then this is the appropriate behavior." According to social learning theory, people not only learn behaviors from observing others but also learn about consequences. An individual who sees, for example, that acting aggressively produces certain desired results might develop the expectation: "If I act aggressively, then I will get such and such." According to social learning theory, seeing another person engage in a certain behavior and attain a desired goal provides vicarious reinforcement to the observer. Because of vicarious reinforcement, the likelihood of the observer imitating a certain behavior will increase.

Perhaps the most lasting legacy of social learning theory is the idea that much of human behavior arises from information that we have passively observed. As we'll see in Chapter 14, we do indeed use such information to guide our actions.

Summary and Comment

Early learning theorists such as Watson and Hull suggested that biology provides the energy for behavior but that the direction is mainly due to learning. They argued that persistence has its roots in our biology but even persistence can be modified. The main advantage of these theories over instinct theories was their ability to account for individual differences.

Although Watson developed behaviorism theory, Hull and Skinner were its two most influential proponents. Hull argued that the energy and persistence of behavior derive from drives, but the direction of behavior comes from learning (habits). Skinner abandoned the concept of drives. In doing so, he also abandoned the idea that our biology is a main determinant of our behavior. Skinner even suggested that to produce adaptive behaviors we merely need to arrange appropriate reinforcement contingencies. In two popular books, he argued that it is possible to create a utopian society by systematically employing principles of reinforcement.

Social learning theory has shown that humans process a great deal of information about the environment and that such information provides the source (energy) and direction of our actions. Both Skinner's theory and social learning theory represent a movement away from motivation theorists' initial focus on behavior as an attempt to adapt to the environment. Adaptive behavior is typically viewed within the context of the underlying biology, which was of no particular interest to Skinner or the social learning theorists.

What is important to remember is that each of these theories has at its core the idea that behaviors, once acquired, exert a profound effect on our daily lives. We commonly refer to these behaviors as habits to emphasize the fact that they are acquired behaviors rather than being hardwired.

Implicit in the idea of learning is the idea that if behaviors (habits) are acquired (learned) they can also be altered. But that does not mean an individual is free to alter his or her responses to a stimulus at will. An underlying assumption of these theories is the idea that learning is basically passive. According to Hull and Skinner, for example, external reinforcement strengthens or weakens a response. According to Social Learning theory, we tend to imitate (process information) about what important people normally do in certain situations (e.g., parents). According to this view, drives, tissue needs, instincts, and conflicts from childhood push each of us. What we do, therefore, is not what we want to do but what we have been taught to do. Because events called "stimuli" have been linked to responses, we behave in a certain way each time a certain stimulus appears. In the next section, we will look at what are sometimes called pull theories. Rather than being "pushed around" we are pulled by something that is aroused by our interaction with the environment and our need to adapt to the environment (Seligman & Csikszentmihalyi, 2000).

Growth and Mastery Motivation Theories

Exploration, Curiosity, and Mastery

Growth motivation theories grew out of the idea that animals and humans are motivated by their need to successfully interact with the environment (Dember & Earl, 1957; Piaget, 1970; White, 1959). One underlying concept of growth theory is that humans are not born with fully developed abilities. To adapt and succeed, humans need to develop those abilities. Central to all growth theories is the idea that humans need to

process information and acquire skills—in other words, to develop *mastery*. To successfully deal with the environment, organisms need to learn as much as they can about the environment and to develop their skills to their maximum.

In growth theories, the mechanism that motivates growth and mastery is a discrepancy between where the individual is and where the individual needs to be to successfully adapt to the environment. This discrepancy creates a tension inside the organism. To reduce this tension, the individual needs to reduce the discrepancy, by developing skills and intellect. The concept of tension is a motivational concept intended to capture the idea that a mildly to moderately negative affective state is associated with a discrepancy, something like an itch or a hunger pang, and it is this negative state that motivates the individual to engage in an appropriate action. According to Piaget, organisms must develop cognitive structures that enable them to process vast amounts of information quickly and efficiently. The term *cognitive structure* is used to capture the idea that the ability to process information depends on the development of higher order mental processes such as categories. Using categories, such as bear, fruit, shelter, for example, people do not have to deal with the details of each new object they encounter, and as a result, they can process information quickly by using an existing category. What is lost, of course, is detail but that is often not important. According to growth theorists, animals explore because the environment is a source of novelty. That novelty creates a discrepancy, which in turn creates a tension. To reduce that tension, organisms explore their environment and process all the information contained in it. When the environment is no longer novel, the tension subsides and exploratory behavior stops. Some theorists have suggested that organisms are designed to feel best when there is an optimal level of incoming stimulation for them to process (Berlyne, 1960). If the immediate environment does not provide enough stimulation, they will seek out a novel environment to satisfy their need for stimulation.

The idea of tension is reminiscent of Hull's drive concept. Like drives, tensions have a compelling quality. Tensions motivate the organism to do things that will return it to a tension-free state. With growth motivation, these tensions are only reduced when the individual develops skills or cognitive structures sufficient to deal effectively with the environment.

Growth theorists do not fully agree about whether it is best to account for growth motivation through approach or avoidant mechanisms. Many growth theorists suggest that the discrepancy between what is out there in the environment and what is inside the individual (such as knowledge or skills) creates motivation. However, discrepancies can be conceptualized as the basis for experiencing challenge (an approach state) or tension (an avoidant state). A growing body of data suggests that some people react to a discrepancy as though it were a challenge (approach motivation), whereas others react to a discrepancy as though it were a threat (avoidant motivation). On this basis, theorists have made a distinction between people who are mastery-oriented and those who are ego-oriented (Nicholls, 1984). As it turns out, this distinction has far-reaching implications for explaining the differences in individuals' reactions to the same situation.

Why do people react so differently? It has been suggested that some people adopt a mastery orientation, which means, in broad terms, they are motivated to learn everything they can about the environment in which they live. What we have learned from years of research is that this type of orientation seems to flourish in a supportive/safe environment. If we are constantly threatened in some way, we often come to develop a very different orientation—what has been called an *ego orientation.* The ego orientation means, in broad terms, that individuals only learn only about those things in the environment that are of immediate use to them and their survival. In contrast to the mastery orientation, people with an ego orientation develop a much narrower or limited view of the world. It has been suggested that such an orientation develops in an environment that is characterized by threat.

Some theorists have argued that the environment in isolation doesn't necessarily produce these differences; rather, these differences have their roots in genetics. That is, some individuals are born with a disposition to develop a mastery orientation or an ego orientation. According to this way of thinking, genetics creates a disposition to react to the environment as benign/safe or as threatening. Still other theorists have argued that our reactions are determined largely by how we label our experiences.

In the next section, we consider humanistic theories, which were also concerned with the question of growth.

Humanistic Theories

Abraham Maslow (1943, 1970) and Carl Rogers (1902–1987) (1959) originally proposed the humanistic approach. Humanistic psychologists base their theories on the premise that humans are basically good and possess an innate (biological) tendency to grow and mature. They further believe that each of us is unique. A central humanist concept is the need for self-actualization, which depends on a highly developed self-concept.

Carl Rogers (1951) suggested that organisms have one basic tendency, which is to "actualize, maintain and enhance the experiencing self." Although Rogers recognized that humans have needs, he stressed the inherent tendency of the individual to coordinate those needs to develop the self. He saw the self as constructed from basic sensory experiences and from the individual's interaction with the world. Though the tendency to actualize was seen as innate, he recognized that the route to self-actualization is frequently characterized by pain and suffering.

Rogers believed that people have within themselves the capacity to judge what is good for them and what is not. Individuals value positively those experiences perceived as maintaining and enhancing the self and value negatively those perceived as undermining growth. Thus, what we approach and what we avoid depends on our perception of what promotes the development of the self.

Rogers suggested that, as we interact with the environment, we develop the *need for positive regard*—the need to receive approval, to be accepted, and to be loved. The need for positive regard also makes us sensitive to the criticism and praise of others. He suggested that positive regard eventually becomes internalized and, as a result, we come to develop *positive self-regard.* Rogers believed strongly that people need to have positive self-regard to realize their potential.

However, Rogers pointed out a potential problem with internalizing positive regard: If we determine our behavior on the basis of what pleases others, we lose sight of what is good for the development of the self.

Rogers believed that the movement towards socialized worth and away from inherent worth was antithetical to self-actualization. People need to listen to their inner voices—to their innate capacity to judge what is good for the self; he called this the *organismic valuation process*. His child-rearing advice to parents was that, rather than offering conditional love—that is, withholding love until children comply with behaviors that the parents value—they should embrace unconditional love; in other words, they should love their children for all their choices and behaviors, out of respect for their inherent ability to do what is best for themselves.

Even though Maslow and Rogers were never part of mainstream empirical psychology, their ideas received wide acceptance outside the mainstream. In recent years, as psychologists have begun to explore the nature of the self and the possibility that people can self-regulate their behavior, there has been a resurgence of interest in the ideas of Maslow and Rogers.

Summary and Comment

Growth and mastery theories grew, in part, from a backlash against learning theories that suggest all behavior is learned. A fundamental assumption of growth theories is the idea that we have a biological disposition to master our environment. This idea is consistent with an evolutionary approach to behavior that assumes our ability to adapt has not been left to chance but, rather, is guided by our biology. The focus of growth theories has been to uncover the process or mechanisms that guide the tendency to master. Most, if not all, of the theories of mastery and growth assume that the tendency to master develops from a fundamental curiosity or exploratory need. Thus, the focus of early researchers was on curiosity and exploratory behavior.

One surprise of the early researchers was the discovery that this disposition to explore is often fragile. Specifically, it was found that when individuals are anxious or stressed, they do not engage in exploratory behavior, rather, they tend to seek out the familiar. As it turns out, this makes a lot of sense from an evolutionary perspective. According to evolutionary principles, immediate threats to the individual must always be dealt with first to ensure survival. After one deals

with immediate threats, that person is free to deal with long-term adaptation. Stress and anxiety are often aroused when an individual experiences some immediate threat. Various researchers such as Nicholls have argued that people can be differentiated into those types that tend to habitually respond to the world as threatening (ego types) and those who habitually respond to the world as benign (mastery types). In other words, the tendency to be mastery oriented or ego oriented depends on underlying mechanism that we variously refer to as anxiety, arousal, stress, or emotionality. In recent years, there has been a tendency to think of the underlying mechanism as having its origin in one's perception of the world. In evolutionary terms, this means that some people are more prepared than are others to treat new events (novelty) as a source of threat.

The idea that humans have a disposition to master was picked up by the humanists who elaborated on some basic ideas found in empirical research. Although their theories were appealing and widely accepted, they have not always withstood the tests of scientific scrutiny.

Cognitive Theories

Cognitive theories of motivation have their roots in work done by learning theorists such as Edward Tolman (1886–1959) (1932), personality theorists such as Kurt Lewin (1890–1947) (1938), and developmental theorists such as Jean Piaget (1896–1980) (1970). These theorists argued that mental representations formed by humans and animals play a central role in guiding their behavior. Traditional learning theorists such as Watson and Hull argued that behavior could be explained simply by the strengthening of a habit or association, without invoking the idea of mental representations; for many people, the idea that animals—especially rats—have mental representations was simply going too far. The early cognitive theorists designed a number of studies that were difficult to explain on the basis of traditional learning theory. For example, in the latent learning studies, one group of animals (typically rats) was allowed to explore a maze in the absence of any rewards (preexposure phase), while the control group was not provided with the opportunity to explore. Both groups of animals were then made hungry and rewarded when they got from one point to another. The animals given the preexposure learned the correct path much more quickly than did the controls. Cognitive theorists argued that the rats formed some type of mental map during the preexposure phase and used that map to find their way around when the rewards were introduced.

Expectancy-Value Theories

The idea of mental representations took hold in the 1950s and was incorporated into a number of theories in the field of motivation and elsewhere. One type of mental representation is an *expectancy*, a judgment about the likely outcome of some behavior, formed because of past experiences. If I ask my boss for a raise, for example, what is the likelihood that I'll get it?

Expectancy is not a motivational construct by itself; however, it proves very useful when coupled with the motivational construct called *value*. The resulting expectancy-value theories suggest that people not only have expectations about what might happen in response to a particular behavior but can also assign a value to the outcome. According to expectancy-value theories, people choose between different tasks by simultaneously assessing expectation and value for each. Suppose I want a game of tennis. I might form an expectation about my likelihood of beating my neighbor, as against the likelihood of beating her five-year-old son. If I conclude that I might be able to beat both of them, would it be more satisfying (of greater value) to beat my neighbor or her son?

Expectancy-value theories are hedonistic. They assume that we will select the alternative likely to arouse the greatest feeling of pleasure (positive affect). If the alternatives are all perceived as unattractive, we might select the option that produces the least pain. Expectancy-value theories were also called cognitive-choice theories or decision theories (Edwards, 1961). Tests of the expectancy value theory involved determining which of two or more alternatives a person would select given the probability of achieving a certain outcome (winning the lottery) and the reward magnitude (amount of money). In other words, what are the trade-offs that an individual makes when confronted with these two variables?

Goal-Setting Theories

The idea that humans can form expectations about the future played a key role in the development of goal-setting theories. According to Locke and Latham (1990), humans can motivate themselves by setting future goals. They suggest that goals affect behavior in four ways: (1) they direct attention; (2) they mobilize effort to the task; (3) they encourage persistence; and (4) they facilitate the development of strategies (Locke, 1968). Their research indicates that goals should be both difficult and specific; saying, "Do your best" is not an effective way to motivate people. An important underlying moderator of goal setting is commitment. Unless we are committed to our goals, we will not put forth the effort necessary to achieve them. Psychologists have found that one way to increase commitment is to allow people to set their own goals.

Social-Cognitive Theories of Goal Setting

Whether people will set difficult goals for themselves (or commit themselves to such goals) depends on whether they perceive that they have, or can develop, the abilities they will need to attain the goals. Albert Bandura (1991a, 1991b) writes about people's *self-efficacy*, defined as expectations that focus on beliefs about their capabilities to organize and execute the behaviors requisite for attaining the outcome. Notice that, in expectancy-value theories, expectancy relates to outcomes corresponding to a specific level of effort, whereas self-efficacy expectations focus on our beliefs about our capacities. Ultimately, such beliefs relate back to our self-concept. In other words, in Bandura's theory, the nature of the self plays a role in goal setting. As we'll see in Chapter 14, the visualization of possible selves can play an important role in determining the kinds of goals that people set.

Summary

Cognitive theories grew out of the idea that humans can form mental representations of their environment, which they can then use to guide their behavior. Moreover, humans can make choices between alternatives. According to cognitive theorists, behavior is not merely the result of a habit that propels us blindly forward.

Cognitive-choice theories were designed to explain how and why people make immediate choices. One of the most prominent early motivational theories was expectancy-value theory, which suggested not only that humans have expectations about outcomes, but that they attach values to these outcomes. According to expectancy-value theories, expectancies and values are multiplicative.

Goal theories grew out of the idea that humans have expectations about the future and that one way to make these expectations happen is to set goals. According to Locke and Latham (1990), these goals help provide the direction and persistence that characterizes goal attainment.

Social-cognitive theories of goal setting incorporate the idea that people have perceptions not only about their present level of skills, but also about their ability to develop skills. Thus, the future goals that people set for themselves depend on their self-concept.

Biological, Learned, and Cognitive Forces

In this review of some major theories of motivation, we have seen that motivation theorists have viewed the cause of behavior in terms of biology, principles of learning, and principles of cognition. In this book, we will examine several motivational systems. In each system, we will see that learning and cognition modify the expression of the underlying biology. Freud recognized a long time ago that human biology does not automatically aim a person in the right direction. Forces of society also play a role. For example, there is considerable evidence that one of the causes of bulimia (the tendency to binge and purge) in North American society is our obsession with thinness and dieting. There is also evidence that learning can short-circuit adaptive behavior. People sometimes use alcohol, for example, to help them block out the pain of loneliness or poor self-esteem. Consequently, they develop the habit of drinking when faced with loneliness or feelings of inadequacy.

The focus in this book is to explain not only why people do what they do but also how they can change through self-regulation. A growing body of research indicates that people can change their behavior if they learn how to set goals and to ward off self-doubt. Advice based on research showing that people can change is presented throughout the following chapters; much of it involves principles of learning and cognition.

Learning to Make Use of the Internet

In the past we often looked to books, especially textbooks, to provide us with the information that we needed to know on a particular topic. Over the years, there has been a virtual explosion of information and now most texts can now only provide a general overview. The way most of us are going to stay abreast of things is to learn how to constantly access what is new and different. It appears that the main way most of us are going to do this is through the Internet. For that reason I have decided to make using the Internet a feature of this book. Throughout this book, I am going to suggest a number of questions that you might want to pursue using the Internet. I think this is a good learning experience, and I think it is fun.

One problem with using the Internet to answer questions is trying to sort through all the junk (what we more formally call noise). To help students get where they need to go quickly and efficiently, while avoiding noise, Thomson Learning has created an information base that is updated continually. Not all the questions that I pose or that might occur to you can be answered by that database, but most can.

Main Points

1. There are two types of motivation: approach and avoidant motivation.
2. Eight themes underlie contemporary motivation: Behavior represents an attempt to adapt; it is important to determine what arouses and energizes behavior; it is necessary to understand what governs direction; it is important to understand persistence; feelings are important; there are individual differences; humans often can self-regulate their behavior; humans have limited volition.
3. Darwin suggested that the behavior of animals and humans is caused by their underlying biology.

4. Early psychologists such as McDougall attempted to explain all human behavior as a limited set of instincts that provided not only the energy but also the direction of behavior.

5. Need theorists such as Murray suggested that humans can be characterized by a set of needs that provide the energy for behavior and the direction as well.

6. Maslow suggested that needs can be arranged in a hierarchical fashion.

7. Recently, researchers have shown through factor analytic procedures that there are five basic personality factors: extraversion, neuroticism, agreeableness, conscientiousness, and openness to experience.

8. Hull suggested that the energy for behavior was the result of drives and went on to suggest that behavior is caused by the multiplicative effect of drives times habit (B = D × H).

9. Skinner abandoned the idea of drive but retained the concept of reinforcement.

10. Social learning theorists suggested that many behaviors (habits) can be acquired in the absence of rewards: for example, people could learn to be violent simply by watching violence on television and by seeing the consequences of this behavior (vicarious reinforcement).

11. Growth motivation theories developed from the idea that organisms need to learn how to successfully interact with their environment.

12. Growth theorists suggested that the reason animals explore their environment is to gain mastery over it.

13. According to goal-orientation theories, people adopt different orientations to the environment depending on whether they are threatened. When threatened, they adopt an ego orientation; otherwise, they adopt a mastery orientation.

14. According to expectancy-value theories, organisms have expectations about whether they are likely to attain particular goals. People will choose the option with the best combination of expectancy and value.

15. According to social-cognitive theories of goal setting, whether people are inclined to set specific attainable goals depends on their feelings of self-efficacy.

Chapter Two

Components of Motivation

■ *What are the components of motivation?*

■ *Why is it necessary to talk in terms of components?*

■ *Why have scientists tended to study behavior from a single perspective?*

■ *What are the implications of adopting a single perspective?*

■ *What are some of the implications of viewing behavior from multiple perspectives (biological, learned, and cognitive)?*

■ *How does a multiple-perspective (components) approach help us understand such things as why people run?*

Motivation theorists are concerned with the origins or causes of action. They are interested in why people do any number of things—eat, seek out sexual partners, take drugs, retaliate when threatened, make friends, care for children, set goals, solve problems, create. Early motivation theorists hypothesized that needs cause action (e.g., Murray, 1938). Their main focus was the identification and measurement of needs. It soon became apparent, however, that two different people with the same need—such as the need to achieve—did not expend the same energy nor did they persist equally. Obviously other factors were at work. Over the years, it has become apparent that a number of factors moderate and enhance needs. Self-esteem, for example, plays an important role in determining whether people persist in the face of adversity or give up. In response to these findings, psychologists have reconceptualized needs not as direct causes of action but rather as dispositions to action (Atkinson & Birch, 1978; de Rivera, 1982; Raynor, 1974; Weiner, 1974). Needs give us a push or nudge in a certain direction but they do not, by themselves, supply all the energy, nor do they fully provide the direction. The energy and the final direction come from other processes or systems.

These other processes or systems can be classified as biological, learned, or cognitive. Brain circuits are activated, learned responses are triggered, or we take control by making plans. I refer to these processes as *components of behavior* or *components of motivation*. Research shows that behavior is not caused solely by a biological, a learned, or a cognitive process but, rather, by the interaction of all three (Kleinginna & Kleinginna, 1981b). Thus, the basic approach I have adopted in this book is that, in studying motivation, we are concerned with understanding how dispositions lead to action through the joint operation of biological, learned, and cognitive processes.

The Biological Component

When we talk about biology, our main focus is going to be on the structure and design of the brain. Our brain is largely responsible for our survival, our happiness, our health, our ability to attain success and do all those things that we do. Over the years, researchers have begun to better understand some aspects of that design

and in doing so we have come to better understand why we do what we do.

It is beyond the scope of this book to talk about the details of the design. We are going to focus, nevertheless, on some of the design features that pertain to motivation. We will also explore some of the theory and research that pertains to the question of why our brain is designed as it is. Let's begin by talking about why researchers believe our brain is designed the way it is.

Origins of Human Brain Design

A new branch of psychology, called evolutionary psychology, has emerged in recent years to address the question of why our brain is designed the way it is. This discipline has its roots in Darwinian evolutionary theory and can be summarized in terms of four basic assumptions (Nicholson, 1997).

The first assumption is that the human community as we know it today has resulted from years of evolution. Our earliest hominid ancestor has been traced back some 4 to 5 million years, and our present species goes back about 250,000 years. It is important to note that species tend to evolve rapidly for some time and then stabilize without evolving further (Eldredge & Gould, 1972). The second assumption is that just as we have adapted physically, we also have an adapted mind—one that is capable of learning and problem solving. Specifically, this mind is designed to help us survive and reproduce. The term *mind*, as opposed to *brain*, is often used by evolutionary psychologists to emphasize the idea that the brain is made up of a number of "intelligent" systems that work together with the body to produce our actions. The third assumption is that our bodies and mind are adapted for a world in which we no longer live. Our bodies and minds emerged when global cooling converted tropical forests into a more arid savanna environment. The emergence of an upright bipedal stance and the development of a hunter gatherer society were two adaptations that allowed our ancestors to deal with this new climate change and the new food supply that came as a result of that climate change. The fourth assumption is that under new circumstances, adaptations of the brain can be used for purposes other than those for which they were designed. This extended adaptation allows us to use a brain that was designed some 150,000 to

250,000 years ago to deal with our present environment. Take remembering phone numbers or driving a car, for example. It has been argued that while we can do those things very well, the reason is not because the brain adapted to remember phone numbers or drive cars but, rather, at one point in time, perhaps 150,000 to 250,000 years ago, the brain made an adaptation that now makes it possible for us to do these things (Sherry & Schacter, 1987).

One interesting and important feature of evolutionary psychology is the proposition that humans are essentially social animals, a design feature caused by our ancestors needing to becoming hunters and gatherers to survive. In that environment, it has been argued, our ancestors needed to cooperate, and as a result, the brain adapted to meet those environmental demands giving it a very distinctive social quality.

It should be noted, if it is not already apparent, that to understand the design of our brain we need to go back to our ancestors to discover the problems they faced. In that context we can discover why a certain kind of brain design emerged rather than another. It is important to remember that evolution is incapable of looking forward and thereby preparing us for a life to come (Nicholson, 1997). Evolution helps us survive the present and, in doing so, gives us the opportunity to carry our brain design forward. Whether that brain design will survive in future generations depends on how well it can deal with new problems.

This theory should not be confused with the selfish gene theory that has come to be called sociobiology theory (see Richard Dawkins's [1990], *The Selfish Gene*). According to this theory, we are motivated to propagate our own genes in future generations to preserve ourselves in some way. According to evolutionary psychology, people don't selfishly spread their own genes, rather, their genes spread themselves. "They do it by the way they build our brains. By making us enjoy life, health, sex, friends, and children, the genes buy a lottery ticket for representation in the next generation, with the odds that were favorable in the environment in which we evolved (because healthy, long-lived, loving parents did tend, on the average, to send more genes into the next generation)" (Pinker, 1997, p. 94). Pinker also points out: "Sometime the most selfish things a gene can do is build a selfless brain—for ex-

ample, one that gives rise to a loving parent or a loyal friend (Pinker, 1997, p. 94).

Theorists such as Buck (1999) have suggested that we can think of humans as having two central complimentary drives (minds): one being self-preservation and the other being preservation of the species. Because of this dual nature we sometimes act selfishly and sometime selfless. That doesn't mean to imply that we are unpredictable. As we will see, in some situations it is appropriate for us to act in a selfish manner and in other situations it is appropriate for us to act in a selfless manner. As Buck points out, our genes cause us to act appropriately given the situation. Our genes influence, persuade, and even cajole us to act as we do.

The Example of Temperament

Temperament refers to how we react to the world (reactivity) and how we self-regulate ourselves (self-control) in the face of certain environmental demands (Rothbart, Ahadi, & Evans, 2000). In laypeople terms, we sometimes talk about how some people react in a bold manner while others react in a more timid manner. The fascinating thing is that at birth we come into the world with a predisposition to react in one way or another (Kagan & Snidman, 1991; Rothbart, Ahadi, & Evans, 2000) and then maintain that approach for the rest of our lives (McCrae et al., 2000). That is not to say we don't change in often subtle but important ways. It is generally agreed that although temperament provides the disposition to act in a certain way, other factors modify that tendency to some degree. We call the outcome personality (Rothbart, Ahadi, & Evans, 2000).

Temperament can best be described as three broad factors. The first factor has to do with having a disposition toward high activity, a preference for intense stimulation (e.g., loud noises), and a proclivity for taking risks. Children who have these qualities, it has been found, are typically at ease in social situations. The second factor has to do with having a disposition toward negativity—to be fearful and/or sad and to be angry when frustrated, for example. Children who are low in negativity tend to be more curious, open to new experiences, happy, and not readily frustrated. The third factor has to do with the ability to regulate attention and behavior—something that has been called "effortful control." Children who can focus their attention or behavior are more likely to achieve or overcome obstacles and as a result experience pleasure factors (Rothbart, Ahadi, & Evans, 2000).

Take a minute to think about how you would describe yourself and others using these three factors and how this explains some of your preferences. If you like to take risks, are not inclined to worry (are not fearful or do not see the negative in things), and can focus your attention and behavior, you might be a person who would like to climb rocks or perhaps start a business. Alternatively, if you do not like to take risks, have a tendency to worry (see the negative side of things), but are good at focusing your attention, you might like to play chess or write an article about the environment, capitalizing on your tendency to anticipate what can go wrong.

In recent years, researchers have shown that personality can be broadly described by three to five underlying factors: extraversion (positive emotionality), neuroticism (negative emotionality), agreeableness, conscientiousness, and openness to experience (see Chapter 1). Cross cultural studies have shown that irrespective of where you were born or how you were raised (Plomin & Daniels, 1987), these factors are sufficient to account for a wide range of individual differences (McCrae et al., 2000) during what appears to be the life span of an individual (Caspi, 2000). This is not to say that parenting makes no difference. What parenting appears to do is help children, irrespective of their temperaments, learn how to best deal with the world given their temperaments (McCrae et al., 2000). In this context, temperament only accounts for about 40 to 50% of the variance. This emphasizes the idea that learning and cognition also play important roles. Together, these different factors can account for the great diversity amongst people.

It has been argued that each of these five dimensions has their roots in our genes. That is, when you look at the descriptions of various temperaments and the descriptions of the big five personality factors, they often refer to the same thing. Moreover, when you measure each independently, there is a high correlation between certain types of temperament and one or more of the five personality types (Rothbart, Ahadi, & Evans, 2000).

One might assume from an evolutionary perspective (think of our ancestors living in a hostile environment), that it would be adaptive if we all had temperaments that made us inclined to avoid risks, to be on guard, and to be highly in control of everything we do. Some have argued, however, that our very survival depended to some degree on taking risks (such as in hunting), on not being too cautious (so that we could explore and find new food) and not always being in perfect control (so that we could be open to new information or ideas, as well as act creatively). One underlying principle of evolutionary theory is the idea that diversity is adaptive (Wilson, 1994). By being different we have unique qualities that are useful in the search of a partner, friends and functioning in a complex social environment (Nicholson, 1997).

Earlier I said that evolution does not prepare us for the future. Although that is true, it is also important to remember that one thing that evolution must not do if we are to survive as a species is to make us so specialized that when a change in the environment does come we are unable to adapt. It appears from the work on temperament and personality differences that humans have a diverse gene pool. We assume those diverse genes are largely responsible for our survival as a species.

Monozygotic and Dizygotic Twins

One main technique used by scientists to determine whether a certain behavior is caused by genes is to compare monozygotic twins with dizygotic twins. Monozygotic twins result from a division of a single egg and, as a result, have exactly the same set of genes. Dizygotic twins, in contrast, result from the fertilization of two different eggs by two different sperm. As a result, they are just like any two siblings from the same family; that is, while some of their genes may be the same, others are different. By comparing monozygotic twins with dizygotic twins, it is possible to control for the effects of the environment, the effects of having two children that are exactly the same age, and gender-related differences. For each set of twins, the environment is going to be largely the same. Siblings might have differences because of parents' experience in child-rearing, parents' job-related stress, marital conflict, the political climate in society, and so forth. Also, gender-related differences can be caused by different genes on the X and Y chromosomes and differences in socialization. Finally, because evidence indicates that twins react differently to each other than to older or younger siblings, it is important to control for this effect as well.

To determine if individual differences have a genetic basis, rates of obesity, for example, are calculated for monozygotic and dizygotic twins. If obesity is caused by genetic processes, the weights of monozygotic twins should be closer than the weights of dizygotic twins. Indeed, this is what has been found. Nevertheless, there is still considerable variability among monozygotic twins, especially if they have been raised in different environments. This suggests that, along with genetic processes, the environment also plays an important role. One important experimental procedure to understand the role of learning and cognition is to observe the effects of raising monozygotic twins in different environments.

Brain Design and Motivation

Brain Structure and Brain Circuits

Our brain contains a number of structures linked by nerve pathways. When our sensory receptors are stimulated, these nerve pathways carry the incoming information to various parts of the brain. This incoming stimulation typically triggers memories, which allow us to recognize things that are familiar and important to us; they tell us how to respond appropriately to a given situation or a certain set of demands.

Brain structures generally work in conjunction with one another. When different structures, together with connecting pathways, are aroused simultaneously, we refer to them as *brain circuits*. The current view is that brain circuits cause emotions. For example, the activation of a certain circuit causes fear, the activation of another circuit causes anger, and still another causes euphoria. In other words, each emotion has a distinct brain circuit.

Usually, the activation of a certain brain circuit does not cause behavior or action but, rather, creates the disposition to action. How the individual actually acts

will be influenced by both learned and cognitive variables. With anger, for example, my disposition to retaliate might be modified by such things as memories of how my father dealt with provocations or rules of behavior that I have developed from my own experiences.

Some Examples of Brain Design

Many of the brain systems in humans are general systems. They may have evolved as a specific adaptation; however, there is good reason to believe that they have extended capacity, meaning they can be used for other things. This idea has been called "extended adaptation" and has important implications for understanding why humans can do a number of things including such things as building a high tech society (Nicholson, 1997). In this section we are going to look at a number of brain systems that are important in helping us to understand why we do a wide variety of things including why we are inclined to take drugs, for example.

The Disposition to Experience Pleasure: Reward Systems in the Brain

As well as brain circuits for specific emotions, others appear to facilitate the acquisition of adaptive behaviors. More than 40 years ago, James Olds (1955) found that animals would learn a wide variety of responses to receive electrical stimulation to certain areas of the brain, initially called reward centers. The system of reward centers is now called the *reward pathway* (Figure 2-1). Experience with electrodes inserted in the brain to treat depression indicates that electrical activation of the reward pathway generally—although not always—produces very positive feelings in humans. Drugs such as amphetamines that activate this system are known for their ability to produce feelings of euphoria. Correspondingly, considerable evidence indicates that activation of these pathways tends to reinforce behavior; that is, organisms will quickly learn behaviors that activate this system (Olds & Milner, 1954; Panksepp, 1981).

One of the most basic principles of psychology is that humans (and animals) are motivated to perform actions that produce positive feelings (positive affect).

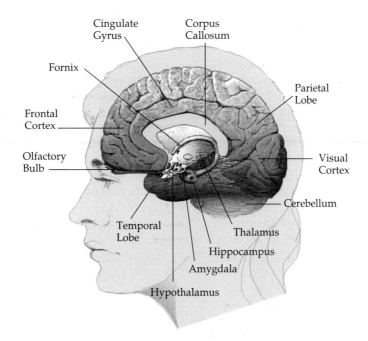

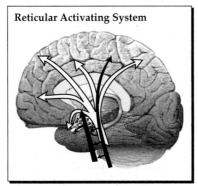

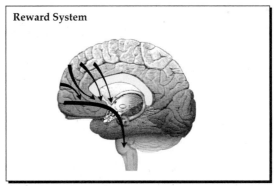

Figure 2-1.   Major structures of the human brain and their relationship to the reward pathway and the reticular activating system.

This mechanism helps humans to learn highly adaptive behavior, such as finding food, but also some less adaptive behavior. For example, recreational drug use produces positive affect but is typically not adaptive (Chapter 7).

The reward pathway is not the only system that is responsible for producing feelings of pleasure. The *limbic system,* a set of interconnected structures deep within the brain that regulates emotions such as fear, love, and anger, is believed to be involved not only in the activation of behavior (dispositions) but also in its reinforcement. Note that the limbic system is triggered in somewhat different circumstances than is the reward pathway. In other words, these systems help us adapt to different environmental demands. (For more details on the limbic system, see Chapter 5.)

Identifying and understanding those biological systems is important because so much of human action seems to be motivated by the desire to experience positive affect (Watson, Wiese, Vaidya, & Tellegen, 1999). With an understanding of these systems, psychologists might be able to help people give up maladaptive behaviors by teaching them to substitute more adaptive ones. Rather than telling teenagers to say no to drugs, which they could find hard to do, it would be better to teach them to get high by engaging in behaviors that have less destructive outcomes. What this often means, for example, is looking for activities that involve elements such as risk and challenge (something we will discuss in greater detail later in this book). Researchers have suggested that it was adaptive for our ancestors to take risks, such as when hunting, and that brain structures or circuits, like the reward center, evolved to ensure our ancestors hunted (Buck, 1999). In effect, when we teach people to select activities that will make them high (experience positive affect), we are telling them to look for the same elements of activities that made our ancestors high (Higgins, 1997). Because general mechanisms evolved rather than specific ones, we do not necessarily have to hunt to get the same high as our ancestors got when they hunted. We can, for example, substitute rock climbing.

The Disposition to Process Information: The Reticular Activating System

To survive, we need to be vigilant in detecting anything that threatens us. We also need to master our environment. We do that by processing information and developing skills. Through mastery, for example, we learn to obtain food and water and gain the opportunity to reproduce. Being vigilant and mastering the environment are generally viewed as highly incompatible activities. Because we only have a limited ability to process information, we don't have the resources to both scour the environment for potential threats and process new information. In addition, we don't have unlimited energy. Keeping two systems activated all the time would take an enormous amount of energy. Ideally, the brain's information-processing systems would respond to immediate demands and then shut down to conserve energy and to do routine maintenance such as rebuilding cells and restoring depleted chemicals.

This energy-saving arrangement is made possible by the reticular activating system (RAS), located at the top of the brainstem (Moruzzi & Magoun, 1949). When there is no incoming information, the RAS shuts down the brain. When the sensory receptors are stimulated, however, the RAS activates the brain and insures that incoming information is analyzed. The RAS does not always activate the brain completely. When the incoming information is very familiar, for example, the brain is only partially activated. If a threat arises, however, the brain is fully activated to deal with it.

New or novel information of any kind almost always activates the brain. The brain analyzes new developments for any signs of a threat and also for purposes of gaining mastery over the environment. In this way, our brain maximizes our chances of survival.

Other systems within the brain that are devoted to arousal include the limbic system, which is thought to be more involved in rewards, whereas the RAS is more involved in neuronal organization (Routtenberg, 1968).

The Role of Neurotransmitters in Information Processing

Information is transmitted in the brain via nerve pathways. Interestingly, these nerve pathways are not continuous but are made up of short lengths of nerve fiber separated by gaps called *synapses*. Information must somehow cross these gaps to travel along the pathway. Researchers have found that, when the nerve pathway is activated, chemicals called neurotransmitters are released and carry the information across the synapse (Figure 2-2).

Figure 2-3 presents a classification of the many neurotransmitters in the brain. We will mainly be concerned with the biogenic amines. Note that, for each type of neurotransmitter, there are several different receptors. For example, there are ten types of receptors for serotonin, at least five for dopamine, and several alpha and beta types for norepinephrine. The combination of different neurotransmitters and different receptors

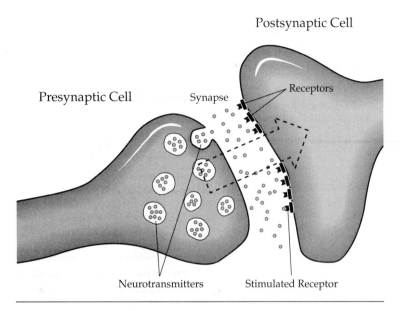

Figure 2-2.   Neurotransmitters are released from presynaptic cells into the synapse to stimulate receptors on the postsynaptic cells.

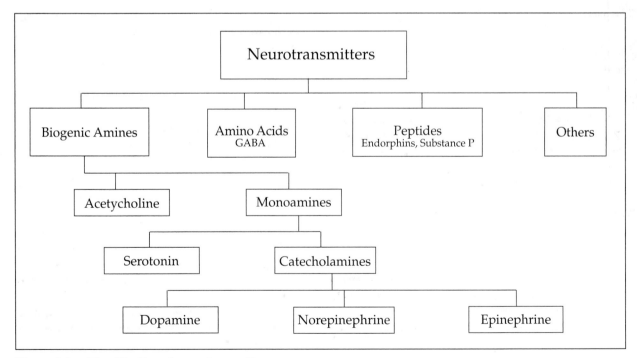

Figure 2-3.   Classification of neurotransmitters.

Table 2-1. The effect of certain neurotransmitters on moods.

Neurotransmitter	Some Effects on Mood
1. Serotonin	Low levels linked to negative mood (depression); high levels linked to positive mood (euphoria).
2. Dopamine	Low levels linked to negative mood (depression); high levels linked to positive mood (euphoria). Many recreational drugs (such as amphetamine) trigger dopamine release.
3. Norepinephrine (also known as noradrenaline)	Low levels linked to negative mood (depression); high levels linked to positive mood (euphoria).
4. Epinephrine (also known as adrenaline)	High levels linked to brain activation; no direct link to mood.

helps account for the ability of the brain to perform a wide range of complex functions (Kalat, 1995).

An important feature of neurotransmitters is that, once they have carried a message across the synapse, they are typically inactivated; this ensures that they do not excite the postsynaptic neuron indefinitely. The inactivated neurotransmitter is reabsorbed by the presynaptic neuron, synthesized back into an active state, and stored in vesicles ready for release. In certain cases, the synthesis of a neurotransmitter involves proteins from foods that we eat. In other words, diet can play a role in the availability of neurotransmitters.

Neurotransmitters and Moods

Many neurotransmitters are also involved in the regulation of moods. Norepinephrine, for example, has been linked to feelings of euphoria and depression. When the norepinephrine level at the synapse is high, we feel euphoric; when it is low, we feel depressed. Various drugs, such as the tricyclic antidepressants and cocaine, create a positive mood by maintaining a high level of norepinephrine in the synapse. Table 2-1 summarizes some of the mood effects linked to neurotransmitters.

GABA (gamma-aminobutyric acid), an amino acid neurotransmitter, plays an important role in regulating anxiety and information processing. (The relationship between anxiety and information processing is discussed in Chapter 5.) Two of the peptide neurotransmitters, endorphins and substance P, play an important role in the experience of pain. Endorphins have analgesic (painkilling) properties and have also been linked to positive moods. Heroin and morphine trigger endorphin release (Chapter 7). Substance P is involved in the transmission of pain information; painkillers block its action.

We are only beginning to understand how mood and adaptive behaviors are linked. In general, negative moods tend to be associated with attention to, or memory of, threatening stimuli, whereas positive moods tend to be linked to attention to, or memories of, opportunities and possibilities (for example, exploratory behavior). Which comes first is not clear. Perhaps both are triggered by the activation of a certain brain circuit (Buck, 1999).

Because they are relatively easy to monitor, moods can play an important role in helping us to understand and redirect our behavior. The ability to monitor moods is important in stress management, for example. By recognizing our moods and understanding what causes them, we can learn to alter our behavior or environment to regulate our moods and attention. Moods, in other words, might have evolved to help us self-regulate. Thus, rather than curse at negative moods, we should view them as something to be cherished because they give us feedback that something is amiss (Buck, 1999).

Summary

Motivation is concerned with understanding how dispositions can lead to actions, through the interaction of biological, learned, and cognitive processes. These processes are known collectively as components of motivation. Ample evidence from a variety of sources indicates that human behavior is not infinitely flexible, as some learning theorists have argued, nor is it totally preprogrammed.

Evolutionary psychologists suggest that our behavior is due to the design of our brain, a design that evolved to help our ancestors adapt to their environment some 150,000 to 250,000 years ago. According to the principle of extended adaptation, we are able to use this "old" brain to adapt to our present environment.

Temperament is a good example of what is meant by brain design. Temperament presumably was an adaptation that allowed our ancestors to better deal with a hostile world. We know from research that what starts out as temperament becomes personality. Although personality has its roots in temperament, and therefore bears a certain resemblance to temperament, it is more complex and because of that complexity, we are better able to respond appropriately to our present environment.

Two important general brain systems that are involved in a wide range of motivated behaviors are the reward system and the arousal system. The existence of general reward systems and arousal systems suggests that humans are capable of learning a number of new behaviors not specifically dictated by their genetic structure. In addition to these two systems are the neurotransmitters. Neurotransmitters have been implicated in a wide range of motivated behaviors and therefore it is important for us to understand what they do.

The Learned Component

Attention and Learning

What we learn is governed, to a very large degree, by attention. For psychologists, attention consists of three interrelated processes. First, humans need to focus their sensory receptors on a source of information (stimulation) to analyze that information. We sometimes call this type of attention *attending* or *receptor orientation*. Second, even when organisms focus their attention on a given source of information, they selectively process only part of the incoming information. This is called *selective attention;* it is related to the individual's mindset. If I'm hungry, for example, I'm likely to process food-related information, even though other information is present. Third, because we are limited in our ability to process information, we often cannot deal effectively with vast amounts of information or complex topics. One way we deal with vast amounts of information is to look for the underlying organization. Among other things, we look for things that can be grouped or chunked. One reason we hire guides when we travel is to help us deal with the complexity of the new environment. Guides help us to focus on what they think we should see and learn (selective attention). In addition, they often provide information that helps us to organize and make sense out of the information impinging on our receptors. We use words such as *perception, meaning,* and *understanding* to denote the idea that we are grasping the underlying organizational properties of the situation. What we remember are images, themes, and stories; rarely do we remember random, unrelated pieces of information (Kahneman, 1973; Navon & Gopher, 1979; Norman & Bobrow, 1975; Wickens, 1984).

Good teaching involves maximizing all three types of attention. First, a teacher aligns the desks toward the front of the room to ensure sensory receptors are oriented on what the student is supposed to learn. Second, the teacher tells the students what they need to focus on and what to ignore. Finally, the teacher helps students to organize the material—for example, by providing lists or themes that link various elements of the material in some way. The teacher may also encourage her students to create their own organization by looking for personal meaning. A good way to link things together so that you can remember them is to create a story.

Associative and Cognitive Learning

Generally, when we talk about learning, we mean what psychologists call associative learning. Historically, psychologists have conceptualized these processes as *S-R learning,* the connection or association of stimuli and responses. Such learning processes depend on the first two types of attention and form the subject of the present section.

In the next section, I will discuss cognitive learning, which is the process of organizing information to construct meaning. This type of learning, studied by cognitive psychologists, depends on the third type of attention. As individuals, we often start to make sense out of the world through associative learning processes but, as things become more complex, we find it necessary to rely more and more on cognitive processes.

Let's now turn our attention to associative learning and the types of attention on which it depends: receptor orientation and selective attention.

Is Attention Under Voluntary Control?

Attention is only partially under voluntary control. When something new is introduced into the environment, for example, attention will typically shift to that new source of stimulation. If we cannot process the information because we lack the ability to comprehend it, our attention is likely to move on. Likewise, if we have processed the same information on some previous occasion, our attention will shift to something else. When this happens, we subjectively report that we are bored. When our attention shifts, so does our learning. Thus, managing attention is the key to effective learning.

To the best of their ability, teachers attempt to present material at the optimum pace: not so fast that they lose the slow learner and not so slow that they lose the fast learner. Children with attention deficit/hyperactivity disorder are extremely distractible. Among other things, they seem unable to ignore most external stimuli. As a result, they often cannot learn in a regular classroom setting. Bright children sometimes have difficulty maintaining their attention in class because they shift their focus to other things when they have extracted all the information presented to them.

Practical Application 2-1

Becoming Aware of Your Biological Processes

People can become aware of many of their biological processes. Peter Suedfeld (1975) found that people who spent long periods of time under conditions of sensory deprivation often became aware of some of their physiological responses, such as their heart rate and respiration (see Chapter 3). He suggested that, under conditions of sensory isolation, people begin attending to their physiological responses because they have nothing else to arouse their attention. More important, perhaps, he found that, as a result of their sensory isolation experience, they were less affected by stress at a later time. The reason they experienced less stress, he argued, was that they had learned to control those responses. In short, they had learned the basic techniques of relaxation, one of the main ways to alleviate stress.

Considerable research shows that one of the first steps in learning to control your physiological responses is to become aware of them. In relaxation training, for example, people are often first taught to contract a certain set of muscles (in their arm, for example) and then to relax them. In contracting and then relaxing a group of muscles, people typically become aware of those muscles and how to control them. As a result, when they become tense, they can focus on those muscles and relax them at will. People can even learn to monitor and control their brain waves. When hooked to a machine that records brain waves (an electroencephalograph, or EEG) and allowed to monitor their brain waves on a screen, they can learn to produce alpha waves, which have been linked to a state of relaxed awareness. To produce alpha waves at will, people can learn to recreate the psychological state that is linked to alpha waves. Thus, when they are in a state of relaxed awareness, they know, based on past learning, that their brain is likely to be producing alpha waves.

We can become directly aware of our heart rate, respiration, and the tenseness of our muscles, but we can only become indirectly aware of certain other biological processes. Take, for example, the reward pathway in the brain. This pathway has been linked to moods: When it is activated, we experience positive moods or feelings of euphoria, whereas when it is not active, we tend to experience negative moods or even feelings of depression. One way to become indirectly aware of your reward pathway is to monitor how positive or negative you feel.

Chemicals called neurotransmitters carry messages across synapses in the brain. Without them, it would be impossible to think or process information. These neurotransmitters tend to become depleted as a result of intense mental activity, stress, or even drinking alcohol. When this happens, thinking becomes sluggish. By monitoring

Because attention is not always under our control, psychologists make a distinction between deliberate (intentional) and incidental (passive) learning. At times, we deliberately set out to learn something. For example, I might deliberately focus my attention on the way a person swings a golf club; or I might deliberately rehearse a phone number so that I can recall it at a later time. At other times, our learning is more incidental. Relaxing in front of the television, for example, I might learn how to rescue someone who has fallen in a fast-moving stream or how to cook squash. Neither of these two pieces of information might have any immediate interest to me; nonetheless, I might store them away and draw on them later when I need them.

Because the amount of information we can process is limited, we often shift our attention back and forth to learn two things simultaneously. In a conversation, for example, we might shift our attention to a person entering the room and then shift back to the person talking. During that brief time, we might fail to process part of the conversation. Then we either try to fill in the missing portion or apologize for our lapse. We are not always aware that our attention is shifting in this way.

To some degree, we can learn to attend to two different sources of stimulation by this technique. For example, we can focus on something in the foreground while monitoring something in the background; or we

your ability to think clearly, you can indirectly monitor the release of neurotransmitters in your brain. At various times throughout the day, estimate how well you can think or process information. This will give you some idea of the level of your neurotransmitters.

Another interesting exercise is to try to fire neurons in your brain by creating visual images (Crick & Koch, 1992). Because neurons fire only when an electrical threshold is crossed, you will be more likely to fire neurons in your visual cortex if your images are very detailed. First, create an image that you find very relaxing, such as sitting by a creek in summer, and then monitor your heart rate, your respiration, and your mood. Next, imagine a situation that would cause a stress response, such as seeing a spider walk across your arm or leaning over a balcony on the 40th floor of a building. Again, monitor your heart rate, your respiration, and your feelings. Try alternating between a relaxing and a stressful image and see how your reactions change. In this exercise, you are not only firing neurons in your brain, but also inducing the release of a variety of chemicals that have been linked to relaxation and to stress. The more you practice doing this, the more you will become aware of your own biology.

People in the western hemisphere are raised to ignore their biological processes or to treat them as distinct from mental processes. This is sometimes called the dualistic

paradigm (Langer, 1989). We begin to become more aware of our biological responses when we understand that they are directly linked to our mental processes.

One thing that characterizes humans is their ability to monitor affective states (feelings). Buck (1999) has suggested affective states can be viewed as voices of the genes. He argues that the way genes influence, persuade, or cajole us to do all the things we do is by creating affect. While we normally ignore these affective states, because they are at a low intensity, we nonetheless can monitor them. As Buck points out, when they are at high intensity, they are difficult to ignore and, as a result, we feel compelled to react. If affect is a voice of our genes we can come to know a great deal about our genes by deliberately focusing on our affective states. Buck suggests that there are two classes of affect: selfish affect and prosocial affect. Try focusing on your selfish affect and see if you can label some of your feelings. Are you sad, happy, frustrated, content, energized, for example? Next, try focusing on your prosocial affect. Prosocial affect is normally aroused in a social context. See if you can label some of your emotions. Ask yourself if you are experiencing any guilt, shame, empathy, envy, or jealousy.

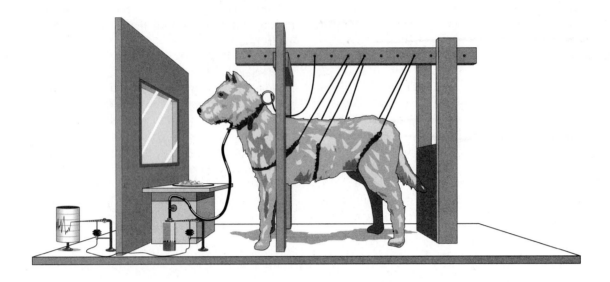

Figure 2-4.   A typical Pavlovian setup.

can focus our eyes on one thing while listening to something else. Our ability to do so is limited mainly by the amount of information contained in the two sources of stimulation and the amount of time available. If the foreground provides considerable information to process, for example, we will not process information in the background. If we are presented with complex visual information, we might have little attention left over for auditory stimulation. Given unlimited time, people will often demonstrate that they can readily do two or even more things simultaneously.

The point I want to emphasize is that learning depends on attention processes and therefore, to understand what people learn, we need to understand what controls and limits attention. Because attention is governed partly by motivational processes, what we learn can often be understood, at least partly, in motivational terms (Simon, 1994).

Now it's time to begin our survey of learning theories, with Pavlov's classic work on conditioning.

Classical Conditioning

Ivan Pavlov (1849–1936) (1927) discovered classical conditioning when he found that dogs could be taught to salivate at the sound of a bell if the bell was rung whenever food was presented (Figure 2-4). According to Pavlov's analysis, food is conceptualized as an unconditioned stimulus (US) that naturally leads to the unconditioned response (UR) of salivation. The bell does not normally elicit salivation but, when paired with food (preferably a half-second before the food is presented), it acquires the ability to do so, because it is a reliable predictor that food is forthcoming. Pavlov found that, after several pairings of bell and food, the bell elicited salivation even when no food was presented. In such circumstances, we say that the bell has become a conditioned stimulus (CS). The response elicited by the CS is called the conditioned response (CR). In general, the CR is not as strong as the UR. If the CS (the bell) is repeatedly presented in the absence of the US (the food), it will eventually lose its ability to elicit the response. The procedure of repeatedly presenting the CS in the absence of a reward or the US is called *extinction*.

Note that experiments demonstrating classical conditioning in the laboratory were arranged to increase the likelihood that the experimental subject (in this case, the dog) would attend to the relevant stimuli (in this case, the food, and the bell). For example, animals were restrained so that they faced a given direction, and extraneous forms of stimulation were removed. Think of trying to replicate this experiment in the forest with rabbits running about.

Conditioning and Adaptive Behavior

Classical conditioning is crucial for adaptive behavior. Many organisms, including humans, depend on relatively innocuous signals to warn of threats to survival. Thus, it is imperative to accurately identify those signals. According to current thinking, classical conditioning involves more than simple S-R associations (e.g., Rescorla, 1988). The study of humans and animals suggests that organisms often act as sophisticated statistical evaluators of information; they select out those aspects of the situation that predict the presence or absence of other significant events (e.g., Basic Behavioral Science Task Force, 1996).

An interesting feature of conditioning is illustrated by a phenomenon known as *blocking*. If an animal is given a tone as a signal for a forthcoming electric shock, it will quickly learn to associate the tone with the shock. It will learn, for example, to make an avoidance response when the tone is presented. If a light is then presented together with the tone, the animal is inclined to treat the light as redundant and not to respond when the light is presented alone. In other words, the prior association of the tone and the shock will block the learning of the light-shock association (Kamin, 1968). This is consistent with other studies showing that the information value of the stimulus is what produces learning (Rescorla, 1988). The simple pairing of two events is not sufficient to produce classical conditioning. What is needed to account for learning is some additional concept—such as attention or information processing—that describes how organisms selectively attend or selectively process information (e.g., Kahneman, 1973; Navon & Gopher, 1979; Norman & Bobrow, 1975; Wickens, 1984).

Context and Conditioning

Associations are formed not just between the primary events that psychologists present, such as the CS and the US, but also between these events and the situation in which the conditioning takes place. This finding has helped us to understand a wide variety of findings, including research on drug addiction. Perhaps one of the most interesting findings about drug addiction is that drug effects are, to a very large degree, under situational control. The urge to use drugs, for example, appears to be triggered by the environment. Change the environment and the urge seems to disappear. Following the Vietnam war, only 15% of heroin users in the U.S. military became addicted again after returning to their homes (Basic Behavioral Science Task Force, 1996). It is also known that users need greater amounts of the drug to experience a high when they are in a familiar environment than they do in a new environment. In fact, heroin users taking their usual dose of the drug in a new environment have been known to die from an overdose. According to the opponent process theory of drug addiction, heroin and related drugs trigger an opponent process that neutralizes their effects. Research suggests that this opponent process can be conditioned to environmental cues. Thus, when a heroin user enters a familiar environment, the opponent process will immediately be triggered. This means the user will have to take greater amounts of heroin to override the opponent process. Should that same drug user inject heroin in an unfamiliar environment, the initial effects of the heroin would be strong because the opponent process would not be in place. The heroin itself would eventually trigger the opponent process, but it might be too late to prevent an overdose.

Instrumental Learning

In instrumental learning, organisms learn that certain environmental events, such as receiving rewards or punishments, depend on their own behavior. Certain foods can be rewarding (reinforcing) to an animal if it is hungry or if the food stimulates one of the sensory systems associated with food intake. Figure 2-5 compares classical conditioning and instrumental learning. What is particularly interesting about rewarded behavior is that, in many cases, the behavior will continue at a high rate even if the reward is removed. A nonrewarded response will eventually diminish in rate or strength. This process is called extinction. One way to make a response continue in the absence of reward is to offer *partial reinforcement* of the behavior—that is, instead of rewarding the behavior on every trial, to reward the behavior on only some of the trials.

Secondary Rewards and Instrumental Learning

If a reward is to be effective, it must be applied as soon as possible after the desired behavior has occurred. *Primary reinforcers* such as food are often very effective as rewards for behavior, especially in training animals. A

Classical Conditioning	Instrumental Learning
Teaching a dog to salivate to a bell	*Teaching a dog to sit on command*

UCS (food)	→	UCR (salivation)	S ("Sit")	→	R (dog sitting), reward
CS (bell)	→	CR (salivation)			

1. The optimal conditions for producing conditioning are to present the CS (conditioned stimulus) about 0.5 sec before the UCS (unconditioned stimulus).

2. In this type of learning, the CS becomes a signal that the UCS is about to be presented. The UCR (unconditioned response) is automatically elicited by the UCS. The CR (conditioned response) is typically weaker, but it is the same response.

3. If the UCS (food) is not presented, the response will eventually extinguish.

1. The optimal conditions for producing instrumental learning are to present the reward immediately after the desired R (response) is made.

2. In this type of learning, the S (stimulus) becomes the signal to perform an R. Getting the R to occur may require shaping (for instance, putting the dog into a sitting position).

3. If the reward is not presented, the response will eventually extinguish.

Figure 2-5. Comparison of classical conditioning with instrumental learning.

---

primary reinforcer is something with the capacity to increase a response independently of any previous learning. Thus, we do not have to be taught the reward value of eating food, particularly when we are hungry. However, primary rewards are not very practical as reinforcers of many human behaviors. It's hard to imagine a university professor offering little pieces of candy to a student each time the student does well on a test. For humans, *symbolic* or *secondary rewards*—for instance, writing "Very good" or a big A on a test paper —often prove more effective than primary rewards.

Why do these symbolic or secondary rewards actually work? There are at least two lines of thinking. One is that various forms of praise acquire reward value because they have been associated with the presentation of a primary reward. For example, when your dog sits up and you offer a little piece of meat as a reward, you may say, "Good dog." After a time, the phrase "Good dog" acquires reinforcing properties, through the principles of classical conditioning, because it has been paired with the presentation of the primary reward. For this reason, researchers have suggested that we can refer to secondary rewards as "conditioned incentives" (White, 1996). When you were a child, your parents did the same thing when they fed you. As a result, when they express praise for you now,

it makes you feel good, just as the food you ate as a child made you feel good. The second line of argument is simply that, as a thinking being, humans know that "Very good" or an A at the top of their paper means that they are acquiring a skill that has value. This skill can be used to earn money or simply to earn love and respect from people who matter to them.

Social Incentive Theory

The principles of classical conditioning and instrumental learning form the basis of social incentive theory. According to social incentive theory, positive (rewarding) experiences often occur when we do what others want us to do. For example, we often experience approval in connection with primary rewards such as money, food, clothing, affection (for example, hugging) and permission to watch television. Approval, in other words, takes on great significance; it signals that other primary rewards are forthcoming. Similarly, disapproval takes on great significance. Typically, we experience disapproval in connection with such things as withdrawal of money, having to go without dinner, physical punishment, and withdrawal of privileges such as watching television. Therefore, we learn to avoid disapproval, because it signals the withdrawal of primary rewards (Bandura, 1991b).

Seeking approval and avoiding disapproval are assumed to be central motivators for humans. One reason for their durability as motivators is that they are somewhat unpredictable (Bandura, 1991a). Research has shown that, when reinforcement is intermittent, stimuli retain their ability to act as motivators. Later in life, we continue to seek approval and avoid disapproval. Disapproval can arouse in us the fear that we will lose our job or privileges, while approval arouses in us the expectation that rewards such as promotions or pay raises will be forthcoming.

Much of what we have called the learned component of motivation has its roots in social incentive theory. For example, some children learn to eat more than others do because it earns them approval from a parent

who eats too much. Some people use physical aggression to get their way because they received social approval for such behavior as children. We learn to control our sexual impulses, at least in part, from a desire to please parents or significant others in society.

Once we have learned something, it is often difficult to change our behavior. Practical Application 2-2 points out some reasons why it is difficult to change and how we can use intention to help us change.

Learning and Memory

For some time scientists have been interested in establishing the links between learning and memory. Some of the questions that have been addressed over the years are these: Are there several memory systems or is

Practical Application 2-2

The Need for Intention and Planning When Changing Unwanted Habits—Taking Charge Through Self-Regulation

We talk a great deal in motivation about the fact that acquired behaviors (habits) are often difficult to change. There are three basic reason for this. First, old habits are not only easy to initiate but easy to execute. Second, they are often cued by the environment, which means they are automatically initiated and executed when we find ourselves in a certain environment. Third, habits are often consistent with short-term motivation (Ouellette & Wood, 1998). It feels good to smoke, for example. Thus, even with good intentions we often find ourselves a slave to our pasts.

One thing that we need to do to change a behavior is to somehow impede existing habits while we are forming new ones that will eventually replace them. Otherwise, what we will find is that we automatically execute the old habit before we have a chance to practice the new one (Ouellette & Wood, 1998). Take, for example, something as simple as learning to take your shoes off when entering your house. If that is something you have not done in the past, it might take some time for you to notice that you are wearing

your shoes as you move about your house. One way to impede the old habit would be to deliberately leave something, like an umbrella, on the floor of your entry. It would be difficult not to step on, so it would be a reminder that you need to remove your shoes.

We execute many habits without thinking. The process by which we learn to take charge of our behavior is called self-regulation. One of the many things we do in self-regulation is set new goals. To achieve those goals we often need to develop new habits, which means, among other things, giving up old habits. Later in this book (Chapter 14) I will talk more about how to implement intentions. For now, let me simply point out that intentions can and often do play an important role in the learning process, something that psychologists are coming more and more to accept.

The fact we can intervene in our own learning is a good illustration of how various components of motivation and interact and work together to produce adaptive behavior.

there only one memory system? Where is/are these memory systems located in the brain? If there is more than one system, do they communicate? What is the relationship of memory and motivation? What is the relationship between memory and cognition?

Multiple Memory Systems

Current evidence indicates there are at least three memory systems and that they can communicate with each other. Further, it appears that each of these systems has evolved to serve a somewhat different function. According to a model that has its roots in empirical research, White and MacDonald (in press), suggest that incoming information flows through each system but each system only extracts and stores certain information depending on what the system was designed/ evolved to do. The fixed processing style of each system determines what can be stored in that system. According to this model, these systems can work in concert to meet the demands of a particular situation. As a result, individuals are equipped to deal with a wide range of situations.

Hippocampal System (S-S Learning)

This system is involved in forming relationships among cues or events. This system allows the individual to link together stimulus dimensions such as color, size, smell, taste, location, and time. As a result of this system, we can form a representation of the environment that we sometimes call a spatial map. This form of learning was originally referred to as "cognitive" learning because it did not require the acquisition of a response (Tolman, 1948). S-S traditionally refers to the association or linking of one or more stimuli, such as in the formation of a spatial map.

From a motivational perspective, this system is valuable because it allows us to engage in "win-shift" behavior. Should I run out of food in one location, for example, I can shift to another, or should I find one escape route blocked, I can use another. Unlike conventional reward learning, where a person tends to keep going to the same location until such behavior is extinguished, the individual can quickly shift his or her di-

rection of behavior by drawing on stored information that pertains to the location of various incentives.

The theory suggests that organisms are capable of selecting among the various alternatives by weighing their respective incentive value. Thus, the hippocampal system not only acts as a store, it assists the individual in making choices.

Dorsal Striatum System (S-R Learning)

This system is important in forming habits (instrumental learning). Psychologists have for some time viewed the formation of habits as integral to survival. In the formation of habits we practice and perfect new behaviors so they will occur with a high probability. After executing a response repeatedly in the presence of a certain stimulus, this response more or less becomes automatic (not dependent on conscious thought). This is the type of learning that Hull (1943) investigated and described in his theory.

From a motivational perspective, it is very adaptive to develop habits. When behavior becomes automatic, the individual is free to think about and even do other things. Moreover, habits ensure that the individual will perform an adaptive response when a particular stimulus arises. Habits not only ensure we engage in adaptive approach behaviors (such as going to the refrigerator when hungry) but that we also engage in adaptive avoidance behaviors (learning not to touch a hot stove). In contrast to win-shift, this kind of learning can be characterized as "win-stay." It worked in the past, so do it again.

Amygdala System (S-Rf Learning)

This system is important for conditioning both approach and avoidance responses. It corresponds to Pavlov's (1927) system and is commonly referred to as classical conditioning. This system differs from S-R learning in that the response does not have to be performed or learned. This system differs from S-S learning because the stimuli involved are single cues or stimulus arrays that are treated as single cues.

As some researchers have noted, Pavlovian conditioning is a form of S-S learning that is restricted to associations between neutral stimuli and reinforcers (Rescorla, 1988). Thus, it has been labeled Rf learning. In this type of learning, for example, a fuzzy stuffed animal (S), after being paired with a loud noise that elicits fear (Rf), has the power to trigger the fear response.

From a motivational perspective, this system ensures that an individual will quickly learn to make either approach or avoidance responses. The amygdala has been implicated in the rapid acquisitions of behaviors that are based on biologically significant events. As we will discuss in more detail in Chapter 8, the amygdala is a "quick and dirty system" that can give us an edge when it comes to survival, for example, by telling us to "freeze" or "flee" when threatened.

Memory and Cognition

Viewed in this context, memory is not a passive activity but, rather, an active one. Memory is not simply registering events/information but, rather, is involved in filtering, sorting, and representing that information in some form. As such it acts more like a cognitive process. Further, memory determines to some degree what is or is not significance, and it determines what we do or do not do. As a result of this, the distinction that we often make between learning and cognition is becoming more and more blurred. For this reason, I often combine research pertaining to learning and cognition under a single heading even though they have traditionally been treated as two distinct processes. Until the research that has led to this and other theories filters down into the mainstream, we will likely retain this distinction a bit longer. In the next section, we will discuss some of the traditional views of what we mean when we use the term *cognitive*.

Summary

Most learning theorists agree that all learning is governed by attention. We cannot attend to everything, so we learn certain things but not others. Attention is only partially under our control; we have been programmed, to some degree, to attend to things that might threaten our survival.

Learning is an associative process. Two important forms of associative learning are classical conditioning and instrumental learning. Contrary to the assumption that only contiguity between stimulus and response is important for classical conditioning to take place, researchers have shown that information value and not contiguity is the critical feature. This is consistent with the idea that attention is important in learning. However, the fact that context affects the strength of a conditioned response suggests that individuals are conditioned to the situation and not simply to a specific cue or to part of the situation.

Instrumental learning depends on administering a reward. Many things acquire the ability to reward (become secondary reinforcers or conditioned incentives) because they have been associated with a primary reward such as food.

Social incentive theory has its roots in classical conditioning and instrumental learning theories. According to social incentive theory, the desire for social approval is a powerful human motivator. Nonetheless, a great deal of research suggests that we also learn for intrinsic reasons.

Once we have acquired certain habits, it is not always easy to replace those old habits with new, more up-to-date or desired habits. Intentions by themselves often fail to produce the desired response.

Research suggests that three memory systems are involved not only in what is processed but also in what is stored. These memory systems can be viewed as active systems that have many cognitive qualities.

The Cognitive Component

In psychology, cognitive processes are those associated with knowing. Cognition, therefore, involves thinking, perceiving, abstracting, synthesizing, organizing, or otherwise conceptualizing the nature of the external world and the self. Cognitive theories are typically framed in terms of having or developing cognitive structures that allow us to make sense of the complexity of the world.

Cognitive processes are often conceptualized by the third aspect of attention discussed earlier. Humans are unable to process limitless amounts of information.

Therefore, we need to develop cognitive structures that will reduce the complexity of the information we encounter. We do this by finding higher-order relationships, structures, principles, and rules. In other words, we process something other than the raw sensory information that falls on our receptors; we process the inherent order that summarizes that raw sensory information. Memories, therefore, have to do with order and structure.

Where do we get this organization and structure? Some is given to us by our sensory system; we are born with the ability to see a figure as distinct from a background, for example. Part of it comes from learning; we are taught relationships, structure, and rules. Much of it comes, however, from personal discovery. We are brilliantly equipped to find redundancy, for example; this allows us to discard everything but the essential elements. We are also equipped with the ability to create stories that link elements of our experience. It seems that, when we have a story, we don't need to remember the details; we can fill in the details based on schemata stored in our memories.

Cognitive Theories

Jean Piaget's (1896–1980) theory of development is a good example of a cognitive theory. Piaget contended that children are motivated to develop cognitive structures because they need to interact with and master the environment. They begin, he suggested, by simply processing information by whatever structures they have. Piaget called this process *assimilation*. When these structures are no longer complex enough for the child to make complete sense of his or her interactions with the world, the child begins to experience confusion or incomprehension, a state that Piaget simply called *disequilibrium*. He suggested that this state of disequilibrium motivates the child to develop new cognitive structures to make sense of the complexity, a process Piaget called *accommodation*. Development, according to Piaget, is a lifelong process in which we continually move between disequilibrium and equilibrium.

Most, if not all, cognitive theories state or imply that the development of cognitive structures is linked to motivation processes. Most theories suggest that motivation can be conceptualized as some kind of discrepancy between what the individual can presently

Jean Piaget

comprehend and what the individual needs to comprehend to make sense out of the world or simply to fully know. Early cognitive theorists focused on how we can come to know our external world, but recently several cognitive theorists have focused their attention on how we come to know ourselves and how this can lead to the self-regulation of behavior, as we discussed briefly at the end of Chapter 1.

The Nature of Cognitions

In recent years, there have been numerous demonstrations that how we think about ourselves and the world has a profound impact on how we behave. Without attempting a complete overview of this work, the present section offers some basic examples of how cognitions affect behavior.

Note that cognitions are often based on past learning. As children, we learn to categorize, and we develop beliefs and attitudes by imitating and modeling our parents. As we develop, however, we often modify these cognitive structures. Using our own experiences, listening to the experience of others, or studying a carefully designed discourse (a lecture or a book, for example), we alter our beliefs. These changes are typically the result of a cognitive process. One interesting aspect of cognition is the tendency to make things consistent. We modify beliefs and attitudes so that they are consistent with our values. The result is a new set of cognitive structures that incorporate those values. Although these cognitive structures may seem very similar to those we acquired as children, they often differ from our parents' in subtle but important ways.

This section is organized around the idea that humans are inclined to organize information according to certain rules, principles, and theories that allow them to see the world as consistent and predictable. According to attention theory, we see the world as consistent and predictable because we have developed structures for processing all incoming information. We do not wake up each morning and attempt to view the world through the raw sensory information falling on our receptors; rather, we see it with the same eyes that saw it yesterday, last week, last year. It takes a great deal of change in the environment before we change our ideas. Sometimes, we need to be faced with some adversity before we will take a second look. The bottom line is that, once our cognitive structures are formed, they are very resistant to change. In a sense, we have learned to be lazy. We trust our cognitive structures even when they are no longer in harmony with the world.

Categories and Labels

The brain has evolved to identify the main characteristics of incoming stimulation. By this process, for example, infants learn to recognize the faces of their parents. So that we can make sense out of the complex world in which we live, the brain has been designed or organized not only to isolate features (a figure as opposed to a background, for example) but also to identify abstract qualities that define a thing or group of things.

For example, the defining attributes of the category comprised of animals include life, legs, and a body. Horses, cows, and dogs are subsets of this category, each with their own defining characteristics. Behavioral neuroscientists suggest that, when a distinct combination of neurons is repeatedly fired, it forms an interconnection (or a pattern in the brain), to which we attach a name. These distinct patterns are not just the product of the external environment, but also involve memories. When we can't see something—perhaps because another object is blocking our view—we fill in the missing information by drawing on our generic memory (a collection of schemata), which contains the essential or defining features of a category (Crick & Koch, 1992). Categories, in other words, allow us to summarize complex information into more generic forms, thereby freeing us from the necessity of having to keep track of endless pieces of specific information. We label these categories appropriately as house, dog, mountains, and so forth. This is where learning enters the picture.

Categories and labels not only help us identify objects or things, but also help us identify dispositions, emotions, or behaviors—anger, happiness, sadness, or aggression, for instance. Think for a minute how important it is that we are able to do this. Let's say that I am standing in the hallway and someone steps on my toe. I ask myself how I should classify and label this behavior. If I label it as clumsy, I can forget it. If I label it as aggressive, however, it is quite a different matter. Humans, for the most part, feel that they must retaliate for an aggressive act. If I don't retaliate, I may be forced to regard myself as a victim. Thus, how I label someone else's behavior has important implications for how I react to them. If I label another person's behavior as selfish rather than altruistic, I might be inclined to provide a poor job recommendation for that person, especially if the job involved helping children with disabilities. If that same person were applying for a job as a construction worker, however, my perception of the person as more selfish than altruistic might have no effect on my recommendation.

Even more important, perhaps, is how I categorize and label my own behavior. Stanton Peele (1989) has argued that, when people label themselves as alcoholic, they begin to behave like an alcoholic; they lose control of drinking, for example. In his view, it is the label, and not the alcohol, that creates the behavior. Research has shown that people who drink as heavily but do not label themselves as alcoholic behave differently; they do not lose control of their drinking, for example. Peele argues that, in our culture, there is an association between being an alcoholic and the tendency to lose control when drinking alcohol. Thus, the label I use to describe myself can be very important because labels carry with them a wide range of prescribed behaviors that I will unwittingly follow.

Cognitive psychology suggests that we have the power to select labels. That is, we can discover what is associated with a label and so determine whether it is useful. Thus, cognitive psychology does not deny past learning but contends that we need not be governed solely by it. We can redefine what a label means, just as we redefine our beliefs and attitudes.

Beliefs, Attitudes, and Values

As we develop, we learn many of our beliefs, attitudes, and values from our parents. We come to believe, for example, that a certain political party is best for us and our country because we have listened to the arguments of our parents and observed how they voted. We may come to value the family or the church because our parents valued them.

Many beliefs, attitudes, and values, however, are based on our own experiences and desires. Take, for example, the question of values—that is, those things that we believe are important to achieving success, happiness, health, and fulfillment. As we experiment with the values of our parents, we might be inclined to change them. We might come to believe, for example, that it is more important to live a full life than a long life. As a result of our new principle, we will begin to behave in very different ways.

Considerable evidence suggests that children and adolescents are actively involved in their own development (Lerner, 1984). An adolescent might, for example, come to appreciate that his or her behavior is leading to the destruction of the environment, which, in turn, will eventually reduce the length or quality of life. As a result, the teenager decides to adopt a lifestyle with a less negative impact on the environment—for example, to recycle bottles and cans, to buy products only from companies with good environmental practices, or to eat organic foods. By changing values, the individual hopes to achieve new goals, not only on a personal level but also for society at large.

According to this distinction, some beliefs, attitudes, and values result from learning (imitation and modeling), whereas others result from cognitive processes (active construction). This distinction is important, although not always easy to make in practice. To change behavior, we often need to change beliefs, attitudes, and values. One way of doing this is to become more mindful of why we are doing or saying something (Langer, 1989). In particular, we can learn to make finer and finer distinctions. Instead of saying, "I hate person X," I might try to identify what it is about person X that I dislike. I might find that I dislike only a couple of things—X's habit of chewing gum and X's hairstyle. Once I can get past those things, I might notice some of X's more likable attributes—kindness and a sense of humor, for example.

One important feature of learning is the tendency to generalize a response learned in one situation to other situations. Generalization has obvious adaptive benefits, but it can also be highly nonadaptive. We can use cognitive processes to eliminate nonadaptive generalizations. Stereotypes (African Americans are good dancers; men are aggressive; women are complainers; Italians are criminals) are classic examples of response generalization. They arise when we try to generalize from a very limited number of instances. Because Michael Jackson is a good dancer doesn't mean that all African Americans are necessarily good dancers. Because we have been exposed to a rash of newspaper articles about homicidal men doesn't mean that all men are violent. Because women on a particular TV show complain a lot doesn't mean that all women are complainers. Because there is a predominance of Italians in the Mafia doesn't mean that all Italians are criminals. Stereotypes, in other words, are a special class of category.

Stereotypes typically arise in the absence of relevant personal knowledge. We simply adopt the beliefs and attitudes of other people. Many of our stereotypes come from parents, teachers, and other significant people in our lives. We have stereotypes about many things, such as how people should or will act at different ages, how people will act if they are religious, and how people will act if they are rich or poor.

Although stereotypes are often relatively stable, considerable research indicates that they can change. They disappear, for example, when we encounter new examples that do not fit the expected category. In that case, we are forced to make finer and finer distinctions. As this happens, the original stereotype (category) proves hopelessly inadequate and the brain rejects it. For a good description of what happens, see Langer (1989). The breakdown of a stereotype is also a good illustration of Piaget's theory of cognitive development.

Cognitive Dissonance Theory

Cognitive dissonance theory has its roots in the idea that people need to experience cognitive consistency (Festinger, 1957). This theory helps to explain why categories, beliefs, attitudes, values, and stereotypes are highly resistant to change. According to cognitive dissonance theory, humans are inclined to process information in such a way that it will be consistent with existing categories, beliefs, attitudes, values, stereotypes, and behavior—in other words, to ignore information that does not fit with existing beliefs and to seek out information that does fit. If we have a stereotype about old people, for example, we will be inclined to ignore exceptions and to process only those examples that are consistent with our beliefs.

One major area of research that grew out of cognitive dissonance theory concerns people's behavior when they have already committed to an action that is inconsistent with their cognitions. For example, what do people do when they have purchased a car and they discover that it is defective? Research has shown that they are inclined to disregard such information or to seek out more positive information. In other words, they are inclined to do whatever is necessary to make their beliefs and attitudes consistent with their actions. A study of smokers' reactions to evidence that smoking is linked to cancer provides a particularly good example. Although nonsmokers were inclined to believe the evidence was reasonably conclusive, smokers were not (Festinger, 1957).

Cognitive dissonance theory has been able to explain, for instance, why people are inclined to become committed to an organization or an individual, even if that organization or individual does not treat them well. One study found that students' liking for a fraternity went up as the severity of the initiation increased. Having consented to behave in ways that are inconsistent with their beliefs about themselves and how they should be treated, individuals need to explain to themselves why they joined that fraternity (e.g., Aronson & Mills, 1959). Their reasoning, it has been suggested, goes something like this: "Why did I dress in that silly outfit and eat raw eggs, oatmeal, and hot sauce while they hurled insults as me? It must be because this is a great fraternity."

Implicit Theories

It has been suggested (Dweck, 1991; Epstein, 1990) that people develop *implicit theories*—hypotheses, models, and beliefs about the nature of the external world (world theories) and about what we need to do to satisfy our desires in this world (self theories). They are called implicit theories because they often exist at the preconscious level. In psychology, if we act at the conscious level, we are fully aware of the reasons for our actions. If we are operating at the preconscious level, by contrast, we could become conscious of the reasons for our actions given the right guidance or perhaps the right set of circumstances (Epstein, 1990).

Unlike scientific theories, which are rational and designed to make sense out of an existing body of facts, implicit theories often involve more irrational and intuitive thinking. Epstein has proposed that implicit theories often come out of a different system for processing information—the *experiential system*.

In the past, psychologists used the concept of expectations to explain why people with different desires, needs, or experiences would see things differently (Bruner, 1992). In recent years, it has become apparent that the concept of expectations is too narrow to explain the complex thought patterns that link individuals' actions to their perceptions of the external world and their conceptualizations of their skills and abilities. Consequently, emphasis has shifted to the concept of implicit theories.

Although they can be learned—at least in part—from modeling the behaviors of others, listening to the views of others, and reading what others have to say, implicit theories are thought to result mainly from our own experiences, our own interactions with the world, and our own successes and failures. In short, they are very personal. More important, perhaps, we think of them as constructed. Presumably, if we constructed them, we can change them.

Habits, Automatic Behavior, and Cognition

Psychologists make a distinction between habits and automatic behavior. *Habits* result from the repetition of some response or sequences of responses. Although some theorists (for instance, Hull) have argued that a drive must be reduced for a habit to be strengthened, others argue that habits simply come from repeating a response over and over and that rewards merely act as an incentive for engaging in repetition (Hull, 1943).

Where do habits come from? According to learning theorists, they grow out of existing behavior. The ability to find food, for example, is assumed to grow out of some type of random behavior. When the organism consistently finds food in one location, the accompanying responses are strengthened over time, and a habit develops.

By contrast, *automatic behavior* has its origins in intentional or planned behavior (e.g., Bargh & Gollwitzer, 1994; Langer, 1989). If I am trying to find my way to a certain part of the city, for example, I might consult a mental map or even write out a set of instructions that tell me how to get there. Interestingly, after repeating the behavior over and over, I no longer need to think about what I intend to do; it becomes automatic. Alternatively, I might construct a set of implicit rules that I will follow when I meet someone new, so that I won't offend him or her. Again, over time I no longer need to think about my intentions.

Automatic behavior is highly adaptive. It allows me to use my limited attention to do other things. For example, while driving to some destination, I can think about what I am going to say when I get there. Sometimes, automatic behavior has amusing outcomes. I have, on occasion, left my house to go downtown and ended up in my parking spot at the university. Initially, the route is the same, and, if I happen to get absorbed in thought, automatic behavior takes me to the university.

Some theorists use automatic behavior as a more inclusive term to denote both habits and automatic behaviors that derive from planned behavior. According to current concepts regarding the nervous system, both types of behavior come from the strengthening of neural circuits in the brain. Existing technology cannot distinguish between circuits in the brain that had their origins in planned or intentional behaviors and those that came from the strengthening of some existing response; perhaps they are the same.

For people new to psychology, it might appear that the distinction between habit and automatic behavior is unnecessary. However, this distinction grows out of a long debate among scientists about whether humans can actually create new behaviors or are simply creatures of conditioning. The concept of automatic behavior, with its aspects of planning and intention, implies that humans can take charge of their own behavior and create a new life for themselves (Higgins, 1997). Early in this chapter, under the section on The Learned Component, we noted that intention, when combined with planning, can be an effective way to replace old habits with new ones. The role of intention and planning, in other words, is setting the stage for learning rather than causing the learning to take place.

An Example: What Causes Happiness?

It has been suggested that happiness depends on whether or not the environment is providing us with satisfying rewards. According to this view, the way to increase happiness in the world is to create a perfect environment. This is one of the basic assumptions of Skinner's learning theory. But what is a perfect environment? To answer that question, you need to ask people what would make them happy. However, people do not agree on the answer.

Cognitive theorists do not focus on changing the environment. They argue that, though obviously important, the environment is often very difficult or even impossible to change. The best thing to do under those circumstances is to change the way you view the environment. This idea was summarized centuries ago by the Roman emperor Marcus Aurelius, who said, "If you are pained by the external things, it is not they that disturb you, but your own judgment of them. And it is in your power to wipe out that judgment now."

According to cognitive theories, what you see or feel depends to a very large degree on your beliefs, attitudes, values, and implicit theories. In our society, we often hold the view (an implicit theory) that we cannot be happy unless our stomachs are full. Yet in countries where there is a chronic shortage of food, people learn to be happy even though their stomachs are not always full. They take pleasure, for example, in being with their families or in laughing when their children tell jokes.

Happiness, in other words, is highly subjective. People often erect barriers that limit their ability to experience happiness. They say to themselves: "I will be happy when I retire" or "I will be happy when I have a sports car" or "I will be happy when I am married."

Many people have decided that they want to experience happiness as often as possible. As a result, they find happiness in simple things such as a cat chasing its tail, a wild flower, rainfall, children playing, a good night of sleep. Some of the happiest people in the

Practical Application 2-3

Becoming Mindful of Your Cognitive Processes

In her book *Mindfulness,* Ellen Langer (1989) makes the case that our behavior is often mindless. We set out for work without thinking about how to get there, yet we arrive safely and on time. Although mindless or automatic behavior is useful, because it frees our conscious mind to think about other things, it often means that we get into ruts; we don't change our habits even when we should. If we want to change, we need to become mindful of our cognitions. When we become mindful, we gain the power to change and to control things. As we'll see later, the ability to control or simply the belief that we can control our destiny is important for physical and psychological health.

How can you become mindful of your cognitions? Here's a simple step: Each time you decide to do something, ask yourself if there is something else you might do instead. Several things happen when you do this.

1. You learn to generate alternatives. Generating alternatives is a creative act and is the basis for all behavioral change. It makes you aware that you have choices.
2. You gain a sense of control. When you make decisions, you become aware that life is not just happening to you; you are making it happen.
3. You learn *how* to make decisions. Decision making takes practice. Once you learn to make decisions about simple things, you will eventually develop

the ability to make decisions about important things.
4. You learn to take control of your thinking process. The more you analyze your thinking, the more you will become aware of your thinking and able to control it.

By forcing yourself to make a conscious decision about things that you do, you slowly become aware that you often do things for reasons. The next time you turn on the television, ask yourself: "Why am I turning on the television? Is there something else I could do?" You can use this technique in every area of your life. If you find yourself making a value judgment such as "I hate living in this city," ask yourself exactly what it is you don't like and if you want to do something about it. This forces you to make finer and finer distinctions. In doing so, you learn to identify what it is that you don't like. Using this approach, you might discover that you don't dislike the city you are living in but rather the neighborhood in which you live, the house, or even the level of traffic. If you come to realize that you hate your neighborhood, rather than the city, you have gained a great deal of power. Now, instead of having to quit your job and leave your friends to be happy, you only have to move to a new house or apartment. You have turned what appeared to be an insurmountable problem into a very manageable one. It all happened because you learned to become aware of your cognitions.

world have come to appreciate simply being alive and experiencing the world after recovering from a serious accident or illness.

According to cognitive theories, happiness is a state of mind; it is the result of decisions we make. We know, for example, that optimists tend to be happier than pessimists do. In general, optimists tend to see what is good, whereas pessimists tend to see what is bad. Research suggests that optimism can be learned. In his book *Learned Optimism,* Martin Seligman (1990), a leading psychologist, describes how we can become more optimistic. It may well be, as Seligman and others have argued, that optimism is the result of our learning a new way of explaining events to ourselves so that bad outcomes do not undermine self-esteem and good outcomes build self-esteem.

Does this mean the external world is not important? Quite the contrary. We gain happiness through our senses, through exercising skills, through mastery, and through social interactions. But we each decide what aspects of the external world will make us happy. There are many ways to stimulate our senses, to exercise competency, and to experience the joys of social relations. If we accept the message of the advertising industry that happiness depends on wearing the right clothes, driving the right car, or drinking the right beverage, we cut ourselves off from many sources of happiness. Many people have found that happiness does not require an abundance of material things. They have learned that happiness can be found, for example, in enjoying nature, in developing friendships, and in helping other people (Myers, 2000).

Individual Differences

The main problem with most early theories of motivation was their failure to account for individual differences. Many theories of the 1950s were about so-called average humans. (A notable exception was Atkinson's theory of achievement motivation; see Chapter 13.) Data averaged from random samples of rats, pigeons, and humans were used to describe how the average person learned. Since then, we have come to realize that most of us don't behave in this way. Humans differ by gender, age, temperament, past conditioning, cognitive structures, momentary stress, goals, and recent failures and successes. These are the factors that we need to understand if we are to explain why different humans do quite different things under the same environmental conditions.

Attribution Theory: Perceiving the Causes of Behavior

Attribution theory is concerned with how humans come to perceive the causes of behavior. To what cause does a person attribute a given behavior? How does a particular individual account for the fact that he failed? How does he account for the fact that he succeeded? When an individual notices that her heart is beating faster, how does she account for that? Will her interpretation affect her subsequent behavior? If someone's perceptions (interpretations) about the cause of behavior affect subsequent behavior, then we have good evidence that cognitive factors are not just secondary or incidental but play a central role in the arousal, direction, and persistence of behavior.

An experiment by Nisbett and Schachter (1966) illustrates how cognitive factors can affect behavior. They showed that humans could be made to tolerate high levels of shock by persuading them that their autonomic responses, such as fast heart rate, were not caused by the shock but, rather, by a pill they had taken. In their experiment, Nisbett and Schachter asked subjects to take a series of electric shocks of steadily increasing intensity and to indicate (1) when the shocks became painful and (2) when the shocks became too painful to tolerate. Before receiving the shocks, the subjects were given a pill. Some were told that the pill would produce hand tremors, palpitations, and other autonomic responses. Others were told that the pill would produce a variety of symptoms that were not autonomic. Actually, the pill was a placebo; it had no physiological effects.

Attribution theory suggests that people are inclined to look for reasonable explanations for their behavior, including autonomic responses. If that is correct, then the subjects who thought the pill would increase autonomic activity would be inclined to attribute their autonomic responses to the pill, whereas the other subjects would be inclined to attribute their autonomic responses to the shock. Subjects who did not attribute their autonomic responses to the shock should be less sensitive to it and willing to tolerate higher levels of shock. Nisbett and Schachter found that, indeed, subjects who were told the pill would produce autonomic responses tolerated shock levels four times as great as did the other subjects. These results indicate that cognitive factors play an important role even in something as basic as the perception of pain.

Because people come from different backgrounds, because they have different experiences, and because they learn to think differently, they react very differently to the same event. Whether they are optimists or pessimists, for example, has important implications for how they will react. In this book, we will repeatedly address the question of individual differences. Let's begin by talking about the distinction between people known as internals and externals.

Locus of Control Theory: Internal and External Causes

Heider (1958) suggested that people can be divided into two categories: those who tend to identify internal causes of their behavior (internals) and those who tend to identify external causes (externals). Internals perceive that the cause of behavior lies within themselves, whereas externals believe that it lies outside themselves. These two groups are said to differ in their locus of control.

One difference between external and internal determinants of behavior is that only actions with internal causes can be regarded as intentional. For example, if I step on your toe, you might arrive at two different conclusions: that I did it intentionally (internal causation) or that it was an accident (external causation). How you assess the situation will, of course, affect how you respond.

Externals are more likely to use an external frame of reference to label an event, whereas internals are more likely to use an internal frame of reference. Because of this difference, internals and externals often react differently to the same environmental event. We will return to this difference later.

Context and Cognition

Humans show a great deal of sensitivity to the situation or context (Bargh & Gollwitzer, 1994). The kinds of things I say, for example, are often tailored to the situation. What I say to my parents is often very different from what I say to friends. Beginning as an adolescent, I might take pleasure in provoking my parents. Later, I

might decide I'd rather soothe them, on the grounds that they have a right to their opinions, just as I have a right to mine. Why not try to make our relationship as good as possible? What is interesting is that, over time, my new behavior becomes automatic. Even though I might fall back into my habit of provoking them, I become steadily better at making good on my original intention. According to the principles of cognition, my behavior could change because I developed a new way of viewing the situation (a new implicit theory).

Earlier, in discussing the learned component of motivation, we saw that drug effects and drug use are influenced by the context and that this could be understood in terms of the principles of classical conditioning. Could my attitudes toward my parents also be explained by the principles of classical conditioning? No, because there is an important distinction between intentional and unintentional (or passive) learning. The learning was initially intentional in the parental example, whereas it was unintentional in the drug use example.

Not everybody is equally sensitive to situational or interpersonal cues. Snyder (1979) has suggested that some people, called *high self-monitors,* are much more sensitive to situational and interpersonal cues and, therefore, are inclined to adjust their behavior to the demands of the situation. *Low self-monitors,* in contrast, tend to be oblivious to situational and interpersonal cues; they tell inappropriate stories or bore you to death with their preoccupations. Although we are not certain of the origins of these two approaches to the world, we do know that the tendency to be a high or a low self-monitor is habitual or automatic; it is something people do without having to think about it. According to self-regulation theories, we learn one pattern or the other (Bandura, 1991a).

Social Incentive Theory and Cognitive Theory

There is a fine line between social incentive theory and cognitive theory. Seeking approval, which is the main theoretical construct within social incentive theory, is viewed as passively conditioned or learned, rather than being intentional. Bandura assumed that people simply imitate or model because they have been reinforced for such behavior. Cognitive theorists, by contrast, assume that people engage in forethought (Bandura, 1991a); they think, analyze, create hypotheses, formulate plans, and set goals. Collectively, we refer to these activities as intentions. We call behavior that results from intentions cognitive.

Summary

Cognition involves thinking, perceiving, abstracting, synthesizing, organizing, or any other process that allows the individual to conceptualize the nature of the external world and the self. According to attention theory, one reason that we develop cognitive structures is that we have limited ability to process information.

Cognitive processes give rise to categories, to which we attach labels. Cognitive processes also give rise to beliefs, attitudes, and values. Stereotypes are categories that develop out of limited information or the tendency to adopt the beliefs and attitudes of other people, especially role models. Beliefs, attitudes, values, and stereotypes are often very resistant to change. One explanation for this can be found in cognitive dissonance theory, which suggests that humans are inclined to process incoming information so that it is consistent with existing cognitions and behavior.

Implicit theories are hypotheses, models, and beliefs that we have about the nature of the external world (world theories) and about what we need to do to satisfy our desires in this world (self theories). Although we are often not fully aware of them, they guide our behavior. Implicit theories can, for example, play an important role in feeling happy or contented.

According to attribution theory, humans have a natural tendency to look for the causes of their behavior. Nisbett and Schachter illustrated the importance of the attribution process in their study of pain (shock). They showed that misattribution (mislabeling) of the source of increased autonomic activity was sufficient to decrease a person's sensitivity to pain (shock). Compared with controls, subjects who thought that their elevated arousal level was due to a placebo pill, rather than to the shock itself, tolerated shock levels four times as high as the controls did.

Humans tend to differ in their tendencies to attribute events to internal factors as opposed to external factors. This tendency helps to account for the wide range of individual differences that we observe. The labels people use frequently provide a clue to the way

What motivates people to run?

they perceive or interpret the cause of an event. Research has shown that the way we label an event—such as someone stepping on our toe—can affect not only how we feel but how we react.

An Example of a Components Approach

To illustrate a components approach to motivation, let's examine the motivation for running.

Motivation for Running

On the surface, running appears to be a straightforward activity. People state that they decide to run to get into shape, to lose weight, or to improve their health. However, there are also less obvious reasons. Some people run, they confess, to get away from their spouses or to avoid having lunch with their colleagues or to escape from the confines of their office or home. So far, all these explanations are couched in avoidance terms. What about the positive reasons? It is hard at first for most people to see the pleasure in puffing and sweating on a hot day or freezing on a cold day but, after they have had a chance to experience the effects of running for some time, they tend to report that it makes them feel good and is a pleasant activity. The question that presents itself is how an activity that appears to demand so much effort—and sometimes pain —can be pleasant.

To answer this question, we need to understand that why people do something initially and why they continue to do it may be unrelated. For instance, most of us have good intentions that somehow fail to get translated into long-term behavioral change. I call this the New Year's resolution phenomenon. People will change their behavior for a day, a week, or even a month, but then fall back to their previous patterns. Once the initial motivation fades, there is nothing to maintain the new behavior.

What, then, is the motivation that maintains running, as distinct from the motivation for taking up running? Although not everyone who tries running persists with it, some people develop signs of being addicted. If they stop running for a few days, they experience a negative physiological or psychological state analogous to drug withdrawal together with a compulsion to engage in the activity on a regular basis (Conboy, 1994). The obvious question is whether running produces in this group of people some kind of chemical output that has motivating and possibly addicting properties.

The answer is a qualified yes. It appears that running or any aerobic exercise—such as swimming, cycling, walking, rowing, and cross-country skiing— stimulates the output of several chemicals. Norepinephrine output, for example, will increase to as much as 4.5 times normal levels (Davis, 1973; Howley, 1976). Increased norepinephrine levels have been implicated in elation and euphoria, whereas low levels have been implicated in depression (Buck, 1999), so it seems that people may run to experience increased outputs of this or related chemicals. Can people become addicted to norepinephrine? Again, the answer is a qualified yes. Addiction to amphetamines, which produce arousal and euphoria, has been documented

for some time. Among other effects, amphetamines stimulate the output of norepinephrine and dopamine, and it has been hypothesized that people take amphetamines specifically for this purpose. It makes sense, therefore, that people will continue to perform a response, such as running, that stimulates the output of one of these chemicals (Pedersen & Hoffman-Goetz, 2000).

Several studies have shown that aerobic exercise alleviates anxiety (e.g., Leedy, 2000; Raglin, 1997) and depression (Leedy, 2000; Martinsen & Morgan, 1997).

Although considerable evidence suggests that running is a rewarding activity for many people and helps many people to cope with such things as anxiety, depression, stress, fatigue, and other negative mood states, it is not clear that running can be classified as an addiction (Leedy, 2000). Some people seem to show a form of withdrawal (report more negative moods) when they can't run, but they don't necessarily show that they will run even though running might have adverse effects on their health, work, social, and family relations (Leedy, 2000). One of the main characteristics of addiction is the tendency to engage in a behavior to the detriment of things such as health, work, social relations, and the family. Nonetheless, evidence indicates that people do run to cope with a variety of negative psychological states. Thus, it seems clear that running can be a highly rewarding activity because running alleviates negative mood states and produces positive ones. As such, running can be viewed as a learned activity that has it roots in a number of powerful biological reward mechanisms. It can be viewed as a habit, one that is triggered by a variety of internal cues (perhaps negative mood states) as well as by external cues (time of day, for example).

So far we have talked about the biology and the learned aspects of running. What about cognition? Many people run or engage in some form of aerobic activity for cognitive reasons, for example health benefits that come from exercise. A growing body of research shows we can decrease the likelihood or progression of a number of health disorders such as heart disease (Gottlieb, 2000) and cancer (Hoffman-Goetz & Husted, 1995). Researchers believe the health of the immune response plays a critical role in cancer. What the exercise research shows is that the immune response is strengthened as a result of exercise and that the effects likely cannot be duplicated with a vitamin supplement (Pedersen & Hoffman-Goetz, 2000). High output of epinephrine and norepinephrine are important in the recruitment of cancer fighting cells (Pedersen & Hoffman-Goetz, 2000). It also appears that exercise does many different things that are beneficial to the heart. Having a good immune response is important given that some heart disease has a bacterial origin. Compelling evidence demonstrates that exercise does reduce cholesterol levels, something that has been implicated for some time in heart disease (Rimmer & Looney, 1997). There is also a growing body of research that indicates exercise can slow down the aging process. In one study, for example, researchers found that men who exercised on a regular basis showed minimal cardiovascular losses over 33 years (Karsch et al., 1999). As we discussed earlier, a form of learning called automatic learning has it roots in intention. Because we have a cognitive goal, we set out to do something because we believe it will result in something positive. We do it even though there might be no immediate biological reward. If there is an immediate reward, it would be more cognitive in nature, a feeling of being virtuous; for example, because I believe I am doing something important. Intentional behavior often results in a habit that we call automatic behavior. After a time we engage in a behavior without having to even think about why we are doing it.

The point I want to emphasize is that because we have scientific research (a knowledge base) that indicates certain behaviors are adaptive, we learn to engage in certain behavior, often in the absence of immediate biological reward. Although many people exercise, what is perhaps regrettable is that many do not. More than 60% of Americans are not regularly active, and 25% are not active at all (Harvard Heart Letter, 2001). In short, it does not appear that we have been biologically programmed to be active. Perhaps what kept our ancestors as healthy as they were, given all the dangers they faced, were the constant demands by the environment to be active. Without those demands we become inactive.

Why don't people exercise if it is so rewarding, and why don't they exercise given that it is so good for us? Let's begin by addressing the first question. Considerable evidence indicates that there are wide individual differences when it comes to experiencing positive affect as a result of running. Among other things, some people are born with low levels of an enzyme called monoamine oxidase and as a result they can experience a greater high from running than others do (Zuckerman, 1994). Some people are born with lower levels of anxiety and depression, which means they would not experience the pleasurable reduction in those negative states should they run. The answer is not as clear for the second question. We are only beginning to understand why some people are better able to fully understand and capitalize on information. As we discussed earlier, people who are not inclined to exercise, for one reason or another, are more likely to disregard information that is inconsistent with their behavior because of cognitive dissonance. Also, some people seem to better understand how to go about implementing intentions. This has to do with the ability to self-regulate behavior.

In the final analysis, when we see someone running, we cannot be sure why they are doing it unless we ask them about their motives. If we talk with them over a period of time, we will find that some do it for the sheer pleasure associated with the activity of running (the chemicals that are released), some do it because of the consequences of running (reduction in anxiety and depression, feeling better or looking better), some because it has become a habit, and some because they have come to believe that in running they will enjoy a healthier and longer life.

Consistent with the idea that the best way to maintain a behavior is to make it rewarding, psychologists often look for ways to get people to somehow enjoy an activity that is good for them. Sometimes people seem to discover on their own why they do an activity. One of the curious and interesting things about humans is that they often come to enjoy the things they do on a regular basis. As I indicated earlier in connection with cognitive dissonance, people are inclined to find reasons why they are doing something that they may not have initially thought worthy of their efforts. People who run for example, talk about the enjoyment they get from being outdoors or how they have come to enjoy the scenery or the company of those with whom they run. That is perhaps why automatic behaviors are often maintained in the absence of the cognitions that gave rise to them. Virtually any activity has some good qualities that can be identified if one looks for them.

Summary

This example illustrates why it is necessary to consider biological, learned, and cognitive factors when we try to explain a particular behavior. Although present in most—if not all—behaviors, biological factors can never be viewed as the sole determinants of human behavior. Humans are exposed to a wide variety of external rewards, which we know have a profound effect in modifying the direction of their behavior. Further, we must recognize that biological factors frequently find their expression because humans have learned a response that stimulates a biological mechanism. Humans also acquire behaviors based on a cognitive analysis of what is good for them. The intentions they implement often become automatic behaviors.

Main Points

1. In studying motivation, we are concerned with understanding how dispositions can lead to action through the interaction of biological, learned, and cognitive processes or components.
2. Evolutionary psychologists are attempting to answer the question of why the brain is designed the way it is.
3. In contrast with sociobiologists, evolutionary psychologists have argued that our social nature has emerged as an adaptation to becoming hunters and gatherers.
4. The disposition to experience pleasure has been linked to reward systems in the brain.
5. The reticular activating system plays an essential role in helping us to process information important to our survival.
6. Neurotransmitters are important not only for information transmission but also for creating the moods we experience.
7. What we learn is largely governed by attention.

8. Attention is not completely under our control and is limited.
9. There are two types of learning: classical conditioning and instrumental learning.
10. Psychologists use the term *cognitive* to refer to processes that have to do with knowing. Cognition, therefore, involves thinking, perceiving, abstracting, synthesizing, organizing, or any other process that allows the individual to conceptualize the nature of the external world and the self.
11. Many of our beliefs, attitudes, and values are often initially copied from our parents; however, they are also based on our own experiences and our own desires.
12. Cognitive dissonance theory has its roots in the idea that people need to experience cognitive consistency. According to cognitive dissonance theory, humans are inclined to process information in such a way that it will be consistent with existing categories, values, beliefs, and behavior.
13. Implicit theories are hypotheses, models, and beliefs that we have about the nature of the external world (world theories) and about what we need to do to satisfy our desires in this world (self theories).
14. Automatic behavior refers to intentional behaviors that have become habitual.
15. Analysis of why people run indicates that all three components—biological, learned, and cognitive—can be important in motivating a behavior.

InfoTrac® College Edition

A great deal of evidence indicates that there are many benefits associated with cooperating. Other than instructing people to cooperate, what can you do to get people to cooperate? Using InfoTrac®, find out what other people have done. (Search word: cooperativeness)

Based on empirical research, various authors have argued that you can achieve greater happiness. Use InfoTrac® to identify five things you can do to achieve greater happiness. (Search words: happiness, joy, enthusiasm)

Chapter Three

Hunger and Eating

- How do humans come to avoid foods that might poison them?
- Why do pregnant women develop aversions to certain foods?
- Why are some foods more appealing than others?
- What makes us feel satisfied or full after we eat?

- Why do so many people tend to become overweight?
- Why do people who have become overweight have difficulty shedding those extra pounds?
- Why is food often associated with celebrations and social gatherings?

From a biological perspective, we eat for three basic reasons. First, we need to have a source of energy. One major source of energy is fat which we get from foods such as milk, meat products, and cooking oils. Another source of energy comes from carbohydrates (also referred to simply as starches and sugars), which we get from eating such foods as bread, pasta, cakes, desserts, and fruits. Finally, proteins, which we get mainly from meat, beans, nuts, and seeds, are a major source of energy.

Second, we need to have the necessary elements for rebuilding cells and manufacturing the various chemicals, hormones, and enzymes that make it possible for the body to perform a variety of functions. The basic element for building cells and manufacturing neurotransmitters is the amino acids that are found in abundance in meats but are also plentiful to some degree in beans and seeds. Proteins also provide a source of vitamins, minerals, and trace elements, but these can also be found in carbohydrates and to some degree in fats. Third, we need be able to remove toxins that often are a by-product of eating various foods. In recent years, we have come to recognize the important role that certain foods such as red fruits and green tea play in removing the toxins from the body. High levels of toxins in the body have been linked to such things as the development of cancer (Weil, 2000).

In addition to the biological function of food, we eat for various social and psychological reasons. We eat, for example, to socialize. Throughout history, food has been integral to the process of celebrating, be it a marriage, a birth, or some achievement or milestone. Food has been integral in forming friendships and reaffirming relationships and commitments. Although the focus of this chapter will be on the basic psychology of eating, we will briefly address the important social and psychological aspects of eating at the end of this chapter.

In this chapter, we are going to focus on four basic issues or questions.

1. How is it that humans rarely die of food poisoning, even though our environment is filled with toxic substances? How do children, for example, learn to avoid toxins? Given that many of the foods we eat harbor toxins either because they have been absorbed by the plant or animals or are carried on the surface, how do we get rid of them?

2. How do humans select foods that will give them the energy they need, as well as provide the constituents necessary for growth and day-to-day functioning? In addition, how do we come to eat foods that aid in toxin removal?

3. Why is it that humans are inclined to become obese? One of the greatest problems linked to eating today is the problem of obesity. Moreover, once one has gained weight, it is not easy to get rid of it. Why is it that people cannot get rid of those extra pounds?

4. Food is often at the center of family gatherings and celebrations. What is the social significance of food?

How Do Humans Avoid Toxins?

In addition to toxins that humans have created, various plants and animals have natural toxins that can make humans sick and even kill them in large amounts. It has been argued from an evolutionary perspective that the reason some plants and animals create toxins was to ensure their own survival (Buss, 1999). In short, if you are not eaten, you can reproduce and pass along your genes.

The Biological Component

Humans have evolved a number of mechanisms to guard against eating natural toxins. The first line of defense is smell and taste. Things that humans find bad smelling or disgusting are often a source of toxins such as human waste or food that has become contaminated or has spoiled (Rozin, 1996). The second line of defense is the gagging, spitting, and vomiting response, which is not random (Buss, 1999). That children dislike vegetables such as broccoli and Brussels sprouts is not an accident. Both vegetables contain allylisothiocynate, a toxic substance for young children (Nesse & Williams, 1994).

During pregnancy, women frequently become nauseated by certain foods and avoid them. Nausea, it has been argued, is a protective mechanism against eating toxins. Instead of digesting foods that make us sick, we involuntarily eject them from the stomach before they can do harm. Through simple conditioning, we learn to avoid similar foods in the future. From this perspective, it follows that perhaps the reason women become nauseated when encountering certain foods is a way of protecting a developing fetus from those foods that might not harm the mother but could harm the offspring (Pinker, 1997).

Research, indeed, supports this hypothesis. Profet (1992) found from synthesizing hundreds of studies that (1) plant toxins that can be tolerated by adults are linked to birth defects and spontaneous abortion; (2) pregnancy sickness is at its highest when the embryo's organ systems are being laid down and tend to wane once they are nearing completion; (3) women with pregnancy sickness tend to avoid bitter, pungent, highly flavored, and novel foods, which are those that are most likely to tend to contain toxins; (4) women's sense of smell tends to be hypersensitive during that period of time they experience pregnancy sickness; (5) pregnancy sickness is universal across all cultures; (6) women who experience greater pregnancy sickness are less likely to bear offspring with birth defects.

Evolutionary theorists have argued that protecting the offspring is of primary importance because that ensures the survival of the species or, more precisely, survival of one's genes. It is interesting to note in this context that in many mammals, the newly born offspring get all their food from the mother's milk; this protects them from eating toxins.

The Learned Component

Many years ago, John Garcia and his colleagues (Garcia & Koelling, 1966; Garcia, McGowan, Ervin & Koelling, 1968) undertook a series of studies to examine some parameters of how organisms learn to avoid things that make them sick. In these studies, the animals were presented with a variety of stimuli that preceded induced sickness, caused by large doses of irradiation (X-ray). It has been known for some time that when patients are treated for cancer using X-rays, they experience nausea and vomit. By using X-rays in these studies they could manipulate sickness without causing death of the animals. In these studies, researchers placed the animal, in this case a laboratory rat, into a small area (apparatus) where the animal was presented with either a visual stimulus, an auditory stimulus or a taste stimulus (food with a certain taste). The rats were then given a large dose of X-ray that would cause them to get sick in about six hours. The next day, the rats were tested to see if they had learned to avoid the stim-

ulus that had been paired with the X-ray. What they found was that after a single training session, the group of animals that had been given taste/food as a cue avoided that stimulus but that the other animals given the visual and auditory stimulus never learned to avoid those cues. The fact the animals given the visual and auditory stimulus did not show any learning is not surprising in many ways. For conditioning to occur, the response normally needs to be contingent (or at least fairly close in time) with the stimulus. A six-hour delay can hardly be considered contingent. What is surprising, therefore, is that the animals in taste/food cue learned so quickly. This finding suggests that animals are biologically prepared (prewired) to make certain associations and not others (Garcia & Koelling, 1966; Garcia et al., 1968).

When it comes to our survival, we often have only one chance. Humans as well as many animals have a natural tendency to avoid new or novel foods but will sample them from time to time, especially when hungry (Rozin, 1976). This is highly adaptive behavior. Taken in small amounts potentially toxic foods might only make us sick, and through simple conditioning, we can learn to avoid them in the future. Eaten in large amounts, toxic foods could kill us. Dogs will often eat large amounts of a tainted food but they also have the capacity to quickly regurgitate such food.

Why should there be room for learning? Why not simply prewire animals to avoid all potentially toxic foods. From an evolutionary perspective, it is important that the food supply not be too restrictive. Equipping the animal through prewiring has the potential of doing just that. Thus, it appears that we have the best of both worlds. We have a relatively unrestricted food supply but are equipped with the mechanisms necessary to make us sample so that we can learn to avoid potentially toxic foods. Humans have come to cook much, if not most, of their foods. The tendency to cook and perhaps even overcook has a sound basis. A number of roots, seeds, stems, and leaves contains toxins that are neutralized when cooked (Weil, 2000). Mushrooms, for example, contain toxins that can be removed by cooking. Meat, as most people know, can readily become contaminated with bacteria when left out for even short periods of time. Proper cooking, however, will typically kill such bacteria. Although there are disadvantages of overcooking, such as removing the vitamins from vegetables or creating toxins that can cause cancer (e.g., blackened animal flesh is carcinogenic), it appears from an evolutionary perspective that the benefits of cooking outweighed the costs (Weil, 2000). We assume that our ancestors initially learned to cook through the process described by Garcia and his associates. That is, they learned to cook because when they didn't cook they got sick. The reason people cook today is likely the result of what might be called cultural conditioning. By that I mean our food preferences are largely learned and that the mechanism that governs these preferences is taste. By learning to eat only those foods that have been offered to us by our caretakers, we can avoid the risk of eating things that might kill us. In other words, it is a safe route to take. Cultural conditioning obviously has it roots in the process of imitation, but it goes beyond mere imitation because we come to use taste as our guide. In short, we develop a taste preference that is more general than the specific food we initially ate.

We are not entirely slaves to our past, however. People who move to new locations often do eventually acquire new taste preferences, but it often takes time. The best explanation of what is happening is that we are limited somewhat by our evolutionary past. Specifically, we need to go through the process of sampling. This mechanism makes sure we don't poison ourselves. If new foods don't make us sick and provide us with nutrients, they become accepted and, over time, can even become preferred. In many parts of the world, as cultures come together, they readily eat foods of other cultures. They might, for example, try foods in a new restaurant in their neighborhood, or they might come to be served new foods when they make new friends. With time, they come to enjoy and even prefer the new or novel foods that they initially might have avoided.

The Cognitive Component

With the advent of chemistry and the ability to create a wide variety of chemicals, including pesticides and herbicides, animals and humans have been faced with the daunting task of how to avoid those chemicals that might kill them. Evolution has not prepared us for this task. For example, antifreeze tastes good but is toxic. As a result, we are faced on a daily basis with a wide variety of warnings designed to draw our attention to the fact that certain chemicals are dangerous, not only if ingested but even when we breath them or our skin is exposed to them. Research is ongoing into how humans can be protected through such things as warnings or lids that make it difficult for children to open those containers. As more and more toxins are getting into the food chain, it becomes increasingly important to ensure that foods are constantly monitored for toxicity levels. The problem facing us today is that toxins often exist in small amounts in the food we eat but not enough to trigger one of our natural defenses. The problem with many toxins is they tend to build up in the body and as the levels slowly rise, they begin to have an effect. Researchers have suggested that one way for us to deal with this problem is to ingest more natural antioxidants (Weil, 2000).

Summary

Considerable evidence indicates that humans have evolved mechanisms that help protect them against a variety of toxins. The clearest evidence comes from studies of pregnant women who often become nauseated by certain foods containing toxins that could harm the embryo. Learning has also been shown to play an important role. What is particularly interesting is that humans can learn to avoid toxic foods after a single experience with a food that produces sickness. This finding suggests that evolution has prepared humans to learn to associate taste with sickness. Evolution has not, however, prepared humans to deal effectively with all the new toxins that are becoming part of the food chain. As a result, we are becoming increasingly dependent on research that can tell us what is or is not safe for us to eat.

Food Selection

Humans eat not only for the energy they need but also to build cells and create all the complex chemicals that are necessary for daily living. Humans are omnivores, which means they eat all foods. In this section, we will examine, among other things, why we are omnivores.

Humans eat not only to satisfy hunger needs but for the sensory experience food provides.

It is important, as we will see shortly, to make a distinction between food as a source of energy and food as a source of nutrients. The two are interlinked, so let's start with a discussion of the basics.

Food and Energy: Fats, Carbohydrates, and Proteins

When we ingest food, our stomach and intestines—the gastrointestinal (GI) tract—breaks down the food into more basic units that can be used for energy, as well as for rebuilding the body cells and manufacturing the chemicals needed to run the body (Table 3.1). *Carbohydrates,* also referred to simply as starches and sugars—which we get from eating such foods as bread, pasta, cakes, desserts, and fruits—are broken down into glucose, fructose (fruit sugar), and galactose (a milk sugar), which are a source of immediate energy. Glucose can be oxidized (metabolized) and used for energy or it can be converted to glycerol and stored in the liver and muscles for short-term energy use. In the ab-

sence of carbohydrates in the diet, the glycerol stores can maintain blood sugar for 48 hours in a sedentary person. Exercise rapidly depletes these stores causing athletes to experience what has come to be called "hitting the wall" as their bodies shift from glycerol metabolism to fat metabolism. It should be noted that the specialized cells of the brain prefer glucose, and the body will manufacture glucose from protein should there be an insufficient supply in the absence of carbohydrates (such as in the low carbohydrate diet). Unfortunately, as I will discuss shortly, our bodies tend to digest our own muscle to get that glucose, even if there is protein in the digestive tract. *Fats,* which we get from such foods as meats, milk products, seeds/grains (from which cooking oils are made), are broken down into fatty acids. Fatty acids are converted to energy through a process called fatty acid oxidation, a process that is not as efficient as converting glycerol to glucose. Fatty acids that are not used for immediate energy are stored under the skin as an energy reserve for hard times in such places as the stomach, hips, thighs, arms. We can readily make fat from glucose and do so when

Table 3-1. Endocrine glands and brain systems involved in hunger, eating, and energy mobilization.

Gland	Hormone	Action/Function
Endocrine Glands		
Stomach	Gastin	Stimulates release of hydrochloric acid. Increases gastric activity.
Duodenum (small intestine)	Secretin	Triggers release of pancreatic juices.
	Cholecystokinin	Digestion, absorption, and metabolism. Release linked to satiety.
Pancreas		Pancreatic juices essential for digestion of food.
	Insulin	Triggered by the intake of carbohydrates. Increases glucose uptake and converts to glycogen, which is then stored in the body cells. Promotes synthesis of fat and proteins. Release linked to satiety.
Adrenal cortex	Glucocorticoids	Convert stored fats and proteins to carbohydrates. Increases glucose levels in the blood. (Important in the mobilization of energy, especially under stress.)
Adrenal medulla	Epinephrine (adrenaline)*	Increases heart rate, oxygen consumption, and glycogen mobilization. (Again, important for the mobilization of energy.)
	Norepinephrine (noradrenaline)*	Increases blood pressure, constricts blood vessels.
Thyroid	Thyroxin (T4)	Regulates cell growth. Regulates metabolic rate.
Brain		
Hypothalamus	Various	The hypothalamus directs and monitors a number of endocrine functions.
Lateral		Monitors the taste and texture of food. Good taste and texture increases food intake.
Ventromedial		Monitors glucose levels (glucoreceptors). Lesioning presumably reduces the ability to detect low glucose levels.

*Also produced in the brain, where they act as neurotransmitters. Increased levels of norepinephrine in the brain have been implicated in positive moods.

caloric intake exceeds energy expenditure; however, we cannot readily convert fat to glucose, which means that once we have converted excess glucose to fat, it is not immediately available for energy. This has important implications for people with weight problems. Gram for gram, fats contain twice as many calories as carbohydrates (Weil, 2000). This means it can be an excellent source of long-term energy. *Proteins*, which we get from such foods as meats, beans, nuts and seeds, are broken down into amino acids, many of which can

in turn be readily broken down in glucose, turned into glycogen, or converted to fat for storage, depending on energy needs. These more basic units are absorbed into the bloodstream. After a big meal, it typically takes several hours for all the food in the intestines to be digested and absorbed. Thus, the intestines act as excellent storehouse for energy.

Amino acids and sugars go directly to the liver, which has the first choice of nutrients before passing them along to the rest of the body. The liver regulates the amino acid level in the blood. There are 20 different amino acids, which are used by the body for growth, repair, and energy. Amino acids are derived from proteins, and the best source is meat. Most plants are low in amino acids, and many do not contain the full complement of the 20 amino acids that the body needs to function normally.

That meat is a good source of amino acids has important ramifications for vegetarians. It is critical that vegetarians eat a wide range of beans, nuts, seeds, and vegetables to ensure all the various amino acids are ingested. Although some people have argued that you cannot get all the essential amino acids from a pure vegetarian diet and, therefore, need meat, others have questioned this conclusion (Weil, 2000).

Food and Nutrients

We also eat to obtain all the nutrients that we need to function properly. It is well beyond the scope of this chapter, however, to review all that research. What we know is that humans need a balanced diet that should contain about 50 to 60% carbohydrates, 10 to 20% fat, and 10 to 20% proteins. With this balance, we will not only have a good supply of energy but we will also be able to manufacture all the enzymes, hormones, chemicals that we need to function on a daily basis.

Humans Evolved as Meat Eaters

Humans, like many primates, are omnivores (which means they eat both plants and animals). Incidentally, it is interesting to note that although we have some incisors, like those of carnivores, our back teeth (molars) are more like those of herbivores. This is one of many facts that suggests that we have been omnivores for some time (Buss, 1999). It has been argued from an evolutionary perspective that there was a distinct advantage for our ancestors to be omnivores; it meant they were not dependent on one type of food source. Should one supply run out, they could readily shift to another source. For our ancestors, however, there was a problem with being an omnivore: Being an omnivore increased the odds of being poisoned (Rozin, 1996). The more foods that one ate the greater was the likeli-

hood of being poisoned. As we have already indicated, certain mechanisms evolved to help us deal with toxins. Several theorists have argued that the reason humans gave up some of the flexibility of being an omnivore wasn't the toxin problem. Specifically, researchers have argued that we came to be increasingly dependent on meat. First, let's look at the evidence that we became meat eaters. An estimated 20 to 40% of the human diet comes from meat, the highest estimate of some 222 primate species (Tooby & DeVore, 1987). Interestingly, nutritionists have suggested that we only need 10 to 20% meat in our diet. One might argue that this represents a preference rather than necessity. The evidence, however, strongly suggests that meat (at least protein) is essential to our diet. This argument is based on several important facts. First, it is extremely difficult for humans to get all the essential nutrients, such as cyanocobolamin, from an exclusively vegetarian diet (Tooby & DeVore, 1987). Second, the human body cannot produce Vitamins A and B_{12}, even though these vitamins are essential for human survival. These two vitamins are found in meat (Allman, 1994). The body also needs thiamine, which comes from pork and organ meat; vitamin K, which comes from meats; vitamin A, which comes from milk and butter; and vitamin D, which comes from cod liver oil. Third, the amino acids contained in proteins provide the basic components that our body needs to manufacture, for instance, the neurotransmitters (such as norepinephrine and serotonin) that our brains need to function (Wurtman, 1982). Amino acids also contain the components necessary for cell repair. Fourth, the human gut is dominated by small intestines, which distinguishes it from all other primates. In the small intestines, proteins are rapidly broken down and nutrients are absorbed (Allman, 1994). The ape's gut, in contrast, is mainly a colon suitable for vegetarian diet. Fifth, fossil evidence of our ancestors' teeth is consistent with the idea they were meat eaters. Sixth, various researchers who have studied large quantities of bones that are more than two million years old, have independently corroborated the fact that these bones had cut marks consistent with the idea that humans ate meat (Leaky & Lewin, 1992). That our ancestors ate meat has been taken as evidence that meat eating is part of our evolutionary past and does not reflect a new development that could be confused with developing a taste preference.

Why did we become meat eaters? Was it simply convenience or was it something more? Stanford has suggested that the reason humans became more dependent on meat grew out of the evolutionary advantage associated with developing of a large brain (1999). Although most evolutionary biologists agree that what makes humans unique is our brainpower, Stanford's hypothesis is both appealing and controversial. It is appealing because it would explain both the trend toward a larger brain and the trend toward more meat in the human diet. It is controversial because he suggests meat is a source of power and that because males are the hunters, they have more power. I will return to this issue later.

The Biological Component

The Role of Taste in Food Selection

As we discussed, taste plays an important, if not critical, role in food aversions. Taste also plays an important role in selecting what we should eat. Humans have two important unlearned taste preferences: sweet and fatty and perhaps a third, salty, that I will treat as learned following the lead of others. We appear to be born with the preference for sweet foods and perhaps fatty foods (Rozin, 1996). Both preferences make sense from an evolutionary perspective, whether present at birth or emerge later, as might be the case for fatty foods. For example, foods that are sweet are less toxic (Rozin, 1976) and tend to be a good source of calories (Weil, 2000). Most sweet foods are carbohydrates, a valuable source of glucose, which is an efficient and the preferred fuel of the body. In fact, the brain will only use glucose, a point I will elaborate shortly. Carbohydrates also contain many of the important nutrients including vitamins and minerals. A mother's milk is sweet (contains lactose). When you combine sweet with the sucking response, you ensure that the offspring will quickly get the nourishment they need.

People who deliberately restrict their carbohydrate intake (when they go on a low-carbohydrate diet, for example) often develop a condition called ketosis. This occurs when the body can no longer supply the brain with glucose and is forced to burn ketone bodies. The body can manufacture glucose from protein, but this is not a highly efficient way to get the glucose the body

needs. This might be because for humans to develop a highly specialized brain (one that prefers glucose to all other fuels), we had to give up some of our flexibility of being able to substitute one food for another, as is implied by the word omnivore. Instead, we became dependent on having a balanced diet.

As I indicated earlier, when people diet (such as when they go on a low-carbohydrate diet), much of their weight loss is muscle mass rather than fat. Even when their protein intake is high, this tendency persists. Why this happens is not immediately clear. It might be that when glycerol is used, the body switches into some kind of emergency mode that involves, among other things, digesting muscle to provide the amino acids necessary for manufacturing neural chemicals and energy. In other words, even though we might have protein (meat) in the gut, the body acts as though we are in a state of starvation. Another possibility is that we have become dependent on carbohydrates as a catalyst for digesting food. There might be something in the carbohydrates that help convert protein in the gut to amino acids. Consistent with this idea is the observation that meat is not completely digested when people reduce their carbohydrate intake. Whatever the exact explanation, the presence of carbohydrates in our diet is important and explains why nutritionists say that carbohydrates should account for at least 50 to 60% of our diet. The fact that we need carbohydrates is consistent with the argument that when we developed a large brain, our digestive system changed in some very important ways to meet the demands of running this complex neural system (Stanford, 1999). The point I want to emphasize here is that as we adapted over centuries, we came to be an animal that needed both protein and carbohydrates. Later in this chapter, I will talk about how this can explain some of our food-sharing practices that characterize our current behavior.

Nutritionists suggest that 15% of our diet should be fat. Fats contain a number of essential ingredients that are essential to good health (Weil, 2000). Also, as I have already pointed out, gram for gram, fat contains twice as many calories as carbohydrates. This alone would have been important for our ancestors who had to expend a great deal of energy just to survive. Fat is contained in meat, so having a preference for fat would have served a dual function of ensuring not only that we had fat in our diet but meat as well. What this means is that with two basic preferences, sweet and fatty, we would be inclined to eat all the three basic food groups—that is, because carbohydrates tend to have a sweet taste and meats tend to have a fatty taste as well as contain fat, following our taste preferences will ensure we eat carbohydrates, meat and fat.

The Learned Component

The eating preferences of different ethnic groups provide compelling evidence that learning plays an important role in diet. The Italians are known for their love of pasta, the French for their garlic, the Mexicans for their hot peppers, the Japanese for their raw fish, and so on. Where do these different preferences come from?

From an evolutionary perspective, it would be highly adaptive if humans could learn to eat different foods depending on what was available. To do this, they would need to be able to identify not only which foods were nutritious but also which ones would make them ill. Considerable evidence indicates that humans, as well as other organisms, quickly learn to avoid foods that are lacking in nutrition and are toxic (make you sick); however, learning to select nutritious foods takes considerably longer. Research by John Garcia and others suggests that, to detect that a food is not providing nutrition, the organism must get sick. In other words, food selection comes from learning to avoid all those foods that produce some type of aversive state (Garcia & Koelling, 1966; Garcia et al., 1968; Nachman, 1970). In these circumstances, the development of taste preferences in the early stages of food intake would be highly adaptive. Specifically, by modeling their parents and thereby developing preferences, individuals would eliminate the need to go through a long trial-and-error learning process with its attendant dangers.

Because the availability of foods changes, this learning process would need to be flexible, so that individuals could try new foods in the absence of their preferred diet. That people develop new tastes, albeit over a considerable period, is consistent with this idea. Again, many of these new preferences are linked to taste and texture rather than to nutritional value.

Humans appear to prefer salt. We know this from a variety of sources. One simply can look at the amount of salt used by the manufacturers of fast foods to understand how much we like salt. Research with rats suggests that this is a learned preference (Rozin, 1976, 1996). If rats are deprived of salt, they immediately show a preference for salt. What is curious is that they do not show this same quick learning when they are deprived of Vitamin A and other essential nutrients. We do know that salt is very important in our diet and that when it is not present in sufficient amounts we quickly experience an aversive state. It takes much longer for us to experience a general malaise when we are deprived of thiamin. In addition, salt has a distinctive taste but thiamin does not. To quickly condition an internal state to a stimulus, it is necessary to have a distinctive stimulus and a distinctive internal state. Not only is salt a distinctive taste but the deprivation of salt also produces a highly aversive and life threatening state. Thus, the quick learning that comes from salt deprivation makes sense. Consistent with this explanation is the finding that although rats can learn to eat foods containing nutrients they are lacking (e.g., thiamin) by using taste to guide their selection, when the taste cue is switched to a food that now lacks that nutrient, they eat the deficient food rather than a food that contains the nutrient (Rozin, 1976, 1996).

Many of the junk foods that we have come to prefer are high in sugar, fat, and salt. We are inclined to eat them even when they are not high in nutrients. In view of what we have already said, this is not surprising. It appears that our evolutionary past has predisposed us to depend on taste to tell us what is good for us. This is well known by the manufacturers of fast foods. As a result, we are being enticed to eat foods that are lacking in basic nutrients.

The Cognitive Component

In recent years, there has been extensive research on which foods we should or should not eat based on scientific research. This research has largely focused on the question of what is good for our health; for example, what we should eat to prevent such things as heart disease or reduce the risk of cancer. It is beyond the scope of this chapter to summarize that research, but some good popular books provide a summary. Andrew Weil (2000), for example, in his book entitled

Eating Well for Optimum Health, talks about what fats we should or should not eat and which foods can help reduce the risk of cancer or coronary heart disease.

The point I want to make here is simply that in our modern society we have come to depend more and more on our ability to think and reason (e.g., scientific research) to tell us what we should or should not eat. Although our evolutionary past has provided us with some basic mechanisms to help guide food selection, those mechanisms have not kept pace with current food production practices. For example, the use of herbicides and pesticides, which are toxins, do not seem to trigger those mechanisms designed to make us avoid certain foods likely due to the fact we tend to ingest them in very small amounts.

The advent of fast foods and junk foods is another problem. Most fast foods and junk foods taste good because they are sweet, fatty or salty but many of them do not provide basic nutrients. In the early 1970s, researchers discovered that many of the breakfast cereals were completely lacking in basic nutrients. This led to a public outcry, and the government responded by writing laws that forced manufacturers to list the contents of their cereals on the boxes. This allowed consumers to decide what to buy based on the ingredients, not what simply tasted good. Manufacturers quickly responded and began to fortify their cereals with various vitamins to lure back disgruntled shoppers who felt they had been misled.

Summary

Research indicates that one thing that guides food selection is taste. Humans are born with a preference for sweet, which not only helps them to avoid toxins (which are typically bitter) but also to eat carbohydrates, the main fuel of our brain and body. Humans also show a preference for fat; a preference that ensures we eat protein in addition to fat.

Research also indicates that we can learn to select foods using the taste mechanism. Some of the best evidence comes from the observation that we develop a food preference that corresponds to the culture in which we were raised.

Evolution has not prepared us to deal with modern foods that contain small amounts of toxins that can accumulate in the body or foods that taste good but are lacking in essential nutrients.

Distinguishing Between Hunger and Eating

There are also many psychological reasons for eating. We might eat out of habit—because it is lunchtime, for example; we might eat because we want the pleasant sensory experience provided by food; we might eat because others are eating; or we might eat because we are bored.

Most researchers think it is important to distinguish between the concepts of hunger and eating. Hunger is a biological need. Eating too much of the wrong things results in being overweight and the associated health disorders, so eating is the problem.

This distinction also involves issues of control. If we say that we only eat because we are hungry, we aren't taking responsibility for our behavior; we're blaming our biology. When we accept the idea that we eat for reasons other than hunger, we implicitly make the assumption that we have some control. At the same time, there is also a danger in assuming that we have complete control. It is important to know what we can and cannot change.

A common assumption is that people stop eating when they are full—in other words, that the state of satiety is what causes us to stop eating. Like hunger, satiety is a biological state. It has been linked to chemicals such as insulin and cholecystokinin that are released in the course of digestion (Table 3-1). As we will see, people often eat well beyond biological satiety. They continue to eat, for example, until they have finished what is on their plate.

Eating as a Sensory Experience

Eating is a sensory experience. Not only do we eat foods because we enjoy their taste, we eat food to experience the texture. We do this even when foods lack nutritional value (Schachter, 1971a). The tendency to select foods based on their sensory qualities has been linked to obesity. The role of sensory cues in the eating patterns of obese individuals was demonstrated in a

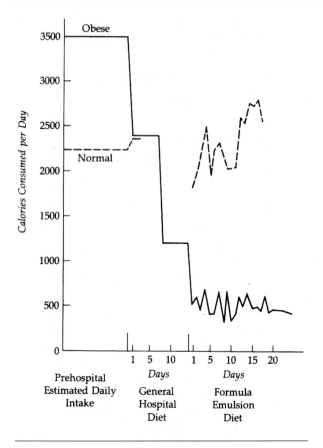

Figure 3-1. Effect of a formula emulsion diet on the eating behavior of an obese and a nonobese subject. (From *Emotion, Obesity and Crime*, by S. Schachter. Copyright © 1971 by Academic Press. Reprinted with permission.)

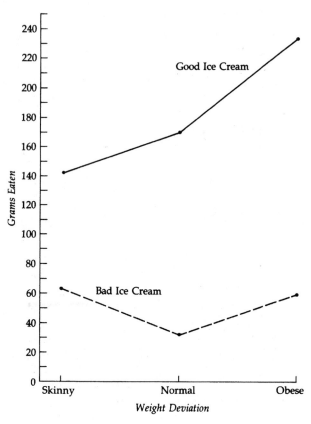

Figure 3-2. Effect of a formula emulsion diet on the eating behavior of an obese and a nonobese subject. (From *Emotion, Obesity and Crime*, by S. Schachter. Copyright © 1971 by Academic Press. Reprinted with permission.)

study that compared extremely obese men and women with nonobese controls (Hashim & Van Itallie, 1965). The researchers prepared a bland, homogenized liquid diet similar in taste and composition to the vanilla flavors of commercial preparations such as Nutrament and Metrecal. The subjects, who were confined to a hospital, were allowed to eat as much of this diet as they wanted, but consumption was in a situation with no social interaction. The nonobese individuals continued to consume their daily average of about 2400 calories, but obese subjects reduced their intake to 500 calories a day, about 3000 calories less than their daily average before admission to the hospital (Figure 3-1).

Although other studies have not shown so dramatic an effect, the same general finding seems to hold even in very tightly controlled studies. In an experiment that asked subjects to evaluate taste (Nisbett, 1968), obese subjects ate significantly more than did nonobese and skinny subjects when the food tasted good, but ate about the same amount when the food tasted bad. Again, this indicates that obese people are strongly influenced by the positive sensory qualities of food (Figure 3-2). Similar results have been obtained with cake and milk (Schachter, 1971b).

The Question of Overweight and Obesity

One of the most important issues today in North America concerning food is obesity. Unfortunately, there is no easy way to define obesity. The term has been used to refer to people who have a very moderate amount of fat and to those who are extremely overweight. In many studies, individuals are categorized as obese if they exceed the average weight for their height, build, age, and gender by a given percentage—for example, 25%. This means that a person whose target weight is 150 pounds would be classified as obese at 180 pounds. Thus, among the people with whom we interact daily, some are obese. Many of us experience excessive weight gain sometime during our lives. Within us, there lives the potential obese person, ready to emerge if given the opportunity.

To understand the complex issue of overweight and obesity, we need to understand the role of insulin in digestion and eating because insulin levels seem to be at the center of everything that we will be discussing.

When carbohydrates are ingested, acids in the stomach initially break down the food and then enzymes are released that begin the conversion of carbohydrates into glucose. When glucose levels begin to rise in the blood, the pancreas releases insulin to maintain the glucose at an optimal level. When glucose levels become too high they create a condition called hyperglycemia; a toxic condition that must be cleared rapidly to maintain normal functioning. The failure to produce sufficient insulin is called diabetes, a serious disorder that can lead to vascular and retinal damage.

Without insulin, glucose levels continue to rise, and the kidneys draw water into the urine, resulting in an excessive output of diluted urine. To compensate for the lack of glucose, fat is mobilized, fatty acids are oxidized, and protein is used as a source of energy. As a result of the lack of protein, repair of injured tissue is slowed, and resistance to infection is low. Diabetics have particular difficulty breaking down carbohydrates, a condition that can be easily treated by daily injections of insulin and restricted intake of carbohydrates (Sherman & Sherman, 1989).

One of the main culprits in obesity is not lack of insulin but, rather, the opposite: too much insulin, a condition called hyperglycemia. When insulin levels are high several things can happen. Among other things glucose in the blood is reduced, more glucose is converted to glycerol, and there is greater conversion of glucose to fat (Rabinowitz & Zierler, 1962). The consensus is that hunger is linked to low blood glucose, so people who have high insulin levels will experience hunger and begin eating. At the same time, they will be converting more glucose to fat. The net effect is they will tend to get fatter and fatter. When people become overweight, they develop a chronic condition called hyperinsulinemia. As a result, they have chronically low blood glucose and are constantly hungry (Williams, 1960).

People can do a couple of things to reverse this condition: one is exercise and the other is adjusting their diets. Let's begin by looking at the whole question of energy use.

The Biological Component

The Genetic Factor

To distinguish what is inherited from what is acquired through experience, it is necessary to control for either the environment or our genes. It is usually difficult to control the environment, so scientists have traditionally studied adopted versus natural children and identical versus fraternal twins. These studies have shown that adopted children tend to resemble their biological parents in weight far more than they resemble their adoptive parents (Stunkard et al., 1985) and that identical twins, even when reared apart, are closer in weight than are fraternal twins or other siblings (e.g., Stunkard, Foch, & Hrubec, 1985). In other words, genes appear to play a central role.

One thing that might be inherited is metabolic rate; a person with a high metabolic rate tends not to become obese. Other inherited factors were suggested by a study in which children of overweight parents not only preferred sweeter solutions but were more responsive to external cues in their environments (Milstein, 1980). People who are external are highly susceptible to the taste and texture of food; we'll return to this topic later in the chapter.

Energy Expenditure

The three components. Energy expenditure has three main components: the *basal metabolic rate* (BMR),

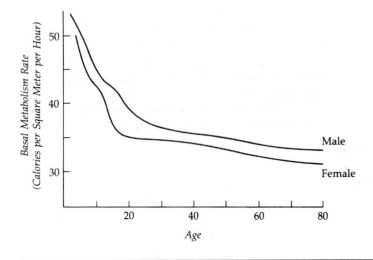

Figure 3-3. Changes in basal metabolic rates with age. (From *Slim Chance in a Fat World*, by R. B. Stuart and B. Davis. Copyright © 1972 by the Research Press Company. Reprinted with permission.)

physical activity, and the *specific dynamic action* (SDA) of food. The *BMR* is the amount of energy we use in a given period in relation to our body size. It is measured as the number of calories we burn per square meter of body surface per hour when we are resting. About one-third of our energy use is attributable to exercise and about two-thirds to our BMR (Rodin, 1981). SDA is the increase in energy expenditure following the ingestion of food. It can increase the BMR by as much as 20% for a few hours after a meal. Certain foods, such as proteins, produce the greatest increase (Powers, 1982). The actual proportions of energy expended in exercise and metabolism obviously depend on individual exercise patterns. What is interesting about BMR is that it declines quite rapidly from birth to about age 20 (Figure 3.3), and there are wide individual differences (Rose & Williams, 1961).

Obesity and Anorexia as Malfunctions of the Hypothalamus

A tiny brain structure called the hypothalamus is involved in a wide variety of motivational functions, including hunger and eating (see Figure 2-1). Two areas of the hypothalamus have been linked to eating behavior: Lesions of the ventromedial nuclei in the hypothalamus produce overeating, which leads to obesity (Teitelbaum, 1961) and lesions of the lateral hypothalamus lead to a failure to eat, a state called *anorexia*.

Lesions of the ventromedial nuclei. Teitelbaum (1961) noted that animals with lesions of the ventromedial nuclei (VMN) show the following characteristics:

1. They are unresponsive to normal satiety cues, which are presumably mediated by glucose.
2. They will not work as hard as normal animals to obtain food.
3. They will stop eating adulterated foods (such as food laced with quinine) sooner than will animals with no lesions of the VMN.
4. They will eat large amounts of highly palatable foods.

Recent research has shown that VMN lesions produce a hyperinsulinemia, a condition that precedes the development of obesity (Suga et al., 1999). This finding is consistent with the observation that obese people are characterized with chronic hyperinsulinemia. When people overeat for a time, the brain acts as though this is a normal state. How does this happen?

It has generally been accepted that satiety is linked to high levels of leptin (a blood borne peptide secreted from the adipose [fat] tissue) in the VMN. It has been suggested lesions of the VMN destroy the leptin receptors, which would account for the overeating. It has been observed that people who develop chronic hyperinsulinemia have high levels of leptin circulating in the brain. This has lead to the speculation that high levels of insulin in the brain, a condition that precedes obesity, may somehow reduce the sensitivity of the leptin receptors in the brain, which would account for the chronic state of obesity. According to this line of thinking, it would be difficult if not impossible to reverse the state of obesity (Sorensen, Echwald, & Holm, 1996).

Researchers have identified an obesity gene called the leptin gene (Caro, Sinha, Kolaczynski, Zhang, & Considine, 1996). What has aroused considerable interest is that this gene has been shown to mutate, which would help explain why obesity will arise spontaneously in some families. Evidence indicates that people are born with different rates of metabolism, which would help explain why some people stay thin even when they eat large amounts of food.

Lesions of the lateral hypothalamus. Lesions of the lateral hypothalamus (LH) have been shown to produce effects analogous but complementary to those in the VMN. Specifically, lesions of the LH result initially in the cessation of eating. After such animals have lost considerable body weight, they begin to eat again, but at a much-reduced rate. This reduced rate of eating tends to be very stable. While palatable foods tend to result in increased eating and weight gain, as in animals with no lesions, animals with LH lesions continue to maintain their weight well below the prelesion level. The degree of anorexia that the animals display is related to the size of the lesion (Keesy & Powley, 1975).

The lesions studies do not imply that hypothalamus lesions cause anorexia and bulimia in humans. What these studies point out is simply the possibility that these areas in the brain play some type of mediating role in these and perhaps other eating disorders.

Set-Point Theory

Based on the findings from studies of the hypothalamus, Keesy and Powley (1975) have proposed the set-point theory of weight level—specifically, that the hypothalamus sets our weight. Some of us will have close to average weight, some will tend toward obesity, and some will tend toward anorexia. This hypothesis is summarized in Figure 3-4.

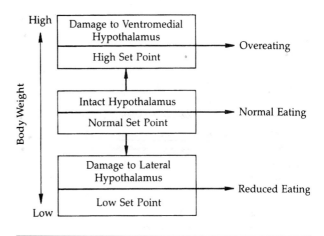

Figure 3-4. Damage (or lesions) to the ventromedial hypothalamus raises the set point, while damage (or lesions) to the lateral hypothalamus lowers the set point. (Based on R. E. Keesy and T. L. Powley, "Hypothalamic Regulation of Body Weight," *American Scientist*, 1975, *63*, 558–565.)

Keesy and Powley argue that their theory of weight level can readily account for the tendency of people who are inclined to overweight to fall off their diets. Because such people have a high set point, they would feel hungry, and to satisfy their hunger they would be inclined to overeat. Eventually, their weight would match their set point and, at that time, their food consumption would level off. Only by deliberately restraining their eating would they be able to keep their weight down. Any failure to restrain their eating would immediately result in a tendency to overeat.

The Yo-Yo Effect and the Famine Hypothesis

People who diet to achieve the slim figure that wins social approval often experience a phenomenon labeled the *yo-yo effect.* Once they have achieved their desired weight, they find it virtually impossible to keep the weight off and after a short time are again overweight, at least according to their standards. Obsessed with the desire to be slim, they again diet but again put on weight after achieving their desired weight. To their dismay, such dieters often find that, each time they put on weight following a diet, they not only regain all the weight they lost but put on a little more. Slowly but surely, they get heavier on each upswing. Why do they put on more weight each time they diet? No one is certain, but one explanation comes from the famine hypothesis.

According to the famine hypothesis, obesity can be understood as an adaptive mechanism from our evolutionary past gone awry because we are no longer faced with periodic food shortages. By this theory, the adipose tissue evolved to protect humans against food shortages (Margules, 1979; Margules, Moisset, Lewis, Shibuya, & Pert, 1978) and, now that such shortages are rare, we tend to continue adding to an already adequate reserve. In short, people are inclined to progress from a comfortable reserve to a state of obesity. Extending this hypothesis, we can construct an explanation for the yo-yo effect: When people diet, the body responds as though it is going through a famine. If the weight loss caused by the diet pushes the body below the set point, the body says to itself at the end of the diet: "I didn't have enough fat reserves to handle this last famine, so I must put on more weight than before, so that I'll be prepared for the next famine." When the person diets again and achieves his or her desired weight (again pushing the body below its set point), the body says: "The last time I put on extra weight it wasn't enough, so next time I'll have to put on even more." As a result, each time the individual's weight dips below the set point, the body becomes even more determined to prevent this from happening again and works to protect the individual against the next, inevitable famine by increasing the fat reserves even more. Obviously, the body doesn't talk to itself. Some type of mechanism must signal the body to put on more weight.

The Yo-Yo Effect and Reduced Metabolism

One consequence of reduced food intake is a reduction in the rate of metabolism. It has been argued that this response to reduced food intake is highly adaptive, because it allows the individual to survive a famine. It may be that the yo-yo effect is simply the result of decreased metabolism. In other words, people might simply tend to eat the same amount following a diet

but, because the body's metabolism has slowed because of dieting, the same food intake produces greater weight gains.

The Learned Component

Statistics indicate that overweight children are likely to have overweight parents (Garn & Clark, 1976). Further, there is evidence that overweight children tend to become overweight adults (Eden, 1975; Hirsch, Knittle, & Salans, 1966). Although these findings support the idea that obesity may be genetically determined, there are reasons to question this conclusion. First, the child's weight tends to be more highly correlated with the mother's weight than with the father's (Garn & Clark, 1976). If the cause were purely genetic, the correlations should be equal. Second, the resemblance in the weight of siblings, even identical twins, decreases in later life. This suggests that factors other than the genes must be responsible for weight patterns.

How do we account for these findings? The reason that a child's weight tends to be correlated with the mother's might be that the mother largely controls the eating behavior of her children or simply the availability of food. Because of her own tendency to overeat, for example, the mother might fill her children's plates with more food than they require or simply make food available. If they are encouraged to eat all the food on their plates or to snack, the children will eventually convert the extra food into fat. If this behavior becomes a habit, it could help to explain their tendency to overeat in later life.

Another possibility is that fat mothers like to prepare appealing foods. Children who eat such foods might learn to associate eating with certain cues. Thus, foods with a particular taste, texture, or smell would tend to elicit the eating response. The presence or availability of such foods would determine whether such a person became obese. In any environment where such foods were readily available, the individual would be likely to overeat.

The finding that some people eat more when emotionally upset or under stress can be explained in a similar way. If a mother tries to comfort her children with food when they are upset, for example, the child might learn to eat under these conditions. Later in life, such people turn to food for comfort, just as they turned to their mother in childhood.

Finally, the tendency to eat more than is necessary could eventually result in hyperinsulinemia. To deal with the oversupply of food the body learns to produce large amounts of insulin in response to repeated occurrences of high food intake.

The Cognitive Component

Do we eat more when we are depressed, anxious, or stressed? No direct link has been established between emotional disorders and overeating. Typically, depression is characterized by weight loss rather than overeating. When a depressed state was induced in subjects high in self-restraint, however, they ate significantly more than did similarly depressed subjects who were low in self-restraint (Frost, Goolkasian, Ely, & Blanchards, 1982). This finding makes sense if we assume that the ability to control eating is greater in people who have more self-control and that they lose their ability or desire to exercise control when they become depressed. Typically, people who are depressed feel they have lost control of their lives.

Considerable evidence indicates that overweight people are more depressed than normal weight people are. It cannot be concluded from such studies, however, that depression is the cause of overweight. People who are overweight might be more inclined to become depressed as the result of becoming overweight. The depression could be caused, for example, by feelings of loss of control, one of the known antecedents of depression. The only way to show that depression causes overweight is to undertake a prospective study. This involves selecting a sample of normal weight people and assessing levels of depression, and then at a later time, looking at the same people to see if the more depressed individuals of the sample have become overweight. One study using this design failed to confirm the widely held view that depression leads to weight gains. In fact, it was found that, as a rule, the overweight individuals were initially less depressed than normal weight individuals (Smoller, Wadden, & Stunkard, 1987). This finding is consistent with the general conclusion that depression results in an overall reduction in motivation, including the motivation to eat (see Chapter 10).

Summary

Obesity is commonly defined as weight in excess of some norm, usually by approximately 25%. The tendency to obesity appears to be at least partly genetically determined. First, people who are overweight often come from overweight parents. Second, adopted children are more likely to resemble their biological parents than their adoptive parents in weight, and identical twins, even when raised apart, are closer in weight than fraternal twins are. Two possible explanations are that they inherit a similar metabolism rate or a propensity to eat in response to external cues.

Energy expenditure can also contribute to overweight. Energy expenditure has three main components: the BMR, physical activity, and SDA. Our BMR, which accounts for about two-thirds of our energy expenditure, decreases as we age. It slows fairly abruptly at around the age of 20, which could explain why some people tend to put on weight around that age.

Set-point theory suggests that the weight of each individual is governed by a set point determined by the hypothalamus. This theory is based on research showing that lesions in the hypothalamus can produce obesity and anorexia in animals

It is generally accepted that leptin is important for satiety. Recent research suggests that some people become obese because their leptin receptors are not sensitive to the release of leptin, a condition that might be genetic.

Margules has argued that obesity is an adaptive mechanism gone astray: We prepare for a famine that never comes. The famine hypothesis can account for the yo-yo effect. Each time individuals bring their weight below their set points, the body responds as though the famine has come. If food is available, as it tends to be in North America, individuals will be motivated to eat and prepare for the next famine.

Several factors suggest that overweight is due, at least in part, to learning. Because a child's weight is more likely to resemble the mother's weight than the father's, it has been argued that children of overweight mothers learn not only to overeat but also to eat foods high in calories.

Researchers have observed that overweight people tend to be depressed, but prospective studies suggest that depression is likely the result not the cause of obesity.

Theories of Overweight and Obesity

Internal-External Theory of Hunger and Eating

One of the major theories about why people are overweight is linked to the observation that some people seem to eat in response to *external* cues, such as the sight and smell of food and the time of day, whereas other people seem to depend on *internal* cues, such as stomach contractions, glucose levels, and fat levels. This led Stanley Schachter to propose the internal-external theory of overweight and obesity. This theory generated a great deal of research and has been the cornerstone for much research.

Stomach Activity and Hunger

One of the first systematic demonstrations that obese and nonobese people respond to different cues was made by Stunkard (1959). He arranged for both obese and nonobese subjects, having gone without food overnight, to enter the laboratory at 9 A.M. Each volunteer was asked to swallow a gastric balloon (filled with water) that was attached to a mechanical device to record stomach contractions. Every 15 minutes for four hours, the volunteers were asked to report whether they were hungry. It was found that the nonobese were more likely to report hunger when the stomach was active than were the obese. This suggests that feelings of hunger are associated with internal stimuli for the nonobese but not for the obese. Since we would expect hunger to be associated with internal cues, the question is why the obese fail to respond to these cues. If they are not responding to internal cues, what cues are eliciting their reports of hunger?

Schachter (1971a) demonstrated that, whereas the nonobese person tends to respond to internal cues such as stomach motility or hypoglycemia (low blood glucose), the obese person tends to respond more to external cues. An obese person who is accustomed to eating at a certain time, for example, will feel hungry when the clock indicates mealtime. The nonobese person will be less influenced by the time on the clock, unless it happens to coincide with his or her internal cues. To test this prediction, Schachter had volunteers come to the laboratory under the pretense of studying "the relation between physiological reactions and psychological characteristics which require base level measurements of heart and sweat gland activity" (Schachter & Gross, 1968, p. 99). Electrodes were attached, presumably to measure heart rate and galvanic skin response. Half the obese and half the nonobese subjects were then left for a period of time (ostensibly to establish a baseline) with a rigged clock that over 50 minutes would be 15 minutes slow. The other half were left for the same period with a rigged clock that would be 30 minutes fast. The first group finished this phase of the study when its clock said 5:20 P.M., the second when its clock said 6:05 P.M. The experimenter returned at this point with a box of crackers from which he was snacking and offered some to the volunteer. The experimenter also asked the subject to fill out an irrelevant questionnaire. If obese persons are more affected by clock time than by real time, they would be expected to eat more in the condition where the clock time was fast than in the condition where it was slow, because the apparent time in the fast-time condition was either near or past the subject's regular eating time. The results (Table 3-2) supported the hypothesis. On the average, obese subjects ate more crackers in the fast-time condition than in the slow-time condition, whereas nonobese subjects ate more in the slow-time condition. Why was there a reversal for the nonobese subjects? Schachter notes that, when the nonobese subjects in the fast-time condition refused crackers, they said "No, thanks. I don't want to spoil my dinner." Apparently, cognitive factors were responsible in this case.

The Air France study. These findings are consistent with those obtained by more naturalistic methods

Table 3-2. Amount of crackers eaten (in grams) by Schachter's subjects in four conditions.

	Time	
Weight	Slow	Fast
Obese	19.9	37.6
Nonobese	41.5	16.0

Source: From *Emotion, Obesity and Crime,* by S. Schachter. Copyright © 1971 by Academic Press. Reprinted with permission.

(Goldman, Jaffa, & Schachter, 1968). An airplane crosses several time zones when it flies from Paris to New York, so that a passenger's internal cues will fail to correspond with clock time after a flight. Because obese people respond to clock time rather than internal cues, they should adjust quickly to the local eating time. The nonobese, in contrast, should find it much more difficult to adjust their eating habits to local time. Interviews with Air France personnel assigned to transatlantic flights indicated that those who were overweight had less trouble adjusting to local eating time than those who were average in weight (Figure 3-5).

Aspects of Externality

Is externality innate or learned? According to Schachter's theory, as we have seen, some people come to depend on external cues to tell them when to eat, whereas other people depend on internal cues to tell them when to eat. Whether this is an innate or learned pattern of behavior has never been clearly established. Many diet clinics encourage their clients to listen to their bodies' needs (internal orientation) rather than allowing themselves to be controlled by the sensory qualities of food (external orientation). Despite this commonsense suggestion, evidence suggests that, if you are an external, it is very difficult to learn to become an internal.

Externality and nonobese individuals. We might conclude from Schachter's work that only obese people are sen-

sitive to cues in the environment associated with eating. Work by Rodin and her colleagues indicates that this is not always true. They have shown that many nonobese people are sensitive to such environmental cues and that many obese people are not (e.g., Rodin, 1981; Rodin & Slochower, 1976). Further, they have shown that losing weight is not accompanied by a decrease in responsiveness to those cues (Rodin, Slochower, & Fleming, 1977). An obese person who salivates at the sight of a steak will have the same response even after losing considerable weight. Rodin's work indicates that, although externality might be associated with the motivation to eat, there is no one-to-one correspondence between that motivation and a person's weight. This lack of correspondence is undoubtedly caused by three factors: differences in metabolic rates; differences in self-control; and differences in the availability of food, especially palatable foods.

Sensory cues, externality, and the insulin response. In a series of studies, Rodin (1981) has explored the hypothesis that sensory cues such as taste and smell are sufficient to stimulate the release of insulin in externals. As discussed earlier, high insulin levels have been linked to hunger, presumably because high levels of insulin reduce glucose levels in the blood. If, indeed, sensory cues are capable of triggering the release of insulin in externally responsive people but not in internally responsive people, then we have a mechanism that can explain why externals tend to eat more and become obese. To test this hypothesis, Rodin first determined the subjects' degree of externality by a battery of measures that did not involve eating. Next, she asked the subjects to fast for a period of 18 hours. When they arrived at the laboratory, a steak was in the process of being grilled. They could see it, smell it, hear the crackling sound of it. At the same time, a blood sample was drawn to measure their insulin levels. The externally responsive subjects, whether overweight or not, showed the greatest insulin response to the sight, smell, and sound of the grilling steak. In another study, Rodin examined whether the insulin response would increase as a function of palatability. As expected, the increase in insulin response was greater in externally responsive subjects.

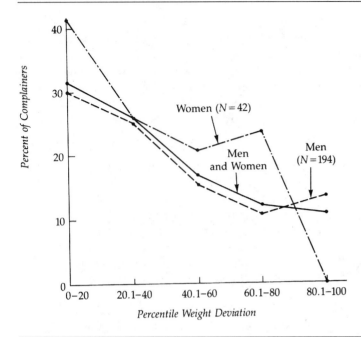

Figure 3-5.   Relation of weight deviation among Air France personnel to complaints about the effect of time-zone changes on eating. (From *Emotion, Obesity and Crime*, by S. Schachter. Copyright © 1971 by Academic Press. Reprinted with permission.)

Field studies of the insulin theory. According to Rodin's theory, if different foods trigger different amounts of insulin, people might be able to control their weight and not feel hungry by carefully selecting the foods they eat. Because it was found that glucose triggers a greater insulin release than does fructose, it follows from Rodin's theory that, if people eat food containing fructose (for instance, fruits) rather than food that results in high levels of glucose (such as breads), they will feel less hungry at a later time. In a study by Spitzer (cited in Rodin, 1984), subjects were asked to drink lemon-flavored water that contained either fructose, glucose, or glucose made to taste as sweet as fructose. Two and one-quarter hours later, subjects were presented with a buffet containing a very large variety of foods and asked to eat whatever they liked until they were comfortably full. Subjects in both glucose conditions ate significantly more than did subjects in the fructose condition. Extrapolating to what might happen if subjects ate as they had done during the experiment over the course of a year, Rodin calculated that a given individual would gain (or lose) up to 50 pounds.

These results provide compelling evidence for the idea that insulin levels play an important role in gov-

erning food intake. If more insulin is present in the bloodstream when we load up our plates, we will put more on the plate.

Boundary Theory of Hunger, Eating, and Obesity

Janet Polivy and Peter Herman have proposed a boundary model of hunger and eating (Polivy & Herman, 1983; Herman & Polivy, 1984). According to this model, two separate mechanisms control hunger and eating, one for hunger and one for satiety (Figure 3-6a). Both mechanisms are assumed to have a physiological basis. Following the lead of other theorists, Polivy and Herman assume that, if we fail to eat or if we eat too much, we will experience an aversive state. Between these two boundary points is a range that is not under direct physiological control. Once we become hungry and begin to eat, the amount we eat will be controlled by such factors as social expectations and the taste and texture of the food. They argue that, within these boundaries, eating is under cognitive rather than biological control.

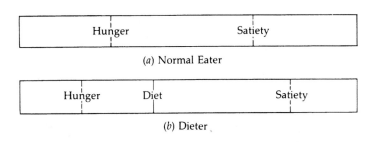

(*a*) Normal Eater

(*b*) Dieter

Figure 3-6.   Hunger and satiety boundaries of dieters and nondieters. (The diet boundary is purely cognitive.) (Adapted from "A Boundary Model for the Regulation of Eating," by C. P. Herman and J. Polivy. In A. J. Stunkard and E. Stellar (Eds.), *Eating and Its Disorders*. Copyright © 1984 Raven Press. Reprinted with permission.)

They further suggest that the upper and lower boundaries vary from person to person. They suggest that the lower hunger boundary is lower in dieters (Figure 3-6b) than in nondieters (Figure 3-6a), and the upper satiety boundary is higher in dieters than in nondieters. They further argue that, because dieters want to control their weight, they impose on themselves an upper boundary well below the biological satiety boundary. This is a purely cognitive boundary. This particular idea is an outgrowth of work on dieters and nondieters, which led Polivy and Herman to distinguish between restrained and unrestrained eaters.

Restrained and Unrestrained Eaters

Dieters, Polivy and Herman have found, tend to be *restrained eaters*. Even though they often feel hungry, think a great deal about food, and are readily tempted by the sight and smell of food, they consciously attempt to control their impulse to eat. If they do overeat or eat high-calorie foods (a no-no for dieters), they feel guilty. Nondieters, in contrast, tend to be *unrestrained eaters*. They do not experience persistent feelings of hunger, do not think about food as much as restrained eaters do, and are not so readily tempted by the sight and smell of food. More important, they are not constantly trying to control their food intake, nor do they feel guilty when they overeat.

Polivy and Herman have developed a scale to determine whether or not people are restrained or unrestrained (normal) eaters. They argue that the ideal weight, as prescribed by society, is often below the lower limit of a person's natural range. If such people are to achieve this ideal weight, they must constantly restrain their natural urges. In other words, the problem for the restrained eater is the need to deal more or less constantly with hunger and attraction to food. To see if you are a restrained eater, take the test in Table 3-3. The higher your score, the more restrained an eater you are.

The Preloading Studies

Some of the most convincing evidence for Polivy and Herman's theory come from what can be called the preloading studies. They gave dieters and nondieters either one or two milkshakes (preloading) and then asked them to judge the tastes of three varieties of ice cream. Control subjects got no milkshake. Experimental subjects in the preloading condition were told that the purpose of the preloading was to determine how a previous taste affected subsequent taste perception. However, the real purpose was to determine whether preloading would affect the amount of ice cream that dieters and nondieters would eat. As dieters are restrained eaters who avoid such foods as ice cream, they should feel guilty and consequently make fewer taste tests (that is, eat less) than nondieters. The initial study (Figure 3-7) showed that, as preloading increased, the amount of ice cream the dieters ate in the course of the taste test also increased (Herman & Mack, 1975). In a subsequent study, subjects were told that the caloric content was high or low. When they were told that the caloric content was high, the effect was even greater (Polivy, 1976). These results are contrary to what we might intuitively expect. As we will see momentarily, however, they are consistent with the theory of Herman and Polivy.

The Disinhibited Eater

Herman and Polivy have suggested that, when dieters fail to restrain their eating (in this case, because they

Table 3-3.   Eating restraint scale.

1. How often are you dieting?
   Never; rarely; sometimes; often; always. *(Scored 0–4)*

2. What is the maximum amount of weight (in pounds) that you have ever lost within one month?
   0–4; 5–9; 10–14; 15–19; 20+. *(Scored 0–4)*

3. What is your maximum weight gain within a week?
   0–1; 1.1–2; 2.1–3; 3.1–5; 5.1+. *(Scored 0–4)*

4. In a typical week, how much does your weight fluctuate?
   0–1; 1.1–2; 2.1–3; 3.1–5; 5.1+. *(Scored 0–4)*

5. Would a weight fluctuation of 5 pounds affect the way you live your life?
   Not at all; slightly; moderately; very much. *(Scored 0–3)*

6. Do you eat sensibly in front of others and splurge alone?
   Never; rarely; often; always. *(Scored 0–3)*

7. Do you give too much time and thought to food?
   Never; rarely; often; always. *(Scored 0–3)*

8. Do you have feelings of guilt after overeating?
   Never; rarely; often; always. *(Scored 0–3)*

9. How conscious are you of what you are eating?
   Not at all; slightly; moderately; extremely. *(Scored 0–3)*

10. How many pounds over your desired weight were you at your maximum weight?
    0–1; 2–5; 6–10; 11–20; 21+. *(Scored 0–4)*

Source: From *Breaking the Diet Habit: The Natural Weight Alternative,* by J. Polivy and C. P. Herman. Copyright © 1983 by J. Polivy and C. P. Herman. Reprinted by permission of the author.

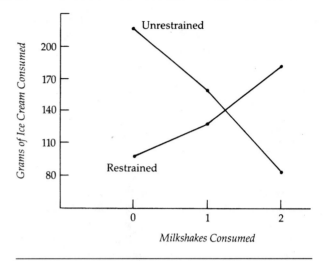

Figure 3-7.   Effect of preloading (milkshake consumption) on subsequent ice cream consumption in restrained and unrestrained eaters. (From "Perception of Calories and Regulation of Intake in Restrained and Unrestrained Subjects," by J. Polivy. *Addictive Behavior,* 1976, *1,* 237–243. Reprinted by permission of the author.)

have agreed to serve in an experiment that requires them to break their usual strict rules), they adopt a what-the-hell attitude. They become disinhibited. They say to themselves, "As long as I've already lost control, I might as well eat as much as I want." What has happened, Herman and Polivy contend, is that, having for the moment abandoned their diet boundary, they are left with only their biological satiety boundary, which is higher than the nondieter's. That the effect increases when they are told that the preload is high in calories provides compelling evidence that the diet boundary is indeed cognitive rather than biological. How long does the dieter remain in this disinhibited state? Many dieters consider the next day a new beginning, and restrained eating is again the rule. However, the disinhibition effect can also be markedly reduced if their attention is called to their behavior (either by themselves or by someone else) (Polivy, Herman, Hackett, & Kuleshnyk, 1986).

Research indicates that stress can affect eating and that it does so differently for restrained and unrestrained eaters. In one condition, a group of men and women were shown a film about industrial accidents (stress condition) or a pleasant travelogue (control condition) while they had access to sweet, salty, and bland snack foods. While stress markedly decreased food consumption in men, women under stress ate nearly twice as much sweet food as did their control counterparts, along with more bland food (Grunberg & Straub, 1992). The reason that, under stress, women ate more than did men might be that more women than men tend to be restrained eaters. If preoccupied with stress, they might fail to monitor their eating or simply not be motivated to control food intake. As a result, they would become disinhibited eaters.

Although the boundary theory appears to be able to explain the behavior of dieters (especially the characteristic disinhibition effect), it has been criticized because it fails to contribute to a better understanding of why people actually become obese (Ruderman, 1986).

Summary

Internal-external theory developed from the observation that obese people often eat in response to external cues, whereas nonobese people eat in response to internal cues. Several studies have shown that obese people tend to respond to time of day, palatability of food, and other external cues, whereas nonobese individuals tend to respond to internal cues. In a fascinating study, Rodin has shown that the insulin response to the sight and smell of food is greater in externally responsive people than in internally responsive people. Field studies have shown that, indeed, insulin does seem to govern the amount we eat.

Boundary theory proposes that we have two boundaries, one for hunger and one for satiety. Polivy and Herman suggest that restrained eaters have a very high satiety boundary and, as a result, tend to overeat. To maintain their weight, dieters set a cognitive boundary. If circumstances should induce them to exceed their cognitive boundaries, they tend to become disinhibited eaters for a time, usually the remainder of the day.

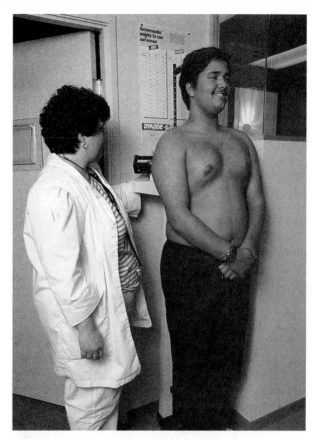

Many humans are faced with the problem of overweight early in life.

Difficulties Confronting Dieters

Anyone who has attempted to lose weight can attest to the difficulty and frustration involved. Why is dieting so difficult? Once again, let's consider the biological, learned, and cognitive components of this question.

The Biological Component

Anabolism (Caloric Thrift) and Catabolism (Caloric Waste)

According to the famine hypothesis, humans have developed several mechanisms to ensure survival in conditions where the food supply is unreliable:

1. A mechanism to deal with the lack of food. This mechanism turns down the thermostat so that we don't use as much energy (Apfelbaum, 1975; Garrow, 1978). The deceleration of metabolism is referred to as *anabolism* or *caloric thrift*.
2. A mechanism to store food when it is available. The extra food is stored in the form of fat.
3. A mechanism to prevent the buildup of excessive amounts of fat. Excessive fat would hinder the individual's mobility and thus be nonadaptive. This mechanism is the acceleration of metabolism, which is referred to as *catabolism* or *caloric waste*. In this state, energy is spent more freely (Polivy & Herman, 1983).

These mechanisms might have been adaptive in a world where food was scarce, but they haunt the overweight person who decides to diet. When the dieter begins to cut down on food, the body responds with a reduced metabolic rate (anabolism), which hinders weight loss. To overcome this regulatory mechanism, the dieter must cut down intake still further. The body responds by further reducing the metabolic rate. Moreover, overweight individuals are used to eating large quantities of food with relatively little weight gain, thanks to catabolism, and so dieting means they have to break entrenched habits of food consumption.

Dieters must also contend with the dynamics of insulin production. As indicated earlier, overweight people tend to develop hyperinsulinemia.

The Learned Component

The Cultural Ideal

Various researchers have noted that the ideal body enshrined in current cultural norms is extremely lean. Fashion magazines such as *Vogue,* for example, show the ideal female as very slim; typically, the models in fashion photographs are well below normative weight. Perhaps not surprisingly, about 70% of women in North America say they feel fat, but only 23% are truly overweight. The lean ideal is promoted by a diet industry valued at more than $30 billion per year, which supplies diet books, programs, videos, foods, pills, and devices (Brownell & Rodin, 1994). This obsession with thinness has emerged only since the Industrial Revolution. Before then, the larger a man's wife the more he was perceived as a good provider. During the Industrial Revolution women saw thinness as a way of differentiating themselves from the lower classes (Brumberg, 1989). Western cultures are now exporting this obsession around the world (*Mclean's,* 2000).

Can people actually lose weight to achieve this culturally ideal weight? And if it is possible, is it advisable for health reasons? As we have seen, considerable evidence suggests that we are born with a set point that is difficult to alter.

Behavior Modification and Weight Control

Although the antidieting movement that emerged in the early 1990s argues that all diets fail (e.g., Garner & Wooley, 1991; Wooley & Garner, 1991), evidence implies that some diets can work. Programs combining very low-calorie food with intensive education and behavior modification seem to work best (e.g., Jeffery et al., 1993).

Behavior modification practitioners suggest that the main problem for the overweight person is to learn new patterns of eating that will not only lead to an immediate weight loss but also maintain the new weight. Dieters need a plan that will enable them to acquire a new set of habits. Many diets can result in weight loss; the problem is to keep from gaining the weight back again. Weight Watchers, probably the most famous behavioral program, was developed from the belief that the best way to treat overweight is to teach new eating habits.

To illustrate this approach, Practical Application 3-1 presents a series of rules that a person in such a program might be required to follow and summarizes the reasons that these rules should lead not only to weight loss but also, over time, to a new set of eating habits that will maintain the weight loss. These rules, which are logical extrapolations from the research literature on hunger and eating, are similar in some respects to those in books on how to alter eating habits (e.g., Jeffrey & Katz, 1977; Mahoney & Mahoney, 1976; Stuart, 1978). There is nothing magical about these rules; they simply show how we can use our current knowledge to keep our weight under control. Note, however, that our knowledge about weight control is still incomplete. Not all overweight people are overweight for the same reason, as Rodin (1981) and others have repeatedly emphasized. Nevertheless, there is considerable agreement that, whatever the exact cause of the problem, overweight people must learn to reorganize their lives if they are to lose their unwanted weight and keep it off.

The Cognitive Component

Although individuals should not be held responsible for their weight and shape, evidence suggests that being a self-determined person—having a sense of autonomy—plays an important role in dieting. People with a stronger sense of autonomy tend, for example, to attend weight-loss programs more regularly, to lose more weight in the course of the program, and to maintain the weight loss longer (Williams, Grow, Freedman, Ryan, & Deci, 1996). Self-determination, therefore, plays an important role in dieting and dieting outcome. Goal setting has also been shown to be an effective way to help people to lose weight (Bagozzi & Edwards, 1998). People in weight-loss programs need to be educated about their contribution to the outcome. Often dieters attribute their failure to the program, rather than to their own levels of commitment or their sense that change is possible.

Health Implications of Weight Loss and Obesity

Obesity has been associated with diabetes, hypertension, cardiovascular disease, and cancer (Bray, 1992). Obesity is responsible for 5.5% of all health care costs in the United States—about $39 million annually (Colditz, 1992). At the same time, most researchers agree that current cultural norms regarding the ideal body put enormous pressure on people to become rigid, lean, and contoured. Indeed, North Americans tend to be prejudiced against fat people (Crandall, 1994). For many dieters, achieving the cultural ideal is difficult, if not impossible, and consequently they are subjected to a great deal of physical and psychological stress.

Increasingly, psychologists are taking an active role in informing the public about issues surrounding weight loss and about behaviorally sound methods for losing weight (Brownell & Rodin, 1994). The following are some conclusions from existing research:

1. Society needs to accept greater variability in shapes and weight.
2. Losing weight usually, but not always, prolongs life.
3. Modest weight losses can have significant health benefits.
4. Dieters should avoid drastic weight fluctuations.

Summary

There are two primary obstacles to dieting. First, when the body is deprived of food, the metabolic rate tends to decline, thereby frustrating the dieter's attempt to lose weight. Second, dieting often produces a craving for restricted foods, often high-calorie foods.

The current cultural ideal calls for an extremely lean body, which is impossible for many people to achieve. However, weight loss is possible within limits. The best method for losing weight involves changing our eating habits and exercising. Self-determination plays a central role in weight loss.

Society needs to accept people as they are and to appreciate their diversity. Weight loss usually improves the health of obese people, but this is not always the case. Nonetheless, maintaining a normal weight often does have important health benefits. Some evidence demonstrates that drastic weight fluctuations have negative health implications, but recent research suggests that this is not necessarily so.

Food Sharing and Eating as a Social Event

Eating is often but not always a social event. It is common for us to eat with other people—be they family, friends, work associates, or business associates. Weddings, graduations, promotions, and even death are a time when we come together to eat and drink. In the process of coming together, we often share food. This is something we do not observe in other animals and has lead psychologists to think of eating as something more than just replenishing fuel and nutrients (McGrew & Feistner, 1992).

The Biological Component

A major theme that comes from an evolutionary analysis of behavior is the idea that sharing food constituted a major advance for humans. Let's begin with the story the biologists tell about our ancestors. According to that story, our ancestors were hunters and gatherers. We assume, from what we now know, that the reason for having both hunters and gatherers was that we needed both types of food. Considerable evidence from a wide variety of sources suggests that humans have become dependent on having a balanced diet that includes the three basic food groups. It is generally assumed in the evolutionary analysis of behavior that males were the hunters and females were gatherers. Because they were specialized and, further, because they each needed what the other had, they needed to learn how to share (Tooby & DeVore, 1987). What emerged was a tendency to share, something that changed the course of human history.

Some writers have argued that sharing emerged because we became meat eaters (Stanford, 1999). The essence of the argument is that when we became meat eaters, perhaps an adaptation associated with developing a larger brain, men gained a power advantage. According to this argument, because meat was a valuable commodity, they were in a better position to broker for what they wanted, whether other types of food, sex, or choice of work. In other words, this was the origin of patriarchal society. I don't think the facts necessarily support that conclusion. As we have seen, carbohydrates tend to be the greater part of our diet. If the males were busy hunting, they would not have had time to gather food, also a time consuming activity. It could be argued, therefore, that females had the advantage. This would be especially true if they also did the food preparation. What is clear is that humans have for some time required a balanced diet. Developing a means of sharing, therefore, was essential (Tooby & DeVore, 1987). Perhaps the emergence of a patriarchal society resulted from some other adaptation.

The Learned Component

Sharing could have emerged in several ways. It has been argued that when humans first began to share food it was with family. Only when the needs of the

Practical Application 3-1

Some Rules for Dieting

Rule 1: *Eat in only one place and at regular times.* This rule is intended to help you stop snacking, by limiting the number of places where you eat and ensuring that you eat at appropriate intervals rather than by impulse. People are typically not good at monitoring their food intake, and many overweight people have become overweight because they snack. If you eat at regular times, your body will have the necessary calories and nutrients to keep you going. Eat *nothing* between meals.

Rule 2: *Use small plates.* Overweight people tend not only to fill their plates but also to eat what is on them. Therefore, when you use a smaller plate, you tend to eat less.

Rule 3: *Eat slowly.* You should accomplish three things by eating slowly. First, the pleasure you get from eating will be maximized. Second, since the mouth provides feedback about the amount we have eaten, we can signal the brain that we have eaten a great deal by carefully chewing our food and making the eating process last as long as possible. Third, when we eat slowly, our digestive system has time to absorb some of the food, and this process should help to stimulate our satiety mechanism. I call this the *fon-*

due phenomenon. A meat fondue is made at the dining table, not in the kitchen. Each diner immerses little pieces of meat, one at a time, in a pot of near-boiling oil. When one piece is eaten, another goes into the pot. The process may take a couple of hours. People often report that they feel full long before all the meat is gone, even when the quantity of food eaten is quite small.

Rule 4: *Eat in the company of others.* People tend to eat slowly and to eat less when they are in the company of others. Besides, conversation tends to extend the eating time, an important factor in reducing food intake (see rule 3).

Rule 5: *If you eat alone, don't read or watch television.* The purpose of this rule is to help you learn to respond to internal cues as well as to help you monitor what and how much you are eating. When you are doing something else, you not only fail to monitor your intake but tend to eat quickly.

Rule 6: *Limit the availability of fattening foods.* If you can't resist cookies, candy, cake, and other high-calorie foods, limit the amounts that are available. Remember that overweight people are often externals, and the mere sight of such food can stimulate the output of insulin.

immediate (genetic) family had been met did the sharing extend to other members such as relatives (Isaac, 1978). But there is also evidence that sharing went beyond the family: Our ancestors hunted big animals, and they likely shared their surplus. Meat tends to spoil quickly, so it would be prudent to share with the local community as well as with the family.

An abundance of meat, for example, would provide a good opportunity for many people to come together. Sharing food in this context meant you were part of a larger family or community; a community that might come to your assistance in times of trouble or hardship. We now have things like potlucks, dinner parties, banquets. Like our ancestors, these gatherings symbolize we are a part of some larger family unit.

This tendency to share sharply contrasts with our closest primate relative, chimpanzees, who eat what they gather (Silk, 1978). Researchers have suggested that because chimpanzees do not need meat in their diets the demand for sharing was never as important. Any sharing that has been observed in chimpanzees is typically limited to mother sharing with her offspring (McGrew & Feistner, 1992).

Sharing of food has emerged in recent times as an event that goes beyond simply ensuring that family members have the energy and nutrients they need to survive. It appears that as social animals, we take pleasure in the others' company and use food as a way of creating and maintaining such friendships. We also use food to create and cement alliances. Even when people

Rule 7: *Allow for variety.* When we eliminate from our diet certain foods that we normally eat, we often develop a craving for those foods. When the craving becomes strong, we have a tendency to eat large quantities of those foods, if they are available. So if you are accustomed to eating pastas, for example, don't try to eliminate them altogether; just cut down.

Rule 8: *Don't try to lose weight too quickly.* When we do, our body often responds with a reduced metabolic rate. This response not only interferes with our ability to lose weight but can cause problems when we have reached our ideal weight. Another disadvantage of trying to lose weight very quickly is that, when we fail to meet our short-term goal, we tend to give up.

Rule 9: *Eat a balanced diet.* The goal of dieting should be not only to lose weight but also to keep that weight off. Sometimes you can lose weight very rapidly by following a diet that requires you to eliminate certain types of food. Not only do such diets often precipitate health problems, but they also fail to teach us how we should eat after we have reached our desired weight. The goal of dieting is simply learning to eat less while staying healthy.

Rule 10: *Combine your diet with exercise.* Since basal metabolism can account for one-third of our energy expenditure, and exercise increases the BMR, exercise is useful not only for getting rid of excess fat but for maintaining our desired weight. The most effective program calls for at least 20 minutes of exercise three times a week and involves an activity that uses 300 calories and raises the heart rate to 60 to 70% of its maximum (McArdle, Katch, & Katch, 1991). Ideal activities are running, swimming, bicycling, walking upstairs, or any other aerobic activity that induces us to take in large amounts of oxygen. (Oxygen is required to burn calories.) Sustained exercise (over several hours) is an ideal way to burn off fat. Remember that fat is a long-term fuel reserve and before we burn fat we need to use up other available fuels such as glycerol.

Exercise is very important when dieting because in the absence of exercise the body tends to use muscles as fuel. Exercise appears to instruct the body not to use muscle when food is in short supply but rather to use fat reserves. It makes sense that the body would not use muscle as fuel when they are needed. The bottom line is that if you want to get rid of fat, you need to exercise.

are not "close" friends, they will come together to share a meal, such as at a potluck dinner for the neighborhood or at a banquet for a political organization. In these cases, sharing of food is often associated with sharing common values.

There are many historical examples of sharing. Along the northwest coast of North America natives from nearby communities have, for at least a hundred years, come together to "potlatches." These gatherings historically served, among other things, to cement relationships with neighbors. The host was expected to provide more food than the guests could eat (Piddocke, 1965). The word *feasting* is often used when describing these gatherings. Researchers have suggested that offering food to others in large amounts is a way of showing respect and kinship (Peabody Museum, 1999).

The Cognitive Component

From time to time researchers have suggested that acts of sharing are nothing more than expressions of instinctive altruism or empathy (see Cosmides & Tooby, 1992). That explanation, however, doesn't adequately explain why we use food sharing to make friends or cement alliances. Another goal that is independent of the need for energy and nutrients might apply to friendships and alliances. Food creates a basic sense of well-being and trust and we might capitalize on that. Alternatively, food might create a sense of indebtedness. The point is that people systemically use food for reasons other than to supply energy and nutrients.

The cognitive revolution of the 1960s and 1970s developed from the premise that humans are essentially thinking machines. They process information and they engage in creating models and strategies; qualities that make them problem solving organisms (Pinker, 1997). What food sharing represents, researchers have suggested, is the emergence of a thinking machine—one that has the ability to construct abstract models and develop strategies (Fiske, 1991). Recall that researchers have argued that humans became dependent on a balanced diet to create their large brains. This large brain allowed humans to become thinking machines.

These mental models or strategies were adaptations that not only made it possible for humans to

share food but also made it possible for humans to engage in a wide variety of human exchanges; for example, exchanging food for tools. One implication of the theory that humans' sharing came from more abstract mental models and strategies is that sharing could have many different forms depending on the situation's complexity (Cosmides & Tooby, 1992). Whether or not we share, for example, could be linked to short-term and long-term availability of food, which are two very different things. Whether or not we share might also be linked to whether or not we had been deprived in the past. Finally, we might begin to use surpluses as a commodity that would enable us to engage in exchanges and, in doing so, allow us to exercise power and control over others to establish social status (Barkow, 1992).

Food sharing, according to this theory, is about human relationships (Fiske, 1991). This could explain why we use food in so many situations. Whenever we want to establish good relationships we retrieve the models or strategies that emerged to make it possible for us to share food. Perhaps that model or strategy is not as unlinked to food as some theorists have argued. As a result, whenever we use that model or strategy, we have an underlying tendency to use food. The tendency to sharing food, in other words, is a remnant of our past. Subjectively, it seems natural for us to offer food when we want to establish good human relationships and receive food when people reach out to us.

Summary

Researchers have argued that a major step forward in the evolutionary advance of humans was food sharing and that initially sharing was limited to the immediate family. At some point, however, sharing became more extensive and included a larger family unit such as the immediate community. Today, sharing food is a way of establishing friendships and cementing alliances. Evolutionary psychologists have suggested that sharing was made possible through the evolution of a larger brain. The new and bigger brain made it possible for humans to create mental models or strategies that could deal with the complexities of food sharing. The mental models or strategies that emerged to make it possible to share food are the same basic mental models that allow us to engage in a variety of social exchanges. It is perhaps, not surprising, therefore, that we find it quite natural to use food whenever we want to establish a good social exchange or to establish a social relationship.

Main Points

1. Humans are born with a number of mechanisms to guard against ingesting toxins.
2. We can also learn to avoid toxins because we are designed to associate taste and sickness.
3. A balanced diet should consist of protein (10–20%), carbohydrates (50–60%), and fats (10–20%).
4. Humans prefer foods that taste sweet, fatty, and salty.
5. Evidence suggests that one main reason we eat is for the sensory qualities that food provides.
6. Obesity is defined as weight about 25% or more in excess of normal.
7. About two-thirds of our energy expenditure is caused by the basal metabolic rate and one-third by exercise.
8. Set-point theory suggests that the hypothalamus sets our weight.
9. According to internal-external theory, one reason that people become overweight is that their food intake is controlled by external cues.
10. Boundary theory proposes that two separate mechanisms control our eating, one for hunger and one for satiety.
11. Dieters tend to be restrained eaters who set a cognitive boundary.
12. Metabolism tends to slow down during deprivation (anabolism) and increase after weight gain (catabolism).
13. Self-determined (autonomous) people are more successful at dieting.
14. Excess weight has been linked to health problems such as diabetes, hypertension, and cardiovascular disease.
15. Researchers have suggested that food sharing is not only an important adaptation but was made possible by the development of a large brain.

 ## *InfoTrac® College Edition*

Considerable research indicates that people who are obese are more likely to develop diabetes. Does that mean if someone is overweight, he or she is likely to develop diabetes as well? See what the relationship is between overweight, insulin output, and diabetes and determine if you or perhaps your friends might be prone to diabetes. (Search words: diabetes, obesity, insulin)

Do you like eating foods from other cultures? Some people like eating foods from other cultures but others don't. Is it simply a matter of taste or is something more involved, such as your willingness to embrace the ideas and people of another culture? See what you can learn from researchers and writers by logging onto the Internet and decide for yourself where you fit. (Search words: food and culture)

Chapter Four

Passion, Love, and Sexual Behavior

- *From a physiological perspective, what constitutes sexual arousal or passion?*
- *What produces sexual arousal in females and males?*
- *What is the function of sexual fantasies?*
- *How is love different from sexual arousal or sexual passion?*
- *Why do people fall in love?*
- *Can we learn to fall in love or is that beyond our control?*
- *How do male and female mating strategies differ?*
- *How important are hormones? What do they do?*
- *Is homosexuality biologically determined, is it learned, or does it come from choices that people make?*
- *Can people change their sexual orientation?*

The study of sexual behavior is a controversial topic. The controversy involves traditional values: Is it appropriate to discuss sex openly? Is sex only for reproduction? Is sex only for marriage? Or, perhaps, is sex merely to have fun? The controversy also involves the question of equity: Are males and females presented evenhandedly? Are stereotypes about male and female behavior being perpetuated? It involves women challenging the old male dogma and introducing their own. It involves debates about the role of biology and the environment.

In this chapter, we will examine four major topics. First, we will look at the underlying physiology of passion. Second, we will look at how passion and love differ and what leads people to fall in love and form long-term relationships. Third, we will examine the role that hormones play not only in sexual behavior but also in producing male and female differences. Fourth, we will review the research pertaining to the origin of sexual orientation.

Human Sexual Arousal (Passion)

Before Masters and Johnson's pioneering book *Human Sexual Response* (1966), no solid scientific information was available about the nature of human sexual arousal—what we commonly call passion. This seems extraordinary in view of the vast number of publications purporting to inform the professional and the layperson about human sexual motivation. For example, a leading medical text stated unequivocally that women were nonorgasmic and rarely, if ever, had sexual feelings (cited in Masters & Johnson, 1966). Two books by Alfred Kinsey and his associates—*Sexual Behavior in the Human Male* (Kinsey, Pomeroy, & Martin, 1948) and *Sexual Behavior in the Human Female* (Kinsey et al., 1953)—caused a storm of controversy. In these books, Kinsey objectively reported the results of interviews with male and female volunteers, which indicated not only that women enjoy sex, as do men, but that both sexes seem to enjoy a wide variety of sexual practices; that is, they like to have sex in different locations and in different positions. At the time, many people regarded the idea of variation in the sexual response as perverse. Among other things, Kinsey was

attacked for the procedures he followed to obtain his sample. The basic argument was that his volunteers were not representative of the general population— that individuals willing to talk to strangers about their sexual practices must be deviant or abnormal. Although there were problems with Kinsey's sampling procedures, time has more or less vindicated him. Humans enjoy sex, and a large number of them enjoy variations in their sexual behavior.

The Biological Component

The consensus that has emerged from Masters and Johnson's work is that human sexual behavior occurs in two major stages: a nontactile stage followed by a tactile stage. In the heterosexual paradigm, the person becomes interested in a member of the opposite sex because of visual, auditory, olfactory, or even cognitive cues. A woman, for example, may arouse the interest of a man by the shape of her body, her clothes, the way she smiles, the quality of her voice, the way she smells, or what she says. If she in turn finds the man attractive, she may agree to spend some time in proximity to him. They may go to a movie, have dinner together, walk together, and so on. If this first stage of proximity is satisfying for both, they move on to the second stage, which involves tactile stimulation. It usually begins with touching or holding hands, proceeds to petting, and gradually becomes more intimate unless inhibitions prevent the natural progression. The eventual aim is usually to have intercourse, with orgasm.

Masters and Johnson focused their research on the tactile phase of sexual behavior. In general, they held that human sexual behavior can be described as a sensory event. They argued that sex is rewarding because it provides a pleasurable sensory experience. Therefore, we need to understand exactly how the structure of this system facilitates the sensory events that motivate human sexual behavior.

There is remarkable similarity between the female and the male sexual response. In other words, from a biological perspective, the sexual response seems to be organized in much the same way for males and females. Any differences seem to be due largely to learned and cognitive factors.

The Female Sexual Response

Masters and Johnson (1966) corrected certain misconceptions about the female sexual response: that women do not derive any pleasurable sensation from sex; and that women do not experience orgasm. In fact, they never found a case in which a woman who was properly stimulated did not experience an orgasm. Misconceptions about the female sexual response are probably caused by comparisons with the male response. The differences that exist do not necessarily make a woman's response less intense or less satisfying than a man's response.

To describe the patterning of physiological and psychological responses, Masters and Johnson have divided the female sexual response into four stages: (1) the excitement phase; (2) the plateau phase; (3) the orgasmic phase; and (4) the resolution phase.

The female sexual response involves physiological changes that occur (1) outside the genital area, (2) in the clitoris, and (3) in the vagina. The diagram of the female pelvic area in Figure 4-1 will be useful in the following discussion.

It is beyond the scope of this chapter to describe all the varieties of stimulation that will produce a female orgasm. For most women, tactile stimulation in the genital area is the most effective. Stimulation of the female genital area produces a more or less uniform pattern of physiological and psychological responses, as summarized in Table 4-1.

According to Masters and Johnson (1966), the clitoris is unique among organs in the human body in that its only function is pleasure. They argue that it exists solely for the purpose of receiving and transforming sensual information. Although no one denies that stimulation of the clitoris produces pleasure, some have argued that it is analogous to the penis (e.g., Morris, 1969). Masters and Johnson maintain that it is unique because it has nothing to do with reproduction and might not be necessary for orgasm, although it obviously plays some role in sexual pleasure and is usually involved in orgasm.

The Male Sexual Response

Figure 4-2 shows a lateral view of the male pelvic area; Table 4-2 summarizes male responses at various stages.

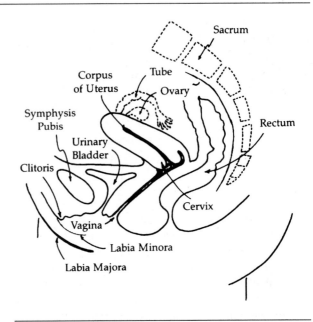

Figure 4-1. Female pelvis: normal anatomy. (From *Human Sexual Response,* by W. H. Masters and V. E. Johnson. Copyright © 1966 by Little, Brown and Company. Reprinted with the permission of the publisher and authors.)

Although both the penis and the clitoris serve as important receptor systems for sensual stimulation, the penis has other functions not shared by the clitoris: The penis is essential for reproduction; and it plays an important role in stimulating the female.

One of the first signs of sexual arousal in the male is penile erection, which results from vasocongestion in the penis. The tissue structure of the penis is such that the increased supply of blood results in its elongation and distention. Continued stimulation of the penis typically produces ejaculation.

The Learned Component

Researchers have been interested in the question of what is sexually arousing for some time. They have found that pictures of nude members of the opposite sex can elicit sexual arousal and that pictures showing a member of the opposite sex in a state of sexual arousal or two persons engaged in sexual acts elicit sexual arousal more effectively than do simple pictures

Table 4-1. The human female sexual response.

Phase	Site of Reaction		
	Extragenital	Clitoris	Vagina
Excitement	Nipple erection Enlargement of breasts Sex flush (breasts) Involuntary muscle contractions Contractions of rectal sphincter	Size of clitoris increases (wide variation among individuals)	Vaginal lubrication Lengthening and distention of vagina Retraction of cervix and corpus of uterus into false pelvis
Plateau	Nipple erection continues Breasts enlarged Sex flush may spread to lower abdomen, thighs, buttocks Involuntary muscle contractions (hands and feet) Hyperventilation Increased heart rate Increased blood pressure	Entire clitoris retracts from normal overhang position	Marked vasocongestion near vaginal opening
Orgasm	Nipple erection continues Breast enlargement continues Sex flush terminates abruptly Involuntary muscle contractions Continued hyperventilation Peaking of heart-rate increase Peaking of blood pressure increase	Clitoris remains in retracted position	Rhythmic contractions near vaginal opening (area of vasocongestion)
Resolution	Decrease in all the above; also perspiratory reaction	Clitoris returns to normal overhang position	Rapid dispersal of vasocongestion Relaxation of vagina

Source: Based on W. H. Masters and V. E. Johnson, *Human Sexual Response*, 1966.

of nudity (e.g., Griffith, May, & Veitch, 1974; Mosher & Abramson, 1955). Several studies have shown that the stimulus does not have to be visual; verbal descriptions of sexual behavior are sufficient to elicit sexual arousal in most volunteer subjects (e.g., Heiman, 1977). The ability to fantasize may be an important mediator of this phenomenon, because subjects can become sexually aroused through fantasy (e.g., Heiman, 1975, 1977; Masters & Johnson, 1966). People who are prone to fantasize or who have some sexual experience find it relatively easy to produce sexual fantasies (Carlson & Coleman, 1977).

Romantic themes and lust themes apparently produce the same amount of arousal (e.g., Fisher & Byrne, 1978; Heiman, 1977; Osborn & Pollack, 1977). It has long been held that women are not aroused by explicit erotic material, whereas men are (e.g., Abelson, Cohen, Heaton, & Suder, 1971), and that, compared with men,

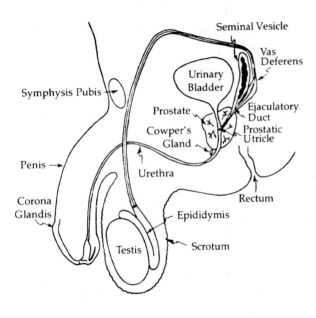

Figure 4-2. Male pelvis: normal anatomy. (From *Human Sexual Response,* by W. H. Masters and V. E. Johnson. Copyright © 1966 by Little, Brown and Company. Reprinted with the permission of the publisher and authors.)

women are more sexually aroused by romantic themes. Research does not support these beliefs. It appears that, in the past, women have been reluctant to admit that they are aroused by pornography because of cultural proscriptions (Gebhard, 1973).

The theme of chance encounter appears to increase sexual arousal in response to pornographic material. This finding is consistent with the literature on romantic attraction, which we will discuss later.

Why are nudity, romantic narratives, and the theme of chance encounter so arousing? Gagnon (1974, 1977) has suggested that these responses are learned—specifically through the creation of sexual scripts. According to Gagnon's analysis, sexual scripts govern all human sexual behavior.

Sexual Scripts

Sexual scripts are mental schemata of how an interpersonal sexual episode should be enacted (Gagnon, 1974, 1977; Simon & Gagnon, 1986). A sexual script is analo-

gous to a movie script in which the actors have motives and feelings. Part of this movie script requires the actors to say certain things and to engage in certain nonverbal actions (Gagnon, 1974). Thus, in any sexual encounter, each individual is guided by a personal script.

Simon and Gagnon argue that sexual scripts initially arise from information to which children are exposed, rewards and punishment they receive, and the process of imitation and modeling. Until adolescence, sexual scripts mainly involve gender-appropriate behaviors. Sexual scripts tell young boys and girls how they should react to and treat each other in nonsexual encounters.

With the onset of adolescence, these scripts begin to incorporate sexual feelings. Gagnon has suggested that, during masturbation, males coordinate or integrate their sexual feelings and activities with their gender roles. This coordination leads them to develop a sexual script that tells them how they should respond in actual sexual intercourse. As they experience each phase of the sexual response (excitement, plateau, orgasm, and resolution), they see themselves engaging in certain sexual behaviors (certain physical activities) and communicating (engaging in appropriate verbal and nonverbal responses). As the sexual script becomes more sophisticated, each phase becomes more clearly differentiated, so that the appropriate sexual behaviors (physical activity) and appropriate communication pattern coincide more closely to each phase of the sexual response.

It has been suggested that females have more difficulty learning to coordinate or integrate sexual feelings into their sexual scripts because fewer females masturbate in early adolescence. Also, relative to male scripts, female sexual scripts in early adolescence contain less information that is purely sexual. Female scripts tend to focus on falling in love, whereas male scripts tend to focus mainly on sexual activity. Although falling in love may involve the excitement phase of the sexual response, it typically does not involve the other phases, which are more closely linked to sexual activity. Later in adolescence, female sexual scripts do incorporate the entire four-stage sexual response.

Gagnon (1974) suggests that, when adolescents begin to date, the script begins to shift from a fantasy-based masturbatory script to a more interpersonal and

Table 4-2.   The human male sexual response.

Phase	Site of Reaction		
	Extragenital	Penis	Scrotum and Testes
Excitement	Nipple erection (60% of males) Some sex flush Involuntary muscle contractions Involuntary contraction of rectal sphincter	Penile erection (vasocongestion) Urethra lengthens	Localized vasocongestion Contraction of smooth-muscle fibers Thickening of scrotal skin Testicular elevation
Plateau	Nipple erection Greater sex flush (25% of males) Involuntary muscle contraction Involuntary contraction of rectal sphincter Hyperventilation Increased heart rate Increased blood pressure	Vasocongestive increase in penile diameter Penile urethral bulb enlarges	As in previous stage, plus greater elevation of testes and increase in testicular size
Orgasm	Continued nipple erection Continued sex flush Involuntary contraction of rectal sphincter Hyperventilation Increased heart rate Increased blood pressure	Ejaculatory reaction (regular contractions of muscles) Seminal fluid expelled through involuntary muscle contractions Urethra contracts in rhythm	As in previous stage
Resolution	Very gradual retraction of nipples Rapid disappearance of sex flush Perspiratory reaction	Penile detumescence (two stages): rapid decrease in vasocongestion followed by slow decrease in vasocongestion	Either rapid or delayed return to normal state

Source: Based on W. H. Masters and V. E. Johnson, *Human Sexual Response,* 1966.

interdependent sexual script. In the course of petting, young couples begin to explore sexual arousal through touching each other while fully clothed. This behavior is experienced as exciting, but it does not typically produce orgasm. What is learned at this stage is to coordinate the feeling of being touched by another person with the excitement phase of the sexual response. In other words, the fantasy gives way to interpersonally instigated sexual excitement that comes largely through touch. Eventually, the female begins to adjust her script to include sexual arousal, which lays the groundwork for eventual orgasm.

As dating continues, the partners learn a number of other skills, such as mutual disrobing, how to obtain privacy, and how to better focus attention on the other person. Gagnon points out that, at this stage, sexual performance is often awkward, clumsy, and anxiety-ridden. With repeated practice and with greater mutual sensitivity, couples learn to coordinate their sexual scripts so that both can achieve sexual pleasure. Once

As the sex drive increases in adolescence, interest in sexual material also increases. Males have been found to be particularly interested in visual material.

a satisfactory solution has been worked out, sexual behavior often becomes semiritualized (Simon & Gagnon, 1986).

The Interaction of Biological and Learned Factors

Because of the important role of sexual scripts, it can be argued that sexual pleasure is the result of an interaction of biological (sensory) and learned factors. The pleasure that originally came only from self-stimulation eventually is shifted to the other person. According to this interpretation, sexual arousal comes to depend on sensory awareness of the sexual partner. Characteristics of the other person—including the sight, smell, and touch of that person—come to act as the source of sexual arousal. Through the process of generalization, other people can also act as sources of sensory arousal. Because images, fantasies, and scripts have also become linked to sexual arousal, the degree to which another person elicits these images, fantasies, and scripts will determine, in part, that person's potential for eliciting sexual arousal. In that respect, sex-

ual arousal is in the eye of the beholder; people are aroused by what they perceive will happen.

The Reward Value of Sex

The reward value of sex seems to depend on participating in a satisfying sexual script. Women and men show a great deal of agreement on the typical sequence of heterosexual behaviors that lead to coitus. Fourteen behaviors have been identified as part of this script, including kissing, caressing, manual stimulation, oral stimulation, and penetration. Where the sexes differ is in the degree of arousal they experience from each of the fourteen behaviors in the script. Male arousal tends to build linearly with each subsequent step (behavior) in the sequence, culminating with the greatest arousal at penetration, whereas female arousal does not build in this way but, rather, is highly variable. What females found most arousing was being stimulated by males, not penetration. Thus, even though males and females agree on the script, they tend to react differently to the same sexual behaviors (Geer & Broussard, 1990). This could account for the finding that females tend to show less interest in sex than do males (Hite, 1976; Zilbergeld, 1978).

Over the years, there has been continuing speculation about the nature of the female orgasm and conjecture about why sexual arousal is different in women and men. Learning theorists suggest that differences in sexual arousal are linked to the individual's focus. Females tend to focus on being stimulated by the male rather than on penetration, so it follows that their greatest feelings of sexual arousal would be linked to being stimulated, rather than, as in the male, to orgasm associated with penetration.

The Cognitive Component

Adults' sexual scripts are influenced by the beliefs and attitudes they hold. Where do these beliefs and attitudes come from? They come in part from the society at large, from peer groups and from internalized values and ideals. Without reviewing all the data on the role of belief systems, let's look at a few interesting topics.

Liberal and Conservative Attitudes Toward Sex

From the 1950s to the early 1980s, North American society became more sexually permissive, especially toward premarital sexual experiences (D'Emilio & Freedman, 1988). Since then, sexual attitudes have become somewhat more conservative, perhaps as a result of a concern over sexually transmitted diseases and a broader cultural trend toward conservatism (Gerrard, 1987). The period from the 1950s to the 1980s was also characterized by a decline in the sexual double standard—the idea that premarital sex is socially acceptable for males but not for females (Brooks-Gunn & Furstenberg, 1989). As a result, despite the trend to conservatism, couples are having sex earlier and more frequently. They have become more open in their attitudes about sex.

Beliefs About the Sex Drive

Both males and females tend to believe that the sex drive is stronger in males than in females (e.g., Byrne, 1977) and, consequently, that sex is more important and more enjoyable for men than for women. This belief could account, in part, for the persistent double standard that sexual promiscuity is more acceptable in males than in females. As an exercise, think about some further implications of this belief.

The Meaning of Sexual Experience

Perhaps one of the strongest differences between males and females is the meaning they attach to sex. Females tend to connect sex with feelings of affection and closeness, whereas males tend to perceive sex as an achievement, an adventure, a demonstration of control and power, or a purely physical release. Consistent with this is the finding that men are less likely than women are to be romantically involved with their first sexual partner. Women tend to value intercourse because it gives them a sense of shared feelings, emotional warmth, and being wanted. Men, in contrast, tend to isolate sex from other aspects of the relationship. They are more inclined to focus on arousal, for example (Basow, 1992).

Remember, however, that these general tendencies reflect statistical differences. Like men, women sometimes perceive sex as an achievement, adventure, a demonstration of control and power, or a purely physical release; like women, men might associate sex with affection and closeness. Indeed, most men prefer that love and sex go together; like women, they value love far ahead of sex in overall importance in their lives (Chassler, 1988: Pietropinto & Simenauer, 1977). As men get older, love and intimacy become the main motivators of sex (Sprague & Quadagno, 1987).

Summary

Masters and Johnson's pioneering work has provided us with a scientific description of the physiological events that result from sexual stimulation. The sexual response of both females and males can be divided into four phases: excitement, plateau, orgasm, and resolution. Although important differences in the reactions of females and males have been known for some time, Masters and Johnson have shown that there are many similarities.

Material that is sexually arousing for both males and females includes pictures of nude members of the opposite sex, people engaged in sexual acts, and verbal descriptions of sexual behavior. The ability to fantasize plays an important role in determining the degree to which different types of material will be sexually arousing.

Gagnon suggested that human sexual behavior is largely the result of sexual scripts. These mental representations or schemata help guide the individual through a sexual episode. It has also been suggested that, during masturbation, males and females coordinate or integrate their sexual feelings and activities with their gender roles. In this way, they develop a sexual script that tells them how they should respond during sexual activity with another person. With the onset of dating, the fantasy-based script is gradually transformed to a more interpersonal and interdependent sexual script. This transition is often characterized by awkwardness, clumsiness, and anxiety—by trial-and-error behavior. Because of the important role of sexual scripts, it can be argued that sexual pleasure is the result of an interaction of biological (sensory) and learned factors. According to this analysis, mature sexual arousal—sexual arousal that comes from others rather than the self—results from an increased awareness of the sexual partner's sensory characteristics.

Our sexual scripts are influenced by our beliefs, attitudes, and values. It is not surprising that, as a more liberal attitude toward sex became prevalent, premarital sex increased. The persistent belief that the sex drive is stronger in males than in females helps account for the double standard in our society relative to sexual promiscuity.

One of the strongest differences between males and females is the meaning they attach to sex. Females associate sex with feelings of affection and closeness, but males tend to perceive sex as an achievement, an adventure, a demonstration of control and power, or a purely physical release. Note, however, that these are statistical differences and do not reflect individual differences. Like women, most men prefer that love and sex go together and value love far ahead of sex in overall importance in their lives.

Attraction, Passion, Love, and Reproduction

Consider the following scenario. You are walking on a college campus and an attractive person of the opposite sex says: "Would you have sex with me?" If you are like the women in one study, 100% of you would

say no. You would find such a comment offensive or perhaps puzzling. If you were a male on the other hand, 75% of you would say yes. Most men feel flattered. Many of the 25% who declined were apologetic, often citing a previous commitment (Clarke & Hatfield, 1989). This study illustrates males and females tend to approach sexual behavior from a very different perspective. In this section, we will examine some of the ways males and females differ.

The Biological Component

From an evolutionary perspective, the purpose of sexual behavior is to produce offspring. That will help ensure our genes survive in future generations. From that perspective, the pleasure we experience is simply an evolutionary mechanism that emerged to motivate us to engage in sexual behavior on a repeated basis. Love, similarly, is another mechanism that helps us to focus our attention on a particular mate or potential mate with the ultimate purpose that we repeatedly have sex with that person.

One of the basic problems linked to human evolution was how best to adapt to raising offspring that could survive and thus ensure that our genes would survive. When humans developed large brains capable of great feats of learning, they also became very dependent on others to ensure they could survive during the early stages of development. For humans to develop a large brain, one capable of thinking and planning, we had to give up our dependence on more instinctive (hardwired) response patterns (Pinker, 1997). As a result, the human offspring is highly vulnerable at birth. This is necessary for the parent to take an active role in protecting offspring and to teach them how to survive. To do this, researchers have argued that it was necessary for both parents to become involved (Geary, 2000). In many species, parenting is left solely to the mother. Within this context, evolutionary psychologists have argued that humans developed a whole new strategy for ensuring their genes survived. The core of this strategy involved the emergence of sharing in the raising of offspring (Mann, 1992). Many other species also share in the raising of the offspring, but researchers have argued that among primates, this strategy has emerged to a much higher level and is more complex. Conception, in other words, is only the beginning of the process. Because it takes humans a long time to survive on their own, we need to be motivated to devote a large part of our life to the process of ensuring our offspring survive. In other words, humans have evolved to prefer raising their offspring with a mate that is willing to commit to a long-term relationship (Geary, 2000).

Evolution and Biology of Love

Establishing a long-term relationship has not been left to chance. One mechanism that has evolved to ensure humans establish a long-term relationship is love. When people are in love they experience a psychological state close to euphoria. Research has shown that love has been linked to dopamine and norepinephrine, which have both been implicated in euphoria. In addition, love is especially linked to phenylethylanine (PEA), which "gives you that silly smile that you flash at strangers. When we meet someone who is attractive the whistle blows at the PEA factory" (Walsh, 1991). Phenylethylanine does not last forever, however; after two or three years, it begins to fall. This is consistent with the observation that, in 62 different cultures, the divorce rate peaks around the fourth year of marriage (Fisher, 1992).

Why do many marriages last beyond that point? It appears that the initial attraction stage gives way to an attachment stage, mediated by endorphins (Fisher, 1992). Endorphins (discussed in more detail in Chapter 7) are the equivalent of the body's own morphine; they not only reduce pain but also produce feelings of well-being. Growing evidence indicates that endorphins are released not just in pain or fear, as originally thought, but also by other emotions; for instance, laughter is linked to endorphin release. Endorphins also play a critical role in maintaining the immune system. It is perhaps not surprising that the immune system tends to decline dramatically following the death of a spouse (Chapter 11).

Oxytocin has also been implicated in love. This chemical, produced by the brain, sensitizes nerves and stimulates muscles. It is thought to promote cuddling and to enhance orgasm. In a study of men, oxytocin levels increased by a factor of 3 to 5 during climax. Fisher (1992) suggests that oxytocin produces feelings of relaxed satisfaction and attachment.

Love might be what cements a relationship, but it appears that we do not fall in love with just anybody. Evidence suggests that we fall in love with members of the opposite sex who possess certain important physical and psychological traits that will increase the likelihood our genes will survive in future generations. Evolutionary psychologists argue that we have evolved mating strategies that will make certain potential mates more attractive than others. We will begin by discussing female mating strategies.

Long-Term Female Mating Strategies

Given that both males and females have evolved a preference for a mate who will make a long-term commitment to raising the offspring, what characteristics are most adaptive to females and which for males? Keep in mind that the underlying motivation is to ensure that one's genes survive in future generations.

Researchers have suggested that women need a mate who (1) has or can obtain the resources to invest in raising the offspring, (2) is willing to invest those resources, (3) has the capacity to physically protect both her and her offspring, (4) has or can develop good parenting skills, (5) is a mate who is compatible, and (6) is healthy (Buss, 1999).

Consistent with the argument that it is adaptive for women to seek out a mate who has the potential to obtain adequate resources, it has been found that women prefer males who have good financial prospects (Buss, Abbot, Angleitner, Asherian, Biaggio & 45 others, 1990; Buss & Schmitt, 1993); prefer men with greater social status (which would give them more access to resources) (Buss & Schmitt, 1993); prefer older men (older men on the average have more power, prestige, and control) (Buss & Schmitt, 1993); and prefer men who are more ambitious (more motivated to obtain resources) (Kyl-Heku & Buss, 1996). Consistent with the argument that it would be adaptive for women to prefer men who are willing to invest their resources, it has been found that women look for dependability and stability in potential mates (Buss et al., 1990). These two characteristics suggest that resources will be provided consistently over time. Not surprising, women also look specifically for commitment. Consistent with the argument that it would be adaptive for women to have mates who could protect them, it has been found that women have a preference for taller, stronger, and more athletic men (Barber, 1995). Consistent with the argument that it would be adaptive for women to select mates who have good parenting skills is the finding that women rate males who show affection toward children more attractive (La Cerra, 1994). Consistent with the argument that women are attracted to males who are compatible are numerous studies of marital satisfaction that have shown that there is greater satisfaction in relationships where the partners have similar interests and values (Gibson, Franken, & Rowland, 1989). Finally consistent with the argument that women prefer men who are healthy are studies that show women prefer men with symmetrical bodies and faces (Gangestad, Thornhill, & Yeo, 1994). Symmetry, it has been found, is a good health cue (Buss, 1999).

Long-Term Male Mating Strategies

Sociobiology theories have argued that the best strategy for males is to mate with as many females as possible. Doing so, researchers have argued, would increase the probability of ensuring ones' genes survive in future generations. In other words, let the female take responsibility for raising the offspring. Even if there might be an advantage to having two partners raise the offspring, there is a greater advantage for males to have sex with many different partners and to depend on them to care for the offspring. The problem with this argument is that it assumes females will tend to acquiesce to such an arrangement. Further, it assumes males are in control of sexual encounters. But are they in control? Considerable evidence suggests that females exert a great deal of control. Moreover, a female who forms a long-term relationship has an advantage because that relationship will give her the help she needs to raise the offspring. Thus, there is a distinct advantage for females to look for commitment. The net effect is that if females look for commitment, the pool of women available to men who do not want to commit is limited (Buss, 1999). The way to get access to this larger pool is, obviously, to commit. From a female perspective, it would be nice if the male would be willing to invest resources as well as provide protection. In short, it would be advantageous for females to seek out males with those qualities as well as being willing to commit. Females compete with other females, just as males compete with

other males, so it is not simply a matter of holding out until one gets what he or she wants. There must be some kind of trade off. This is the point at which males who are willing to commit, willing to invest resources and willing to offer protection, gain an advantage. They are in a position to gain greater access to the pool of women and, thus, are in a better position to choose among females that will produce offspring who will survive (Buss, 1999). In other words, instead of going for quantity, which we have just seen has limitations, they are in a position to go for quality because by selecting for quality they improve the chances the offspring will be superior and thus survive. We will turn to those qualities momentarily, but first, let me point out a couple of additional advantages to forming long-term relationships.

One additional advantage of entering a long-term relationship is to gain greater sexual access (often exclusive access), thereby increasing the likelihood of producing offspring (Kenrick, Keefe, Gabrielidis, & Cornelius, 1996). Another advantage is the increased likelihood the offspring will survive (Kenrick et al., 1996). Evidence indicates that children who are raised by two parents gain a distinct advantage not only in their own survival but also in being willing and able to produce their own offspring (Hill & Hurtado, 1996).

Given the advantage for males who commit to a long-term relationship, with whom should they mate? It has been suggested that the main thing males focus on is fertility or reproductive value (i.e., the ability to produce many offspring). Consistent with this, researchers have found that males prefer young attractive women. Young women are more likely to be healthy (capable of producing offspring) and will have a longer period of fertility. Considerable evidence that attractiveness is a sign of health. Attractiveness is typically considered such things as full lips, clear skin, smooth skin, clear eyes, lustrous hair, good muscle tone, and a symmetrical face. In addition, males appear to focus on the waist to hips ratio (WHR). Researchers have shown that men prefer WHRs of .70 (Singh, 1993; Singh & Luis, 1995; Singh & Young, 1995). The significance of this is the finding that healthy, reproductively capable women have WHR of .67 to .80. It is interesting to note in this context that the WHRs of *Playboy* centerfolds and winners of beauty contests over the past 30 years (even though models became thinner over the years) have remained constant at .70. It is also interesting to note that plumpness is an unreliable characteristic of attractiveness when taken out of context. The context that needs to be considered is food supply. In societies where food is scarce, plumpness signals wealth, health, and adequate nutrition during development (Rosenblatt, 1974). In societies where food is relatively abundant, such as the United States and Europe, the relationship between plumpness and status is reversed (Symons, 1979). In North America women think that men like them to be thin but studies have shown that men prefer average women (Rozin & Fallon, 1988).

The Learned Component

Although evolutionary psychology provides a powerful theory for explaining the motivation for sex and what makes a mate attractive, a considerable body of research indicates a wide range of factors play a role in sexual motivation and sexual attraction. Take, for example, falling in love. The phrase "falling in love" implies that becoming emotionally attracted to another person is often outside our immediate control, a process that can be rapid or gradual. Research shows that we frequently fall in love with somebody other than our ideal. In one study, only 40% of the subjects reported that their most intense experience of love was with a person close to their ideal (Averill & Boothroyd, 1977). In other words, falling in love depends on factors other than those we think we are looking for.

Certain common elements have been identified. Thoughts about the other person and dating frequency seem to be important factors (Kleck & Rubenstein, 1975; Tesser & Paulhus, 1976). Interestingly, chance meeting appears to be among the conditions most conducive to falling in love (Averill & Boothroyd, 1977), perhaps because the phrase itself suggests an accidental quality, so unexpected encounters make us more attuned to the possibility.

Sternberg (1991) argues that whether or not we fall in love is largely under our control. It has to do with our cognitive set: If we are set or prepared to fall in love, we will. According to Sternberg, love does not have to be accidental; it can be planned. You fall in love through your actions, and you can stay in love through your actions.

Perhaps not surprisingly, falling in love tends to cause very positive changes in our self-concept. Among other things, people who have fallen in love are found to experience increased self-esteem and increased feelings of self-efficacy, which is a measure of individuals' perceptions of their ability to mobilize resources and meet a challenge (Aron, Paris, & Aron, 1995).

Arousal and Attraction

Perhaps one of the most fascinating chance phenomena that plays a role in attraction is arousal. Consider the following scenario. You are on an elevator and it begins to fall. After falling for several floors it comes to an abrupt halt. As you wait for help, you make eye contact with an attractive person of the opposite sex. You are immediately attracted and one of you suggests you go for a cup of coffee as soon as you can get out. This is followed by several dates and eventually you marry. Sound absurd? Research suggests quite the contrary. It appears to be a very reliable phenomenon. Numerous studies have shown that arousal increases attraction to an attractive opposite sex target and decreases attraction to an unattractive opposite-sex target (Foster, Witcher, Campbell, & Green, 1998). The results can be best explained by "response facilitation" theory (Allen, Kenrick, Linder, & McCall, 1989). According to this theory arousal heightens a specific dominant response. Specifically, it increases the attractiveness of an attractive person as well as increases the aversiveness of the unattractive person. One practical implication of this research is if you want someone who is already attracted to you to fall in love with you, you need to take that person on a fast spin on a motor cycle, dancing, or anything that would produce a high level of arousal.

Intimacy

Intimacy has to do with feelings of closeness, connectedness, and being bonded. It pertains more to the social and psychological aspects of love than to physical sex. Intimacy is something that people must learn. In the intimacy literature, long-term commitment is often used as one of the defining characteristics of true intimacy. Sternberg (1991) carefully distinguishes between intimacy and commitment. Commitment is a decision; it is a cognitive activity.

Intimacy, on the other hand, is a skill; it is something that you learn.

It is often thought that intimacy takes time to develop, but this need not be the case. One way that people establish intimacy is to engage in self-disclosure. In self-disclosure, a person discloses something personal or private, in the expectation that, in return, the other person will disclose something personal or private. If self-disclosure proceeds rapidly, intimacy can quickly be established.

Research has linked willingness to self-disclose to a sensation-seeking personality type. According to Zuckerman (1979), sensation-seeking personalities need a high degree of novelty and complexity in their lives and are willing to take risks to meet this need. Research from a variety of sources has shown, among other things, that high sensation seekers tend to have more sexual partners than do low sensation seekers. It is interesting to ask, therefore, whether high sensation seekers tend to engage in self-disclosure. Do they use self-disclosure or do they use some other strategy? A study on this question found that high sensation seekers are inclined to self-disclose information about their sexual motivation and behavior (Franken, Gibson, & Mohan, 1990). This suggests that sensation seekers not only use self-disclosure to establish intimate relationships but also use a form of self-disclosure that signals their motives to the other person early in the relationship.

Sexual Self-Schemas

Sexual self-schemas are derived from our experiences and manifest themselves is sexual cognition. Researchers have shown that self-schemas play a key role in romantic attachment (Cyranowski & Andersen, 1998; Griffin & Bartholomew, 1994). For purposes of research, schemas have often been viewed as being positive, thereby facilitating sexual attachment, or negative, interfering or inhibiting sexual attachment. A positive self-schema has two important components. First, it involves having a positive view of our ability to become attached. Researchers have suggested this positive view has its roots in how we were treated as children. If we were consistently loved, for example, we would develop a nonanxious view about our ability to become attached; however, if we were treated inconsistently, we would be more inclined to develop an anxious view. We might say to ourselves, for example

that because we were not loved consistently as children, we do not possess qualities that will allow us to establish a strong attachment. The second component involves our view of whether or not others are available or supportive. If we believe that we can form a strong attachment and that others are available and supportive, we will be inclined to engage in approach behavior. Alternatively, if we have a negative (anxious) view of ourselves and do not see others as readily available, we will be inclined to avoid getting involved in close relationships. Research has been found that engaged women who have a positive versus a negative self-schema: have had more extensive histories of previous romantic relationships, were more likely to be in a current relationship, and were more likely to describe that current relationship in positive terms (Cyranowski & Andersen, 1998).

The Cognitive Component

According to Robert Sternberg (1991), staying in love depends on making the decision that you love someone, and that you are willing to invest the time and energy necessary to stay in the relationship. It is ultimately your decision whether you stay in love or fall out of love.

Commitment involves, among other things, the realization that love involves satisfying the needs of two distinct individuals. It also involves accepting that there are going to be differences or problems and that, if love is to endure, they must be resolved to the mutual satisfaction of both parties. In the final analysis, Sternberg contends, commitment is not just a desire or wish but rather the willingness to invest time and energy—in particular, the time and energy required to develop problem-solving skills. (We will return to this question in Practical Application 4-1.)

Having examined the biological, learned, and cognitive components of love, let's turn to a model that integrates all three.

Sternberg's Interaction Model

Sternberg (1991) suggests that love involves three primary components: passion, intimacy, and commitment. Sternberg's model of love (Figure 4-3) is a true interaction model. It is interesting to consider what happens to relationships that lack some of the three primary components in his theory. Sternberg has offered the following:

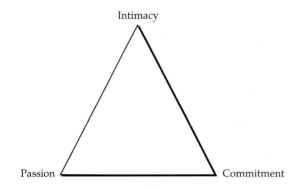

Figure 4-3. Sternberg's love triangle. (From *Love the Way You Want It*, by R. J. Sternberg. Copyright © 1991 by Bantam Books. Reprinted with permission.)

Passion alone = infatuated love. Infatuations often arise unexpectedly—simply as the result of a look, a touch, a word. They are characterized by bodily sensations, a tingling, a heightened heart rate, a warm sensuous feeling. Sometimes people act on their infatuations (also called attractions); sometimes they don't. Infatuations are often the grist for fantasies.

Sometimes infatuations become obsessive. Teens, for example, might become so infatuated with a movie star or a rock star that they cannot pursue real relationships. Because infatuations are so limited, they are unfulfilling. Unless we can get beyond infatuation, we can never be truly happy.

Intimacy alone = liking. Liking occurs when you feel close and connected but without the need for passion or commitment. Relationships at work can be of this type; they are not important outside the context of work. Friendship is generally based on liking. We enjoy sharing our ideas and feelings because it gives us a sense of being in tune with another person.

Commitment alone = sterile love. We often see commitment alone at the end of a long-term relationship, when partners are no longer physically attracted to each other and have lost their emotional involvement with each other. In societies where marriages are arranged, sterile love often characterizes the beginning of a relationship and is followed by the development of passion and intimacy.

Passion + intimacy = romantic love. Romantic lovers experience more than just physical attraction. They enjoy the emotion that comes with being together, experiencing the same feelings, sharing their closeness. They do not, however, have any sense that it will last or that they particularly want it to last. Sometimes romantic love starts with passion and the partners become close. Sometimes it starts with a friendship that over time grows into passion. It could be a shipboard romance or a summer fling.

Passion + commitment = fatuous love. Fatuous love is like the proverbial Hollywood marriage. After a whirlwind courtship, the couple gets married, without taking the time to develop intimacy. After a glorious honeymoon, they go their separate ways, in the conviction that their love will cross continents. Because there was no intimacy, however, true commitment never develops. When the passion fails, there is nothing to hold them together.

Intimacy + commitment = companionate love. Companionate love might best be described as a long-term committed friendship. Sometimes, as the passion in marriage subsides, people retain a strong sense of intimacy and commitment. Family relationships are often characterized by both intimacy and commitment, as are cherished friendships.

Intimacy + passion + commitment = consummate love. Consummate love is the combination of intimacy, passion, and commitment. It is hard to attain and harder still to keep. People strive for consummate love, but it often eludes them (see Practical Application 4-1).

Summary

According to evolutionary psychologists, the ultimate reason for engaging in sexual behavior is to produce offspring that will carry our genes into future generations. Attraction, passion, and love are merely adaptive components that ensure that we engage in sexual behavior on a repeated basis thereby increasing the chances our genes will be carried into future generations. According to evolutionary theory and research, it has become highly adaptive for humans to form long-term relationships. Because females must invest so much time and advantage in producing and raising offspring, it is adaptive for them to seek males who are willing to commit, invest resources and protect. Because females are more likely to mate with males who commit, willingness to commit increases the pool of females available to males who will commit. Males who are willing to commit, invest resources and protect have a distinct advantage over males lacking those qualities because they have a larger pool of females from which they can select and they can select for those qualities that are likely to lead to offspring who have a better chance of survival.

In addition to what evolutionary psychologists have pointed out, several other things play roles in attractiveness, love, and sexual behavior. Chance meeting has been found to be a major determinant of why people fall in love. Perhaps because the idea of falling in love suggests an accidental quality, some people seem predisposed to fall in love with an attractive person whom they meet by chance. The perceived availability of the imagined partner also plays a role. This suggests that calculations of the energy required to attain a goal form part of feelings of attraction.

If you find someone attractive, increases in arousal have been shown to heighten those feelings. If you are willing to disclose to someone you find attractive you will be more inclined to establish intimacy, an essential component of consummate love. Positive sexual self-

Practical Application 4-1

Striving to Attain Consummate Love

Sternberg argues that people can learn to attain consummate love. The first thing they need to recognize is that consummate love is like any other goal. They must consciously choose it as a goal and decide that they are willing to work toward it.

Many people in our society are not willing to commit themselves to this goal. They might decide, for example, that intimacy is not desirable or possible or that commitment to another person is inconsistent with their desire to be free or to be an individual. As a result, they might decide to satisfy their passion by pursuing endless sexual relationships. As one relationship fades, they look for another sexual encounter.

Sternberg points out that, if people commit themselves to the goal of consummate love, they need to recognize the obstacles and challenges that they must overcome. First, people have different tastes, different beliefs, and different habits. As a result, there are bound to be conflicts and problems. To deal with such differences, people need to learn problem-solving skills. One of the first things to learn is how to identify a problem. A good starting place is to simply identify the category to which it belongs. Does the conflict have to do with, for instance, money, running the household, sexual preferences, friends, religion, or political beliefs? Identifying the category helps to define the problem. Unless two people both agree on the problem, there is no point in trying to find the so-

lution. Identifying the problem helps focus communication on the problem and prevents people from bringing in unrelated arguments. ("And furthermore, you never put the cap back on the toothpaste.") Sometimes it may be important to seek the help of other people. When people learn to focus on the problem and treat it as a mutual problem, they are less likely to blame each other.

Sternberg argues that people who have made the decision to attain consummate love need to learn to recognize the pitfalls—what he calls love villains—in relationships. All of us, he argues, hide behind a mask from time to time. When we feel vulnerable or afraid, we may try to hide our feelings, by putting forth an image that is the opposite of what we really feel. This is likely to cause problems in the relationship. Sternberg has identified ten villains or masks: the controller, the typecaster, the pious fraud, the procrastinator, the conflict avoider, the yes-sayer, the expert, the righteous accuser, the pretender, and the blamer.

People who wish to attain consummate love must accept that relationships are never perfect and are never cast in stone. People change, so we must learn to accept such change. People make mistakes, so we must learn to forgive. In the final analysis, we need to see obstacles as challenges and to see the possibility for growth and optimism in the future.

schemas play a key role in determining whether or not you will be inclined to engage in an approach strategy.

According to Sternberg, love—consummate love, as he calls it—has three major components: passion, intimacy, and commitment. Passion has to do with the physical and emotional aspects of love—with being attracted to another person and a desire for romance. Intimacy has to do with feelings of closeness, connectedness, and being bonded; it is a skill that people must learn if true love is to be achieved. Commitment involves a decision that your partner in love is worth the time and effort to make the relationship work. Much of that effort will be invested in acquiring the necessary problem-solving skills. Sternberg shows that relationships in which one or more of these components are missing are something less than consummate love. He argues that people can attain consummate love and offers several ideas about how to do it.

Biological Differences Between Men and Women

How genetically different are males and females? In 1990, British scientists identified a single gene of the Y chromosome that determines maleness. Without this gene, all embryos would develop into females. The role of this gene is to activate a host of other genes, which guide the complex task of turning a fetus into a boy. The sex hormones are essential to this process.

Sex Hormones

Males and females have the same sex hormones but in different amounts. These hormones play a critical role in ensuring that we have two sexes, male and female. They have also been implicated in a wide range of behaviors.

Some of the research on hormones grows out of work that is still in its infancy, though it has been going on for more than 25 years. This tremendously exciting research might eventually help us come to a better understanding of individual differences. Right now, much of the focus is on differences between males and females because, at least in animals, they are very stereotypical and therefore relatively easy to quantify. This work does indicate that there are biological differences between males and females, but its significance relates, in my view, to the more basic question of how the brains of males and females develop.

Three Major Categories of Sex Hormones

The major category of hormones that govern male sexual behavior consists of *androgens*, the most important of which is testosterone. The two main categories of hormones that govern female sexual behavior consist of *estrogens* and *progestins*. The major estrogen is estradiol, and the major progestin is progesterone. Though we speak of androgens as male sex hormones and of estrogens and progestins as female sex hormones, this distinction is not entirely accurate. Androgens can be converted into estrogens and progestins, just as progestins can be converted into androgens. Estrogens and progestins circulate in the blood of men as well as women, and androgens circulate in the blood of women (Hoyenga & Hoyenga, 1979). Estrogen levels in males have been found to range from 2% to 30% of the level found in females, while the androgen levels in females has been found to range from 6% to 30% of the level found in males (Money, 1980). The main difference between the sexes, therefore, is simply the degrees of concentration of these hormones. One reason that the range is so large is that the levels of all hormones change constantly. As we shall see, both internal and external factors can dramatically alter these levels.

The Production of the Sex Hormones

The sex hormones are produced by the adrenal glands and the gonads. The male gonads are the testes; the female gonads are the ovaries. The male gonads produce mainly androgens, whereas the ovaries produce mainly estrogens and progestins. The adrenal glands produce mainly androgen. It has been estimated that about half of the androgen found in females is produced by the adrenal glands and about half by the ovaries.

The amount of each sex hormone present at any moment is governed by the pituitary gland, which is ultimately controlled by the hypothalamus. The pituitary releases as many as 10 hormones that act in various ways to excite, inhibit, and generally modulate the complex patterns involved in the arousal and direction of the sexual response (Whalen, 1976). Most research has focused on the two gonadotropic hormones: follicle-stimulating hormone (FSH), which induces maturation of the ovarian follicles in the female and stimulates production of sperm in the male; and luteinizing hormone (LH), which induces ovulation in the female and stimulates the output of androgen by the testes of the male. Androgen influences the mating response of male animals and is generally regarded as one of the hormones that governs the arousal of sexual interest in the human male.

Androgen is produced more or less continuously in males. The output increases suddenly in early adolescence, which largely accounts for the sudden awakening of sexual interest in adolescent boys, and declines gradually through adulthood and old age. The decline in sexual interest with increasing age might be caused by the decrease in androgen production (Bancroft, 1987), as well as other factors such as lack of variety and even the self-fulfilling prophecy that, as we grow older, we lose interest in sex.

The female hormones, in contrast, are produced in accordance with a 28-day cycle linked to egg production. The ovaries have a dual function: They produce both egg cells and hormones. The cycle begins when an anterior-pituitary hormone (follicle-stimulating hormone) initiates the growth of an ovarian follicle—an ovum and the surrounding cells. This growth continues for half the cycle. Because the follicle cells secrete estrogen, the amount of estrogen produced increases with growth of the follicle. About halfway through the cycle, the ovum breaks through the wall of the follicle and the ovary. This phenomenon is called *ovulation*. For the few days surrounding ovulation, the female is fertile; that is, the ovum is capable of being fertilized by male spermatozoa. Once the ovum breaks through the wall of the follicle and the ovary, estrogen production diminishes quickly, although estrogen continues to circulate in the bloodstream for some time.

Receptivity in many lower animals is linked to estrogen levels, but receptivity in the human female is relatively independent of estrogen levels. Various researchers, such as Masters and Johnson (1975), have argued that one of the primary functions of sexual behavior in humans is to create a pleasure bond. Within the context of this pleasure bond, couples produce and care for their offspring (see also Morris, 1969).

In humans, ovulation ceases in the late 40s and early 50s, on the average. Simultaneously, of course, estrogen production dwindles. This change in physio-

logical functioning is called *menopause*. As we have seen, estrogen is not closely tied to receptivity in humans and, although some women report a decline in sexual interest in the age range from 40 to 50, just as many report no decline or even an increase.

Sex Hormones and Differences in Physical Characteristics

For about one month after the egg has been fertilized, male and female embryos cannot be differentiated. In the second month, sex differences begin to appear. If the egg has been fertilized with an X chromosome, the gonads (the two collections of germ cells) begin to develop into ovaries. As the male ducts disintegrate, the female ducts thicken and become the womb, the fallopian tubes, and the upper two-thirds of the vagina.

If the egg has been fertilized with a Y chromosome, development moves in a very different direction during the second month. H-Y antigens, believed to be produced by the Y chromosome, change the ovaries into testicles, which produce various hormones: one that absorbs the female parts, such as the womb; testosterone, which thickens the spermatic cord; and dihydrotestosterone, which promotes the formation of the penis (Goy & McEwen, 1980; Haseltine & Ohno, 1981; Wilson et al., 1981; see also Durden-Smith & de Simone, 1983, for a very readable discussion of the material in this section).

To demonstrate that hormones are indeed responsible for the development of sex organs, female rats have been injected with the male hormone testosterone. Their female offspring are then found to be modified in several ways. They are born with an external vagina, often have a penis, and exhibit few mating responses in adulthood (Beach, 1976).

Ethical considerations prevent such manipulations with humans, but a great many data indicate that human hormones work in the same way. Some evidence comes from observations of people who have undergone a voluntary sex change. Candidates for sex-change operations are injected with either testosterone (for a female-to-male change) or estrogen (for a male-to-female change). A male transsexual who receives estrogen (the family of hormones related to estradiol) can expect to grow breasts and add fat at the hips and thighs. Conversely, if androgen (the family of hormones related to testosterone) is given to a female transsexual, she develops an enlarged clitoris and grows facial hair, her voice deepens, and her musculature becomes more masculine (Rubin, Reinisch, & Haskett, 1981; CIBA Foundation Symposium, 1979).

Sex Hormones and Intellectual Functioning

Men and women do not differ in terms of intellectual functioning (for example, IQ scores), but they do seem to differ in certain specific ways. Males tend to be superior on visual-spatial tasks such as tracking a moving object (e.g., Law, Pellegrino, & Hunt, 1993), mental rotation (e.g., Masters & Sanders, 1993), navigating their way through a route, and guiding or intercepting projectiles (Kimura, 1992). The difference may be as large as $d = 1.0$ standard deviation, depending on the test used (Voyer, Voyer, & Bryden, 1995). Females show superior performance on synonym tasks and verbal fluency (Gordon & Lee, 1986; Hines, 1990). The effect size is in the range $d = 0.5-1.2$ standard deviations. In addition, women do better than men on perceptual speed tasks— that is, identifying and matching items (Kimura, 1992). Females tend to have a clear quantitative advantage in the early years, but this effect reverses itself before puberty (Hyde, Fennema, & Lamon, 1990). After puberty and into old age, males maintain their superiority.

Researchers have found that at least some of these differences can be linked to testosterone levels. For example, Kimura (1992) has found that women with high testosterone perform better on a spatial task (rotating figures) than women with low levels of testosterone, and that men with low levels outperform men with high levels (see top panel of Figure 4-4). Moreover, it has been shown that older men given testosterone improve their performance on visual-spatial tests (Janowsky, Oviatt, & Orwoll, 1994).

On tests of mathematical reasoning, men with low levels of testosterone perform better than do men with high levels (e.g., Christiansen & Knussman, 1987; Kimura, 1992), but in women mathematical reasoning is unrelated to testosterone level (Kimura, 1992) (see middle panel of Figure 4-4). On perceptual speed tasks —tasks in which women are typically superior—there is no relationship between testosterone and performance (see bottom panel of Figure 4-4).

Kimura has not been able to find any differences on vocabulary tests and tests of verbal reasoning. This is consistent with the work of Hyde and Linn (1988), who did a meta-analysis of 165 studies involving about 1 million subjects and found no differences between the sexes. Kimura has, however, found differences between men and women in mathematical abilities. This topic is still controversial. In a meta-analysis of 100 studies, Hyde, Fennema, and Lamon (1990) concluded that "gender differences in mathematics are small" (p. 139). In particular, they found that this difference has decreased dramatically over the past two decades, which suggests the influence of environmental factors. The largest sex differences in mathematical ability tend to be at the upper end of the distribution (in the gifted population), where males outnumber females 13 to 1 (Benbow & Stanley, 1980, 1983). Hyde, Fennema, and Lamon (1990) have argued, however, that it is inappropriate to generalize from samples such as those studied by Benbow and Stanley. Benbow herself has acknowledged this point.

Intellectual functioning is influenced by many factors other than hormones. For an excellent summary of what is known and not known about intelligence, see Neisser et al. (1996).

Sex Hormones and Play

Some of the strongest evidence that sex hormones cause differences in behavior comes from research on play (for a review of these studies, see Collaer & Hines, 1995). The general finding is that females who have had prenatal exposure to high androgen levels show a tomboy pattern, characterized by rough, active outdoor play and by relatively high interest in practical clothing, in toys typically preferred by boys (cars, guns, building materials), and in boys as playmates. In addition, these females show relatively low interest in feminine clothing, makeup, jewelry, doll play, and rehearsal of the adult maternal role. Males who have experienced prenatal exposure to progestin-based progesterone show the reverse effect, but less dramatically.

Summary

Males and females share the same basic sex hormones, but they produce them in different amounts. These different concentrations of sex hormones appear to be responsible not only for many of the physical differences between males and females, but for some of the psychological differences as well. On the physical side,

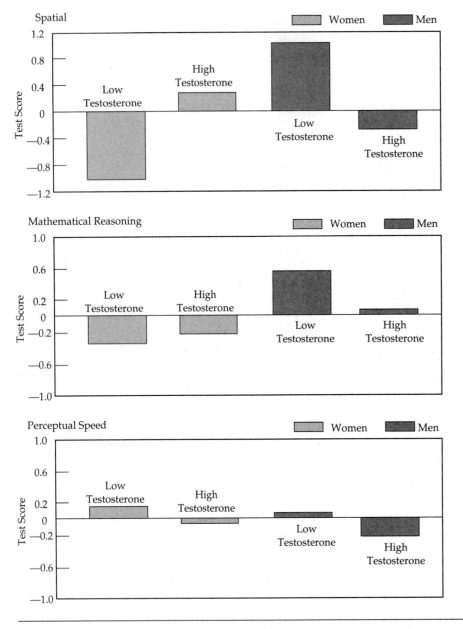

Figure 4-4. Testosterone levels can affect performance on some tests. Women with high levels of testosterone perform better on a spatial task *(top)* than do women with low levels; men with low levels outperform men with high levels. On a mathematical reasoning test *(middle)*, low testosterone corresponds to better performance in men; in women, there is no such relation. On a test in which women usually excel *(bottom)*, no relation is found between testosterone and performance. (From "Sex Differences in the Brain," by D. Kimura. *Scientific American*, 1992, *267*, 118–125. Copyright © 1992 by Scientific American. All rights reserved.)

testosterone has a masculinizing effect. Among other things, testosterone is responsible for the development of the male penis, facial hair, and a deep voice. Injections of testosterone in females tend to produce an enlarged clitoris. Conversely, estrogen tends to have a feminizing effect. Among other things, it produces breast development and stimulates the body to store fat on the hips and thighs. In transsexual operations, estrogen is injected into males, with similar effects.

Kimura (1992) has shown that women with high testosterone levels tend to perform better on certain spatial tasks (tasks in which men tend to outperform women) than do women with low testosterone levels. On mathematical reasoning tasks, men with low testosterone levels tend to outperform those with high levels (Christiansen & Knussman, 1987; Kimura, 1992), whereas no relationship was found between testosterone levels and mathematical reasoning in women (Kimura, 1992). Some of the clearest evidence for the role of hormones in sex differences comes from the examination of play in young children.

Sexual Dimorphism in the Brain

Dimorphism means the existence of two distinct forms. Evidence for sexual dimorphism comes from the observation that particular structures in the brain are different in size, number of neurons, and dendritic branching for females and males (Gorski, 1991).

Many researchers believe that these structural differences are associated with certain behavioral differences. These structures can often be altered by pre- or postnatal administrations of sex hormones. This suggests that differences in the male and female brain are due, at least in part, to the effects of sex hormones. Evidence that the environment can also alter these structures indicates a complex interaction between hormones and the environment.

Some Examples of Dimorphism

The hypothalamus. Considerable research indicates that the hypothalamus is involved in sexual and reproductive behavior. Researchers have found, for instance, that the number of neurons in an area of the hypothalamus called the sexual dimorphic nucleus is greater in male rats than in female rats. These nuclei are 5–7 times larger in the male than in the female. Prenatal injections of testosterone will increase the number of neurons in the dimorphic nucleus of a female rat, so that the hypothalamus more closely resembles that of a male, and prenatal administration of antitestosterone drugs to a male rat will reduce the number of nuclei in the dimorphic nucleus (Gorski, 1974, 1985, 1991; Haseltine & Ohno, 1981; Wilson et al., 1981).

Research has shown similar differences in the human brain (Swaab & Fliers, 1985). The hypothalamus is shown in Figure 4-5, together with some other brain structures in which sexual dimorphism has been found. Later in this chapter, when we discuss sexual orientation, we will review an interesting study by LeVay (1991) on dimorphism in the hypothalamus.

The cerebral cortex. The term cerebral cortex refers to the outer layer of the brain that starts at the front of the brain (frontal cortex) and extends around and back to the rear of the brain (visual cortex). Studies of this outer layer indicate the right cortex is thicker than the left in male rats but not in female rats (Diamond, Dowling, & Johnson, 1981). The right hemisphere is thought to be involved in spatial abilities. We know that these differences are due, at least in part, to sex hormones because they can be produced artificially by injecting testosterone in the female infant rat at a critical stage—usually at birth or shortly thereafter—or by castrating the male infant rat at birth (Beach, 1976; Haseltine & Ohno, 1981; Wilson et al., 1981). The work of Stewart and Kolb (1988) indicates that androgens suppress development of the left cortex. However, the environment also affects the development of these structures in rats (Diamond, 1988). Animals provided with an enriched environment will show an increase in certain structures of the cortex.

Similar results have been obtained in human fetuses, where the right hemisphere is larger than the left in males but not in females (LaCoste et al., cited in Kimura, 1992). The evidence for humans is still meager, however, and needs to be treated with caution.

The corpus callosum. The corpus callosum is thought to be involved in the coordination of the two sides of the brain. Researchers have suggested that, if one sex is found to have more connecting fibers in the corpus callosum, that sex should have a greater capacity to coordinate the two sides of the brain (e.g., Kimura, 1992). In humans, the corpus callosum—more precisely, the posterior portion—is larger and more bulbous in females than in males (Allen, Richey, Chai, & Gorski, 1991). Verbal fluency correlates positively with the size of a region of the corpus callosum (mainly defined by the splenium) and that another region of the corpus callosum (the posterior callosum) correlates negatively with language lateralization (Hines, Chiu, McAdams, Bentler, & Lipcamon, 1992). Because the area of the corpus callosum linked to superior language skills was larger in females, researchers believe that the reason females often perform better than males do on certain language tasks is the result of the difference in the brain structure of females and males. This research uses a new method called magnetic resonance imaging

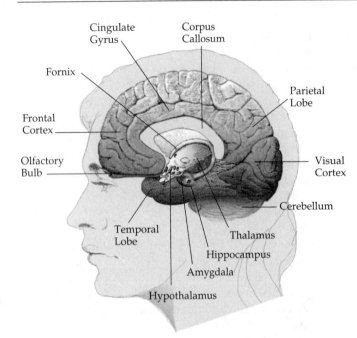

Figure 4-5. Cross section of the human brain, with some of the structures in which sexual dimorphism has been found.

(MRI), which permits measurement of the intact (living) brain. Previously, researchers had to rely on patients with neural lesions, a method that is highly limited.

There is still no clear evidence indicating at what stage in development the corpus callosum becomes sexually dimorphic, nor has it been clearly shown to be affected by sex hormones. All sexually dimorphic structures examined thus far have been influenced by prenatal hormones, however, so Gorski (1991) suggests such effects will probably be found for the corpus callosum.

Evidence also demonstrates that early experience can alter this dimorphism (Berrebi et al., 1988; Juraska & Kopcik, 1988).

Other regions. The anterior commissure is larger in human females than in males (Allen & Gorski, 1991). There are also differences in subregions of the amygdala (Hines, Allen, & Gorski, 1992), a region in the brain that has often been linked to sex, aggression, gonadotropic secretion, and integration of olfactory information. Finally, recent brain imaging studies have found what could be differences in the lateralization of language (Shaywitz et al., 1995).

Although these differences in brain structure could be of genetic or hormonal origin, they could also be the result of experience. Certain patterns of thought or behavior could stimulate certain areas of the brain to develop. Further, as various theorists have suggested, a bidirectional effect could be at work: Because a certain area of the brain is more highly developed, an individual might be disposed to engage in activities involving that area of the brain, and the increased use of that area may stimulate it to develop more.

Critical Periods of Sexual Differentiation

When does sexual dimorphism develop? Considerable research suggests that brain structures can be masculinized only at certain stages of development and that to reverse them at a later stage is impossible.*

---

* Masculinization is an unfortunate word. It's known that, without testosterone, the brain would tend to develop in its female form. Females also produce small amounts of testosterone, however, and research with both animals and humans suggests that even small amounts of testosterone alter the development of the female brain. In other words, one reason why various structures of the female brain differ from those of the male brain is that the female brain was exposed to testosterone at some critical stage of development. Until someone suggests a better word, however, I will continue to speak of masculinization.

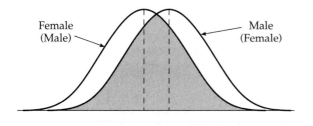

Figure 4-6. Normal distribution curves representing the differences between males and females. In most cases, the differences between males and females are small. These curves show that, when there are small differences, the vast majority of males and females tend to be alike rather than different (shaded area). Thus, when people talk about differences, they are talking about a very small proportion of the general population (unshaded area).

There is evidence, for example, that, after a certain critical period, injections of testosterone will no longer alter the hypothalamus (Haseltine & Ohno, 1981; Wilson et al., 1981). This critical period occurs either shortly before birth or shortly after birth. If the hypothalamus governs sexual orientation, as some people have suggested, the idea of critical periods means that, once sexual orientation has been established in the brain, it is very difficult, if not impossible, to alter that orientation.

In the case of the cerebral cortex, on the other hand, extensive evidence suggests that sexual dimorphism can occur much later. This suggests a greater potential for environmental input to some structures than to others.

Sexual Dimorphism and Individual Differences

Gorski and others often point out, in connection with their work on sexual dimorphism in the brain, that there are large individual differences. Individual differences are generally larger than group differences (differences between males and females). In practical terms, this means that many female brains look more like typical male brains than like typical female brains and, similarly, that many male brains look more like typical female brains than like typical male brains. As Figure 4-6 illustrates, the general finding is that most differences in brain structure and abilities between men and women are quite small compared with the large individual differences within the populations of

men and of women. In some cases, such as the hypothalamus, these differences within each population are particularly large.

The Politics of Biological Difference

Research on differences between men's and women's brains is highly contentious (Eagly, 1995), because the existence of biological differences between men and women has sometimes been claimed as evidence of male superiority (Tavris, 1992) or the lack of certain abilities among women (Lotti, 1996). Research findings that males may be superior to females in certain areas might be used to buttress the argument for continued male dominance in certain occupations. This is sometimes characterized as the argument that biology is destiny. Many women scholars have taken issue with this argument and have pointed out that most of the differences are small and, in many cases, might be caused by environmental factors rather than by biology (Lotti, 1996).

Because biological differences between men and women are often small, some scholars have argued that they have no practical significance and may be ignored. Small biological differences are often responsible, however, for large individual differences. By aiming an organism in one direction rather than another, these biological differences influence what the organism sees, hears, experiences, and thinks and even the self-schemata that are constructed. For an excellent review of the politics of comparisons between women and men, see Eagly (1995).

Summary

Substantial research indicates the existence of sexual dimorphism of the brain—differences in certain brain structures of males and females. Such sexual dimorphism appears to be caused by the hormone testosterone. For example, prenatal injection of testosterone will increase the number of neurons in the female rat's hypothalamus, so that it more closely resembles that of a male. Injections of testosterone increase the thickness of the right hemisphere in the female brain, so that it more closely resembles that of the male. Interestingly, it has been shown that the environment can produce these differences as well. Recent evidence indicates that sexual dimorphism of the corpus callosum might be linked to brain lateralization. Finally, ample evidence indicates that such sexual dimorphism can only develop during critical periods of brain development.

Sexual Orientation

Researchers have suggested that all human beings have a sense of being female, male, or somewhere in between and that humans are inclined to publicly present themselves as female, male, or ambivalent. Our private inner experience is sometimes called our *gender identity,* and our public outward expression is our *gender role* (Money, 1987a, b). There is good reason to believe that gender identity and gender role arise in different ways. In the following section, we will be talking mainly about gender identity.

Where do feelings about femaleness and maleness come from? Research on the sexual dimorphism of the brain suggests that such differences include a biological component. Hormones don't predetermine our feelings of femaleness and maleness, but they do seem to point us more in one direction than another. Whether we come to see ourselves as female or male also depends on learned and cognitive factors. Let's look at the biological, learned, and cognitive components of sexual orientation and, more specifically, homosexuality.

The Biological Component

Sexual Dimorphism of the Hypothalamus and Male Sexual Orientation

Some of the first hard scientific evidence that male homosexuality has a biological basis came from the work of LeVay (1991), a neurobiologist at the Salk Institute in San Diego. LeVay found that a speck of neurons in the hypothalamus that is known to be linked to sexual behavior is more than twice as large in men as in women. The area is too small to study in living humans, so he used the autopsied brains of 19 homosexual men and 16 heterosexual men. He found the oval cluster in homosexual men to be half the size of that in heterosexual men; sometimes, it was even missing. His focus on the hypothalamus was prompted by the

knowledge that, when the hypothalamus is damaged in male monkeys, they lose interest in females but they do not lose their sex drive, as indicated by their continued tendency to masturbate.

LeVay's research is consistent with evidence that male rats, if castrated at birth and thus deprived of testosterone, will never try to mate with females and will allow other males to mount them (Gorski, 1974, 1985, 1991). It is also consistent with evidence that testosterone is responsible for the development of the hypothalamus (Gorski, 1988; Haseltine & Ohno, 1981; Wilson et al., 1981). Note, however, that the nuclei that LeVay examined were not the same as the nuclei studied in the rat research. The significance of this difference has yet to be clarified.

Some researchers have called for further work to verify LeVay's findings. Because his sample of gay men consisted of men with AIDS, the differences observed in the hypothalamus might have been caused by AIDS. Concerns have also been expressed about the small size of the sample.

Despite LeVay's findings, neurobiologists do not believe that structural changes in the hypothalamus are the sole cause of homosexuality. First, other research indicates that the anterior commissure, a nerve network connecting the two hemispheres, is larger in females than in males and is larger in homosexual men than in heterosexual men (e.g., Allen & Gorski, 1991). Further, as we will see shortly, the environment also plays an important role.

Twin Studies and Male Sexual Orientation

Recent evidence indicates that genetic factors are important in determining individual differences in sexual orientation. Heritability estimates range from 31% to 74% (Bailey & Pillard, 1991). Using 110 fraternal and identical twins and 46 adoptive men and their brothers, this study found that, if one brother in a pair was homosexual, the likelihood that the other brother would be homosexual increased with the degree of genetic similarity.

The researchers advertised for homosexual and bisexual men who had a male twin or an adoptive or genetically unrelated brother with whom they started living by the age of 2. The brothers in 52% of the 28 sets of identical twins were both gay; those in 22% of the 27 sets of fraternal twins were both gay; and 11% of the adopted brothers were both gay. Since identical twins have the same genes, fraternal twins only share some genes, and the adopted brothers should have virtually none of the same genes, the evidence clearly points to a role of genetics in homosexuality.

Consistent with this is the recent discovery of a link between homosexuality in males and the long arm of the X chromosome (Hamer, Hu, Magnuson, Hu, & Pattatucci, 1993; Hamer & Copeland, 1994; Hu et al., 1995). If the gene for homosexuality were carried on the Y chromosome, homosexuality might be expected to disappear over time, because homosexuals tend to produce fewer offspring. If carried on the X chromosome, however, the trait would tend to be maintained over time. Research indicates that homosexuality has been prevalent for some time, exists independent of culture, and is behaviorally similar (Whitam & Mathy, 1986); these findings are consistent with the idea that it has a genetic basis.

Twin Studies and Female Sexual Orientation

Studies of twins have found similar results for lesbians (Bailey, Pillard, Neale, & Agyei, 1993). In a study of 71 sets of identical twins, 37 sets of fraternal twins, and 35 sets of adoptive sisters, it was found that 48% of the identical twins who said they were homosexual or bisexual had twins who were lesbian, compared with 16% of the fraternal twins and 6% of the adopted sisters. Heritability estimates ranged from 27% to 76%. These results closely parallel those found for gay men. No linkage between homosexuality and the X chromosome has yet been found for lesbians (Hu et al., 1995).

Congenital Adrenal Hyperphasia and Female Sexual Orientation

When researchers deprived male rats of testosterone (for instance, by castration) and treated female rats with estrogen, which can have a masculinizing effect, they found that the genetic males behaved like females and the genetic females behaved like males (Williams, cited in Kimura, 1992). Because this same research cannot be done with humans, researchers have to depend on "experiments of nature" to determine whether or not hormones affect sexual orientation. Experiments of nature are much like laboratory

experiments, except that the manipulation was not planned but occurred by accident. Because of a genetic defect, some women produce abnormally high levels of adrenal androgens—a condition called congenital adrenal hyperphasia (CAH). To assess whether the female offspring of these women tend to be more bisexual or homosexual, their responses to erotica have been examined. The reason for using responses to erotica comes from the idea that erotica is perhaps less governed by social pressure to conform than is something like gender identity. Ehrhardt and Meyer-Bahlburg (1981) reported that in studies using such measures, approximately half the dreams of CAH-affected women were bisexual (none were homosexual). There were no control groups, however, so the researchers said they could not draw any definitive conclusions from this measure. Their conclusions were undoubtedly affected by the fact they also found that CAH-affected women tend to adopt the gender identity they were assigned at birth; that is, they saw themselves as female. In a more highly controlled study, evidence was found for the idea that CAH-affected women tend to be more bisexual or homosexual (Money, Schwartz, & Lewis, 1984). In a sample of 30 CAH-affected women, 37% rated their sexual imagery and activity as bisexual or homosexual, 40% as heterosexual, and 23% were noncommittal. In a control group of 27 women with other endocrine disorders, 7% rated their erotic imagery and activity as bisexual whereas the remainder rated it as heterosexual.

Because CAH-affected girls often have more masculinized genitalia, some researchers have attributed the results to a more masculine upbringing of girls with CAH (Quadagno, Brisco, & Quadagno, 1977). This point has been contested by Ehrhardt and Meyer-Bahlburg (1981), who note that, if anything, parents of such children tend to encourage femininity—that is, stereotypical female behavior.

Ehrhardt and Meyer-Bahlburg (1981) also found that CAH-affected girls showed: (1) "a combination of intense active outdoor play, increased association with male peers, long-term identification as a 'tomboy' by self and others, probably all related to high energy expenditure" and (2) "decreased parenting rehearsal such as doll play and baby care, and a low interest in the role rehearsal of wife and mother versus having a career" (p. 1314).

Other researchers have shown that CAH-affected adult females score significantly higher than do controls on tests of spatial ability (Resnick, Berenbaum, Gottesman, & Bouchard, 1986) and that, in highly controlled studies, CAH-affected girls have been found to play more with stereotypical boy toys and less with stereotypical girl toys (Berenbaum & Hines, 1992). Finally, prenatal exposure to sex hormones has been shown to affect certain immune systems (Geschwind & Galaburda, 1987; Halpern & Cass, 1994).

DES-Affected Women and Female Sexual Orientation

There is also data from women who were exposed prenatally to diethylstilbestrol (DES), a synthetic estrogen (formerly used to maintain pregnancy) that can have masculinizing effects on the brain but does not produce masculinizing effects on the genitalia (Dohler et al., 1984; Hines, Alsum, & Roy, 1987). In a sample of 30 DES-exposed women, 21% rated themselves as having bisexual or homosexual responsiveness compared to none in a control group (Ehrhardt et al., 1985). Twelve of the DES-exposed had unexposed sisters, so it was possible to compare them with their sisters. Whereas 42% of the DES-exposed rated themselves as bisexual or homosexual, only 8% of their sisters rated themselves similarly. DES does not masculinize the genitalia, so it is difficult to argue that the effects are caused by the parents' decision, based on the size of the genitalia, to raise their daughters more male-like (see section on sex assignment at birth for a more complete description of this hypothesis). The work on the CAH-affected and DES-exposed is not without critics. Fausto-Sterling (1985) has offered a detailed critique of the work on CAH as well as other work that has been put forth as evidence for a biological basis for sex differences.

The Learned Component

For a long time, there has been a bias toward viewing sexual orientation as acquired. Historically, homosexuality was assumed to be the result of pathology. When researchers began to investigate this hypothesis, they could find no evidence to support it. In his study of 30

homosexual and 30 heterosexual men, Hooker (1957) concluded, "Homosexuality as a clinical entity does not exist. Its forms are as varied as those of heterosexuality" (p. 30). Lacking any evidence for the pathology hypothesis, the American Medical Association and the American Psychological Association no longer list homosexuality as a clinical disorder.

As research begins to show that there is a strong biological component, other learning interpretations have come under much closer scrutiny. It is no longer self-evident that homosexuality is acquired or is the result of choice. If homosexuality is acquired, as some people argue, what conditions lead to it? In the following section, I will examine some hypotheses that have been advanced over the years.

Psychoanalytic Theory

According to psychoanalytic theory, homosexuality in males grows out of a family constellation characterized by a close-binding overprotective mother and a detached, absent, or openly hostile father (Bieber et al., 1962). Such parents inhibit the expression of heterosexual feelings in the son. In addition, the absence of an effectual father means that the child has no good role model from whom to learn appropriate heterosexual behavior. The consensus is that support for the psychoanalytic interpretation is not good; no research has been able to clearly link domineering mothers and ineffectual fathers to homosexuality.

Chance-Learning Hypothesis

According to this hypothesis, a young person seduced by someone of the same gender would learn to associate the pleasures of sex with the gender of the seducer. No evidence has been put forth in support of this hypothesis; moreover, recent studies of young females and males who have been sexually seduced—or sexually abused—indicate that, if anything, the result is the opposite. The following study by the Kinsey Institute suggests that there is little or no evidence to support the chance-learning hypothesis.

The Kinsey Institute Study

In one of the most extensive studies of the origins of homosexuality, a group of researchers at the Kinsey Institute interviewed 979 homosexual men and women and 477 heterosexual men and women (Bell,

Weinberg, & Hammersmith, 1981). The researchers asked a number of questions from a variety of theoretical orientations. Based on their research, they drew the following conclusions regarding the origins of sexual orientation.

1. Sexual orientation is determined before adolescence, even when youngsters have not been particularly sexually active. (Numerous other studies have shown that most homosexual males become aware of their orientation during childhood or adolescence; Dank, 1971; Reiche & Dannecker, 1977; Whitam, 1977).
2. Homosexual behavior emerges from homosexual feelings—feelings that occur about three years, on average, before any overt homosexual experience.
3. Homosexual women and men tend to have a history of heterosexual experiences in childhood and adolescence but have found these experiences not to be satisfying.
4. Identification with either parent played no significant role in the development of sexual orientation.
5. There was no evidence that any particular type of mother produces homosexual children. A slightly higher proportion of homosexuals had poor relationships with their fathers, but it was impossible to determine if this was a causative factor.

Sex Assignment at Birth

One of the main hypotheses regarding gender identity is the role of sex assignment at birth. This model is presented in Figure 4-7.

According to this hypothesis, boys and girls are treated differently as they grow up. After dressing girls in pink and boys in blue, for example, parents give boys toy cars and trucks and reward them for boy activities but give girls dolls and reward them for girl activities. According to this hypothesis, sex assignment is the key to differences between men and women because sex assignment determines how children are rewarded (Tavris & Wade, 1984). Although considerable evidence indicates that boys and girls are rewarded differently, most of the studies are correlational. Next, we'll examine a noncorrelational study that relates to the hypothesis of sex assignment at birth.

Before we do so, it is important to make a distinction between sexual orientation and core gender iden-

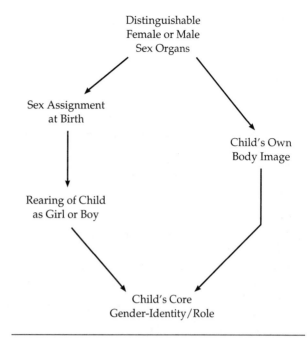

Figure 4-7. Environmental and cultural factors that influence the development of a child's gender identity/role. (From *Sexuality Today: The Human Perspective,* 3rd ed., by G. F. Kelly. Copyright © 1992 by The Dushkin Publishing Group, Inc., Guilford, CT. All rights reserved. Reprinted with permission.)

tity. Whereas sexual orientation has to do with preference for a sexual partner, core gender identity has to do with the sense of being male or female. We will be mainly concerned with core gender identity (Hines & Green, 1991).

Rearing Boys as Girls and Core Gender Identity

Individuals with a genetic deficiency of the enzyme 5-alpha-reductase produce less dihydrotestosterone from testosterone, beginning in utero. This leads to female-appearing genitalia, because dihydrotestosterone is necessary for the prenatal development of the penis. In a sample of 18 such individuals, all raised as girls, 17 professed male identity in adolescence. Note that, at puberty, they developed male genitalia under the influence of testosterone (Imperato-McGinley et al., 1974, 1979). According to the hypothesis of sex assignment at birth, they should have adopted a gender identity corresponding to their assigned sex.

An enzymatic deficiency (17-beta hydroxysteroid dehydrogenase) produces female-appearing genitalia at birth; this is followed by considerable phallus growth and excessive hair growth in adolescence. A study of 25 such individuals found that they generally adopted a male identity during adolescence despite having been raised as females (Rosler & Kohn, 1983).

Status of the Learning Hypothesis

Although there is still relatively little evidence for the three main hypotheses of sexual orientation—psychoanalytic, chance-learning, and sex assignment at birth—evidence from twin studies indicates that learning plays an important role. If biology is the main determinant of homosexuality, we would expect identical twins to be of the same orientation—either both homosexual or both heterosexual. That is clearly not the case. Only 30 to 70% of the variance in the study of male twins can be directly attributed to heredity. This leaves considerable scope for the role of learning or cognition (Bailey & Pillard, 1991). Further, considerable evidence suggests that male sexual orientation is a matter of degree. If it were simply biological, there should be more evidence for greater similarity between homosexuals (Haslam, 1997).

It seems clear at this point that, individually, none of the learning hypotheses provides a very complete explanation. To explore sexual orientation further, what we need, rather than studies that pit learning theories against each other or pit learning against biology, are experiments to elucidate the different kinds of learning experiences that might push an individual toward homosexuality.

Learning and the Expression of Sexual Orientation

Even if we knew beyond doubt that sexual orientation was completely biologically determined, it would still be important to consider the role of learning. Substantial evidence indicates that, like anyone else, gay men and lesbians select role models to help guide their development. One consistent complaint from the gay and lesbian community has been that the mainstream media do not offer them a range of role models. Gay men are often presented in the media as stereotyped effeminate individuals who are passive and often promiscuous. Lesbians complain that they are presented as very masculine, aggressive, and man-hating.

A particular sexual orientation can be expressed in many ways. Most likely, what determines its expression is the same for homosexuals as for heterosexuals. In other words, learning plays just as important a role in the expression of a homosexual orientation as it does in the expression of a heterosexual orientation.

The Cognitive Component

Is homosexuality a choice? Do people decide to become homosexuals because it offers them an attractive and fulfilling lifestyle?

There is little or no evidence that homosexuality is actively chosen, except in unusual circumstances—in particular, in prison. In fact, many individuals have reported that, when they finally came to accept the possibility that they were gay or lesbian, they felt distraught and experienced psychological symptoms including anxiety, depression, suicidal ideation, and stress.

Nonetheless, extensive evidence suggests that cognitive factors play an important role in how homosexuals come to think about themselves and express themselves. Cass's theory of homosexual identity formation provides a good summary of what we know about cognitive aspects of homosexual identity.

Cass's Six Stages of Homosexuality

Cass's (1990) description of the six stages of homosexual identity formation suggests that, for the process of homosexual identity formation to begin, the individual must experience some degree of sexual attraction or interest in someone of the same sex. As we see from the following account, the development of a homosexual identity involves a range of cognitive processes, including changes in attitudes, the development of new expectations, and the construction of a gender schema.

Stage 1: Identity confusion. In this stage, individuals begin to realize that information about homosexuality may somehow relate to them. They often experience persistent dreams and fantasies about members of the same sex but typically avoid homosexual behavior.

Stage 2: Identity comparisons. In this stage, individuals begin to examine the broader implications of what it means to be a homosexual. They deal with the question of how the acceptance of such an identity might affect their relationships with their families and their friends and how will they fit into society. They often experience a profound sense of loss, as they realize their alienation from heterosexual society. Some devalue heterosexuality; others turn their sexual identity confusion into antihomosexual attitudes and even exaggerated heterosexual behavior, while still entertaining homosexual fantasies.

Stage 3: Identity tolerance. As they accept their homosexuality, they begin to realize that sexual, social, and emotional needs go with being a homosexual. Typically, individuals become more involved with other homosexuals at this stage. As they accept that they have special sexual, social, and emotional needs, they develop a greater tolerance of their homosexual identities.

At this stage, individuals must decide how open they wish to be about their sexual orientation. The process in which individuals acknowledge their homosexuality and communicate it to others has been called coming out of the closet, or simply coming out.

Stage 4: Identity acceptance. In this stage, there is typically greater involvement with the gay and lesbian subculture and the development of a positive attitude toward other homosexuals. Individuals move from tolerating their homosexual self-image to fully accepting it.

Stage 5: Identity pride. As individuals accept the accomplishments of the gay and lesbian community and realize that there are standards of comparison other than those of the heterosexual community, they develop a sense of pride and abandon attempts to hide their homosexuality. This stage is often characterized by anger.

As they become more conscious of the discrimination and homophobia that prevent them from living a full life, individuals often become politically active, in an attempt to change attitudes and laws that have a negative impact on gay men and lesbians.

Stage 6: Identity synthesis. In the last stage, individuals begin to accept that the world is not divided into warring factions of homosexuals and heterosexuals and that all heterosexuals need not be regarded as enemies. The anger that characterizes stage 5 gives way to a greater self-acceptance as a gay man or lesbian and the acknowledgment of a wide range of personality attributes and interests.

Partner Preferences of Gays and Lesbians

A common stereotype is that gays are more feminine and that lesbians are more masculine. An extension of this stereotype is that gays, therefore, prefer more feminine partners and that lesbians prefer more masculine partners. Although on the average gay men are somewhat feminine and lesbians somewhat masculine, there are large variations within both groups. When it comes to partner preference, studies of personal advertisements show that, on the average, gay men prefer partners who describe themselves as masculine and that lesbians, on the average, prefer partners who describe themselves as feminine (Bailey, Yim, Hills, & Linsenmeier, 1997).

Sexual Plasticity in Humans

Considerable evidence from cross-cultural work indicates that the sexual behavior of humans is often highly plastic; humans adapt themselves to the conditions in which they find themselves. For example, when confined to prison, many men will engage in same-sex behavior even though they regard themselves as heterosexual. Money and Ehrhardt (1972) offer many examples of such plasticity. They point out that, in some cultures, young males go through a period in which they adopt a homosexual orientation, for example. This plasticity, however, applies only to behavior; it does not affect the individual's core gender identity.

Summary

Evidence from a range of sources indicates that there is a biological basis for a homosexual orientation. Specifically, sexual dimorphism of the hypothalamus appears to be responsible. Work on CAH-affected women and women exposed to DES suggests that exposure to androgens during critical stages of brain differentiation could be responsible, at least in part, for female homosexuality. That is not to say that homosexuality in men or women is hardwired, but that biology points the individual in a certain direction. Learning and cognition appear to affect the development of a homosexual orientation. The influence exerted by the selection of role models and value systems on individual development is undoubtedly as important for homosexuals as for heterosexuals.

Little evidence indicates that sexual orientation and core gender identity are the result of sex assignment at birth. Good evidence, however, suggests that core gender identity has a biological basis. Heritability estimates account for 30 to 70% of the variance. This leaves considerable scope for the contribution of learned and cognitive components.

A compelling argument that male homosexuality is not a conscious choice but is biologically based has been presented by some gay men. Who would willingly choose, they ask, a lifestyle characterized by job discrimination, homophobic violence, a high risk of AIDS, and wholesale rejection by friends, family, and society?

Main Points

1. Masters and Johnson have identified four more or less distinct phases in the sexual response of males and females.
2. Masters and Johnson argue that the clitoris is unique among human organs in that its only function is pleasure.
3. Sexual behavior in humans is thought to be largely the result of sexual scripts.
4. With the onset of adolescence, sexual scripts become coordinated with sexual feelings aroused through masturbation.
5. The sexual scripts that people come to use are influenced by the beliefs and attitudes they hold.
6. Women tend to value sexual activity because it provides a sense of shared feelings, emotional warmth, and being wanted, whereas men often focus more on arousal.
7. Evolutionary psychology suggests that the involvement of both parents in the raising of offspring emerged because we developed a large brain—one that was less tuned to immediate survival.
8. It appears that attraction is at least partly the result of phenylethylanine (PEA), whereas attachment is due, at least in part, to endorphins.
9. Mate selection for both females and males evolved as an adaptation to ensure our genes would survive in future generations.
10. According to Sternberg, love—what he calls consummate love—involves three components: passion, intimacy, and commitment.
11. Situational factors (e.g., arousal) causes us to fall in love, but Sternberg argues that we can make love happen.
12. Sternberg's model accounts for the complexity of love and provides an explanation of why people who do not share a common definition of love may find it difficult to maintain a long-term relationship.
13. Three main categories of sex hormones: androgens (mainly male), estrogens (mainly female), and progestins (mainly female) are responsible for producing a wide number of physical and psychological characteristics of females and males.
14. Much of the sexual dimorphism of the brain has been linked to the presence of sex hormones during critical stages of development.
15. Three examples of sexual dimorphism of the brain can be found in the hypothalamus, the cerebral cortex, and the corpus callosum.
16. There is considerable evidence that hormones play a central role in determining sexual orientation.
17. It has yet to be demonstrated that the core gender identity of an individual can be changed merely by rearing the child according to cross-gender norms.
18. Cass has described six distinct stages of homosexual identity formation: identity confusion, identity comparisons, identity tolerance, identity acceptance, identity pride, and identity synthesis.

InfoTrac® College Edition

How do you know you are in love? Using InfoTrac®, identify at least four characteristics of people in love. (Search words: love, how to tell you are in love)

There is an ongoing debate about whether the gay/lesbian lifestyle is a choice or is biologically determined. I have made the argument that there is considerable scientific data to suggest a biological component. What are the arguments that it is a matter of choice? (Search words: gay, lesbian, homosexuality)

Chapter Five

Arousal, Attention, and Peak Performance

- *What is peak performance?*
- *Can people achieve peak performance in all areas of their lives?*
- *What role does arousal play in peak performance?*
- *Can anxious people ever achieve peak performance?*
- *What role does attention play in peak performance?*

- *Can people learn to control attention?*
- *Can people achieve peak performance when they are threatened?*
- *How does evaluation affect our ability to perform at peak levels?*

Peak performance means doing the very best that we are capable of. It means being able to fully focus on the task in front of us and to persist in the face of distractions and adversity. For an athlete, it means being able to execute a skill while ignoring the presence of an audience, thoughts about failure, and feelings of fatigue.

One of the main things that prevents us from achieving peak performance is our inability to control our attention. The direction and organization of attention, it turns out, seems to be governed to a large degree by arousal. Research indicates that, when arousal shifts, attention tends to shift. Thus, to control attention, we need to gain control of our arousal.

The degree to which our attention is under voluntary control is a topic of great controversy. Those who argue that attention is controlled by arousal are saying that it is under involuntary control. They often go on to argue, however, that we can gain control over arousal and, thus, we are indirectly in control of attention.

Let's begin by discussing the nature and measurement of arousal.

Definition of Arousal

Arousal is the activation of the brain and the body. When we are aroused, body and brain are in a state of readiness, so that we are prepared to engage in adaptive behaviors. Electrical activity in the brain increases, the heart beats more rapidly, and blood is redirected to the brain and muscles. Muscle tonus increases, in preparation for quick and efficient response. The activation of the brain and the body can be viewed as a state of energization. When we are aroused, the brain and the body are prepared to make use of chemicals—stored in various parts of the body—that facilitate information processing, planning, and the expenditure of physical energy.

There are two primary arousal systems: the cortical arousal system and the autonomic nervous system. The reticular activating system (RAS) is largely responsible for cortical arousal. The autonomic nervous system arouses the body.

Cortical and autonomic arousal often function independently (Neiss, 1988). It makes sense that there are occasions when we should be cortically aroused but not autonomically aroused—for example, when we are engaging in intellectual activities. At other times, we should be autonomically aroused but not cortically aroused—for instance, during routine but physically demanding activities. Finally, there are situations in which we need to be both cortically and physically aroused—for example, during a sporting activity, in battle, or during a musical or theatrical performance. To conserve energy and reduce wear and tear on the body, these systems are only activated when needed.

Let's begin our discussion of arousal with a look at cortical arousal.

Cortical Arousal

The Reticular Activating System (RAS)

Each of the various sensory receptors (visual, auditory, tactile, and so on) is connected to a sensory area in the brain via an afferent nerve pathway that ascends to the cortex via a specific projection system. Fibers branching from these pathways ascend to the reticular formation (Figure 5-1). When sensory information stimulates this system, it responds by activating the brain. Research on the RAS has shown that, unless the cortex is aroused, sensory signals going to the cortex will not be recognized or processed. If the cortex is optimally aroused, it will quickly recognize signals and efficiently process incoming information. In one study (Fuster, 1958), rhesus monkeys were required to learn to discriminate between two objects (to learn which object had a food reward hidden under it) when the objects were presented tachistoscopically (for a fraction of a second at a time). In the experimental condition, the animals were electrically stimulated in the RAS through a permanently implanted electrode; control animals received no stimulation. The experimental animals learned faster, and they had faster reaction times.

The RAS also has a descending tract, which influences motor functions. There is good reason to believe that the descending tract of the RAS might be partly responsible for the improvement in the speed and coordination of reactions under higher levels of arousal.

As a result of being put in this state of readiness, people can process more information (visual, auditory,

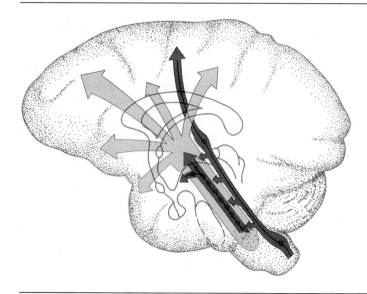

Figure 5-1.   Ascending reticular activating system (reticular formation) schematically projected on a monkey brain. (From *Handbook of Psychology: Neurophysiology,* by D. B. Lindsley, Vol. 3, 1960. Copyright © 1960 by the American Psychological Society. Reprinted with permission.)

tactile, and so on) and can process it better. Furthermore, they are able to better identify important features in the environment and integrate that information with memories or schemata stored in the brain. Finally, because the motor cortex has been activated, they are prepared to make an appropriate response or responses both rapidly and accurately.

Measuring Cortical Activity

Electroencephalograms

The brain is composed of many interconnecting nerve pathways. Electrical impulses generated by chemical processes travel along these pathways. The electroencephalograph (EEG) was designed to amplify these impulses so that a permanent record could be made of the activity of various brain structures. It is technically possible to obtain records of activity in any brain structure, but EEG recordings on humans are typically taken from structures on the outer perimeter of the brain.

EEG readings have shown that changes in brain activity are characterized by abrupt rather than gradual changes in the amplitude and frequency of the impulses (brain waves). In general, as a particular brain structure becomes more active, the amplitude (wave height) decreases and the frequency (number of peaks

per second) increases. Figure 5-2 shows some examples of cortical activity corresponding to various behavioral and mental states.

Positron Emission Tomography

For about 100 years, researchers have known that the regulation of blood supply to the brain is tightly coupled with local neuronal activity in the brain. About 40 years ago, researchers began tracing circulation by infusing radioactive material. Positron emission tomography (PET) is a refinement of this approach. A PET scanner is composed of hundreds of detectors that circle the brain. Using mathematical averaging techniques, the distribution of an isotope in the tissue can be measured. PET results in a very plastic and changing image that reflects neuronal activity in various regions of the brain (Raichle, 1988).

Let's look at a few of the important findings established by PET. Semir Zeki (1992) has used PET to explore which areas of the brain become active when people are exposed to various forms of visual stimulation. His work shows, among other things, that different regions in the brain become active in response to different dimensions of a stimulus—for instance, its color, form, and movement. From this we conclude that the brain tends to break down images into their component parts.

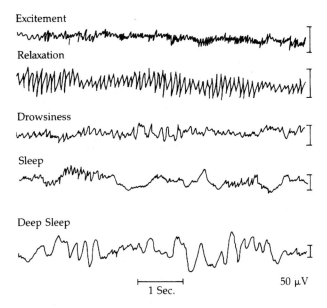

Excitement

Relaxation

Drowsiness

Sleep

Deep Sleep

1 Sec.   50 µV

Figure 5-2. EEG patterns ranging from sleep to wakefulness to excitement. (From "Electroencephalography," by H. H. Jasper. In W. Penfield and T. C. Erickson (Eds.), *Epilepsy and Cerebral Localization*, 1941. Copyright © 1941 by Charles C Thomas, Publishers. Reprinted with permission.)

Other studies have been able to locate which area of the brain is used to detect signals. Through a series of converging experiments, it has been established that the right prefrontal cortex is part of an attentional system that is engaged when a subject is looking for a particular signal (e.g., Petersen, Fox, Posner, Mintun, & Raichle, 1988; Posner, Peterson, Fox, & Raichle, 1988). Richard Gur (1992) of the University of Pennsylvania has noted that men and women use different parts of the brain when solving problems and that men have difficulty detecting emotions in facial expressions, especially the facial expressions of women.

This work complements the work on the RAS. Not only does the brain as a whole become generally more active in response to external stimulation, but different areas of the brain become selectively more active in response to specific task demands. Perhaps even more important is the finding that, as people operate on information in certain ways, different areas of the brain

become involved (e.g., Petersen et al., 1988; Posner et al., 1988).

The Autonomic Nervous System

Although cortical activity has frequently been used as a measure of arousal, many other physiological changes occur when a person is in a state of arousal. The autonomic nervous system is responsible for these changes. A wide array of stimuli trigger activity in the autonomic nervous system. For example, physical exertion, exposure to a loud noise or novel stimulus, injury to the body, anxiety, apprehension, or certain drugs will elicit a rather predictable pattern of responses. Heart rate increases, and blood vessels constrict. Together, these two reactions produce an increase in blood flow. The liver releases glucose for immediate energy, and the spleen releases red corpuscles, which are important for carrying oxygen. Digestion halts; however, fats are released into the bloodstream for conversion to energy. Perspiration increases, which is important for cooling when the person is expending great amounts of energy. Secretion of saliva and mucus decreases, giving a dry-mouth feeling. The muscles tense, the pupils dilate, and the senses are improved.

This pattern of responses, which is generally accompanied by increased cortical activity, is caused by the hypothalamus, which triggers two parallel and complementary reactions: It stimulates activity in the autonomic nervous system and in the endocrine (glandular) system (Levine, 1960). Figure 5-3 shows the pathways in the sympathetic nervous system, a division of the autonomic nervous system. Most of the physiological changes associated with arousal can be traced to the activity of the sympathetic nervous system. In addition, the autonomic nervous system stimulates the adrenal medulla, which then secretes epinephrine or norepinephrine. Both epinephrine and norepinephrine produce RAS arousal. RAS activity is often associated with general arousal, which mediates sensory thresholds, muscle tonus, and other responses. It has been suggested that the release of epinephrine and norepinephrine provides a long-lasting chemical backup to the immediate action of the sympathetic nervous system. Epinephrine and norepinephrine have also been implicated in human emotional reactions.

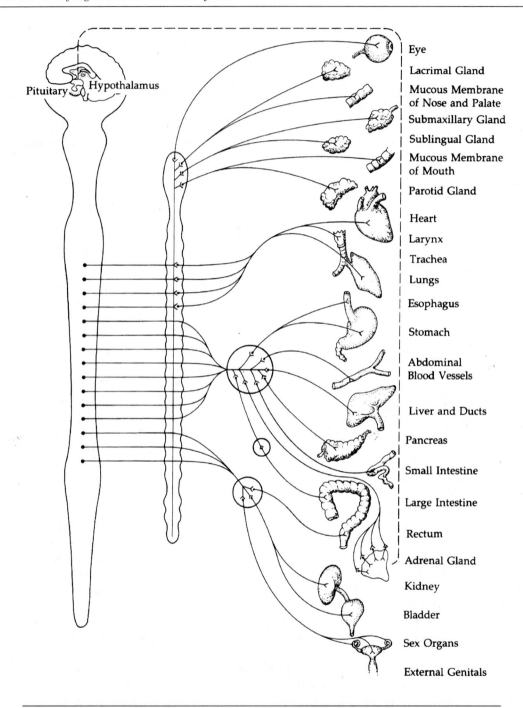

Figure 5-3. Schematic diagram of the sympathetic nervous system (solid lines) and the action of the pituitary on the adrenals via the bloodstream (dashed line). (From "Stimulation in Infancy," by S. Levine. *Scientific American*, May 1966, *214*, 84–90. Copyright © 1966 by Scientific American, Inc. All rights reserved.)

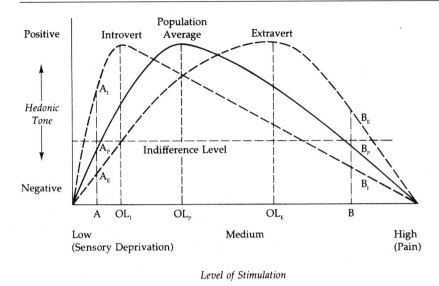

Figure 5-4. Relation between level of stimulation (arousal) and hedonic tone (affect) as a function of personality. (From *Experiments with Drugs,* by H. J. Eysenck. Copyright © 1963 by Pergamon Press Ltd. Reprinted with permission.)

Arousal, Affect, and Performance

Arousal and Affect

For some time, theorists have accepted the idea that arousal and affect are best described by an inverted U-shaped function (Figure 5-4). According to this theory, affect is negative or neutral at low levels of arousal, highly positive at some intermediate level of arousal, and negative (aversive) at very high levels of arousal. Further, it has been suggested that organisms are inclined to seek out new information that will produce positive affect. In other words, the motivation to explore, process information, and master the environment is assumed to be governed by a preference for moderate levels of arousal (Berlyne, 1960; Eysenck, 1967). Over the years, this theory came to be called the *optimal stimulation theory* of behavior. Within stimulation theory, it is generally assumed that individuals come to a particular situation with different baseline levels of arousal. As a result, what is optimal stimulation for one individual is not optimal for another. That is because it is assumed that arousal produced by incoming stimulation adds to baseline arousal. Accordingly, individuals with high baseline levels of arousal should prefer lower levels of stimulation or lower levels of complexity whereas individuals with low baseline levels of arousal should prefer higher levels of incoming stimulation or higher levels of complexity.

Some evidence suggests that the inverted U-shaped function describes the relationship between autonomic arousal and affect, but its relevance to cortical arousal has been disputed (Matthews, Davies, & Lees, 1990). Considerable evidence suggests that the relationship between cortical arousal and affect is linear; people often find high levels of cortical arousal highly pleasurable—for example, when they are thinking or problem solving or even in a sporting competition.

Even high levels of autonomic arousal can be quite pleasurable, at least for short periods, as in a sporting competition. When autonomic arousal remains high for long periods, however, it is experienced as negative. As we will see in Chapter 9, when autonomic arousal is prolonged, the stress response emerges.

Arousal and Performance

After reviewing all the data relating behavioral efficiency to arousal, Donald Hebb (1955) proposed an inverted-U-shaped function to describe the relation between arousal and performance (Figure 5-5). This is also commonly known as the Yerkes-Dodson principle, based on 1908 observations by Yerkes and his student Dodson. According to the Yerkes-Dodson law, high

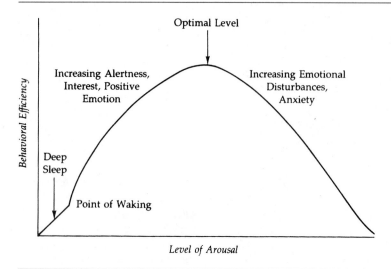

Figure 5-5. Hypothetical relation between behavioral efficiency (performance) and level of arousal. (From D. O. Hebb, "Drive and the C.N.S. (Conceptual Nervous System)." *Psychological Review,* 1955, *62,* 243–254. Copyright © 1954 by the American Psychological Association.)

arousal tends to facilitate performance on easy or simple tasks whereas low arousal tends to facilitate performance on difficult or complex tasks.

Again, it has been disputed that the inverted U-shaped function always describes the relationship between arousal and performance (Matthews et al., 1990). Substantial research indicates that people are often better at detecting signals or identifying cues when cortical arousal is high. Similarly, it has been found that motor performance is often superior at high versus moderate levels of arousal.

To understand why theorists have postulated an inverted U-shaped function for both affect and performance, we need to consider two main lines of research: sensory deprivation and anxiety.

Research on Sensory Deprivation

Studies of sensory deprivation suggest that humans find low levels of stimulation aversive. Donald Hebb and his students at McGill University were the first to undertake systematic studies of sensory deprivation (Bexton, Heron, & Scott, 1954). Woodburn Heron (1957), one of Hebb's associates, paid male college students a substantial sum of money to lie on a bed for as many days as they could. To restrict visual stimulation, the students had to wear special translucent visors. To restrict auditory stimulation, they had to rest their heads on rubber pillows next to an air conditioner that put out a steady hum. To reduce tactile stimulation, the

students were required to wear cotton gloves and cardboard forearm cuffs. The fingers are a rich source of stimulation and can be used to stimulate the body, by rubbing and kneading. The experimental setup is shown in Figure 5-6.

The effects of sensory deprivation began to show up after about a day. Subjects indicated that they had trouble thinking clearly. Many indicated that they simply ran out of things to think about. When they did try to think about something, they had trouble concentrating for any length of time. After 48 hours, most of the subjects found they were unable to do even the most basic mathematical computations (1 + 2 + 3 + 6 = ?).

Many subjects found that they began to see images; nearly all reported that they had dreams or visions while awake. Hallucinations were common and were likened to those produced by drugs. Most subjects tried to entertain themselves by thinking about certain things or activities, but many found it difficult to concentrate. Most of the participants welcomed activities that normally held no interest for them—having the opportunity to read stock market reports, for example. Such findings are consistent with Berlyne's (1960) view that, when people are underaroused, they will attempt to generate stimulation as best they can or focus on what is available.

All the subjects found the experience very aversive. Even though they were being paid a substantial sum of money for each day of the experiment, most left after the second or third day.

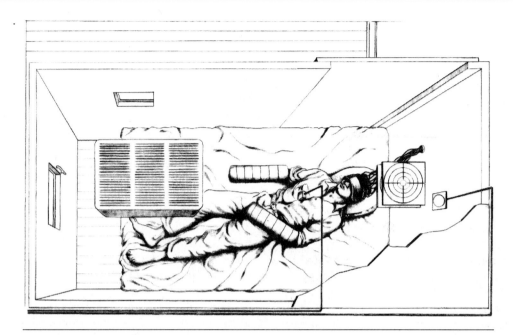

Figure 5-6.   Sensory deprivation chamber used by the McGill University group. (Adapted from E. Mose, "The Pathology of Boredom," by W. Heron. *Scientific American,* January 1957, p. 52. Copyright © 1957 by Scientific American, Inc. All rights reserved.)

This research is consistent with the inverted U-shaped function. However, it took a day or two for the lack of sensory stimulation to produce the intellectual deficits and for the aversiveness of the experience to emerge. The inverted U-shaped function suggests that the effects should have been experienced immediately. According to optimal stimulation theory, the moment-to-moment changes in arousal govern stimulation-seeking behavior.

Research on Anxiety

Research on anxiety indicates that chronically high levels of arousal are aversive (Barlow, 1988; Barlow, Chorpita, & Turovsky, 1996). Considerable evidence also indicates that, when people are anxious, their intellectual functioning becomes impaired. Among other things, they have difficulty in learning and concentrating and are easily distracted. Such research is consistent with the inverted U-shaped function.

Chronically high arousal does not mean that arousal is always high. People who have been classified as anxious often experience periods in which they do not experience high arousal. The research evidence

seems to suggest that anxious individuals are more reactive than are nonanxious people to certain types of environmental stimulation; that is, they show greater increases in arousal. Among other things, anxious individuals are more reactive to novelty and to cues that signal dangers or threats. One consequence of this reactivity is that anxious people often experience high levels of arousal when there are high levels of stimulation.

Many theorists contend, however, that anxiety is not merely a state of hyperarousal (e.g., Barlow, 1988; Barlow et al., 1996). They argue that the difference between anxious and nonanxious people is more qualitative; that is, the reason anxious people experience more negative affect is not simply because of high arousal but rather because they see the world in more negative terms (Watson & Clark, 1984).

Optimal Stimulation and Individual Goals

Apter (1982) has argued that the level of stimulation that people prefer depends on their goals. He has suggested that, rather than preferring some moderate level of arousal, people sometimes prefer high arousal and at other times prefer low arousal; that is, sometimes people like to experience excitement and at other times they like to relax. According to this theory, people tend to swing back and forth between these two states. Nevertheless, some people tend to be primarily in the high arousal state, and others tend to be primarily in the low arousal state (Apter, 1982).

Apter (1982) further argues that people also shift between two types of motivational goals. At certain times, people are motivated by the need for achievement; they focus on what are called *telic goals*. They plan their activities carefully and tend to complete them to receive the satisfaction that comes from achieving a goal. Their behavior is marked by efficiency rather than by pleasure. In this state, they are serious-minded and future-oriented; they plan. At other times, the same individuals are motivated by a desire to experience pleasure in the here and now; they focus on *paratelic goals*. They are inclined to prolong activities as long as they are producing high levels of pleasure. They tend to be playful and spontaneous (Svebak & Murgatroyd, 1985).

The crux of the theory is that the affect associated with arousal can shift abruptly, as individuals switch between telic and paratelic goals. In other words, satisfaction comes not from high or low arousal but the level of arousal appropriate to current goals (Figure 5-7). When we are in the achievement state, low arousal can be pleasant; we call it relaxation. When we are in the pleasure-seeking state, we call the same low level of arousal boredom. Similarly, high arousal can be very unpleasant (anxiety) in the achievement state and very pleasant (excitement) in the pleasure-seeking state. Note that, if you take the average of these two states, you come up with an inverted U-shaped function (the dotted curve in Figure 5-7).

Conclusion

There is no clear evidence that momentary high or low levels of arousal are aversive. It seems that prolonged periods of either high or low arousal are aversive. Although high arousal and negative affect seem to characterize anxious people, it does not automatically follow that arousal is the source of the negative affect or the poor performance that often characterizes anxious people. There is good reason to believe that the negative affect experienced by anxious people is due to their negative view of the world.

Arousal and Attention

Arousal and Selective Attention

Easterbrook (1959) has proposed that, at low levels of arousal, our attention is broad (we attend to many things) and inclusive (we process a great deal of information). At high arousal—beyond the optimal level—our attention becomes narrow (we attend to few things) and exclusive (we ignore everything but survival-related stimuli). At high arousal, in other words, we practice *selective attention*. According to Easterbrook, arousal governs attention and information processing. We are hardwired, so to speak, to perceive certain things when arousal is low and other things when it is high.

The environment is very complex, and humans have only a limited capacity to be aware of, and process, what is going on around them. To deal with their limited capacity, humans constantly shift their attention—not only the orientation of their receptors (eyes and ears) but the internal perspectives from which they examine incoming information. Theorists have suggested that humans attempt to classify all incoming information using existing broad categories. As I watch someone execute a series of movements, for example, I look for an existing category that can summarize those movements. I might say the person is playing tennis, or running.

When we must devote our attention to some task, our ability to process information about the environment is further restricted. Suppose that I'm trying to find my way to a particular location in a strange city. Because I must concentrate on identifying key reference points on my route, I may not process very much about other things along my path—the buildings or the people I am passing.

Arousal and the Reorganization of Attention

According to Easterbrook (1959), high arousal can also lead to the reorganization of attention. According to his theory, when arousal becomes very high, our attention is directed toward the location and identification of things in the environment that might threaten our survival.

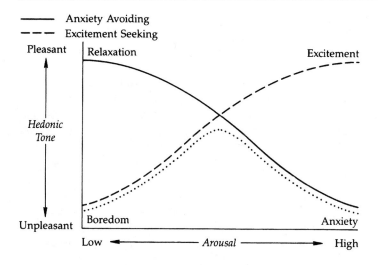

Figure 5-7. The hypothesized relationship between arousal and hedonic tone (affect) for the achievement state and the pleasure-seeking state. (From *The Experience of Motivation: Theory of Psychological Reversals*, by M. J. Apter. Copyright © 1982 by Academic Press. Reprinted by permission.)

Easterbrook does not clearly indicate when attention will narrow and when it will become reorganized. Barlow (1988) and others suggest that, as arousal increases, attention first becomes narrower and eventually is reorganized. Barlow has suggested that arousal and the narrowing of attention are mutually reinforcing. Narrowing often increases arousal, which, in turn, provokes further narrowing of attention. Once reorganization begins, Barlow contends, there is a similar dynamic between reorganization and arousal. As people focus more and more on threat cues, they become more aroused, which makes them more inclined to focus on threat cues.

Two Activation Systems

Many current researchers have concluded that we have two activation systems: a negative one and a positive one. The negative activation (NA) system is an avoidance system. From an evolutionary perspective its adaptive function is to keep organisms out of trouble. It does this by inhibiting behaviors that might lead to pain, punishment, or some other negative consequence. The positive activation (PA) system is an approach system: Its function is to direct individuals to situations and experiences that could offer pleasure and reward. From an evolutionary perspective, the adaptive function of this system is to ensure organisms obtain the resources essential for survival of both the individual and the species (Gray, 1982; Watson, Wiese, Vaidya, & Tellegen, 1999).

Although we assume that these two systems evolved more or less independently of each other to serve two different functions, that doesn't mean the two systems don't work together in some way. Research suggests that the PA system tends to govern most of our daily behavior except when we are momentarily threatened in some way. When that happens, the PA system shuts down and the NA system takes over. This arrangement makes a great deal of sense. It ensures that when we are threatened we give our full attention to dealing with that threat (Watson, Wiese, Vaidya, & Tellegen 1999).

Conclusion

Conceptualizing the origins of arousal/activation as two separate systems is more in line with our current understanding of how the brain works. That doesn't invalidate in any way Easterbrook's and Barlow's theories. Their theories were designed to describe how attention becomes reorganized when there are certain changes in arousal/activation. Where that arousal came from was not their immediate concern.

We are still faced with an interesting and important question. According to Easterbrook's theory, arousal directs attention. Attention is not governed by higher-order cognitive processes—such as the individual's implicit theories about the world—but directly by arousal itself. In other words, arousal is more or less hardwired to attention processes. According to this view, the only way to gain control over attention is to gain control over arousal. Indeed, many theorists have approached the problem of attention from the perspective that humans need to learn how to control arousal.

Considerable evidence suggests that how we think about and conceptualize the world plays an important role in the activation of the various arousal systems. The implication of this research is that we are not completely at the mercy of arousal; rather, we can control arousal through the way we think about things. Nonetheless, such approaches generally accept Easterbrook's contention that arousal plays a directive role in attention. From an evolutionary perspective, the reason arousal is hardwired is to ensure that we respond even if it might be a false alarm: Better to be safe than dead (Buss, 1999).

Summary

Because arousal plays a central role in the direction of attention, it is often necessary to manage arousal in order to achieve peak performance. The two main arousal systems are the cortical arousal system and the autonomic arousal system.

Overall cortical arousal is largely caused by the RAS. Studies using the EEG, which measures and records brain activity, have shown that changes in brain activity are abrupt rather than gradual. Research using PET indicates that not all areas of the brain are equally active.

Bodily arousal is caused by the autonomic nervous system, which prepares the body to take action; this produces a number of bodily changes that prepare the individual to expend great amounts of energy. Most of the bodily changes are produced by a branch of the autonomic nervous system called the sympathetic nervous system. In addition, the pituitary gland activates the adrenal glands, which secrete epinephrine and norepinephrine. These chemicals provide the long-term

backup for the more immediate action of the sympathetic nervous system.

Research from a variety of sources suggests that arousal and affect can be related by an inverted U-shaped function. Studies of sensory deprivation, for example, suggest that low levels of stimulation are aversive. Conversely, studies of anxious people suggest that high levels of stimulation are aversive. Other research indicates, however, that whether high levels of stimulation are aversive depends on what goals people are pursuing and whether arousal is prolonged.

Arousal alters attention. Among other things, researchers have argued that arousal restricts and even reorganizes attention. Specifically, under high arousal, our attention becomes directed toward survival-related cues in the environment.

Two main criticisms of arousal theory are that it has failed to treat the origins of arousal as important and that traditional arousal theorists have neglected the distinction between cortical and autonomic arousal.

Challenges for Performance Theory

In the remainder of this chapter, we will examine arousal within the context of individuals' attempts to obtain peak performance. As we begin, let's look at some of the challenges a theory of peak performance must face.

Unexplained Arousal

One of the central problems for performance theorists is to deal with the whole question of unexplained arousal (Neiss, 1988). A long line of research indicates that arousal has few psychological implications when people can explain the source of arousal, but has quite important psychological implications otherwise (Schachter & Singer, 1962). For example, if I have been running, I know that is why my heart is beating rapidly, and my heart rate is of no concern to me. However, if I notice that my heart is beating rapidly and I don't know why, I will begin at once to search for an explanation, and I may become quite alarmed.

Generally, people tend to look for explanations through whatever motivational system is currently active. If I am with someone I love, I will tend to attribute any indicators of high arousal to my being in love. If something I am doing frightens me, I will tend to attribute high arousal to my fears.

Reconceptualizing the Link Between Arousal and Performance

Over the years, the concept of arousal has become central to our thinking about affect and performance. Recently, however, various researchers have challenged some of the traditional views on this topic. Although accepting that arousal is important, they argue that we need to reconceptualize its role (e.g., Neiss, 1988; Reisenzein, 1994). One criticism is that, traditionally, arousal has been given too large a role and that we need to also consider the role of learned and cognitive variables (Neiss, 1988).

Systems Involved in Peak Performance

Several systems have been implicated in peak performance. These systems are more or less functionally independent, according to the research literature. I refer to them as *arousal systems*. To attain peak performance, each of these systems must be operating optimally.

Traditionally, psychologists have made a distinction only between trait and state arousal. *Trait arousal* characterizes the individual more or less independently of the situation (or across situations), whereas *state arousal* arises out of the individual's interaction with the environment. Studies have shown that a wide variety of factors, both learned and cognitive, give rise to state arousal. We will limit our discussion to a few of the better-known systems.

Table 5-1 summarizes the main features of the most important systems that govern the performance of a skill. The first system in Table 5-1 is trait arousal. High trait arousal is often called anxiety or negative emotionality. The vast literature on anxiety and negative emotionality indicates that people differ in whether they chronically experience low, moderate, or high arousal. In general, chronically high arousal appears associated with negative affect. Further, research suggests that these individuals with chronically high arousal attend to very different things in their environment than do individuals with lower arousal. Not only

Table 5-1.   Arousal systems that govern the performance of a skill.

Type of Arousal	Related Research Areas	Effect on Attention	Effect on Performance Outcome
Trait arousal			
Anxiety	Anxiety	Restriction or narrowing	Avoidant behavior
	Timidity	Reorganization (to threat)	Distraction of attention
	Emotionality	Self-evaluative focus	Apprehension
	Reactivity		
	Negative affectivity		
State arousal			
I. Sensory overload arousal	Sensory complexity	Restriction or narrowing	Failure to process
	Stress	Reorganization (to threat)	Inability to deal with complexity
II. Cognitive dissonance arousal	Cognitive conflict	Restriction or narrowing	Failure to process
	Counterattitudinal behaviors		Inability to deal with complexity
III. Evaluation arousal			
A. Test anxiety	Test taking	Intrusive thinking	Failure to focus on task
B. Competition	Competition	Self-focused ego concerns	Failure to focus on task
	Interpersonal rivalry	Performance concerns	Distraction
	Self-focused attention		Impaired judgments

do individuals with high arousal focus on threats, but they also tend to focus on their perceived lack of ability to deal with such threats. The negative affect and the accompanying shifts of attention are inconsistent with peak performance. As a result, such people are likely to engage in avoidant behavior or to experience apprehension.

The second system involved in peak performance is state arousal. *State anxiety* has been defined as a transitory emotional response involving feelings of tension and apprehension, whereas *trait anxiety* has been defined as a personality trait determining the likelihood that a person will experience anxiety in stressful situations (Spielberger, 1983). Stress comes from a person-environment interaction and often comes from overstimulation and the inability to process the accompanying information. This corresponds to sensory overload arousal (Table 5-1). Researchers have repeatedly shown that environmental complexity tends to cause an increase in cortical arousal. When cortical arousal increases beyond some optimal point (beyond the individual's ability to process that information, for example), various mechanisms within the body automatically reduce information input. As we will see, individuals often learn to control input so that it matches their ability to process information. This is Easterbrook's (1959) narrowing concept.

A second type of state arousal involves cognitive dissonance arousal. When two pieces of information are in conflict, the individual responds, among other things, with increased arousal (Elkin & Leippe, 1986). This increased arousal can alter performance on subsequent tasks. The research is consistent with Easterbrook's view that increases in arousal narrow attention.

A third type of state arousal involves evaluation arousal. This type of arousal is more or less specific to evaluative situations, such as taking a test or performing in a competition. Sarason (1984) and others have shown that, when put in a testing situation, many people show high levels of autonomic arousal. This is known as test anxiety. In this state, they experience *intrusive thinking*—thinking that focuses on themselves rather than on the task. Competition also leads to arousal. Competitiveness appears to be a learned orientation and has been linked with the need to win. Indirect evidence suggests that people with a strong need to win tend to become highly aroused in competitive situations (Franken & Brown, 1996). Other research indicates that people dislike competitive situations because they cause distraction and give rise to self-image concerns (Franken & Prpich, 1996).

Test anxiety does not correlate significantly with dislike of competition, so these could be viewed as two distinct systems, each with its own antecedents. We will now consider trait arousal and the various types of state arousal in more detail.

Trait Arousal (Anxiety)

The Biological Component

High arousal has been found to characterize people with negative emotionality, anxiety, and neuroticism, whereas low arousal has been found to characterize people who are low in emotionality, engage in meditation, or have mastered the relaxation response (Benson, 1975). Anxiety is a common emotion and is thought to be normal as long as it does not become completely debilitating. Estimates indicate that 7% of the U.S. population experiences debilitating anxiety (Katz, 1990). Anxiety is debilitating when there is no known cause and when it is completely out of proportion to the danger. Panic attacks, phobias, and obsessive-compulsive disorders are all examples of debilitating anxiety. On the average, twice as many females as males experience debilitating anxiety (11.0% of females and 5.1% of males); most of that difference is because of the higher incidence of phobias (8.0% of females and 3.4% of males).

Twin studies of clinically anxious people have shown a significant genetic component. Slater and Shields (1969) found, for example, that the concordance scores for generalized anxiety were 65% in monozygotic twins and 13% in dizygotic twins. Studies of normal personality, which typically isolate a factor referred to as anxiety, neuroticism, or negative emotionality, have also repeatedly shown that anxiety tends to be highly correlated in monozygotic twins but not in dizygotic twins (Young, Fenton, & Lader, 1971; Kendler, Heath, Martin, & Eaves, 1986). The underlying physiology that characterizes anxiety and negative emotionality is a state of hyperarousal (Lader, 1975, 1980a, b). This state has been shown to be stable over time, which is another indication that it is a trait (e.g., Izard, Libero, Putnam, & Haynes, 1993).

Kagan's Timidity Theory

Jerome Kagan (Kagan & Snidman, 1991) has been studying timidity for more than a decade. Studies of young children and infants indicate that, although some children are inclined to approach unfamiliar people and objects, others are not. Kagan has distinguished between inhibited and uninhibited children. One distinction is their sympathetic reactivity (autonomic arousal); inhibited children are characterized by higher levels. He argues that inhibited and uninhibited children possess different thresholds for excitability in the amygdala and its varied projections and that this difference results in their disposition to be inhibited or uninhibited. He points out that uninhibited and inhibited children represent not merely two ends of a continuum but two distinct types with a distinct genetic origin. He and his colleagues have taken the position that this is only a disposition and, therefore, it is necessary to consider the role of learning and cognition.

Eysenck's Extraversion/Introversion Theory

Hans Eysenck (1967) has suggested that arousal, or activation, is one of the main continuums on which people can be differentiated. Some people, he has suggested, have an arousal level that is relatively low (extraverts), whereas others have an arousal level that is moderate to high (introverts). The key to understanding the difference between extraverts and introverts, according to Eysenck, is understanding how these two types of people maintain optimal stimulation. On the average, he argues, extraverts need more stimulation than introverts do. Socialization is a key source of arousal, so extraverts would be more inclined to socialize than introverts would. Because introverts tend to have a moderate to high arousal level, they are motivated either to maintain existing arousal levels or to reduce arousal levels. Therefore, in contrast to extraverts, who seek out social stimulation, introverts tend to avoid social contacts to prevent any further increase in arousal (see Figure 5-8).

Another axis in Eysenck's theory runs from neuroticism to stability. Neurotic individuals are characterized by high autonomic nervous system reactivity, which would also influence limbic system activity. According to Eysenck, anxious individuals have high standing levels of cortical and autonomic arousal. Extraversion and neuroticism are the first two of the five factors isolated to describe personality by factor analytic procedures.

Even though Eysenck assumes that biology plays a central role, he believes that there is an interaction between biology and learning. As a result, the expression of personality involves understanding the nature of this interaction. Many of his experiments focused on changing behavior using the principles of learning and led others to credit him with being one of the founders of behavioral therapy.

Gray's Behavioral Inhibition Model

Extending Eysenck's theory, Jeffrey Gray (1982) proposed that personality and emotions are determined by two affective-motivational systems. The primary system is the behavioral inhibition system, which involves the septal-hippocampal systems of the brain, its monamine afferents, and the frontal cortex. Like Kagan (Kagan & Snidman, 1991), Gray argues that specific stimulus inputs such as punishment, nonreward, and novelty trigger the inhibition system, which suppresses ongoing behavior and redirects attention to relevant stimuli. According to Gray, people with an active behavioral inhibition system—anxious individuals—would reflect a combination of Eysenck's introversion and neuroticism. At the other end of Gray's axis is an approach system—sometimes called impulsivity—that reflects a combination of extraversion and stability (Figure 5-8).

Barlow's Anxious Apprehension Model

David Barlow has offered a model suggesting that anxiety tends to make people more and more dysfunctional as a result of a bidirectional effect between arousal and attention (Barlow, 1988; Barlow, Chorpita, & Turovsky, 1996). What happens, according to Barlow, is that the negative affect causes a shift in attention to a *self-evaluative focus*. This results in further increases in arousal and a further narrowing of attention. Instead of attention being broad and open, the individual shifts to a hypervigilant state in which attention becomes focused on the recognition of potential threats. The psychological state that accompanies this is intense worry.

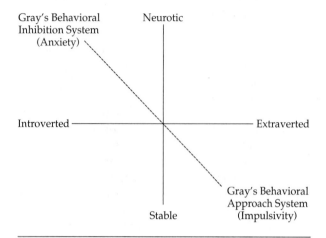

Figure 5-8. Eysenck's introversion-extraversion and neuroticism-stability axes, with Gray's anxiety-impulsivity axis superimposed. (Adapted from *The Biological Basis of Personality*, by H. J. Eysenck (Ed.). Copyright © 1967 by Charles C Thomas Publisher, Ltd.)

At this point, anxiety can take on a highly dysfunctional quality. Intense worry is highly aversive, so the individual could be consumed by avoidance behaviors. The most common avoidant response would be to leave the situation. Barlow's model of anxious apprehension is shown in Figure 5-9.

In Barlow's theory, anxious people tend to account for unexplained arousal in terms of their negative view of the world. In other words, when arousal increases, the world takes on an even gloomier look.

Conclusion

Each of these theories uses slightly different language. What they have in common is the idea that, because of an underlying biological disposition, individuals react differently to the environment. The key factors in the theories—reactivity, timidity, inhibition, or apprehension—all have their roots in the individual's biological makeup. Dispositions do not cause behavior, thus, whether dispositionally high levels of trait arousal will direct attention in a certain way or provoke certain patterns of thought depends on the individual's underlying principles of learning and cognition. In short, trait anxiety interacts with learning and cognition to determine behavior.

The Learned Social Component

There is considerable evidence that most, if not all, of the anxiety disorders—such as irrational fears, phobias, panic reactions, and obsessive-compulsive behaviors—have their roots in generalized anxiety (Barlow, 1988). It has been suggested that, when people are anxious, they are prepared to make certain types of associations rather than others. Specifically, they are prepared to associate stimuli that signal things are threatening and dangerous. For example, people who experience their highly aroused (anxious) state as highly aversive will be inclined to associate a wide variety of stimuli with this state. It seems that certain classes of stimuli are more likely than are others to become associated with this aversive state. This has been referred to as a state of preparedness (Seligman, 1971).

One of the key features of anxiety is the tendency to be constantly vigilant for potential dangers or threats. Various theorists have argued that, although our biology may predispose us to be alert to dangers and threats, the tendency to be chronically preoccupied with dangers and threats results from the interaction of biology and the principles of learning and cognition (Watson & Clark, 1984). According to Beck (1985), the affective system leads people to process the environment in a distorted way. When we are highly aroused or the behavioral inhibition system is activated, for example, we tend to focus on things that are potentially dangerous. The result is that we tend to process only negative information. This view is very similar to Barlow's view that high arousal tends to shift attention to threat and danger cues. Beck goes on to suggest that, if we process mainly negative information, we will be inclined to develop a schema or implicit theory of the world that involves more bad things than good things. The development of this negative schema would then determine how we are likely to process information in the future. In other words, even if arousal levels were lowered, we would continue to search for dangers and threats. Beck argues that anxious people not only distort information about the world but also distort information about how effectively they deal with the world. Because it is a bad world and they are unable to make

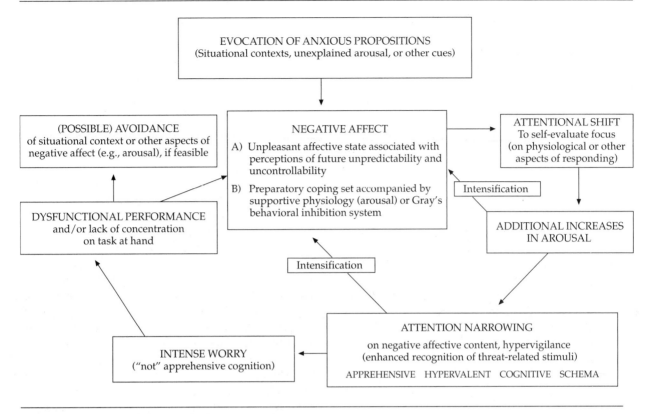

Figure 5-9. Barlow's model of anxious apprehension. (From *Anxiety and Its Disorders: The Nature and Treatment of Anxiety and Panic,* by D. H. Barlow. Copyright © 1988 by Guilford Press. Reprinted by permission.)

it good, they tend to see themselves as ineffective. Over time, anxious individuals come to believe that they lack the ability to deal with a bad world. This becomes the basis for depression.

Beck has argued that appraisal has its root in past information processing, which came about because of some affective system. By contrast, the social learning theorists can account, at least in part, for differences in information processing in terms of principles such as imitation and modeling. Living with parents who keep alerting us to dangers in our environment or telling us how bad things are could bias our information processing so that we tend to see more bad than good. Also, constantly being given a biased view of the world by the media could dispose us to develop an implicit theory of the world that is negative. There could even be a spiral effect: As our view of the world becomes more negative, we might be more inclined to buy papers that

present a negative picture consistent with our view. This could induce publishers of papers to present even more bad news, on the principle that they are giving the public what it wants.

The Cognitive Component

Many theorists have argued that the experience of anxiety depends on how the individual appraises the world (e.g., Spielberger, 1985). Most of these theorists start with the idea that some event, often accompanied by autonomic arousal, causes us to carefully examine our situation. If the situation is appraised as dangerous or threatening, we will respond with fear or anxiety. If, on the other hand, we appraise the situation as challenging, we will respond with a very different set of emotions, such as mastery or involvement. According to cognitive theories, the affective reaction (arousal) is a very diffuse autonomic discharge that is experienced as neither good or bad; rather, our appraisal of it causes our subjective experience.

According to cognitive theories, anxiety is a personality trait. These theories account for differences in anxiety provoked by different situations, but they typically fail to say where these differences in appraisal come from. In Beck's theory, the different schemas or implicit theories are thought to have their origins in our affective reactions. One major problem for the cognitive theories is their inability to account for irrational anxiety. Often people know their reactions are inappropriate or irrational but are unable to control them.

Despite such problems, cognitive theories tell us something very important about the mental processes necessary to achieve peak performance. To deal with new challenges or with failure, we need to find ways of seeing the situation that will encourage us to redouble our efforts at learning and coping. How we appraise the situation determines whether we will engage in approach/adaptive behaviors or avoidant/nonadaptive behaviors.

Beck suggests that schemas are learned, but his methods for changing those schemas are cognitive. In working with clients, Beck teaches people how to think in more adaptive ways. He argues that, because people have developed faulty thinking, they are inclined to appraise situations in negative or nonadaptive ways. In his research, he has shown that, when people are given cognitive retraining on how to appraise a situation, they respond in a more adaptive manner.

A large body of research has linked anxiety to cognitive judgments about the predictability or controllability of a situation. The research indicates that the anxiety reaction is likely to vary in proportion to the degree that the situation seems predictable and controllable (e.g., Seligman, 1975). Consequently, broad belief systems involving hope and optimism are important in mitigating anxiety.

High Trait Arousal and Performance

High trait arousal is viewed as a major obstacle to attaining peak performance. One main problem for anxious individuals is not being able to focus their attention on the task. Instead, they tend to focus on potential threats and on their ineffectiveness in dealing with those threats.

To prevent such a reorganization of attention, anxious people must train themselves to appraise the world in positive terms. In other words, people born with a disposition to be anxious can learn to see the world in more positive terms. To do so, they need to change their schemata or implicit theories of the world. If anxious individuals develop a positive implicit theory in which the world is benign, they should be less inclined to respond to everything they encounter as a potential threat.

An aspect of anxious individuals' negative outlook is that they tend to overgeneralize following failure. Instead of accepting failure as the outcome of a specific situation and moving on, they are inclined to expect that all subsequent situations will also end in failure. Developing a positive implicit theory should help with this problem. Anxious individuals also need to develop the belief that they can be effective in making changes. They need to believe that they can make a difference. Research has consistently shown that people with good coping skills experience far less anxiety than do people with poor coping skills.

In addition, anxious individuals need to accept that high arousal is necessary for peak performance. Also, high arousal can be experienced as a positive emotion. Whether we experience high arousal as negative or positive often depends on whether we view the situation as a threat or a challenge. Peak performance involves rising to the challenge. Thus, learning to appraise the situation in more positive ways can help anxious individuals to deal with their high arousal.

Finally, individuals need to learn how to rest and relax. When our arousal level is too high for too long, we are likely to develop a stress reaction.

Summary

Twin studies indicate that anxiety has a genetic component. Kagan distinguished between inhibited and uninhibited children based on their responses to unfamiliar situations and found that inhibited children are characterized by greater sympathetic reactivity (autonomic arousal). Eysenck has proposed that differences in arousal predispose people to be extraverted or introverted. He suggests that, to produce an optimal level of arousal, extraverts seek out stimulation, whereas introverts seek out a nonchanging environment to keep stimulation at tolerable levels. According to Gray, emotions are primarily determined by the behavioral inhibition system.

Barlow postulates a bidirectional effect between arousal and attention. The net result is that arousal not only narrows attention but also reorganizes attention, so that anxious individuals tend to worry all the time. Worry is highly aversive, so anxious individuals are inclined to engage in avoidant behavior. When people are anxious, they are prepared to make certain types of associations rather than others and, as a result, are more inclined to develop certain types of disorders, including panic, phobias, and obsessive disorders.

A key feature of anxiety is the tendency to be constantly vigilant for potential dangers or threats. According to Beck, the negative affect associated with anxiety leads people to process the environment in a distorted way. The negative schemata that result from such processing then determine how they are likely to process information in the future. Social learning theorists account for this effect through such principles as imitation and modeling.

Many theorists have argued that our experience of anxiety depends on how we appraise the world. Differences in appraisal, according to these theories, are associated with differences in personality. Cognitive judgments about predictability and controllability are also important in determining how much anxiety we experience.

A major problem for anxious individuals is their tendency to react to everything as danger or threat. One way for them to change that perception is to develop a more positive view of the world. In addition, they need to see themselves as competent individuals capable of coping with the problems they encounter. Finally, they need to accept the idea that high arousal is a necessary condition for peak performance.

We now turn to state arousal, which results from a person-situation interaction. We will consider three basic types of state arousal.

State Arousal: Sensory Overload

Arousal is constantly changing in response to biological rhythms and to incoming environmental stimulation. In this section, we will consider the effect of envi-

Aircraft controllers must often deal with sensory overload, also called information overload.

ronmental stimulation on attention and, hence, on peak performance.

Note that one consequence of sensory overload, especially when prolonged, is stress, which is highly debilitating physically and emotionally. Thus, managing environmental stimulation is critical for peak performance.

The Biological Component

Sources of Arousal

First, let's review the two factors responsible for fluctuations of arousal.

1. **Rhythmic activity of the nervous system.** Arousal—especially cortical arousal—is under the control of certain biological rhythms. Michel Jouvet's (1967) work

suggests that the alternating activity of the raphe nuclei, which secrete the neurotransmitter serotonin, and the locus coeruleus, which secretes the neurotransmitter norepinephrine, governs arousal and alertness in humans. Jouvet found that serotonin is associated with reduced cortical activity (reduced arousal), and norepinephrine is associated with increased cortical activity (increased arousal). All of us are more alert at some times than at others. All normal people experience these involuntary changes in arousal (alertness), and they often experience them at certain predictable times of the day. So-called morning people, for example, experience greater alertness in the mornings; night people experience greater alertness at night. Still others have a mixed pattern—a period of alertness in the morning, followed at midday by a drop in alertness, which is followed, in turn, by another period of increased alertness. Not surprisingly, people with this pattern are likely to take a nap.

2. **Stimulation of the sensory systems.** Stimulation of any of the sensory systems—visual, auditory, olfactory, or tactile—is accompanied by an increase in arousal. The increase in arousal allows humans to maximize the input of incoming information. There is considerable evidence, however, that humans have a limited capacity to process incoming information. In other words, even when the brain is fully activated, we are unable to process all the incoming data. As a result, we begin to experience confusion and distraction, which can be interpreted as anxiety.

The Concept of Sensory Overload

Our ability to process information is linked, at least in part, to the cognitive structures (schemas) that we have developed. Researchers have suggested that as the result of developing schemas we increase our ability to process information because we have developed a rule or type of organization that allows us to summarize information. G. A. Miller (1956) suggested that we refer to these units of information as "chunks" and argued that we are limited to dealing with a maximum of perhaps seven chunks at a time, a relatively limited amount of information. As a result, we often experience sensory overload in complex environments. Humans tend to experience sensory overload as highly aversive and stressful, perhaps because it represents a loss of predictability and control. From our perspec-

tive, we are interested in sensory overload because it produces fundamental shifts in attention that can interfere with peak performance.

Mechanisms to Reduce Sensory Overload

Lacey and Lacey's attention/rejection model. Research indicates that a couple of systems are designed to help humans deal with sensory overload. One appears to be linked to increases in heart rate. Acceleration of the heart produces pressure on receptors in the carotid sinus and aortic arch, and this pressure has been shown to reduce RAS activity (Bonvallet & Allen, 1963). Accordingly, Lacey and Lacey (1970, 1978) have suggested that changes in heart rate determine reticular activity, at least in part. Most arousal theorists take the opposite position—that the RAS controls heart rate.

Lacey and Lacey have suggested that such a feedback system has important psychological significance. According to their model, the reduced RAS activity resulting from heart-rate acceleration would block a certain portion of the incoming stimulation and thereby reduce cognitive overload. Similarly, when the person was not working to capacity, deceleration of the heart would signal the RAS to increase activity and thereby allow the individual to process more information.

In one test of Lacey and Lacey's model, subjects had to do three tasks (Lacey, Kagan, Lacey, & Moss, 1963). The first task required the subjects to pay close attention to external stimulation; the second involved mental problem solving, which presumably would be disturbed by external stimulation; the third task involved both internal and external stimulation. The results showed that the heart decelerated when the task called for careful attention to external stimulation, and accelerated when the task called for the momentary rejection of external stimulation. In the combined task, there was no change. The Laceys and their colleagues argued that the task in which the subject had to concentrate simultaneously on external and internal information produced a conflict, which explains why there was no change.

The GABA system. GABA (gamma-aminobutyric acid) is a naturally occurring inhibitory neurotransmitter (Cooper, Bloom, & Roth, 1982; Tallman, Paul, Skolnick, & Gallager, 1980). That means that GABA somehow reduces the flow of neural transmission.

We will consider GABA in detail in Chapter 7, so here we will simply note that the GABA system also appears to be designed to help protect us against sensory overload.

The Learned Component

Young children deal with sensory overload simply by covering their eyes or ears with their hands. As adults, we learn similar ways of dealing with sensory overload. We seek out a quiet place, or we listen to soothing music. Some businesses have instituted brief periods of relaxation at the beginning of the day, to ensure that employees are not so highly aroused that they cannot work efficiently. Coffee breaks often serve a similar function.

In Chapter 9, we will deal with a variety of procedures that are very effective in reducing arousal, including biofeedback, relaxation, and meditation. One such technique is restricted environmental stimulation technique (REST). REST is an effective treatment for excessive environmental stimulation, which, if chronic, can produce physical as well as psychological disorders (Suedfeld, 1975; Suedfeld & Kristeller, 1982).

Two basic methods have been used in the REST research. One involves secluded bed rest in a completely dark, soundproof room for 24 hours. A second method is to have the individual float for approximately an hour in a shallow tank filled with a solution of Epsom salts and water.

The REST technique has been found to increase the power of more standard stress-management techniques, such as biofeedback (Plotkin, 1978). When REST was used as a component in the treatment of essential hypertension, clinically significant drops in systolic and diastolic blood pressure were found (Suedfeld & Kristeller, 1982). REST has also been successfully used to help people stop smoking, lose weight, and reduce drug dependency.

Why does REST work? Studies have shown that REST has not only an immediate but a long-term effect. Suedfeld and Kristeller (1982) have suggested that REST may help people to shift their attention away from external cues to internal cues. High arousal, as we'll see shortly, often directs attention to survival-related cues, which are usually external because threats to our survival are typically external. It follows that people exposed to excessive environmental stimulation may learn to habitually attend to the external environment. REST may help such people to shift their attention to internal cues. As a result, they tend not only to monitor those cues more closely but also to deal with them before they produce serious health problems.

Another interpretation of the REST research is that, during these sessions, people learn how to account for their arousal. As a result, unexplained arousal becomes explained and is no longer seen as a threat.

The Cognitive Component

Whenever we interpret an event as threatening or potentially exciting, we are likely to experience an increase in arousal, both cortical and autonomic. When we are threatened, the body must be prepared to deal with that threat, both mentally and physically. Similarly, when we select some challenging activity, our body must be prepared for it. If we are going scuba diving, for example, we need to be both physically and mentally prepared for it. An increase in arousal, in other words, is associated with a wide variety of forthcoming activities.

The important point to remember about this kind of arousal is that it is anticipatory; it occurs before some anticipated event (Spinks, Blowers, & Shek, 1985). Because it is based on our cognitive interpretation, it might be inappropriate. I may anticipate that I am going to be fired, for example, when nothing of the sort is about to happen. Sometimes the magnitude of the arousal we experience is not appropriate. I may have good reason to experience a very high level of arousal if I am asked to address a large audience, but it would be inappropriate to experience the same level of arousal if I were asked to introduce a friend to someone else I know.

The magnitude of our arousal is generally proportional to the importance of the forthcoming event. If we have a number of important things to do, we are likely to experience substantial anticipatory arousal. Like environmental arousal, anticipatory arousal is thought to be additive. If, on a particular day, we realize that we have too much to accomplish and too little time, for example, we may experience anticipatory arousal that exceeds some optimal level.

Dealing with Sensory Overload

Setting Priorities

One way of reducing sensory overload is to make lists of what we are going to do and what tasks are most important. Further, we need to promise ourselves that we are only going to focus on one task at a time. In this way, we avoid the tendency to think about everything at once. Unless I make a list when I have a lot of things to do, I tend to jump from one thing to the next. Even though much of our attention is outside of our control, research on goal setting (Locke & Latham, 1990) indicates that we can take charge of certain things. When we decide something is important, that becomes the focus of our attention. Only when we have not decided what is important is our attention governed by the arousal system.

We must be very careful about what we decide is important because that will become the focus of our attention. Deciding not to fail, for example, may have serious consequences. We could become so obsessed with not failing that we became paralyzed. We will return to this topic shortly.

Managing Information

The best way to manage a complex environment is to become completely familiar with it. When we are familiar with something, we have processed all the information contained in it (Berlyne, 1960). When we process information, we typically also develop schemata, categories, and rules that summarize that information. Those schemata are useful when we are placed in a new situation.

Very often, when we attempt to become familiar with something, we become overwhelmed. To avoid becoming overwhelmed, we need to break it down into manageable units (Horowitz, 1979). When I am writing, I can become overwhelmed and stressed if I attempt to do too much. If I keep my focus narrow, however, I find I can master a block of information and write about it. One way of knowing whether or not something is manageable is to monitor my feelings. If I feel stressed, I've tried to tackle something that is too big.

Sensory Overload and Performance

Arousal caused by sensory overload can lead to the narrowing of attention (Easterbrook, 1959). One problem associated with the narrowing of attention is the failure to perform at optimum levels. Moreover, evidence suggests that sensory overload not only causes increases in arousal but can cause a stress reaction. Stress typically produces marked performance losses, especially if the immediate task demands sustained attention. Prolonged stress may trigger the reorganization of attention (Easterbrook, 1959). It may direct attention toward survival cues in the environment rather than to the immediate task. Under these conditions, individuals rarely learn anything new, apparently because they are focusing their attention on threat and survival cues. (We will return to this topic in Chapter 12.) The overall picture that emerges is that, when people are experiencing sensory overload, their performance on tasks suffers.

The focus of techniques to deal with sensory overload is to reduce how much information must be processed in a given period. Sometimes people use drugs to deal with sensory overload, but this approach is counterproductive because it further reduces our ability to process information. The best way to deal with sensory overload is to become familiar, over time, with that information. The way we become familiar with something is simply to interact with it. The human brain has been built to create schemata that will enable us to summarize very complex sources of information. Once those structures are in place, we will have the capacity to deal with vast amounts of information. Under those conditions, arousal will be lowered and attention will be broad and inclusive.

Summary

Sensory overload can result not only in high arousal but also in stress. Biological mechanisms can help control arousal. One of these systems appears to be linked to increased heart rate; another involves the GABA system.

Considerable evidence suggests that we can learn to control our arousal. The most obvious—and perhaps most efficient—way is to restrict incoming stimulation. We can also learn to focus our attention in ways that restrict incoming stimulation. An interesting side effect of our ability to anticipate events is that we sometimes experience high levels of anticipatory arousal.

To manage sensory overload, we need to decide what is important rather than simply allowing ourselves to be bombarded with information. Also, we need to break information down into manageable units.

Sensory overload has been linked to performance deficits. These deficits can be mediated by increases in arousal that accompany sensory overload.

State Arousal: Cognitive Dissonance

When we encounter new information that is inconsistent with our existing ways of thinking about the world, a state of cognitive dissonance typically arises. It has been postulated that cognitive dissonance creates a motivational state within us that disposes us to look for ways of reducing it (Festinger, 1957). To do this, we can add new cognitions or change existing ones, seek information that is consistent with existing cognitions, or simply avoid information that is inconsistent with existing cognitions.

The Biological Component

Festinger (1957) conceptualized cognitive dissonance in two distinguishable ways. He suggested that it leads to psychological discomfort and alluded to dissonance as a bodily condition analogous to a tension or drive state. Many early researchers who examined the motivational properties of cognitive dissonance focused on its drive-like properties. They conceptualized cognitive dissonance as arousal and conducted studies designed to see if cognitive dissonance did in fact produce physiological arousal. A number of studies suggested that cognitive dissonance leads to increases in arousal (Croyle & Cooper, 1983), but one of the first definitive studies used the counterattitudinal essay induction technique (Elkin & Leippe, 1986). In this technique, typically, individuals are asked to write an essay that is inconsistent with some belief or attitude. Students might be asked, for example, to write an essay about why their tuition should increase, despite their opinions to the contrary. Elkin and Leippe (1986) found in two different studies that the galvanic skin response (GSR) was elevated following a freely written counterattitudinal essay. This finding has been replicated in other studies (e.g., Losch & Cacioppo, 1990).

It is not surprising that arousal has been closely linked to cognitive dissonance. When people need to process information, to think about some issue, or to resolve some conflict, the brain typically becomes active. When the brain is highly aroused in one task, it performs other tasks less well. In a later section, we will consider the implications of this phenomenon.

The Learned Component

Festinger (1957) suggested that perceptions of an inconsistency among an individual's cognitions generates psychological discomfort—intrapersonal tension—and that this aversive state motivates individuals to take remedial action. Recently, in an experiment designed to examine this idea, participants were induced to write a counterattitudinal or proattitudinal essay about a 10% tuition increase the next term. Subsequently, they were asked to indicate how uncomfortable, uneasy, and bothered they were. The results provided data consistent with Festinger's motivational hypothesis (Elliot & Devine, 1994). When participants wrote counterattitudinal essays they indeed experienced psychological discomfort. When an attitudinal shift occurred, however, their psychological discomfort returned to baseline levels.

What is interesting from a learning perspective is that the strategies used to reduce dissonance are reinforced. When these strategies are employed, psychological discomfort decreases, and therefore individuals are inclined to use those strategies again when they experience cognitive dissonance. This explains why people can be presented repeatedly with certain information and yet never accept it—such as why a cigarette smoker is able to discount evidence regarding the negative health effects of smoking.

The Cognitive Component

As we have seen, cognitive dissonance theory can explain why people are inclined to maintain their existing beliefs. Cognitive dissonance theory also suggests that it is possible to change other people's attitudes. For one reason or another, people sometimes engage in behaviors that are not consistent with their underlying beliefs and attitudes. When that happens, they will sometimes change their attitudes to match their behavior. Festinger (1957) argued that, since they cannot go back and change their behavior, the only thing they can do to reduce cognitive dissonance is to change their beliefs. The counterattitudinal essay is one way of producing this effect in the laboratory.

Volunteer organizations often use this phenomenon. They ask people to perform seemingly innocuous tasks, such as stuffing envelopes with information about a political organization. Eventually, people need to rationalize to themselves why they are working for a political party. Often they conclude that the organization is not only worthwhile but also needed to address a particular problem in society.

This strategy will only work if people freely engage in the behaviors. If they are coerced or paid, they might rationalize that they did it for those reasons. Bem (1967) suggests that people infer attitudes based on observations of their own behavior. If they are paid for writing a counterattitudinal essay, for example, they might be inclined to attribute their behavior to being paid. As a result, they would experience no cognitive dissonance and no pressure to change their attitudes.

Cognitive Dissonance and Performance

Considerable research indicates cognitive dissonance can lead to performance decrements. Among other things, it has been shown that, although cognitive dissonance can facilitate performance on subsequent overlearned tasks, cognitive dissonance often interferes with performance on subsequent difficult or complex tasks (e.g., Pallak & Pittman, 1972). The basic interpretation of these and other findings is that cognitive dissonance increases arousal, and the increased arousal mediates these effects. According to an attentional model, increases in arousal narrow attention. Although narrowed attention can facilitate performance on an existing highly practiced skill, high arousal would interfere with learning that required broad rather than narrow attention. Further, if high arousal tends to focus attention on survival-related cues, it would be difficult for the individual to integrate new information that did not pertain to survival.

Cognitive dissonance can make it difficult for people to focus or concentrate, so they sometimes attempt to control this type of arousal by managing information input. Actors, for example, might decide to put off reading their reviews until they have a block of time to

think about them and put them in perspective. In the course of a sporting competition, an opponent might attempt to use cognitive dissonance to distract an individual—by saying, for instance, "My grandmother can run faster than you" or "Your team always folds under playoff pressure."

Summary

Festinger conceptualized cognitive dissonance in two ways. He suggested that it leads to psychological discomfort, on the one hand, and to a drive-like state, on the other. He contended that the psychological discomfort motivates individuals to implement remedial strategies. Researchers have interpreted the drive-like state as arousal. Several studies have provided convincing evidence that cognitive dissonance does produce physiological arousal. Not only that, these increases in arousal have been shown to facilitate performance on overlearned tasks and to interfere with performance on difficult or complex tasks. The results of such studies suggest that the arousal produced by cognitive dissonance is more or less the same as that responsible for narrowing of attention and ultimately reorganization of attention.

State Arousal: Evaluation Arousal

Peak performance is closely linked to evaluation arousal. Many people find that, when they are being evaluated, their performance deteriorates. In this section, we will examine why evaluation can lead to deterioration in performance, in the context of two lines of research—test anxiety and dislike of competitive situations.

Test Anxiety

For some time now, we have had evidence that tests are often perceived as a threat and this perception produces a high level of arousal. If the arousal is prolonged—for instance, when students have to take several tests—it can cause a stress reaction. The high level of arousal associated with tests has been linked to a deterioration in performance. Note that not everybody

Exams are often a source of anxiety and stress.

responds to tests as a threat; some people respond to tests as a challenge.

The Biological Component

Various physiological changes occur when students prepare for and take an examination. For example, glucose levels rise before an exam and decline significantly during the exam. Lactic acid, too, is elevated before an exam but, unlike glucose, continues to increase during the exam (Hall & Brown, 1979); both of these responses are indicative of the stress level. Norepinephrine levels rise, while levels of immunoglobin A (a compound in the blood that indicates the activity level of the immune system) decline, especially in people with a strong power motive (McClelland, Ross, & Patel, 1985). McClelland has argued that the power mo-

tive reflects, among other things, the need to control. People with a strong power motive tend to be most highly aroused by situations in which they fear loss of control, such as examinations. This research suggests that, following an examination (or loss of control), an individual might be more susceptible to infection.

The Learned Component

Sarason (1984) has argued that test anxiety is largely a problem of *self-preoccupying intrusive thinking* (p. 929). A preoccupation with our own thoughts interferes with task-focused thinking. What kinds of thoughts? They seem generally to be responses that arise from a self-assessment of personal deficits in the face of certain situational demands. Neurotic individuals are particularly prone to such thinking. Bolger (1990) found that neuroticism increases preexamination anxiety and that neurotics are prone to engage in wishful thinking and self-blame, among other things.

Can we learn to reduce the interference that comes from such thinking? Sarason has shown that self-preoccupying intrusive thinking is reduced when we focus on the task. He argues that helping people focus on the task is a much better way of helping them to deal with test-induced stress than is simply attempting to reassure them. Once again, note that, although attention is sometimes governed by arousal, humans can often redirect their attention. Simply learning that it is important to focus on the task seems to be a highly effective procedure for dealing with test-induced high arousal.

The Cognitive Component

There are large individual differences in the amount of stress induced by an examination. This is not surprising because the outcome of the exam will have different implications for different individuals. Students who need a certain grade to get into graduate school, for example, could perceive the stakes as very high indeed. Individuals also differ in the amount of control they feel as they prepare for the exam, wait for the day to arrive, and finally take the exam. Their perceptions of the exam's difficulty vary as well. We will look at the effects of perceived difficulty later.

When students see the exam as a threat, how do they respond? Typically, they use a combination of problem-focused and emotion-focused coping strategies. (We will discuss this distinction in more detail in Chapter 9.) In the anticipatory stage, they tend to prepare for the examination. During such problem-focused coping, they experience positive emotions, such as hopefulness. Just before the exam, during the final waiting stage, their emotions begin to turn negative. Having reviewed the material to be covered by the exam, they are no longer as actively preparing, and they have time to appraise the adequacy of their efforts (Folkman & Lazarus, 1985).

Test Anxiety and Performance

Considerable evidence indicates that test anxiety causes poorer performance on tests. The poor performance of test-anxious individuals appears to be linked to their tendency to focus attention on the intrusive thoughts. Armed with this hypothesis, Sarason (1984) set out to help text-anxious individuals by teaching them to focus on the test and not on their thoughts. His research provides data consistent with the view that the performance deficits are mediated by attention and are not caused by any loss of memory or intellectual capacity.

Summary

Although wide individual differences exist, test taking tends to produce a number of physiological changes, including increases in autonomic arousal. Attentional shifts have been found to be directly linked to these changes in arousal. In particular, people experience self-preoccupying intrusive thinking. The effect seems to depend on what is at stake for the individual. This finding indicates that cognitive processes play an important role.

Competition Arousal

A second form of evaluative arousal is the arousal associated with competition. Competition arousal and test arousal may be regarded as separate sources of evaluative arousal, because they are not significantly correlated (Franken & Prpich, 1996).

Research from various sources indicates that a competitive orientation often leads to a deterioration in performance. Some of the best work comes from Spence and Helmreich (1983), who hypothesized that three factors are linked to achievement: mastery, work, and competitiveness (Table 5-2). Research with their Achievement scale indicated that, contrary to their initial hypothesis, work and mastery predict achievement in various situations, but competitiveness does not. In fact, having a competitive orientation seems to undermine achievement. Let's look at three studies that showed this effect.

Predicting GPA. To see if their scale could predict academic achievement, as measured by a student's cumulative grade-point average (GPA), Spence and Helmreich (1983) administered their scale to more than 1300 students. The results pointed to an interaction of GPA with the three subscales. To determine how the students with higher GPAs differed from those with lower GPAs, the investigators divided the students by gender and then, within each gender, formed a group with GPAs above the median (the high-GPA group) and another group with GPAs below the median (the low-GPA group). Thus, they now had four groups. The results (Figure 5-10) indicate that the students with the highest GPAs were high in work and mastery and low in competitiveness. If competitiveness contributes to achievement, as Spence and Helmreich initially thought, why didn't students who were high in work and mastery and high in competitiveness get the highest GPAs? It appears from these results that being high in competitiveness tends to undermine the performance of those who are also high in work and mastery.

Predicting annual income. Annual income is often taken as an indication of achievement in the business world. To explore the possibility that competitiveness is detrimental to performance in the business world (at least as measured by income), a group of businesspeople were given the Achievement scale (Saunders, 1978). Businesspeople tend to score relatively high on competitiveness, which is consistent with the idea that a competitiveness orientation is necessary to survive in the business world. If we look at who makes the most money (Figure 5-11), however, we see that competitiveness has a detrimental effect. The people who make the most money are high in work and mastery and low in competitiveness.

Table 5-2. Items from the first part of the Achievement scale. The items are to be answered using a four-point scale that goes from *Not at all like me* to *Very much like me.* The items that measure competitiveness, mastery, and work are labeled with the letters C, M, and W. Items that are to be reverse-scored are marked with an asterisk (*).

1. I would rather do something at which I feel confident and relaxed than something which is challenging and difficult. (M)*

2. It is important to me to do my work as well as I can even if it isn't popular with co-workers. (W)

3. I enjoy working in situations involving competition with others. (C)

4. When a group I belong to plans an activity, I would rather direct it myself than just help out and have someone else organize it. (M)

5. I would rather learn easy fun games than difficult thought games. (M)*

6. I find satisfaction in working as well as I can. (W)

7. It is important to me to perform better than others on a task. (C)

8. If I am not good at something, I would rather keep struggling to master it than move on to something I may be good at. (M)

9. There is satisfaction in a job well done. (M)

10. I feel that winning is important in both work and games. (C)

11. Once I undertake a task, I persist. (W)

12. I find satisfaction in exceeding my previous performance even if I don't outperform others. (M)

13. It annoys me when other people perform better than I do. (C)

14. I prefer to work in situations that require a high level of skill. (M)

15. I like to work hard. (W)

16. I try harder when I'm in competition with other people. (C)

17. I more often attempt tasks that I am not sure I can do than tasks that I believe I can do. (M)

18. Part of my enjoyment in doing things is improving my past performance. (M)

19. I like to be busy at all times. (W)

Source: J. T. Spence and R. L. Helmreich, "Achievement-Related Motives and Behavior." In J. T. Spence (Ed.), *Achievement and Achievement Motivations,* 1983. W. H. Freeman. Reprinted with permission.

Predicting scientific productivity. One way of measuring the worth of a scientific contribution is to count the number of times a scientific article has been cited by other scientists in their publications; this is called a citation index. A study of the citation indices of male academic psychologists suggests that the Achievement scale can also predict scientific attainment (Helmreich, Beane, Lucker, & Spence, 1978; Helmreich, Spence, Beane, Lucker, & Matthews, 1980). The people who make the most contributions are high in work and mastery and low in competitiveness (Figure 5-12). The consistency between the findings for students, businesspeople, and academics is particularly striking.

As usual, we'll now review the biological, learned, and cognitive components of competition arousal.

The Biological Component

There is considerable evidence that competition creates high autonomic arousal not only in physical sports but also in interpersonal activities such as discussions and debates. Although some question how much of the arousal in sports is caused by physical activity and how much by interpersonal rivalry, interpersonal rivalry can lead to increases in arousal (Cratty, 1989). Note also that interpersonal conflict has been

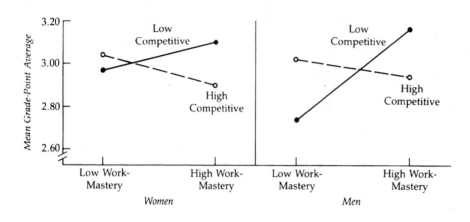

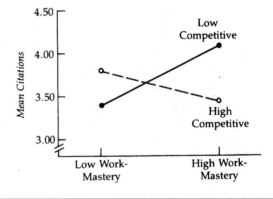

Figure 5-10. Mean grade-point average in the four achievement-motive groups of male and female undergraduates. (From "Achievement-Related Motives and Behavior," by J. T. Spence & R. L. Helmreich. In J. T. Spence (Ed.), *Achievement and Achievement Motivations.* Copyright © 1983 by W. H. Freeman and Company. Used with permission.)

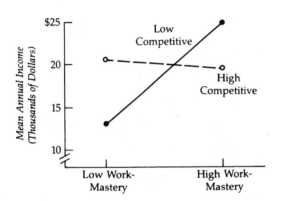

Figure 5-11. Income in four achievement-motive groups of businesspeople, corrected for years of experience. (From "Achievement-Related Motives and Behavior," by J. T. Spence & R. L. Helmreich. In J. T. Spence (Ed.), *Achievement and Achievement Motivations.* Copyright © 1983 by W. H. Freeman. Reprinted with permission of the editor.)

Figure 5-12. Citations to published research in four achievement-motive groups of male academic scientists. (From "Achievement Motivation and Scientific Attainment," by R. L. Helmreich, W. E. Beane, G. W. Lucker and J. T. Spence. *Personality & Social Psychology Bulletin,* 1978, 4(2), 222–226. Copyright © 1978 by Sage Publications, Inc. Reprinted with permission.)

linked to arousal and stress (Lazarus & Folkman, 1984). According to another study, informing people that their performance outcome is very important increases their arousal levels and impairs their ability to make difficult judgments (Pelham & Neter, 1995). The need to perform at high levels and the need to win appear to be major sources not only of arousal but also of stress.

The Learned Component

In *No Contest: The Case Against Competition,* Alfie Kohn (1986) makes the case that competition is largely learned. As he points out, there are no data to support the idea that competitiveness is part of human nature. Kohn provides numerous examples of cultures where cooperation is the norm and reviews extensive research findings that children will adopt a cooperative model, rather than a competitive model, if appropriate reward contingencies are arranged (Johnson & Johnson, 1985). Finally, he discusses evidence that competing is often not the best way to achieve happiness.

"Winning isn't everything; it is the only thing." That famous line has been attributed to Vince Lombardi, former coach of the Green Bay Packers football team. As it turns out, Lombardi never said that. What he said (at a speech in Milwaukee in 1968) was, "Winning isn't everything. Trying to win is." According to biographer Michael O'Brien (1987), Vince Lombardi later commented, "I wished to hell that I had never said that damned thing. I meant the effort. . . . I meant having a goal. . . . I sure as hell didn't mean for people to crush human values and morality."

Virtually all the evidence suggests that interpersonal rivalry tends to undermine rather than enhance personal performance (Kohn, 1986). For people to perform at their personal best, they cannot afford to divert their attention from the task at hand. Interpersonal rivalry can lead to the reorganization of attention; that is, people can become more focused on undermining the competition than on performing at their personal best. Some evidence indicates that, when people have a highly developed skill, competition can motivate them to put forth more effort (Franken & Brown, 1995). Most likely, however, what is important is the arousal and not the interpersonal rivalry. In short, if competition only leads to arousal, it may facilitate performance by narrowing attention; however, if competition diverts or reorganizes attention (as in interpersonal rivalry), it can and often does undermine performance.

The Cognitive Component

Highly competitive people have a strong need to win. In an extension of Spence and Helmreich's work, a colleague and I developed three factors that correlated highly with their factors. We renamed the competitiveness scale the need-to-win scale because our factors contained mainly items that pertained to winning (Franken & Brown, 1995). Note, however, that not all people who like competitive situations have a high need to win; some highly skilled (mastery-oriented) people appreciate a competitive situation because it motivates them to perform at a high level (Franken & Brown, 1995).

To better understand those competitive individuals characterized by a high need to win, we studied a group of university students. They were asked to fill out a variety of personality assessment measures, including the need-to-win scale and a couple of questionnaires designed to assess their reactions and attitudes (Franken & Brown, 1996). One questionnaire we administered was the COPE scale, which was designed to identify those personal and behavioral qualities that have been shown to make people resistant to the effects of stress (Carver, Scheier, & Weintraub, 1989). We found that people with a strong need to win have very poor coping strategies relative to people with a low need to win and people with a mastery orientation. Among other things, people with a high need to win have poor active coping skills, tend to have poor social support systems, tend to face stress with denial and behavioral and mental disengagement, and tend to be low in acceptance, positive reinterpretation, and growth. In short, they tend to possess virtually none of the qualities that help people to resist the effects of stress (Carver, Scheier, & Weintraub, 1989).

The students' responses to a second questionnaire, designed to assess their implicit theories of the world, implicit theories of themselves, and theories of success, suggested that people with a strong need to win tend to lack those positive behavioral attributes that have been linked to success. For example, people with a strong need to win tended to endorse such statements as: "It is a dog-eat-dog world," "Some people are winners and some are losers," "I take as much as I can get," and "I am inclined to hoard information."

How do they view themselves? Compared with people with a mastery orientation, those with a need to win are low in hope, optimism, and self-esteem. Further, they tend to see abilities as fixed, whereas people with a mastery orientation generally perceive that they can improve their skills and abilities through effort. People with a need to win also see themselves as "aggressive" and "forceful" (Franken & Brown, 1995). Finally, they see the route to success as modeling others. They endorsed such statements as "Modeling others is a good way to get ahead" and "Appearance plays an important role in success."

The overall picture that emerges is fairly dismal: People with a strong need to win have a fairly negative view of themselves and a negative view of the world. Moreover, they lack the fundamental skills necessary to deal with the daily stresses of life. Because optimism and hope have been linked to health and stress has a negative impact on health, their future does not look good.

Competition Motivation and Performance

Many people dislike competition. Research indicates there are two main reasons (Franken and Prpich, 1996):

1. Competition arouses self-image concerns (ego concerns)—about not meeting the expectations of others, being seen as a loser, receiving negative comments from others, and so on.
2. Competition arouses performance concerns, including self-consciousness, apprehension, and nervousness. To determine if being evaluated might be one of the reasons people dislike competition, Prpich and I constructed 20 questions designed to assess various reasons why people might dislike being evaluated. Factor analysis of those items resulted in a single factor, which we called distraction of attention. The participants in our study indicated that, when they are being evaluated, they become distracted from what they are doing, lose their ability to concentrate, become self-conscious, and think about their faults and weaknesses. At a more global level, these results indicate that people dislike competition because it interferes with their ability to perform at their maximum. We also found that the personality traits of positive self-esteem and hope tend to mitigate these deleterious effects of competition (Franken & Prpich, 1996).

These results suggest that performance decrements are likely to result from self-image concerns and performance concerns. Research on self-focused attention has shown that, when attention is directed at the self—by having the subject work on a task in the presence of mirrors, for example—performance often deteriorates in low self-esteem individuals (Shrauger, 1972). Taken as a whole, the research on competitiveness suggests that having a competitive orientation is counterproductive for high levels of performance. It appears that having a competitive orientation diverts attention away from the task.

Evolutionary Considerations

Earlier I discussed the idea that arousal/activation might be due to two different activation systems, a positive (PA) system and a negative activation (NA) system. According to that distinction, cooperation comes from the PA system and competitiveness comes from the NA system (Watson et al., 1999). What this means is that people who are chronically competitive have a more active NA system whereas people who are chronically cooperative have a more active PA system. Although we could argue that it would be better for society if there was less competitiveness, we must remember that from an evolutionary perspective it is adaptive for a species to be characterized by diversity. With diversity people can assume different roles and in doing so we can meet the broad needs of our species (Pinker, 1997).

Coping with Evaluation Arousal

Research from a variety of sources indicates that, in the long run, the best way to prepare for evaluation is by developing skills and knowledge to their fullest (Dweck & Leggett, 1988). Moreover, when people are prepared, they are less likely to experience anxiety (e.g., Folkman & Lazarus, 1985) and less likely to experience distraction of attention (Franken & Prpich, 1996). Despite being well prepared, some people still experience evaluation anxiety. In that case, they need to learn how to bring down arousal levels through relaxation. In Chapter 9 we will examine more fully when to use problem-focused versus emotional-focused coping.

Summary

Several experimental studies have provided evidence that a competitive orientation (high need to win) interferes with the individual's ability to attain peak levels of performance. Although the effect might be partly caused by the high levels of arousal that characterize competition, learning and cognition probably play key roles. Evidence from a number of sources indicates that a competitive orientation is largely learned. Further, evidence indicates that individuals with a competitive orientation see the world in more negative terms and see themselves as lacking in the ability to effect change. A particularly interesting finding is that people with a competitive orientation have poor skills for coping with stress.

Many people dislike competition because it arouses performance concerns and self-image concerns. Self-report data suggest that being evaluated not only affects attention (individuals lose their ability to concentrate or become distracted) but causes self-doubt (they begin to think about their strengths and weaknesses). Procedures that create self-focused attention have confirmed that it produces performance decrements.

State Arousal and Performance: Some Concluding Comments

Arousal and Performance on an Immediate Task

As we have seen, arousal often arises out of a person-situation interaction. When trying to deal with a complex environment, for example, people often experience sensory overload; the result is high arousal. Cognitive dissonance also increases arousal. Finally, when people are being evaluated, they experience increases in arousal. In all these cases, it has been shown that increases in arousal lead to a narrowing of attention. If arousal reaches high levels, there is typically a reorganization of attention: Attention shifts to threat cues. For example, considerable evidence indicates that during evaluation, attention shifts to self-image concerns; people become worried about being seen in a negative way.

Narrowing of attention can be highly adaptive: In sensory overload, it helps reduce the amount of incoming information. In cognitive dissonance, it helps the individual focus on the cognitive inconsistency. In evaluation, it can help the individual to focus on the task.

What is the adaptive function of the reorganization of attention? Generally, the reorganization of attention involves a shift of attention to survival-related cues or to self-image concerns. Both humans and animals seem to have been designed to err on the side of caution when arousal exceeds some optimal level; they shift their attention at once to survival-related cues. This has important implications for performance. In general, when attention shifts to survival-related cues or to self-image concerns, performance on specific tasks will deteriorate.

Arousal and Performance on a Subsequent Task

Research indicates that, once arousal is elevated to meet the demands of a given task, it often persists after the challenge of the task has been met. This persistence has been demonstrated for sensory overload, for example. Sensory overload can even trigger a stress reaction; to manage that stress, the individual needs to learn how to relax. The work on REST supports this idea. Also, even after an attitude shift has been induced by cognitive dissonance, arousal persists for a time (Elkin & Leippe, 1986). Finally, there is evidence that arousal persists for a time following evaluation.

If arousal persists, then it can affect performance on a subsequent task. There have been only a few controlled studies to test this hypothesis (e.g., Zillman, Katcher, & Milavsky, 1972), but the idea that arousal transfers from one activity to another is very prevalent in the psychological literature. It is also a common theme in sports psychology. Athletes are often encouraged to prepare for a forthcoming competition by isolating themselves from activities or information that might lead to increases in arousal. Even actors, politicians, and business executives often operate on that principle and will find a quiet place to help prepare them for a forthcoming challenge.

Pooled Arousal

There is considerable evidence for the idea of *pooled arousal*—the idea that arousal from different sources is additive. We know, for example, that trait-anxious people are often more reactive to sensory overload or to evaluation. In fact, one way researchers determine individual differences in trait anxiety is to see how reactive subjects are to situations that produce state arousal. If arousal is pooled, as many theorists believe, all the arousal systems will affect each other (Neiss, 1988).

One implication of this idea is that, to achieve peak performance, people need to learn to identify and then manage each of these different sources of arousal. Let's look at how this might be done.

Self-Regulation of Arousal and Attention

Some theorists have argued that the best way to attain peak performance is to learn how to manage arousal—in other words, how to relax. Their position is that, by learning to manage arousal, we can learn to manage attention. Other theorists advocate managing attention more directly. They start from the position that high arousal is often necessary to achieve peak performance. Thus, trying to manage—usually, to reduce—arousal could be counterproductive because we might reduce the arousal necessary to perform a certain task. Most practitioners, including sports psychologists, believe that both positions have merit. The following is a brief summary of the thinking that comes from sports psychology.

To perform at a high level, an individual must minimize residual arousal—dispositional trait anxiety, prior sensory overload, arousal caused by cognitive dissonance, and so on. However, no attempt should be made to reduce or eliminate the arousal that comes from a person-task interaction. When focused on a task, the brain needs to become aroused to maximize its ability to process information.

It appears that intrusive thoughts—about how others might be thinking about you, for instance—and a tendency to focus on threat cues are universal. In our evolutionary history, such thoughts developed for their survival value. However, they can be a source of annoyance when we attempt to achieve peak performance on a certain task. Skilled performers must learn to manage those thoughts. We will return to this subject later. For the moment, growing evidence indicates that we can come to control such thoughts. If these thoughts are not controlled, they tend to become the focus of our attention, and performance deteriorates, often radically.

Main Points

1. Arousal is produced by two primary mechanisms: the reticular activating system (RAS) and the autonomic nervous system.
2. Epinephrine and norepinephrine, which are secreted by the adrenal glands, provide the long-term backup for the more-immediate action of the sympathetic nervous system.
3. The relationship between arousal and affect can be described as an inverted U-shaped function. Studies of anxiety and sensory deprivation provide evidence for this hypothesis.
4. According to Apter's theory, people are sometimes motivated by a desire for achievement (by telic goals) and at other times by a desire to experience pleasure in the here and now (by paratelic goals).
5. According to Easterbrook, our attention is broad and inclusive at low levels of arousal and becomes narrow and exclusive at high levels.
6. Eysenck's theory describes how trait arousal interacts with environmental arousal to produce optimal hedonic states (affect).
7. Whether we experience anxiety has been linked to how we are inclined to appraise situations.
8. According to Lacey and Lacey's attention/rejection model of sensory overload, the heart provides feedback that affects activity in the reticular activating system (RAS).
9. Restricted environmental stimulation technique (REST) is useful in helping people deal with excessive environmental stimulation. This technique appears to work by helping people to focus their attention on internal rather than external cues.
10. Sensory overload can lead to increases in arousal that lead to narrowing and reorganization of attention.
11. Psychological discomfort—also called intrapersonal tension—motivates individuals to implement strategies that will alleviate that state.

12. Test anxiety increases arousal and causes self-preoccupying intrusive thinking.

13. Sarason indicated that people can control intrusive thinking by focusing on the task.

14. Several laboratory studies have shown that a competitive orientation (high need to win) tends to undermine performance.

15. Studies suggest that people with a strong need to win not only see the world as threatening but see themselves as lacking the skills to successfully cope with the world. Among other things, they have poor skills for coping with stress.

16. Evaluation appears to lead to distraction of attention. People report that evaluation makes them self-conscious, induces them to lose concentration, and leads them to think about their faults and weaknesses.

InfoTrac® College Edition

People frequently experience anxiety in connection with giving a speech or performing (stage fright). Using the information you find on InfoTrac®, what are some things you can do to overcome or deal with such anxiety? (Search words: stage fright, anxiety, performance evaluation)

What can you do to help reduce test anxiety? Several good sites are available on the Internet to help with this question. (Search words: test anxiety)

Chapter Six

Wakefulness, Alertness, Sleep, and Dreams

- Why do we fall asleep?
- Why do we wake up?
- Why can't we fall asleep any time we want to?
- How much sleep do we need?

- How should we deal with jet lag?
- Why do we dream?
- What is the significance of dreams?
- What causes insomnia?

Why do we feel tired and drowsy at some times but rested and alert at others? We all know from experience that these states are related, at least in part, to how long ago and how well we slept. Typically, as our normal sleep time approaches, we feel somewhat tired. Shortly after waking, we usually feel rested and alert—sometimes with the aid of a cup of coffee—unless, of course, we did not sleep well. We also know from experience, however, that feelings of drowsiness and alertness can be somewhat independent of how long and how well we slept. We sometimes feel drowsy even though we have slept recently, or alert even though it is well past our normal sleep time. We also know that it is difficult to shift our normal sleep patterns. As anyone who has tried to get up earlier than usual can attest, such a shift requires more than just going to bed earlier. Moreover, people who cross several time zones in their travels often have difficulty adjusting to a new clock time. Such experiences seem to suggest that humans have an internal clock that can only be reset with some difficulty. There is also the question of dreams. What is the function of dreams? Are they important for mental health, processing information, or what?

Years of controlled laboratory research have begun to provide answers to these and other fascinating questions about wakefulness and sleep. As we'll see, wakefulness and sleep involve physiological and psychological mechanisms that work together in a complex manner. Although the states of wakefulness and sleep are not so distinct as we might think, we cross a very important line when we pass from one to the other; we lose consciousness—awareness of the external environment. Typically, loss of consciousness is fairly abrupt, although at times we seem to enter a detached intermediate state that might reflect what Vogel (1978) calls *sleep-onset mentation.*

Origins of Sleep: Evolutionary Considerations

Sleep is ubiquitous in mammals, birds, and reptiles. From work with rats, it appears that sleep is essential for life. In one set of studies, researchers have shown that if rats are deprived of sleep they will die in about two to three weeks. If they are selectively deprived of REM (which only constitutes about 7% to 10% of the adult rat's existence) they die in about five weeks (Rechtschaffen, 1998). At this point it is not clear what causes death. The immune system is impaired when organisms are sleep deprived, so researchers have suggested that this might explain why sleep-deprived rats die (Everson, 1993).

Research has shown that sleep plays a role in a wide range of physiological functions such as metabolic rate, heart rate, respiration rate, blood pressure, secretions of insulin, testosterone, and glucose levels. Sleep also plays a central role in a wide range of psychological functions such as attention, information processing, memory, mood regulation, problem solving, and creativity (Rechtschaffen, 1998). Perhaps one of the most interesting findings is that sleep is critical for development, which may help explain why children need so much sleep to develop normally (Rechtschaffen, 1998; Roffwarg, Muzio, & Dement, 1966).

Even though sleep has been linked to several physiological and psychological functions, we don't know why sleep evolved. In evolutionary terms, the question is how we conceptualize sleep as an adaptation. If one of our main drives is to procreate, the fact that we sleep goes against the logic of natural selection. When we sleep, we don't procreate, therefore, sleep must serve some equal or more important function. Perhaps the best way to understand the evolution of sleep is to assume that at some point sleep emerged as an adaptation to an environmental problem and that subsequently other functions were shifted to the sleep period to maximize our fitness (to create a brain design that would optimize our ability to deal with environmental demands). Assume, for the moment that it was important for our ancestors to conserve energy because there was insufficient food or that it took a great deal of time and effort to obtain food. Under those conditions, our ancestors might have retreated to a safe location and slept. Because it might also have been adaptive for our ancestors to have a brain in the waking state that was able to deal with threats, it would have been adaptive for them to use the sleep period to ready the brain for the next day. Consistent with this argument, it has been found that we conserve energy when we sleep and that sleep prepares the brain for the next day by replenishing glycogen supplies in the brain (Benington & Heller, 1995).

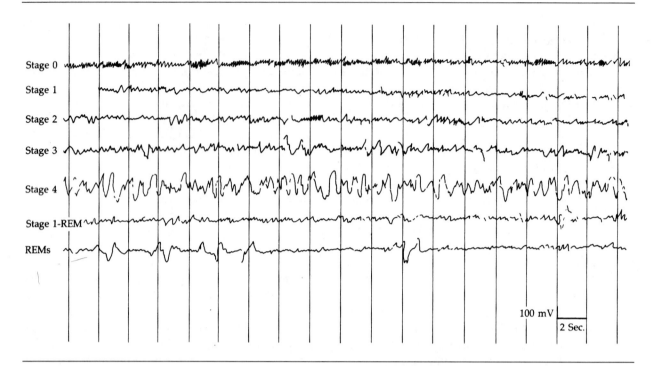

Figure 6-1.   EEG tracings of the sleep stages. State 0 is wakefulness. (From *Sleep: The Gentle Tyrant,* by W. B. Webb. Copyright © 1975 by Prentice-Hall, Inc. Reprinted by permission of the author and the University of Florida Sleep Laboratories.)

Even though this argument is appealing given that the two main themes associated with our ancestors were obtaining food and avoiding predators, it is important to note that sleep serves a wide range of important functions, many but not all of which we will discuss in this chapter. Thus, we cannot necessarily conclude sleep was an adaptation to conserve energy. What we can conclude, however, is that at some point sleep became one of our most important adaptations (Rechtschaffen, 1998).

It is interesting to note in this context that various species had made certain accommodations to sleep in order to deal with other problems they face. Dolphins, for example, need to periodically surface to breathe. To both sleep and carry out this important function they sleep with one half of the brain at a time (Oleksenko, Mukhametov, Polyakova et al., 1992). Even though

muscle tonus is typically low during sleep, perching birds maintain muscle tonus while sleeping (Amlaner & Ball, 1994).

Wakefulness, Sleep, and EEG Activity

Correlates of Sleep and Wakefulness

The best index of wakefulness, drowsiness, and sleep in humans is cortical activity (Webb, 1975). Figure 6-1 shows the types of EEG activity during the various stages of sleep. A typical night of sleep consists of gradual progress from stage 0 (wakefulness) through stages 1, 2, 3, and 4 and then backward through stages 3, 2, and 1 into what is called stage 1-REM. This cycle,

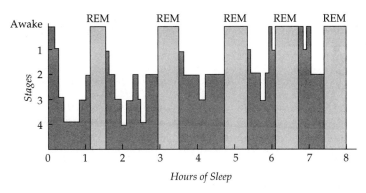

Figure 6-2. A plot showing the pattern of REM sleep, NREM sleep, and the four stages of NREM sleep for an individual over the course of one entire night of sleep. (From *Some Must Watch While Others Must Sleep*, by William C. Dement. Copyright © 1972, 1974, 1976 by William C. Dement and the Stanford Alumni Association. Reprinted with permission.)

which takes about 90 to 120 minutes, then repeats itself. In the course of 7–8 hours of sleep, we go through this cycle about five times. Individuals tend to show minor variations from this pattern. Figure 6-2 shows the EEG chart of a typical individual over the course of a night. Note that, although an individual bypasses certain stages from time to time, a rhythm (pattern) can nevertheless clearly be observed.

REM is an acronym for rapid eye movement. In studying electrical recordings of eye movements, Aserinsky and Kleitman (1953) found that rapid eye movements occurred in conjunction with low-voltage mixed brain-wave frequencies and that when people were awakened on such occasions they regularly reported vivid dreams. Four years later, Dement (1972) found that dreams and REM were, indeed, related. Since then it has been common to refer to this pattern as REM sleep and to all other patterns as NREM (non-REM) sleep. Periods of REM sleep are identified in Figure 6-2. Although it was initially thought that REM sleep was synonymous with dreaming, it has since been shown that humans dream during other stages of sleep as well and sometimes fail to experience dream content during REM.

Periods of REM typically occur in conjunction with stage 1 sleep. REM bursts, as they are sometimes called, occur about 90 minutes after we go to sleep and then recur every 90 minutes, on average (the time varies between 70 and 110 minutes). Interestingly, REM sleep tends to lengthen as the night progresses until it lasts as much as an hour at a time. As a result, an adult who sleeps 7.5 hours generally experiences 1.5 to 2 hours of REM sleep (Dement, 1972). Researchers have found that, during REM, blood flow goes up by 40%, metabolism increases, spontaneous firing of nerve cells increases beyond the waking level and the kidneys produce less urine, but it is higher in concentration.

Jouvet's Model of Sleep

Why do EEG patterns fluctuate during sleep? Probably the most widely held view is that EEG activity during sleep is governed by the reticular activating system (RAS). Michel Jouvet (1967) has shown that changes in EEG activity during sleep are due to the alternating activity of two sites in the RAS. The raphe nuclei, which secrete serotonin when active, have been shown to increase NREM sleep in cats. Jouvet has suggested that the onset of sleep is caused by the increased activity of the raphe nuclei. The locus coeruleus, which secretes norepinephrine when active, has been shown to increase REM sleep. Increased EEG activity during REM sleep is typically associated with dreaming in humans, so Jouvet has suggested that the onset of dreams is caused by increased activity of the locus coeruleus. Because the activity of these two sites tends to alternate, Jouvet's model can readily account for the rhythmic nature of sleep—its fluctuation between deep and light sleep. Exactly why these two sites alternate in activity is not clear. One good possibility is that, after a time, activity in one center stimulates activity in the other center (J. M. Siegel, 1979).

Hobson's Model of Sleep and Dreams

J. Allan Hobson (1994) has provided a somewhat different (but not necessarily inconsistent) model. What Hobson has attempted to do is not only explain why we go back and forth between REM and NREM but also why our mental processes in the REM state are so different from waking and the NREM state. His explanation is based on the relative activity of the two main chemical systems of the brain: the aminergic system and the cholingeric system. When we fall asleep, our brain enters the NREM state, a state that is characterized by inactivity of the cerebral cortex and reduced activity of the aminergic system—a system that comprises the monoamine transmitters, norepinephrine, and serotonin. The amines help us to decide how to make decisions when we are awake. When these amines are secreted at a high level, they inhibit the cholingeric system. When we fall asleep, the aminergic system plunges and the cholingeric system becomes active. Left unchecked by the aminergic system, the cholingeric system begins to activate the visual and motor cortex, eventually creating the dream state called REM. In this state, the visual cortex is active and the individual experiences visual images that are best described as "hallucinations" because they do not come from stimulation of the visual system via our eyes. The stream of images often violates rules of time and place, so we often refer to dreams as being bizarre. We call these images bizarre when we reflect on them, rather than when we are experiencing them in our dreams. The reason they do not seem bizarre when we are dreaming is because the amines are at a low level. Amines, among other things, allow us to determine what is real or not real by assessing information by our past experiences. In the absence of amines, we can no longer determine if the visual images we are experiencing are coming from our eyes or from something else such as memories, emotions, and thoughts.

Like Jouvet, Hobson views the ebb and flow of NREM and REM as being due to the cyclical natures of different brain systems operating in a complimentary and interdependent fashion. What neither Jouvet nor Hobson tells us, however, is why after about eight hours of sleep, going back and forth between REM and NREM, we wake up, and then why after about 16 hours of wakefulness, we fall asleep. In short, why do we move from a conscious to an unconscious state?

Why We Fall Asleep and Why We Wake Up

At least three sets of factors determine when we fall asleep and when we wake up. As we'll see, each set of factors interacts with the others.

Circadian Rhythm

One essential factor that determines when we fall asleep is our circadian rhythm. The word *circadian* comes from the Latin *circa diem,* "about a day." People who have been left to establish their own routines in caves, bunkers, or specially designed laboratories tend to adopt a 25-hour cycle, rather than a 24-hour circadian rhythm (Aschoff, 1965). The tendency to follow a 24-hour cycle appears largely to be the synchronizing effects of events in our environment. Because we generally have regular times for eating, watching TV, going to bed, and so on, we tend to constantly reset our biological clocks so that they are attuned to the 24-hour day. When we free ourselves from the normal synchronizing effects of the environment—for instance, on a weekend or vacation or any time that we stay up late, sleep in, and eat when we like—we often experience great difficulty getting back into our normal routine. The Monday-morning blues might be a direct result of letting ourselves shift to our natural 25-hour biological rhythm. If we follow our internal biological clock on the weekends, by going to bed one hour later each night, we might find that, when Monday morning comes around, we are sleep-deprived when the alarm wakes us, and we don't become alert until two hours later than normal. Dement and Vaughn (1999) have argued that many people suffer from chronic sleep deprivation because we sleep according to clock time rather than our need for sleep.

What produces this rhythm? The time we fall asleep, the soundness of our sleep, and the length of time we sleep are linked to the output of epinephrine (adrenaline) by the adrenal glands. When the epinephrine level declines, we tend to fall asleep; when it rises, we tend to wake up (Nishihara, Mori, Endo, Ohta, & Kenshiro, 1985). Going back one step further, researchers have suggested that the rhythm of the adrenal glands is controlled by the hypothalamus. Ultimately, in other words, the circadian rhythm is caused by some rhythmical activity of the hypothalamus. (See Practical Application 6-1 for a discussion of jet lag.)

Environmental Arousal

When we are under stress, our body moves into a state of high arousal. Under these conditions, we often find that we cannot go to sleep or that we have trouble staying asleep. Drugs that increase arousal, such as stimulants, also disturb sleep onset and interfere with the ability to stay asleep. An exciting event often produces increases in arousal and also tends to interfere with sleep onset and good sleep. Environmental arousal is situational, so the sleep disturbance usually disappears when the stimulating event is over.

Sleep Deprivation

One important factor that determines if and when we go to sleep is the length of time that has passed since we last slept. When people are deprived of a night's sleep, they tend to go to sleep sooner and to stay asleep longer, regardless of environmentally induced arousal. We'll return to this topic shortly.

Individual Differences in Sleep Cycles

Personality variables might predict the rhythm of daily patterns. Extraversion and introversion measures, for example, can predict fluctuations in body temperature and in performance on vigilance tasks (Taub, Hawkins, & Van de Castle, 1978). Extraversion is associated with higher body temperature and better performance in the evening, and introversion is associated with higher body temperature and better performance in the morning. Researchers have suggested that these two personality types develop from biological differences. In other words, the underlying biology is ultimately responsible for this effect.

Other Sleep Rhythms

The Half-Day Rhythm

Studies have shown that when subjects are first deprived of sleep and then allowed to sleep for an extended period of time, there is a significant return of slow-wave sleep (SWS) after 12.5 hours of sleep (Gagnon, De Koninck, & Broughton, 1985). These findings are consistent with the observation that people tend to become less alert and sleepy around noon

Practical Application 6-1

Adjusting to Jet Lag

Let's say you left New York on a plane bound for Paris at 6 P.M. Eastern Standard Time. The flight time is about 8 hours. Therefore, when you arrive in Paris it's 10 A.M. Paris time, but your circadian clock is telling you it's 2 A.M. (two hours past your bedtime). What should you do—take a nap or stay up till midnight Paris time? The answer depends on whether you want to see Paris nightlife or be a regular tourist. If you go to your hotel and sleep, you're likely to sleep for 7 to 8 hours, so you'll wake up at 6 P.M. That will give you plenty of time to have a leisurely dinner, close down the last nightclub, and sip a brandy with or after breakfast, before retiring for 8 hours. But, if you want to be a regular tourist, then you should stay up until midnight. By midnight you will be experiencing the effects of sleep deprivation and you should have little or no difficulty getting to sleep and sleeping most of the night, even though you are not synchronized with your circadian rhythm. A night's sleep will help to reset your circadian rhythm. Remember that one of the factors that determines when you will next be sleepy is the time elapsed since you last slept. Even a short nap is not a good idea because it will reduce some of the effects normally associated with sleep deprivation, and consequently you will not be able to sleep as long when you do go to sleep.

(Richardson, Carskadon, Orav, & Dement, 1982). In many cultures, the norm is to take an afternoon siesta. The phenomenon of afternoon napping, according to Gagnon and his colleagues, "may reflect a biological propensity to re-enter the psychological state that accompanies SWS" (Gagnon, De Koninck, & Broughton, 1985, p. 127). SWS refers to stage 3 and 4 sleep.

The Basic Rest/Activity Cycle

A basic rest/activity cycle (BRAC) that lasts about 90 to 120 minutes has been found in such waking activities as performance on various sensory tasks, vigilance tasks, and fantasy tasks. The ability to fall asleep during the day is determined by this cycle. That is, it is easier to fall asleep when we are in the rest part of the cycle.

The regularity of REM sleep every 90 minutes raises the interesting possibility that REM is somehow controlled by BRAC. Researchers have shown, for example, that people tend to dream at the same time every night (McPartland & Kupfer, 1978) although some researchers have supplied evidence that seems to contradict this conclusion. They have shown, for example, that REM tends to occur 90 minutes after sleep onset (McPartland & Kupfer, 1978; Moses, Naitoh, & Johnson, 1978). If REM is controlled by sleep onset, then it cannot be controlled by some natural BRAC rhythm that is independent of sleep onset. This apparent inconsistency disappears when we recognize that people often don't go to sleep until they are in a certain phase of their BRAC. In other words, our overall circadian rhythm and our BRAC rhythm affect our inclination to go to sleep.

The Left Brain/Right Brain Cycle

The brain has two hemispheres, each of which performs slightly different functions. The right hemisphere tends to be involved in fantasy and intuitive thought, and the left hemisphere tends to be involved in verbal and intellectual thought. What is fascinating is that each hemisphere has a cycle lasting 90–100 minutes that is 180° out of phase with the other hemisphere. Thus, we tend to swing back and forth between fantasy/intuitive thought and verbal/intellectual thought (Klein & Armitage, 1979). REM dreams tend to be more fantasy/intuitive in character, whereas NREM dreams tend to be more verbal and intellectual. It

might be that, before I can have REM dreams or NREM dreams, I need to be in the right mental state; that state is determined by my BRAC.

Effects of Sleep Loss

Because considerable evidence indicates that lack of sleep can do irreparable harm, it would be unethical to deprive people of sleep against their will. An alternative approach is to study people who for one reason or another get less sleep than normal.

Voluntary Sleep Reduction and Sleep Stages

Studies of voluntary sleep reduction found that subjects were unable to reduce their sleep below 4.5 hours per night, suggesting biological limits to sleep reduction (Mullaney, Johnson, Naitoh, Friedmann, & Globus, 1977). It has been found that voluntary sleep reduction to 4.5 to 5.5 hours a night does not produce significant personality changes or reduce performance on certain types of tasks, but it tends to produce persistent feelings of fatigue (Friedmann et al., 1977). As we'll discuss shortly, sleep reduction produces a number of performance deficits, especially when the task is complex or demands sustained attention. It appears, however, that people can often rise to the challenge for short periods on tasks that are more familiar or practiced.

As sleep time is reduced, the pattern of sleep undergoes several changes. Although there is no reduction in the amount of stage 3 and stage 4 sleep (Figure 6-1), there is a significant reduction in REM and stage 2 sleep (Mullaney et al., 1977; Webb & Agnew, 1975a). When the regimen of partial sleep deprivation is maintained, REM sleep begins to occur earlier in the sleep period, thereby attenuating the REM deficit. However, REM sleep rarely replaces stage 4 in order of appearance, and it never achieves normal levels.

This tendency to make up for certain types of sleep when sleep time is curtailed is probably one of the important reasons that lack of sleep does not have a greater impact on our normal functioning. As we shall discuss in more detail shortly, stage 4 sleep and REM sleep seem to help maintain physiological and psychological integrity. Thus, it makes sense that such sleep would be the priority. Tilley (1985) suggested that "obtaining a daily stage 4 quota acts as the primary drive mechanism of the sleep system" (p. 129).

Voluntary Sleep Reduction and Feelings of Sleepiness and Fatigue

Until recently the general consensus was that although sleep loss produces feelings of sleepiness (a craving or desire for sleep) and fatigue (a general lack of motivation or energy), there were no serious long-term consequences (e.g., Hartse, Roth, & Zorick, 1982). Further, they can be reversed in a single night's sleep (Carskadon & Dement, 1981). That position has radically changed in recent years. Many prominent researchers are now arguing that many of us are constantly sleep deprived and this has important implications for how we function in a wide range of activities (Dement & Vaughn, 1999). Researchers have suggested that two-thirds of adults in the United States are not getting adequate sleep. Sleep loss reduces performance, and it can be downright dangerous. Researchers have estimated that more than 100,000 automobile accidents are the result of sleep deprivation (Brink, 2000). In addition numerous airline close calls and crashes have been linked to sleep deprivation of pilots (Dinges, 1995). Considerable evidence now indicates that sleep deprivation also leads to an impaired immune response (Dinges, Douglas, Hamarman, Zaugg, & Kapoor, 1995). Let's begin by looking at some of the research pertaining to impaired performance following sleep deprivation.

Environmental and Cultural Sleep Reduction and Deterioration in Performance

Field studies have shown that people who work at night not only complain of sleepiness but perform less well than they do during the day (Åkerstedt, Torsvall, & Gillberg, 1982). The reason night workers perform less well is because night workers have difficulty adjusting their circadian rhythm to coincide with their new schedule. Interestingly, older subjects seem more affected by sleep loss than are younger ones (Webb & Levy, 1982).

Here are some of the basic changes that occur as a result of sleep loss (Dinges, 1989; Dinges & Kribbs,

1991). These decrements tend to arise from about 3 A.M. to 5 A.M.

1. **Lapsing.** Lapsing refers to the unevenness in performance with sleep deprivation. Whereas people typically respond immediately to a signal or a crisis, sleep-deprived people may respond quite slowly at times, but normally at other times. As people become more sleep-deprived, lapsing becomes more of a problem, and performance gradually deteriorates. In situations where people need to react quickly, lapsing is a major safety concern (Dinges & Kribbs, 1991).

2. **Cognitive slowing.** When people are sleep deprived, there is a reduction in the number (speed) of their cognitive responses in a self-paced task. This cognitive slowing, originally attributed to lapses, is now thought to be caused by *microsleeps*—very short sleep episodes interjected into an otherwise wakeful state. Microsleeps appear to increase in number as sleep deprivation increases. Consequently, people tend to show greater cognitive slowing as sleep deprivation increases (Dinges & Kribbs, 1991).

3. **Memory problems.** Sleeplessness is often accompanied by reduction in immediate recall, which could be caused by a combination of factors, including lapses and failure to encode information properly. In many studies, memory loss is not significant until wakefulness has exceeded 30 hours (Dinges & Kribbs, 1991).

4. **Vigilance decrements and habituation.** As a general rule, the impact of sleep deprivation on performance will increase with an increase in task duration. In other words, performance decrements caused by sleep loss might not be apparent at the start of the workday, but will surface as the shift proceeds (Dinges & Kribbs, 1991). This has important implications for people who must monitor devices and make periodic adjustments at nuclear reactors and gas plants, for instance.

5. **Optimum response shifts.** In many situations, there is a limited time period during which people must respond with sustained attention to prevent some adverse consequence. Researchers thought for some time that sleep-deprived people could rise to these occasions, but more recent data suggest they

may not (Dinges & Kribbs, 1991). This has important implications for pilots, doctors, and others who experience sleep loss on the job.

The extent to which any of these changes will be observed depends somewhat on feedback and the complexity of the task. Evidence suggests that feedback can improve performance, but it is unlikely to totally override the effects of sleep loss. Feedback that reports on whether the subject is succeeding or failing is better than feedback that merely provides information about speed and accuracy (Dinges & Kribbs, 1991).

A growing body of data shows sleep deprivation leads to performance loss on a wide range of tasks. One study showed, for example, that when subjects are deprived of sleep for one night, their driving performance is similar to having a blood alcohol content of .07% (Fairclough & Graham, 1999). In another study, researchers demonstrated that college students who were deprived of a night of sleep performed significantly worse on a cognitive task than did nondeprived subjects (Pilcher & Walters, 1997). In still other studies, researchers have demonstrated both short-term and long-term effects of sleep deprivation, especially on complex tasks (Hockey, Wastell, & Sauer, 1998).

How much sleep do we need? Researchers are now advocating people have at least eight hours of sleep a night and that feelings of sleepiness and fatigue are warning signals that we are not getting enough sleep (Dement & Vaughn, 1999).

The Compensatory Model of Sleep Reduction

Much of what has been found can be accounted for by what is called the compensatory model, which was developed to explain how people under stress react to complex or demanding tasks. This model postulates that under high performance demands people who are sleep deprived attempt to compensate for their lack of ability to fully process incoming information by, among other things, focusing their attention on high priority goals while neglecting low priority goals. According to the compensatory model, this requires greater effort (greater attention/executive control), which leads to greater fatigue. To compensate for this,

sleep-deprived individuals shift to less complex information processing strategies that demand less dependence on attention/executive processes (Hockey, 1997).

Studies of PET scans following sleep deprivation have provided evidence consistent with this model. When subjects were sleep deprived and then asked to memorize a short list of words, they showed greater activity in the prefrontal cortex as well as in the parietal lobes compared with a control group. The prefrontal cortex has been identified as being involved in attention/executive functions, so the greater activity in the prefrontal cortex suggests that sleep deprived subjects were having more difficulty attending/organizing than were non–sleep-deprived subjects. The greater activity of the parietal lobes, a structure that has been implicated in arithmetic, might further reflect the recruitment of other brain structures to compensate for the cognitive losses caused by sleep deprivation (Drummond et al., 2000). (See Practical Application 6-2 for a discussion of the value of cat naps.)

Sleep Apnea and Fragmented Sleep

Some people suffer a form of sleep loss because they cannot breath properly when they fall asleep, a condition called sleep apnea. As a result, they tend to wake up repeatedly, sometimes as many as 500 times a night. People who suffer from this disorder not only experience feelings of fatigue and sleepiness, they tend to show a wide range of performance deficits. To understand this disorder, researchers have simulated this disorder by repeatedly awakening experimental participants (after every minute of sleep). The result was a severe reduction in SWS (stages 3 and 4) and REM sleep, a decline in performance, and reports of sleepiness equivalent to those found after sleep loss of 40–64 hours (Bonnet, 1985). It should be noted that the subjects managed to sleep a great deal of the time. From this it can be concluded that SWS and REM are critical not only for reducing or eliminating feelings of sleepiness and fatigue but also for ensuring people can perform at an optimum level. As already noted, when people go on reduced sleep regimens, they typically compensate for the loss of sleep by increasing REM and SWS at the expense of other states of sleep. It appears, therefore, that the reason people can perform reasonably well on reduced sleep regimens is because they can get enough SWS and REM to get by. The reason I say "get by" is because current research, as I have already indicated, points to the idea most people appear to need at least eight hours or more of sleep each night to perform at an optimal level (Dement & Vaughn, 1999).

Some Paradoxical Effects of Sleep Deprivation

Not all the research has demonstrated that sleep deprivation is bad. Studies conducted in clinical laboratories suggest that mild to moderate antidepressant effects can follow just one night of sleep deprivation in 30 to 60% of endogenously depressed individuals—that is, individuals whose depression cannot be linked to a specific life event (Gerner, Post, Gillin, & Bunney, 1979). Studies using PET, have found that depressed people have very high levels of brain activity in certain areas of the brain that regulate emotions and that when they were sleep deprived, the metabolic rate in those areas of the brain that regulate emotions was reduced (Haugen, 2000). What this research suggests, for reasons that are not entirely clear, is that sleep deprivation reduces the high activity that has been linked to depression. As we have known for some time, people can be too sensitive to cues that would arouse certain emotions. Later in this chapter we will discuss Vogel's theory to explain why sleep deprivation reduces depression in the endogenous depressed.

Summary

Sleep is ubiquitous in mammals, birds, and reptiles and appears to be essential for life. Sleep serves a number of important physiological and psychological functions. EEG activity has a rhythmic pattern during sleep; Jouvet has suggested that these rhythms are controlled by the RAS. When we fall asleep and when we wake up are influenced by various biological rhythms (the circadian rhythm, the 12.5-hour cycle, and the BRAC). Hobson has argued that the stages of sleep can be understood as the ebb and flow of the two chemical systems of the brain, the aminergic system and the cholingeric system. Although it is not altogether clear why we fall asleep and why we wake up, empirically we know that sleepiness depends largely on the time that has elapsed

since we last slept, and wakefulness depends on the time that has elapsed since we went to sleep.

Reduced sleep produces feelings of sleepiness and fatigue and impairs performance on tasks that require sustained interest and attention. Although people can learn to get along with as little as 4.5 to 5 hours of sleep per day, their bodies need to maintain a certain minimal level of SWS and REM.

This research emphasizes what sleep consultants have said for some time: To go to sleep, maintain sleep, and have quality sleep, it is important to have a routine. Routines not only synchronize our biological rhythms with our daily performance demands but also allow us to have reasonably continuous sleep. Even when sleep must be reduced, a routine enables the body to schedule SWS and REM soon after we fall asleep, thereby ensuring that we get enough of them.

One very good way to make up for lost sleep is with catnaps. People who do not get adequate sleep because of their occupations or because of situational demands—such as the need to complete an important task—often use catnaps to compensate for lost sleep.

The Function of REM Sleep

From the earliest beginnings of sleep research, researchers have been interested in REM sleep. The reason is that REM in humans is typically associated with dreams, a topic that never fails to fascinate.

So, why do we dream? To answer this question, researchers have studied the effects of REM deprivation. Before we look at that research it is important to know something very special about REM sleep: when we have REM sleep we become paralyzed.

Paralysis During REM

We know that the brain and the entire central nervous system tend to become very active during REM, so why don't people walk, talk, and engage in other motor responses when they begin to dream? The answer is very simple. In each period of REM sleep, the action of the spinal cord motor neurons that cause skeletal muscles to contract is inhibited. As a result, the muscles are atonic (without tone); they are paralyzed. The mechanisms that control this inhibition and the release from it are located in the reticular formation (Morrison, 1983). One reason for research interest in these mechanisms is that some people experience a condition called narcolepsy, which causes them suddenly and unexpectedly to pass from wakefulness to REM sleep without losing consciousness. As a result, they experience paralysis but can do nothing to control it. If they are sitting, they may find they can do nothing to stop themselves from falling. Consequently, narcolepsy may be not only stressful but dangerous.

REM Deprivation in Humans

Researchers can selectively deprive subjects of a particular type of sleep—say, REM—by continuously monitoring their EEGs and waking them whenever that

sleep pattern appears. In that way, it is possible to study the effects of REM or other types of sleep deprivation on various activities. In these studies, one group of subjects is typically awakened after they enter REM, and a control group of subjects is awakened during NREM. Using such a procedure, we can be assured that the effects are not simply due to being awakened.

The REM Rebound Effect

Early studies of REM deprivation showed that people deprived of REM sleep for one or more nights show a *REM rebound*; that is, if allowed to sleep without interruption for a whole night, they spend more time in REM sleep than usual. This observation led researchers to conclude that REM must indeed be important for

Practical Application 6-2

Shift Work, Sleepiness, and Catnaps

Shift work is a major problem in our society. The problem is worse for people who work night shifts (usually from 11 P.M. to 7 A.M.). Catastrophes such as those at Three Mile Island and Chernobyl took place in the early hours of the morning. Later afternoon shifts (4 P.M. to 12 P.M.) are also a problem, but to a lesser degree.

There are two basic problems. First, people who work night shifts and later afternoon shifts are often out of phase with their normal circadian rhythms. As a result, even though they are awake, they are not alert. As we know, temperature and alertness are correlated. People who work night shifts often show a drop in temperature in the early hours of the morning (3 A.M. to 5 A.M.), a time when many accidents occur (Dinges, 1984).

People often learn to shift their circadian rhythms, but that can take a considerable time. It's still not clear why some people can shift to a new circadian rhythm relatively quickly, but others cannot. When people cannot adjust, they experience feelings of sleepiness. This leads us to the second problem, which is sleep deprivation. Considerable evidence indicates that people who work night shifts are also experiencing chronic sleep loss, which also leads to

feelings of sleepiness. Many find it difficult to sleep during the day and, therefore, they are chronically sleep-deprived.

Pilots may find themselves in a particularly difficult situation because they often must make a return after as little as 8 to 12 hours of rest. Many find they cannot sleep. Therefore, when they make their return flight, they are experiencing sleep loss.

What Is the Best Way to Deal with Shift Work?

People who work later afternoon and night shifts often perform poorly and are accident-prone. This is particularly worrying in such occupations as pilot, train engineer, doctor, or nuclear plant operator because it raises questions of public safety. Accordingly, much research has addressed the best ways for people to deal with shift work or with jobs that require them to perform at times when they are not normally at their peak.

The question is how best to help people who work later afternoon and night shifts to get the amount of sleep they need. One reason these people are chronically sleep-deprived is that they attempt to maintain their social relations and family obligations, although they are out of sync normal functioning. Consistent findings were obtained in a study of sleep patterns in subjects who were permitted to sleep for 30-minute periods separated by 60 minutes of forced wakefulness (Carskadon & Dement, 1977). Sleep-onset REM periods occurred frequently during the 30 minutes of sleep, although REM sleep normally begins 90 minutes after sleep onset. This indicates that the lack of REM for any significant period will trigger some mechanism to override the normal sleep schedule to ensure that the body gets adequate REM sleep.

REM Deprivation in Animals

All mammalian species that have been studied have REM sleep. In addition, a sizable percentage of avian predators (such as hawks and eagles) have REM. Only a negligible amount of REM occurs in other birds, and reptilian species show no REM (Ellman & Weinstein, 1991).

The main technique for REM sleep deprivation of small mammals, such as rats, is to place them on a small elevated platform above a tank of water. The rat will become paralyzed when it goes into REM sleep and will fall off the platform into the water. The experience of falling into the water and climbing back onto the platform appears to provide powerful motivation for rats to learn to avoid REM sleep. As we noted earlier, when rats are deprived of REM they will die—not as fast as when they are completely deprived of sleep but, nevertheless, they die (Rechtschaffen, 1998).

with other people. Interestingly, people who work late afternoon shifts and night shifts are often not aware that they are sleep-deprived (Dinges, 1989). Thus, it is important to educate people about their sleep needs and help them plan a sleep schedule that will enable them to get enough sleep as well as to satisfy their other needs. Even when people know they should get more sleep, they sometimes find it difficult to do so because their circadian rhythms tell them it is time to be awake.

How can people adjust their circadian rhythms to the demands of the task? Researchers in chronobiology have addressed that topic, which is the scientific study of rhythms of life that are an outgrowth of biology. There are several important considerations.

First, because it takes time to adjust circadian rhythms, a general rule of thumb is that people should not be required to change their shifts too often. As they settle into a shift, they can synchronize their biological rhythms with the demands of the task (Coleman, 1986). How long this takes varies greatly from individual to individual. Sleep deprivation is a good way to speed up this process (as we saw in discussing jet lag in Practical Application 6-1). Coleman (1986) has suggested that, under certain conditions, sleep deprivation combined with sleeping pills might be justified as a means of speeding up the adjustment time.

Second, when workers' shifts are changed, they should be moved from morning to afternoon to night and not in the reverse direction. Studies have found that people find it much easier to move in this direction (Coleman, 1986), because there is a natural tendency for the circadian rhythm to drift to a later time. That is, we are inclined to go to bed later and get up earlier because our circadian rhythm is about 25 hours.

Third, it might be advisable for shift workers to take catnaps.

Making Up for Loss of Sleep with Catnaps

A great deal of evidence indicates that people should use catnaps to make up for loss of sleep. Most people can go without one night of sleep without much loss in performance, but attempts to go beyond that typically result in significant performance drops. Research has shown that, young or old, people can achieve complete or virtually complete recovery after one full night of sleep (Bonnet & Rosa, 1987). A catnap of any length is highly effective in helping to restore full functioning after a shortened sleep time. If we know ahead of time that we will need to forego

(continued on next page)

Motivation Theories of REM

Ellman's Motivation Theory of REM

The essence of Steven Ellman's theory is that, during both sleep and wakefulness, the positive reward system—also called the intracranial self-stimulation (ICSS) system—needs to be periodically fired. (We discussed this system in Chapter 2.) The ICSS system is assumed to maintain motivation when we are not involved in behaviors such as eating, drinking, sex, and aggression and is turned off when we are involved in these behaviors. During sleep, according to the theory, the REM state is responsible for periodically firing the ICSS system.

How can this be related to the content of REM dreams? Implicit in Ellman's theory is the idea that the environment is a rich source of stimulation that will periodically fire the ICSS (although it can also be fired by the BRAC or another rhythm). In sleep, the body needs to generate similar stimulation that will fire the ICSS. If the ICSS is to be activated, this stimulation needs to be as vivid and compelling as the environ-

ment. To produce such vivid and compelling stimulation, Ellman further argues, we need to momentarily set aside self-reflection. The net result is that REM dreams have a vivid and compelling quality, like that of the external environment, but can also have some strange organizational characteristics (bizarre qualities) when we reflect on them in a waking state (Ellman & Weinstein, 1991).

One fascinating feature of Ellman's theory is that it can explain why infants spend so much time in REM. In the absence of external stimulation, they need to generate stimulation that will keep the ICSS in a state of motivated readiness. If organisms were not in a state of readiness, their threshold for motivated behavior would increase, a highly nonadaptive state much like that observed in depressive individuals. Ellman and Weinstein (1991) go so far as to argue that the lack of REM in infancy could slow down the maturational process. In other words, REM in infancy is critical to maturation. Dement and Vaughan cite a case in which an infant who suffered sleep apnea failed to develop. When proper breathing was re-

Practical Application 6-2 (continued)

sleep for a long period—for instance, for an entire night—we can prepare ourselves for it with a catnap (the longer the better, but any length will help) (Dinges, as reported in Saltus, 1990).

People who need to complete a lot of work over a short period might consider changing their sleep regimen so that they break up what sleep they can get into short naps. During his creative period, Leonardo da Vinci would reduce his sleep regimen to six catnaps of 15 minutes each. Many famous people, including Winston Churchill, Napoleon, and Thomas Edison, are reported to have survived on catnaps. Laboratory studies have shown that it is indeed possible for people to survive for as long as two weeks on such a schedule. In the animal world, catnapping is widespread and might even be more normal than the sleep/wakefulness cycle that modern humans attempt to maintain. The industrial revolution forced us into a sleep cycle that is not consistent with our history as humans. In many cultures, the afternoon

siesta is common; it allows people to get up early and party late.

People who cannot get adequate sleep because of jet lag (for instance, pilots), interrupted sleep (for instance, combat soldiers or doctors), or the need to be on alert (for instance, combat pilots) might learn to use catnaps as a means of making up for the losses they experience because of their jobs. It has been shown that older people who find it difficult to sleep for 8 hours straight can benefit greatly from catnaps. Since many researchers believe that most people in North America—if not the industrialized world—do not get enough sleep, all of us should consider catnaps as a way of getting more sleep. Evidence indicates that people who have good sleep regimens are not only healthier but live longer (Hoth et al., 1989).

Although there are strong arguments for catnaps, they can also contribute to sleep disturbances such as insomnia if they begin to replace normal sleep. I discuss this problem in Practical Application 6-4.

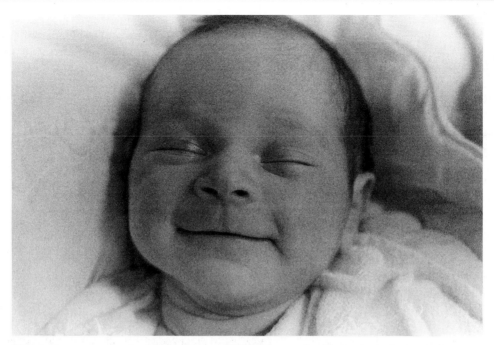

This infant seems to be having a good REM dream, but because infants can't verbalize their mental processes, we cannot assess the content of their REM dreams.

stored development resumed (Dement & Vaughn, 1999).

Vogel's Motivation Theory of REM

Gerald Vogel (1979) has suggested that neural activity is heightened during REM sleep and prevented or inhibited by REM deprivation. As a result, REM deprivation leads to greater neural activity or excitability during the waking state. (Neural excitability is a hypothetical state of neural readiness necessary for efficient and effective response to events in the environment. It is generally assumed to be caused by some chemical process that readies the cells to fire.) Because there is evidence that greater neural excitability increases such drive-motivated behaviors as sex, aggression, pleasure seeking, food seeking, and grooming, Vogel argues that, under certain conditions, REM sleep can have a detrimental effect on certain waking behaviors. It is possible, he argues, that depression results from excessive neural disinhibition during REM sleep. That is,

REM sleep dissipates too much accumulated neural excitability. As a result, depressives lose interest in, or fail to engage in, those activities that tend to provide positive rewards. According to this view, it is easy to understand why REM deprivation would lead to improved mood in depressed persons. Since such deprivation would prevent the discharge of neural excitability, depressed persons would again become more sensitive to their drive states and would engage in behaviors that produced rewards associated with these drive states. In short, they would experience the positive affect that typically flows from adaptive behaviors.

Vogel's theory is concerned with endogenous depression, which occurs for unknown reasons, rather than with reactive depression, which is typically precipitated by some traumatic event—for example, the loss of a spouse, a child, or a job. According to Vogel's theory, endogenous depression occurs when, for still-unknown reasons, there is excessive neural disinhibition during REM sleep. Normally, he argues, neural activity is not allowed to dissipate completely. He believes that some inhibitory mechanism exists to prevent complete discharge and serves an important survival function by ensuring that the person is in a stage of readiness to respond to drive stimuli.

Vogel (1975) has reviewed some research showing that drugs can frequently alleviate symptoms of depression. The most effective drugs, he notes, are those that produce a dramatic and sustained reduction of REM sleep—the major antidepressants (monoamine oxidase inhibitors and the tricyclics). In other words, he maintains, these drugs work because they block REM sleep, which is assumed to be responsible for the dissipation of neural excitability.

Ellman's theory is essentially an extension of Vogel's theory. Ellman suggests that REM deprivation is able to alleviate depression because it ensures that motivation remains high (Ellman, Spielman, Luck, Steiner, & Halperin, 1991).

Neural Organization Theories of REM

REM Sleep and the Consolidation of Memory

One of the most actively pursued hypotheses concerning sleep is that REM sleep is important for the consolidation of memory. According to the consolidation theory, it takes time for recently learned material to be transferred from immediate or short-term memory to long-term memory. Evidence indicates that the REM state facilitates this transfer (Grosvenor & Lack, 1984; McGrath & Cohen, 1978). Additional evidence suggests that REM is also involved in the active integration of complex information with previously learned information (Scrima, 1982).

REM Deprivation and Learning in Animals

Considerable data from animal studies indicate REM deprivation interferes with learning and retention (Ellman et al., 1991). Shuttle box avoidance learning, for example, depends on REM sleep (Smith & Butler, 1982; Smith & Young, 1980). Shuttle box avoidance learning involves putting an animal in a rectangular box that is designed to deliver a shock to half the box via a grid floor (the side on which the animal is standing). Prior to the shock being delivered, the animal is given a signal (often a tone or light) that indicates shock is forthcoming in a few seconds. By going to the other side of the box when the signal is presented (the side that is not electrified), the animal can learn to avoid the shock altogether. The word *shuttle* refers to the fact that the animals must learn in this apparatus to go back and forth on successive trials because there is always a safe area in this type of apparatus. It typically takes several days of training before an animal such as a rat will perform flawlessly.

Other studies have shown that whether REM deprivation disrupts learning depends on whether animals are in an emotional state. Emotionality in animals is typically determined by such behavioral indicators as amount of defecation and urination, which have been shown to be linked to autonomic arousal. If the animals are emotional when training takes place, REM deprivation disrupts learning; if not, REM deprivation has no effect (Koridze & Nemsadze, 1983; Oniani, 1984).

REM Deprivation and Learning in Humans

REM sleep and memory. REM sleep seems to facilitate most kinds of learning, but it is particularly beneficial for certain kinds of tasks. In general, the REM deprivation literature shows consistent benefits from REM sleep on the learning and retention of more complex or emotionally loaded tasks. In one study that demonstrated beneficial effects of REM sleep (Cartwright et al., 1975), subjects were required to Q-sort adjectives as descriptive of themselves and of their ideal selves and were then tested for immediate and delayed (by 7 hours) recall of the words. In a Q-sort task, the subject places cards bearing descriptive words into stacks according to how well they describe some particular item —in this case, their actual and ideal selves. Subjects were divided into four groups, which were treated in different ways during the retention interval: the subjects in group 1 were maintained awake day and night; those in group 2 were allowed undisturbed sleep; those in group 3 were allowed to sleep but were REM-deprived; and those in group 4 had their REM sleep reduced by 25%. After the retention intervals, subjects were asked to recall as many of the adjectives as they could. For our purposes, the most important finding is that the REM-deprived subjects tended to recall more self-affirming items, whereas the normal-sleep subjects tended to recall more items indicating personal dissatisfaction; that is, REM sleep facilitated memory for items related to personal dissatisfaction.

One interpretation of these findings is that it takes more time or effort to process emotionally laden information, especially information that doesn't readily fit with an existing view of the self (an existing cognitive structure) (Hockey, 1997). If sleep deprivation reduces the ability to process information, it follows that people who are sleep deprived would have more difficulty processing views that were inconsistent with their self-view but might still be able to process information that was consistent with their self-view.

Timing of REM. Numerous studies in both animals and humans have found evidence that an essential function of sleep is the strengthening of memories; evidence that is consistent with the consolidation hypothesis (Cipolli, 1995). But as we noted earlier, there are different kinds of learning and different kinds of memory. To better understand the relationship between memory and sleep, researchers have begun to examine in greater detail the link between different kinds of memory and the timing of REM. One recent study looked at declarative memory (paired-associate learning) and procedural memory (mirror-tracing learning) in relationship to the timing of REM sleep. The results showed that although sleep (compared with no sleep) improved both types of memory, early nocturnal sleep (which contains five times more SWS sleep) facilitated declarative learning more than did procedural memory and that later nocturnal sleep (which contains twice as much REM as early nocturnal sleep) facilitated procedural memory more than did declarative memory (Plihal & Born, 1997).

Animal studies suggest that declarative memory, more than any other type of memory, depends on hippocampal mechanisms supporting consolidation. Researchers have suggested that the process involves the hippocampal replay of previously encoded information allowing the information to be transferred to the neocortex (Wilson & McNaughton, 1994).

REM Sleep and Stress

Sleep researchers have more or less consistently argued that sleep is an important time for the brain to organize or reorganize information in such a way that the individual will be prepared to deal effectively with the coming day. In this regard, one thing that would help is if the information that caused stress could somehow be dissipated rather than consolidated. That REM sleep can dissipate the emotion caused by a stressful or noxious stimulus has been clearly demonstrated in a variety of studies including one by Greenberg, Pillard, and Pearlman (1972). After watching a stressful movie, subjects were allowed (1) undisturbed sleep, (2) REM-deprived sleep, or (3) NREM-deprived sleep. After sleeping, the subjects were shown the movie again and their reactions to it were assessed. REM-deprived subjects showed the greatest anxiety, suggesting that the opportunity to experience REM sleep had produced some dissipation or adaptation to the emotion caused by the stressful events in the movie.

Ernest Hartmann has suggested that during REM sleep emotional content is, indeed, reduced or dissipated. He argues that the process is very different from how we normally conceptualize consolidation. Instead of replaying the same thing over and over new connections are made. The essence of the theory is this: When we are no longer under the control of the aminergic system, the brain is free to make all kinds of connections. Guided by the emotion we are experiencing, many connections are made based on some underlying relevance. As a result of forming new or strengthening weak connections, the piece of information that gave rise to the emotion is shared and distributed throughout the brain. The net effect is that the emotion is dissipated. A central assumption of Hartmann's theory is that when information that creates an emotion is isolated from the rest of our experiences that piece of information can be a powder keg, ready to be ignited at any moment. If, however, that information has been integrated with our life experiences (what he calls contextualized), it loses its isolation and loses its ability to create a strong emotion. According to Hartmann, it is not so much that we have become insensitive to or have lost interest in that information but, rather, that we have learned to accept that information within a broader context, that being our life experiences (Hartmann, 1998).

REM Sleep and Divergent (Creative) Thinking

If REM sleep facilitates the processing of information, especially information that must be integrated with existing information, the mental activity of REM sleep should be consistent with such a task. Indeed, there is evidence for such a position. Lewin and Glaubman (1975) have found that REM sleep is characterized by mental activity that is extremely flexible and divergent, rather than integrative and consolidating. However, it has been argued that the flexible and divergent aspects of REM mental activity would facilitate the integration of new, complex, emotional, or unusual information. A replication of Lewin and Glaubman's original study with somewhat different procedures again found that REM sleep facilitates divergent thinking (Glaubman et al., 1978). Subjects were assigned a divergent-thinking task in the evening and told they would have to perform the task in the morning. The task required them to tell what the consequences would be if gravity disappeared, for example, or if all people went blind. During the night, subjects were deprived of either REM or NREM sleep. NREM-deprived subjects gave not only more original responses but also numerically more responses (both are indexes of degree of divergent thinking). Interestingly, the NREM-deprived subjects gave more positive consequences than did the REM-deprived subjects. For example, asked what would happen if all people went blind, NREM-deprived subjects were more likely to say that wars would be abolished than that all people would die.

Some studies have shown that even small amounts of sleep loss will produce impairments in creative and complex thinking that are more than simple fatigue or lapses of attention. These studies suggest that sleep is important for maintaining higher order mental processes including creative mental processes. These results are consistent with the finding that sleep deprivation has a greater effect on complex tasks rather than simple tasks (Rechtschaffen, 1998).

Individual Differences in the Need for REM Sleep

Research has established a clear pattern of variation in the amount of REM sleep across the life cycle. Infants have twice as much REM sleep as adults do. As adults age, the percentage of REM sleep remains the same, but the absolute amount of REM is less in older adults (Table 6-1). Given this overall pattern, we might ask whether there are individual differences in the need for REM sleep.

If the amount of REM sleep under nondeprivation conditions is used as a measure, the evidence that different people have different needs is meager. Most studies have found equivocal results. Although researchers have demonstrated that retardates with

Table 6-1.   Change in sleep patterns.

	Sleep	REM	Absolute
Infancy (3 months)	14.0	40%	5.6
Maturity	7.5	20%	1.5
Old age (70s)	6.0	20%	1.2

lower IQ scores need less REM sleep (e.g., Castaldo & Krynicki, 1973) and that older people with lower IQ scores also need less (Feinberg, Koresko, Heller, & Steinberg, 1973), these results must be treated with caution. Individuals with schizophrenia appear to show little or no increase in REM sleep following REM deprivation (e.g., Gillin & Wyatt, 1975) but, because of the complexity of the topic and various questions raised regarding these studies (Vogel, 1975), the significance of this finding remains unclear.

There is good evidence for individual differences, however, if increased REM sleep following REM deprivation (REM rebound) is used as a measure of need. Let's consider some of the evidence.

Field Dependence and REM Rebound

It has been shown that field-independent people exhibit greater REM rebound than do field-dependent people (Cartwright, Monroe, & Palmer, 1967). Field dependence or independence is an aspect of cognitive style. Field-independent people tend to use an internal frame of reference in organizing incoming information; they generally relate information to the self, so this style represents a very active form of information processing. Field-dependent people, in contrast, tend to use external frames of reference; they are not likely to involve the self and thus take a more passive approach to information processing (Goodenough, 1978).*

According to the consolidation hypothesis of learning, it takes some time to transfer information from a temporary memory system into a more long-term storage system. It follows that dealing actively with infor-

---

*This distinction derives from studies on visual perception. Some people, it was found, would use themselves (their bodies) as reference points when making judgments about the direction in which a light is moving, for example (field-independent people), while other people would use some feature of the environment as a reference point (field-dependent people).

mation—organizing it with reference to the self—would not only be a more complex task, but would take more time and, consequently, field-independent subjects would tend to need more REM sleep. The data on REM rebound are consistent with this reasoning.

REM Sleep and Ego Threat

Greiser, Greenberg, and Harrison (1972) showed that ego-threatening manipulations affect memory. In their study, subjects were given anagrams preselected to ensure that about half could be solved in the allotted time. To threaten the subjects' self-concept (ego), subjects were told that the task was a measure of intelligence. The subjects were then exposed to sleep manipulation. The results showed that, compared with NREM sleep deprivation, REM sleep deprivation disrupted recall of failed anagrams but did not affect recall of solved anagrams. These results suggest that REM sleep facilitates the processing of material that draws the individual's self-concept into question or is inconsistent with that self-concept.

What would explain better recall of material inconsistent with or threatening to the individual's self-concept? One obvious explanation is that the person is motivated to resolve the discrepancy. We know from other work that this form of cognitive dissonance tends to produce arousal and that people are motivated to reduce such dissonance (Kiesler & Pallak, 1976). If a person fails to reduce the dissonance before sleep onset, REM sleep may offer an opportunity to accomplish this task.

Other researchers have threatened subjects' egos by giving them a difficult test that could not be completed in the allotted time and intimating that the test measured intelligence. Control subjects were given an easier version of the test that they could complete in the time allowed. The study found that ego threat did produce stress and that one night of uninterrupted sleep resulted in significant adaptation to the stress (Koulack, Prevost, & De Koninck, 1985). Further, subjects who recalled more of the stressful event in their dreams showed less adaptation upon awakening. These findings suggest that the adaptive value of sleep is the resolution or partial resolution of the stressful event (ego threat). Subjects who did not resolve the stressful event—that is, who showed less adaptation

on awakening—continued to have elements of the stressful event represented in their REM-state dreams.

Neuroticism and REM Rebound

People who score high on neuroticism (sensitizers) show less REM rebound following deprivation than do low-neuroticism people (repressors) (e.g., Nakazawa, Kotorii, Kotorii, Tachibana, & Nakano, 1975). In neuroticism research, a *repressor* is defined as someone who tries to deny or minimize a threat or avoids thinking about its consequences, whereas a *sensitizer* tries to control the danger by dwelling on its potential consequences (Bell & Byrne, 1978). In one study, subjects were deprived of either REM or NREM sleep early in the sleep period to determine the effects on REM episodes later in the period (Pivik & Foulkes, 1966). Repressors showed increased dreamlike fantasy during these later REM periods; sensitizers did not. Finally, Cohen (1977) showed that repressors have a greater need for REM sleep.

Why do repressors need more REM sleep? We know that a repressor tends to deal with threat by denying it. Considerable cognitive activity will be required to resolve the dissonance associated with such a strategy; a good or adequate solution could involve the generation of a series of hypotheses. In that sense, the repressor might be behaving like Greiser's subjects who were subjected to ego-threatening manipulations (Greiser et al., 1972).

The REM rebound data considered in this section are consistent with the suggestion that REM sleep is necessary for the consolidation of learning that involves the "assimilation of unusual information" (Greenberg & Pearlman, 1974, p. 516).

Summary

All mammalian species that have been studied and many avian predators (such as hawks and eagles) have REM sleep. In research with animals, it has been established, under controlled laboratory conditions, that REM sleep is linked to lowering of the threshold for motivated behaviors such as sex and eating. According to Ellman's theory, REM sleep is important for periodically firing the ICSS system. The function of REM dreams is to create the stimulation that can fire this system. According to Ellman, the explanation for infants' high level of REM is that, in the absence of external stimulation, the brain creates the stimulation needed for its own development. Early findings that deprivation of REM sleep produced anxiety, irritability, and difficulty in concentrating have not been replicated in more recent studies. In fact, Vogel has found that REM deprivation often alleviates the related symptoms of endogenous depression. Lack of REM sleep frequently leads to feelings of sleepiness and affects certain moods, such as friendliness and aggression. Considerable evidence indicates that REM sleep facilitates learning, especially learning that is complex or emotionally loaded. Consistent with the consolidation hypothesis, the timing of REM has been found to be important. Evidence also indicates that REM sleep increases adaptation to stressful and noxious events and enhances divergent thinking. Greenberg and Pearlman (1974) have argued that REM sleep is necessary for the consolidation of learning that involves the "assimilation of unusual information" (p. 576).

Not all people have the same need for REM sleep. Field-independent people, people who are ego-threatened and repressors tend to need more. These findings are consistent with the hypothesis that certain cognitive styles or certain habitual ways of dealing with problems or events require a divergent approach that can be augmented through REM sleep.

Dreaming

Various sleep researchers such as Hartmann (1998) have argued that REM sleep and dreams have overlapping but different functions. In this section, we are going to focus on what various researcher have said about dream content.

Hobson's Activation/Synthesis Theory

We talked earlier about Hobson's theory of sleep cycles. Here we are going to talk in more in depth about his work. Let me start by going back to some of his basic ideas.

In Hobson's activation-synthesis theory, activation is provided by the brainstem, while synthesis is provided by the forebrain (a part of the brain that is concerned with such things as thinking and planning).

One interesting feature of activation phase is the shutting down of a group of neurons in the brainstem called the *aminergic cells*, which are linked to attention and memory. Unlike most brain cells, the aminergic cells rest during sleep, especially during REM sleep. The modulatory or inhibitory activity of the aminergic cells makes it possible for humans to focus their attention, process information, and systematically retrieve memories. When these cells shut down, other brain cells spontaneously become active. In this state, the brain operates free of external stimulation and internal inhibition. We are free to dream. Because the motor system is disabled during REM, the activity of the brain does not result in motor responses. This helps explain, in part, the unusual nature of the dream state (Hobson, 1994).

Hobson suggests the REM state makes possible but does not determine the content of dreams. To make sense of dreams, we must link the various elements of information in some logical and coherent manner. To accomplish this, the brain changes the way it normally processes information. Among other things, both external and self-reference systems are set aside. This allows the brain to link pieces of information that normally have not been linked or cannot be linked. For example, it allows me to incorporate images of my deceased brother into a current part of my life. According to Hobson, synthesis is story telling. He argues that we are born with the tendency to make sense out of nonsense by creating stories (themes) that link unrelated pieces of information. Together, these two parts of the dream state can account for five important features of dreams (Hobson, 1994):

1. **Dreams as hallucination.** Although external sensory input and motor output produce our sensory experiences, the mental activity we experience in sleep arises from a special excitatory signal that activates the higher neurons in the visual system. The net effect is that the visual system responds to memories as though the signal came from the outside world, and we see memories as though they were produced from external sensory input and motor output. Fantasy, in contrast, does not involve this excitatory process and, consequently, fantasies lack the vivid and compelling quality of dreams.

2. **Dreams as delusions.** What makes these hallucinations so fascinating is that we tend to accept them as

Dreams are often characterized by bizarreness.

reality. Hobson argues that the internally generated signals grow from memories that are synthesized into extraordinary stories. These stories, which link the vivid and compelling sensory experiences (the hallucinations), allow the past to be experienced as present. Like Ellman, Hobson believes that the extraordinary stories can occur because the synthesis system bypasses or momentarily sets aside the self-reference system.

3. **Distortions in time, place, and person.** In REM sleep, multiple sensory channels are simultaneously activated by multiple memories. This is very different from the waking stage, in which attention is focused sequentially on different sensory inputs. Hobson argues that, despite the great difference from the waking state, the brain still attempts to synthesize this information. To accomplish this feat, it must allow for distortions affecting the time, place, and characters of the dream. In other words,

it sets aside certain fundamental rules that would govern perceptions in the waking state. If this did not happen, the brain would not be able to create a unifying story or theme to tie the elements of the dream together. Hobson has referred to this tendency of the forebrain to synthesize information differently in dreaming and waking as *mode switching.*

4. **Intensification of emotion.** Hobson argues that the activation produced by the brain stem is responsible for physiological changes such as increased heart rate or increased activity in some part of the limbic system, which is linked to emotions. In attempting to account for this physiological activity, the brain ascribes each physiological response to an emotion such as anxiety, surprise, fear, or elation. In other words, the brain creates an emotion that accounts for the increased physiological activity of the body and, at the same time, helps link the various memories into a unified theme or story.

5. **The failure of memory.** Hobson accounts for the failure of memory as follows:

> In dreaming, the brain-mind follows the instructions: "Integrate all signals received into the most meaningful story possible; however farcical the results, believe it; and then forget it." The "forget" instruction is most simply explained as the absence of a "remember" instruction. (Hobson, 1988, p. 214)

According to this interpretation, we can train our mind to remember our dreams. Many dream researchers have done so, by keeping a journal of their dreams.

The Meaning of Dreams

From the layperson's point of view, probably the most interesting question is, "Do my dreams have any meaning?" Over the years, some theorists have argued they do and others that they don't, and still others suggest that the content of dreams needs to be viewed in terms of the larger question of the neurophysiology of the brain.

Let's review some of the more important dream theories.

Freud: Symbolic and Disguised Dreams

Freud (1900/1953) conceptualized dreams as arising from unfulfilled needs. He believed that the purpose of dreams is to act as a safety valve that would allow these unfulfilled needs to be filled; dreams drain off energy that otherwise might build and lead to actions provoking interpersonal conflicts, guilt, or anxiety.

Freud argued that dreams can be important in understanding unconscious motivation. In his view, the unfulfilled needs underlying our dreams express themselves as wishes, often sexual, which were assumed to be a product of the id (the more biological part of the personality) and buried deep in the unconscious. Many of these motives are in direct conflict with the conscience or the superego (the social and moral part of the personality), which therefore exerts a strong counterforce to push them back into the unconscious. According to Freud's theory, these wishes will continue to grow in strength and eventually force their way into the conscious, where they find expression. Freud hypothesized that, to avoid this conflict, the ego transforms the unacceptable images that arise from needs into more acceptable images—specifically into universal symbols. Thus, if the individual were motivated to view a penis, the ego might transform the image of a penis into a pencil or a telephone pole (presumably depending on how large a penis the individual might be motivated to see). Similarly, someone who was motivated to have sex might instead have an image of being engaged in an up and down motion—for example, being in an elevator or riding a horse. The idea that there are universal images for things meant that anyone who knew the symbols that the unconscious used could understand the contents of his or her dreams.

Freud did not believe that universal symbols existed for all manifest dream content, however. He often asked patients to free-associate to the manifest content of their dreams so he could identify the underlying or latent content. Unlike some more recent theorists, Freud believed that dreams are highly meaningful and that it is possible to analyze even the most-minute detail of a dream to find its meaning.

Hobson: Transparent and Unedited Dreams

Hobson (1988, 1994) starts from the position that dreams are caused by a neuronal state (REM state) and that the content of dreams emerges after the individual enters this REM state. The sensory experiences or hallucinations initially arise from memories, and then the brain attempts to make sense of them with a story or narrative. These narratives are viewed as creative story telling. Although the stories might resemble other stories used in the past, they are typically unique, even though the underlying theme of different stories might be the same.

According to Hobson, dreams are transparent and unedited. He suggests that they are also meaningful, undisguised, and often rich in conflictual impulses. This contrasts with Freud's view that dreams are obscure and disguised. Hobson believes that dreams are a mirror of our inner stories. To understand dreams, we need to look at the narrative that holds the diverse content together. He also believes that dreams are creative. During sleep, new ideas and new solutions are derived consciously or unconsciously from our inner mental world. Finally, Hobson believes that dreams are there to entertain us. We therefore need to accept them and enjoy them.

Crick and Mitchison: Meaningless Dreams

According to Crick and Mitchison, the content of dreams has little or no meaning. They maintain that dreams are simply the utilization of stored memories to make sense of random activation. They argue that the random activation accounts for the bizarreness, discontinuity, and incoherence of dreaming. Although the content of dreams is assumed not to be important, they believe that REM sleep is, nevertheless, an important process that is "designed to make storage in an associative net more efficient" (Crick & Mitchison, 1983, p. 112). They proposed that the function of sleep

> is to remove certain undesirable modes of interactions in network of cells in the central cortex. We postulate that this is done in REM sleep by a reverse learning mechanism, so that the trace in the brain of the unconscious dream is weakened, rather than strengthened. (Crick & Mitchison, 1983, p. 111)

In a second paper, they suggested that dreams were important to reduce fantasy and obsession in the waking state (Crick & Mitchison, 1986). In other words, although they do not think that the content of dreams is important, they do believe that dreams serve a very important function in preparing the brain for optimal functioning in the waking state.

Cartwright: Dreams as Information Processing

Studies of dream content indicate that dreams are regular and orderly (Kramer, 1982). Dream content exhibits consistent patterns from night to night and within a single night. Rosalind Cartwright (1990) has shown that this regular and orderly nature of dreams tends to be linked to the dreamer's affective state. She argues that these affective states trigger a network of memories and thus, over the course of a night, the content of different dreams will reflect a common theme. The implication is that, by sampling a night of dreams, we will be able to identify that theme.

Cartwright found that latencies for REM are shorter when an individual is in a highly emotional or affective state. This implies that there is some urgency for us to enter REM sleep when we are in a highly emotional state—for example, when our self-concept is threatened. Note that these findings are consistent with the research reviewed earlier on the role of REM sleep when the ego is threatened (Greiser et al., 1972).

Cartwright (1999) has shown that dreams can play an important role in alleviating negative moods. She found that participants who went to bed feeling low often woke up in the morning feeling much better. Interestingly, the content of their dreams reflected this change in mood. When they first went to sleep, the content was initially more negative but during the course of the night, the content became more neutral and eventually more positive, so that when they awoke, they reported feeling good. In a replication using depressed subjects, Cartwright found a similar pattern for a number of subjects but not for all. Those that showed the negative to positive shift during the night tended to show a reduction in depression, and one year later 72% of the participants were much less depressed that they had been a year earlier. Those that still had negative dreams at the end of the night, Cartwright suggested, are people who need to seek help to resolve their problems. The good news is that many people seem to have within themselves the capacity to resolve their problems. All they need is a good night of sleep.

Kramer: The Meaning of Nightmares

Nightmares are fairly common in children of ages 3 to 5. By the age of 5, most children outgrow them. Nonetheless, adults experience nightmares from time to time. Kramer (1990) has studied nightmares in males diagnosed with posttraumatic stress disorder as a result of their Vietnam combat experience. The dreams of this group had a high proportion of military content.

Kramer has argued that the veterans' dreams, compared with a control population, reflected a common attempt to assimilate their military experience, which they perceived as profoundly threatening to their self-concepts. One factor hindering resolution—and thus prolonging the nightmares—was that many of the veterans had engaged in violent acts in Vietnam and needed to come to terms with that after returning to a society where violence is not condoned.

Kramer (1990) has argued that dreams often involve more than just assimilating information; they also involve the process of accommodation. In accommodation, we develop new cognitive structures to deal with the complexity of the information in our lives. For many of the soldiers, the underlying theme of the dreams was how to move ahead and get on with life. Kramer views this as a metaphor for all dreams. In dreams, we attempt to come to terms with experiences and, in doing so, are able to move forward.

Hartmann's New Theory of Nightmares and Dreams

Earlier we discussed some aspects of Hartmann's new theory of dreams in connection with stress. According to Hartmann's new theory, the immediate function of dreams is to spread out the excitation of an emotion by forming new connections in the brain. This serves as an immediate calming effect. Forming new connections also help prepare the individual to deal with similar situations in the future. Because these connections have been strengthened, should an individual find him- or herself in a similar situation in the future, the emotion will be automatically dissipated (Hartmann, 1998).

According to Hartmann's theory, the content of the dream reflects the formation of new connections. To understand the meaning of dreams one should look at them as a metaphor in which there is a dominant emotion. If someone dreams of running to escape from an attacker, the likely emotion that caused that dream is fear. If one dreams that he or she is unable to complete a task or is lost, the likely emotion is helplessness. What might seem bizarre to us when we recall a dream is simply the brain's way of making connections. Viewed in that perspective, dreams become a wonderful glimpse of how the brain goes about regulating emotions.

Many researchers have come to accept the idea that sleep with all its different forms plays a critical role in regulating our emotions. Subjectively, most of us know that after a good night of sleep, we often feel rested and emotionally prepared to deal with whatever challenges we might face.

Status of Theories

What I have done in this section is to discuss a variety of interesting approaches to the question, "Do dreams have meaning?" As I look at this research, it seems that although dreams are clearly story telling, the stories we tell are more than just entertainment. What is needed is a broad theory that can incorporate some of the divergent lines of evidence which, at one level, seem to contradict each other.

Lucid Dreaming

Although we are typically passive observers in our dreams, evidence suggests that we can learn to actively participate in the dream state as though we were awake and aware; we seem to be fully conscious in the sensory world that characterizes dreams. In this state—called *lucid dreaming*—we can make decisions about what we want to do with the hallucinations we are experiencing. If we are walking down a hall, for example, we can decide to turn right or left or to open a door and see what is inside. We can talk to people and ask them to do things; we can leave if we don't like what is happening; we can do battle with a threatening figure (Gackenbach & Bosveld, 1989a, b; LaBerge, 1985).

In lucid dreaming, we can engage in extraordinary physical and psychological feats because we are not bound by the laws of physics. We can fly, jump over skyscrapers, throw trucks through the air, or jump from one continent to another with no loss of time. People who have learned to become lucid dreamers often look forward to going to sleep, so that they can enter a world where they are in complete control.

Studies of lucid dreaming reveal not only its entertainment value but also its role in self-discovery and self-mastery.

Lucid Dreaming as Empowerment

In lucid dreaming, people, situations, and things seem less threatening. As a result, we can confront threatening people, situations, and things and learn how to deal with them. For example, individuals who are unable to confront their parents in normal waking life can use lucidity to deal with them. It appears that, having learned to deal with their parents in their dreams, they can transfer that learning to the waking state.

Because it is possible to manipulate dream content, dreamers can actively get in touch with places, times, situations, or persons that are a source of anxiety or conflict. They can then use lucidity to resolve the anxiety or the conflict. It is even possible for people to get a new perspective on a situation by occupying another person's body. There are clinical reports of people detaching themselves from their own body in dreams, floating over to another person's body, and occupying it (Gackenbach & Bosveld, 1989a).

Lucid Dreaming and Health

Lucid dreaming appears to have great potential as a vehicle to improved health. It has been linked to improved self-confidence, feelings of control, and optimism, all of which have been linked to good health (LaBerge, 1985). The evidence, which is mainly anecdotal, needs to be confirmed by controlled laboratory studies. (See Practical Application 6-3 for guidelines for becoming a lucid dreamer.)

Hartmann's Theory of Sleep

The Function of REM and NREM Sleep

Hartmann (1973, 1996) has suggested that REM sleep and NREM sleep serve two distinct and important functions: NREM sleep serves a general physiological restorative function, whereas REM sleep serves a more specialized reprogramming function. Because of the complexity of our daily lives, he argues, we have much unfinished business, such as stress, conflict, and unorganized information. REM helps deal with this unfinished business and plays a general role in maintaining the systems that underpin the processes of alertness and attention.

Electrical Activity During REM and SWS

In a study involving patients with implanted electrodes that monitored the activity of 13 deep subcortical structures, researchers found that changes in electrical activity in the various areas were asynchronous (not related to activity in other areas) during SWS

(NREM) sleep but were highly synchronous during REM (Moiseeva, 1979). This finding is consistent with Hartmann's theory that, during SWS, each of the various areas of the brain is undergoing repair, whereas, during REM, the various areas work together to reprogram the individual so that the individual will be prepared for the following day.

REM Sleep and Catecholamines

Hartmann has specifically argued that information processing depletes catecholamines and that REM sleep replenishes them. According to his theory, when we are awake, we are able to maintain our attention because of subtle feedback systems that allow us to block out irrelevant information or focus on relations that make the situation meaningful. These feedback-modulated guidance systems weaken with extended use (because of catecholamine depletion), and REM sleep restores these systems to their proper level. In effect, Hartmann argues that these systems are bypassed while they are under repair. From this perspective, he suggests, we can understand the nature of dreams. During dreams, he notes, we are often unable to focus attention; we simply experience a pattern of environmental events. Sometimes these events even violate laws of time and space. We might put two things together that normally don't go together, or perceive two events occurring simultaneously when in fact they occurred at different times. For example, we might dream that two persons who have never met, although we know them both, are talking to each other as though they were old acquaintances. This can happen because the feedback systems are not operative.

In a test of this theory, Hartmann and Stern (1972) deprived rats of REM sleep, thus producing a decrement in acquisition of an avoidance task. When the rats were then injected with a drug that increased the availability of catecholamines, this deficit was reversed; that is, the rats learned normally when the catecholamine level was raised. Since their original work, numerous studies have confirmed this finding (Hartmann, 1996).

Summary

According to Freud, dreams are the result of unfulfilled wishes. To avoid a conflict with the conscious, the ego transforms unacceptable images into more acceptable symbols. Dreams, therefore, are both disguised and symbolic. Crick and Mitchison argue that the content of dreams is random and, therefore, dreams have no meaning. According to their theory, REM sleep reverses learning and prepares the individual for optimal functioning. According to Hobson, dreams are meaningful, undisguised, and often rich in conflictual impulses. Hobson suggests that the brain has a natural tendency to synthesize the images produced when the inhibiting action of the aminergic cells is interrupted. It synthesizes the images by creating a story. The meaning of dreams is to be found in the story that our brain creates. According to Cartwright's theory, dreams that have been triggered by a strong affect have the most meaning as far as the self is concerned. She argues that dreams reflect normal information processing. Kramer's work on nightmares also suggests that dreams reflect an attempt to assimilate information. Nightmares might reflect the need not only to assimilate but also to accommodate.

In lucid dreaming, individuals participate in the dream as though awake and aware. Some researchers view lucid dreaming as a potential means of attaining empowerment and health.

Hartmann has proposed that REM and NREM sleep serve two distinct functions: a reprogramming function and a restorative function.

Sleep Disorders

The best way to determine the exact nature of a sleep disorder is to take EEG measures during one or more nights of sleep in a sleep clinic. Often people who complain of a sleep disorder are unable to explain its exact nature, or they perceive a problem that in fact doesn't exist. With objective data, it is possible to chart a course of action that might alleviate the problem (Dement & Vaughn, 1999).

Insomnia

One of the most common categories of sleep disorders is insomnia. Insomnia is any failure of sleep. It can involve inability to get to sleep, inability to stay asleep, periodic awakenings, or light sleep, a condition in which the person has difficulty staying asleep and tends to have a high proportion of stage 1 sleep and a low proportion of stage 4 sleep (Webb & Agnew,

1975b). Large-scale surveys have found that about 14% of the population feel they have some difficulty with sleep. These studies indicate that difficulties with sleep are independent of racial origin, socioeconomic status, and nationality (Webb & Agnew, 1975b). Age, however, has been found to be a major predictor. As many as half of the older people questioned indicated they experienced troubled sleep from time to time.

Drug-Related Insomnias

In the past, insomnia was commonly treated with barbiturates. Barbiturates will increase sleep time at first, but larger and larger doses are typically required to maintain this pattern. Eventually, most people who use barbiturates develop a very disturbed sleep pattern. They can initially go to sleep with the aid of the barbi-

turates, but they have difficulty staying asleep. The reason has become clear. Initially, barbiturates suppress REM sleep. In larger and larger doses, barbiturates suppress not only REM sleep but also stages 3 and 4. Because the absence of REM and stage 4 sleep produces deficits that need to be made up, people who take barbiturates are in a state of continuous REM and stage 4 sleep deprivation. The many bursts of cortical arousal observed among barbiturate users during sleep can be interpreted as attempts to enter stage 3, 4, or REM sleep (Dement & Villablanca, 1974). More recently, muscle relaxants have been used to treat insomnia. Tense muscles increase arousal and arousal is incompatible with sleep (Dement & Vaughn, 1999).

The effects of alcohol on sleep are similar in many respects to those of barbiturates. In single doses, alco-

Practical Application 6-3

How to Become a Lucid Dreamer

If you are willing to persist and to exercise a bit of patience, you can probably become a lucid dreamer. Sampling my students, I find that about 15 to 20% of them have experienced lucid dreams without trying to do so. We do not fully understand the nature of lucid dreams, but the following five rules may help you to experience them.

1. **Practice dream recall.** As soon as you awake, you should record your dreams in a dream journal. The act of recording your dreams instructs the brain that you want it to store your dreams in memory. The natural tendency of the brain is to *not* store dreams in memory. When you start recording your dreams, you will find that you remember more and more of them. Learning to remember your dreams is the first step toward recognizing that you are dreaming. The ability to recognize that you are dreaming will make you a lucid dreamer.

When you get up in the morning, you should ask yourself, "What did I dream?" Even if the answer does not come immediately, don't give up. After a short time, you will likely find that you can recall some fragments. As time passes, these fragments will evolve into complete dreams. It takes time for the

brain to clearly understand that you want to be able to record your dreams in some detail, rather than simply having some indication that you did dream.

Often your feelings and thoughts first thing in the morning are linked to the dreams you had during the night. By focusing your attention on these thoughts and feelings, you may be able to trigger your dream memories.

Make sure that you do not let other things interfere with recording your dreams. If you don't record them immediately, you won't remember them in as much detail, and you will tend to record them in a more waking like form. These dream records are important not only because they teach you to remember, but also because they will provide you with the information you need to recognize that you are dreaming.

2. **Teach yourself to recognize that you are in a dream.** Start by asking yourself 5 to 10 times a day "Am I dreaming?" This will help you ask the question at night. Before going to bed, make it your intention to recognize dreams. If you wake up in the night, use LaBerge's (1985) MILD (mnemonic induction of lucid dreams) technique. Say to yourself, "Next time I am dreaming, I want to remember to recognize I am dreaming." LaBerge suggests that you

hol reduces REM sleep, while sometimes slightly increasing slow-wave sleep. Chronic alcohol use typically produces fragmented sleep characterized by a reduction of REM and SWS. Withdrawal of alcohol following chronic use often results in hallucinations. Delirium tremens (the DTs) can result when REM sleep breaks into the waking state (Webb & Agnew, 1975b).

Mild stimulants such as caffeine—found, for example, in coffee, tea, some soft drinks, and NoDoz—produce a mild disruption of sleep. The equivalent of 3 to 4 cups of coffee before retiring lengthens the time it takes to get to sleep, produces more awakenings, and generally leads to the subjective evaluation of poor sleep. Strong stimulants such as amphetamines have a much more pronounced effect. They increase the time it takes to get to sleep and the number of awakenings

and reduce REM and SWS. Withdrawal from chronic use results in REM rebound and associated nightmares.

Antidepressants and some tranquilizers also decrease REM sleep, as do some nonprescription sleeping pills. The ultimate benefit of these drugs as far as sleep is concerned is therefore questionable.

Non–Drug-Related Insomnias

Webb and Agnew (1975b) have suggested five categories of non–drug-related insomnias: situational, benign, and arrhythmic insomnias, sleep anomalies, and secondary sleep disorders.

Situational insomnias. These insomnias are produced by a response to some event in the waking world, such as excitement about a new business opportunity or a

---

should generate this intention either immediately after waking from a REM period or following full wakefulness. In his research, he has found this technique particularly effective in triggering the recognition of dreams.

Learn to ask, "Am I dreaming?" whenever you experience a strong emotion or when something seems strange, bizarre, or has any of the other characteristics associated with dreams. Leaning to ask this question whenever you detect something similar to a dream in the waking state will increase the probability that you will ask this question when you are dreaming.

Read your dream journal so that you will become familiar with the characteristics of your dreams. This will help train your brain to recognize when you are in a dream. Identify any unique characteristic about your dreams, so that you will be able to more readily recognize that you are in a dream. Actively practice linking these and other characteristics of dreams to the idea that you are dreaming. Say to yourself, for example, "When two people from two different parts of the country are talking as old friends, it means I am probably dreaming." The more you become aware of the characteristics that differentiate dreams and the waking state, the better you will be at recognizing that you are dreaming.

3. **Learn to confirm to yourself that you are dreaming.** One of the easiest tests to determine whether you are dreaming is to see if you can violate the laws of gravity by floating, flying, or jumping 6 feet in the air. Sometimes people suspect they are dreaming but, in the absence of direct evidence, they fail to fully acknowledge the fact. In short, they fail to become fully lucid when they are on the threshold of lucidity.

4. **Plan ahead of time what you intend to do when you become lucid.** There are two reasons why this is a good practice. First, when you make plans, you give your brain the message that you want to know when you are in a dream, so that you can carry out some goal. Second, although lucid dreams can be highly entertaining, they can also be used to deal with specific problems or to achieve goals. To make sure you will fully exploit lucidity, you need to plan.

5. **Practice the necessary skills as often as possible.** As with any learned skill, the more you practice, the better you will become. Whether you acquire this skill will be largely determined by your motivation.

new love, the death of a loved one, guilt, or failure. The passage of time will often resolve a situationally induced sleep disorder.

Benign insomnias. In this case, people perceive they have poor sleep although in fact their sleep patterns are well within normal limits. Perhaps the person simply doesn't need to sleep as long as he or she imagines. Such a person may simply need to be made aware that there are great variations not only in the length of sleep but also in its timing.

Arrhythmic insomnias. These problems are caused by irregular sleep patterns. Going to bed or getting up at irregular hours eliminates some of the cues that normally control sleep. As a consequence, a person might

have difficulty going to sleep or might not get enough sleep because of the tendency to wake up early. Following a regular sleep pattern will usually control, if not eliminate, such forms of insomnia.

Sleep anomalies. One kind of sleep anomaly involves the intrusion of sleep into the waking state (narcolepsy and hypersomnia). These disorders are frequently disruptive but can be treated by sleep clinics. A second kind involves the presence of wakelike behaviors during sleep (sleepwalking, night terrors, nightmares, and enuresis). These sleep disorders are age-related and typically disappear by mid-childhood.

Secondary sleep disorders. Some sleep disruptions occur because of some form of pathology. Treatment requires

Practical Application 6-4

Some Common Reasons for Insomnia

Many of us suffer from insomnia from time to time. There are at least four common reasons for difficulty in going to sleep.

Sleeping In

If we have stayed up late or if we have not been getting enough sleep, we are often inclined to sleep in. According to Kleitman, the grandfather of sleep research, one of the best predictors of the time we will go to sleep is the length of time we have been awake, because the body tends to alternate between sleep and wakefulness in a very orderly fashion. Because our circadian rhythm lasts 25 hours, the body will quickly adjust to any new pattern that puts us to bed later and gets us up later. To maintain a 24-hour rhythm, then, we must constantly reset the cycle by getting up at the same time each day. When we interrupt the pattern by sleeping in, our body adopts a new arousal (alertness) pattern that finds us staying alert longer in the evening and being less alert in the morning. Alertness (arousal) in the evening makes it very difficult to get to sleep. The Monday-morning blues that many people experi-

ence might simply be the result of letting their bodies get out of synchrony with the 24-hour world in which they live. On Sunday night, they discover that they cannot readily fall asleep. When they finally do fall asleep, they simply do not have time to get enough REM and stage 4 sleep, and they haven't reset their alertness cycle to match the working day.

Engaging in High-Arousal Activities Before Sleep

I find that if I lecture for three hours in the evening—say, from 7 to 10 P.M.—I have great difficulty getting to sleep. The reason is fairly simple. Certain activities—in my case, lecturing for three hours—tend to produce a high level of arousal, which takes time to diminish, and even moderately high levels of arousal are incompatible with sleep. That is why people who win lotteries or suffer the death of a loved one typically cannot sleep. Students who must take an exam the following day often have difficulty sleeping. When we think about some forthcoming activity, especially if it is challenging, we often experience fairly high levels of arousal.

an attack on the primary cause. Once the primary pathology has been removed, sleep typically returns to normal. For example, a person who has difficulty sleeping because of guilt feelings must deal with the guilt before normal sleep can be achieved.

See Practical Application 6-4 for some common reasons for insomnia.

Sleep Apnea

To be classified as suffering from sleep apnea, a person must stop breathing for an interval of about 10 seconds on 30 or more occasions during the night. In some cases, people will stop as often as 500 times a night. Although this condition is reasonably rare (Bixler et al.,

1982), it is considered life threatening because it can cause severe hypoxia (oxygen deficiency in the body tissues) and cardiac arrhythmias (irregular heartbeat). Sleep apnea was once considered a common cause of insomnia in adults, but controlled laboratory studies have not confirmed this belief (Kales et al., 1982). Cessation of breathing typically awakens the sleeper, who experiences fragmented sleep (which we have already discussed). Daytime sleepiness is a common consequence (Stepanski, Lamphere, Badia, Zorick, & Roth, 1984). The mechanism by which this disorder is produced is not completely understood. The condition has been successfully eliminated by surgery that increases the ability to take in air. Consumption of alcohol before bedtime can increase sleep apnea (Scrima, Broudy, Nay, & Cohn, 1982).

Irregular Bedtime

People who do not go to bed at the same time each night often experience insomnia, especially on a night when they try to go to bed early. The reason is that we thrive on regularity; our body attempts to synchronize itself with the demands or expectations that we place on it. When we tend to stay up late, our body attempts to accommodate that demand. Then, if one night we go to bed early, we find that our body is still operating at a higher level of arousal than is compatible with sleep. The net effect is that we lie awake waiting for our body to shut down.

Our bodies tend to respond to internal clocks (rhythms), but we can reset those clocks by adopting a new pattern of waking and sleeping. Some people can adjust their rhythms quickly, but others find the task difficult. Most researchers agree that the best way to produce a good internal rhythm is to adopt a set schedule. When you do not stick to a schedule, your body fails to develop a consistent rhythm, and you might have occasional difficulty getting to sleep.

Napping

The ability to fall asleep is determined to a very large degree by the time that has passed since you last slept, so a relatively long afternoon nap—as distinct from a catnap, of no more than 30 minutes—can make it very difficult for you to fall asleep at your regular bedtime. People who are inclined to nap in the evening can also suffer a form of insomnia. Sometimes the body treats such naps as part of the sleep cycle. Since awakening is largely determined by the length of time we have slept, people who nap in the evening tend to wake up very early. Not surprisingly, they then have difficulty getting back to sleep. The best way to cure this problem is to discontinue the evening naps. This is often very difficult because people in the habit of taking such naps tend to fall asleep involuntarily while reading or watching TV. A nap serves to maintain the pattern they have established: early to sleep and much too early to wake. Not all people have trouble with naps; the body can learn to accommodate naps in the daily waking/sleeping cycle. This indicates that, to some degree, the sleep/wakefulness pattern can be trained.

Summary

Insomnia is one of the most common sleep disorders that can be caused by a wide variety of chemicals, including barbiturates, alcohol, and caffeine. Insomnia can also be produced by environmental conditions. Benign insomnia is a condition in which a person complains of sleep disruption but has sleep patterns within the normal range. There are several kinds of sleep anomaly, such as intrusion of sleep into waking state or the presence of wakelike behaviors during sleep. Though disruptive, many of these disorders can be treated. Sleep apnea, characterized by cessation of breathing for 10 seconds on 30 or more occasions during the night, is a life-threatening disorder.

Main Points

1. The best index of wakefulness, drowsiness, sleep, and dreams is cortical EEG activity.
2. During the course of a night (7–8 hours), an individual goes through approximately five sleep cycles; each cycle consists of four stages of sleep plus stage 1-REM.
3. REM sleep episodes lengthen as the sleep period continues; the total is about 1.5–2.0 hours of REM sleep per night.
4. According to Jouvet's model of sleep, serotonin controls the onset of sleep and norepinephrine produces REM sleep.
5. If people are left to establish their own sleep/wakefulness cycles (circadian rhythm), they tend to adopt a 25-hour cycle.
6. People who reduce the total time they sleep to 4.5–5.5 hours experience less REM and stage 2 sleep than normal but the same amount of stage 4 sleep.
7. Sleep reduction tends to reduce performance in tasks that demand persistence and attention but not in tasks that demand precision and cognitive functioning.
8. Fragmented sleep, defined as sleep from which the individual is awakened repeatedly, can produce deficits similar to those that accompany total deprivation of sleep.
9. According to Ellman's theory, REM sleep is important for periodically firing the ICSS system.
10. Vogel has provided evidence that REM deprivation could benefit people experiencing endogenous depression.
11. REM facilitates the learning not only of complex tasks but also of emotionally loaded ones.
12. REM sleep appears to play a particularly important role in dealing with material that is threatening to the ego.
13. According to Hobson, dreams are meaningful, undisguised, and often rich in conflictual impulses.
14. Hartmann suggested that NREM sleep has a restorative function and that REM sleep has a reprogramming function.
15. There are three categories of insomnia in addition to the kind related to drugs: situational, benign, and arrhythmic insomnia.

 ## InfoTrac® College Edition

Are you getting enough sleep? What are some of the indicators of lack of sleep? How would you rate yourself relative to some of these indicators? (Search words: sleep, sleep deprivation)

There are many Web sites devoted to sleep disorders. Log on to one of the following or InfoTrac® and see what you can find about ways of dealing with sleep apnea (Search words: sleep apnea):

SleepNet: www.sleepnet.com

American Sleep Disorders Association: www.asda.org

National Sleep Foundation: www.sleepfoundation.org

Sleep Medicine Home: www.users.cloud9.net/~thorpy/

The Sleep Well: www.stanford.edu/~dement/

Chapter Seven

Drug Use and Drug Addiction

■ *What is drug addiction?*

■ *Is there an addictive personality? Why do some people fail to become addicted?*

■ *What is the difference between drug abuse and drug addiction?*

■ *What are some of the biochemical explanations of the effects of drugs?*

■ *What role does learning and cognition play in the addictive process?*

■ *Is abstinence the only cure for alcohol addiction, or can people who have become addicted learn to use alcohol responsibly?*

■ *Is having a couple of drinks a good way to relax?*

■ *How do people quit addictions?*

When we speak of addiction, we typically mean the use and abuse of drugs—alcohol, stimulants, heroin, marijuana, nicotine, or even caffeine.

In this chapter, I will try to answer a number of basic questions: Why are people more likely to become addicted to some drugs than to others? Why is it that some people become addicted and others do not? Can the addiction process be reversed? If so, how? Let's begin by briefly discussing the evolutionary origins of drug addiction.

Evolutionary Considerations

Drug use is clearly not an adaptation to some environmental problem. What years of research have told us is that drug use allows people to co-opt a system or systems that were designed for something else. By co-opt, I mean we have learned how to activate that system by using drugs.

What is that system or systems? One underlying system appears to work in conjunction with several other systems to produce somewhat different reactions for different drugs. The main system is referred to variously as the reward pathway system, the dopaminergic system, or simply the dopamine system. At its broadest level, the dopaminergic system gives rise to feelings of euphoria (high, buzz, rush), a system that is sometimes referred to as the pleasure-seeking system (Nutt, 1996; Powledge, 1999).

One interesting implication of having a common system is that it becomes meaningless to distinguish between drugs by referring to them as soft or hard, treatable or nontreatable, legal or nonlegal. That is not to say that different drugs don't have a greater capacity to activate the dopaminergic system or that different drugs don't have unique and serious side effects. What it means, in very simple terms, is that it is a bit hypocritical to condemn those who smoke pot and take heroin while you are smoking a cigar and drinking a glass of scotch.

What was the dopaminergic system designed for? We know from a wide range of studies that it can be activated in a variety of ways besides using drugs. Most notably, we know that it can be activated when we take risks while exercising control. Mountain climbers, for example, talk about the rush they get from climbing a

difficult rock face that demands their complete concentration or race car drivers talk about the buzz they get from overtaking and passing another driver at high speeds. Looking backward, as evolutionary psychologists are forced to do, has led to the suggestion that systems like the dopaminergic system likely emerged to encourage or motivate our ancestors to do various things such as hunt. Hunting is an activity that not only involves risks but also involves exercising control. Moreover, hunting is important for survival and, thus, it is important that hunting was rewarded (Buss, 1999).

Many theorists have concluded that the dopaminergic system is not just a pleasure system but is important for learning a wide range of behaviors that enable us to survive (Powledge, 1995, 1999). Hunting, at one level of evolutionary analysis, makes little sense because hunting increases our chance of being killed. But if hunting increases our access to food, hunting would increase our chances of survival. Researchers have argued that the dopaminergic system provides pleasure and helps focus attention on those events that produce reward. This idea is consistent with the belief that the dopaminergic system emerged to ensure our ancestors repeatedly engaged in hunting as well as in other adaptive behaviors (Buss, 1999).

Today, the dopaminergic system exists as a system that provides pleasure when we eat and do all those things that are adaptive. This system makes us creatures of habit and, thus, helps ensure we sustain life (Powledge, 1999). The paradox, of course, is that the very system that emerged to sustain life is the system that also promotes and sustains drug addiction.

Let's begin by examining some basic terms and concepts relating to drug addiction.

Some Basic Terms and Concepts

Drug Addiction: The World Health Organization Definition

The World Health Organization has defined *drug addiction* as "a state of periodic or chronic intoxication produced by repeated consumption of a drug" (Swinson & Eaves, 1978, p. 56). Characteristics of drug addiction described by the World Health Organization are presented in Figure 7-1.

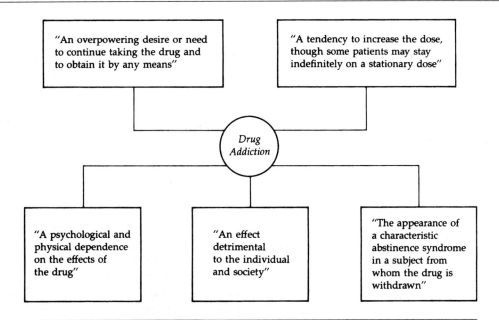

Figure 7-1.   Characteristics of drug addiction as defined by the World Health Organization. (Based on R. P. Swinson and D. Eaves, *Alcoholism and Addiction.* Copyright © 1978 by Macdonald and Evans, Ltd., Estover, Plymouth.)

The World Health Organization has recognized that there are many problems with this definition and, as a result, has suggested that the term might be counterproductive and should be dropped (Worick & Schaller, 1977). Because of its wide currency, however, it is unlikely to fade from use.

The main problem with this definition is that it identifies only the final stages of addiction. Often by the final stages—for instance, in confirmed alcoholism—serious health problems have set in and it is virtually impossible to reverse the process. There could also be serious psychological dependency on the drug. Prolonged use can dramatically alter a person's ability to cope with the real world. Years of failing to exercise normal coping responses can leave the person without any. In short, the drug might have changed the person both physically and psychologically. To understand drug addiction, we need to know the motivation for drug use, not just its effects. What we need to know is why people initially take drugs and, further, why they continue to take drugs. What roles are played by biological factors, the environment, and personality?

Substance Abuse

The one common factor in most, if not all, instances of drug addiction is drug abuse or what has come to be called *substance abuse* (Lowinson, Ruiz, & Millman, 1997). Substance abuse refers to the tendency to use a substance to excess—either more than was prescribed by a doctor or more than the person can handle without physical and psychological ill effects. It also refers to any tendency to use substances indiscriminately without regard for our need to function as members of society. The question that we need to answer, therefore, is why some people can use a drug or substance in moderation, so that it does not markedly affect their health, their performance, or their interpersonal relationships, but other people use the drug or substance to excess, so that it causes problems in these areas of their lives.

Psychoactive Drugs

A *psychoactive drug* affects mood, consciousness, or both. It might be a prescription drug such as Valium, or it could be a nonprescription drug such as marijuana.

This concept is generally viewed as important in the drug abuse literature because people tend to abuse psychoactive drugs but not nonpsychoactive drugs. In short, because a drug can alter psychological functioning, people tend to use and abuse it.

Dependency

Most drugs produce a variety of physiological and chemical changes in the body. A drug that produces addiction has altered normal body functions to such a degree that further doses of the drug are required to maintain a state of normal well-being. This state of drug *dependency* is generally assumed to be physiological, even though the main symptoms associated with the absence of the drug are often psychological. For example, a drug might produce a very pronounced feeling of euphoria or general well-being. Once a dose of the drug has run its course, the person might suffer intense depression or anxiety. Because more of the drug is required to return the person to a normal psychological state—let alone to a state of euphoria—the person is regarded as having a physical dependency on the drug, even though the main indicator is psychological (Nutt, 1996).

Tolerance

People often need to use increasing amounts of a particular drug to obtain the same psychological effects. In the drug literature, this process is generally referred to as *tolerance*. Evidence indicates that tolerance to many—if not all—drugs is caused by the physiological changes they produce. That people tend to develop a tolerance has been taken as clear evidence that drug addiction is caused by physiological changes that result from repeated use of a drug (Nutt, 1996).

Solomon's Opponent Process Model of Tolerance

Richard Solomon noted that a person who experiences an increase in positive affect is likely to experience a sharp increase in negative affect a short time afterward (Solomon, 1980; Solomon & Corbit, 1974). Similarly, an increase in negative affect is likely to be followed by a sharp increase in positive affect. He argues that the hu-

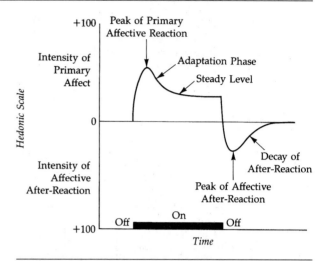

Figure 7-2. The standard pattern of affective dynamics, showing the five distinctive features: the peak of the primary affective reaction, the adaptation phase, the steady level, the peak of the affective after-reaction, and finally the decay of the after-reaction. The heavy black bar represents the time during which the affect-arousing stimulus is present. The ordinate represents two hedonic scales, each departing from neutrality, one for the primary affect, the other for the affective after-reaction. (From "The Opponent-Process Theory of Acquired Motivation," by R. L. Solomon, *American Psychologist*, 1980, 35, 691–712. Copyright © 1980 by the American Psychological Association. Reprinted with permission of the author.)

man is designed so that, whenever affect departs from a baseline, an *opponent process* is triggered to return the person to baseline. He suggests that the opponent process is rather sluggish and requires time to exert its full effect. When the opponent process does exert its effect, it produces for a time the affective state opposite to the one that triggered it. This sequence is illustrated in Figure 7-2.

Solomon holds that the opponent process is strengthened by use and weakened by disuse. He suggests that, because the opponent process tends to increase in strength each time it is triggered, the initial affective reaction will be shortened and the opponent affective reaction will grow stronger. Thus, for people to experience the same effect of the drug, they need to take larger amounts. According to Solomon, this mechanism accounts for the tolerance effects observed when people use opiates, barbiturates, amphetamines, and a number of other drugs.

Withdrawal

Withdrawal refers to the physiological and psychological symptoms that follow the cessation of drug use/intake (Nutt, 1996). Although withdrawal is typically referred to in negative terms such as shakes, headaches, pain, depression, or anxiety, withdrawal can be experienced as positive. Alcohol, for example, produces cognitive impairment and when people stop using alcohol they can, typically after a short period of recovery, think more clearly and process information more efficiently. Heroin produces a relaxed or even lethargic state that some people find interferes with their ability to fully enjoy arousal-producing activities such as climbing, cycling, dancing. Cocaine can produce a state of agitation, anxiety, and even paranoia that some people find highly aversive and inconsistent with the need to feel safe, secure, and relaxed.

Researchers have suggested that part of the motivation for the continued use of drugs is to avoid the negative symptoms or states that occur when people stop using drugs (Nutt, 1996). Although few people disagree with this idea, negative symptoms of withdrawal are only one of many reasons that people use drugs. Withdrawal does not explain why people use drugs in the first place or why people re-addict themselves after going through a period called drying out—a period of time that allows the body to remove the drug.

To understand fully why people use drugs and why people often re-addict themselves, we must recognize that people often use drugs as a form of self-medication. Researchers have found, for example, that people sometimes use alcohol or heroin to deal with stress, smoke cigarettes to deal with depression or various forms of negative affect, or use cocaine to enhance performance or self-esteem. What this means is that when they quit using a drug they often must deal with the original negative emotion that motivated them to use a particular drug in the first place (Carroll, 1997). This phenomenon makes the whole question of withdrawal very complex because we cannot be sure, in many cases, if the motivation to continue using a drug or the tendency to re-addict is caused by withdrawal symptoms produced by a drug or to the aversive psychological state the people experience when they give up a drug.

One way of demonstrating that the motivation for using a drug is caused by some psychological condition that preceded drug use and not by withdrawal symptoms is to remove the psychological condition that has been linked to drug use. Take cigarette smoking, for example. Researchers have established that many smokers use nicotine to alleviate various negative affective states. Research with smokers who have tried to quit smoking demonstrates that the negative affect associated with giving up a drug seems to play a key role in making it difficult for smokers to quit and in the tendency to relapse (Piasecki, Kenford, Smith, Fiore, & Baker, 1997). Many treatment programs have built into them some ways for addicts to deal with the negative affect that comes from giving up certain drugs such as alcohol and nicotine (Carroll, 1997).

Craving

Craving refers to the strong desire to ingest a drug or drugs and the preoccupation with obtaining and ingesting a drug or drugs. *Preoccupation* refers to the narrowing or focusing of attention and thought about how to obtain a drug or drugs and the pleasure that ingesting a drug or drugs will bring. This preoccupation can result in the neglect of other important activities such as job, family, and friends. For example, an alcoholic may spend a great deal of time thinking about when and where he will get his next drink and, in the process, neglect job and family.

The term *craving* is often used in two related contexts: (1) pre-consummatory and consummatory phases of drug use and (2) relapse.

The term *consummatory* is often used in the drug literature to emphasize the idea that ingesting a drug is a goal-directed activity. People have a goal to ingest a drug or drugs, and they have a goal relative to how much of that drug or drugs they wish to have—something called intoxication level. Although some people are satisfied with a moderate level of intoxication, others prefer a high level of intoxication. Those who prefer a state of high intoxication exhibit behavior that is characterized by repeated ingestion of the drug (several drinks, several joints, several injections) until the desired level is reached. A cocaine user, for example, might spend hundreds of dollars over a short period of time if his or her goal is to become highly intoxicated (sometimes called wasted). Although some people have argued that repeated ingestion of a drug (having several drinks for example) is an unlearned response and is caused by the activation of some brain system that takes control of behavior, the evidence does not support such a conjecture. First, clear evidence indicates that people can learn to use drugs moderately. That is, most people can learn to control intake. Second, it has yet to be demonstrated that when people are introduced to a drug for the first time they lose control. Third, considerable evidence indicates that people who are inclined to seek high levels of intoxication have a history of doing so. That is, once they start simply using a drug, they engage in a pattern of behavior that has become habitual. As we will discuss in more detail later, there are a number of reasons why people do or do not seek high levels of intoxication or why they limit their drug use in one situation but not in another. Guided by those reasons (the context), they come to use drugs at a certain level. The habit that is formed within that context becomes a memory. Later, when the contextual cues are present, a memory is activated, including the affective state that was experienced in that context, and the individual reenacts the memory (Goldman, 1999).

People who have decided they want to use a drug at a lower level of intoxication often find it not that difficult. That is, because they have developed new expectations about the link between intoxication level and desired outcome. Others, who do find it more difficult, can learn to achieve lower intoxication levels by systematically substituting new habits for old ones (Peele, 1998). At a theoretical level, researchers have suggested that people are forming competing memories of how a drug should be used in a particular context (Goldman, 1999).

One of the most perplexing problems associated with drug use is why people relapse after drying out. They no longer have withdrawal symptoms, so what motivates their behavior? What drug users report is they relapse because of a strong craving. Research has shown that the positive affect associated with drugs can be conditioned (Wikler, 1980). As a result, cues in the environment, even memories, can trigger an affective state. Once triggered, the individual shows all the

characteristics associated with that affective state including the pre-consummatory and consummatory behaviors linked to that affective state. Relapse, according to this conceptualization, is a psychological problem rather than a physical one. What the people must do at this point is learn how to deal with the emotion/motivation, making sure they do not allow themselves to actually use the drug that produced that affective state. This is where a good treatment program can help by teaching people how to develop new habits to effectively deal with such a situation (Piasecki et al., 1997; Shiffman, Paty, Gnys, Kassel, & Hickcox, 1996). If extinction is to occur, it is important that rewards are not forthcoming. The whole idea behind using various chemical blockers to treat drug addiction is based on the premise that people will give up drugs if they no longer experience reward (Nutt, 1996).

Summary

Addiction typically involves abuse of such drugs as alcohol, stimulants, heroin, marijuana, nicotine, and even caffeine. In recent years, research has focused on attempts to determine what motivates people to use drugs rather than on the effects of drugs. This shift in emphasis comes from the perception that it makes more sense to prevent addiction than to devise methods for treating it.

Drug dependency is generally thought to be physiological, even though the main symptoms associated with the absence of the drug are often psychological. People often need to use increasing amounts of a particular drug to obtain the same psychological effects; this process is usually called tolerance. When people stop using a drug they often experience withdrawal symptoms. Negative symptoms of withdrawal appear to motivate people to continue drug use, positive symptoms often motivate people to stop using a drug. Habitual users of drugs often report a craving when they stop using a rewarding drug. Craving appears to be a psychological state that triggers the disposition to think about and use drugs. Cravings can be triggered by the environment or by memories of what the drug does.

Solomon's theory can account for the dependency and tolerance in connection with drug use and for the observation that a marked mood shift—either very positive or very negative—is likely to be followed by the opposite mood. According to Solomon, an opponent process is triggered whenever there is a marked shift in mood. The opponent process is sluggish but, when it does exert its effect, it can be powerful, depending on experience, and can push the mood not only back to baseline but even in the opposite direction.

Why People Become Addicted

Approach and Avoidant Motivation

Who uses drugs and who becomes addicted are separate but related questions. Many people use drugs for years and do not become addicted; however, some people become addicted after only a short period. There is no simple explanation for this difference if you assume that the drug causes the addiction.

It appears that people are more likely to become addicted if they use drugs to escape a noxious or aversive mood state, such as anxiety and depression, than if they use drugs to enhance an already positive mood state—that is, if they are seeking excitement. This general principle has its origins in the work of Kolb (1962), who noted that two more or less distinct types of people take drugs: The hedonist takes drugs to obtain a euphoric effect; the psychoneurotic takes drugs to obtain relief from anxiety.

As we have seen, avoidant motivation is more compelling than is approach motivation. The reason for this, researchers have suggested, is that avoidant motivation often signals a threat to our survival. As a result, we are designed to learn quickly those reactions that will take us out of the threatening state. This general principle is used to explain why painkillers and antianxiety drugs are so addictive.

See Practical Application 7-1 for a discussion of factors that affect drug use.

A Motivational Model

A recent study clearly illustrates that people often use drugs for different reasons and that the underlying reasons for their drug use determine whether they are likely to abuse that drug (Cooper, Frone, Russell, & Mudar, 1995). This study focused on alcohol use, but

its findings are thought to provide a good model for thinking about other drugs because drugs activate the same underlying system.

The study grew out of a model of alcohol use suggesting that people are inclined to use drugs to regulate moods and that people drink for two distinct reasons: to enhance positive emotional experiences—for example, to feel more friendly or caring—and to reduce a negative mood, such as anxiety. According to the model, people who use drugs to cope with negative experiences are more likely to have drinking problems.

To test the model, various measures were taken to assess factors such as mood, expectations, and sensation seeking, for adolescent and adult samples. The results for the adolescent sample are presented in Figure 7-3.

The results confirmed that there are two distinct reasons why people drink: drinking to enhance and drinking to cope. Note that there is a positive relationship between drinking to enhance and drinking to cope; that is, people who drink to enhance are also likely to drink to cope. Such people simply drink more in all conditions. The overall finding is that drinking for any reason tends to lead to drinking problems. But note the direct path from drinking to cope to drinking problems. This is consistent with the general finding that people who drink for avoidant reasons are more likely to abuse alcohol and to become addicted.

The relatively small correlations found in this model between negative mood and drinking to cope indicate that negative moods themselves do not trigger drinking. Expectations were found to have a far greater predictive value. People are inclined to drink because of both social and emotional enhancement expectations and tension reduction expectations. Expectations come not only from our experiences but also from what we have heard from other people or from the media—for example, that sex is more fun if you use alcohol or that alcohol reduces stress. There are strong indications that the reason adolescents first use drugs is to experience those expectations that have been handed down to them. Even if those expectations are not confirmed through the adolescents' own experiences, they might still play a significant role in their lives for some time. One possible reason for the maturing-out process—people's tendency to use fewer drugs or quit as they get older (Peele, 1989)—could be that drugs gradually lose their motivational impact when they fail to fulfill users' expectations.

The Initial Motivation to Use Drugs

It follows from the model just considered that, if we use drugs on a regular basis, we are more likely to abuse drugs or become addicted. From this perspective, it follows that, the earlier we start using drugs the more likely we are to abuse drugs and perhaps become addicted. The key question, therefore, is why people use

drugs in the first place. Let's consider the biological, learned, and cognitive components of this question.

The Biological Component

Children in urban areas in the United States often begin to experiment with drugs (tobacco and alcohol) at about 12 years of age (Kandel & Yamaguchi, 1985; Robins & Przybeck, 1985; Wills, DuHamel, & Vaccaro, 1995). To assess whether this initial tendency to use drugs is linked to our biology, researchers have examined the correlations between drug use and tempera-

Practical Application 7-1

Factors That Influence Drug Use

Commitment to other activities. In *The Meaning of Addiction*, Peele (1998) argues that, although there is very little evidence for an addictive personality per se, considerable evidence suggests that the addiction process is linked to social, cultural, and parental influences, together with a desire to satisfy certain needs. He has argued that lack of commitment to nondrug activities often plays an important role in the process. If drugs interfere with activities that people value, they will limit their drug use or abstain, to maximize the rewards of the nondrug activity. In their therapy program, Cox and Klinger (1988) attempt to help people develop nonchemical goals as a means of developing a satisfying way of life.

Social class. A strong relationship has been found between socioeconomic level and alcohol addiction. Subjects of lower socioeconomic backgrounds are three times more likely to be addicted to alcohol than are middle-class subjects (Vaillant, 1983). As we'll see, these differences could be due not to socioeconomic class per se but, rather, to other characteristics associated with the various classes. Personal values, for example, could be the important factor.

Peer and parental influences. Peers have consistently been found to play an important role in initiating drug use. Research studies have shown that the effect of peer pressure is greatest in regard to mari-

juana, somewhat less in regard to alcohol, and least in regard to hard drugs (Kandel, Kessler, & Margulies, 1978). Peers might be influential in the initial experimentation with drugs, but it is questionable whether peer pressure can account for the tendency of a given individual to abuse drugs. In fact, peers might provide role models for moderation. For example, groups that encourage controlled use of heroin tend to limit the use of drugs to certain specific occasions, while encouraging the maintenance of social, scholastic, and professional interests (Jacobson & Zinberg, 1975).

Culture and ethnicity. Membership in a particular ethnic group seems to exert an influence on the likelihood of drug abuse. Several studies indicate that cultures or ethnic groups vary widely in the attitudes they foster and that these attitudes influence drinking patterns. There are wide cultural and ethnic differences regarding the acceptability of drunkenness, the tolerance of aggression in a drunken person, the idea of drinking as an expression of masculinity, and so forth. For example, Jews as a group tend to be moderate drinkers, whereas the Irish tend to drink to excess (Vaillant, 1983). Researchers have suggested that this difference is linked to the Jewish tradition of high regard for rationality and self-control (Keller, 1970) and an Irish ethos that alcohol is both magical and tragic (Bales, 1946). The Irish, that is, treat drinking not as something that we may choose to do or not do, but rather ment—in particular, mood temperament, activity temperament, and novelty-seeking temperament.

Mood Temperament

Mood is generally conceptualized as a continuum that ranges from negative affect to positive affect. Anxious or neurotic people are grouped at the negative end of the continuum. The individuals at the positive end of the continuum, according to Lerner and Lerner (1986), laugh and smile frequently, are generally cheerful, and enjoy life. We discussed the genetic basis for anxiety in Chapter 5.

Considerable evidence indicates that cigarette smokers and alcoholics tend to be more anxious and neurotic (e.g., Barnes, 1979; Sher, Walitzer, Wood, & Brent, 1991). These results are consistent with the hypothesis that people use drugs to manage moods. We'd expect that, if people are already in a positive mood state, they will be less inclined to use drugs (Tarter, 1988).

Activity Temperament

Activity temperament is conceptualized as a continuum from low activity—represented by individuals

as something that can bring magic into our life. The Japanese and Chinese tend to be moderate drinkers, whereas Native Americans and Inuits tend to be excessive drinkers (Klausner, Foulkes, & Moore, 1980). The incompatibility between excessive drinking and commitment to achievement might be responsible for the moderate drinking of the Japanese and Chinese (Peele, 1983).

Moderation as a life value. Researchers have suggested that drug abuse reflects a tendency to excessive behavior (Gilbert, 1981) and, conversely, that people for whom moderation is the central organizing principle will be less inclined to develop drug dependence (Peele, 1983). Individuals might be more likely to endorse moderation if they place a high value on health, which may be learned from parents or social peers (Becker, 1974).

Achievement motivation and fear of failure. Evidence from a variety of sources indicates that people characterized by strong achievement motivation are less likely to become addicted than are people who lack such motivation. People with strong achievement motivation tend to work hard and generally have good opinions of their abilities. People with a strong fear of failure tend to have a low opinion of their abilities, and tend to avoid situations that could demonstrate their ineptitude. To avoid looking bad, they look for easy problems or problems that are so difficult that no one would reasonably expect them to succeed. In short, their lives revolve around attempts to escape the need to

perform (to test their skills). One means of escape is to take drugs, often a highly ritualized activity that requires little skill and therefore offers no threat to low self-esteem. Birney, Burdick, and Teevan (1969) have suggested that the rise in drug use in the 1960s grew out of this learned fear of failure. Peele (1982) has included this kind of drug use among the coping strategies he calls *magical solutions.* Although such a coping strategy enables the individual to escape the immediate problem, it has no long-term survival value because it keeps the individual from facing reality.

Alienation from society. When people become alienated from their society, they have an increased tendency to become addicted. Researchers have found, for example, that the use of marijuana is associated with alienation from social institutions (Kandel, 1984). When people become alienated from their society, they no longer feel bound by its rules. As a consequence, they see no value in the principle of moderation or the standards by which other people judge the appropriateness of behavior. The lack of activities designed to lead to achievement or other rewards valued by the society makes these people susceptible to the drug experience (Jessor, 1979). It makes sense that, when people experience no rewards from the society in which they live, they might look elsewhere for a rewarding experience.

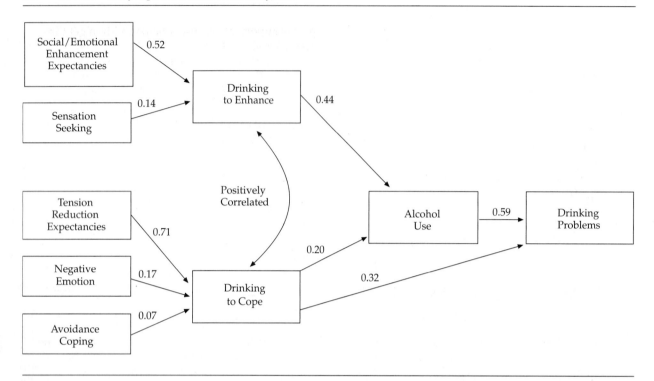

Figure 7-3.   People drink for two distinct reasons: drinking to enhance and drinking to cope. The above model shows the correlations for an adolescent sample. (From "Drinking to Regulate Positive and Negative Emotions: A Motivational Model of Alcohol Use," by M. L. Cooper, M. R. Frone, M. Russell and P. Mudar, *Journal of Personality and Social Psychology,* 1995, *69,* 990–1005. Copyright © 1995 by the American Psychological Association. Reprinted by permission of the author.)

who pursue more sedentary pursuits—to high activity—represented by individuals who tend to be restless and who frequently move around and can't sit still, such as hyperactive individuals. According to optimal arousal theory, hyperactivity can be conceptualized as resulting from a chronic state of underarousal (Zentall & Zentall, 1983). To experience optimal arousal, hyperactive children engage in activities that will increase momentary arousal. Motor activity is a very good way of increasing momentary arousal; feedback from the muscles stimulates the RAS, which in turn activates the cortex. Researchers also believe that the impulsivity and short attention span characterizing hyperactive children result from the tendency of such children to seek out new and different experiences. When we are confronted by new stimuli or new information, the brain automatically becomes aroused to process it. Once the new information has been processed, the

brain relaxes. Thus, to maintain momentary arousal at an optimal level, the hyperactive child must continually seek out new stimulation.

Most drugs that people use for recreation tend to increase arousal. It is not surprising, therefore, that hyperactive children are more likely to use drugs than are normal children (Wills, DuHamel, & Vaccaro, 1995) and that impulsivity has been linked to drug use (Cloninger, Sigvardsson, & Bohman, 1988). Note that Ritalin, the main drug used to treat hyperactivity (also called attention deficit disorder), is a central nervous system stimulant. Thus, these individuals' drug use might be considered a form of self-medication.

Novelty-Seeking Temperament

Considerable evidence links drug use to the trait called novelty seeking (Donohew et al., 1999; Wills, Vaccaro, & McNamara, 1994). Novelty seeking is one aspect of sensation seeking. Zuckerman (1979) has defined sensation seeking as "a trait defined by the need for varied, novel and complex sensations and experiences and the willingness to take physical and social risks for the sake of such experiences" (p. 10). According to Zuckerman (1979), one reason sensation seekers find drug use so reinforcing is that their low levels of the enzyme monoamine oxidase allows them to experience greater affect than do people with high levels of monoamine oxidase (Chapter 12). Researchers have suggested that many hyperactive children become sensation seekers to increase their arousal (Tarter, Moss, & Vanyukov, 1995).

The Learned Component

Various researchers have suggested that the learned pattern of coping plays an important role in drug use (e.g., Rothbart & Ahadi, 1994; Tarter, 1988). The general argument is that children with certain temperaments, such as high activity, experience greater anger and helplessness in problem-solving situations and therefore might be more inclined to use drugs as a method of dealing with these emotions. If these children could learn to better cope with their problems, they might be less prone to use drugs as a way of managing their avoidant motivation (Wills, DuHamel, & Vaccaro, 1995).

Several research studies support this argument. First, considerable evidence indicates that, as children get older, individual differences tend to increase; that is, some children show a greater disposition to use drugs, while others show less. One reason that some children are less inclined to use drugs might be that they have learned to cope better with their environments. As a result, they experience fewer feelings of anger and helplessness. What about those who tend to show an increase in drug use? Researchers have suggested that, as a result of their temperaments, some children tend to gravitate toward a social network of nonnormative peers, which provides initial access to drugs such as alcohol and tobacco and social reinforcement for their use (Donohew et al., 1999; Patterson, DeBaryshe, & Ramsey, 1989).

Second, research indicates that children with difficult temperaments often feel they have less family support (Wills, Vaccaro, & McNamara, 1992). Family support is important because it helps children get through difficult times. Children with active and negative temperaments might be partially responsible for their lack of support. Parents who find that their actions have little effect on the child—at least as compared with other children—find it less rewarding to deal with such children (Rothbart & Ahadi, 1994). In this scenario, a split grows between the child and the parents.

It follows that, as their parents become less supportive, children are more likely to turn to their peers for support. If those peers are nonnormative, the children would drift into a culture that rewards them for drug use.

The Cognitive Component

Self-control (or generalized self-regulation ability), which is an important predictor of success, is also related to drug use. The general finding is that drug abuse tends to be linked to undercontrol or lack of control. One study identified self-control as one of the main factors involved in drug use. Children with poor self-control also lacked coping skills and, consequently, experienced more anger and helplessness (Wills, DuHamel, & Vaccaro, 1995).

People are not born with self-control. Self-control is a developmental construct; it results, at least in part, from our own self-analysis. As a result of self-monitoring, people realize that they can and do have control over many situations in their lives. This process is obviously much more difficult for children with an active or negative temperament. Because they are often at odds with their parents and society, these children are more likely to entertain the belief that they are out of control. Their drug use might reinforce that belief. Indeed, researchers have shown that perceptions of self-control are negatively related to temperaments such as activity and negative mood (Wills, DuHamel, & Vaccaro, 1995).

Summary

People who use drugs to escape a noxious or aversive situation are more likely to become addicted than are those who use drugs for entertainment. According to one model of addiction, people use drugs to regulate

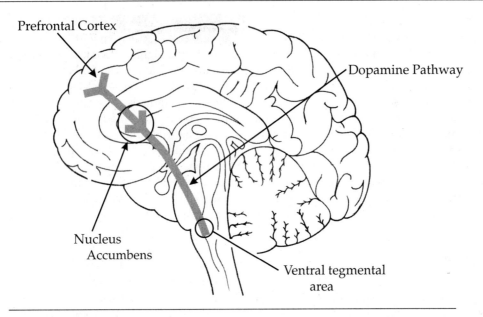

Figure 7-4.   The primary circuit for drug addition is the dopamine pathway, which starts in the ventral tegmental area, runs through the nucleus accumbens to the prefrontal cortex.

moods. They are more likely to become addicted, however, if they use drugs to cope.

Considerable evidence suggests that mood temperament, activity temperament, and novelty-seeking temperament are responsible for initial drug use. Learned and cognitive factors can reduce or increase this tendency.

Why Drugs Are Addictive

Most of the drugs we will be discussing activate the dopaminergic system, so it is important to have a basic understanding of that system.

Within the limbic system (considered an old part of the brain from an evolutionary perspective) is a pathway (often called the reward pathway) that runs from the ventral tegmental area (VTA) through the nucleus accumbens to the prefrontal cortex. Dopamine release in either the nucleus accumbens, prefrontal cortex, or both, is produced by all the misused drugs including heroin, cocaine, marijuana, alcohol, and nicotine (see Figure 7-4). Unlike most events that only activate the

system momentarily, drugs often keep the system active for long periods by interfering with the normal process of degradation or re-uptake. Degradation refers to the process whereby enzymes break down the neurotransmitter into more basic elements so that they can be re-synthesized to create new neurotransmitters. Re-uptake refers to a process by which neurotransmitters released at the synapses are reabsorbed into the synapse and stored for later release. What the additive drugs typically do is interfere with the process of degradation and re-uptake, and as a result, dopamine concentrations at the synapses increase far beyond what they would normally be. The main consequence is the reward pathway remains active for long periods of time, allowing users to experience euphoria for long periods of time. These prolonged periods of euphoria sharply contrast with those more fleeting periods of euphoria that might come from something as simple as eating an ice cream cone. When we eat an ice dream cone the dopamine that is released is quickly degraded or reabsorbed. Researchers generally believe that the brain was designed to carefully regulate dopamine because when there is too much or it is too prolonged, there can be serious consequences. How much dopamine is released must be proportional to the situation and to the demands associated with the situation (Powledge, 1995, 1999). In hunting, for example, it might have been appropriate for dopamine to be released in large quantities over a period of time to ensure the hunt was completed. Such a response would not have been appropriate, however, for eating an apple.

Heroin and Morphine

Biological Component

The most common mood change associated with heroin is euphoria, although panic and anxiety are not uncommon. The maximum effect is reached in about two hours, and the effect begins to wear off in five hours. Heroin is often the preferred drug of many drug addicts because it stimulates the release of abnormally high amounts of dopamine and stimulates other systems that seem to compliment the use of heroin (Powledge, 1999). Morphine is the same drug, but it is less preferred because of something called "drug efficacy" (Nutt, 1996). Most users want to experience the effects of the drug as quickly as possible and heroin is in a form (lipophilic) that allows it to enter the brain much faster than morphine can. To accelerate the process even more, addicts will often inject a drug directly into a vein so that it will be transported quickly to the brain. This unfortunate practice has led to the sharing of needles, which has increased the spread of HIV and hepatitis viruses (Nutt, 1996).

The Dopamine System Plus the Opioid System

The consensus is that the main effects of heroin are caused by the activation of the dopaminergic system. In addition, considerable research indicates the involvement of the opioid system. We have already discussed the dopaminergic system, so let's turn to the opioid system.

Endorphins: Natural Opioids of the Brain

In 1973, researchers discovered that the brain has specific receptors for opiates (Pert & Snyder, 1973; Snyder, 1977a, b). Subsequent research revealed that the body manufactures its own opiates, which are called *endor-*phins (from *endogenous morphine*). The brain produces two opiate-like peptide neurotransmitters: met-enkephalin and leu-enkephalin (Hughes, Smith, Kosterlitz, Fothergill, Morgan, & Morris, 1975) that interact with the same receptors as morphine does. These two chemicals (concentrated in the periaqueductal gray area) block substance P and, thus, have been implicated in the relief of pain. In addition, the pituitary gland produces two hormones with opiate-type effects: beta-endorphin and dynorphin. Collectively these are known as endorphins (Kalat, 1995). In addition to killing pain, endorphins alter mood and remove symptoms of stress. Their more subtle effects are to slow respiration, induce constipation, constrict the pupils, lower body temperature, and alter the functioning of the pituitary (Fincher, 1979). That humans and animals show a marked tolerance to morphine suggests that an opposing metabolic process or antagonist is at work to counteract the effects of morphine. Heroin acts at the same sites as the natural opioids, but because heroin has greater efficacy, it appears to be able to "high jack" the system. As a result, heroin produces an exaggerated response (Nutt, 1996).

The discovery of opiate receptor sites and of endorphins has provided us with a much clearer idea of why people become addicted to opiates such as morphine, heroin, and methadone. The existence of natural opiates (endorphins) suggests that somehow it was necessary for vertebrates to evolve these chemicals—that they were important for survival. (Endorphins are found only in vertebrates and the ancient hagfish.)

Psychological and Social Needs and the Power of Opioids

Although animals are sometimes used to study addiction, Vincent Dole (1980) states that "most animals cannot be made into addicts" (p. 142). This suggests that the drug itself is not the cause of addiction. Indeed, special conditions must often be met to produce addiction in animals. Specifically, animals need to be deprived of the opportunity to express basic needs or drives.

For instance, a comprehensive research program at Simon Fraser University has shown that rats must be housed under very restricted conditions (very little space, no social interaction, virtually nothing to explore) to produce morphine addiction (Alexander et al., 1985). Nichols (1965) devised a technique to produce withdrawal symptoms, one of the conditions that has been hypothesized to motivate drug use. As expected, this technique did produce increased morphine consumption but, interestingly, the effect was much greater in the animals housed under restricted conditions than in those housed under more natural conditions (more space, opportunity for social interaction, and availability of objects to explore). In other words, even under conditions of withdrawal, the tendency to select morphine is modified by housing conditions. One interesting finding was that female rats tended more than male rats to prefer morphine under restricted conditions. This effect was magnified after the rats were trained with Nichols' procedure. As we'll see, this might have something to do with the female rat's greater need for social contact or opportunity for activity. Subsequent studies have shown that the combination of space and social contact rather than either space or social contact alone produces the addictive results.

How can we account for these effects? Researchers have suggested that morphine interferes with complex rodent activity. If we assume that these activities are rewarding for rodents, it makes sense that rats in an environment that provided those rewards might tend to avoid morphine.

Expectations and the Power of Opioids

Researchers have repeatedly demonstrated that placebos can be just as effective as active drugs. In one study, a placebo killed pain as effectively as morphine (Lasagna, Mosteller, Von Felsinger, & Beecher, 1954). It has also been shown that the withdrawal symptoms people experience depend largely on their knowledge that heroin can produce withdrawal symptoms and on knowing what these symptoms are (Peele, 1998). Note that, often, these expectations are not based on direct experience but, rather, on knowledge acquired through reading and talking. It appears that, from a biological perspective, opioids are not as powerful as we have been led to believe. They will not necessarily produce strong and uncontrollable withdrawal symptoms and that, as a consequence, once we use heroin, we will be under its power.

The Learned Component

Conditioning of the Heroin Response

Individuals who inject opiates intravenously—sometimes called mainliners—report a rush (intense pleasure) shortly after an injection. According to the principles of classical and instrumental conditioning, if a drug that produces reinforcing effects is used in the presence of certain stimuli, those stimuli will, over time, become associated with the internal state that those drugs produce and will control drug-taking behavior (S. Siegel, 1979; Wikler, 1980). Some addicts can get a high simply by inserting a needle into their arms (in the absence of any drug effect), presumably because they associate the insertion of a needle with the euphoric feeling that typically follows an injection of heroin.

The Power of Reinforcement: Short-Circuiting of Biological Drives

Because heroin will effectively reduce a variety of discomforts—including hunger, fatigue, anxiety, and pain (Nutt, 1996)—the heroin addict may fortuitously learn to use heroin to reduce such discomforts. For example, a person who used heroin at one point to eliminate withdrawal symptoms might learn, through continued use, that heroin is an effective way of coping with anxiety. Nichols (1965) originally suggested this possibility when he pointed out that morphine can short-circuit many biological drives, such as hunger, thirst, and sex. Note that the relapse rate for heroin addicts has been reported to be as high as 90% (Dole, 1980). This finding is consistent with Nichols' suggestion that heroin use becomes a habit that is probably triggered by a wide variety of stimuli in the environment.

The Vietnam War Study

Until the Vietnam war, the only data we had on human addiction to morphine (heroin) came from studies of street users. Data from street users are problematic, however, because these individuals do not represent a cross section of society. Many are on the street because they are disturbed; they have been abused as children; they lack basic skills that would allow them to be employed; they are constantly having to deal with lack of shelter; they are often subjected to threats from other street people, as well as from the police; they are not

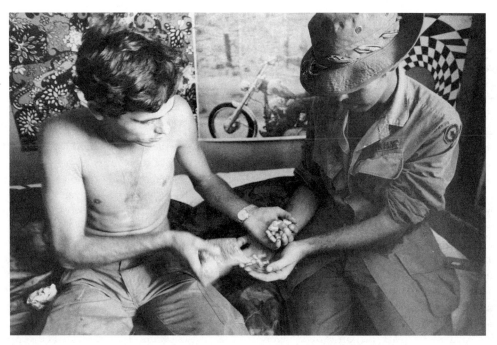

Drug use was common during the Vietnam war and paved the way for many soldiers to become heroin addicts.

eating properly, they are exposed to disease and do not have access to proper medical treatment; they are stressed; and so forth. In other words, it's hard to know if data on street users reflect the effects of the drug or the effects of all the other circumstances of their existence. Attempts to locate other users failed because of people's fears about losing their jobs, being harassed by the police, and so forth. Would you admit that you were using heroin if a researcher came to your door and asked you?

When it became apparent that soldiers in the Vietnam war were using heroin, the conditions necessary for obtaining good data seemed possible. Because they were a captive group who could be tested at will by the army, it proved relatively easy to identify a group of heroin addicts. The army was alarmed that the group of users was so large. Given the expected re-addiction rate of around 90%, there was concern about turning loose such a large group of potential addicts into the population. To the surprise of both the army and re-

searchers, only 15% of the heroin users re-addicted themselves. After careful analysis of the results, researchers discovered that the 15% who re-addicted themselves had all used drugs before going to Vietnam. The 85% who did not re-addict themselves returned to environments (their homes, for example) where drug use was not accepted or not the norm (Siegel, 1983).

The basic interpretation of this finding is that the context controlled drug use. The 15% who re-addicted themselves returned to environments where drug use was accepted or the norm. However, most theorists have argued that much more is involved (e.g., Davis, Goodwin, & Robins, 1975; Peele, 1989; Robins, Davis, & Goodwin, 1974). The model of drug addiction outlined in this chapter provides a good vehicle for coming to a broader understanding of what happened. Let's take a look.

The Vietnam war was very unpopular. Many of those serving were not fully committed to the official goal of the war—to stop the spread of communism in Asia—and were critical of the way the war was being waged. They felt there was too much dependence on ground forces and not enough emphasis on air strikes. Troops suspected that they were not there to win but rather to force a stalemate. As a result, many felt it was a stupid and pointless war. The ability of the Viet Cong to infiltrate and selectively kill U.S. soldiers was a source of constant stress. Although the war was technically between North and South Vietnam, it was virtually impossible to distinguish the enemy from allies. Away from family and friends, young soldiers were lonely. In short, the conditions for becoming addicted were ideal, at least according to the model in which an avoidant state is a precondition of addiction.

We know that social disapproval is one of the factors that inhibits drug use. In the late 1960s, however, the use of marijuana and other drugs by young people, especially university students, was the norm rather than the exception. In other words, the prohibitions against using drugs—at least certain drugs—were more or less absent for this group of soldiers. Further, heroin was readily available, and availability has repeatedly been shown to be a factor in drug use.

The model outlined in this chapter suggests that drug use does not necessarily lead to drug addiction, even if drugs are used to avoid or cope with negative emotions. We can assume from the Vietnam study that the GIs used drugs to manage their emotions. If these same emotions were not present when they returned, however, the internal conditions that would cue them to use the drugs would also not be present.

Those who did re-addict themselves had all previously used drugs. If they had used drugs in the past to manage their emotions, returning to the same environment would be likely to arouse the same emotions, and, with them, the risk of addition.

Finally, the model suggests that whether people use drugs will depend partially on their expectations. Soldiers from environments where drugs were viewed as a route to happiness would be inclined to use drugs once they returned to that environment. In contrast, soldiers from environments where other activities were seen as a route to happiness would be more inclined to engage in those other activities.

Thus, based on our model, it makes sense that only a certain portion of soldiers would become addicted again on returning home.

The Cognitive Component

Giving Up an Addiction

How do people give up a heroin addiction? Several circumstances are relevant here.

First, because many people use drugs to manage emotions—in particular, powerful aversive feelings—addicts need to learn other ways to manage those emotions.

Second, as is clear from Alexander's work with rats (Alexander et al., 1985), addicts must make efforts to identify activities that will fulfill their psychological needs, because drug abuse "depends on what behavior opportunities are available in life's situations, and whether the individual is prepared to exploit those opportunities" (Falk, 1983, p. 390). The Vietnam veterans who returned to lives they found satisfying and rewarding found no need to use drugs. If our only happiness has come from using drugs, then we will continue to use drugs.

Those who depend heavily on drugs to make them happy must find new activities that will provide them with happiness and satisfaction. A problem here is that new activities often depend on developing new skills. Nonetheless, the only true route to giving up drugs is to find such activities.

Interestingly, many people voluntarily give up drugs when they realize that their drug use is interfering with other positive and rewarding activities in their life, such as their job or their relationships (e.g., Peele, 1989). With many people, a good starting point is to ask them to assess whether the drug they are using is living up to their expectations. Is it providing happiness or interfering with their happiness? People often conclude that the drug is not helping. For many people, the benefits of drug use are more of an illusion than a reality.

There is a growing consensus that the best way to help people deal with drugs is to get them involved early in life in activities that are rewarding and satisfying. Out of those experiences, they find activities that make them immune to drugs. In other words, telling people to just say no is not enough. Drugs will be attractive to those who don't have meaningful alternatives.

Beliefs About Self-Control

A growing body of data suggests that people are most likely to give up an addiction when they make a clear decision to do so (Peele, 1998; Peele & Brodsky, 1991); that is, when they say to themselves that they can control their behavior, they change. The success rate is typically much higher for self-initiated change than for other-initiated change. When people are placed in programs designed to educate and train them, without making a commitment to themselves that they will change, they often fail. Success in beating addictions seems to start with the belief that we can control our behavior and the decision that we want to change our behavior. Unless we believe that we can change our behavior, we can't; if we don't want to change our behavior, we won't. The Vietnam veterans' experience indicates that, once we're addicted to a drug, we don't have to stay addicted. We have a choice.

Summary

Heroin and morphine, which are opioids, typically produce feelings of euphoria and suppress the aversive qualities of pain (analgesic properties). Opioids are thought to produce their effects through a number of neurotransmitter systems, as well as through substance P, which transmits pain signals. The discovery of receptor sites for morphine led scientists to conclude that the body produces its own morphine (endorphins).

Rats can be induced to become addicted to morphine if they are subjected to very restricted living conditions. The reason, researchers have suggested, is that, under restricted living conditions, the rats are unable to experience natural rewards. One implication of this research is that people will have a tendency to become addicted in environments that prevent them from experiencing natural rewards.

Many habits that humans acquire become controlled by internal or external stimuli. As a conse-

quence, certain behaviors are performed in the absence of the motivating state that originally established the habit. Nichols' research shows that even animals will learn to use a drug out of habit. Because morphine can short-circuit various biological drives, people sometimes use morphine when they should be eating, drinking, and establishing social relationships.

The Vietnam war provided an excellent opportunity to determine some of the conditions that lead to addiction. The fact that only 15% of users re-addicted themselves after the war attests to the importance of psychological variables in the addiction process. This finding has been explained in terms of learning principles.

Addictions can be viewed as attempts to manage moods or to provide personal satisfaction. Individuals with psychologically rewarding lives are unlikely to become addicted. Correspondingly, if people are to give up an addiction, they will typically need something to replace it. Beliefs about self-control have also been found to play an important role in determining whether people can give up an addiction.

Stimulants: Cocaine and Amphetamines

Although heroin and cannabis have been reported to induce euphoria, controlled studies comparing heroin and cannabis with amphetamines and cocaine have shown that amphetamines and cocaine produce euphoria more reliably and that the euphoria is far more intense (Ellinwood, 1992; Grinspoon & Hedblom, 1975).

Cocaine and the amphetamines are two of the best known stimulants (euphoria-producing drugs). They work in a very similar way.

The Biological Component

Cocaine is a naturally occurring chemical found in significant quantities in the leaves of two species of the coca shrub. It reliably produces positive feelings in most people. Researchers have found that people have difficulty discriminating small doses (less than 10 mg) of cocaine from a placebo. At moderate to high levels (25–100 mg), people who take cocaine intranasally reliably report euphoria within 15–30 seconds. Some people may experience anxiety, depression, fatigue, and a desire for more cocaine 45–60 minutes after taking a 100-mg dose. There is often a crash period of extreme discomfort after a large amount of cocaine is smoked or injected. This effect is less common when cocaine is taken intranasally. As with many other drugs, the adverse effects (discomfort or disturbing thoughts) appear to be associated with higher doses (Van Dyke & Byck, 1982). Over the years cocaine has been progressively refined from paste, to powder and finally to lipophilic free-base crack (Nutt, 1996).

Under the influence of amphetamines, people tend to experience feelings of reduced fatigue and of increased efficiency, endurance, and perseverance. The effect lasts for approximately 10 to 12 hours compared with 45 minutes for cocaine (King & Ellinwood, 1992). Note, however, that individuals' behavior might not be consistent with those feelings; they could, in fact, behave very inefficiently and exhibit little energy. Under certain conditions, though, amphetamines can lead to more energetic and efficient behavior. For example, they have been shown to improve performance in swimming, running, and cognitive problem-solving tasks. Faster conditioning and decreases in reaction time have also been reported (Barr, 1969; Grinspoon & Hedblom, 1975; Kalant, 1973; Swinson & Eaves, 1978).

The Dopamine System Plus the Norepinephrine

Heroin works by stimulating the output of large amounts of dopamine, but cocaine works mainly by blocking the re-uptake of dopamine. Figure 7-5 conceptualizes what happens when cocaine blocks the re-uptake pump. Amphetamines block the re-uptake of dopamine and stimulate the additional release of dopamine (Powledge, 1999).

Norepinephrine is also released when people use stimulants (Nutt, 1996). Norepinephrine plays an important role in processing information and may explain why stimulants are the preferred drug when people want to be mentally alert. One reason people sometimes choose amphetamines over cocaine is because amphetamines are less expensive (Selden, 1991).

To maximize feelings of euphoria, users prefer smoking and intravenous injections to oral intake.

The Learned Component

Experimental evidence suggests that dopaminergic activity can be conditioned (Schiff, 1982). In a series of studies, rats were administered amphetamine or apomorphine, which are known to affect dopamine metabolism, and placed in a novel environment. These drugs produced certain predictable behavioral changes in head bobbing, sniffing, activity levels, amount of rearing, and so forth. After ten training trials, rats were given a test trial in which a placebo was administered. It was found that when the animals given the placebo were placed in the novel environment (the CS), they showed the distinctive pattern of behaviors that tend to be produced by injections of amphetamine or apomorphine, while the controls, which were given drug treatment but not placed in the novel environment, did not. To determine if this pattern of responses was mediated by changes in dopamine metabolism, the animals were sacrificed, so that certain chemicals in the brains could be carefully analyzed. The results of this analysis provided support for the idea that the conditioned responses to cues previously associated with amphetamine and apomorphine (the novel environment) were mediated by increased dopamine turnover.

The results have important implications. An abundance of data shows that medically cured addicts— people who have gone through a drying-out period and have received drug counseling—will often become addicted again on returning to an environment in which they previously used drugs. This could be the result of conditioning. If the environment stimulates dopaminergic activity, this can be sufficient to reinstate the habit of taking a drug (Schiff, 1982). Research has shown that rats will reinitiate drug administration following self-induced abstinence if they are given a small dose of the drug (Pickens, 1968). Note in this context that a basic tenet of incentive motivational theory is that reinforcers have response-instigating as well as response-reinforcing effects (Bindra, 1974).

The tendency for people to renew their addiction in response to a particular mood—such as stress, anxiety, or depression—can also be understood in terms of con-

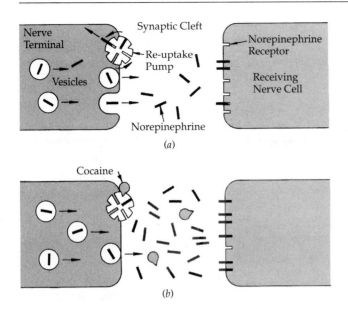

(a)

(b)

Figure 7-5. Cocaine blocks the re-uptake of neurotransmitters such as norepinephrine at synapses of the sympathetic nervous system. (The sympathetic nervous system controls heart rate, blood pressure, and other functions.) When the neurotransmitter molecules are released from vesicles in the nerve terminal (*a*) they cross the synaptic cleft and stimulate the succeeding nerve cell. Ordinarily, some of the neurotransmitter molecules in the cleft are pumped back into the nerve that released them. In the presence of cocaine, the action of the re-uptake pump is blocked (*b*), and the stimulation by the neurotransmitter molecules increases as their concentration in the synaptic cleft builds up. (From "Cocaine," by C. Van Dyke and R. I. Byck. *Scientific American*, March 1982, *246*, 128–141. Copyright © 1982 by Scientific American, Inc. All rights reserved.)

ditioning. If that mood has been linked to the habit of drug taking, then there will be a tendency for the habit to be evoked whenever that particular mood arises.

The Cognitive Component

Expectations

Different people report different effects from taking amphetamines or cocaine, including a wonderful sense of euphoria, a sense of control, a sense of power, improved sexual performance, increased creativity, and no effect at all. The most common reaction reported is a sense of euphoria. The feelings and thoughts that people experience when they take drugs such as amphetamines or cocaine depend largely on their expectations (Peele, 1998). If individuals expect some effect before they take the drug, they usually experience that effect, whatever it is. Although there is little evidence of withdrawal symptoms for cocaine, some people do report negative withdrawal symptoms. Some people show tolerance effects, even though the research demonstrates that cocaine sensitizes rather than desensitizes the dopamine system (Vezina, Kalivas, & Stewart,

1987). Some data even show that the magnitude of the reported reaction increases with increase in the cost of the drug.

Relapse

One of the central issues in all drug research is the problem of relapse. It appears that relapse is linked to our memory of the drug's effects. When we remember the experience we had with a drug, we might develop a craving for it (Wise, 1988). According to this interpretation, we are not compelled to take the drug; rather, we have some control over the process. For example, we might be able to recognize the consequences of indulging our craving. Alternatively, we could learn to substitute other memories of good experiences in activities unrelated to drugs.

Summary

Both cocaine and amphetamines are known for their ability to produce feelings of euphoria, their ability to reduce feelings of fatigue, and their ability to increase feelings of efficiency. They are sometimes used to enhance both physical and mental performance. Cocaine and amphetamines appear to work by increasing the concentration of neurotransmitters such as norepinephrine and dopamine at the synapses. The general consensus is that the dopamine system activates the self-reward system in the brain, which produces the euphoria linked to cocaine and amphetamines. Cocaine and amphetamines do not produce a tolerance effect and do not produce withdrawal symptoms, but they are habit-forming.

Evidence indicates that the dopaminergic system can be conditioned. One implication of this is that a particular mood, if elicited, could prime the dopaminergic system and lead to re-addiction.

The wide range of reactions to cocaine and amphetamines appears to be largely the result of particular users' expectations. The main explanation proposed for relapse is that users' pleasant memories of the drug's effects prompt them to try it again.

The Hallucinogenics: Cannabis and LSD

The Biological Component

Cannabis (Marijuana, Hashish)

Cannabis produces a number of rather mild physical symptoms, including increased pulse rate, rise in blood pressure, dilation of the pupils, redness of the eyes (caused by dilation of the conjunctival blood vessels), and occasionally breathlessness, choking, and some neurological changes reflected in unsteadiness, muscular twitches, tremors of the tongue, and changes in the deep reflexes (Lowinson, Ruiz, & Millman, 1997).

Psychologically, cannabis produces a wide variety of reactions. Naive subjects often experience anxiety and apprehension. These reactions, however, might not reflect the action of the drug as much as fear of the unknown. Generally, the effects of the drug are agreeable: a general feeling of euphoria, distortions of time and space, illusions, and even hallucinations. Often there are changes in body image, together with a feeling of depersonalization (Joyce, 1970; Lowinson, Ruiz, & Millman, 1997; Paton & Crown, 1972).

Dopamine Plus Anandamide

Although less is known about marijuana than about drugs such as heroin and cocaine, the consensus seems to be that dopamine plays a central role in producing the euphoria that is linked to marijuana use. In addition, researchers have found that anandamide is involved and works by blocking the re-uptake of dopamine (Adams & Martin, 1996; Travis, 1999). The changes in perceptions of time and space, on the other hand, could involve still another neurotransmitter, serotonin.

LSD (Lysergic Acid Diethylamide)

LSD produces a number of changes, including a rise in blood pressure, sweating, dilation of the pupils, increase in muscle tension (sometimes accompanied by nausea), headaches, and lightheadedness (Swinson & Eaves, 1978). These changes are caused by the drug's stimulant action on the reticular activating system (RAS). In addition, LSD often produces changes in perceptual processes associated with all sense modalities. The most dramatic changes typically occur in connection with visual perception. Objects appear to change in color, shape, and size. Two-dimensional objects suddenly appear to be three-dimensional. Under certain conditions, people will experience fully formed hallucinations of objects, events, or even people. There are typically alterations in perception of time or the ability to gauge time. The ability to reason is often disturbed, as is the ability to plan.

Dopamine Plus Serotonin

Evidence indicates that LSD depresses the activity of the serotonin-containing neurons in the raphe nuclei. Because serotonin normally inhibits certain kinds of visual and other activities of the brain, the net effect is that LSD disinhibits activity of the neurons in the visual system, the limbic system (the area of the brain linked to emotions), and other brain areas (Jacobs, 1987; Jacobs & Trulson, 1979). Drugs that increase the level of serotonin in the human brain have been found to reduce the effects of LSD, and drugs that block serotonin magnify its effects. Note that psilocybin (the active component of what recreational drug users call magic mushrooms) seems to work by the same mechanism.

The Learned Component

Dependency on or craving for cannabis and LSD does not appear to be a major problem. In reviews of addiction to drugs, cannabis and LSD often receive only passing attention (e.g., "Models of addiction," 1988). That is not to say that people cannot become dependent. In our society, however, relatively few people have become dysfunctional because of cannabis or LSD addiction in comparison with alcohol, heroin, and cocaine addiction (Hall & Solowij, 1998).

In general, people rarely become addicted to drugs they use infrequently. LSD tends to be used infrequently, partly because it renders users virtually incapable of doing anything else for a period of many hours, so its use requires some forethought. Cannabis, in contrast, can be used more casually as part of daily life and tends to be used more frequently, with a correspondingly larger risk of addiction.

The Cognitive Component

Altered Perceptions

Cannabis and LSD are mainly known for their ability to alter perception, especially visual perception. Psychedelic designs produced in the 1960s represented the visual experiences of cannabis and LSD users; some were made while under the influence of the drugs. Auditory, tactile, and other sensory systems are also altered. Since the 1960s, some artists and musicians have used cannabis and LSD to see the world differently—for instance, to increase their comprehension of music, heighten their perception of color and form, and help them focus on artistic endeavors (Grinspoon & Bakalar, 1993).

Memory and Attention Deficits

Cannabis produces dose-related impairment of various motor and cognitive functions similar to that found for alcohol. For example, researchers have found that impairment for driving is similar to that found for people with blood alcohol levels of .07% to 10%. Impairment is greater for tasks that are complex and tasks that demand sustained attention. Various memory, attention, and cognitive functions are impaired when someone is intoxicated, but no evidence indicates that long-term

use of cannabis results in severe impairment of memory, attention, and cognitive function, even though some researchers feel it could have subtle effects that have not been identified yet. Evidence indicates, however, that long-term use of cannabis results in certain health problems such as respiratory problems (Hall & Solowij, 1998).

Ecstacy (Adam, XTC)

Ecstacy, also known as MDMA (methylenedioxymethamphetamine), is a synthetic psychoactive drug with amphetamine-like and hallucinogenic properties. It has received a great deal of media attention in recent years and has been targeted as a recreational drug of abuse (National Institute of Drug Abuse, 2001). One of the main concerns of those who have studied the drug is the drug's potential for causing brain damage. Research has found that MDMA produces lasting effects on the serotonergic neurons in primates (Ricaurte, Martello, Katz, & Martello, 1992) and in human beings (McCann, Szabo, Scheffel, Dannals, & Ricaurte, 1998). Many of the risks are similar to those found with the use of amphetamines, including psychological difficulties (confusion, depression, sleep problems, severe anxiety, and paranoia), physical symptoms (muscle tension, blurred vision, nausea, chills, and sweating), and increased heart rate and blood pressure (National Institute of Drug Abuse, 2001).

Summary

Cannabis and LSD have stimulant or euphoric properties and distort perceptions of time and space. LSD also produces powerful distortions of the sense modalities, especially vision. Although some evidence indicates that cannabis and LSD are addictive, they are not generally regarded as a major concern. Cannabis is often used to create feelings of well-being and to treat a wide range of physical and psychological symptoms. The use of LSD is not very prevalent today, but cannabis is the most widely used recreational drug after alcohol and nicotine. Cannabis is used by people of virtually all ages and all economic levels, for a wide variety of reasons, including to reduce awareness of current problems and to create feelings of well-being (Grin-spoon & Bakalar, 1993).

Health Considerations: Treating People with Persistent Pain

Recently, media attention has focused on the medical properties of cannabis. It helps to relieve the chronic pain associated with cancer and other diseases and has been found useful by individuals with glaucoma, epilepsy, multiple sclerosis, paraplegia and quadriplegia, AIDS, migraines, menstrual cramps, and labor pains. Many people use cannabis to self-medicate for depression and various mood disorders (Grinspoon & Bakalar, 1993). With the growing interest in its potential to manage pain, researchers are examining the health implications to see if and what health problems might be associated with its use. The general consensus seems to be that although marijuana can cause certain health problems, such as respiratory problems, it is a very effective pain killer for many disorders such as cancer and HIV (Hall & Solowij, 1998).

Nicotine

The Biological Component

Nicotine appears to activate both the dopamine system and the opioid overproduction systems (Powledge, 1999). Evidence also indicates that nicotine activates acetylcholine—a system that has been implicated in learning and memory (Wonnacott & Lunt, 1993). The fact that nicotine stimulates several systems may account for its paradoxical effects—its ability to both arouse and relax. Although some people report they smoke to relax, others report they smoke to stimulate or arouse themselves. People who report they smoke to relax smoke more than do those who report they smoke to stimulate themselves. Researchers have suggested that in small doses, nicotine acts as a stimulant and in large doses as a relaxant (Armitage, Hall, & Sellers, 1969; Gilbert, 1979). The arousal elicited by nicotine appears to be very similar to that elicited by amphetamines, caffeine, LSD, and other stimulants (Eysenck, 1973).

The Learned Component

Considerable evidence indicates that smoking behavior is largely controlled by cues in the environment, both external and internal. Interestingly, heavy smokers appear to respond primarily to internal cues (nicotine levels), and light smokers respond to external cues. Light smokers can be made to smoke as much as heavy smokers if the external cues for smoking are made more prominent (Herman, 1974).

It is fascinating that people will often report that they didn't enjoy the cigarette they just smoked or will put out a cigarette shortly after lighting it. In other words, people often smoke even without experiencing a craving. Conversely, when people do experience a craving, they will go to great lengths to have a cigarette. Now that entire buildings have been designated as nonsmoking in many cities, it's common to see a crowd of people smoking outside an office building on a winter's day, as snow falls around them. We can conclude that, although often the result of a habit, smoking also has a biological basis.

For most smokers, many cues elicit smoking. This creates problems when people attempt to quit. Even after smokers have successfully weaned themselves from their nicotine dependence, the urge to smoke could be triggered by one of those cues. This abundance of cues, which partly reflects the wide social acceptance of smoking until recently, helps to explain the very high relapse rate for smokers. A single cigarette is often enough to reestablish the smoking habit in ex-smokers.

People report that, even after months or even years of not smoking, they will suddenly get the urge to smoke in a situation with some prior link to smoking. Such situations elicit memories of the pleasure of smoking (Wise, 1988). Thus, even in the absence of a biological need, the urge to smoke can be triggered.

The Cognitive Component

People who enter a smoking program are often asked to keep track of when they smoke, so that they can become aware of the cues that control their smoking. By their nature, habits are automatic; we don't need to make a conscious decision each time we smoke a cigarette. If people are forced to make a conscious decision each time they take a cigarette, however, perhaps they will gain control over the habit (Langer, 1989). In the process, people can then replace old behaviors with new behaviors. For example, if my habit is to have a cigarette each time I drink a cup of coffee, I might decide to instead have a piece of gum after each cup of coffee. Unfortunately, such substitution procedures often lead to new habits: I might learn to chew gum after drinking coffee. Indeed, I have a friend who successfully quit smoking but is now a habitual gum chewer. Eventually gum chewing should disappear because gum does not have the same reinforcing properties of nicotine (at least as far as we know).

It is important for people to learn to deal with the wide range of cues that elicit their behavior. Then, even if they relapse, they will have acquired an important set of skills related to a particular aspect of their addiction; those skills will eventually help them deal with their total addiction. In other words, relapse, which is so common in drug addiction (Niaura et al., 1988), can be regarded as part of a process of acquiring the skills that are necessary for eventual success; after each relapse, the individual is not starting from scratch, but is already farther along the path.

Many smokers who are also drinkers tend to relapse when drinking alcohol, probably because of alcohol's disinhibition effect. Eventual success, therefore, demands that they learn how to deal with this situation.

Summary

In small to moderate doses, nicotine typically acts as a stimulant; in larger doses, it can have a calming effect. Smoking often increases in stressful situations. Researchers have suggested that nicotine, like many other drugs, works by activating the dopaminergic system, the opioid system and the cholingeric system. Evidence also indicates that urinary acidity mediates the tendency to smoke. When urinary acidity levels go up, nicotine is excreted more rapidly from the body, so smoking increases. Stress leads to increases in urinary acidity levels, which could trigger the desire to smoke.

Smoking appears to be triggered by cues in the environment—usually to a diverse and extensive set of environmental cues. Teaching people to become aware of the cues that trigger their smoking habit and encouraging them to learn other ways of responding to these cues has been suggested as an important method of capitalizing on the power of cognition.

Alcohol

Without question, the drug that has received the most attention by researchers is alcohol. Alcohol is widely used and widely abused in our society and in many parts of the world. People often find it very difficult to quit drinking, and numerous programs have been developed to help people control their drinking or stop drinking altogether.

The Biological Component

In low doses, alcohol stimulates the central nervous system. In moderate doses, however, it depresses brain activity. This leads to a disinhibition effect, which will be discussed shortly. The heart rate rises with moderate doses, and the mechanical efficiency of the heart as a pump is reduced. In large doses, alcohol temporarily increases the level of blood glucose. Later, the blood glucose level falls, often to disastrously low levels. Alcohol tends to decrease the formation of glucose in the liver and accelerate the deposition of fat in the liver; this gives rise to cirrhosis. Large amounts of alcohol affect the cerebellum, which results in motor impairment (Lowinson, Ruiz, & Millman, 1997).

The euphoria produced by alcohol appears to be caused by the release of dopamine and opioids. Because alcohol suppresses activity of the cortex, its effects are experienced as somewhat different from heroin. As we will discuss shortly, suppression of the cortex reduces one's ability to make reasoned judgments, which can profoundly affect how people behave under these two drugs.

Expectations and the Effects of Alcohol

It appears that how people behave after drinking alcohol depends, in part, on their expectations about its effects. People given a placebo in place of alcohol often

Alcohol is readily available in our society and is often used in a social context. Whether or not people become addicted depends to a large degree on whether or not they use alcohol to avoid an aversive or negative state.

experience a wide range of volitional behaviors, which they are willing and able to control, and nonvolitional behaviors, which they are unwilling or unable to control (Kirsch, 1985). For example, sober people become more aggressive and sexually aroused when they believe that they have been drinking alcohol (Wilson, 1981). Alcoholics even lose control when misinformed that they have been drinking alcohol (Engle & Williams, 1972). This suggests that it is alcoholics' belief about what alcohol does rather than the alcohol itself that leads to loss of control. After reviewing studies on the role of expectancy, Hull and Bond (1986) concluded, "Expectancy increases the incidence of illicit social behaviors and has few effects on nonsocial acts. Such a pattern of behavior is consistent with the hypothesis that expectancy provides an attributional excuse to engage in desired but socially prohibited acts" (p. 358). Note in this context that alcohol has consistently been implicated in physical assault (Scott,

Schafer, & Greenfield, 1999). Consistent with the idea that the tendency to assault is not caused by alcohol but rather is an excuse for aggression comes from research that shows that intoxicated individuals provided with cues of self-awareness and socially appropriate behavior behave in a nonaggressive manner (Taylor, 1986).

A novel approach to getting people to cut down on their alcohol consumption involves challenging people's expectancies. Many people believe that alcohol facilitates such things as social interaction and their ability to perform on various tasks. When it is demonstrated to them that these beliefs are false, they often reduce drinking (Goldman, 1999).

Depression and Alcoholism

Researchers have repeatedly found a link between alcohol abuse and depression. Until recently, it was thought that people drink to reduce their depression. In other words, depression somehow leads to drinking. There is now good evidence that the reverse is true. Vaillant (1983) started tracking a group of 600 adolescents before any drinking problems had arisen. He concluded, among other things, that a difficult life was rarely a major reason for developing alcohol dependence. In a *Nova* segment broadcast on public television, Vaillant said, "I found to my surprise that alcoholics are depressed because they drink; they don't drink because they are depressed." This finding, of course, is consistent with the observation that alcohol leads to the depletion of dopamine and norepinephrine.

Alcohol and the Disinhibition Effect

Because one of the main functions of the cortex is to inhibit behavior (Eysenck, 1973), the depressant action of alcohol on the cortex (and the reticular activating system) produces a state of disinhibition. That is, behaviors that are normally inhibited are freely expressed under the influence of alcohol. Masserman and Yum (1946) first showed this phenomenon. Cats that showed no inclination to drink alcohol were trained to obtain food from a closed feeding box. Once this habit was well learned, the cats were given an air blast when they opened the box. This noxious stimulus disrupted the cats' normal feeding pattern and produced a number of emotional responses that Masserman and Yum labeled experimental neurosis. When the cats were given alcohol, they approached the food box and persisted despite the noxious air blast. Many of these cats came to prefer a milk-alcohol mixture to plain milk. Other work has confirmed that alcohol tends to reduce anxiety in the type of situation that Masserman and Yum created (Smart, 1965).

Masserman and Yum's situation is a classic approach/avoidance conflict, so Conger (1956) decided to determine whether alcohol was increasing the tendency to approach or decreasing the tendency to avoid. Conger first taught rats to eat at a particular location and then introduced shock at the feeding site. After measuring the rats' tendency to approach the food site under normal and alcoholic states, Conger concluded that alcohol reduced the avoidance gradient. His findings can be summarized in the form of a general model that includes approach and avoidance gradients (Figure 7-6). Not all research has confirmed

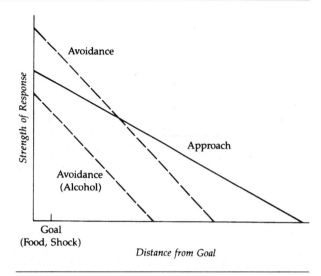

Figure 7-6. Approach and avoidance gradients for appetitive and aversive goal stimuli. Alcohol produces a general reduction in the tendency to avoid, while leaving the tendency to approach unaffected. (Based on J. J. Conger, "Reinforcement Theory and the Dynamics of Alcoholism." *Quarterly Journal of Studies on Alcohol,* 1956, *17,* 296–305.)

these findings (e.g., Weiss, 1958), but considerable evidence suggests that alcohol does reduce emotional reactivity in frustrating situations and leads to a greater persistence of goal-directed behavior in such situations (Barry, Wagner, & Miller, 1962).

Alcohol is frequently used in connection with sex. In small amounts, alcohol seems to facilitate sexual interest and performance, presumably because it reduces sexual inhibitions. In large amounts, alcohol lowers testosterone output in males, thereby interfering with sexual interest and performance (Farkas & Rosen, 1976).

The Learned Component

Situational Factors

Studies have shown that not only the tendency to use a drug but also the amount of a drug that we use and where we use it are governed by situational factors— that is, by our perceptions of the appropriateness or social desirability of a behavior in a specific situation.

Our tendency to develop a drinking problem can be predicted from the amount our companions drink and the extent to which our life revolves around drinking (Cahalan & Room, 1974).

Multiple Determinants of Alcohol Use

According to the principles of learning, any time a behavior occurs in the presence of a stimulus, the behavior will tend to come under the control of that stimulus. In other words, an association tends to develop between a stimulus and a behavior. In this way, a given behavior can become controlled by a wide variety of stimuli. A person who tends to drink alcohol when anxious, for example, will develop the habit of drinking alcohol at the onset of anxiety. Similarly, a person who tends to drink with dinner will develop a habit of drinking with dinner.

Alcoholism in France and Italy

France has a good climate for grapes and a thriving wine industry. It has been customary in many households to drink wine throughout the day—with breakfast, lunch, and dinner and between meals—either to quench thirst or to lubricate social occasions (Swinson & Eaves, 1978). Thus, the average French citizen has ample opportunity to experience the wide range of reinforcing effects that alcohol produces in various situations and, thus, to form multiple associations of alcohol intake with internal and external cues.

Italy also has a good climate for grapes and an extensive wine industry, but its rate of alcoholism is relatively low (Swinson & Eaves, 1978). The reason for this difference is that most Italians drink wine only with the evening meal and drunkenness is not condoned. Accordingly, for Italians, drinking is restricted to a particular time and a particular setting, and they tend to drink moderately (Swinson & Eaves, 1978). Thus, Italians have less opportunity than do the French to learn to associate alcohol with a wide variety of internal and external cues.

Family Environment

Symptoms of conduct disorder and antisocial personality disorder have been repeatedly linked to alcohol and drug abuse. These disorders appear to have their roots in certain families, so the question is whether it is caused by genetics or by the behavior of the family members. Research indicates that when the family members are themselves dysfunctional there is a greater tendency towards addiction (Taylor & Carey, 1998). These results suggest that treating an individual without treating the family could be difficult. As we will discuss in the next section, one's culture plays a significant role in drug use.

Cultural Factors

Stanton Peele (1984, 1985) has reviewed some of the data on the role of cultural factors in drug use. He points out that the Zuñi and Hopi Indians used alcohol in a ritualistic and regulated manner until the coming of the Spanish, after which they used it in a destructive and generally addictive manner. Peele further points out that the use of alcohol leads to antisocial aggressive behaviors in certain cultures (including Native American, Inuit, Scandinavian, Eastern European, and Anglo-American) but fails to do so in other cultures (including Greek, Italian, American Jewish, Chinese, and Japanese). These and other differences appear to relate to the beliefs people hold about what drugs do—not personal beliefs but cultural and societal beliefs.

Treating Alcoholism

There has been growing interest in using learning principles to treat addicts, especially alcoholics (Miller & Muñoz, 1976). The basic aim is to teach individuals to restrict their drinking to particular situations, and then to limit the amount they drink in those situations. If they associate with people who drink excessively, they are encouraged to find new friends; if they go to a place where alcohol is readily available, they are encouraged to seek out places where it is more restricted. In essence, the goal of such programs is to put drinking under external control, as it is difficult for alcoholics to learn internal control.

The Cognitive Component

Alcohol and Myopia

Expectation seems to play an important role in the effects people experience, but Steele and Josephs (1990) have argued that expectations alone do not explain the effects. They point out that, under the influence of alcohol, the same person can be aggressive and belligerent one night, amiable and generous another night, and morose and withdrawn a third night. If expectation alone were responsible, we would expect greater consistency.

Steele and Josephs argue that alcohol causes *myopia*. Myopia is characterized by short-sighted information processing, in which people ignore certain pieces of information that would normally inhibit their behavior. Instead of attending to all the relevant cues, they attend to only the most salient. Suppose we meet our boss at a cocktail party on the same day as a negative encounter with the boss. Still reeling from this encounter, we are very aware of our feelings of injustice and anger. Normally, we would decide not to chew out the boss because this could result in embarrassment, another unpleasant encounter, and even the loss of our jobs. In other words, normally we are able to deal with the complexity of the situation and act appropriately. Under alcohol, however, as Steele and Josephs argue, we are limited in our ability to deal with the complexity or the amount of information. As a result, we focus only on what is most salient—our feelings of anger. We do not consider the possible consequences.

What makes this theory so appealing is that it can explain why alcohol sometimes leads not only to increased aggression but also to a self-inflated ego (conceit). For most of us, the realization that we do not always measure up to our ideal teaches us modesty. Under the influence of alcohol, however, people often show an inflated ego; they brag about themselves. According to Steele and Josephs, when we drink, we are inclined to focus only on the more salient cues, one of which is our ideal self. In a study by Banaji and Steele (1989), subjects rated the importance of 35 traits pertaining to their real and ideal selves before and after they drank alcohol or a placebo. Since the differences between the real and the ideal self could be minimal or very large, Banaji and Steele distinguished between two groups: individuals with large differences that they viewed as important (individuals with high inhibition conflict), and individuals with small differences that they viewed as not important (individuals with low inhibition conflict). They found that alcohol had a

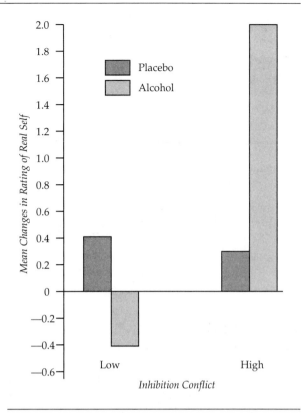

Figure 7-7. Changes in self-rating under the influence of alcohol for individuals characterized by low and high inhibition conflict. (From "Alcohol Myopia: Its Prized and Dangerous Effects," by C. M. Steele and R. A. Joseph, *American Psychologist,* 1990, *45,* 921–933 (Figure 3). Copyright © 1990 by the American Psychological Association. Reprinted with permission of the author.)

significant effect on self-ratings in the case of high inhibition conflict; specifically, it greatly increased the self-ratings (Figure 7-7). On the basis of these results, Banaji and Steele concluded that alcohol has a myopic effect that can result in a form of self-conceit. After drinking alcohol, the participants in this study ignored the relevant information about their limitations and saw only their strengths. In short, they lost the ability to temper or inhibit their positive self-image based on a realistic assessment of their weaknesses.

To summarize, according to Steele and Joseph's model, the pharmacological effects of alcohol restrict our attention to the most salient cues. Increase in alcohol consumption is associated with greater restriction of attention (greater myopia). What is salient is determined by cognitions linked to our current thinking, attention, and motivation. Whether there will be marked behavioral change is assumed to depend on the amount of conflict in our cognitions. The greater the conflict, the greater the tendency for people to see those qualities that are central to their thinking, attention, and motivation. People seem to be motivated to see themselves in the best possible light, so it is not surprising, for example, that they are inclined to see only their good qualities and ignore their limitations when intoxicated.

Beliefs About Control

People often have a great deal of information, correct and incorrect, about drug addiction. Much of this information comes from conversation, newspapers, and TV. You might have read, for example, that alcoholics lose control once they start drinking, or have a drink every day, or show a tendency to become aggressive when they drink, or find it impossible to quit, or drink progressively more as time goes on. These pieces of information then provide the basis for your belief system. There are two important things to note here. First, few people share precisely the same belief system. Second, two people could have similar drinking patterns, yet one might fit the criteria of addiction, whereas the other does not.

If belief controls behavior, then individuals who come to the conclusion that they are alcoholics will begin to behave in a manner consistent with that label: they will tend to lose control when they drink, find it virtually impossible to quit, and exhibit all the other behaviors that they associate with alcoholism. Individuals who do not label themselves as alcoholics, on the other hand, might drink just as much but manage not to lose control and find it less difficult to quit. Indeed, data suggest that those who do not perceive themselves as alcoholics (or who perceive themselves as having at least some control) respond much better to

rehabilitation programs that involve control of alcohol rather than total abstinence (e.g., Skinner, Glaser, & Annis, 1982). Conversely, individuals who perceive themselves as alcoholics (or as having no control) do not fare well in such programs but do benefit from programs that focus on abstinence (Miller, 1983). That makes sense; if you think you can't control your drinking, then the best solution is to not drink.

Alcoholics Anonymous (AA) is based on the principle that certain people can never learn to control their drinking and must recognize that fact if they are ever to live normal lives. AA members are required to openly identify themselves as alcoholics. This makes them admit to themselves that they have lost control and further reinforces the idea that they can never drink again. The message that they have lost control could be very damaging if AA members were to generalize it to other parts of their lives. However, the tendency to generalize is held in check by AA members' belief that alcoholism is a disease. Belief that it is a disease means, however, that you can never be cured. Scientific evidence for the disease theory of alcohol remains generally negative.

Finally, individuals who label themselves alcoholics run the risk of relapse. If alcoholics are unable to control their drinking, then individuals who accept an alcoholic identity will expect to lose control when they drink (Heather, Winton, & Rollnick, 1982; Peele, 1998). Controlled studies comparing cognitive theories to 12-step theories have found support for the idea that behavioral change is most likely to result from rational choices and goal-setting (Bell, Montoya, Richards, & Dayton, 1998). Abstinence programs have success rates of only 5 to 10% (Emrick & Hansen, 1983). One reason for this low figure is that many people tend to "fall off the wagon." This is not to say that 12-step programs are not useful or effective. Research shows they are effective but only if they are attended on a weekly basis (Fiorentine, 1999). When people fail to attend on a regular basis, they are more likely to take a drink and relapse.

Studies of therapeutic treatment programs show that the most important factor in determining success is readiness for treatment (DeLeon, Melnick, & Kressel, 1997). Further, researchers have found that to change people need to carefully plan how they are going to replace an old habit with a new one so that intention can be translated into action. When new habits are intentionally repeated they tend to become automatic. When this happens, people are freed from their past conditioning (Ouellette & Wood, 1998).

Taking Control by Cutting Down

Can people who are abusing alcohol (drinking too much) learn to cut down the amount they drink? Recent research (e.g., Miller & Muñoz, 1976; Sobell & Sobell, 1976), although it has come under vigorous attack, has found evidence that some people who have been classified as alcoholics—that is, uncontrolled drinkers—can learn to drink in moderation. In fact, Miller (1983) has reported that 23 of 24 studies on this question have found the reduced drinking technique superior to other treatment techniques for a range of alcohol abuse problems, and that no study has shown that abstinence is more effective overall than moderation. We still do not know what determines whether a person can return to a pattern of moderate drinking. Values, beliefs about control, and stress are just some of the factors that need to be explored further in this context.

Researchers have suggested that perhaps not everybody can learn to control their drinking. In a 10-year follow-up of the subjects treated by Sobell and Sobell (1976), a group of researchers found that, of the 20 subjects treated, only one was drinking without problems, eight were drinking excessively, six were abstinent, four were dead for reasons related to alcohol consumption, and one could not be located (Pendery, Maltzman, & West, 1982). Faced with criticism that they were promoting a life-threatening procedure, the Sobells pointed out that the follow-up did not include the initial control group. When the Sobells did that follow-up, they found that the mortality rate for the control group was 30%, as against 20% for the controlled drinking subjects. The long and the short of this is that, although controlled drinking does not work for some, there is no evidence that people are worse off for having tried the procedure. One reason for the low success rate in the Sobells' study might be that they were attempting to treat people who had been abusing alcohol for some time. Studies in which people have been treated earlier in their pattern of abuse consistently find higher rates of success.

Beliefs About Self-Change

There are numerous accounts of people who, after drinking heavily for years, have suddenly altered their drinking patterns. A father who one day notices that his son is modeling his drinking suddenly stops drinking; a mother who realizes that she is slurring her speech at the dinner table abruptly stops having her usual three or four cocktails before dinner. Peele (1983) has noted that people frequently alter their drinking pattern when it begins to interfere with things they value. Although some individuals might indeed be unable to control their drinking, many can. Vaillant (1983) presented evidence that alcohol problems regularly reverse themselves without medical intervention. In other words, it is incorrect to speak of an inevitable progression affecting all alcoholics and drug users.

See Practical Application 7-2 for a discussion of how people quit additions.

Summary

Alcohol is a stimulant in small to moderate amounts. The euphoric effect might be caused by its ability to stimulate the dopaminergic system and the endorphin system. Researchers believe that alcohol creates depression rather than being the result of depression; this is consistent with the idea that alcohol stimulates the release and eventual depletion of dopamine and the endorphins, which seem to be the source of positive feelings. The disinhibition effect of moderate to high levels of alcohol consumption is well known. In an approach avoidance conflict, this effect is associated with a reduced tendency to avoid; the tendency to approach is not affected.

According to the learning model, if a drug is used in the presence of many different stimuli, all those stimuli will come to control that behavior, as a comparison of the addiction rates for the French and Italians illustrates.

Cognitive factors play an important role in alcohol use and abuse. Expectations about the effects of a drug seem to play a large part in determining how individuals respond. According to Steele and Josephs, however, expectation alone cannot account for many of the effects observed with alcohol. They argue in their interaction model that the pharmacological effects of alcohol produce restricted attention, in which people under the influence of alcohol attend to only the most salient cues. As a result, people react to a situation without considering certain important pieces of information;

they demonstrate what Steele and Josephs call a myopic approach to the world. Situational factors—for instance, whether a behavior is perceived to be appropriate—also largely determine how people behave when they use drugs. Differences in cultural beliefs regarding the effects of drugs and appropriate behaviors are reflected in differences in the effects of drugs. The disease model of alcoholism links loss of control directly to the disease of alcoholism, not to cognitive variables.

Practical Application 7-2

How People Quit Addictions

Data from people who quit addictions indicate that most people do it on their own. The success rate from formal treatment programs tends to be very poor. Survey data about smoking, for example, indicates that millions of people quit smoking and most of these (as many as 95%) do so on their own (Cohen et al., 1989). In fact, 30% of adult Americans are now ex-smokers (Peele, 1989). Abstinence rates from formal treatment programs tend to cluster around 20% (Cohen et al., 1989). The same patterns have been found for alcohol. Peele (1998) notes that most alcohol abusers overcame their alcohol problem by either cutting back or quitting altogether. Very few of those who licked their drinking problem sought formal treatment. Of those who chose to abstain, 60% had no contact with AA. Those who simply cut back did not contact AA, an organization based on the concept that the only way to deal with alcohol abuse is through abstinence. Abstinence programs have success rates of only 5% to 10% (Emrick & Hansen, 1983). Even when it comes to losing weight, doing it on your own is more likely to work than if you join a formal program. Schachter and Rodin (1974) found in a study of two different populations that 62% of those who had tried to lose weight had succeeded. They had succeeded in losing weight (the average weight loss was 34.7 pounds), and they had kept it off (11.2 years). The data for heroin and cocaine again suggest that quitting on your own works best (Peele, 1989).

Granfield and Cloud (1996) put it very well when they point out that the success rate of self-regulators is "the elephant that no one sees."

How do people do it? They seem to do it by designing their own programs. But before you can design your own program, you need to believe that you can quit and you need to have a reason to quit. After that, it is often a trial-and-error procedure that eventually results in success. Researchers have described it as a dynamic process, rather than a discrete event (Cohen et al., 1989).

1. **Readiness to change.** People often quit drugs because of such things as the threat of divorce, the possibility of losing their jobs, or court proceedings. Quitting under these conditions is often temporary, motivated only by the possibility of some immediate negative consequence. Research has shown the most people change only when they have internalized the need for change, called *readiness to change*. Readiness to change is more than just the intention to change, it involves opening oneself up to help. It is important to recognize that giving up drugs is difficult and that a number of programs have been developed that can help people by teaching them to develop new habits (DiClemente, 1999).

2. **Belief that one can quit.** Believing you can quit on your own is one of the most important factors. If you believe that you can only quit through a formal program, you give responsibility to an external agent. Should you fail, it is the program's fault and not yours. The formal programs

Factors influencing drug use include commitment to other activities, social class, peer and parental influences, culture and ethnicity, a respect for the value of moderation, the need to achieve, the fear of failure, and the degree of alienation from society.

It appears that the best way to give up an addiction is to do it on your own. At least six factors have been linked to self-quitting: believing that it is possible to quit, developing feelings of self-efficacy, learning how to interpret failure, valuing health, developing interest in new activities, and maturing out.

Main Points

1. Because drug addiction is usually preceded by drug abuse, the current strategy for studying addiction is to identify the factors that lead to drug abuse.

that work best seem to be those that convince the individual they can succeed, and then put the responsibility on the individual (Bandura, 1999; DiClemente, 1999).

3. **Developing self-efficacy.** When people take responsibility for designing their own programs and succeed, their self-efficacy improves. Even small successes can improve feelings of self-efficacy. If someone tells you what to do and you succeed, you cannot take responsibility and, as a result, your self-efficacy will not improve. When people's self-efficacy improves, it reinforces their initial belief that they can quit. Perceived self-efficacy exerts its effect on all phases of drug addiction—making the decision to change, designing a way to change, and overcoming relapse (Bandura, 1999).

4. **Learning how to interpret failure.** Because it is common for people to relapse, we might expect that self-efficacy would be undermined following failure. Whether or not it is undermined depends on how people interpret failure. If they interpret failure as a flaw in the design they have created, and not in themselves or their ability to quit, they learn how to focus on the design and improve it. For example, if they find they are inclined to drink too much, they might set a limit beforehand and then resolve to quit when they reach that self-imposed limit. Some people learn to drink one beer and then fill the bottle with water and drink that before having a second beer. When you begin to ask people how they have learned to succeed, you get literally hundreds of different answers. Different

things work for different people. Each person needs to find out what works for him or her. It is important to note that the number of previous unsuccessful attempts is unrelated to future success in quitting (Cohen et al., 1989).

5. **Changing existing self-views**. Negative self-views often characterize drug users; however, changing negative self-views is very difficult. People often work to maintain self-views, even when they are incorrect. People maintain self-views by selectively rejecting information that is consistent with a positive self-view and confirming information that is inconsistent, even if the information is correct. Several different approaches have been suggested for helping people to create a more positive self-view that would enable them to better deal with giving up drug use. These techniques range from writing scripts about what one might become to logically confronting negative self-views (Linehan, 1997).

6. **Valuing health.** When people value health, they are less inclined to use drugs such as alcohol and nicotine because of the negative health implications. As people get older they often realize that if they are going to live a long productive life, they need to take care of their health. There are many examples of people who drank heavily or used drugs in their younger years, then suddenly cut down or quit altogether (Peele, 1989, 1998).

(continued on next page)

2. Dependency refers to the need to take drugs to maintain normal feelings of well-being.

3. Tolerance refers to the fact that people need to take increasing amounts of a drug to achieve the same feelings of well-being.

4. Activation of the dopaminergic system appears to be the motivation behind most, if not all, drug use.

5. The discovery of opiate receptors in the brain has led researchers to suggest that the use of opiates is a means of tapping into certain naturally occurring reward and survival mechanisms.

6. Considerable evidence points to the idea that humans, as well as animals, only become addicted to drugs such as heroin if basic psychological and social needs are not being met.

7. Researchers have argued that social acceptability often plays an important role in the addiction process, especially to such drugs as heroin.

8. Beliefs about control play an important role in one's ability to recover from an addiction such as heroin.

9. Amphetamines do not produce tolerance or withdrawal, but they can become habit-forming.

10. Research indicates that the hallucinations produced by LSD work via the serotonin-containing neurons in the raphe nuclei.

11. Adolescents who have experimented with marijuana but who have not become users tend to be well-adjusted.

12. In low doses, alcohol stimulates the central nervous system. In moderate doses, it depresses activity of the brain by direct action on the brain. This leads to a disinhibition effect.

13. The link between alcohol and depression can be explained by the tendency of alcohol to produce depression through the depletion of dopamine and norepinephrine stores.

14. The different rates of alcohol addiction in France and Italy illustrate the idea that drinking can be conditioned to a wide range of stimuli.

15. That people's reactions to drugs vary with the situation and with the drug taker's culture raises serious questions about the disease model of addiction.

Practical Application 7-2 (continued)

7. **Developing interests in new activities or coming to value activities.** When people value their work, their family, and the various activities they do, they often refrain from drinking or taking drugs to better appreciate those things. It is common to hear people say that they have had enough to drink or they are not going to take drugs tonight because tomorrow they want to get up early to engage in a cherished activity. It is when people have no other reason for living they fill their lives with drugs. One reason for the high addiction rate in the slums is that many of these people do not have positive things on which they can focus their attention. One primary reason athletes abstain from drugs is that virtually all drugs interfere with high-level athletic performance. Only those athletes who do not value doing their very best will typically fall prey to drugs. When people's

lives are filled with activities they cherish, they have little reason for taking drugs (Cox & Klinger, 1988; Peele, 1998).

8. **Maturing out.** As a general rule, people tend to cut down or quit using drugs altogether as they get older (Peele, 1989). This reduction in drug use or quitting has been explained in many ways, ranging from the loss of reinforcing powers that drugs have on people as they get older (a biological explanation) to conscious control that results from such things as health concerns (a more cognitive explanation). Whatever the explanation, the idea that the longer you use drugs the more likely it is that you will become addicted is not the general rule. Quite the contrary, the general rule is that people seem to give up drugs after years of use. Quitting, in other words, is very natural.

16. Beliefs about control and ability to change play an important role in determining whether a person becomes addicted.

17. Factors influencing drug use include commitment to other activities, social class, peer and parental influences, culture and ethnicity, attitudes toward moderation, degree of achievement motivation and fear of failure, and commitment to the values of society.

18. There is considerable evidence that when people quit on their own they are more likely to succeed.

 InfoTrac® College Edition

There has been a great deal of concern about the large numbers of people in our society using drugs (especially adolescents). What appears to be the reason for the wide use of drugs in our society? (Search words: drug abuse, motivation for drug abuse, adolescence and drug abuse, environment and drug abuse)

How effective are drug treatment programs? (Search words: drug abuse, drug abuse resistance education, drug prevention)

Chapter Eight

Aggression, Coercive Action, and Anger

■ *Are there different kinds of aggression?*

■ *Is aggression in our genes?*

■ *How do our bodies respond when we become angry?*

■ *Does testosterone make males aggressive? What about females?*

■ *To what degree is aggression learned?*

■ *Can we learn to control our aggression?*

■ *Does viewing aggression on television and in movies lead to aggressive behavior?*

■ *What is coercive action?*

■ *Can people learn to control their anger?*

■ *Does anger have implications for our health?*

Human aggression did not emerge as a specific adaptation to deal with a specific problem but rather emerged an adaptation to deal with a number of different problems pertaining to human survival (Buss, 1999). Some time ago Moyer (1976) identified at least eight different kinds of aggression in animals, all of which can be found, in one form or another, in human behavior. Moyer has argued that these types of aggression are distinct, although there is some overlap. Among other things, each type involves somewhat different brain structures. Here are Moyer's eight kinds of aggression.

Kinds of Aggression

1. **Predatory aggression:** Attack behavior that an animal directs against its natural prey. Many of our human ancestors hunted to feed themselves. More recently, we have domesticated a variety of animals to feed us. Nonetheless, even today, many recreational hunters like to track and kill animals, including deer, elk, moose, bear, pheasants, ducks, and geese. Others fish for food or sport.
2. **Intermale aggression:** Threat, attack, or submissive behavior by a male in response to a strange male. In the United States, 87% of those arrested for murder and aggravated assault were males (Tedeschi & Felson, 1994).
3. **Fear-induced aggression:** Aggressive behavior that occurs when an animal is confined. Attack behavior is usually preceded by an attempt to escape. Like animals, humans do not like to be confined. To prevent attempts at escape, convicted criminals and prisoners of war are typically held within highly fortified structures and guarded at all times. Attacks on guards sometimes occur, despite the threat of reprisals. We seem to be biologically programmed to resist any type of confinement. Infants who are physically restrained (by holding their wrists) show anger (Stenberg & Campos, 1990). At three months, they show signs of distress; at four months, they look angrily at the hand holding the wrist; and, at seven months, they look angrily at the face of the person holding the wrist.
4. **Territorial aggression:** Threat or attack behavior when an intruder is discovered on home-range territory or submissive and retreat behavior when an animal is confronted while intruding. Homes, offices, yards, and private land are all territories that humans tend to protect. The most valued and protected territory is our homes. Any uninvited intrusion by friends or strangers into our homes is viewed as very serious. Our laws recognize our right to protect our territory: An owner who shoots and kills an intruder is unlikely to be charged.

   Businesspeople often prefer to make deals on their own territory—at their office—because they feel at an advantage there. Negotiations between hostile parties are typically conducted on neutral territory. When U.S. President Reagan and Soviet Premier Gorbachev decided to have discussions during the Cold War, they flew to Iceland, a country regarded as neutral by both parties.
5. **Maternal aggression:** Attack or threat directed by the female toward an intruder when her young are present. Human mothers are known for their tendency to protect their offspring. Should someone attempt to harm her children in any way, the mother will do whatever is in her power to protect them.
6. **Irritable aggression:** Attack or destructive behavior directed toward any object as the result of frustration, pain, deprivation, or any other stressor. For humans, frustrations only lead to aggression when they are large and unexpected. We have learned to expect certain frustrations, such as having to wait in line or to sit in a traffic jam. Should your new $30,000 car break down on the way home from the dealer, however, you will probably become angry and even aggressive. Pain and deprivation are highly compelling motivational states. Berkowitz (1993) has argued that when negative feelings are evoked, they often lead to aggression and even rage in humans. Aggression is typically not an appropriate response to such events, so humans often need to learn more adaptive reactions.
7. **Sex-related aggression:** Aggressive behavior elicited by the same stimuli that elicit sexual behavior. A person who sexually excites us can also make us feel jealous and aggressive if, for example, we see that person flirting with someone else. Evolutionary psychologists argue that jealousy is linked to our desire to preserve our genes in future generations (Buss, 1994). When a person whom we regard

as a potential sexual partner shows interest in a third party, the potential for us to reproduce with that person is threatened. The survival of our genes is a primary motive, so we are alert to cues that inspire jealousy. Verbal and even physical aggression can accompany such feelings.

8. **Instrumental aggression:** Aggressive behavior that has previously resulted in some kind of reward. Much of human aggression is instrumental aggression. We will look at how humans use coercive action to help them achieve their goals when we discuss the cognitive component of aggression. As we'll see, aggression is very common in everyday human behavior.

It is beyond the scope of this chapter to deal in detail with all these forms of aggression. Instead, we will focus on a few areas of research. Historical evidence indicates that humans have an enormous capacity for violence. Despite incidents of genocide and mass warfare, however, we often live in remarkable harmony because of our capacity to inhibit our aggression. Our natural tendency to act aggressively in a wide variety of situations can be socialized and, given the right set of conditions, we can live in peace with one another.

The Traditional Definition of Aggression

Traditionally, psychologists have defined aggression as behavior against another person with the intention of committing harm (Geen, 1990). Note that this definition refers to socially unacceptable behavior. In our everyday speech, aggression is used more broadly to refer to socially unacceptable behavior and to certain forms of socially acceptable behavior. A person who works long and hard to win a business contract, a person who competes with others to become the executive of a large company, or an athlete who manages to become the top scorer on the team is often viewed in our society as aggressive in an acceptable and desirable way. By contrast, drivers who honk their horns at slower cars or individuals who challenge others to a fight to settle an argument are typically regarded as aggressive in a socially unacceptable or undesirable way.

In addition, aggression is not defined by harm but by the coming together of intention and harm. Unintentional harm can occur in a variety of situations. A driver might accidentally hit another car, a clerk might inadvertently short-change a customer, or a professor might err in grading a student's essay. That these acts were unintentional means that they were not acts of aggression. In contrast, drivers who honk their horns at slower cars intend to goad another person to precipitate action, which could conceivably have fatal consequences.

Research on Aggression

Early Laboratory Research

The initial focus of laboratory research was to test the idea that aggression arises from an intent to harm. The main question was how to operationalize harm: Was it sufficient to simply observe a negative verbal exchange, or was it necessary to actually show that subjects will inflict physical harm on another person? In the end, many researchers felt that, to be sure that subjects were motivated by the intent to harm, it was necessary to show that they would in fact inflict physical harm. To this end, researchers decided to operationalize intent to harm by whether participants would deliver a painful shock to another person (Baron, 1977).

These studies demonstrated that indeed individuals will deliver a painful shock to others. In most of the studies, the task was disguised. Individuals were told, for example, that they were part of a scientific study to determine whether giving people electrical shocks when they made mistakes would help them to learn. In these studies it was found that participants would deliver shocks even when they thought the shocks would be extremely painful (Milgram, 1963, 1974).

In a number of studies, participants were provoked by means of a negative evaluation (an unearned F for an essay they were asked to write) or insulted by the research assistant in the course of the experiment. They were then allowed to retaliate by delivering one or more shocks (often up to ten) to the research assistant who had been the source of the poor evaluation or the insult. Participants were typically told that delivering shocks was a way of evaluating the performance of the research assistant. Participants were not only will-

Scenes from Stanley Milgram's study of obedience to authority: the "shock genera-tor" (top left), the "learner" being strapped to his chair (top right), a subject being told to administer a severe shock (bottom left), and the subject refusing to continue (bottom right). Despite some objections, most subjects obeyed the experimenter.

ing to deliver shocks to the research assistant but were also inclined to deliver more shocks to those research assistants who had been more severe in their evalua-tion or who had been more insulting (Baron, 1977). One of the main conclusions of these studies is that in-dividuals usually need to be provoked in some way before they will retaliate.

Other studies found that, if they have been physi-cally harmed—by a series of unprovoked shocks, for example—individuals normally retaliate in kind; that is, a recipient given a certain number of shocks is likely to return the same number (e.g., Borden, Bowen, & Taylor, 1971; Dengerink & Bertilson, 1974; Dengerink & Myers, 1977; Taylor, 1967). Evidence also indicates that when subjects believe that they will not experience fu-

ture retaliation (perhaps because they are anonymous in the study), they tend to inflict more shocks than they received (Zimbardo, 1969, 1972).

On certain occasions, people are inclined to engage in massive retaliation. Patterson (1976) has observed that, within the family setting, one family member will often use aggressive behavior to stop the attacks of an-other. He has further observed that, when one family member suddenly increases the intensity of the ag-gressive exchange, the other is likely to terminate his or her attack; that is, whereas gradual escalation of the at-tack might increase an aggressive exchange, a sharp in-crease (massive retaliation) might decrease or end it. Evidence from other sources is consistent with this ob-servation. For example, when the threat of retaliation for aggressive behavior is high, the tendency to initiate an attack is reduced (Baron, 1973; Dengerink & Levendusky, 1972; Shortell, Epstein, & Taylor, 1990). There is one important exception. When the person is very angry, the threat of retaliation—even severe retaliation—does not reduce the tendency to initiate an attack (Baron, 1973).

Aggression in the Real World

These studies have been criticized on the basis that participants knew they were in a laboratory as opposed to the real world. Even then, the studies had to be disguised. In many instances, the participants were told that the immediate pain that they inflicted would have long-term benefits for humankind. Another criticism was that, when provoked, participants were normally only allowed to use physical aggression. In the real world, we often have other alternatives at our disposal. As a result, researchers questioned the high rate of physical aggression observed in the laboratory. The current focus is to examine aggression in the real world. Such studies don't always provide the level of control necessary to establish cause and effect, but they are essential if we are to understand the aggression that occurs on a daily basis.

New Concepts Regarding Aggression

In preparing this chapter, I was faced with the task of how broadly or how narrowly I should approach the topic of aggression and whether or not I should start with a clear definition or a general discussion of how psychologists have traditionally thought about aggression. In the end I decided it was necessary to provide the context that leads psychologists to conceptualize aggression in fairly narrow terms but with broad implications for understanding exactly why humans often behave aggressively. As we will discuss, the discovery that people have a strong need to control leads psychologists to reconceptualize what motivates aggression.

Although the laboratory studies provided a wealth of empirical data concerning the conditions under which individuals will and will not engage in physical acts of aggression, they largely failed to ad-

dress the question of motivation. Obviously, the intent to harm must come from something more basic than a need to retaliate. It must come, researchers have argued, from our need to survive and adapt.

The Need to Control

Various researchers have suggested that the underlying motivation for acts of aggression is the human need for control. The need to exert control over events or people seems to be a fundamental human characteristic (Rotter, 1972). Many religious wars have been justified on the basis that, if people can be forced to behave in certain ways and to hold certain beliefs and attitudes, it will be a better world for all of us.

Hans Toch (1969, 1993) pointed out that violent criminals often lack the basic social skills necessary to control people and events in the environment and tend to use force as a means of compensating for this deficiency. Young children often use physical violence but eventually develop more socially acceptable methods of control (Patterson, 1976). If individuals fail to develop such skills, physical aggression is the only method of control available to them. Toch believes that teaching physically aggressive criminals appropriate social skills for controlling events in the environment would reduce their tendency to initiate physical attacks on others.

One of the most influential theories of crime is based on the premise that people who commit crimes have low self-control (Gottfredson & Hirschi, 1990). This theory can explain why people commit crimes and why people engage in a wide variety of antisocial and aggressive behaviors (Brannigan, 1997).

A Working Definition of Aggression

If we start from the proposition that aggression grows out of a need to control others, and we assume that people differ in the strength of this need, we can define aggression as the willingness to engage in physical and psychological acts of harm to control the actions of other people. This definition retains all the essential features of the traditional definition but extends it in three important ways. First, it incorporates the idea that aggression involves psychological as well as physical harm. Even though the traditional definition of aggression does not exclude the idea of psychological harm, experiments that developed from this definition typically operationalized aggression as physical harm. Second, the definition specifies that the motivation underlying aggression is to gain control over the behavior of other people. Third, this definition defines aggression as a disposition. If aggression is a disposition, learning and cognitive factors must play an important role in its expression. As we'll see, the tendency to act aggressively is frequently inhibited.

Note that this definition fails to explain unprovoked aggression, random acts of violence, and vandalism. It can be argued that such behaviors have their roots in anger, as we'll see when we look at Berkowitz's concept of generalized anger and rage.

Anger and Aggression

According to our working definition, aggression is an instrumental behavior that develops from an underlying need to control. This should not be confused with anger, which is typically conceptualized as an emotion. As an emotion, anger can and often does interact with instrumental aggression. Among other things, anger lowers the threshold for instrumental aggression. Although there is a strong positive correlation between anger and aggression, people often feel angry without becoming aggressive and often become aggressive without feeling angry. For example, people may feel anger when they become sick, when they are frustrated in their attempts to achieve a goal, or when a relationship fails, but they do not strike out at someone else. Similarly, without feeling angry, people will act aggressively to achieve a desired goal—for instance, to win a sporting competition, to gain advantage in a political contest, or to exercise power. In the Milgram (1963) study, the participants who administered high levels of shock did so without experiencing anger.

Thus, we can distinguish instrumental aggression, which is goal-directed and not associated with anger, from angry or affective aggression.

Summary

Moyer has identified eight kinds of aggression in animals; most of these can be found in humans. In psychology, aggression has traditionally been defined as

behavior intended to harm another person. It does not apply to accidental harm, out of negligence or in the normal course of competitive behavior (for example, in an athletic contest).

The initial focus of laboratory research was to verify that aggression arises from an intent to harm. In experiments, whose purpose was often disguised, it was repeatedly demonstrated that people will deliver a painful shock to another human being. Studies of retaliation suggest that people are normally inclined to retaliate in kind but will increase the level of retaliation if they perceive that they are protected against any future consequences such as when they are anonymous. Massive retaliation is often a message to the opponent to cease the aggressive exchange.

According to our working definition, aggression is the willingness to engage in physical and psychological acts of harm to control the actions of other people. This definition incorporates the essential features of the traditional definition and specifies the underlying motivation for aggressive behavior.

Although there is a strong positive correlation between anger and aggression, people often feel angry without becoming aggressive and often become aggressive without feeling angry. Accordingly, it is useful to distinguish between instrumental aggression, which does not involve anger, and affective aggression, which is characterized by anger.

Measuring Human Aggression

Casual observation of human behavior suggests that humans differ in their tendency to act aggressively. To determine whether some individuals tend to engage in more acts of aggression or have greater feelings of anger and hostility, researchers have constructed and validated self-report inventories. The frequently used Hostility Inventory developed by Buss and Durkee (1957) has been shown to predict a wide range of aggressive behaviors. More recently, Buss and Perry (1992) constructed a new inventory. Factor analysis of the items in this inventory has identified four factors or components: physical aggression, verbal aggression, anger, and hostility. Physical aggression and verbal aggression, which involve hurting other people, represent the instrumental component. Anger, which involves physiological arousal, represents the emotional or affective component. Hostility, which involves feelings of ill will and injustice, represents the cognitive component of aggression (Buss & Perry, 1992).

Now let's examine the biological, learned, and cognitive aspects of aggression.

The Biological Component of Aggression

Genetic Processes

Several studies have compared monozygotic and dizygotic twins based on self-reported inventories of aggression. Although some have found a genetic factor for aggression, others have not (Tedeschi & Felson, 1994). One study of 573 twin pairs, found a correlation of 0.40 for monozygotic twins and no correlation for dizygotic twins, results that indicate a strong genetic effect (Rushton, Fulker, Neale, Nias, & Eysenck, 1986).

A meta-analysis of data from 24 studies that used various personality measures of aggression found that genetics can account for as much as 50% of the variance (Miles & Carey, 1997). The data review suggests that the expression of aggression in children is more closely linked to the environment but that in later years the expression of aggression is more closely linked to genetics. In other words, when the early environmental constraints are removed, genetics asserts itself.

Studies have also shown that the temperamental trait of impulsivity is related to aggressive and antisocial behavior (Coccaro, Bergeman, & McClearn, 1993; Karli, 1991). Serotonin levels in the brain may mediate this tendency. Increased serotonin has been shown to produce response inhibition, whereas decreased serotonin has been shown to produce hyperactivity in associated brain structures. Researchers have been particularly interested in linking temperament to aggression as a step toward tracking the developmental progression that leads to full-blown delinquent or criminal behavior. Remember that an individual with a temperamental disposition to act aggressively will not necessarily become a delinquent or a criminal. Perhaps the reason for the link between impulsivity and aggression is that we appear to inhibit the majority of our aggressive impulses. Impulsive people, who are unable to do

so, would, therefore, be more inclined to act aggressively. We will return to the whole question of impulsivity, self-control, and crime later in this chapter.

Hormones and Aggression

Hormones and Male Aggression

One of the main hormones linked to aggression is testosterone. Two research designs have been used to determine whether testosterone causes aggression: In one, testosterone levels are increased, and aggression is monitored; in the other, testosterone levels are decreased, and aggression is monitored.

Because it would be unethical to administer testosterone for experimental purposes, researchers have tried to identify individuals who self-administer drugs —such as steroids—that lead to increases in testosterone levels. A comparison of weight lifters who use steroids with nonsteroid users on the basis of the Buss-Durkee Hostility Inventory found that steroid users had higher levels of hostility (Yates, Perry, & Murray, 1992). This study doesn't rule out the possibility that being aggressive caused the steroid use. Note, however, that animal studies involving random assignment have shown that steroids increase aggressive behavior (Haug, Brain, & Kamis, 1985).

Studies on the effects of castration provide further evidence that testosterone plays an important role in aggression. Follow-up studies of castrated sex offenders have indicated that castration not only reduces the sex drive but also reduces hostility and aggressive tendencies (Bremer, 1959; Hawke, 1950; Sturup, 1960). Injections of testosterone in castrated males have been shown to restore the previous aggressive tendencies (Hawke, 1950). Therefore, the reduction of aggression was probably caused by a decrease in testosterone level and was not simply a by-product of the trauma of castration or the accompanying therapy. Testosterone antagonists have also been used to treat sexual offenders. The findings are generally consistent with the idea that decreases in testosterone result in decreased aggression (e.g., Money, 1980; Sturup, 1968).

After examining all the research on the relationship of testosterone and aggression, Sapolsky (1997) concluded that testosterone does not cause aggression but is important for its expression. What the data show is that if you suppress testosterone, aggressive behaviors are reduced but not eliminated, and if you pump up testosterone, aggressive behaviors are increased or exaggerated. Thus, aggression must be triggered by something else. It takes more than testosterone to explain why people pull the trigger of a gun (Sapolsky, 1997).

In a recent study, testosterone levels were linked to social success rather than physical aggression. Specifically, researchers found that testosterone increased when boys were socially challenged and decreased when they lost status (Schaal, Tremblay, Soussignan, & Susman, 1996). These findings are consistent with the idea that testosterone does not cause aggression per se but rather serves as a chemical backup system that provides the motivation for maintaining such things as status and dominance (Buss, 1999).

Hormones and Female Aggression

Attempts to link female aggression to high levels of testosterone or estradiol have generally been inconclusive (Gladue, 1991) so many researchers have looked for animal models to better understand the role of hormones in female aggression.

Androstenedione and Aggression in the Female Hyena

Female spotted hyenas not only look and act like males, but they force their dominance over males through their size and aggression. Researchers have found, for example, that a single female will dominate the dominance hierarchy (the so-called pecking order). Studies have shown that levels of testosterone and related androgens are higher in this dominant female than in the average male and six times higher than in the average female (Hopson, 1987).

What has particularly intrigued scientists about the female spotted hyena is the enlarged clitoris, which looks strikingly like the male penis. It turns out that this large clitoris is linked to a prehormone called androstenedione, which is produced in the gonads and adrenal glands of all mammals. Androstenedione is the last chemical in the chain of chemical reactions before it splits into the production of either male hormones or female hormones. As a result, this chemical might have the capacity to determine gender. It has been shown, for example, to induce bisexuality in male rats. When male rats were castrated, to remove their normal source of testosterone, and then injected with an-

drostenedione, they displayed both female posturing and male mounting. When pregnant female rats were injected with androstenedione their offspring, whether genetically female, were born with a phallus and exhibited male-type sexual activity.

Researchers have suggested that the pattern of aggressive behavior evolved to give the female hyena and her offspring an evolutionary advantage. They suggest that masculinized genitals could have been an accidental by-product of this evolutionary process (Hopson, 1987).

Studies with humans have found that higher levels of androstenedione in both male and female adolescents is related to a variety of problem behaviors, including lying, disobedience, tendency to explode, talking back to parents and teachers (in boys), and taking an angry and dominating attitude toward parents (in girls) (Hopson, 1987).

How important is it for us to understand the role of hormones? Researchers have estimated that 20 to 25% of aggression could be due to endocrine factors (Gladue, 1991). Although this is a significant proportion, we obviously need to look also at the role of learned and cognitive factors.

Sex Differences in Males and Females

In view of the positive correlation between testosterone and male aggression, it might be concluded that males are more aggressive than females. Although crime statistics clearly show that males commit most crimes, research studies find little difference between male and female aggression.

After reviewing studies using different measures of aggression, researchers concluded that although males, on the average, are more aggressive than females, the difference is quite small (Eagly & Steffen, 1986). In a meta-analysis of 143 studies, Hyde (1986) found that the difference between males and females was about one-half of a standard deviation ($d = 0.50$). This means that 63% of the males were above average in aggression and 38% of the females were above average. Hyde's meta-analysis indicated that gender accounted for only 5% of the difference. A recent comparison of males and females using the Aggression Questionnaire found that men scored slightly higher on verbal aggression and hostility, much higher on physical aggression, and were equal on anger (Buss & Perry, 1992).

A fundamental problem when using averages to determine whether males or females are more aggressive is that a preponderance of one type of measure of aggression—physical or psychological, for example— can skew the data. In the studies reviewed by Eagly and Steffen (1986), a preponderance used the teacher-learner paradigm, which is more likely to elicit aggression in men than in women and tends to elicit greater aggression toward men than women. Eagly and Steffen point out that the magnitude of the difference between males and females is related to their tendency to use physical harm. Women, it has been speculated, are more cautious than males are about using any form of physical aggression because they are more aware of the consequences. Further, women appear to experience more guilt and anxiety in connection with the decision to retaliate. Finally, considerable evidence indicates that females might be more motivated to turn off or deescalate aggression, especially in aggressive exchanges with males.

Some Additional Differences

1. Females find aggressive acts more reprehensible than do males (Harris & Knight-Bohnhoff, 1996).
2. Even when they do the same thing, aggression of males is considered worse than aggression from females (Harris & Knight-Bohnhoff, 1996).
3. Aggression toward females is worse than aggression toward males (Harris & Knight-Bohnhoff, 1996).
4. Irrespective of sex, older and educated people find aggression more reprehensible (Harris & Knight-Bohnhoff, 1996).
5. Males who endorse the masculine stereotype (as measured by Bem's Sex Role Inventory) are more openly aggressive (Weisbuch, Beal, & O'Neal, 1999).
6. Aggressive sexual behavior exhibited by some males has been linked to misplaced aggression toward their mothers (McCollaum & Lester, 1997).

Neuromechanisms

Gray (1991) has identified three neurobiological structures that are involved in aggression—two that are involved in the instigation of aggression and one that is involved in the inhibition of aggression.

1. **The Fight-Flight System (FFS).** This system is activated when we experience pain and frustration. Such events stimulate the amygdala, hypothalamus, and midbrain; with the brain stem, these produce defensive behavior. We are going to talk in more detail about this system in the chapter on stress and health.
2. **The Behavioral Activation System (BAS).** This system is activated in connection with frustration. To overcome obstacles or stifle punishment, individuals must engage in instrumental behavior. Instrumental behaviors are governed by the BAS system, which is capable of producing rewards. One main component of this system is the dopaminergic system, which we discussed in the previous chapter.
3. **The Behavioral Inhibition System (BIS).** This system is referred to as the "stop look and listen system" (Gray, 1991). The ability to inhibit behavior comes from the activation of this. This system is activated by novel stimuli and by stimuli that are associated with the potential of punishment or the cessation of reward. Several brain structures are involved in this system. When this system is activated there is increased arousal and attention becomes focused on the threatening stimuli. As we talked about earlier (Chapter 2), arousal appears to automatically focus attention on threatening cues. We will talk more about this system in Chapter 10 on negative emotions.

Explaining Trait Aggression

Considerable evidence indicates that people differ in trait aggression. Researchers have suggested that the differential tendency of people to act aggressively results from being born with different thresholds for activating each of these systems. Take verbal aggression, for example. According to this conceptualization, people who are inclined to be verbally aggressive are people who have a low threshold for BAS activity, a low threshold for activation of the FFS and a high threshold for BIS activity. In concrete terms, "individuals high in verbal aggression are highly motivated to achieve goals through interpersonal interaction, quickly turn to aggressive tactics when initial attempts fail, and without sufficient inhibition, become highly aggressive. The attention focus which accompanies system activation promotes persistent focus on the goal and mini-

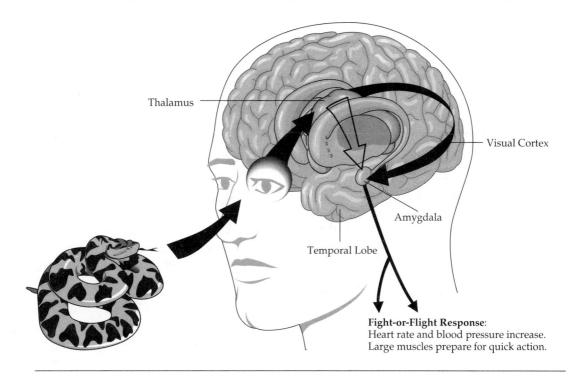

Figure 8-1.   Some important brain structures involved in aggressive behavior.

mizes focus on potential negative consequences of aggressive symbolic action" (Beatty & McCoskey, 1997, p. 450). The concept of thresholds is an important feature of the theory because it suggests that even people who are low in trait aggression could become verbally aggressive when environmental events are sufficient to activate the FFS and the BAS but insufficient to trigger the BIS.

Amygdala

The amygdala, one of the central structures of the FFS, is a structure within the limbic system, a system that has been implicated in a wide range of emotional behaviors (Figure 8-1). The limbic system is often referred to in connection with emotions. The extensive system involves several structures including the cingulate gyrus, hippocampus, the thalamus, hypothalamus, pituitary (the traditional neuroendocrine system), the septal nuclei and the olfactory bulbs, and the mammillary bodies. Within that system, the amygdala triggers the body's fight-or-flight hormones, mobilizes the cen-

ter for movement, activates the cardiovascular system, triggers the release of norepinephrine, and generally makes us more alert (LeDoux, 1986, 1992, 1993, 1996). LeDoux has suggested that the amygdala plays a pivotal role in governing our behavior because it can initiate actions before our thinking (rational) brain has been fully able to comprehend an incoming signal. The essence of his argument is that a sensory signal first goes to the thalamus, then is routed to two different locations: the amygdala and the neocortex. Because the signal takes longer to reach the neocortex, the amygdala is free to act—at least for a few milliseconds—before the neocortex can evaluate and confirm the nature of the incoming signal. He suggests, as other theorists have, that humans are prepared to treat a novel stimulus as a potential threat to our survival. He goes on to argue that, because of this delay, some emotional reactions and memories can be formed without any conscious or cognitive participation. What we have, in short, is two memory systems: one for ordinary events and one for emotionally charged events.

The problem is that memories in the amygdala might be faulty guides to the present. They might prime us to perceive harmless stimuli as threatening and therefore to act aggressively. LeDoux also points out that this emotional system sustains its own activity once activated. As a result, we will be primed—at least for some period—to see things as threatening. When we perceive that we are threatened, we are more dispositionally inclined to act aggressively.

The essence of impulsivity is acting without complete information. LeDoux's findings explain the initial tendency to act impulsively and indicate why this tendency resists change. His findings also help us to understand why impulsivity is likely to lead to antisocial behavior and even violence. Unless this system is somehow retrained, it tends to push people toward more aggressive and antisocial behavior (Dozier, 1998).

Although there are numerous studies on brain structures and aggression in animals, there are very few studies of humans. An often-reported case involves Charles Whitman, an introspective young man with no previous history of violence, who one night killed his wife and his mother. The next morning he went to the University of Texas administration building, where he killed the receptionist and barricaded himself in the tower. From the top of the tower, he used his high-powered rifle to shoot anyone he saw through the telescopic lens. During the next 90 minutes, he killed 14 persons and injured another 24. His shooting spree ended only when the police were able to kill him. The autopsy showed a brain tumor, whose exact location was difficult to pinpoint because of the wounds inflicted by police bullets. The evidence seemed to indicate, however, that a tumor on the medial part of the temporal lobe was exerting pressure on the amygdala (Dozier, 1998).

Considerable evidence from animal work indicates that lesions or ablations of the amygdala produce a calming effect (Grossman, 1967; Pribram, 1976). Although psychosurgery is a radical treatment, it has been used with humans who experience outbursts of violence and aggression. Using animal research as a model, surgeons have cut away part of the temporal lobes and the amygdala. The results of such surgery have shown that it is partially effective in reducing aggression (Dozier, 1998).

Summary

Using self-report inventories, individuals can be differentiated by dispositional aggression. Although some studies of monozygotic and dizygotic twins have shown a genetic component to aggression, others have not. Studies of temperament have shown that impulsivity is linked to aggressive and antisocial behavior. Serotonin levels in the brain could mediate this tendency. A large body of data links male aggression to testosterone, but data linking female aggression to testosterone or to changes in the ratio of estrogen and progesterone are inconclusive. Research with hyenas suggests that androstenedione could be an important source of aggression in females as well as in males.

Using a variety of measures of aggression, persistent differences between men and women have been found. Males tend to be slightly higher on verbal aggression and hostility and much higher on measures of physical aggression. It appears that the expression of aggression—especially physical aggression—is more inhibited in females, who also experience more guilt and anxiety about aggression.

Considerable evidence links animal aggression to various brain structures, but human data do not permit solid inferences yet. Results from psychosurgery indicate that removing the temporal lobes and the amygdala has a marked calming effect. LeDoux has argued that the amygdala plays a central role in aggression by triggering the fight-or-flight response and initiating defensive actions without the full involvement of the neocortex. His model explains the link between impulsivity and antisocial behavior.

Considerable evidence from animal research indicates that removing the amygdala produces a calming effect.

The Learned Component of Aggression

The Concept of Frustration

Frustration has long been regarded as a major cause of aggression. According to the frustration hypothesis, the tendency to become aggressive increases when goal-directed behavior is blocked (Berkowitz, 1962, 1969; Miller, 1941). Thus, such everyday events as finding that a favorite restaurant is closed, having to wait in line to see a movie, or not getting a good grade on a test might produce frustration, which, in turn, would increase the tendency to engage in aggressive behavior. Frustration can be viewed as having its roots in the need to control or need to be in control. When that need is thwarted in some way, the individual becomes aroused (has feelings of frustration). What the individual does depends on a variety of other social and cultural factors. One interesting and important feature of frustration is that it must become quite intense before it actually triggers an aggressive act. What this suggests is that some threshold must be exceeded before aggression occurs.

Although many studies have produced results consistent with the frustration hypothesis (e.g., Berkowitz & Geen, 1966; Burnstein & Worchel, 1962; Geen, 1968), others have not (e.g., Buss, 1963; Kuhn, Madsen, & Becker, 1967; Taylor & Pisano, 1971). After a careful examination of the conflicting results, Baron (1977) has concluded, "frustration can indeed facilitate later aggression" (p. 91) but is likely to do so only when frustration is (1) "quite intense" and (2) "unexpected or arbitrary in nature" (p. 91). Thus, having to wait in line might fail to facilitate aggression because the accompanying frustration is not intense enough. In fact, most of us learn that at times we will have to wait and, as a result, we tend to experience little or no frustration in that situation. Whether a student's failure to receive the expected grade will facilitate aggression might be affected by the student's perception of whether the grading was fair.

Frustration and the Direction of Behavior

Despite what we might expect, frustrated people often do not attack the source of the frustration, for several reasons; the attack might result in retaliation, for example. When frustrated, however, people will engage in a range of behaviors. Because frustration is a negative motivational state, the reduction of frustration should be highly rewarding, and any behavior that has that effect is likely to occur more often in the future.

In a recent reexamination of research on the frustration hypothesis, Berkowitz (1989) suggested that frustration generates aggressive inclinations to the degree that it arouses negative affect. Situations in which people do not act aggressively when frustrated fail to arouse negative affect, according to Berkowitz. Whether a situation arouses negative affect depends partially on our cognitive processes—for example, on whether we perceive that we have been blocked deliberately or accidentally. If we perceive that someone else deliberately blocked us from reaching our goal, we are more likely to react with anger and aggression.

The Concept of Displacement

If we are frustrated by something, it makes sense to attack the cause. However, it's not always possible to attack the source of the problem. If I have to wait in line at a bank, the source of the problem is often the manager, who has failed to assign enough tellers to handle the volume of people; however, that might not stop me from snapping at the teller. When I was a graduate student, I saw how rats responded to nonreward. In an experiment, rats were rewarded on a full reinforcement schedule for a time and then switched to a partial reinforcement schedule. When nonrewarded trials were introduced, the rats would bite the food dish or attack some other nearby portion of the cage. When I removed the rat from the apparatus, it would often try to bite me as well. I was obviously the source of the problem, but the frustration was initially displaced toward other things because I wasn't available. Sometimes we aren't even sure what the source of the problem is; in that case, we might strike out indiscriminately (Tedeschi & Felson, 1994).

Generalization and Inhibition

Following intense frustration, humans typically do not strike indiscriminately. Both animal and human data indicate that we are equipped with inhibitory mechanisms that enable us to use aggression selectively or to suppress it altogether, when it is in our interest to do so (Brannigan, 1997; Lore & Schultz, 1993). The principle of *generalization* has been invoked to explain why we strike out selectively. According to this principle, stimuli can be ranked along a continuum of their similarity to one another. Regarding aggression, the principle of generalization says that, if the target of our frustration is unavailable, we will direct our actions toward those stimuli that are most similar to the target. Thus, if we are forced to stand in line and the bank manager is unavailable, the next best target is the teller. In a job setting, we might find it very difficult to strike out at anybody. As a result, we might strike out at other people who somehow symbolize our frustrated state. A spouse is often the first available target after a frustrating day at work. Some people take out their frustrations by cutting off people in traffic.

Our actions are also governed by the principle of *inhibition*. Early in life, we discover that, when we engage in certain behaviors—such as physically attacking another person who has frustrated us—we will be punished. If frustrated children bite, hit, or kick their parents, such acts usually incur quick and often painful consequences; as a result, children learn to inhibit such behaviors. Acceptable responses to frustration depend on culture, economic status, gender, and other factors. Males are often taught to channel their aggressive energy into sports; females are often taught to deal with aggression by sharing their feelings with someone else. Because of these early experiences, we learn to do certain things rather than others.

By understanding the principles of generalization and inhibition, we can better understand why frustration leads to different behaviors in different people.

Blind Rage: Generalized Anger and Aggression

With no apparent provocation, certain individuals commonly respond to negative situations with anger and aggression; they lash out at anything and everything in sight. Berkowitz (1990) explains this phenomenon in terms of generalization.

Berkowitz starts with the observation that anger and aggression can be provoked by a range of unpleasant experiences, including foul odors, high temperatures, exposure to pain, cold water, getting sick, and getting caught in a traffic jam. Sometimes people become angry when they are sad—when a close friend dies, for example—or when they are depressed—after losing their jobs, for instance. Berkowitz suggests that the tendency to become angry and aggressive in response to a wide range of stimuli is largely learned. Once people learn to associate a wide range of negative feelings with anger and aggression, they become angry and might become aggressive whenever they experi-

ence those feelings. Specifically, he suggests that negative affect activates ideas, memories, and actions associated with anger and aggression. As a result, when we begin to experience negative affect, we are put in a state of readiness to experience anger and to engage in a variety of aggressive acts.

Cognitive theorists maintain that certain kinds of beliefs are necessary before the emotion of anger can arise, but Berkowitz disagrees. Consider the example of a person who develops a toothache, asks, "Why me?" and angrily kicks a door. To explain such incidents, Berkowitz argues that pain elicits memories of previous negative feelings, such as anger, and the associated actions, such as aggression. As a result, people come to express their anger and engage in aggression whenever they experience pain, even from a toothache. Note that, in this theory, the negative affect is the common mediator of the two distinct emotions. Clearly, in this way, a wide range of negative emotions might, over time, come to elicit aggression.

Berkowitz does acknowledge the role of cognitions; in fact, he calls his theory a cognitive-neoassociationistic approach. Most people, he argues, have a rudimentary idea (prototype) of the primary emotions and what factors are involved in these emotions (sensation, thoughts, memories, and so on). As a result, there is a limit on the degree to which negative emotions can become linked to anger and aggression. According to his theory, as we learn to differentiate emotions we come to define our prototypes more clearly. As a result, we are less inclined to generalize and therefore less inclined to respond to pain with anger and aggression.

The strength of Berkowitz's theory lies in its ability to account for two things: (1) why certain negative emotions can come to elicit anger and aggression even though these responses are not adaptive, at least from a biological perspective; and (2) why people who have learned to differentiate their emotions do not show this maladaptive tendency.

According to this theory, teaching people how to better differentiate their emotions should reduce generalized aggression in our society. Biologists maintain that emotions evolved to make us adaptive. To maximize our adaptiveness as humans, we must learn to differentiate our emotions, so that we respond appropriately to each of the emotions we experience.

Social Learning Theory

According to social learning theory, the environment often plays an important role in the acquisition, expression, and maintenance of aggressive behavior (Bandura, 1973, 1986, 1997).

Modeling and Imitation

One of the main ways children learn aggression is through observation and imitation. We know, for example, that how people discipline their children is often very similar to how they were disciplined as children (Patterson, 1980). Those raised with strict discipline tend to employ strict discipline with their children; those raised more leniently tend to be lenient. We also know that physical and sexual abuse is often passed on from generation to generation; this has been called the cycle of violence.

The Cycle of Violence

Parents who abuse their children often know that it is wrong by the standards of society but continue anyway. They seem unable to break the habit. The consensus among experts in the field is that, unless it can be broken, this pattern will continue into succeeding generations. This is a powerful example of the role learning plays in the acquisition and maintenance of an aggressive behavior pattern.

Research on the cycle of violence indicates that not all children who grow up in homes characterized by violence and neglect become violent or abuse their children (Widom, 1989a, b). Unfortunately, at this point we do not know why the cycle is broken in some cases but not in others. As DiLalla and Gottesman (1991) point out, important biological and genetic factors have been implicated in the transmission of violence from generation to generation. The individual might have to possess a certain biological temperament, for example, before such learning takes place.

Aggression and TV Violence

Does watching violent TV shows promote violent behavior? Despite extensive research, the answer is still not clear. It seems that, once exposed to violence on TV, some individuals are more inclined to engage in aggressive behaviors if they are provoked. This does not mean, however, that exposure to TV violence causes

Children frequently model aggression they see from watching television.

aggressive behavior in the absence of provocation. Rather, TV violence might act indirectly to increase aggressiveness (e.g., Fenigstein, 1979). At least four explanations have been offered: (1) modeling and imitation of aggression; (2) release—or disinhibition—of aggressive impulses; (3) elicitation of aggressive actions that have been previously learned; and (4) an increase in arousal produced by watching aggressive activities (Bandura, 1973; Geen, 1976).

A large proportion of the children who watch violence on television do not show increased aggressiveness. Why is that? One important factor is how the parents view violence. If the parents do not endorse

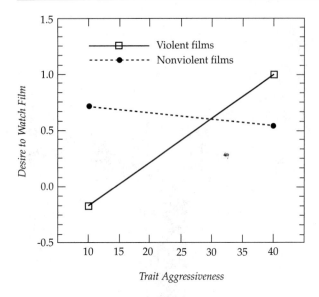

Figure 8-2. The moderating role of trait aggressiveness on desire to watch the violent and nonviolent films.

violence as a means of settling disputes, achieving goals, and so on, children who watch violence on television tend not to be affected by it (Dominick & Greenberg, 1971). Another relevant factor is whether a given child prefers violence. Not all children, it appears, like to watch violence. Those who do prefer violence on TV tend to be more innately aggressive (Bushman, 1995; Eron, Huesmann, Lefkowitz, & Walder, 1972; Fenigstein, 1979). Consequently, the correlation found between watching violence on TV and aggressive behavior might simply reflect a greater preexisting inclination to aggression in children who enjoy TV violence. Figure 8-2 shows that, as the trait of aggressiveness becomes stronger, so does preference for violent films. Parental attitudes may again play an important role in facilitating or inhibiting this tendency. Finally, it appears that TV violence can be a very powerful contributor to aggression, at least for a short time, when a person is angry (Doob & Climie, 1972). This finding suggests that TV violence has a general arousal effect that facilitates aggressiveness, rather than a specific modeling effect.

In a study comparing American cities that had television and those that did not, no effect was found for the presence or absence of television (Hennigan et

al., 1982). Further, when cities without television obtained it, violent crimes did not increase. Thus, there is no evidence for the idea that viewing television leads to aggressive behavior.

Pornography and Aggression

Does aggression in pornographic films lead to increasing violence toward women, especially rape? The extensive research on this topic (Donnerstein & Linz, 1986; Malamuth & Donnerstein, 1984) has focused on the distinction between erotica that involves no violence or force and pornography that does portray violence and force. A film showing a woman being raped or tortured, for example, differs substantially from a film depicting sexual activity between two lovers. The research has shown that erotic images do not seem to lead to an increase in male aggression toward women, but violent pornography with scenes of rape may lead to an increase in the tendency to rape. These studies have not shown that the male volunteers have actually raped as a result of watching scenes of rape; however, they have shown rather that the men tended to see rape as having little or no serious or harmful effect on women, possibly because, in pornographic films, the woman typically offers only token resistance to rape before she is swept away by passion for her attacker. Men who fail to understand that rape is a terrifying and traumatic experience for a woman could be misled by these portrayals. As a result of viewing films in which women are represented as enjoying rape, men could come to view rape not as the infliction of harm on another person but as the delivery of pleasure. As a result, their inhibitions around rape are lowered.

If men's inhibitions about rape are reduced as a result of the way women are portrayed in pornographic films, rather than by the depiction of sexual activity, we might conclude that it is important to consider how the media in general portray women. Researchers have suggested that violence toward women is endemic in TV shows, films, and advertising. At this point, very little work has been done to evaluate the effects of these violent images.

In 1987, the Attorney General's Commission on Pornography concluded that there is a causal relationship between exposure to pornography and several antisocial behaviors, including violence toward women (Linz, Donnerstein, & Penrod, 1987), and called for more stringent law enforcement. Some scientists whose work was used by the commission have argued that some of the extrapolations made by the commission are unwarranted and that some of the findings are inconsistent with research data. These critics argue that we should be concerned with violent images throughout the media, not just in pornography, and design educational programs to prevent all forms of violence, including sexual violence (Linz, Donnerstein, & Penrod, 1987).

Summary

According to the frustration hypothesis, the tendency to become aggressive increases when goal-directed behavior is blocked. If frustration is to cause aggression, it must be quite intense, unexpected, or arbitrary. Frustration does not give direction to aggressive behavior; rather, frustration gives rise to a negative motivational state that, when reduced, will reinforce behavior. Much of the aggression that occurs as a result of frustration is displaced because humans have learned to inhibit aggressive attacks toward certain targets. Berkowitz has suggested that negative affect is one main source of anger and aggression, arguing that negative affect activates ideas, memories, and actions associated with anger and aggression. As a result, when we begin to experience such negative feelings, we are in a state of readiness to experience anger and engage in aggressive acts. Berkowitz points out that people who learn to better differentiate their emotions are less likely to engage in this maladaptive tendency to respond to all negative affect with anger and aggression.

Social learning theory suggests that the environment plays an important role in the acquisition, expression, and maintenance of aggressive behavior, through the mechanisms of modeling and imitation. The cycle of violence is thought to be an example of learned behavior. After many studies, we have little evidence of a causal link between TV violence and aggression. TV violence could, however, send the message that violence is an acceptable way of settling conflicts. Researchers have also been unable to establish a clear causal link between pornography and violence against women, but argue that any portrayal of violence toward women is a source of concern. Research on this topic should not be limited to studies of pornography.

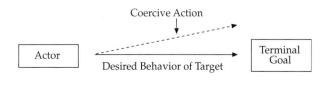

Figure 8-3.   Model of coercive action.

The Cognitive Component of Aggression

Tedeschi and Felson (1994) proposed a theory of coercive action that focuses on the social functions of harm-doing—both physical harm and psychological harm. Tedeschi and Felson start from the perspective that people use threats and punishment to achieve certain goals or to preserve certain values they hold. In other words, coercive behavior is not simply reactive, but is intentional. They define a *coercive action* as an action taken with the intention of imposing harm on another person or forcing compliance.

Coercive action takes many forms. Coercive action is designed to get another person to comply and often involves threats and punishments. In a parent-child relationship, where the parent is most likely to use coercive action, it might involve such things as scolding the child, withdrawing of privileges (such as watching television), or physical punishment. At work, where the boss is most likely to use coercion, it might involve giving a suggestion, berating, or withholding a promotion. In a romantic relationship, where either party might use coercive actions, it might involve insults, withholding of affection, or even physical abuse.

A Model of Coercive Action

Let's begin with three important concepts within the theory of coercive action. First, the *actor* is the person who evaluates information and makes decisions about what to do under a variety of different circumstances. Second, the *targets* are people who are threatened by the actor or do not fall in line with the actor's desires. Finally, the *terminal goal* represents the motives and values that cause the actor to think in certain ways and decide on certain courses of action (Figure 8-3).

There is no need for coercive action when the behavior of the target is consistent with the motives and values of the actor (solid line). Coercive action only arises when the behavior of others is not in line with the wishes of the actor (dashed line). The point of the coercive action is to bring that behavior back into alignment with the desired behavior (the solid line). When parents look at the behavior of their child—how tidy the child's room is, for example—they decide whether it matches their expectations. If it does, there is no need for coercive action. If not, the parents will engage in some form of coercive action—perhaps a simple scolding.

The Costs of Coercive Action

The theory of coercive action is designed to account for a wide range of behavior. For example, consider the behavior of bank robbers during a holdup. As long as the bank employees and the hostages follow the robbers' instructions (the solid line), there would be no need to engage in coercive action. Should someone not follow their instructions (the dashed line), they would have to consider some kind of coercive action; they might threaten to hit or even kill the noncomplying individual. The terminal goal, of course, is to get the money from the bank vault. They can only achieve that goal if others comply.

The nature of the coercive action chosen by an actor is largely determined by costs. In the theory, there are at least four types of costs:

1. *Opportunity costs.* Actors ask themselves whether it is worth the time, effort, and energy to engage in coercive behaviors.
2. Potential *retaliation costs.* Actors evaluate, perhaps based on previous experiences with the target, whether the target is likely to retaliate or to comply. If the retaliation costs are too high, the actor might decide against coercive behavior. If the target is likely to comply, however, the costs would be minimal.
3. *Costs of noncoercion.* Sometimes the target is faced with a no-win or least-of-evils choice. An employee faced with unacceptable conditions might decide it would be better to quit than to comply. The employer must then weigh how important is it to keep this person against how important is it to make the employee comply.
4. *Third-party costs.* For example, what if a parent disciplines a child and the neighbors or the police in-

tervene? If there are substantial third-party costs, the actor might decide not to engage in coercive behavior.

Evidence indicates that, as people get older, they perceive that the costs associated with criminal activity increase. This would account for the negative correlation between age and criminal activity.

The Relationship Between Skills and Costs

According to the model, actors who see themselves as highly skilled are inclined to feel that the costs of securing compliance are relatively low. An actor who has mastered the art of telling people what they want to hear or giving them what they want might feel confident about securing the target's compliance by means of those skills. The underlying theme of the actor's presentation in that case might be this: "If you do that for me, I can get this for you." An actor who knows that the most important thing for me is my children might do something for my children and attempt to use the leverage of indebtedness to gain compliance. In all these cases, the actor's strategy is calculated from the outset.

Irrational Coercive Action

The theory of coercive action proposes that people make rational decisions about how to get what they want by means of coercive action. Like other rational models, this theory assumes complete information processing. That means that the actor is inclined to analyze all aspects of the situation and consider all the possible alternatives. In reality, people are rarely completely rational. Tedeschi and Felson acknowledge that people often take coercive actions without complete information processing. They recognize that we often engage in mindless repetitive behaviors or simply behaviors copied from others. They argue that one of the main reasons for incomplete information processing is that, as humans, we have a limited ability to process information. Because we are preoccupied with other things, we fail to fully appreciate what is necessary and appropriate. What we need to do, it appears, is discover ways of ensuring that people have better and more complete information.

Alcohol and Coercive Action

There is a strong correlation between alcohol and criminal behavior. One study, for example, found that, in 64% of the criminal homicides studied, one of the parties was drinking alcohol (Wolfgang & Strohm, 1956). As we saw in Chapter 7, one of the most significant effects of alcohol consumption is disinhibition. After several drinks, people's behavior becomes less constrained.

The general interpretation of disinhibition is that our ability to process information is impaired under the influence of alcohol. For example, our attention is narrowed. As a result, we fail to consider certain important information when making decisions. We may fail to consider how others will evaluate us, for example.

Steele and his colleagues (Banaji & Steele, 1989; Steele & Josephs, 1990) have suggested that alcohol produces a kind of myopia in which people tend to ignore, disregard, or downgrade certain pieces of relevant negative information when making judgments, especially judgments about the self (Chapter 7). As a result, people tend to see themselves in a more positive light (more like their ideal self). This is analogous to what happens in the approach/avoidance conflict when people use alcohol; approach motivation is left more or less unchanged under the influence of alcohol, but avoidant motivation is markedly reduced. The net effect is that people are more willing to act based on their positive motives or feelings. Often, the consequences of ignoring negative motives are not fully understood until some later time. A person who insults a co-worker at an office party, for example, might not realize the likely consequences until the next day.

Using this argument, Tedeschi and Felson argue that people are more coercive under the influence of alcohol because they fail to fully consider the costs of engaging in a coercive act, which, in turn, is because their alcohol-induced myopia leads them to ignore or disregard negative information. As the apparent costs decline, the tendency to engage in coercive action increases. When people are encouraged to take responsibility for their behavior (to become more self-focused), aggression is reduced, which suggests that it is not entirely the pharmacological effects of alcohol that produces aggression (Ito, Miller, & Pollock, 1996).

The decision to take coercive action often involves considerations of justice. Justice is a value that we acquire early in life from our interactions with parents, teachers, and other role models. We are taught that, if we do something now, we can expect something else to happen later—for example, that, if we do our chores, we can expect an allowance at the end of the week. In a longer time frame, we are told that, if we get good grades in school, we can expect a job when we graduate from high school. Lerner (1977) has suggested that, if certain promises are kept when we are young, we will come to believe in a just world. In such a world, we can live without undue anxiety about our future. When the time comes, there will be a job and money to live.

In a just world, we need to follow certain rules of conduct. One simple but important rule of conduct is that we need to wait our turn. The fundamental idea is that, if everybody abides by this rule, then we will all get what we deserve. Waiting in line is a good example. If even one person is allowed to go to the head of the line, others may do the same. If that happens, I can no longer be assured that I will get what I deserve.

The rules of conduct can be understood as norms. Take borrowing, for example. Should I refuse to return a borrowed book, I would be in violation of a norm. If I violate one norm, however, I prompt the suspicion that I will violate others. If I don't return a book, can I be trusted to return a borrowed car? In the end, I will be deprived of the privilege of borrowing.

The rules of justice involve not only obeying norms, but also taking responsibility for our actions. If we all take responsibility for our actions, we can be assured that we will not be harmed, for example, or that others will not take more than their fair share. We make allowances within our implicit theories of justice for mental and physical disability, age, and even gender. Again, norms come into play. Even though I may think that certain people should not receive welfare, the larger group of which I am a part might not operate on this norm. As a result, I am obliged to go along with the norm.

Different groups of people often hold different norms. Some believe that women have a right to decide whether to abort an unwanted child, whereas others fiercely disagree. Political parties are often based on beliefs regarding which norms are good and which are bad and will sometimes attempt to force one norm on all people. The current debate about welfare involves norms: To what degree should people be required to take responsibility for their own well-being?

Retributive Justice

Retributive justice refers to the belief that blameworthy behavior should be punished. According to retributive

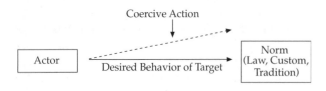

Figure 8-4.   Model of retributive justice.

justice, people whose behavior deviates from the norm (norm violation) need to be punished to bring compliance with the norm (Figure 8-4). Figure 8-4 resembles Figure 8-3, except that the terminal goal is labeled as a norm. Conceptually, norms and terminal goals are very similar. They both represent what we want for ourselves or what we think is right.

Three Types of Norm Violation

Interestingly, all the various types of norm violations can be summarized under three types.

1. **Distributive justice** refers to the fair allocation of resources, the fair distribution of duties, and recognition of the amount of effort and level of performance. Children often fight over the division and use of property: Who gets the best room? Who gets to use the car? They also fight over duties that they must perform: Are two sets of chores equivalent in time, effort, and skill required? Distributive justice plays an important role in employee satisfaction. If workers perceive that resources are not being distributed fairly, they are likely to be resentful and even retaliate.
2. **Procedural justice** refers to the means or procedures that are used to resolve conflicts of interest. We typically try to resolve such differences by having the two aggrieved parties tell their respective stories to a neutral party. Within the legal system, we have a highly formalized set of rules that govern this process.
3. **Interactional justice** involves conformity to norms about demeanor, respect, and politeness toward other people. The more common forms of perceived interactional injustice include lack of loyalty, lack of regard for the feelings of others, selfishness, hostility, and failure to keep agreements (Mikula, Petri, & Tanzer, 1989). Research in-

dicates that this is by far the most important category of unjust events because it is intimately linked to our self-identities.

Justice as Self-Worth

Folger (1991) has suggested that all three aspects of justice are important because they reflect on our perceived self-worth. Violations of our sense of justice are perceived as a direct attack on our value as a person. Businesses, schools, and governments must ensure that standards of justice are met because our willingness to work and cooperate is linked to feelings of self-worth.

Attribution of Blame

How do we decide that some behavior is blameworthy? Researchers have suggested that, whenever we observe unwanted or unexpected behaviors, we search for an explanation (Wong & Weiner, 1981). As we see in Figure 8-5, the attribution of blame can be viewed as a series of steps at which inferences are made (Rule & Nesdale, 1976).

According to Figure 8-5, the observer initially makes a judgment about whether or not some external actor caused the negative outcome. If the decision is made that the actor caused the outcome, the observer then considers whether the outcome was intended or unintended. If the wrong was intended, the observer then decides whether the actor's intention was justified or unjustified. If the action was justified, no blame is assigned; however, if the action was not justified, blame is assigned. Being reprimanded for not doing something they were never instructed to do (such as making sure a certain setting was used before starting a machine) would be considered an unjustified act and therefore worthy of blame. Had they been told ahead of time to use a certain setting, the reprimand would not be viewed as justified and therefore no blame would be assigned. Note that according to this decision tree, even if an act is not intended but some consequence is foreseeable, there is justification for assigning blame. Knowing that a certain lever setting should be used before starting a machine and allowing someone to proceed would be blameworthy. According to this framework, what leads people to consider an act as aggressive is linked to whether or not some type of injustice occurred.

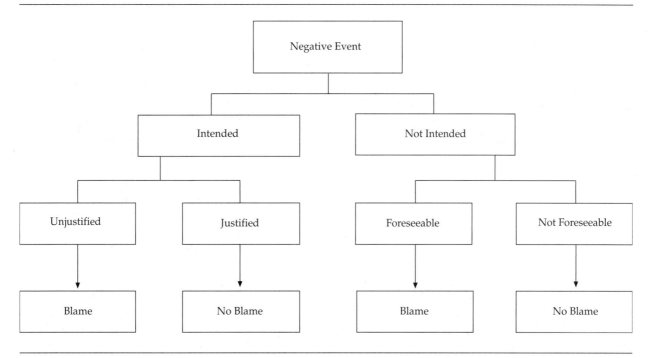

Figure 8-5. The series of inferences that lead to the attribution of blame.

Interpersonal Violence

The Link Between Control and Power

Controlling other people is highly instrumental in achieving our goals and preserving our values. Feminist, multicultural, and gay and lesbian scholars have suggested that attempts to control others through violent means can often be understood as the link between power and control (e.g., Walker, 1989). A common theme in that literature is that people who have power or perceive that they have power will be inclined to exercise it on their own behalf and to maintain their power base because they believe that they have the right to control others, even to the extent of using violent means.

What triggers acts of violence? According to psychological control theory, it is the threat of loss of power (control). Parents who abuse their children do so because they want to retain power. Lacking the skills to control their children's behavior through more socially accepted means, they resort to physical violence. Similarly, individuals who engage in spousal abuse are motivated by the desire for power; again, lacking the skills to maintain control, they resort to physical abuse.

Some theorists have suggested that violence against people of color, gay men, and lesbians reflects a struggle for power. As oppressed groups try to free themselves from the control of those in power and to take charge of their lives, they threaten existing power structures and the way resources are distributed. Consequently, oppressed groups' attempts at empowerment trigger acts of violence against them (Staub, 1996). According to this analysis, one approach to reducing such violence would be a public education campaign to explain that the empowerment of one group does not necessarily mean that other groups will lose their power.

Politics has to do with gaining and maintaining power. Through the political system, people attempt to ensure that resources are distributed fairly and that they are treated in a fair and just way. It is not surprising that people who do not see themselves as having fair access to resources or being treated fairly will often reject the government and its laws and resort to violence.

Violence as the Last Resort

According to the coercive action model, aggression must be understood within the larger context of how people attempt to gain control of others. For most of us, physical acts of aggression are the last in a chain of strategies designed to gain compliance. However, people who lack other means of control are inclined to become aggressive and violent. Anger and alcohol are among the factors that can short-circuit the normal constructive ways that people use to gain control.

Summary

Tedeschi and Felson proposed a theory of coercive action on the basis that individuals use threats and punishment to achieve certain goals or preserve certain values. According to this theory, we don't need coercive action when the target complies with our wishes. When the target fails to comply, however, we engage in coercive action to bring the target's behavior in line with what we want. Tedeschi and Felson have identified four costs associated with coercive action: opportunity costs; potential retaliation costs; noncoercion costs; and third-party costs.

Their model is a rational model of how people should act if they process all the available information. However, people sometimes fail to process all the information and do not act in a completely rational manner. Alcohol provides an interesting example of how people behave when they fail to consider certain important pieces of information.

Many coercive actions are motivated by the value of justice. Retributive justice refers to the belief that blameworthy behavior—behavior that departs from some norm—should be punished. Three other important aspects of justice are distributive justice, procedural justice, and interactional justice. Researchers have suggested that the attribution of blame involves a series of inferential steps that result in judgments of blame or no blame. Anger commonly accompanies the attribution of blame. There is good reason to argue that the high arousal that comes with blame is responsible, at least in part, for the poor decisions and the escalation of aggression that often accompanies a sense of injustice.

Researchers have suggested that violence against women, people of color, and gay men and lesbians can be understood as the link between power and control. People who believe that they have the right to control another person will often resort to acts of coercion, in-

cluding physical aggression. People often resort to physical aggression when verbal means of control fail.

Youth Violence

Although violence is not the same thing as aggression and perhaps doesn't belong in a chapter on aggression, many people tend to equate violence and aggression. For this reason I thought it was important to consider, at least briefly, the nature of violence. Violence often has its roots in feelings of being wronged or mistreated. Sometimes it has its roots in feelings of loss of control.

Youth violence in the United States has increased significantly during the past decade (Eron, Gentry, & Schlegel, 1994). For example, the homicide rate for young men in the United States is 7 times that of Canada and 18 times that of the United Kingdom (Tedeschi & Felson, 1994). There are several possible explanations for this. Some researchers have pointed out that poverty increased in this period and suggest that poverty is the best predictor of violence, including homicide (Hill, Soriano, Chen, & LaFramboise, 1994). Many children who grow up in poverty, however, do not become violent. San Francisco's Chinatown is one of the poorest areas of the city and yet the murder rate there remains extremely low (Staub, 1996). Researchers have also suggested that those abused in childhood will be more inclined toward violence and aggression, especially against their own children, but only about 30% of those abused children show this trend (Staub, 1996). Although abused children often display other forms of aggression in their teens and later life, the pattern is not universal. As a result of such findings, researchers have concluded that early experiences of abuse only creates a disposition toward violence. High rates of violence on TV and elsewhere in the media have been cited as a possible cause of youth violence; however, many children who watch such violence do not themselves become violent.

Many factors promote and inhibit violence. The model in Figure 8-6 summarizes some of the research findings on the development of violence. It includes two paths: One leads to antisocial and criminal behavior, and the other leads to noncriminal behavior. Starting at the same point, these paths diverge more and more as children have different experiences. The

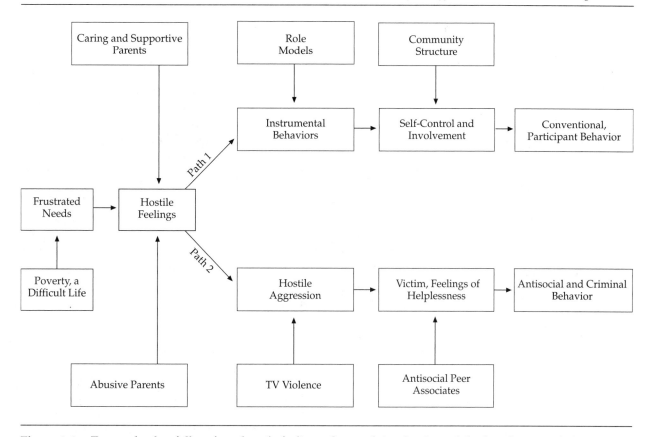

Figure 8-6.   Two paths that follow from hostile feelings. One path is adaptive, while the other is maladaptive.

model is based on the idea that biological, learned, and cognitive factors interact. In the model, they move broadly from the biological on the left to the cognitive on the right.

The lower path consists of risk factors for antisocial, criminal behavior. Individuals with more risk factors will be more likely to engage in criminal behaviors. The upper path consists of factors that give rise to more conventional participant behavior.

The Biological Component

According to Berkowitz (1993, 1994), frustration and other negative affects give rise to aggression. This proposal has its roots in the idea that humans are motivated to survive and that they come into the world with general mechanisms and systems to help them survive. One of those is the tendency to take what we need and to use force if necessary. The noxious cry of

babies when their biological needs are not met ensures that we attend to their needs. Staub (1996) has argued that, when basic needs are frustrated, a very powerful force is set loose. When such frustration is combined with difficult life conditions, the stage is set for aggressive behaviors to develop.

In the model in Figure 8-6, frustration does not lead immediately to aggression; it leads to hostile feelings. Feelings of hostility are very basic; they do not have to be learned. Hostility and anxiety are part of the fight-or-flight response, which is triggered by the amygdala in response to a perceived threat. As we've seen, this process often does not involve the brain's rational systems.

If, as the model in Figure 8-6 suggests, frustrated needs are the first step toward criminal behavior, does it make sense that youth violence is much higher in the United States? Remember that frustration is relative to what is possible. If everyone is poor, there should be little frustration because the discrepancy between individuals is small. Frustration will be greater where there is a large discrepancy between rich and poor. In some societies, individuals are born into a certain class and stay there. In that case, the frustration for a poor person should be low. In the United States, however, everyone is encouraged to realize the American Dream —to become enormously wealthy. For the poor, the discrepancy between their circumstances and what is possible is very large.

Considerable research indicates that hostile feelings can be modified by other experiences. On the one hand, adults who have grown up in caring homes with a great deal of nurturance do not show the same level of aggression as those who experienced little nurturance (Staub, 1996). On the other hand, children who were abused tend to be more aggressive, other things being equal (Dodge, 1993; Widom, 1989a, b). It makes sense that, if counteracting forces—such as love, understanding, and acceptance—are at work, perceptions of threat will be reduced. Conversely, individuals whose needs are not being met and who are also being physically beaten and psychologically rejected will experience greater feelings of hostility.

The Learned Component

Responses to Threat

On different occasions, animals use very different methods of dealing with threats and pain. Sometimes, they physically attack the source of threat; at other times they engage in instrumental behaviors that put distance between themselves and the object of threat. Humans show a similar pattern (Pinel, 1993).

In the model in Figure 8-6, hostile feelings can take two different directions. On the one hand, they motivate the individual to engage in instrumental behaviors to escape the threat. Children from abusive families may run away from home, for example. On the other hand, hostile feelings can motivate an individual to attack the threat. Some children attempt to fight back when their parents abuse them, for example.

Not all instrumental behaviors are equally effective. Research indicates that children who have good guidance, good role models, and good education are more likely to escape from their plight. For example,

by engaging in certain adaptive instrumental behaviors, they are able to fulfill their basic needs and remove themselves from an environment that is harsh and difficult.

Many children, however, fall into a pattern involving helplessness and hostile aggression. They watch violence on television, which confirms their belief that it is a bad world. They join gangs, which reinforce the view that the only way to get what we want is to act in a violent and aggressive manner (Hammond & Yung, 1993). Many male youth assume a macho role characterized by insensitivity, dominance, and hostility to women (Sanday, 1981). Typically, gang members regard the world as hostile and threatening. It perhaps is not surprising that gangs often confine themselves to a very limited territory. Many find the world too frightening to venture outside those self-imposed boundaries.

Empathy

People who tend to be more empathetic, as indicated by self-report, are less inclined to be aggressive (Miller & Eisenberg, 1988). As might be expected, abusive parents tend to score lower than other parents do on measures of empathy (Feshbach, 1987). Further, children who were abused tend to exhibit less empathy than nonabused children do. In fact, considerable evidence indicates that abusive parents' lack of empathy has long-term negative implications for the socioemotional development of these children. This lack of empathy and generally poor emotional development could account for the cycle of violence. Miller & Eisenberg (1988) have suggested empathy training as a way of helping to break this cycle of violence.

The Cognitive Component

The model in Figure 8-6 suggests that, if people have nurturing parents, good guidance, and good role models, they are more likely to develop a positive self-concept characterized by self-control. Alternatively, individuals exposed to violence from their parents and deviant role models will come to see themselves as victims.

Many theorists have argued that, ultimately, people need to develop a sense of control, which often has its roots in beliefs about competence and justice. A sense of control allows people to believe that they can deal with their unfulfilled needs.

These perceptions tend to grow out of a strong, well-functioning community. When there is structure, there are rules. Participants within such a system can expect certain things to happen should they do certain things. Researchers have suggested that a good way to help children who might otherwise fall into criminal behavior is to get them to participate in their community. In the process of participating, they will come to see that they can have an effect (control) and that the route to that control is learning the rules. In other words, they learn that there is justice, provided they respect certain norms.

People come to see themselves as victims when they have no sense of real control, and they attribute this and their misfortunes to their past history. A consistent finding in the aggression research literature is that individuals tend to be highly influenced by those with whom they associate and from whom they seek approval (Staub, 1996). Individuals who live in the larger world composed of communities and nations will be sensitive to all the diverse needs of other people; however, those whose only world is their antisocial friends will allow their antisocial friends to define their values.

Summary

Violence in youth can be understood by two paths: one leads to more conventional, participant behavior; the other leads to antisocial and criminal behavior. According to the model, frustrated needs lead to hostile feelings. Whether these hostile feelings are channeled into more instrumental and adaptive behaviors or into hostile aggression behaviors depends largely on how the parents treat the child. Further, role models, both positive and negative, reinforce those initial differences in direction. If the disposition to act in an adaptive way is reinforced in schools and the community, youth can develop a sense of self-control and involvement. This is the basis for conventional and participatory behavior. If the disposition to act in a more hostile way is supported by antisocial peers, youth can develop a

sense of being helpless victims. This is the basis for antisocial and criminal behavior.

Aggression and Crime

When people think of aggression, they often think of it relative to crime. Because our jails are filled and overflowing, the media argue aggression is on the rise in our society. Most people who are in jail, however, are not there because they are aggressive. They are there because they have done such things as used drugs, stolen things, failed to pay a bill, engaged in fraud. Jails do contain people who have committed acts of violence, but many of those acts of violence were not precipitated by aggression but, rather, for economic reasons—wiping out an adversary such as can happen when two gangs attempt to gain control of the drug traffic. Let's examine how people involved in conceptualizing crime view the origins of crime.

An Integrated Theory of Crime

The integrated theory of crime that we are going to discuss has its roots in control theory. The underlying assumption is that people who commit crimes are low in the ability to control their impulsivity. Impulsivity, within the integrated theory of crime, is a word that is used to describe a complex of personality characteristics that include (1) the need for immediate gratification of desires; (2) the desire to avoid great outputs of time or energy (money without work, sex without courtship); (3) preference for activities that are exciting, thrilling, or risky; (4) the absence of long-term commitment be it interpersonal or economic (e.g., investments); (5) the absence of planning; and (6) insensitivity to the pain or discomfort of others (Gottfredson & Hirschi, 1990).

These six traits should be viewed as overlapping, rather than as distinct. Clearly, if one is driven by immediate gratification for doing exciting things, there will be little or no commitment to the expenditure of time, energy, planning, or commitment.

Not all people who are impulsive commit crimes because some have developed the ability to delay gratification and to satisfy their needs for risk in sociably acceptable ways. That this is learned rather than inherited comes from research that shows people with low self-control come from families that are dysfunctional. Research indicates that the family structure, rather than poverty, predicts crime. Poverty is often the result of being impulsive, rather than being the cause. According to an integrated theory of crime, what prevents crime is conformity to social structure.

A good theory of crime needs to address two issues: (1) gender differences and (2) something called the age-curve. Age curve refers to the fact that acts of crime begin in early adolescence, peak in late adolescence, and then decline in early adulthood. Although some variation exists between the sexes and among different cultures, it is essentially an invariant characteristic (Gottfredson & Hirschi, 1990). Gender differences refer to the finding that a disproportionate number of crimes are committed by males. Although evidence indicates that female children receive more supervision from their parents (something that should lead to more conformity), this does not appear to account for the sex differences (Brannigan, 1997).

Researchers have suggested that the age curve and gender differences can be understood through evolutionary psychology. Specifically, researchers have suggested that "males gain reproductive success by commanding and displaying resources that exceed their subsistence needs" (Daly & Wilson, 1988, p. 179). As a result researchers have suggested males are attracted to crime. The age curve corresponds to the period of sexual maturation starting at puberty and trailing off around the first marriage (Brannigan, 1997).

The reason some males do not become criminals, researchers have argued, is because their socialization stresses such things as delay of gratification, empathy, planning, and work. In the absence of such supervision, the default setting appears to be impulsiveness.

One final point. The research suggests that the acquisition of prosocial behaviors occur in the first 6 to 8 years (Gottfredson & Hirschi, 1990). Thus, if we are to reduce crime, we need to start early. I point this out because many writers have documented the failure of our penal system in deterring crime and why rehabilitation programs that offer jobs typically fail. They fail, researchers have argued, because they do not address the underlying personality of the criminal (Brannigan, 1997).

Aggression and Self-Esteem

It has become popular in recent years to view many societal problems, including aggression and violence, as caused by low self-esteem. As a result, the media have praised the virtues raising self-esteem and governments have become involved in programs to nurture self-esteem (California Task Force, 1990). The guiding model behind the idea that low self-esteem leads to aggression is the compensatory model that hypothesizes people are motivated to engage in aggression and violence because they lack self-esteem (e.g., Toch, 1993). The evidence, however, does not support that idea. In fact, considerable evidence indicates that aggression and violence are linked to a form of high self-esteem. Specially, researchers have suggested that aggression and violence are linked to egotism—a term used to refer to "favorable appraisals of self and to the motivated preference for such favorable appraisals, regardless of whether they are valid or inflated" (Baumeister, Smart, & Boden, 1996, p. 6).

One interesting characteristic of the self-concept is that people normally resist modifying their self-concept even when external evidence indicates that they are not viewing themselves objectively. That is true for people with both high and low self-esteem. In concrete terms that means people with low self-esteem maintain a sense of low self-esteem even when they are succeeding and receiving the approval of others and that people with high self-esteem maintain that sense of high self-esteem even when they are not succeeding and when other people are not giving them approval. We will discuss this paradox more in Chapter 14. For now, let me simply point out that, for whatever reason, people are inclined to maintain their existing level of self-esteem or self-appraisal. Of particular interest to us here is that people with high self-esteem attempt to maintain that high self-esteem even when it seems unwarranted.

It is important to understand the distinction between positive self-appraisal that is earned versus not earned. When positive self-appraisal is based on skills and accomplishments, we say it is earned. When it is based on such things as birth, race, sex, membership in some group, we say it is not earned. For example, feeling superior because one is white is not earned. Feeling superior because one is born into the upper classes is not earned. Feeling superior because one belongs to a gang that espouses their superiority is not earned.

Humans seem to be highly motivated to defend their favorable self-view, so what are the implications of this distinction? If we have skills and are challenged, we can defend ourselves by exercising our skills. If we don't have skills, the situation is entirely different. Now we are faced with a very different task. It appears from the research that one way some people deal with this situation is by engaging in aggression and violence. They defend their cherished view of themselves by attacking others who might challenge that view. Researchers have suggested that the motivation for so fiercely defending their self-view comes from the consequences of not defending that self-view. When people feel they need to give up a cherished view, they typically experience feelings of anxiety, sadness, and dejection (Heatherton & Polivy, 1991b).

It is possible to view self-esteem as a zero sum game in which to gain self-esteem you need to take it from others or a nonzero sum game in which everybody can succeed. People who come to see themselves as superior, but not based on competence, appear to view self-esteem as a zero sum game. They get their self-esteem by taking it from others. People who see themselves as competent, on the other hand, get their self-esteem from exercising competence and feel good about themselves by exercising their competence.

Not everybody with high self-esteem is prone to aggression and violence. This tendency appears to be more related to (1) having an inflated self-view rather than an accurate self-view and (2) having an unstable self-esteem level. As noted earlier, people have a tendency to maintain a consistent perception of their self-esteem levels, irrespective of external input. If, however, a person has managed to develop a more favorable view of him or herself, such as by joining a gang, they are inclined to embrace that view and defend it against any contrary information that might force them to give it up.

Researchers have suggested that when people are faced with the choice of accepting or rejecting negative appraisal they need to make a choice—to either accept it or withdraw. Figure 8-7 provides a schematic of what happens. Note in this schematic that negative emotions give rise to feelings of threat. This perception of threat arouses the FFS that we discussed earlier.

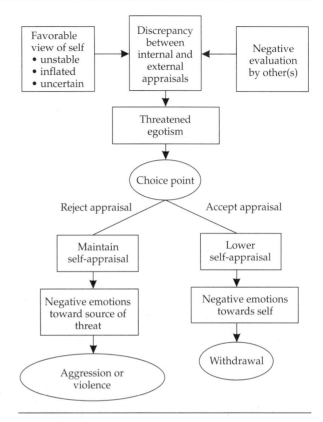

Figure 8-7. Schematic representation of the relation of threatened egotism to violent behavior. (From "Relation of Threatened Egotism to Violence and Aggression: The Dark Side of High Self-Esteem," by R. F. Baumeister, L. Smart, and J. M. Boden, *Psychological Review*, 1996, *103*, 5–33. Copyright © 1996 by the American Psychological Association. Reprinted by permission of the author.)

This model has the potential to explain a wide range of violent behaviors that are sometimes difficult to explain by the theory of control (Gottfredson & Hirschi, 1990).

1. **Alcohol and aggression.** Alcohol gives rise to favorable self-appraisal (Banaji & Steele, 1989). Thus, people who are intoxicated might be more prone to aggression.
2. **Assault.** Men who have been imprisoned for assault often have a good self-appraisal. Research

suggests that the reason they assault is they are excessively prone to regard the remarks of others as insulting or belittling (Berkowitz, 1978).

3. **Bullying.** There is no evidence that bullies suffer low self-esteem. Indeed, it appears they have very good opinions of themselves. The act of bullying appears to be how some individuals assure themselves they are superior (Olweus, 1994).

4. **Dueling.** Dueling in European history took place among the upper class. It was often precipitated by inflated notions of honor, virtue, entitlement, and respect (Kierens, 1989).

5. **Rape.** Evidence suggests that male rapists have a belief in male superiority. Further, one study found that one pattern of rape was precipitated by threats to the rapist's ego (Groth, 1979).

6. **Domestic violence.** Considerable evidence indicates that abusive husbands often endorse the traditional views about family—especially male privilege and responsibility for the family (Gondolf, 1985).

7. **Elder abuse.** Victims of elder abuse tend, on the whole, to be more independent and in control. Abusers, on the other hand, tend to be more dependent and are embarrassed by their lack of independence. Their refusal to accept their dependent role and their aggression fits with the pattern of high but threatened self-esteem (Baumeister et al., 1996).

Practical Application 8-1

Learning to Manage Anger

Anger is the bridge both to physical and verbal aggression and to hostility (Buss & Perry, 1992). Accordingly, we need to learn how to manage anger if we are to reduce our aggression and hostility. Research has shown that it is possible for people to learn to control their anger, even following relatively brief training sessions (Snyder, Kymissis, & Kessler, 1999).

Anger can be a very powerful source of positive energy if it is properly channeled. The civil rights movement and the feminist movement both grew out of a strong sense of injustice fueled by feelings of anger. Although some people in both movements allowed their anger to turn to aggression and violence, most directed their anger toward changing the system. As Martin Luther King reported, "When I am angry I can write, pray, and preach well, for then my whole temperament is quickened, my understanding sharpened, and all mundane vexations and temptations gone." In your own experience, a critical comment from a professor on a paper you wrote might have angered you but also stirred you to think more clearly and argue more precisely. That has been true for me.

When not properly directed or managed, however, anger can be a very destructive emotion. If we allow it to fester inside us, it can lead to physical problems such as hypertension. On the other hand, if we ventilate it—if we strike out at the source of our anger—we often make matters worse. There is little evidence to support the idea that ventilation is a good way of draining off hostile energy. Many people who ventilate experience shame and loss of control. In the heat of an angry exchange, they do things that they later regret. In addition, yelling or shouting escalates the negative bodily reactions; anger turns to rage, and we are left in a state of heightened negative emotion. If we learn to control our anger—to cool down—we are less likely to fall prey to this problem.

Learning to cool down—by counting to ten, for example—might not be the best long-term solution, however, especially for people who are chronically angry. Many chronically angry people interpret the actions of others as motivated by anger and aggression. As a result, they feel constantly provoked. When a person on a bus rings the bell twice, for example, a chronically angry bus driver might interpret the response as a deliberate act of provocation. It could be, however, that the person who rang twice is merely anxious about missing the next stop.

How do we learn to change our perceptual habits without becoming totally passive and helpless? Here are some suggestions. (For more on this topic, see Tavris, 1989.)

1. **Look for another explanation.** When people are critical or act in ways that violate our norms or expectations, they could be distracted or under stress. On one occasion, a car

8. **Violent gangs and juvenile delinquency.** Researchers have suggested that "Violent youth seem sincerely to believe that they are better than other people, but they frequently find themselves in circumstances that threatened or challenge these beliefs, and in those circumstances they tend to attack other people (Baumeister et al., 1996, p. 22).

9. **Political terror.** Political terror is often correlated with a favorable view of oneself. If you feel your views are correct, then one way of dealing with those who disagree is to attack them (Baumeister et al., 1996).

10. **Genocide.** A psychological analysis of four major genocides found that the aggressor had a sense of being superior and the event of genocide was precipitated by a threatening condition challenging that idea (Staub, 1989).

Summary

According to the integrated theory, crime has its roots in an impulsive personality that has not been socialized to conform to the norms of our society. These norms would include such basic things as the need to delay gratification and the need to work, plan, and expend energy. Finally, we must develop a sense of empathy

---

ran a stop sign and forced me to slam on my brakes. In the process it sliced off my front license plate. Not surprisingly, I felt angry. However, when the driver apologized and explained that his wife had just been diagnosed with cancer, my anger quickly subsided.

2. **Distract yourself.** One of the best ways to reduce anger is to get involved in some absorbing activity. Some people find exercise works; others read or watch TV; still others become involved in their favorite hobby.

3. **Look for the humor.** Humor is a way of recasting a situation to find the incongruity or the absurdity in it. When we can do that, our anger will subside because humor is incompatible with anger. Learning to laugh at our reactions helps relieve our anger and communicates to others that we understand our reactions were inappropriate.

4. **Determine what triggers your anger.** Keep a diary of your anger, so that you can discover what types of situations make you angry. Some people, for example, find that criticism makes them angry; others find that certain behaviors of others make them angry; and so forth. Once you understand what triggers your anger, you can develop plans to deal with such situations (Novaco, 1985).

5. **Create an inner dialogue that reduces anger.** Most people carry on inner dialogues with themselves. Although some people have dialogues that reduce anger, others have dialogues that escalate or maintain their anger (Jacobs, cited in Tavris, 1989). After a divorce, couples might stay angry with each other for years. They might, for example, dwell on one thing, such as an affair their spouse had, and still be trying to extract the kind of apology they thought they deserved. By becoming aware of our inner dialogue, we can begin to change it.

6. **Learn to recognize that life is not always fair.** Unless we accept that the world is less than perfect, we will become angry at anything and everything—being treated impolitely, breaking a leg because we tripped on a broken sidewalk, finding we weren't invited to a party, having a flat tire on our way to work, and so on. Whether to become angry or not can be a decision. This is a decision that we can learn to make both consciously and unconsciously. We can develop the habit of accepting the fact that life is unfair.

7. **Learn to talk it out and negotiate.** Anger often accompanies conflict. One way to decrease anger is to engage in a dialogue that will enable us to see how the other party views the situation. Although we might not always agree, talking provides the basis for negotiating some kind of solution or compromise. Most of us do not like to compromise but, once we learn that compromise is better than prolonging anger, we can appreciate the fine art of compromise as a means for living happier and more stress-free lives.

toward others. Researchers have suggested that age-curve and gender differences can be explained by principles of evolutionary psychology. Various crimes, researchers have suggested, are attractive to young males because they can display excess resources—a condition favorable for attracting females and propagating.

One current myth is that aggression and violence have their roots in low self-esteem. In reality, it appears that aggression and violence have their roots in a form of high self-esteem has been referred to as egotism. This form of high self-esteem is characterized as an inflated view but unstable view of the self. The basic concepts of the theory account for aggression and violence in a wide range of situations.

Main Points

1. Moyer has identified at least eight types of aggression in animals, all of which can also be found in humans.
2. Human aggression is traditionally defined as behavior against another person with the intention of committing harm.
3. Much of aggression has its roots in our need to control the actions of others.
4. According to our working definition, aggression is the willingness to engage in physical and psychological acts of harm to control the actions of other people.
5. An aggressive act motivated by the desire to achieve a desired goal, rather than by the desire to harm another person, is called instrumental aggression.
6. The prehormone androstenedione has been linked to female aggression.
7. About 20 to 25% of aggression can be linked to endocrine factors.
8. Frustration might motivate people to strike out at the source of the frustration, but often behavior is

displaced to a safer goal object. The principles of generalization and inhibition can account for this phenomenon.
9. Modeling and imitation are thought to account for the cycle of violence.
10. According to the theory of coercive action, people are inclined to use threats and punishment to achieve certain terminal goals.
11. Coercive actions are motivated by the value of justice. Three aspects of justice have been distinguished: distributive justice, procedural justice, and interactional justice.
12. People who are chronically unable to get what they want through verbal means will sometimes resort to violence.
13. Researchers have suggested that youth violence has its roots in frustrated needs that give rise to hostile feelings.
14. Whether these hostile feelings lead to instrumental and adaptive behaviors depends on parental attitudes and the available role models.
15. One of the underlying assumptions of the Integrated Theory of Crime is that people who commit crimes are low in their ability to control their impulsive natures.
16. Through socialization, an individual can learn to delay gratification, make plans for the future, and develop empathy.
17. High, unstable self-esteem has been linked to aggression and violence.

 ## InfoTrac® College Edition

What are some of the current findings pertaining to reasons for there being differences in male and female aggression? (Search words: aggressiveness [Psychology], male aggression, female aggression)

Chapter Nine

Emotions, Stress, and Health

- ■ *Do we have any control over our emotions?*
- ■ *Why is stress regarded as an emotion?*
- ■ *Why is stress often linked to health?*
- ■ *Why is stress often referred to as the fight-or-flight response?*
- ■ *What chemicals are released when we are under stress, and what do these chemicals do?*
- ■ *Why is stress often linked to diseases such as cancer?*
- ■ *Do certain personality types experience more stress?*
- ■ *How can people make themselves more resistant to stress and disease?*

Stress is typically viewed as a uniquely human emotion that results from the way we appraise the world. For most humans stress is a negative source of affect that gets in the way of our doing things that we want to do. Among other things, stress interferes with our ability to focus our attention. For some people, when stress becomes very high, the sole focus of life becomes escaping from stress. In recent years, stress has been linked to a wide range of health disorders. When we experience negative emotions, the immune system weakens, and when we experience positive emotions the immune system strengthens (Salovey, Rothman, Detweiler & Steward, 2000). From a motivational perspective, therefore, it is important to understand what gives rise to stress and how to manage stress so it does not interfere with achieving goals. Although we will not discuss emotions in much detail, it is nevertheless important to have a rudimentary understanding of what emotions are and how emotions and motivation interact.

The main thing I want to emphasize is that emotions often have their roots the way we appraise the environment and our reactions to it. As we will see, humans often come to appraise things as threats to their survival when, in fact, those things are not threats. As a result, the fight-flight response is activated. Many people also come to see large portions of the environment (such as their jobs, their neighborhoods) as sources of threat. As a result, the fight-flight response is activated for long periods. What we have discovered is that when the fight-flight response is activated for long periods, many physiological and psychological things happen. Physiologically, our immune system shuts down, which makes us prone to all kinds of diseases that we can normally ward off. For example, people who are dealing with severe stressors for longer than a month are substantially more susceptible to colds (Cohen et al., 1998). Psychologically, we find we have difficulty focusing our attention and often develop a negative mood state; a condition that undermines our ability to cope as well as to ward off disease (Salovey et al., 2000).

In the previous chapter, we discussed anger and aggression as also having their roots in the perception of threat. That threat was relatively specific, for example, a threat that was aroused by another person or persons. Moreover, the threat was often short-lived. In stress, however, the perceived threat that leads to what we call the stress response is typically a more generalized one and as a result the stress is more difficult to eliminate (Dozier, 1998); thus, we experience a prolonged fight-flight response. In other words, even though we start at the same point when we talk about aggression and anger, the outcome of stress is generally quite different and the variables that are involved are quite different.

In this chapter, we will focus on understanding how and why humans develop this kind of generalized perception of threat and how humans can change or manage such perceptions when they are not adaptive. Let's start by looking at the link between emotions and motivation.

Emotions and Motivation

In recent years, researchers have come to believe that we cannot think about emotions without considering motivation and that we cannot think about motivation without considering emotion (Frijda, 1988; Lazarus, 1991a, b, c). This has not always been the case. In the 1930s and 1940s, motivation was conceptualized in terms of needs. Needs were thought to provide the impetus (energy), the direction, and the persistence of behavior. Little was said about the role of emotions. In the 1950s and 1960s, motivation was conceptualized as caused by the existence of drives. In these early theories, drives provided the energy or impetus for behavior, and learning provided the direction (Hull, 1943). According to the drive theorists, emotions were thought to be mainly a by-product of motivation but not integral to motivation. Berlyne (1960), for example, conceptualized motivation as the drive for optimal arousal and regarded affect as a by-product of satisfying that drive. Within drive theory, persistence was conceptualized as largely learned. According to Amsel's (1958, 1972) theory, for example, persistence was largely caused by the counterconditioning of stimuli linked with frustration, and frustration represented a very limited concept of emotion—an emotion that grew out of failure to receive a reward.

In the later 1960s and early 1970s, psychologists began to talk about motivation in terms of action. Motives and needs were central in this conceptualization, but needs were conceptualized very differently than in the 1930s and 1940s. Psychologists began to view needs not as causing action, but merely as dispositions to action. What created actions were goals and threats; goals were conceptualized as positive incentives and threats as negative incentives (Atkinson & Birch, 1978; de Rivera, 1982; Raynor, 1974; Weiner, 1974).

Conceptualizing motivation in terms of goals proved to be a powerful theory (Locke & Latham, 1990; Pervin, 1989; Snyder et al., 1991), but it became apparent to a number of theorists that goals and threats, although perhaps the impetus to immediate action, often failed to account for long-term action. Although some people persisted in their goal-directed behavior, others did not. What seemed to differentiate people in their persistence was their emotions. Those who could remain optimistic in the face of threats and difficulties persisted, whereas those who developed feelings of pessimism and self-doubt often abandoned their goals (Seligman, 1990).

Despite differences of emphasis, most contemporary theorists agree that emotions play a critical role in motivation. This observation led some psychologists to stress the self-regulation of emotions. As Albert Bandura (1991a) pointed out, "Talent is only as good as its execution." To achieve their goals, he argued, people need to learn how to manage their emotions, especially self-doubt (Bandura, 1997).

In the beginning of this chapter, we will discuss some of the basic emotions that have been implicated in goal-directed behavior. The major focus is on how people can learn to develop emotions that sustain goal-directed behavior and to neutralize or deflect emotions that tend to undermine goal-directed behavior.

The Definition of Emotions

Probably because emotions are so complex, many different definitions have been proposed over the years. Paul Kleinginna and Anne Kleinginna (1981a) have proposed a definition that incorporates the key elements of previous definitions. According to this consensual definition, emotions occur as a result of an interaction between subjective factors, environmental factors, and neural and hormonal processes. In support of this definition, they make the following points:

1. Emotions give rise to affective experiences, such as pleasure or displeasure.
2. Emotions stimulate us to generate cognitive explanations—to attribute the cause to ourselves or to the environment, for example.
3. Emotions trigger a variety of internal adjustments, such as increased heart rate.
4. Emotions elicit behaviors that are often, but not always, expressive (laughing or crying), goal-directed (helping or avoiding), and adaptive (removal of a potential threat to our survival).

As we see, this definition acknowledges that emotions result from the interaction of biological, learned, and cognitive processes.

Another very important function of emotions is to reward and punish behavior. When people experience a very positive emotion, they are likely to engage in behaviors that will produce that emotion again. Similarly, when people experience a very negative emotion, they will avoid behaviors that will cause them to feel that emotion again. In other words, emotions act as reinforcers of behavior (Thorndike's law of effect; Thorndike, 1913).

The Universal Nature of Emotions

Core Relational Themes

Various theorists argue that emotions result from our attempts to adapt to the environment. Evidence suggests that all humans experience a common set of emotions. Lazarus (1991a) has suggested that these emotions can be described by their *core relational themes* (Table 9-1). By adopting this term, Lazarus emphasizes that our emotional responses grow out of our interactions with the environment (are relational); are highly cognitive; and are often complex, frequently involving two or more emotions operating simultaneously. Identifying the various core themes in an emotional response would obviously help us to reduce its complexity.

Summing up his approach, Lazarus (1991c) states:

> The fundamental premise is that in order to survive and flourish, animals (humans in particular) are constructed biologically to be constantly evaluating (appraising) their relationships with the environment with respect to significance for well-being. (p. 825)

Table 9-1.   Core relational themes for various emotions.

Emotion	Core Relational Theme
Anger	A demeaning offense against me and mine.
Anxiety	Facing uncertain, existential threat.
Fright	Facing immediate, concrete, and overwhelming physical danger.
Guilt	Having transgressed a moral imperative.
Shame	Having failed to live up to an ego-ideal.
Sadness	Having experienced an irrevocable loss.
Envy	Wanting what someone else has.
Jealousy	Resenting a third party for loss of or threat to another's affection.
Disgust	Taking in or being too close to an indigestible object or idea (metaphorically speaking).
Happiness	Making reasonable progress toward the realization of a goal.
Pride	Enhancement of one's ego-identity by taking credit for a valued object or achievement.
Relief	A distressing goal-incongruent condition that has changed for the better or gone away.
Hope	Fearing the worst but yearning for better.
Love	Desiring or participating in affection, usually but not necessarily reciprocated.
Compassion	Being moved by another's suffering and wanting to help.

Source: Adapted from *Emotion and Adaptation*, by R. S. Lazarus, p. 122. Copyright © 1994 by Oxford University Press, Inc. Used by permission of Oxford University Press, Inc.

Facial Expressions

Studies of facial expressions reveal that certain basic emotions, such as happiness, anger, distress, and disgust, can be identified in a wide range of cultures. This supports the idea that there are core relational themes underlying emotions. Based on data on facial expressions, some researchers have even argued that most—if not all—emotions are a product of heredity. Whether this is true is still being hotly debated because other re-

searchers view emotions as largely the product of learning and culture (Ekman, 1994; Russell, 1995).

What seems quite clear is that, when people experience an emotion, they are inclined to wear that emotion on their faces. Further, evidence suggests that, when people deliberately put on a happy or a sad face, they tend to trigger the emotion that corresponds to the facial expression (e.g., Izard, 1990). Noting the close link between emotions and facial expression, Izard has suggested that people can learn to regulate their subjective feelings by learning to control their facial expressions (Izard, 1990). The bottom line is that, if you want to be happy, you put on a happy face.

The Role of Appraisal in Emotions

According to Lazarus (1991c) whether we experience a certain emotion depends on how we appraise a situation. For example, we might ask ourselves, "What emotion is appropriate for this situation, given my goals, my motives, and my concerns?" The idea that appraisal plays an important role in our emotions suggests, of course, that cognitions are central to emotions. If cognitions (ways of thinking) are important, then the implicit theories that people hold are also important. For example, people who tend to be optimistic and those who tend to pessimism will experience very different patterns of emotions; people are happier if they think optimistically. As we will see, how much stress people experience depends largely on whether they appraise a situation as a threat or a challenge. Because people are inclined to appraise situations differently, large individual differences in emotion often occur.

Summary

Like aggression and anger, stress has it roots in the perception that our survival is somehow threatened. Stress differs from aggression and anger, however, in that stress seems to come from a more generalized perception of threat.

Although early theorists conceptualized motivation in terms of drives, current theorists conceptualize motivation in terms of needs, which are viewed as dispositions. Whereas goals are often the impetus for action, sustained action appears to depend on positive emotions such as optimism. It seems that people can learn to regulate their emotions and thus sustain goal-directed behavior.

According to the definition proposed by Kleinginna and Kleinginna, emotions give rise to affective experiences, stimulate the individual to generate cognitive explanations, trigger a variety of internal adjustments, and elicit expressive, goal-directed, and adaptive behaviors.

Evidence from a variety of sources suggests that humans share a common set of emotions, which can be described by their core relational themes. This idea is consistent with the work on facial expression. Whether we experience a certain emotion depends on how we appraise a situation.

What Is Stress?

The Definition of Stress

Stress has to do with adapting to threat, or, to use a more positive word, adapting to challenge (Friedman, 1992). In our daily lives, we speak of stress in connection with, for instance, taking examinations, the breakup of a marriage or relationship, struggling to pay our bills, commuting on congested roads, and dealing with people we dislike. Notice that stress has come to describe a diverse set of negative feelings. Failing an examination produces feelings of humiliation and shame; the breakup of a relationship may lead to a deep sense of loss and remorse; not being able to pay our bills can be frustrating and irritating; driving on a crowded road can produce both frustration and anger; conflicts in interpersonal relationships can lead to contempt and disgust.

Although laypeople generally use the term *stress* to refer to various negative feelings, the scientist thinks of stress somewhat differently—as a set of neurological and physiological reactions that serve some ultimate adaptive purpose. How the individual responds to those reactions determines whether they produce feelings of *distress* (a negative feeling) or *eustress* (a positive feeling). In general, when people view an event as threatening, they experience distress; when they view it as challenging, they experience eustress.

Current research indicates that, when people interpret an event as challenging their health is not adversely affected; however, when they interpret it as threatening, their health can be adversely affected. In general, people who interpret an event as challenging engage in coping responses, which might be responsible for the different health outcomes of the two interpretations. This implies that simply learning appropriate coping responses will lead to improved health (Cohen & Williamson, 1991; Friedman, 1991). We will consider the links between stress and health later in the chapter.

Stress as a Sustained Fight-or-Flight Response

When people talk about the stress reaction, they frequently refer to it as the fight-or-flight response. This label grows out of an evolutionary analysis. Animals have two basic ways of dealing with threats: they fight or they flee. Rabbits are designed to flee to stay alive even though they sometimes fight. Lions, in contrast, are designed to fight to stay alive even though they sometimes flee. Whether we fight or flee, certain basic requirements must be met. First, we need to expend a great deal of energy. Second, we have to keep our head. Third, we frequently have to deal with injury. The stress reaction clearly meets these requirements (Figure 9-1). To maximize energy needs, blood rushes to the sites where it is needed (the muscles and brain); fats are released into the bloodstream; we perspire to cool ourselves; and so forth. The high level of arousal that we experience helps us focus our attention on survival cues. To help us deal with injury, our blood thickens, and chemicals are released to enable our body to deal with injury, should it occur.

In our lives today, we do not have to expend as much physical energy as our foraging ancestors did, nor are we normally threatened with injury when we experience stress. We no longer need to have so much fat released in our blood; we do not need to perspire; our blood pressure need not skyrocket; our blood need not thicken to guard against an injury; we do not need chemicals circulating in our blood to attack some foreign body that might enter our system. Nevertheless, each time we experience stress, our body prepares itself as though we were still living as our ancestors lived.

Let's consider the biological, learned, and cognitive components of stress.

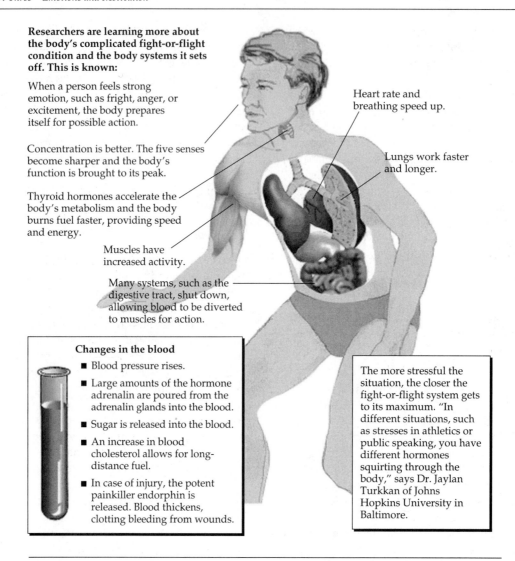

Researchers are learning more about the body's complicated fight-or-flight condition and the body systems it sets off. This is known:

When a person feels strong emotion, such as fright, anger, or excitement, the body prepares itself for possible action.

Concentration is better. The five senses become sharper and the body's function is brought to its peak.

Thyroid hormones accelerate the body's metabolism and the body burns fuel faster, providing speed and energy.

Muscles have increased activity.

Many systems, such as the digestive tract, shut down, allowing blood to be diverted to muscles for action.

Heart rate and breathing speed up.

Lungs work faster and longer.

Changes in the blood

- Blood pressure rises.
- Large amounts of the hormone adrenalin are poured from the adrenalin glands into the blood.
- Sugar is released into the blood.
- An increase in blood cholesterol allows for long-distance fuel.
- In case of injury, the potent painkiller endorphin is released. Blood thickens, clotting bleeding from wounds.

The more stressful the situation, the closer the fight-or-flight system gets to its maximum. "In different situations, such as stresses in athletics or public speaking, you have different hormones squirting through the body," says Dr. Jaylan Turkkan of Johns Hopkins University in Baltimore.

Figure 9-1.   Stress can be viewed as a fight-or-flight response. Psychologists define stress as a set of neurological and physiological reactions that are ultimately adaptive. (Adapted from "Stress Reaction," by Rob Struthers. Copyright © *The Calgary Herald*. Reprinted with permission.)

The Biological Component of Stress

The Sympathetic/Adrenal and Pituitary/Adrenal Responses

When people are challenged, they tend to mobilize a great deal of effort to deal with that event. Similarly, when people lose control, they might try to reassert control. Under these conditions, the body makes a sympathetic/adrenal response. The sympathetic system allows us to respond to the immediate demands of the situation by activating the body: our heart rate accelerates, our blood pressure rises, and we become more alert. In short, we become aroused (Chapter 5). To provide a longer-term chemical backup to the immediate action of the sympathetic system, the adrenal

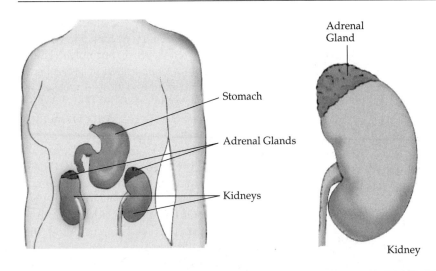

Figure 9-2. The location of the adrenal glands in the body. (From K. B. Hoyenga and K. T. Hoyenga, *Motivational Explanations of Behavior.* Copyright © 1984 by Wadsworth, Inc.)

glands (Figure 9-2)—specifically, the adrenal medulla (the inner part of the gland; Figure 9-3)—release epinephrine and norepinephrine.*

Whereas the sympathetic/adrenal system takes care of arousal, the pituitary/adrenal system is more closely associated with what is traditionally called the stress reaction—our fight-or-flight responses. The adrenal cortex (the outer part of the gland) secretes two main types of hormones: the mineralocorticoids and the glucocorticoids (including cortisol and corticosterone). The release of these hormones is linked to the release of other chemicals, as we'll see shortly. Under stress, the sympathetic/adrenal and the pituitary/adrenal responses typically occur together. However, these two systems operate separately in some circumstances—generally when we attempt to gain control over stress by engaging in some kind of adaptive behavior. As we gain control, the cortisol level frequently drops, while the epinephrine level remains high (Frankenhaeuser, Lundberg, & Forsman, 1980). Cortisol is frequently used as a measure of the action of the pituitary/adrenal system, whereas urinary epinephrine is a measure of the activity of the sympathetic/adrenal system. The endocrine glands and hormones associated with stress responses are summarized in

Table 9-2. We explored the sympathetic/adrenal system in Chapter 5. Let's now turn to the pituitary/adrenal system.

The Pituitary/Adrenal Response

The hypothalamus initiates activity in the pituitary/adrenal system (Figure 9-3) by secreting corticotropin-releasing factor (CRF), which stimulates the pituitary. The pituitary, in turn, secretes adrenocorticotropic hormone (ACTH). Although we commonly use the term pituitary in this context, the anterior portion of the pituitary is involved.

Experimental findings suggest that ACTH plays a central role in our ability to respond to threatening stimuli. Curiously, ACTH stimulates another hormonal reaction that is responsible for terminating further ACTH secretion. Specifically, ACTH stimulates the adrenal cortex, which then secretes glucocorticoids. When the glucocorticoid level is elevated, the central nervous system shuts down the processes that lead to ACTH secretion (de Wied, 1967, 1980; Vernikos-Danellis & Heybach, 1980).

Animal research indicates that ACTH is released approximately 10 seconds after a stressful event. The slowness of this reaction—relative to the central nervous system, which acts immediately—suggests that the endocrine system is probably involved in longer-term survival reactions, rather than in the immediate survival responses of fight-or-flight. For example,

*Epinephrine and norepinephrine are also referred to as adrenaline and noradrenaline, respectively, especially when they are released to the periphery of the system rather than to the brain. This distinction is often ignored, however.

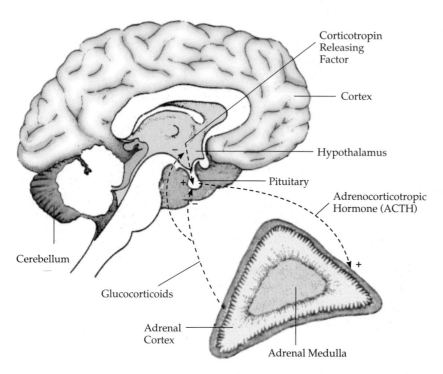

Corticotropin
Releasing
Factor

Cortex

Hypothalamus

Pituitary

Adrenocorticotropic
Hormone (ACTH)

Cerebellum

Glucocorticoids

Adrenal
Cortex

Adrenal Medulla

Figure 9-3. The interaction of the pituitary, hypothalamic, and adrenal cortical hormones. The brain is illustrated in a so-called midsagittal section—that is, as if sliced down the middle, halfway between the ears, from front to back. Corticotropin-releasing hormone from the hypothalamus stimulates secretion of ACTH from the pituitary. ACTH stimulates the secretion of the corticosteroids from the adrenal cortex into the bloodstream. In turn, the glucocorticoids inhibit both the hypothalamic and pituitary secretion of hormones. This is an example of a negative feedback loop. (From K. B. Hoyenga and K. T. Hoyenga, *Motivational Explanations of Behavior.* Copyright © 1984 by Wadsworth, Inc.)

ACTH stimulates fatty acid release and glucose utilization, thereby providing the energy to deal with a threat (White, Handler, & Smith, 1964). It takes between 15 minutes and 1 hour for the glucocorticoids to reach a level sufficient to terminate ACTH secretion (Vernikos-Danellis & Heybach, 1980). Thus, once set in motion, the stress reaction continues for a time. The glucocorticoids remain active much longer than the ACTH does. The continued presence of glucocorticoids in the blood could account for some poststress reactions, such as weight loss, changes in body temperature, and increased secretion of stomach acid (Weiss, 1968).

Prolonged stress seems to result in a breakdown of the adrenal system, accompanied by susceptibility to a variety of diseases. We'll return to this topic shortly.

Endorphins and Stress

Beta-endorphin is mobilized from the pituitary gland during stress in approximately the same quantities as ACTH (Rossier, Bloom, & Guillemin, 1980). This could explain why stress tends to induce analgesia (Akil, Madden, Patrick, & Barchas, 1976). In addition, endor-

phins produce feelings of euphoria, apparently by altering the concentrations of neurotransmitters that activate the reward pathways in the brain (Smith, Freeman, Sands, & Lane, 1980). A striking example of how pain is alleviated and euphoria is activated during stress is the reaction of a football player who breaks his collarbone. Instead of reporting pain, he insists to his coach that he wants to continue playing.

Laboratory studies of endorphins indicate that the endorphin response can be triggered not only by physical stressors, such as shock, but also by fear (Bolles & Fanselow, 1982). This could explain why people expose themselves to situations that elicit fear, such as parachuting and mountain climbing.

Stress and the Immune System

During the past 30 years, numerous studies have demonstrated how stressors cause changes in the immune system (Maier, Watkins, & Fleshner, 1994). Specifically, stressors seem to turn off the immune response. For example, researchers have demonstrated

Table 9-2. Endocrine glands involved in stress, distress, and coping.

Gland	Hormone	Action/Function
Hypothalamus	Corticotropin-releasing hormone	Stimulates the pituitary to release ACTH. The hypothalamus is initially triggered by the thalamus, but that action can be inhibited by the cortex.
Pituitary	ACTH (adrenocorticotropic hormone)	Stimulates the adrenal cortex to release glucocorticoids.
Adrenal Cortex	Glucocorticoids:	The glucocorticoids are also important in energy metabolism.
	Cortisol	Antiinflammatory, antiallergy (important in the fight-or-flight response).
	Corticosterone	Suppresses the immune system (important for keeping the immune response in check).
Adrenal Medulla	Epinephrine	Released following environmental extremes (for example, cold), physical exertion, fear. Increases heart rate, oxygen consumption, and glycogen mobilization.
	Norepinephrine	Released during coping, especially when coping response is vigorous. Increases blood pressure and constricts blood vessels.

that stress makes us more susceptible to infections and common colds (Cohen et al., 1998). There is still some question about the role of stress in cancer, but a number of researchers assert, mainly on the basis of correlational studies, that there is a link (Andersen, Kiecolt-Glaser, & Glaser, 1994). These findings need to be replicated using designs that can establish a causal link.

This research has wide-ranging implications for our health. Why would the immune system not work at maximum efficiency when we need it most? To answer that question, let's look at how the immune system operates.

Two Immune Systems

The immune system is very complex and is divided into two systems: nonspecific (innate) and specific (acquired). The nonspecific immune system is present from birth and, as its name suggests, operates in a nonspecific way, without regard to particular pathogens (for example, bacteria). The specific immune system is an acquired system; it learns to recognize foreign substances. T and B lymphocytes play a critical role in this system, which is involved in fighting such things as cancer and AIDS. The specific system has evolved more recently and involves some of the same mechanisms as the nonspecific system has.

Let's begin by examining the bidirectional effects between stress and nonspecific immunity and nonspecific immunity on stress. Understanding bidirectional effects allows us to understand such things as how and why such coping improves our mental health as well as our physical health. Following that discussion I will discuss some of the current thinking on how and why stress affects the specific system. My purpose is to show that there is, indeed, good reason to argue that if we want to be physically healthy, we need to develop certain health-enabling behaviors, including coping.

Stress and the Nonspecific Immune System

Links between the central nervous system and the immune system. To illustrate that immunity cannot be explained simply in physical terms, consider an experiment done with rats (Fleshner, Laudenslager, Simons, & Maier, 1989). When male rats are housed in groups, one—called the alpha rat—will become dominant. If a stranger is introduced, the alpha rat will attack the intruder. The intruder typically engages in defensive behaviors but, in the end, makes submissive responses (defeat postures). In this experiment, the intruder was administered an antigen (an agent that triggers an antibody response) before being introduced. Measurements of antibody activity indicated that being introduced into an established territory—even for brief periods—markedly reduced antibody activity. The reduction in antibody levels lasted as much as three weeks. To meet the objection that being bitten or attacked could explain the change in antibody activity, the experimenters measured the time spent in defeat postures and attacks. The results clearly showed that defeat postures were linked to antibody activity ($r = -0.80$). A small number of animals did not submit and received numerous bites; antibody activity in these animals was unaffected.

In humans, both *acute stressors,* such as final examinations, battle task vigilance, and sleep deprivation, and *chronic stressors,* such as divorce and bereavement, have been shown to affect the immune response. In addition, researchers have shown that depression, anger, and anxiety affect the immune system (Maier et al., 1994). Note, however, that different stressors cause different mixes of autonomic activation and hormone activity. Thus, we must study each stressor to determine how it affects us. As we'll see shortly, many things moderate the effects of stressors.

Links between the immune system and the central nervous system. Before the brain can participate in the immune response, it must receive information that an immune response is occurring. Indeed, considerable evidence indicates that both electrical and chemical activity does change when the immune response is activated. For example, researchers have shown that the level of the neurotransmitter norepinephrine changes in the hypothalamus (Carlson, Felten, Livnat, & Felten, 1987). Evidence also indicates that the immune response activates the pituitary/adrenal response by triggering the release of CRF in the hypothalamus (Maier et al., 1994). In other words, considerable evidence indicates that the central nervous system somehow monitors what is happening in the periphery of the body and then participates in the process.

It appears that an activated immune response triggers circuitry in the central nervous system to increase our sensitivity to pain. Sensitivity to pain is thought to have adaptive value during the recuperative process; for example, it helps us avoid reinjuring ourselves. Further research is needed to determine how mood, emotional reactivity, and attention are affected by the immune response.

We refer to the interplay between the stress response and the immune response as a bidirectional effect. What this means is that the two systems communicate in some way to produce an outcome that is favorable to the individual.

Functional significance of the bidirectional effects. Perhaps the best way to understand the functional significance of this bidirectional system involving stress and our immune responses is to consider inflammation, which is one of the most important aspects of the nonspecific immune response. Inflammation is a highly localized reaction that is designed to limit the damage resulting from tissue injury to one location and to prevent the invasion of infection and other irritants. In the inflammation process, agents are called to the site to remove pathogens and repairs are initiated. Inflammation lasts 1 to 2 hours and is followed in 8 to 12 hours by the acute phase response.

The acute phase response involves processes such as the production of agents to fight pathogens; the removal of the nutrients necessary for pathogens to grow; the synthesis of proteins involved in scavenging and removing cellular debris; and fever. Fever is highly adaptive. Elevated body temperature enhances a number of enzymatic reactions important for repairs and the proliferation of immune cells but suppresses the replication of unwanted microbes (Maier et al., 1994). The acute phase also involves reduced activity; being lethargic has benefits for recuperation. The hypothalamus is responsible for the regulation of temperature, so the involvement of the central nervous system is important in the acute phase response.

Stress, Energy, and Immunity: Evolution of the Stress Response

Under stress, the body's energy is redistributed. When we perceive that we are threatened, cardiac output is increased, blood from the digestive tract is shunted to the muscles, the muscles become more receptive to blood, the brain becomes active, pupils dilate for better distance vision, and so forth. It is highly adaptive to put those things that do not immediately threaten our survival on hold and to shift our energy resources to survival-related behavior.

Similarly, wouldn't it be productive to take the considerable energy going to the immune response and shift that to survival-related functions? Moreover, when dealing with a threat, we don't want to experience enhanced pain, fever, and reduced activity. In fact, it would be useful to experience analgesic effects, which is what happens under stress.

If energy is the key to maximizing survival, we would expect that the systems responsible for energy production will be mobilized. The glucocorticoids have been implicated not only in shutting down—or regulating—the inflammation process but in the mobilization of energy. The inflammation system appears to be very old, in evolutionary terms. The fight-or-flight response emerged much later, when organisms had developed the capacity to detect predators or other dangers, the motor capacity to take necessary action, and the ability to integrate these two functions. Evolution often works by using old systems for new purposes, so theorists have suggested that, when the fight-or-flight response emerged, it simply used the inflammation system (Maier et al., 1994). All that was required was to ensure that the system reacted immediately, and not 8 to 12 hours later when the acute phase of the inflammatory process normally begins.

What this means is that our immune response is now under the control of the stress response. Although this could be viewed as an unfortunate by-product of our evolutionary history, we have good reason to be optimistic. Because there are links between not only behaviors and the immune system but also thinking and the immune system, we can compensate for this loss. The answer lies in learning how to think and act in appropriate ways when stressed. If we learn such adaptive responses, our immune system will continue to do what it was designed to do.

Summary

A physical or psychological threat provokes a characteristic pattern of responses called the stress response. A series of chemical reactions set in motion by the hy-pothalamus alters, in a predictable way, our response to events in the environment. Most researchers have conceptualized the stress response as a fight-or-flight response, in which the body and brain are mobilized to deal with a threat. The stress response is thought to be caused by the action of the pituitary/adrenal system. This system causes the release of endorphins and the glucocorticoids, the hormones that have been implicated in the downgrading of the immune system.

Research has shown a bidirectional effect between the central nervous system and the immune system. This bidirectional action is important for regulating such things as the inflammation response. The impact of stress on the immune response has been explained as the evolutionary advantage of shutting down the immune response when threatened to shunt the associated energy to the fight-or-flight response. The net result is that our immune system has come under the control of the stress response.

The Learned Component of Stress

In this section, we focus on how people deal with brief periods of stress. Brief stresses are often associated with threats to our survival or sensory overload. In many respects, this form of stress is hard to distinguish from anxiety. Anxiety, however, is typically defined in more existential terms; it has more to do with our perceptions about the future. Stress is here and now; it has to do with what is affecting us at the moment.

Unpredictability and Stress

Whether we experience stress depends on several psychological factors. In particular, researchers have shown repeatedly that exposure to aversive events is much more likely to produce stress and disease if the events are unpredictable than if they can be foreseen. From an evolutionary perspective, unpredictability is a signal that something has changed. Because survival depends on things to be predictable (known), we must be sensitive to change (Dozier, 1998). Compared with predictable stress, unpredictable stress produces higher levels of corticosterone (Weiss, 1970, 1971a), more severe stomach ulceration (Caul, Buchanan, & Hays, 1972; Weiss, 1971a), greater weight loss (Weiss, 1970), alterations in the levels of glucose and free fatty acids (Quirce, Odio, & Solano, 1981), and myocardial dysfunction (Miller, Grossman, Richardson, Wistow, & Thomas, 1978).

In exploring the role of unpredictability, researchers have examined three main factors that influence whether an aversive event will lead to stress: discrimination of stress cues; availability of a coping response; and repeated experience with the aversive stimulus. Let's look at these factors.

Discrimination of Stress Cues

Research has shown that, if an organism experiences intermittent stress, knowing when that stress will come helps the organism prepare for the stress just before onset and to relax after the stress has ended. The problem for the organism, therefore, is to learn to discriminate the cues that predict the onset of stress. Laboratory research has confirmed that this is an important factor. In one study (Weiss, 1970), rats were given a warning signal that they were about to receive a tail shock. A yoked control group received the same duration and pattern of shocks but without a warning signal. Intermittent shocks produce not only a reliable stress reaction but also lesions in the stomach (thought to be a precursor to ulcers). The question was whether signaled or unsignaled shock would produce more lesions. As we see in Figure 9-4, unsignaled shocks are more stressful than signaled shocks. The analogy with humans is obvious. For instance, scheduled tests are difficult enough; unscheduled tests are even more stressful because they do not allow the student to relax. In the office, knowing when the boss is scheduled to arrive or when things normally go wrong can have important implications for learning to deal with stress.

Several studies have failed to show that signaled shock leads to less stress (Averill, 1973). Commenting on these studies, Averill notes that signaled shock seems to work only if the signal tells the subject not only when the shock will come but also when the subject can relax. The key, in other words, is knowing when to relax.

Availability of a Coping Response

Monkeys in a shock-avoidance situation show somewhat different levels of various catecholamine in their blood when they can and cannot avoid shock (Brady, 1975). Weiss (1968, 1971a) found that animals that learn

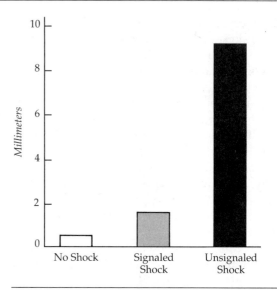

Figure 9-4. Total length of stomach lesions produced by shocks that are signaled, so that rats can learn a discrimination, and shocks that are unsignaled, so that no discrimination is possible. (From "Somatic Effects of Predictable and Unpredictable Shock," by J. M. Weiss, *Psychosomatic Medicine*, 1970, *32(4)*, 397–408. Copyright © 1970 by Elsevier North-Holland, Inc. Reprinted with permission.)

an avoidance response not only experience fewer lesions of the stomach but show less stress (as measured by level of plasma corticosterone) than do yoked control subjects with no opportunity to make an avoidance response. Exactly why coping responses reduce stress is not altogether clear. Studies have ruled out the possibility that their effectiveness is caused by the greater activity (exercise) that accompanies active avoidance (Weiss, Glazer, & Pohorecky, 1976). As we'll see in the next section, evidence indicates that the effect is cognitively mediated, at least partially.

If it is to be effective, the coping response must be fairly easy, as well as free of conflict. In one study, rats had to perform either an easy coping response (a single bar press) or a more difficult response (several bar presses) to avoid shock. Animals with an easy response had fewer stomach lesions than did their yoked partners (Tsuda & Hirai, 1975). In another experiment, rats had to experience a brief shock while making an avoidance response that prevented a longer train of

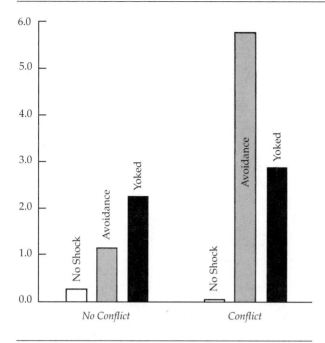

Figure 9-5. Total length of stomach lesions produced by an avoidance task when the avoidance response involves conflict and when it does not. The rat that learned the avoidance (coping) response suffered fewer stomach lesions than did yoked control subjects when the task was simple and clear-cut but considerably more when the task involved conflict. (From "Effects of Punishing the Coping Response (Conflict) on Stress Pathology in Rats," by J. M. Weiss, *Journal of Comparative and Physiological Psychology*, 1971, 77, 14–21. Copyright © 1971 by the American Psychological Association. Reprinted with permission of the author.)

shocks. In this situation, the coping group developed more stomach lesions than did the yoked control subjects, as we see in Figure 9-5 (Weiss, 1971b).

In everyday life, we learn to experience less stress if we know what to do. Say, for example, that your job is to deal with customer complaints. How can you learn to deal with constant exposure to customers' anger? Many training programs have been designed to deal with such situations. After training, most people experience very little stress. What these programs teach is how to diffuse the anger and solve the problem. This involves two steps. First, employees need to accept that the customer has been inconvenienced and so has a right to be angry, but that such anger is not directed at them personally. In accepting the anger, they communicate to the customer that they understand how the customer feels and are sympathetic. Second, they need to turn their attention to solving the problem. Once people see that someone is willing to help them, their anger often subsides and they too become involved in helping to solve the problem. People who learn this technique well can often turn a bad situation into a positive one for both themselves and the customer.

We'll return to the role of coping when we discuss moderators of stress.

Repeated Experience with the Aversive Stimulus

Studies have shown that an acute stress reaction depletes norepinephrine (Miller, 1980). Animals are slow to learn after an acute stress reaction, and researchers have suggested that the failure to learn is caused by the norepinephrine depletion (Dozier, 1998).

In a study to determine if the stress response can be habituated, rats were exposed to acute stress for 15 consecutive days. Control rats were exposed to acute stress on only one day, with no prior exposure. After exposure, indices of norepinephrine metabolism in the rats' brains were examined. The prior-exposure animals had higher levels of enzymes involved in norepinephrine synthesis than did the no-exposure animals (Weiss, Glazer, Pohorecky, Brick, & Miller, 1975).

Marianne Frankenhaeuser (1980) has argued that repeated exposure to a stressor will reduce the stress reaction (particularly the activity of the adrenal medulla) only if there is a decrease in psychological involvement. For example, she notes that parachute jumping never becomes routine. Catecholamine output during jump periods tends to remain high even after several jumps (Bloom, von Euler, & Frankenhaeuser, 1963). Probably the reason is that parachute jumping demands constant attention and concentration. In other words, when a high degree of psychological readiness is required, the stress reaction remains high.

Prior exposure is often used as a training procedure to help people in a variety of situations deal more effectively with stressful stimulation. Training soldiers for combat duty typically involves exposing them to acute stress over a period of time. Mountain climbers train extensively, by exposing themselves to the conditions that they could encounter in an important climb, such as cold, rain, wind, and prolonged physical exertion. Pilots are trained in simulators to react to a wide range of emergencies. In all these situations, the goal is to train the stress reaction and to teach the person to correctly evaluate the nature of the stimulus that is a potential stressor. Certain patterns of stimulation should elicit the stress reaction and others should not.

Learning How to Respond to Stress

As a general rule of thumb, it is not a good idea to make decisions or engage in a variety of behaviors when under stress. Here are two suggestions for functioning under stress.

1. **Learn a prescribed set of rules for making decisions under stress.** Why do people tend to make bad decisions under stress? Research indicates that it is largely because they fail to fulfill an elementary requirement of the decision-making process, which is to systematically consider all the relevant alternatives (Keinan, 1987). To ensure sound decision making—for example, when controllers are guiding planes into an airport for a landing—people are carefully trained to make sure they follow a prescribed set of rules. Sometimes, they are required to actually check off each function as they complete it.

2. **Learn not to react.** It is not just poor decision making that leads to poor performance under stress. Stress has been shown to disrupt behavior that we consider automatic or habitual. After being told that his wife has cancer, a man drives through a stop sign on his way home; after being refused a loan by her banker, a woman forgets to pick up her purse. The reasoning behind learning not to react immediately is that humans tend to process information with two systems: one is a quick and dirty system that does not fully process all the information and the other is a more thorough system that involves rational thought processes (LeDoux, 1993). Individuals who feel pressured to respond quickly, such as when threatened, are inclined to use the quick and dirty system, a system that evolved to help us deal with emergencies; this system is, however, based on incomplete information processing.

One way to help people deal with emergencies is to teach them a pattern of response that they can auto-

matically use in an emergency. Airplane pilots are given special training in simulators to ensure that in the event of an emergency, they will know what to do without having to think. Astronauts are trained not to respond until they have first consulted ground control. Because of the complexity of a spaceship, it is necessary to use a computer to analyze all the implications of a particular response before it is executed. In our daily lives, we would do well to resist the temptation to respond to stress with a hasty action and instead allow our more thorough information processing system to help us decide a proper course of action.

Social Factors and Stress: The Workplace Example

The stress reaction is elicited by a variety of psychosocial stimuli—stimuli associated with our jobs, our residences, our social interactions, and the activities we engage in. Because they are part of our daily lives, they can elicit a prolonged stress reaction, which could precipitate a variety of adaptive diseases. To illustrate social factors, let's look at stress in the workplace.

Conflict-Prone and Conflict-Resistant Organizations

Stokols (1992a) suggests that the physical arrangements and the social conditions of an organization can predispose their members toward chronic conflict and resultant health problems. Table 9-3 presents the qualities of conflict-prone and conflict-resistant organizations, under three general categories: (1) the social-psychological qualities of groups; (2) organizational structure; and (3) environmental conditions. Stokols argues that the conflict-prone organization is often a major source of stress and illness in people.

The Individual-Environment Interaction

In his work on organizations, Stokols (1992a) argues that more attention needs to be paid to the physical environment and the sociocultural environment. In the past, researchers have focused on the individual's ability to adapt as the main source of difficulty and have put the blame more or less on the individual for his or her stress. Although an individual with a disposition toward optimism, hardiness, and high self-esteem, for example, will tend to be less affected by stress, these

Table 9-3.   Qualities of conflict-prone and conflict-resistant organizations.

Levels of Organizational Analysis	Tendencies Toward Conflict or Cohesion	
	Conflict-Prone Organizations	*Conflict-Resistant Organizations*
Social-psychological qualities *(norms, goals, and role expectations)*	Absence of shared goals among group members.	Presence of and commitment to shared goals among group members.
	Incompatible styles and role assignments among group members.	Compatible style and role assignments among group members.
	Presence of rigid ideologies; low tolerance for diverse points of view.	Absence of rigid ideologies; high tolerance for diverse points of view.
Organizational structure *(interrelations among roles and resources)*	Existence of competitive coalitions.	Absence of competitive coalitions.
	Nonparticipatory organizational processes.	Participatory organizational processes.
	Overstaffed organization.	Adequately staffed organization.
	Pervasive competition among members for scarce roles and resources.	Minimal competition among members for roles and resources.
	Ambiguous organization of space and territory among group members.	Clear-cut territorial organization and use of space among group members.
	Relatively unstable role structure and membership.	Relatively stable role structure and membership.
	Absence of formal and informal dispute-resolution mechanisms.	Availability of formal and informal dispute-resolution mechanisms.
Environmental conditions	Local and remote environmental resources for meeting organizational goals are inadequate.	Ample environmental resources for meeting organizational goals are available.
	Environment external to the organization is anomic and turbulent.	Environment external to the organization is cohesive and nonturbulent.

Source: From "Conflict-Prone and Conflict-Resistant Organizations," by D. Stokols. In H. S. Friedman (Ed.), *Hostility, Coping and Health* (Table 5-1). Copyright © 1992 by the American Psychological Association. Reprinted with permission of the author.

factors alone might not be sufficient to eliminate work-related stress. If the environment plays havoc with people who have relatively positive dispositions, how much more impact will it have on people with more negative dispositions (toward hostility, anger, and low self-esteem). As yet, we do not have any direct estimates, but indirect evidence gives cause for concern. Indeed, some people's jobs are killing them, and it is worse for those who have more negative dispositions.

Note that people who have a competitive orientation tend to react poorly to stress. Among other things, they tend to engage in denial and to behaviorally and mentally disengage; show poor active coping skills; do not seek out social support, (which is important in

dealing with stress); and tend not to accept or interpret events in an adaptive manner (Franken & Brown, 1996). Since all of these characteristics have negative health implications, it is not surprising that organizations that promote a competitive atmosphere are typically characterized by poor employee health. By contrast, people who hold an exchange orientation (the general expectation of reciprocity) and a communal orientation (a positive regard for the needs and feelings of others) tend to experience less stress in organizational settings (Buunk, Doosje, Jans, & Hopstaken, 1993).

These principles apply not only to the workplace but also to marital relationships, family functioning, interactions with friends, and casual interactions. It would be a useful exercise to analyze such everyday situations in terms of the principles in Table 9-3.

Summary

Learning can modify both the nature of the stress reaction and the way a person or animal tends to respond under stress. Learning to predict when a stressor will come allows the individual to relax when the stressor is absent. Short periods of relaxation appear to help ward off the effects of stress. In addition, learning a coping response seems to reduce some of the adverse effects of stress, such as ulcers. Habituating a response under stress seems to mobilize the body to provide the necessary physiological base for good performance. Evidence from a wide variety of sources indicates that, under stress, automatic and habitual responses deteriorate. The failure to make good decisions under stress is an example of how stress disrupts performance, probably by disrupting attention.

Social interactions—especially social conflicts—can be a significant source of stress. Studies of conflict-prone and conflict-resistant organizations indicate that stress tends to be higher in organizations characterized by a lack of shared goals, a rigid structure that is intolerant of diverse viewpoints, competitiveness, unstable roles and structure, and the absence of adequate resources. Correspondingly, stress tends to be less in organizations characterized by commitment to shared goals, a structure that tolerates and even encourages diversity, absence of competitiveness, and ample resources. One of the main dividends from working in a stress-resistant organization is good health.

The Cognitive Component of Stress

Richard Lazarus and his colleagues (Coyne & Lazarus, 1980; Folkman, 1984; Folkman, Lazarus, Dunkel-Schetter, Delongis, & Gruen, 1986; Folkman, Schaefer, & Lazarus, 1979; Lazarus, 1981, 1991a, b, c; Lazarus & Launier, 1978) have developed one of the most comprehensive theories about the role of cognitive factors in stress. According to this theory, how an individual appraises an event plays a fundamental role in determining not only the magnitude of the stress response

but the kind of coping strategies that the individual employs to deal with the stress. Appraisal occurs in two stages.

1. **Primary appraisal.** At this stage, we determine whether a stressful event represents harm/loss, threat, or challenge. *Harm/loss* refers to injury or damage that has already taken place, such as loss of a limb, loss of a job, or simply loss of self-esteem. *Threat* refers to something that could produce harm or loss. *Challenge* refers to the potential for growth, mastery, or some form of gain. As we'll see, numerous factors, both personal and situational, are involved in an individual's appraisal of a situation. From this perspective, the origins of stress cannot be assessed by looking solely at the nature of the environmental event that precipitates it. Rather, stress involves the interaction of the individual with the environment.

2. **Secondary appraisal.** After determining whether a stressful event represents harm/loss, threat, or challenge, we evaluate our coping resources and options; we ask what we can do. Generally, we have access to physical, social, psychological, and material coping resources. Physical resources include health and energy, social resources include family and friends, psychological resources include self-esteem and problem-solving abilities, and material resources include money and equipment.

Problem-Focused and Emotion-Focused Coping

According to Lazarus's theory, *coping* refers to cognitive and behavioral efforts to master, reduce, or tolerate the internal and external demands created by the stressful transaction (Folkman, 1984). Note that, by this definition, coping refers to efforts to manage rather than to the outcome of those efforts. In other words, having or developing a positive attitude is a form of coping, even if that positive attitude ultimately fails to resolve the situation.

The theory makes an important distinction between two ways of reducing stress. In *problem-focused coping,* we engage in some kind of problem-solving behavior designed to resolve the stressful transaction. If I'm experiencing stress on the job because of another person, for example, I might be able to reduce that stress by asking to be transferred to another department, arranging for the other person to be transferred, or devising some strategy to change the other person's behavior. In *emotion-focused coping,* by contrast, we focus on controlling the symptoms of stress. If I cannot avoid the other person, for example, I might deliberately take time out after every encounter to relax and think about the positive aspects of the job or to talk with some other person who might provide sympathy.

Over the years, considerable support has been found for the idea that the best ways of dealing with stress that arises from loss of control is to use a combination of problem-focused coping and emotional-focused coping. This combination reduces stress and leads to improved health (Terry & Hynes, 1998).

Situational Factors and Personal Control

Whether an individual tends to focus on the problem or on the emotion in dealing with stress depends largely on whether the individual appraises the situation as controllable and on whether the situation is, in fact, controllable. Some stressful situations are uncontrollable, such as living near a nuclear reactor, perhaps, or working as a police officer, or having a friend who is dying of cancer. Other situations are subject to control (controllable), such as having an examination scheduled next week, perhaps, or having a tire on your car that has a slow leak, or having no money but having a job that permits you to work overtime. Note that circumstances could make what appears to be an uncontrollable situation controllable and vice versa. More important, people sometimes appraise a situation as uncontrollable that is really under their control and, conversely, appraise a situation as controllable when it is not.

Potentially Controllable Situations

When people are faced with a forthcoming examination, they tend to appraise that event as either challenging or threatening (Folkman & Lazarus, 1985). When people appraise an event as challenging, two things typically happen. First, they engage in problem-solving behavior. Second, they develop a positive emotion (excitement, eagerness, hopefulness) that acts as a motivational support for their problem solving. In other words, two complementary processes lead to effort. When people appraise an event as threatening,

however, something quite different happens; they experience a negative emotion. Negative emotions are indicators that something is wrong—at least that is our traditional way of viewing negative emotions. Whatever the exact reason, humans experiencing a negative emotion tend to focus on that emotion, and the time and effort devoted to coping with it distract the individual from activities better calculated to solve the problem. Note that people tend to appraise a situation as threatening when they perceive that it may not be altogether controllable.

Getting a promotion or simply having a high-level job can be perceived as both challenging and threatening. What makes a promotion threatening is the possibility that we might not succeed in the job. As long as the job is perceived as challenging, we are likely to handle it effectively. When feelings of threat arise, however, we will tend to waste time and effort in coping with those feelings. Management systems that use threats to motivate people obviously undermine the employees' motivation.

Situations Unlikely to Be Controllable

Faced with events over which we are unlikely to gain much control, we may do best to accept this fact, rather than to treat the situation as potentially controllable. This might seem like bad advice because we know that viewing a situation as a challenge leads to a positive psychological state. But what happens when people make repeated attempts to control a situation that, in fact, is not controllable? A study of residents of Three Mile Island, the site of a major nuclear accident (Collins, Baum, & Singer, 1983), suggests that people who engage in problem-focused coping to deal with such an uncontrollable situation develop more psychological symptoms than do people who rely on more emotion-focused coping. When we are faced with a problem that is truly beyond our control, it seems to make more sense simply to deal with our emotions.

Controllability and Longevity

Apparently, perceived controllability even promotes longevity. In a long-term study, two groups of older people in institutions with different levels of opportunity for control and responsibility were compared.

Those given more control became more active and reported being happier. Their reduced levels of corticosteroids suggested that these subjects were experiencing less stress. After two years, this group was significantly healthier than the comparison group was. Moreover, in that period, half as many people died in this group as in the comparison group (Rodin & Langer, 1977).

Summary

Primary appraisal, according to Lazarus's theory, involves classifying or labeling a stressful event as representing either harm/loss, threat, or challenge. Secondary appraisal involves the evaluation of the relevant coping resources and options that are available. In general, coping strategies are either problem-focused or emotion-focused. According to Lazarus's theory, whether an individual tends to use problem-focused or emotion-focused coping depends on two additional factors: whether the threat is potentially controllable and, if so, whether the individual perceives that he or she has the skills to deal with it.

Moderators of Stress

A moderator of stress tends to reduce the stress response. Stress moderators can be broken down roughly into biological, learned, and cognitive factors. Although the fit is not perfect, these categories emphasize the idea that moderators work in different ways to achieve their final common goal, which is to reduce stress.

The Biological Component

Social Support and Stress

According to current thinking, humans need to be viewed as social beings rather than as individuals. This way of thinking about humans develops from the idea that we evolved in a social context in which we needed, among other things, to cooperate with others to survive. Consequently, we are inclined to look to others not only for help but also support when we feel threatened. The presence of others reassures us that we

can and will survive (Buss, 1999). Thus, it is not surprising that social support has consistently emerged as a moderator of life stress (Vaux, 1992; Veiel & Baumann, 1992). Three dimensions of social support have been identified (Schwarzer, Dunkel-Schetter, & Kemeny, 1994; Vaux, 1992):

1. Emotional support (intimacy and reassurance), which can come from family, friends, spouses or partners, volunteers, and community groups such as churches.
2. Tangible support (the provision of aid and service), which involves receiving such necessities as clothing, food, and shelter, as well as help with daily chores such as cleaning, shoveling snow, raking leaves, and banking.
3. Informational support (advice and feedback), which involves receiving information and advice about how to take care of ourselves and having someone who will listen in an empathetic manner.

Whether social contacts are beneficial depends on whether they are discretionary or obligatory (Bolger & Eckenrode, 1991). If it is apparent that someone is only helping out of a sense of duty, we are not likely to experience a reduction in stress. What we are looking for is genuine, rather than superficial commitment.

The Repressive Personality Type and Social Support

It appears that certain people who resist seeking out social support appear to be susceptible to a number of physical diseases, particularly cancer (Eysenck, 1988). These people, who are said to have a *repressive* personality, are characterized by their tendency to chronically defend themselves against negative affects, particularly anger and anxiety, and to deny that they are distressed (Derakshan & Eysenck, 1997; Emmons, 1992). Of particular interest is evidence that repressors tend to experience difficulties in interpersonal functioning. They seem to be preoccupied with issues of relatedness and are troubled by feelings of dependency and ambivalence in their relations with others (Bonanno & Singer, 1990).

Considerable evidence indicates that social support has beneficial effects for (1) cardiovascular system, (2) endocrine functioning (e.g., catecholamines), and (3) a strong immune response (Uchino, Cacioppo & Kiecolt-Glaser, 1996). In view of such findings, people must reach out to others to provide them with emotional support and learn to be open to the emotional support that others might offer. We might say that it is important to go back to our roots.

Social Support and Bereavement

Can social support help us to cope with the considerable stress associated with the death of a loved one? Some theorists contend that bereavement can be compensated by a strong social support network (e.g., Stroebe & Stroebe, 1987), but attachment theory suggests that no amount of social support can make up for such losses (Bowlby, 1979). Tests of these two opposing views indicate that attachment theory is a better explanation of the research findings (Stroebe, Stroebe, Abakoumkin, & Schut, 1996). When a loved one dies, we experience emotional loneliness, which cannot readily be compensated by reducing social loneliness.

Some research has demonstrated that when people find meaning in the death of others (e.g., purpose or a reason to live), they experience a strengthened immune response and overall better health. Researchers have suggested that the ability to find meaning is a way of regaining a sense of control over one's life (Taylor, Kemeny, Reed, Bower, & Gruenewald, 2000).

The Learned Component

Managing Stressful Information

Horowitz (1979) argues that, to deal with life stressors, we must avoid becoming overwhelmed. To do this, we engage in a variety of control operations that allow us to keep the stress within bounds. For example, we might use denial to regain composure or we might focus on only one aspect of the event. Horowitz speaks of breaking the stressful information down into a series of micro-intervals, so that it is within our ability to deal with it. In this way, we master a stressful event by sequentially attacking each of its units. Failure to put the stressful information under tight control, Horowitz

Practical Application 9-1

Pet Ownership and Health

As people get older, their health often deteriorates, and they seek doctors to help them. This puts a great burden on the medical system. A great deal of anecdotal lore suggests that pets can improve the psychological outlook of patients and can even help sustain life in times of physical and psychological stress. Research by Judith Siegel (1990) confirms these benefits. In a prospective study of 938 Medicare enrollees in a health maintenance organization over the span of one year, she found that people with pets visited their physicians less, and that pets helped them to deal better with stressful events. People with pets, for example, experienced less stress associated with the loss of companionship. In this sample, 26% experienced the death of a close friend. More than 75% of the pet owners mentioned that their pet provided them with companionship and comfort, and 25% indicated that they felt more secure with their pets, and 21% said they felt loved by the pet. In other words, owning a pet seems to help meet people's companionship needs. Siegel suggests that one reason people go to see their doctor is to satisfy their need for companionship.

Which is the best pet to own? The results indicated that only a dog is a stress buffer. Finer analysis of the data indicated that dog owners spent more time outdoors with their dog and talked more with their dog. Once again, this provides evidence that the pet is a source of companionship. Siegel controlled for health status in all her data analyses, so it appears that dog ownership influences social and psychological processes rather than physical health. Nonetheless, we know that psychological health is often a good predictor of physical health. Two studies of older individuals found that those who felt more attached to their pets were in better physical health (Garrity, Stallones, Marx, & Johnson, 1989; Ory & Goldberg, 1983); this indicates a positive relationship between psychological and physical variables.

Dogs are not only good companions, but they are also good for your health.

---

says, might lead to information overload, which could precipitate a total breakdown. In computer language, we might say that the system would crash.

Epstein's Theory

Epstein's theory is largely cognitive, but the way people think is habitual. As we'll see in this section, we experience stress because we learn to think about things in certain ways. By learning to think differently, we gain control over stress.

The search for universal coping strategies. For some time, coping has been regarded as one of the main moderators of stress. Despite a great deal of anecdotal evidence linking individual coping strategies to reduction in stress, psychologists have had difficulty identifying universal coping principles or styles of coping that underlie these diverse individual strategies. Along with Folkman and Lazarus (1985), whose work we have already discussed, Seymour Epstein and his associates at the University of Massachusetts have moved us closer

to identifying such universal strategies. In a nutshell, Epstein's theory is that people who are effective in dealing with stress tend to think more *constructively* when faced with problems, whereas those who tend to experience stress think more *destructively* (Epstein & Meier, 1989).

Intelligence and adjustment. Epstein's theory grew out of his work on practical intelligence. Like others before him, he has observed that academic intelligence does not predict adjustment. Specifically, academic intelligence does not predict mental health, physical health, good family relations, good social relations, satisfactory romantic relations, or success at work. According to Epstein's cognitive-experiential self-theory (CEST), people have three semi-independent systems that help them deal with daily life: a rational system, roughly corresponding to academic intelligence; an experiential system, which we will consider shortly; and an associationistic system, observed in altered states of consciousness. Epstein believes that the experiential system gives rise to good mental and physical health, good relationships, and success at work. Note that, although academic intelligence predicts grades and is therefore indirectly related to success at work, many people who are successful at work do not have high academic intelligence. Academic intelligence does not predict who makes the most money, who gets promoted, and other indicators of success at work (Epstein, 1990).

To test this theory, Epstein and Meier (1989) created an inventory to measure experiential abilities—the Constructive Thinking Inventory (CTI). This inventory provides an index of the degree to which people tend to be constructive thinkers rather than destructive thinkers when dealing with daily problems. It contains a global measure of coping, plus six specific measures or scales: emotional coping, behavioral coping, cate-gorical thinking, superstitious thinking, naive optimism, and negative thinking. The first two scales—emotional coping and behavior coping—are the best predictors of coping and correspond to Lazarus's emotion-focused coping and problem-focused coping. Often, the best way to understand what a scale measures is to examine some of the items (Table 9-4). Scales such as this typically contain positively and negatively worded items, and subjects are asked to indicate, using a five-point scale, the degree to which they think the item is like them or not like them. A minus sign (–) beside the item indicates that the item is reverse-scored; that is, if a person scores the item as 1, it will be recorded as 5 when computing the final score.

The four remaining scales—categorical thinking, superstitious thinking, naive optimism, and negative

Table 9-4. Examples of items from constructive thinking inventory scales.

Emotional Coping

> I worry a great deal about what other people think of me. (–)
> I don't let little things bother me.
> I tend to take things personally. (–)

Behavioral Coping

> I am the kind of person who takes action rather than just thinks or complains about a situation.
> I avoid challenges because it hurts too much when I fail. (–)
> When faced with upcoming unpleasant events, I usually carefully think through how I will deal with them.

Categorical Thinking

> There are basically two kinds of people in this world, good and bad.
> I think there are many wrong ways, but only one right way, to do almost anything.
> I tend to classify people as either for me or against me.

Superstitious Thinking

> I have found that talking about successes that I am looking forward to can keep them from happening.
> I do not believe in any superstitions. (–)
> When something good happens to me, I believe it is likely to be balanced by something bad.

Naive Optimism

> If I do well on an important test, I feel like a total success and that I will go very far in life.
> I believe that people can accomplish anything they want to if they have enough willpower.

Negative Thinking

> When I am faced with a new situation, I tend to think the worst possible outcome will happen.
> I tend to dwell more on pleasant than unpleasant incidents from the past. (–)
> I get so distressed when I notice that I am doing poorly in something that it makes me do worse.

Source: "Constructive Thinking: A Broad Coping Variable with Specific Components," by S. Epstein & P. Meier, *Journal of Personality and Social Psychology,* 1989, *57,* 332–350. Copyright © 1989 by the American Psychological Association. Reprinted with permission.

thinking—all measure nonadaptive thinking. The underlying finding of Epstein and others is that, to act adaptively, we need to think accurately. None of these four types of thinking gives us a realistic view of the world. *Categorical thinking* is a type of black-and-white thinking that has been linked to rigid and intolerant people. In reality, most things are neither black nor white. The ability to recognize gray is useful in seeing the world as it is. *Superstitious thinking* is irrational thinking in which doing or saying certain things is believed to produce certain outcomes. It can sometimes be seen in children's play—for instance, the game in which children avoid cracks in the sidewalk as they say: "If you step on a crack it will break your mother's back." *Naive optimism*—also called Pollyanna thinking—is another kind of irrational thinking, rooted in the idea that all you have to do to succeed is think positively. *Negative thinking* is a tendency to expect the worst. For many people, negative thinking becomes a self-fulfilling prophecy.

Differences between constructive and destructive thinkers. Work with the CTI scales (especially the global scale) has provided some indication of how people who are good constructive thinkers differ from poor constructive thinkers. The main difference, it appears, relates to dealing with negative outcomes. Both good and poor constructive thinkers tend to respond favorably to good outcomes (they remain positive and optimistic about future performance), but poor constructive thinkers tend to overgeneralize about the self after negative outcomes. Among other things, their self-esteem plummets, they feel depressed, and they assume a helpless attitude about future performance. Interestingly, these symptoms also characterize depressed individuals.

Origins of destructive thinking. Why do some people develop such a profound negative self-view following poor performance, but others do not? Epstein (1992) speculates that this might be linked to self-schemata within the implicit self theory that we developed as children. Like many others before him, he suggests that, when love is withdrawn for poor performance or when love is made conditional on good performance, we tend to develop, as part of our implicit self theory, the idea or belief that making mistakes or performing

poorly will result in the withdrawal of love. Since the withdrawal of love is one of the most profound and devastating experiences that a child can experience, making mistakes or performing poorly takes on much greater significance than it should. Even though, as adults, we might conclude that our reactions are inappropriate, we often have difficulty learning how to respond more appropriately. Why we have difficulty unlearning this belief and replacing it with a more rational or reasonable one is not altogether clear. Among other things, researchers have suggested that the experiential system does not work by rules of reason or logic and, therefore, to change requires something more than just understanding the source of our problem (Epstein & Meier, 1989).

Poor constructive thinking and stress. In laboratory studies where stress was induced by having subjects subtract 7s from 300 or engage in mirror-tracing and constantly telling them of their errors, poor constructive thinkers reported more negative thoughts—both related and unrelated to the experiment—and experienced more negative affect (Katz & Epstein, 1991). Physiological measures of poor constructive thinkers also indicated that they experienced greater stress than did good constructive thinkers. Epstein concluded that poor constructive thinkers contribute to the stress they experience by spontaneously generating negative thoughts in the absence of external stressors and that they appraise external stressors as more threatening.

Constructive thinking and success in life. Epstein's theory is relevant to managing stress and to achieving success. In Chapter 13, we will discuss the importance of developing the kind of thinking that has been used by successful people.

Emotion-Focused Coping Strategies

Strategies that have been advocated for dealing with stress include meditation, relaxation, exercise, and even biofeedback training. Let's review some of the research assessing the effectiveness of these techniques.

Meditation. Maharishi Mahesh Yogi introduced transcendental meditation (TM) to North America in the 1960s. More than half a million people have already been trained, and their numbers continue to grow.

Countless books and articles advocate the use of meditation to overcome stress and increase inner energy (e.g., Bloomfield, Cain, Jaffe, & Kory, 1975; Goleman, 1995; Schwartz, 1974).The various techniques for meditation seem to be equally effective in lowering anxiety and countering the effects of stress. Each of these techniques retrains attention in some way, according to Daniel Goleman (1976), who has offered the following simple procedure for meditation:

> Find a quiet place with a straight-back chair. Sit in any comfortable position with your back straight. Close your eyes. Bring your full attention to the movement of your breath as it enters and leaves your nostrils. Don't follow the breath into your lungs or out into the air. Keep your focus at the nostrils, noting the full passage of each in- and out-breath, from its beginning to its end. Each time your mind wanders to other thoughts, or is caught by background noises, bring your attention back to the easy, natural rhythm of your breathing. Don't try to control the breath; simply be aware of it. Fast or slow, shallow or deep, the nature of the breath does not matter;

your total attention to it is what counts. If you have trouble keeping your mind on your breath, count each inhalation and exhalation up to 10, then start over again. Meditate for 20 minutes; set a timer, or peek at your watch occasionally. Doing so won't break your concentration. For the best results, meditate regularly, twice a day, in the same time and place. (p. 84)

The evidence showing that meditation does reduce the stress reaction is impressive. Researchers have shown, for example, that meditation will reduce high blood pressure (Benson & Wallace, 1972) and the frequency of headaches, colds, and insomnia (Wallace, Benson, & Wilson, 1971). One series of studies showed that transcendental meditation practiced by volunteer subjects produced a decrease in oxygen consumption (Wallace & Benson, 1972). These results (Figure 9-6) are particularly impressive because oxygen consumption reflects metabolic rate, a physiological response that cannot be altered through voluntary efforts. We might ask whether meditators can reduce the activity of the adrenal cortex. It appears that meditation does reduce

Practical Application 9-2

Becoming a Constructive Thinker

Epstein's work suggests that those who think destructively focus their negative thinking not only on the self but also on the outside world. As a result, they see themselves as inadequate and the world as threatening. Research suggests these two tendencies are different but highly related and probably have a common origin in the implicit theories that people have constructed about their ability to deal with the external world. All behavior involves, at least to some degree, an attempt to interact with the environment. To interact successfully involves an assessment of our abilities (the self) and the challenge offered by the environment.

How do we learn to deal successfully with the external world? First, we need to believe that we can succeed and then we need to learn the skills that will enable us to succeed. Many people never make the effort to develop the skills they need because they don't believe they can succeed. The first step, therefore, is to develop a more positive attitude about our

abilities to deal with the environment. The second thing, of course, is to see the world as an opportunity—as a source of pleasure rather than as pain. Many psychologists are regarding thinking styles as habits that we have developed. If they are habits, we can learn to change them through the principles of reinforcement. In other words, we have reason to be optimistic that we can all become constructive thinkers.

The idea that our thinking consists of habits helps me understand why I often have difficulty changing the way I think. Even when I know, at a rational level, that I need to think differently, I find myself falling back into my previous mode of thinking. It seems easier and more natural—more me. Eventually, however, I feel very comfortable with my new way of thinking.

It has been my experience that, when I do change the way I think—often after repeated attempts—the world looks very different to me; it is a better world.

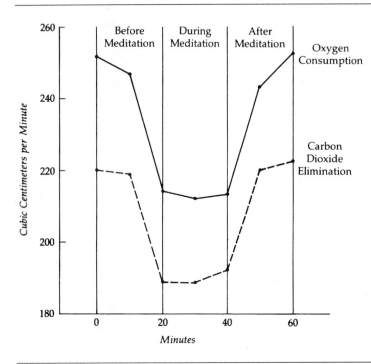

Figure 9-6. Effect of meditation on subjects' oxygen consumption (solid line) and carbon dioxide elimination (dashed line), recorded in 20 and 15 cases, respectively. After the subjects were invited to meditate, both rates decreased markedly. Consumption and elimination returned to the premeditation level soon after the subjects stopped meditating. (From "The Physiology of Meditation," by R. K. Wallace and H. Benson, *Scientific American,* February 1972, 84–90. Copyright © 1972 by Scientific American, Inc. All rights reserved.)

adrenocortical activity, as indicated by reduced cortisol levels (Jevning, Wilson, & Davidson, 1978).

Goleman (1976) has noted that meditators typically recover rapidly from stress and suggests that fact is the key to understanding why meditators successfully resist the effects of stress. If a person can relax after each stressful event, the aversive effects associated with stress are kept to a minimum, and the person has greater reserves of energy to deal with future stressful events. Rather than letting each stressful event add to the previous one, the person treats each event more or less separately. As we have noted, stress seems to have a damaging effect only if it is prolonged. It appears that, because meditators recovery so rapidly, they do not experience prolonged stress.

Relaxation. If the beneficial effects of meditation are caused by the increased relaxation that it produces, then other forms of relaxation might be just as effective. Indeed, several studies have shown that to be the case (Beary, Benson, & Klemchuk, 1974; Cauthen & Prymak, 1977; Fenwick et al., 1977; Holmes, 1984;

Morse, Martin, Furst, & Dubin, 1977). Relaxation is found to be effective in reducing both systolic and diastolic blood pressure (e.g., Fey & Lindholm, 1978; Mount, Walters, Rowland, Barnes, & Payton, 1978). In *The Relaxation Response,* Herbert Benson (1975) tells how relaxation can be readily learned and used.

Exercise. Research data on exercise relate mainly to anxiety, which is often associated with stress. A study comparing the effects of exercise and meditation found that, although exercise reduced certain somatic aspects of anxiety, it did not necessarily reduce the cognitive aspects (Schwartz, Davidson, & Goleman, 1978). These researchers argue that exercise, if combined with relaxation, could enhance the beneficial effects of relaxation, but exercise cannot be substituted for relaxation. Nonetheless, considerable evidence suggests that physical fitness does moderate the negative health effects of life stress (Brown, 1991; Dubbert, 1992). This might be partially because exercise has been found to be a good way to reduce negative mood (Mondin et al., 1996). As we discussed earlier, negative moods have been linked to a weakening of the immune response (Salovey et al., 2000).

Biofeedback. Since the discovery that involuntary responses mediated by the autonomic nervous system can be altered through operant conditioning procedures, there has been considerable interest in using these procedures to reduce the stress reaction. After reviewing the relevant research, Tarler-Benlolo (1978) found no evidence that biofeedback is better than relaxation for dealing with a variety of stress-induced disorders, including migraine headaches and elevated blood pressure. Each technique might be particularly suited to certain people or certain disorders, but more data are required before specific conclusions can be drawn. There could be reasons to use both techniques at once (Cuthbert, Kristeller, Simons, Hodes, & Lang, 1981; Fey & Lindholm, 1978).

The Cognitive Component

Trauma and Thought Suppression

Individuals who have suffered from a variety of traumas in childhood are far more likely to become ill if they never talk about the traumas (Pennebaker, 1992; 1997). Several studies have confirmed that talking or writing about a trauma not only reduces stress but also leads to health benefits. Among other things, people who wrote about their traumas visited the doctor less and had an improved immune response (Pennebaker, 1990). Conversely, researchers have shown that thought suppression leads to a decrease in the immune response (Petrie, Booth, & Pennebaker, 1998). When people who have suffered a trauma become stuck in the past, they experience elevated psychological distress but when they take a future orientation, one in which life is better or more hopeful, they are less likely to experience stress (Holman & Silver, 1998).

Pennebaker argues that although inhibition can be highly adaptive, because inhibition allows us to control our thinking and behavior (as in goal-directed behavior), inhibition of traumatic events is very harmful. Over time, he argues, the constant injunction to not think about the trauma creates stress. To reduce this stress, people need to deal with the trauma and put it to rest. Various theorists have argued that, when peo-

ple actually translate an experience into language, they can *assimilate* it (Horowitz, 1976). Whatever the actual process, talking and writing seem to reduce the tension associated with constantly repressing something that affected us deeply.

Personal Control and Meaning

Although researchers have accepted for some time that beliefs about personal control helps protect mental health, current research indicates that beliefs about personal control also affect physical health. Research has shown, for example, that breast cancer proceeds more slowly in women who believe they can personally control the cancer and that HIV progresses more slowly in men who believe they can personally control the disease. Further, researchers have found that when people can somehow find meaning in their health disorder, such as having cancer or HIV, or in the health disorder and even the death of loved ones, their diseases progress more slowly. Meaning here refers to discovering that life has purpose or that life is something to be appreciated (Taylor et al., 2000).

In her work, Taylor and her associates have documented that having unrealistically high optimism, having strong beliefs about personal control, and being able to find meaning in the face of death are adaptive. These positive illusions, as she refers to them, go against the idea that people should be realistic when it comes to such things as their health. Her work indicates that when people hold positive illusions, their immune systems function at higher levels and as a result, diseases such as cancer and HIV progress more slowly (Taylor et al., 2000). In one study, for example, researchers demonstrated that optimism is associated with better mood and high number of T cells and high killer cell cytotoxicity (Segerstrom, Taylor, Kemeny, & Fahey, 1998). Of particular interest was the finding that situational optimism, rather than trait optimism, is the better predictor of the immune response. What this means in a practical sense is that we need to work at being optimistic, especially when we are sick.

How do we account for the fact that positive illusions can lead to better health in view of what Epstein has found about accurate thinking? Although the mechanism is not known, it might be linked to the role that positive emotions play in the immune response. We turn to that next.

Positive Emotional States and Evolution

Considerable evidence indicates a direct link between positive emotional states and physical health. One important implication of this finding is that such things as optimism, positive illusions, meaning, and humor all follow a common pathway to health by creating a positive emotional state. From an evolutionary perspective, researchers have argued that perhaps positive emotions are an adaptation that provide us with not only the information about the state of our immune system but also the motivation necessary for us to do those things that are necessary to developing a strong immune response (Salovey et al., 2000). From a practical perspective, this means that we should try to become attuned to our emotions and work actively to promote positive emotions.

Researchers have suggested that one problem with people in the Western world is their tendency to suppress or ignore their emotions. Researchers have argued that this is an outgrowth of our tendency to think of body and mind as separate entities—one physical and one mental. Further, researchers have argued, those in the Western world have a tendency to value a rational-nonemotional approach to life as superior to one that involves considering the importance of emotions in our daily functioning. As a result, we are no longer attuned to our emotions. One of the many consequences is poor health. To overcome this tendency we need to become more mindful of our emotions (Langer, 1989).

The Hardy Personality

People who remain healthy after experiencing high degrees of life stress often exhibit a distinctive personality profile—the *hardy personality,* with three main characteristics (Kobasa, 1979a, b, 1982; Kobasa, Maddi, & Kahn, 1982):

1. *Control*—the belief that one can influence the course of life events.
2. *Commitment*—the belief that life is meaningful and has a purpose.

3. *Challenge*—the attitude that difficult or onerous events are normal and can provide an opportunity for mastery and development.

The concept of hardiness could account for other moderators of stress, such as the locus of control and sensation seeking, which we will discuss shortly (Kobasa & Puccetti, 1983). Suzanne Kobasa has shown that people with a hardy personality profile are less likely to become ill after experiencing stress. The work of Hull, Van Treuren, and Virnelli (1987) suggests that hardiness should be treated as three separate phenomena: They found that only commitment and control were significantly related to health outcome.

The concept of a hardy personality has generated a great deal of interest. A number of studies have been designed to determine exactly how and why the hardy personality leads to lower rates of illness. The bulk of the evidence seems to indicate that hardy people see the world as less threatening and see themselves as more capable of dealing with stressful events by means of problem-solving and support-seeking strategies (Florian, Mikulincer, & Taubman, 1995). When confronted with stress, hardy people show less frustration (Wiebe, 1989) and offer more positive self-statements and fewer negative self-statements (Allred & Smith, 1989), as illustrated in Figure 9-7.

Summary

One of the most fundamental moderators of life stress is social support. It seems that certain people who resist seeking out social support—repressive types—are susceptible to a number of physical diseases, particularly cancer. Interestingly, owning a pet—especially a dog—has significant health benefits. However, social support does not appear to mitigate the stress associated with bereavement.

Coping appears to be a major moderator of stress. According to Epstein's theory, people who are effective in dealing with stress tend to think more constructively when faced with problems, whereas those who tend to experience stress think more destructively. The Constructive Thinking Inventory (CTI) contains a global measure of coping, plus six specific measures or scales: emotional coping, behavioral coping, categorical think-

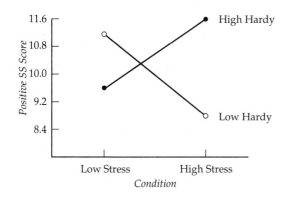

Figure 9-7. Effects of stress and hardiness on positive self-statements (SS). (From "The Hardy Personality: Cognitive and Physiological Responses to Evaluative Threat," by K. D. Alfred and T. W. Smith, *Journal of Personality and Social Psychology*, 1989, *56*, 257–266. Copyright © 1989 by the American Psychological Association. Reprinted with permission of the author.)

ing, superstitious thinking, naive optimism, and negative thinking. Work with the CTI indicates that constructive thinkers tend to deal effectively with negative outcomes. They score high on emotional and behavioral coping measures. Researchers have suggested that the destructive thinking style emerges early in life and could result from the withdrawal of parental love following poor performance. People can become constructive thinkers by learning to change how they think about themselves and the world.

Among the emotion-focused coping strategies, transcendental meditation has been shown to be effective. Researchers such as Goleman have concluded that all forms of meditation are equally effective. It appears that meditation teaches people to relax following a stressful event and thus allows them to reduce the adverse effects of a prolonged stress reaction. Some researchers have suggested that relaxation can be taught directly, without meditation. Exercise has also been advocated as a way of reducing stress. Although exercise reduces certain somatic components, it does not appear to be a substitute for relaxation. Biofeedback is effective, but it appears to be no better than relaxation. Exactly why relaxation is so effective is not clear. Research is needed to determine whether relaxation af-

fects only bodily reactions or both bodily and cognitive reactions.

Researchers have argued that keeping a threatening event suppressed, such as a trauma, is a continuing source of stress for the individual. One way of reducing the stress and gaining better health in the process is to write about the trauma. Optimism, beliefs about personal control, and finding meaning have all been implicated in a strengthened immune response. The hardy personality, characterized by control, commitment, and challenge, has been shown to lead to good health. Most research on hardiness suggests that the effects are caused by the way hardy people appraise their interactions with the environment: Specifically, they see the world as less threatening and see themselves as more capable of coping. A strong link has been found between a positive emotional state and a strong immune response. From an evolutionary perspective, this means we have been equipped with a system that provides the information and motivation for maintaining good health.

Stress and Health

Hans Selye, a pioneer of stress research, was initially interested in understanding the adaptive role of stress in the repair of injuries and the body's ability to resist disease. Within a short period, he discovered that a wide range of events can provoke the stress response, including psychological events such as the loss of a job or the death of a family member. He conceptualized the stress response as involving three stages: the alarm reaction, the stage of resistance, and the stage of exhaustion (characterized by collapse of the adrenal system and death). He came to believe that diseases of adaptation take place in the stage of resistance. Diseases of adaptation include insomnia, headaches, sinus attacks, high blood pressure, gastric and duodenal ulcers, certain somatic or allergic afflictions, and cardiovascular and kidney diseases (Selye, 1974).

Since these early studies, a great deal of research on the role of stress in disease has indicated that there is a bidirectional effect. Although disease typically causes stress, the progression of a disease is largely governed by the magnitude of the stress response. Because a wide range of behaviors can control stress, we ultimately can learn to control the progression of a disease (Andersen et al., 1994). This has broad implications not only for quality of life and life expectancy following disease onset but also for our ability to remain immune from a wide range of diseases.

The Cancer Model

Cancer is a major health problem that accounts for 23% of all deaths in the United States. Death rates caused by heart disease, strokes, and other conditions have been decreasing, but deaths caused by cancer have risen by 20% in the last 30 years (American Cancer Society, 1994). Extensive research into the nature of this disease suggests that we might be able to control the progression of cancer, at least to some degree, by developing a range of behaviors that ultimately strengthen the immune system.

Current research indicates that cancer tends to develop, at least in part, from the failure of the immune system. Specifically, the development of cancer is linked to lower natural killer (NK) cell activity and to B- and T-cell activity. Knowing this has allowed researchers to determine how a range of variables can affect the progression of cancer. For example, if researchers can show that certain behaviors cause an increase in NK activity, then we can conclude that those behaviors affect cancer via the immune system.

The immune system is affected both directly and indirectly by a number of systems and behaviors. Indirect effects are not necessarily less important. Often we

Practical Application 9-3

Some Rules for Dealing with Stress

A variety of organizations and educational institutions are offering courses designed to help people deal with unwanted stress. Some teach methods for reducing the magnitude of the stress reaction, including meditation, relaxation, exercise, and biofeedback. Others help people plan their lives so that they encounter fewer stressors or the stressors come at times when they are physically and psychologically prepared to deal with them. Here are seven rules for dealing with unwanted stress.

1. **Plan activities to reduce or eliminate stressors.** Our daily routine exposes many of us to a wide variety of stressful events, such as traffic snarls on the way to and from work, periodic interruptions, noise, the need to make quick decisions, requests for assistance in areas that are not our responsibility, criticisms of the quality or quantity of our work, and involvement in hostile exchanges. Although some of these events are unavoidable, it is often possible to reduce the number or magnitude of such stressors. For example, arranging to go to work earlier and leaving earlier could allow us to avoid traffic jams, to work at least for a time without interruptions, and to experience less noise. This could also limit the opportunity for people to make unwarranted requests and reduce hostile exchanges. If we can do at least part of our job before the other employees arrive, we might have more time to make decisions and to respond tactfully to criticisms and requests. The resulting reduction in stress could decrease irritability and arousal and, thus, make us less sensitive to other potential stressors. It could also lead to improved performance, with further reduction in criticisms and the possibility of rewards and promotions.

2. **Plan activities so that stressors come at times when they are easier to handle or tolerate.** The same event could induce a more intense stress reaction at certain times than at others. For example, a common source of stress results from interruptions that occur when we are trying to complete a task—a ringing telephone, a person dropping by to ask questions or simply to chat, or certain distracting noises. It is often possible to reduce or eliminate this source of stress by systematic planning. Turning off the telephone ringer, telling the secretary to hold all calls, putting up a "Do Not Disturb" sign, or moving to a location where such interruptions are unlikely are some possible solutions. People often find that after an important task is completed, distracting events are less stressful or not stressful at all. Alternatively, we might take care of

have more control over things that indirectly affect cancer and thus, by identifying those indirect routes, we can develop behaviors that will impede the development of cancer.

The following behavioral model is directed toward ensuring that people engage in behaviors that will strengthen their immune systems. Again, we will consider the biological, learned, and cognitive components in turn.

The Biological Component

Direct Effects

Both the central nervous system and the neuroendocrine system have direct effects on the immune system. As we saw earlier in this chapter, considerable evidence indicates that the central nervous system monitors what is happening in the periphery of the body and then participates in the process—in particular, by activating the stress response. Unfortunately, as we have also seen, the suppressed immune response appears to be due directly to the activation of the stress response—specifically to the release of one of the glucocorticoids, corticosterone. Nevertheless, the existence of direct effects suggests that humans can learn to influence the immune system by engaging in behaviors that will lead to decreased stress.

Indirect Effects

Diet, exercise, quality of sleep, alcohol consumption, and other factors have an indirect effect on our health.

---

details early in the day, so that a block of time is available later in the day to work at certain tasks.

3. **Learn to relax between activities.** Some people tend to experience less stress than others do in the course of a demanding or rigorous schedule. Although constitutional differences might play a role here, another contributory factor is the way people pace themselves. Shutting down the stress reaction periodically by relaxing appears to keep stress under control. Research from a variety of sources suggests that stress becomes distressful when it is allowed to become intense. Unless we shut down the stress reaction periodically, the stress of one activity tends to add to the stress of another. At some point, stress becomes our enemy. It is likely to have an adverse affect on our health and on our performance. We can reduce these effects by learning to relax between activities. It might also be easier to reduce low stress than high stress. When the stress reaction becomes very intense, it frequently provokes a psychological state of helplessness; we feel that we no longer have control over events. Such a feeling can, of course, act as a primary source of stress. Because stress can interfere with our ability to cope, we are caught in a vicious circle, in which the experience of stress becomes a stimulus for further stress.

4. **Learn to recognize the early signs of stress.** Because humans are dynamic, their reactions to events are always affected by previous activities. This means that at certain times an event might cause only mild stress, but at other times it might cause intense stress. If we are to gain control of the stress reaction before it becomes too intense, we must be able to recognize when stress is starting to exceed some *safe limit*. This is not an easy task for many people, who can recognize stress only when it has reached a high intensity. Biofeedback training can help such people understand the stress reaction and teach them how to intervene when it starts to exceed some safe limit.

5. **Learn to treat stress as a challenge.** Stressful events often demand that we react. We can react with fear and helplessness, or we can rise to the challenge. If we treat a stressor as a challenge, we will trigger a norepinephrine response, which not only helps supply us with energy but also provides us with positive affect. In other words, it appears that norepinephrine has evolved to help us cope with stress. To tap that adaptive chemical, we must rise to the challenge. We must view stress as an opportunity to exercise our adaptive responses or to develop such responses.

(continued on next page)

Individuals who are being treated for cancer tend not to eat properly. This is not surprising in that distressed individuals often have appetite disturbances and correspondingly eat meals of less nutritional value (Andersen et al., 1994). Getting cancer patients to eat properly is important for many reasons. Because their bodies are in a highly distressed state, they need enormous energy to fight the disease. Further, they need vitamins and minerals as the building blocks for a properly functioning immune system. Eating fruits and vegetables is especially important because they have been found to decrease the likelihood of developing various types of cancer. Moreover, poor nutrition has been associated with a variety of immunological impairments (Chandra & Newberne, 1977). Thus, the hope is that, through proper education, people can

learn to eat foods that will strengthen their immune systems.

Substantial research indicates that exercise is positively related to mental and physical health, good sleep, and positive mood and negatively related to anxiety and depression (Dubbert, 1992). All these factors have been linked in one way or another to the immune system, cancer, or both. Exercise seems to lower the overall stress response and, in one study, has been shown to assist breast cancer patients (MacVicar, Winningham, & Nickel, 1989). Exercise has also been implicated in sound sleep, most likely because it reduces stress.

Drugs such as alcohol and nicotine have been negatively implicated in cancer. The mechanisms by which they act are still not completely understood. Alcohol might exert its effect by such routes as disturb-

Practical Application 9-3 (continued)

Failure to rise to the challenge will only undermine our self-concept and our natural tendency to control stressful events in our environment.

6. **Learn to prevail by becoming problem-focused.** Considerable research emphasizes that people need to learn how to manage self-doubt because it is an important aspect of learning to prevail. As Bandura (1991a) points out, everybody experiences self-doubt from time to time, especially when faced with a negative life event. What differentiates those who prevail from those who give up is how they deal with such self-doubt. People who fail typically ruminate on their self-doubts, rehearse all their past failures, and count all their inadequacies. Those who succeed, in contrast, learn to rehearse their past successes and to enumerate their strengths.

The key to managing self-doubt is learning to become problem-focused. When attention is focused on the problem, some change may happen; that is the basis for hope and optimism. When people become self-focused, by contrast, they tend to focus on the negative and to accept that nothing can change because the source of their difficulty lies in their personal inadequacies. The more they ruminate, the more distressed they become, and the harder it is for

them to think about a solution to their problem (e.g., Wood, Saltzberg, Neale, Stone, & Rachmiel, 1990).

To become more problem-focused, start by thinking of how you succeeded in the past under similar circumstances. In other words, give yourself a pep talk. Next, look for ways that other people succeeded under similar circumstances. This will get your thinking off yourself. Finally, ask people to help you find a solution. This is a good way to establish social relations and make use of the considerable skills that other people have.

7. **Actively develop those personality characteristics that will ward off stress.** Your personality is largely a matter of your attitude toward the world and yourself. People who are healthy are positive and optimistic, accept themselves, take charge of their lives, have a sense of humor, and have good social relations. Most people cannot change their personalities overnight. But people do change; personality is not carved in stone (Chapter 14). One of the most powerful reasons I can think of for wanting to change is to be physically healthier and, as a result, live longer. Stress is not inevitable. We can keep it to a minimum if we are willing to create an environment that is conducive to harmony, cooperation, and support.

ing sleep, altering metabolism, and depleting certain catecholamines.

The Learned Component

Direct Effects

The relaxation response is a learned response; once acquired, however, it can be effectively used in a variety of situations. For some time, psychologists have used relaxation to help people reduce stress. In a study to determine if relaxation training would affect the immune system, older adults (with a mean age of 74 years) were randomly assigned to a relaxation group, a contact group, and a no-contact group. Analysis of psychological measures indicated that relaxation treatment improved affect and sleep. Moreover, it produced a significant increase—about 30%—in NK cell activity (Kiecolt-Glaser & Glaser, 1992). Such data indicate the importance of managing the stress response in cancer.

Indirect Effects

Let's look at three indirect effects that have been examined in the research literature.

Social support. Social support has long been linked to improved mental and physical health. There appear to be several mechanisms (Uchino et al., 1996). One suggestion is that social support helps us to address fears and anxieties. When we do so, we often experience reduced stress. If perceived threat determines the magnitude of the stress response, anything that alters our perceptions of threat might be viewed as a direct effect. Research suggests that this is a highly effective tool for people dealing with cancer (e.g., Cain, Kohorn, Quinlan, Latimer, & Schwartz, 1986). Although we have previously used the term *direct effect* to refer only to behaviors that reduce the stress response once it has been triggered, there is no reason to exclude variables that reduce the initial magnitude of the stress response. We will return to this question when we consider the cognitive component.

Coping skills. Teaching people behavioral and emotional coping skills has been proposed as an important component of any treatment program (Andersen et al., 1994). We have already discussed coping skills at

length; again, as we'll see shortly, they might be regarded as direct effects.

Compliance. It is important to induce cancer patients to comply with the treatment program. Failure of cancer patients to take their medications as scheduled or to show up for treatments as scheduled is a very significant problem for cancer treatment. The patient's willingness to comply is critical to the effectiveness of any treatment program and, hence, to the recovery of the patient's immune system (Andersen et al., 1994). Many cancer patients fail to comply because of negative moods or because they believe treatment is futile. Compliance is more likely within a larger context of social support and education about the disease and the importance of good health and exercise (Andersen et al., 1994). Effective goal-setting is also important (Bandura, 1998).

The Cognitive Component

Distinguishing Between Direct and Indirect Effects

Do cognitions have a direct effect on health? To answer that question, researchers must control for the indirect effects of certain cognitions. Considerable evidence suggests, for example, that perceived control has positive health implications; however, people who believe they can control something also tend to engage in positive coping behaviors. One way of thinking about this question is to ask if these people would engage in the same behaviors if they did not hold the same beliefs. In other words, would the same effect be obtained if people were simply conditioned to engage in the same behaviors, or is it necessary for people to believe in what they are doing?

We have already discussed indirect effects. As we saw, the process of education shows that there are many indirect effects. We will now review the evidence—from cancer research and beyond—that there could be direct links between cognition and the immune system.

The Evidence for Direct Effects

Researchers have assumed for some time that stress is the cause of a diminished immune response, but we now have good reason to challenge that assumption.

The diminished immune response might be caused by negative cognitions. In studying depression, Seligman (1990) noted that depletion of the catecholamines triggers an endorphin response, which then shuts down the immune system. Although stress often depletes the catecholamines, the immune system often shuts down in the absence of stress. If negative cognitions are the cause of a diminished immune response, this would explain why researchers have not been able to consistently predict poor health based on stress markers, such as high blood pressure, and why indicators of negative cognitions often predict poor health.

Another piece of evidence relates to interaction of implicit theories and stress. It appears that people who have a malevolent implicit theory of the world tend to experience more stress than do people who have a benign or benevolent implicit theory of the world (e.g., Epstein, 1990). Likewise, a recent study found that individuals who believe in a just world had a more benign cognitive appraisal of stress tasks, rated experimental tasks as less stressful, and had autonomic reactions more consistent with challenge than threat (Tomaka & Blascovich, 1994). According to Lazarus, there are two distinct steps in the appraisal process: primary appraisal, which assesses threat and harm, and secondary appraisal, which assesses coping skills. Numerous studies have found that primary appraisal and secondary appraisal account for different portions of the variance (e.g., Florian, Mikulincer, & Taubman, 1995). According to Lazarus's (1991c) theory, primary and secondary appraisal are distinct processes. Primary appraisal occurs first and produces the initial stress reaction to threat or harm, although secondary appraisal follows and modulates that initial reaction. If we perceive that our coping skills are good, the stress reaction should go down; if not, it should remain the same. This is consistent with the idea proposed by LeDoux (1996)—and discussed in Chapter 8—that incoming threat information is relayed from the thalamus to two different locations, the amygdala and the neocortex. The amygdala produces the stress reaction (the fight-or-flight response), although the neocortex provides an inhibitory function (regulating the fight-or-flight response). In other words, our perception of the threat activates the stress response, but our cognitive assessment of the threat—in relation to our coping skills, in particular—determines whether the stress response continues.

According to Lazarus's theory, we do not actually have to engage in coping responses to reduce stress. Simply knowing that we have coping responses seems to be sufficient. Again, this suggests that the effect is highly cognitive. These people typically do have coping responses; however, so it could be argued that this is merely a conditioned effect. That is, because stress was reduced in the past when people used their coping responses, the thought of coping in the past (memory, if you like) is sufficient to trigger a lowered stress response.

To determine which interpretation is correct, we need to find people who believe they can cope even before they have acquired or used coping responses. Considerable research has shown that beliefs about control—beliefs about being able to cope or to develop coping skills—tend to reduce stress. People often experience less stress when they simply decide to see a therapist, for example. Because they believe the therapist is going to help them, there is a so-called placebo effect. Further, substantial research indicates that people will talk themselves into believing they can control things even before they have developed the necessary coping skills. This research—known variously as research on need for control, desire for control, or illusion of control (e.g., Friedland, Keinan, & Regev, 1992; Law, Logan, & Baron, 1994; Taylor et al., 2000)—shows that such beliefs exert a powerful positive influence on health.

Hope, optimism, and constructive thinking have repeatedly been linked to health. It appears that people with a positive view of the world and of themselves tend to bounce back relatively easily from adversity. They typically engage in behaviors that will get them out of their present predicaments. A study of HIV-positive men found that those characterized by dispositional optimism engaged in more positive health-related coping behaviors and experienced less distress, even though the virus they were carrying would almost certainly kill them in due course (Taylor et al., 1992). The ability to think positively not only reduces the magnitude of the stress response but leads to the development of coping skills. Both are important for strengthening the immune response. In this example, as in many of the others, we cannot rule out indirect effects. Nonetheless, we cannot rule out the idea there could be direct effects. Obviously, further research is needed.

A long-term study comparing optimists and pessimists on various health measures found that, although they did not show any differences in health at the age of 25, health differences began to emerge after about the age of 45 (Peterson, Seligman, & Vaillant, 1988). People who were more pessimistic began to show more health disorders, although people who remained optimistic often showed little deterioration. In other words, people who are more negative might ultimately pay the price for their pessimism.

We know positive thinking is important, but we still don't completely understand why. Perhaps this is because positive thinking leads to coping. In other words, the key to good health might boil down to doing the right things, something that seems to come naturally to optimistic people. Another possibility is raised by Ellen Langer (1989), who has suggested, based on her research, that the effects of physical and psychological aging are moderated by remaining mindful—staying in touch with the world as an active decision maker and an active learner. In the past, many researchers viewed such activities as stressful. Perhaps all this shows is that we need to experience optimal stress for good health.

Benson (1987), who for many years has advocated learning the relaxation response as a means of reducing stress, has recently suggested a bidirectional effect between relaxation and cognition. For example, he has found that, as a result of learning to relax, people often come to perceive the world as less threatening and perceive themselves as more in control. Obviously, a life that is relatively free of threat is very important if we are to reduce stress and remain healthy. In recent years, there have been many reports that meditation can improve individuals' views of the world and can play a significant role in helping them to give up their addiction to drugs.

The question that remains to be answered is whether these research findings represent direct effects of cognitive patterns on health, or simply indirect effects.

Summary

The first studies of the stress response focused on the role of stress in adapting to disease. However, Selye discovered that stress is not only involved in adapting to injury and diseases but also has other health implications, which he referred to as diseases of adaptation.

Considerable evidence indicates that there are bidirectional effects between stress and disease. For example, cancer triggers stress, and stress itself plays a central role in the progression of cancer. One implication of this is that anything we can do to reduce stress will slow the progression of a disease such as cancer.

The immune system is affected both directly and indirectly by a number of systems and behaviors. Stress has a direct effect. Thus, lowering stress through relaxation, for example, can have a direct effect. Diet, exercise, and alcohol seem to have a more indirect effect.

Some evidence indicates a direct effect between certain patterns of thought—for example, optimism—and the immune system, but more research is needed on this topic. However, even if there is no direct effect, optimistic thinking clearly has positive health benefits.

Main Points

1. Although early motivation theorists conceptualized motivation as drives or needs that lead directly to action, current theorists conceptualize motivation as dispositions. Whether these dispositions will result in action often depends on emotions, which can undermine or sustain goal-directed behavior.

2. According to the Kleinginnas' definition, emotions give rise to affective experiences, stimulate us to generate cognitive explanations, trigger a variety of internal responses, and elicit behaviors that are expressive, goal-directed, and adaptive.

3. Two separate systems—the sympathetic/adrenal and the pituitary/adrenal—are involved in the stress response.

4. Endorphins are mobilized from the pituitary and are important for their analgesic and euphoric properties. The stress response triggers the release of endorphins.

5. There are two immune systems—the innate (nonspecific) and acquired (specific) systems.

6. One of the main reasons immunity is downgraded during stress is to free up energy for the flight-or-fight response.

7. Generally, the stress response is more likely to be triggered by unpredictable events than by predictable events.

8. In primary appraisal, we assess three categories: harm/loss, threat, and challenge.
9. Secondary appraisal involves the evaluation of coping resources and options and may be either problem-focused or emotion-focused.
10. One good way to manage stress is to break information down into manageable units.
11. Emotion-focused strategies for coping with stress include meditation, relaxation, exercise, and biofeedback.
12. Optimism, beliefs about persona control and finding meaning strengthen the immune response.
13. The personality profile of people who remain healthy after experiencing high degrees of life stress—known as the hardy personality—is distinguished by three main characteristics: control, commitment, and challenge.

14. Diet, exercise, drugs, social support, coping strategies, and compliance are thought to have an indirect effect on the immune system.
15. How we think about the world—in particular, whether we view it positively or negatively—could have a direct effect on the magnitude of the stress response.

 ## InfoTrac® College Edition

What are some organizations doing to decrease stress in the workplace? (Search words: stress, management of stress)

What are five things that you can do to reduce stress? (Search words: stress [Psychology], management of stress)

Chapter Ten

Goal-Incongruent (Negative) Emotions

- *What are goal-incongruent emotions?*
- *What is the difference between fear and anxiety?*
- *What is the relationship between anxiety and depression?*
- *What is the relationship between pessimism and depression?*
- *When people become depressed, why do they often feel helpless?*
- *Can people get rid of depressed feelings by changing the way they think?*
- *What is the difference between guilt and shame?*
- *Why do some people experience more guilt and shame than others do?*
- *Is it adaptive to experience no guilt or shame?*

Lazarus (1991a, b) has suggested a distinction between goal-incongruent emotions, which thwart the attainment of personal goals, and goal-congruent emotions, which facilitate the attainment of personal goals: Goal-incongruent emotions are generally negative (associated with negative affect), whereas goal-congruent emotions are generally positive. This way of classifying emotions is consistent with recent approaches to motivation in which goals are central (Locke & Latham, 1990). Within this framework, emotions that are involved in goal-directed behaviors are of most interest, from a motivational perspective.

The phrase "negative emotions" (often used by psychologists and implied by the title) is an oxymoron. If emotions evolved to ensure our survival, as we believe they did, they cannot be negative. I simply inserted the word negative into the title because writers frequently refer to them as negative. When we use the term *negative emotion* what we are simply saying is that these emotions produce negative affect. We are not saying that they are something to be shunned.

It is very important to distinguish feelings and emotions because although we might not like a certain feeling, that feeling might nonetheless be invaluable for telling me about my emotional state. When I am under stress, for example, I might be vulnerable to a heart attack but by listening to my feelings, I can learn to intervene and thus avert a heart attack.

It has become fashionable to ignore negative feelings and, when they arise, to distract oneself by putting on a happy face. Although this idea has some merit, there are also some pitfalls. In this chapter, I am going to show that although certain emotions can be momentarily unpleasant and get in the way of goal directed behavior, they are nonetheless worth listening to. Feelings are the voices of our emotions and as such they are the "voices of our genes" (Buck, 1999). The better we listen, the more likely we will survive.

Fear and Anxiety

Is there a distinction between fear and anxiety? Some theorists have suggested that the two are the same (Izard & Tomkins, 1966; Rosen & Schulkin, 1998); others suggest they are quite different, involving different brain structures. The consensus seems to be they are quite different, so we are going to follow that path.

Current research suggests that fear can be conceptualized as an emotional system that is sensitive to cues, unlearned or learned, that signal physical punishment (pain). Anxiety, in contrast, can be conceptualized as an emotional system that is attuned to situations characterized by uncertainty, social comparison, personal failure, and negative evaluation of personal worth. According to this distinction, fear evolved to ensure our immediate physical survival and anxiety evolved to ensure our social survival (White & Depue, 1999).

As noted in the previous chapter, psychologists have come to view humans as social beings. This idea came from an evolutionary analysis that argues our ancestors' survival depended on being attuned to the needs of the group. Those not attuned to the needs of the group jeopardized the survival of the group and were likely ostracized—an act that meant almost certain death. Thus, it follows that evolutionary pressures gave rise to the capacity to be sensitive to social evaluative stimuli. Possessing such a capacity would ensure both material and social support for the individual. According to this conceptualization, anxiety is a negative emotion that alerts us to potentially threatening situations. Among other things it (1) helps us focus on social-evaluative stimuli and (2) activates reverberating circuits that give rise to ruminative thoughts. *Reverberating circuits* refer to the phenomenon that once a neurological (brain) circuit has been activated, it tends to stay activated for a period in the absence of the stimulus that triggered it in the first place. In this context, *ruminative thoughts* refers to thinking about ways of preventing social rejection and ostracization (White & Depue, 1999). Later, we are going to talk more about the role of rumination in both anxiety and depression. For now, simply be aware that the word *rumination* (which also means chewing the cud) refers to excessive analysis of our actions.

Trait anxiety appears to fall along a continuum, so people high in trait anxiety can be viewed as people who are "overly" sensitive and those low in trait anxiety as "underly" sensitive. One of the problems for people high in trait anxiety is that even though they might not be in a social situation, they tend to engage in ruminative thinking. In short, they more or less continually think about situations in which they were ostracized or about future situations in which they could be ostracized (White & Depue, 1999).

The overlap between anxiety and depression has been estimated at 20 to 70% (Petersen et al., 1993). It is not surprising, therefore, that many of the same psychological antecedents that underlie anxiety also underlie depression. For example, both anxious individuals and depressed individuals are characterized by negative implicit theories of the world (e.g., Brief, Butcher, George, & Link, 1994), a tendency to be self-critical (Blatt, 1995), and a perceived sense of loss of control (Chorpita & Barlow, 1998). One important thing that differentiates depression from both anxiety and pessimism is that depressed people tend to entertain thoughts of suicide.

The Biological Component

Considerable evidence suggests the heritability of trait anxiety. According to Gray's model, what is inherited is a tendency or disposition for a certain area of the brain to be highly active (Gray, 1982; Gray & McNaughton, 1996). Gray has argued that fear is caused by the activation of the fight-flight system and that anxiety is caused by the activation of the behavioral inhibition system (BIS). We have already discussed the fight-flight system in some detail in the previous chapter, so let's turn to the BIS system. The BIS consists of the septal-hippocampal system and the closely related Papez circuit. The Papez circuit includes the ascending adrenergic (from the locus coeruleus) and serotonergic (from the raphe nuclei) pathways that innervate the septal-hippocampal system and neocortical structures. When this system is activated, there is an increase in nonspecific arousal, and the organism directs its attention to environmental stimuli (Chorpita & Barlow, 1998).

This survival system is activated by both unconditioned and conditioned stimuli. At the unconditioned level, the survival system is activated by innate fears, as we might expect, and also by novelty. Why should novelty activate this system? Researchers have argued that organisms need complete knowledge about their immediate environment to survive. A rabbit, for example, will explore all the available escape routes, thus preparing for a time that it might encounter an enemy such as a coyote. Any change in that environment constitutes a potential threat and, therefore, the rabbit will attend to that new source of information. In Gray's terms, the rabbit will stop, look, and listen when it encounters a novel stimulus.

Gray makes a fundamental distinction between the BIS and the fight-or-flight system (Chapter 9). He points out that antianxiety drugs affect the BIS system but not the fight-or-flight system. This finding is central to his argument that anxiety is mediated by the BIS rather than the fight-or-flight system. Gray notes that all antianxiety drugs exert their influence by deactivating the BIS. The net result is that when under the influence of antianxiety drugs, people are less inclined to stop, look, and listen, and more inclined to carry on with task-related behaviors.

According to Gray, the fight-or-flight system is activated by pain. This is an unconditioned reaction rather than a conditioned one. Gray feels that a wide range of responses currently ascribed to stress should more accurately be called anxiety. Because antianxiety drugs are so widely used in our society, let's briefly discuss how they work.

Antianxiety Drugs

Estimates indicate that 7% of the U.S. population experience anxiety to the degree that it becomes debilitating (Katz, 1990). The prevalence of debilitating anxiety has prompted considerable interest in producing antianxiety drugs. Two commonly used antianxiety drugs, chlordiazepoxide (Librium) and diazepam (Valium), belong to a class of drugs called benzodiazepines. In addition to decreasing anxiety, these drugs produce sedation (which tends to wear off in a couple of days), muscle relaxation, and anticonvulsant activity.

The consensus is that the effect of the benzodiazepines is caused by the actions of the gamma-aminobutyric acid (GABA), a naturally occurring inhibitory neurotransmitter (Cooper, Bloom, & Roth, 1982; Tallman, Paul, Skolnick, & Gallager, 1980). When GABA binds to receptor sites, GABA reduces the flow of neural transmission. The ability of GABA to bind, however, appears to depend on the presence of benzodiazepines. Benzodiazepines themselves have receptor sites and, when they bind to these sites, they increase the ability of GABA to bind. The net effect is that the potency of GABA is momentarily enhanced. The existence of receptors for drugs such as Librium and Valium suggests that the body probably produces its own

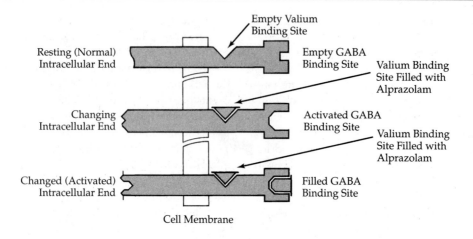

Figure 10-1. Valium/GABA receptor. This simplified schematic drawing shows three stages in the activation of the receptor complex: (1) The receptor, lodged in a cell membrane, has unfilled binding sites for GABA and a benzodiazepine (Valium, alprazolam, etc.) molecule. (2) When alprazolam binds to its site, like a key in a lock, it opens (activates) the GABA site, allowing the site to bind a GABA molecule. (3) Once both alprazolam and GABA are bound and active, the intracellular end of the receptor may change its shape, setting off a chemical domino effect that can transmit a message inside the cell. (From "Valium/GABA Receptor," by S. M. Fishman and D. V. Sheehan, *Psychology Today*. Reprinted with permission from Psychology Today Magazine. Copyright © 1985 by Sussex Publishers, Inc.)

benzodiazepines, though naturally produced benzodiazepines have not yet been isolated. When Valium binds with its receptor site, like a key in a lock, it changes the shape of the GABA site, as we see in Figure 10-1, and thus allows the GABA to bind. In other words, benzodiazepines must be present if GABA is to be effective. The next step in this chain of events is that GABA receptors trigger the opening of chloride channels. These chloride channels lead to a decreased firing rate of critical neurons in many parts of the central nervous system (Dykstra, 1992). The consequence of these actions is reduced activity of the BIS.

Benzodiazepines are typically prescribed to help people deal with a wide range of aversive or noxious situations, including anxiety, death of a friend or relative, and all types of stress. As already noted, when people use a drug that will allow them to escape a noxious or aversive situation (a negative reinforcer), they become very susceptible to the reinforcing effects of that drug (Woods, Katz, & Winger, 1987).

Prefrontal Cortex and the Regulation of Emotion

Brain imaging has shown that positive, outward reaching emotions are linked to activity in the left prefrontal cortex and negative, inhibiting emotions are linked to activity in the right prefrontal cortex. Most people have activity on both sides, depending on things such as in the situations they are in or how they are responding. In anxious and depressed people, however, the right side seems to be active a disproportionate amount of time. It is not clear at this time whether the right side simply comes to dominate the left or if the left side somehow fails to assert itself (Robbins, 2000).

The general belief among scientists is that the left cortex normally listens to but does not act on the messages from the amygdala—a brain structure that constantly monitors the environment for dangers and more or less constantly sends signals to the cortex of possible dangers. (See Chapter 8 for a more complete discussion of the amygdala.) What the prefrontal cortex seems to do is analyze the information it monitors both from the amygdala and other brain systems to determine if the danger is real and immediate, as well as weigh the possible alternative courses of action one could take. In other words, the prefrontal cortex provides alternatives other than merely to fight or give flight. In the absence of a strong prefrontal cortex, the amygdala appears to run unchecked and, consequently, a person is flooded with fear, despair and feelings of helplessness (Dozier, 1998). Indeed, researchers demonstrated some time ago that severing the prefrontal lobes from the rest of the brain (done in the belief that such surgery would help patients with psychiatric disorders) reduced anxiety but increased social inappropriate behavior (Kalat, 1998). What this research suggests is that the tendency to be anxious (what we sometimes refer to as temperament) could reside in the prefrontal cortex. This finding has led to the idea that perhaps we should focus on changing the activity of the prefrontal cortex. Some preliminary research indeed suggests that it might be possible to train the left prefrontal cortex to become more active and thereby reduce the dominance of the right prefrontal cortex in people who are depressed (Robbins, 2000). We need to be cautious, however, in viewing the prefrontal cortex as the seat of anxiety. Gray and others have clearly implicated the BIS in anxiety. What we need to understand more clearly is how the BIS system works in concert with the prefrontal cortex. Only then will we fully understand the roots of anxiety and the experience of negative affect.

The Learned Component

Conditioned Stimuli and Gray's Model

Gray argues that the BIS can be conditioned to two general classes of stimuli (Gray, 1982; Gray & Mc-Naughton, 1996): cues that signal punishment is forthcoming, or cues that signal rewards will be withheld (frustrative nonreward). According to Gray, a child who has been punished in the past for touching an expensive vase will learn to feel anxiety at the idea of touching that vase again.

Gray's model is summarized in Figure 10-2. Like others, Gray has argued that anxiety is essentially an anticipatory response to the possibility of an aversive outcome. Because aversive outcomes are a threat to our survival, it is important to deal with them immediately; however, being too vigilant means that we fail to get on with other goal-directed activities.

Phobias and Panic Attacks

Considerable research has linked anxiety to impaired performance. If anxiety is an adaptive emotion, how does it become maladaptive? For example, in what circumstances does it interfere with goal-directed activities? To answer this question, we need to examine some clinical disorders of anxiety. Within this literature, we can find the conditions that give rise to maladaptive anxiety and the conditions that will enable people to manage maladaptive anxiety.

The development of phobias. According to Mineka (1985), phobia is a persistent and recognizable irrational fear of an object or situation and is characterized by distress and a compelling desire to avoid that object or situation. The thing that differentiates phobias from fear is the irrational aspect of phobias. For example, people often come to fear such things as spiders or snakes even when they know they are harmless.

Phobias can be viewed as the product of classical conditioning; however, classical conditioning alone does not explain why people are inclined to become fearful of certain things but not of others (Mineka, 1985). It could be that, because we needed to avoid spiders and snakes in our evolutionary past, we are biologically prepared to make certain associations more readily than others (Seligman, 1971). Research has shown that, even if a phobic reaction is not elicited when spiders and snakes are initially presented, it is very easy to condition a fear reaction to these stimuli (Seligman, 1971).

Gray has argued that we have evolved a "quick and dirty system" to help us deal with threats to our survival. As he points out, "Failing to respond to danger is more costly than responding inappropriately to a benign stimulus" (Gray & McNaughton, 1996, p. 104). Thus, we are biologically prepared to develop phobias even though they can be maladaptive. Within this context, it is not too hard to understand why people might

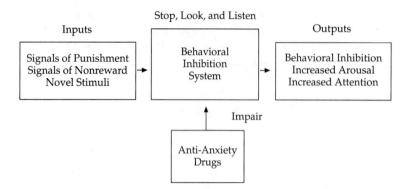

Figure 10-2. Gray's model of the behavioral inhibition system.

develop a variety of phobias such as claustrophobia (fear of enclosed places) or acrophobia (fear of heights).

Treating phobias with systematic desensitization. Systematic desensitization is a very effective procedure for eliminating fears. It is possible to rank-order stimuli along a continuum ranging from those that elicit only mild fear (usually symbolic stimuli) to those that elicit extreme fear (usually concrete stimuli). People who are afraid of spiders, for example, usually respond with only mild fear to the word spider, with greater fear to pictures of spiders, and with intense fear to an actual spider. Typically, before systematic desensitization training begins, the therapist teaches the patient how to become fully relaxed. Then the therapist presents a stimulus that normally elicits mild fear. Presented when the patient is relaxed, the mild stimulus often loses its ability to elicit the fear reaction. The therapist then moves to a stronger stimulus and repeats the procedure. Eventually, the therapist moves to the strongest stimulus. This procedure is based on the idea of counterconditioning; that is, the client is being conditioned to experience a feeling of relaxation and a sense of control to the stimuli that originally elicited fear.

An important feature of this procedure is that the subject is not allowed to make an avoidance response. If the subject is able to make an avoidance response, the procedure is not nearly as effective. The persistence of the avoidance response appears linked to the anxiety reduction that accompanies it. From learning theory, we know that, if a response is continuously rewarded, it will be maintained at a very high level. To

get rid of the response, we need to eliminate the ongoing reward.

The development of panic attacks. Panic attacks (traditionally considered an anxiety disorder) are characterized by somatic symptoms, fear of dying, and fear of losing control. Like Gray, Barlow has argued that panic attacks can be understood as a conditioned fight-or-flight response (Barlow, 1988; Barlow, Chorpita, & Turovsky, 1996). Barlow distinguishes between two types of anxiety: anxious apprehension and fear. Fear, according to Barlow, is governed by the alarm reaction—the first stage of the fight-or-flight response, which involves the activation of the sympathetic nervous system. Anxious apprehension, by contrast, is governed by the BIS system, or something like it. Anxious apprehension prepares the individual to cope with challenges of everyday life. This state involves high arousal, negative affect, perceptions of helplessness and loss of control over future events, and something called worry. Barlow has identified four risk factors for anxious apprehension: (1) a high level of biologically based stress reactivity of genetic origin; (2) the perception that negative events are neither predictable nor controllable; (3) an absence of good coping skills; and (4) inadequate social support. As we see in Figure 10-3, anxious apprehension plays a mediating role in panic-related disorders.

The alarm reaction is normally triggered in life-threatening situations (when it is considered a true alarm) but can also occur spontaneously (when it is considered a false alarm). Subjectively, the two re-

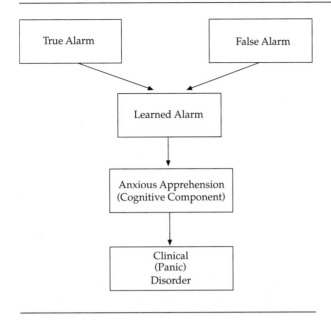

Figure 10-3. Origins of panic-related disorders.

sponses are the same—somatic symptoms, fear of dying, fear of losing control—but, in the case of false alarms, we cannot identify what triggered the response. Barlow argues that the alarm reaction can be conditioned. In other words, we develop learned alarm reactions. Going into our office, for example, could trigger the alarm reaction if it has been a source of stress in the past.

Research indicates no obvious external cues for panic attacks. They occur under a wide variety of conditions—at home, at work, or on a bus, for example. Given the human propensity to look for causes of their behavior, it might be that, in the absence of external cues, humans will be inclined to look for internal ones. This hypothesis is consistent with the finding that panic patients are more sensitive to internal cues (Barlow, 1988).

If panic attacks are truly false alarms, they should occur for virtually everyone. Why, then, do only a few people become disabled by panic attacks? Why does a certain portion of the population decide to stay home and avoid going out? Research shows that people who experience panic attacks find it more stressful to experience the panic attack in situations where they feel trapped or where they would be embar-

rassed. Their focus, in other words, shifts from the panic attack to being embarrassed. The fear of having a panic attack in public is often sufficient to imprison such individuals in their own homes (Chambless & Gracely, 1989).

Panic attacks, when left untreated, often increase over time. Researchers have suggested that when left untreated certain brain systems become sensitized to cues in the environment that normally trigger a fear response. As a result, a panic attack, rather than a controllable fear response, occurs (Rosen & Schulkin, 1998). In other words, although panic attacks look like false alarms, they are the result of an overly sensitive fear detector.

Treating panic attacks with information. People who experience panic attacks are typically perplexed and troubled by them and come to believe that they might die or lose control in an attack. Thus, one way to help such people is to provide them with some basic information about the nature of panic attacks. Research has shown that three things are useful. First, convincing people that they are not going to die or experience a major medical problem because of a panic attack is often sufficient to stop them from having full-blown attacks (Salkovskis, Clark, & Hackmann, 1991). Second, convincing them that the attacks are no more likely to occur in public than at home tends to reduce their need to stay at home. Third, convincing them that they will not lose control or embarrass themselves if they have a panic attack in public lessens the anxiety associated with leaving their homes.

These findings are consistent with the idea that people's emotional reactions can be understood, in part, through a normative approach—that is, through what is perceived as normal or expected. That normative arguments can affect anticipated emotions, such as panic attacks, indicates that people are inclined to bring their emotional responses in line with what they believe to be appropriate or normal (Baron, 1992).

It is important for all of us to understand that some of the anxiety we experience has been learned. When we realize that our reactions are inappropriate or irrational, we might decide to design a program—perhaps with professional help—that will help us bring our behavior in line with what is useful and appropriate.

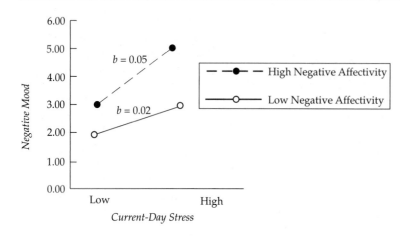

Figure 10-4. Mood across day as a function of current-day stress and negative affectivity, while holding all other variables constant at zero. (From "Daily Stress and the Trajectory of Mood: Spillover, Response Assimilation, Contrast, and Chronic Negative Affectivity," by C. A. Marco and J. Suls, *Journal of Personality and Social Psychology*, 1993, *64*, 1053–1063. Copyright © 1993 by the American Psychological Association. Reprinted by permission of the author.)

The Cognitive Component

Cognitive factors play an important role in the arousal of fear and anxiety. Let's look at a few of these.

Viewing the World as Threatening

Several research approaches indicate that anxious people have a bias toward viewing the world as threatening.

1. **Negative affectivity**. Negative affectivity is a mood or dispositional tendency. People high in this quality (a) are more likely to experience stress and dissatisfaction as they interact with the environment, (b) tend to dwell on their failures more, (c) tend to see the world in negative terms, and (d) have a poor self-concept, characterized by dissatisfaction with themselves and their lives (Watson & Clark, 1984).

As we see in Figure 10-4, people high in negative affectivity experience more stress, often at the beginning of a day, and are also more reactive to increases in stress—that is, they show greater cumulative effects of the many stressful events encountered in the course of a day (Marco & Suls, 1993). Researchers also found that people high in negative affectivity tend to have slower recovery rates from stress. These results demonstrate that the environment alone does not cause stress. How much stress we experience depends on how we interpret the environment. These results are consistent with the idea that cognitions play a key role in understanding negative moods and emotions such as anxiety. If stress were solely the result of environmental stressors,

there would be no differences between people with different cognitions. Remember that most theories of stress are based on the premise that stress results from seeing the world as a potential source of threat to the individual's well-being.

2. **Bias in interpreting ambiguous stimuli**. Considerable evidence indicates a positive relationship between anxiety and the tendency to see the world as threatening, but what does that mean? Does our interpretation of the world give rise to anxiety, or does anxiety make us see the world as threatening? To answer this question, McNally (1996) has undertaken some laboratory experiments with clinically anxious individuals. He has concluded that anxious people have an interpretive bias; they are inclined to interpret ambiguous stimuli as threatening. If the situation were not ambiguous, you would not expect differences to emerge, and they don't.

3. **Attentional bias to process threat cues**. A person who holds an implicit theory that the world is a source of constant threat is likely to develop a mental set to identify those threats. This follows directly from the assumption of evolutionary psychologists that humans are programmed at birth to attend to their survival needs first. Using a variety of paradigms, various researchers have provided evidence that "patients with anxiety disorders exhibit an attentional bias favoring the processing of threat cues" (McNally, 1996, p. 223).

The research on cognitive bias indicates that healthy control subjects are often characterized by biases in the opposite direction from those exhibited by anxious patients. These people tend to see the world as benevolent (Chapter 12).

One obvious implication that follows from this research is that anxious people must learn to see the world as less threatening if their symptoms are to abate. Although antianxiety drugs can create the perception that the world is less threatening, that perception seems to be almost completely drug-dependent. That is, the less-threatening perception does not carry over into the nondrug state.

Unwanted or Intrusive Thoughts

Unwanted or intrusive thoughts—also known as automaticity—are typically associated with anxiety. Intrusive thoughts are a problem for clinical populations and are also commonly found in nonclinical populations (Kelly & Kahn, 1994). The content of intrusive thoughts is different in a panic state, an obsessive-compulsive state, or merely a generalized anxiety state. Panic patients experience thoughts about imminent insanity, death, and loss of control in the midst of their attacks. Obsessive-compulsive patients experience intrusive thoughts about violence, contamination, and other upsetting themes. People with a generalized anxiety disorder often ruminate about possible misfortunes (McNally, 1996).

Several researchers have examined whether people can learn to suppress intrusive thoughts using techniques such as distraction. In some studies, people have successfully learned to suppress intrusive thoughts (e.g., Kelly & Kahn, 1994), but in others attempts to suppress have resulted in a rebound effect (e.g., Wegner, 1989). Evidence from various sources suggests that people can learn to reduce and even eliminate unwanted thoughts—for example, by undergoing therapy (McNally, 1996). Perhaps the answer lies in getting people to think in new ways about important events in their lives. We will return to this topic when we discuss depression.

Loss of Control

Considerable evidence indicates that perceived loss of control is linked to the expression of anxiety. Control here refers to "the ability to personally influence events and outcomes in one's environment, principally those related to positive or negative reinforcement" (Chorpita & Barlow, 1998, p. 5). We talk about perceived control because there are individual differences in what

people think they can or cannot control. Where do such differences come from? The evidence suggests early experience with control plays a central role. Researchers have found, for example, that people who experienced diminished control as children tend to have a bias toward interpreting events as out of their control. Because of this bias, they tend to be vulnerable to anxiety (Chorpita & Barlow, 1998).

Ruminative Thoughts About Loss of Control

A central feature of anxiety is ruminative thoughts about personal failure (Mikulincer, 1994). Ruminative thoughts are like unwanted thoughts—they focus attention on self-inadequacy. As such, they tend, among other things to create negative affect and undermine self-esteem (Bodner & Mikulincer, 1998). We will talk more about rumination when we talk about depression. For now, simply make a mental note that rumination is a central feature in many negative emotions. Although it is normal to ruminate to some degree, when rumination takes over one's life, it can and often does become highly debilitating.

Inability to Make a Coping Response

Lazarus (1991a, b) has argued that the inability (or the perceived inability) to make an adaptive response to a threatening event or the fact (or perception) that no such response is available will lead to feelings of anxiety. Lazarus points out that ambiguity is the main consideration here, because it prevents the elaboration of clear action patterns (coping strategies) that would allow the individual to deal with the threat.

Lazarus suggests that transforming anxiety into fear might be a useful way of getting people to cope with a threat. Once they know what is threatening them, they can devise a pattern of action to deal with it. When they don't know what the threat is, they are left in limbo; they experience anxiety but don't know what to do about it.

Top-Down and Bottom-Up Theories of Subjective Well-Being

Researchers have suggested that the opposite of anxiety is subjective well-being. Theories of subjective well-being adopt two very different perspectives:

■   Bottom-up theories start with the assumption that happiness comes from a summation of pleasurable

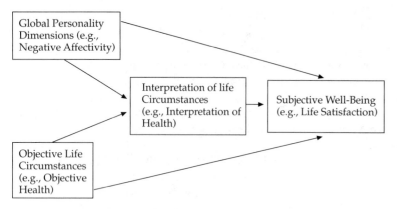

Figure 10-5.   An integrated approach to subjective well-being. (From "Integrating Bottom-Up and Top-Down theories of Subjective Well-being: The Case of Health," by A. P. Brief, A. H. Butcher, J. M. George, and K. E. Link, *Journal of Personality and Social Psychology*, 1993, *64*, 646–653. Copyright © 1993 by the American Psychological Association. Reprinted by permission of the author.)

and unpleasurable experiences. According to this line of thinking, if you have more pleasurable than unpleasurable experiences during the day, you will be happy.

- Top-down theories assume that individuals are happy because they tend to see the world and themselves in a positive way.

There is evidence for both theories. A study designed to examine the relative contributions of bottom-up and top-down variables found that both make an important contribution (Brief, Butcher, George, & Link, 1994). On the one hand, if individuals think about the world and themselves in negative terms, they will become anxious but, if they think of the world in positive terms, they will experience subjective well-being. On the other hand, if individuals have bad experiences, such as poor health, they will experience anxiety but, if they have good experiences, such as good grades, they will experience subjective well-being. The results of this experiment are consistent with the model in Figure 10-5.

The implication of this research is that individuals need to develop the following:

1. Beliefs and attitudes that will engender a positive mental set about the world and themselves, so that they see the world as a place where goals can be attained and they can grow and experience satisfaction and meaning.
2. Habits that will ensure their daily lives are filled with good experiences—that is, habits that will give them good health, minimal stress, and reduced conflict.

3. Friends and social support networks to which they can turn when things look bleak.

Summary

The consensus is that fear and anxiety represent the operation of two distinct systems. Evolutionary psychologists have argued that fear evolved to ensure our immediate survival and anxiety evolved to ensure our long-term survival based on the existence of a well-tuned community. Gray has argued that fear is caused by the activation of the fight-flight system and anxiety is caused by the activation of the behavioral inhibition system (BIS). The system is activated by both unconditioned stimuli—innate fears and novelty—and conditioned stimuli—signals indicating punishment or nonreward. Gray makes a fundamental distinction between the BIS and the fight-or-flight system. He points out that antianxiety drugs affect the BIS system but not the fight-or-flight system. Gray argues that phobias are learned and have their roots in the BIS, whereas panic has its roots in the fight-or-flight response. Barlow has made a distinction between true and false alarms as ways of thinking about panic. Desensitization has been found to be highly effective in helping people to deal with phobias. Although it is difficult to eliminate panic attacks, giving people information about the origins of panic attacks has proven effective in helping them to deal with their attacks.

Anxious individuals tend to view the world as threatening. They have a bias to interpret ambiguous stimuli as threatening and to attend to threatening stimuli first. Unwanted or intrusive thoughts are a major problem for anxious people, because they perpetuate feelings of threat and negative emotion. Perceived loss of control and perceived absence of a coping response also tends to create feelings of anxiety. Research indicates that subjective well-being, the opposite of anxiety, comes from two classes of variables: a positive mental attitude toward the world and a set of well-developed habits that ensure good physical and mental health.

Pessimism and Depression

The concepts of pessimism and depression are closely linked. The study of depressed individuals shows that most tend to use a pessimistic explanatory style, and considerable data indicate that people who use a pessimistic explanatory style are more likely to become depressed (Seligman, 1990). Nevertheless, the differences are important to note. Although people who are depressed are characterized by loss of motivation (loss of interest in food, sex, work, social relationships, achievement, and so on) and loss of interest in life (they are often suicidal), pessimistic people generally remain motivated, despite their limited tendency to embrace and interact with the outside world. Let's start by looking at the concept of depression.

Types of depression. There are three kinds of depression: normal, unipolar, and bipolar. Bipolar depression has also been called a manic-depressive disorder because it is characterized by both manic episodes and depressive episodes. Bipolar depression is much more heritable than is unipolar depression and is very responsive to lithium carbonate. We have good reason to believe that bipolar depression is not the result of pessimistic thinking but, rather, is caused by a genetic disorder (Seligman, 1990).

The prevailing view is that normal depression is simply a passing demoralization, whereas unipolar depression is a chemical or clinical disorder and needs to be treated with drugs, psychotherapy, or both. Taking exception to this view, Seligman (1990) points out that the two cannot be distinguished based on their symptomatology. He argues that those with normal depres-

sion are more likely to recover because they are not as severely depressed.

According to the American Psychiatric Association's (1994) *Diagnostic and Statistical Manual of Mental Disorders (DSM-IV)*, a major depressive episode is characterized by at least five of the following criteria, including depressed mood or loss of interest. They typically must occur on a daily basis.

1. Depressed mood most of the day.
2. Markedly diminished interest or pleasure in usual daily activities.
3. Significant weight loss when not dieting, or weight gain, or decrease or increase in appetite.
4. Insomnia or hypersomnia.
5. Psychomotor agitation or retardation.
6. Fatigue or loss of energy.
7. Feelings of worthlessness or excessive or inappropriate guilt.
8. Diminished ability to think or concentrate or indecisiveness.
9. Recurrent thoughts of death and/or recurrent suicidal ideation (with or without plan).

How prevalent is depression? Some years ago, in a survey to determine the prevalence of depression among university students, 78% of the students reported that they had experienced depression at some time during the academic year, and 46% of those indicated that their symptoms had been severe enough to warrant psychiatric help (Beck & Young, 1978). As already noted, when people are depressed, they frequently entertain thoughts of suicide; of the 9 to 10 million people in the United States and Canada who experience depression in any given year, more than 150,000 (about 1.5%) eventually commit suicide (Rosenfeld, 1985).

Beck and Young (1978) reported that depression is generally twice as high among university students as in a comparable group of nonstudents. Women are 2 to 5 times more prone to depression than men. In the past, depression tended to occur more frequently at midlife (the 40s or 50s), but recently it has also been occurring earlier; many people in their 30s, 20s, and even teens are experiencing depression. Between 1960 and 1988, for example, adolescent suicides increased from 3.6 to 11.3 per 100,000 population. This represents a 200% increase, as compared with a general population increase of 17%. Although not all these suicides could be linked to depression, depression was clearly the most direct psychiatric antecedent. Completed suicides were typically precipitated by a shameful or humiliating experience such as an arrest, a perceived failure at school or work, or rejection or conflict in an interpersonal or romantic relationship (Garland & Zigler, 1993).

Modern Individualism and the Rise of Depression

Seligman has argued that depression can be linked, at least in part, to modern individualism. He notes that the rate of depression has increased 10 times in the United States over the last two generations, but there has been no increase in depression among the Amish, a closely knit religious community of 10,000 farmers, who use no electricity, shun modern technology, and use no drugs or alcohol. Research indicates that depression is prevalent mainly in technologically advanced countries. In a study of one primitive tribe, the Kaluli of New Guinea, scientists were unable to find any signs of depression at all (Seligman, 1988).

Martin Seligman has suggested that this prevalence of depression in technologically advanced countries is the result of a new form of individualism that is highly susceptible to depression. Individualism has deep roots in North American history (Bellah, Madsen, Sullivan, Swidler, & Tipton, 1985; de Tocqueville, 1835/1969) and has had many positive consequences. However, Seligman and others have suggested that, in modern society, some people have pursued individualism at the expense of obligation (for example, to the family), commitment (for example, to marriage), and involvement (for example, in the community). The two basic characteristics of modern individualism are autonomy and self-reliance.

Seligman (1988) points out that the modern individual has also been encouraged to embrace consumerism. We have been told that we can find happiness by owning objects, which can provide pleasure but do not demand commitment, obligation, or feeling; they do not threaten autonomy and self-reliance. Drugs and sex have also been marketed as part of this new consumerism. To be happy, you simply need more and better drugs and sex.

If the complete focus on the self is causing problems, why don't we return to a more traditional lifestyle? One reason may be a reluctance to give up our autonomy and self-reliance, two attributes that we have come to value (Bellah et al., 1985). However, many writers have concluded that we must acknowledge that we are social animals (e.g., Buck, 1999). We need other humans to experience certain basic emotions such as love and worth, for example.

Deci and Ryan (1991) distinguish between self-reliance and self-determination. Although they encourage people to become self-determined, they do not encourage people to become more self-reliant. Self-reliant means that we do not need other people. Self-determined by contrast, means making choices, developing competencies, and adapting to our social environment, so we can take charge of our lives (Deci & Ryan, 1985, 1991).

Let's examine the biological, learned, and cognitive components of depression.

The Biological Component of Depression

The Heritability of Depression

A long line of evidence indicates that depression runs in families (Weissman, Lear, Holzer, Meyers, & Tischler, 1984). Perhaps the best data comes from twin studies. Identical twins are 4 to 5 times more likely to show concordances for major depressive disorders than are fraternal twins (Kendler, Heath, Martin, & Eaves, 1986; Wender et al., 1986). The genetic loading for childhood and adolescent depression might be greater than that for depression occurring in adulthood, and earlier onset appears to predict more frequent and severe episodes (Petersen et al., 1993). Note, however, that most family studies have failed to disentangle genetic and environmental influences. As a result, it is still not clear what role learning and cognition play; the only thing we really know is that there is a significant genetic component.

Researchers have found that depressed individuals show relatively more electrical activity in the right hemisphere of the brain. It's possible that chronic activation of the right hemisphere predisposes individuals to depressive or anxiety disorders as well as to other types of illness (National Advisory Mental Health Council, 1995). As I cautioned earlier, we need to better understand how the right hemisphere, especially the prefrontal cortex, works in concert with other brain systems before we can completely understand the implications of this finding.

Type A Depression: Catecholamine Depletion

After analyzing the relationship between affective disorders and catecholamines, Schildkraut and Kety (1967) formulated the catecholamine hypothesis of affective disorders. Because drugs that deplete or block norepinephrine and also, to some extent, dopamine, produce sedation and depression, whereas drugs that increase norepinephrine relieve depression and produce elation and euphoria, Schildkraut and Kety concluded that norepinephrine and dopamine are the chemicals primarily involved in the mood changes that characterize various affective disorders. According to their hypothesis, excessive amounts of norepinephrine and dopamine produce the manic state—the high end of the manic-depressive continuum—and a deficiency of norepinephrine and dopamine produces the depressive state at the low end.

Buck (1999) has argued that failure to meet environmental challenges often leads to burnout, despair, and type A depression (characterized by norepinephrine depletion). One consequence of norepinephrine depletion is the inability to experience reward. This would explain such things as why individuals who are depressed show diminished pleasure in usual daily activities. Norepinephrine has been implicated in attention and memory, so depletion of norepinephrine would account, in part, for reduced attention.

Type B Depression: Serotonin

Indolamines—especially serotonin (also called 5-HT)—are also implicated in depression. As with norepinephrine, it is depletion that seems to be a major antecedent.

Buck (1999) argues that Type B depression results from the inability to meet social challenges, something that can result in a subordinate status. According to Buck, the best way to understand depression is to view depression in how our ancestors evolved to survive.

Survival and the Two Biological Affects

Buck (1999) has proposed that two affective systems evolved to ensure our survival. The first system is called the selfish affect and is involved in self-preservation. The second is called prosocial affects and is involved in the preservation of the species. We have already talked at various points in this book about selfish affect, which mainly involves the behavioral activation system (BAS), a system that is important in rewarding behavior. When we attain goals or meet challenges we experience positive affect, which provides the incentive for engaging in such adaptive behaviors. Within Buck's system affects (those positive and negative feelings we experience) are viewed as "voices of the genes." These affects tell us what we are doing right as well as what we are doing wrong. Depression within this context is telling us that we are failing to meet certain demands. Depression, therefore, is a wake-up call for us to initiate adaptive behaviors. Paradoxically, this extreme affective state seems to cause catecholamine depletion. As a result, we lack the chemicals that play a central role in providing the positive affect (the incentive) to act adaptively. Researchers have suggested that this might also be adaptive. There is a point when it is prudent to give up when a goal is unattainable. What we need to do is rethink what we are doing, set new goals if necessary, and then move forward.

As indicated earlier, there is growing acceptance of the idea that human survival depends on acting selfishly and acting prosocially. Buck uses the concept of attachment when talking about prosocial behavior. He argues that we are biologically designed to bond with others. Within this system are two types of social motives: (1) the need to follow or exceed expectations that come from the group and (2) the need to be loved. Group expectations refers to such things as helping obtain food, provide shelter, and fend off enemies. When we follow or exceed expectations, we experience strong feelings of social acceptance, bonding and love, whereas when we fail we experience feelings of social rejection, distress, and panic. Negative affect (depression) that results from failing to meet or exceed expectations is, as before, the voice of the genes telling us we are not on the right track—that we need to correct our behavior.

Buck's system emphasizes the need for children to experience attachment. He argues that the experience of attachment provides a sense of belonging, whereas the lack of attachment gives rise to a sense of isolation. Figure 10-6 provides a summary of the overall theory. Note that social affects and cognitive affects give rise to moral affects. Moral affects have to do with things such as justice and our perceptions that people are being

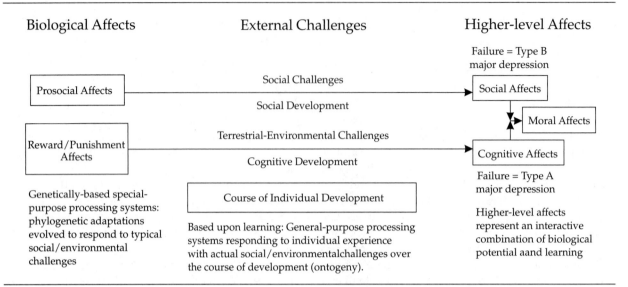

Figure 10-6. Hypothesized relationships between biological affects and higher-level affects. (From "The Biological Affects: A Typology," by R. Buck, *Psychological Review*, 1999, *106*, 301–336. Copyright © 1999 by the American Psychological Association. Reprinted by permission of the author.)

treated fairly and equitably (Buck, 1999). Within any community, there needs to be justice if people are going to cooperate.

Using Drugs to Treat Depression

Depression is often initially treated with drugs. Research indicates that 60 to 80% of patients treated with drugs experience significant short-term improvement. In the long term, however, people often fall back into a negative mood state, together with negative thinking unless cognitive therapy is combined with drug therapy (Hollon, DeRubeis, & Evans, 1990).

Traditionally, tricyclic antidepressants, such as Tofranil and Elavil, were preferred for the initial treatment of symptoms of depression. The tricyclics work in the same way that cocaine works; they help to block the reuptake of norepinephrine and serotonin at the receptors, thereby increasing the concentration of norepinephrine and serotonin at the receptor sites. Monoamine oxidase inhibitors (MAOI), such as Narplan, Nardil, and Parnate, are also used as antidepressants, especially if the tricyclics fail to work or have severe side effects. Monoamine oxidase (MAO) is an enzyme important in the regulation of catecholamines such as norepinephrine and serotonin. When the

monoamine oxidase level is high, it somehow reduces the levels of norepinephrine and serotonin. As the MAOI inhibits monoamine oxidase, the norepinephrine and serotonin levels rise.

Prozac, as well as a whole family of new drugs, selectively block the reuptake serotonin and for a period of time, became the preferred drug to treat depression (mainly because it has fewer side effects). The effectiveness of Prozac, although less than that of the tricyclics in some cases, has led some researchers to speculate that serotonin is an essential regulator of mood and that depression often represents a shortage of serotonin. It is now possible to tailor drugs to produce the different desired effects (e.g., reduced serotonin uptake, reduced dopamine uptake, etc.). Although many of these drugs are used in connection with depressive symptoms, they are also prescribed for anxiety disorders including obsessive-compulsive disorder. Remember that the overlap between anxiety and depression is about 20 to 70%. Figure 10-7 shows how researchers think some of the antidepressants work.

Stress and Depression

Numerous studies have found a link between stress and depression. One laboratory technique for inducing

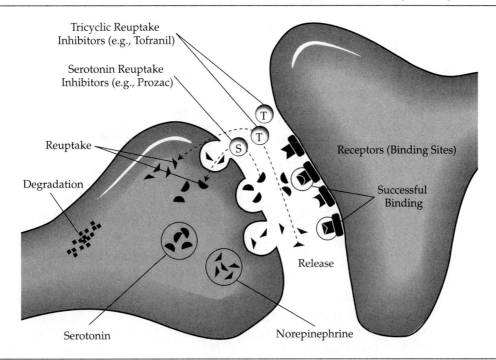

Tricyclic Reuptake
Inhibitors (e.g., Tofranil)

Serotonin Reuptake
Inhibitors (e.g., Prozac)

Reuptake

Degradation

Receptors (Binding Sites)

Successful
Binding

Release

Serotonin

Norepinephrine

Figure 10-7. Serotonin and norepinephrine are neurotransmitters that carry messages across the synapses from one nerve cell to another. After carrying a message across a synapse, a process that involves binding, they are reabsorbed through a process called reuptake. Researchers have suggested that some antidepressants plug the reuptake pump, which is responsible for the reabsorption. Although tricyclics appear to block the reuptake of both norepinephrine and serotonin, serotonin reuptake inhibitors (such as Prozac) simply block the reuptake of serotonin. The net result is that concentrations of norepinephrine and serotonin are high at the synaptic gap, a phenomenon that has been linked to elevated mood. The monoamine oxidase inhibitors (MAOI) work in a very different way. They block the action of monoamine oxidase (MAO), an enzyme involved in the regulation of these neurotransmitters. When MAO levels are high, norepinephrine and serotonin levels are low. Blocking the action of MAO allows levels of norepinephrine and serotonin to rise, and mood is elevated. Note that this diagram ignores the role of dopamine, which might also be involved in depression.

stress is to expose humans or animals to uncontrollable shock. When animals are exposed to uncontrollable shock, norepinephrine is released at a high rate from the locus coeruleus, an area in the brainstem that we discussed in connection with sleep and dreams (Chapter 6). Apparently, the receptors in the brainstem do not use all the available norepinephrine, and the unused norepinephrine is reabsorbed by the neuron and destroyed. The store of norepinephrine is then depleted. Once the body cannot synthesize norepinephrine as quickly as it is being released, the norepineph-

rine level in the locus coeruleus is lowered. This lowered level of norepinephrine is believed to result in feelings of depression (Buss, 1999).

The Learned Component of Depression

Seligman's Model of Learned Helplessness

While doing research on the relation between fear conditioning and instrumental learning, Martin Seligman and two colleagues discovered a striking phenomenon

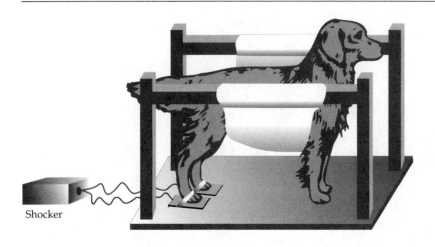

Figure 10-8. Experimental apparatus used to study the effects of inescapable and uncontrollable shock in dogs. (From *Discovering Psychology,* by N. Carlson. Copyright © 1988 by Allyn and Bacon. Reprinted by permission.)

Shocker

that came to be called learned helplessness (Overmier & Seligman, 1967; Seligman & Maier, 1967). Initially, they restrained dogs in a harness to administer moderately painful but not physically damaging shock (Figure 10-8). Although their original intent had not been to study inescapable shock, that is in fact what they had fortuitously arranged for the dogs. Nothing the dogs did could affect the onset, the offset, the duration, or the intensity of the shocks. From the perspective of the dogs, the shocks were uncontrollable.

The second phase of the experiment was designed to study how these dogs behaved in a shuttle box (Figure 10-9). Normally, when naive (untrained) dogs are placed in the shuttle box and the shock is turned on, they frantically jump about the box and accidentally scramble over the barrier to the safe (no-shock) side. In a very few trials, these dogs learn to jump as soon as the shock begins, thereby drastically limiting the amount of shock they experience at any given trial. Typically, it takes several more trials before the dogs will begin to avoid the shock by jumping at the onset of the signal rather than the onset of the shock. They eventually learn this very important adaptive response, which enables them to avoid the painful stimulus altogether.

Much to the surprise of Seligman and his colleagues, the dogs given the inescapable-shock training showed a markedly different pattern of responses. Initially, they behaved like naive dogs; they frantically ran around the shuttle box when the shock was turned

on. After 30 seconds, however, their behavior suddenly changed. They stopped jumping and running, lay down on the shock grid, and whined. When the animals failed to make any further responses for 60 seconds, the shock was turned off. They had, of course, failed to make an escape response. The same pattern of behavior occurred in the next trial. The animal struggled at first and then gave up, passively accepting the shock. On succeeding trials, the behavior followed a similar pattern, with increasing passivity toward the shock. On none of the trials did the animal attempt to escape.

To make sure the effects observed were caused by lack of control over the shock, Seligman and his colleagues designed an experiment to isolate the effects of controllability from the effects of the shock itself. The design involved three groups.

The first group of dogs received pretreatment shock that they could control by some response. In one study, the dog was able to limit the shock's duration by pressing a panel with its nose (Seligman & Maier, 1967) and, in another study, by not moving (Maier, 1970). A second group consisted of yoked controls. These dogs received the same pattern of shock but had no way of controlling it. Thus, the second group experienced exactly the same amount of shock as the first but without the critical factor of control. In both conditions, the animals were restrained by a hammock to prevent them from jumping or running. A third group was given no pretreatment.

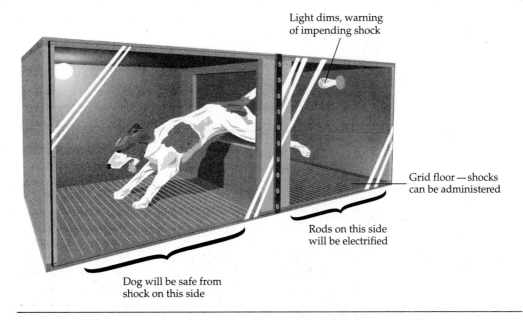

Light dims, warning
of impending shock

Grid floor — shocks
can be administered

Rods on this side
will be electrified

Dog will be safe from
shock on this side

Figure 10-9. Shuttle box used to study avoidance learning in dogs. (From *Discovering Psychology*, by N. Carlson. Copyright © 1988 by Allyn and Bacon. Reprinted by permission.)

After 24 hours, the dogs were given escape-avoidance training in a shuttle box. The no-pretreatment group and the group allowed to control the shock during pretreatment readily learned the task. They jumped over the barrier at the onset of shock and then learned to avoid the shock. The group given uncontrollable shock performed much more poorly. Most of the dogs failed to jump the barrier at the onset of shock. These results clearly show that the deficit was not the result of the shock itself but of the inability to control the shock. Maier's (1970) study makes it impossible to argue that the animals were simply learning to be active; in Maier's study, the animals were learning to be inactive.

Learned Helplessness in Humans

The phenomenon of learned helplessness is by no means restricted to dogs. Learned helplessness has been demonstrated in cats (e.g., Thomas & Balter, cited in Seligman, 1975), in fish (e.g., Padilla, Padilla, Ketterer, & Giacalone, 1970), in rats (e.g., Maier, Seligman, & Solomon, 1969; Seligman, Maier, & Solomon, 1971), and in primates (e.g., Seligman, 1975). How-

ever, learned helplessness in humans has attracted most interest.

In one study using human subjects, Hiroto (1974) replicated almost exactly the findings obtained by Seligman and his colleagues. Subjects in his controllability group were exposed to a loud noise, which they could turn off by pushing a button. His no-control group received the same loud noise but could not control it. After this pretreatment, the subjects were tested in a finger-shuttle box that simply required them to move their hand from one side to the other to escape the noise. As in the dog experiments, the no-pretreatment and controllability groups quickly learned the escape problem, but the no-control group failed to learn it. Most of the subjects in the no-control condition sat passively and accepted the noxious noise.

Hiroto also studied the influence of two additional variables on the subjects' responses. First, half of the subjects in each of the three groups were told that their performance in the shuttle box was a test of skill; the others were told that their scores were governed by chance. As expected, subjects who received the chance

Feelings of helplessness and loss of control are major antecedents of depression.

The results of Hiroto's study confirm that humans react to lack of control in the same way as animals do and emphasize the cognitive nature of helplessness in humans. This is consistent with Seligman's suggestion that helplessness reflects a belief about the effectiveness of responding. Helpless individuals do not believe that their responses will have any effect on aversive or noxious events, whereas those who have not learned to be helpless believe that their responses will be effective in terminating such events.

Immunization

If exposure to uncontrollable events is sufficient to produce learned helplessness, then is it possible to immunize people against learned helplessness by teaching them that events are often controllable? Early successes (Maier & Seligman, 1976) have been confirmed by more recent findings that giving people a controllable experience produces a proactive interference against attempts to induce helplessness (Ramírez, Maldonado, & Martos, 1992). This makes a great deal of sense. When people view two things as linked it is very difficult for them to change that perception or when they see two things as not linked it is very difficult to change that perception (Ouellete & Wood, 1998). These results explain why children who experience diminished control in childhood are less likely to believe they can control events in their lives.

The Cognitive Component of Depression

For a decade, Seligman's theory seemed to be a plausible explanation of why some people get depressed when placed in situations that they were unable to control. The major problem with the theory, as John Teasdale of Oxford pointed out, was that the helplessness training procedure that had been used to demonstrate the validity of the theory only seemed to work on two out of three people; a third of the people resisted the training procedure and showed no inclination to become helpless (Seligman, 1990). This observation, together with doubts expressed by two of his own graduate students, led Seligman and his critics to recast the theory in more cognitive terms.

The Reformulated Theory of Learned Helplessness

One of the main contributing forces behind the reformulation of the learned helplessness theory came from

instructions tended to respond more helplessly in all the conditions.

Hiroto also decided to examine personality differences. Using a personality inventory measure, he divided his subjects into two groups corresponding to externals and internals. As we have seen, externals believe that events in their lives are governed largely by events over which they have little or no control, whereas internals believe that events can be controlled and that the application of skills can bring about positive outcomes (Rotter, 1966). As predicted, externals were more inclined to become helpless than were internals. As we will see shortly, the distinction between internal and external became a major organizational construct in Seligman's reformulated theory of learned helplessness.

Bernard Weiner (1972, 1974) of the University of California at Los Angeles, who had been studying people's explanatory styles (attributions) in achievement situations. Weiner found that whether people are inclined to persist at a task in the face of failure is linked, for example, to whether they have concluded that the failure is simply caused by a lack of effort on their part or is caused by something over which they have no control (Weiner et al., 1971). The reformulated theory expanded some of Weiner's ideas to help explain why some people become depressed and others never do (Abramson, Seligman, & Teasdale, 1978; Miller & Norman, 1979). The reformulated theory suggests three basic reasons why some people fail to become depressed when they experience bad events (Peterson & Seligman, 1984).

According to the reformulated theory, individuals' propensity to become depressed is associated with their personal explanatory styles. In other words, whether individuals become depressed in challenging situations depends on how they explain bad events and good events. There are three main patterns, which relate to evaluations of permanence, pervasiveness,

and personal responsibility (personalization). Let's look at these three issues.

Permanence

Explaining bad events. People who give up and become helpless believe that the causes of bad events that happen to them are permanent. People who do not give up, in contrast, believe that bad events are temporary. If we believe that something is temporary, then we have reason to persist. Here are some examples (based on Seligman, 1990).

Permanent/Stable (Pessimistic):	Temporary/Unstable (Optimistic):
"I'm all washed up."	"I'm exhausted."
"Diets never work."	"Diets don't work when you eat out."
"The boss is a bastard."	"The boss is in a bad mood."

Failure tends to make almost everyone momentarily helpless. The people who succeed, however, are those who pick themselves up and try again. The finding that persistence is one of the major characteristics

Practical Application 10-1

How to Ward-Off Depression

Considerable evidence indicates that depression has its roots not only in the way we think but also in how we approach the inevitable problems that arise in our daily lives. The worst thing people can do if they are faced with a problem is to behave as though nothing happened, try to ignore it, expect the worst, withdraw (hoping the problem will go away), or vent their frustration by shouting, crying, slamming doors, and so forth. A study of adolescents who used such coping strategies found that they tended to become depressed (Seiffge-Krenke & Klessinger, 2000). The best thing people can do to ward off depression, this study found, was to immediately share the problem or concern with others, try to solve the problem (often with the help of others), accept the idea that it might be necessary to compromise, and try not to worry based on the belief that things will work out or

that they can find a solution. One finding from this study is that to ward off depression, people need to accept that they are not perfect and that they do not live in a perfect world.

The participants in this study were adolescents, and many of them reported that they shared their problems with their parents. One main theme of this book is that we are social animals whose lives are inextricably inter-linked with those around us, especially our families. Therefore, to live a happy and productive life we need to strengthen those bonds and make productive use of them. In that context, we can learn to live happy and productive lives.

You might create a little poster for yourself with the words: Accept, Share, Solve, and Move On. When you allow yourself to become stuck, you can become depressed.

of success is so consistent that it might be called the law of success: People who persist will eventually succeed. Unless we persist in the face of difficulty, we will never learn how to do something correctly and thus attain a goal. As we persist, we alter our responses systematically so that we can discover how to reach a goal.

Explaining good events. When good things happen to pessimists, they see that outcome as temporary. Optimists, by contrast, see that outcome as more or less permanent.

Permanent/Stable (Optimistic):	Temporary/Unstable (Pessimistic):
"I'm always lucky."	"It's my lucky day."
"I'm talented."	"I try hard."
"My rival is no good."	"My rival got tired."

People who believe that good events have permanent causes try harder after success, whereas people who believe good events are caused by temporary causes tend to give up. If we believe good events are temporary, we will regard what happened as a fluke. We gambled and won, and now we'll take our earnings and quit.

Pervasiveness

Explaining bad events. Although permanence is about time, pervasiveness is about space. When pessimists experience a bad event, they allow it to affect all parts of their life; they view the bad event as universal. When a relationship breaks up, for example, they are inclined to stop eating, stop seeing their friends, stop working, and so forth. All of us might be affected by such events for a few days, but pessimists tend to wallow in their sadness and allow it to affect every other part of their life, until they are totally depressed. Optimists, in contrast, might initially feel that life is not worth living but, after a few days, they begin to bounce back; they see the bad event as specific and localized. Realizing that life has much else to offer, they might, for example, make special efforts to see their friends, throw themselves into their work, or decide to learn a new language. It is as though optimists see life as made up of many little boxes, each of which contains a little treasure they need to preserve. Pessimists, in contrast, seem to see life as one big box, where everything is mixed together. When one little treasure gets broken, all the other treasures in the box get broken as well.

As we've seen, pessimists allow themselves to wallow in their misery. One of the most exciting new ideas that has come out of therapy is that people can learn to stop themselves from sinking deeper and deeper into depression. Optimists, it seems, have learned to do this on their own. We will examine how to become an optimist in the next chapter.

Here are some examples of how pessimists and optimists explain bad events.

Universal/Global (Pessimistic):	Specific/Local (Optimistic):
"All teachers are unfair."	"Professor Franken is unfair."
"I'm repulsive."	"I'm repulsive to him."
"Books are useless."	"This book is useless."

Explaining good events. The way pessimists and optimists explain good events is just the opposite of how they explain bad events.

Specific/Local (Pessimistic):	Universal/Global (Optimistic):
"I'm smart at math."	"I'm smart."
"My broker knows oil."	"My broker knows Wall Street stocks."
"I was charming to her."	"I was charming."

Pessimists explain good events by transient causes, such as mood and effort, and optimists explain good events by permanent causes, such as traits and abilities. One says *sometimes*; the other says *always*.

The nature of hope and hopelessness. In Seligman's theory, hope and hopelessness grow out of the two dimensions of pervasiveness and permanence. To be characterized as hopeful, people need to respond to bad events as specific and temporary causes. People who are hopeless, in contrast, respond to bad events as permanent and universal.

Personalization: Internal versus External

Explaining bad events. When bad things happen, people are inclined to either blame themselves (internalize) or blame someone else (externalize). One day, when I had left my sailboat in the driveway, my son backed our car into it and caused some minor damage. My son blamed me for not putting the boat away; I blamed him for not watching where he was going. Further, I argued, he should have remembered that I had gone sailing, to which he replied, "Why am I supposed to keep track of what you are doing?" Psychologists have established that people with low self-esteem blame themselves when something goes wrong, whereas people with good self-esteem tend to blame others. I guess my son and I are both on the right track for good self-esteem.

Here are some examples of how low self-esteem and high self-esteem people are inclined to respond to bad events.

Internal (Low self-esteem):	External (High self-esteem):
"I'm stupid."	"You're stupid."
"I have no talent at poker."	"I have no luck at poker."
"I'm insecure."	"I grew up in poverty."

Explaining good events. Again, the style for explaining good events is the opposite to that of explaining bad events. Here are some examples.

External (Pessimistic):	Internal (Optimistic):
"A stroke of luck."	"I can take advantage of luck."
"My teammates' skill."	"My skill."

When people believe they cause good things to happen, they like themselves; when they believe that good things come from some circumstances over which they have no control, they are less inclined to like themselves.

A caveat about responsibility. Seligman (1990) is careful to point out that, despite the clear benefits of an external belief system, he does not advocate that people should switch from being internals to externals because individual responsibility is important. However, sometimes people assume too much responsibility. For example, if I blame the fact that my wife did not get a promotion on something I said, I might be taking too much responsibility. In the final analysis, people must learn to take responsibility for those things they can control and not to take responsibility for those things they can't control (Weiner, 1995).

Status of the Theory

Although considerable research supports the reformulated theory of depression, various researchers have ar-

gued that the theory could have greater predictive power if it incorporated other important psychological principles. Let's consider two areas of research.

One of the reasons people give up (become disengaged from a task) is not because they believe they are incompetent (have lost control) but, rather, because there are obstacles over which they have no immediate control. One implication of this argument is that people might not get depressed when they experience personal failure because they do not see themselves as the cause of their problem. Consistent with this line of argument, researchers have shown that personal failure can lead to depressivelike responses or paranoidlike responses depending on whether failure is viewed as a personal deficiency or is caused by the actions of another person (Bodner & Mikulincer, 1998). This finding cannot be easily handled by the broad distinction between internal and external because it has to do with perceived obstruction, which is very different from the belief that failure is caused by personal inadequacy. This finding has important implications for people who feel they are being discriminated against for reasons of such things as age, sex, race, religion, or even appearance. Attributing failure to obstruction might help ward off depression, but it might not be adaptive from the perspective of developing competence and ultimately succeeding.

A second line of research that needs to be incorporated into the reformulated theory of depression to increase its predictive power comes from research that shows people come to tasks with very different goal orientations. Research has shown that people can be differentiated into two types: those who are growth seeking and those who are validation seeking. According to this distinction, validation-seeking rather than growth-seeking individuals would be more threatened by failure because failure of the validation-seeking individuals indicates they are not living up to their beliefs about who they are. Consistent with this idea, researchers have shown that validation-seeking individuals experience greater anxiety, depression, self-esteem loss and task disengagement. Growth-seeking individuals are not threatened by failure but, rather, use failure as a guide to where they must focus their efforts to grow. Consistent with this idea is the convergent finding that compared with validation-seeking individuals, growth-seeking individuals are less anxious, are less depressed, show little or no self-esteem loss, and show little or no task disengagement (Dykman, 1998).

Pessimism as a Cause of Depression

How can we demonstrate that pessimism is the cause of depression? One way is to take people who tend to think more pessimistically and see what happens when they experience bad events. Seligman has shown that people who think more pessimistically are more likely to become depressed. In a study of students who did not perform as well as they expected on an examination, he found that people with a more pessimistic thinking style were more likely to demonstrate the symptoms of depression. In another case, he studied prisoners. Prisons consistently produce depression in people who tended not to show depression before they were sentenced. Seligman found that pessimists sentenced to prison were inclined to develop deeper depression than did optimists (Abramson, Metalsky, & Alloy, 1989; Seligman, 1990; Sweeney, Anderson, & Bailey, 1986).

A second way to demonstrate a link between pessimism and depression is to change subjects' pessimistic thinking style to a more optimistic one and to observe whether their symptoms of depression then wane. A great deal of research shows that teaching people to think more optimistically does result in the lessening—and often the elimination—of their depression.

Is there any difference between people treated with antidepressant drugs and those who have learned to think more optimistically? The general finding is that drugs will often work for a period of time, but people who have been given only drug treatment tend to relapse, whereas people who have been given drugs and also taught how to think differently are much less inclined to relapse (Hollon et al., 1990).

Pessimism and Rumination

One main characteristic of depressed people, like anxious people, is that they tend to engage in excessive analysis, or rumination. Because of their pessimistic thinking style, depressed people who ruminate tend to create a highly negative world for themselves. Optimists might also ruminate but, when they do so, they create a highly positive world for themselves.

Research shows that people who tend to be pessimists but not ruminators are less likely to become depressed. In other words, the combination of being pessimistic and being a ruminator is very likely to produce depression (Kuhl, 1981; Nolen-Hoeksema, 1990).

Pessimism and Health

Pessimism has been linked to a number of health indicators. First, pessimists tend to report more health complaints (Scheier, Carver, & Bridges, 1994). Second, pessimistic cancer patients were found to be more likely to die during a follow-up period compared with less pessimistic counterparts (Schulz, Bookwala, Knapp, Scheier, & Williamson, 1996). Third, pessimists show both greater systolic and diastolic blood pressure, two important health indicators (Räikkönon, Matthews, Flory, Owens, & Gump, 1999). Although the mechanism for these diverse findings are not immediately clear, the findings are not unexpected and reinforce the idea we need to maintain positive mental states.

Beck's Theory of Depression

Aaron Beck (1967, 1976, 1991), a pioneer of cognitive approaches to depression, has proposed that the thinking patterns of depressed people play a critical role in initially producing depression and in maintaining it. He has pointed out that depressed people tend to view their current and future situations in negative terms. Such thinking is characterized by three tendencies. First, depressed people tend to view situations as negative even when a positive interpretation is possible. Second, they view interactions with the environment in terms of deprivation, disease, and defeat. Third, they tend to tailor facts to fit their negative conclusions. They might even ignore external input that is not consistent with their conclusion that life is essentially bad.

Beck argues that depressed people tend to develop an organized and stable schema, or representation of themselves, and they process information based on this schema. They screen, differentiate, and code the environment in accordance with the representation they have formed of themselves.

Beck emphasizes that the thinking process of depressed people often leads to cognitive distortions. Because depressed people have a systematic bias against the self, such that they compare themselves unfavorably with other people, they develop feelings of deprivation, depreciation, and failure. These cognitive distortions can be viewed as errors in thinking. Beck identified four kinds of errors of thinking:

1. Exaggeration: exaggerating the negative aspects of our experiences. We might say, "I made a complete

fool of myself," when we simply made a social error in an otherwise impeccable performance.

2. Dichotomous thinking: viewing a partial failure as complete failure. We might say, "My talk was a total bomb," when the only problem with our talk was the lack of a good ending.

3. Selective abstraction: seeing only the negative aspects of an experience and using that information to make an inference about our ability. We might say, "Nobody liked my performance," when one person raised an objection and most people voiced their approval.

4. Overgeneralization: using one outcome to make inferences about our ability. We might say, "I have no ability whatsoever to do that kind of thing," when we have a great deal of ability but we didn't do so well in one particular situation.

Beck (1983, 1991) has distinguished between two types of individuals who are prone to become depressed after a negative experience. The autonomous individual, who is motivated by the need for independent achievement, mobility, and solitary pleasures, is prone to become depressed after an autonomous stressor such as failure, immobilization, or enforced conformity. The sociotropic individual is motivated by acceptance and attention from others and is prone to become depressed by sociotropic traumas such as social deprivation or rejection.

According to this distinction, the lack of good social relationships would not affect the autonomous type but would affect the sociotropic type. Indeed, this is what has been found (Hokanson & Butler, 1992). Note that this distinction is similar to the one made by Buck (1999). As we noted, Buck argues there are two sources of depression, one closely linked to individual achievement and another linked to social failure.

Perfectionism and Depression

Humiliating events, failures, and rejection are common antecedents of suicide. However, a significant number of talented and successful people commit suicide each year. One of the underlying characteristics of these people is an intense perfectionism (Blatt, 1995). Perfectionism—satisfaction from attaining a very high standard of excellence—is an admirable quality but, when people set unrealistically high standards for themselves, they may find it impossible to find satisfaction

in a job well done and instead experience humiliation and defeat.

In a recent study it was clearly shown that perfectionistic thinking leads to high levels of depressive symptomatology and anxiety. One important finding of this study was the high level of rumination amongst people with perfectionistic thinking (Flett, Hewitt, Blankstein, & Gray, 1998).

Summary

Studies of twins indicate that depression can be inherited. Strong evidence demonstrates that depression is linked to the depletion of catecholamines (norepinephrine and dopamine) as well as of serotonin. Buck suggests there are two types of depression, one triggered by failure to meet environmental demands and the other by the failure to meet social demands. Further evidence for the link between neurotransmitters and depression comes from work done with monoamine oxidase inhibitors (MAOI). MAO is an enzyme that regulates neurotransmitters in the brain. Various people have argued that depression should be viewed as an adaptive mechanism that can be valuable to us in dealing with a changing environment.

According to Seligman's model, when animals or humans are presented with an aversive stimulus such as shock, and are unable to escape that stimulus, they develop a sense of helplessness. In contrast, when animals or humans are presented with an aversive stimulus that they can learn to escape, they do not develop a sense of helplessness. Individuals who develop a sense of helplessness fail to initiate behaviors that will allow them to learn how to escape an aversive situation. By contrast, those who fail to develop a sense of helplessness are inclined to initiate behaviors that will allow them to learn how to escape an aversive situation. As Seligman has pointed out, evidence from various sources indicates that experiencing two events as independent (noncontingent) makes it very difficult at some later time to learn that they are dependent, or related, when they have been made contingent. As a result, the individual who has experienced noncontingency will tend to behave as though there is no contingency.

Although Seligman suggests that experiencing noncontingencies is the basis for learned helplessness, not all experiences of noncontingencies will necessarily lead to feelings of helplessness. If, for example, an individual has previously learned that two events are contingent, suddenly making them noncontingent will not result in feelings of helplessness. It appears that the previous contingency training is sufficient to immunize the individual against helplessness training. Some people get depressed when exposed to helplessness training procedures, but others do not. According to the reformulated theory of learned helplessness, these differences are linked to differences in individuals' explanatory style. People who are inclined to see bad events as temporary, specific, and external are less in-

Practical Application 10-2

Cognitive Therapy and Depression: Learning the Art of Constructive Thinking

Cognitive therapy can be summarized by six tactics that we can use to take charge of our thinking (Beck, 1983; Seligman, 1990). These tactics should prove helpful to anyone who is prone to pessimism and depression.

1. **Learn to recognize destructive automatic thoughts.** When things go bad, people often hear themselves repeat short phrases or sentences. A mother who has lost her temper, for example, might hear herself say, "I'm a terrible mother." A student who has done poorly on an exam might hear himself say, "I should be shot, I'm such an idiot." A teenager who feels embarrassed after a social blunder might hear herself say, "I wish I were dead." The curious thing about such fleeting thoughts is that they seem to come from somewhere inside us and yet we know that we haven't consciously created them. They are therefore called *automatic thoughts.*

2. **Learn to dispute destructive automatic thoughts.** Most people fail to challenge their automatic thoughts. They accept them as coming from somewhere deep inside themselves and therefore as fair and valid commentary. At the same time, most people find these thoughts to be disturbing and are perplexed by their occurrence. Why they arise is not clear.

   Most cognitive therapists argue that these thoughts are not fair commentary and that it is critical that we learn to dispute them. The best way to dispute them is to marshal contrary evidence. A mother who has lost her temper is not necessarily a bad mother; she likely does a number of good things. To deal with such disturbing thoughts, she needs to enumerate her good qualities. Similarly, the student who has performed poorly needs to say to himself, "I didn't do as well as I expected, but they don't shoot people for doing poorly." In addition, he needs to recount the number of times he performed admirably.

3. **Learn to avoid using destructive explanations.** Many of the fleeting comments that people experience are characterized by permanence and pervasiveness. People need to learn to find an explanation that is more temporary and situation-specific. The mother might learn to say, "I'm a good mother most of the time but, later in the afternoon when it gets hot or I'm tired, I tend to become irritable. And that little rascal is not in such a great mood when it gets hot either." The student might say, "I had a bad day. The exam was different than I expected, and I guess I ended up studying the wrong thing." The teenager who made a social blunder might say, "I was thinking about something else and I slipped up. If someone had videotaped that one, it would get a lot of laughs on TV."

4. **Learn to distract yourself from depressive thoughts.** Becoming involved in an activity is a very good way of distracting yourself from depressive thoughts. As we have seen, men are more inclined than women are to adopt this strategy. Among the numerous activities that will work are reading a book, going for coffee with a friend, becoming involved in a hobby, going to a movie, or simply imagining yourself in some activity that you might like.

5. **Learn to create less self-limiting happiness self-statements.** Many people put limits on what will allow them to be happy. They say such things as

   "I won't be happy until I have a new car."

clined to become helpless and depressed. Considerable evidence supports the idea that depression is the result of a pessimistic explanatory style. In particular, researchers have shown that people who are more pessimistic are more likely to become depressed, and that people given antidepressant drugs plus cognitive ther-

apy are more likely to recover from depression than are people given only drugs.

Beck has noted that depressed people tend to view the present and future in negative terms. This negative style of thinking arises from a stable internal representation, or schema. Depressed people, Beck argues,

---

"I'll be happy when I fall in love."

"I can't be happy unless I know that everybody likes me."

"I'll be happy when I retire."

Each of these statements puts severe limits on when or how we can be happy. As a result, they prime us for depression. There is nothing wrong with wanting a new car or wanting to be in love or looking forward to retirement. The problem lies in saying that we can't be happy until those conditions have been met.

When people engage in this form of inner dialogue, the statements they make to themselves become rules or principles. As a result, they find themselves unable to experience happiness until these self-imposed conditions have been met. Unfortunately, when the conditions are met, people often experience only momentary happiness, because happiness is rarely found in reaching a goal. Rather, happiness tends to be found in the process of working toward a goal.

To become less susceptible to depression, you will need to assess and redesign your inner dialogue. First, take some time to analyze your inner dialogue to see if you are setting limits on your happiness. Give yourself time to become aware of your automatic thoughts. Whenever you become aware of one, write it down, so that you can analyze it rationally.

Having recognized these negative self-statements, you will need to replace them with more positive versions. Here is how you might redesign the statements noted earlier to preserve the goals but permit happiness in the interim.

"This is a good car for now but my goal is to buy a new one eventually."

"I am enjoying dating and look forward to falling in love."

"I'd like to be viewed as a sensitive and considerate person but, because my values are different from other people's, I need to learn that others may not always understand or appreciate where I am coming from."

"It is great to be healthy and earning a good living, both of which are going to make retirement rewarding."

6. **Learn to make your inner dialogue process-oriented.** You might go one step further and turn each of your happiness statements into a process goal, which focuses more on the process and less on the end goal. Most people seem to get their happiness from the process, perhaps because humans are inclined to become habituated to static emotions very quickly (Frijda, 1988). Here are some examples of how to turn the original happiness statements into process statements.

"I get a great deal of enjoyment out of cars, and I hope to own several fine cars in my lifetime."

"Love and being loved is a skill. I am going to work hard at making love a central focus of my life."

"My goal is to gain the respect and admiration of many people in my life. It is a skill that others before me have nurtured and developed, and I am determined to see if I can emulate them."

"To be truly happy in retirement takes a great deal of work and planning. I am going to study people who are happy in retirement so that, when I retire, I can be truly happy."

have a bias against the self that leads to errors in thinking, such as the tendency to overgeneralize and to make inferences without consideration of alternative points of view.

Beck has distinguished between two types of people who are prone to become depressed—the sociotropic and the autonomous. Among other things, his theory predicts that good social relationships are important for the sociotropic type but less so for the autonomous type. The link between perfectionism and suicide indicates the role of cognitive variables in depression and suicide. Similar to anxiety, depressed individuals show that rumination is a central feature of depression.

To take charge of our thinking, we need to (1) learn to recognize automatic thoughts, (2) learn to dispute destructive automatic thoughts, (3) learn to avoid using destructive explanations, (4) learn the art of distracting ourselves, (5) learn to create less self-limiting happiness self-statements, and (6) learn to make our inner dialogue process-oriented.

Guilt and Shame

Guilt and shame are usually treated as overlapping emotions. Until recently, there was little empirical information on the nature and origins of these emotions (Zahn-Waxler & Kochanska, 1990). As more data accumulate, the consensus is that these emotions are implicated in a wide range of human motivated behaviors. There are at least five important points about guilt and shame.

1. Guilt and shame are uniquely human emotions, although some have argued that canines are capable of guilt.
2. Guilt and shame play a role in a wide variety of behaviors, including sexual abuse, rape, eating disorders, stress-related physical disorders, alcoholism, divorce, and emotional illness. As research continues, further links between these emotions and motivated behaviors are expected to emerge.
3. Shame and, in particular, guilt have been linked to pessimism and depression. People who are more depressed experience more guilt and shame. Some researchers believe that guilt and shame cause depression (Zahn-Waxler & Kochanska, 1990).

4. The capacity for these emotions is innate, but their mode of expression is learned (Zahn-Waxler & Kochanska, 1990). Among other things, this means that individuals differ greatly how they express these emotions because of their developmental experiences. Moreover, if the mode of expression is learned, it can be redirected more adaptively.
5. Like virtually all other negative emotions, guilt and shame tend to disrupt adaptive behavior when they become excessive. Hence, if people want to achieve goals, they must learn how to manage these emotions. Many researchers now feel that this is a distinct possibility (Thompson, 1990).

Guilt and shame can elicit and sustain certain behaviors (such as achievement and cooperation) but inhibit others (such as anger and aggression). From an adaptive perspective, this is very important. The proper execution of any response typically demands the excitation and inhibition of various emotions. Businesspeople who are negotiating a contract, for example, might need to inhibit expressions of anger or dislike.

It is also important to distinguish between acts of commission (such as becoming angry and aggressive, belittling someone's achievements, or criticizing) and acts of omission (failure to achieve a goal, failure to provide for our family, failure to live up to a family value). Recognizing this distinction, Lazarus (1991a) has suggested that the core relational theme for guilt is having transgressed a moral imperative, whereas the core relational theme for shame is having failed to live up to an ego-ideal. Researchers have suggested that the opposite of guilt is empathy (Zahn-Waxler & Kochanska, 1990). Whereas we often feel guilt after being insensitive to the feelings or needs of others (acting in our own self-interest), empathy involves being sensitive to the feelings and needs of others. In the next chapter, we will deal with empathy and with worth, two important emotions that seem to play a fundamental role in helping and acts of altruism.

Both guilt and shame are involved in goal-directed behavior. In our desire to achieve our goals, we might do various things that cause us to feel guilty. For instance, we might take short-cuts, hoard information to prevent others from finding the solution, take the ideas of others and pass them off as our own, or undermine the attempts of others. Similarly, we could experience shame for not having achieved the level we think we

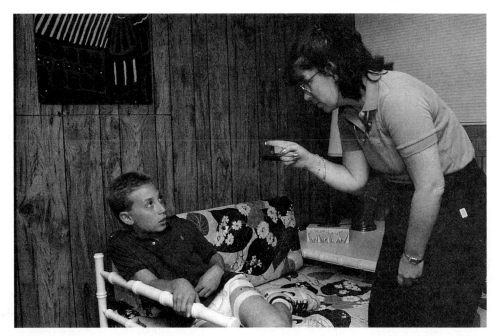

Parents play a central role in creating a sense of guilt and shame in their children.

should have, for not having worked as hard as we might have, for not having won the praise that we thought we should have, and so forth.

Although researchers have suggested from time to time that shame and guilt are similar and overlapping emotions, a recent study indicates differences (Tangney, Miller, Flicker, & Barlow, 1996). The most substantial difference is that shame is more intense and aversive and involves more physiological change. Young people who experienced shame felt more isolated, diminished, and inferior to others and were more compelled to hide and less inclined to admit what they had done. Contrary to the suggestion that shame is more public than guilt, research indicates that both emotions are experienced in public and in private.

The Biological Component

Guilt and Shame as Adaptive Emotions

Numerous writers agree that guilt and shame are basically adaptive emotions; they serve to ensure good social relationships (Buck, 1999; Kagan, 1984). The maintenance of good social relationships is important from

an evolutionary perspective because the survival of the individual often depends on conditions in the larger group to which the individual belongs.

Researchers have suggested that maintaining good social relations depends on two complementary processes: being sensitive to the needs of others, and being motivated to make amends or make reparations when a transgression does occur. In short, maintaining good social relations depends on the capacity for guilt. Hoffman (1982), who has focused on the guilt that comes from harming others, suggests that the motivational basis for this guilt is empathetic distress. Empathetic distress occurs when people realize their actions have caused harm or pain to another person. Motivated by feelings of guilt, they are inclined to make amends for their actions. Making amends serves to repair damaged social relations and restore group harmony.

Discrete Emotions Theory

In Izard's (1977) theory, guilt is viewed as a discrete emotion—that is, as one of the primary constituents or components of motivation. According to Izard, discrete emotions involve three basic elements: a neural substrate, a characteristic facial pattern (or neuromuscular expressive pattern), and a distinct subjective feeling. The cardiovascular, endocrine, respiratory, and other systems are also involved and are presumably governed by the neural substrate. According to the theory, emotions evolved as an adaptive function, and the communication of emotions take place via the recognition of facial expression.

The main adaptive function of guilt, according to Izard, is to prevent waste and exploitation. Taking responsibility and making amends for wrongdoing have survival value for individuals and relationships and ultimately ensures the survival of societies and civilization. Guilt inhibits aggression and encourages people to make reparations—a key method of restoring harmony. Note that this evolutionary view emphasizes the survival of the group, rather than the survival of the individual. This view is similar to that proposed by Buck (1999). As we have already noted, according to Buck, our survival is largely caused by the evolution of prosocial affect. In other words, emotions such as guilt and shame are highly adaptive and critical to understanding human behavior. These emotions are designed to counter or balance our self nature.

The Learned Component

Social learning theorists avoid using such mentalistic terms as guilt and shame to explain social conduct and good social relations. They prefer concepts such as rewards, punishment, extinction, discrimination, and generalization. According to social learning theorists, good social behavior—including the appropriate expression of aggression—has its origins in our social interactions, especially those with our parents. These theorists argue that, when our parents show disappointment and disapproval, we experience a negative emotion (a punishment), which we come to associate with the initiating event. Whenever we find ourselves engaging in the same behaviors, these negative feelings are automatically elicited. Engaging in these behaviors could even trigger memories and images of our parents. When we feel guilty for some transgression, for example, we see our mother frowning in disapproval. When we experience shame for not having lived up to some ideal, we might see our father's face bathed in disappointment. Guilt, in this analysis, does

not involve any mentalistic or cognitive elements; it is simply a conditioned negative feeling (Zahn-Waxler & Kochanska, 1990).

The learning theorists have focused mainly on affectively driven guilt (empathetic guilt and anxiety- or fear-based guilt). In their approach, they have examined factors such as the timing and severity of punishment, the specific techniques used, and the quality of the affective relationship between parent and child (Zahn-Waxler & Kochanska, 1990). Let's review the portion of their research that focuses on discipline and parental love.

Discipline Techniques

Three types of discipline techniques can be distinguished (Hoffman, 1970b, 1982):

1. Power assertion—physical punishment, threats, deprivation of privileges or objects, and direct control.
2. Love withdrawal—nonphysical expressions of dislike and anger, in which the parent shows disapproval by techniques such as turning away, refusing to communicate, and threatening separation.
3. Induction—providing explanations so that the child can understand why his or her behavior is a cause for concern (for instance, "It makes Sally unhappy when you tease her").

Naturalistic studies of children have shown that power assertion leads to low levels of moral development, as measured by, for example, ability to resist temptation, feelings of guilt, or confession. Induction, in contrast, has been linked to high levels of moral development. Love withdrawal has been found to be related to moral development but less consistently than has induction (Hoffman, 1970b).

Love Withdrawal and Induction

Some studies have shown that love withdrawal and induction lead to different kinds of guilt. Hoffman (1970a), for example, distinguished between two types of children, representing two types of guilt: humanistic-flexible children, who were concerned about the harm they had done to others, and conventional-rigid children, who were more concerned with whether or not they had violated institutionalized norms. Hoffman suggests that the humanistic-flexible children are motivated by feelings of empathy, whereas the conventional-rigid are motivated more by their lack of impulse control. The conventional-rigid type corresponds closely to the psychoanalytic concept of guilt. When Hoffman examined the socialization of these two types, he found that humanistic-flexible children had been socialized more by induction, whereas conventional-rigid children had been socialized more by love withdrawal.

Quality of the Affective Relationship Between Parent and Child

In general, researchers have found that a positive relationship between parental warmth and the development of conscience and guilt in children. One reason for the inconsistent effects of love withdrawal on guilt might be linked to whether the parents tend to be warm and affectionate. Some evidence suggests that love withdrawal will only be effective if the parent tends to be warm and affectionate in general.

The Cognitive Component

According to the cognitive theorists, guilt is a conscious process that involves a well-developed self-structure. Feelings of guilt occur when the process of self-reflection (also called self-judgment) leads us to conclude that our behavior failed to meet some internal standard of conduct. As we have seen, Lazarus (1991a, b) views shame as growing out of the self-concept (the ego-ideal).

Where do internal standards of conduct come from? Most cognitive theorists take the position that internal standards result partially from learning or role-taking (for example, we accept the beliefs and values of our parents, or we accept norms) and, in part, to rational construction that arises from self-reflection—a process that involves an analysis of a body of facts about the external world and our belief about those facts. For example, we could decide, after reading several articles on the state of the environment, that proper conduct includes the recycling of waste. We might decide on this conduct even though our parents and friends do not share our view.

It is important to distinguish between acts of commission (for which we feel guilt) and acts of omission (for which we feel shame). Although acts of commission often grow out of transgressions against others, acts of omission grow more out of our failure to work toward our goals, whether given to us by our parents

("You should become an engineer") or selected for ourselves ("I don't want to become an engineer because I hate math" or "I think I should become a doctor because I like the life sciences and I like helping people"). In everyday language, we tend to speak of guilt in relation to both acts of commission and acts of omission. As psychologists, however, we need to be aware of the distinction between guilt and shame.

Cognitive theorists hold the view that we not only construct standards but also change them through a process of self-reflection. We could, for example, decide to alter our goals when we acknowledge that our talents do not match our goals. I have a friend who entered a university with the ultimate goal of becoming an engineer, like his uncle. When he realized that he was not particularly interested in engineering but found economics fascinating, he decided to abandon his previous goal, which had largely been given to him by his parents, and set a new goal for himself. In due course, his parents came to terms with his new goal and gave him their wholehearted support.

If we can construct new and different standards of conduct for ourselves, we could manage our guilt and shame by modifying our standards (see Practical Application 10-3).

The Link Between Guilt and Depression

Guilt and depression have been explicitly linked in the theories of Beck and Seligman. In Beck's (1967) model, depressives are likely to assume personal responsibility for events with negative outcomes that result in feelings of guilt, self-blame, self-deprecation, and dejection. In Seligman's reformulated model (Seligman, 1990), the self is also held responsible for negative outcomes and these self-attributions of responsibility are permanent, pervasive, and consistently internal. One obvious conclusion is that guilt comes from taking far too much responsibility for negative outcomes.

Negative Emotions and Goal-Directed Behavior

All the negative emotions discussed in this chapter tend to undermine goal-directed behavior. When people see the world as threatening—when they are troubled by fear and anxiety, for example—they are less inclined to initiate goal-directed behaviors. Rather, they tend to pull back and focus their energies on protecting themselves from a world that they perceive as hostile to their intentions. In contrast, as we'll see in the next chapter, people who view the world as more benign or benevolent are more willing to explore the world and to master and shape the environment so that it can provide them with pleasure.

Similarly, when people interpret any failure in their attempts to master and shape the world as evidence that they are helpless victims—as in the case of

pessimists and depressives—they are inclined to discontinue their goal-directed efforts. In contrast, as we'll see in the next chapter, optimists are not debilitated by failure and are inclined to carry on in the face of obstacles.

Finally, people who set excessively high standards for themselves can feel overwhelmed by guilt or shame. In contrast, as we'll see in the next chapter, people with a strong sense of self-worth take joy in

Practical Application 10-3

Managing Excessive Guilt and Shame

Many people experience excessive guilt and shame—that is, guilt and shame that are totally out of proportion to the situation. For example, a woman might feel guilty when two members of her family get into an argument. Because she knew that they are prone to conflict, she blames herself for not having intervened. Children sometimes feel guilty when their parents break up and divorce because they reason that something they did provoked the split. A man may feel guilty when his wife is fired. He reasons that if he had been friendlier toward his wife's boss, even though he disliked the man, his wife would not have been fired.

A similar thing happens with shame. When a student receives a B+ instead of the A she expected, she reasons that she has failed not only herself but also her family. A father who takes great care to teach his children honesty experiences sharp pangs of shame each time he remembers the day he was called into the principal's office because his son had copied someone else's work. The head of a company feels a sense of despair as the company she heads loses money in the middle of a recession. She reasons that she should have been better prepared to deal with the recession.

Often, people realize that the guilt and shame they experience are unwarranted but still find they are unable to do anything about their feelings. They feel trapped. Frijda (1988) explains this by proposing the law of conservation of emotional momentum as a restriction on the law of habituation: He suggests that, under certain conditions, "emotional events retain their power to elicit emotions indefinitely, unless

counteracted by repetitive exposures that permit extinction or habituation, to the extent these are possible" (p. 354).

Various writers have suggested that two parallel systems control our behavior. The conscious system is generally conceptualized as more abstract and rational; it involves logical explanations, for instance. The unconscious system, in contrast, is generally conceptualized as more sensory-based—operating by way of images, memories, and the principles of associative learning, such as classical conditioning (e.g., Lazarus, 1991b)—or more experientially based, operating by way of concrete images, metaphors, and narratives (e.g., Epstein, 1990). In the more sensory-based system described by Lazarus, images and memories are thought to become linked to feelings, so that certain images, when elicited, automatically trigger certain feelings. In the sensory-based system, guilt might be elicited by something as simple as a frown. If my mother frowned in the past when she disapproved of some transgression, I might feel pangs of guilt at the sight of a frown on anyone's face. Presumably, the precise feeling would depend on the feeling that I experienced when caught in a transgression. That feeling could be loss of love, pain that comes from punishment, or simply the negative emotion associated with conflict. The feeling component can be somewhat different for different people.

What about the feelings that come from the more rational system? Some theorists contend that these feelings can be very different from those appearing in the sensory-based system. Hoffman (1982) suggests, for example, that the rational system is more likely to be based on empathetic distress. Rather than reexperiencing our own pain, we learn to experience the pain or distress of others.

their encounters and can forgive themselves for their shortcomings.

Summary

According to Lazarus, guilt is defined as having transgressed a moral imperative, and shame is defined as having failed to live up to an ego-ideal. The biological theorists have argued that guilt is innate and universal and that its modes of expression are learned. Working from an adaptive framework, they argue that guilt is designed to maintain good social relations. According to Izard, the main adaptive function of guilt is to prevent waste and exploitation. This has survival value not only for the individual but also for the larger group.

The learning theorists have focused on affectively driven guilt (empathetic guilt and anxiety- or fear-

---

In general, most theorists seem to believe that the feelings that come from the sensory- or narrative-based system are much more difficult to alter than are those from the rational system (e.g., Epstein, Lipson, Holstein, & Huh, 1992; Epstein, 1990). In theory, it should be possible to extinguish (habituate) these feelings by repeatedly exposing an individual to the stimuli that cause them. However, we often do things that in some way remove the stimuli that caused our guilt feelings. When a person frowns, for example, we might stop what we were doing, so that the frown disappears. As a result, the guilt feelings never become full-blown, and therefore cannot extinguish or habituate (Frijda, 1988). Most theorists seem to agree that, for habituation to occur, a response must be allowed to run its course; it must be allowed to wear out, so to speak. Also, acts of reparation are positively reinforcing because they reduce or remove the negative feeling of guilt. As a result of this repeated positive reinforcement, we are inclined to perpetuate acts of reparation and, thus, never put ourselves in a situation that would allow the emotions to habituate. Because we work hard to ensure that our parents are not upset, we continue to feel guilt in their presence. Only by allowing our parents to become upset can we allow habituation to take place. It is apparent from this example that guilt minimizes conflict, even though it might cause a great deal of internal stress. The question of excess might best be conceptualized as a problem of rumination. People who experience guilt or shame often ruminate about their feelings, and in the course of ruminating, they become debilitated.

Note that feelings of guilt and shame are often reinforced in our society. We tell people how important it is for them to be considerate of the feelings and wishes of other people, especially their parents, even when it undermines their own ability to deal with important events in their lives. We also praise people for taking full responsibility for their actions.

Is there any hope for the person who is experiencing too much guilt? Probably the best solution is to tackle the problem at the rational (thinking) level. Epstein argues that when we operate out of the experiential system we tend to overgeneralize. Often we need to learn that our reactions to other people, such as our parents, have not been thought through rationally but have been learned through our experiential system.

We can better manage feelings of guilt and shame if we adopt a new explanatory style that is relatively free of permanence and pervasiveness. Instead of attempting to get rid of guilt and shame (to habituate them), we need to make them more situation- and time-specific, as both Beck and Seligman suggest. Most people experience pangs of guilt from time to time, and there is nothing wrong with being sensitive to social conflict and wanting to make amends for our acts of transgression (sins of commission) or lapses in sensitivity or empathy (sins of omission). Those who lack a desire to maintain good social relations or to experience feelings of empathy are often psychopaths. We need to view feelings of guilt and shame as simple reminders that we are social beings. Making quick and simple corrections or reparations has always been the mark of socially sophisticated people. The key is not to expect perfection in ourselves or to think that we can please everybody.

based guilt). The study of discipline techniques has shown that the highest level of moral development comes from a technique called induction, and the worst comes from power assertion. Love withdrawal has been found to be inconsistently related to moral development. The work of Hoffman suggests that love withdrawal leads to two different kinds of guilt—humanistic-flexible and conventional-rigid—each of which has been linked to different socialization processes.

Cognitive theorists have focused on symbolic and representational skills such as role-taking and self-reflection in their analyses of guilt. They have argued that guilt and shame come from the internal representation of norms (often through role-taking) and through rational construction of standards (through self-reflection). Through self-reflection, people can change their standards.

Guilt and shame have been explicitly linked to depression by Beck and Seligman. Learning to deal with excessive guilt and shame plays an important role in reducing depression.

Main Points

1. Gray has proposed that anxiety is caused by the activation of the behavioral inhibition system (BIS).
2. The BIS can be activated by both conditioned and unconditioned stimuli.
3. The BIS can be conditioned to two classes of stimuli: those that signal punishment is forthcoming, and those that signal rewards will be withheld (frustrative nonreward).
4. Unwanted or intrusive thoughts have been linked to anxiety.
5. Loss of control and inability to make a coping response have been linked to feelings of anxiety.
6. Converging research indicates that people who view the world as threatening tend to be more prone to debilitating anxiety.
7. Researchers have found that depletion of certain catecholamines and serotonin are linked to depression.
8. According to Buck, there are two types of depression: one precipitated by failure to meet environ-

mental demands and one by failure to meet social demands.
9. The reformulated model of learned helplessness suggests that people are inclined to become depressed if they use an explanatory style characterized by permanence, pervasiveness, and personalization.
10. The idea that pessimism causes depression is supported by the research finding that people who tend to use a pessimistic explanatory style are more likely to become depressed when they experience bad events.
11. According to Beck, depression results from a negative thinking style that alters the way people screen, differentiate, and code the environment. Their bias against the self leads to cognitive distortions or errors in thinking.
12. Beck has distinguished between two subtypes of depression and their associated personality types. Sociotropic individuals are motivated by acceptance and attention from others, whereas autonomous individuals are motivated by the need for achievement, control, and the avoidance of interpersonal impediments.
13. According to evolutionary theory, the emotions of guilt and shame are critical to human survival.
14. Cognitive approaches to guilt and shame emphasize the role of self and link guilt to self-reflection.
15. Getting rid of guilt and shame may not be altogether desirable, however, because excessive guilt and shame tend to undermine goal-directed behavior, people often need to learn how to manage these emotions.

 InfoTrac® College Edition

Some people are more socially anxious than others are. Why and what can they do about it? (Search words: anxiety, social)

Depression is becoming increasingly common in adolescence. How can you spot depression in adolescent youth? (Search words: depression, adolescence, symptoms)

Chapter Eleven

Goal-Congruent (Positive) Emotions

- What is happiness?
- What makes people happy?
- Can people learn to create happiness?
- Why does taking risks make some people happy?
- What is the difference between optimism and hope?
- Are some people born optimists, or can anybody learn to be an optimist?

- What role does early experience play in such things as happiness and optimism?
- Why are people with good social support systems happier and healthier?

oal-congruent emotions are those that facilitate and sustain the attainment of personal goals (Lazarus, 1991b). In this chapter, we'll briefly survey some of these emotions, to get an idea of their power in our daily lives. In Chapter 13, we will examine another goal-congruent emotion, pride.

Happiness is a prime example of a positive emotion. Lazarus defines happiness as making reasonable progress toward the realization of a goal (Lazarus, 1991b, p. 121). According to Lazarus, emotions such as happiness represent a person-environment interaction. The emotion of happiness is our cognitive evaluation of that interaction.

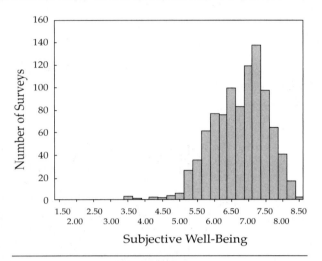

Figure 11-1. As self-reported in 916 surveys of 1.1 million people in 45 nations (with answers calibrated on a 0 to 10 scale, with 5 being neutral and 10 being the high extreme). Average subjective well-being was 6.75. (Figure by Ed Diener, from data collated by Ruut Veenhoven and reported in "The Pursuit of Happiness," by D. G. Myers and E. Diener, *Scientific American*, 1996, *274*, 54–56. Copyright 1996 Ed Diener. Adapted with permission.)

Happiness

Happiness has been operationally defined in two ways. Some researchers simply ask people to rate on a scale of 1 to 10 how good or positive they feel at a given moment. To get an average measure of someone's positive affect they may be randomly signaled, by a pager that sends a vibration, for example, to indicate how good or positive they are feeling at that moment. The average of those ratings would be their overall happiness score. The more preferred measure has come to be called subject welling-being (SWB), a measure that assesses, through a series of questions, how people evaluate their lives both affectively and cognitively. Studies of people who are characterized by high SWB experience the following: (1) many positive emotions, (2) few negative emotions, (3) tendency to be involved in interesting activities, and (4) satisfaction with their lives (Diener, 2000). Research has found that people high in SWB have many desirable qualities. They participate in more community organizations, are more liked by others, are less likely to get divorced, tend to live slightly longer, perform better at work, and earn higher incomes (Diener, 2000).

Cultural differences have been found in how people decide they are happy and satisfied with their lives. People in individualistic nations (such as the United States) consult their feelings—using positive affect as a reasonable predictor of life satisfaction. In contrast, people from collective societies (such as South Korea)

tend to consult norms for whether they should be satisfied. Among other things, they are more likely to consider the appraisal of family and friends in evaluating their lives (Suh, Diener, Oishi, & Triandis, 1998).

Two Myths About the Origins of Happiness

1. The Myth That Life Is Difficult and Few People Are Happy

Historically, many writers—from novelists such as Albert Camus and Tennessee Williams to philosophers such as Bertrand Russell (1930/1985)—have offered the view that few people are happy and to achieve success is a difficult task. Some psychologists have even suggested that only 10 to 20% of people are truly happy (Hart, 1988; Winokur, 1987). When people are asked, however, a very different picture emerges. Figure 11-1 is based on 916 surveys of more than 1.1 mil-

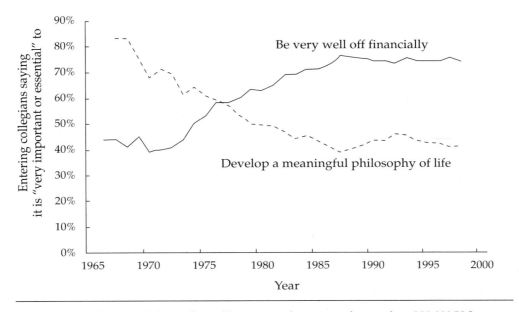

Figure 11-2.   Changing Materialism. (From annual surveys of more than 200,000 U.S. students entering college [total sample approximately 6.5 million students]. (From "Funds, Friends, and Faith of Happy People," by D. G. Myers, *American Psychologist*, 2000, *55*, 56–67. Copyright © 2000 by the American Psychological Association. Reprinted by permission of the author.)

lion people in 45 nations, which represents most of the world. What this figure indicates is that, overall, people are quite happy (Myers, 2000).

2. The Myth That Money Makes People Happy

In the belief that money will make them happy, people buy lottery tickets, enroll in universities to take courses to improve their jobs prospects, and change jobs. Indeed, evidence suggests that money is important. Money is what provides the basics of life—such things as food, shelter, clothing. What is interesting, however, is that in nations with a gross national product of $8,000 per person, the positive correlation between wealth and well being disappears (Myers, 2000). This suggests that once the basic necessities of life have been satisfied, increasing income does not lead to greater happiness. David Lykken (1999) observed, based on his own studies, "People who go to work in their overalls and on the bus are just as happy, on the average, as those in suits who drive to work in their own Mercedes" (p.17).

Studies of people who have suddenly become wealthy shows that such good luck does elevate feelings of happiness but that those feelings are short lived (Brickman, Coates, & Janoff-Bulman, 1978). As Myers (2000) points out, "Thanks to our capacity to adapt to even greater fame and fortune, yesterday's luxury can soon become today's necessities and tomorrow's relics" (p. 60).

Although little evidence indicates that money per se brings happiness, considerable evidence indicates that people do believe money is important, if not essential, to the good life. A study that compared how college students rated "Being very well off financially" and "Develop a meaningful philosophy of life," as important or essential for a good life found that during the past 35 years there has been a shift toward materialism (Figure 11-2) (Sax, Astin, Korn, & Mahoney, 1998). Researchers have suggested the media has played a central role by making the pitch that "consuming" a variety of goods will make us happy (Diener, 2000).

The Biological Component

Studies of twins adopted into different households indicate that about half of the variance in subjective well-being in American society is the result of heritability (Tellegen et al., 1998). Studies of people who differ in happiness have found that happiness is positively related to the personality trait of extraversion and negatively related to the personality trait of neuroticism (Heady & Wearing, 1992; Lucas, Diener, Grob, Suh, & Shao, 1998). In addition, researchers have found that happiness is positively related to good social relationships (DeNeve & Cooper, 1998; Myers & Diener, 1995).

This pattern of findings suggests that happiness is linked to both the behavioral activation system (BAS) and behavioral inhibition system (BIS). Recall that the BAS system is capable of producing reward and is important for instrumental behavior. One of the main subsystems is the dopaminergic system that gives rise to positive affect. Recall that the BIS system is referred to as the "stop, look and listen system." This system is activated by novel stimuli and stimuli that are associated with the potential of punishment or the cessation of reward. This system has been closely linked to neuroticism. Neuroticism has consistently been found to be negatively related to happiness, so it has been argued

Practical Application 11-1

Improving Human Happiness

Numerous writers have suggested that we have the capacity to improve our happiness and the happiness of others. In this section, I am going to discuss some suggestions that arise from our current understanding of what makes people happy. I am going to avoid talking about things that are not well grounded in the psychological research literature.

One main thing I want to focus on in this practical application is the importance of developing good social relations. This idea has its roots in personality research. In a meta-analysis, happiness was positively linked to both extraversion and agreeableness. Extraversion, it has been suggested, is linked to the *quantity* of friends, whereas agreeableness is linked to the *quality* of friends (DeNeve & Cooper, 1998). Other writers who have examined the literatures on happiness have concluded there is overwhelming support for the idea that social relations are central to happiness (Myers, 1993, 2000)

Various writers have suggested that we have strayed from our biological roots (Buss, 2000). Although there are several possible reasons, let's consider two. First, it appears that we have become enamored with the concept of self-interest, a concept that has its roots in individualism (Miller, 2000). We have a long history in the western world of thinking in terms of individualism, which is not necessarily bad by itself. The problem, it seems, is that somewhere along the line we have abandoned our social

relations. Miller and others have suggested that media, especially advertising, has been successful in selling the idea that happiness comes from consuming. Further, advertising has been somewhat successful in selling the idea that good social relations come from consuming products that make us look better and smell better, rather than developing good social skills, including things such as empathy and caring.

Buss (2000) has suggested four things at which we need to work. His ideas arise from the assumption that we survived because our fate was linked to the fate of the group something Sober and Wilson (1998) called "shared fate." Some of these suggestions have their basis in the work of others in the field.

1. **Increase closeness of extended kin.** Buss has argued that we need to go back to our roots. We need to go back and examine how our ancestors lived. He argues that one of the things that gave them a sense of security was the presence of kin, people who would be there in times of stress. He acknowledges that it is not always possible or even practical to move close by but that shouldn't stop us from maintaining contact with mail, phones, email, and such. As some advertising slogans have said, we can stay connected.

Having extended kin increases happiness, and research suggests that when kin are close by certain forms of abuse, especially wife battering, decreases (Figueredo, 1995).

the disposition to be happy comes from an active BAS and a relatively inactive BIS (Larsen & Ketelaar, 1991).

The links to good social relationships also makes sense in terms of Buck's suggestion that there are two forms of positive affect, selfish affect, and social affect. The idea that part of the positive affect we experience is based on good social relationships has it roots in the concept of "shared fate" (Sober & Wilson, 1998). According to this idea, any failure by our ancestors means we would not be here today. Ancestors, in this context, refers to the community from which our ancestors came. The cooperative success of the community allowed our parents to survive and reproduce. Practical

Application 11-1 suggests how you can become happier by returning to your roots.

Positive emotions have been linked to an active left prefrontal cortex and negative emotions have been linked to the right prefrontal cortex (Davidson & Hugdahl, 1995; Dozier, 1998). Buck (1999) has suggested that the positive-negative distinction should be replaced by a prosocial/selfish distinction. Accordingly, the left hemisphere would be viewed as prosocial and the right hemisphere as selfish. It is not altogether clear at this point whether having a more active left or right prefrontal represents a temperamental disposition or whether this represents a

---

2. **Development of deep friendships.** Tooby & Cosmides (1996) have argued that many people suffer a dearth of friendships in modern urban society. It is not easy to develop deep friendships because fair-weather friends can mimic true friends. The essence of forming deep friendships is to find people who are like you, who appreciate you as an individual, who value your unique skills and abilities. The way to develop such friendships is for you to become the person you would like to have as a friend.

3. **Reduce competitive feelings and increase cooperative feelings**. Buss (2000) has argued that humans have evolved mechanisms to inflict costs on others to gain an advantage at the expense of others, to delight in the downfall of others, and to envy people who are more successful at achieving their goals. Research has indeed found that people often do take delight in the downfall of others (Feather, 1994). It has also been argued that humans evolved mechanisms to engage in acts of cooperation. The tendency to cooperate seems to be aroused when we share a common fate (Sober & Wilson, 1998). From this perspective, it follows that in the long run we are better off to cooperate. From such a perspective, it makes good sense to follow the advice of Axelwood (1984) who recommends that we do four things:

i. *Enlarge the image of the future.* If you can think beyond the moment you might be inclined to act differently. For example, instead of retaliating when you felt demeaned by another person, you might say

nothing thereby keeping open the door to future interactions.

ii. *Teach reciprocity.* Cooperators tend to survive whereas people who are exploiters tend to be shunned and even ostracized. No one likes to be taken advantage of.

iii. *Insist on equity.* If you don't insist on getting more than you give, people are more likely to cooperate. Again, people have a sense of being treated fairly and with respect.

iv. *Develop a reputation as a reciprocator.* When you do that people will seek you out as a cooperator. If you develop a reputation as an exploiter, people will shun you.

4. **Fulfill basic wishes.** Humans have been found to have a basic set of wishes that provide a good evolutionary fit and lead to happiness. These include the desire for health, professional success, helping friends and relatives, achieving intimacy, feelings of confidence to succeed, satisfying the taste for high quality food, securing personal safety, and having the resources to attain these things (King & Broyles, 1997; Petrie, White, Cameron, & Collins, 1999).

To the degree we can achieve all these wishes or desires, at least to some degree, we can experience contentment. People experience happiness in fully living their lives.

learned response. It probably is both. That is, although we might be born with a certain asymmetry, we are not doomed to live our lives with that disposition—such as being excessively fearful. As indicated earlier, only 50% of SWB has been linked to genes.

Happiness as an Adaptive Behavior

Happiness has been inextricably linked to leading a full and productive life (Csikszentmihalyi, 1999). Buss (2000) has identified eight basic wishes or goals that people have. These wishes or goals indicate that people (at least certain people) have a desire for good health, want professional success, are interested in helping friends and relatives, wish to achieve intimacy, want to experience feelings of confidence that would help them to succeed, want to experience the satisfying taste that comes from high quality food, want to be secure and safe, and want to have the resources to attain these things (King & Broyles, 1997; Petrie, White, Cameron, & Collins, 1999). Buss (2000) has suggested these wishes or goals are consistent with an evolutionary analysis of what is in our best interests. In other words, our wishes have their roots in our genes.

That humans are even able to think about such goals is quite an achievement. Not that long ago, our ancestors were focusing mainly on daily survival needs. The question we need to address, therefore, is what happened that made this possible. We need to discuss two things: One is our ability to manage fear. The other is our ability to make plans.

The Learned and Cognitive Component

The Conquest of Fear

Some of the new and exciting ideas on the links between happiness and adaptive behavior have come from attempts to integrate knowledge that we have about the structure of the brain to concepts in learning and cognition. Some of these ideas are speculative, but they represent an important step in bridging knowledge from different disciplines. What these concepts do is help us to better understand not just what happiness is from a neuroscience perspective but where it comes from in the first place. By knowing where it came from, scientists believe that we will be in a better

position to know how to help people experience it. We start by taking an evolutionary perspective.

Most evolutionary theorists do not believe that the changes we have observed in humans during the past 150,000 to 250,000 years can be explained by genetics alone (Pinker, 1997). In fact, many argue that the changes are the result of cultural evolution rather than genetic evolution (e.g., Dozier, 1998). Let's start with our ancestors' conquest of fire.

Most animals have an innate fear of fire, something that appears to have been hardwired in most animals because it is important for survival. That our ancestors were able to conquer the fear of fire is therefore a remarkable feat. By learning to conquer fear, our ancestors were able to do many things. This ability allowed them, for example, to eat more diverse foods because they had the ability to grasp the concept that some foods, if cooked, could be incorporated into their diet. Researchers have observed, for example, that animals with highly developed brains tend to have more diverse diets (Dozier, 1998). The conquest of fire also meant our ancestors could venture to and live in colder climates. In more recent times, conquest of fire allowed manufacturing to emerge using coal and other fuels to fire the furnaces of the industrial revolution. Fire even allowed our ancestors to protect themselves from predators: By sitting around a fire they could warm themselves and keep their enemies at bay. Think for a moment what our lives would look like if our ancestors never learned to conquer the fear of fire.

Humans have, for the most part, come to conquer many innate fears, including such things as the fear of heights, the fear of enclosed spaces, the fear of wide open spaces, and the fear of drowning. How did our ancestors manage to do this? To understand this, we need to understand how the human brain is designed and why it is designed that way.

One fascinating feature is that the human brain more or less constantly analyzes our environment for threats to our survival. The main system that is responsible for this is the amygdala. Were it not for the cortex, especially the prefrontal cortex, the amygdala would likely put us in a state of fight or flight many times throughout the day. But it doesn't. The reason is that the cortex has the capacity to inhibit or block the signals that come from the amygdala to activate the fight-flight response. As we discussed earlier (Chapter 8), the amygdala is a quick and dirty system that evolved to protect us from all sorts of threats (LeDoux, 1996). Although this system is very fast, it lacks the ability to make fine discriminations. As a result, the amygdala often produces false alarms. To reduce false alarms, a system capable of making finer analyses of incoming stimulation was necessary. That system is the prefrontal cortex. The prefrontal cortex compares all incoming stimulation against memories and other information stored in the brain and then decides if the threat is real and, if so, how it can be managed by engaging in some type of coping response. If the prefrontal cortex decides that threat is real and can find no coping response to activate, it will allow the fight-flight response to become full-blown. If it decides it can be managed or that there is no real threat, it shuts down the fight-flight response.

The whole process is analogous to how the military defends against enemy aircraft and missiles. By attaching powerful computers to sensitive radar systems the military does not have to initiate a defense system, such as launching planes, whenever something is detected in the sky. Like the prefrontal cortex, the computer compares the images it receives with other images stored in its memory and only when it cannot rule out an enemy attack, does it make the decision to launch or not launch a defensive response.

The Ability to Make Plans

The prefrontal cortex does a lot more than just make decisions about when we are or are not threatened. The prefrontal cortex has also been implicated in the ability to create and manipulate images. At a functional level that means we can reflect on an outcome and make plans for the future. Being able to think several steps in advance meant that our ancestors could develop contingency plans such as "if this doesn't work do this." Researchers have argued that because of their large prefrontal cortexes, our ancestors were able to learn how to deal with threats in a whole new way. In the case of enemies, our ancestors learned at some point that they could reduce the threat of their enemies by building physical defenses, such as blocking the en-

trance to a cave with rocks. Over time, that simple strategy evolved into primitive fortresses, castles, and eventually walled cities. Today we have locked doors, all kinds of security devices, and as a last resort, the police. Our ancestors were likely nomadic (following the food supply), so this change meant they had to make several other changes such as learning how to store food, raise their own food, domesticate animals. They probably also had to learn to cook to adapt to a more limited food supply. As a result of these new adaptations our ancestors were less preoccupied with threat. Culture flourished in those early castles.

Castles and walled cities did not mean that our ancestors were self-imposed prisoners. Castles and walled cities provided a safe retreat. People learned they could work in the shadow of the walls and sleep peacefully at night. Armed groups could make forays into the forests as they always had, not having to worry about the safety of their spouses and offspring. They had sentries who could spot their enemies in the distance from high towers.

The main point I want to make here is that as a result of learning to conquer fear and make plans, our ancestors were less under the direction of the fight-flight response. Thus, they likely came to experience positive emotions more of the time. In other words, the emotion of happiness likely provided the incentive to think and plan.

I am not saying we have lost our capacity for fear. That is right under the surface for most of us. The amygdala is alive and still working continuously as it always has. What is important is what we have gained: the capacity to create an environment in which we are not constantly threatened.

The ability to make plans makes it possible for humans to self-regulate. We no longer assume that happiness is something we discover by chance. Happiness results, on the one hand, from making use of self-regulatory processes that ensure we avoid pain and, on the other hand, from making use of self-regulatory processes that help us achieve goals (Higgins, 1997). In Chapter 14, we are going to talk self-regulation in some detail. For now, let me simply point out that because we have this large prefrontal cortex, we have the capacity to achieve high levels of happiness through self-regulation.

Why Did Humans Evolve a Large Prefrontal Cortex in the First Place?

I have already suggested indirectly the answer to this question, so let me just briefly summarize. In broad terms, it can be argued that it was adaptive for our ancestors to become sensitized to potential threats. Fear, in short, evolved to help them survive (Dozier, 1998). The problem for them, however, was that fear likely had a tendency to overwhelm or immobilize them. In short, they became too sensitized. Therefore, it became essential to have another system that would allow our ancestors to determine which of those potential threats were real, which of them could be dealt with by exercising some coping response, which of them were not a threat because something else nullified the threat (such as a fence in the case of a lion, for example), and so forth. Had they not evolved such a system, they would not have survived. The bottom line is that both the amygdala and the prefrontal cortex emerged to deal with the same problem—threats to our survival. As such, they likely evolved together.

The Motivation for Creating Plans

If the conquest of fear and the ability to make plans was not because of genetic evolution, what was and is the motivation for making plans and then passing them along to our relatives?

First, let's look at the question of motivation. Various theorists have argued that positive emotions are responsible for self-interest and for our personal survival (Buck, 1999). Thus, the pursuit of happiness is a universal quality of humans. It is not an epiphenomenon but, rather, is at the heart of human survival and human evolution. In other words, the emotion of happiness motivated and still motivates us to make plans.

Researchers have suggested that humans are strongly motivated, because of the need for group survival, to ensure this information is passed along to subsequent generations. In other words, this isn't simply altruism at work, it is prosocial affect, which like selfish affect, is at the heart of human survival and human evolution (Buck, 1999). Researchers have suggested that each succeeding generation refines the knowledge it has been given and then passes that knowledge to the next generation. The motivation underlying this process is "shared fate." Thus, the capacity we show

today as humans is not something that can be thought of as hardwiring but, rather, must be thought of as shared knowledge. Dozier (1998) has suggested that the feeling of shared fate likely led the United States to be the first country in the world to institute public education.

What we have been talking about is something called cultural evolution. Because of the humans' large brain and because they learned how to communicate rather complex ideas, humans developed the capacity to pass along chunks of cultural information that are important for the survival of future generations.

The Flow Experience and Happiness

Csikszentmihalyi (1990, 1999) has written extensively about the flow experience that he has linked to feelings of happiness. His work is the outgrowth of thousands of interviews asking people to describe what makes them feel good. His work suggests that what gives people the greatest happiness does not come from working for money or recognition (extrinsic motivation) but, rather, from doing things that are satisfying for themselves (intrinsic motivation). The flow experience might come from writing songs, painting a picture, designing a garden, climbing a mountain, or anything that can totally capture one's attention so that nothing else seems to exist or nothing else is more important.

There are several common characteristics to the flow experience. First, people who experience flow are completely aware of everything they are doing. They completely understand the steps that are involved and can progress even though they don't always know where they are going. Second, they are able to get immediate feedback. They know at each step they are going in the right direction or making the right choices. Third, they feel their abilities match the task before them. They are neither anxious nor bored but, rather, feel completely challenged.

Csikszentmihalyi points out that happiness is not something that is experienced during flow but rather occurs most strongly when people have finished a flow activity. In that regard, happiness seems to be more of a cognitive evaluation. One important thing to note, given that we have been talking at length about the role of fear in our daily lives, is that people in the flow experience seem to be totally free of fear and anxiety.

Humans, it can be argued, experience flow because they have a prefrontal cortex that allows them to manage fear and anxiety, on the one hand, and manipulate images, on the other hand.

How does one achieve flow? Flow is achieved by allowing oneself to become completely absorbed in an activity be it an athletic activity, an artistic activity, or an intellectual activity. It means setting aside ego (not worrying about what others might think), and freeing oneself from distractions. It means letting an activity become your complete and total focus without regard for time or other commitments. Once involved in flow activity, people need to increase its complexity so that it will continue to challenge and absorb them. As a result, people can come to enjoy flow over and over again (Csikszentmihalyi, 1990, 1999).

Happiness and Coping

As much as we would like to have constant flow, this state is not always easy to achieve. The main reason for this is that in our daily lives we need to deal with an external world that is often characterized by threats and demands that exceed our immediate skills. We often say that life is stressful, which is another way of saying that many of our interactions with the outside world resulted in the activation of the fight-flight response. The word *coping* is often used in connection with the word *stress*. *Coping* was coined to capture the idea that sometimes the best that we can do is make reasonable progress toward dealing with external demands as well as goals. We might not, for example, have the full complement of skills that are required by the task. Unlike being in flow, we often don't know what the next step should be, let alone the path that we should follow.

The important thing that I want to point out is that even in this state of ambiguity, people can and do experience happiness, which is one of the main reasons why Lazarus defined happiness as making reasonable progress toward a goal (Lazarus, 1991b).

Myers and Diener (1995, 1996) identified four main qualities linked to feelings of happiness: extraversion, optimism (which we will talk more about shortly), self-esteem, and personal control. Three of these—optimism, self-esteem, and personal control—are closely linked with the tendency to engage in coping responses. When people are optimistic they believe that good things are going to happen. Self-esteem—which is measured by such questions as "I feel good about myself," "I am fun to be with," "I have good ideas"—reflects self-confidence and has a long history of being linked to coping and success. Finally, personal control is a belief that I can muster the resources that one needs. What this suggests is that believing in oneself plays an important role. Simply believing that one will likely succeed can make a difference. Let's look at the biological, learned, and cognitive components of coping.

The Biological Component

One of the basic paradigms that has been used to study coping is the avoidance paradigm that we discussed in the previous chapter. What we know from years of research is that when animals are shocked in an apparatus, they show all the physiological reactions that characterize the fight-flight response. Among other things, they show high outputs of various catecholamines such as epinephrine and norepinephrine (Frankenhaeuser, Dunne, & Lundberg, 1976; Hansen, Støa, Blix, & Ursin, 1978).

Once learning occurs, however, the chemical output changes radically. There tends to be a dramatic decrease in the output of such chemicals as epinephrine and arousal drops dramatically. One chemical that tends to remain high is norepinephrine, a chemical that has been linked to making adaptive behaviors and a chemical that has been implicated in the activation of the reward pathways of the brain. Such findings have led psychologists to conclude that once learning takes place stress is markedly reduced. This finding is consistent with the view that many if not most of our daily interactions can be characterized as moving between fear and happiness (Dozier, 1998). What reinforces behavior is triggering of positive affect. Evidence from a wide variety of sources indicates that, when people make a coping response, they experience a wide range of emotions. They might, for example, feel gratified, pleased, elated, euphoric, or triumphant (Lazarus, 1991b). If they had to acquire a new skill in the process of exercising control, they might even experience a sense of pride or self-efficacy (a sense of being able to deal effectively with the demands of the task).

The Learned/Cognitive Component

If you study the same animal in different avoidance learning situations, what you find is they tend to learn faster in subsequent situations. We talked about this briefly in the last chapter in connection with immunizing rats against learned helplessness. What many psychologists have come to believe is that animals develop some kinds of generalized belief or expectation such that if they were able to cope in one situation they can cope in another situation. In humans, we have called these feelings of personal control, self-esteem, and optimism. Bandura has referred to such beliefs as feelings of self-efficacy. In Bandura's case, however, feelings of self-efficacy are more situation specific.

One implication of all this is that the threat associated with the need to cope loses some of its negativity. If you believe that you can cope with a variety of situations based on your past successes, you aren't going to judge new situations as that threatening to your survival. Let me refer back to the flow experience. The reason people can experience flow is because they believe their skills are consistent with the demands and they are doing it for themselves. In other words, there is no external threat, something that exists when we need to cope.

Summary

Goal congruent emotions are those that facilitate the attainment of personal goals. Contrary to the myth that life is difficult, most people say they are relatively happy. Contrary to myth that money makes people happy, that relationship is weak at best. Research with twins suggests that 50% of happiness is heritable. The rest comes from such things as coping and beliefs that coping will work. Researchers have suggested that one thing that has allowed humans to experience greater happiness comes from their conquering a number of fears, such as the fear of fire. Another thing is their ability to make plans. Both the ability to conquer fears and the ability to plan have been linked to the emergence of a large prefrontal cortex. Although humans share 98% of their genes with their closest relative, the chimpanzee, humans have a considerably larger prefrontal cortex, which might help us understand why we seem to differ so greatly.

The word *coping* is often used when talking about stress. Considerable evidence indicates that successful coping can arouse the emotion of happiness. Researchers have found that people who have developed generalized beliefs about their ability to cope tend to be happier than are those who have not developed such generalized beliefs.

The Question of Uncertainty and Coping

Happiness from Confronting Fear and Uncertainty: Developing a Bias for Action

One thing that characterized our daily interactions with the environment is the lack of certainty in how we should deal with a new situation. Uncertainty has been a major concept in the field of coping. Researchers have suggested that one of the major reasons we experience stress is because we don't have a coping response available.

From an evolutionary perspective, lack of certainty is a major problem. When there is no certainty, one's survival is threatened. To survive, people need to know about their environment and how to effectively interact with the environment which psychologists simply call *coping*.

Often, we refrain from doing what we believe will bring us happiness because of the fear and uncertainty associated with taking action. Fear alerts us to threats to our survival, so it makes sense not to do what we fear. Uncertainty is a cognitive state in which we are unable to fully understand something or to fully know the outcome of an act. Not surprisingly, researchers have found that uncertainty leads to high arousal, which can lead to the reorganization of attention (Chapter 5). To survive, we need to be fully informed about our environment. Uncertainty alerts us that we are not fully prepared to deal with our environment and typically elicits anxiety. Thus, it makes sense that uncertainty predisposes us to inaction.

In the previous chapter, we noted that acts of omission and commission that pertain to moral transgressions trigger feelings of guilt and shame. Acts of omission and commission can also trigger other feelings such as embarrassment, sadness, and yearning. For example, we might experience embarrassment when we have failed to prepare for a speech ("I made a fool of myself and will never be able to show myself in public again"), or we might experience sadness if we failed to seize the moment and allowed a potential life partner to slip away ("I wish I had answered that letter"), or we might experience yearning if we failed to attend university and thus do not have the qualifications to practice medicine ("I wish I could somehow help those people"). Gilovich and Medvec (1995) suggest that acts of omission refer to not living up to our potential, whereas acts of commission refer to not being prepared. These feelings have collectively been referred to as feelings of regret. Although acts of commission generally affect us immediately and can dominate our attention (not being prepared for a speech, for example), acts of omission tend to become important over time (not going to university, for example).

The most common regret is that of inaction (Erskine, 1973; Gilovich & Medvec, 1995). One of the common reasons people fail to take action is because they are anxious or afraid. When people do confront their fears, they are often rewarded handsomely. Again, let's look at the biological, learned, and cognitive aspects of taking action.

The Biological Component

To study uncertainty in the laboratory, psychologists have created situations that are not completely controllable. The way you make a shock avoidance situation partially controllable is to introduce nonsignaled shocks into an avoidance learning paradigm. What this means, from the animals' perspective, is that even if they learn to associate shock with the onset of a light, and learn to make a response that will prevent them from being shocked when they are signaled by a light, sometimes they will get shocked anyway. In short, they

can do nothing to make the situation completely controllable. Despite the fact that the situation is not completely controllable, animals do learn. When they do learn, they show a strong output of norepinephrine. Even though they learn, epinephrine levels remain high. What this suggests is that the animals are continuing to experience stress even though they are experiencing reward.

Some time ago, Schildkraut and Kety (1967) suggested what has come to be a widely accepted view (see Buck, 1999):

> Increased epinephrine excretion seems to occur in states of anxiety or in threatening situations of uncertain or unpredictable nature in which active coping may be required but has not been achieved. In contrast, norepinephrine excretion may occur in states of anger or aggression or in situations which are challenging but predictable and which allow active and appropriate behavioral responses to the challenge. Under various conditions, increase of either epinephrine or norepinephrine or of both of these catecholamines may represent specific adaptive responses. (Schildkraut & Kety, 1967; p. 23)

To deal with unpredictability, humans typically engage in behaviors that will make things more predictable. If we are faced with an imminent attack, for example, we might attempt to build defenses that will protect us. Psychologists call such acts *behavioral coping.* Whenever we engage in behavioral coping, norepinephrine is released in large amounts and our mood improves. Later we will talk about cognitive coping, which is somewhat different. As a rule, when we engage in behavioral coping, our emotions change from anxiety to hope.

The Learned/Cognitive Component

A great deal of evidence indicates that people get significantly more self-satisfaction from exercising a coping response when the task is difficult than when it is easy (Bandura, 1991a; Locke & Latham, 1990). In learning terminology, the reward value of being able to control the outcome in a very demanding situation is greater than that of being able to control the outcome in a less demanding situation. Personal control over threatening events appears to be a powerful source of motivation for humans, and inability to control such events is often a source of stress (Bandura, Cioffi, Taylor, & Brouillard, 1988). It is perhaps not surprising that we experience less stress when we perceive our coping behavior to be high in effectiveness.

There is generally a positive relationship between the difficulty of coping and the magnitude of the norepinephrine response (Frankenhaeuser & Johansson, 1976), perhaps because people must put forth more effort when the response is more difficult. As extensive research has shown, organisms are inclined to redouble their efforts when situations become uncontrollable. Efforts to control a situation have typically been linked to high outputs of norepinephrine, as long as the response is potentially adaptive. As humans, when we get feedback that we cannot control a situation, we are inclined to redouble our efforts to regain control. Similarly, it can be argued that the reason for the high norepinephrine output in the shock-avoidance study is that the monkeys were attempting to gain control of a situation that was only partially controllable.

It appears that people can reframe or reinterpret a negative situation by adopting a positive perspective (Lazarus & Launier, 1978). A rock climber, for example, could decide to focus on the self-satisfaction associated with successfully executing a climb, rather than on the potential dangers. If individuals view a situation from a positive perspective, they typically experience a positive emotion. Such findings attest to the role of cognitions in motivation and emotion.

What remains to be determined is the amount of control that people have over their perceptions. We will return to the question shortly.

Before we move on to our next topic, we should note one last point. The research that we have just reviewed tells us that deciding to take action triggers a number of mechanisms that will reinforce our behavior. What this research doesn't tell us is why people are inclined to take action in the first place. Why should anyone struggle to overcome fear and uncertainty? Gilovich and Medvec (1995) have suggested that, as humans, unless we learn to seize the moment, we could end up at some point with a list of regrets. We need to understand that, although making mistakes may produce momentary pain, in the long haul, regrets tend to outweigh any memory of failure. In short, we need to develop a bias for action.

The Motivation for Thrill Seeking

Thrill-seeking or risk-taking behaviors have captured the attention of psychologists because they seem to represent a form of irrational behavior. It is easy to understand why people should learn to overcome fear of public speaking or fear of failure, but why should someone learn to overcome a fear that seems to serve a clear adaptive function, such as reducing the likelihood of death?

In this section, we will consider an interpretation of thrill seeking based on the interaction of biological, learned, and cognitive factors.

The Interaction of Biological, Learned, and Cognitive Variables

We know from studies of sky diving, hang gliding, mountain climbing, and other thrill-seeking activities that norepinephrine and epinephrine are commonly released in the course of such activities (Zuckerman, 1979). We also know from self-reports that risk-takers experience a psychological high when they take risks (e.g., Fenz & Epstein, 1969). These results can be understood in terms of Schachter and Singer's (1962) theory of emotions.

Most thrill-seeking activities involve the acquisition of a set of skills. Rock climbers, for example, need to acquire a number of appropriate hand and foot movements. Psychologists typically view these as behavioral coping skills. The idea is consistent with the finding that engaging in thrill-seeking behaviors triggers the release of norepinephrine, a chemical that has been linked to positive mood.

This explains why people might develop and execute a set of skills; however, it doesn't explain why people take risks to engage in these behaviors. To understand that, we should first note that many risk activities involve speed, height, or both, which typically trigger an innate fear or anxiety response and thus give rise to a dramatic increase in arousal. According to the Schachter and Singer theory, increases in arousal can increase the intensity of an emotion. Thus, it could be argued that thrill seekers learn—perhaps through trial and error—to use fear as a means of increasing their arousal level, to experience a psychological high.

Thus, in this interpretation, people make use of fear or uncertainty to trigger arousal, which ultimately gives them their psychological high. Because they have good coping skills, they do not in fact experience much fear. Instead, they experience the self-satisfaction associated with exercising a highly developed coping skill in the face of uncertainty. One problem with this interpretation is the idea that, more or less at will, people can get rid of the cognitive component of fear and anxiety—the negative thoughts and feelings of apprehension. In practice, that might not be an easy task. Let's look at some means of controlling anxiety.

Self-Efficacy Theory and the Dual Route to Anxiety Control

We know that some people are more likely than others are to confront their fears and anxieties. Why is that? Bandura (1989) suggests that one reason people initiate actions is because they have feelings of *self-efficacy*. According to Ozer and Bandura (1990), perceived self-efficacy is concerned with people's beliefs in their capabilities to mobilize the motivation, cognitive resources, and courses of action needed to exercise control over given events (p. 472). Self-efficacy determines what challenges people undertake, how much effort they will expend, how long they will persevere, and how much stress and despondency they will endure in the face of difficulties and failures (Bandura, 1991a). People must ask themselves if they have the skills, the energy, and the ability to endure the fear and anxiety they will experience from thrill seeking. A second reason people initiate a certain course of action is linked to *outcome efficacy*—that is, their beliefs about how satisfying it will be to achieve a certain goal. The thrill seeker might ask whether engaging in a particular risk-taking activity will produce the desired emotional outcome. According to self-efficacy theory, people carefully weigh the various elements—personal and situational—that are involved in taking action.

Bandura (1991a) has suggested that, people avoid potentially threatening situations not because they experience anxiety and arousal but, rather, because they fear that they will be unable to cope, either behaviorally or cognitively. In behavioral coping, people engage in behaviors that will prevent or at least curtail the threat; although in cognitive coping, people operate under the belief that they can manage their thinking or cognitions. According to Bandura (1991a), one of the greatest sources of threat at the cognitive level is the inability to deal with perturbing thoughts that often arise in the face of fear and threat. One reason that people with agoraphobia are reluctant to leave their homes is that they are afraid they will have a panic attack in a new or strange situation. The possibility of not being in control terrifies them.

Thus, according to self-efficacy theory, whether we choose to engage in a particular activity depends on whether we perceive that we have behavioral coping skills and that we can control our thinking. Evidence for this idea comes from a variety of sources but is perhaps best illustrated by a study of women who were fearful of being assaulted (Ozer & Bandura, 1990). In the study, women were taught how to fend off potential attackers (mastery training). The women were asked to indicate to what degree they felt their feelings of self-efficacy had changed as a result of the training. The results indicated that this training led women to perceive that they could better cope behaviorally with an assault, and that they were less fearful of going to places that previously aroused a great deal of anxiety. In short, they felt less constricted and less threatened as they went about their daily activities.

There is a strong link between feelings of self-efficacy and catecholamines such as norepinephrine and epinephrine (Figure 11-3). When feelings of self-efficacy are strong, catecholamines are typically at a low level. As self-doubt begins to increase (at moderate levels of self-efficacy), the level of these two catecholamines increases markedly. When people refuse to participate in a potentially threatening activity (when self-efficacy is weak), the level of these two catecholamines goes down (Bandura, Taylor, Williams, Mefford, & Barchas, 1985). Figure 11-3 reflects cognitive coping, as opposed to behavioral coping. Typically, behavioral coping leads to an increase in norepinephrine. Thus, as self-doubt increases, there are

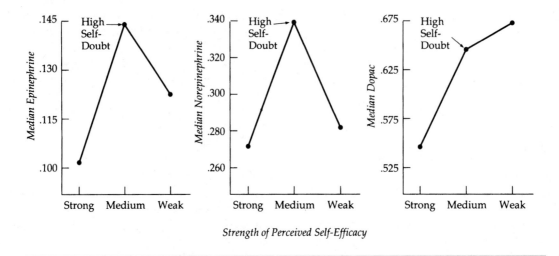

Figure 11-3. Median level of plasma catecholamine (epinephrine, norepinephrine, and dopamine) secretion as a function of perceived coping self-efficacy. (From "Catecholamine Secretion as a Function of Perceived Coping Self-Efficacy," by A. Bandura, C. B. Taylor, S. L. Williams, I. N. Mefford, & J. D. Barchas. *Journal of Consulting and Clinical Psychology,* 1985, *53,* 406–414. Copyright © 1985 by the American Psychological Association. Reprinted with permission.)

marked changes in catecholamine levels, which, as we know, are closely linked to feelings.

To identify the causal structure underlying the tendency to participate in various activities (approach motivation), even though there might be a potential threat to their safety (avoidant motivation), Ozer and Bandura (1990) undertook a path analysis of their results. The results of this path analysis for women who have received mastery training—that is, training to help them deal with a potential assault—are shown in Figure 11-4. Let's look at the top pathway. Following mastery training (called coping efficacy in Figure 11-4), the women felt less vulnerable and were better able to discern if a particular situation was risky. Because they felt less vulnerable and were better at discerning risk, the tendency to approach (get involved in activities) increased, and the tendency to avoid (not get involved) decreased. Note that sometimes people do not get involved in activities because of apathy, for example, and not simply because they are afraid. For this reason, Ozer and Bandura took separate measures to determine the degree to which people are likely to get involved (approach behavior) or not (avoidant behavior).

The lower pathway of Figure 11-4 links mastery training (coping efficacy) with increased cognitive con-

trol efficacy. Ozer and Bandura measured cognitive control efficacy by asking women to indicate how easy or difficult it was for them to turn off thoughts about sexual assault. It makes sense that mastery training would lead to increased cognitive control efficacy. If the women felt they could fend off an attack, there would be less reason to worry. Following the lower pathway, we see that, when cognitive control efficacy was high, negative thoughts were low and, when negative thoughts were low, the tendency to avoid was also low. Considerable research shows that negative thoughts tend to be closely linked to avoidant behaviors (Bandura, 1991a). In the path analysis, negative thoughts, rather than anxiety, caused women to avoid becoming engaged in activities. Although the women did experience anxiety, that anxiety was the result of two things: negative thought and perceived risk. The finding that anxiety did not by itself inhibit action is consistent with other research that shows that even though anxiety often makes us apprehensive, it is often not the primary reason that we fail to act (Barlow, 1988). Remember that anxiety is a complex emotion that has both an arousal and cognitive component. What anxiety causes us to do is to be cautious—to stop, look, and listen before proceeding. What this model shows is that before we can gain control over our

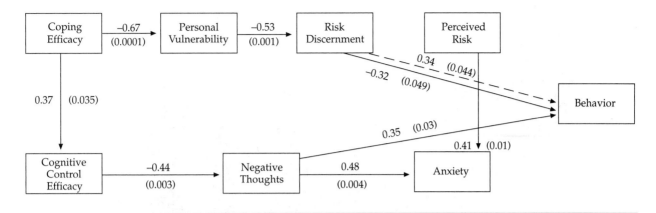

Figure 11-4. Path analysis of causal structures at the follow-up stage (after mastery training). The numbers on the paths are significant standardized path coefficients; the numbers in parentheses are the significance levels. The solid line to behavior represents avoidant behavior; the dashed line represents participant behavior. Path coefficients in the model that fell below the 0.10 significance level are not shown. (From "Mechanisms Governing Empowerment Effects: A Self-efficacy Approach," by E. M. Ozer and A. Bandura, *Journal of Personality and Social Psychology*, 1990, 58, 472–486. Copyright © 1990 by the American Psychological Association. Reprinted by permission of the author.)

actions, as well as our anxiety, we need to gain control over our negative thoughts. One thing that can help us gain control over our negative thoughts is to become competent, what Ozer and Bandura refer to in their model as having or developing coping efficacy.

Self-Efficacy Theory and Thrill Seeking

Making Use of Arousal

The self-efficacy model provides a good framework for understanding thrill-seeking behavior.

We have already considered the possibility that thrill seekers attempt to use the arousal component of fear and anxiety to increase the intensity of their emotions. To do so, according to Ozer and Bandura's model (Figure 11-4), thrill seekers would need to be able to discern risk and also to control their negative thoughts because both of these factors lead to avoidant motivation. The self-efficacy model suggests that they can attain both of those goals by acquiring the skills necessary for the particular activity. In short, people come to control their fears and anxiety through mastery training.

I once told a student of mine, an avid hang glider, that, according to a newspaper article I'd read, hang gliding is, on a per capita basis, the sport most likely to

result in death. He replied, "It's only dangerous if you are not careful." He went on to point out that he was skilled and had the best equipment that money can buy; for him, there was no risk. Previously, he had indicated to me that he loved to hang glide because it made him feel fully aware and fully conscious. This anecdote illustrates that fear is closely linked to our perceptions of our skills.

In many ways, the essence of being happy is to be highly aroused without being afraid. One reason that people take amphetamine, an arousal-producing drug, is that it produces a state of relaxed awareness—that is, an arousal high without feelings of anxiety.

Why are people attracted to bungee jumping, which doesn't involve a complex set of skills? It can be argued that what keeps people from bungee jumping is their negative thoughts. Should they be able to control those thoughts—and to feel reasonably confident in the equipment—they would be in a position to enjoy effects of high arousal without anxiety.

Increasing the Level of Risk

One characteristic of thrill-seeking behaviors is that people are inclined to increase the level of risk as their

There is a large sport industry devoted to helping people get high by taking risks under careful supervision.

skills improve. This makes sense. A situation must include some uncertainty to elicit fear and anxiety, without which arousal would remain relatively low. Thus, to get the increased arousal, it is necessary to increase the level of risk. What this means is that thrill seekers appear to be constantly endangering their lives. From the thrill seekers' perspective, the level of risk might not be that high. Thrill seekers know there is some risk but accept that a certain level of risk is necessary to be happy (Rowland, Franken, & Harrison, 1986).

Some Concluding Remarks

The perspective adopted in this section integrates various approaches. Our starting point is that people take risks to trigger a variety of chemical reactions. In other words, people engage in certain behaviors with no apparent adaptive function for the sake of hedonic enjoyment. However, goals are also important. Setting and achieving goals gives rise to feelings of self-efficacy and self-satisfaction and also plays a role in triggering the release of certain chemicals. A shortcoming of cog-

nitive interpretations is that they fail to recognize that we are biological creatures and that our feelings are linked to the release of chemicals in our brain. However, the hedonistic interpretation fails to address how we deal with our perturbing thoughts, which so often prevent us from doing things. Learning interpretations, by contrast, fail to adequately acknowledge the importance of chemicals released in the brain and the role of cognitions in determining behavior.

Summary

Research indicates that the most common regret is the regret of not taking action when the opportunity presented itself. One main reason for inaction is the fear and uncertainty associated with taking action. Research has shown that, when we are confronted with uncertainty, epinephrine levels typically rise. Epinephrine has been linked not only to arousal but also to anxiety and stress. Whether people experience anxiety and stress seems to be linked to whether they have developed a coping response that will enable them to deal with the aversive stimulus. That people can reframe a negative situation in positive terms has important implications for understanding why some people are more likely to confront fear and uncertainty than are others.

Thrill-seeking behaviors can be understood as an interaction of biological, learned, and cognitive variables. According to Schachter and Singer's theory of emotions, one reason people put themselves into situations that elicit fear is to intensify the positive emotion that results from successful coping. The main problem with this interpretation is that it ignores the complexity of emotions such as fear and anxiety; they have both an arousal component—which appears to be neutral as far as approach and avoidant behaviors are concerned—and a cognitive component—such as personal vulnerability, risk, and negative thoughts—which has been linked to avoidant behaviors. Research by Ozer and Bandura suggests that people can come to manage many of the cognitive aspects of anxiety. Thus, it may be possible for people to experience the high arousal that often comes with fear and uncertainty, without the accompanying negative motivation. This interpretation overcomes some of the major problems associated with wholly biological or wholly cognitive approaches.

Optimism and Hope

When people see desired outcomes as attainable, they are inclined to continue to exert efforts to attain those outcomes; however, when they see outcomes as unattainable, whether this is caused by something they lack or to external constraints, people reduce their efforts and eventually give up (Scheier & Carver, 1988). In other words, outcome expectancies play an important role in determining whether people are inclined to continue or give up.

Optimists and hopeful people tend to view all desired outcomes as attainable, even in the midst of failures and setbacks. They tend to persist, and even put forth more effort, when things are presently going against them. Some people have suggested that they tend to be very unrealistic (e.g., Alloy & Abramson, 1979) or that they live in an illusionary world (e.g., Taylor, 1989) because they fail to accept that things are not going well. They refuse to acknowledge that the best predictor of the future is how things are going right now. Why can't these people accept that and get on with their lives?

The paradox, of course, is that people who refuse to give up often end up accomplishing great things. Even though the idea of a light bulb was not new when Edison began his work, it took him and a staff of scientists nearly three years before they found the combination of features that would make the light bulb a viable commercial product.

When things are going well, there is not a great deal of difference between optimists and pessimists—hopeful and hopeless people. When things start to go badly, however, pessimistic and hopeless people tend to give up, whereas optimists and hopeful people tend to persist. In this section, we will examine why some people refuse to give up.

Note that giving up is not all that bad. Being too hopeful is both a blessing and a curse. As Tillich (1965) said, "Hope is easy for the foolish, but hard for the wise. Everybody can lose himself in foolish hope, but genuine hope is something rare and great" (p. 17).

Definitions

Conceptualizations of optimism and hope include definitions in terms of biological variables; learning approaches, adopted by Seligman and others, in which optimism is regarded as the result of a particular explanatory style; and more cognitive approaches (e.g., Synder et al., 1991), in which optimism is defined in terms of the self-concept that people have.

For a working definition of optimism, we will adopt that offered by Scheier and Carver (1985): Optimism is a generalized expectancy that good, as opposed to bad, outcomes will generally occur when confronted with problems across important life domains. Using their Life Orientation Scale (LOT), Scheier and Carver (1985) have been able to demonstrate a positive relationship between optimism, health, and recovery from surgery (Scheier et al., 1989).

We will discuss definitions of hope in more detail after we have reviewed some of the work on optimism. In general, optimism denotes a positive attitude or disposition that good things will happen, regardless of our ability, whereas hope is associated with goal-directed behavior. The concept of hope implies that we can find the path to our goal, often by using our skills or ability or perhaps by persisting (e.g., Snyder et al., 1991).

Optimism and Pessimism

Are optimism and pessimism two ends of the same continuum? If they were, then there would be little reason to have separate measures of these two constructs. Research indicates that they are not (Marshall, Wortman, Kusulas, Hervig, & Vickers, 1992; Robinson-Whelen, Kim, MacCallum, Kiecolt-Glaser, 1997). Pessimism seems to be principally associated with neuroticism and negative affect, whereas optimism is principally linked with extraversion and positive affect. Among other things, this seems to indicate that, although optimists tend to be open to new experiences or new stimulation, pessimists tend to be more withdrawn and inhibited in their interactions with the world.

Remember that happiness has also been linked to positive affect and extraversion. The main difference between happiness and optimism is that optimism has to do with expecting good things to happen in the future even when things are not going particularly well right now.

The Biological Component

Lionel Tiger (1985) offers an evolutionary perspective on optimism. He argues that, when our ancestors left the forest and became plains animals, they were faced with the task of obtaining food by killing other animals. In the course of hunting, they doubtless experienced many adverse circumstances; many of them must have suffered a variety of injuries. Learning principles tell us that humans tend to abandon tasks that are associated with negative consequences. So why did hunters carry on in the face of such adverse conditions? Tiger argues that it was biologically adaptive for our ancestors to develop a sense of optimism. Optimism would carry them through adverse circumstances, even injury.

By what mechanisms did optimism develop? Tiger suggests that one mechanism involved the endorphins. When we are injured, our bodies typically release endorphins. Endorphins have at least two important qualities (Chapter 7): They have analgesic properties (the ability to reduce pain), and they produce feelings of euphoria. Tiger contends that it was adaptive for our

hunting ancestors to experience a positive emotion when they were injured because that would reinforce their tendency to hunt in the future. It would have been disastrous, he argues, if our ancestors had abandoned the tendency to hunt. More recently Tiger (1999) has argued there are likely many neurochemicals associated with the feelings of hope and optimism, including such chemicals as serotonin.

Tiger emphasizes the utility of a sense of optimism. When things go wrong, it is important not to give up. He points out that optimism is a positive and active emotion. It makes us turn to our environment for the resources that we need. Such an attitude, he argues, was very important for our ancestors' survival, especially in the face of hardships and setbacks.

Researchers who have written about the evolution of hope emphasize that hope is not a selfish emotion but, rather, is a social emotion (e.g., Nesse, 1999). To be hopeful, in an evolutionary sense, means that one is concerned with establishing good social relations and cares about the environment. Only then can we take solace in the future.

The Learned/Cognitive Component

Optimism as an Acquired Thinking Style

A number of researchers are beginning to conceptualize thinking styles as habits. This has proven a very powerful way to conceptualize the behavior of optimists and hopeful people. If optimism and hope are merely ways that people have learned to think about the world and do not reflect deep underlying personality attributes, it should be relatively easy to change such thinking styles. Indeed, this is the premise on which Seligman's thinking program is based.

As we saw in Chapter 10, Seligman (1990) has taken the approach that optimism grows out of people's explanatory style. Optimists regard setbacks, failures, and adversity as temporary, as specific to a given situation, and as caused by external causes. Similarly, hope involves an explanatory style in which problems are regarded as temporary and specific to a given situation. Thus, within Seligman's system, optimism is a more inclusive concept; it contains three elements, whereas hope contains only two. As we'll see later, other theorists view hope as the more global of these two concepts.

Evidence for Seligman's Theory

There is considerable support for Seligman's theory in the research literature. Let's review a few examples that illustrate the diverse areas in which the theory is applicable.

Success at sales. Selling life insurance is a very tough job because salespeople are faced with repeated rejections. Typically, after a period of time, many salespeople quit. Over the years, insurance companies have developed a variety of tests to assess the suitability of applicants because it is very expensive to train new salespeople. To determine whether measures of optimism might be good predictors of sales success, Seligman compared his test of optimism with the Career Profile tests developed by Metropolitan Life to select their sales staff. The salespeople in the control group (the regular group) were hired using the Career Profile. The salespeople in the special force group, as they were called, were hired using two criteria: they had to have high optimism scores (in the top half), and they had to have failed the Career Profile.

The salespeople in the regular group were also given Seligman's Attribution Style Questionnaire (ASQ), which measures optimism and pessimism, so that it would be possible to look at the role of optimism independently of the Career Profile. At the end of the first year, the optimists in the regular force outsold the pessimists by only 8%. At the end of the second year, however, the optimists had outsold the pessimists by 31%.

What about the special force group? They outsold the pessimists in the regular force by 21% in the first year and 57% in the second year. They even outsold the average of the regular force over the two years by 27%. As a result of this study, Metropolitan Life began to use optimism scores as their main hiring criteria (Seligman, 1990; Seligman & Schulman, 1986).

Academic success. Although academic intelligence is a reasonably good predictor of success in school, educators have argued for some time that intelligence scores by themselves fail to account for the wide range of achievement that teachers observe daily. Clearly, many educators have argued, motivation plays a critical role. Those children who persist get the top marks. More recently, educators have observed that one reason performance in the classroom dives is because children get depressed.

In a study to examine their reactions to failure, two groups of schoolchildren with different explanatory styles—helpless children (pessimists) and mastery-oriented children—were given solvable and unsolvable problems. Before failure was introduced, the two groups showed no difference in their problem-solving skills. After failure, however, the problem-solving skills of the pessimistic children deteriorated to the first-grade level. When the mastery-oriented students failed, their problem-solving skills stayed at the fourth-grade level (Dweck & Licht, 1990).

In a longitudinal study to examine the role of optimism and pessimism on depression and intellectual achievement, researchers found that there were two major risk factors for poor achievement: pessimism and bad life events (parents separating, family deaths, family job loss). In addition to being predictors of poor achievement, these factors are predictors of depression in children (Seligman, 1990).

To assess whether optimism plays any role in success at a university, first-year students were given the ASQ. They had already submitted their Scholastic Aptitude Test (SAT) scores as part of the admission procedure, so at the end of the first semester when the grades were submitted, they could determine if optimism played any role in their performance. The results showed that students who did better than their SAT scores would predict were optimists. It appears that being optimists prepared them to deal with this new environment and the challenges it presented.

Optimism and Health

Numerous studies have shown that optimistic people are healthier than pessimistic people are. For example, Peterson (1988) monitored the health of 150 students for a year. He found that, compared with optimists, pessimists had twice as many infectious illnesses and made twice as many visits to their doctors. Optimists also seem to survive cancer longer than do pessimists (Seligman, 1990).

Over the years, the idea that an explanatory style can influence the progression of a disease such as cancer has provoked considerable skepticism. The assumption in our society has been that disease progression is independent of mental processes. If anything, a disease should undermine our mood, rather than the reverse.

To determine if a disease such as cancer can be affected by psychological states, Visintainer, Volpicelli, and Seligman (1982) decided to produce helplessness in rats using the helplessness training procedure that Seligman had used with his dogs (see Chapter 10). The main difference in her study was that she used rats that had been implanted with a few cells of sarcoma under each flank the day before she began her helplessness training procedure. The tumor she selected was one that invariably leads to death if it grows and is not rejected by the animal's immune system.

At the end of a month, 50% of the rats not given helplessness training (not shocked) had died, and the other 50% had rejected the tumors. She had determined ahead of the experiment just how much of the cancer cells needed to be implanted to produce a 50% death rate. Of the rats given mastery training, 70% rejected the tumor compared with only 27% of those given helplessness training. What Visintainer and her associates showed conclusively in this well-controlled study is that helplessness training reduced the ability of the body to reject the cancer cells (Visintainer et al., 1982) This finding is consistent with the idea that helplessness training produces a reduction in the immune response.

Considerable evidence indicates that optimism promotes health in a variety of ways, including an improved immune response (Scheier et al., 1999; Segerstrom, Taylor, Kemeny, & Fahey, 1998), reduction in negative mood (Weisse, 1992), and better health-promoting behaviors (Peterson, Seligman, Yurko, Martin, & Friedman, 1998).

Status of the Optimism Concept

Some researchers have expressed concern that optimism is becoming viewed by many people as the panacea for everything that ails society and that in the rush to help people achieve happier and less stressful lives they are being encouraged to simply adopt a more optimistic thinking style (Peterson, 2000). Two specific concerns follow from this general concern: The first concern is that we might be neglecting other important moderators of behavior, including negative emotions such as pessimism. Research indicates that emotions such as pessimism also predict various adaptive behav-

iors (Robinson-Whelen, 1997). It is sometimes good to be cautious and heed the voice of negative emotions that tell us bad things can and do happen. Optimists and pessimists do not differ when it comes to primary appraisal but do differ when it comes to secondary appraisal. Optimists are more inclined, compared with pessimists, to consider their coping alternatives (Chang, 1998). What this suggests is that what we need to teach people is how to make plans in the face of setbacks and challenges. In the next section on hope, we will discuss the importance of making plans.

The second concern is that advocating optimism could play into some of the individualism or self-interest at the expense of the group. As we have discussed before, there is good reason to be aware of our "shared fate." Perhaps, as Peterson (2000) has suggested, we need to think in some concept as group optimism, which has to do with creating an environment in which we can all live and be happy. One downside of optimism is that it can lead to greed (Peterson, 2000). As we discussed before, the satisfaction of material needs does not ensure happiness.

The Concept of Hope

Feelings of hope, as we will show, are also closely linked to a wide range of adaptive behaviors. Let's start by looking at the definition of hope.

Snyder's Definition of Hope

Snyder and his colleagues define hope in terms of two major elements that they conceptualize as forms of thinking (Curry, Snyder, Cook, Ruby, & Rehm, 1997; Snyder et al., 1991). First, there is pathway thinking that involves conceptualizing one or more routes to a desired goal. Second, there is agentic thinking that involves thoughts that have to do with initiating movement along one's chosen path. This very generalized belief—a belief in oneself—can be summarized by the saying, "Where there's a will, there's a way."

Snyder and his colleagues regard the relationship between agency and pathways as reciprocal. Hopeful people believe, on the one hand, that they can attain goals (agency) and, on the other, that they can generate the alternatives (pathways) needed to achieve those goals. In their theory, these two elements are interdependent.

They contrast their theory with that of Scheier and Carver (1985), who argue that outcome expectancies are the best predictors of behavior. According to Scheier and Carver, optimism is a generalized expectancy or disposition that good outcomes will generally occur across important life domains. Snyder argues that putting all the emphasis on outcomes fails to adequately account for behavior.

Empirical Support Consistent with Snyder's Theory

Hope and negative feedback. According to Snyder's model, hope sustains people in the presence of a stressor, such as an obstacle to a goal. In a study to test this prediction, participants were divided into groups characterized by high, medium, and low hope. Each group was divided into negative-feedback and no-feedback conditions. Those in the negative-feedback condition were asked to imagine the following scenario:

Although you have set your goal of getting a B, when your first examination score—worth 30% of your final grade—is returned, you have received a D. It is now one week after you have learned about the D grade.

They were then asked to respond to five agency questions on a seven-point scale:

1. How much effort are you exerting to reach your goal (no effort to extreme effort)?
2. When you think about this goal, do you feel energized (not at all to extremely)?
3. How confident are you of reaching your goal (not at all to extremely)?
4. How important is receiving this grade goal to you (not at all to extremely)?
5. What is the probability of reaching this goal (0% to 100%)?

Subjects were also asked five pathways questions, which involved listing potential strategies for reaching the grade goal of B.

With respect to the agency measure, the results showed that, unlike the high-hope individuals, medium- and, especially, low-hope individuals reported less agency in the negative feedback condition than in the no-feedback condition. With respect to the pathways measure, the high-hope individuals reported more pathways than medium-hope individuals, who, in turn, reported more pathways than the low-hope individuals. To summarize, when confronted with a setback or an obstacle, high-hope individuals exhibited sustained agency and pathway behaviors, whereas low-hope individuals showed decreased agency and pathway behaviors (Yoshinobu, 1989).

Hope and number of goals. Snyder's model also predicts that people with enhanced goal agency and a sense of pathways to goals would pursue a greater number of goals in their lives. A study of people in their 20s, 30s, and 40s found that, indeed, people who are high in hope tend to have more goals (Langelle, 1989).

Hope and preferred difficulty of goals. Snyder's model also predicts that, because high-hope people have a stronger sense of agency and pathways, they should set more difficult goals. Two studies (Harris, 1988; Sigmon & Snyder, 1990) have provided clear evidence that high-hope people are more inclined to select difficult tasks. Scheier and Carver's LOT scale was not as good a predictor. This is consistent with the idea that goal-directed behavior is mediated by the interaction of agency and pathways.

Hope and goal attainment. Do high-hope people actually meet the more difficult goals they set for themselves? The results of a study in which students were asked to set a realistic goal for their final grade indicated that (1) compared with low-hope students, high-hope students said they would get higher grades, (2) they were more successful at attaining those higher grades even when early feedback suggested they might not, and (3) they actually did obtain the higher grades they set for themselves (Anderson, 1988).

Hope and athletic performance. A recent series of studies showed that hope is a good predictor of academic success and of athletic success as well (Curry et al., 1997). One interesting and important finding was that hope is a better predictor of athletic success than is self-esteem. What these results emphasize is the need to focus on how to attain goals rather than just feeling good about oneself.

Summary

Scheier and Carver define optimism as a generalized expectancy that good outcomes will generally occur across important life domains. According to Tiger, optimism provides the motivation for acting (engaging in adaptive behavior) and rewards behaviors that have an adaptive function. According to the learning theorists, optimism can be viewed as an acquired thinking style. Seligman has suggested that optimists view (explain) setbacks, failures, and adversity, as temporary, specific to a given situation, and caused by external causes. Evidence for Seligman's theory is extensive. Among other things, the theory has been successful in predicting the success of life insurance salespeople, academic success, and health. Together with Hollon and Freeman, Seligman has developed the ABCDE program, which is designed to change pessimistic thinking styles into more optimistic thinking styles. This program trains people to dispute their negative thinking by asking four questions: (1) What evidence do I have for my interpretation? (2) What alternative interpretations are there? (3) What are the implications if I take this position? (4) How useful is my belief?

Cognitive theorists such as Snyder and his colleagues have argued that hope involves both a sense of agency and a sense of pathways. They have offered a series of convincing studies to show that, indeed, there is a reciprocal relationship between a sense of agency and a sense of pathways. They have shown that their measure of hope, which taps into both agency and pathways, predicts behavior in response to negative feedback, the number of goals that people set for themselves, the difficulty of the goals that they select for themselves, the attainment of goals, academic success, and athletic success.

The Role of Early Experience: The Question of Attachment

Parent-child interaction plays an important role in a wide range of adaptive emotions such as happiness, optimism, and self-worth as well as in adaptive behaviors such as coping with stress and self-regulation of motivation (Bowlby, 1980; Mikulincer, Florian, & Weller, 1993: McIntyre & Dusek, 1995; Strage, 1998).

The main theoretical model that has emerged to account for the positive as well as the negative effects of various parenting styles is attachment theory (Ainsworth, Blehar, Water, & Wall, 1978; Bowlby, 1980). According to attachment theory, the ability of parent and child to form a secure bond fundamentally affects the child's approach to the world. From the security of having a close bond, the child explores, develops feelings of confidence, and learns how to interact socially (Bretherton & Waters, 1985). Research has confirmed that the benefits of secure bonding last well into adolescence and adulthood (Strage, 1998). Thus, the attachment experience seems to be very important.

The Biological Component

Evolutionary psychologists argue that the mother, father, family and even the extended family (sometimes called the tribe) are perceived as important sources of protection for the child who, at birth, has few defenses. For this reason researchers have suggested that human infants evolved a number of mechanisms to securely bond with parents and caretakers. These mechanisms, such as crying, smiling, hugging, have their roots in what Buck has called the prosocial affect system that we referred to earlier (Buck, 1999). They ensure bonding occurs.

Buck argues that two fundamental social motives emerge from attachment: the need to follow or exceed expectations and the need to be loved. Both have their roots in the need to conform to the group. Only if the individual can ultimately perform valuable functions is the individual useful to the group. What the group does not need is an independent maverick who is unresponsive to the group needs. What is required by the group, therefore, is a person who can carry out certain survival related functions (meet and exceed expectations) and be responsive to emerging needs (the need to be loved). Implicit in the idea of having a need to be loved is the idea that one needs to be attuned to the greater needs of the group and anticipate these needs if possible. In being attuned, the individual becomes an esteemed member of the group. Conversely, the more esteemed one is, the more the group is going to protect that individual. Thus, there is a reciprocal relationship between the group and the individual. Buck argues that these two social motives are the strongest of all the human motives and are responsible for the flexibility we observe in human behavior.

As we discussed earlier in the chapter, the flow experience occurs when we are free of fears and anxiety. It occurs when we are not preoccupied by thoughts of survival such as the need to please others and the need to be loved. At the core of attachment theory is the proposition that humans learn to reduce their fears and anxieties by becoming securely attached. It was in our ancestors' best interests to learn how to conquer various fears so they could focus their attention on other things. It is not surprising, therefore, that securely attached children explore more and are better able to cope with a variety of life distresses. Because of knowledge that they have or can develop secure attachments they are able to do other things than simply focus on survival.

The Learned/Cognitive Component

Although it may be in the best interest of the child to become securely attached, not all parents appear to be motivated to form such secure attachments. As a result, different types or degrees of bonding have been documented. I will return to these shortly, but first let me point out something important.

Given the principle that parents are motivated to ensure their genes survive in future generations, shouldn't they also be motivated to form secure attachments? Wouldn't that be the optimal strategy? Chisholm (1996) has addressed this question and has pointed out that there are a variety of reasons why this likely didn't happen in the past and perhaps wouldn't happen today. First, our ancestors often didn't have the resources needed to provide for an offspring. Thus, they had to divide their energy accordingly, making decisions about what was optimal and even neglecting certain offspring, much like the mother dog ignoring the runt of the litter. Even today, as a result of having limited means, parents will often chose to provide higher education for only some of their children. Second, Chisholm, argues that our ancestors likely had different mating strategies. Although we talked earlier as though there were an optimal strategy for each of the sexes, we know that there are variations. Although

we argued that humans are generally motivated by quality, not all are. If you are motivated by quantity rather than quality, you might be less willing to form secure attachments with your offspring.

One way to better understand the advantages of being securely attached is to look at what happens when there are different parenting styles that result in some children being less securely attached than others.

Three Attachment Styles: What happens when children are not securely attached?

Researchers have suggested three distinctive attachment styles develop in children as a result of how they were treated by their mothers (Ainsworth et al., 1978).

1. **Secure attachment style.** When a mother is sensitive and responsive to the child's need to contact, the child comes to feel safe in the environment. As a consequence the child explores the environment, coming back to the mother periodically to establish contact before venturing forth once again. Such children are characterized by self-confidence and emerging independence.

2. **Anxious/ambivalent attachment style.** When mothers are inconsistent in meeting the child's need for contact, sometimes ignoring them and at other times forcing their affection on them, the child become anxious and fearful, more concerned with becoming attached than exploring the environment. Such children tend to be inhibited, dependent, and characterized by low self-confidence.

3. **Avoidant attachment style.** When mothers avoid or reject their child's need for contact, the child comes to ignore and avoid the mother. Although these children appear to show normal exploratory behavior, such behavior seems to be motivated more by a desire to avoid their mother than a true desire to explore.

That the securely attached child is more inclined to explore is consistent with the idea that the tendency to learn is often greater when fear and anxiety are low. As we will discuss in more detail in the next chapter, exploratory behavior is inconsistent with fear and for very good reason. Although we might get something that looks like exploration in the avoidant attachment style, it does not appear to be driven by the motivation to learn about the environment in the same way we talk about the securely attached learning about the environment. This behavior is more like that of the person whose motivation to run comes from a desire to escape his or her spouse.

Attachment in Adults

Researchers have suggested that the need for attachment in children is a prototype of the adult need for attachment (Hazan & Shaver, 1987; Shaver, Hazan, & Bradshaw, 1988). Although the exact mechanism has not been identified it likely resulted in humans coming to view the world as more nonthreatening and open to enjoyment and satisfaction. Consistent with this idea is the finding that securely attached adults (as measured by self-reports) have the highest interest in their jobs, experience the greatest job satisfaction, and are the lowest in terms of being fearful about evaluation. Anxious/ambivalent attached adults, in contrast, tend to treat work largely as a search for approval, express feelings of not being appreciated on the job, and prefer working with others rather than working alone. Finally, avoidant attachment adults, tend to regard work primarily as a means of getting away from undesired social contacts.

As we will talk about later, the secure attachment adults appear to intrinsically motivated. These are people who can find satisfaction in doing a good job. These people are likely to have the flow experience. Although some people might work well because of their unresolved neurotic feelings (anxiety and such), they appear to be the minority.

Attachment History, Stress, and Seeking Social Support

If the family and extended family (sometimes called the tribe) were a source of comfort and protection in the formative years, one might expect people who had experienced such a protective environment would be inclined to seek out that or a similar community when distressed. As we have already discussed in the chapter on stress, good social support systems reduce the stress response. Consistent with this idea, research shows that securely attached adults are indeed more inclined to seek social support (Greenberger & McLaughlin, 1998).

Social Support Systems and Health

When things are going well, social support systems don't seem to be that important. In the face of adversity, however, people who have a strong social support system—family or community—tend to recover more quickly than do those who do not (Cohen & McKay, 1984; Taylor, 1990).

Social support involves emotional support, informational support, tangible assistance, and appraisal support (feedback on the accuracy of our evaluations of the environment). Researchers have argued that different types of support are needed in different situations. Tightly knit communities, such as the Amish community, embody a comprehensive network system in which different people within the community provide different types of support when they are needed.

McClelland (1989) has found that affiliative trust (a willingness to cooperate with others), together with a sense of agency, is linked to a strong immune response and good health. This is consistent with a growing body of evidence that people with good social support systems tend to be healthier.

Providing social support to another person will not necessarily reduce stress in that person. Social support has been found to interact with various personality attributes and with constitutional difference. For example, researchers have shown that the support of a spouse is more important than is a friend's support (Schuster, Kessler, & Aseltine, 1990). Researchers have also shown that the stress-buffering effects of perceived support is higher in people with an internal locus of control (Lefcourt, Martin, & Saleh, 1984). Finally, researchers have shown, using twins, that genetics play a key role. It has been found, for example, that genetics can explain between 28% and 52% of the variance on certain support measures (Kessler, Kendler, Heath, Neale, & Eaves, 1992). One important conclusion that we can draw from this research is that social support is more in the eye of the beholder than the provider. That is, people who are open to receiving social support can benefit greatly from it; however, those who close themselves off, for whatever reason, are the

Feelings of attachment and belongingness typically give rise to happiness, self-confidence, and good health.

losers. In short, you can't help people unless they are open to support. As I indicated earlier, there is good reason to argue that we need to encourage people to develop good support systems. Practical Application 11-2 summarizes some suggestions Buss (2000) made about how to become happier that are equally applicable to becoming healthier.

Attachment, Belongingness, and Faith

Freud argued that religion resulted in an obsessional neurosis characterized by guilt, repressed sexuality, and suppressed emotions. Empirical studies have not found much support for his conclusions. Myers (2000) points out that people who have a strong spiritual faith (a belief in god, for example) tend to be happier than are people who do not have a strong faith. A survey of the National Opinion Research Center found higher levels of very happy people among those who reported they feel extremely close to God. It is not immediately clear why this is the case, however, evidence suggests that it has to

do with a faith community providing social support (Ellison, Gay, & Glass, 1989). Whether this can completely account for the results is not clear. Perhaps, as Myers (2000) points out, faith meets a number of important human needs, including a sense of meaning and purpose.

Summary

Parent-child bonding has been found to play an important role in feelings of happiness and self-worth. Attachment research suggests that the degree of security and confidence that children feel determines their willingness to explore, learn, and take on new challenges. When we develop secure attachments (mainly with our mother), we see the world as less threatening and hostile and, as a result, we are less vulnerable to adversity. Attachment theory emphasizes the role of parents in the development of traits such as self-confidence but acknowledges that other attachments later in life can

How to Become an Optimist: The ABCDE Method

Considerable evidence indicates that people who are inclined toward depression—that is, who use an explanatory style characterized by permanence, pervasiveness, and personalization—can learn to change to a more optimistic style. The ABCDE method is designed to help people think more accurately when they are faced with adversity. This method, developed by Seligman (in conjunction with Dr. Steven Hollon of Vanderbilt University and Dr. Arthur Freeman of University of Medicine and Dentistry of New Jersey), is based on the ideas and work of Albert Ellis, an early pioneer in cognitive therapy.

To understand this method, we'll break it down into two parts: ABC and DE. Let's start with ABC.

Step 1: Identifying Adversity, Belief, and Consequences (ABC)

As we've seen, what differentiates optimists from pessimists is how they deal with adversity. The reason optimists are more successful is that they do not fall apart, as pessimists do, when they encounter adversity. Instead of giving up, optimists tend to persist. Thus, the focus of this method is to help people better deal with adversity by analyzing the accompanying inner dialogue.

Humans tend to engage in a perpetual dialogue that is often just below our level of awareness. Ellis, Beck, Seligman, and others have discovered that, by asking the right questions, we can become fully aware of our inner dialogues. They start by pointing out that it is common for people to encounter setbacks, failures, obstacles, and frustrations, which fall under the general heading of *adversity* (A). Next they point out that adversities tend to trigger interpretations or explanations that fall under the general heading of *belief* (B). Finally, our interpretations give rise to feelings, which fall under the heading of *consequences* (C). Let's look at some examples of adversity and the accompanying thinking process.

Example 1: Jeff

Jeff left his small hometown to attend a large university in the city. He missed his old friends and was feeling lonely as he began his studies. He suggested to Chris, a student he met in one of his classes, that they might go hiking on the weekend, and Chris seemed genuinely interested. They agreed to go on Saturday. When he stopped by to pick up Chris on Saturday morning, Chris's roommate told him that Chris had decided to go home for the weekend. As Jeff walked down the sidewalk toward his Jeep, he said to himself: "It's going to be a very lonely year for me. I'm never going to make any friends. I should never have decided to come to this university. I come from a small town and people probably think I'm a hick. Maybe I should pack my bags and go home." When Jeff was asked to analyze this adversity into the three components, he offered the following.

Adversity: "I want to develop some friendships but I haven't been able to do so."

Belief: "I lack the ability to make friends."

Consequence (feeling): "I am feeling more lonely than ever."

If we look carefully at his inner dialogue, we see that it contains all the elements typical of a pessimist. The failure has led to an explanatory style that is permanent (I can't make friends), pervasive (I will never make friends), and personal (I lack the ability to make friends).

Example 2: Mary

Mary was one of the top students in her high school and had no difficulty being admitted to a top university. She expected to get As at university, as she had in the past but, when she got her first essay back, it was only a B+. As she returned to her room, she found herself thinking: "I really blew this one. I thought I was bright, but maybe I have been fooling myself. Now I'm in the big leagues, and that's what counts. Probably the reason I got the grades I did in high school was because I was one of those polite kind of people who teachers reward for being nice. With those grades, I will never be able to get into Med school. I probably shouldn't even be here. All these people are much smarter than I am. Maybe I should quit at the end of this year."

When Mary was asked to analyze her adversity into the three components, she offered the following.

Adversity: "I want to go into medicine but I don't think I will be able to get into Med School."

Belief: "I am not as smart as I thought I was."

Consequence: "I feel awful and wish I could drop out of the university."

If we look carefully at her inner dialogue, we see that it too contains all the elements typical of a pessimist. The failure leads to an explanatory style that is permanent (I can't get the grades I think I need), pervasive (I will never get those grades), and personal (I lack the ability to get good grades).

Keeping a Record of Adversities

If you want to determine if you are prone to pessimistic thinking and might like to change your thinking style, you should collect at least five examples of adversity over a period of a few days. There are many possibilities: for example, someone not returning your phone call; someone not returning something you loaned them; discovering that you lost your parking stall because your check was misplaced; discovering that someone dented your car and did not leave a note or contact you; getting a poor mark on a test; not being able to get a course that you need to graduate; finding your bicycle has been stolen; discovering that the dry cleaner damaged your favorite coat; or finding that your bank made a mistake and, as a result, one of your checks bounced.

Once you have collected your examples, write down your interpretation or explanation (beliefs), followed by your feelings (consequences). Analyze these examples to see if they reflect a pessimistic thinking style. You might discover that your style is not completely pessimistic but has elements of pessimism. Most people respond inconsistently—sometimes with pessimism, sometimes with optimism.

Step 2: Distraction and Disputation (D) and Energization (E)

Jeff's and Mary's stories are not that unusual. Having friends and doing well in college are important to people. As a result, they often respond dramatically to adversities when these domains of their lives are threatened.

Seligman identifies two ways of dealing with pessimistic thinking: *distraction* and *disputation* (D). If we don't distract ourselves or dispute our thinking, we are inclined to ruminate. As we saw in Chapter 10, one of the worst things that people can do is to allow themselves to ruminate about adversity.

Distraction means that you try to think of something else or simply get involved in something else. Some time ago, Ellis suggested that people should simply say "No" or "Stop" when they do not want to think about something. This has proven to be a fairly effective way of eliminating unwanted thoughts. You should feel free to say "No" or "Stop" out loud or to write these words in bold letters on a card and put it in front of yourself. After you have practiced saying "No" or "Stop," you will find that you can indeed stop some of this negative thinking.

Disputation involves learning how to argue with yourself. You need to ask yourself four questions.

1. What evidence do I have for my interpretation? When Jeff was asked what evidence he had that he couldn't make friends, he could only cite this one example. It was the same for Mary. This was a one-shot deal.
2. What alternative interpretations are there? As it turned out, the reason Chris was not there when Jeff arrived was that he left in a hurry because his mother was ill. Chris's roommate failed to pass that information along because he assumed that Jeff already knew that Chris's mother had been ill. Mary found out that the best mark for that particular paper was a B+. It was standard practice for this particular professor to give low grades on the first paper to chasten new students. Before you jump to a conclusion, you should investigate other possible explanations for what has happened.
3. What are the implications for me if I take this position? Even if my belief is correct, what does it mean? Is it really that important? When Jeff was asked to think about the implications, he began to realize that life was not over just yet. So what if Chris is irresponsible? Surely there were plenty of people at the college like those he knew in his hometown. When Mary was asked to consider the implications of her adversity, she too decided things weren't as bad as they initially looked. She knew she had worked as hard as she could have. Further, she had often thought that pursuing a career in arts would be far more exciting than medicine, even if she would likely be poor.
4. How useful is my belief? Life is not always fair, nor does it always work out as we plan. It would be nice if life worked out just as we had planned.

(continued on next page)

also provide the basis for feelings of security. The theory suggests that people are particularly important to us in times of adversity.

Evolutionary psychologists argue that the infant is designed to form secure attachments because a secure attachment provides the child with a sense of protection—a feeling or emotion that frees them from fears and threats. Not all parents are willing to provide a secure attachment and as a result some children develop what is called anxious/ambivalent attachment, and others develop avoidant attachment. Research evidence indicates one's early attachment experience becomes the prototype for adult attachment. Those who were able to form secure attachments as children tend as adults to develop good social support systems that

lead to improved health. Finally, there is evidence that that religious faith can lead to greater happiness.

Main Points

1. Goal-congruent emotions facilitate and sustain the attainment of personal goals.
2. Lazarus suggests that the core relational theme of happiness is making reasonable progress toward the realization of a goal.
3. Twin studies indicate that 50% of happiness is inherited. Although cognitive theorists view happiness as a means to an end (goal), hedonists conceptualize happiness as an end (goal).

Practical Application 11-2 (continued)

But how realistic is that? Besides, much of the excitement in life comes from the unexpected.

Jeff began to realize as the year progressed that people were more competitive at the university than at his high school. They were also less tolerant of, or less interested in, some of his more rural ways of having fun. But others found him fresh and sincere. One person said, "Jeff's a genuine article." The friends he developed turned out to be far more interesting and diverse than he had anticipated. Chris, he discovered, was a nice person but lacked imagination.

Mary learned that good grades were tougher to get than she had thought. "Everybody is smart here," she concluded. She began to discover that, by using her social skills, she could get the help and guidance she needed to rise to the top. By the end of the year, she was close to being a straight-A student. Because she asked so many questions, she was offered a summer job as a research assistant by one of her professors, who told her, "I like you because you aren't afraid to ask tough questions."

Energization (E)

Energization involves summarizing your thoughts and actions and planning where you will go next. It is

important to gain some degree of closure, so that you can put this event behind you and move ahead. This will help to prevent further rumination and set the stage for further adaptive actions. You might like to view energization as an internal pep talk in which you are your own coach.

Let's return to Jeff and Mary and look at their finished ABCDE records after their first adversity. Their disputation is particularly important because that is where their thinking changes. (Their use of the four questions is noted in the disputation sections.)

Jeff's ABCDE Record

Adversity: "I want to develop some friendships but I haven't been able to do so."

Belief: "I lack the ability to make friends."

Consequence (feeling): "I am feeling more lonely than ever."

Disputation: "I was disappointed when I found out that Chris had gone home and was upset that he hadn't called me [evidence]. He probably didn't realize how important it was for me [alternative]. The fact that he didn't call was inconsiderate of him, but there may be some explanation [alternative]. I really shouldn't let one event get me so upset [usefulness]. It's not as though this is the last person in the world [implications]. I think I have a pretty good record for making friends [implications]."

4. Happiness has been linked to our conquest of various fears and our ability to make plans.

5. The flow experience is often used as an example of what is involved in the happiness experience.

6. Research indicates that norepinephrine is released when organisms make coping responses and that making coping responses typically leads to a reduction in stress and anxiety.

7. Bandura has argued that people do not avoid potentially threatening situations because they experience anxiety and arousal but, rather, because they fear they will not be able to cope either behaviorally or cognitively.

8. Ozer and Bandura have suggested that there is a dual route to controlling anxiety. Their research suggests that the main route to anxiety control comes from developing skills (mastery training).

9. Optimists and hopeful people tend to view all desired outcomes as potentially attainable.

10. Seligman has suggested that optimism arises from people's explanatory style. Optimists view (explain) setbacks, failures, and adversity as temporary, specific to a given situation, and caused by external causes.

11. Seligman has proposed the ABCDE method as a means of becoming an optimist. This method involves first identifying adversities, beliefs, and consequences. Next, people must learn to distract themselves and dispute their thinking, then to act, which will result in energization.

Energization: "There will undoubtedly be more opportunities for making friends this coming week. Who knows, I might be able to meet someone tonight if I go to the local coffeehouse or possibly the bar. I hate going by myself but maybe it's time to put aside my pride and admit that I'm lonely. I can't be the only person at this university who is feeling lonely tonight. Surely there is nothing wrong in admitting that you are lonely."

Mary's ABCDE Record

Adversity: "I want to go into medicine but I don't think I will be able to get into Med School."

Belief: "I am not as smart as I thought I was."

Consequence: "I feel awful and wish I could drop out."

Disputation: "It was a real shock for me to receive a B+ because I always did very well on papers in high school [evidence]. I guess I thought that I could put forth the same effort I did in high school and get the same grades [implication]. I wonder if I really understood the assignment [alternative]. Perhaps the professor was looking for something different [alternative]. If worse comes to worse, I can pursue one of my other strengths [alternative/usefulness]. I really should stick it out a little longer before I decide I don't have the ability [implication]. I may be working myself into a snit over nothing [usefulness]."

Energization: "The first thing I must do is make an appointment with my professor, so I can get his honest appraisal. I've heard for years that it is much tougher to get As at the university than in high school. I know I can put forth more effort if that is what's required. I've always been good at asking questions, so now it is time to make use of those skills."

Catastrophizing and Decatastrophizing

These two examples illustrate how people often jump to conclusions or *catastrophize*. When we catastrophize, we see the worst-case scenario. Disputation serves, among other things, to *decatastrophize*. This is important because it allows us to think about other alternatives and eventually to think about positive ways of producing the results we want. The world is not always as we would like it to be. Armed with a sense of openness and a willingness to learn, however, we can often succeed in ways that we had not expected or planned.

For a more detailed discussion of how to become an optimist, read Martin E. P. Seligman's (1990) book *Learned Optimism*.

12. Snyder and his associates have defined hope as based on two reciprocal elements: a sense of agency and a sense of pathways.

13. Being able to form secure attachments with parents or caregivers has been found to play an important role in such emotions as happiness, self-worth, and in coping with stress.

14. Considerable evidence indicates that people who have good social support systems are less prone to depression and tend to be healthier than are people without such social support systems.

15. People with a strong religious faith are not only happier but healthier.

 ## InfoTrac® College Edition

What are some of the positive outcomes associated with being a risk taker and what are some of the negative outcomes of being a risk taker? (Search words: risk taking)

What are some of the immediate and long-term advantages of being optimistic and hopeful? (Search words: optimism, hope)

Chapter Twelve

From Curiosity to Creativity

- *What motivates people to explore a new city?*
- *Is this exploratory behavior learned or innate?*
- *Why do people believe that exploratory behavior is motivated by the curiosity drive?*
- *What is sensation seeking?*
- *Is the trait of sensation seeking learned or acquired, or is it something we are born with?*

- *What motivates people to be creative?*
- *Why is it that people sometimes feel creative and at other times, they do not?*
- *Do people have to be inspired to be creative or can people be creative at will?*
- *Are younger people more creative than older people?*

Before 1950, researchers generally believed that much of what we learn results from being taught —that is, that learning is extrinsically motivated, rather than intrinsically motivated. In the 1950s, a group of researchers challenged that idea with a series of well-designed studies that clearly showed that much of what we learn and master is intrinsically motivated and has its roots in curiosity and exploratory behavior.

Those early studies provided, in many ways, the impetus for two lines of research. The first is work on sensation seeking. Sensation seekers are characterized by a strong curiosity drive and by a willingness to take risks to satisfy that curiosity drive. What makes sensation seekers so interesting is that they develop distinct personalities.

The second line of research that developed from the early work on curiosity and exploratory behaviors was the study of competency. To become successful and happy, humans need to become competent in a variety of domains. Becoming competent, it turns out, involves taking the talents that we have and developing them to their fullest. To do that, people need to be free of anxiety and to develop mental attitudes that will support the development of competency. Because competency is so important, we will devote the next chapter to various facets of competency, including predictability and control, achievement mastery, and self-esteem.

In the last part of this chapter, we look at the motivation for creativity. Creative performance involves the generation of novel ideas and behaviors that meet a standard of quality or utility. Creative people, it turns out, need to have a base of knowledge (competency) and need personality attributes that will allow them to generate novel ideas and behaviors. The creative process, in many ways, represents the coming together of competency with qualities that are possessed by the sensation seeker.

Curiosity and Exploratory Behavior

Children like to explore their environments. Young children might take the pots and pans out of the kitchen cupboard or rummage through a book of old photos that they find in a box in the basement. They might disassemble a watch and find that they can't put it back together.

As children grow up, they begin to explore other areas, such as the neighborhood in which they live. They develop friendships and learn to play games. This exploratory behavior seems to occur without very much encouragement from their parents. In fact, parents often try to discourage children from their interest in the contents of closets and cupboards and from wandering too far from home. Although most developmental psychologists argue that, by exploring, children become knowledgeable about their environments and competent in dealing with them (e.g., Piaget, 1952; White, 1959), the motivation for this has been the basis for much discussion and debate.

Before the 1950s, the behaviorists argued that primary drives, such as hunger, energized the organism to engage in random behavior. When the organism encountered the appropriate goal object during such random movements, the drive would be reduced. As a result, the preceding behavior would be reinforced. Through learning, the organism would become increasingly more efficient at finding the appropriate goal object when a given drive state had been activated.

Novelty, Curiosity, and Exploratory Behavior

In the 1950s, this idea was challenged by researchers who believed that although we may learn to do many things as a result of reinforcement, the tendency to explore is not one of those behaviors. To determine if organisms have an innate curiosity drive, researchers created a variety of situations to see what would happen if you introduced an individual to a novel environment or situation. What these studies showed is that organisms are motivated to interact with new or novel objects and they learn in the process. Harlow (1953) showed, for example, that monkeys will learn to solve various kinds of mechanical puzzles when no motivation is provided other than the presence of the puzzles. He observed the monkeys had a persistent tendency to carry out the solution in a flawless manner, which suggests the development of some kind of competency. Butler (1953) put monkeys in a room with four windows that they could open to see a toy train, various other objects, or other monkeys. These monkeys spent a great deal of time simply looking at things, and they learned which window provided which kind of stimulation.

Corinne Hutt (1966) gave children a novel object in which a lever was connected to a set of counters and the numbers on the counters changed as the lever was moved. In one condition, the children could see the counters move; in another, the counters were covered. As expected, when the counters were visible, the children spent more time pressing the lever. Also as expected, their interest in the counters diminished with repeated trials.

The fact that interest in novel things diminishes with repeated exposure led many researchers to conclude that what motivated exploratory behavior initially was novelty. By definition, novelty means new, and something is only new as long as it contains information that hasn't been completely processed. This led researchers to the idea that if something contained more information, it would maintain interest longer, and thus, the concept of complexity arouse.

The Preference for Complexity

If animals are given a choice between two novel stimuli, one of which is more complex, they will choose the more complex stimulus (Earl, Franken, & May, 1967). Humans also show a preference for complexity. Robert Earl (1957) had children work on block-design puzzles of moderate complexity and then gave them the opportunity to select a new block-design puzzle. The children could choose either more complex or simpler designs. Most selected a design that was somewhat more complex than the design they had just been working on. They did not, for the most part, select either a design that was simpler or a design that was much more complex. This tendency to select a slightly more complex puzzle indicates that human exploratory behavior is highly systematic. Humans, it appears, do not explore their environment haphazardly.

Earl's findings have been duplicated by Richard May (1963), who had preschool children look at checkerboard designs of moderate complexity and then gave them the opportunity to look at a pile of simpler or more complex checkerboard designs. Like Earl, May found that most of the children selected the more complex designs.

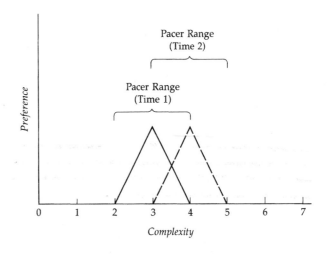

Figure 12-1. The pacer range. According to Dember and Earl's theory, an organism that has adapted to the level of complexity represented by point 2 on the complexity dimension will be inclined to respond only to stimuli enclosed by points 2 and 4; maximum attention will be directed toward stimuli at point 3. Interacting with stimuli at point 3 will lead to a new adaptation level corresponding to point 3. As a result, there will be a new pacer range, enclosed by points 3 and 5. Thus, as long as there are stimuli corresponding to those in the pacer range, over time the individual will systematically interact with all the stimuli in its environment.

Dember and Earl's Theory of Exploratory Behavior

To account for these and other findings, Dember and Earl (1957) created a theory of exploratory behavior that was, in many ways, the prototype for present theories. The theory is based on the assumption that organisms are motivated to experience optimal complexity. This word was used to capture the idea that stimuli contain information that can be processed. One important feature of their theory is the concept of a *pacer range* (Figure 12-1). They suggest that an individual becomes accustomed, or habituated, to a certain level of complexity (called an *adaptation level*) and is motivated to explore stimuli that are slightly more complex than this adaptation level. This concept is intended to explain why exploratory, curiosity, and play behaviors tend to be systematically directed toward more complex levels of stimulation and also why individuals prefer certain stimuli to others. The appeal of the theory is its simplicity: It predicts that individuals will always select stimuli slightly more complex than those to which they have adapted and that, over time, individuals will come to prefer increasingly complex stimulation.

The measure of any theory, however, is how well it can account for the research findings. Several tests of the theory have shown that, indeed, many forms of stimulation can be ordered by their psychological complexity and, further, that preferences are systematically related to psychological complexity. For example, preference for auditory stimuli appears to be determined by their complexity (Vitz, 1966a, b). The same is true of preference for visual stimuli (e.g., Munsinger & Kessen, 1964; Smith & Dorfman, 1975).

Competence and Exploratory Behavior

Implicit in Dember and Earl's theory, as well as in many other theories of exploratory (e.g., Berlyne, 1960), is the idea that interacting with stimuli in the environment increases competency. Individuals can and do respond to more complex stimuli because they interact with stimuli as their competency is increasing. Some theorists, such as Berlyne (1960) viewed competency as ability to process information. That is not necessarily the only component, however. It is probably best to think of exploratory behavior as involving a multifaceted set of skills. One early theorist, Robert White (1959), suggested that exploratory behavior has its roots in the intrinsic need to deal with the environment. He argued that effective interactions with the environment are intrinsically rewarding, something he called "effectance motivation." His ideas of concerning effectance motivation are intended to capture the idea that competency is being developed while one is exploring the environment.

What Is the Motivation to Explore?

Motivation from an Evolutionary Perspective

From an evolutionary perspective, animals explore to help ensure their survival. To escape a predator they need to know escape routes, to eat they need to know food supplies, to reproduce they need to know the location of potential mates, and so forth. It is particularly important to respond to any change in the environment

because change can be a source of potential danger. Anything that is not known or is not expected must therefore be investigated. The motivation, therefore, is to know everything that might affect one's survival.

Some theorists have argued that the motivation is no longer tied directly to specific survival needs but, rather, has its roots in a more generalized drive, the need for self-determination, that emerged as an evolutionary adaptation. This need, as we will discuss more later, ensures that individuals will process important information and develop skills (competencies) that will help protect the individual in a wide range of domains (Ryan, Kuhl, & Deci, 1997). Most current theories assume that the generalized need to explore is not linked to any specific biological drive.

Motivation from a Psychological Perspective

The theories that we will be discussing in the remainder of this chapter conceptualize exploratory behavior as arising from a generalized adaptive drive. Dember and Earl (1957) suggested that the motivation for exploration had its roots in a curiosity drive. They suggested that curiosity is aroused by novelty and argue that novelty is in the eye of the beholder. We could have seen something many times before but, as the result of having new skills or competency, we discover new or different aspects of that object. This is very important for understanding why people will often return to explore things that they explored before or do things they have done before. In our daily lives, for example, we might decide to listen to a piece of music that we have listened to many times. By returning to that music with a new or fresh perspective, perhaps as a result of listening to other music, we find something new and interesting. One reason people can play a card game such as Bridge over and over is because no matter how many times you have played the game, it will be different in some way. Moreover, as their skills improve, people have new facets of the game to explore.

Like most of the models of exploratory behavior, the motivation within the Dember and Earl theory is best described as a positive feedback loop. As a result of developing competency, things in the environment are new or novel, which motivates the individual to interact with them. As a result of this interaction, new or novel things become familiar and other things become new or novel, which motivates me to interact with them. Thus, in a complex environment, the individual

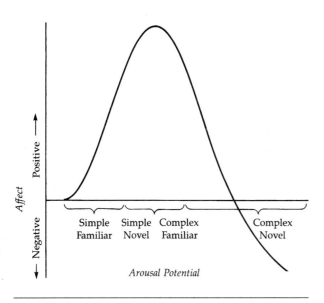

Figure 12-2. The relation between affect and the arousal potential of a stimulus, according to Berlyne's theory. Note that positive affect is greatest when a stimulus is moderately complex or moderately novel. (From "Novelty, Complexity and Hedonic Value," by D. E. Berlyne. *Perception and Psychophysics*, 1970, 283. Copyright © 1970 by the Psychonomic Society, Inc. Reprinted with permission.)

will systematically attend to all the various features of that environment.

Berlyne (1960) suggested that the basic mechanism underlying exploratory and play behaviors is the level of arousal. He proposed that the relation between arousal and hedonic tone can be described as an inverted U-shaped function, such that hedonic tone is greatest when arousal is moderate (Figure 12-2). He argued that either a very low level of stimulation or very complex stimulation produces low affect and that high complexity or novelty can even lead to negative affect. According to Berlyne's theory, organisms are motivated to seek out positive affect and avoid negative affect. Therefore, a person experiencing low arousal—in a situation that has low arousal potential—will seek out situations that will increase arousal, whereas a person experiencing high arousal—in a situation that has high arousal potential—will seek out situations that will lower arousal.

According to Berlyne, the tendency to process new information is governed by the ability of the new stimulus to elicit arousal. When we encounter a new stimulus that departs in some way from the standard, the discrepancy will elicit arousal. The greater the discrepancy, the greater the arousal. If the discrepancy is moderate, it will elicit moderate arousal, and because moderate arousal is pleasurable, the person will try to maintain contact with the stimulus. Because organisms are inclined to process the information contained in a stimulus, however, it is simply a matter of time before the essential features of the new stimulus have been abstracted. As a result, a novel stimulus becomes familiar, a surprising stimulus loses its ability to elicit surprise, and an incongruous stimulus becomes ordinary and predictable. Because organisms are motivated to maintain moderate arousal, they will be inclined to seek out new stimuli that depart from the standard to experience moderate arousal once again. In this way, the organism tends, over time, to learn more and more about different parts of its environment.

The Concept of Challenge

It should be noted that in recent years motivation theorists have come to conceptualize exploration as a person-environment interaction in which the environment (and getting to know it) provides a challenge to the individual. In response to that challenge, the individual develops a wide range of competencies. Play in children, for example, is often viewed as a way for the child to learn how to interact with other children (Buck, 1999). One doesn't have to look very long at a group of children to realize that some are much more adept than others are at getting along. We talk about this as acquiring social skills. Considerable research has shown that during play, a wide range of social skills more or less automatically emerge.

Anxiety and Exploratory Behavior

One important finding from the early research on exploration was that exploration decreases or stops altogether when the individual is anxious. Years ago we undertook a study that clearly illustrates this (Franken & Strain, 1974). In that study we used a large multiunit maze that permitted certain sections to be changed from white to black or black to white between

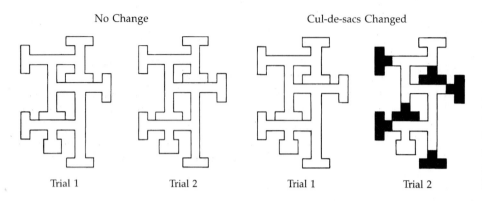

Figure 12-3. The maze used by Franken & Strain (1974) in studies of exploratory behavior, showing the changes between trials 1 and 2.

the two daily trials. Figure 12-3 shows the arrangement of the maze, together with the changes made between trials 1 and 2. If exploratory behavior is motivated by the tendency to seek out novelty, animals high in that tendency should select and respond to the changed parts of the maze. To determine whether this tendency might decrease when an animal is highly aroused, half of the animals (rats) were injected with methamphetamine between the two daily trials, and the other half were injected with saline solution (an inert substance).

A quick note about drugs such as methamphetamine: At low to moderate doses, drugs in the amphetamine family tend to increase arousal and produce positive affect. At moderate to high dose levels they tend to produce anxiety. We initially chose a relatively high dose level and found that our animals would never leave the start box. They would poke their noses out but quickly withdraw. We lowered the dose levels until we found a level where the animals would actually leave the start box and transverse the entire maze.

As expected, the animals injected with saline solution (low-arousal/anxiety animals) responded to the changes in the maze. These animals entered somewhat more cul-de-sacs on trial 2 than on trial 1 even when the cul-de-sacs were not changed. When they were changed, the animals entered many more of them. The results for the methamphetamine-injected (aroused/anxious) animals are almost opposite to those of the saline animals. When the cul-de-sacs were changed, the animals tended to avoid them. They entered fewer cul-de-sacs on trial 2 than on trial 1. These results (Figure 12-4) clearly show that arousal mediates the tendency to respond to novelty. In similar experiments, Berlyne has manipulated arousal/anxiety with drugs and has obtained results consistent with his theory (Berlyne, 1969; Berlyne, Koenig, & Hirota, 1966).

These results are consistent with other results that show that emotional animals explore less, but when they have been tamed their tendency to explore increases (Denenberg, 1967). These results are also consistent with research showing that securely attached infants explore more (Frodi, Bridges, & Grolnick, 1985). What this and other research clearly demonstrates is that exploratory behavior can be readily disrupted. If exploratory behavior has survival value, why is it so easily disrupted? Shouldn't it be highly resistant to anxiety? The answer to these questions lies in understanding that two distinct things are happening when the individual explores. A general system rewards individuals for approaching new or novel stimuli, and another system alerts individuals to potential dangers. It isn't that individuals have stopped exploring or processing information when they are aroused; rather, they have shifted their attention. Recall in Chapter 5 we talked about how arousal increases attention shifts to more survival-related cues when arousal increases.

The Biological Component

Some time ago, researchers found that children vary in their tendencies to approach novelty (Thomas, Chess, & Birch, 1970). Children with relatively stable temperaments are more receptive to new situations. Children who are less receptive to new experiences will eventu-

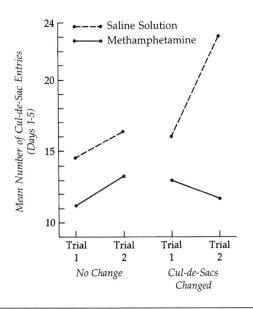

Figure 12-4. Number of cul-de-sacs entered by rats injected with methamphetamine and rats injected with saline solution when cul-de-sacs were changed in color between trials and when they were not. Methamphetamine reduced exploration (number of cul-de-sacs entered) as well as the tendency to approach the changed cul-de-sacs on the second trial. (Reproduced with permission of the publisher from "Effect of Increased Arousal on Response to Stimulus Change in a Complex Maze," by R. E. Franken and A. Strain, *Perceptual and Motor Skills*, 1974, *39*, 1076–1078. Copyright © 1974 Perceptual and Motor Skills.)

ally respond to these experiences, explore, and adapt to new situations, once they have become secure in their environment. As discussed in Chapter 5, Kagan and Snidman (1991) have been doing research on timidity for more than a decade. They have found that, although some children are inclined to approach unfamiliar (novel) people and objects, others are not. Kagan and Snidman made a distinction between what they call inhibited and uninhibited children. Their research indicates that these two temperaments are inherited.

Extraversion has also been linked to the tendency to select variety, novelty, and complexity. Researchers have repeatedly shown that extraversion is inherited,

at least to some degree, so these results are consistent with the idea that preference for variety has a biological basis.

Research from these and other sources suggests that the tendency to explore must be viewed within a hierarchical motive system. The motive to explore seems to be only fully aroused when fear and anxiety are at some minimal level (White, 1959). Researchers have suggested that, when anxiety and arousal are high, attention is focused on survival cues. Only when survival needs have been met do other motives become activated, and only then does attention shift elsewhere.

Note that virtually all the temperamental dispositions that have been linked to reduced curiosity and exploratory behavior in humans are characterized by higher than normal levels of anxiety or arousal. Thus, anxiety is probably responsible for the reduced tendency to explore.

Considerable evidence indicates that exploratory behavior has its roots in two complimentary systems, the behavioral activation system (BAS) and the behavioral inhibition system (BIS). The BAS system is activated by the reward systems together with arousal. The general consensus is that organisms are motivated to increase activity in this system. Among other things, as we have already seen, activation of this system produces positive affect. To keep this system active organisms seek out rewarding activities. They would, according to the theories of exploratory behavior, systematically respond to novelty or new challenges (Buck, 1999).

Among other things, the BIS acts as a "comparator," continually comparing actual with expected stimulation. As long as there is a match between actual and expected, the BIS remains in a checking mode. Under these conditions, behavior is controlled elsewhere. In the case of the flow experience, for example, behavior might be under the control of the right prefrontal cortex. If the comparator discovers that the actual and the expected do not match, the BIS is activated and behavior is inhibited. The subjective experience is a feeling of anxiety. Remember that the BIS is what Gray (1982) calls the stop, look, and listen system.

In exploratory behavior, these two systems work in concert. What propels the individual to begin exploring is the BAS; a system is activated by the novelty or challenge that is triggered by a stimulus or situation.

If the situation is new or novel, the BIS is also activated. As a result, you typically see a more cautious or timid approach by most animals in a new situation. After repeated exposures to the environment the timidity or cautiousness disappears. Should something new or novel be introduced, most animals become somewhat timid and cautious when they get near the thing changed or introduced.

What these two systems are doing as they work in concert is motivate individuals to explore while making them cautious. More anxious types are less inclined to explore, at least initially, because the BIS system is more active. Once timid children become familiar with a new environment, it is virtually impossible to distinguish them from less timid children— until you introduce something new again (Thomas, Chess, & Birch, 1970).

The Learned/Cognitive Component

Age and Preference for Complexity

Considerable evidence suggests that experience, or competency as we tend to call it now, plays a central role in the tendency to respond to variety, novelty, and complexity. In the early literature on novelty and complexity, experience or competency was typically described in information-processing terms. According to such a model, organisms become familiar with something by abstracting information. Those researchers assumed that information processing was more or less directly linked to attention. As we attend more closely to something, we process more of the information in that stimulus. The information-processing model, such as that proposed by Piaget (1970) and others, also assumes that we tend to develop more highly differentiated or complex cognitive structures as the result of processing information. In other words, as we grow older, we can process more complex cognitive stimuli. If humans are motivated to process new information and develop competency, it follows that older individuals will prefer more complex stimuli.

Experience, Competency, and Preference for Complexity

According to the information-processing hypothesis, if individuals are repeatedly exposed to a stimulus, they will lose interest in it because they will exhaust all the information that it contains. To test this hypothesis,

Smith and Dorfman (1975) divided their study participants into three groups, who were to be exposed to low, medium, and high levels of complexity. The individuals in each of these complexity groups were further divided into four subgroups, which were shown a stimulus, respectively, 1, 5, 10, and 20 times. According to the information-processing hypothesis, it would take very little time to extract all the new information contained in a stimulus of low complexity, and therefore individuals would quickly lose interest in such a stimulus with repeated exposures. Stimuli of medium complexity might require individuals to develop new cognitive structures, so such stimuli might not be preferred initially but would come to be preferred once the individuals had developed the cognitive structures necessary to process them. Having developed such structures, however, the individuals would then lose interest in those stimuli, just as they had lost interest in stimuli of low complexity. Because it would take even longer for individuals to develop the cognitive structures necessary to process the information contained in a stimulus of high complexity, it should take even more exposures before individuals come to prefer high-complexity stimuli. The results of this study (Figure 12-5) are consistent with the information-processing hypothesis.

Munsinger and Kessen (1964) argued that, because art students tend, on the average, to have had more experience with complex visual stimuli, they should already possess the cognitive structures to process complex visual stimuli and therefore they should, on the average, tend to prefer more complex visual stimuli. This is exactly what they found when they compared art students with nonart students.

Arkes and Boykin (1971) have further shown that children who participated in a Head Start program came to prefer more complex stimulation. There have been numerous demonstrations that animals also tend to select more complex stimulation after being exposed to moderate complexity. The fact that a variety of animals respond in the same way as humans do provides evidence for the generality of this phenomenon.

Intrinsic Motivation

In the 1970s, the term *intrinsic motivation* became widely used in place of *exploratory behavior*. Intrinsic motivation has been defined as "the inherent tendency

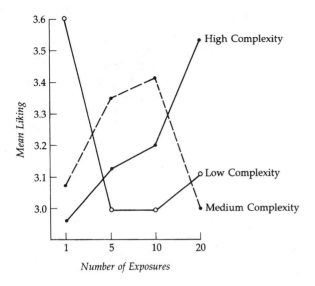

Figure 12-5. Mean preference ratings at three levels of stimulus complexity as a function of number of exposures to the stimulus. (From "The Effect of Stimulus Uncertainty and the Relationship between Frequency and Exposure and Liking," by G. F. Smith and D. D. Dorfman, *Journal of Personality and Social Psychology,* 1975, *31,* 150–155. Copyright © 1975 by the American Psychological Association. Reprinted with permission.)

to seek out novelty and challenge, to extend and exercise one's capacities, to explore and learn" (Ryan & Deci, 2000, p. 70). We are still talking about the person-environment interaction but in a more extended way. Words such as *challenge* and *capacities* have been introduced to better capture the idea that things such as exploratory behavior involve subjective evaluation of people's abilities relative to the tasks and situations facing them.

Self-Determination Theory

Two of the main theorists in this movement, (Deci, 1975; Deci & Ryan, 1985, 1991; Ryan & Deci, 2000), developed self-determination theory. Their goal was to develop a theory that incorporated personality into a theory of curiosity and exploratory behavior. Based on research findings, they argued that humans have three innate needs: competence, relatedness, and autonomy.

Two of these needs, competence and autonomy, form the basis for understanding intrinsic motivation. Like other theorists, Deci and Ryan argue that feelings of competence are central to the motivation to explore and respond to challenge. They argue, however, that before people can experience a sense of competency they must experience feelings of autonomy.

Autonomy is perhaps best understood in the context of what controls behavior. One reason we behave as we do is because something, learned or unlearned, influences or compels us to respond in certain ways. We might, for example, respond in a certain way because of rewards and praise or because we were raised with certain cultural traditions that were enforced in the formative years of our lives. In contrast, autonomy pertains to behavior that has arisen in the absence of such external controls or influences. This behavior is free of external controls. Using the language of locus of control theory, this means having an internal rather than an external frame of reference.

A wide range of both laboratory and field studies have provided support for the theory, especially autonomy. When autonomy is encouraged students show greater intrinsic motivation, curiosity, and drive for challenge (e.g., Deci, Nezlack, & Sheinman, 1981; Flink, Bogiano, & Barrett, 1990; Ryan & Grolnick, 1986). When control is emphasized initiative decreases, and students learn less effectively, especially when learning requires conceptual and creative processing (Amabile, 1996; Grolnick & Ryan, 1987; Utman, 1997).

The premise of self-determination theory is that humans are innately inclined to systematically respond to novelty and challenge and, in the process, to develop competency. Humans can self-regulate, which means, among other things, they can set goals, find paths to goals, and activate mental capacities that are important for meeting challenges (see Chapter 13). To better understand why people often fail to manifest intrinsic motivation, Deci and Ryan focused on the conditions that tend to undermine intrinsic motivation. Like some of the other theories of exploratory behavior that we have already discussed, Deci and Ryan view the tendency to explore, learn, and develop competency as having a certain fragile quality, something that is relatively easy to undermine. Within this context, Deci and Ryan have tried to identify what those conditions might be so that it will be possible to construct an environment that is conducive to promoting intrinsic motivation.

Although it is beyond the scope of this chapter to review all their findings, one area of particular interest is the research that pertains to what happens when you reward people for engaging in activities that have their roots in intrinsic motivation. This gets at the heart of what it means to have autonomy. The prediction that comes from reward theory is that the application of rewards should increase such behavior. In fact, it does just the opposite. In these studies participants were presented with an interesting task designed to arouse intrinsic motivation. One group was left to work without any external demands or suggestions, and another group was given a reward for their efforts (e.g., Deci, 1972; Deci & Ryan, 1985). The rewards used in these studies are typically a monetary reward or some other tangible reward, rather than praise. Invariably, when rewards are given, interest diminishes, and participants cease their involvement or interaction with the task they had been working on. A recent meta-analysis of 128 studies designed to study the effects of extrinsic reward on an intrinsically interesting task, found that reward had a detrimental effect (Deci, Koestner, & Ryan, 1999). One implication of such research is that if you reward intrinsically motivated individuals you will undermine their motivation. For people in business as well as education this is an important question.

Fortunately, there are ways to get around this problem. One is finding ways of giving people greater autonomy. Within the bounds of what needs to get done in business, for example, people can be given greater autonomy for what they do, how they do it, when they do it, and so forth. Another way of getting around this problem is to get people to identify with and internalize the goals of the company (make the company goals their own). Ryan and Deci (2000) have suggested that through the process of internalization people experience a greater sense of autonomy. Mission statements can help, as can giving people a share in the company through stock options. In the academic world, students need to be encouraged to internalize the value associated with fully understanding a topic. Remember that Ryan and Deci suggested there are three basic human needs, competence, relatedness, and autonomy. We have already talked about how competence and autonomy needs are expressed, so the question is how the relatedness need comes into the picture.

A sense of relatedness, they suggest, grows out of feelings of being connected or having a sense of belonging. To achieve such feelings, people internalize many of the important rules that govern cooperative behavior. Thus, the need to be related or belong provides the motivation for internalizing values such as being an important member in a group. Remember that the process of internalization can and often does give rise to feelings of autonomy. As Ryan and Deci point out, autonomy doesn't mean to be independent, detached, or selfish but, rather, to having feelings of volition that can accompany any act. When people become involved with a cause, such as the environment, they often work with people who share their concerns. Rather than feeling that the group controls them, they feel they are at the core of change. Remember that social motives such as relatedness have their roots in a sense of "shared fate."

Summary

Research with animals has indicated that the tendency to explore is motivated by novelty. In fact, it appears that animals are motivated by the opportunity to explore the visual, auditory, tactile, and olfactory properties of objects and that they will learn behaviors that allow them to experience the stimulation that comes from interacting with various objects. Like animals, humans are motivated by the variety and novelty of objects we encounter. Considerable evidence indicates that animals and humans are motivated by the complexity of objects. Researchers have shown that children tend to select increasingly complex objects. Apparently, as children's ability to handle more complex forms of stimulation increases, they have a natural preference for more complex stimuli. Dember and Earl argue that organisms are motivated to seek a level of complexity slightly above their current level. According to Dember and Earl, only a certain range of stimuli (the pacer range) will be acceptable. Berlyne has suggested that the mechanism underlying exploratory and play behaviors is arousal. When arousal is low, organisms are motivated to increase arousal by interacting with novel stimuli in their environment; stimuli that can provide optimal arousal will become the objects of attention. According to Berlyne's theory, attention to an object is sufficient to produce information processing. Once all the information has been processed, the individual will be inclined to seek out new stimuli.

The tendency to explore is often markedly reduced when organisms are anxious. Research with humans suggests that some individuals have a temperamental disposition, often characterized by anxiety, that markedly reduces their tendency to explore. The tendency to explore appears to be the result of the BAS and the BIS working in concert. Anything that activates the BIS results in a marked reduction or the cessation of exploratory behavior. Considerable evidence indicates that the tendency to explore novel and complex stimuli increases as a result of exposure to certain kinds of stimuli, emphasizing the role the competency plays in exploratory behavior.

Because individuals often differ in arousal and anxiety, there are also great differences in their tendency to explore. Teachers and parents might be able to increase children's tendency to explore by creating an environment that is relaxed and free of anxiety.

According to self-determination theory, humans need competence, autonomy, and relatedness. When people experience feelings of autonomy, they are inclined to engage in intrinsically motivated behavior; that is, to seek out novelty and challenge, to extend and exercise capacities, and to explore and learn. When such things as extrinsic rewards undermine feelings of autonomy, intrinsic motivation tends to decrease or cease altogether. To increase intrinsic motivation, people should be given more control over their efforts and be encouraged to internalize the values of the group.

Sensation Seeking (Thrill Seeking)

According to Berlyne's (1960) model, humans are strongly motivated to process information in the environment to maintain optimal arousal. If stimulation falls below some optimal level, the individual will experience negative affect. To explore the role of stimulation, various researchers have studied the effects of depriving people of all stimulation. As a graduate student, Marvin Zuckerman (1979) conducted various studies on sensory deprivation that required volunteers to stay for an extended period under conditions of minimal stimulation. He noticed that the people who volunteered for his experiments had certain common characteristics: They were very curious, liked to have new experiences, and were willing to take certain risks to have those experiences. Most of them had volunteered for his experiments because that was something they had never done before. He wondered if these people represented a personality type that could be measured. After talking with them, he created a questionnaire called the Sensation Seeking Scale (SSS). People who score high on this scale are typically referred to as high sensation seekers, whereas those who score low are referred to as low sensation seekers or sensation avoiders. To find out if you are a high, medium, or low sensation seeker, take the test in Practical Application 12-1.

According to Zuckerman (1979), sensation seeking "is a trait defined by the need for varied, novel and complex sensations and experiences and the willingness to take physical and social risks for the sake of such experiences" (p. 10). Note that one of the key elements of sensation seeking is the willingness to take risks. Work on exploratory behavior suggests that organisms tend to avoid exploration (the search for new sensations and new experiences) when it entails risks. Risks are thought to arouse anxiety, which is incompatible with exploratory behavior. Several theories of exploratory behavior assume that anxiety produces high levels of arousal. If organisms explore to increase arousal, it makes sense that organisms experiencing fear will not explore because they are already at an optimal level of arousal. Alternatively, researchers have suggested that high arousal tends to shift attention to more survival-related cues, which is incompatible with exploratory behavior. It is interesting, therefore, that Zuckerman has been able to identify people who are willing to take risks to explore.

Zuckerman's SSS is based on four related but independent factors that were derived through factor analytic procedures. These factors denote slightly different aspects of sensation seeking.

1. **Thrill and adventure seeking.** Some people are inclined to seek excitement through risky but socially acceptable activities such as parachuting or driving fast, even if they haven't engaged in such activities.
2. **Experience seeking.** Some people desire to seek sensation by engaging in activities outside a conventional lifestyle. They might travel, seek out

unusual friends, engage in artistic endeavors, experiment with drugs, and in general lead less conventional lives.

3. **Disinhibition.** Those who choose to follow a conventional lifestyle might periodically escape by engaging in social drinking or gambling or by pursuing a variety of sexual partners. They drink to free themselves from the social inhibitions that are part of their conventional lifestyles.

4. **Boredom susceptibility.** Some people have a much lower tolerance for repetition and sameness. They tend to seek out stimulation and change to escape the monotony of everyday life. These people are inclined to engage in sensation-seeking activities.

The Biological Component

Monoamine Oxidase and Sensation Seeking

What is the origin of the sensation-seeking trait? Researchers have shown that sensation seeking as well as impulsiveness is negatively correlated with monoamine oxidase (MAO) levels (Zuckerman, 1979, 1993, 2000). That is, levels of MAO are low in high sensation seekers and high in low sensation seekers. MAO is an enzyme that is important in the regulation—and therefore the ultimate availability—of amine neurotransmitters such as norepinephrine, dopamine, and serotonin. When the MAO level is high, little of the amine neurotransmitters are available; however, when the MAO level is low, considerable amine neurotransmitters are available (Buck, 1999). The level of amines in the brain is linked to whether or not the reward centers of the brain can be activated (BAS system). Because sensation seekers are characterized by low MAO levels, their levels of norepinephrine tend to be high; and the brain's reward centers are available for activation. That means that high sensation seekers are likely to experience greater pleasure, or greater reward, when they take drugs such as cocaine, which stimulate the reward centers. As a result, high sensation seekers are likely to use drugs again. Conversely, because of their different brain chemistry, low sensation seekers do not experience the same level of reward when they use those drugs and therefore are less likely to use them again.

Practical Application 12-1

Are You a High or a Low Sensation Seeker?

To test your own sensation-seeking tendencies, try this shortened version of one of Marvin Zuckerman's earlier scales. For each of the 13 items, circle the choice, A or B, that best describes your likes or dislikes or the way you feel. Instructions for scoring appear at the end of the test.

1. A. I would like a job that requires a lot of traveling.
   B. I would prefer a job in one location.
2. A. I am invigorated by a brisk, cold day.
   B. I can't wait to get indoors on a cold day.
3. A. I get bored seeing the same old faces.
   B. I like the comfortable familiarity of everyday friends.
4. A. I would prefer living in an ideal society in which everyone is safe, secure, and happy.
   B. I would prefer living in the unsettled days of our history.

5. A. Sometimes I like to do things that are a little frightening.
   B. A sensible person avoids activities that are dangerous.
6. A. I would not like to be hypnotized.
   B. I would like to have the experience of being hypnotized.
7. A. The most important goal of life is to live it to the fullest and experience as much as possible.
   B. The most important goal in life is to find peace and happiness.
8. A. I would like to try parachute-jumping.
   B. I would never want to try jumping out of a plane, with or without a parachute.
9. A. I enter cold water gradually, giving myself time to get used to it.
   B. I like to dive or jump right into the ocean or a cold pool.

There seems to be general agreement that the amine neurotransmitter serotonin is directly linked to impulsiveness (Buck, 1999). Thus, when we talk about sensation seeking we are often talking about someone who is more inclined to be impulsive—a word that we sometimes use in connection with the idea of becoming disinhibited.

The Heritability of Sensation Seeking

Where do these differences in MAO level come from? Zuckerman (1979, 1983, 2000) has argued that they are inherited. Twin studies have indeed supported the hypothesis that the monoamine level has a genetic component. Research indicates that 60% of the sensation seeking trait can be attributed to genetics. Frank Farley (1986) has pointed out, however, that sensation seeking has also been linked to testosterone level. Whatever the exact mechanism, he also endorses the hypothesis that sensation seeking is inherited.

Animal research has shown that exploratory behavior is inherited. Exploratory behavior has been linked to the need for variety and change, so such data provide converging evidence that the sensation-seeking need, or the need to experience novelty and change, may indeed be inherited.

Gender and Age Differences

For reasons that are not altogether clear, levels of sensation seeking tend to be higher in men than in women. It has also been found that the sensation-seeking trait tends to diminish with age. Although biological factors may be at work here, these findings could also be because one of the scales used to measure sensation seeking contains a large number of sports interest items.

The Learned/Cognitive Component

Although the disposition for sensation seeking has a biological basis, learning and cognition must play an essential role in its development and expression.

Research indicates that when they administer punishment, fathers do not suppress their children's

---

10. A. When I go on a vacation, I prefer the comfort of a good room and bed.
    B. When I go on a vacation, I prefer the change of camping out.
11. A. I prefer people who are emotionally expressive even if they are a bit unstable.
    B. I prefer people who are calm and even-tempered.
12. A. A good painting should shock or jolt the senses.
    B. A good painting should give one a feeling of peace and security.
13. A. People who ride motorcycles must have some kind of unconscious need to hurt themselves.
    B. I would like to drive or ride a motorcycle.

Scoring. Count one point for each of the following items that you have circled: 1A, 2A, 3A, 4B, 5A, 6B, 7A, 8A, 9B, 10B, 11A, 12A, 13B. Add up your total and compare it with the following norms.

0–3	Very low on sensation seeking
4–5	Low
6–9	Average
10–11	High
12–13	Very high

Although the test gives some indication of a person's rating, it is not a highly reliable measure. One reason, of course, is that the test has been abbreviated. Another is that the norms are based largely on the scores of college students who have taken the test. As people get older, their scores on sensation seeking tend to go down.

(From "The Search for High Sensation," by M. Zuckerman, *Psychology Today*, February, 1978, *11*(9), 38–46. Copyright © 1978 by the American Psychological Association. Reprinted with permission.)

sensation-seeking motives (Zuckerman, 1994), although they might play a key role in giving direction to motives. Peers play an important role in nurturing the motive and in giving direction to it (Farley, 1986; Zuckerman, 1994). In a more delinquent peer group, motives might be expressed in behaviors such as drug taking and law breaking. In a more conventional peer group, by contrast, motives might be expressed in behaviors such as risky sports or even the arts.

The sensation-seeking motive can be satisfied in a variety of ways. High sensation seekers tend to be more unconventional and rebellious than low sensation seekers are, so their behaviors might appear foolish and even stupid to others. Let's briefly review some of the ways in which the sensation-seeking motive is satisfied.

Sports

Sensation seekers tend to get involved in sports, especially those regarded as risky. They climb mountains, hang glide, scuba dive, and go downhill skiing, for example. However, there is no evidence that they are attracted to danger for its own sake. It appears, rather, that sensation seekers do not let risk stand in the way of new experiences. Rowland, Franken, and Harrison (1986) found that high sensation seekers more quickly get bored with a given sport and try something new. Over time, then, they tend to participate in more sports than do low sensation seekers. Sooner or later, high sensation seekers are likely to try high-risk activities. High sensation seekers are not put off by risk, so it is not surprising that more high than low sensation seekers tend to get involved in risky sports.

Experience Seeking

Sensation seekers satisfy their need for new experiences in many ways—by traveling, making new friends, and becoming involved in new activities, for example (Zuckerman, 1994). They value variety. For instance, they are inclined to have a broad set of friends with diverse views about the world. Sensation seekers are also inclined to become involved in artistic activities. They seek out music that is new and different and take pleasure in poetry and humor (Zuckerman, 1994). High sensation seekers tend to be open to all new forms of artistic endeavor.

Drug Use, Sexual Behavior, and Uninhibited Behaviors

Abundant evidence indicates that sensation seekers tend to use alcohol, marijuana, and cocaine (e.g., Huba, Newcomb, & Bentler, 1981). As we have seen, this has been attributed to their biological constitution—specifically, their brain chemistry. Research also shows that sensation seekers like to have sex frequently and with a variety of partners (Zuckerman, 1979). Finally, a great deal of evidence indicates that sensation seekers like parties, especially parties characterized by uninhibited behavior. Parties provide a wealth of sensory stimulation. They typically include food (olfactory and gustatory stimulation), music (auditory stimulation), dancing (tactile and kinesthetic stimulation, arousal), conversation (social stimulation, arousal), sexual stimuli, and alcohol or other drugs.

Openness, Unconventionality, and Undependability

Someone who is open to new experiences might also be less constrained by conventions—by what other people think or say. Further, if one is open and drawn to new experiences, it follows that he or she might be quite willing to break previous commitments. Indeed, this is what research shows (Franken, 1987). Thus, the undependable nature of sensation seekers seems to have its roots in a persistent need to have new and different experiences.

Researchers have noted that sensation seeking can lead to delinquency, on the one hand, and creativity, on the other (Farley, 1986). The direction people take seems to be molded by a variety of factors, nonetheless, delinquent and creative people share a common motive, an openness to new ways of doing and seeing things, a disdain for convention and tradition, and a lack of commitment to the ways other people think and act.

Thinking Styles and Creativity

Creative people are able to view things in new ways or from a different perspective and to generate new possibilities or alternatives. Tests of creativity measure the number of alternatives that people can generate and the uniqueness of those alternatives. The ability to generate new alternatives or to see in new ways is linked to other, more fundamental qualities of thinking, such as flexibility, tolerance of ambiguity or unpredictability, and the enjoyment of novelty. Sensation seekers have all of these qualities (Farley, 1986; Franken, 1987).

Decision-Making Styles and Sensation Seeking

Peters and Waterman (1982) have studied the planning and decision-making styles of the top executives of the best-run companies in the United States. They point out that these executives like to make decisions, like to make them quickly, can make them without having complete information, and are willing to abandon plans that are not working. In short, the executives have the capacity to stay on the cutting edge of their fields by following their hunches. These characteristics are also typical of sensation seekers (Franken, 1988). Sensation seekers' personality styles make them adept at working in environments where change is a way of life.

Sensation Seeking and Commitment

Sensation seekers cannot afford to become committed to any one activity because they need to be able to explore any new and more interesting opportunities that come along. To ensure that they can take advantage of change, they need to be vigilant about keeping their options open. One study found clear evidence consistent with this hypothesis. Among other things, sensation seekers are inclined to make decisions at the last minute; make only short-term commitments; do not feel guilty when they break commitments because something more interesting came up; do not make plans but rather let things happen; and do not carefully consider the consequences before they act (Franken, 1993). Sensation seekers even indicate that keeping their options open is more important than being viewed as dependable.

Although sensation seekers are inclined to self-disclose (a quality that has been linked to intimacy), they are not inclined to commit themselves to long-term relationships (Franken, Gibson, & Mohan, 1990). Although evidence suggests that high sensation seekers are inclined to marry high sensation seekers and that low sensation seekers are inclined to marry low sensation seekers, researchers have found that sensation seeking has more of a negative impact on marital satisfaction in high-sensation-seeking women (Gibson, Franken, & Rowland, 1989). One explanation is that high-sensation-seeking women experience more pressure to conform to the traditional wife role in a marital relationship than high-sensation-seeking men experience to conform to the traditional husband role. As a result, high-sensation-seeking women would experience less satisfaction with marriage than high-sensation-seeking men would.

Summary

Sensation seeking "is a trait defined by the need for varied novel and complex sensations and experiences and the willingness to take physical and social risks for the sake of such experiences" (Zuckerman, 1979, p. 10). High sensation seekers tend to be open and unconventional people. This trait can lead to creativity or, if it is not properly channeled, to delinquency.

Twin studies provide considerable evidence that the sensation-seeking trait is inherited. Zuckerman has argued that sensation seeking is governed by MAO levels. High sensation seekers have low monoamine oxidase levels, whereas low sensation seekers have high monoamine oxidase levels. Farley has suggested that testosterone also plays an important role in motivating sensation seeking. Consistent with this interpretation is the finding that men score higher than women do on Zuckerman's Sensation Seeking Scale. The sensation-seeking trait, as measured by Zuckerman's scale, has been shown to decline with age. Factor analytic studies have identified four distinct factors that characterize the sensation-seeking motive: thrill and adventure seeking, experience seeking, disinhibition, and boredom susceptibility.

High sensation seekers are inclined to get involved in a variety of high-risk sports activities, apparently because of their interest in new experiences rather than because of any attraction to risk itself. High sensation seekers also tend to use drugs, have a variety of sex partners, and seek out situations—such as parties—where they can behave in an uninhibited manner.

High sensation seekers like to make decisions, like to make them quickly, and are willing to make them with incomplete information. In addition, they are willing to abandon plans that are not working. High sensation seekers tend to keep their options open. Among other things, they are unwilling to make long-term commitments. Sensation seekers are inclined to self-disclose, but they are not inclined to commit to long-term relationships.

Creativity

Creativity is closely linked to curiosity and exploratory behavior. It is also closely linked to sensation seeking—the desire to do new and different things.

Why are people motivated to engage in creative acts? There are at least three reasons.

1. **The need for novel, varied, and complex stimulation.** One way to meet this need is to create or find new things that will stimulate our senses (for instance, new recipes, new art, or new cars) or challenge our intellects (for instance, books, computers, or movies). Berlyne (1960) has attributed the creation or appreciation of beauty to this need.

2. **The need to communicate ideas and values.** Concerned that children are dying of starvation, a photographer triggers our compassion with a picture of an emaciated child. A politician wanting to make a difference writes a book to challenge our beliefs and stimulate us to action.

3. **The need to solve problems.** As we encounter new diseases or our business begins to fail, we search for answers that can give us hope.

Definition. A great deal of controversy surrounds the definition of creativity (Mumford & Gustafson, 1988). Some writers have argued that creativity should be defined by problem-solving ability (Cattell, 1971; Klahr & Simon, 1999). By that definition, some of the world's most famous paintings or novels might not be viewed as creative products. Other writers have suggested that it is a personality trait (MacKinnon, 1962). Such a definition suggests that some people are creative and others are not. Some writers have suggested a definition based on the production of ideas (Guilford, 1967), which would exclude people who, although not good at producing ideas themselves, can recognize a creative idea or product when they encounter it. Other writers have suggested that the definition should include the recognition of ideas (Tyler, 1978). In that case, a movie producer or publisher who makes truly creative products available to the public also plays a creative role.

Artists constantly strive to find new ways of expressing an idea or emotion.

All these various definitions offer useful ways of thinking about creativity. For our purposes, creativity is defined as the tendency to generate or recognize ideas, alternatives, or possibilities that can be useful in solving problems, communicating with others, and entertaining ourselves and others. Our focus in this section is to better understand the role that motivation plays, compared with such things as intelligence.

The Biological Component

Researchers have suggested that creativity is linked to an active right prefrontal cortex. The right prefrontal cortex allows us to manipulate images as well as see things as a whole (Dozier, 1998). This ability to manipulate images allows us to appreciate such things as the ordering of events and the formation of objects and to recombine things in new and different ways. Even at an early age children take delight in putting one animal's head on the another's body or putting the feet of one animal on another. Children will often draw things to explore what happens when they combine things in new and different ways rather than to represent reality.

Creativity has also been linked to positive affect. It has been suggested that the positive affect is caused by elevated dopmaine levels and that the elevated dopamine levels of the cingulate gyrus increase cognitive flexibility and facilitate the selection of different cognitive perspectives that result in people seeing things in different ways (Ashby, Isen, & Turken, 1999).

Creativity is often viewed as a playful activity in which we allow ourselves to reorder or recombine things in new and different ways. Researchers who have studied creativity often point out that creative people tend to act in similar ways to children. Creative people seem to have a sense of disinhibition (Klahr & Simon, 1999). Many writers have stressed that what prevents many of us from such acts of playfulness is the natural tendency to combine things in the way we have learned they are combined (DeBono, 1970, 1987). People who have studied creativity and documented the mental processes used in creativity have concluded that creativity is a mental phenomenon that results from ordinary cognitive processes (Smith, Ward, & Finke, 1995; Ward, Smith, & Vaid, 1997). Nonetheless, evidence demonstrates that certain intellectual and dispositional traits are inherited (Bouchard, 1994; Eysenck, 1995).

Taken together, the existing research suggests that one of the main factors in creativity is motivation, so therefore, creativity is open to anyone who is willing to develop the resources that are important for creativity to occur. Creativity is often viewed as a flow experience; it is an experience that brings joy and happiness (Csikszentmihalyi, 1997). As such, creativity appears to have its roots in the BAS. As we will see, we have good reason to argue that one thing that gets in the way of creativity is an active BIS when people feel anxious and threatened. In that sense, creativity is very similar to exploratory and play behavior. It is difficult to be creative (to be interested in what is new or novel) when your survival is threatened.

Intelligence and Creativity

Early research using standard IQ tests indicated individuals need to have a certain level of intelligence to manifest creativity, but beyond that level there is no correlation between intelligence and creative behavior (Barron & Harrington, 1981). In recent years several writers have argued that there are multiple intelligences. According to Gardner (1993), people differ with respect to such things as musical, bodily-kinesthetic, interpersonal, and intrapersonal intelligences. Further, he argues that each intelligence is associated with a specific manifestation of creativity such as painting, choreography, or psychology.

Personality and Creativity

For some time, researchers have argued that a dispositional personality style leads to greater creativity. Over the years, numerous researchers have conducted studies in an effort to identify this style (e.g., Martindale, 1989; Simonton, 2000). The research indicates that the creative people are disposed to be independent, nonconformist, unconventional, and even bohemian in their ways. Further, they are characterized by wide interests, greater openness to new experiences, conspicuous behavioral and cognitive flexibility, and the tendency to take more risks (Simonton, 2000). Finally, one study found that in addition to being more open to experience, creative individuals, as compared with controls, were more neurotic (Gelade, 1997).

Zuckerman's (1979) finding that people high in the sensation-seeking motive tend to be more creative than do people low in this motive suggests that creativity helps sensation seekers to satisfy their need for variety and change. When you look at the overlap between sensation seeking and creativity, it is clear that the two have their roots in some of the same underlying systems.

The Learned/Cognitive Component

The Tyranny of Old Habits

Edward DeBono (e.g., 1970, 1987) has written extensively about creativity and has taken the position that the brain evolved to isolate predictability and consistency. As organisms explore their environments, they link together various elements of a stimulus. This enables them to form an image of the stimulus at some later time, even though they might have seen only one element. For example, a rabbit needs to see only the head of a dog and not the whole body before it engages in flight. Obviously, this is highly adaptive.

The problem, DeBono argues, is that, if we view elements only as parts of something larger, it is difficult for us to combine them in new and different ways. How, then, do people learn to recombine elements? DeBono has devoted much of his life to designing exercises that help people to do this.

Ellen Langer (1989) has used a similar line of reasoning to account for lack of creativity. She argues that many of our behaviors become habitual, automatic, and unconscious. As a result, we behave in a mindless (thoughtless) rather than a mindful (thoughtful) way. Like DeBono, she acknowledges that it is highly adaptive for us to perform routine tasks without actively thinking about them. Among other things, it frees our brain to focus on other things. The downside to having well-ingrained habits, however, is that they may come to control our behavior. As our environment changes, we continue to engage in the same responses, even though they are no longer adaptive. To break out of our routine behavior patterns, we need to become mindful, but how do we do that? Langer suggests that the first step is to become aware that we have the choice to behave differently. The next step is to become aware of what our alternatives are. That involves generating alternatives based on our assessment of the situation.

Langer believes that people can become mindful at will. This parallels DeBono's conviction that people can learn to become creative. To do so, they need motivation and also a set of techniques for generating new possibilities. For Langer, that means learning to make new distinctions and create new categories. For DeBono, it means learning to recombine elements in new ways or to see them from a different perspective.

Creativity as Disinhibition

Convention and tradition. Researchers have suggested that people often have a tendency to act creatively but inhibit such tendencies for fear of rejection by society (Franken, 1990). Such people might be motivated more by the need to be accepted or to belong than by a need to experience variety and change. As a result, they become conventional and traditional in their views. Instead of questioning the values of society, as more creative people do, they go along. Research on creativity suggests that, to be creative, we need to be able to let go of conventional perspectives (Strickland, 1989)—in other words, to become disinhibited. We need to feel free to recombine things in new and different ways, even if those combinations seem silly or even wrong.

Rigidity. Many people are afraid of change or motivated to avoid it. They might be anxious, fearful, or highly aroused. To manage those feelings, they look for consistency and predictability in their environments. People who are chronically anxious or aroused often develop a behavior pattern characterized by excessive rigidity. To become creative, these people need to throw off their rigidity, although that will not be easy for them (e.g., Berlyne, 1960).

Rigidity can also occur simply because we have allowed ourselves to become creatures of habit, as Langer (1989) pointed out. Of course, being rigid is inconsistent with creativity.

Psychological Climate and Creativity

Researchers have shown that otherwise uncreative people will suddenly demonstrate creativity in certain conditions (Mumford & Gustafson, 1988). For example, if people know that creativity is expected, they will perform better on divergent-thinking measures of creativity (Harrington, 1981; Torrence, 1965). In tests of divergent thinking, people are typically presented with a question or stimulus and asked to generate as many ideas and associations as possible, without reflecting on the usefulness or practicality of their responses. They might be asked, for example, to think of things to do with a piece of chalk. Their divergent-thinking score increases with the number of ideas that they generate. Sometimes people are given a higher score if they generate more unusual ideas—throwing the chalk to get someone's attention, rather than using it to write, for instance.

Studies indicate that scientific productivity is enhanced when the organizational climate provides physical support for creative efforts and encourages independent action—that is, when a company is committed to creativity and innovation, rewards creative people, and attempts to provide whatever might assist people to become more creative (Andrews, 1975; Taylor, 1972). These data are consistent with that finding that support and recognition of creative effort, particularly in the early stages of a project, lead to innovation (e.g., Lind & Mumford, 1987). A wealth of research suggests that removing inhibitions on the expression of creativity—such as undue reliance on custom and tradition—and rewarding creativity can unleash creativity in virtually anyone. Again, it appears that creativity is actively inhibited in certain environments.

Some evidence indicates that people tend to be more creative when affect is positive. It appears that positive affect facilitates cognitive organization—specifically, it increases our tendency to combine things in new ways and to see relatedness among divergent stimuli (Isen, Daubman, & Nowicki, 1987).

Adverse Psychological Climate and Creativity

Research findings indicate individuals faced with adversity, or who are faced with the need to deal with new people, can turn out to be more creative (Simonton, 2000). This research points out two things. First, when people are forced to deal with new situations—something that has been referred to as diversifying experiences—they are forced to break down old ways of thinking and acting. No longer constrained by past socialization, they can think in new ways. Second, people often learn, especially when faced with adversity, the importance of persevering (Simonton, 2000). When a person is faced with not getting a job, for example, but eventually succeeds, he or she learns that it pays to keep trying.

Rewards and Creativity

As we discussed earlier, several researchers have suggested that extrinsic rewards inhibit the development of intrinsic motivation. Accordingly, it has also been suggested that extrinsic rewards inhibit creativity. Eisenberger and Cameron (1996) argue that this idea is largely a myth. When people are rewarded repeatedly for high creativity in one task, creativity in a subsequent task is enhanced (Eisenberger & Selbst, 1994). It appears that rewards only reduce creativity in a subsequent task if people are repeatedly rewarded for low creativity. Eisenberger and Cameron (1996) argue that, under these conditions, people are essentially being rewarded for being lazy or uncreative. The key to promoting creativity is to make rewards contingent on high creative output.

Critics of Eisenberg and Cameron have pointed out that it is erroneous and misleading to suggest that the detrimental effects of rewards only occur under limited conditions. Although these critics agree it is possible to train people not to respond to rewards, they point out that rewards generally undermine creativity (Hennessey & Amabile, 1998), probably for the reasons pointed out by Ryan and Deci.

Self-Image and Creativity

Barron and Harrington (1981) have linked creativity to various personality traits including a creative self-image. How might a creative self-image lead to greater creativity? Consider the following possibility. If I value creativity, I might learn to become more tolerant of ambiguity in my life or I might become more inclined to keep an open mind because I have learned that these are key elements of the creative process. Similarly, to be more creative, I might learn to see myself as autonomous, independent, and creative. To buffer myself or to make myself less sensitive to criticism, I might adopt a more unconventional attitude or even begin to question tradition. Because creativity demands that I become highly involved with my materials, I might develop an achievement orientation. According to this interpretation, the traits that characterize creative individuals emerge over time because of individuals' desires to maximize their creativity.

According to this model of creativity, two interdependent and opposing forces are at work: the reward that comes from acting creatively and the punishment that acting creatively sometimes brings. Teenagers are often acutely aware of the punishment (criticism) that comes when they dress differently or when they invent a new vocabulary to communicate their experiences. Similarly, academics are acutely aware of the punishment (criticism) that they could experience when they attempt to put forth a new theory (e.g., Seligman, 1990). To become truly creative and enjoy the rewards that come with creativity, individuals need to learn how to reduce the punishment (criticism) they often experience. They do this by attaching less importance to others' opinions. An unconventional attitude will also help buffer them from criticism.

Early Experiences and Creativity

The work on early experiences suggests that learning plays an important role in developing the kind of personality that makes people more prone to be creative as adults. First, researchers have shown that the intellectual values that characterize creative individuals seem to come from their families. Families that foster intellectual development tend to produce more creative individuals (Mumford & Gustafson, 1988). Second, the autonomy and independence that characterize creative individuals also come from their early upbringing. Researchers have shown, for example, that scientists who are more creative were subjected to less structure and less discipline (Stein, 1968), that their parents were less controlling and more likely to encourage openness to experience (Getzels & Jackson, 1962), and that the family environment gave them a firm sense of self as a creative entity (Trollinger, 1979). This research is consistent with the idea that creativity is largely learned.

Later Experiences and Creativity

Considerable evidence indicates that creativity is often fostered later in life through mentors and teachers. This research suggests that, at least in the sciences, what teachers and mentors do is to help novices internalize exacting professional standards along with a sense of excellence, achievement, and self-confidence (Zuckerman, 1974). The themes of excellence, achievement, and self-confidence run through much of the research on later influences. Mentors seem to teach—often through their example—the conditions that are necessary for creativity to emerge.

Birth Order and Creativity

In a fascinating book on birth order and family dynamics, Sulloway (1996) provides considerable evidence that later-borns are more creative than first-borns are. He sets forth the proposition that, because first-borns tend to be the initial recipients of parents' attention, they are highly motivated to preserve their special position when other siblings come into the family. They do this by complying with the wishes of the parents and carrying on the traditions of the family. In short, they try to maintain the status quo. Later-borns, he argues, feel excluded from the position of privilege occupied by the first-born and, as a result, are inclined to rebel against the repressive power of the first-born sib-lings and devise strategies that will provide them with recognition and privilege. Thus, the later-borns nurture their creative abilities and their tendency to rebel against conventions and traditions. This is consistent with Sulloway's finding that later-borns tend to be characterized by openness to experience, a personality trait associated with being unconventional, adventurous, and rebellious. Sulloway argues, in essence, that openness is an acquired personality trait that grows out of the perception of being treated as a downtrodden underdog.

He offers some interesting historical information in support of his theory. For example, later-borns were 9.7 times more likely than first-borns were to endorse the theory of evolution before the publication of Darwin's books. During the Reformation, later-borns were 46 times more likely to be burned at the stake than first-borns were. Left-wing revolutionaries are 18 times more likely than are right-wing revolutionaries to be later-borns.

The Process of Creativity

In this section, we will see that it is possible to increase creativity. By understanding the conditions that lead to greater creativity, we can learn how to motivate people to become more creative.

Let's look at some of the important components of creativity: delineating the problem, knowledge, the ability to construct images or categories, the ability to synthesize, and the willingness to withhold judgment.

Delineating the problem. Delineating or defining the problem gives direction to our thinking. When we know the problem, we can immediately recognize which of the various patterns that our brain generates are potentially important or useful. Movie producers, publishers, and CEOs of large companies often depend on others for the solutions they require. Unless they know what the problem is, they are unable to determine which of the solutions that are constantly being offered to them are worth considering. Generally spending time to define the problem speeds up the subsequent creative process. By delineating and defining, we tell the brain what is and is not important. Obviously, the brain can arrive at a solution more quickly when it has less to deal with.

The process of creativity typically involves the application of existing knowledge to a carefully delineated problem.

Knowledge. To generate new alternatives or new ideas, we need a well-developed information or knowledge base. Ideas do not arise spontaneously; they are typically the result of synthesizing information (Langley, Simon, Bradshaw, & Zytkow, 1986). Accordingly, creativity is moderately related to intelligence because we need a certain basic level of intelligence to acquire a knowledge base. Given that basic level of intelligence, what differentiates those who are creative from those who are not is their motivation to gather that information or acquire the knowledge base they need.

Recently, there has been a trend to teach creativity without providing the necessary knowledge base. People will encourage children to write creative stories or will hire a facilitator to help them solve problems. However, it is a misconception that creativity is independent of knowledge. If there is no depth to our knowledge, our creativity will blossom and then die, just as a flower will die without soil to nourish it.

New ideas are frequently the elaboration, extension, or new application of an existing idea. For example, Steve Jobs and Steve Wozniak, the co-inventors of the Apple Computer, used ideas and technology from a variety of sources to create the first personal computer (Young, 1988). Jazz composer Dave Brubeck used basic themes from Chopin and Japanese music to create some of his most successful songs (Calgary, 1997). If creativity is the extension of existing ideas, it makes a great deal of sense to go out and systematically research what has been done before. That knowledge base could well provide the ingredients to create something new and different. To invent a commercial light bulb, Thomas Edison brought together a group of engineers who systematically tested a variety of ideas and principles. The greatest ideas in the world typically come from people who are best educated. It is no coincidence that the United States, with some of the best universities in the world, has produced proportionally more Nobel prizes than any other country has (*Business Week, Special Issue,* 1989). To compete with the United States, Japan has adopted a principle of making endless small improvements, a principle that has been adopted by many industrialized countries throughout the world (*Business Week, Special Issue,* 1989).

Constructing images and categories. Pieces of information can be regarded as involving groups of patterns or components. Thinking about the sky, for example, fires a group of cells that correspond to the sensory experience I get when I look at the sky. I can also ask my brain to activate several memories or patterns simultaneously and thereby create a new image. For example, I can superimpose some clouds, perhaps add an airplane, and even insert the funnel of a tornado into my image of the sky. In each step, my image of the sky abruptly changes. I can also create images that no one has seen by combining patterns. I can, for example, insert a flying elephant into my sky if I wish. Dreams, researchers have suggested, are nothing more than several patterns of neurons firing in the brain simultaneously (Hobson, 1988).

A verbal category, such as dog or silverware, can also be viewed as a pattern, even if I don't get a visual image. Thinking about the word *dog* fires a group of cells that correspond to the attributes that define the corresponding category. If I try to think simultaneously of several different animals, such as dogs, cats, bears, and wolves, I would probably activate the superordinate category of animals or perhaps mammals.

Synthesis. Synthesis involves putting together components to create a whole. How does this happen? It can happen spontaneously, through what we call insight or creativity, or it can be approached in a very logical way, at least according to DeBono (1970, 1987), a specialist in how to become more creative. DeBono conceptualizes the brain as a highly sophisticated problem solver that looks for redundancy. When it finds that redundancy, a new pattern emerges in the brain. This model is consistent with the way behavioral scientists regard the emergence of distinct images.

According to DeBono, we can speed up this process of finding redundancy by deliberately activating various patterns in the brain. DeBono calls this *lateral thinking* (1987). According to him, we do not have to learn how to see new patterns when they emerge. As soon as a new pattern emerges, it will be recognized immediately as something new and distinct. Patterns are the basis for categories. The only thing left for us to do when a pattern emerges is to assign a name to the new pattern, so that we can retrieve it at will. Note that the early writers described creativity as an "aha" or insight experience. It happened when people suddenly recognized that two disparate things were related because they shared certain common features.

Redundancy is the basis for perception and meaning. For example, when we can see something—a chair, perhaps—as distinct from the background, we have a perception. Meaning typically involves intention. Thus, if I take another person by the arm and lead him or her across the street, we say the act has meaning; it was intended to help or assist.

Obviously, the idea that the brain is designed to search for redundancy among patterns is consistent with the finding that creativity is linked to the willingness to tolerate ambiguity—the willingness to simultaneously entertain various pieces of information that do not seem related. Likewise, this idea is consistent with the link between creativity and openness to information. The brain is always alert for new information to include in its search for redundancy.

We can use lateral thinking to generate alternatives when we are problem solving. Instead of waiting patiently for an idea to emerge, we actively generate possibilities, often using past experience. If I want to get a ball off a roof, I might think of various possibilities, the most obvious being a ladder. In the absence of a ladder, I might become more creative and entertain possibilities such as throwing rocks at it, using the force of the water from a garden hose to dislodge it, climbing a tree near the house and jumping over to the roof to get it, hiring a helicopter, and so forth. Obviously, some of these ideas are better than others are, and I can simply select from among the alternatives. Another example of lateral thinking is to open the dictionary at random and start reading words, in the hope that one of the words will stimulate me to come up with an answer. The words are intended to activate various patterns in the brain.

Hobson (1988), whose ideas on dreaming we discussed in Chapter 6, has suggested that the brain has a natural tendency to link these different patterns by creating a story. Other theorists have suggested that the brain creates categories that allow us to summarize the essential features contained in a body of information (Langer, 1989). Still others have argued that some type of reorganization or reintegration allows us to make sense out of information or gain insight into it (Kaha, 1983). If you are in New Orleans, for example, you might wonder why there are costumed people in the street; realizing that it is Mardi Gras would make sense of that information. These various ideas—storytelling, the creation of categories, and reintegration—all imply some type of synthesis.

Suspension of judgment. Making judgments will stop the creative process—that is, stop synthesis (Strickland, 1989). People with strong opinions often have difficulty being creative because they are inclined to short-circuit the creative process by making premature judgments. Langer (1989) has identified premature judgments as a cause or characteristic of mindlessness. Hobson (1988) has suggested that, to dream (which is a kind of creative storytelling), people need to set aside their self-referent or self-reflection systems. Some researchers have suggested that being introspective or self-focused can interfere with making good decisions. For example, Wilson and Schooler (1991) found that, when people were made aware of the reasons for their choices, they adopted nonoptimal strategies, presumably because their attention shifted away from the more global problem at hand. Before categories can emerge spontaneously, we need to free the brain from constraints. We need to learn to suspend judgment long enough for the creative process to run its course.

Adopting a playful attitude is a good way of suspending judgment. The very nature of play is to have fun without the need to achieve a goal or find closure. Play allows us to deal with uncertainty and ambiguity and to incorporate fantasy. In its purest form, creativity involves the complete suspension of judgment.

Learning to Be Creative

If the brain is designed to synthesize, then it should be possible to promote creativity by simply juxtaposing certain pieces of information in our brain. Extensive data supports this idea.

Remote associations. An interesting study showed that giving people moderately remote word associations rather than highly remote associations produced greater creative achievements (Gough, 1976; MacKinnon, 1962). A moderately remote association involves words with some overlap, whereas a highly remote association involves words with little overlap. In the context of designing a building, for example, the name of a shape, such as pyramid, would represent a moderately remote association, whereas the name of a fruit, such as pear, would represent a highly remote association. It is not hard to imagine the relevance of a pyramid to the design of a building; the relevance of a pear is much less clear.

According to DeBono (1987), exercises that encourage individuals to make remote associations can trigger their creativity. He has invented a number of such exercises (see Practical Application 12-2). If the techniques used to solve these exercises become habitual, people can learn to be creative. This idea is consistent with the finding that the dreams of creative professionals were more implausible and unrealistic than were the dreams of less creative professionals (Sladeczek & Domino, 1985). Perhaps, as DeBono has suggested, some people learn to make more remote associations, and that style of thinking is found in their dreams as well as their waking states.

Brainstorming and Group Creativity. Brainstorming was initially introduced into small groups to promote group problem solving and has become a very popular technique in industrial and organization settings (Farr, 1990). It can be useful if people are carefully instructed and guided (Simonton, 2000). With the growth of the Internet, researchers are optimistic that brain storming can occur with people in distant locations. Brainstorming refers to the generation of ideas. Typically, one rule of brainstorming is that no idea is to be viewed as silly, absurd, or wrong. When people are encouraged to freely associate in an atmosphere of nonjudgment, they tend to generate more ideas. Further, ideas that initially seem silly or even absurd often stimulate the generation of more workable ideas.

Creativity Across the Life Span

In various areas of endeavor, major contributions tend to be made by people in young adulthood, whereas minor contributions tend to peak at middle age (Lehman, 1966). There are at least three possibilities:

creativity declines with age, motivation changes with age, or younger people are more likely to make remote associations.

Few psychologists believe that the capacity for creativity decreases with increasing age. Often, middle-aged people have an excellent knowledge base and, therefore, they should be able to make major contributions. Further, the fact that they often make good minor contributions suggests they have the capacity for dealing with complex material. Finally, considerable evidence indicates that many older people remain highly creative throughout their lives.

However, it appears that motivational concerns can shift from youth to middle age. For example, as people reach middle age, they come to value pragmatic achievements, perhaps because they are more concerned with career development than are younger people (e.g., Vaillant, 1977). Data also indicate that the generation of ideas is more important to younger individuals than to older individuals (Macon, 1987).

What about the ability to make remote associations? Again, this may simply be a matter of motivation. Although young adults often produce a number of highly creative solutions—for instance, to a problem requiring mechanical ingenuity—middle-aged adults produce more workable solutions. With experience, people might learn which types of associations have a higher payoff (Owens, 1969). Alternatively, with experience, people might tend to rely more on tried and true procedures, which could inhibit reintegration by virtue of their stability, prior use, and automaticity (Barsalou, 1993).

Summary

People engage in acts of creativity for at least three reasons: to satisfy their need for novel and varied stimulation, to improve their ability to communicate ideas and

Practical Application 12-2

Motivating Creativity by Asking, "What If?"

The brain tends to resist forming new ideas. When people try to think creatively, their brains only generate solutions that are consistent with socially accepted ideas of what is true or correct. As a result, people find that, when they attempt to be creative, their brains only offer them a rehash of everything they already know. The problem, therefore, is to get the brain to break out of existing patterns and entertain new ones.

At least three conditions are necessary to trigger the emergence of new patterns (DeBono, 1970). First, we need to juxtapose two seemingly unrelated ideas, so the brain will look for new ways of relating that information. Although juxtaposing two pieces of unrelated information is not that difficult, the brain's initial tendency is to ignore the juxtaposition. If the pieces of information haven't been perceived as related in the past, the brain is inclined to make the judgment that they are unrelated and should remain

so. Thus, the second thing we need to do is to induce the brain to withhold this kind of premature judgment. Sometimes, simply telling the brain to withhold judgment is sufficient to increase creativity. The third thing we must do is to allow the brain time to do its job. Considerable evidence indicates that, given enough time, the brain will find areas of similarity, no matter how remote those similarities might be. During this time of incubation, as it is often called, the brain appears to ruminate—to look at ideas from many perspectives. This process of rumination allows the brain to discover relationships. Sometimes people have access to this process via their inner dialogue. They will hear themselves say, for example, "If I did X, then maybe Y would occur and perhaps, if I did Y, then Z would happen." If rumination is to occur, we must learn to tolerate ambiguity and uncertainty. By demanding certainty and predictability at all times, we will certainly short-circuit the process.

values, and to help them to solve problems. The various definitions of creativity offered over the years have all been useful in helping us to understand the nature of creativity.

DeBono takes the position that the brain evolved to isolate predictability and consistency and, as a result, is highly resistant to forming new patterns. Similarly, Langer argues that many behaviors become automatic (habitual) and that, as a result, we tend to become mindless. Like DeBono, she argues that it is highly adaptive for us to be able to do things without thinking about them. Unfortunately, as our environment changes, we continue to do the same things, even though they are no longer adaptive. To break out of our habitual behavior patterns, we need to become mindful.

Numerous researchers have suggested that many people, although potentially creative, inhibit creative behavior because it conflicts with conventional or traditional opinions. People characterized by rigidity might inhibit creativity because of their strong need for predictability. The idea that all people are potentially creative is consistent with the observation that, when the right conditions exist, generally uncreative people will suddenly demonstrate that they can be creative and that creativity can be increased through rewards.

Personality characteristics that have been linked to creativity include intellectual and artistic values, breadth of interests, attraction to complexity, high energy, a concern with work and achievement, independence of judgment, autonomy, intuition, self-confidence, tolerance for ambiguity, a willingness to resolve conflict, creative self-image, and openness to new experiences and new ways of viewing things.

It can be argued that, because they find creativity so rewarding, people learn to adopt certain orientations to the world and themselves—certain beliefs and attitudes—that increase the likelihood of their being creative. Work on the effect of early and later experiences is consistent with this hypothesis.

In *Lateral Thinking*, DeBono (1970) suggests a number of techniques to facilitate the formulation of juxtapositions and to inhibit the brain's natural tendency to reject such juxtapositions. One technique he suggests is the random-word method. If we get stuck on a problem, we can simply pick up a dictionary and randomly read out words. The goal of this technique is to stimulate the brain to activate patterns that were previously inactive, in the hope that they will provide the link between two seemingly remote ideas on our path to a solution. In addition, the random-word technique seems to elicit a playful attitude, which can help to inhibit the judgment process.

DeBono emphasizes that solutions to problems often involve a series of steps; this idea is contrary to the popular myth that the correct solutions to problems emerge suddenly and in their final form. He argues that the key to problem-solving and creativity is to induce the brain to do what it does naturally—find links between things that initially seem unrelated.

By forcing the brain to look for these relationships and learning to tolerate ambiguity in the process, we should be able to become more creative. According to DeBono, we need to learn to withhold judgment, to accept as many divergent views as possible, and to feel comfortable with ambiguity. We need to learn to ask, "What if?"

By adopting this playful attitude, we free ourselves from the rules of convention, the rules of tradition, the rules of closure, the rules of consistency, the rules of logic, the rules of time, and the rules of place. In short, we put ourselves in a position to juxtapose anything we like, in any way we like. When we do this, we provide the brain with the ideal set of conditions for doing what it has been designed to do: to generate new possibilities, new alternatives, and new realities.

Creativity involves at least five important steps: delineating or defining the problem, gathering information and knowledge, constructing images or categories, synthesizing, and withholding judgment. Many writers have suggested that we can learn to be more creative. An interesting study on this topic showed that people produced greater creative achievements when confronted with moderately remote word associations, rather than highly remote associations.

Major creative contributions tend to be made in young adulthood, whereas minor contributions tend to peak at middle age. The evidence suggests that motivation changes with age; younger people are more inclined to make remote associations. Research on birth order indicates that later-borns are more likely to be creative than first-borns are.

According to DeBono, we can learn to be more creative (1) by learning to juxtapose information or ideas, (2) by learning to withhold our natural tendency to reject the juxtaposition of two things because past experience suggests that they are unrelated, and (3) by giving ourselves time.

Main Points

1. The early behaviorists suggested that exploratory behavior was learned.
2. Various studies have shown that animals and humans are motivated to seek out optimal complexity.
3. When animals are anxious or emotional, they tend not to seek out novelty or complexity.
4. Considerable evidence indicates that the tendency to explore has a genetic basis. Individuals with a temperamental disposition characterized by low curiosity and exploratory behavior are usually also characterized by high anxiety.
5. The preference for complexity increases with age and the degree of previous exposure to various levels of complexity.
6. Extrinsic motivation reduces the tendency to explore and undermines intrinsic motivation.
7. We can facilitate intrinsic motivation by giving people the freedom to organize tasks as they want and by reducing or eliminating competing motives.

8. High sensation seekers are motivated by a need for varied, novel, and complex sensations and experiences and are willing to take physical and social risks to get them.
9. High sensation seekers have low monoamine oxidase levels, whereas low sensation seekers have high monoamine oxidase levels.
10. High sensation seekers tend to be involved in a wide range of sports, tend to use drugs, to have a variety of sex partners, and to like situations that allow them to behave in an uninhibited manner.
11. People are motivated to be creative by, in particular, the need for novel, varied, and complex stimulation; the need to communicate; and the need to solve problems.
12. Creativity is defined as the tendency to generate or recognize ideas, alternatives, or possibilities that could be useful in solving problems, communicating with others, and entertaining ourselves and others.
13. Creativity can be increased by a psychological climate that encourages creativity or by being forced to have diversifying experiences.
14. There are four important components of creativity: knowledge, the ability to construct images and/or categories, the ability to synthesize, and the willingness to withhold judgment.
15. Major creative contributions tend to be made by younger people, whereas minor creative contributions are more likely to be made by older people.

InfoTrac® College Edition

Businesses have become very interested in promoting innovation, which has its roots in the concept of creativity. What are some things businesses are doing to facilitate innovation and creativity? (Search words: business creativity)

What are some of the things that tend to undermine innovation in the workplace? (Search words: business creativity)

Brainstorming can be a very useful way to solve problems. What are some of the steps for successful brainstorming? (Search words: group problem solving)

Chapter Thirteen

Need for Control, Mastery, and Self-Esteem

- *Does everybody have a need for predictability and control?*

- *Is it a good thing to have a need to control?*

- *Does the need for control make people more successful?*

- *Can people develop the motivation to achieve?*

- *How do success and failure experiences affect the tendency to achieve?*

- *Why do some people set difficult goals, and others do not?*

- *Where do our feelings of self-esteem and self-worth come from?*

- *Is it normal for people to experience self-doubt when they fail?*

- *If we are to experience high self-esteem, what kind of self-concept do we need?*

To survive, succeed, and go where no person has gone before, organisms need to develop competence. Competence is more than simply having or developing a set of skills. It involves being able to successfully deal with threats, being able to successfully interact with the environment, being able to set goals, and being able to see oneself as capable of going where no other person has gone before. In this chapter we look at some basic human needs that pertain to the development of competence. First, we look at the need to control. Researchers have suggested that the need to control arises from our need for a predictable environment. This need ensures that we can deal efficiently and effectively with the world in which we live. Research indicates that when we lose control we begin to experience negative emotions such as anxiety, depression, and stress. Conversely, when we have control, we experience a sense of well-being, together with good physical and psychological health. Next, we discuss the need to achieve and the need to master. These needs or dispositions are fundamental to developing the knowledge and skills that allow us to interact successfully with the environment as well as get what we need and want from life. Much of human behavior, at least in the Western world, is devoted to going beyond satisfying survival needs. Humans have aspirations, they set goals, and they experience the satisfaction that comes from doing what no other person has done before. Finally, we will consider self-esteem. Because humans are self-reflective by nature, they can experience self-esteem. Research indicates that when people have a good opinion of their ability to deal with important things in their lives (good self-esteem), they are inclined to take charge of their lives, to set difficult goals for themselves, and to aspire to do things that no other person has done before. Good self-esteem, in other words, is central to developing competence. Without it, people often fail to realize their potential.

The Need for Predictability and Control

The need to control might be one of the most fundamental of all human needs (Shapiro, Schwartz, & Astin, 1996). Individuals' ability to gain and maintain control is essential for their survival (Averill, 1973). Furthermore, the need to control appears to be linked to our need for predictability.

At birth, the infant's focus is almost solely on survival. The baby is only interested in food, comfort, and safety and attempts to make those elements predictable by crying whenever they are absent (Hoffman, 1982). Once these basic needs of survival are predictable, the infant turns to other things, such as exploring the environment. As we saw in Chapter 12, some theorists suggest that mastery is the outcome of such exploratory behavior. This implies that mastery only arises when the individual is free of anxiety, but it seems likely that mastery also takes place under conditions of anxiety. Sternberg (1991) has suggested that we need to recognize different kinds of competency that arise from different situational demands.

Research indicates that personal control provides the cognitive basis for experiencing optimism and hope. More fundamentally, personal control is linked to health.

Control and Health

Psychological Health

Control appears to be one of the most critical variables involved in psychological health and well-being (e.g., Bandura, 1989; Seligman, 1990). In fact, feelings of loss or lack of control have been implicated in a wide range of disorders, including stress, depression, anxiety, drug addiction, and eating disorders (Shapiro et al., 1996). Comparisons of clinical and nonclinical populations have shown that nonclinical individuals "overestimate the amount of control they have in a situation, are more optimistic about their ability to control and believe they have more skills than they actually do" (Shapiro et al., 1996, p. 1214). Such results point to the importance of having a sense of control to function normally and successfully within our society. Without that sense of control, people lose their ability to cope effectively with even the smallest difficulties.

The stress literature also indicates the importance of control. Laboratory studies have shown that it is relatively easy to trigger the stress response by first giving people control over an aversive stimulus, such as shock, and then removing that control. When the ability to control is restored, the stress response typically

We attempt, to the best of our abilities, to make our lives relatively predictable.

subsides (e.g., Glass, 1977a). The stress literature indicates that, when people are able to make coping responses, they are far less inclined to experience stress. Interestingly, they benefit even if the attempts to cope do not work. This suggests that the individuals' belief that they are in control is of primary importance.

Physical Health

People who have greater perceived control over their lives tend to live longer. In an oft-cited study by Rodin and Langer (1977), nursing home residents who were given control over such things as the time and nature of meals and the choice of movies were healthier, and lived longer, than did those in a matched comparison group.

Studies of cancer patients have shown that low perceived control and a sense of helplessness are strong predictors of recurrence of the disease and of death. Similarly, low perceived control has been implicated in cardiovascular disease (Shapiro et al., 1996). Although a sense of control often does not reverse the course of a disease, at least in its final stages, perceived control has been linked to individuals' adjustment to the disease and overall quality of life.

Laboratory studies suggest that low perceived control might suppress the immune function (Kamen, Rodin, Seligman, & Dwyer, 1991). Numerous studies have shown that both acute and chronic stress suppress the immune response (Kiecolt-Glaser & Glaser, 1992). Hassenfeld (1993) has suggested that the link between stress and the immune system is mediated by feelings of loss of control.

Now that we have some preliminary understanding of the need for control, let's analyze its biological, learned, and cognitive components.

The Biological Component

Is there a genetic basis for individuals' sense of personal control? To answer this question we need a way of measuring personal control. One of the most widely used instruments, Rotter's Locus of Control Scale, provides a score indicating the degree to which individuals are internal—that is, believe the cause of behavior lies within themselves—or external—that is, believe the cause of behavior lies outside themselves. Recall that we talked about locus of control in Chapter 2 and again in Chapter 10 in connection with Seligman's theory of depression. Among other things we noted that people with an internal locus of control are inclined to view both good and bad outcomes as something they caused whereas externals are inclined to view both good and bad outcomes as things outside their control. Twin studies using Rotter's scale have found that genetics accounts for about 30% of the variance associated with personal control and with how responsible people felt for misfortunes in their lives (Pedersen, Gatz, Plomin, Nesselroade, & McClearn, 1989). These results indicate that there is a genetic basis for feelings of personal control.

When we obtain measures of internal and external while doing research, these measures indicate where people are and not where they can necessarily go. Some people might have already reached their upper limits of perceived control or lack thereof (as determined by their underlying genetics), but others have not. Considerable evidence indicates that humans can and often do reach higher or lower levels of either internal or external control as a result of learning and cognition.

The Learned Component

Rotter's (1966) distinction between internal and external personality types has its roots in reinforcement theory. He suggests that people adopt an internal locus of control if they perceive, as a result of their past experiences, that taking control produces certain anticipated or desired results. Conversely, if they perceive that taking control does not produce certain anticipated or desired results, they will perceive that things that happen to them lie outside their control. He recognizes that individuals might feel more control in certain situations than in others, but he argues, nonetheless, that they come to develop a generalized belief that they are the cause of events in their lives including their misfortunes (internal locus) or that the cause of such events lie outside themselves (external locus).

More recently, researchers have concluded that beliefs about cause and control are not determined solely by the individuals' past reinforcement history. In Western cultures, we are inclined to think of *active control*—that is, what I can do to change the external environment. If we are experiencing stress, for example, we are inclined to engage in behaviors that will remove the stressors from our lives. If we cannot remove the stressors, we might decide to distance ourselves from them. In some Asian cultures, people are more inclined to think of *self-control*. Rather than actively trying to get rid of stressors, they would be inclined to reduce the impact of the stressors by engaging in self-control strategies (Shapiro et al., 1996).

These two approaches to control are very different. Moreover, they imply different approaches to helping those who are experiencing a loss of control. In Western cultures, a therapist might encourage such people to become more assertive. This approach grows out of a philosophy of individualism that encourages self-determination. In Asian cultures, a therapist might be more inclined to train people to accept loss of control and to use self-control strategies such as meditation, relaxation, and cognitive modification to reduce the impact of the stressor. This approach grows out of a philosophy that emphasizes the collective or the community (the larger group) rather than the individual (Shapiro et al., 1996). When I use the terms *Western* and *Asian,* I am not referring to specific individuals. Many Westerners think in terms of self-control and, likewise, many Asians think in terms of active control.

More recently, many western theorists have incorporated more Asian ideas into their theories. For example, Lazarus, whose work we considered in Chapter 9, distinguished between two forms of coping: one involves mastery or problem-solving (active coping), and the other involves controlling our autonomic responses by meditation, relaxation, or biofeedback (Lazarus, 1991a). Similarly, when people from Asian cultures come to the United States, they often find it necessary to become more assertive. In Western society, assertiveness is viewed not only as adaptive but as essential.

The key point here is simply that our attitudes to control issues are shaped by how our parents thought and acted, by how they trained us to think and act, and by how our cultures taught us to act.

The Cognitive Component

We live in a world in which we can control some things but not others. We can, for example, generally control when we go to bed, what we eat, and who become our friends. We can't control, however, things such as what others eat, the weather, or traffic. What if I find that I might miss an important appointment because traffic is particularly heavy? Should I attempt to see if I can make up time by cutting in and out and running a few red lights, or should I simply accept it? Alternatively, what if I discover that I lost some important points on a test that was returned. Should I simply ignore it, or should I point this out to my professor?

Researchers have established that individuals react very differently to situations involving issues of control (Evans, Shapiro, & Lewis, 1993). Some people realize that they can control some situations but not others. Others react inappropriately, however: those with a high need to control might attempt to control the uncontrollable; those with a low need to control might make no attempt to control a situation that is actually controllable.

When people try to control situations that are essentially uncontrollable, they are inclined to experience high levels of stress. Thus, suggesting that they need to take active control is bad advice in those situations. What they need to do is to accept that some things are beyond their control. Similarly, teaching people to accept a situation that could readily be changed could be bad advice; sometimes the only way to get what you want is to take active control. Research has shown that, when people who feel helpless fail to take control, they experience negative emotional states such as anxiety and depression. Like stress, these negative emotions can impair the immune response. We can see from this that health is not linearly related to control. For optimum health, people should be encouraged to take control to a point but to recognize when further control is impossible.

The internal and external dimensions of Rotter's Locus of Control Scale are independent (Levenson, 1981). That means we can be high on both, low on both, or high on one and low on the other. Recall that, according to Seligman's theory, an internal orientation is more likely to result in depression, whereas an external orientation could be a defense against depression. As Seligman was careful to point out, he did not mean that people should give up their attempts to control; rather, they should come to understand that there are benefits from not taking too much control.

A famous prayer sums up this issue: "Please, God, give me the courage to change what can be changed, the serenity to accept what I cannot, and the wisdom to know the difference."

Control and Mastery

The research literature indicates that believing that we have control is essential if we are to engage in mastery and achievement behaviors. Without this generalized belief, we will not be inclined to initiate such behaviors.

Bandura's research indicates that behavioral control and cognitive control are necessary to initiate new behaviors, something we discussed in detail in Chapter 11 (Ozer & Bandura, 1990). Bandura's (1997) concept of cognitive control corresponds to Rotter's inter-

nal orientation. That orientation is what allows people to initiate mastery behaviors. As we saw in Chapter 11, considerable evidence also indicates that people only initiate new behaviors when they have optimism and hope. The bottom line is that people will not be motivated to work toward mastery and achievement unless they believe that their behavior will effect some desired outcome.

Summary

The need for control plays an essential role in determining such things as whether or not people will initiate new behaviors. The need for control has been implicated in psychological and physical health and in our ability to get what we want from life. Twin studies have shown that about 30% of the variance associated with personal control is the result of genetics. Cultural differences in attitudes to control have been noted: in Western societies, the emphasis is on active control, whereas Asian societies value self-control. Although both active control and self-control can be effective procedures, we need to match our control strategy to the demands of the situation. Attempting to control an uncontrollable situation tends to produce stress, whereas not attempting to take charge of a controllable situation has been linked to anxiety and depression.

Mastery and Achievement Motivation

Mastery involves acquiring knowledge and developing skills. It also denotes complete learning. To master something, you learn everything there is to know about it or you develop the skill to its highest possible level. *Achievement* involves attaining a goal such as a university degree. Mastery is usually implicated in high levels of achievement, but not always; some people achieve things without complete mastery.

Achievement often calls on us not only to master a certain set of skills or acquire a certain body of knowledge but also to learn how to deal with our emotions, including self-doubt. In other words, although mastery might be important for achievement, it does not guarantee that you will achieve your goals. Being an optimist, for example, might be the most important factor in achieving goals.

The function of mastery is to ensure that the individual develops competence in various areas. *Competence*, among other things, involves skill, ability, capacity, proficiency, or fitness. These are some qualities we need to interact with the environment and to get what we want from life. Take social competency as an example. To be socially accepted or to work in certain social situations, we need a basic set of social skills and knowledge. Without social competency, we might be excluded from certain jobs or social events. It might even be difficult or impossible to marry and raise children unless we possess some basic level of social competency.

Mastery and achievement can be contrasted with a laissez-faire approach to life. Instead of searching for a job, the laissez-faire person simply waits for a job to come along. As we have seen, whether an individual initiates mastery and achievement behaviors will depend on his or her beliefs about control.

People with a mastery and achievement orientation have a sense of *agency* (Bandura, 1989, 1997). They take action so that they get what they want from life. Psychologists often characterize the person who is inclined to make things happen as *instrumental*. To make things happen, such individuals set goals and make plans to attain those goals. Moreover, as Bandura and others have pointed out, these individuals are not undermined the first time they fail to attain their goals. Instead, they adjust their plans or simply make new plans. In the final analysis, people who take control also take responsibility for their actions. They take responsibility for their successes and for their failures.

Achievement Motivation

Henry Murray (1938), a pioneer in this field, defined the need to achieve as a desire or tendency to "overcome obstacles, to exercise power, to strive to do something difficult as well as and as quickly as possible" (pp. 80–81). As we see from this definition, Murray saw achievement as a generalized need. Like others, he believed that the pleasure of achievement is not in attaining the goal but, rather, in developing and exercising skills. In other words, the process provides the motivation for achievement. As we'll see shortly, many other theorists have come to the same conclusion.

For more than four decades, David McClelland has been doing research related to the achievement motive. His extensive contributions are summarized in his book *Human Motivation* (McClelland, 1985). To measure the achievement motive with more precision, McClelland and his colleagues adapted the Thematic Apperception Test (TAT) and developed a precise method for scoring the achievement motive (McClelland, Atkinson, Clark, & Lowell, 1953). The TAT involves showing people pictures and having them write stories about those pictures. The theory behind the test is that people will identify with one of the characters in the pictures and in doing so will tell stories about themselves and their motives. Several studies to assess the validity of the TAT measure have shown that a generalized motive or disposition does exist and that it can predict behavior in a wide variety of situations (e.g., Atkinson, 1953; French, 1956; Mischel, 1961).

The Biological Component

Although researchers have not been able to identify an obvious biological link to a brain center or a neurotransmitter, McClelland and others have argued that achievement motive grows out of a more basic incentive to "do something better"—not to gain approval or any other kind of external reward, but "for its own sake" (McClelland, 1985, p. 228). McClelland points out that the development of this natural incentive is shaped by the environment. For example, parents play an important role, often by providing the kind of environment that allows the achievement motive to flourish. We'll return to this topic shortly.

Theories of Competence

Robert White (1959), discussed in the last chapter, published one of the most influential articles on the nature of mastery and competence. He argued that the tendency to explore is based on a more general motive, which he called *effectance motivation*. This motive, White suggested, is directed toward understanding the nature of the environment and the order inherent in it.

Feelings of *efficacy* occur when the individual comes to understand or know that he or she is able to affect the environment. Such feelings, White argues, can act as a reward. An infant who discovers that, whenever she kicks her feet, the mobile hanging above her head moves, for example, will experience feelings of efficacy. She might smile, laugh, or show some other outward sign of her internal state. Most important, she will gain a sense of mastery. Another theorist who has had a profound impact on the understanding of competency is Jean Piaget, whose ideas we discussed in Chapter 2. Like White, Piaget believed that the need to interact with the environment forces the child to engage in the process of mastery (Piaget, 1970).

Conclusions

Although theorists have argued that an underlying biology governs mastery and competency, none have tried to single out certain brain structures or neurotransmitters. Within Gray's (1982) theory it would be mainly the behavioral activation system (BAS) together with the behavioral inhibition system (BIS), the same systems that we suggested were involved in curiosity and exploratory behavior. White and others have pointed out that anxiety plays an important role in the mastery process. Perhaps, rather than saying that anxiety eliminates the tendency to master, we should say that anxiety alters individuals' focus. When they are anxious, their focus tends to narrow and become restrictive; it is directed toward survival cues. When individuals are free of anxiety, by contrast, their focus tends to be broad and inclusive; it is directed more toward general learning.

As already noted, researchers are tending to turn their attention away from general mastery and instead are analyzing the factors that give rise to particular competencies. Using that strategy, researchers will be able to better incorporate the concept of talent. *Talent* is a capacity for doing or learning something. Considerable evidence indicates that people are born with different talents for music, athletics, and academics, for instance (Gardner, 1983). Even within those broad areas, there appear to be differences in talent. Researchers need to examine how talent interacts with learned and cognitive variables to produce high levels of achievement.

The Learned Component

Social Learning Theory

According to social learning theory, children learn from their observation of adults that one way to get what they want from life is to gain knowledge and develop skills. They might notice, for example, that an athlete they admire receives a great deal of money and approval from society. As a result, children begin to model those whom they admire. They dress like their heroes and begin to imitate the behavior. To facilitate this process, children might buy books and magazines and they try to watch the athlete as often as they can, on television or at a sporting event. According to social learning theory, modeling and imitation are the processes by which individuals secure what they want from life. The motivation is provided by money, social approval, and other rewards.

Social learning theory provides a broad framework that allows us to understand why individuals in our society are inclined to select particular goals and how individuals acquire the skills they need. What this theory doesn't tell us is why people often develop a generalized need state called—by Murray and others—the need to achieve or the need to master. Why are some people inclined to engage in achievement and mastery behaviors for their own sakes? According to McClelland, we come to internalize certain values, and this internalization process is what gives rise to the disposition to achieve. Let's look at some research that has its roots in McClelland's theory.

Independence and Mastery Parenting

Several studies in the experimental literature show that, when parents emphasized or encouraged early independence and mastery, children scored higher on need for achievement. In these studies, need for achievement was measured by asking children to produce imaginative stories and coding the stories by a procedure designed to assess the amount of achievement imagery. McClelland and his colleagues employed this procedure, which is rather time-consuming but essentially reliable and valid, because they were unable to construct questionnaires that were consistently valid (McClelland, 1985).

Other studies used different techniques to determine whether certain parenting methods resulted in high need achievement scores. One study established that children who scored high on need for achievement had parents who had encouraged them, for instance, to do well in school, to look after their possessions, and to try hard things by themselves (Winterbottom, 1958). In another study, children who were high and low in need for achievement were blindfolded and asked to stack blocks as high as they could with their left hands, while their parents watched. The parents were asked how well they thought their children would do. As predicted, children with a high need to achieve were more likely to have parents who had high expectations (Rosen & D'Andrade, 1959). One study showed that even putting children on a feeding schedule and requiring them to regulate their sphincters in a socially appropriate manner led to increased achievement motivation (McClelland & Pilon, 1983).

What these and other studies showed is that, when children are encouraged to be independent and to master, they tend to develop a higher need to achieve. To assess whether this motive tends to grow and develop over time and is the result of the cumulative number of demands, McClelland and his colleagues looked at the strength of the need to achieve motive at different ages. As Figure 13-1 shows, considerable evidence indicates that the motive is linked to independence and mastery (McClelland et al., 1953).

The general theory that McClelland (1985) has offered for these findings is that children have an inborn capacity to experience satisfaction (reward) because of *progressive mastery*. If the individual repeatedly experiences that satisfaction, the corresponding inborn motive state will be strengthened.

McClelland argues that the achievement motive can be aroused directly by challenging the individual or by presenting the individual with a situation that would offer the opportunity to master. What is aroused, presumably, are anticipatory feelings of satisfaction that could come from engaging in mastery behaviors.

Conclusions

Learning theorists have attempted to show that the tendency to achieve, master, or gain competence can be largely understood through principles of learning. Although social learning theorists have focused on why people learn certain behaviors rather than others, theorists such as McClelland have focused on how the behavior expressing the motive for achievement is acquired through the principles of reinforcement. According to McClelland, we are not born with the motive to achieve and master. We discover the underlying rewards of mastery in the process of achieving goals as children. When parents encourage us, they help us to discover that gaining mastery is rewarding. Consequently, we continue to set goals throughout our lives to experience the rewards associated with mastery.

The Cognitive Component

Atkinson's Cognitive-Choice Theory

John Atkinson, who collaborated with McClelland in some early work on the achievement motive, developed a distinctively cognitive theory of achievement motivation that retained the basic idea of McClelland's theory—that people select and work toward goals because they have an underlying need to achieve.

Atkinson (1957) made two important additions. First, he argued that the need to achieve is always tempered by another fundamental need, the need to avoid failure. He suggested that, if the need to achieve is stronger than the need to avoid failure, the individual will engage in approach behavior; however, if the need to avoid failure is stronger than the need to achieve, the individual will engage in avoidance behavior. Second, Atkinson suggested that these two fundamental needs interact with expectations and values in a multiplicative fashion. He suggested that when expectation of success was high or low, the incentive value was low. If it was high the individual wouldn't expect to succeed and therefore had no reason to put forth effort, and if it was low, there was no challenge and again no reason to put forth effort. In a complimentary way he argued that when the expectation of failure was high, there was high negative incentive and therefore reason to avoid the task, and when it was low there was, paradoxically, also good reason to avoid the task. He suggested that because failing at an easy task would be embarrassing or humiliating, the individual with a need to avoid failure would be inclined to avoid easy tasks.

Perhaps the most lasting contribution of Atkinson's work was his suggestion that people are not only characterized by the need to achieve but by the need to avoid failure. We will return to this topic shortly be-

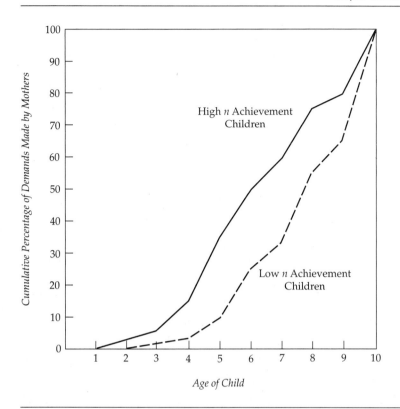

Figure 13-1. Cumulative curves showing the proportion of total demands made up to each age level as reported by mothers of children scoring high and low on *n* achievement (McClelland, Atkinson, Clark, & Lowell, 1953, after Winterbottom, 1958).

cause this distinction has been revived in a more recent theory of achievement motivation.

Dweck's Theory of Competence Development

Carol Dweck and her colleagues have suggested that we can understand differences in achievement and competency by understanding the implicit theories that people have about the origins of achievement and competency. She argues that some people view competency as the skills and knowledge they now possess. They say to themselves, "This is what I am, and therefore this is what I can do." Other people, she argues, view competency as their ability to acquire skills and knowledge. They say to themselves, "Look what I've accomplished so far. That's a good indication of what I can do in the future." Individuals of the first type subscribe to what she calls an *entity* theory; they see intelligence as fixed. Individuals of the second type subscribe to an *incremental* theory; they see intelligence as changeable (Dweck, 1991; Dweck & Leggett, 1988). For reasons that are still not completely clear, some people

believe that learning stops at a certain age or that their capacity to learn is limited and that, therefore, no matter how hard they work, there is little hope for real change. Such people regard their possibilities as limited. People who hold the incremental theory, on the other hand, believe that the only thing that limits their ability to learn and develop new skills is their willingness to work. They regard their possibilities as virtually unlimited; how much they learn depends on how much they think they can learn. Our nervous system places limits on us, of course. Nonetheless, researchers have shown that one major factor determining how far we go is how persistent we are, and how persistent we are is linked to our beliefs about whether we can learn and develop.

Research with people who perceive that they have ability indicates that, when given a choice among tasks of various levels of difficulty, people who hold an incremental theory tend to choose challenging tasks—tasks that call on them to stretch themselves—whereas people who ascribe to an entity theory tend to choose

Table 13-1. Dweck and Leggett's theory of the relationship between implicit theories of intelligence and the behavior patterns of mastery and helpless types.

Theory of Intelligence	Goal Orientation	Perceived Present Ability	Behavior Pattern
Entity theory (intelligence is fixed)	Performance orientation; the goal is to gain positive judgments and to avoid negative judgments of competence.	High	Mastery; the individual seeks challenge and is high in persistence.
		Low	Helplessness; the individual avoids challenge and is low in persistence.
Incremental theory (intelligence is changeable)	Learning orientation; the goal is to increase competence.	High or low	Mastery; the individual seeks challenge that fosters learning and is high in persistence.

Source: From "A Social-Cognitive Approach to Motivation and Personality," by C. S. Dweck and E. L. Leggett, *Psychological Review*, 1988, *95*, 256–273. Copyright © 1988 by the American Psychological Association. Reprinted with permission.

tasks that are more in line with their abilities. People who perceive themselves to be low in ability and who hold an entity theory are inclined to choose relatively easy tasks because they are likely to succeed in such tasks and, consequently, they can avoid judgments about their lack of competency. Should they fail, of course, it would be devastating to their already low self-image. The net result is that people with low perceived ability who hold to an entity theory are inclined to avoid challenges and to choose easy tasks.

Dweck and Leggett (1988) contend that avoiding a challenging activity is a maladaptive strategy, whereas the tendency to select challenging tasks is adaptive. Because most achievement involves overcoming obstacles, acquiring skills, and persisting in the face of setbacks, they argue, it is important to be dispositionally disposed to select challenging tasks. Dweck and Leggett's theory is summarized in Table 13-1. Note that people with low perceived ability are prone to helplessness (Chapter 10).

To end this discussion of Dweck's ideas, let's compare the consequences of believing in the entity theory or the incremental theory.

Consequences of believing in the entity theory. According to Dweck's model, people who believe in the entity

theory are motivated to select goals that will indicate they do have intelligence and to avoid goals that might provide evidence that they lack intelligence. Research indicates that, when these people experience failure, they tend to attribute it to lack of intelligence (e.g., Elliott & Dweck, 1985, cited in Dweck, 1986). If I believe I lack intelligence, why should I put forth effort? People who reason this way have to select their tasks very carefully because any failure confirms their lack of intelligence. After reviewing the research literature on the way children react to success and failure, Dweck has suggested that even a single encounter with failure can make a person helpless.

Thus, failure can be devastating to people who hold to the entity theory. For this reason, they learn to avoid challenges. These people might become low achievers to avoid the failure they fear.

Consequences of believing in the incremental theory. According to Dweck, people who believe in the incremental theory tend to select goals that will enable them to increase their competence (e.g., Nicholls, 1984). If intelligence is something that we can acquire, it is important to select goals that maximize learning. To maximize learning, we must be careful not to select goals based on certainty of success. Sometimes we can learn a great deal in situations where failure is likely. For instance, we can't learn the skills needed to be good at the ring-toss task by simply standing next to the post and dropping the ring over it. This obvious observation is not always clear to the person obsessed with the need to avoid failure.

The development of competence at any task usually requires persistence, so belief in the incremental theory of intelligence turns out to be very adaptive in the process of setting and attaining goals. Both rewards and failure simply provide feedback to the individual.

Note that Dweck's theory incorporates the idea that people with a generalized belief that they can control important things in their lives are inclined to engage in mastery behaviors.

A Hierarchical Model of Approach and Avoidance Motivation

The two approaches to achievement motivation that we have just discussed represent parallel approaches to the question of motivation. Recently, researchers have proposed a conceptualization of motivation that incorporates their two approaches. The result is a partitioning of achievement motivation into three orientations (Elliot & Harackiewicz, 1996).

1. Mastery goal—focused on the development of competence and task mastery.
2. Performance approach goal—focused on the attainment of favorable judgments and competence.
3. Performance avoidance goal—focused on avoiding unfavorable judgments of competence.

Practical Application 13-1 provides some sample items that the reader might use to determine what orientation they typically use.

The theory incorporates the idea that people have the capacity to self-regulate, so they will be inclined to engage in behaviors that will be consistent with their orientations. Accordingly, the mastery goal and performance approach orientations will seek positive outcomes that will result in task mastery and feelings of competence while the performance avoidance orientation (often characterized by anxiety) will seek to avoid task engagement, something that leads to a helpless pattern of behavior.

Experiments designed to test the theory have found good support. Among other things, researchers have shown that the mastery goal and performance approach orientations lead to intrinsic motivation whereas the performance avoidance orientation undermines intrinsic motivation (Elliot & Harackiewicz,

Practical Application 13-1

Determining Your Achievement Orientation

I have generated these sample items to help you to determine which of the three orientations is most like you. For each question assign a number from 1 to 5, with the number 1 referring to not being like you and 5 being very much like you. Add up your scores to see which one is highest. That is your dominant achievement orientation.

Mastery Goal

It is important to me to completely understand whatever I am doing (such as the content of a course).

I like to have a broad and deep understanding of things that arouse my curiosity.

Performance Approach Goal

It is important for me to do better than others.
I am motivated by the desire to do better than others.

Performance Avoidance Goal

I often worry that I won't do well at a task I undertake.
I often think to myself when I approach a task, "what if I do badly?"

1996). Given our discussion in the last chapter on the tendency for external control and extrinsic rewards to undermine self-directed behavior, the question arises as to why both the mastery and the performance approach lead to similar levels of intrinsic motivation. Shouldn't intrinsic motivation be higher among people who have a mastery orientation? Subsequent research has indeed shown that intrinsic motivation is more closely linked to a mastery orientation (Elliot & Church, 1997). The reason why this didn't show up as clearly in the first studies is partly because of the complexity of goal-directed behaviors. In addition to the variable that we have already discussed, we must consider perceived feelings of competency, what Bandura has called perceived self-efficacy. When perceived competence is high, people are much more inclined to engage in goal-directed behavior. Thus, whether or not one adopts a particular orientation appears to depend on how that person expects to perform. Being good at math can have a profound effect, for example, on how one might expect to perform in a statistic course rather than in some other course. Indeed, it might shift one's orientation from performance avoidance to performance approach.

Consistent with the theory, researchers found that the mastery goal orientation has it roots in the need to achieve and the performance avoidance orientation in the need to avoid failure. Also consistent with the theory, it was found that the performance orientation can lead an individual in different directions. Depending on the situation, such as taking a particular course that has different facets, both the need to achieve and the need to avoid failure could be aroused. As a result, there could be times or days when behavior has its roots in the need to avoid failure and other times or days in which behavior has its roots in the need to confirm one's competency. The direction of one behavior, therefore, can shift or change.

Although we tend to emphasize the importance of adopting mastery goals because they tend to be linked to complete learning, one study found that students who adopted performance goals achieved higher grades than did students who adopted mastery goals. We can interpret these findings in at least two ways: One is that performance goals in the context of being graded relative to one's peers arouse a greater need for more complete or "deeper" learning. The other inter-

pretation is that students with performance goals focus at a more superficial level, memorizing definitions and other material that they think will be on a forthcoming test. Further research is needed to answer this important question. It is hard to argue that we shouldn't encourage complete or deep learning, nor that we should suggest they do not adopt strategies that can lead to success.

In the next section, we are going to examine the question of self-esteem, a concept that has been closely linked to feelings of competency. As we will see, people with a mastery orientation tend to have high self-esteem.

Conclusions

Cognitive theorists suggest that people come to achieve, master, or gain competence because they have the capacity to anticipate the future—that is, because they have expectations about what might be. Various theories have suggested that, when people have positive expectations, they are inclined to put forth effort. Conversely, they are unlikely to put forth effort if they do not believe that the effort will pay off—for instance, if they perceive that they lack ability.

Summary

The initial impetus for work on achievement motivation came from Henry Murray, who recognized that people vary in their desires or tendencies to "overcome obstacles, to exercise power, to strive to do something difficult as well as and as quickly as possible." To measure the achievement motive with more precision, McClelland and his colleagues adapted the TAT and developed a precise method of scoring the achievement motive.

White has proposed that competence grows out of curiosity and exploratory behaviors, which are based on a general motive he has called effectance motivation. This motive is directed toward understanding the nature of the environment and the order inherent in it. Feelings of efficacy occur, he suggests, when individuals come to understand that they are able to affect the environment. Piaget has argued that individuals are motivated to integrate the information contained in their environment. McClelland has shown that, when parents encourage independence and mastery, their children develop a stronger need to achieve. He argues that engaging in mastery behaviors results in feelings of satisfaction that strengthen the need to achieve.

One of Atkinson's important and fundamental contributions was his suggestion that the need to achieve is always tempered by another fundamental need, the need to avoid failure. These two motives interact with expectations to produce either approach or avoidance motivation.

According to Dweck's model, people who believe in the entity theory are motivated to select goals that will indicate that they do have ability and to avoid goals that might provide evidence that they lack ability. People who believe in the incremental theory tend to select goals that will enable them to increase their competence. If ability (intelligence) can be acquired, it is important to select goals that can maximize learning.

What are the consequences of believing in the entity model or the incremental model? People who believe in the entity model of intelligence are motivated to select goals that will put them in a favorable light. Should they fail, they tend to attribute their failure to lack of ability (intelligence). This perception tends to undermine any future desire to put forth effort. People who hold to the incremental model of intelligence tend to set a goal that will increase their competence. When these people fail, they tend to interpret failure not as lack of ability but as feedback that tells them how well they are performing. They often interpret failure as an indication that they did not put forth the necessary effort, and so they are motivated to work harder.

According to the hierarchical model of approach and avoidance motivation, achievement can be partitioned into three orientations: mastery goal, performance approach, and performance avoidance.

Both the mastery and performance orientation can lead to intrinsic motivation, however, the performance avoidance orientation tends to consistently undermine intrinsic motivation. Consistent with the theory researchers have shown that the mastery goal orientation has its roots in the need to achieve and the performance avoidance has its roots in the need to avoid failure. The performance approach orientation is less straight forward since it can be aroused both by the need to achieve and the need to avoid failure.

Self-Esteem

Self-esteem has been positively linked to a wide range of behaviors, including mastery and achievement, subjective well-being, and health. Low self-esteem has been identified as a risk factor for aggression, delinquency, drug use, depression, poor school performance, spousal abuse, child abuse, and so forth. Recently, some politicians and school boards have suggested that schools and other social agencies should design programs to raise self-esteem, on the assumption that self-esteem is the cause, rather than the effect, of societal problems, that it exists independent of a specific situation, and that it can be elevated by external interventions.

In this section, we will review some research findings on self-esteem and consider how feasible it is to raise self-esteem.

The Definition of Self-Esteem

There are many definitions of high self-esteem. All of them try to capture in one way or another the positive feelings or beliefs that people enjoy when they experience high self-esteem. Rarely can one find definitions of low self-esteem, even though low self-esteem has been the main focus of therapists and the self-esteem movement. Let me define both high and low self-esteem.

High Self-Esteem

High self-esteem is "pride in oneself in which one becomes aware and accepting of one's imperfections while cherishing one's inherent strengths and positive qualities" (proposed by Andrea Parecki as quoted in Lazarus, 1991c, p. 441).

A key element in this definition is pride. We feel pride when we can take responsibility for producing a socially valued outcome or for being a socially valued person (Mascolo & Fischer, 1995). Storm and Storm (1987) suggest that pride can be grouped with other positive emotions such as the feelings of being triumphant, victorious, accomplished, special, brave, and courageous. Lazarus (1991c) suggests that the core relational theme for pride is enhancement of our ego-identity by taking credit for a valued object or

People who can believe in themselves can often accomplish the impossible.

achievement, either our own or that of some person or group with whom we identify. This emphasizes the important role of pride in the emergence of the self both as an individual and as a member of a group. Like Lazarus, others have suggested that pride is important for the emergence of traits linked with high self-esteem, such as confidence, independence, curiosity, and initiative (Harter, 1990). From being able to experience pride (to take credit), people gain a strong sense of their own power and agency; pride provides them with the unshakable belief that they can effect change and thereby cope.

Pride can help sustain goal-directed behavior. People sustain themselves in the face of adversity because they are convinced that their actions will eventually make a difference. Persistence is learned; it is based on developing an unshakable belief that, over the long haul, our abilities will make a difference. People who have a sense of agency and pathways have hope (Snyder et al., 1991), and, as we saw earlier, those with hope persist and succeed.

Children need to experience pride because it gives them a sense of autonomy, power, and self-confidence (Deci & Ryan, 1985). Can anyone prevent them from experiencing pride? It appears so. Parents or teachers who take credit for things that children have done rob them of this powerful emotion. In addition, some children are raised in environments that prevent them from doing things on their own. It seems that pride is nurtured when people make their own choices and receive full credit for their accomplishments but are not blamed for their shortcomings.

Another key aspect of high self-esteem is that we must accept our imperfections. As we saw in Chapter 10, perfectionists set themselves up for depression by not allowing themselves to fail. People who can accept that they are less than perfect can better deal with adversity and setbacks.

Researchers have suggested that self-esteem is not a global attribute that applies to all situations but, rather, is specific to certain situations (domains). To emphasize that feelings of self-worth come from competencies in different domains, Susan Harter (1990) prefers to speak of *global self-worth*. She has pointed out that feelings of self-worth are essential to a wide range of behaviors, including establishing and maintaining social relationships.

Low Self-Esteem

Low self-esteem may be defined as the shame that comes from appraising ourselves as lacking skills and abilities important to valued others.

An essential element of this definition is shame. Low self-esteem is not simply the absence of pride; it is a highly negative emotional state. The emotion that most closely approximates that state is shame (Tangney, Burggraf, & Wagner, 1995). Mascolo and Fischer (1995) suggest that we feel shame when we have failed to live up to the standards of worth in valued others: "In shame the entire person seems to be experienced as unworthy" (p. 68).

Another key element of low self-esteem is that individuals believe they are lacking in important skills and abilities. As a result, they feel a persistent sense of hopelessness.

Although self-esteem often drops momentarily as the result of negative feedback, individuals' levels of self-esteem for each particular domain seem to be relatively stable over time. Most researchers emphasize the role of early experiences in establishing these relatively stable levels of self-esteem (Heatherton & Polivy, 1991b) but they could be, at least partially, the result of genetics.

In my view, low self-esteem is a highly overused term. This term is frequently used to refer to people who lack high self-esteem or simply lack confidence; people who do not know if they can do something or have feelings of apprehension; and people who have self-doubt, which we all experience from time to time when we set difficult goals (Bandura, 1991a). However, some people truly suffer from low self-esteem. They are plagued with feelings of guilt and shame.

The Origins of Self-Esteem

We can identify three major sources of self-esteem.

1. **Self-evaluation.** The consensus is that feelings of self-esteem grow out of self-evaluation (e.g., Osborne, 1996; Swann, 1996). Self-evaluation is most likely to occur when individuals experience success or failure. Intuitively, we might expect that people would experience pride when they succeed and shame when they fail. Curiously, as we will discuss later, individuals with high self-esteem tend to experience feelings of pride when they succeed but fail to experience feelings of shame when they fail. The research indicates that they have developed effective ways of appraising failure that minimize its impact. Conversely, people with low self-esteem tend to experience feelings of shame when they fail but rarely experience feelings of pride when they succeed. They have developed ways of appraising success that prevent them from experiencing pride. As a result, they tend to maintain their low self-esteem.

2. **Successes in valued domains.** Different domains are important to different people. For some people, physical attributes are important; for others, athletic performance is important; for still others, academic success is important. As a result, individuals attach more importance to successes in certain domains than in others. If I value sports, for example, I will experience greater pride—and self-esteem—from winning at some sporting event than from getting a good grade on a test. Likewise, failing at something I value will produce greater shame than will failing at something that I do not value.

At least three distinct domains have been identified: performance, social skills, and appearance (Heatherton & Polivy, 1991b). Research to measure these domains showed that people's self-esteem for each of these domains often drops momentarily when they experience private failure on a task (performance self-esteem), when they experience public failure on a task (social self-esteem), or when they have concerns about their physical appearance (physical self-esteem). Other research suggests that there are many more domains and that they change with age (Harter, 1990).

3. **Societal values.** What people value is often a reflection of societal values, parental values, and peer values. In our society, material success is valued. From the day we are born, we hear about the American Dream. As Swann (1996) has pointed out, we are told not simply that we can become wealthy but that we should. Thus, when we don't become rich, we might be inclined to develop lower self-esteem. If we don't buy into this value, on the other hand, we will not experience lower self-esteem as a result of not becoming rich.

Parental values are also important because children are likely to internalize their parents' values. If parents value education, for example, their children will be inclined to value education. Consequently, their self-esteem will be more affected by their performance at school than by their performance in other domains.

Peers also shape our values. Part of the developmental process involves separating ourselves from our parents. This theme is particularly strong in adolescence. During that stage, adolescents often look to their peers to tell them how to behave. Adolescents who decide not to buy into the values of their peers—not to smoke, for example—might find it difficult to experience high self-esteem.

The important point is that our self-esteem results largely from our appraisal of our behavior relative to some standard or value. People who do not have the skills they need to achieve that standard will experience low self-esteem. One way for them to experience high self-esteem would be to rethink what is important. Do they need to be rich to be happy? Do they need to succeed at school to be successful? Do they need to be good at sports to experience pride? Sometimes when people follow their strengths, rather than some standard given to them by society, their parents, or their peers, they begin to develop high self-esteem. In our society, artistic skills are often not valued. As a result, people who excel in the arts but not in other domains could experience lower self-esteem. For some of these people, discovering a group of artists who appreciate their skills can result in a rapid improvement in self-esteem.

Gender Differences

Meta-analyses to examine gender differences in global self-esteem have found there is a small but significant gender difference favoring males (Kling, Hyde, Showers, & Buswell, 1999). The exact reasons for such a difference is unclear. One problem with comparing males and females is that they seem to get their self-esteem in different ways—males by taking an agentic (action) orientation and females by a communal (social) orientation.

The Perpetuation of Low Self-Esteem

People with low self-esteem engage in behaviors that perpetuate low self-esteem. First, although most theorists believe that humans are inherently motivated to experience positive self-regard or high self-esteem (e.g., Rogers, 1959), the research literature indicates that people with low self-esteem do not accept positive feedback but do accept negative feedback. Told that they have done something well, they will disregard that compliment as invalid. Told that they have done poorly, however, they will accept and process that information as correct and fair. This makes no intuitive sense. It also means that they are doomed to experience low self-esteem for the rest of their lives.

Second, people with low self-esteem set low goals. According to Dweck (1991), one reason for this is to avoid disapproval caused by failure. Third, they engage in *self-handicapping*; that is, they set up obstacles to successful performance—for example, by getting drunk the night before an exam or failing to prepare for a presentation at work.

Because self-esteem is linked to such behavior, theorists have argued that self-esteem involves an entire way of relating to the world. Among other things, it involves strategies for setting goals, strategies for reacting to challenges, and strategies for dealing with failures and setbacks (Swann, 1996). The curious thing is that these strategies seem designed to perpetuate low self-esteem. Why is that? Researchers have proposed at least three explanations:

1. **The need for predictability**. It appears that the need for predictability, which we discussed at the beginning of this chapter, takes precedence over the principles of reinforcement. This could explain why the individual with low self-esteem ignores positive feedback and the individual with high self-esteem ignores negative feedback.

2. **The need for self-verification**. Self-verification is linked to the maintenance of the individual's self-concept. Research suggests that the self-concept emerges as early as the first year of life. At that time, individuals become aware of themselves as distinct and separate from the environment. Swann (1983) has suggested that the need for self-verification would enhance or maximize the need for predictability.

3. **The need to avoid shame**. Shame carries with it the possibility of exclusion from the group or collective. Because this has profound implications for the individual's survival, shame might take precedence over pride in human motivation. Thus, when people with low self-esteem set easy goals for themselves, they could be protecting themselves against the shame associated with failure.

Note that people who have a mastery orientation tend to be relatively high in self-esteem, whereas people with a performance orientation tend to be low in self-esteem (e.g., Franken & Prpich, 1996). This finding is consistent with the view that people with low self-esteem are motivated by the need or desire to avoid shame and that people with high self-esteem are motivated by the need or desire to experience pride.

Self-Esteem and Reactions to Success and Failure

Research has consistently shown that, whereas people with high self-esteem perform equally well following success and failure, people with low self-esteem perform significantly less well after failure. Research by Brockner (1979), however, indicates that this is only true under self-focusing stimulus conditions. That is, when subjects were encouraged to focus on their performance or simply tended to be self-conscious about their performance, subjects with low self-esteem tended to perform poorly after a previous failure. These findings are consistent with Carver's (1979) model, which suggests that fear or anxiety cues will disrupt performance if they become salient. According to Carver, when such cues become salient, the person is inclined to assess the likelihood of completing the task. Subjects whose expectations are positive—for instance, after a success—will be motivated to match their behavior against the standard. If they begin to think that they will not be able to complete the task, however, they will respond with passivity and withdrawal. Subjects with low self-esteem tend to have a low opinion of their abilities, so they will be more inclined to respond to failure with reduced motivation. Tests of this model have shown that, in comparison with negative expectations, positive expectations do lead to greater persistence or performance, but only when there is self-focused attention (Carver, Blaney, & Scheier, 1979a, b).

The finding that individuals with high self-esteem and those with low self-esteem respond differently to failure is consistent with the idea that individuals with low self-esteem are more motivated by the need to avoid shame than are those with high self-esteem. In the next section, we will see why.

Interestingly, both individuals with high self-esteem and those with low self-esteem tend to experience self-doubt when they fail. An approach to managing self-doubt is outlined in Practical Application 13-2. It should also be noted that people with low-self esteem tend to overgeneralize following failure. Practical Application 13-3 talks about this tendency and what you can do to overcome this tendency.

The Development of Self-Esteem

As we have seen, levels of self-esteem tend to be relatively stable over time and highly resistant to change. Moreover, a number of studies have shown that the individual's level of self-esteem develops relatively early in life. Let's examine the biological, learned, and cognitive aspects of that process.

The Biological Component

People with high self-esteem tend to be low in anxiety, whereas people with low self-esteem tend to be high in anxiety (e.g., Franken & Prpich, 1996). Because considerable evidence indicates that anxiety has a strong genetic component (Chapter 5), there is reason to believe that anxiety could be partly responsible for low self-esteem. As we have seen, anxious people tend to be apprehensive about the future (Barlow, 1988). Among other things, they have a bias to process threat cues (Chapter 10) and tend to seek out the familiar and predictable (Chapter 12). In contrast, people who are low in anxiety tend to have a bias toward processing new stimuli (Chapter 12). Moreover, individuals with low anxiety are more inclined to engage in mastery behaviors. This pattern of behavior is very similar to that for individuals with low and high self-esteem, respectively (Osborne, 1996).

Though the two patterns of behavior are similar, most researchers recognize that self-esteem is a higher-order construct that involves anxiety and our conceptions about the world.

The Learned Component

The self-esteem movement has arisen from the assumption that individuals will have high self-esteem if their life experiences are mainly positive. To produce high self-esteem, then, the individual needs an environment in which successes are more likely than failures. One approach, of course, would be to lower the standards for success. The self-esteem movement also assumes that, if the balance between positive and negative experiences is shifted, individuals with low self-esteem will automatically begin to behave in the same way as do those with high self-esteem; low self-esteem individuals will suddenly begin to select difficult tasks, and so forth. Such a transformation would be almost magical. That idea might be what made the self-esteem movement so appealing. It appears to bypass all the complicated stuff about teaching people to set goals, encouraging them to be independent, and encouraging

them to persist. Research has found little support for this approach (Osborne, 1996). In fact, it can backfire. One study found that children who were given easy tasks to ensure success had lower confidence in their ability than children not given easy tasks (Meyer, 1982).

Research on high self-esteem strongly indicates that it develops from a mastery orientation. Among

Practical Application 13-2

Managing Self-Doubt After Failure: Downward Comparison

One of the things most likely to undermine goal-directed behavior is failure. All individuals, whether high or low in self-esteem, experience self-doubt following failure and tend to reduce their efforts markedly as a result. Interestingly, although people with low self-esteem often give up following failure, those with high self-esteem bounce back as though nothing happened.

Why is that? It appears that, following a failure, people with high self-esteem lower their expectations, at least momentarily. Specifically, instead of comparing themselves to high performers—those who have already achieved difficult goals—they compare themselves to low performers—people whom they have already passed on the road to success. As a result, they feel much better about themselves. Instead of seeing themselves in the bottom of the high group, they see themselves in the top of the low group. In short, they see themselves as winners; they take pride in what they have already achieved.

Those with low self-esteem are not inclined to do this. They continue to compare themselves with people in the high-performance group and come to feel that they have not achieved much. As a result, they cannot take pride in their past accomplishments and they begin to see themselves as losers (e.g., Gibbons & McCoy, 1991; Wills, 1981, 1991).

We might ask why anyone would want to select the high-performance group as a standard of comparison in the first place? Why not select the low-performance group? Wouldn't that ensure good self-esteem?

In practice, that doesn't work for most people, for at least two reasons. First, people are normally well aware that they are part of a larger society, and they know that, in the long run, they are going to be judged by what the larger group has done. Second, certain people take a great deal of satisfaction in maximizing their skills and becoming the best. To know what it means to be the best, they look to others around them. Whether this inclination to excel is learned or innate remains unclear.

Research indicates that, after a failure, individuals with high self-esteem will eventually select the high performers as their standard of comparison again, because high performers motivate them to develop their skills.

Note that some people never select the high-performance group as their standard. By selecting low performers as their standard of comparison, low achievers attempt to maintain their self-esteem. To select the high performers would be devastating for such people.

The key, perhaps, to making personal use of this information is to understand that we need to select role models that are better than we are but not so much better that we can never hope to match their successes. If possible, we should attempt to find models who will share with us what they do to succeed. Success, is not the result of chance but, rather, comes from attending to all those various facets that work together in concert to produce a final outcome.

other things, people with high self-esteem tend to select difficult tasks (e.g., Franken & Prpich, 1996). McClelland's (1985) work shows that people with a strong need to achieve also tend to have high self-esteem. Although the self-esteem movement has generally argued that self-esteem causes achievement, McClelland's research suggests that achievement has its roots in independence training. The same conclusion follows from a classic study by Coopersmith, which we will look at next.

Self-esteem and parental guidance. Stanley Coopersmith (1967) concluded that individuals with high self-esteem differ in a number of important ways from individuals with low self-esteem. Those with high self-esteem set more difficult goals, are less troubled by

anxiety, experience less stress and fewer psychosomatic symptoms, are less sensitive to failure and criticism, experience greater feelings of control and fewer feelings of helplessness, tend to be more enterprising in approaching problems, and tend to explore more—show more curiosity toward themselves and their environment. They are intrinsically motivated people who tend not only to be competent but also to have a positive attitude toward themselves.

Coopersmith's research indicates that self-esteem can be nurtured and that parents play a primary role in that nurturing process. Parents of children with high self-esteem are characterized by total acceptance of, and respect for, the child; a tendency to set clearly understandable limits on what the child is permitted and not permitted to do; and a tendency to allow the child

Practical Application 13-3

Learning Not to Overgeneralize After Failure

The tendency of people with low self-esteem to overgeneralize following failure results from lack of differentiation. Overgeneralization is the tendency of negative outcomes to trigger other feelings of personal inadequacy in domains that are unrelated to the initial negative outcome (Kernis, Brockner, & Frankel, 1989). What this means is that, when people experience a negative outcome at work, say, they are inclined to generalize that negative outcome to other domains in their life—for example, to their social relations, appearance, and intelligence. In other words, the criticism makes them question not only their abilities to do the job but also their intelligence, their appearance, and their social skills. The process seems to involve rumination. As they think about what they did wrong, they begin looking for other instances where they failed in their life. They could conclude, based on the examples they dredge up while ruminating, that they are not worthy of positive self-regard. As a result, their self-worth plummets.

What happens to people with high self-esteem when they receive negative feedback? First, presumably because they have highly differentiated self-

concepts, the negative feedback does not cross into other domains of their lives; it remains highly compartmentalized. If the work domain itself is highly differentiated, they might be able to further compartmentalize the negative feedback into a subcategory of that domain. The net result is that people with high self-esteem simply reconfirm something they already knew about themselves before they received the negative feedback.

Note that negative feedback creates self-doubt in everyone. Whereas those low in self-esteem overgeneralize when this happens, however, those high in self-esteem do not. The tendency to overgeneralize is the source of the problem. This is reminiscent of the antecedents of pessimism and depression.

One thing people can do to guard against the tendency to overgeneralize is to focus on what went wrong in this particular instance and then make plans about what they will do in similar circumstances in the future. Such active problem-solving strategy distracts one from the tendency to ruminate and helps reestablish beliefs that events are, for the most part, controllable.

Graduating from a university is a major accomplishment that can and often does open to new and exciting possibilities.

great latitude to explore and test within those limits. Coopersmith argues that parents of children with high self-esteem create a climate that frees the child from anxiety and doubt. Within such an environment, the child can explore freely and, in so doing, gain competence. Coopersmith notes that parents of children with high self-esteem encourage the children to become responsible and competent and to accept the independence and diversity of expression that accompany the emergence of such behavior. In other words, the children learn from their parents—a significant source of acceptance and love—that they are important individuals, who can expect continued acceptance by their parents and by society at large even if they occasionally fail or if their behavior deviates somewhat from

the norm. The children react to that signal, Coopersmith finds, by continuing to set high goals and working hard to attain them.

Coopersmith's work indicates that self-esteem can mediate, in part, the tendency to achieve. It also suggests that individual differences in self-esteem are acquired early in life. As we noted earlier, one reason that changing achievement behavior is difficult is that it involves changing individuals' perceptions of their abilities. If self-esteem affects their perceptions of their abilities (competence), then their self-esteem must also be changed. The work on changing achievement motivation suggests that we need to focus on both self-esteem and perceptions of ability (control) because they influence each other.

Coopersmith's research suggests how to maximize feelings of pride in children and, in the process, to nurture high self-esteem. When children are viewed as independent, autonomous, and capable of making choices, they learn, in their own small ways, that they can be victorious and triumphant. That gives them the confidence to accept challenges later in life.

Carl Rogers considered the parental role in the development of self-esteem within a somewhat different framework—that of conditional and unconditional love. Let's look at Rogers' approach.

Self-esteem and unconditional love. Rogers (1959) assumed that we are innately motivated to develop high self-esteem, which he calls positive self-regard. Whether we develop positive self-regard, Rogers suggested, is linked to whether we are raised with unconditional or conditional love. If we are raised with conditional love, we will have difficulty experiencing positive self-regard. Conditional love is dependent on our acting in an acceptable way. Instead of being loved for who we are or for what we believe, we are loved for what we do or what we accomplish. According to Rogers, conditional love often produces a negative self-image. When parents or other significant people in our lives emphasize the importance of achieving important goals or acting in a certain way, we develop unrealistic ideas about what we must do before we can think positively about ourselves. Rogers maintained that, if we are to be able to think positively about ourselves, we need to have a sense of worth that is not conditional on a specific behavior. All of us make mistakes; we all fail sometimes. Faced with this reality, we often develop a sense of conditional worth: "When I act in a certain way, I am worthy but, when I don't act in that way, I am not worthy." Conditional worth eventually leads to a negative self-concept. According to Rogers, the realization that we can never achieve certain goals—never live up to our ideals—leads to a sense of futility.

Unconditional love, in contrast, leads to positive self-regard. If love is not dependent on acting in prescribed ways, it doesn't matter if we sometimes fail or make mistakes. Rogers maintained that, when mistakes and failures are not linked directly to feelings of worth, they can be viewed in a more realistic and less destructive way. We can view our mistakes simply as part of the process of maturing or as feedback about our progress. When parents withdraw love to indicate their disapproval, it creates enormous anxiety in the child because the parent is the child's primary means of survival. If, on the other hand, parents do not withdraw their love when they disapprove, the child is not overpowered with feelings of anxiety.

This argument recalls Dweck's (1991) suggestion that people who have learned to seek approval from others develop an other-directed performance orientation, rather than a learning orientation, in which the goal is to increase personal competence. This is also consistent with Coopersmith's findings that children with high self-esteem come from environments characterized by acceptance and that such environments tend to produce a mastery orientation.

The Cognitive Component

A number of recent studies have examined how people's ideas about themselves and their relationship to the world influence their self-esteem. Let's begin by considering the role of the individual's locus of control.

Self-concept and self-esteem. It appears that, as the result of certain early experiences, people construct a self-concept that is either good at enhancing and maintaining their self-esteem or is not. Let's look at some of the differences in self-concept between individuals with high and low self-esteem.

Substantial evidence indicates that people with high self-esteem have a clearly differentiated self-concept (Campbell, 1990; Markus & Nurius, 1986). Among other things, that means that these people have a clear idea of the life domains that are important to them and of their strengths and weaknesses in these domains. As a result, they have a clear and stable view of themselves so they can deal with both positive and negative feedback. Those with low self-esteem, in contrast, seem to have no clearly defined idea of the life domains that are important to them nor of their strengths and weaknesses in these domains. As a result, they are unable to deal with negative feedback.

Remember that high self-esteem involves learning to acknowledge and accept our weaknesses. This seems to lessen the impact of negative feedback. As Baumgardner (1990) has pointed out, "To know oneself is to like oneself" (p. 1062). When people know themselves, they can maximize outcomes because they know what they can and cannot do. For example, they can find ways of compensating for their weaknesses. In contrast, people who don't know their strengths and weaknesses are not in a position to take effective action. As a result, they experience a sense of insecurity.

One strategy of people with low self-esteem—or unstable self-esteem, that is, a view of themselves that is positive but fragile—is to resist or ward off evaluative feedback (Kernis, Gannemann, & Barclay, 1989). Although it might spare them some negative feedback, this strategy prevents them from forming a clear idea of who they are and robs them of valuable information that they need to improve their behavior. People are more likely to learn and develop when they are willing to seek out evaluation and assistance.

Showers (1992) has found that some people compartmentalize their self-knowledge into positive and negative categories. If they activate one of these categories, access to the other is temporarily blocked. As a result, if people activate the positive category, they will feel good about themselves; if they activate the negative category, they will feel bad about themselves. In general, people high in self-esteem are more inclined to perceive their positive qualities or strengths, so they tend to feel good about themselves most of the time. People low in self-esteem, in contrast, tend to perceive their negative qualities or weaknesses and tend to feel bad about themselves much of the time.

Showers (1992) also found that having a highly differentiated self-concept—that is, having many distinct categories—tends to reduce the impact of negative feedback.

Increasing Self-Esteem

As we have seen, research indicates that people with high self-esteem are characterized by optimism and hope (Franken & Prpich, 1996). According to Seligman (1990), optimism allows individuals to take credit for their successes and to avoid shame when they fail. According to Snyder and his colleagues, hope gives people a sense of agency and of pathways (Snyder et al., 1991). Agency is a tendency to take the initiative, to engage in coping behaviors, or to take control. Deci and Ryan (1991) refer to this as self-determination. A sense of pathways is the awareness that there are many ways to get to a goal. If one path doesn't work, there is always another.

Conversely, people with low self-esteem are characterized by pessimism and despair (Franken & Prpich, 1996). How can we replace pessimism with optimism, and despair with hope? Most researchers (e.g., Osborne, 1996) argue that, if people are to achieve high self-esteem, they must identify their core strengths—strengths that can bring them a sense of pride and accomplishment. They need to develop a mastery orientation.

Individuals who are unable to experience love and acceptance at home often develop low self-esteem. Adolescents who do not experience self-worth at home often turn to their friends. Children with low self-esteem are at risk for drug use and crime (Chapter 8) because they will be attracted to any group, delinquent or not, that satisfies their craving for acceptance.

A persistent theme in the literature is that our self-esteem is linked to getting what we want from life. If people see themselves as possessing the skills and abilities that they need to get what they want, they are likely to be high in self-esteem. This anticipatory cognition, based on beliefs about control, allows people to set goals and persist in the face of failure. One central reason people are low in self-esteem seems to be that they don't see themselves as having the skills and abilities to realize their goals (e.g., Osborne, 1996).

To increase individuals' self-esteem, it is necessary to change their self-concept. They need to perceive themselves as possessing the resources to get the important things that they want from life. Much of what people want reflects the values of society, parents, and peers. If they have skills consistent with those values, they are more likely to experience high self-esteem (Harter, 1993). Should their strengths lie elsewhere, they might need to change their values, so that they can derive self-esteem from the skills that they have.

There is no quick fix for low self-esteem. Nonetheless, researchers feel that it is possible for people to change. Many of us can improve our self-esteem by becoming more optimistic, by becoming more hopeful, and by becoming aware of our strengths and weaknesses. Ultimately, perhaps, the best approach is to help people become more mastery-oriented.

Summary

According to Parecki, high self-esteem is "pride in oneself in which one becomes aware and accepting of one's imperfections while cherishing one's inherent strengths and positive qualities." The core relational theme for pride, according to Lazarus, is enhancement of our ego-identity by taking credit for a valued object or achievement, either our own or that of some person or group with whom we identify. When children experience pride, they gain a sense of autonomy, power, curiosity, and self-confidence. On that basis, they can see themselves as agents capable of initiating change. Lazarus has argued that children who are able to experience pride develop high self-esteem.

Low self-esteem is the "shame in oneself that comes from appraising oneself as lacking skills and abilities important to valued others." Research indicates that feelings of self-esteem come from self-evaluation and from succeeding and failing in important domains. Further, they come from internalizing the values of society.

A consistent research finding is that individuals with low self-esteem tend to perpetuate their low self-esteem. At least three explanations have been offered to account for this finding: that individuals are motivated by predictability, that individuals are motivated by self-verification, and that individuals are motivated to avoid shame.

Because individuals who experience low self-esteem tend to be anxious, and because anxiety has a genetic basis, it can be argued that low self-esteem has its roots in our biology. Considerable evidence indicates, however, that self-esteem can be increased with mastery training. Coopersmith's work suggests that parents who create an atmosphere that is characterized by acceptance and freedom from anxiety tend to promote the development of high self-esteem. Such an atmosphere, it appears, tends to encourage curiosity and exploratory behaviors. Rogers has argued that people who are raised with unconditional love tend to develop positive self-regard.

Self-esteem appears to come from having a self-concept that is good at maintaining self-esteem. It is particularly important to have a highly differentiated or complex self-concept. One consistent theme in the research literature is that to change self-esteem people must learn to honor their strengths so they can experience pride.

Finally, people with high self-esteem are more inclined to make a downward comparison, a strategy that enhances their self-esteem.

Main Points

1. Twins studies have shown that about 30% of the variance associated with personal control (internality) is caused by genetics.
2. We can distinguish between two styles of personal control: active control and self-control. Different cultures tend to favor different styles.
3. Murray defined the need to achieve as the desire or tendency to "overcome obstacles, to exercise power, to strive to do something difficult as well as and as quickly as possible."
4. McClelland has argued that the achievement motive develops from a more basic incentive to "do something better"—not to gain approval or any other kind of external reward, but "for its own sake."
5. Social learning theory has suggested that achievement can be explained by the processes of modeling and imitation.
6. According to Atkinson, resultant achievement motivation is a joint function of the need to achieve and the need to avoid failure.
7. People have different implicit theories of intelligence. Some people see intelligence as fixed; this is called the entity model. Others see intelligence as changeable; this is the incremental model.
8. People who believe in the entity model of intelligence are motivated to select goals that will put them in a favorable light, whereas people who hold to the incremental model of intelligence tend to set a goal that will increase their competence.
9. Parecki has defined self-esteem as "pride in oneself in which one becomes aware and accepting of one's imperfections while cherishing one's inherent strengths and positive qualities." Low self-esteem can be defined as the shame that comes from appraising ourselves as lacking skills and abilities important to valued others.
10. People with high self-esteem have a bias to perceive their positive qualities or strengths, whereas people with low self-esteem, in contrast, have a bias to perceive their negative qualities or weaknesses.
11. Three factors—acceptance by parents, having limits, and having the opportunity to explore—appear to be important in the development of self-esteem, which, Coopersmith suggests, influences a child's tendency to achieve.
12. Rogers has suggested that unconditional love is likely to result in high self-esteem.
13. People with high self-esteem typically have clearly differentiated self-concepts and mastery orientations.
14. Overgeneralization refers to the tendency of negative outcomes to trigger other feelings of personal inadequacy in domains that are unrelated to the initial negative outcome.

InfoTrac® College Edition

What are some things that parents and educators can do to increase children's self-esteem? (Search words: self esteem, psychological aspects)

How can you learn to increase self-control? (Search words: self-control)

Chapter Fourteen

Self-Regulation of Motivation

- What does it mean to self-regulate?
- Are there any constraints on our ability to self-regulate?
- Should we set long-term goals for ourselves?
- Is it important to have short-term goals?
- Does goal-directed behavior ever become a habit (automatic) or do we continually have to work at it?

- Is it normal to experience self-doubt?
- Which is more important for success—ability or motivation?
- How do we learn to maintain an optimistic outlook when things are not going well?
- Do we need a good self-concept to succeed?
- Can we change our self-concepts?

Self-regulation refers to the ability to make use of knowledge we have about the lawfulness of human behavior and use that knowledge to achieve goals that we think are in our best interest or simply goals that will make us happy. Researchers have known for some time that good intentions are not enough. Good intentions need to be translated into action, a process, as we have discussed in the previous chapters, that depends on recognizing the forces of biology on the one hand and the powers of learning and cognition on the other hand.

The Self-Regulation of Behavior

Self-regulation theories have their roots in social-cognitive theories of behavior. Self-regulation involves three processes: (1) self-observation (self-monitoring); (2) self-evaluation, (self-judgment); and (3) self-reaction (self-incentive) (Bandura, 1991b).

1. **Self-observation (self-monitoring).** Before we can change a behavior, we need to become aware of it. This involves monitoring our behavior. The more systematically we monitor our behavior, the more quickly we will become aware of what we are doing. If we attend carefully to our performance, we will be inclined to set goals that lead to progressive improvement. If we want to improve our social skills, for example, we might start by making a list of things we do in social situations (for example, compliment, criticize, complain). Next, we might observe how often we do these things and under what conditions. Finally, we might set goals that will help us to become the persons we want to be.
2. **Self-evaluation (self-judgment).** The next step is to decide if what we are doing is congruent with what we want or, more generally, our personal standards. Personal standards are developed from information that we gain from significant others. Note that we do not passively absorb standards from others; rather, we construct them by reflecting on those behaviors and the effects that they produce. We ask ourselves whether it makes sense to criticize those with whom we want to develop a friendship, for example.

Social-cognitive theory assumes that most of us possess considerable knowledge about the best course of action to achieve a certain outcome but do not have

a clear idea of what we are presently doing. That's why we need to begin by self-monitoring. Once aware of our behavior, we need to determine whether to change that behavior. By focusing on consequences, we can assess whether or not we have produced the effect we want. By focusing on the consequences of our behavior, we can determine, for example, whether we tend to be overly critical or unduly passive.

Having decided what we need to do, we set a goal and then attempt to match our behavior to that goal. By continuing self-evaluation, we can determine if we are on the right track.

3. **Self-reaction (self-incentive).** Self-judgments are typically accompanied by affective reactions. When we succeed or do well, we typically experience pleasure or satisfaction; however, when we fail or perform poorly, we typically experience a negative mood or dissatisfaction. These self-reactions can lead us to set higher goals or to abandon a goal.

To achieve our goals, we need to pursue a course of action that produces positive self-reactions and avoid courses of action that produce self-censure. When we make self-satisfaction contingent on certain accomplishments, we motivate ourselves to expend the energy needed to attain our goals. Those who succeed in regulating their motivation make effective use of self-incentives—for instance, by making self-satisfaction contingent on performing a certain prescribed set of actions, such as those necessary to achieve their goals (Bandura, 1991b).

The Biological Component

The Evolution of Consciousness

Although many researchers have conceptualized consciousness as something you have or don't have it is perhaps more conceptually powerful and accurate to think of consciousness as levels that go from low to high (Damasio, 1999). From this perspective, levels of consciousness can be defined in terms of various qualities or characteristics that reflect the dynamic quality of how we think and react to the world around us. This is consistent with the subjective view that at times we feel very aware of everything that is happening around us, but at other times we do not. To the degree that animals share some of these qualities that give rise to consciousness, they too can be considered to have consciousness, even though it might be at a lower level and different than that characterizing human consciousness. According to Antonio Damasio (1999), consciousness has its roots in wakefulness and the ability to generate images of objects. He suggests that to have core consciousness, we also need to have a sense of the self. This sense of self arises from observations that the images have a relationship to the person. From an evolutionary perspective, it was highly adaptive to be able to form images and map those images in relation to the self. Think of what it would be like if you couldn't form images of objects. If a predator was behind a rock, for example, it would be gone and, thus, no threat. By being able to create images of the predator that lasted for short periods, our ancestors developed the capacity to maintain their vigilance even if their receptors were not being stimulated by the predator's image. Think of what it would be like not to have a sense of self. Knowing that a predator was approaching or leaving had important implications for survival. For mapping to take place there has to be a reference point and that reference became the person or self.

According to Damasio, higher levels of consciousness (including the autobiographical self) require lasting images (long-term memory) that we can retrieve at any time, not simply those fleeting images that helped our ancestors to remain vigilant. Like others, he argues that this high level of consciousness that allows humans to use the past and the future to guide one's actions was made possible by humans' large brains, especially the development of long-term memory. A large memory allows humans to draw on their past experiences to help them make decisions. A large memory also allows humans to use the stored experiences of others to help them make decisions. It was also important for humans to have the capacity to entertain several alternative possibilities more or less simultaneously. Researchers suggest that our large forebrain makes this possible. For example, the prefrontal cortex has been linked to such things as problem-solving and creativity.

Damasio (1999) calls this higher level consciousness extended consciousness. It involves both core consciousness and a large working memory. It can give rise to the autobiographical self that includes memories about our lived life and our planned life. What links all these memories about the self together are stories that we create. Damasio views humans as natural story tellers. At the core of these stories is the self. The self maps all our experiences and produces our uniqueness.

Although most researchers seem to agree that our large brains make it possible for us to have and enjoy a high level of consciousness (Damasio, 1999), to engage in self-observation (Ornstein, 1991) and to become efficient problem solvers (Pinker, 1997), researchers don't agree about why we developed large brains in the first place. One argument is that the cortex grew large as an adaptation to cool the brains of our ancestors (Ornstein, 1991). Others have argued that it grew large as an adaptation to becoming problem solvers (Pinker, 1997). There are many advantages to becoming a "thinking machine." Instead of having to wait for multiple generations of humans to adapt to a new situation, the thinking machine/problem-solving organism could process and store information about the environment and then use that information to make decisions. This allows us to use past experiences to help guide our behavior. By developing language, we could pass that experience along to our offspring and thereby increase their chances of survival (Pinker, 1997; Tooby & Cosmides, 1992). Despite all these wonderful arguments, evolutionary theory works from the perspective that adaptations, such as developing a large brain, occurs because of some problem faced by our ancestors. What was that problem? We are not certain.

The argument—that the large brain emerged to cool the body (Ornstein, 1991), to allow us to become problem solvers (Pinker, 1997), or to allow us to develop consciousness—are not incompatible. According to current thinking, even if our large brains evolved to meet a specific adaptation, nothing would prevent the brain from being used for other purposes (Nicholson, 1997). In other words, if the brain tissue designed to cool the brain could be simultaneously used to do other things without destroying its original function, it could simultaneously cool and provide the mass of neural tissue that would be needed to allow us to become a thinking machine.

What seems to make the human brain so unique is that it appears to be able to process information at a much higher level than that of our close relatives—chimpanzees—with whom we share 98% of our genes. Robert Ornstein (1991) argues that this ability to process large amounts of complex information makes it possible for us to engage in self-observation. But self-observation alone does not make it possible for us to self-regulate. To self-regulate we need to be able to take control of all our behaviors—even those that are deeply rooted in our basic biology—including such things as hunger, sex, and the fight-flight response.

Most if not all evolutionary psychologists believe that complete self-control (the ability to completely self-regulate or become completely rational) is not possible (Nicholson, 1997; Pinker, 1997). The best we can hope for is the ability to inhibit, redirect, and refine some of our behaviors. Researchers have argued that what governs behavior is many independent systems (sometimes called minds) and that each of these systems has a unique evolutionary path. Among other things, this means these systems do not necessarily communicate or cooperate with other systems. It, therefore, is a daunting task for humans to self-regulate their behavior. Various people have argued, nonetheless, that we can move in this direction but that it takes a great deal of time and effort. In short, self-regulating our behavior is something that we can learn to do (Langer, 1989).

The Learned Component

Although we have the capacity for self-observation (presumably because of spare or excess capacity), it does not appear that we are necessarily predisposed to use that ability. This is consistent with the idea that consciousness (self-observation) did not come about as an adaptation per se but, rather, is something that is possible because we evolved large brains. One important implication of this idea is that if we want to make use of that capacity, it needs to be developed. Taking the time and effort to develop the capacity implies that we think there will be some benefit. Most who have written about the evolution of consciousness have come to the conclusion there is a benefit. Clearly, the people who have worked on self-regulation have made this assumption (Ornstein, 1991).

How do we come to develop consciousness so that we can engage in self-observation? Various writers have suggested that the first step is to recognize that there are many different systems or minds vying for control. These different motivation systems include

such things as our energy system (food), our reproductive system (sexual behavior), and our fight-flight system (stress). In addition, all the emotions have their roots in our biology. Second, we need to recognize that these systems and emotions evolved more or less independently of one another but that each evolved to help us survive in some way. Thus, like egocentric children, each system and emotion attempts to take center stage. To self-regulate, we need to recognize the existence of these systems but not necessarily allow them to control our actions. This means, among other things, that we do not have to become angry, we do not have to feel guilty, we do not have to feel rejected, and we do not have to experience low self worth.

The Cognitive Component

What consciousness (self-observation) allows us to do, in other words, is to refine our actions. We need to recognize that although our emotions evolved to help us adapt, they are sometimes wrong or inappropriate. Evolution has helped us to survive by making us overreact. It is clearly better to overreact than under react. It is better to make sure we are a safe distance from a bear than risk being attacked by a bear. What we need to do, therefore, is constantly ask ourselves what is the right thing to do—are we overreacting?

Does that mean we should attempt to ignore our feelings? No, our feelings are a very good source of information. Remember that our feelings evolved to be correct most of the time, not all the time (Ornstein, 1991). What we need to do is ask if our feelings are appropriate, and if they are appropriate, what is the best reaction. In short, we need to realize that for everything we do, we could do alternative things (Langer, 1989). Our goal is to strive to become fully conscious. To do that we need to ask ourselves constantly what other alternatives are possible. When we have been verbally attacked, for example, we need to ask ourselves if we should retaliate and if so how. A verbal attack does not threaten our survival, so physically retaliating might not be in our best interest. Through experience or training, most of us have learned not to retaliate physically. In many cases, it isn't even worth our time to become angry. If we do become aroused, we are likely to fret for some time about how to retaliate in some way. In many situations, it is in our best interest to not experience anger and to simply exit from the situation. When we can do that, we are operating as though we were fully conscious.

Summary

Self-regulation of behavior is an outgrowth of social-cognitive theories. Self-regulation involves three steps: (1) self-observation (self-monitoring), (2) self-evaluation (self-judgment), and (3) self-reaction (self-incentive). From an evolutionary perspective, it was adaptive for our ancestors to develop the ability to create images of objects and to map the world using themselves as reference points. This rudimentary ability is what has given rise to core consciousness. Extended consciousness was made possible by the evolution of a large brain that could store and manipulate large amounts of information. Autobiographical self refers to the lived and to the planned self. The autobiographical self emerged out of the natural tendency of humans to tell stories.

The consensus seems to be that humans need to work at developing consciousness. Through the process of becoming fully conscious we can learn to self-regulate. Among other things, learning to self-regulate means we do not have to be servants to our emotions. Through self-regulation we can redirect our behavior, and in doing so, bring our behavior in line with what we believe is in our best self-interest.

Setting Goals

In this chapter we are going to focus mostly on what might simply be called attaining personal success. We start by discussing how we can use goals to achieve what we want from life. As we will discuss, the cornerstone of attaining personal success is mastering the art and science of goal-setting.

Under the right conditions, goals (1) arouse effort, (2) give rise to persistence, (3) provide direction, and (4) motivate strategy development (Bandura, 1991a; Locke & Latham, 1990). The first three effects derive from traditional motivation theory, but the fourth has its roots in cognitive motivation theory. Strategy devel-

opment involves finding routes to our goals. According to cognitive motivation theory, we take an active role in determining the best route to a particular goal. To do so, we need to acquire knowledge, to generate alternatives, to make plans, and so forth. Cognitive motivation theorists maintain that goals create the motivation to engage in these activities.

Proximal and Distal Goals

It is important to distinguish between different kinds of goals. To create action, a goal must be proximal rather than distal. Proximal goals relate to the immediate future. By meeting proximal goals, we will eventually achieve our distal goals. By achieving the proximal goal of writing a term paper, for example, I move toward my distal goal of obtaining a postsecondary degree. Distal goals are sometimes referred to as aspirations.

A general rule of thumb is that distal goals are useless without proximal goals, and proximal goals are useless without distal goals. Distal goals are typically associated with greater anticipatory emotion. Thinking about being a doctor, for example, produces greater feelings of satisfaction than thinking about finishing a term paper. As a result, distal goals have the capacity to sustain motivation even when we are pursuing a boring or time-consuming proximal goal. We often use distal goals to sustain motivation when the proximal goal is unable to do so. The image of being a doctor, for instance, will sustain a student through a difficult chemistry class.

Distal goals also keep us on course. Without them, we are inclined to drift off in other directions. We turn our attention to a more interesting proximal goal, for example. Extensive anecdotal evidence indicates that those without distal goals are inclined to change their direction often, whereas those with a clear distal goal are more inclined to stay the course.

Distal goals without proximal goals tend to result in no action. When we talk about doing something one day, we typically fail to get on with the task. The proximal goal motivates us to action. A proximal goal is what we plan to do today or tomorrow. My experience is that, without a game plan for the immediate present, I tend to do very little. On days when I make a list, I get things done.

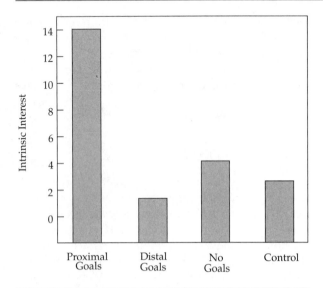

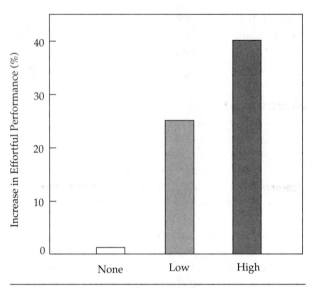

Figure 14-1. Level of intrinsic interest in arithmetic activities shown by children in different goal conditions when given free choice of activities. (From "Cultivating Competence, Self-Efficacy and Intrinsic Interest through Proximal Self-Motivation," by A. Bandura & D. H. Schunk, *Journal of Personality and Social Psychology*, 1981, *41*, 586–598. Copyright © 1981 by the American Psychological Association. Reprinted by permission.)

Figure 14-2. Mean increases in motivational level under conditions of performance feedback for people who continue to perform the activity without goals and those who spontaneously set low or high goals for themselves. (From "Self-Regulation of Motivation through Anticipatory and Self-Reactive Mechanisms," by A. Bandura. In R. A. Dienstbier (Ed.), *Perspectives of Motivation. Nebraska Symposium on Motivation*, 1991, 69–164 (Figure 6). Copyright © 1991 by University of Nebraska Press. Reprinted with permission.)

Evidence from a range of sources attests to the importance of having immediate goals. For example, the data in Figure 14-1 show the level of interest in arithmetic activities expressed by children with different types of goals, when given a free choice of activities (Bandura & Schunk, 1981). Albert Bandura (1991a) argues that meeting proximal goals or subgoals generates self-satisfaction. These immediate subgoals offer a continuing source of motivation, quite apart from the loftier superordinate goals.

People may be reluctant to set goals—difficult goals, in particular—because they fear the regret that will come if they do not achieve those goals. To put it another way, people do not set goals for themselves because they are motivated to protect their self-esteem. Research has shown that people with low self-esteem are inclined to minimize opportunities for regret (Josephs, Larrick, Steele, & Nisbett, 1992).

Setting Difficult but Attainable Goals

According to Edwin Locke and Gary Latham (1990), we should set difficult but attainable goals for ourselves. Most of us have the capacity to determine whether we can or cannot do something. Research indicates that, once we have decided that we can attain a particular goal, we are inclined to put forth effort and persist until we reach it. If the goal is not sufficiently difficult, it will fail to motivate. Alternatively, if the goal is perceived as unattainable, we will not put forth effort.

Bandura (1991a) has compared the effort expended, under the action of feedback, by people with no goals and those who spontaneously set low or high goals. Figure 14-2 indicates that goal difficulty plays a critical role in the amount of effort people are willing to put forth. (As we'll see shortly, feedback is a critical variable in performance.) When people are not given goals, they often spontaneously set goals for themselves (Locke & Latham, 1990). Many people have learned, it appears, that setting goals is a good way to motivate themselves.

Why do some people set easy goals for themselves, but others set difficult goals? As a general rule, people do not like to be viewed as lacking in competence. To avoid that possibility, some individuals select only easy tasks. By failing to stretch themselves, however, they impede the development of a sense of competence. Individuals with an entity theory of intelligence (Chapter 13) tend to select easy tasks because failure would further undermine their already fragile sense of competence.

Feedback

Within Bandura's theory, feedback is essential if motivation is to be maintained at a high level (Bandura, 1991a). Bandura and Cervone (1983) found that motivation is highest in the presence of both goals and feedback (Figure 14-3). These results are consistent with the idea that we are motivated to meet a certain standard of performance that we have set for ourselves. Without feedback, we cannot determine how well we are doing and, consequently, we cannot easily assess whether we need to put forth more effort, to persevere, or even to analyze our behavior.

Self-Set Goals, Assigned Goals, and Commitment

Bandura and others have argued that self-set goals tend to produce greater motivation than assigned goals do. There are at least two reasons for this. First, we are in the best position to create an optimal goal because we are the best judges of our own capacity for a given task. Second, we tend to be more committed to decisions that we have made ourselves. Thus, it makes sense that self-set goals will maximize motivation.

Locke and Latham (1990) demonstrated that assigned difficult goals can motivate people, but only when people become committed to the goal. Much of their research has been done in a work setting, where people are already committed to putting in time. In

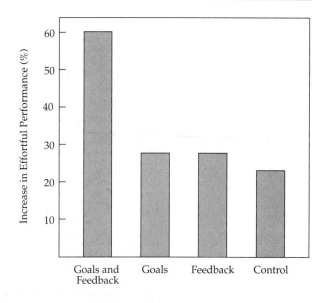

Figure 14-3. Mean percentage change in level of motivation under four conditions: goals with performance feedback, goals alone, feedback alone, and none of these factors (control). (From "Self-Evaluative and Self-Efficacy Mechanisms Governing the Motivational Effects of Goal Systems," by A. Bandura & D. Cervone, *Journal of Personality and Social Psychology*, 1983, *45*, 1017–1028. Copyright © 1983 by the American Psychological Association. Reprinted with permission.)

that situation, committing to a difficult goal might simply be perceived as an opportunity for greater satisfaction. In addition, assigning a difficult goal could communicate to workers the idea that their boss is confident in their ability to complete the task. Research indicates people are more inclined to select difficult goals if they perceive that they have ability to attain those goals. Teachers often set difficult goals for students to communicate to them the belief that they have or can develop competence.

The Need for Challenging Goals

It was popular for a time to tell people to do their best rather than to assign difficult goals. As we saw in Chapter 13, this approach grew out of a model in which self-esteem is assumed to depend on the sum to-tal of positive and negative events. This model suggests that reducing negative events will improve self-esteem and hence performance.

Research shows that individuals told to do their best do no better than those with no goals (Locke & Latham, 1990). It appears that, when people are told to do their best, they interpret these instructions to mean "Stay the course." Unless they are challenged, they assume that they are doing their best. As we see in the next section, if a goal is to motivate behavior, it must create a discrepancy. It appears that saying "Do your best" fails to do that.

Discrepancy Hypotheses

Most goal-setting theories argue that goals create a discrepancy between where the individual is and where the individual would like to be and that the tension created by this discrepancy leads to action. However, the theories describe this discrepancy in different ways.

1. **Large Discrepancy.** According to discrepancy theory, which typically focuses on proximal goals, people need to create a discrepancy large enough to motivate them to action. The larger the discrepancy, the greater the motivation. Although some evidence indicates that effort increases as goal difficulty increases, there is an upper limit to the effort (Locke & Latham, 1990).

2. **Optimal Discrepancy.** Optimal-discrepancy theory emerged to define more precisely what kinds of proximal goals motivate behavior. According to optimal-discrepancy theory, a task should be neither so difficult that the individual cannot hope to achieve it nor so easy that it does not challenge the individual. Most optimal-discrepancy theories are concerned with what challenges an individual. They have their roots in cognitive processing theory, which describes how people process information and develop competence. Optimal-discrepancy theories assume that mastery involves the incremental development of the motor or cognitive structures that underlie competence (Bandura, 1991a; Dember & Earl, 1957).

3. **Normative Discrepancy.** It is sometimes suggested that people with a performance or ego orientation are

motivated to achieve a level of a skill that will meet normative standards (Locke & Latham, 1990). According to this approach, people are motivated by the discrepancy between where they are and some level of skill possessed by an important referent group. In sports, for example, participants must meet important standards before they can win.

Self-Efficacy Theory

Bandura (1997) has put forth a comprehensive overview of goal setting, as follows. First, the individual assesses whether the distal goal will provide some desired reward or satisfaction. (For example, "If I lose weight, will I really be more attractive or healthier?") Bandura describes this step as *outcome expectations*, defined as "a person's estimate that a given behavior will lead to certain outcomes." If outcome expectations are low, then the individual will not be motivated to select that goal. If expectations are high, the individual might then move to the next step—assessing whether he or she can mobilize the resources necessary to achieve the desired outcome. If I have become convinced that the only way to achieve my weight objectives is through exercise, I must then assess whether I can put in the time and effort required to achieve that goal. Bandura calls this judgment *feelings of self-efficacy*, defined as "the conviction that one can successfully execute the behavior required to produce the outcomes." In research, participants are simply asked if they believe they can do something. The resulting judgment can be thought of as a measure of *subjective difficulty*. One person might foresee little difficulty in pursuing an exercise program, but another might find the idea almost impossible.

Feelings of self-efficacy are assumed to be stable across time, but they are not stable across different situations. Unlike global feelings of competency, self-efficacy is situation-specific. Thus, we must measure feelings of self-efficacy for each new situation.

According to Bandura's theory, then, behavior is governed both by feelings of self-efficacy and by outcome expectations. If I have strong outcome expectations and strong feelings of self-efficacy, I will be inclined to put forth the effort necessary to achieve the desired outcome.

Bandura argues that goal-directed behavior is driven by the discrepancy between outcome expectations and where the individual is now, but the anticipated satisfaction is mediated by feelings of self-efficacy. If feelings of self-efficacy are low, I will not be inclined to make an effort or persist in the face of poor progress toward the goal. Feelings of self-efficacy will be affected by outcome expectations. If my goals are very high, my efficacy feelings might be lower as a result. If my outcome expectations are low, my feelings of self-efficacy are likely to be higher. In tests of the theory, self-efficacy ratings are typically used to predict performance. Most tests have shown that such feelings tend to be good predictors of a wide range of behaviors.

According to Bandura, discrepancies are reduced through a process called concept matching. When we set a goal, we create an image of the anticipated outcome. Failure to match the image sustains our motivation. Once the image has been matched, Bandura suggests, the motivation will subside. If my image is a slim and athletic torso, I would be inclined to maintain my efforts longer than if my image is only a moderately lean and athletic torso. What makes Bandura's theory so elegant is that it incorporates the idea that people have different goals and different beliefs about their ability to attain those goals. As a result, the theory can predict the wide individual differences that we typically observe when studying motivational processes.

Self-efficacy theory has proven very powerful in predicting a wide variety of behaviors such as adherence to exercise programs and stop-smoking programs (Schwarzer & Fuchs, 1995), athletic performance (Bandura, 1997), complex decision-making (Bandura & Jourden, 1991), self-empowerment (Ozer & Bandura, 1990), and health functioning (Bandura, 1997), to mention a few. The theory was originally proposed to account for the effectiveness of programs for the treatment of anxiety. In these programs, people were given specific skills to deal with specific anxiety-provoking or fearful situations. Thus, a person anxious about public speaking would be provided with the skills to effectively handle such a situation—for instance, how to structure a talk, how to speak clearly and dramatically, and how to manage any accompanying anxiety. Studies show that, once they have the skills they need,

people are less anxious and their self-efficacy typically increases. In short, when people perceive that they have the skills to deal with a specific situation, they feel empowered and self-confident.

Automaticity of Goal-Directed Behavior

Goal-directed behavior has traditionally been viewed as intentional; this means, among other things, that goal directed behavior results from conscious intentions or exercising our wills. An abundance of evidence indicates goal-directed behavior can and often does become unconscious or, simply, automatic. William James tells the story of getting ready for a dinner party, undressing, washing and then climbing into bed (Langer, 1989, p. 43). When people become distracted, they often follow a more familiar routine. I have on a couple of occasions found myself driving into the University parking lot on a Saturday when my intention was to go to some other place. In those instances, my thoughts were on something else.

A variety of researchers have argued that because the conscious is limited in its ability to process information, it is convenient and often necessary for humans to make better use of the unconscious to execute a variety of behaviors. This frees up the conscious to do other things such as generate ideas, make plans, organize activities, solve problems, and reflect on behavior. Experiments have shown that perhaps 95% of all goal-directed behavior is automatic (see Baumeister, Bratslavsky, Muraven, & Tice, 1998; also Baumeister & Sommers, 1997). Does that mean we should delegate all goal-directed behavior to the unconscious? As it turns out, it depends on whether or not the goal-directed action is in need of further refinement. Once actions are delegated to the unconscious they are no longer available for further refinement; thus, before delegating actions to the unconscious, they need to be well designed. Consistent with this argument, experiments have shown that automaticity of goal directed behavior occurs when the same choice is made repeatedly and consistently in a situation (Bargh & Chartrand, 1999). What is so intriguing about automatic behavior is that it is fast, efficient, and effortless (Bargh & Chartrand, 1999). What often slows down a response

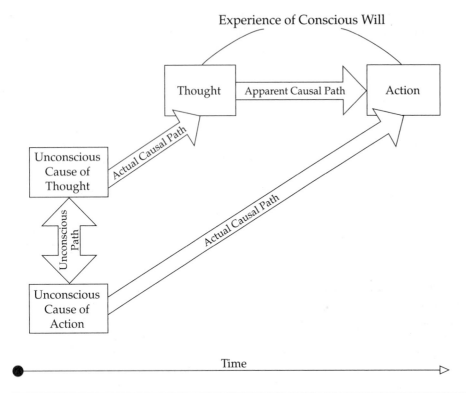

Figure 14-4.   A model of conscious will. (Note: Will is experienced to the degree that an apparent causal path is inferred from thought to action.) From "Apparent Mental Causation: Sources of Experience of Will," by D. M. Wegner and T. Wheatley, *American Psychologist*, 1999, *54*, 480–491. Copyright © 1999 by the American Psychological Association. Reprinted by permission.

and makes it so effortful is the need to make decisions; that is, to select among a variety of alternatives. One reason why pilots are trained in a simulator is to ensure that all the things they need to do in an emergency are under automatic control. In an emergency, there isn't time to recall what was said in the manual and then make decisions about what or what not one should do.

The Illusion of Conscious (Willful) Control

The idea that our actions come from unconscious thought processes rather than conscious thought processes often seems to contradict our subjective experience that our conscious intentions are what cause our actions. Researchers who have addressed this question have come to the conclusion that the subjective belief we experience about the causal link between thought and action is our interpretation (Wegner &

Wheatley, 1999). Figure 14-4 shows a model of what seems to happen. According to this model, the unconscious causes action and causes thought. Because we have experienced thoughts in conjunction with action, we interpret the contingency as evidence that our intentions (thoughts) were the cause of our actions.

Using Automatic Behavior to Accomplish Goals

The main problem that most people encounter when they attempt to translate goals into action is the failure to get started, becoming distracted, or falling into old habits (a word we often use to denote automaticity). It has been suggested that people can make strategic use of automatic process to secure goals attained by engaging in what has been called implementation intentions. Implementation intentions are plans that specify what an individual intends to do when a certain situation arises (what I will do when I get up in the morning). What these intentions do is delegate the initiation of goal directed behavior to anticipated situation cues (e.g., time, place, circumstances), that when encountered, will automatically trigger a desired behavior. These implementation intentions must be carefully designed so they will, in fact, trigger the desired behavior. For example, an implementation intention that includes a precise time someone will do something, such as 9:00 in the morning rather than sometime tomorrow, is much more effective. The more specific the cue is, the more likely the response will be triggered.

Harnessing Imagination in the Pursuit of Goals

Pop psychologists and others have suggested that an effective way to motivate yourself to achieve a goal is to imagine how you might think and feel when you have actually achieved your goal. If your goal, for example, is to become a doctor, you would think about such things as the respect you would enjoy, the comfortable life you would have, the exhilaration you would get from driving a new sports car, and so forth. The unfortunate thing about this very appealing idea is that it doesn't work (Taylor, Pham, Rivkin, & Armor, 1998). What does work, however, is thinking about what you need to do to achieve your goal. Specifically, this means using a process called mental simulation.

Mental simulation has been defined as the representation of some event or series of events (Taylor & Schneider, 1989). This could involve the replay of an event, such as athletes and others often do when they try to discover what led them to make an error or how they might have performed better. It could involve generating hypothetical scenarios of how one is going to act in the future, such as how one might ask for a date or how one might go about asking for a raise. What differentiates mental simulation from simple planning is that mental simulation makes things seem more real by creating images (Taylor et al., 1998).

Mental simulation is effective, researchers suggest, because it addresses the two fundamental tasks of self-regulation and coping, namely, the management of emotions and the ability to plan and solve problems. Not all forms of mental simulation are useful. For example, ruminating about a past painful event or substituting fantasy for reality can be counterproductive. Mental simulation works when it is used to simulate the process of achieving a goal. In mental simulation, the person sees him or herself succeeding by engaging in a series of carefully planned actions. Thus, when the time comes to actually execute a series of goal directed responses, it is as though one has already done this before. An ice skater might use mental simulation to create a new program or element to a program. To create a new element, the skater might imagine what would happen if he linked various existing skills together (jumps, turns, arm movements) in a new and different way. The next step, of course, would be executing the mental image.

Mental simulation can also be a useful way of dealing with past failures. Someone who has suffered a painful event in the past might successfully use mental simulation to help her deal with that event by rerunning the past event with an important difference; in the rerun the individual would prevent the painful outcome by engaging in some alternative course of action. Doing this would accomplish two things: It would reduce feelings of self-doubt while preparing the individual to succeed in the same or similar situations in the future. A politician who has suffered a humiliating defeat in a debate might rerun the debate inserting better arguments into the debate at those points where the previous arguments had been inefficient or weak.

When Outcome Expectancies Are Incongruent with Process Motivation

People often adopt goals, such as becoming a doctor or a lawyer, based on outcome expectations (which might or might not be realistic) without ever considering the process. For example, a person might think about the financial rewards of becoming a doctor without carefully considering the process necessary to achieve that goal. People might, for example, fail to consider that they dislike the sciences or that it will take many years to achieve their goals, or that when they do achieve their goals they will need to put in long hours and demanding work to receive the financial reward that initially appealed to them. That people often select goals based on some perceived outcome rather than on the process (the actions necessary to achieve their goal) could explain why it has been repeatedly found that motives and goals often do not correlate (Schultheiss & Brunstein, 1999). It is reassuring to know, however, that when goal imagery has been momentarily aroused, there is a positive relationship between implicit motives and explicit goals. What this research tells us is that people must align goals with motives (process motivation) rather than the reverse. We experience satisfaction and happiness when we are pursuing goals that are consistent with what we like to do. As it has been suggested from time to time, "The journey is the reward."

When Goal Intentions
and Good Implementation Plans Don't Work

Even if people have learned how to deal with such things as procrastination and distraction by forming good implementation intention plans, there could still be the problem of other competing automatic responses (what we often call bad habits) being triggered by the situation that undermine or get in the way of executing an intention. For example, even when people have carefully planned a speech, for example, they might experience anxiety. Kirsch and Lynn (1999) have suggested that these unwanted and nonadpative responses can be conceptualized as response sets that arise from response expectancies. The term *response expectancies* is intended to emphasize the idea that these unwanted and nonadaptive responses are thoughts (cognitions) rather than conditioned responses. If this is the case, the appropriate way to modify them is to modify the thought that triggers them.

One reason many psychologists think that response sets, such as an anxiety response, arise from our thoughts comes from a diverse set of research findings. Take for example, the placebo effect. Because people believe that a drug will often improve some mental or physical condition, they get better even when they haven't been given an active drug. As a result, it has become routine in the evaluation of drugs, especially psychoactive drugs, to determine how much of the improvement is caused by the drug and how much is caused by the placebo effect. In a study to examine the effectiveness of Prozac on depression, two different types of placebos were used: the normal control placebo, that gave participants an inactive substance, and a second control that gave participants an active substance: a drug that has not been linked to reducing the symptoms of depression but produced side effects (Kirsch & Sapirstein, 1999). The reasoning behind us-

ing this second type of placebo is that it is necessary to control for the fact that many drugs produce perceptible side effects. In the absence of perceptible side effects, researchers have argued, participants might conclude they had been assigned to the placebo condition whereas if they experienced perceptible side effects, they might conclude they had been assigned to the drug condition. If they were more inclined to believe they were in the experimental group, the placebo effect might be larger. As in previous research, this study found that Prozac was effective in alleviating symptoms of depression. What was interesting about this study was the fact 75% of the Prozac effect was duplicated by the administration of the inert placebo. But even more interesting, for our purposes, was the finding that participants given an active placebo showed the same improvement as subjects given a variety of antidepressants including Prozac (Kirsch & Sapirstein, 1999). This research does not claim to say that antidepressants aren't an effective tool in the treatment of depression. Rather, what this particular study shows is that expectancies can play a very powerful role in such things as feelings of depression.

If response sets are caused by thoughts, as research seems to show, how should these nonadaptive response expectancies be changed? As it turns out, this is not an easy question to answer. People who experience such thoughts often know they are not adaptive and consequently use distraction as a means of reducing such thoughts. Research has shown that such coping strategies are doomed to failure (Hayes & Gifford, 1997). No matter how hard people try to distract themselves, the negative thoughts return. To understand why distraction is often not effective, we need to understand the role that self-doubt plays in goal-directed behavior.

Dealing with Self-Doubt

Virtually everybody suffers from self-doubt. Some people, however, are able to manage self-doubt and do not let it overwhelm them. As Bandura (1991a) noted, "You cannot prevent the birds of worry and care from flying over your head. But you can stop them from building a nest in your head" (p. 135).

Self-doubt often results when we cannot turn off negative thoughts that intrude into our thinking. Irwin

Sarason (1984) has found that intrusive thinking is one of the major components of test anxiety. It prevents us from focusing our attention on the task at hand. Apparently, what produces this stress is not the intrusive thoughts themselves nor their frequency but, rather, our inability to turn them off (Churchill & McMurray, 1990; Kent, 1987). Evidence from many sources indicates that dwelling on our coping deficiencies causes distress and impairs our level of functioning and performance (Bandura, 1988; Lazarus & Folkman, 1984; Meichenbaum, 1977). Failure to control intrusive thinking can also result in depressive rumination, which again impairs performance and diminishes perceptions of competency (Chapter 10).

Research indicates that people with strong self-efficacy beliefs are less troubled by self-doubt, tend to handle adversity better, and tend to organize their thinking better (Bandura, 1991a, 1997). In other words, they do not need to spend as much time managing negative thinking.

Within Bandura's theory, there is a dual route to emotional control: through our perception that we have the ability or skills to cope with a specific situation, and through our perception that we can deal with intrusive negative thoughts. As discussed earlier (Chapter 11), research by Ozer and Bandura (1990) showed that negative thoughts not only lead to feelings of anxiety but also to avoidant behavior. In their research, which focused on empowering women who were fearful of sexual assault, Ozer and Bandura found that mastery training greatly reduced negative thoughts. Are there other ways to decrease negative thought? Various theorists have argued that it is often possible to gain control over negative thoughts by employing various self-regulation processes.

Suppressing unwanted thoughts implies that people have some kind of volitional control over their thinking. Research on this topic indicates that, indeed, people can control their thinking but that there are limitations. Research has found that although people can suppress unwanted thought for a period of time, there can be a rebound effect such that there is an increase in unwanted thoughts at a later time (Macrae, Bodenhausen, & Milne, 1998; Muraven, Tice, & Baumeister, 1998). This suggests that volition is a limited resource, much like limited energy. In one series of studies, researchers found that when volition is used for one activity, it reduced the ability to control behavior in a subsequent activity. One study showed, for example, that suppressing eating of chocolates (which takes a great deal of will power) rather than radishes (which takes much less will power) reduced persistence in a subsequent problem solving activity. Another study showed that suppressing an emotion reduced persistence in a later activity (Baumeister, Bratslavsky, Muraven, & Tice, 1998).

Gaining Control over Negative Thoughts

Ellis and Grieger (1977) have suggested three methods of gaining control of negative intrusive thoughts: monitoring self-talk; cognitive restructuring; and substituting other thoughts. A fourth method involves distancing.

Monitoring Self-Talk

People often engage in self-talk when they are trying to accomplish a task (Helmstetter, 1986). They might say to themselves, for instance, "This is too hard for me," "I'm never going to make it," "If I can just get around the next corner, I'm home free," or "I think I'm going to win this one." Where does this self-talk come from, and what does it mean? Self-talk comes from our assessment of our abilities relative to the difficulty of the task. Because self-talk changes quite dramatically as we proceed from the beginning of a task to the end, it is obviously not a stable estimate of our abilities. For example, people will start by saying, "I think I am going to do well"; then, when things get tough, they say, "I don't think I can do this"; and toward the end, they say, "If I can just hang in there, I'll make it."

Motivation is typically at a low point when our self-talk becomes negative. Negative self-talk generally reflects a momentary downward shift in feelings of self-efficacy. As a result, we are inclined to give up because the discrepancy between perceived abilities and goals is no longer optimal. Can we learn to control our self-talk, to prevent a slump in our motivation? It appears so. We must learn first to monitor our self-talk and then to alter it so that it is more congruent with goal-directed behavior. In short, we need to engage in positive self-talk, such as "I know I can do it," "I know I can succeed," "I have been here before and succeeded."

Cognitive Restructuring

Once we have learned to substitute positive for negative self-talk, the next step is to become aware of the dynamics of success. If we are aware, for example, that we tend to experience self-doubt when we push ourselves, we can regard the emergence of self-doubt as an indicator that we are indeed pushing ourselves to new heights. When athletes—especially body builders—want to overcome plateaus, they will often remind themselves, "No pain, no gain." It appears that many of the limits on our performance that we accept are purely psychological. After Roger Bannister broke the four-minute mile, for instance, many other athletes matched his achievement. Obviously, their bodies weren't limiting them—their minds were.

Substituting Other Thoughts

One reason that competing against other people can push us to new levels is that our attention shifts away from our pain and fatigue and toward the idea of winning. Considerable evidence indicates that, when we are thinking pleasant thoughts, our bodies respond favorably. The trick is to learn to control our thinking so that we do not fall prey to lower motivation.

Distancing Oneself from Negative Thoughts

Recent research suggests that an excellent way to get rid of negative thoughts or negative response expectancies, or at least reduce their impact, is to first accept them and then to distance oneself from them (Kirsch & Lynn, 1999). Distancing oneself means to view such thoughts as not of one's own making but, rather, as thoughts that we have come to adopt from some other source such as our parents or our society. Recall that according to evolutionary psychology, we have many minds. To successfully self-regulate, we need to accept they exist but not necessarily allow them to take control of our actions.

Developing Good Thinking Habits

One route toward the self-regulation of motivation is to develop good thinking habits. As Martin Seligman (1990) has noted, "Habits of thinking need not be forever. One of the most significant findings in psychology in the last twenty years is that individuals can

choose the way they think" (p. 8). Because all of us—no matter how skilled we are or how carefully we plan—will encounter frustrations and setbacks, we need to learn to become optimistic. We examined the differences between optimists and pessimists at length in Chapters 10 and 11, along with ways of becoming an optimist. The important point is that becoming an optimist, like becoming a constructive thinker, is a self-regulation process—a process that we can learn.

Ellen Langer (1989) has made a similar point in her book *Mindfulness*. She argues people often allow themselves to be guided by images that they have stored in their unconscious. When we become old, for example, we might allow ourselves to be guided by images that we have stored earlier about what old people can and cannot do, never questioning whether these images are accurate or useful. As a result, we might do things that reflect what we think we should do and not what we are capable of doing. Based on her research, she has argued that one reason people act old, such as not making decisions or not carrying heavy things, is not because they cannot make decisions or are not capable of carrying heavy things but because their images tell them they can't. In one experiment, she induced older men to adopt a more youthful set of images and found that this manipulation produced not only many outward changes, such as a younger posture and gait, but also several more basic changes such as improved eyesight, better mental functioning, and improved memory (Langer, 1989).

Langer argues that people need to question the images they have about how to behave in certain situations or at different ages and, if necessary, to change those images so that they are congruent with a happy and productive life. She argues that we do not have to behave mindlessly; we can become mindful by reflecting on our own behavior.

The Need to Live Consciously

I don't want to leave this section on goal setting, automaticity, and self-doubt without a few words of caution. Even though it appears that making goal-directed behavior automatic is highly desirable, an alternative body of research says we should attempt to live our lives consciously. As we discussed previously, in her work on aging, Langer (1989) showed that when people are given challenges or when they are required to make decisions, they are healthier and happier. I like Langer's suggestion that we should constantly ask ourselves two questions: Why am I doing this and what else could I be doing? Times change and as a result we need to ensure our behavior is appropriate to the present demands. Then we are acting in an adaptive manner. Research has shown that it takes both time and energy to live at a conscious level, but the rewards for making this extra effort appear to be numerous. A large body of data indicates that successful living is living consciously (Damasio, 1999; Langer, 1989; Ornstein, 1991).

Summary

According to goal-setting theory, goals (1) arouse effort, (2) give rise to persistence, (3) provide direction, and (4) motivate strategy development. A distinction has been made between distal and proximal goals. Although both are important, they serve different functions. As a general rule, people should set difficult but attainable goals. The motivation to work toward assigned goals appears to be mediated by commitment. Interestingly, people who are instructed to do their best do no better than people with no goals. According to goal-setting theory, there should be optimal discrepancy; that is, the task should be neither so difficult as to be unachievable nor so easy as to be no challenge.

Self-efficacy theory involves two major constructs: outcome expectations, and feelings of self-efficacy. According to the theory, motivation is created by self-set goals. The mechanism that governs the termination of motivation is concept matching. Goal-directed behavior has traditionally been viewed as intentional, but considerable evidence suggests it can and often does become automatic. An effective way of facilitating goal-directed behavior is to make use of mental simulation—a process that helps reduce emotions, such as self-doubt, and create the motivation to solve problems and make plans. It follows from this work and the work on implementation intentions that for us to work efficiently and effectively, we should make as much of our behavior as possible automatic (under unconscious control). In saying that, I must warn the reader that automatic behavior can turn us into mindless robots. It must be remembered that much of the

joy we get from life is arousing and managing our emotions as well as acting creatively. The trick is to find the right balance. The ideal is to ensure that much of our behavior is on automatic pilot so that we can free our conscious minds to deal with important things (the things we want or need to do to be happy). If we don't have a routine of some sort, we will have to spend all our energy dealing with mundane daily things. Trying to be constantly spontaneous, in other words, has its limits, as does routine.

Managing our emotions is important for goal attainment. We can learn to manage self-doubt by managing intrusive thinking. According to Bandura, there is a dual route to emotional control: People need to learn how to control their thinking and how to develop coping skills. Self-defeating thoughts can be managed by monitoring self-talk, by cognitive restructuring, by substituting positive thoughts, and by distancing.

Self-Regulation and the Self-Concept

Research shows that our success is not predicted by our intelligence but, rather, by how we think about the world (Epstein, 1991; Seligman, 1990). Some people have learned to think in ways that lead them to succeed; others think in more destructive ways that ultimately result in failure.

Many theorists believe that our self-concept ultimately determines the goals that we set, how we evaluate progress toward those goals, and the impact of success and failure on our future goal-directed behavior. In short, the self is the cornerstone of self-regulation. Certain individuals, for example, are inclined to set difficult goals for themselves because their self-concept allows them to entertain the belief that they can reach those goals. Perhaps their self-concept incorporates the idea they have the capacity to learn, or the capacity to work hard, or the capacity to find the right path. Armed with such beliefs, they can visualize themselves reaching their goals, and they decide to put forth effort.

The self-concept can be conceptualized as self-knowledge. It embraces how we think about the external world and how we think about our ability to deal with it. Growing out of our attempts to make sense of our own behaviors, our self-concepts represent the past, the present, and the future. Self-concept determines, for instance, how we process information, the feelings we experience, the dreams we have, our motivation to act, our reactions to feedback, and how we reflect on success and failure (Deci & Ryan, 1991; Dweck, 1991; Markus & Wurf, 1987).

The self-concept might or might not be conscious; that is, we might or might not be aware of the principles by which it operates. For example, we might or might not be aware that we ascribe to an entity theory of intelligence or an incremental theory of intelligence. Nevertheless, having decided at some level of consciousness to endorse one of these theories, we will behave in highly predictable ways. If we believe in an incremental theory, for example, we will be more inclined to put forth effort.

The self-concept has three main functions:

1. **To provide information.** The self-concept provides information that will enable us to make judgments about what we can or cannot do. The information contained in the self-concept, however, is not always well-grounded in reality, and much of it has not been confirmed by social experience (Markus & Nurius, 1986). Individuals whose self-concept underestimates their skills and talents could find it difficult and even impossible to develop aspirations that might motivate them to set difficult goals.

2. **To provide context.** Humans are inclined to view feedback regarding their behavior in the context of their enduring aspirations and goals. Receiving a grade of B might mean very little for someone whose only wish is to graduate but a great deal for someone who wants to be admitted to medical school. Similarly, a broken lunch date could have very different implications for us, depending on whether we feel lonely or we simply hoped to gain some interesting information from our prospective companion.

3. **To provide integration.** The self-concept is a storehouse of information about the self and provides the global integration of that information (Higgins, 1996). From that integration of information comes our sense of identity. Some time ago Eric Erikson (1950) pointed out our sense of identity provides us with the ability to experience the self as something that has both continuity and sameness. Interestingly, this sense of continuity and sameness may make it difficult for us to change

because changing means that we must give up, at least momentarily, the sense of who we are or who we are destined to be.

According to many current theorists, the self is both learned and constructed (Deci & Ryan, 1991). The self is learned by internalizing the beliefs and attitudes of those around us, such as our parents and teachers; it is constructed by developing new beliefs as a result of our interactions with the environment. Even though my parents were not concerned about the environment, I might learn to care because of what I see happening around me. Politically, I could have learned from my parents to favor government social programs but, because of my perceptions about the growing national debt, I might come to favor fewer and less generous government programs.

Self-Knowledge and Self-Regulatory Functions

Self-knowledge is unique because it pertains to our survival and because it must be continually regulated to be as current as possible, again for reasons of survival (Higgins, 1996). Self-knowledge is also selective; it tends to keep track of those aspects that are important for survival, such as our strengths and weaknesses. In the final analysis, the self exists to help us interact with the environment.

Three components of the self with three distinct self-regulatory functions have been distinguished: (1) the instrumental self, (2) the expectant self, and (3) the monitored self.

1. **The instrumental self.** The instrumental self provides information about what will happen if we behave or fail to behave in certain ways—for instance, "If I don't give this phone message to my boss, she'll get annoyed" or "If I reciprocate the generosity of a friend, the friendship will endure." This information often pertains to the consequences of meeting—or failing to meet—the desires and expectations of significant others—for example, "Being kind to others would please my mother" or "If I procrastinate, I know my father will be upset." Thus, in a work setting, for instance, our behavior will be influenced not only by what we think is important and appropriate there but also by what we carry with us from our past (Higgins, 1996).

2. **The expectant self.** The expectant self provides information about what is likely to happen if we engage in a certain activity. If I ask someone for a date, for example, I will expect a certain outcome, depending on a variety of factors, based on my experience in the past. Similarly, if I get involved in a game of tennis, I will have some idea of what is going to happen, again depending on the context. Representation of certain competencies has a clear survival function. By knowing what to expect, I can prepare myself for the outcome. If I expect failure, for example, I will know what to do next.

The expectant self is more than just a summary of our experiences. It provides the motivation for contingency plans—for instance, the tendency to shift to a less difficult task when we begin failing at an easy task. E. Tony Higgins (1996) suggests that the expectant self should be conceptualized as a dispositional state. It gives rise to action, but the specific action is determined by other parts of the self.

3. **The monitored self.** The monitored self provides information about how well we are doing in relation to some goal or desired state. In other words, the monitored self exists to help reduce the discrepancy between the current and ideal selves. Should a person develop a new desired self, perhaps because of a new intimate relationship, the monitored self would become involved in creating this new *emergent self*. The survival value of a monitored self is obvious. Because the discrepancy between the ideal and the existing is assumed to motivate behavior, ensuring that the individual focuses on this discrepancy would facilitate achieving a particular goal (Higgins, 1996).

These three selves are complementary. The instrumental self provides information about how the world responds to us, the expectant self provides information about how we respond to the world, and the monitored self provides information about how we are doing in relation to certain desires and demands. Each of these pieces of information enables us to choose the most appropriate action in the given circumstances. The existence of these more or less distinct systems should enhance our survival.

Two Aspects of the Self

William James (1890) made a distinction between the "I" and the "me" of the self. Edward Deci and Richard Ryan (1991) characterized these two aspects of the self as, respectively, an agent and a repository (a storage place) of society's values. The repository part of the self (the "me") involves values, such as family, justice, and sharing and regulatory processes, such as persisting, following rules, and abstaining from aggression. We internalize both values and regulatory processes because, as social beings, we have a need for relatedness. To gain that sense of relatedness or acceptance, we internalize the beliefs of people who are important to us, such as our parents and friends. The agent side (the "I") is autonomous and needs to be in control. When the autonomous side of the self is allowed to develop skills and competence by mastering the environment, the individual gains a sense of self-determination. The agent side is responsible for actively integrating information (rather than absorbing it) and for generating rules and principles to guide our actions. According to this distinction, the agent side actively constructs the repository side. Over time, I will adjust my values and my self-regulatory processes so that they are congruent with the self-determined part of the self. I could decide, for example, to give up the idea that I must have children because it is inconsistent with my desire to pursue certain plans I have selected, such as sailing around the world.

Self-Discrepancy Theory

According to Higgins' (1987, 1996) self-discrepancy theory, there is a discrepancy between the *actual self*, which represents the attributes we think we possess, and the *ideal self*, which represents our hopes, wishes, and aspirations. In this model, the ideal self is viewed as a *self-guide;* it gives us direction. This ideal self is also a source of affect; although living up to an ideal can be a source of positive affect—for instance, self-satisfaction—failure to live up to an ideal can be a source of negative affect. This model suggests that there is a single core self and a single ideal self. However, other theorists have suggested that there can be many ideal selves and that they could have their roots in rethinking the core self (Higgins, 1996).

Possible Selves

Self-knowledge, by itself, does not automatically lead to growth and development. According to Hazel Markus and Paula Nurius (1986), the possible selves that we construct for ourselves create motivation and are therefore the basis for change. These possible selves are closely linked to our self-concept. When we think about what we might become, we draw heavily on self-knowledge. We ask ourselves, for example, whether we have the skill or ability to do something, whether we can develop that skill or ability, whether we are willing to put forth the effort and persist, and whether we are willing to give up other activities. In other words, we don't arbitrarily pull possible selves out of the air; rather, we create them from information contained in the self. These images are very real, because they come out of very personal information—our self-knowledge. Like aspirations, however, they have an abstract, conditional quality. They are possibilities that might follow from certain actions.

Possible selves are created selectively based on our experience in a given domain of expertise. As we become aware of our own abilities or talents, we develop an enduring sensitivity to tasks in which those abilities or talents might be relevant (Nicholls, 1990). If we know that we are smart in school, for example, we will remain sensitive to issues of intelligence and achievement in school. If we know that we are good at dealing with others, we will remain sensitive to occupations in which we can make use of those talents. The self also contains sociocultural and historical information (Stryker, 1984). This information can be both liberating and limiting. If I am from a poor background and I learn that someone with a similar background became president of the United States, I may realize that, despite my background, I don't have to set limits on my goals. If I know that no one from my family has ever experienced great success, however, I may unconsciously conclude that I cannot hope for success.

Possible Selves and Goals

Researchers have suggested that possible selves link the self-concept to goals (Markus & Nurius, 1986; Markus, Cross, & Wurf, 1990): "The inclusion of a sense of what is possible within the self-concept allows it to become dynamic" (Markus & Nurius, 1990, p. 960).

Possible selves represent the future-oriented component of the self-concept. They range from the ideal self that we would like to become—the successful self, the creative self, the rich self, the thin self, the loved self, the respected self—to the self that we are afraid

we might become: the alone self, the depressed self, the incompetent self, the alcoholic self, the unemployed self. If we're aware that we enjoy using drugs, for example, a possible self might be a drug addict. If we're aware that we cannot make decisions, a possible self might be a person who depends on others to get through life.

Possible selves might or might not be an immediate source of motivation. Sometimes we have no real intention of acting on a certain possible self. The impetus that pushes us from possible selves to creating aspirations is not altogether clear. It could be as simple as a word of encouragement from another person or as complex as a careful assessment of the pros and cons. In the final analysis, it involves making a decision.

Developing a Range of Possible Selves

Individuals who wish to achieve great things need to develop a self-concept that will permit the elaboration of a range of possible selves. As Markus and Nurius (1986) point out, possible selves do not simply happen; rather, they grow out of a well-defined self-concept. There are at least three characteristics of a well-defined self-concept: highly differentiated, positive, and linked to perceptions of competencies. Let's look at each of these aspects in turn.

1. **A highly differentiated self-concept.** As we saw in Chapter 13, people with highly differentiated or diverse self-concepts tend to be more likely to achieve difficult goals. Markus and Nurius (1986) suggest that individuals who view themselves as having numerous categories for the self (numerous possible selves) are able to achieve more goals, because they perceive that they can assume more roles. Linville (1987) has suggested that people who have *self-complexity*—that is, a range of conceptions of their identity—are better able to achieve goals and to deal with a wide variety of negative events. Because they can see themselves in a wide variety of situations, they can rise to new challenges and cope with new situations. Jennifer Campbell (1990) argues that people with high self-esteem have greater clarity of self-concept. Using confidence measures, she has found that people with high self-esteem are more certain of self-attributes. Ann Baumgardner (1990) suggests that it is important to have depth or certainty about a particular trait dimension. Certainty about a trait—being athletic or creative, for instance—

is important, she argues, because it is the basis for self-esteem, which, in turn, is the basis for attempting new and different things. As we have already noted, Baumgardner (1990) concludes that "to know oneself is to like oneself" (p. 1062). She argues that a strong self-concept, characterized by depth or certainty, promotes a sense of control over future outcomes and thus leads to positive affect and self-confidence.

2. **A positive self-concept.** Campbell (1990) found that people with high self-esteem describe themselves with more positive attributes. Extensive research has shown that people with high self-esteem possess attributes that are linked to success and tend to cope well with change and stress. For example, children identified as having high self-esteem are characterized by two sets of attributes: (1) confidence, curiosity, independence, and self-initiative; and (2) the ability to adapt to change and stress. Children with low self-esteem, in contrast, are characterized by (1) failure to show confidence, curiosity, independence, and initiative; and (2) inability to adapt to change (Harter, 1990). A consistent theme in the self-concept literature is that people with good self-concepts are motivated by challenges and can deal with stress (e.g., Epstein, 1992). Another common theme in the experimental literature is that people with good self-esteem tend to react positively to new challenges (Seligman, 1990). Substantial evidence suggests that, to be positive, people need to view the world as benevolent. In a benevolent world, people can take risks.

3. **A self-concept linked to perceptions of competencies.** Ultimately, the self-concept is linked to competencies (Nicholls, 1990) and perceptions of competencies (Langer & Park, 1990). If we have a clear perception that we are competent in a given domain, we are likely to set more difficult goals for ourselves. There is some reason to believe that taking an optimistic view of our competencies is a good idea (Seligman, 1990). Those who believe that they can do something will often try and, in the process of trying, they will often succeed. That is what it means to be an optimist.

The Creation of Possible Selves

Possible selves do not just happen. They result from combining and recombining elements of the self in new ways. Sometimes, they emerge from acts of fantasy in which we entertain a wide variety of images of ourselves. Sometimes they are constructed on the basis of decisions about what we should or should not do. Values that we hold or principles that we have come to accept as important can shape those decisions. Deciding that we'd prefer a long life to an exciting life, for example, might affect our selection of an occupation (Kendall, Learner, & Craighead, 1984; Learner, 1982).

If possible selves are created and constructed, we can take personal responsibility for motivating ourselves to change. Many theorists take the position that possible selves are only the starting points for change. In the final analysis, we need to set clearly defined goals for ourselves. However, those goals, it appears, must be congruent with our values or else we are unlikely to achieve them. A study by Langer and Thompson (cited in Langer, 1989) illustrates that people find it difficult to change behaviors that they value. The study participants were presented with a list of negative traits—such as rigid, grim, and gullible—and asked whether they had tried to change these behaviors and if they had succeeded or failed. Later, the participants were asked how much they valued such traits as consistency, seriousness, and trust. The researchers found that the participants had difficulty changing certain negatively phrased traits if they valued those traits. For example, people generally do not like to see themselves as rigid but, if they value consistency, they might find it difficult to become spontaneous. Similarly, people generally don't like to see themselves as gullible but, if they value trust, they might have difficulty becoming suspicious or cynical.

Although our possible selves are closely linked to our self-concept, we can begin to create new possible selves (see Practical Application 14-1).

Implicit Theories

The self houses our implicit theories. We have many implicit theories about many things. Two classes of implicit theories are relevant to goal-setting: implicit theories about the world, and implicit theories about ability. These are sometimes called simply world theories and self theories. Let's examine these in turn.

Implicit Theories About the World

A number of self theorists suggest that everyone develops an implicit theory of reality (e.g., Dweck & Leggett, 1988; Epstein, 1990). It appears that people not only have a world theory and a self theory but also have beliefs and ideas about the relationship between the self and the world. For example, people might believe that, because they live in a bad world, they cannot control most things that happen to them or that, because it is a good world, events are controllable (Epstein, 1990). In this section, we consider three prototypes of how people conceptualize the world and how those concepts shape their ideas about what they can or should do.

Prototype 1: The world as threatening or malevolent. Some people are inclined to view the world in negative terms (Epstein, 1990; Watson & Clark, 1984). They see the world as threatening or malevolent. When they wake up each morning, they dread to enter the world that waits outside their front doors. Apprehensive that the world is going to harm them, they experience stress in preparation for fight or flight. Their hearts might speed up and their blood pressure might rise. Sometimes they are angry, on the unspoken assumption that, in a hostile world, the best defense is an offense. Alternatively, they could become very passive, in the hope of being left alone.

These people are pessimists. They expect bad things to happen and sometimes seem pleased when bad things happen to others because such events confirm their view of the world and their survival strategy. These people have little sense of agency or control; they are reactive. They think of survival of the fittest in a dog-eat-dog world.

At least two dimensions characterize this implicit theory of the world. First, these people tend to have what Watson and Clark (1984) called a disposition toward negative affectivity. All their experiences are focused around deprivation and defeat. They are anxious, fearful, unhappy, and distressed. According to Watson and Clark (1984), a wide variety of personality scales that purport to measure trait anxiety, neuroticism, repression-sensitization, ego strength, and general maladjustment appear to measure the same underlying personality trait—the disposition toward negative affectivity. Following up on this work, people who are anxious and fearful tend to view the world as threatening (Franken, Gibson, & Rowland, 1992). They are inclined to limit their interactions with the world because it is a threat to their physical and psychological well-being.

Practical Application 14-1

How to Create Possible Selves

Sometimes people get into a rut. Because their parents told them they should become doctors like Uncle George, they never entertain any other alternative. Years ago, I had a friend who had decided, with encouragement from his parents, to emulate his uncle by pursuing a career in engineering. Not having the aptitude, he struggled and failed. At that point, he had to face the possibility that his chosen career might not be right for him. When he began to explore other options, he suddenly realized that his interests were in the social sciences. One success followed another and eventually, after graduating from Oxford, he set up his own research institute.

How do you go about creating possible selves without having to wait for failure? Start by making a list of things that you are good at doing or things that you have done well. Make sure this list contains things that are not part of your school experiences, such as bargaining or making friends. Also, write down some of the skills that you think you might acquire with some effort. For example, perhaps you think you could learn how to repair a bicycle or to play an instrument.

Next, find the category under which such a skill could be found. For example, if you have worked at a swimming pool and been left in charge from time to time, the corresponding category is manager. If you have organized a school dance, you would put that in the category of producer or organizer. If you have won an athletic contest, you would call yourself a winning athlete. Take each of these category names and put them into a new list. The purpose of this exercise is to get you to think in broader terms. When you do that, a whole new world will open

People who are anxious also tend to have low self-esteem (Franken, Gibson, & Rowland, 1992). For example, they are easily discouraged, they are inclined to give up when things aren't working, they get nervous in new situations, they have poor opinions of themselves, they do not see life as satisfying, and they often wish they were someone else.

Second, people who view the world as threatening tend to be aware only of limited possibilities. For example, people who are anxious do not select new or different activities but, rather, select activities that are more familiar to them (e.g., Berlyne, 1960; White, 1959). Evidence also indicates that people who can be characterized as fearful perceive more activities as dangerous, risky and therefore psychologically unavailable to them (Franken, Gibson, & Rowland, 1992).

Prototype 2: The world as benevolent. Some people have the disposition to view the world in positive terms (Scheier & Carver, 1985, 1988; Seligman, 1990; Snyder et al., 1991). They see the world as benevolent—as good and generous. When these people wake up in the morning, they are convinced that good things are going to happen to them; they are optimists. They exude

confidence and seem unaffected by setbacks. Their sense of agency is highly developed. They feel that they have the ability to find the right path and to claim their rightful reward. They think, "This is my day" or "Something good is going to happen to me today."

Again, two dimensions characterize these people. First, they have a disposition to experience positive affect. They see themselves not only as successful but also as happy people. Seligman (1990) views optimism as the opposite of depression. Whereas negative mood and negative affect characterize depression, positive mood and positive affect characterize optimism.

Second, these people believe that the world offers many positive opportunities or possibilities. For instance, research on anxiety shows that people who are low in anxiety are more inclined to explore their environments, more inclined to respond to new stimulations, and more inclined to try new activities (e.g., Berlyne, 1960; White, 1959). Research on optimism and hope also indicates that optimists are open to new experiences and challenges (Seligman, 1990) and that people who are hopeful tend to have a strong sense of agency (goal-directed determination) and awareness of pathways (ability to plan routes to goals) and are able

for you. You will say to yourself, I'm a manager, an organizer, and an athlete. Often people do not realize that the skills they acquire in one task will generalize to other situations. Armed with these new categories, you can suddenly see yourself doing many things.

With this new list, think of things that you might do. Write down all of them, even if they wouldn't make money or make you famous. Over the next weeks or even month, write down other things that come to mind. From this list, generate as many possible selves as you can. It is not important whether you actually want to pursue them. The point of this exercise is to make you aware that there are many possibilities. You might be surprised to see many options that you have never considered before.

A very good technique is to ask your friends what they think a person with the skills from your category list

might do. We are often blind to new alternatives because our self-concept works hard to prevent us from entertaining new alternatives. In fact, when presented with a new alternative, we often say, "That isn't me." Nevertheless, when people make suggestions, we tend to incorporate those ideas into our unconscious. It is amazing how a simple act of encouragement can alter our motivation. If someone else can believe we can do it, why can't we? Psychologists have known about this phenomenon for some time and systematically use suggestions and encouragement to get people to try new things. Often, when people try new things, they succeed, which is the basis for further strivings.

Many people have turned to T'ai Chi and other forms of martial arts to help them train their minds and their bodies.

to set more goals and more difficult goals (Synder et al., 1991).

Further evidence comes from work with sensation seekers—people who are motivated by the need for novel and complex stimulation and are willing to take risks to experience such stimulation (Zuckerman, 1979). My colleagues and I did a study with sensation seekers to explore their tendencies to take risks. Risk is defined by Webster's dictionary as the possibility of loss or injury. If an activity is perceived to be risky, it follows that we should avoid it. But what makes something risky? Is there some objective measure of risk? Perhaps everything we do is risky if viewed from a certain perspective. From our research, we can see that some people willingly participate in activities traditionally labeled as dangerous. It is important to remember that labeling something as dangerous or risky is based on norms. If we were to use only anxious people to define what is risky, then the norms for what is risky would be very different than if we used nonanxious people or sensation seekers. If very anxious people were the norm, leaving the house at all might be viewed as a risky activity.

My colleagues and I wanted to explore why some people are willing to engage in activities that have traditionally been labeled as risky whereas others are not. In our study, we gave participants Zuckerman's Sensation Seeking Scale, Wolpe and Lange's Fear Schedule Survey, a Danger Assessment Questionnaire, and an Attitudes Toward Risk Questionnaire. The Attitudes Toward Risk Questionnaire asked people to indicate on a five-point scale whether items were "like me" or "not like me." A factor analysis of this scale identified two distinct factors: one that pertained to taking psychological risks, which we called *disregard of social approval;* another that pertained to taking physical risks, which we called *disregard of danger.* The items for the two factors are presented in Table 14-1.

We found that people high in the sensation-seeking motive tended to be less fearful, tended to perceive a variety of activities as less dangerous, and indicated that they like to take both physical and psychological risks (Franken, Gibson, & Rowland, 1992). These results indicate that fear, danger, and risk may be in the eye of the beholder.

Table 14-1. Items from the Attitudes Towards Risk Questionnaire. In the original scale administered to the study participants, the items were mixed together; they have been rank-ordered in this table according to which item loaded greatest on that particular factor.

Factor 1: Psychological Risks: Disregard of Social Approval

1. While I don't deliberately seek out situations or activities that society disapproves of, I find that I often end up doing things that society disapproves of.
2. I often do things that I know my parents would disapprove of.
3. I often think about doing things that are illegal.
4. I do not let the fact that something is considered immoral stop me from doing it.
5. I often think about doing things that I know my friends would disapprove of.
6. I often seek out situations or activities that society does not approve of.
7. I do not let the fact that something is illegal stop me from doing it.
8. I often think about doing things that I know my parents would disapprove of.
9. I often think about doing things that I know society would disapprove of.
10. I often think about doing things that are immoral.

Factor 2: Physical Risks: Disregard of Danger

11. I like the feeling that comes with taking physical risks.
12. I consider myself a risk-taker.
13. Being afraid of doing something new often makes it more fun in the end.
14. The greater the risk, the more fun the activity.
15. I like to do things that almost paralyze me with fear.
16. I like the feeling that comes with taking psychological or social risks.
17. While I don't deliberately seek out situations or activities that involve physical risk, I often end up doing things that involve physical risk.
18. I like the feeling that comes from entering a new situation.
19. I often think about doing activities that involve physical risk.
20. I often think about doing things that would arouse a great deal of fear or anxiety in me.

Source: Reprinted from "Sensation Seeking and the Tendency to View the World as Threatening," by R. E. Franken, K. J. Gibson, & G. L. Rowland, *Personality and Individual Differences*, 1992, *12*, 31–38 (Appendix 3, p. 37). Copyright © 1992. Reprinted with kind permission from Pergamon Press Ltd, Headington Hill Hall, Oxford OX3 0BW, UK.

Prototype 3: The world as benign. There are people who view the world as neither threatening nor benevolent. For these people, pleasure and satisfaction are not the result of something good happening or of preventing something bad from happening but rather derive from their own actions—more precisely, from exercising competence. These people wake up in the morning with a goal they want to accomplish. Perhaps they have decided that they want a bigger house in a new location. In time, they buy an old house, tear it down, and build their dream house.

Thus, for these people, pleasure comes from operating on the world and changing it. To do so, they must develop skills or competence. Through exercising skills and competence, they experience satisfaction. They say to themselves, "I will develop the skills so that I can make it into what I want" or "I want to be free to do it my way."

This view of the world has its origins in the philosophy of individualism. According to this philosophy, people should be treated as autonomous and self-reliant. Further, they must be given freedom to exploit the world because people gain happiness through exercising their skills and changing things.

The idea that some people view the world as benign is reflected in the theory of Deci and Ryan (1991), who suggest that people are born with three needs: the need for autonomy, the need for competence, and the need for relatedness. Satisfying these needs brings happiness and satisfaction.

What about the dimensions of affect and possibilities that we used to characterize the other two world theories? People who view the world as benign do not see it as the source of either positive or negative affect. They see positive and negative affect as consequences of their actions, which, in turn, are a product of their goals. The main positive emotion that Deci and Ryan talk about is pride, which results from exercising competence or gaining mastery. Negative affect results from the inability to experience autonomy and self-determination. Frustration would be one of the main negative emotions. They also talk about the need for relatedness, which, they suggest, provides the primary impetus for internalizing values and regulatory processes.

What about possibilities? Possibilities come from within the self and have little or no direct link to the external world. The self acts on the world and creates something new by molding or shaping the world according to our needs or desires. The ultimate basis for all possibilities is competence. With competence, anything is possible; without it, nothing is possible.

This does not mean, however, that people who view the world as benign have nothing to fear, nor that they gain no pleasure from the external world. Deci and Ryan acknowledge that the external world can be a source of both pleasure and pain, but they do not see this as the focus of the self. It is unfortunate that we have to deal with, for instance, crime, pollution, and divorce in the course of exercising competence, but these are not of central concern to the self; they are peripheral. The self is concerned with autonomy, self-determination, and relatedness.

Self-regulation and world theories. The obvious implication of all this is that whether people will set difficult goals for themselves is linked to their implicit theory of the world. That is, the more people believe the world is benevolent or even benign, the more likely they are to construct broad and well-defined possible selves and, consequently, the more likely they are to set difficult goals.

From a survival perspective, seeing the world as malevolent is adaptive because we are sensitized to cues that might threaten our survival. Because of our defensive posture, however, we fail to set difficult goals or take risks. In short, we end up living a life of quiet desperation; always alert to danger, we never really enjoy ourselves or embrace new challenges.

To change, we need to view the world differently. Instead of seeing the world as a source of threat, we need to see it as a source of challenge. Numerous experiments by social psychologists show that, when people change the way they label things, their perceptions and actions change as well. Take the concept of challenge, for example. Research using a stress paradigm has shown that, if people view something as challenging, they are less likely to experience stress than if they view it as a threat (Higgins, 1996). Such research suggests that people might be able to self-regulate by monitoring their thought processes and learning how to replace self-defeating views with self-facilitating views. This is often called *cognitive reframing* or *restructuring*. By taking a different view of the situation, people react to it differently. Numerous researchers, including Beck, Epstein, and Seligman, have argued that, through self-regulation, people can learn to change the way they think about their interactions with the world.

Implicit Theories of Competence

To understand how people view the self, we need to observe how they cope, adapt, shape, or embrace the external world—collectively called *strategies*. Most people do not simply react mindlessly; they respond with carefully devised strategies.

Of the many strategies that people use, two seem to be very pervasive across many situations: the *mastery strategy* and the *performance strategy*. It's helpful to think of these strategies as *orientations*. Like a disposition, an orientation points us in a certain direction.

The mastery strategy and the performance strategy have been discussed by various theorists—most notably, Carol Dweck (Dweck, 1991; Dweck & Leggett,

1988). These concepts have their roots in the early literature on the mastery motive (e.g., White, 1959) and in Carl Rogers' (1959) work on conditional and unconditional love.

These strategies are not rational or conscious; rather, they are implicit theories that we develop through processes such as modeling, instruction, and construction. We are not locked into one strategy or another but, rather, can learn to change our orientation by adjusting our focus.

The mastery strategy. The mastery strategy can be defined as a general belief system that involves three interrelated beliefs: the belief that we can acquire the skills necessary to survive, the belief that we can control the environment through the development of skills, and the belief that we have the capacity to create happiness and health. In Dweck's (1991) theory, the mastery strategy arises from the belief that intelligence is incremental. Through work and effort, people can change their intelligence and their ability to adapt to the world.

Some writers fail to emphasize that people with a strong mastery motive are typically very skilled. In addition to believing that they can control things, they actually have a large repertoire of skills that enable them to control things. For example, they often have the ability to acquire the information they need, they know how to organize the information they acquire, they know how to apply that information, and they have the social skills necessary to be truly effective. The mastery motive, in other words, combines attitudes and beliefs with a set of generalized skills.

People who develop a mastery strategy learn to take credit for their actions. Further, they come to develop a generalized belief that they can effect change through their ability to learn and develop new skills. Their continued development of new skills is rewarded and sustained by the feelings of self-efficacy that accompany the development of each new skill. Typically, they feel pride at their achievements.

The performance strategy. The performance strategy can also be defined as a belief system that involves three interrelated beliefs: that we can achieve what we want by learning the rules for winning, that winning is an acceptable way to get ahead, and that happiness is the result of winning. The important distinction is that the performance-oriented person tends to be concerned

Success comes to those who have embraced the importance of mastery.

with the *outcome,* whereas the mastery orientation is concerned with the *process.*

As we have seen, mastery-oriented individuals are sustained by the feelings of self-efficacy they gain from effectively dealing with the world; the process is the source of their motivation. Performance-oriented individuals, in contrast, are sustained by winning—that is, by the outcome. Although skills are often involved in winning, performance-oriented individuals do not necessarily view themselves as having skills. Rather, they see themselves as using tactics, such as undermining other people. As a result, it is more difficult for them to take credit for their successes.

This distinction does not mean that mastery types do not like to win, nor that performance types are not interested in experiencing feelings of self-efficacy, but they have a different focus or emphasis. Considerable evidence indicates that experiencing feelings of efficacy is the more powerful motivator of behavior in the long run (Deci & Ryan, 1991).

Self-regulation and self theories. The obvious implication of all this is that whether people will set difficult goals for themselves is linked to their implicit theories about competence. That is, the more people are mastery-oriented, the more likely they are to set difficult goals for themselves. How does a person become more mastery-oriented?

One of the most important things people can learn is that competency isn't something they have or don't have; rather, competency is something they must develop. Although there are obvious biological limitations, they account for much less than people often think. In a study mentioned earlier, Langer (1989) asked her students to evaluate the intelligence of scientists who had achieved an impressive intellectual outcome, such as discovering a new planet or inventing a new drug. When she described the achievement of a series of steps, they judged the scientists to be less intelligent than when she simply named the achievement. When they saw the steps, the accomplishments did not seem that difficult. Thus, the key to becoming mastery-oriented is to recognize that a series of well-defined steps leads to every accomplishment. If we can discover those steps, we can become competent.

By recognizing that each achievement involves a series of steps, Japanese industrialists have made great strides in manufacturing quality products such as cars and electronic equipment. They have learned to view manufacturing as a process made up of many components. To improve the overall product, they focus their energy on trying to improve each of the components and the links between those components. Whenever they learn how to produce a better component, they introduce the change as soon as possible, whereas North American manufacturers tend to wait for a model change. As a result, the Japanese are usually slightly ahead of their competition. This approach has come to be called continuous improvement.

The continuous improvement concept is a good metaphor for creating personal competency. Like the manufacturing process, competency is made up of a series of components. Each component can be improved and then reintroduced into the chain that makes up the competency. Athletes often use this approach. For a time, they work on one component. Having perfected that component, they reintroduce it into the chain to ensure that it harmonizes with the other components. Next, they work on another component and then reintroduce that component into the chain, and so on. Change is incremental in the short run, but it is often very dramatic in the long run.

By breaking processes down into components and then reassembling them, athletes can create a variety of skills out of a few basic components. Standup comics use a similar approach. They have a series of components—skits and jokes—that they can string together in various ways depending on the particular audience.

The Relationship Between World Theories and Self Theories

Seymour Epstein (1990) has suggested that individuals' world theories and self theories are linked by certain propositions. As yet, we don't have a clear idea of these propositions. All we really know is that world theories seem to vary independently of self theories. That is, if we know that a person has adopted the view that the world is threatening, we cannot predict whether that person has a mastery orientation or a performance orientation.

Some psychologists have suggested that world theories and self theories are linked by superordinate categories. Each of us has an underlying principle that guides our life—a guiding phrase, for example. Let's say that my guiding phrase is "I want to make this a better world." This phrase can embody the idea that, although I perceive the world as malevolent—a source of pain and threat, at least for some people—my goal is to help relieve that pain, perhaps by entering politics, creating a new drug, or writing a book. Let's say that my guiding phrase is "I am going to enjoy life to the fullest." This phrase may embody the idea that it is a benevolent world and that I intend to enjoy it, by adopting either a mastery or a performance orientation.

Becoming a Process-Oriented Person

Most current motivation theorists hold that, to succeed, we need to focus on the process, rather than on the goal. Virtually all the work reviewed in this chapter stresses the importance of the process, rather than the outcome. In his book *Flow,* Csikszentmihalyi (1990) argues that optimal experience occurs when we undertake challenging tasks with clear goals and immediate feedback. In such situations, he argues, we lose all self-doubt and experience a sense of control. That experience is so strong, he argues, that we are willing to put forth whatever effort is needed to develop the skills we require.

Many motivation writers have argued that the main reward or satisfaction from achievement is associated not with reaching the goal but with working toward the goal—not with being there but with getting there. When Torvil and Dean won their gold medal in the Olympics for pair figure skating, Dean said he felt that he had achieved his dream; it was wonderful. In the next sentence, he talked about how difficult it would be to go back to work. Achieving a dream is exciting, but the pleasure is often short-lived. To continue enjoying life, we need new dreams to sustain us. One of our more celebrated dreamers and achievers is Apple Computer co-founder Steve Jobs; fittingly, his biography is subtitled, *The Journey Is the Reward* (Young, 1988).

Performance goals should not be ignored in this process. If we are to make important contributions to society and to gain recognition, we must be attuned to the wants and needs of other people. Knowing that we have made a difference to our society can be a great source of self-satisfaction. Mother Teresa is a good example of a person who learned the importance of creating something that transcends ourselves.

Using Reflection to Replace Rumination

I recently ran across a fascinating piece of research that addressed the question of distinguishing between rumination and reflection. The term *rumination* is frequently used in connection with the thinking styles of depressive individuals; specifically, the tendency for depressives to engage in negative or pessimistic thinking (see Chapter 10). Research indicates that the tendency to ruminate is motivated by perceived threats, losses, or injustices to the self (Trapnell & Campbell, 1999). As in the previous section, the tendency to ruminate is linked with an implicit theory of the world as malevolent as well as linked to the personality trait of neuroticism. In contrast, reflection is motivated by cu-

riosity or interest in understanding the self and has been linked to the personality trait of openness to experience (see Chapter 11). Openness to experience is linked to the implicit theory of the world as benevolent. Openness to experience leads to growth and to creativity. People high in openness value authenticity, uniqueness, and autonomy whereas people low in this trait tend to value authority, propriety, and tradition. Thus, people who are caught up in the act of doing and living tend to be characterized by reflection.

As we have discussed earlier, considerable research suggests that curiosity is a positive trait and neuroticism is a negative trait as far as growth and success are concerned. Because the traits of openness and neuroticism are independent (people can be high in both, low in both, or high in one and low in the other); the obvious implication is that people can simultaneously reflect more and ruminate less (Trapnell & Campbell, 1999). Not only can they, but from our perspective they should. How does one reflect more and ruminate less? Research suggests that, perhaps, people can do this by focusing their attention on an activity. What the research shows is that when people are focused on an activity they not only reflect more they experience fewer intrusive negative thoughts. It has been suggested that the reason people experience fewer intrusive negative thoughts is because attention is limited. Another thing that people can do is direct their attention to making a plan. Making plans demands attention, and it seems to demand that attention be directed in a positive way. For example, making plans involves, among other things, thinking and researching (e.g. reading, using the Internet, talking to other people); making use of problem-solving skills, organizing. Making plans should also lead to increased feelings of self-efficacy because a plan provides positive feedback to the individual that a goal can actually be achieved by the formation of a viable plan (see Bandura, 1997; Langer, 1989).

Summary

Research on the self-regulation of behavior has led to a renewed interest in the concept of self. Our self-concept is determined both by how we view the external world and by how we view our ability to deal with it. The self can be thought of as self-knowledge that provides both information and context. Higgins has argued that the self has three distinct self-regulatory functions that correspond to three selves: an instrumental self, an expectant self, and a monitored self. Going back to William James, a distinction has been made between two aspects of the self: as a repository of information ("me") and as an agent ("I").

Possible selves have been suggested as the link between the self-concept and goals. The first step of self-motivation, therefore, is to create possible selves. Possible selves are the future part of our self-concept. Possible selves are closely linked to the self-concept, and therefore, self-knowledge plays an important role in their creation. Possible selves are created selectively based on our experience in a given domain of expertise, but they also contain sociocultural and historical information, which provides the necessary context. If we are to create diverse possible selves, we need a highly differentiated self, a positive self-concept, and a self that is linked closely to perceptions of competencies. Through goal-setting, possible selves create action.

The psychological literature includes at least three prototypes describing how people view the external world. People who perceive the world as threatening (prototype 1) are dispositionally inclined to experience negative affect and tend to see the world as limited in opportunities or possibilities. Anxious and neurotic people are examples of this prototype. People who view the world as benevolent (prototype 2) are dispositionally inclined to experience positive affect and tend to view the world as offering many opportunities or possibilities. Optimists and hopeful people are examples of this prototype. People who view the world as benign (prototype 3) value autonomy and self-determination. In shaping the external world through the application of autonomy and self-determination, they experience the pleasure that comes with exercising competence. The outside world is neither a source of pleasure or pain, nor a source of opportunity. Individualists are examples of this prototype. Finally, a distinction can be made between people who hold a mastery orientation and those who hold a performance orientation. Whereas the mastery orientation is motivated by the process— the feelings of self-efficacy that accompany the exercise of skills—the performance orientation is motivated by outcome.

Main Points

1. Growing evidence indicates that humans can self-regulate their motivation.
2. Goals arouse effort, give rise to persistence, provide direction, and motivate strategy development.
3. There are two basic classes of goals: distal goals and proximal goals.
4. Within Bandura's theory, outcome expectations are defined as "a person's estimate that a given behavior will lead to certain outcomes," and self-efficacy is defined as "the conviction that one can successfully execute the behavior required to produce the outcomes."
5. Mental simulation is an effective way of facilitating goal-directed behavior.
6. Learning to manage self-doubt is important because self-doubt tends to undermine feelings of self-efficacy.
7. Four methods have been suggested to deal with self-doubt: monitoring self-talk, cognitive restructuring, substituting more positive thoughts, and distancing.
8. The self-concept can be thought of as self-knowledge. It is based on our experiences in a given domain and reflects sociocultural and historical information.
9. The self-regulatory self can be conceptualized as made up of three distinct components (selves): the instrumental self, the expectant self, and the monitored self.
10. The repository side of self (the "me") involves values and regulatory processes, whereas the agent side of the self (the "I") is autonomous and needs to be in control.
11. If we are to construct diverse possible selves, we need a self-concept that is highly differentiated, positive, and closely linked to perceptions of competency.
12. The three different prototypes of self-awareness and environmental awareness are (1) that the world is hostile and threatening, (2) that the world is benevolent, and (3) that the world is benign.
13. People with a mastery strategy deal with the world by developing competency; feelings of efficacy reward the development of competency.

14. People with a performance strategy deal with the world by learning the rules of winning.
15. Mastery-type individuals tend to be process-oriented; performance types tend to be outcome-oriented.

 InfoTrac® College Edition

When it comes to goal-setting and performance, what are the advantages and disadvantages of having an ego-orientation? (Search words: goal-setting, psychological aspects)

What are some of the things parents and teachers can do to improve the self-concept of children and adolescents? (Search words: self-perception, psychological aspects)

References

ABELSON, H., COHEN, R., HEATON, E., & SUDER, C. (1971). National survey of public attitudes toward and experience with erotic materials. In *Technical Report of the Commission on Obscenity and Pornography* (Vol. 6). Washington, DC: Government Printing Office.

ABRAMSON, L. Y., METALSKY, G. L., & ALLOY, L. B. (1989). Hopelessness depression: A theory-based process-oriented subtype of depression. *Psychological Review, 96,* 358–372.

ABRAMSON, L. Y., SELIGMAN, M. E. P., & TEASDALE, J. D. (1978). Learned helplessness in humans: Critique and reformulation. *Journal of Abnormal Psychology, 87,* 49–74.

ADAMS, I. B., & MARTIN, B. R. (1996). Cannabis: Pharmacology and toxicology in animals and humans. *Addiction, 91,* 158614.

AINSWORTH, M. D. S., BLEHAR, M. C., WATER, E., & WALL, S. (1978). *Patterns of attachment: A psychological study of the strange situation.* Hillsdale, NJ: Erlbaum.

ÅKERSTEDT, T., TORSVALL, L., & GILLBERG, M. (1982). Sleepiness and shift work: Field studies. *Sleep, 5,* S95–S106.

AKIL, H., MADDEN, J., IV, PATRICK, R. L., & BARCHAS, J. D. (1976). Stress induced increase in endogenous opiate peptides: Concurrent analgesia and its partial reversal by naloxone. In H. W. Kosterlitz (Ed.), *Opiates and endogenous opiate peptides.* Amsterdam: Elsevier North-Holland.

ALEXANDER, B. K., PEELE, S., HADAWAY, P. F., MORSE, S. J., BRODSKY, A., & BEYERSTEIN, B. L. (1985). Adult, infant, and animal addiction. In S. Peele, *The meaning of addiction* (pp. 73–96). Lexington, MA: Lexington Books.

ALLEN, J. B., KENRICK, D. T., LINDER, D. E., & MCCALL, M. A. (1989). Arousal and attraction: A response facilitation alternative to misattribution and negative-reinforcement models. *Journal of Personality and Social Psychology, 57,* 261–270.

ALLEN, L. S., & GORSKI, F. A. (1991). Sexual dimorphism of the anterior commissure and massa intermedia of the human brain. *Journal of Comparative Neurology, 312,* 97–104.

ALLEN, L. S., RICHEY, M. F., CHAI, Y. M., & GORSKI, R. A. (1991). Sex differences in the corpus callosum of the living human being. *Journal of Neuroscience, 11,* 933–942.

ALLMAN, W. F. (1994). *The stone age present.* New York: Simon & Schuster.

ALLOY, L. B., & ABRAMSON, L. Y. (1979). Judgement of contingency in depressed and nondepressed students: Sadder but wiser. *Journal of Experimental Psychology, General, 108,* 441–485.

ALLRED, K. D., & SMITH, T. (1989). The hardy personality: Cognitive and physiological responses to evaluation threat. *Journal of Personality and Social Psychology, 56,* 257–266.

AMABILE, T. M. (1996). *Creativity in context.* New York: Westview Press.

American Cancer Society. (1994). *Cancer facts and figures—1993.* New York: Author.

American Psychiatric Association. (1994). *Diagnostic and statistical manual of mental disorders* (4th ed.). Washington, DC: Author.

AMLANER, C. J. J., & BALL, N. J. (1994). *Avian sleep.* In M. H. Kryger, T. Roth, & W. C. Dement (Eds.), *Principles and Practice of Sleep Medicine.* Philadelphia: W. B. Saunders.

AMSEL, A. (1958). The role of frustrative nonreward in noncontinuous reward situations. *Psychological Bulletin, 55,* 102–119.

AMSEL, A. (1962). Frustrative nonreward in partial reinforcement and discrimination learning: Some recent history and a theoretical extension. *Psychological Review, 69,* 306–328.

AMSEL, A. (1972). Behavioral habituation, counterconditioning, and a general theory of persistence. In A. H. Black & W. F. Prokasy (Eds.), *Classical conditioning: Vol. II. Current research and theory.* New York: Appleton-Century-Crofts.

ANDERSEN, B. L., KIECOLT-GLASER, J. K., & GLASER, R. (1994). A biobehavioral model of cancer stress and disease course. *American Psychologist, 49,* 389–404.

ANDERSON, J. F. (1988). *The role of hope in appraisal, goal-setting, expectancy, and coping.* Unpublished doctoral dissertation. University of Kansas, Lawrence.

ANDREWS, F. M. (1975). Social and psychological factors that influence the creative process. In I. A. Taylor and J. W. Getzels (Eds.), *Perspectives in creativity* (pp. 117–145). Chicago: Aldine.

APFELBAUM, M. (1975). Influence of level of energy intake on energy expenditure in man: Effects of spontaneous intake, experimental starvation, and experimental overeating. In G. A. Bray et al. (Eds.), *Obesity in perspective* (DHEW Publication No. NIH 75–708, Vol. 2). Washington, DC: U.S. Government Printing Office.

APTER, M. J. (1982). *The experience of motivation: Theory of psychological reversals.* New York: Academic Press.

ARKES, H. R., & BOYKIN, A. W. (1971). Analysis of complexity preference in Head Start and nursery school children. *Perceptual and Motor Skills, 33,* 1131–1137.

ARKIN, A. M., ANTROBUS, J. S., ELLMAN, S. J., & FARBER, J. (1978). Sleep mentation as affected by REMP deprivation. In A. M. Arkin, J. S. Antrobus, & S. J. Ellman (Eds.), *The mind in sleep: Psychology and psychophysiology.* Hillsdale, NJ: Erlbaum.

ARMITAGE, A. K., HALL, G. H., & SELLERS, C. M. (1969). Effects of nicotine on electrocortical activity and acetylcholine release from the cat cerebral cortex. *British Journal of Pharmacology, 35,* 152–160.

ARON, A., PARIS, M., & ARON, E. N. (1995). Falling in love: Prospective studies of self-concept change. *Journal of Personality and Social Psychology, 69,* 1102–1112.

ARONSON, E., & MILLS, J. (1959). The effect of severity of initiation on liking for a group. *Journal of Abnormal and Social Psychology, 59,* 181–188.

ASHBY, F. G., ISEN, A. M., & TURKEN, A. U. (1999). A neuropsychological theory of positive affect and its influence on cognition. *Psychological Bulletin, 106,* 529–550.

ASCHOFF, J. (Ed.). (1965). *Circadian clocks.* Amsterdam: North-Holland.

ASERINSKY, E., & KLEITMAN, N. (1953). Regularly occurring periods of eye mobility and concomitant phenomena during sleep. *Science, 118,* 273–274.

ATKINSON, J. W. (1953). The achievement motive and recall of interrupted and completed tasks. *Journal of Experimental Psychology, 46,* 381–390.

ATKINSON, J. W. (1957). Motivational determinants of risk-taking behavior. *Psychological Review, 64,* 359–372.

ATKINSON, J. W., & BIRCH, D. (1978). *An introduction to motivation* (rev. ed.). New York: Van Nostrand.

AVERILL, J. R. (1973). Personal control over aversive stimuli and its relationship to stress. *Psychological Bulletin, 80,* 286–303.

AVERILL, J. R., & BOOTHROYD, P. (1977). On falling in love in conformance with the romantic ideal. *Motivation and Emotion, 1,* 235–247.

AXELWOOD, R. (1984). *The evolution of cooperation.* New York: Basic Books

BAEKELAND, F. (1970). Exercise deprivation: Sleep and psychological reactions. *Archives of General Psychiatry, 22,* 365–369.

BAEKELAND, F., & LASKY, R. (1966). Exercise and sleep patterns in college athletes. *Perceptual and Motor Skills, 23,* 1203–1207.

BAGOZZI, R. P., & EDWARDS, E. A. (1998). Goal setting and goal pursuit in the regulation of bodyweight. *Psychology and Health, 13,* 593–621.

BAILEY, J. M., & PILLARD, R. C. (1991). A genetic study of male homosexual orientation. *Archives of General Psychiatry, 48,* 1089–1097.

BAILEY, J. M., PILLARD, R. C., NEALE, M. C. I., & AGYEI, Y. (1993). Heritable factors influence sexual orientation in women. *Archives of General Psychiatry, 50,* 217–223.

BAILEY, J. M., YIM, P. Y., HILLS, A., & LINSENMEIER, J. A. W. (1997). Butch, Femme, or Straight Acting? Partner preferences of gay men and lesbians. *Journal of Personality and Social Psychology, 73,* 960–973.

BALES, R. F. (1946). Cultural differences in the rate of alcoholism. *Quarterly Journal of Studies on Alcohol, 6,* 380–499.

BANAJI, M. R., & STEELE, C. M. (1989). The social cognition of alcohol use. *Social Cognition, 7,* 137–151.

BANCROFT, J. (1987). A physiological approach. In J. H. Geer & W. T. O'Donohue (Eds.), *Theories of human sexuality* (pp. 411–421). New York: Plenum.

BANDURA, A. (1973). *Aggression: A social learning analysis.* Englewood Cliffs, NJ: Prentice-Hall.

BANDURA, A. (1986). *Social foundations of thought and action: A social cognitive theory.* Englewood Cliffs, NJ: Prentice-Hall.

BANDURA, A. (1988). Self-efficacy conceptions of anxiety. *Anxiety Research, 1,* 77–98.

BANDURA, A. (1989). Human agency in social cognitive theory. *American Psychologist, 44,* 1175–1184.

BANDURA, A. (1991a). Self-regulation of motivation through anticipatory and self reactive mechanisms. In R. A. Dienstbier (Ed.), *Perspectives on Motivation.* Nebraska Symposium on Motivation (pp. 69–164). Lincoln: University of Nebraska Press.

BANDURA, A. (1991b). Social cognitive theory of self-regulation. *Organizational Behavior and Human Decision Processes, 50,* 248–287.

BANDURA, A. (1997). *Self-efficacy: The exercise of control.* New York: Freeman.

BANDURA, A. (1998). Health promotion from the perspective of social cognitive theory. *Psychology and Health, 13,* 623–649.

BANDURA, A. (1999). A sociocognitive analysis of substance abuse: An agentic perspective. *Psychological Science, 10,* 214–217.

BANDURA, A., & CERVONE, D. (1983). Self-efficacy mechanisms governing the motivational effects of goal systems. *Journal of Personality and Social Psychology, 45,* 1017–1028.

BANDURA, A., CIOFFI, D., TAYLOR, C. B., & BROUILLARD, M. E. (1988). Perceived self-efficacy in coping with cognitive stressors and opioid addiction. *Journal of Personality and Social Psychology, 55,* 479–488.

BANDURA, A., & JOURDEN, F. J. (1991). Self-regulatory mechanisms governing the impact of social comparison on complex decision making. *Journal of Personality and Social Psychology, 60,* 941–951.

BANDURA, A., & MISCHEL, W. (1965). Modification of self-imposed delay of reward through exposure to live and symbolic models. *Journal of Personality and Social Psychology, 2,* 698–705.

BANDURA, A., & SCHUNK, D. H. (1981). Cultivating competence, self-efficacy and intrinsic interest through proximal self-motivation. *Journal of Personality and Social Psychology, 41,* 586–598.

BANDURA, A., TAYLOR, C. B., WILLIAMS, S. L., MEFFORD, I. N., & BARCHAS, J. D. (1985). Catecholamine secretion as a function of perceived coping self-efficacy. *Journal of Consulting and Clinical Psychology, 53,* 406, 414.

BARBER, N. (1995). The evolutionary psychology of physical attractiveness: Sexual selection and human morphology. *Ethology and Sociobiology, 16,* 395–424.

BARGH, J. A., & CHARTRAND, T. L. (1999). The unbearable autonomy of being. *American Psychologist, 54,* 462–479.

BARGH, J. A., & GOLLWITZER, P. M. (1994). Environmental control of goal-directed actions: Automatic and strategic contingencies between situation and behavior. In W. D. Spaulding (Ed.), *Integrative views of motivation, cognition and emotion: Nebraska Symposium on Motivation* (Vol. 41, pp. 71–124). Lincoln: University of Nebraska Press.

BARKOW, J. (1992). Beneath new culture is old psychology; Gossip and social stratification. In J. H. Barkow, L. Cosmides, & J. Tooby (Eds.), *The adapted mind: Evolutionary psychology and the generation of culture* (pp. 623–637). New York: Oxford University Press, 1995.

BARLOW, D. H. (1988). *Anxiety and its disorders: The nature and treatment of anxiety and panic.* New York: Guilford Press.

BARLOW, D. H., CHORPITA, B. F., & TUROVSKY, J. (1996). Fear, panic, anxiety and disorders of emotion. In R. A. Dienstbier (Ed.), *Perspectives on anxiety, panic, and fear. Nebraska Symposium on Motivation* (Vol. 43, pp. 251–328). Lincoln: University of Nebraska Press.

BARNES, G. (1979). The alcoholic personality: A reanalysis of the literature. *Journal of Studies on Alcohol, 40,* 571–634.

BARON, J. (1992). The effect of normative beliefs on anticipated emotions. *Journal of Personality and Social Psychology, 63,* 320–330.

BARON, R. A. (1973). Threatened retaliation from the victim as an inhibitor of physical aggression. *Journal of Research in Personality, 7,* 103–115.

BARON, R. A. (1977). *Human aggression.* New York: Plenum.

BARR, T. (1969). *Psychopharmacology.* Baltimore: Williams & Wilkins.

BARRON, F., & HARRINGTON, D. M. (1981). Creativity, intelligence, and personality. In M. R. Rosenzweig & L. W. Porter (Eds.), *Annual review of psychology* (pp. 439–476). Palo Alto, CA: Annual Reviews.

BARRY, H., III, WAGNER, A. R., & MILLER, N. E. (1962). Effects of alcohol and amobarbital on performance inhibited by experimental extinction. *Journal of Comparative and Physiological Psychology, 55,* 464–468.

BARSALOU, L. W. (1993). Ad hoc categories. *Memory and Cognition, 11,* 211–227.

Basic Behavioral Science Task Force of the National Advisory Mental Health Council, Rockville, MD (1996). Basic behavioral science research for mental health: Perception, attention, learning, and memory. *American Psychologist, 51,* 133–142.

BASOW, S. A. (1992). *Stereotypes and Roles* (3rd ed.). Pacific Grove, CA: Brooks/Cole.

BAUMEISTER, R. F., BRATSLAVSKY, E., MURAVEN, M., & TICE, D. M. (1998). Ego depletion: Is the active self a limited resource? *Journal of Personality and Social Psychology, 74,* 1252–1265.

BAUMEISTER, R. F., SMART, L., & BODEN, J. M. (1996). Relation of threatened egotism to violence and aggression: The dark side of high self-esteem. *Psychological Review, 103,* 5–33

BAUMEISTER, R. F., & SOMMERS, K. L. (1997). Consciousness, free choice, and automaticity. In R. S. Wyer, Jr. (Ed.), *Advance in social cognition* (Vol. X, pp. 75–81). Mahwah, NJ: Erlbaum.

BAUMGARDNER, A. H. (1990). To know oneself is to like oneself: Self-certainty and self-affect. *Journal of Personality and Social Psychology, 58,* 1062–1072.

BEACH, F. A. (1976). Hormonal control of sex-related behavior. In F. A. Beach (Ed.), *Human sexuality in four perspectives* (pp. 247–267). Baltimore: Johns Hopkins University Press.

BEARY, J. F., BENSON, H., & KLEMCHUK, H. P. (1974). A simple psychophysiologic technique which elicits the hypometabolic changes in the relaxation response. *Psychosomatic Medicine, 36,* 115–120.

BEATTY, M. J., & McCROSKEY, J. C. (1997). It's in our nature: Verbal aggressiveness as temperamental expression. *Communication Quarterly, 45,* 446–460.

BECK, A. T. (1967). *Depression: Clinical, experimental, and theoretical aspects.* New York: Harper & Row.

BECK, A. T. (1976). *Cognitive theory and emotional disorders.* New York: International Universities Press.

BECK, A. T. (1983). Cognitive therapy of depression: New approaches. In P. Clayton & J. Barrett (Eds.), *Treatment of depression: Old and new approaches* (pp. 265–290). New York: Raven Press.

BECK, A. T. (1985). Theoretical perspectives on clinical anxiety. In A. H. Tuma & J. D. Maser (Eds.), *Anxiety and anxiety disorders.* Hillsdale, NJ: Erlbaum.

BECK, A. T. (1991). Cognitive therapy: A 30–year retrospective. *American Psychologist, 46,* 368–375.

BECK, A. T., & YOUNG, J. E. (1978, April). College blues. *Psychology Today,* pp. 80–92.

BECKER, M. (Ed.). (1974). *The health belief model and personal health behavior.* Thorofare, NJ: Charles B. Slack.

BELL, A., WEINBERG, M. S., & HAMMERSMITH, S. K. (1981). *Sexual preference: Its development in men and women.* Bloomington: Indiana University Press.

BELL, D. C., MONTOYA, I. D., RICHARDS, A. J., & DAYTON, C. A. (1998). The motivation for drug abuse treatment: testing cognitive and 12-step theories. *American Journal of Drug and Alcohol Abuse, 24,* 551–565.

BELL, P. A. & BYRNE, D. (1978). Repression-sensitization. In H. London & J. E. Exner, Jr. (Eds.), *Dimensions of personality*. New York: Wiley.

BELLAH, R. N., MADSEN, R., SULLIVAN, W. M., SWIDLER, A., & TIPTON, S. M. (1985). *Habits of the Heart*. New York: Harper & Row.

BEM, D. J. (1967). Self-perception: An alternative interpretation of cognitive dissonance phenomenon. *Psychological Review, 74*, 183–200.

BENBOW, C. P., & STANLEY, J. C. (1980). Sex differences in mathematical ability: Fact or artifact? *Science, 210*, 1029–1031.

BENBOW, C. P., & STANLEY, J. C. (1983). Sex differences in mathematical reasoning ability: More facts. *Science, 222*, 1029–1031.

BENET, V., & WALLER, N. G. (1995). The big seven factor model of personality description: Evidence for its cross-cultural generality in a Spanish sample. *Journal of Personality and Social Psychology, 69*, 701–718.

BENINGTON, J. H., & HELLER, H. C. (1995). Restoration of brain energy metabolism as a function of sleep. *Progress in Neurobiology, 45*, 347–360.

BENSON, H. (1975). *The Relaxation Response*. New York: Avon Books.

BENSON, H. (1987). *Your Maximum Mind*. New York: Avon Books.

BENSON, H., & WALLACE, R. K. (1972). Decreased blood pressure in hypertensive subjects who practiced meditation. *Circulation*, Suppl. 2, 516.

BERENBAUM, S. A., & HINES, M. (1992). Early androgens are related to childhood sex-typed toy preferences. *Psychological Sciences, 3*, 203–206.

BERKOWITZ, L. (1962). *Aggression: A social psychological analysis*. New York: McGraw-Hill.

BERKOWITZ, L. (1969). The frustration-aggression hypothesis revised. In L. Berkowitz (Ed.), *Roots of aggression* (pp. 29–34). New York: Atherton Press.

BERKOWITZ, L. (1978). Is criminal violence normative behavior? Hostile and instrumental aggression in violent incidents. *Journal of Research in Crime and Delinquency, 15*, 148–161.

BERKOWITZ, L. (1989). Frustration-aggression hypothesis: Examination and reformulation. *Psychological Bulletin, 106*, 59–73.

BERKOWITZ, L. (1990). On the formation and regulation of anger and aggression: A cognitive-neoassociationistic analysis. *American Psychologist, 45*, 494–503.

BERKOWITZ, L. (1993). *Aggression: Its causes, consequences, and control*. New York: McGraw-Hill.

BERKOWITZ, L. (1994). Guns and youth. In L. Eron, J. H. Gentry, & P. Schlegel (Eds.), *Reason to hope: A psychosocial perspective on violence and youth* (pp. 251–279). Washington, DC: American Psychological Association.

BERKOWITZ, L., & GEEN, R. G. (1966). Film violence and the cue properties of available targets. *Journal of Personality and Social Psychology, 3*, 525–530.

BERLYNE, D. E. (1960). *Conflict, arousal, and curiosity*. New York: McGraw-Hill.

BERLYNE, D. E. (1969). The reward value of indifferent stimulation. In J. T. Tapp (Ed.), *Reinforcement and behavior*. New York: Academic Press.

BERLYNE, D. E., KOENIG, I. D. V., & HIROTA, T. (1966). Novelty, arousal, and the reinforcement of diversive exploration in the rat. *Journal of Comparative and Physiological Psychology, 62*, 772–796.

BERREBI, A. S., FITCH, R. H., RALPHE, D. L., DENENBERG, J. O., FRIEDRICH, V. L., JR., & DENENBERG, V. H. (1988). Corpus-callosum: Region-specific effects of sex, early experience and age. *Brain Research, 438*, 216–224.

BEXTON, W. H., HERON, W., & SCOTT, T. H. (1954). Effects of decreased variation in the sensory environment. *Canadian Journal of Psychology, 8*, 70–76.

BIEBER, I., DAIN, H. J., DINCE, P. R., DRELLICH, M. G., GRAND, H. G., GUNLACH, R. H., KREMERS, M. V., WILBUR, C. B., & BIEBER, T. B. (1962). *Homosexuality: A psychoanalytic study*. New York: Vintage.

BINDRA, D. A. (1974). Motivational view of learning, performance, and behavior modification. *Psychological Review, 81*, 199–213.

BIRNEY, R. C., BURDICK, H., & TEEVAN, R. C. (1969). *Fear of failure*. New York: Van Nostrand.

BIXLER, E. O., KALES, A., SOLDATOS, C. R., VELA-BUENO, A., JACOBY, J. A., & SCARONE, S. (1982). Sleep apnea in a normal population. *Research Communications in Chemical Pathology and Pharmacology, 36*, 141–152.

BLATT, S. J. (1995). The destructiveness of perfectionism: Implications for the treatment of depression. *American Psychologist, 50*, 1003–1020.

BLOOM, G., VON EULER, U. S., & FRANKENHAEUSER, M. (1963). Catecholamine excretion and personality traits in paratroop trainees. *Acta Physiologica Scandinavica, 58*, 77–89.

BLOOMFIELD, H. H., CAIN, M. P., JAFFE, D. T., & KORY, R. B. (1975). *TM: Discovering inner energy and overcoming stress*. New York: Dell.

BLUM, K., HAMILTON, M. L., & WALLACE, J. E. (1977). Alcohol and opiates: A review of common neurochemical and behavioral mechanisms. In K. Blum (Ed.), *Alcohol and opiates: Neurochemical and behavioral mechanisms*. New York: Academic Press.

BODNER, E., & MIKULINCER, M. (1998). Learned helplessness and the occurrence of depressive-like and paranoid-like responses: The role of attentional focus. *Journal of Personality and Social Psychology, 74*, 1010–1023.

BOLGER, N. (1990). Coping as a personality process: A prospective study. *Journal of Personality and Social Psychology, 59*, 525–537.

BOLGER, N., & ECKENRODE, J. (1991). Social relationships, personality, and anxiety during a major stressful event. *Journal of Personality and Social Psychology, 61*, 440–449.

BOLLES, R. C., & FANSELOW, M. S. (1982). Endorphins and behavior. *Annual Review of Psychology, 33*, 87–101.

BONANNO, G. A., & SINGER, J. L. (1990). Repressive personality style: Theoretical and methodological implications for health and pathology. In J. L. Singer (Ed.), *Repression and dissociation* (pp. 435–470). Chicago: University of Chicago Press.

BONNET, M. H. (1985). Effect of sleep disruption on sleep, performance, and mood. *Sleep, 8,* 11–19.

BONNET, M. H., & ROSA, R. R. (1987). Sleep and performance in young adults and older normals and insomniacs during sleep loss and recovery. *Biological Psychology, 25,* 153–172.

BONVALLET, M., & ALLEN, M. B., JR. (1963). Prolonged spontaneous and evoked reticular activation following discrete bulbar lesions. *Electroencephalography and Clinical Neurophysiology, 15,* 969–988.

BORDEN, R. J., BOWEN, R., & TAYLOR, S. P. (1971). Shock-setting behavior as a function of physical attack and extrinsic reward. *Perceptual and Motor Skills, 33,* 563–568.

BORING, E. G. (1950). *A history of experimental psychology* (2nd ed.). New York: Appleton-Century-Crofts.

BOUCHARD, T. J., JR. (1994). Genes, environment and personality. *Science, 264,* 1700–1701.

BOWLBY, J. (1979). *The making and breaking of affectional bonds.* London: Tavistock.

BOWLBY, J. (1980). *Attachment and Loss: Vol. 3. Loss: Sadness and Depression.* New York: Basic Books.

BRADY, J. V. (1975). Towards a behavioral biology of emotion. In L. Levi (Ed.), *Emotions: Their parameters and measurement.* New York: Raven Press.

BRANNIGAN, A. (1997). Self control, social control and evolutionary psychology: towards an integrated perspective on crime. *Canadian Journal of Criminology, 39,* 403–431.

BRAY, G. A. (1992). Pathophysiology of obesity. *American Journal of Clinical Nutrition, 55,* 488S–494S.

BREMER, J. (1959). *Asexualization: A follow-up study of 244 cases.* New York: Macmillan.

BRETHERTON, I., & WATERS, E. (1985). Growing points of attachment theory and research. *Monographs of the Society for Research in Child Development, 50,* (1–2, Serial No. 209).

BRICKMAN, P., COATES, D., & JANOFF-BULMAN, R. (1978). Lottery winners and accident victims: Is happiness relative? *Journal of Personality and Social Psychology, 36,* 917–927.

BRIEF, A. P., BUTCHER, A. H., GEORGE, J. M., & LINK, K. E. (1994). Integrating bottom-up and top-down theories of subjective well-being: The case of health. *Journal of Personality and Social Psychology, 64,* 646–653.

BRINK, S. (2000). Sleepless society. *U.S. News & World Report, 129,* 62.

BROCKNER, J. (1979). The effects of self-esteem, success-failure, and self consciousness on task performance. *Journal of Personality and Social Psychology, 37,* 1732–1741.

BROOKS-GUNN, J., & FURSTENBERG, F. F., JR. (1989). Adolescent sexual behavior. *American Psychologist, 44,* 249–257.

BROWN, G. M. (1983). Endocrine alterations in anorexia nervosa. In P. L. Darby, P. E. Garfinkel, D. M. Garner, & D. V. Coscina (Eds.), *Anorexia nervosa: Recent developments in research* (pp. 231–247). New York: Alan R. Liss.

BROWNELL, K. D., & RODIN, J. (1994). The dieting maelstrom: Is it possible and advisable to lose weight? *American Psychologist, 49,* 781–791.

BRUMBERG, J. J. (1989). *Fasting Girls: The surprising history of anorexia.* Toronto: Penguin Books of Canada.

BRUNER, J. (1992). Another look at New Look 1. *American Psychologist, 47,* 780–783.

BRUNER, J. S., MATTER, J., & PAPANEK, M. L. (1955). Breadth of learning as a function of drive level and mechanization. *Psychological Review, 62,* 1–10.

BUCK, R. (1999). The biological affects: A typology. *Psychological Review, 106,* 301–336.

BURNSTEIN, E., & WORCHEL, P. (1962). Arbitrariness of frustration and its consequences for aggression in a social situation. *Journal of Personality, 30,* 528–540.

BUSHMAN, B. J. (1995). Moderating role of trait aggressiveness in the effects of violent media on aggression. *Journal of Personality and Social Psychology, 69,* 950–960.

Business Week, Special 1989 Bonus Issue (1989). *Innovation in America.*

BUSS, A. H. (1963). Physical aggression in relation to different frustrations. *Journal of Abnormal and Social Psychology, 67,* 1–7.

BUSS, A. H., & DURKEE, A. (1957). An inventory for assessing different kinds of hostility. *Journal of Consulting Psychology, 21,* 343–349.

BUSS, A. H., & PERRY, M. (1992). The aggression questionnaire. *Journal of Personality and Social Psychology, 63,* 452–459.

BUSS, D. M. (1994). *The evolution of desire.* New York: Basic Books.

BUSS, D. M. (1999). *Evolutionary psychology: The new science of the mind.* Boston: Allyn & Bacon.

BUSS, D. M. (2000). The evolution of happiness. *American Psychologist, 55,* 15–23.

BUSS, D. M., ABBOTT, M., ANGLEITNER, A., ASHERIAN, A., BIAGGIO, A., & 45 other co-authors (1990). International preferences in selecting mates: A study of 37 cultures. *Journal of Cross-Cultural Psychology, 21,* 5–47.

BUSS, D. M., & SCHMITT, D. P. (1993). Sexual strategies theory: An evolutionary perspective on human mating. *Psychological Review, 100,* 204–232.

BUTLER, R. A. (1953). Discrimination learning by rhesus monkeys to visual-exploration motivation. *Journal of Comparative and Physiological Psychology, 46,* 95–98.

BUUNK, B. P., DOOSJE, B. J., JANS, L. G. J. M., & HOPSTAKEN, L. E. M. (1993). Perceived reciprocity, social support, and stress at work: The role of exchange and communal orientation. *Journal of Personality and Social Psychology, 65,* 801–811.

BYRNE, D. (1977). Social psychology and the study of sexual behavior. *Personality and Social Psychology Bulletin, 3,* 3–30.

CAHALAN, D., & ROOM, R. (1974). *Problem drinking among American men* (Monograph 7). New Brunswick, NJ: Rutgers Center of Alcohol Studies.

CAIN, E. N., KOHORN, E. I., QUINLAN, D. M., LATIMER, K., & SCHWARTZ, P. E. (1986). Psychosocial benefits of a cancer support group. *Cancer, 57,* 183–189.

Calgary (1989). Comments at a concert. June 23, 1997.

California Task Force to Promote Self-Esteem and Personal and Social Responsibility (1990). *Toward a state of self-esteem.* Sacramento: California State Department of Education.

CAMPBELL, J. D. (1990). Self-esteem and clarity of the self-concept. *Journal of Personality and Social Psychology, 59,* 538–549.

CARLSON, E. R., & COLEMAN, C. E. H. (1977). Experiential and motivational determinants of the richness of an induced sexual fantasy. *Journal of Personality, 45,* 528–542.

CARLSON, S., FELTEN, D. L., LIVNAT, S., & FELTEN, S. Y. (1987). Alternations of monoamines in specific autonomic nuclei following immunization in mice. *Brain, Behavior, and Immunity, 1,* 52–64.

CARO, J. F., SINHA, M. K., KOLACZYNSKI, J. W., ZHANG, P. L., & CONSIDINE, R. V. (1996). Leptin: The tale of an obesity gene. *Diabetes, 45,* 1455–1462.

CARROLL, K. M. (1997). Listening to smoking researchers: Negative affect and drug treatment. *Psychological Science, 8,* 190–193.

CARSKADON, M. A., & DEMENT, W. C. (1977). Sleepiness and sleep state on a 90–min schedule. *Psychophysiology, 14,* 127–133.

CARSKADON, M. A., & DEMENT, W. C. (1981). Cumulative effects of sleep restriction on daytime sleepiness. *Psychophysiology, 18,* 107–113.

CARTWRIGHT, R. (1990). A network model of dreams. In R. R. Bootzin, J. F. Kihlstrom, & D. L. Schacter (Eds.), *Sleep and cognition* (pp. 179–189). Washington, DC: American Psychological Association.

CARTWRIGHT, R. A. (1999). Dreaming up a good mood. *Psychology Today, 32,* 20.

CARTWRIGHT, R. D., LLOYD, S., BUTTERS, E., WEINER, L., McCARTHY, L., & HANCOCK, J. (1975). Effects of REM time on what is recalled. *Psychophysiology, 12,* 561–568.

CARTWRIGHT, R. D., MONROE, L. J., & PALMER, C. (1967). Individual differences in response to REM deprivation. *Archives of General Psychiatry, 16,* 297–303.

CARTWRIGHT, R. D., & RATZEL, R. (1972). Effects of dream loss on waking behaviors. *Archives of General Psychiatry, 27,* 277–280.

CARVER, C. S. (1979). A cybernetic model of self-attention processes. *Journal of Personality and Social Psychology, 37,* 1251–1281.

CARVER, C. S., BLANEY, P. H., & SCHEIER, M. F. (1979a). Focus of attention, chronic expectancy, and responses to a feared stimulus. *Journal of Personality and Social Psychology, 37,* 1186–1195.

CARVER, C. S., BLANEY, P. H., & SCHEIER, M. F. (1979b). Reassertion and giving up: The interactive role of self-directed attention and outcome expectancy. *Journal of Personality and Social Psychology, 37,* 1859–1870.

CARVER, C. S., SCHEIER, M. F., & WEINTRAUB, J. K. (1989). Assessing coping strategies: A theoretically based approach. *Journal of Personality and Social Psychology, 56,* 267–283.

CASPI, A. (2000). The child is father of the man: Personality continues from childhood to adulthood. *Journal of Personality and Social Psychology, 78,* 158–172.

CASS, V. C. (1990). The implication of homosexual identity formation for the Kinsey model and scale of sexual preference. In D. P. McWhiter, S. A. Sanders, & J. M. Reinisch (Eds.), *Homosexuality/heterosexuality: concepts of sexual orientation* (pp. 239–266). New York: Oxford University Press.

CASTALDO, V., & KRYNICKI, V. (1973). Sleep patterns and intelligence in functional mental retardation. *Journal of Mental Deficiency Research, 17,* 231–235.

CATTELL, R. B. (1971). *Abilities: Their structure, growth and action.* Boston, MA: Houghton Mifflin.

CAUL, W. F., BUCHANAN, D. C., & HAYS, R. C. (1972). Effects of unpredictability of shock on incidence of gastric lesions and heart rate in immobilized rats. *Physiology and Behavior, 8,* 669–672.

CAUTHEN, N. R., & PRYMAK, C. A. (1977). Meditation versus relaxation: An examination of the physiological effects of relaxation training and of different levels of experience with transcendental meditation. *Journal of Consulting and Clinical Psychology, 45,* 496–497.

CHAMBLESS, D. L., & GRACELY, E. J. (1989). Fear of fear and the anxiety disorders. *Cognitive Therapy and Research, 13,* 9–20.

CHANDRA, R. K., & NEWBERNE, P. M. (1977). *Nutrition, immunity, and infection: Mechanisms of interaction.* New York: Plenum.

CHANG, E. C. (1998). Dispositional optimism and primary and secondary appraisal of a stressor: Controlling for confounding influences and relations to coping and psychological and physical adjustment. *Journal of Personality and Social Psychology, 74,* 1109–1120.

CHASSLER, S. (1988, December). What teen boys think about sex. *Parade,* p. 1617.

CHISHOLM, J. S. (1996). The evolutionary ecology of attachment organization. *Humans Nature, 7,* 1–39.

CHORPITA, B. F., & BARLOW, D. H. (1998). The development of anxiety: The role of control in the early environment. *Psychological Bulletin, 124,* 3–21.

CHRISTIANSEN, K., & KNUSSMANN, R. (1987). Sex hormones and cognitive functioning in men. *Neuropsychobiology, 18,* 27–36.

CHURCHILL, A. C., & McMURRAY, N. E. (1990). *Self-efficacy and unpleasant intrusive thought.* Manuscript, University of Melbourne.

CIBA Foundation Symposium. (1979). *Sex hormones and behavior.* Amsterdam: Excerpta Medica.

CIPOLLI, C. (1995). Sleep, dreams, and memory: An overview. *Journal of Sleep Research, 4,* 2–9.

CLARKE, D. H. (1975). *Exercise physiology.* Englewood Cliffs, NJ: Prentice-Hall.

CLARKE, R. D., & HATFIELD, E. (1989). Gender differences in receptivity to sexual offers. *Journal of Psychology and Human Sexuality, 2,* 39–55.

CLONINGER, C. R., SIGVARDSSON, S., & BOHMAN, M. (1988). Coping, expectancies, and alcohol abuse: A test of social learning formulations. *Journal of Abnormal Psychology, 97,* 218–230.

COCCARO, E. F., BERGEMAN, C. S., & McCLEARN, G. E. (1993). Heritability of irritable impulsiveness: A study of twins reared together and apart. *Psychiatry Research, 48,* 229–242.

COHEN, D. B. (1977). Neuroticism and dreaming sleep: A case for interactionism in personality research. *British Journal of Social and Clinical Psychology, 16,* 153–163.

COHEN, D. B. (1979). Dysphoric affect and REM sleep. *Journal of Abnormal Psychology, 88,* 73–77.

COHEN, S., FRANK, E., DOYLE, W. J., SKONER, D. P., RABIN, B. S., & GWALTNEY, J. M., JR. (1998). Types of stressors that increase susceptibility to the common cold in healthy adults. *Health Psychology, 17,* 214–223.

COHEN, S., & McKAY, G. (1984). Social support, stress and the buffering hypothesis: A theoretical analysis. In A. Baum, J. E. Singer, & S. E. Taylor (Eds.), *Handbook of psychology and health* (Vol. 4, pp. 253–267). Hillsdale, NJ: Erlbaum.

COHEN, S., & WILLIAMSON, G. M. (1991). Stress and infectious disease in humans. *Psychological Bulletin, 109,* 5–24.

COLDITZ, G. A. (1992). Economic costs of obesity. *American Journal of Clinical Nutrition, 55,* 503S–507S.

COLEMAN, R. M. (1986). *Wide Awake at 3:00 A.M.: By choice or by chance.* New York: W. H. Freeman.

COLLAER, M. L., & HINES, M. (1995). Human behavioral sex differences: A role for gonadal hormones during early development. *Psychological Bulletin, 118,* 55–107.

COLLINS, D. L., BAUM, A., & SINGER, J. E. (1983). Coping with chronic stress at Three Mile Island: Psychological and biochemical evidence. *Health Psychology, 2,* 149–166.

CONBOY, J. K. (1994). The effects of exercise withdrawal on mood states in runners. *Journal of Sport Behavior, 17,* 188–203.

CONDRY, J. C. (1977). Enemies of exploration: Self-initiated versus other-initiated learning. *Journal of Personality and Social Psychology, 35,* 459–477.

CONGER, J. J. (1956). Reinforcement theory and the dynamics of alcoholism. *Quarterly Journal of Studies on Alcohol, 17,* 296–305.

COOPER, J. R., BLOOM, F. E., & ROTH, B. H. (1982). *The biochemical basis of neuropharmacology* (4th ed.). New York: Oxford University Press.

COOPER, M. L., FRONE, M. R., RUSSELL, M., & MUDAR, P. (1995). Drinking to regulate positive and negative emotions: A motivational model of alcohol use. *Journal of Personality and Social Psychology, 69,* 990–1005.

COOPER, M. L., SHAPIRO, C. M., & POWERS, A. M. (1998). Motivations for sex and risky sexual behavior among adolescents and young adults: A functional perspective. *Journal of Personality and Social Psychology, 75,* 1528–1558.

COOPERSMITH, S. (1967). *The antecedents of self-esteem.* San Francisco: W. H. Freeman.

COSMIDES, L. & TOOBY, J. (1992). Cognitive adaptations for social exchange. In J. H. Barkow, L. Cosmides, & J. Tooby (Eds.), *The adapted mind: Evolutionary psychology and the generation of culture* (pp. 163–228). New York: Oxford University Press, 1995.

COSTRA, P. T., JR., & McCRAE, R. R. (1992). Four ways five factors are basic. *Personality and Individual Differences, 13,* 653–665.

COX, W. M., & KLINGER, E. (1988). A motivational model of alcohol use. *Journal of Abnormal Psychology, 97,* 168–180.

COYNE, J. C., & LAZARUS, R. S. (1980). Cognitive style, stress perception, and coping. In I. L. Kutash & L. B. Schlesinger (Eds.), *Handbook on stress and anxiety: Contemporary knowledge, theory, and treatment* (pp. 144–158). San Francisco: Jossey-Bass.

CRANDALL, C. S. (1994). Prejudice against fat people: Ideology and self-interest. *Journal of Personality and Social Psychology, 66,* 882–894.

CRATTY, B. J. (1989). *Psychology in contemporary sport.* Englewood Cliffs, NJ: Prentice Hall.

CRICK, C., & MITCHISON, G. (1983). The function of dream sleep. *Nature, 304,* 111–114.

CRICK, C., & MITCHISON, G. (1986). REM sleep and neural nets. *The Journal of Mind and Behavior, 7,* 229–250.

CRICK, F., & KOCH, C. (1992, September). The problem of consciousness. *Scientific American,* pp. 153–159.

CROYLE, R., & COOPER, J. (1983). Dissonance arousal: Physiological evidence. *Journal of Personality and Social Psychology, 45,* 782–791.

CSIKSZENTMIHALYI, M. (1990). *Flow: The psychology of optimal experience.* New York: Harper & Row.

CSIKSZENTMIHALYI, M. (1997). *Finding Flow.* New York: Basic Books.

CSIKSZENTMIHALYI, M. (1999). If we are so rich why aren't we happy? *American Psychologist, 54,* 821–827.

CURRY, L. A., SNYDER, C. R., COOK, D. L., RUBY, B. C., & REHM, M. (1997). Role of hope in academic and sport achievement. *Journal of Personality and Social Psychology, 73,* 1257–1267.

CUTHBERT, B., KRISTELLER, J., SIMONS, R., HODES, R., & LANG, P. J. (1981). Strategies of arousal control: Biofeedback, meditation, and motivation. *Journal of Experimental Psychology: General, 110,* 518–546.

CYRANOWSKI, J. M., & ANDERSEN, B. L. (1998). Schemas, sexuality and romantic attachments. *Journal of Personality and Social Psychology, 74,* 1364–1379.

CZAYA, J., KRAMER, M., & ROTH, T. (1973). *Changes in dream quality as a function of time into REM.* Paper presented at the meeting of the Association for the Psychophysiological Study of Sleep, San Diego, CA.

D'EMILIO, J., & FREEDMAN, E. B. (1988). *Intimate matters: A history of sexuality in America.* New York: Harper & Row.

DALY, M., & WILSON, M. (1988). *Homicide.* New York: Aldine de Gruyter.

DAMASIO. A. (1999). *The feeling of what happens: Body and emotion in the making of consciousness.* New York: Harcourt Brace.

DANK, B. (1971). Coming out in the gay world. *Psychiatry, 34,* 180–197.

DARWIN, C. (1872). *The expression of the emotions in man and animals.* Chicago: University of Chicago Press, 1965.

DAVIDSON, R. J., & HUGDAHL, K. (Eds.). (1995). *Brain asymmetry.* Cambridge. MA: MIT Press.

DAVIS, B. (1973). *Norepinephrine and epinephrine secretions following rest and exercise in trained and untrained males.* Unpublished doctoral dissertation. University of Illinois at Urbana-Champaign.

DAVIS, D. H., GOODWIN, D. W., & ROBINS, L. N. (1975). Drinking amid abundant illicit drugs. *Archives of General Psychiatry, 32,* 230–233.

DAWKINS, R. (1990). *The selfish gene.* Oxford.

DE RIVERA, T. (1982). *A structural theory of emotions.* New York: International University Press.

De TOCQUEVILLE, A. (1969). *Democracy in America* (G. Lawrence, Trans.; J. P. Mayer, Ed.). New York: Doubleday, Anchor Books. (Original work published 1835)

De WIED, D. (1967). Opposite effects of ACTH and glucocorticoids on extinction of conditioned emotional behavior. In L. Martini, F. Fraschini, & M. Motta (Eds.), *Proceedings of the second international congress on hormonal steroids* (pp. 945–951). Amsterdam: Excerpta Medica.

De WIED, D. (1980). Pituitary-adrenal system hormones and behavior. In H. Selye (Ed.), *Selye's guide to stress research* (Vol. 1, pp. 252–279). New York: Van Nostrand Reinhold.

DeBONO, E. (1970). *Lateral thinking.* London: Penguin Books.

DeBONO, E. (1987). *Six thinking hats.* New York: Penguin Books.

DECI, E. L. (1972). Effects of externally mediated rewards on intrinsic motivation. *Journal of Personality and Social Psychology, 22,* 113–120.

DECI, E. L. (1975). *Intrinsic motivation.* New York: Plenum.

DECI, E. L., KOESTNER, R., & RYAN, R. M. (1999). A meta-analytic review of experiments examining the effects of extrinsic rewards on intrinsic motivation. *Psychological Bulletin, 125,* 627–668.

DECI, E. L., NEZLAK, J., & SHEINMAN, L. (1981). Characteristics of the rewarder and intrinsic motivation of the rewardee. *Journal of Personality and Social Psychology, 40,* 1–10.

DECI, E. L., & RYAN, R. M. (1985). *Intrinsic motivation and self-determination in human behavior.* New York: Plenum.

DECI, E. L., & RYAN, R. M. (1991). A motivational approach to self: Integration in personality. In R. A. Dienstbier (Ed.), *Perspectives on motivation* (pp. 237–288). *Nebraska Symposium on Motivation.* Lincoln: University of Nebraska Press.

DeLEON, G., MELNICK, G., KRESSEL, D. (1997). Motivation and readiness for therapeutic community treatment among cocaine and other drug abusers. *American Journal of Drug and Alcohol Abuse, 23,* 169–189.

DEMBER, W. N., & EARL, R. W. (1957). Analysis of exploratory, manipulative, and curiosity behaviors. *Psychological Review, 64,* 91–96.

DEMENT, W. C. (1972). *Some must watch while some must sleep.* San Francisco: W. H. Freeman.

DEMENT, W. C., & CARSKADON, M. A. (1982). Current perspectives on daytime sleepiness. *Sleep, 5,* S56–S66.

DEMENT, W. C., & VAUGHN, C. (1999). *The promise of sleep.* New York: Dell.

DEMENT, W. C., & VILLABLANCA, J. (1974). Clinical disorders in man and animal model experiments. In O. Petre-Ouadens & J. Schlag (Eds.), *Basic sleep mechanisms.* New York: Academic Press.

DENENBERG, V. H. (1967). Stimulation in infancy, emotional reactivity, and exploratory behavior. In D. C. Glass (Ed.), *Neurophysiology and emotion.* New York: Rockefeller University Press & Russell Sage Foundation.

DeNEVE, K., & COOPER, H. (1998). The happy personality: A meta-analysis of 137 personality traits and subjective well-being. *Psychological Bulletin, 124,* 197–229.

DENGERINK, H. A., & BERTILSON, H. S. (1974). The reduction of attack instigated aggression. *Journal of Research in Personality, 8,* 254–262.

DENGERINK, H. A., & LEVENDUSKY, P. G. (1972). Effects of massive retaliation and balance of power on aggression. *Journal of Experimental Research in Personality, 6,* 230–236.

DENGERINK, H. A., & MYERS, J. D. (1977). The effects of failure and depression on subsequent aggression. *Journal of Personality and Social Psychology, 35,* 88–96.

DERAKSHAN, N., & EYSENCK, M. W. (1997). Interpretive biases for one's own behavior and physiology in high-trait-anxious individual and repressors. *Journal of Personality and Social Psychology, 73,* 816–825.

DEY, F. (1970). Auditory fatigue and predicted permanent hearing defects from rock-and-roll music. *New England Journal of Medicine, 282,* 467–469.

DIAMOND, M. C. (1988). The interaction between sex hormones and environment. In M. C. Diamond (Ed.), *Enriching heredity* (pp. 115–177). New York: Free Press.

DIAMOND, M. C., DOWLING, G. A., & JOHNSON, R. E. (1981). Morphologic cerebral cortical asymmetry in male and female rats. *Experimental Neurology, 71,* 261–268.

DICLEMENTE, C. C. (1999). Motivation for change: Implications for substance abuse. *Psychological Science, 10,* 209–213.

DIENER, E. (2000). Subjective well-being: The science of happiness and a proposal for a national index. *American Psychologist 55,* 34–43.

DIENER, E., SUH, E., LUCAS, R., & SMITH, H. (1999). Subjective well-being: Three decades of progress. *Psychological Bulletin, 125,* 276–302.

DILALLA, L. F., & GOTTESMAN, I. I. (1991). Biological and genetic contributions to violence: Widom's untold tale. *Psychological Bulletin, 109,* 125–129.

DINGES, D. F. (1984).The nature and timing of sleep. *Transactions & studies of the College of Physicians of Philadelphia, 6,* 177–206.

DINGES, D. F. (1989). The nature of sleepiness: Cause, contexts, and consequences. In A. J. Stunkard & A. Baum (Eds.), *Perspectives in behavioral medicine: Eating, sleeping, and sex* (pp. 147–179). Hillsdale, NJ: Erlbaum.

DINGES, D. (1995). An overview of sleepiness and accidents. *Journal of Sleep Research, 4,* 4–11.

DINGES, D. F. DOUGLAS, HAMARMAN, ZAUGG, & KAPOOR, (1995). Sleep deprivation and human immune function. *Advances in Neuroimmunology, 5,* 97–100.

DINGES, D. F., & KRIBBS, N. B. (1991). Performing while sleepy: Effects of experimentally induced sleepiness. In T. M. Monk (Ed.), *Sleep, sleepiness and performance* (pp. 97–127). New York: Wiley.

DODGE, K. A. (1993). Social cognitive mechanisms in the development of conduct disorder and depression. *Annual Review of Psychology, 44,* 559–584.

DOHLER, K.-D., COQUELIN, A., DAVIS, F., HINES, M., SHRYNE, J. E., & GRRSKI, R. A. (1984). Pre- and postnatal influence of testosterone propionate and diethylstilbestrol on differentiation of the sexually dimorphic nucleus of the preoptic area in male and female rats. *Brain Research, 302,* 291–295.

DOLE, V. P. (1980). Addictive behavior. *Scientific American, 240*(6), 138–150.

DOMINICK, J. R., & GREENBERG, B. S. (1971). Attitudes toward violence: The interaction of television exposure, family attitudes, and social class. In G. A. Comstock & E. A. Rubinstein (Eds.), *Television and social behavior: Vol. 3. Television and adolescent aggressiveness* (pp. 314–335). Washington, DC: Government Printing Office.

DONNERSTEIN, E. L., & LINZ, D. G. (1986). The question of pornography. *Psychology Today, 20,* 56–59.

DONOHEW, R. L., HOYLE, R. H., CLAYTON, R. R., SKINNER, W. F., COLON, S. E., & RICE, R. E. (1999). Sensation seeking and drug used by adolescents and their friends: Models for marijuana and alcohol. *Journal of Studies in Alcohol, 60,* 622–631.

DOOB, A. N., & CLIMIE, R. J. (1972). Delay of measurement and the effects of film violence. *Journal of Experimental Social Psychology, 8,* 136–142.

DOZIER, R. W. (1998). *Fear itself.* New York: Thomas Dunne Books.

DRUMMOND, S. P. A., BROWN, G. G., GILLIN, J. C., STRICKER, J. L., WONG, E. C., & BUXTON, R. B. (2000). Altered brain response to verbal learning following sleep deprivation. *Nature, 403,* 655–657.

DUBBERT, P. M. (1992). Exercise in behavioral medicine. *Journal of Consulting and Clinical Psychology, 60,* 613–618.

DURDEN-SMITH, J., & DE SIMONE, D. (1983). *Sex and the brain.* New York: Warner.

DWECK, C. S. (1986). Motivational processes affecting learning. *American Psychologist, 41,* 1040–1048.

DWECK, C. S. (1991). Self-theories and goals: Their role in motivation, personality, and development. In R. A. Dienstbier (Ed.), *Perspectives on Motivation.* Nebraska Symposium on Motivation (pp. 199–235). Lincoln: University of Nebraska Press.

DWECK, C. S., & LEGGETT, E. L. (1988). A social-cognitive approach to motivation and personality. *Psychological Review, 95,* 256–273.

DWECK, C. S., & LICHT, B. (1990). Learned helplessness and intellectual achievement. In J. Garber and M. Seligman (Eds.), *Learned helplessness: Theory and application* (pp. 197–222).

DYKMAN, B. M. (1998). Integrating cognitive and motivational factors in depression: Initial tests of a goal-orientation approach. *Journal of Personality and Social Psychology, 74,* 139–158.

DYKSTRA, L. (1992). Drug Action. In J. Grabowski and G. R. Vanden Bos (Eds.), *Psychopharmacology: Basic mechanisms and applied interventions* (pp. 59–66). Washington, DC: American Psychological Association.

EAGLY, A. H. (1995). The science and politics of comparing women and men. *American Psychologist, 50,* 145–158.

EAGLY, A. H., & STEFFEN, V. J. (1986). Gender and aggressive behavior: A metaanalytic review of the social psychological literature. *Psychological Bulletin, 100,* 309–330.

EARL, R. W. (1957). *Problem solving and motor skill behaviors under conditions of free choice.* Unpublished doctoral dissertation, University of Michigan, Ann Arbor.

EARL, R. W., FRANKEN, R. E., & MAY, R. B. (1967). Choice as a function of stimulus change. *Perceptual and Motor Skills, 24,* 183–189.

EASTERBROOK, J. A. (1959). The effect of emotion on cue utilization and the organization of behavior. *Psychological Review, 66,* 183–201.

EDEN, A. (1975). *Growing up thin.* New York: David McKay.

EDWARDS, W. (1961). Behavioral decision theory. In P. R. Farnsworth (Ed.), *Annual review of psychology* (Vol. 12, pp. 473–498). Palo Alto, CA: Annual Reviews.

EHRHARDT, A. A., & MEYER-BAHLBURG, H. F. L. (1981). Effects of prenatal sex hormones on gender-related behavior. *Science, 211,* 1312–1318.

EHRHARDT, A. A., MEYER-BAHLBURG, H. F. L., ROSEN, L. R., FELDMAN, J. F., VERIDIANO, N. P., ZIMMERMAN, L., & McEWEN, B. S. (1985). Sexual orientation after prenatal exposure to exogenous estrogen. *Archives of Sexual Behavior, 14,* 57–77.

EISENBERGER, R., & CAMERON, J. (1996). Detrimental effects of reward: Reality or myth? *American Psychologist, 51,* 1153–1166.

EISENBERGER, R., & SELBST, M. (1994). Does reward increase or decrease creativity? *Journal of Personality and Social Psychology, 66,* 1116–1127.

EKMAN, P. (1994). Strong evidence for universals in facial expression: A reply to Russell's mistaken critique. *Psychological Bulletin, 115,* 268–287.

ELDREDGE, N., & GOULD, S. J. (1972). Punctuated equilibria: An alternative to phyletic gradualism. In T. J. Schopf (Ed.), *Models in paleobiology.* San Francisco: Freeman, Cooper.

ELKIN, R., & LEIPPE, M. (1986). Physiological arousal, dissonance, and attitude change: Evidence for a dissonance arousal link and a "don't remind me" effect. *Journal of Personality and Social Psychology, 51*, 55–65.

ELLIOT, A. J., & CHURCH, M. A. (1997). A hierarchical model of approach and avoidance motivation. *Journal of Personality and Social Psychology, 72*, 218–232.

ELLIOT, A. J., & DEVINE, P. G. (1994). On the motivational nature of cognitive dissonance: Dissonance as psychological discomfort. *Journal of Personality and Social Psychology, 67*, 382–394.

ELLIOT, A. J., & HARACKIEWICZ, J. M. (1996). Approach and avoidance achievement goals and intrinsic motivation. A mediational analysis. *Journal of Personality and Social Psychology, 70*, 968–980.

ELLIS, A., & GRIEGER, R. (1977). *Handbook of rational emotive therapy.* New York: Springer.

ELLISON, C. G., GAY, D. A., & GLASS, T. A. (1989). Does religion contribute to individual life satisfaction? *Social Forces, 68*, 100–123.

ELLMAN, S. J., SPIELMAN, A. J., LUCK, D., STEINER, S. S., & HALPERIN, R. (1991). REM deprivation: A review. In S. J. Ellman & J. S. Antrobus (Eds.), *The mind in sleep: Psychology and psychophysiology* (2nd ed., pp. 329–376). New York: Wiley.

ELLMAN, S. J., & WEINSTEIN, L. N. (1991). REM sleep and dream formation: A theoretical integration. In S. J. Ellman & J. S. Antrobus (Eds.), *The mind in sleep: Psychology and psychophysiology* (2nd ed., pp. 466–488). New York: Wiley.

EMMONS, R. A. (1992). The repressive personality social support. In H. S. Friedman (Ed.), *Hostility, coping and health* (pp. 141–150). Washington, DC: American Psychological Association.

EMRICK, C. D., & HANSEN, J. (1983). Assertions regarding effectiveness of treatment of alcoholism: Fact or fantasy. *American Psychologist, 38*, 1078–1088.

ENGLE, K. B., & WILLIAMS, T. K. (1972). Effect of an ounce of vodka on alcoholics' desire for alcohol. *Quarterly Journal of Studies on Alcohol, 33*, 1099–1105.

EPSTEIN, S. (1990). Cognitive-experiential self-theory. In L. A. Pervin (Ed.), *Handbook of personality: Theory and research* (pp. 165–191). New York: Guilford Press.

EPSTEIN, S. (1991). Cognitive-experiential self-theory: An integrative theory of personality. In R. Curtis (Ed.), *The relational self convergences in psychoanalysis and social psychology* (pp. 111–137). New York: Guilford Press.

EPSTEIN, S. (1992). Coping ability, negative self-evaluation, and overgeneralization: Experiment and theory. *Journal of Personality and Social Psychology, 62*, 826–836.

EPSTEIN, S., LIPSON, A., HOLSTEIN, C., & HUH, E. (1992). Irrational reactions to negative outcomes: Evidence for two conceptual systems. *Journal of Personality and Social Psychology, 62*, 328–339.

EPSTEIN, S., & MEIER, P. (1989). Constructive thinking: A broad coping variable with specific components. *Journal of Personality and Social Psychology, 57*, 332–350.

ERIKSON, E. H. (1950). *Childhood and society.* New York: Norton.

ERON, L. D., GENTRY, J. H., & SCHLEGEL (Eds.). (1994). *Reason to hope: A psychosocial perspective on violence and youth.* Washington, DC: American Psychological Association.

ERON, L. D., HUESMANN, L. R., LEFKOWITZ, M. M., & WALDER, L. Q. (1972). Does television violence cause aggression? *American Psychologist, 27*, 253–263.

ERSKINE, H. (1973). The polls: Hopes, fears, and regrets. *Public Opinion Quarterly, 37*, 132–145.

EVANS, G. E., SHAPIRO, D. H., & LEWIS, M. (1993). Specifying dysfunctional mismatches between different control dimensions. *British Journal of Psychology, 84*, 255–274.

EVERSON, C. A. (1993). Sustained sleep deprivation impairs host defense. *American Journal of Physiology, 265*, R1148–1154.

EYSENCK, H. J. (1967). *The biological basis of personality.* Springfield, IL: Charles C. Thomas.

EYSENCK, H. J. (1973). Personality and the maintenance of the smoking habit. In W. L. Dunn (Ed.), *Smoking behavior: Motives and incentives* (pp. 113–146). Washington, DC: Winston.

EYSENCK, H. J. (1988). Personality and stress as causal factors in cancer and coronary heart disease. In M. P. Janisse (Ed.), *Individual differences, stress, and health psychology* (pp. 129–145). New York: Springer.

EYSENCK, H. J. (1991). Dimensions of personality: 16, 5, or 3? Criteria for a taxonomic paradigm. *Personality and Individual Differences, 12*, 773–790.

EYSENCK, H. J. (1995). *Genius: The natural history of creativity.* Cambridge: Cambridge University Press.

FAIRCLOUGH, S. H., & GRAHAM, R. (1999). Impairment of driving performance caused by sleep deprivation or alcohol: A comparative study. *Human Factors, 41*, 118–127.

FALK, J. L. (1983). Drug dependence: Myth or motive? *Pharmacology Biochemistry and Behavior, 19*, 385–391.

FARKAS, G. M., & ROSEN, R. C. (1976). Effect of alcohol on elicited male sexual response. *Journal of Studies on Alcohol, 37*, 265–272.

FARLEY, F. H. (1986, May). The big T in personality. *Psychology Today*, pp. 44–52.

FARR, J. L. (1990). Facilitating individual role innovation. In M. A. West & J. L. Farr (Eds.), *Innovation and creativity at work: Psychological and organizational strategies* (pp. 207–230). New York: Wiley.

FAUSTO-STERLING, A. (1985). *Myths of gender: Biological theories about women and men.* New York: Basic Books.

FEATHER, N. T. (1994). Attitudes toward achievers and reactions to their fall: Theory and research concerning tall poppies. *Advance in Experimental Social Psychology, 26*, 1–73.

FEINBERG, I., KORESKO, R. L., HELLER, N., & STEINBERG, H. R. (1973). Sleep EEG and eye-movement patterns in young and aged normal subjects and in patients with chronic brain syndrome. In W. B. Webb (Ed.), *Sleep: An active process.* Glenview, IL: Scott, Foresman.

FELDMAN, R. S., & BERNSTEIN, A. G. (1978). Primacy effects in self-attribution of ability. *Journal of Personality, 46,* 732–742.

FENIGSTEIN, A. (1979). Does aggression cause a preference for viewing media violence? *Journal of Personality and Social Psychology, 37,* 2307–2317.

FENWICK, P. B., DONALDSON, S., GILLIS, L., BUSHMAN, J., FENTON, G. W., PERRY, L., TILSLEY, C., & SERAFINOWICZ, H. (1977). Metabolic and EEG changes during transcendental meditation: An explanation. *Biological Psychology, 5,* 101–118.

FENZ, W. D., & EPSTEIN, S. (1969, September). Stress: In the air. *Psychology Today,* pp. 28–29, 58–59.

FERN, R. W. (1976). Hearing loss caused by amplified pop music. *Journal of Sound and Vibration, 46,* 462–464.

FESHBACH, N. D. (1987). Parental empathy and child adjustment/maladjustment. In N. Eisenberg & J. Strayer (Eds.), *Empathy and its development* (pp. 271–291). New York: Cambridge University Press.

FESTINGER, L. (1957). *A theory of cognitive dissonance.* Evanston, IL: Row, Peterson.

FEY, S. G., & LINDHOLM, E. (1978). Biofeedback and progressive relaxation: Effects on systolic and diastolic blood pressure and heart rate. *Psychophysiology, 15,* 239–247.

FIGUEREDO, A. J. (1995). *Preliminary reports: Family deterrence of domestic violence in Spain.* Unpublished manuscript. Department of Psychology. University of Arizona.

FINCHER, J. (1979, January). Natural opiates in the brain. *Human Behavior,* pp. 28–32.

FIORENTINE, R. (1999). After drug treatment: Are 12-step programs effective in maintaining abstinence? *American Journal of Alcohol and Drug Abuse, 25,* 93–114.

FISHER, H. (1992). *Anatomy of love: The natural history of monogamy, adultery and divorce.* New York: Norton.

FISHER, W. A., & BYRNE, D. (1978). Sex differences in response to erotica? Love versus lust. *Journal of Personality and Social Psychology, 36,* 117–125.

FISKE, A. P. (1991). *Structure of social life: The four elementary forms of human relationships.* New York: Free Press.

FLESHNER, M., LAUDENSLAGER, M. L., SIMONS, L., & MAIER, S. F. (1989). Reduced serum antibodies with social defeat in rats. *Physiological Behavior, 45,* 1183–1187.

FLETT, G. L., HEWITT, P. L., BLANKSTEIN, K. R., & GRAY, L. (1998). Psychological distress and frequency of perfectionistic thinking. *Journal of Personality and Social Psychology, 75,* 1363–1381.

FLINK, C., BOGIANO, A. K., & BARRETT, M. (1990). Controlling teaching strategies: Undermining children's self-determination and performance. *Journal of Personality and Social Psychology, 59,* 916–924.

FLORIAN, V., MIKULINCER, M., & TAUBMAN, O. (1995). Does hardiness contribute to mental health during a stressful real-life situation? The roles of appraisal and coping. *Journal of Personality and Social Psychology, 68,* 687–695.

FOLGER, R. (1991). Justice as worth. In J. Meindl (Chair), Justice in the workplace: Interpersonal processes (II). Symposium conducted at the Third International Conference on Social Justice, Utrecht, the Netherlands, July.

FOLKMAN, S. (1984). Personal control and stress and coping processes: A theoretical analysis. *Journal of Personality and Social Psychology, 46,* 839–852.

FOLKMAN, S., & LAZARUS, R. S. (1985). If it changes it must be a process: Study of emotion and coping during three stages of a college examination. *Journal of Personality and Social Psychology, 48,* 150–170.

FOLKMAN, S., LAZARUS, R. S., DUNKEL-SCHETTER, C., DELONGIS, A., & GRUEN, R. J. (1986). Dynamics of a stressful encounter: Cognitive appraisal, coping and encounter outcomes. *Journal of Personality and Social Psychology, 50,* 992–1003.

FOLKMAN, S., SCHAEFER, C., & LAZARUS, R. S. (1979). Cognitive processes as mediators of stress and coping. In V. Hamilton & D. M. Warburton (Eds.), *Human stress and cognition: An information processing approach* (pp. 265–298). New York: Wiley.

FOSTER, C.A., WITCHER, B. S., CAMPBELL, W. K., & GREEN, J. D. (1998). Arousal and attraction: Evidence for automatic controlled processes. *Journal of Personality and Social Psychology, 74,* 86–101.

FOULKES, D. (1966). *The psychology of sleep.* New York: Scribners.

FOULKES, D., SPEAR, P. S., & SYMONDS, J. D. (1966). Individual differences in mental activity at sleep onset. *Journal of Abnormal Psychology, 71,* 280–286.

FRANKEN, R. E. (1987). *Sensation seeking and beliefs and attitudes.* Unpublished manuscript, University of Calgary, Canada.

FRANKEN, R. E. (1988). Sensation seeking, decision making styles, and preference for individual responsibility. *Personality and Individual Differences, 9,* 139–146.

FRANKEN, R. E. (1990). *Thinking styles of sensation seekers.* Unpublished manuscript, University of Calgary, Canada.

FRANKEN, R. E. (1993). Sensation seeking and keeping your options open. *Personality and Individual Differences, 14,* 247–249.

FRANKEN, R. E., & BROWN, D. J. (1995). Why do people like competition? The motivation for winning, putting forth effort, improving one's performance, performing well, being instrumental, and expressing forceful/aggressive behavior. *Personality and Individual Differences, 19,* 175–184.

FRANKEN, R. E., & BROWN, D. J. (1996). The need to win is not adaptive: The need to win, coping strategies, hope and self-esteem. *Personality and Individual Differences, 20,* 805–808.

FRANKEN, R. E., GIBSON, K., & MOHAN, P. (1990). Sensation seeking and disclosure to close and casual friends. *Personality and Individual Differences, 11,* 829–832.

FRANKEN, R. E., GIBSON, K. J., & ROWLAND, G. L. (1992). Sensation seeking and the tendency to view the world as threatening. *Personality and Individual Differences, 13,* 31–38.

FRANKEN, R. E., & PRPICH, W. (1996). Dislike of competition and the need to win: Self-image concerns, performance concerns and the distraction of attention. *Journal of Behavior and Personality, 11,* 695–712.

FRANKEN, R. E., & STRAIN, A. (1974). Effect of increased arousal on response to stimulus change in a complex maze. *Perceptual and Motor Skills, 39,* 1076–1078.

FRANKENHAEUSER, M. (1980). Psychoneuroendocrine approaches to the study of stressful person-environment transactions. In H. Selye (Ed.), *Selye's guide to stress research* (Vol. 1). New York: Van Nostrand Reinhold.

FRANKENHAEUSER, M., DUNNE, E., & LUNDBERG, U. (1976). Sex differences in sympathetic-adrenal medullary reactions induced by different stressors. *Psychopharmacology, 476,* 1–5.

FRANKENHAEUSER, M., & JOHANSSON, G. (1976). Task demand as reflected in catecholamine excretion and heart rate. *Journal of Human Stress, 2,* 15–23.

FRANKENHAEUSER, M., LUNDBERG, U., & FORSMAN, L. (1980). Dissociation between sympathetic-adrenal and pituitary-adrenal responses to an achievement situation characterized by high controllability: Comparison between Type A and Type B males and females. *Biological Psychology, 10,* 79–91.

FRENCH, E. G. (1956). Motivation as a variable in work-partner selection. *Journal of Abnormal and Social Psychology, 53,* 96–99.

FREUD, S. (1934). *A general introduction to psychoanalysis.* New York: Washington Square Press. (Original work published 1915)

FREUD, S. (1947). The ego and the id. In *The standard edition of the complete psychological works of Sigmund Freud* (Vol. 19). London: Hogarth Press. (Original work published 1923)

FREUD, S. (1949). Formulations regarding the two principles of mental functioning. In *Collected papers of Sigmund Freud* (Vol. 4). London: Hogarth Press. (Original work published 1911)

FREUD, S. (1949). Instincts and their vicissitudes. In *Collected papers of Sigmund Freud* (Vol. 4). London: Hogarth Press. (Original work published 1915)

FREUD, S. (1953). *The interpretation of dreams.* London: Hogarth Press. (Original work published 1900)

FRIEDLAND, N., KEINAN, G., & REGEV, Y. (1992). Controlling the uncontrollable: Effects of stress on illusory perceptions of controllability. *Journal of Personality and Social Psychology, 63,* 923–931.

FRIEDMAN, H. S. (1991). *Self-healing personality: Why some people achieve health and others succumb to illness.* New York: Henry Holt.

FRIEDMAN, H. S. (1992). Understanding hostility, coping, and health. In H. S. Friedman (Ed.), *Hostility, coping and health* (pp. 3–9). Washington, DC: American Psychological Association.

FRIEDMAN, M., & ROSENMAN, R. H. (1974). *Type A behavior and your heart.* New York: Knopf.

FRIEDMANN, J., GLOBUS, G., HUNTLEY, A., MULLANEY, D., NAITOH, P., & JOHNSON, L. (1977). Performance and mood during and after gradual sleep reduction. *Psychophysiology, 14,* 245–250.

FRIJDA, N. H. (1988). The laws of emotion. *American Psychologist, 43,* 349–358.

FRODI, A., BRIDGES, L., & GROLNICK, W. S. (1985). Correlates of mastery-related behavior: A short-term longitudinal study of infants in this second year. *Child Development, 56,* 1291–1298.

FROHMAN, L. A., GOLDMAN, J. K., & BERNARDIS, L. L. (1972). Metabolism of intravenously injected 14C-glucose in weanling rats with hypothalamic obesity. *Metabolism: Clinical and Experimental, 21,* 799–805.

FROST, R. O., GOOLKASIAN, G. A., ELY, R. J., & BLANCHARDS, F. A. (1982). Depression, restraint, and eating behavior. *Behavioral Research and Therapy, 20,* 113–121.

FUNKENSTEIN, D. H., KING, S. H., & DROLETTE, M. E. (1974). The direction of anger during a laboratory stress-inducing situation. *Psychosomatic Medicine, 16,* 404–413.

FUSTER, J. M. (1958). Effects of stimulation of brain stem on tachistoscopic perception. *Science, 127,* 150.

GACKENBACH, J., & BOSVELD, J. (1989a). *Control your dreams.* New York: Harper & Row.

GACKENBACH, J., & BOSVELD, J. (1989b, October). Take control of your dreams. *Psychology Today,* pp. 27–32.

GAGNON, J. H. (1974). Scripts and the coordination of sexual conduct. In J. K. Cole & R. Diensteiber (Eds.), *Nebraska Symposium on Motivation* (Vol. 21, pp. 27–59). Lincoln: University of Nebraska Press.

GAGNON, J. H. (1977). *Human Sexualities.* Glenview, IL: Scott, Foresman.

GAGNON, P., DE KONINCK, J., & BROUGHTON, R. (1985). Reappearance of electroencephalogram slow waves in extended sleep with delayed bedtime. *Sleep, 8,* 118–128.

GANGESTAD, S. W., THORNHILL, R., & YEO, R. A. (1994). Facial attractiveness, developmental stability, and fluctuating asymmetry. *Ethology and Sociobiology, 15,* 73–85.

GARCIA, J., & KOELLING, R. A. (1966). Relation of cue to consequence in avoidance learning. *Psychonomic Science, 4,* 123–124.

GARCIA, J., McGOWAN, B. K., ERVIN, F. R., & KOELLING, R. A. (1968). Cues: Their relative effectiveness as a function of the reinforcer. *Science, 160,* 794–795.

GARDNER, H. (1983). *Frames of mind: A theory of multiple intelligences.* New York: Basic Books.

GARLAND, A. F., & ZIGLER, E. (1993). Adolescent suicide prevention: Current research and social policy implications. *American Psychologist, 48,* 169–182.

GARN, S. M., & CLARK, D. C. (1976). Trends in fatness and the origins of obesity. *Pediatric, 57,* 443–455.

GARNER, D. M., & WOOLEY, S. C. (1991). Confronting failure of behavioral and dietary treatments for obesity. *Clinical Psychology Review, 11,* 729–780.

GARRITY, T. F., STALLONES, L., MARX, M. B., & JOHN-SON, T. P. (1989). Pet ownership and attachment as supportive factors in the health of the elderly. *Anthrozoos, 3,* 35–44.

GARROW, J. (1978). The regulation of energy expenditure. In G. A. Bray (Ed.), *Recent advances in obesity research* (Vol. 2). London: Newman.

GEARY, D. C. (2000). Evolution and proximate expression of human parental investment. *Psychological Bulletin, 126,* 55–77.

GEBHARD, P. H. (1973). Sex differences in sexual responses. *Archives of Sexual Behavior, 2,* 201–203.

GEEN, R. G. (1968). Effects of frustration, attack, and prior training in aggressiveness upon aggressive behavior. *Journal of Personality and Social Psychology, 9,* 316–321.

GEEN, R. G. (1976). Observing violence in the mass media: Implications of basic research. In R. G. Geen & E. C. O'Neal (Eds.), *Perspectives on aggression.* New York: Academic Press.

GEEN, R. G. (1990). *Human Aggression.* Pacific Grove, CA: Brooks/Cole.

GEER, J. H., & BROUSSARD, D. B. (1990). Scaling sexual behavior and arousal: Consistency and sex differences. *Journal of Personality and Social Psychology, 58,* 664–671.

GELADE, G. A. (1997). Creativity in conflict: The personality of the commercial creative. *Journal of Genetic Psychology, 158,* 67–78.

GERNER, R. H., POST, R. M., GILLIN, J. C., & BUNNEY, W. E. (1979). Biological and behavioral effects of one night's sleep deprivation in depressed patients and normals. *Journal of Psychiatric Research, 15,* 21.

GERRARD, M. (1987). Sex, sex guilt, and contraceptive use revisited: The 1980s. *Journal of Personality and Social Psychology, 52,* 975–980.

GESCHWIND, N., & GALABURDA, A. M. (1987). *Cerebral lateralization: Biological mechanisms, associations, and pathology.* Cambridge, MA: MIT Press.

GETZELS, J. W., & JACKSON, P. W. (1962). *Creativity and intelligence: Exploration with gifted students.* New York: Wiley.

GIBBONS, F. X., & McCOY, S. B. (1991). Self-esteem, similarity, and reactions to active versus passive downward comparison. *Journal of Personality and Social Psychology, 60,* 414–424.

GIBSON, K. J., FRANKEN, R. E., & ROWLAND, G. L. (1989). Sensation seeking and marital adjustment. *Journal of Sex and Marital Therapy, 15,* 57–61.

GILBERT, D. G. (1979). Paradoxical tranquillizing and emotion-reducing effects of nicotine. *Psychological Bulletin, 86,* 643–661.

GILBERT, R. M. (1981). Drug abuse as an excessive behavior. In H. Shaeffer & M. E. Burglass (Eds.), *Classic contributions in the addictions.* New York: Brunner/Mazel.

GILLIN, J. C., & WYATT, R. J. (1975). Schizophrenia: Perchance a dream. *International Review of Neurobiology, 17,* 297–342.

GILOVICH, T., & MEDVEC, V. H. (1995). The experience of regret: What, when, and why. *Psychological Review, 102,* 379–395.

GLADUE, B. A. (1991). Aggressive behavioral characteristics, hormones, and sexual orientation in men and women. *Aggressive Behavior, 17,* 313–326.

GLASS, D. C. (1977a). *Behavior patterns, stress, and coronary disease.* Hillsdale, NJ: Erlbaum.

GLAUBMAN, H., ORBACH, J., AVIRAM, O., FRIEDER, J., FRIEMAN, M., PELLED, O., & GLAUBMAN, R. (1978). REM deprivation and divergent thinking. *Psychophysiology, 15,* 75–79.

GLAUBMAN, H., ORBACH, L., GROSS, Y., AVIRAM, O., FRIEDER, L., FRIEMAN, M., & PELLED, O. (1979). The effect of presleep focal attention load on subsequent sleep patterns. *Psychophysiology, 16,* 467–470.

GOLDMAN, M. S. (1999). Risk for substance abuse: Memory as a common etiological pathway. *Psychological Science, 10,* 196–198.

GOLDMAN, R., JAFFA, M., & SCHACHTER, S. (1968). Yom Kippur, Air France, dormitory food, and eating behavior of obese and normal persons. *Journal of Personality and Social Psychology, 10,* 117–123.

GOLEMAN, D. (1976, February). Meditation helps break the stress spiral. *Psychology Today,* pp. 82–86, 93.

GOLEMAN, D. (1995). *Emotional intelligence.* New York Bantam.

GOLLWITZER, P. M. (1999). Implementation intentions: Strong effects of simple plans. *American Psychologist, 54,* 493–503.

GONDOLF, E. W. (1985). *Men who batter.* Holmes Beach, FL: Learning Publications.

GOODENOUGH, D. R. (1978). Field dependence. In H. London & J. E. Exner, Jr. (Eds.), *Dimensions of personality* (pp. 165–216). New York: Wiley.

GORDON, H. W., & LEE, P. (1986). A relationship between gonadotropins and visuospatial function. *Neuropsychologia, 24,* 563–576.

GORSKI, R. A. (1974). The neuroendocrine regulation of sexual behavior. In G. Newton and A. H. Riesen (Eds.), *Advances in Psychobiology* (Vol. 2, pp. 1–58). New York: Wiley.

GORSKI, R. A. (1985). Sexual dimorphisms of the brain. *Journal of Animal Science, 61,* 38–61.

GORSKI, R. A. (1988). Hormone-induced sex differences in hypothalamic structure. *Bull TMIN, 16,* Suppl. 3, 67–90.

GORSKI, R. A. (1991). Sexual differentiation of the endocrine brain and its control. In M. Motta (Ed.), *Brain endocrinology* (2nd ed., pp. 71–104).

GOTTFREDSON, M., & HIRSCHI, T. (1990). *A general theory of crime.* Stanford, CA: Stanford University Press.

GOTTLIEB, S. (2000). Short, sharp bout of exercise good for the heart. *British Medical Journal, 321,* 589–590.

GOUGH, H. G. (1976). Studying creativity by means of word association tests. *Journal of Applied Psychology, 61,* 348–353.

GOY, R. W., & McEWEN, B. S. (1980). *Sexual differentiation of the brain.* Cambridge, MA: MIT Press.

GRANFIELD, R., & CLOUD, W. (1996). The elephant that no one sees: Natural recovery among middle-class addicts. *Journal of Drug Issues, 26,* 45–61.

GRAY, J. A. (1982). *The neuropsychology of anxiety: An enquiry in the functions of the septo-hippocampal system.* Oxford: Oxford University Press.

GRAY, J. A. (1991). The neuropsychology of temperament. In J. Stelau & A. Angleitner (Eds.), *Explorations in temperament* (pp. 105–128). New York: Plenum.

GRAY, J. A., & McNAUGHTON, N. (1996). The activation and regulation of fear and anxiety. In R. A. Dienstrier (Ed.), *Perspectives on anxiety, panic, and fear. Nebraska Symposium on Motivation* (Vol. 43, pp. 61–134). Lincoln: University of Nebraska Press.

GREENBERG, R., & PEARLMAN, C. A. (1974). Cutting the REM nerve: An approach to the adaptive role of REM sleep. *Perspectives in Biology and Medicine, 17,* 513–521.

GREENBERG, R., PILLARD, R., & PEARLMAN, C. (1972). The effect of dream (stage REM) deprivation on adaptation to stress. *Psychosomatic Medicine, 34,* 257–262.

GREENBERGER, E., & McLAUGHLIN, C. S. (1998). Attachment, coping and explanatory style in late adolescence. *Journal of Youth and Adolescence, 27,* 121–140.

GREISER, C., GREENBERG, R., & HARRISON, R. H. (1972). The adaptive function of sleep: The differential effects of sleep and dreaming on recall. *Journal of Abnormal Psychology, 80,* 280–286.

GREIST, J. H., KLEIN, M. H., EISCHENS, R. R., FARIS, J., GURMAN, A. S., & MORGAN, W. P. (1979). Running as treatment for depression. *Comprehensive Psychiatry, 20,* 41–54.

GRIFFIN, D., & BARTHOLOMEW, K. (1994). Models of the self and other: Fundamental dimensions underlying measures of adult attachment. *Journal of Personality and Social Psychology, 67,* 430–445.

GRIFFIN, S. J., & TINDER, J. (1978). Physical fitness, exercise, and human sleep. *Psychophysiology, 15,* 447–450.

GRIFFITH, W., MAY, J., & VEITCH, R. (1974). Sexual stimulation and interpersonal behavior. Heterosexual evaluative responses, visual behavior, and physical proximity. *Journal of Personality and Social Psychology, 30,* 367–377.

GRINSPOON, L., & BAKALAR, J. B. (1993). *Marihuana: The forbidden medicine.* New Haven, CT: Yale University Press.

GRINSPOON, L., & HEDBLOM, P. (1975). *The speed culture: Amphetamine use and abuse in America.* Cambridge, MA: Harvard University Press.

GROLNICK, W. S., & RYAN, R. M. (1987). Autonomy in children's learning: An experimental and individual difference investigation. *Journal of Personality and Social Psychology, 52,* 890–898.

GROSSMAN, S. P. (1967). *A textbook of physiological psychology.* New York: Wiley.

GROSVENOR, A., & LACK, L. C. (1984). The effect of sleep before or after learning on memory. *Sleep, 7,* 155–167.

GROTH, A. N. (1979). *Men who rape: The psychology of the offender.* New York: Plenum.

GRUNBERG, N. E., & STRAUB, R. O. (1992). The role of gender and taste class in the effects of stress on eating. *Health Psychology, 11,* 97–100.

GUILFORD, J. P. (1967). *The nature of human intelligence.* New York: McGraw-Hill.

GUR, R. (1992). *Brain sex. Television documentary.* Canadian Broadcasting Company, 1992.

HALL, J. B., & BROWN, D. A. (1979). Plasma glucose and lactic acid alterations in response to a stressful exam. *Biological Psychology, 8,* 179–188.

HALL, W., & SOLOWIJ, N. (1998). Adverse effects of cannabis (includes list of resources on the health of marijuana (Seminar). *Lancet, Nov 14,* 1611–1161.

HALPERN, D. F., & CASS, M. (1994). Laterality, sexual orientation, and immune system functioning: Is there a relationship? *International Journal of Neuroscience, 77,* 167–180.

HAMER, D. H., & COPELAND, P. (1994). *The science of desire.* New York: Simon & Schuster.

HAMER, D. H., HU, S., MAGNUSON, V. L., HU, N., & PATTATUCCI, A. M. L. (1993). A linkage between DNA markers on the X chromosome and sexual orientation. *Science, 261,* 321–327.

HAMMOND, W. R., & YUNG, B. (1993). Psychology's role in the public health response to assaultive violence among young African American men. *American Psychologist, 48,* 142–154.

HANSEN, J. R., STØA, K. F., BLIX, A. S., & URSIN, H. (1978). Urinary levels of epinephrine and norepinephrine in parachutist trainees. In H. Ursin, E. Baade, and S. Levine (Eds.), *Psychobiology of stress: A study of coping men.* New York: Academic Press.

HARLOW, H. F. (1953). Mice, monkeys, men, and motives. *Psychological Review, 60,* 23–32.

HARRINGTON, D. M. (1981). Creativity, analogical thinking and muscular metaphors. *Journal of Mental Imagery, 6,* 121–126.

HARRIS, C. B. (1988). *Hope: Construct definition and the development of an individual differences scale.* Unpublished doctoral dissertation, University of Kansas, Lawrence.

HARRIS, M. B., & KNIGHT-BOHNHOFF, K. (1996). Gender and aggression I: Perceptions of aggression. *Sex Roles, 35,* 1–25.

HART, A (1988). *15 principles for achieving happiness.* Dallas, TX: Word.

HARTER, S. (1990). Causes, correlates, and the functional role of global self worth: A life-span perspective. In R. J. Sternberg & J. Kolligian, Jr. (Eds.), *Competence considered* (pp. 67–97). New Haven, CT: Yale University Press.

HARTER, S. (1993). Visions of the self: Beyond the me in the mirror. In J. E. Jacobs (Ed.), *Nebraska symposium on motivation: Vol. 40. Developmental perspectives on motivation.*

Current theory and research in motivation (pp. 99–144). Lincoln: University of Nebraska Press.

HARTMANN, E. (1998). *Dreams and Nightmares: The new theory on the origin and meaning of dreams.* New York: Plenum.

HARTMANN, E. L. (1973). *The functions of sleep.* New Haven, CT: Yale University Press.

HARTMANN, E. L. (1974). The functions of sleep. *Annual of Psychoanalysis, 2,* 271–289.

HARTMANN, E. L., & STERN, W. C. (1972). Desynchronized sleep deprivation: Learning deficit and its reversal by increased catecholamines. *Physiology and Behavior, 8,* 585–587.

HARTSE, K. M., ROTH, T., & ZORICK, F. J. (1982). Daytime sleepiness and daytime wakefulness: The effect of instruction. *Sleep, 5,* S107–S118.

Harvard Heart Letter (2001, January). Vol. 11.

HASELTINE, F. P., & OHNO, S. (1981). Mechanisms of gonadal differentiation. *Science, 211,* 1272–1278.

HASHIM, S. A., & VAN ITALLIE, T. B. (1965). Studies in normal and obese subjects with a monitored food dispensary device. *Annals of the New York Academy of Science, 131,* 654–661.

HASLAM, N. (1997). Evidence that male sexual orientation is a matter of degree. *Journal of Personality and Social Psychology, 73,* 862–870.

HASSENFELD, I. N. (1993). Psychophysiology and psychoneuroimmunology. In F. S. Duerkesm (Ed.), *Behavioral science for medical students* (pp. 399–407). Baltimore: Williams & Wilkins.

HAUG, M., BRAIN, P. F., & KAMIS, A. B. (1985). A brief review comparing the effects of sex steroids on two forms of aggression in laboratory mice. *Neurological Science and Behavioral Reviews, 10,* 463–467.

HAUGEN, P. (2000). Lose some, win some. *Psychology Today, 33,* 12.

HAWKE, C. C. (1950). Castration and sex crimes. *American Journal of Mental Deficiency, 55,* 220–226.

HAYES, S. C., & GIFFORD, E. V. (1997). The trouble with language: Experiential avoidance, rules, and the nature of verbal events. *Psychological Science, 8,* 170–174.

HAZAN, C., & SHAVER, P. (1987). Romantic love conceptualized as an attachment process. *Journal of Personality and Social Psychology, 52,* 511–524.

HEADEY, B., & WEARING, A. (1992). *Understanding happiness: A theory of subjective well-being.* Melbourne, Victoria, Australia: Longman Cheshire.

HEATHER, N., WINTON, M., & ROLLNICK, S. (1982). An empirical test of "a cultural delusion of alcoholics." *Psychological Reports, 50,* 379–382.

HEATHERTON, T. F., & POLIVY, J. (1991a). Chronic dieting and eating disorders: A spiral model. In J. H. Crowther, S. E. Hobfall, M. A. P. Stephens, & D. L. Termenbaum (Eds.), *The etiology of bulimia: The individual and familial context* (pp. 86–108). Washington, DC: Hemisphere.

HEATHERTON, T. F., & POLIVY, J. (1991b). Development and validation of a scale measuring state self-esteem. *Journal of Personality and Social Psychology, 60,* 895–910.

HEBB, D. O. (1955). Drive and the C.N.S. (conceptual nervous system). *Psychological Review, 62,* 243–254.

HEIDER, F. (1958). *The psychology of interpersonal relations.* New York: Wiley.

HEIMAN, J. R. (1975, April). Women's sexual arousal. *Psychology Today,* pp. 91–94.

HEIMAN, J. R. (1977). A psychophysiological exploration of sexual arousal patterns in females and males. *Psychophysiology, 14,* 266–274.

HELMREICH, R. L., BEANE, W. E., LUCKER, G. W., & SPENCE, J. T. (1978). Achievement motivation and scientific attainment. *Personality and Social Psychology Bulletin, 4,* 222–226.

HELMREICH, R. L., SPENCE, J. T., BEANE, W. E., LUCKER, G. W., & MATTHEWS, K. A. (1980). Making it in academic psychology: Demographic and personality correlates of attainment. *Journal of Personality and Social Psychology, 39,* 896–908.

HELMSTETTER, S. (1986). *What to say when you talk to yourself.* New York: Simon & Schuster.

HENNESSEY, B. A., & AMABILE, T. M. (1998). Reward, Intrinsic motivation, and creativity. *American Psychologist, 53,* 674–675.

HENNIGAN, K. M., DEL ROSARIO, M. L., HEATH, L., COOK, T. D., WHARTON, J. D., & CALDER, B. J. (1982). The impact of the introduction of television on crime in the United States. *Journal of Personality and Social Psychology, 42,* 461–477.

HERMAN, C. P. (1974). External and internal cues as determinants of smoking behavior of light and heavy smokers. *Journal of Personality and Social Psychology, 30,* 664–672.

HERMAN, C. P., & MACK, D. (1975). Restrained and unrestrained eating. *Journal of Personality, 43,* 646–660.

HERMAN, C. P., & POLIVY, J. (1984). A boundary model for the regulation of eating. In A. J. Stunkard & E. Stellar (Eds.), *Eating and its disorders* (pp. 141–156). New York: Raven Press.

HERON, W. (1957). The pathology of boredom. *Scientific American, 196,* 52–56.

HIGGINS, E. T. (1987). Self-discrepancy: A theory relating self and affect. *Psychological Review, 94,* 319–340.

HIGGINS, E. T. (1996). Self-knowledge serving self-regulatory functions. *Journal of Personality and Social Psychology, 71,* 1062–1083.

HIGGINS, E. T. (1997). Beyond pleasure and pain. *American Psychologist, 52,* 1280–1300.

HILL, H., SORIANO, F. I., CHEN, A., & LaFRAMBOISE, T. D. (1994). Sociocultural factors in the etiology and prevention of violence among ethnic minority youth. In L. D. Eron, J. H. Gentry, & P. Schegel (Eds.). *Reason to hope: A psychosocial perspective on violence & youth* (pp. 59–97). Washington, DC: American Psychological Association.

HILL, K., & HURTADO, A. M. (1996). *Ache life history: The ecology and demography of a foraging people.* New York: Aldine De Gruyter.

HINES, M. (1990). Gonadal hormones and human cognitive development. In J. Balthazart (Ed.), *Hormones, brains, and human behaviors in vertebrates: Vol. 1. Sexual differentiation, neuroatotomical aspects, neurotransmitters, and neuropeptides* (pp. 51–63). Basel, Switzerland: Karger.

HINES, M., ALLEN, L. S., & GORSKI, R. A. (1992). Sex differences in subregions of the medial nucleus of the amygdala, and the bed nucleus of the stia terminalis of the rat. *Brain Research, 579,* 321–326.

HINES, M., ALSUM, P., ROY, M. et al. (1987). Estrogenic contribution to sexual differentiation in the female guinea pig: Influences of diethylstibestrol and tamoxifen on neural behavior and ovarian development. *Hormones and Behavior, 21,* 402–417.

HINES, M., CHIU, L., McADAMS, L. A., BENTLER, P. M., & LIPCAMON, J. (1992). Cognition and the corpus callosum: Verbal fluency, visuospatial ability, and language lateralization related to midsagittal surface areas of the callosal subregions. *Behavioral Neurosciences, 106,* 3–14.

HINES, M. & GREEN, R. (1991). Human hormonal and neural correlates of sex-typed behaviors. *Review of Psychiatry, 10,* 536–555.

HIROTO, D. S. (1974). Locus of control and learned helplessness. *Journal of Experimental Psychology, 102,* 187–193.

HIROTO, D. S., & SELIGMAN, M. E. P. (1975). Generality of learned helplessness in man. *Journal of Personality and Social Psychology, 31,* 311–327.

HIRSCH, J., KNITTLE, J. L., & SALANS, L. B. (1966). Cell lipid content and cell number in obese and nonobese human adipose tissue. *Journal of Clinical Investigation, 45,* 1023.

HITE, S. (1976). *The Hite report: A nationwide survey of female sexuality.* New York: Macmillan.

HOBSON, A. J. (1994). *The chemistry of conscious states.* Boston: Little Brown.

HOBSON, J. A. (1988). *The dreaming brain.* New York: Basic Books.

HOCKEY, G. R. J. (1997). Compensatory control in the regulation of human performance under stress and high workload. *Biological Psychology, 45,* 73–93.

HOCKEY, G. R. J., DAVIES, S., & GRAY, M. M. (1972). Forgetting as a function of sleep at different times of day. *Quarterly Journal of Experimental Psychology, 24,* 386–393.

HOCKEY, G. R. J., WASTELL, D. G., & SAUER, J. (1998). Effects of sleep deprivation and user interface on complex performance: Multilevel analysis of compensatory control. *Human Factors, 40,* 233–254.

HOFFMAN, M. L. (1970a). Conscience, personality, and socialization techniques. *Human Development, 13,* 90–126.

HOFFMAN, M. L. (1970b). Moral development. In P. H. Mussen (Ed.), *Handbook of child psychology* (Vol. 2, 3rd ed.). New York: Wiley.

HOFFMAN, M. L. (1982). *Development of prosocial behavior.* New York: Academic Press.

HOFFMAN-GOETZ, L., & HUSTED, J. (1995). Exercise and cancer: Do the biology and epidemiology correspond? *Exercise Immunology Review, 1,* 81–96.

HOKANSON, J. E., & BUTLER, A. C. (1992). Cluster analysis of depressed college students' social behaviors. *Journal of Personality and Social Psychology, 62,* 273–280.

HOLLON, S. D., DeRUBEIS, R. J., & EVANS, M. D. (1990). Combined cognitive therapy and pharmacology in the treatment of depression. In D. Manning and A. Francis (Eds.), *Combination drug and psychotherapy in depression.* Washington, DC: American Psychiatric Press.

HOLMAN, E. A., & SILVER, R. C. (1998). Getting "stuck" in the past: Temporal orientation and coping with trauma. *Journal of Personality and Social Psychology, 74,* 1146–1163.

HOLMES, D. S. (1984). Meditation and somatic arousal reduction. *American Psychologist, 39,* 1–10.

HOOKER, E. (1957). The adjustment of the male overt homosexual. *Journal of Projective Techniques, 21,* 18–31.

HOPSON, J. L. (1987, August). Boys will be boys, girls will be.... *Psychology Today,* pp. 60–66.

HOROWITZ, M. J. (1976). *Stress response syndromes.* New York: Jacob Aronson.

HOROWITZ, M. J. (1979). Psychological response to serious life events. In V. Hamilton & D. Warburton (Eds.), *Human stress and cognition: An information processing approach* (pp. 237–263). New York: Wiley.

HOTH, C. C., REYNOLDS, C. F., HOUCK, P. R., HALL, F., et al. (1989). Predicting mortality in mixed depression and dementia using EEG sleep variables. *Journal of Neuropsychiatry and Clinical Neurosciences, 14,* 366–371.

HOWLEY, E. T. (1976). The effect of different intensities of exercise on the excretion of epinephrine and norepinephrine. *Medicine and Science in Sports, 8,* 219–972.

HOYENGA, K. B., & HOYENGA, K. T. (1979). *The question of sex differences: Psychological, cultural, and biological issues.* Boston: Little, Brown.

HOYT, M. F., & SINGER, J. L. (1978). Psychological effects of REM ("dream") deprivation upon waking mentation. In A. M. Arkin, J. S. Antrobus, & S. J. Ellman (Eds.), *The mind in sleep: Psychology and psychophysiology.* Hillsdale, NJ: Erlbaum.

HU, S., PATTATUCCI, M. L., PATTERSON, C., LI, L., FULKER, D. W., CHERNY, S. S., KRUGLYAK, L., & HAMER, D. H. (1995). *Nature Genetics, 11,* 248–256.

HUBA, G. J., NEWCOMB, M. D., & BENTLER, P. M. (1981). Comparison of canonical correlation and interbattery factor analysis on sensation seeking and drug use domains. *Applied Psychological Measurement, 5,* 291–306.

HUGHES, J., SMITH, T., MORGAN, B., & FOTHERGILL, L. (1975). Purification and properties of enkephalin—The possible endogenous ligand for the morphine receptor. *Life Science, 16,* 1753–1758.

HULL, C. L. (1943). *Principles of behavior*. New York: Appleton-Century-Crofts.

HULL, J. G., & BOND, C. F. (1986). Social and behavioral consequences of alcohol consumption and expectancy: A meta-analysis. *Psychological Bulletin, 99*, 347–360.

HULL, J. G., VAN TREUREN, R. R., & VIRNELLI, S. (1987). Hardiness and health: A critique and alternative approach. *Journal of Personality and Social Psychology, 53*, 518–530.

HUNT, J. McV. (1963). Motivation inherent in information processing. In O. J. Harvey (Ed.), *Motivation and social interaction: Cognitive determinants*. New York: Ronald Press.

HUTT, C. (1996). Exploration and play in children. In P. A. Jewell & C. Loizos (Eds.), *Play, exploration, and territory in mammals* (pp. 61–81). Symposia of the Zoological Society of London (No. 18). New York: Academic Press.

HYDE, J. S. (1986). Gender differences in aggression. In J. S Hyde & M. C. Linn (Eds.), *The psychology of gender: Advances through meta-analysis* (pp. 51–66). Baltimore: Johns Hopkins University Press.

HYDE, J., FENNEMA, E., & LAMON, S. J. (1990). Gender differences in mathematics performance: A meta-analysis. *Psychological Bulletin, 107*, 139–155.

HYDE, J. S., & LINN, M. (1988). Gender differences in ability: A meta-analysis. *Psychological Bulletin, 104*, 53–69.

IMPERATO-McGINLEY, J., GUERRERO, L., GAUTIER, T., & PETERSON, R. E. (1974, December). Steroid 5 alpha-reductase deficiency in man: An inherited form of male pseudohermaphroditises. *Science, 186*, 1213–1215.

IMPERATO-McGINLEY, J., PETERSON, R. E., GAUTIER, T., & STURLA, E. (1979). Androgen and the evolution of male-gender pseudohermaphroditises with 5 alpha-reductase deficiency. *New England Journal of Medicine, 300*, 1233–1237.

ISAAC, G. (1978). The food-sharing behavior of protohuman hominids. *Scientific American, 238*, 90–108.

ISEN, A. M., DAUBMAN, K. A., & NOWICKI, G. P. (1987). Positive affect facilitates creative problem solving. *Journal of Personality and Social Psychology, 52*, 1122–1131.

ITO, T. A., MILLER, N., POLLOCK, V. E. (1996). Alcohol and aggression: A meta-analysis on the moderating effects of inhibitory cues, triggering events, and self-focused attention. *Psychological Bulletin, 120*, 60–82.

IZARD, C. E. (1977). *Human emotions*. New York: Plenum.

IZARD, C. E. (1990). Facial expressions and the regulation of emotions. *Journal of Personality and Social Psychology, 58*, 487–498.

IZARD, C. E., LIBERO, D. Z., PUTNAM, P., & HAYNES, O. M. (1993). Stability of emotion experiences and their relations to traits of personality. *Journal of Personality and Social Psychology, 64*, 847–860.

IZARD, C. E., & TOMKINS, S. S. (1966). Affect and behavior: Anxiety as negative affect. In C. D. Spielberger (Ed.), *Anxiety and behavior*. New York: Academic Press.

JACOBS, B. L. (1987). How hallucinogenic drugs work. *American Scientist, 75*, 386–392.

JACOBS, B. L., & TRULSON, M. E. (1979). Mechanisms of action of LSD. *American Scientist, 67*, 396–404.

JACOBSON, R. C., & ZINBERG, N. E. (1975). *The social basis of drug prevention* (Publication SS-5). Washington, DC: Drug Abuse Council.

JAMES, W. (1890). *The principles of psychology*. New York: Holt.

JANOWSKY, J. S., OVIATT, S. K., & ORWOLL, E. S. (1994). Testosterone influences spatial cognition in older men. *Behavioral Neurosciences, 108*, 325–332.

JEFFERY, R. W., WING, R. R., THORSON, C., BURTON, L. R., RAETHER, C., HARVEY, J., & MULLEN, M. (1993). Strengthening behavioral interventions for weight loss: A randomized trial of food provision and monetary incentive. *Journal of Consulting and Clinical Psychology, 61*, 1038–1045.

JEFFREY, D. B., & KATZ, R. G. (1977). *Take it off and keep it off*. Englewood Cliffs, NJ: Prentice-Hall.

JESSOR, R. (1979). Marijuana: A review of recent psychosocial research. In R. L. Dupont, A. Goldstein, and J. O'Donnell (Eds.), *Handbook on drug abuse*. Rockville, MD: National Institute on Drug Abuse.

JEVNING, R., WILSON, A. F., & DAVIDSON, J. M. (1978). Adrenocortical activity during meditation. *Hormones and Behavior, 10*, 54–60.

JOHNSON, D. W., & JOHNSON, R. T. (1985). Motivation processes in cooperative, competitive, and individualistic learning situations. In C. Ames & R. Ames (Eds.), *Research on Motivation in Education* (Vol. 2). New York: Academic Press.

JOSEPHS, R. A., LARRICK, R. P., STEELE, C. M., & NISBETT, R. E. (1992). Protecting the self from the negative consequences of risky decisions. *Journal of Personality and Social Psychology, 62*, 26–37.

JOUVET, M. (1967, February). The states of sleep. *Scientific American*, pp. 62–72.

JOYCE, C. R. B. (1970). Cannabis. *British Journal of Hospital Medicine, 4*, 162–166.

JURASKA, J. M., & KOPCIK, J. R. (1988). Sex and environmental influences on the size and ultrastructure of the rat corpus callosum. *Brain Research, 450*, 1–8.

KAGAN, J. (1984). *Establishing a morality: The nature of the child*. New York: Basic Books.

KAGAN, J., & SNIDMAN, N. (1991). Temperamental factors in human development. *American Psychologist, 46*, 856–862.

KAHA, C. W. (1983). The creative mind: Form and process. *Journal of Creative Behavior, 17*, 84–94.

KAHNEMAN, D. (1973). *Attention and effort*. Englewood Cliffs, NJ: Prentice-Hall.

KALANT, O. J. (1973). *The amphetamines: Toxicity and addiction* (2nd ed.). Toronto: University of Toronto Press.

KALAT, J. W. (1998). *Biological psychology*. Pacific Grove, CA: Brooks/Cole.

KALES, A., BIXLER, E. O., SOLDATOS, C. R., VELA-BUENO, A., CALDWELL, A. B., & CADIEUX, R. J.

(1982). Role of sleep apnea and nocturnal myoclonus. *Psychosomatics, 23,* 589–595, 600.

KAMEN, L., RODIN, J., SELIGMAN, M. E. P., & DWYER, J. (1991). Explanatory style and cell-mediated immunity in elderly men and women. *Health Psychology, 10,* 229–235.

KAMIN, L. J. (1968). Attention-like processes in classical conditioning. In M. R. Jones (Ed.), *Miami symposium on the prediction of behavior: Aversive stimuli* (pp. 9–34). Coral Gables, FL: University of Miami Press.

KANDEL, D. B. (1984). Marijuana users in young adulthood. *Archives of General Psychiatry, 41,* 200–209.

KANDEL, D. B., KESSLER, R. C., & MARGULIES, R. Z. (1978). Antecedents of adolescent initiation into stages of drug use: A developmental analysis. In D. B. Kandel (Ed.), *Longitudinal research on drug abuse* (pp. 73–99). Washington, DC: Hemisphere.

KANDEL, D. B., & YAMAGUCHI, K. (1985). Developmental patterns of the use of legal, illegal, and prescribed drugs. In C. L. Jones & R. J. Battjes (Eds.), *Etiology of drug abuse* (pp. 193–235). Rockville, MD: National Institute on Drug Abuse.

KARLI, P. (1991). *Animal and human aggression.* New York: Oxford University Press.

KARSCH, F. W., BOYER, J. L. SCHMIDT, P. K., WELLS, R. H., WALLACE, J. P., VERITY, L. S., GUY, H., & SCHNEIDER, D. (1999). *Age and Ageing, 28,* 531–536.

KATZ, J. L. (1990). Testimony to Maryland Governor's Prescription Drug Commission.

KATZ, L., & EPSTEIN, S. (1991). Constructive thinking and coping with laboratory-induced stress. *Journal of Personality and Social Psychology, 61,* 789–800.

KEESEY, R. E., & POWLEY, T. L. (1975). Hypothalamic regulation of body weight. *American Scientist, 63,* 558–565.

KEINAN, G. (1987). Decision making under stress: Scanning of alternative under controllable and uncontrollable treats. *Journal of Personality and Social Psychology, 52,* 639–644.

KELLER, M. (1970). The great Jewish drink mystery. *British Journal of Addiction, 64,* 287–295.

KELLY, A. E., & KAHN, J. (1994). Effect of suppression of personal intrusive thoughts. *Journal of Personality and Social Psychology, 66,* 998–1006.

KEMLER, D., & SHEPP, B. (1971). The learning and transfer of dimensional relevance and irrelevance in children. *Journal of Experimental Psychology, 90,* 120–127.

KENDALL, P. C., LEARNER, R. M., & CRAIGHEAD, W. E. (1984). Human development and intervention in childhood psychotherapy. *Child Development, 55,* 71–82.

KENDLER, K. S., HEATH, A. C., MARTIN, N. G., & EAVES, L. J. (1987). Symptoms of anxiety and symptoms of depression: Same genes, different environments? *Archives of General Psychiatry, 44,* 451–457.

KENDLER, K. S., HEATH, A., MARTIN, N. G., & EAVES, L. J. (1986). Symptoms of anxiety and depression in a volunteer population. *Archives of General Psychiatry, 43,* 213–221.

KENRICK, D. T., KEEFE, R. C., GABRIELIDIS, C., & CORNELIUS, J. S. (1996). Adolescents age preferences for dating partners: Support for an evolutionary model of life-history strategies. *Child Development, 67,* 1499–1511.

KENT, G. (1987). Self-efficacious control over reported physiological, cognitive and behavioral symptoms of anxiety. *Behaviour Research and Therapy, 25,* 341–347.

KERNIS, M. H., BROCKNER, J., & FRANKEL, B. S. (1989). Self-esteem and reactions to failure: The mediating role of overgeneralization. *Journal of Personality and Social Psychology, 57,* 707–714.

KERNIS, M. H., GANNEMANN, B. D., & BARCLAY, L. C. (1989). Stability and level of self-esteem as predictors of anger arousal and hostility. *Journal of Personality and Social Psychology, 56,* 1013–1022.

KESSLER, R. C., KENDLER, K. S., HEATH, A., NEALE, M. C., & EAVES, L. J. (1992). Social support, depressed mood, and adjustment to stress: A genetic epidemiologic investigation. *Journal of Personality and Social Psychology, 62,* 257–272.

KIECOLT-GLASER, J. K., & GLASER, R. (1992). Psychoneuroimmuninology: Can psychological interventions modulate immunity? *Journal of Consulting and Clinical Psychology, 60,* 569–575.

KIERENS, V. G. (1989). *The duel in European history.* Oxford: Oxford University Press.

KIESLER, C. A., & PALLAK, M. S. (1976). Arousal properties of dissonance manipulations. *Psychological Bulletin, 83,* 1014–1025.

KIMURA, D. (1992). Sex differences in the brain. *Scientific American, 267,* 118–125.

KING, G. R., & ELLINWOOD, E. H., JR. (1992). Amphetamines and other stimulants. In J. H. Lowinson, P. Ruiz, R. B. Millman, & J. G. Langrod (Eds.), *Substance abuse: A comprehensive textbook* (pp. 247–270). Baltimore: Williams and Wilkins.

KING, L. A., & BROYLES, S. J. (1997). Wishes, gender, personality, and well-being. *Journal of Personality, 65,* 49–76.

KINSEY, A. C., POMEROY, W. B., & MARTIN, C. E. (1948). *Sexual behavior in the human male.* Philadelphia: Saunders.

KINSEY, A. C., POMEROY, W. B., & MARTIN, C. E. (1953). *Sexual behavior in the human female.* Philadelphia: Saunders.

KIRSCH, I. (1985). Response expectancy as a determinant of experience and behavior. *American Psychologist, 40,* 1189–1202.

KIRSCH, I. (1999). *How expectancies shape experience.* Washington, DC: American Psychological Association.

KIRSCH, I. & LYNN, S. J. (1999). Automaticity in Clinical Psychology. *American Psychologist, 54,* 504–515.

KIRSCH, I., & SAPIRSTEIN, G. (1999). Listening to Prozac but hearing placebo: A meta-analysis of antidepressant medication. In I. Kirsch (Ed.), *How expectancies shape experience* (pp. 303–320). Washington, DC: American Psychological Association.

KLAHR, D., & SIMON, H. A. (1999). Studies of scientific discovery: Complementary approaches and convergent findings. *Psychological Bulletin, 125,* 524–543.

KLAUSNER, S. Z., FOULKES, E. F., & MOORE, M. H. (1980). *The Inupiat: Economics and alcohol on the Alaskan North Slope*. Philadelphia: Center for Research on the Acts of Man, University of Pennsylvania.

KLECK, R. E., & RUBENSTEIN, C. (1975). Physical attractiveness, perceived attitude similarity, and interpersonal attraction in an opposite-sex encounter. *Journal of Personality and Social Psychology, 31,* 107–114.

KLEIN, R., & ARMITAGE, R. (1979). Rhythms in human performance: 11/2 hour oscillation in cognitive style. *Science, 204,* 1326–1328.

KLEINGINNA, P. R., JR., & KLEINGINNA, A. M. (1981a). A categorized list of emotion definitions, with suggestions for a consensual definition. *Motivation and Emotion, 5,* 345–379.

KLEINGINNA, P. R., JR., & KLEINGINNA, A. M. (1981b). A categorized list of motivation definitions, with suggestions for a consensual definition. *Motivation and Emotion, 5,* 263–291.

KLEITMAN, N. (1963). *Sleep and wakefulness*. Chicago: University of Chicago Press.

KLING, K. C., HYDE, S. H., SHOWERS, C. J., & BUSWELL, B. N. (1999). Gender differences in self-esteem: A meta-analysis. *Psychological Bulletin, 125,* 470–500.

KOBASA, S. C. (1979a). Personality and resistance to illness. *American Journal of Community Psychology, 7,* 413–423.

KOBASA, S. C. (1979b). Stressful life events, personality, and health: An inquiry into hardiness. *Journal of Personality and Social Psychology, 37,* 1–11.

KOBASA, S. C. (1982). Commitment and coping in stress among lawyers. *Journal of Personality and Social Psychology, 42,* 707–717.

KOBASA, S. C., MADDI, S. R., & KAHN, S. (1982). Hardiness and health: A prospective study. *Journal of Personality and Social Psychology, 42,* 168–177.

KOBASA, S. C., & PUCCETTI, M. C. (1983). Personality and social resources in stress-resistance. *Journal of Personality and Social Psychology, 45,* 839–850.

KOHN, A. (1986). *No contest: The case against competition*. Boston, MA: Houghton-Mifflin.

KOLB, L. (1962). *Drug addiction: A medical problem*. Springfield, IL: Charles C Thomas.

KORIDZE, M. G., & NEMSADZE, N. D. (1983). Effect of deprivation of paradoxical sleep on the formation and differentiation of conditioned reflexes. *Neuroscience and Behavioral Psychology, 82,* 369–373.

KOULACK, D., PREVOST, F., & DE KONINCK, J. (1985). Sleep, dreaming, and adaptation to a stressful intellectual activity. *Sleep, 8,* 244–253.

KRAINES, S. H. (1957). *Mental depressives and their treatment*. New York: Macmillan.

KRAMER, M. (1982). The psychology of the dream: Art or science? *Psychiatric Journal of the University of Ottawa, 7,* 87–100.

KRAMER, M. (1990). Nightmares (dream disturbances) in posttraumatic stress disorder: Implications for a theory of dreaming. In R. R. Bootzin, J. F. Kihlstrom, & D. L. Schacter (Eds.), *Sleep and cognition* (pp. 190–202). Washington, DC: American Psychological Association.

KRAMER, M., CZAYA, J., ARAND, D., & ROTH, T. (1974). *The development of psychological content across the REMP*. Paper presented at the meeting of the Association for the Psychophysiological Study of Sleep, Jackson Hole, WY.

KUHL, J. (1981). Motivational and functional helplessness: The moderating effect of state versus action-orientation. *Journal of Personality and Social Psychology, 40,* 155–170.

KUHN, D. Z., MADSEN, C. H., & BECKER, W. C. (1967). Effects of exposure to an aggressive model and "frustration" on children's aggressive behavior. *Child Development, 38,* 739–745.

KYL-HEKU, L. M., & BUSS, D. M. (1996). Tactics as units of analysis in personality psychology: An illustration using tactics of hierarchy negotiation. *Personality and Individual Differences, 21,* 497–517.

LA CERRA, M. M. (1994). *Evolved mate preferences in women: Psychological adaptations for assessing a man's willingness to invest in offspring*. Unpublished doctoral dissertation, Department of Psychology, University of California, Santa Barbara.

LaBERGE, S. (1985). *Lucid dreaming*. New York: Ballantine Books.

LACEY, B. C., & LACEY, J. I. (1978). Two-way communication between the heart and the brain: Significance of time within the cardiac cycle. *American Psychologist, 33,* 99–113.

LACEY, J. I., KAGAN, J., LACEY, B. C., & MOSS, H. A. (1963). The visceral level: Situational determinants and behavioral correlates of autonomic response. In P. Knapp (Ed.), *Expression of the emotions in man* (pp. 161–205). New York: International Universities Press.

LACEY, J. I., & LACEY, B. C. (1970). Some autonomic-central nervous system interrelationships. In P. Black (Ed.), *Physiological correlates of emotion*. New York: Academic Press.

LADER, M. H. (1975). *Psychophysiology of mental illness*. London: Routledge & Kegan Paul.

LADER, M. H. (1980a). Psychophysiological studies in anxiety. In G. D. Burrows & D. Davies (Eds.), *Handbook of studies on anxiety*. Amsterdam: Elsevier/North Holland.

LADER, M. H. (1980b). The psychophysiology of anxiety. In H. van Praag, M. H. Lader, O. Rafaelsen, & E. Sachar (Eds.), *Handbook of biological psychiatry*. New York: Marcel Dekker.

LANGELLE, C. (1989). *An assessment of hope in a community sample*. Unpublished master's thesis, University of Kansas, Lawrence.

LANGER, E. J. (1989). *Mindfulness*. Reading, MA: Addison Wesley.

LANGER, E. J., & PARK, K. (1990). Incompetence: A conceptual consideration. In R. J. Sternberg and J. Kolligian, Jr. (Eds.), *Competence considered*. New Haven, CT: Yale University Press.

LANGER & THOMPSON, (1987).

LANGLEY, P. W., SIMON, H. A., BRADSHAW, G. F., & ZYTKOW, J. M. (1986). *Scientific discovery: Computational exploration of the creative process.* Cambridge, MA: MIT Press.

LARSEN, R., & KETELAAR, T. (1991). Personality and susceptibility to positive and negative emotional states. *Journal of Personality and Social Psychology, 61,* 132–140.

LARSON, L. A., & MICHELMAN, H. (1973). *International guide to fitness and health: A world survey of experiments in science and medicine applied to daily living.* New York: Crown.

LASAGNA, L., MOSTELLER, F., VON FELSINGER, J. M., & BEECHER, H. K. (1954). A study of the placebo response. *American Journal of Medicine, 16,* 770–779.

LAW, A., LOGAN, H., & BARON, R. S. (1994). Desire for control, felt control, and stress inoculation training during dental treatment. *Journal of Personality and Social Psychology, 67,* 926–936.

LAW, D. J., PELLEGRINO, J. W., & HUNT, E. B. (1993). Comparing the tortoise and the hare: Gender differences and experience in dynamic spatial reasoning tasks. *Psychological Science, 4,* 35–40.

LAZARUS, R. S. (1981). The stress and coping paradigm. In C. Eisdorfer, D. Cohen, A. Kleinman, & P. Maxim (Eds.), *Models for clinical psychopathology* (pp. 177–214). New York: Spectrum.

LAZARUS, R. (1991a). Progress on a cognitive-motivational-relational theory of emotion. *American Psychologist, 46,* 819–834.

LAZARUS, R. S. (1991b). Cognition and motivation in emotion. *American Psychologist, 46,* 352–367.

LAZARUS, R. S. (1991c). *Emotion and adaptation.* New York: Oxford University Press.

LAZARUS, R. S., & FOLKMAN, S. (1984). *Stress, appraisal, and coping.* New York: Springer.

LAZARUS, R. S., & LAUNIER, R. (1978). Stress-related transactions between person and environment. In L. A. Pervin & M. Lewis (Eds.), *Perspectives in interactional psychology* (pp. 287–327). New York: Plenum.

LEAKEY, R., & LEWIN, R. (1992). *Origins reconsidered: In search for what makes us human.* New York: Doubleday.

LEARNER, R. M. (1982). Children and adolescents as producers of their own development. *Developmental Review, 2,* 342–370.

LeDOUX, J. (1996). *The emotional brain: The mysterious underpinnings of emotional life.* New York: Simon & Shuster.

LeDOUX, J. E. (1986). Sensory systems and emotion. *Integrative Psychiatry, 4,* 237–248.

LeDOUX, J. E. (1992). Emotions and the limbic system. *Concepts in Neuroscience, 2,* 169–199.

LeDOUX, J. E. (1993). Emotional memory systems in the brain. *Behavior and Brain Research, 58,* 69–79.

LEDWIDGE, B. (1980). Run for your mind: Aerobic exercise as a means of alleviating anxiety and depression. *Canadian Journal of Behavioral Science, 12,* 126–140.

LEEDY, M. G. (2000). Commitment to distance running: Coping mechanism or addiction. *Journal of Sport Psychology, 23,* 255–263.

LEFCOURT, H. M., MARTIN, R. A., & SALEH, W. E. (1984). Locus of control and social support: Interactive modera-

tor of stress. *Journal of Personality and Social Psychology, 47,* 378–389.

LEHMAN, H. C. (1966). The most creative years of engineers and other technologists. *Journal of Genetic Psychology, 108,* 263–270.

LERNER, J. V., & LERNER, R. M. (1986). *Temperament and social interaction in infants and children.* San Francisco: Jossey-Bass.

LERNER, M. J. (1977). The justice motive: Some hypotheses as to its origin and forms. *Journal of Personality, 45,* 1–52.

LERNER, R. M. (1984). *On the nature of human plasticity.* New York: Cambridge Press.

LEVAY, S. (1991). A difference in hypothalamic structure between heterosexual and homosexual men. *Science, 253,* 1034–1037.

LEVENSON, H. (1981). Differentiating among internality, powerful others, and chance. In H. M. Lefcourt (Ed.), *Research with the locus of control construct: Assessment methods* (Vol. 1, pp. 15–63). New York: Academic Press.

LEVINE, S. (1960, May). Stimulation in infancy. *Scientific American,* pp. 80–86.

LEWIN, K. (1938). *The conceptual representation and the measurement of psychological forces.* Durham, NC: Duke University Press.

LEWIN, L., & GLAUBMAN, H. (1975). The effect of REM deprivation: Is it detrimental, beneficial, or neutral? *Psychophysiology, 12,* 349–353.

LIND, S. K., & MUMFORD, M. D. (1987, March). *Values as predictor of job performance and advancement potential.* Paper presented at the meeting of the Southeastern Psychological Association, Atlanta, GA.

LINEHAN, M. M. (1997). Self-verification and drug abusers: Implications for treatment. *Psychological Science, 8,* 181–184.

LINVILLE, P. W. (1987). Self-complexity as a cognitive buffer against stress-related illness and depression. *Journal of Personality and Social Psychology, 52,* 663–676.

LINZ, D., DONNERSTEIN, E., & PENROD, S. (1987). The findings and the recommendations of the Attorney General's Commission on Pornography. *American Psychologist, 42,* 946–953.

LOCKE, E. A. (1968). Toward a theory of task motivation and incentives. *Organizational Performance and Human Performance, 3,* 157–189.

LOCKE, E. A., & LATHAM, G. P. (1990). *A theory of goal setting and task performance.* Englewood Cliffs, NJ: Prentice Hall.

LORE, R. K., & SCHULTZ, L. A. (1993). Control of human aggression. *American Psychologist, 48,* 16–25.

LOSCH, M., & CACIOPPO, J. (1990). Cognitive dissonance may enhance sympathetic tonis, but attitudes are change to reduce negative affect rather than arousal. *Journal of Personality and Social Psychology, 26,* 289–304.

LOTTI, B. (1996). Politics or science? The question of gender sameness/difference. *American Psychologist, 51,* 155–156.

LOWINSON, J. H., RUIZ, P., & MILLMAN, R. B. (1997). *Substance abuse: A comprehensive textbook.* Baltimore: Williams and Wilkins.

LOWTHER, W. (1979, August 6). Marriage running down. *Maclean's*, p. 43.

LUCAS, R., DIENER, E., GROB, A., SUH, E., & SHAO, L. (1998). *Extraversion and pleasure affect. Analysis from 40 nations*. Manuscript submitted for publication, University of Illinois.

LYKKEN, D. (1999). *Happiness*. New York: Golden Books.

MacKINNON, D. W. (1962). The nature and nurture of creative talent. *American Psychologist, 17*, 484–495.

MACON, D. A. (1987, March). *Age, climate and personality as predictors of scientific productivity*. Paper presented at the meeting of the Southern Psychological Association, Atlanta, GA.

MACRAE, C. N., BODENHAUSEN, G. V. & MILNE, A. B. (1998). Saying no to unwanted thoughts: Self-focus and the regulation of metal life. *Journal of Personality and Social Psychology, 74*, 578–589.

MacVICAR, M., WINNINGHAM, M., & NICKEL, J. (1989). Effects of aerobic interval training on cancer patients' functional capacity. *Nursing Research, 38*, 348–351.

MAHONEY, M. J., & MAHONEY, K. (1976). *Permanent weight control*. New York: W. W. Norton.

MAIER, S. F. (1970). Failure to escape traumatic shock: Incompatible skeletal motor responses or learned helplessness? *Learning and Motivation, 1*, 157–170.

MAIER, S. F., & SELIGMAN, M. E. P. (1976). Learned helplessness: Theory and evidence. *Journal of Experimental Psychology, 105*, 3–46.

MAIER, S. F., SELIGMAN, M. E. P., & SOLOMON, R. L. (1969). Pavlovian fear conditioning and learned helplessness. In B. A. Campbell & R. M. Church (Eds.), *Punishment*. New York: Appleton-Century-Crofts.

MAIER, S. F., WATKINS, L. R., & FLESHNER, M. (1994). Psychoneuroimmuninology: The interface between behavior, brain, and immunity. *American Psychologist, 49*, 1004–1007.

MALAMUTH, N. M., & DONNERSTEIN, E. (1984). *Pornography and sexual aggression*. New York: Academic Press.

MANN, J. (1992). Nurturance or negligence: Maternal psychology and behavioral preference among preterm twins. In J. H. Barkow, L. Cosmides, & J. Tooby (Eds.), *The adapted mind: Evolutionary psychology and the generation of culture*. (pp. 367–390). New York: Oxford University Press, 1995.

MARCO, C. A., & SULS, J. (1993). Daily stress and the trajectory of mood: Spillover, response assimilation, contrast, and chronic negative affectivity. *Journal of Personality and Social Psychology, 64*, 1053–1063.

MARGULES, D. L. (1979). Beta-endorphin and endoloxone: Hormones of the autonomic nervous system for the conservation or expenditure of bodily resources and energy in anticipation of famine or feast. *Neuroscience and Biochemical Reviews, 3*, 155–162.

MARGULES, D. L., MOISSET, B., LEWIS, M. J., SHIBUY, A. H., & PERT, C. B. (1978). Beta-endorphin is associated with overeating in genetically obese mice (ob/ob) and rats (fa/fa). *Science, 202*, 988–991.

MARKUS, H., & NURIUS, P. (1986). Possible selves. *American Psychologist, 41*, 954–969.

MARKUS, H., & WURF, E. (1987). The dynamic self-concept: A social psychological perspective. *Annual Review of Psychology, 38*, 299–337.

MARKUS, H., CROSS, S., & WURF, E. (1990). The role of the self system in competence. In R. J. Sternberg & J. Kolligian, Jr. (Eds.), *Competence considered* (pp. 205–225). New Haven, CT: Yale University Press.

MARSHALL, G. N., WORTMAN, C. B., KUSULAS, J. W., HERVIG, L. K., & VICKERS, R. R., JR. (1992). Distinguishing optimism from pessimism: Relations to fundamental dimensions of mood and personality. *Journal of Personality and Social Psychology, 62*, 1067–1074.

MARTINDALE, C. (1989). Personality, situation, and creativity. In J. A. Glover, R. R. Ronning, & C. R. Reynolds (Eds.), *Handbook of creativity* (pp. 211–232). New York: Plenum Press.

MARTINSEN, E. W., & MORGAN, W. P. (1997). Antidepressant effects of physical activity. In W. P. Morgan (Ed.), *Physical activity and mental health*. Washington, DC: Taylor & Francis.

MASCOLO, M. F., & FISCHER, K. W. (1995). Developmental transformations in appraisals for pride, shame, and guilt. In J. P. Tangney & K. W. Fischer (Eds.), *Self-conscious emotions: The psychology of shame, guilt, embarrassment, and pride*. New York: Guilford Press.

MASLOW, A. H. (1943). A theory of human motivation. *Psychological Review, 50*, 370–396.

MASLOW, A. H. (1970). *Motivation and personality* (2nd ed.). New York: Harper & Row.

MASSERMAN, J. H., & YUM, K. S. (1946). An analysis of the influence of alcohol on experimental neuroses in cats. *Psychosomatic Medicine, 8*, 36–52.

MASTERS, M. S., & SANDERS, B. (1993). Is the gender difference in mental rotation disappearing? *Behavior Genetics, 23*, 337–341.

MASTERS, W. H., & JOHNSON, V. E. (1966). *Human sexual response*. Boston: Little, Brown.

MASTERS, W. H., & JOHNSON, V. E. (1975). *The pleasure bond: A new look at sexuality and commitment*. Boston: Little, Brown.

MATTHEWS, G., DAVIES, D. R., & LEES, J. L. (1990). Arousal, extraversion, and individual differences in resource availability. *Journal of Personality and Social Psychology, 59*, 150–168.

MAY, R. B. (1963). Stimulus selection of preschool children under conditions of free choice. *Perceptual and Motor Skills, 16*, 203–206.

McARDLE, W. D., KATCH, F. I., & KATCH, V. L. (1991). *Exercise physiology*. Philadelphia: Lea & Febiger.

McCANN, U. D., SZABO, Z., SCHFFEL, U., DANNALS, R. F., & RICAURTE, G. A. (1998). McCann-Ricaurte MDMA Neurotoxicity study: Positron emission tomographic evidence of toxic effect of MDMA ("Ecstacy") on brain serotonin neurons in human beings. *Lancet, 352*, No. 9138.

McCLELLAND, D. C. (1985). *Human motivation.* Glenview, IL: Scott, Foresman.

McCLELLAND, D. C. (1989). Motivational factors in health and disease. *American Psychologist, 44,* 675–683.

McCLELLAND, D. C., & PILON, D. A. (1983). Sources of adult motives in patterns of parent behavior in early childhood. *Journal of Personality and Social Psychology, 44,* 564–574.

McCLELLAND, D. C., ATKINSON, J. W., CLARK, R. A., & LOWELL, E. L. (1953). *The achievement motive.* New York: Appleton-Century-Crofts.

McCLELLAND, D. C., ROSS, G., & PATEL, V. (1985). The effect of an academic examination on salivary norepinephrine and immunoglobulin levels. *Journal of Human Stress, 11,* 52–59.

McCOLLAUM, B. & LESTER, D. (1997). Sexual aggression and attitudes towards women and mothers. *Journal of Psychology, 137,* 538–539.

McCRAE, R. R., COSTA, P. T. JR., OSTENDORF, F., ANGLEITNER, A., HŘEBÍČKOVÁ, M., AVIA, M. D., SANZ, J., SÁNCHEZ-BERNARDOS, M. L., KUSDIL, M. E., WOODFIELD, R., SAUNDERS, P. R. & SMITH, P. B. (2000). Nature over nurture: Temperament, personality, and life span development. *Journal of Personality and Social Psychology, 78,* 173–186.

McGRATH, M. J., & COHEN, D. B. (1978). REM sleep facilitation of adaptive waking behavior. A review of the literature. *Psychological Bulletin, 85,* 24–57.

McGRAW, K. O., & McCULLERS, J. C. (1974). The distracting effect of material reward: An alternative explanation for superior performance of reward groups in probability learning. *Journal of Experimental Child Psychology, 18,* 149–158.

McGRAW, K. O., & McCULLERS, J. C. (1975, September). *Some detrimental effects of reward on laboratory task performance.* Paper presented at the meeting of the American Psychological Association, Chicago.

McGREW, W. C. (1975). Patterns of plant food sharing by wild chimpanzees. In S. Kondo, M. Kawai, & A. Ehara (Eds.). *Contemporary primatology* (pp. 304–309). Basel: S. Karger.

McGREW, W. C. & FEISTNER, A. T. C. (1992). Two nonhuman primate models for the evolution of human food sharing: Chimpanzees and Callitrichids. In J. H. Barkow, L. Cosmides, & J. Tooby (Eds.), *The adapted mind: Evolutionary psychology and the generation of culture* (pp. 229–243). New York: Oxford University Press.

McINTYRE, J. G., & DUSEK, J. B. (1995). Perceived parental rearing practices and styles of coping. *Journal of Youth and Adolescence, 24,* 499–509.

MCLEANS (2000). *Distorted Images.* (August 14, pp. 41–42)

McNALLY, R. J. (1996). Cognitive bias in the anxiety disorders. In R. A. Dienstrier (Ed.), *Perspectives on anxiety, panic, and fear.* Nebraska Symposium on Motivation (Vol. 43, pp. 211–250). Lincoln: University of Nebraska Press.

McPARTLAND, R. J., & KUPFER, D. J. (1978). Rapid eye movement sleep cycle, clock time, and sleep onset. *Electroencephalography and Clinical Neurophysiology, 45,* 178–185.

MEICHENBAUM, D. H. (1977). *Cognitive-behavior modification: An integrative approach.* New York: Plenum Press.

METCALFE, J., & MISCHEL, W. (1999). A hot/cool analysis of delay of gratification: Dynamics of willpower. *Psychological Review, 106,* 3–19.

MEYER, L. B. (1961). *Emotion and meaning in music.* Chicago: University of Chicago Press.

MEYER, W. U. (1982). Indirect communications about perceived ability estimates. *Journal of Educational Psychology, 74,* 888–897.

MIKULA, G., PETRI, B., & TANZER, N. (1989). What people regard as unjust: Types and structures of everyday experiences of injustice. *European Journal of Social Psychology, 20,* 133–149.

MIKULINCER, M. (1994). *Human learned helplessness: A coping perspective.* New York: Plenum.

MIKULINCER, M., FLORIAN, V., & WELLER, A. (1993). Attachment styles, coping strategies and posttraumatic psychological distress: The impact of the Gulf War in Israel. *Journal of Personality and Social Psychology, 64,* 817–826.

MILES, D. R., & CAREY, G. (1997). Genetic and environmental architecture of human aggression. *Journal of Personality and Social Psychology, 72,* 207–217.

MILGRAM, S. (1963). Behavioral study of obedience. *Journal of Abnormal and Social Psychology, 67,* 371–378.

MILGRAM, S. (1974). *Obedience to authority.* New York: Harper & Row.

MILLER, D. G., GROSSMAN, Z. D., RICHARDSON, R. L., WISTOW, B. W., & THOMAS, F. D. (1978). Effect of signaled versus unsignaled stress on rat myocardium. *Psychosomatic Medicine, 40,* 432–434.

MILLER, D. T. (2000). The norm of self-interest. *American Psychologist, 54,* 1053–1060.

MILLER, G. A. (1956). The magical number seven, plus or minus two: Some limits on our capacity for processing information. *Psychological Review, 63,* 81–97.

MILLER, I. W., III, & NORMAN, W. H. (1979). Learned helplessness in humans: A review and attribution-theory model. *Psychological Bulletin, 86,* 93–118.

MILLER, N. E. (1941). The frustration-aggression hypothesis. *Psychological Review, 48,* 337–342.

MILLER, N. E. (1980). Effects of learning on physical symptoms produced by psychological stress. In H. Selye (Ed.), *Selye's guide to stress research* (Vol. 1). New York: Van Nostrand Reinhold.

MILLER, P. A., & EISENBERG, N. (1988). The relation of empathy to aggressive and externalizing/antisocial behavior. *Psychological Bulletin, 103,* 324–344.

MILLER, W. R. (1983). Controlled drinking: A history and critical review. *Journal of Studies on Alcohol, 44,* 68–83.

MILLER, W. R., & MUÑOZ, R. F. (1976). *How to control your drinking.* Englewood Cliffs, NJ: Prentice-Hall.

MILLS, J. H. (1975). Noise and children: A review of literature. *Journal of Acoustical Society of America, 58,* 767–779.

MILLS, J. H. (1978). Effects of noise on young and old people. In D. M. Lipscomb (Ed.), *Noise and audiology* (pp. 229–241). Baltimore: University Park Press.

MILSTEIN, R. M. (1980). Responsiveness in newborn infants of overweight and normal weight parents. *Appetite, 1,* 65–74.

MINEKA, S. (1985). Animal models of anxiety-based disorders: Their usefulness and limitations. In A. Tuma & J. Maser (Eds.), *Anxiety and anxiety disorders* (pp. 199–244). Hillsdale, NJ: Erlbaum.

MISCHEL, W. (1961). Delay of gratification, need for achievement, and acquiescence in another culture. *Journal of Abnormal and Social Psychology, 62,* 543–552.

Models of addiction [Special issue]. (1988, May). *Journal of Abnormal Psychology.*

MOISEEVA, N. I. (1979). The significance of different sleep states for the regulation of electrical brain activity in man. *Electroencephalography and Clinical Neurophysiology, 46,* 371–381.

MONDIN, G. W., MORGAN, W. P., PIERING, P. N., STEGNER, A. J., STOTESBERY, C. L., TRINE, M. R., & WU, M-Y (1996). Psychological consequences of exercise deprivation in habitual exercisers. *Medicine and Science in Sports and Exercise, 28,* 1199–1203.

MONEY, J. (1980). *Love and love sickness.* Baltimore: Johns Hopkins University Press.

MONEY, J. (1987a). Propaedeutics of diecious G-I/R: Theoretical foundations for understanding dimorphic gender-identity/role. In J. Reinisch, L. A. Rosenblum, & S. A. Sanders (Eds.), *Masculinity/femininity: Basic perspectives* (pp. 13–28). New York: Oxford University Press.

MONEY, J. (1987b). Sin, sickness, or status: Homosexual gender identity and psychoneuroendocrinology. *American Psychologist, 42,* 384–399.

MONEY, J., & EHRHARDT, A. A. (1972). *Man and woman, boy and girl: The differentiation and dimorphism of gender identity from conception to maturity.* Baltimore: Johns Hopkins University Press.

MONEY, J., SCHWARTZ, M., & LEWIS, V. (1984). Adult erotosexual status and fetal hormonal masculinization and demasculinization: 46 XX congenital virilizing adrenal hyperphasia and 46 XY androgen-insensitivity syndrome compared. *Psychoneuroendocrinology, 9,* 203–207.

MORGAN, W. P., & HORSTMAN, D. H. (1976). Anxiety reduction following acute physical activity. *Medicine and Science in Sports, 8,* 62.

MORRIS, D. (1969). *The naked ape.* New York: Dell.

MORRISON, A. R. (1983). A window on the sleeping brain. *Scientific American, 248,* 94–102.

MORSE, D. R., MARTIN, J. S., FURST, M. L., & DUBIN, L. L. (1977). A physiological and subjective evaluation of meditation, hypnosis, and relaxation. *Psychosomatic Medicine, 39,* 304–324.

MORUZZI, G., & MAGOUN, H. W. (1949). Brain stem reticular formation and activation of the EEG. *Electroencephalography and Clinical Neurophysiology, 1,* 455–473.

MOSES, J. M., JOHNSON, L. C., NAITOH, P., & LUBIN, A. (1975). Sleep stage deprivation and total sleep loss: Effects on sleep behavior. *Psychophysiology, 12,* 141–146.

MOSES, J. M., NAITOH, P., & JOHNSON, L. C. (1978). The REM cycle in altered sleep/wake schedules. *Psychophysiology, 15,* 569–575.

MOSHER, D. L., & ABRAMSON, P. R. (1955). Subjective sexual arousal to films of masturbation. *Journal of Consulting and Clinical Psychology, 45,* 796–807.

MOSSHOLDER, K. W. (1980). Effects of externally mediated goals setting on intrinsic motivation: A laboratory experiment. *Journal of Applied Psychology, 65,* 202–210.

MOUNT, G. R., WALTERS, S. R., ROWLAND, R. W., BARNES, P. R., & PAYTON, T. I. (1978). The effects of relaxation techniques on normal blood pressure. *Behavioral Engineering, 5*(1), 1–4.

MOYER, K. E. (1976). *The psychobiology of aggression.* New York: Harper & Row.

MULLANEY, D. J., JOHNSON, L. C., NAITOH, P., FRIEDMANN, J. K., & GLOBUS, G. G. (1977). Sleep during and after gradual sleep reduction. *Psychophysiology, 14,* 237–244.

MUMFORD, M. D., & GUSTAFSON, S. B. (1988). Creativity syndrome: Integration, application, and innovation. *Psychological Bulletin, 103,* 27–43.

MUNSINGER, H., & KESSEN, W. (1964). Uncertainty, structure, and preference. *Psychological Monographs, 78* (9, Whole No. 586).

MURAVEN, M., TICE, D. M., & BAUMEISTER, R. F. (1998). Self-control as limited resource: Regulatory depletion patterns. *Journal of Personality and Social Psychology, 74,* 774–789.

MURRAY, H. A. (1938). *Explorations in personality.* New York: Oxford University Press.

MYERS, D. G. (1993). *The pursuit of happiness.* New York: Avon.

MYERS, D. G. (2000). Funds, friends, and faith of happy people. *American Psychologist, 55,* 56–67.

MYERS, D. G. & DIENER, E. (1995). Who is happy? *Psychological Science, 6,* 10–19

MYERS, D. G. & DIENER, E. (1996). The pursuit of happiness. *Scientific American, 274,* 54–56.

NACHMAN, M. (1970). Learned taste and temperature aversions due to lithium chloride sickness after temporal delays. *Journal of Comparative and Physiological Psychology, 73,* 22–30.

NAKAZAWA, Y., KOTORII, M., KOTORII, T., TACHIBANA, H., & NAKANO, T. (1975). Individual differences in compensatory rebound of REM sleep with particular reference to their relationship to personality and behavioral characteristics. *Journal of Nervous and Mental Disease, 161,* 18–25.

National Advisory Mental Health Council. (1995). Basic behavioral science research for mental health: A national investment: Emotion and motivation. *American Psychologist, 50,* 838–845.

National Institute of Drug Abuse (2001). Internet access: www.nida.nih.gov/infofax/ecstacy.html.

NAVON, D., & GOPHER, D. (1979). On the economy of the human processing system. *Psychological Review, 86,* 214–255.

NEISS, R. (1988). Reconceptualizing arousal: Psychological states in motor performance. *Psychological Bulletin, 103,* 345–366.

NEISSER, U., BOODOO, G., BOUCHARD, T. J., JR., BOYKIN, A. W., BRODY, N., CECI, S. J., HALPERN, D. F., LOEHLIN, J. C., PERLOFF, R., STERNBERG, R. J., & URBINA, S. (1996). Intelligence: Knowns and unknowns. *American Psychologist, 51,* 77–101.

NESSE, R. M. (1999). The evolution of hope and despair. *Social Research, 66,* 429–452.

NESSE, R. M., & WILLIAMS, G. C. (1994). *Why we get sick.* New York: Time Books Random House.

NIAURA, R.S., ROHSENOW, D. J, BINKOFF, J. A., MONTI, P. M., PEDRAZA, M., & ABRAMS, D. B. (1988), Relevance of cue reactivity to understanding alcohol and smoking relapse. *Journal of Abnormal Psychology, 97,* 133–153.

NICHOLLS, J. G. (1984). Achievement motivation: Conceptions of ability, subjective experience, task choice, and performance. *Psychological Review, 91,* 328–346.

NICHOLLS, J. G. (1990). What is ability and why are we mindful of it? A developmental perspective. In R. J. Sternberg & J. Kolligian, Jr. (Eds.), *Competence considered* (pp. 11–40). New Haven, CT: Yale University Press.

NICHOLS, J. R. (1965). How opiates change behavior. *Scientific American, 212*(2), 80–88.

NICHOLSON, N. (1997). Evolutionary psychology: Toward a new view of human nature and organizational society. *Human Relations, 50,* 1053–1079.

NISBETT, R. E. (1968). Taste, deprivation, and weight determinants of eating behavior. *Journal of Personality and Social Psychology, 10,* 107–116.

NISBETT, R. E., & SCHACHTER, S. (1966). Cognitive manipulation of pain. *Journal of Experimental Social Psychology, 2,* 227–236.

NISHIHARA, K., MORI, K., ENDO, S., OHTA, T., & KENSHIRO, O. (1985). Relationship between sleep efficiency and urinary excretions of catecholamines in bed-rested humans. *Sleep, 8,* 110–117.

NOLEN-HOEKSEMA, S. (1990). *Sex differences in depression.* Stanford, CA: Stanford University Press.

NORMAN, D. A., & BOBROW, D. B. (1975). On data-limited and resource-limited processes. *Cognitive Psychology, 7,* 44–64.

NOVACO, R. W. (1985). Anger and its therapeutic regulation. In M. A. Chesney & R. H. Rosenman (Eds.), *Anger and hostility in cardiovascular and behavioral disorders* (pp. 139–147). Washington, DC: Hemisphere.

NUTT, D. J. (1996). Addiction: brain mechanisms and their treatment implications. *Lancet, 347,* 31–36.

O'BRIEN, M. (1987). *Vince: A personal history of Vince Lombardi.* New York: Morrow.

OLDS, J. (1955). Physiological mechanisms of reward. In M. R. Jones (Ed.), *Nebraska Symposium on Motivation* (Vol. 3). Lincoln: University of Nebraska Press.

OLDS, J., & MILNER, P. (1954). Positive reinforcement produced by electrical stimulation of the septal area and other regions of the rat brain. *Journal of Comparative and Physiological Psychology, 47,* 419–427.

OLEKSENKO, A. I. MUKHAMETOV, L. M., POLYAKOVA, I. G. et al. (1992). Unihemispheric sleep deprivation in bottlenose dolphins. *Journal of Sleep Research, 1,* 40–44.

OLWEUS, D. (1994). Bullying at school: Long-term outcomes for the victims and an effective school-based intervention program. In R. Huesmann (Ed.), *Aggression behavior: Current perspectives* (pp. 97–130). New York: Plenum Press.

ONIANI, T. N. (1984). Does paradoxical sleep deprivation disturb memory trace consolidation? *Physiology and Behavior, 33,* 687–692.

ORNSTEIN, R. (1991). *The evolution of consciousness: Origins of the way we think.* New York: Simon &Schuster.

ORY, M., & GOLDBERG, E. (1983). Pet ownership and life satisfaction in elderly women. In A. H. Katcher & A. Beck (Eds.), *New perspectives on our life with companion animals* (pp. 803–817). Philadelphia: University of Pennsylvania Press.

OSBORN, C. A., & POLLACK, R. H. (1977). The effects of two types of erotic literature on physiological and verbal measures of female sexual arousal. *Journal of Sex Research, 13,* 250–256.

OSBORNE, F. E. (1996). *Self: An eclectic approach.* Boston: Allyn & Bacon.

OUELLETTE, J. A., & WOOD, W. (1998). Habit and intention in everyday life: The multiple processes by which past behavior predicts future behavior. *Psychological Bulletin, 124,* 54–74.

OVERMIER, J. B., & SELIGMAN, M. E. P. (1967). Effects of inescapable shock on subsequent escape and avoidance responding. *Journal of Comparative and Physiological Psychology, 63,* 28–33.

OWENS, W. A. (1969). Cognitive, noncognitive and environmental correlates of mechanical ingenuity. *Journal of Applied Psychology, 53,* 199–208.

OZER, E., & BANDURA, A. (1990). Mechanisms governing empowerment effects: A self-efficacy analysis. *Journal of Personality and Social Psychology, 58,* 472–486.

PADILLA, A. M., PADILLA, C., KETTERER, T., & GIACALONE, D. (1970). Inescapable shocks and subsequent escape/avoidance conditioning in goldfish (*Carassius auratus*). *Psychonomic Science, 20,* 295–296.

PALLAK, M., & PITTMAN, T. (1972). General motivational effects of dissonance arousal. *Journal of Personality and Social Psychology, 21,* 349–358.

PANKSEPP, J. (1981). Hypothalamic integration of behavior. In P. Morgane & J. Panksepp (Eds.), *Handbook of the hypothalamus: Vol. 3, Part B. Behavioral studies of the hypothalamus* (pp. 289–487). New York: Marcel Bekker.

PATON, W. D. M., & CROWN, J. (Eds.). (1972). *Cannabis and its derivatives: Pharmacology and experimental psychology: Symposium proceedings.* London: Oxford University Press.

PATTERSON, G. R. (1976). The aggressive child: Victim and architect of a coercive system. In E. J. Mash, L. A. Hamerlynck, & L. C. Handy (Eds.), *Behavior modification and families* (pp. 267–316). New York: Brunner/Mazel.

PATTERSON, G. R. (1980). Mothers: The unacknowledged victims. *Monograph of the Society for Research in Child Development*, No. 45.

PATTERSON, G. R., DeBARYSHE, B. D., & RAMSEY, E. (1989). A developmental perspective on antisocial behavior. *American Psychologist, 44*, 329–335.

PAVLOV, I. P. (1927). *Conditioned reflexes* (G. V. Anrep, Trans.). New York: Dover.

Peabody Museum (1999). Gifting and feasting in the northwest coast Potlach. Exhibit mounted at the Peabody Museum (www.peabody.harvard.edu/potlach/credits.html)

PEDERSEN, N. L., GATZ, M., PLOMIN, R., NESSELROADE, J. R., & McCLEARN, G. E. (1989). Individual differences in locus of control during the second half of the life span for identical and fraternal twins reared apart and reared together. *Journal of Gerontology, 44*, 100–105.

PEDERSON, B. K., & HOFFMAN-GOETZ, L. (2000). Exercise and the immune system: Regulation, integration, and adaptation. *Physiological Reviews, 80*, 1055–1103.

PEELE, S. (1982). Love, sex, drugs and other magical solutions to life. *Journal of Psychoactive Drugs, 14*, 125–131.

PEELE, S. (1983, September/October). Out of the habit trap. *American Health*, pp. 42–47.

PEELE, S. (1984). The cultural context of psychological approaches to alcoholism. *American Psychologist, 39*, 1337–1351.

PEELE, S. (1989). *Diseasing of America: Addiction treatment out of control*. Lexington, MA: Lexington.

PEELE, S. (1998). *The meaning of addiction*. Lexington, MA: Lexington.

PEELE, S., & BRODSKY, A. (1991). *The truth about addiction and recovery*. New York: Fireside.

PELHAM, B. W., & NETER, E. (1995). The effect of motivation of judgment depends on the difficulty of the judgment. *Journal of Personality and Social Psychology, 68*, 581–594.

PENDERY, M. L., MALTZMAN, L. M., & WEST, L. J. (1982). Controlled drinking by alcoholics? Findings and a reevaluation of a major affirmative study. *Science, 217*, 160–175.

PENNEBAKER, J. W. (1990). *Opening up: The healing power of confiding in others*. New York: Avon Books.

PENNEBAKER, J. W. (1992). Inhibition as the linchpin. In H. S. Friedman (Ed.), *Hostility, coping and health* (pp. 127–139). Washington, DC: American Psychological Association.

PENNEBAKER, J. W. (1997). Writing about emotional experiences as a therapeutic process. *Psychological Science, 8*, 162–166.

PERT, C. B., & SNYDER, S. H. (1973). The opiate receptor: Demonstration in nervous tissue. *Science, 179*, 1011–1014.

PERVIN, L. A. (Ed.). (1989). *Goal concepts in personality and social psychology*. Hillsdale, NJ: Erlbaum.

PETERS, T. J., & WATERMAN, R. H., JR. (1982). *In search of excellence*. New York: Harper & Row.

PETERSEN, A. C., COMPAS, B. E., BROOKS-GUNN, J., STEMMLER, M., EY, S., & GRANT, K. E. (1993). Depression in adolescence. *American Psychologist, 48*, 155–168.

PETERSON, C. (2000). The future of optimism. *American Psychologist, 55*, 44–55.

PETERSON, C., & SELIGMAN, M. (1984). Causal explanations as a risk factor for depression: Theory and evidence. *Psychological Review, 91*, 347–374.

PETERSON, C., SELIGMAN, M., & VAILLANT, G. (1988). Pessimistic explanatory style as a risk factor for physical illness: A thirty-five-year longitudinal study. *Journal of Personality and Social Psychology, 55*, 23–27.

PETERSON, C., SELIGMAN, M. E. P., YURKO, K. H., MARTIN, L. R., & FRIEDMAN, H. S. (1998). Catastrophizing and ultimately death. *Psychological Science, 9*, 49–52.

PETERSON, S. E., FOX, P. T., POSNER, M. L., MINTUN, M., & RAICHLE, M. E. (1988). Positron emission tomography studies of the cortical anatomy of single-world processing. *Nature, 331*, 585–589.

PETRIE, K. J., BOOTH, R. J., & PENNEBAKER, J. W. (1998). The immunological effects of thought suppression. *Personality and Social Psychology, 75*, 1264–1272.

PETRIE, K. J., WHITE, G. R., CAMERON, L. D., & COLLINS, J. P. (1999). Photographic memory, money, liposuction: Survey of medical student's wish list. *British Medical Journal, 319*, 1593–1597.

PIAGET, J. (1952). *The origins of intelligence in children*. New York: International Universities Press.

PIAGET, J. (1970). Piaget's theory. In P. H. Mussen (Ed.), *Carmichael's manual of child psychology* (Vol. 1, 3rd ed., pp. 703–732). New York: Wiley.

PIASECKI, T. M., KENFORD, S. L., SMITH, S. S., FIORE, M. C., & BAKER, T. B. (1997). Listening to nicotine: Negative affect and the smoking withdrawal conundrum. *Psychological Science, 8*, 184–189.

PICKENS, R. (1968). Self administration of stimulants by rats. *International Journal of Addiction, 3*, 215–221.

PIDDOCKE, S. (1965). The potlatch system of Kwakiutl: A new perspective. *Southwestern Journal of Anthropology, 21*, 244–264.

PIETROPINTO, A., & SIMENAUER, J. (1977). *Beyond the male myth: What women want to know about men's sexuality*. New York: Times Books.

PILCHER, J., & WALTERS, A. S. (1997). How sleep deprivation affects psychological variables related to college students' cognitive performance. *Journal of American College Health, 46*, 121–129.

PINEL, J. P. J. (1993). *Biopsychology*. Boston: Allyn & Bacon.

PINKER, S. (1997). *How the mind works*. New York: Norton.

PITTS, F. N., JR. (1969). The biochemistry of anxiety. *Scientific American, 220*(2), 69–75.

PIVIK, T., & FOULKES, D. (1966). Dream deprivation: Effects on dream content. *Science, 153*, 1282–1284.

PLIHAL, W., & BORN, J. (1997). Effects of early and later nocturnal sleep on declarative and procedural memory. *Journal of Cognitive Neuroscience, 9*, 534–547.

PLOMIN, R., & DANIELS, D. (1987). Why are children in the same family so different from each other. *Behavioral and Brain Sciences, 10*, 1–16.

PLOMIN, R., & DeFRIES, J. (1998). The genetics of cognitive abilities and disabilities. *Scientific American, 278*, 62–69.

PLOTKIN, W. B. (1978). Long-term eyes-closed alpha-enhancement training: Effects on alpha amplitudes and on experiential state. *Psychophysiology, 15*, 40–52.

POLIVY, J. (1976). Perception of calories and regulation of intake in restrained and unrestrained subjects. *Addictive Behavior, 1*, 237–243.

POLIVY, J., & HERMAN, C. P. (1983). *Breaking the diet habit: The natural weight alternative.* New York: Basic Books.

POLIVY, J., HERMAN, C. P., HACKETT, R., & KULESHNYK, I. (1986). The effects of self-attention and public attention on eating in restrained and unrestrained subjects. *Journal of Personality and Social Psychology, 50*, 1253–1260.

POSNER, M. I., PETERSON, S. E., FOX, P. T., & RAICHLE, M. E. (1988). Localization of cognitive operations in the human brain. *Science, 240*, 1627–1631.

POST, R. M., LAKE, C. R., JIMERSON, D. C., BUNNEY, W. E., WOOD, J. H., ZIEGLER, M. C., & GOODWIN, E. K. (1978). Cerebrospinal fluid norepinephrine in affective illness. *American Journal of Psychiatry, 135*, 907–912.

POWERS, P. S. (1982). Obesity: Psychosomatic illness review: No. 2. *Psychosomatics, 23*, 1027–1039.

POWLEDGE, T. M. (1995). *Your Brain: How you Got It and How It Works.* New York: Scribner.

POWLEDGE, T. M. (1999). Addiction and the brain. *Bioscience. 49*, 513–519.

PRIBRAM, K. H. (1976). Self-consciousness and intentionality. In G. E. Schwartz & D. Shapiro (Eds.), *Consciousness and self-regulation: Advances in research* (Vol. 1). New York: Plenum.

PROFET, M. (1992). Pregnancy sickness as adaptation: A deterrent to maternal ingestion of teratogens. In J. H. Barkow, L. Cosmides, & J. Tooby (Eds.). *The adapted mind: Evolutionary psychology and the generation of culture* (327–366). New York: Oxford University Press, 1995.

QUADAGNO, D. M., BRISCO, R., & QUADAGNO, J. S. (1977). Effects of perinatal gonadal hormones on selected nonsexual behavior patterns: A critical assessment of the nonhuman and human literature. *Psychological Bulletin, 82*, 62–80.

QUIRCE, C. M., ODIO, M., & SOLANO, J. M. (1981). The effects of predictable and unpredictable schedules of physical restraint upon rats. *Life Sciences, 28*, 1897–1902.

RABINOWITZ, D., & ZIERLER, K. L. (1962). Forearm metabolism in obesity and its response to intra-arterial insulin: Characterization of insulin resistance and evidence for adaptive hyperinsulinism. *Journal of Clinical Investigation, 41*, 2173–2181.

RAGLIN, J. S. (1997). Anxiolytic effects of physical activity. In W. P. Morgan (Ed.), *Physical activity and mental health.* Washington, DC: Taylor & Francis.

RAICHLE, M. I. (1988). Modern imaging approaches to human learning and memory: Establishing a basis for understanding the damaged brain. In *Plasticity and Pathology in the Damaged Brain.* The Second Annual Bristol-Myers Squibb Symposium on Neuroscience Research. University of California, San Diego. Raven Health Care Communications.

RÄIKKÖNEN, K., MATTHEWS, K. A., FLORY, J. D., OWENS, J. F., & GUMP, B. B. (1999). Effects of optimism, pessimism, and trait anxiety on ambulatory blood pressure and mood during everyday life. *Journal of Personality and Social Psychology, 76*, 104–113.

RAMÍREZ, E., MALDONADO, A., & MARTOS, R. (1992). Attributions modulate immunization against learned helplessness in humans. *Journal of Personality and Social Psychology, 62*, 139–146.

RAPOPORT, J. L. (1989). *The boy who couldn't stop washing: The experience and treatment of obsessive-compulsive disorder.* New York: E. P. Dutton.

RAYNOR, J. O. (1974). Future orientation in the study of achievement motivation. In J. W. Atkinson & J. O. Raynor (Eds.), *Motivation and achievement* (pp. 121–154). Washington, DC: Winston.

RECHTSCHAFFEN, A. (1998). Current perspectives on the function of sleep. *Perspective in Biology and Medicine, 41*, 359–391.

REICHE, R., & DANNECKER, M. (1977). Male homosexuality in West Germany: A sociological investigation. *Journal of Sex Research, 13*, 35–53.

REISENZEIN, R. (1994). Pleasure-arousal theory and the intensity of emotions. *Journal of Personality and Social Psychology, 67*, 525–539.

RESCORLA, R. A. (1988). Behavioral studies of Pavlovian conditioning. *Annual Review of Neuroscience, 11*, 329–352.

RESNICK, S. M., BERENBAUM, S. A., GOTTESMAN, I. I., & BOUCHARD, T. J., JR. (1986). Early hormonal influences on cognitive functioning in congenital adrenal hyperphasia. *Developmental Psychology, 22*, 191–198.

RICAURTE, G. A., MARTELLO, A. L., KATZ, J. L., & MARTELLO, M. B. (1992). Lasting effects (±)-3,4–Methylenedioxymetamphetamine (MDMA) on central serotonergic neurons in nonhuman-primates: Neurochemical observations. *Journal of Pharmacology and Experimental Therapeutics, 261*, 616–622.

RICHARDSON, G. S., CARSKADON, M. A., ORAV, E. J., & DEMENT, W. C. (1982). Circadian variations in elderly and young adult subjects. *Sleep, 5*, S82–S94.

RIMMER, J. H., & LOONEY, M. A. (1997). Effects of an aerobic activity program on the cholesterol levels of adolescents. *Research Quarterly for Exercise and Sport, 68*, 74–79.

ROBBINS, J. (2000). Wired for sadness. *Discover, 21*, 76–81.

ROBINS, L. N., DAVIS, D. H., & GOODWIN, D. W. (1974). Drug use by U.S. Army enlisted men in Vietnam: A follow-up on their return home. *American Journal of Epidemiology, 99,* 235–249.

ROBINS, L. N., & PRZYBECK, T. R. (1985). Age of onset of drug use as a factor in drug and other disorders. In C. L. Jones & R. J. Battjes (Eds.), *Etiology of drug abuse* (pp. 178–192). Rockville, MD: National Institute of Drug Abuse.

ROBINSON-WHELEN, S., KIM, C., MacCALLUM, R. C., & KIECOLT-GLASER, J. K. (1997). Distinguishing optimism from pessimism in older adults: Is it more important to be optimistic or not to be pessimistic? *Journal of Personality and Social Psychology, 73,* 1345–1353.

RODIN, J. (1981). Current status of the internal-external hypothesis for obesity. *American Psychologist, 36,* 361–372.

RODIN, J. (1984). Effects of food choice on amount of food eaten in a subsequent meal: Implications for weight gain. In J. Hirsch and T. B. Van Itallie (Eds.), *Recent advances in obesity research* (Vol. 4). Lancaster, PA: Technomic.

RODIN, J., & LANGER, E. J. (1977). Long-term effects of a control-relevant intervention with the institutionalized aged. *Journal of Personality and Social Psychology, 35,* 897–902.

RODIN, J., & SLOCHOWER, J. (1976). Externality in the nonobese: Effects of environmental responsiveness on weight. *Journal of Personality and Social Psychology, 33,* 338–344.

RODIN, J., SLOCHOWER, J., & FLEMING, B. (1977). Effects of degree of obesity, age of onset, and weight loss on responsiveness to sensory and external stimuli. *Journal of Comparative and Physiological Psychology, 91,* 586–597.

ROFFWARG, H. P., MUZIO, J., & DEMENT, W. C. (1966). Ontogenetic development of the human sleep-dream cycle. *Science, 152,* 604–619.

ROGERS, C. R. (1951). *Client-centered therapy: Its current practice, implications, and theory.* Boston: Houghton Mifflin.

ROGERS, C. R. (1959). A theory of therapy, personality, and interpersonal relationships, as developed in the client-centered framework. In S. Koch (Ed.), *Psychology: A study of a science. Study 1: Conceptual and systematic: Vol. 3. Formulations of the person and the social context* (pp. 184–256). New York: McGraw-Hill.

ROSE, G. A., & WILLIAMS, R. T. (1961). Metabolic studies on large and small eaters. *British Journal of Nutrition, 15,* 1–9.

ROSEN, B. C., & D'ANDRADE, R. G. (1959). The psychological origins of achievement motivation. *Sociometry, 22,* 185–218.

ROSEN, J. B., & SCHULKIN, J. (1998). From normal fear to pathological anxiety. *Psychological Review, 105,* 325–350.

ROSENBLATT, P. C. (1974). Cross-cultural perspectives on attractiveness. In T. L. Huston (Ed.), *Foundation of interpersonal attraction* (pp. 79–95). New York: Academic Press.

ROSENFELD, A. H. (1985, June). Depression: Dispelling despair. *Psychology Today, 85,* 29–34.

ROSLER, A., & KOHN, G. (1983). Male pseudohermaphroditism due to 17B-hydroxysteroid dehydrogenase deficiency. *Journal of Steroid Biochemistry, 19,* 663–674.

ROSSIER, J., BLOOM, F. E., & GUILLEMIN, R. (1980). Endorphins and stress. In H. Selye (Ed.), *Selye's guide to stress research* (Vol. 1). New York: Van Nostrand Reinhold.

ROTHBART, M. K., & AHADI, S. A. (1994). Temperament and the development of personality. *Journal of Abnormal Psychology, 103,* 55–66.

ROTHBART, M. K., AHADI, S. A., & EVANS, D. E. (2000). Temperament and personality: Origins and outcomes. *Journal of Personality and Social Psychology, 78,* 122–135.

ROTTER, J. B. (1966). Generalized expectancies for internal versus external control of reinforcement. *Psychological Monographs, 80,* 1–28.

ROTTER, J. B. (1972). An introduction to social learning theory. In J. B. Rotter, J. E. Chance, & E. J. Phares (Eds.), *Applications of a social learning theory of personality.* New York: Holt, Rinehart & Winston.

ROUTTENBERG, A. (1968). The two-arousal hypothesis: Reticular formation and limbic system. *Psychological Review, 75,* 51–80.

ROWLAND, G. L., FRANKEN, R. E., & HARRISON, K. (1986). Sensation seeking and participation in sporting activities. *Journal of Sports Psychology, 8,* 212–220.

ROZIN, P. (1976). The selection of food by rats, humans and other animals. In J. Rosenblatt, R. A. Hinde, & E. Shaw (Eds.). *Advance in the study of behavior. Vol 6* (pp. 21–76). New York: Academic Press.

ROZIN, P. (1996). Towards a psychology of food and eating: From motivation to module to model to marker, morality, meaning and metaphor. *Current Directions in Psychological Science, 5,* 18–24.

ROZIN, P. & FALLON, A. (1988). Body image, attitudes to weight, and misperceptions of figure preferences of the opposite sex: A comparison of men and women in two generations. *Journal of Abnormal Psychology, 97,* 342–345.

RUBIN, R. T., REINISCH, J. M., & HASKETT, R. F. (1981). Postnatal gonadal steroid effects on human behavior. *Science, 211,* 1318–1324.

RUDERMAN, A. J. (1986). Dietary restraint: A theoretical and empirical review. *Psychological Bulletin, 99,* 247–262.

RULE, B. G., & NESDALE, A. R. (1976). Moral judgments of aggressive behavior. In R. G. Geen & E. C. O'Neal (Eds.), *Perspectives on aggression* (pp. 37–60). San Diego, CA: Academic Press.

RUSHTON, J. P., FULKER, D. W., NEALE, M. C., NIAS, D. K. B., & EYSENCK, H. J. (1986). Altruism and aggression: The heritability of individual differences. *Journal of Personality and Social Psychology, 50,* 1192–1198.

RUSSELL, B. (1985). *The conquest of happiness.* London: Unwin. (Original work published 1930)

RUSSELL, J. A. (1995). Facial expressions of emotion: What lies beyond minimal universality? *Psychological Bulletin, 118,* 379–391.

RYAN, R. M., & DECI, E. L. (2000). Self-determination theory and the facilitation of intrinsic motivation, social development, and well-being. *American Psychologist, 55,* 68–78.

RYAN, R. M., & GROLNICK, W. S. (1986). Origins and pawns in the classroom: Self-reports and projective assessments of individual differences in children's perceptions. *Journal of Personality and Social Psychology, 50*, 550–558.

RYAN, R. M., KUHL, J., & DECI, E. L. (1997). Nature and autonomy: Organizational view of social and neurobiological aspects of self-determination in behavior and development. *Developmental and Psychopathology, 9*, 701–728.

SALKOVSKIS, P. M., CLARK, D. M., & HACKMANN, A. (1991). Treatment of panic attacks using cognitive therapy with exposure or breathing restraining. *Behavior Research and Therapy, 29*, 161–166.

SALOVEY, P., ROTHMAN, A. J., DETWEILER, J. B., & STEWARD, W. T. (2000). Emotional states and physical health. *American Psychologist, 55*, 110–121.

SALTUS, R. (1990, July 6). Sleep. *Calgary Herald.*

SANDAY, P. R. (1981). The sociocultural context of rape: A cross-cultural study. *Journal of Social Issues, 37*, 5–27.

SAPOLSKY, R. (1997). *The trouble with testosterone.* New York: Simon & Schuster.

SARASON, I. G. (1984). Stress, anxiety, and cognitive interference: Reactions to tests. *Journal of Personality and Social Psychology, 46*, 929–938.

SAUNDERS, D. (1978). *The relationship of attitude variables and explanations of perceived and actual career attainment in male and female businesspersons.* Unpublished doctoral dissertation, University of Texas at Austin.

SAX, L. J., ASTIN, A. W., KORN, W. S., & MAHONEY, K. M. (1998). *The American freshman: National norms for fall 1998.* Los Angeles: Higher Education Research Institute, University of California, Los Angeles.

SCHAAL, B., TREMBLAY, R. E., SOUSSIGNAN, R., & SUSMAN, E. J. (1996). Male testosterone linked to social dominance but low physical aggression in early adolescence. *Journal of the American Academy of Child and Adolescent Psychiatry, 34*, 1322–1330.

SCHACHTER, S. (1971a). *Emotion, obesity, and crime.* New York: Academic Press.

SCHACHTER, S. (1971b). Some extraordinary facts about obese humans and rats. *American Psychologist, 26*, 129–144.

SCHACHTER, S. (1977). Nicotine regulation in heavy and light smokers. *Journal of Experimental Psychology: General, 106*, 5–12.

SCHACHTER, S., & GROSS, L. P. (1968). Manipulated time and eating behavior. *Journal of Personality and Psychology, 10*, 98–106.

SCHACHTER, S., & RODIN, J. (1974). *Obese humans and rats.* Hillsdale, NJ: Erlbaum,

SCHACHTER, S., SILVERSTEIN, B., & PERLICK, D. (1977). Psychological and pharmacological explanations of smoking under stress. *Journal of Experimental Psychology. General, 106*, 31–40.

SCHACHTER, S., & SINGER, J. E. (1962). Cognitive, social, and physiological determinants of emotional states. *Psychological Review, 69*, 379–399.

SCHEIER, M. F., CARVER, C. S., & BRIDGES, M. W. (1994). Distinguishing optimism from neuroticism (trait anxiety, self-mastery, and self-esteem): A reevaluation of the Life Orientation Test. *Journal of Personality and Social Psychology, 67*, 1063–1078.

SCHEIER, M. F., & CARVER, C. S. (1985). Optimism, coping and health: Assessment and implications of generalized outcomes expectancies. *Health Psychology, 4*, 210–247.

SCHEIER, M. F., & CARVER, C. S. (1988). A model of behavioral self-regulation: Translating intention into action. In L. Berkowitz (Ed.), *Advances in Experimental Social Psychology* (Vol. 21, pp. 303–346). New York: Academic Press.

SCHEIER, M. F., MATTHEWS, K. A., OWENS, J. F., MAGOVERN, G. J., SR., LEFEBVRE, R. C., ABBOTT, R. A., & CARVER, C. S. (1989). Dispositional optimism and recovery from coronary artery bypass surgery: The beneficial effects on physical and psychological well being. *Journal of Personality and Social Psychology, 57*, 1024–1040.

SCHEIER, M. F., MATTHEWS, K. A., OWENS, J. F., MAGOVERN, G. J., SR., LEFEBVRE, R. C., & SCHIFF, S. R. (1982). Conditioned dopaminergic activity. *Biological Psychiatry, 17*, 135–154.

SCHEIER, M. F., MATTHEWS, K. A., OWENS, J. F., SCHULZ, R., BRIDGES, M. W., MAGOVERN, G. J., SR. & CARVER, C. S. (1999). Optimism and rehospitalization following coronary artery bypass graft surgery. *Archives of Internal Medicine, 159*, 829–835.

SCHIFF, (1982)

SCHILDKRAUT, J. J., & KETY, S. S. (1967). Biogenic amines and emotion. *Science, 156*, 21–30.

SCHLEISER-STROPP, B. (1984). Bulimia: A review of the literature. *Psychological Bulletin, 95*, 247–257.

SCHULTHEISS, O. C., & BRUNSTEIN, J. C. (1999). Goal imagery: Bridging the gap between implicit motivates and explicit goals. *Journal of Personality, 67*, 1–38.

SCHULZ, R., BOOKWALA, J., KNAPP, J. E., SCHEIER, M., & WILLIAMSON, G. M. (1996). Pessimism and cancer mortality. *Psychology and Aging, 11*, 304–309.

SCHUSTER, T. L., KESSLER, R. C., & ASELTINE, R. H., JR. (1990). Positive interactions, negative interactions, and depressed mood. *American Journal of Community Psychology, 18*, 423–438.

SCHWARTZ, G. E. (1974, April). The facts of transcendental meditation: Part II. TM relaxes some people and makes them feel better. *Psychology Today*, pp. 39–44.

SCHWARTZ, G. E., DAVIDSON, R. J., & GOLEMAN, D. J. (1978). Patterning of cognitive and somatic processes in the self-regulation of anxiety: Effects of meditation versus exercise. *Psychosomatic Medicine, 40*, 321–328.

SCHWARZER, R., & FUCHS, R. (1995). Changing risk behaviors and adopting health behaviors: The role of self-efficacy beliefs. In A. Bandura (Ed.), *Self-efficacy in changing societies* (pp. 259–288). Cambridge University Press.

SCHWARZER, R., DUNKEL-SCHETTER, C., & KEMENY, M. (1994). The multidimensional nature of received social support in gay men at risk of HIV infection and AIDS. *American Journal of Community Psychology, 22*, 319–339.

SCOTT, K. D., SCHAFER, J., & GREENFIELD, T. K. (1999). The role of alcohol in physical assault perpetration and victimization. *Journal of Studies on Alcohol, 60,* 528–542.

SCRIMA, L. (1982). Isolated REM sleep facilitates recall of complex associative information. *Psychophysiology, 19,* 252–259.

SCRIMA, L., BROUDY, M., NAY, K. N., & COHN, M. A. (1982). Increased severity of obstructive sleep apnea after bedtime alcohol ingestion: Diagnostic potential and proposed mechanism of action. *Sleep, 5,* 318–328.

SEGERSTROM, S. C., TAYLOR, S. E., KEMENY, M. E., & FAHEY, J. L. (1998). Optimism is associated with mood, coping, and immune change in response to stress. *Journal of Personality and Social Psychology, 74,* 1646–1655.

SEIFFGE-KRENKE, I., & KLESSINGER, N. (2000). Long-term effects of avoidant coping on adolescents' depressive symptoms. *Journal of Youth and Adolescence, 29,* 617–628.

SELDEN, L. S. (1991). Neurotoxicity of methamphetamine: Mechanisms of action and issues related to aging. In M. A. Miller & N. J. Kozel (Eds.), *Methamphetamine abuse: Epidemiologic issues and implications* (Research Monograph 115, pp. 24–32). Rockville, MD: National Institute on Drug Abuse.

SELIGMAN, M. E. P. (1971). Phobias and preparedness. *Behavior Therapy, 23,* 307–320.

SELIGMAN, M. E. P. (1975). *Helplessness: On depression, development, and death.* San Francisco: W. H. Freeman.

SELIGMAN, M. E. P. (1988, October). Boomer blues. *Psychology Today,* pp. 50–55.

SELIGMAN, M. E. P. (1989). *Why is there so much depression today? The waxing of the individual and the waning of the commons* (G. Stanley Hall Lecture Series, No. 9). Washington DC: American Psychological Association.

SELIGMAN, M. E. P. (1990). *Learned optimism.* New York: Alfred A. Knopf.

SELIGMAN, M. E. P. & CSIKSZENTMIHALYI, M. (2000). Positive Psychology: An introduction. *American Psychologist, 55,* 5–14.

SELIGMAN, M. E. P., & MAIER, S. F. (1967). Failure to escape shock. *Journal of Experimental Psychology, 74,* 1–9.

SELIGMAN, M. E. P., MAIER, S. F., & SOLOMON, R. L. (1971). Unpredictable and uncontrollable aversive events. In F. R. Brush (Ed.), *Aversive conditioning and learning* (pp. 347–400). New York: Academic Press.

SELIGMAN, M. E. P., & SCHULMAN, P. (1986). Explanatory style as a predictor of performance as a life insurance agent. *Journal of Personality and Social Psychology, 50,* 832–838.

SELYE, H. (1974). *Stress without distress.* Philadelphia: Lippincott.

SHAPIRO, D. H., SCHWARTZ, C. E., & ASTIN, J. A. (1996). Controlling ourselves, controlling our world: Psychology's role in understanding positive and negative consequences of seeking and gaining control. *American Psychologist, 51,* 1213–1230.

SHAVER, P., HAZAN, C., & BRADSHAW, D. (1988). Love as attachment: The integration of three behavioral systems. In R. Sternberg & M. Barnes (Eds.), *The psychology of love* (pp. 69–99). New Haven, CT: Yale University Press.

SHAYWITZ, B. A., SHAYWITZ, S. E., PUGH, K. R., CONSTABLE, R. T., SKUDLARSKI, P., FULBRIGHT, R. K., BRONEN, R. A., FLETCHER, J. M., SHANKWELLER, D. P., KATZ, L., & GORE, J. C. (1995). Sex differences in the functional organization of the brain for language. *Nature, 373,* 607–609.

SHER, K. J., WALITZER, K. S., WOOD, P. K., & BRENT, E. E. (1991). Characteristics of children of alcoholics: Putative risk factors, substance abuse, and psychopathology. *Journal of Abnormal Psychology, 100,* 427–448.

SHERMAN, I. W., & SHERMAN, V. G. (1989). *Biology: A human approach.* New York: Oxford University Press.

SHERRY, D. F., & SCHACTER, D. L. (1987). The evolution of multiple memory systems. *Psychological Review, 94,* 439–454.

SHIFFMAN, S., PATY, J. A., GNYS, M., KASSEL, J. A., & HICKCOX, M. (1996). First lapses to smoking: Within-subjects analysis of real-time reports. *Journal of Consulting and Clinical Psychology, 64,* 366–379.

SHODA, Y., MISCHEL, W., & PEAKE, P. K. (1990). Predicting adolescent cognitive and self-regulatory competencies from preschool delay of gratification. *Developmental Psychology, 26,* 978–986.

SHORTELL, J., EPSTEIN, S., & TAYLOR, S. P. (1990). Instigation to aggression as a function of degree of defeat and capacity for massive retaliation. *Journal of Personality, 38,* 313–328.

SHOWERS, C. (1992). Compartmentalization of positive and negative self-knowledge: Keeping bad apples out of the bunch. *Journal of Personality and Social Psychology, 62,* 1036–1049.

SHRAUGER, J. S. (1972). Self-esteem and reactions to being observed by others. *Journal of Personality and Social Psychology, 23,* 192–200.

SIEGEL, J. M. (1979). Reticular formation activity and REM sleep. In R. Drucker-Colin, M. Shkurovich, & M. B. Sterman (Eds.), *The functions of sleep* (pp. 73–97). New York: Academic Press.

SIEGEL, J. M. (1990). Stressful life events and use of physician services among the elderly: The moderating role of pet ownership. *Journal of Personality and Social Psychology, 58,* 1081–1086.

SIEGEL, S. (1979). The role of conditioning in drug tolerance and addiction. In J. D. Keehn (Ed.), *Psychopathology in animals: Research and clinical implications* (pp. 143–168). New York: Academic Press.

SIEGEL, S. (1983). Classical conditioning, drug tolerance, and drug dependence. In R. G. Smart, F. B. Glasser, Y. Israel, H. Kalant, R. E. Popham, & W. Schmidt (Eds.), *Research advances in alcohol and drug problems.* New York: Plenum.

SIGMON, S. T., & SNYDER, C. R. (1990). *Positive and negative affect as a counterexplanation for the relationship between hope and coping strategies.* Unpublished manuscript, University of Kansas, Department of Psychology, Lawrence.

SILK, J. B. (1978). Patterns of food sharing among mother and infant chimpanzees at Gombe National Park, Tanzania. *Folia primatologica, 29,* 129–141.

SILVERSTEIN, B., KOZLOWSKI, L. T., & SCHACHTER, S. (1977). Social life, cigarette smoking, and urinary pH. *Journal of Experimental Psychology: General, 106,* 20–23.

SIMON, H. A. (1994). The bottleneck of attention: Connecting thought with motivation. In W. D. Spaulding (Ed.), *Integrative views of motivation, cognition and emotion: Nebraska Symposium on Motivation* (Vol. 41, pp. 1–21). Lincoln: University of Nebraska Press.

SIMON, W., & GAGNON, J. H. (1986). Sexual scripts: Permanence and change. *Archives of Sexual Behavior, 15,* 97–120.

SIMONTON, D. K. (2000). Creativity: Cognitive, personal, developmental, and social aspects. *American Psychologist, 55,* 151–158.

SINGH, D. (1993). Adaptive significance of waist-to-hip ratio and female physical attractiveness. *Journal of Personality and Social Psychology, 65,* 293–307.

SINGH, D., & LUIS, S. (1995). Ethnic and gender consensus for the effect of waist-to-hip ratio on judgments of women's attractiveness. *Human Nature 6,* 51–65.

SINGH, D., & YOUNG, R. K. (1995). Body weight, waist-to-hip ratio, breasts, and hips: Role in judgments of female attractiveness and desirability for relationships. *Ethology and Sociobiology,16,* 483–507.

SKINNER, B. F. (1938). *The behavior of organisms: An experimental analysis.* New York: Appleton-Century-Crofts.

SKINNER, B. F. (1948). *Walden two.* New York: Macmillan.

SKINNER, B. F. (1969). *Contingencies of reinforcement: A theoretical analysis.* New York: Appleton-Century-Crofts.

SKINNER, B. F. (1971). *Beyond freedom and dignity.* New York: Knopf.

SKINNER, H. A., GLASER, F. B., & ANNIS, H. M. (1982). Crossing the threshold: Factors in self-identification as an alcoholic. *British Journal of Addiction, 77,* 51–64.

SLADECZEK, I., & DOMINO, G. (1985). Creativity, sleep and primary process thinking in dreams. *Journal of Creative Behavior, 19,* 38–46.

SLATER, E., & SHIELDS, J. (1969). Genetic aspects of anxiety. *British Journal of Psychiatry, 3,* 62–71.

SMART, R. G. (1965). Effects of alcohol on conflict and avoidance behavior. *Quarterly Journal of Studies on Alcohol, 26,* 187–205.

SMITH, C., & BUTLER, S. (1982). Paradoxical sleep at selective times following training is necessary for learning. *Physiology and Behavior, 29,* 469–473.

SMITH, C., & YOUNG, J. (1980). Reversal of paradoxical sleep deprivation by amygdaloid stimulation during learning. *Physiology and Behavior, 24,* 1035–1039.

SMITH, G. F., & DORFMAN, D. D. (1975). The effect of stimulus uncertainty on the relationship between frequency of exposure and liking. *Journal of Personality and Social Psychology, 31,* 150–155.

SMITH, J. E., CO, C., FREEMAN, M. E., SANDS, M. P., & LANE, J. D. (1980). Neurotransmitter turnover in rat striatum is correlated with morphine self-administration. *Nature, 287,* 152–154.

SMITH, S. M., WARD, T. B., & FINKE, R. A. (Eds.). (1995). *The creative cognition approach.* Cambridge, MA: MIT Press.

SMOLLER, J. W., WADDEN, T. A., & STUNKARD, A. J. (1987). Dieting and depression: A critical review. *Journal of Psychosomatic Research, 31,* 429–440.

SNYDER, C. R., HARRIS, C., ANDERSON, J. R., HOLLERAN, S. A., IRVING, L. M., SIGMON, S. T., YOSHINOBU, L., GIBB, J., LANGELLE, C., & HARNEY, P. (1991). The will and the ways: Development and validation of an individual-differences measure of hope. *Journal of Personality and Social Psychology, 60,* 570–585.

SNYDER, K. V., KYMISSIS, P., & KESSLER, K. (1999). Anger management for adolescents: Efficacy of brief group therapy. *Journal of the American Academy of Child and Adolescent Psychiatry, 38,* 1409–1420.

SNYDER, M. (1979). Self-monitoring processes. In L. Berkowitz (Ed.), *Advances in experimental social psychology* (Vol. 12, pp. 85–128). New York: Academic Press.

SNYDER, S. (1977a). The brain's own opiates. *Chemical and Engineering News, 55*(48), 26–35; 266–271.

SNYDER, S. (1977b). Opiate receptors and internal opiates. *Scientific American, 236*(3), 44–56.

SOBELL, M. B., & SOBELL, L. C. (1976). Second year treatment outcome of alcoholics treated by individualized behavior therapy: Results. *Behavior Research Therapy, 14,* 195–215.

SOBER, E. & WILSON, D. S. (1998). *Unto others.* Cambridge, MA: Harvard University Press.

SOLOMON, R. L. (1980). The opponent-process theory of acquired motivation: The costs of pleasure and the benefits of pain. *American Psychologist, 35,* 691–712.

SOLOMON, R. L., & CORBIT, J. D. (1974). An opponent process theory of motivation: I. Temporal dynamics of affect. *Psychological Review, 81,* 119–145.

SORENSEN, T. I. A., ECHWALD, S. M., & HOLM, J. (1996). Leptin in obesity: tells the brain how much fat there is, but in obese people the message may not get through. *British Medical Journal, 313,* 953–954.

SORRENTINO, R. M., & HEWITT, E. C. (1984). The uncertainty-reducing properties of achievement tasks revisited. *Journal of Personality and Social Psychology, 47,* 884–899.

SOSTEK, A. J., SOSTEK, A. M., MURPHY, D. L., MARTIN, E. B., & BORN, W. S. (1981). Cord blood amine oxidase activities relate to arousal and motor functioning in human newborns. *Life Sciences, 28,* 2561–2568.

SPENCE, J. T., & HELMREICH, R. L. (1983). Achievement-related motives and behavior. In J. T. Spence (Ed.), *Achievement and achievement motives* (pp. 7–74). San Francisco: W. H. Freeman.

SPIELBERGER, C. D. (1983). *Manual for the State-Trait Anxiety Inventory* (Form V). Palo Alto, CA: Consulting Psychologists Press.

SPIELBERGER, C. D. (1985). Anxiety, cognition, and affect. A state-trait perspective. In A. H. Tuma & J. D. Maser (Eds.), *Anxiety and the anxiety disorders* (pp. 109–130). Hillsdale, NJ: Erlbaum.

SPINKS, J. A., BLOWERS, G. H., & SHEK, D. T. L. (1985). The role of the orientating response in the anticipation of information: A skin conductance response study. *Psychophysiology, 22,* 385–394.

SPRAGUE, J., & QUADAGNO, D. (1987). Gender and sexual motivation: An explanation of two assumptions. *Journal of Personality and Human Sexuality, 2,* 57–76.

STANFORD, C. B. (1999). *The hunting apes: Meat eating and the origins of human behavior.* Princeton University Press.

STAUB, E. (1989). *The roots of evil: The origins of genocide and group violence.* New York and Cambridge: Cambridge University Press.

STAUB, E. (1996). Cultural-societal roots of violence: The examples of genocidal violence and of contemporary youth violence in the United States. *American Psychologist, 51,* 117–132.

STEELE, C. M., & JOSEPHS, R. A. (1990). Alcohol myopia: Its prized and dangerous effects. *American Psychologist, 45,* 921–933.

STEIN, M. I. (1968). Creativity. In F. Bogarta & W. W. Lambert (Eds.), *Handbook of personality theory and research* (pp. 67–89). Chicago: Rand McNally.

STENBERG, C. R., & CAMPOS, J. J. (1990). The development of anger expressions in infancy. In N. Stein, B. Leventhal, & T. Trabasso (Eds.), *Psychological and biological approaches to emotion* (pp. 247–282). Hillsdale, NJ: Erlbaum.

STEPANSKI, E., LAMPHERE, J., BADIA, P., ZORICK, F., & ROTH, T. (1984). Sleep fragmentation and daytime sleepiness. *Sleep, 7,* 18–26.

STERNBERG, R. J. (1991). *Love: The way you want it.* New York: Bantam.

STEWART, J., & KOLB, B. (1988). Cerebral asymmetry and sex. *Behavior and Neural Biology, 49,* 344–360.

STOKOLS, D. (1992a). Conflict-prone and conflict-resistant organizations. In H. S. Friedman (Ed.), *Hostility, coping and health* (pp. 65–75). Washington, DC: American Psychological Association.

STORM, C., & STORM, T. (1987). A taxonomic study of the vocabulary of emotions. *Journal of Personality and Social Psychology, 53,* 805–816.

STRAGE, A. A. (1998). Family context variables and the development of self-regulation in college students. *Adolescence, 33,* 17–31.

STRICKLAND, B. R. (1989). Internal-external control expectancies: From contingency to creativity. *American Psychologist, 44,* 1–7.

STROEBE, W., & STROEBE, M. (1987). *Bereavement and health: The psychological and physical consequences of partner loss.* New York: Cambridge University Press.

STROEBE, W., STROEBE, M., ABAKOUMKIN, G., & SCHUT, H. (1996). The role of loneliness and social support in adjustment to loss: A test of attachment theory versus stress theory. *Journal of Personality and Social Psychology, 70,* 1241–1249.

STRYKER, S. (1984). Identity theory: Developments and extensions. In *Self and social structure. Conference on self and identity.* Symposium conducted at the meeting of the British Psychological Society, University College, Cardiff, Wales.

STUART, R. B. (1978). *Act thin, stay thin.* New York: Norton.

STUNKARD, A. J. (1959). Obesity and the denial of hunger. *Psychosomatic Medicine, 21,* 281–289.

STUNKARD, A. J., FOCH, T. T., & HRUBEC, Z. (1985). A twin study of human obesity. *JAMA, 256,* 52–54.

STUNKARD, A. J., SORENSON, T. I. A., HANIS, C., TEASDALE, T. W., CHAKRABORTY, R., SCHULL, W. J., & SCHULSINGER, E. (1985). An adoption study of human obesity. *New England Journal of Medicine, 314,* 193–198.

STURUP, G. K. (1960). Sex offenses: The Scandinavian experience. *Law and Contemporary Problems, 25,* 361–365.

STURUP, G. K. (1968). Treatment of sexual offenders in Herstedvester, Denmark: The rapist. *Acta Psychiatrica Scandinavica, 44*(Suppl. 204).

SUEDFELD, P. (1975). The benefits of boredom: Sensory deprivation reconsidered. *American Scientist, 63,* 60–69.

SUEDFELD, P., & KRISTELLER, J. L. (1982). Stimulus reduction as a technique in health psychology. *Health Psychology, 1,* 337–357.

SUGA, A., HIRANO, T., KAGEYAMA, H., KASHIBA, M., OKA, J., OSAKA, T., NAMBA, Y., TSUJI, M., MIURA, M., ADACHI, M., & INOUE, S. (1999). Rapid increases in circulating leptin in ventromedial hypothalamus-lesioned rats. *Diabetes, 48,* 2034–2044.

SUH, E., DIENER, E., OISHI, S., & TRIANDIS, H. C. (1998). The shifting basis of life satisfaction judgments across cultures: Emotions versus norms. *Journal of Personality and Social Psychology, 74,* 482–493.

SULLOWAY, F. J. (1996). *Born to rebel: Birth order, family dynamics and creative lives.* New York: Pantheon Books.

SVEBAK, S., & MURGATROYD, S. (1985). Metamotivational dominance: A multimethod validation of reversal theory constructs. *Personality and Social Psychology, 48,* 107–116.

SWAAB, D. F., & FLIERS, E. A. (1985). A sexually dimorphic nucleus in the human brain. *Science, 228,* 1112–1115.

SWANN, W. B. (1996). *Self-traps: The elusive quest for higher self-esteem.* New York: W. H. Freeman.

SWANN, W. B., JR. (1983). Self-verification: Bringing social reality into harmony with the self. In J. Suls & A. G. Greenwals (Eds.), *Social psychological perspectives on the self* (Vol. 2, pp. 33–66). Hillsdale, NJ: Erlbaum.

SWEENEY, P., ANDERSON, K., & BAILEY, S. (1986). Attributional style in depression: A meta-analytic review. *Journal of Personality and Social Psychology, 50,* 974–991.

SWINSON, R. P., & EAVES, D. (1978). *Alcoholism and addiction.* Estover, Plymouth, England: MacDonald & Evans.

SWITZKY, H. N., & HAYWOOD, H. C. (1974). Motivational orientation and the relative efficacy of self-monitored and externally imposed reinforcement systems in children. *Journal of Personality and Social Psychology, 30,* 360–366.

SYMONS, D. (1979). *The evolution of human sexuality.* New York: Oxford.

TAGGART, P., & CARRUTHERS, M. E. (1971). Endogenous hyperlipidaemia induced by emotional stress of race driving. *Lancet, 1,* 363–366.

TALLMAN, J. F., PAUL, S. M., SKOLNICK, P., & GALLAGER, D. W. (1980). Receptors for the age of anxiety: Pharmacology of the benzodiazepines. *Science, 207,* 274–281.

TANGNEY, J. P., BURGGRAF, S. A., & WAGNER, P. E. (1995). Shame-proneness, guilt-proneness, and psychological symptoms. In J. P. Tangney & K. W. Fischer (Eds.), *Self-conscious emotions: The psychology of shame, guilt, embarrassment, and pride* (pp. 343–367). New York: Guilford Press.

TANGNEY, J. P., MILLER, R. S., FLICKER, L., & BARLOW, D. H. (1996). Are shame, guilt, and embarrassment distinct emotions? *Journal of Personality and Social Psychology, 70,* 1256–1269.

TARLER-BENLOLO, L. (1978). The role of relaxation in biofeedback training: A critical review of the literature. *Psychological Bulletin, 85,* 727–755.

TARTER, R. E. (1988). Are there inherited behavior traits that predispose to substance abuse? *Journal of Consulting and Clinical Psychology, 56,* 189–196.

TARTER, R. E., MOSS, H. B., & VANYUKOV, M. M. (1995). Behavior genetic perspective of alcoholism etiology. In H. Begleiter & B. Kissin (Eds.), *Alcohol and alcoholism* (Vol. 1, pp. 294–326). New York: Oxford University Press.

TAUB, J. M., HAWKINS, D. R., & VAN DE CASTLE, R. L. (1978). Personality characteristics associated with sustained variations in the adult human sleep/wakefulness rhythm. *Waking and Sleeping, 2*(1), 7–15.

TAVRIS, C. (1989). *Anger: The misunderstood emotion.* New York: Simon & Schuster.

TAVRIS, C. (1992). *The mismeasure of woman.* New York: Simon & Schuster.

TAVRIS, C., & WADE, C. (1984). *The longest war: Sex differences in perspective* (2nd ed.). San Diego: Harcourt Brace Jovanovich.

TAYLOR, C. W. (1972). Can organizations be creative too? In C. W. Taylor (Ed.), *Climate for creativity* (pp. 1–15). New York: Pergamon Press.

TAYLOR, J., & CAREY, G. (1998). Antisocial behavior, substance use, and somatization in families of adolescent drug abusers and adolescent controls. *American Journal of Drug and Alcohol Abuse, 24,* 635–646.

TAYLOR, S. E. (1989). *Positive illusions: Creative self-deception and the healthy mind.* New York: Basic Books.

TAYLOR, S. E. (1990). Health psychology: The science and the field. *American Psychologist, 45,* 40–50.

TAYLOR, S. E., KEMENY, M. E., ASPINWALL, L. G., SCHNEIDER, S. G., RODRIGUEZ, R., & HERBERT, M. (1992). Optimism, coping, psychological distress, and high-risk sexual behavior among men at risk for acquired immunodeficiency syndrome (AIDS). *Journal of Personality and Social Psychology, 63,* 460–473.

TAYLOR, S. E., KEMENY, M. E., REED, G. M., BOWER, J. E., & GRUENEWALD, T. L. (2000). Psychological resources, positive illusions, and health. *American Psychologist, 55,* 99–109.

TAYLOR, S. E., PHAM, L. B., RIVKIN, I. D. & ARMOR, D. A. (1998). Harnessing the imagination: Mental simulation, self-regulation, and coping. *American Psychologist, 53,* 429–439.

TAYLOR, S. E., & SCHNEIDER, S. K. (1989). Coping and the simulation of events. *Social Cognition, 7,* 174–194.

TAYLOR, S. P. (1967). Aggressive behavior and physiological arousal as a function of provocation and the tendency to inhibit aggression. *Journal of Personality, 35,* 297–310.

TAYLOR, S. P., & PISANO, R. (1971). Physical aggression as a function of frustration and physical attack. *Journal of Social Psychology, 84,* 261–267.

TEDESCHI, J. T., & FELSON, R. B. (1994). *Violence, aggression and coercive action.* Washington, DC: American Psychological Association.

TEITELBAUM, P. (1961). Disturbances in feeding and drinking behavior after hypothalamic lesions. In M. R. Jones (Ed.), *Nebraska Symposium on Motivation* (Vol. 9, pp. 39–68). Lincoln: University of Nebraska Press.

TELLEGEN, A., LYKKEN, D. T., BOUCHARD, T. J., WILCOX, K. J., JR., WILCOX, K. J., SEGAL, N. L. & RICH, S. (1998). Personality similarity in twins reared apart and together. *Journal of Personality and Social Psychology, 54,* 1031–1039.

TERRACE, H. S. (1969). Extinction of a discriminative operant following discrimination learning with and without errors. *Journal of the Experimental Analysis of Behavior, 12,* 571–582.

TERRY, D. J., & HYNES, G. J. (1998). Adjustment to a low-control situation: Reexamining the role of coping responses. *Journal of Personality and Social Psychology, 74,* 1078–1092.

TESSER, A., & PAULHUS, D. L. (1976). Toward a causal model of love. *Journal of Personality and Social Psychology, 34,* 1095–1105.

THARP, G. D. (1975). The role of glucocorticoids in exercise. *Medicine and Science in Sports, 7,* 6–11.

THOMAS, A., CHESS, S., & BIRCH, H. G. (1970, August). The origins of personality. *Scientific American, 223,* 102–109.

THOMPSON, R. A. (1990). Emotion and self-regulation. In *Nebraska Symposium on Motivation 1988: Socioemotional development* (Vol. 36, pp. 367–467). Lincoln: University of Nebraska Press.

THORNDIKE, E. L. (1913). *Educational psychology: The psychology of learning* (Vol. 2). New York: Teachers College Press.

TIGER, L. (1979). *Optimism: The biology of hope.* New York: Simon & Schuster.

TIGER, L. (1985). *Optimism: The biology of hope* (2nd ed.). New York: Kodansha.

TIGER, L. (1999). Hope springs internal. *Social Research, 66,* 611–617.

TILLEY, A. J. (1985). Recovery sleep at different times of the night following loss of the last four hours of sleep. *Sleep, 8,* 129–136.

TILLICH, P. (1965). The right to hope. *The University of Chicago Magazine, 58,* 16–22.

TOCH, H. (1969). *Violent men.* Chicago: Aldine.

TOCH, H. (1993). *Violent men: A psychological inquiry into the psychology of violence.* Washington, DC: American Psychological Association.

TOLMAN, E. C. (1932). *Purposive behavior in animals and men.* New York: Appleton-Century-Crofts.

TOLMAN, E. C. (1948). Cognitive maps in rats and men. *Psychological Review, 56,* 144–155.

TOMAKA, J., & BLASCOVICH, J. (1994). Effects of justice beliefs on cognitive appraisal of, and subjective, physiological, and behavioral responses to, potential stress. *Journal of Personality and Social Psychology, 67,* 732–740.

TOMPOROWSKI, P. D., & ELLIS, N. R. (1986). Effects of exercise on cognitive processes: A review. *Psychological Bulletin, 99,* 338–346.

TOOBY, J., & COSMIDES, L. (1992). The psychological foundations of culture. In J. H. Barkow, L. Cosmides, & J. Tooby (Eds.), *The adapted mind: Evolutionary psychology and the generation of culture* (pp. 19–136). New York: Oxford University Press.

TOOBY, J., & COSMIDES, L. (1996). Friendship and the banker's paradox: Other pathways to the evolution of adaptations for altruism. *Proceeding of the British Academy, 88,* 119–143.

TOOBY, J., & DEVORE, I. (1987). The reconstruction of hominid behavioral evolution through strategic modeling. In W. G. Kinzey (Ed.), *The evolution of human behavior* (pp. 183–237). New York: State University of New York.

TORRENCE, E. P. (1965). *Rewarding creative behavior.* Englewood Cliffs, NJ: Prentice-Hall.

TRACY, R. L., & TRACY, L. N. (1974). Reports of mental activity from sleep stages 2 and 4. *Perceptual and Motor Skills, 38,* 647–648.

TRAPNELL, P. D., & CAMPBELL, J. D. (1999). Private self-consciousness and the five-factor model of personality: Distinguishing rumination from reflection. *Journal of Personality and Social Psychology, 76,* 284–304.

TRAVIS, J. (1999). Marijuana mimic reveals brain role (tetrahydrocannabinol combines to same brain receptors as lipid molocules anandamide). (Brief article). *Science News, 155,* 215.

TROLLINGER, L. M. (1979). *A study of the biographical and personality factors of creative women in music.* Unpublished doctoral dissertation, Temple University, Philadelphia, PA.

TSUDA, A., & HIRAI, H. (1975). Effects of the amount of required coping response tasks on gastrointestinal lesions in rats. *Japanese Psychological Research, 17,* 119–132.

TYLER, L. E. (1978). *Individuality.* San Francisco: Jossey-Bass.

UCHINO, B. N., CACIOPPO, J. T., & KIECOLT-GLASER, J. K. (1996). The relationship between social support and physiological processes: A review with emphasis on underlying mechanisms and implications for health. *Psychological Health, 119,* 488–531.

UTMAN, C. H. (1997). Performance effects of motivational state: A meta-analysis. *Personality and Social Psychology Review, 1,* 170–182

VAILLANT, G. E. (1983). *The natural history of alcoholism.* Cambridge: Harvard University Press.

VAILLANT, G. L. (1977). *Adaptation to life.* New York: Wiley.

VAN DYKE, C., & BYCK, R. (1982). Cocaine. *Scientific American, 246,* 128–141.

VAUX, A. (1992). Assessment of social support. In H. O. F. Veiel & U. Baumann (Eds.), *The meaning and measurement of social support* (pp. 193–216). New York: Hemisphere.

VEIEL, H. O. F., & BAUMANN, U. (1992). The many meanings of social support. In H. O. F. Veiel & U. Baumann (Eds.), *The meaning and measurement of social support* (pp. 1–9). New York: Hemisphere.

VERNIKOS-DANELLIS, J., & HEYBACH, J. P. (1980). Psychophysiologic mechanisms regulating the hypothalamic-pituitary-adrenal response to stress. In H. Selye (Ed.), *Selye's guide to stress research* (Vol. 1, pp. 206–251). New York: Van Nostrand Reinhold.

VEZINA, P., KALIVAS, P. W., & STEWART, J. (1987). Sensitization occurs to the locomotor effects of morphine and the specific m opioid receptor agonist DAGO, administered repeatedly to the ventral tegmental area but not to the nucleus accumbens. *Brain Research, 417,* 51–58.

VISINTAINER, M., VOLPICELLI, J., & SELIGMAN, M. (1982). Tumor rejection in rats after inescapable and escapable shock. *Science, 216,* 437–439.

VITZ, P. (1966a). Affect as a function of stimulus variation. *Journal of Experimental Psychology, 71,* 74–79.

VITZ, P. (1966b). Preference for different amounts of stimulus complexity. *Behavioral Science, 11,* 105–114.

VOGEL, G. W. (1975). A review of REM sleep deprivation. *Archives of General Psychiatry, 32,* 749–761.

VOGEL, G. W. (1978). Sleep-onset mentation. In A. M. Arkin, J. S. Antrobus, & S. J. Ellman (Eds.), *The mind in sleep: Psychology and psychophysiology* (pp. 97–108). Hillsdale, NJ: Erlbaum.

VOGEL, G. W. (1979). A motivational theory of REM sleep. In R. Drucker-Colin, M. Shkurovich, & M. B. Sterman (Eds.), *The functions of sleep* (pp. 233–250). New York: Academic Press.

VOLPICELLI, J. R. (1987). Uncontrollable events and alcohol drinking. *British Journal of Addiction, 82,* 385–396.

VOYER, D., VOYER, S., & BRYDEN, M. P. (1995). Magnitude of sex differences in spatial abilities: A meta-analysis and consideration of critical variables. *Psychological Bulletin, 117,* 250–270.

WALKER, E. L. (1974, September). *Psychological complexity and aesthetics, or the hedgehog as an aesthetic mediator (HAM).* Invited address to American Psychological Association convention, New Orleans.

WALKER, L. E. A. (1989). Psychology and violence against women. *American Psychologist, 44,* 695–702.

WALLACE, R. K., & BENSON, H. (1972, February). The physiology of meditation. *Scientific American,* pp. 84–90.

WALLACE, R. K., BENSON, H., & WILSON, A. F. (1971). A wakeful hypometabolic physiologic state. *American Journal of Physiology, 221,* 795–799.

WALSH, A. (1991). *The science of love and its effects on mind and body.* Amherst, NY: Prometheus Books.

WANNAMETHEE, G., & SHAPER, A. G. (1990). Weight changes in middle-aged British men: Implications for health. *European Journal of Clinical Nutrition, 44,* 133–142.

WARD, T. B., SMITH, S. M., & VAID, J. (Eds.). (1997). *Creative thoughts: An investigation of conceptual structures and processes.* Washington, DC: American Psychological Association.

WATERMAN, A. S. (1993). Two conceptions of happiness: Contrasts of personal expressiveness (eudaimonia) and hedonic enjoyment. *Journal of Personality and Social Psychology, 64,* 678–691.

WATSON, D., & CLARK, L. A. (1984). Negative affectivity: The disposition to experience aversive emotional states. *Psychological Bulletin, 96,* 465–490.

WATSON, D., WIESE, D., VAIDYA, J., & TELLEGEN, A. (1999). Two general activation systems of affect: Structural findings, evolutionary considerations, and psychobiological evidence. *Journal of Personality and Social Psychology, 76,* 820–838.

WATSON, J. B., & MORGAN, J. J. B. (1917). Emotional reactions and psychological experimentation. *American Journal of Psychology, 28,* 163–174.

WEBB, W. B. (1975). *Sleep: The gentle tyrant.* Englewood Cliffs, NJ: Prentice-Hall.

WEBB, W. B., & AGNEW, H. W., JR. (1975a). Are we chronically sleep deprived? *Bulletin of the Psychonomic Society, 6,* 47–48.

WEBB, W. B., & AGNEW, H. W., JR. (1975b). Sleep efficiency for sleep-wake cycles of varied length. *Psychophysiology, 12,* 637–641.

WEBB, W. B., & AGNEW, H. W., JR. (1977). Analysis of the sleep stages in sleep-wakefulness regimens of varied length. *Psychophysiology, 14,* 445–450.

WEBB, W. B., & LEVY, C. M. (1982). Age, sleep deprivation, and performance.

WEGNER, D. M. (1989). *White bears and other unwanted thoughts.* New York: Viking/Penguin.

WEGNER, D. M., & WHEATLEY, T. (1999). Apparent mental causation: Sources of experience of will. *American Psychologist, 54,* 480–491.

WEIL, A. (2000) *Eating well for optimum health.* New York: Knopf.

WEINER, B. (1995). *Judgments of responsibility.* New York: Guilford Press.

WEINER, B. (Ed.). (1972). *Attribution: Perceiving the causes of behavior.* Morristown, NJ: General Learning Press.

WEINER, B. (Ed.). (1974). *Achievement motivation and attribution theory.* Morristown, NJ: General Learning Press.

WEINER, B., FRIEZE, I., KUKLA, A., REED, L., REST, S., & ROSENBAUM, R. M. (1971). *Perceiving the causes of success and failure.* Morristown, NJ: General Learning Press.

WEISBUCH, M., BEAL, D., O'NEAL, E. C. (1999). How masculine ought I be? Men's masculinity and aggression. *Sex Roles: A Journal of Research, 40,* 583–589.

WEISS, J. M. (1968). Effects of coping responses on stress. *Journal of Comparative and Physiological Psychology, 65,* 251–260.

WEISS, J. M. (1970). Somatic effects of predictable and unpredictable shock. *Psychosomatic Medicine, 32,* 397–408.

WEISS, J. M. (1971a). Effects of coping behavior in different warning signal conditions on stress pathology in rats. *Journal of Comparative and Physiological Psychology, 77,* 1–13.

WEISS, J. M. (1971b). Effects of punishing the coping response (conflict) on stress pathology in rats. *Journal of Comparative and Physiological Psychology, 77,* 14–21.

WEISS, J. M., GLAZER, H. L., & POHORECKY, L. A. (1976). Coping behavior and neurochemical changes: An alternative explanation of the original "learned helplessness" experiments. In G. Serban & A. Kling (Eds.), *Animal models in human psychobiology* (pp. 141–173). New York: Plenum.

WEISS, J. M., GLAZER, H. L., POHORECKY, L. A., BRICK, J., & MILLER, N. E. (1975). Effects of chronic exposure to stressors on avoidance-escape behavior and on brain norepinephrine. *Psychosomatic Medicine, 37,* 522–534.

WEISS, M. (1958). Alcohol as a depressant of psychological conflict in rats. *Quarterly Journal of Studies on Alcohol, 19,* 226–237.

WEISSE, C. S. (1992). Depression and immunocompetence: A review of the literature. *Psychological Bulletin, 111,* 475–489.

WEISSMAN, M. M., LEAR, P. F., HOLZER, C. E., III, MEYERS, J. K., & TISCHLER, G. L. (1984). The epidemiology of depression: An update on sex differences in rates. *Journal of Affective Disorders, 7,* 179–188.

WENDER, P. H., KETY, S. S., ROSENTHAL, D., SCHULSINGER, F., ORTMANN, J., & LUNDE, I. (1986). Psychiatric disorders in the biological and adoptive families of adopted individuals with affective disorders. *Archives of General Psychiatry, 43,* 923–929.

WHALEN, R. E. (1976). Brain mechanisms controlling sexual behavior. In F. A. Beach (Ed.), *Human sexuality in four perspectives* (pp. 215–246). Baltimore: Johns Hopkins University Press.

WHITAM, F. L. (1977). The homosexual role. A reconsideration. *Journal of Sex Research, 13,* 1–11.

WHITAM, F. L., & MATHY, R. M. (1986). *Male homosexuality in four societies.* New York: Praeger.

WHITE, A., HANDLER, P., & SMITH, E. L. (1964). *Principles of biochemistry* (3rd ed.). New York: McGraw-Hill.

WHITE, J. (1982). *Rejection*. Reading, MA: Addison-Wesley.

WHITE, J. A., ISMAIL, A. H., & BOTTOMS, G. D. (1976). Effects of physical fitness on the adrenocortical response to exercise stress. *Medicine and Science in Sports, 8,* 113–118.

WHITE, N. M. (1996). Addictive drugs as reinforcers: multiple partial actions on memory systems. *Addiction, 91,* 921–927.

WHITE, N. M., & MACDONALD, R. J. (in press). Multiple parallel memory systems in the brain of the rat. *Neurobiology of Learning and Memory.*

WHITE, R. W. (1959). Motivation reconsidered: The concept of competence. *Psychological Review, 66,* 297–333.

WHITE, T., & DEPUE, R. A. (1999). Differential association of traits of fear and anxiety with norepinephrine- and dark induced pupil reactivity. *Journal of Personality and Social Psychology, 77,* 863–877.

WICKENS, C. D. (1984). Processing resources in attention. In R. Parasuraman & D. R. Davies (Eds.), *Varieties of attention* (pp. 63–102). New York: Academic Press.

WIDOM, C. S. (1989a). Does violence beget violence? A critical examination of the literature. *Psychological Bulletin, 106,* 3–28.

WIDOM, C. S. (1989b). The cycle of violence. *Science, 224,* 160–166.

WIEBE, D. J. (1989). Hardiness and stress moderation: A test of proposed mechanisms. *Journal of Personality and Social Psychology, 60,* 89–99.

WIKLER, A. (1980). *Opioid dependence*. New York: Plenum.

WILLIAMS, G. C., GROW, V. M., FREEDMAN, Z. R., RYAN, R. M., & DECI, E. L. (1996). Motivational predictors of weight loss and weight-loss maintenance. *Journal of Personality and Social Psychology, 70,* 115–126.

WILLIAMS, R. H. (1960). Hypoglycemosis. In R. H. Williams (Ed.), *Diabetes*. New York: Hoeber.

WILLS, T. (1981). Downward comparison principles in social psychology. *Psychological Bulletin, 90,* 245–271.

WILLS, T. (1991). Similarity and downward comparison. In J. Suls & T. Wills (Eds.), *Social comparison: Contemporary theory and research* (pp. 51–78). Hillsdale, NJ: Erlbaum.

WILLS, T. A., DuHAMEL, K., & VACCARO, D. (1995). Activity and mood temperament as predictors of adolescent substance use: Test of a self-regulation mediational model. *Journal of Personality and Social Psychology, 68,* 901–916.

WILLS, T. A., VACCARO, D., & McNAMARA, G. (1992). The role of life events, family support, and competence in adolescent substance use: A test of vulnerability and protective factors. *American Journal of Community Psychology, 20,* 349–374.

WILLS, T. A., VACCARO, D., & McNAMARA, G. (1994). Novelty seeking, risk taking, and related constructs as predictors of adolescent substance use: An application of Cloninger's theory. *Journal of Substance Abuse, 6,* 1–20.

WILM, E. C. (1925). *The theories of instinct: A study of the history of psychology*. New Haven, CT: Yale University Press.

WILSON, D. S. (1994). Adaptive genetic variation and human evolutionary psychology. *Ethology and Sociobiology, 15,* 219–235.

WILSON, G. T. (1981). The effect of alcohol on human sexual behavior. In N. Mello (Ed.), *Advances in substance abuse: Behavioral and biological research*. Greenwich, CT: JAI Press.

WILSON, J. D., GEORGE, F. W., GRIFFIN, J. E. et al. (1981). The hormonal control of sexual development. *Science, 211,* 1285–1294.

WILSON, M. A., & MCNAUGHTON, B. L. (1994). Reactivation of hippocampal ensemble memories during sleep. *Science, 265,* 676–679.

WILSON, T. D., & LINVILLE, P. W. (1985). Improving the performance of college freshmen with attributional techniques. *Journal of Personality and Social Psychology, 49,* 287–293.

WILSON, T. D., & SCHOOLER, J. W. (1991). Thinking too much: Introspection can reduce the quality of preferences and decisions. *Journal of Personality and Social Psychology, 60,* 181–192.

WINOKUR, J. (1987). *The portable curmudgeon*. New York: New American library.

WINTERBOTTOM, M. R. (1958). The relation of need for achievement to learning experiences in independence and mastery. In J. W. Atkinson (Ed.), *Motives in fantasy, action, and society* (pp. 453–478). Princeton, NJ: Van Nostrand.

WISE, R. A. (1988). The neurobiology of craving: Implications for the understanding and treatment of addiction. *Journal of Abnormal Psychology, 97,* 118–132.

WOLFGANG, M. E., & STROHM, R. B. (1956). The relationship between alcohol and criminal homicide. *Quarterly Journal of Studies on Alcohol, 17,* 108–123.

WOLPE, J. (1969). *The practice of behavior theory*. New York: Pergamon Press.

WONG, W. P. T., & WEINER, B. (1981). When people ask "why" questions, and the heuristics of attributional search. *Journal of Personality and Social Psychology, 40,* 650–663.

WONNACOTT, S., & LUNT, G. G. (1993). *Neurochemisry of drug dependence*. London: Portland Press.

WOOD, J. V., SALTZBERG, J. A., NEALE, J. M., STONE, A. A., & RACHMIEL, T. B. (1990). Self-focused attention, coping responses, and distressed mood in everyday life. *Journal of Personality and Social Psychology, 58,* 1027–1036.

WOODS, J. H., KATZ, J. L., & WINGER, G. (1987). Abuse liability of benzodiazepines. *Pharmacological Review, 39,* 251–413.

WOOLEY, S. C., & GARNER, D. M. (1991). Obesity treatment: The high cost of false hope. *Journal of the American Dietetic Association, 91,* 1248–1251.

WORICK, W. W., & SCHALLER, W. E. (1977). *Alcohol, tobacco, and drugs: Their uses and abuses.* Englewood Cliffs, NJ: Prentice-Hall.

WRIGHT, R. A., TOI, M., & BREHM, J. W. (1984). Difficulty and interpersonal attraction. *Motivation and Emotion, 8,* 327–341.

WURTMAN, R. J. (1982). Nutrients that modify brain function. *Scientific American, 246,* 50–59.

YATES, W. R., PERRY, P., & MURRAY, S. (1992). Aggression and hostility in anabolic steroid users. *Biological Psychiatry, 31,* 1232–1234.

YOSHINOBU, L. R. (1989). *Construct validation of the Hope Scale: Agency and pathways components.* University of Kansas, Lawrence.

YOUNG, J. P. R., FENTON, G. W., & LADER, M. H. (1971). Inheritance of neurotic traits: A twin study of the Middlesex Hospital Questionnaire. *British Journal of Psychiatry, 119,* 393–398.

YOUNG, J. S. (1988). *Steve Jobs: The journey is the reward.* Glenview, IL: Scott, Foresman.

ZAHN-WAXLER, C., & KOCHANSKA, G. (1990). The origins of guilt. In *Nebraska Symposium on Motivation (1988): Socioemotional Development* (Vol. 36, pp. 183–258). Lincoln: University of Nebraska Press.

ZEKI, S. (1992, September). The visual image in mind and brain. *Scientific American,* pp. 69–76.

ZENTALL, S. S., & ZENTALL, T. R. (1983). Optimal stimulation: A model of disordered activity and performance in normal and deviant children. *Psychological Bulletin, 94,* 446–471.

ZILBERGELD, B. (1978). *Mate sexuality: A guide to sexual fulfillment.* Boston: Little Brown.

ZILLMAN, D., KATCHER, A. H., & MILAVSKY, B. (1972). Excitation transfer from physical exercise to subsequent aggressive behavior. *Journal of Experimental Social Psychology, 8,* 247–259.

ZIMBARDO, P. G. (1969). The human choice: Individuation, reason, and order versus deindividuation, impulse, and chaos. In W. J. Arnold & D. Levine (Eds.), *Nebraska Symposium on Motivation* (Vol. 17, pp. 237–307). Lincoln: University of Nebraska Press.

ZIMBARDO, P. G. (1972). Pathology of imprisonment. *Society, 9,* 4–8.

ZUCKERMAN, H. (1974). The scientific elite: Nobel laureates' mutual influence. In R. S. Albert (Ed.), *Genius and eminence* (pp. 171–186). New York: Pergamon Press.

ZUCKERMAN, M. (1978a, February). The search for high sensation. *Psychology Today,* pp. 38–46; 96–99.

ZUCKERMAN, M. (1978b). Sensation seeking. In H. London & J. E. Exner, Jr. (Eds.), *Dimensions of personality* (pp. 487–559). New York: Wiley.

ZUCKERMAN, M. (1979). *Sensation seeking: Beyond the optimal level of arousal.* Hillsdale, NJ: Erlbaum.

ZUCKERMAN, M. (1983). *Biological bases of sensation seeking, impulsivity, and anxiety.* Hillsdale, NJ: Erlbaum.

ZUCKERMAN, M. (1993). P-impulsive sensation seeking and its behavioral, psychophysiological, biochemical correlates. *Neuropsychobiology, 28,* 30–36.

ZUCKERMAN, M. (1994). *Behavioral expressions and biosocial bases of sensation seeking.* Cambridge: Cambridge University Press.

ZUCKERMAN, M. (2000). Are you a risk taker. *Psychology Today, 33,* 52–58.

Author Index

Subject Index

Photo Credits

Chapter 1: 1, © Jeff Greenberg / PhotoEdit; **10,** Mary Evans Pictures, Bettmann / CORBIS; **11,** Photo Researchers, Inc.; **18,** Christopher Johnson / Stock, Boston Inc.

Chapter 2: 26, Pamela R. Schuyler / Stock, Boston Inc.; **44,** Bettmann / CORBIS; **52,** Roberto Soncin Gerometta / Photo 20-20

Chapter 3: 56, Michael Newman / PhotoEdit; **60,** © Pierre Boulat / Woodfin Camp / PictureQuest; **77,** Michael Newman / PhotoEdit

Chapter 4: 84, Michael Newman / PhotoEdit; **90,** Elizabeth Crews / Stock, Boston Inc.

Chapter 5: 114, David Young-Wolff / PhotoEdit; **131,** Rudi Von Briel / PhotoEdit; **137,** Arthur Grace / Stock, Boston Inc.

Chapter 6: 146, © Darren Modricker / CORBIS; **159,** Michael Weisbrot / Stock, Boston Inc.; **165,** kofoto

Chapter 7: 175, © Michael Newman / PhotoEdit; **189,** UPI-Bettmann / CORBIS; **198,** Bachmann / PhotoEdit

Chapter 8: 208, © Michael Newman / PhotoEdit; **211,** Copyright 1965 by Stanley Milgram, from the film OBEDIENCE, distributed by the Pennsylvania State University, PCR. By permission of Mrs. Alexandra Milgram; **221,** Shelley Boyd / PhotoEdit

Chapter 9: 237, © David Young-Wolff / PhotoEdit; **256,** D. Falconer / PhotoLink / PhotoDisc

Chapter 10: 271, Jean-Claude Lejeune / Stock, Boston Inc.; **288,** Suza Scalora / PhotoDisc; **297,** Robert Brenner / PhotoEdit

Chapter 11: 303, Myrleen Freguson / PhotoEdit; **318,** Jeff Greenberg / PhotoEdit; **327,** Tony Freeman / PhotoEdit

Chapter 12: 333, © Jeff Greenberg / PhotoDisc; **348,** Jeff Greenberg / PhotoEdit; **353,** Esbin-Anderson / Photo 20-20

Chapter 13: 359, Christopher Brown / Stock, Boston Inc.; **361,** Dennis MacDonald / PhotoEdit; **372,** Peter Southwick / Stock, Boston Inc.; **378,** Robert E. Franken

Chapter 14: 383, © Michael Newman / PhotoEdit / PictureQuest; **404,** © Gaetano / CORBIS; **407,** Michael Newman / PhotoEdit

SHORT BIKE RIDES® SERIES

Short Bike Rides®

in Central and Western Massachusetts

Third Edition

**BY
HOWARD STONE**

The Globe Pequot Press

Guilford, Connecticut

917.44

Cover design: Saralyn D'Amato-Twomey
Cover photograph: West Stock
Map design: Erin Hernandez
Interior photos provided by the author.

Library of Congress Cataloging-in-Publication Data

Stone, Howard, 1947–
    Short bike rides in central and western Massachusetts / by
Howard Stone. — 3rd ed.
        p.   cm.   — (Short bike rides series)
    ISBN 0-7627-0483-7
    1. Bicycle touring—Massachusetts Guidebooks. 2. Mas-
sachusetts Guidebooks. I. Title. II. Series.
GV1045.5.M4S768   2000
796.6'4'09744—dc21   99–37030
                                                         CIP

Manufactured in the United States of America
Third Edition/First Printing

To the memory of Warren Hinterland,
who inspired me.

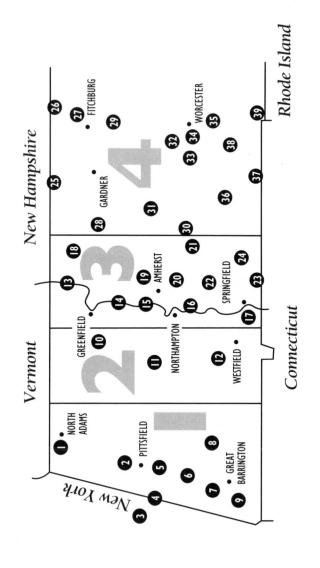

Contents

Acknowledgments

This book could never have come to fruition without a lot of help. My wife, Bernice, provided continual encouragement, support, and late-night snacks. Dominique Coulombe, my supervisor, allowed me to work flexible hours so that I could take advantage of the daylight to research the rides. Jeanne LaFazia helped me interpret the intricacies of the laws of Massachusetts. Carla Kerber helped me type the manuscript. Andy Nosal, owner of The Map Center in Providence, told me about Hot Dog Annie's in Leicester. Dozens of local residents told me about hidden back roads and interesting places to see. I would also like to thank Kevin and Anita Clifford, Alan Moretsky, and Leesa Mann for putting me up overnight at various times.

Some of the photographs in the first edition were supplied by the Massachusetts Department of Commerce and Development, Division of Tourism, which allowed me to look through its photo collection and choose scenes that would best capture the various landscapes of the state. In this edition I have used one of the photographs again.

Preface to the Third Edition

The third edition of *Short Bike Rides in Central and Western Massachusetts* covers the same area as the second edition. The region east of Worcester and Fitchburg is covered in the companion volume *Short Bike Rides in Eastern Massachusetts*. The material follows the same format as the earlier work, with an introductory description, map, and point-to-point directions for each ride. The directions are more concise, but with no loss of clarity, and I've shown more connecting roads on the maps. Many of the rides have been modified slightly to improve scenery and safety, or to avoid badly deteriorated roads. I rerouted most of the Agawam–Suffield–Southwick ride from a counterclockwise to a clockwise direction and routed the South of Worcester ride through the lovely town centers of West Millbury and Sutton.

Introduction

This book is a guide to bicycling in Massachusetts west of Worcester and Fitchburg. The region, along with the sections of neighboring states just over the state line, offers ideal cycling. Massachusetts is blessed with an impressive network of thousands of back roads, most of them paved but not heavily traveled. Beyond the built-up metropolitan areas, which compose a very small percentage of the state, the landscape is rural enough to give the cyclist a sense of remoteness and serenity, and yet the nearest town, village, or grocery store is never more than a few miles away. The terrain is refreshingly varied for a relatively small state.

The Berkshires provide a perfect blend of scenic and cultural wealth—wooded mountains and soft green valleys dotted with lakes, estates, museums, and centers for the performing arts. The hill town region is the most rural part of the state, with rugged hills, deep valleys, and pristine small towns and villages. Central Massachusetts is an inspiring region of broad sweeps of farmland spreading along rugged hills and ridgetops, eventually sloping down to the broad valley of the Connecticut River.

Bicycling is an ideal way to appreciate the New England landscape's unique intimacy, which is not found in most other parts of the United States. The back roads turn constantly as they hug the minute contours of the land, forcing your orientation down to a small scale. Every bend and dip in the road may yield a surprise—a weathered barn, a pond, a stream, a little dam or falls, a hulking old mill right out of the Industrial Revolution, a ragged stone wall, or a pasture with grazing cattle or horses. Most of the smaller town centers are architectural gems, with the traditional stately white church and village green flanked by the town hall, a handsome brick or stone library, and graceful old wooden homes.

Geography of the Region

Western and central Massachusetts form a rectangle that measures about 80 miles from east to west and about 50 miles from north to south. In general, the area is rolling or hilly except for the river valleys. As a result, biking in much of the region involves some effort. Most of the rides traverse at least one or two hills, sometimes steep or long enough that you'll want to walk them. To compensate, however, only a few hills are long enough to be really discouraging, and for every uphill climb there's a corresponding descent. The large majority of the hills you'll encounter are less than half a mile long, the steepest portion limited to a couple of hundred yards or less.

Culturally, Massachusetts has a long and proud history, beginning with the Pilgrim settlement in Plymouth in 1620. The first armed encounters of the Revolutionary War occurred a century and a half later in Concord and Lexington. The deep and sheltered harbors along the coast spawned thriving seaports, fisheries, and maritime commerce in Colonial times and into the nineteenth century. The Industrial Revolution got a head start in Massachusetts when Lowell and Holyoke, two of the first planned industrial cities in the country, evolved before the Civil War. In later years, culminating between the end of the Civil War and the turn of the twentieth century, hundreds of mills were built along the swift-flowing Housatonic, Westfield, Quaboag, and numerous other rivers, employing thousands of immigrants from Europe and Quebec.

Today, hundreds of smaller towns and villages in Massachusetts make up some of the state's most appealing and architecturally fascinating hallmarks. As you bike through a town, try to notice each building along the green. First you'll see the graceful white church, usually built before 1850, often on a little rise, standing proudly above the rest of the town. Next look for the town hall, usually a handsome, white-pillared, colonial-style building or an ornate wooden or stone Victorian one. Near the town hall you'll usually find the library, a gracious brick or stone building dating from the turn of the twentieth century or the two decades before it. The small-town library is almost always recognizable, generally built to appear dignified yet inviting, with wide steps, a portico framing the front door, and often a dome or rounded roof. Another building worth noticing is the schoolhouse. In the smaller towns, the schools are generally handsome old wooden or brick buildings, sometimes with graceful bell towers or cupolas.

Mill towns at first may look depressing, but there is always some architectural beauty to be found. The mills themselves are often fascinating old Victorian structures, forbidding but ornamented with cornices and clock towers. Next to the mill is usually a small millpond with a little dam or falls. Many mill towns have orderly rows of identical two- or three-story wooden houses, originally built for the workers during the late 1800s. Unfortunately, fire, neglect, and vandalism claim several mills each year, but a growing consciousness has arisen about preserving and maintaining these unique and impressive buildings. Many old mills have been recycled into apartments, condominiums, or offices.

Geographically, the region covered in this book is divided into four fairly distinct areas. The Berkshires, in Berkshire County at the western edge of the state, provide surprisingly enjoyable bicycling. Although this region contains the highest mountains in Massachusetts, most of the roads lie in the fertile valleys between them. In general, the grades tend to be long and steady rather than discouragingly steep. Most of the elevations are larger than hills but smaller than mountains, giving the region a gentle and intimate beauty rather than Colorado-like grandeur. Communities vary widely, from gracious college towns (Williamstown) to Victorian mill towns (North Adams, Adams, Lee) to elegant cultural centers (Lenox, Stockbridge) to numerous unspoiled villages. A unique feature of the Berkshires is its concentration of cultural attractions like museums, estates, former Shaker communities, music festivals, and centers for the performing arts, all in strikingly beautiful surroundings. Many writers, including Herman Melville, Nathaniel Hawthorne, and William Cullen Bryant, came to the Berkshires in the mid-1800s, seeking peace and inspiration. Their lyrical descriptions of the region's beauty inspired industrialists, financial barons, and successful political figures to build summer mansions and estates (which they called "cottages") during the gilded age of the 1880s and 1890s, turning the Stockbridge-Lenox area into an inland Newport. In the 1930s three well-known performing arts festivals—the Tanglewood Music Festival, the Jacob's Pillow Dance Festival, and the Berkshire Theater Festival—transformed the Berkshires into a cultural mecca, and dozens more performing arts centers have become established in more recent years.

The area between the western edge of the Connecticut River Valley and Berkshire County comprises the hill towns. This region is the most undeveloped and sparsely populated portion of the state. It was also the last part of Massachusetts to be settled, because the steep slopes and rocky soil were unsuitable for farming and the rugged terrain made transportation difficult. Two-wheeled transportation is equally difficult—you can almost always count on a tough climb between towns. Most of the towns are lovely, with graceful white churches, attractive libraries, and inviting country stores. Scenic highlights of the region include the Bridge of Flowers in Shelburne Falls, a former trolley bridge that is now a pedestrian walkway lined with brilliant floral displays, and Chesterfield Gorge, a rockbound canyon carved by the Westfield River. The homestead of poet William Cullen Bryant in Cummington is the best-known historic site in the hill towns.

The Pioneer Valley, also called the Connecticut River Valley, provides the easiest bicycling in this book until you reach the hills at the valley's eastern edge. In the southern third of the state, the Connecticut River is heavily urbanized by Springfield, Chicopee, and Holyoke; but north of Holyoke it is delightfully rural as the broad, gracefully curving river winds between rich farms and tobacco fields, with the mountains rising dramatically at the edge of the valley several miles away. At the center of the region is a cluster of five colleges, three of them in Amherst. Ten miles south of the Vermont border is Old Deerfield, a restored community of elegant old homes. East of Amherst the landscape becomes very

Doane Falls, Royalston

rural and very hilly—challenging but exciting to bicycle through. At the eastern edge of the region is the immense Quabbin Reservoir, by far the largest lake in the state. As in much of rural Massachusetts, the towns in the Pioneer Valley are for the most part unspoiled gems. Some of the villages in the northern half of the state, such as New Salem, Wendell, and Warwick, seem unchanged from a hundred years ago except for cars in the driveways and pavement on the road.

Central Massachusetts covers the slice of state between the Quabbin Reservoir on the west and Worcester and Fitchburg on the east. This is one of the most rural and inspiringly beautiful parts of the state. The terrain is hilly and challenging for the cyclist, but the scenery more than makes up for it. The region is marked by an endless succession of hills and ridges, many crowned by broad, open farms that provide magnificent views. The Wachusett Reservoir, with its massive dam at the northern end in Clinton, is the second largest lake in the state. Almost without exception, the towns are graceful New England classics. The historic highlight of the region is Old Sturbridge Village, a superb reconstruction of a rural community from the early 1800s.

Massachusetts is fortunate to benefit from an active heritage of preserving its land and historic sites that began in the nineteenth century, before preservation was even considered in many other parts of the country. The state park system, run by the Department of Environmental Management, is admirable. A unique feature of the state park system is its responsibility for renovating old mills and factories, along with their adjacent waterways, into interpretive museums and visitors centers called Heritage State Parks. The names of two organizations, the Trustees of Reservations (TOR) and the Society for the Preservation of New England Antiquities (SPNEA), appear frequently in the descriptions of the rides. The first body is dedicated to acquiring and maintaining scenic areas, and it does the job admirably. TOR reservations are never shabby or shopworn, as so many other public areas are; instead, they are impeccably clean and well landscaped. Some of the finest natural areas in the state are TOR properties. The second body aims to acquire, preserve, and open to the public historic homes and mansions. Like TOR, it does a superb job. SPNEA properties, however, are open only during limited hours, usually afternoons in the summer. Largely a volunteer and member-supported organization, SPNEA simply does not have the funds to keep longer hours. In addition to these two bodies, dozens of other local historical societies and conservationist groups, including the Massachusetts Audubon Society, maintain historic houses and areas of green space.

One final geographic feature you'll encounter across the state is the drumlin, a small, sharp hill left behind by the glaciers. Most drumlins are elliptical like a football sliced lengthwise along the middle. They are usually less than a mile long, less than 200 feet high, and lie along a northwest-southeast or north-south axis, the direction of glacial flow. Clusters of drumlins are scattered across the state; one extensive drumlin region lies between Worcester and Springfield. In rural areas they transform the land into a rippling sea of rolling hills with broad pastures and orchards sweeping up and over them, providing some of the most inspiring and scenic bicycling in the state.

About the Rides

Ideally a bicycle ride should be a safe, scenic, relaxing, and an enjoyable experience that brings you into intimate contact with the landscape. In striving to achieve this goal, I've routed the rides along paved secondary and rural roads, avoiding main highways, larger cities, and dirt roads as much as possible. I've tried to make the routes as safe as possible. Hazards such as very bumpy roads or dead stops encountered while riding down a steep hill have been avoided whenever reasonable alternate routes exist. Dangerous spots are clearly indicated in the directions by a Caution warning. I've included scenic spots such as dams, falls, ponds, mill villages, or open vistas on the rides whenever possible.

Most of the rides have two options—a shorter one averaging about 15 miles long and a longer one that is usually between 25 and 30 miles long. All the longer rides are extensions of the shorter ones, with both options usually starting off in the same way. A few rides, generally in remote areas, have no shorter option, and several have three alternatives. All the rides make a loop or figure eight rather than backtracking along the same route. For each ride I include both a map and directions.

If you've never ridden any distance, the thought of riding 15 or, heaven forbid, 30 miles may sound intimidating or even impossible. I want to emphasize, however, that *anyone* in normal health can ride 30 miles and enjoy it if he or she gets mildly into shape first. You can accomplish this painlessly by riding at a leisurely pace for an hour several times a week for about three weeks. At a moderate pace, you'll ride about 10 miles per hour. If you think of the rides by the hour rather than the mile, the numbers are much less frightening.

To emphasize how easy bicycle riding is, most bike clubs have a 100-mile ride, called a century, each fall. Dozens of ordinary people try their first century without ever having done much biking, and finish it, and enjoy it! Sure, they're tired at the end, but they've accomplished the feat and loved it. (If you'd like to try one, the flattest and most popular century in the Northeast is held in southeastern Massachusetts on the Sunday after Labor Day, starting in Tiverton, Rhode Island—ask at any good bike shop for details.)

If you count short stops but not long ones, a 15-mile ride should take about two hours at a leisurely speed, a 20- to 25-mile ride about three hours, and a 30-mile ride about four hours. If you ride at a brisk pace, subtract an hour from these estimates.

A few of the rides in this book have short (half a mile or less) sections of dirt road. This was occasionally necessary when there was no simple alternate route, or to avoid making the directions needlessly complicated. If you come to a dirt road, get the feel of it first. If it's hard-packed, you can ride it without difficulty; but if it's soft, you should walk because it's easy to skid and fall unless you're on a mountain bike.

For every ride I've recommended a starting point, but you can start anywhere else along the route if it's more convenient. For some of the rides between Worcester and Springfield, you may want to start at the western edge of the ride if you're coming from the Springfield area, or at the eastern edge if you're coming from the Worcester area.

I have intentionally not listed the hours and fees of historic sites because they are subject to so much change, often from one year to the next. If it's a place you've heard of, it's probably open from 10:00 a.m. to 5:00 p.m., seven days a week. Unfortunately, many of the less frequently visited spots have limited hours—often only weekday afternoons during the summer, perhaps one afternoon during the weekend. A few places of historic or architectural interest are open only by appointment because of funding and staffing considerations. Most historic sites are maintained by voluntary contributions and effort, and it's simply impossible to keep them staffed more than a few hours a day or a few months a year. If you really want to visit a site, call beforehand and find out the hours.

Enjoying the Rides

You'll enjoy biking more if you add a few basic accessories to your bike and bring a few items with you.

• **Handlebar bag with transparent map pocket on top** It's always helpful to have some carrying capacity on your bike. Most handlebar bags are large enough to hold tools, a lunch, or even a light jacket. If you have a map or directions in your map pocket (or taped to the top of the bag), it's much easier to follow the route. You simply glance down to your handlebar bag instead of fishing map or directions out of your pocket and stopping to read them safely. You may also wish to get a small saddlebag that fits under your seat or a metal rack that fits above the rear wheel, to carry whatever doesn't fit in the handlebar bag.

Always carry things on your bike, not on your back. A knapsack raises your center of gravity and makes you more unstable; it also digs painfully into your shoulders if you have more than a couple of pounds in it. It may do for a quick trip to the grocery store or campus, but never for an enjoyable ride when you'll be on the bike for more than a few minutes.

• **Water bottle and/or hydration pack** It is vital to carry water with you—if you don't drink enough water you will dehydrate. Bring two or three water bottles and keep them filled. Put only water in your water bottles—it quenches thirst better than any other liquid.

An excellent alternative or addition to water bottles is a hydration pack worn like a backpack. You drink through a tube conveniently positioned in front of you, eliminating the need to reach down and remove a bottle from your bike. Most hydration packs have the capacity of two or three bottles. It is important to allow the inner reservoir to dry when not in use to prevent mold and mildew; you can buy a flexible frame that will hold it open for this purpose.

• **Basic tools** Always carry a few basic tools with you when you go out for a ride, just in case you get a flat or a loose derailleur cable. Tire irons, a 6-inch adjustable wrench, a small pair of pliers, a small standard screwdriver, and a small Phillips-head screwdriver are all you need to take care of virtually all roadside emergencies. A rag and a tube of hand cleaner are useful if you have to touch your chain. If your bike has any Allen nuts (nuts with a small hexagonal socket on top), carry metric Allen wrenches to fit them. Most bike shops sell a handy one-piece kit with several Allen wrenches, along with a standard and Phillips-head screwdriver.

• **Pump and spare tube** If you get a flat, you're immobilized unless you can pump up a new tube or patch the old one. Installing a brand new tube is less painful than trying to patch the old one on the road. Do the patching at home. Pump up the tire until it's hard, and you're on your way. Carry a spare tube in your handlebar bag, or wind it around the seat post, but make sure it doesn't rub against the rear tire.

If you bike a lot and don't use a mountain bike, you'll get flats—it's a fact of life. Most flats are on the rear wheel, because that's where most of your weight is. You should therefore practice taking the rear wheel off and putting it back on the bike, and taking the tire off and putting it on the rim, until you can do both confidently. It's much easier to practice at home than to fumble at it by the roadside.

• **Dog repellent** When you ride in rural areas you're going to encounter dogs, no two ways about it. Even if you don't have to use it, you'll have peace of mind knowing you have something like ammonia or commercial dog spray to repel an attacking dog if you have to. More on this later.

• **Bicycle computer** A bicycle computer provides a much more reliable way of following a route than depending on street signs or landmarks. Street signs are often nonexistent in rural areas or are rotated 90 degrees by mischievous kids. Landmarks like "turn right at green house" or "turn left at Ted's Market" lose effectiveness when the green house is repainted red or Ted's Market goes out of business. Most computers indicate not only distance but also speed, elapsed time, and cadence (pedal revolutions per minute). The solar-powered models last a long time before the batteries need replacement.

• **Bike lock** This is a necessity if you're going to leave your bike unattended. The best locks are the rigid, bolt-cutter-proof ones such as Kryptonite and Citadel. The next best choice is a strong chain or cable that can't be quickly severed by a normal-size bolt-cutter or hacksaw. A cheap, flimsy chain can be cut in a few seconds and is not much better than no lock at all.

In urban or heavily touristed areas, always lock both wheels as well as the frame to a solid object and take your accessories with you when you leave the bicycle. Many a cyclist ignoring this simple precaution has returned to the vehicle only to find one or both wheels gone, along with the pump, water bottle, and carrying bags.

• **Rearview mirror** A marvelous safety device, available at any bike shop, that lets you check the situation behind you without turning your head. Once you start using a mirror, you'll feel defenseless without it. Most mirrors are designed to fit on either a bike helmet or the handlebars. Some fit directly onto the temple piece of eyeglasses.

• **Bike helmet** Accidents happen, and a helmet will protect your head if you fall or crash. Bike helmets are light and comfortable, and most cyclists use them. Helmets are legally required for children in Massachusetts and adjacent states.

• **Food** Always bring some food with you when you go for a ride. It's surprising how quickly you get hungry when you're biking. Some of the rides in this book go through remote areas with no food along the way, and that country store you were counting on may be closed on weekends or out of business. Fruit is nourishing and includes a lot of water. A couple of candy bars, some pastry, or an ice cream cone will provide a burst of energy for the last 10 miles if you're getting tired. (Don't eat candy or sweets before then—the energy burst lasts only about an hour, and then your blood-sugar level drops to below where it was before, and you'll be really weak.)

• **Bicycling gloves** Gloves designed for biking, with padded palms and no fingers, will cushion your hands and protect them if you fall. For maximum comfort, use handlebar padding also.

• **Kickstand** Using a kickstand is the most convenient way to stand your bike upright without leaning it against a wall or other object. Keep in mind that a strong wind may knock your bike over and that in hot weather a kickstand may sink far enough into asphalt to topple your bike.

• **Bike rack** It is easier to use a bike rack than to wrestle your bike into and out of your car or trunk. Racks that attach to the back of the car are most convenient—do you really want to hoist your bike over your head onto the roof? If you use a rack that fits onto the back of the car, make sure that the bike is at least a foot off the ground and that the bicycle tire is well above the tailpipe. Hot exhaust blows out tires!

• **Light** Bring a bicycle light and reflective legbands with you in case you are caught in the dark. Ankle lights are lightweight and bob up and down as you pedal, giving additional visibility.

• **Fanny pack** Since many cycling shorts and jerseys don't have pockets, a small fanny pack is useful for carrying your keys, a wallet, and loose change.

• **Toilet paper**

• **Roll of electrical tape** You never know when you'll need it.

If you are not concerned with riding fast, the most practical bicycle for recreational riding is either a mountain bike or a hybrid between a mountain bike and a sport bike. Most people find them more comfortable than sport bikes because the riding position is more upright. The gearing is almost always lower than it is on sport bikes, which makes climbing hills much easier. (If you buy a mountain bike, be sure to get one with 18 or more speeds.) Mountain bikes usually have thumb-operated shift levers, so you don't have to move your hands when shifting gears. The fatter, thicker tires are very resistant to punctures. Mountain bikes are very stable—you're less likely to skid or fall if you should go off the road into soft dirt or if you hit an obstacle like a sand patch, pothole, sewer grate, or bad bump. Mountain bikes are rugged and resistant to damage; for example, a pothole will often dent the rim of a sport bike but will not usually hurt a mountain bike. The only disadvantage of mountain bikes is that they are a little slower than other bicycles because of the wider tires and less streamlined riding position.

If most of your riding is on pavement, you don't need standard mountain-bike tires, which are about 2 inches wide with a deep, knobby tread. Use narrower tires (often called city tires or cross-training tires), which are 1.375 or 1.5 inches wide with a fairly smooth tread.

Take advantage of your gearing when you ride. It's surprising how many people with 21-speed bikes use only two or three of their gears. It takes less effort to spin your legs quickly in the low or middle gears than to grind along in the higher ones. For leisurely biking, a rate of about 80 revolutions per minute is comfortable. If you find yourself grinding along at fewer than 75 RPMs, shift into a lower gear. Time your RPMs periodically on a watch with a second hand or your bicycle computer—keeping your cadence up is the best habit you can acquire for efficient cycling. You'll be less tired at the end of a ride and will avoid strain on your knees if you use the right gears.

If you have a 10- or 12-speed bike, you'll find it much easier to climb hills if you get a freewheel (the rear cluster of gears) that goes up to 34 teeth instead of the standard 28 teeth. You may also have to buy a new rear derailleur to accommodate the larger shifts, but the expense will be more than worthwhile in terms of ease of pedaling. For the ultimate in hill-climbing ease, you need a bicycle with 18 or more speeds. The smaller the inner front chainwheel, the lower the low gear. I recommend a small chainwheel with 24 or 26 teeth.

When approaching a hill, always shift into low gear *before* the hill, not after you start climbing it. If it's a steep or long hill, get into your lowest gear right away and go slowly to reduce the effort. Don't be afraid to walk up a really tough hill; it's not a contest, and you're out to enjoy yourself.

Here are few more hints to add to your cycling enjoyment: Adjust your seat to the proper height and make sure that it is level. Test for proper seat height by pedaling with your heels. Your leg should barely straighten out (with no bend) at the bottom of the downstroke. If your leg is bent, the seat is too low. If you rock from side to side as you pedal, the seat is too high.

Pedal with the balls of your feet, not your arches or heels, over the spindles. Toe clips are ideal for keeping your feet in the proper position on the pedals; they also give you added leverage when going uphill. The straps should be *loose* (or the spring tension on clipless pedals should be low) so that you can take your feet off the pedals effortlessly. In proper pedaling position, your leg should be slightly bent at the bottom of the downstroke.

Eat before you get hungry, drink before you get thirsty, and rest before you get tired. Two good guidelines are to drink one bottle of water per hour and to take a five- to ten-minute break every hour. (Longer stops are likely to make you feel stiff.) To keep your pants out of your chain, tuck them inside your socks. Wear pants that are as seamless as possible. Jeans or cut-offs are the worst offenders; their thick seams are uncomfortable. For maximum comfort, wear padded cycling shorts with no underwear, and cycling tights that fit over the shorts when the temperature is below sixty or sixty-five degrees. Use a firm, good-quality seat. A soft, mushy seat may feel inviting, but as soon as you sit on it the padding compresses under your weight so that you're really sitting on a harsh metal shell.

If you have to use the bathroom, the simplest solution is to get out of sight off the road. A footpath or one-lane dirt road that curves out of sight into the woods is ideal. Most fast-food restaurants have easily accessible rest rooms. If a restaurant is of the "Please wait to be seated" variety or has facilities "for customers only," either walk in briskly or order a snack. Most gas stations have rest rooms; most convenience stores and country stores do not, but they will sometimes accommodate you if you ask urgently.

About the Maps

The maps are reasonably accurate but are not necessarily strictly to scale. Congested areas may be enlarged in relation to the rest of the map for the sake of legibility. All the maps adhere to these conventions:

• Route numbers are circled.

• Small arrows alongside the route indicate direction of travel.

• The longer ride is marked by a heavy line. The shorter ride is marked by a dotted line where the route differs from that of the longer ride.

• I've tried to show the angle of forks and intersections as accurately as possible.

- Names of towns are in capital letters.

The maps show the main connecting roads, but I have shown them for reference only and not as recommended cycling routes. I must emphasize that I have not inspected most of the connecting roads and cannot vouch for their condition. Some of these roads are heavily traveled, very hilly, in poor condition, or unpaved.

Using the Maps and Directions

Unfortunately, a book format does not lend itself to quick and easy consultation while you're on your bike. The rides will go more smoothly if you don't have to dismount at each intersection to consult the map or directions. You can solve this problem by making a photocopy of the directions and carrying it in your map pocket or taping it to the top of your handlebar bag, dismounting occasionally to turn the sheet over or to switch sheets. Most people find it easier to follow the directions than the map.

In the directions, I have indicated the name of a road if there was a visible street sign at the time I researched the route; I designated the road as "unmarked" if the street sign was absent or not clearly visible. (Many street signs are visible from only one direction or are obscured by tree branches or utility poles.) Street signs have a short life span—a couple of years on the average—and are often nonexistent in rural areas. Any sign with a double entendre, such as Cherry, will be adorning some teenager's room within a week. Very frequently, the name of a road changes without warning at a town line, crossroads, or other intersection.

Using a bicycle computer is virtually essential to enjoying the rides. The directions indicate the distance to the next turn or major intersection. Because so many of the roads are unmarked, you'll have to keep track accurately of the distance from one turn to the next. It is helpful to keep in mind that a tenth of a mile is 176 yards, or nearly twice the length of a football field.

In the written directions, it is obviously not practical to mention every intersection. I have not mentioned most crossroads or traffic lights if the route goes straight, nor have I mentioned forks where one branch is clearly the main road. Always stay on the main road unless directed otherwise.

In addition to distances and a description of the next intersection, the directions also mention points of interest and situations that require caution. Any hazardous spot—for example, an unusually busy intersection or a bumpy section of road—has been clearly indicated by a **CAUTION** warning. It's a good idea to read over the entire tour before taking it in order to familiarize yourself with the terrain, points of interest, and places requiring caution.

In the directions certain words occur frequently, so let me define them to avoid any confusion.

To "bear" means to turn diagonally, somewhere between a 45-degree angle and going straight ahead. In these illustrations, you bear from road A onto road B.

To "merge" means to come into a road diagonally, or even head-on, if a side road comes into a main road. In the examples, road A merges into road B.

A "sharp" turn is any turn sharper than 90 degrees; in other words, a hairpin turn or something approaching it. In the examples, it is a sharp turn from road A onto road B.

Safety

It is an unfortunate fact that thousands of bicycle accidents occur each year, with many fatalities. Almost all cycling accidents, however, are needless and preventable. Most accidents involve children under sixteen and are caused by foolhardy riding and failure to exercise common sense. The chances of having an accident or serious injury can be greatly reduced by having your bike in good mechanical condition, using two pieces of safety equipment (a rearview mirror and a helmet), being aware of the most common biking hazards, and not riding at night unless prepared for it.

Before going out for a ride, be sure your bike is mechanically sound. Its condition is especially important if you bought the bike at a discount store, where it was probably assembled by a high school kid with no training. Above all, be sure that the wheels are secure and the brakes work. If your wheels are fastened with quick-release levers, be certain that they are clamped properly. If you're not sure how to do this, ask someone at a bike shop to show you; your safety depends on it.

Be certain your shoelaces are firmly tied, or use footwear with Velcro closures. A loose shoelace can wrap around the pedal axle or get caught in the chain, trapping you on the bicycle.

Invest in a rearview mirror and a bicycle helmet, both available at any bike shop. Most mirrors attach to either your helmet or your handlebars and work as well as car mirrors when properly adjusted. When you come to an obstacle such as a pothole or a patch of broken glass, a glance in the mirror lets you know whether it's safe to swing out into the road to avoid it. On narrow or winding roads you can always be aware of the traffic behind you and plan accordingly. Best of all, a mirror eliminates the need to peek back over your shoulder—an action that is not only awkward but also potentially dangerous, because you sometimes unconsciously veer toward the middle of the road while peeking.

A bicycle helmet is the cyclist's cheapest form of life insurance. A helmet not only protects your head if you land on it after a fall but also protects against the sun and the rain. All responsible cyclists wear helmets, so you shouldn't feel afraid of looking odd if you use one. They are light and comfortable; once you get used to one you'll never even know you have it on. As mentioned previously, helmets are legally required for children in Massachusetts and adjacent states.

While on the road, use the same plain old common sense that you use while driving a car. Stop signs and traffic lights are there for a reason—obey them. At intersections, give cars the benefit of the doubt rather than trying to dash out in front of them or beat them through the light. Remember, they're bigger, heavier, and faster than you are. And you're out to enjoy yourself and get some exercise, not to be king or queen of the road.

Several situations are inconsequential to the motorist but potentially hazardous for the bicyclist. When biking, try to keep aware of these:

• **Road surface** Not all roads in Massachusetts are silk-smooth. Often the bicyclist must contend with bumps, ruts, cracks, potholes, and fish-scale sections of road that have been patched and repatched numerous times. When the road becomes rough, the only prudent course of action is to slow down and keep alert, especially going downhill. Riding into a deep pothole or wheel-swallowing crack can cause a nasty spill. On bumps, you can relieve some of the shock by getting up off the seat.

• **Sand patches** Patches of sand often build up at intersections, sharp curves, the bottoms of hills, and sudden dips in the road. Sand is very unstable if you're turning, so slow way down, stop pedaling, and keep in a straight line until you're beyond the sandy spot.

• **Storm-sewer grates** Federal regulations have outlawed thousands of hazardous substances and products, but unfortunately they have not yet outlawed the storm sewer with grates parallel to the roadway. This is a very serious hazard, because a cyclist catching the wheel in a slot will instantly fall, probably in a somersault over the handlebars. Storm sewers are relatively rare in rural areas but always a very real hazard.

• **Dogs** Unfortunately, man's best friend is the cyclist's worst enemy. When riding in the country you will encounter dogs, pure and simple. Even though many communities have leash laws, they are usually not enforced unless a dog seriously injures someone or annoys its owners' neighbors enough that they complain— a rare situation because the neighbors probably all have dogs, too.

The best defense against a vicious dog is to carry repellent—either ammonia in a squirt gun or plant sprayer (make sure it's leakproof), or a commercial dog spray called Halt, which comes in an aerosol can and is available at most bike shops. Repellent is effective only if you can grab it instantly when you need it—*don't* put it in your handlebar pack, a deep pocket, or anywhere else where you'll have to fish around for it. For Halt to work you have to squirt it directly into the dog's eyes, but if the dog is close enough to really threaten you, it's easily done.

The main danger from dogs is not being bitten, but rather bumping into them or instinctively veering toward the center of the road into traffic when the dog comes after you. Fortunately, almost all dogs have a sense of territory and will not chase you more than a tenth of a mile. If you're going along at a brisk pace and you're in front of the dog when it starts to chase you, you can probably outrun it and stay ahead until you reach the animal's territorial limit. If you're going at a leisurely pace, however, or heading uphill, or the dog is in the road in front of you, the only safe thing to do is dismount and walk slowly forward, keeping the bike between you and the dog, until you leave its territory. If the dog is truly menacing, or there's more than one, repellent can be comforting to have.

If you decide to stay on the bike when a dog chases you, always get into a low gear and spin your legs as quickly as possible. It's hard for a dog to bite a fast-rotating target. Many cyclists swing their pump at the animal, but this increases the danger of losing control of your bike. Often, yelling "Stay!" or "No!" in an authoritative voice will make a dog back off.

A word of caution about using commercial dog spray: It can be legally argued that dog spray comes under the Massachusetts firearms law, which carries a mandatory one-year jail sentence for carrying an unlicensed firearm. Such a case would probably not hold up in court, but because of the potential hazard, a zealous police officer might give you a hassle if he or she noticed it on your bike. The law states in Section 10 of Chapter 269, "Whoever . . . carries . . . a firearm . . . as defined in Section 121 of Chapter 140 . . . shall be punished by imprisonment. . . ." When you go to the definition in Section 121 of Chapter 140, it says, "Firearm shall mean a pistol, revolver or other weapon of any description loaded or unloaded, from which a shot or bullet can be discharged." A court would have to decide whether dog spray fits this definition.

• **Undivided, shoulderless four-lane highways** This is the most dangerous type of road for biking. If traffic is very light there is no problem, but in moderate or heavy traffic the road becomes a death trap unless you ride assertively. The only safe way to travel on such a road is to stay in or near the center of the right lane, rather than at the edge, forcing traffic coming up behind you to pass you in the left lane. If you hug the right-hand edge, some motorists will not get out of the right lane, brushing past you by inches or even forcing you off the road. Some drivers mentally register a bicycle as being only as wide as its tire, an unsettling image when the lane is not much wider than a car.

Several rides in this book contain short stretches along highways. If traffic is heavy enough to occupy both lanes most of the time, the only truly safe thing to do is walk your bike along the side of the road.

• **Railroad tracks** Tracks that cross the road at an oblique angle are a severe hazard, because you can easily catch your wheel in the slot between the rails and fall. *Never* ride diagonally across tracks—either walk your bike across or, if no traffic is in sight, cross the tracks at right angles by swerving into the road. When riding across tracks, slow down and get up off the seat to relieve the shock of the bump.

• **Oiled and sanded roads** Many communities occasionally spread a film of oil or tar over the roads to seal cracks and then spread sand over the road to absorb the oil. The combination is treacherous for biking. Be very careful, especially going downhill. If the sand is deep or if the tar or oil is still sticky, you should walk.

• **Car doors opening into your path** This is a severe hazard in urban areas and in the center of towns. To be safe, any time you ride past a line of parked cars, stay 4 or 5 feet away from them. If traffic won't permit this, proceed very slowly and notice whether the driver's seat of each car is occupied. A car pulling to the side of the road in front of you is an obvious candidate for trouble.

• **Low sun** If you're riding directly into a low sun, drivers behind you may not see you, especially through a smeared or dirty windshield. Here your rearview mirror becomes a lifesaver, because the only safe way to proceed is to glance constantly in the mirror and remain aware of conditions behind you. If you're riding directly away from a low sun, motorists coming toward you may not see you and could make a left turn into your path. If the sun is on your right or left, drivers on your side may not see you, and a car could pull out from a side road into your path. To be safe, give any traffic that may be blinded by the sun the benefit of the doubt, and dismount if necessary. Because most of the roads you'll be on are winding and wooded, you won't run into blinding sun frequently, but you should be aware of the problem.

• **Kids on bikes** Children riding their bikes in circles in the middle of the road and shooting in and out of driveways are a hazard; the risk of collision is always there because they aren't watching where they're going. Any time you see kids playing in the street, especially if they're on bikes, be prepared for anything and call out

"Beep-beep" or "Watch out" as you approach. If you have a loud bell or horn, use it.

• **Wet leaves** In the fall, wet leaves are very slippery. Avoid turning on them.

• **Metal-grate bridges** When wet, the metal grating becomes very slippery, and you may be in danger of falling and injuring yourself on the sharp edges. If the road is wet, or early in the morning when there may be condensation on the bridge, please walk across.

A few additional safety reminders: If bicycling in a group, ride single file and at least 20 feet apart. Use hand signals when turning—to signal a right turn, extend your right arm. If you stop to rest or examine your bike, get both your bicycle and yourself *completely* off the road. Sleek black bicycle clothing is stylish, but bright colors are more visible and safer.

Finally, use common courtesy toward motorists and pedestrians. Hostility toward bicyclists has received national media attention; it is caused by the 2 percent of discourteous cyclists (mainly messengers and groups hogging the road) who give the other 98 percent—responsible riders—a bad image. Please do not be part of the 2 percent!

Bikeways

There are currently only two bona fide bikeways, or bicycle paths, in the area covered by this book, although others are being planned. Both are in the Amherst-Northampton area. The Norwottuck Rail Trail, also called the Five-College Bike Path, runs for about 10 miles between the eastern edge of Northampton (at the Connecticut River) to Warren Wright Road in Belchertown, following a course that is roughly parallel to Route 9. The other facility, the Northampton Bikeway, runs 2.6 miles from Look Park to State Street north of the downtown area. There is a gap of about a mile between the two bikeways because an active railroad passes between them.

Bikeways are a mixed blessing. If well designed and well maintained, like the Norwottuck Rail Trail or the East Bay Bicycle Path in Rhode Island, they are a pleasure. If poorly designed or maintained, they are much more dangerous than the roads that they're supposed to avoid. Many bikeways are too narrow or have curves that are too sharp, and many have unsafe road crossings. Unless maintenance is vigilant, a bikeway will rapidly fill up with leaves, glass, and debris, and the surface will deteriorate. In good weather, all bikeways in populated areas will be heavily used by pedestrians, joggers, inline skaters, skateboarders, children, dogs, and other noncyclists.

The Massachusetts Bicycle Coalition is actively striving to improve and increase bikeways. If you'd like to join in its efforts, contact the coalition at 44 Bromfield Street, Suite 207, Boston, MA 02108, (617) 542–2453.

Feedback

I'd be very grateful for any comments, criticisms, or suggestions about the rides in this book. Road conditions change, and a new snack bar or point of interest may open up along one of the routes. An intersection may be changed by road construction or improvement, or a traffic light may be installed. I'd like to keep the book updated by incorporating changes as they occur, or modifying a route if necessary in the interest of scenery or safety. Many of the changes I have made in previous editions have been inspired by riders' suggestions (for example, routing the Old Sturbridge Village Ride through the lovely town center of Warren). Please feel free to contact me through The Globe Pequot Press, P.O. Box 480, Guilford, CT 06437 with any revision you think helpful.

Chapter 1: The Berkshires

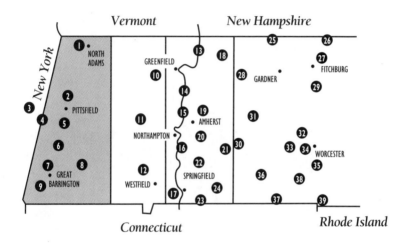

Church in Adams

The Northwest Corner
North Adams–Williamstown–Adams

Number of miles:	26 (15 without Adams extension)
Terrain:	Gently rolling, with several moderate hills.
Facilities:	Restaurants and grocery stores in the towns. Restaurant next to starting point.

The northwest corner of Massachusetts is a fascinating area with three towns of widely contrasting character. Adams and North Adams are well-preserved mill towns brimming with Victorian architecture, while Williamstown is the epitome of the gracious New England college town. All three towns lie at the base of mighty Mount Greylock, which at nearly 3,500 feet is the highest mountain in the state. Dramatic views of the mountain greet you around almost every bend. Although the area is mountainous, the ride is one of the easiest in the Berkshires because all the roads are in the valley of the Hoosic River. (If you really want to bike up Greylock, you may; the route is in Lewis Cuyler's book, *Bike Rides in the Berkshire Hills*.)

North Adams, where the ride starts, is a town of striking visual impact. The downtown area contains 2 blocks of handsome five- and six-story commercial buildings from the late 1800s. Next to the center of town are a cluster of four magnificent churches with tall spires, the turreted public library, and ornate Victorian houses. Along the river lie massive Dickensian mills and rows of duplex and triplex mill houses. The hillside behind the starting point provides a fine view of the town, its church steeples outlined against the mountains to the east.

3

The starting point, Western Gateway Heritage State Park, is a museum devoted primarily to the building of the Hoosac Tunnel between 1851 and 1875. The railroad tunnel, blasted through nearly 5 miles of solid rock, provided a direct route between Boston and the Great Lakes, and ultimately, the developing West. The state park is housed in a complex of former railroad buildings that now contains shops and restaurants as well as museum exhibits.

From North Adams you'll head west to Williamstown on Route 2. Although busy, the road is wide enough to be safe for bicycling. After about 2 miles you'll go through the village of Greylock (part of North Adams), dominated by a large brick mill. As you arrive in Williamstown, you'll loop south through a gracious residential area before passing through the center of town and the lovely campus of Williams College. Shortly before the campus the route passes the Sterling and Francine Clark Art Institute, one of two superb art museums in Williamstown. It has a strong collection of French impressionist paintings. About a mile ahead is the Williams College Museum of Art, which emphasizes American and contemporary art. Also on the campus (which is perfectly integrated into the town) are two large, stately churches and the handsome Williamstown Memorial Library.

The ride returns to North Adams via a secondary road that runs parallel with Route 2 along the north bank of the Hoosic River. As you arrive in town you'll see a huge brick mill complex, which is now the Massachusetts Museum of Contemporary Art, or MoCA. It has the space to show works of enormous size that would be impossible to display in a traditional setting.

The long ride heads south from North Adams for about 5 miles to Adams. This portion of the ride, which follows the eastern edge of the Hoosic River Valley, provides stunning views of · Mount Greylock, which towers 2,500 feet above the valley floor. The flatiron-shaped scar just below the summit was caused by a landslide in 1990 after heavy rains. Like North Adams, Adams has

4

fine brick business buildings in the downtown area, several impressive churches, and an attractive library built in 1897. (The ride does not go through the center of town but comes within a few blocks of it.) As you leave Adams you'll ride past several long, brick rowhouses reminiscent of a Welsh mining town and see limestone quarries etched into the base of the mountainside. You'll return to the starting point along Route 8, a table-flat road with good shoulders.

DIRECTIONS
FOR
THE RIDE

1. Follow Furnace Street to Route 8. Turn left (north) and go less than 0.4 mile to second traffic light (sign points right to Routes 2 and 8).
2. Right for 0.1 mile to end.
3. Right and then immediately right again on Route 2 West at traffic light.

    Go 4.8 miles to Route 43 (Water Street) on left, in Williamstown. It's just after a traffic light where Cole Avenue turns right.

    You ride through Greylock, a mill village that is part of North Adams.

4. Left for 1.1 miles to Gale Road on right, shortly after Ide Road on right.
5. Right for 1.7 miles to Route 2 East on right, immediately after stop sign.

    The Clark Art Institute is on your left after 1.2 miles, at the top of a short hill. When you get to Route 2 East, a small park is on the left. In the center of the park stands the 1753 House, a replica of a small dwelling constructed by Williamstown's original settlers. The reproduction was built in 1953 by volunteers as part of the town's bicentennial celebration.

6. Right for 0.6 mile to Cole Avenue on left, at traffic light.

    You'll pass through the campus of Williams College; most of it is on the left. Spring Street, the town's main

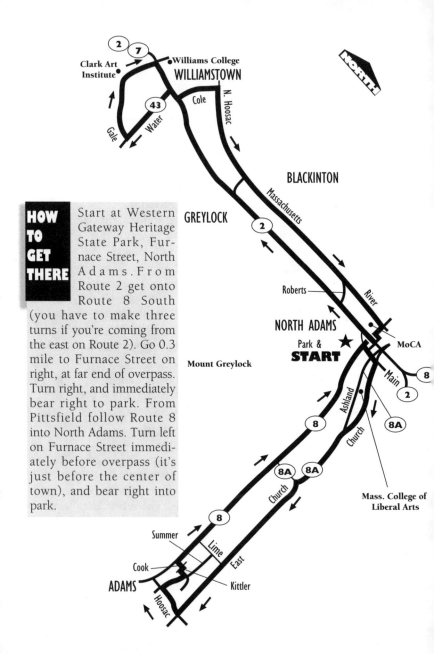

HOW TO GET THERE Start at Western Gateway Heritage State Park, Furnace Street, North Adams. From Route 2 get onto Route 8 South (you have to make three turns if you're coming from the east on Route 2). Go 0.3 mile to Furnace Street on right, at far end of overpass. Turn right, and immediately bear right to park. From Pittsfield follow Route 8 into North Adams. Turn left on Furnace Street immediately before overpass (it's just before the center of town), and bear right into park.

shopping street, is on the right after 0.3 mile. The Williams College Museum of Art is on the right just ahead, immediately before you start to go downhill (it's in Lawrence Hall, set back a short distance from the road). The small, stone, turreted building on the right midway down the hill is a planetarium.

7. Left for 0.8 mile to end (North Hoosac Road). You'll pass a handsome brick church on the left and then an old brick mill on the right just before the end.

8. Right for 3 miles to fork. You'll have good views of Mount Greylock on the right. After about 2 miles you'll ride through the village of Blackinton (part of North Adams), where you'll pass a brick mill and a small stone church on the right and, just ahead, a Gothic-style church built in 1871 on the left.

9. Bear left for 1.5 miles to traffic light (Houghton Street on left, Marshall Street on right). The massive mill complex on the right just before the intersection is the site of the Massachusetts Museum of Contemporary Art, or MoCA.

10. Right for 0.2 mile to second traffic light (Main Street). You pass the main entrance of MoCA on your right.

    The long ride turns left on Main Street, but if you're doing the short ride, continue straight for 0.25 mile to Furnace Street on right, at far end of overpass. Turn right on Furnace Street, and the starting point is just ahead on the right.

11. Left for 0.2 mile to fork where Church Street bears right, at top of short hill.

    You go through downtown North Adams. At the fork, three fine churches cluster around the intersection. The ornate, Victorian building on the far right corner is the public library.

12. Bear right for 1.3 miles to stop sign (merge left on Route 8A). **CAUTION**: Watch for potholes near end. You'll pass

Massachusetts College of Liberal Arts (formerly North Adams State College) on the right after 0.6 mile.

13. Bear left for 1.1 miles to Church Street on left. The main road curves sharply right at the intersection.

14. Left for 2.9 miles to crossroads (East Hoosac Street), at the bottom of a little hill. **CAUTION**: Potholes for the first 0.5 mile. You'll enjoy spectacular views of Mount Greylock on the right.

15. Right for 0.5 mile to crossroads and stop sign (Summer Street), in Adams. A magnificent brick church guards the far left corner. Here the ride turns right, but if you'd like to see the center of town, go straight for 0.3 mile to end (Route 8) and then left for 0.2 mile.

16. Right for less than 0.4 mile to second crossroads (Kittler Avenue).

17. Left for 0.1 mile to end (Crotteau Street).

18. Jog right and then immediately left on Cook Street. Go 0.1 mile to end (Route 8).

19. Right for 4.6 miles to Furnace Street on left, immediately before overpass. **CAUTION**: Dangerous diagonal railroad tracks after 0.75 mile. You'll pass several long, brick rowhouses on your left at the beginning.

20. Turn left, and the starting point is just ahead on the right.

Pittsfield–Cheshire–Adams

Number of miles:	30 (15 without Cheshire-Adams extension, 25 with shortcut omitting Adams)
Terrain:	The short ride is gently rolling with one tough hill and one moderate one. The long rides are hilly. Six-tenths mile of dirt road on the two longer rides.
Facilities:	Grocery and restaurant in Cheshire. McDonald's at end.

The region northeast of Pittsfield, heading toward Adams, is very pleasant for bicycling. The dominant features of the landscape are the Cheshire Reservoir, which is nearly 4 miles long, and stunning views of Mount Greylock to the north. Pittsfield thins out quickly as you head north out of the city, and the secondary roads have very little traffic.

The ride starts in the northeastern part of Pittsfield from a shopping center that strives for uniqueness by planting half a boat vertically in the parking lot. Within a mile the landscape starts to become rural as you climb out of a residential area. A beautiful back road traverses the hillside above the western shore of the Cheshire Reservoir (also called the Hoosac Reservoir), and then descends gradually to Route 8 just south of Cheshire. You'll return to the starting point on Route 8, which hugs the opposite shore of the reservoir closely for the first couple of miles. This road is moderately traveled and has a good shoulder.

The long rides go into the center of Cheshire, an attractive small town with a traditional New England church and a handsome town hall built in 1898. Across the road from the post office is a monument in the shape of a cheese press. It commemorates a 1,235-pound cheese produced in 1801 from local dairy farms and sent to President Thomas Jefferson in Washington. A long climb brings you into the hills east of the town, where you'll see Mount Greylock rising in dramatic splendor beyond the fields of grazing cows. At the top of the ridge is another unusual memorial, the Stafford Hill Monument. It is a circular stone structure with graceful arches built in 1927; a Revolutionary War hero is buried here. Behind the monument is an inspiring view of Mount Greylock. A glorious descent follows with a panorama of the Hoosic River Valley unfolding before you to Adams, North Adams, and beyond to Vermont.

As you approach Adams, you'll ride along an open ridge with magnificent views before plunging steeply downhill into the outskirts of town. The downtown area (just off the route) contains attractive brick commercial buildings from the late nineteenth century, several impressive churches, and a handsome library built in 1897. From Adams the route ascends once again into the hills south of town, loops downhill back into Cheshire, and rejoins the short ride.

DIRECTIONS
FOR
THE RIDE

1. Turn right out of the south end of the parking lot, with McDonald's on your left as you leave the lot. Immediately bear right at stop sign on Crane Avenue (unmarked). Go 0.4 mile to Oak Hill Road on right.

2. Right for 2.8 miles to end. After about a mile you'll climb steeply for 0.3 mile. This is the worst hill of the short ride. Then you'll see Berkshire Mall on the right and Mount Greylock straight ahead. Oak Hill Road becomes Partridge Road.

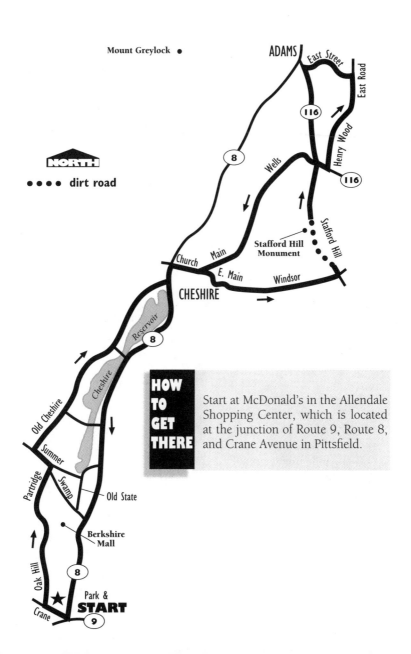

Mount Greylock ●

ADAMS
East Street
East Road

NORTH

●●●● dirt road

116

8

Wells

Henry Wood

116

Stafford Hill

Stafford Hill Monument

Church

Main

E. Main

Windsor

CHESHIRE

Reservoir

8

Cheshire

Old Cheshire

Summer

Swamp

Partridge

Old State

Berkshire Mall

Oak Hill

8

Park & **START**

Crane

9

HOW TO GET THERE

Start at McDonald's in the Allendale Shopping Center, which is located at the junction of Route 9, Route 8, and Crane Avenue in Pittsfield.

3. Left for 0.4 mile to Old Cheshire Road on right.
4. Right for 4.2 miles to end (Route 8). You'll ride through rolling farmland, with glimpses of the Cheshire Reservoir nestled below on the right.

   The 30- and 25-mile rides turn left on Route 8; for the 15-mile ride, turn right on Route 8 for 6.7 miles to shopping center on right. You'll follow the shore of the Cheshire Reservoir for the first 2.5 miles.
5. Left for 0.3 mile to traffic light, in Cheshire. There's a graceful white church on the far right corner.
6. Right for 0.5 mile to fork (Main Street bears left, East Main Street bears right). You pass the town hall on your right and then the Cheese Press Monument on your left across from the post office.
7. Bear left for 0.6 mile to fork where Notch Road bears right and Windsor Road (unmarked) bears left. The second half of this section is a steep climb.
8. Bear left for 2.2 miles to crossroads where Richmond Hill Road turns right and Stafford Hill Road turns left. Most of this stretch is uphill, with two very steep pitches. There are dramatic views of Mount Greylock on your left.
9. Left for 2 miles to end (Route 116). Bear right at large traffic island just before end.

   The road climbs steeply for 0.3 mile, then it levels off and becomes dirt for 0.6 mile. The Stafford Hill Monument is on your left at the point where the pavement resumes; it's 0.1 mile down a one-lane dirt road. The view from the monument is partially obscured by trees; there's a better view from the field behind it. Beyond the monument is a long, steep descent with glorious views.

   The 30-mile ride turns right at the end onto Route 116, but to shorten the ride to 25 miles turn left immediately before the end onto Wells Road. Resume with direction number 14, turning left on Wells Road instead of right.

10. Right for 0.25 mile to Henry Wood Road (unmarked) on left.
11. Left for 2.1 miles to East Street on left.

    At the beginning you'll ascend with wonderful views in all directions, including behind you. Immediately before the intersection you'll see an old white house on the right. Susan B. Anthony, a leader of the women's suffrage movement, was born here in 1820.
12. Left for 0.9 mile to end (Route 116). **CAUTION**: Curving, very steep descent—take it easy. Here the ride turns left, but if you'd like to visit the center of Adams, turn right for 0.3 mile.
13. Left for 2.1 miles to Wells Road on right, shortly after high school on left. Route 116 climbs steeply for the first 0.6 mile.
14. Right for 3.8 miles to traffic light (Route 8), back in Cheshire.

    Most of this section is downhill, with good views of Mount Greylock on the right. You pass the Cheese Press Monument again on your right near the end.
15. Left for 7 miles to shopping center on right. You'll follow the Cheshire Reservoir on your right near the beginning.

Chatham, New York

Chatham, New York

Number of miles:	21
Terrain:	Mostly gently rolling, with one steady climb a mile long and several short hills.
Facilities:	Country store and restaurant in Old Chatham. Restaurant in Chatham, at end.

The Chatham region, about 5 to 10 miles west of the Massachusetts border and 25 miles southeast of Albany, provides superb bicycling past prosperous farms and rolling hillsides. Back roads with very little traffic curl past old barns and soft green meadows where horses and cattle graze. The wonderful Shaker Museum, which you'll visit about halfway through the ride, is a historical highlight.

The ride starts from the center of Chatham, an attractive small town with a brick business block dating from the late nineteenth century, a dignified town hall with pillars framing the doorway, and a weathered old train station that was built in 1887. You'll promptly head into rural countryside, where Route 66 rolls past perfectly groomed horse and dairy farms with hills rising in the distance—the predominant landscape of the ride. After a few miles you'll descend into Chatham Center, a hamlet with a few houses and a graceful white church. From here you'll pedal through the fertile valley of Kinderhook Creek to the hamlet of Malden Bridge, where you'll pass an art gallery, two antiques shops, and a handsome brick house.

An idyllic country lane leads about 2 miles from Malden Bridge to the Shaker Museum. The Shakers, who flourished during the middle of the nineteenth century, are the best known and among the most fascinating of America's communal sects. Their belief in celibacy ensured their eventual demise. Their lifestyle was strictly regimented and spartan, but not to the point of privation or misery. Shaker architecture, artifacts, and furnishings are unique because they combine form and function with almost spiritual simplicity. The museum, which contains several rustic buildings surrounded by fields and horse farms, provides a wonderful opportunity to gain an understanding of the Shaker way of life. In addition to furniture and household implements, the museum also displays a blacksmith shop, a weaving studio, and a schoolroom. Other exhibits pertain to the Shakers' agriculture and medicinal herb industry.

The gracious hamlet of Old Chatham, where an inviting country store and several fine houses cluster around the main intersection, is shortly after the Shaker Museum. You may wish to grab a snack here to boost you up the mile-long hill just ahead. But you'll be rewarded by a steep drop into East Chatham and then a gradual descent for several miles back to Chatham.

DIRECTIONS
FOR
THE RIDE

1. Head north on Route 66. You will immediately come to a fork where Route 295 bears right and Route 66 bears left.

   The clock tower in the middle of the fork was built in 1872.

2. Bear left on Route 66. **CAUTION**: Walk your bike through this dangerous intersection, which has railroad tracks running diagonally through it. Go less than 0.2 mile to a small traffic circle at the far end of the business district.

   Notice the pillared town hall on your right at the traffic circle.

3. Go three quarters of the way around the traffic circle, staying on Route 66 North (**CAUTION** here). Go 4.4 miles to

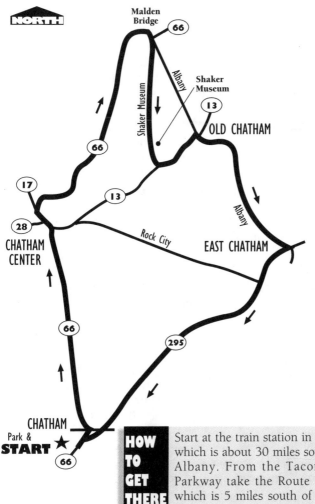

HOW TO GET THERE Start at the train station in Chatham, which is about 30 miles southeast of Albany. From the Taconic State Parkway take the Route 203 exit, which is 5 miles south of the Berkshire spur of the New York State Thruway (I–90). Turn right on Route 203 if you're coming from the south and left if you're coming from the north. Go about 1.5 miles to Route 66, at traffic light, and turn right for 0.3 mile. Park where legal on Route 66 near train station.

fork where County Road 17 goes straight and Route 66 bears right.

The road rolls past horse farms and grassy hillsides. You'll ride through the hamlet of Chatham Center 0.5 mile before the fork. Notice the stately white church, with pillars framing the entrance, on your right.

4. Bear right for 4.4 miles to the intersection where Route 66 turns left, just after a bridge. The hamlet of Malden Bridge, with a handsome brick house on your left and a couple of antiques shops, is just before the bridge.

5. Go straight and then immediately bear right on Shaker Museum Road (unmarked), passing a small church on your left. Notice the bell in front of the church. Go 2.6 miles to end (merge left on County Road 13).

You'll ride past tidy horse farms and come to the Shaker Museum on your left after 2.1 miles.

6. Bear left for 1 mile to end, at top of hill, in the village of Old Chatham. There's a country store on your right at the intersection and a restaurant across the road.

7. Right for 3.1 miles to crossroads and stop sign immediately after railroad bridge (Route 295).

At the beginning there's a steady climb a mile long, but once you're at the top, the rest of the ride is mostly downhill. The road parallels the Berkshire spur of the New York State Thruway on your right. The village of East Chatham is at the end.

8. Right (it's a somewhat sharp right) for 5.3 miles to stop sign (merge left on Route 66). This section is mostly wooded.

9. Bear left (**CAUTION** here), and the train station is immediately ahead on your right.

The Shaker Village Ride
Pittsfield–Richmond–Canaan, New York–New Lebanon, New York

Number of miles:	26 (14 without Canaan–New Lebanon extension)
Terrain:	The short ride is rolling. The long ride is hilly, with a steep, 2.5-mile climb toward the end.
Facilities:	Apple and cider store in Richmond. Convenience store and country store in Canaan. Restaurant in New Lebanon.

The area west and a little south of Pittsfield, straddling the Massachusetts–New York border, provides scenic bicycling past farms with hills and mountains rising in the distance. The rugged Taconic Range, which you'll struggle across on the longer ride, runs along the state line and extends a short distance westward into New York. A historic highlight of the ride are two former Shaker communities—Mount Lebanon Shaker Village, which you'll see on the long ride, and Hancock Shaker Village, which is on the route of both rides.

The ride starts from the west side of Pittsfield, and within a mile you'll leave the built-up part of the city behind. Fortunately for the bicyclist, Pittsfield is a compact city unmarred by urban sprawl. Richmond, the town bordering Pittsfield on the southwest, has a population of less than 2,000; Hancock, which is squeezed between the city and the New York state line, has fewer than 1,000 residents. You'll follow a secondary road southwest into Richmond, passing small farms and an apple orchard. As you approach the state line, the landscape becomes more rolling, with steep little ups and downs that are fun to bicycle over if you use your gears properly. Just before the state line, the route turns north along quiet side roads to Route 20, which will bring you back to Pittsfield.

You'll arrive at Hancock Shaker Village just after you turn east onto Route 20. The Shakers, who flourished during the middle of the nineteenth century, are the best known of America's communal sects (see ride 3 for more detail). The Shaker Village, which contains twenty original buildings surrounded by broad expanses of farmland, provides a wonderful opportunity to gain an understanding of the Shaker way of life. The most distinctive building is a round stone barn about 85 feet in diameter; it was designed to allow one person standing in the center to feed an entire herd of cattle.

From the Shaker Village it's about 3.5 miles back to the starting point along Route 20. The road is moderately traveled, gently rolling, and fairly wide.

The long ride heads farther west across the state line into Canaan, New York. You'll pass through a gap in the Taconic Range, with a short hill followed by a long, steady descent into a valley just west of the border. A back road hugs the shore of Queechy Lake. Then you'll ride gradually downhill through the valley into the village of New Lebanon, which is bordered by beautiful rolling farmland.

East of New Lebanon there is no gap in the Taconic Range, so you'll have to endure a steady, 2.5-mile climb to get across it. After about a mile you can take a break by visiting Mount Lebanon Shaker Village, which is much less visited than the one in Hancock. Mount Lebanon, which also contains about twenty handsome brick and wooden buildings, served as the spiritual center for the entire Shaker movement (analogous to the Vatican for the Catholic Church) between 1820 and 1860. Some of the buildings form the campus of the Darrow School, a small preparatory school. The stone barn was the largest of its kind in North America when it was built in 1851 (it was destroyed by fire in 1972, but the shell remains standing). A small Sufi community, called Abode of the Message, is located beyond the school. The Sufis are Islamic mystics; their ultimate goal is union with God.

The climb continues for nearly 2 miles beyond Mount Lebanon, with a magnificent view just before the top. Then it's all downhill to Hancock Shaker Village, just before which you'll rejoin the short ride.

DIRECTIONS

FOR

THE RIDE

Directions for the ride: 26 miles—

1. Right on Route 20 (left if you're starting from the shopping center) for 0.25 mile to Barker Road on right, immediately after traffic light.

2. Right for 4.5 miles to Summit Road on right, at top of short hill.

    As you're riding along, Lenox Mountain dominates the landscape ahead of you toward the left. You'll pass Bartlett's Orchard, an excellent apple and cider store, on the left shortly before the intersection.

3. Right for 2 miles to end (Route 41). Here the short ride turns right. Summit Road is very rolling, with short, steep ups and downs.

4. Left and just ahead right on Route 295. Go 2.4 miles to traffic light (Route 22).

    There's a short hill at the beginning and a long, relaxing descent at the end. You'll enter New York State 0.8 mile before the intersection. When you get to Route 22 there's a convenience store on the left, but you'll come to a more appealing country store a mile up the road.

5. Straight for 0.9 mile to Queechy Lake Drive (Columbia County Route 30), which turns sharply right. The Canaan Market is on your right at the intersection.

6. Sharp right for 1.4 miles to end (Route 22 again).

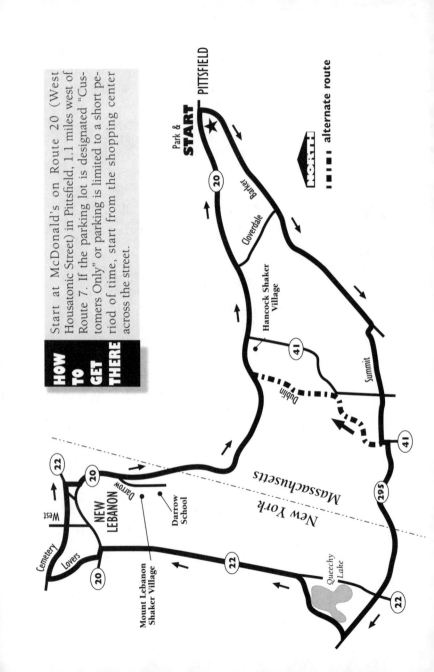

HOW TO GET THERE

Start at McDonald's on Route 20 (West Housatonic Street) in Pittsfield, 1.1 miles west of Route 7. If the parking lot is designated "Customers Only" or parking is limited to a short period of time, start from the shopping center across the street.

PITTSFIELD

Park &
START

20

Baker

Cloverdale

Hancock Shaker Village

41

Dublin

Summit

41

295

NORTH

------ alternate route

New York

Massachusetts

22

20

West

Cemetery

Lovers

20

NEW LEBANON

Darrow

Darrow School

Mount Lebanon Shaker Village

22

Quechy Lake

22

This is a beautiful ride along Queechy Lake. When you come to Route 22, the Berkshire Farm Center, a rehabilitation center for nonviolent juvenile offenders, is on the far side of the intersection.

7. Left for 3.4 miles to end (Route 20), in New Lebanon.

    Most of this section is a gradual descent through a valley, with the Taconic Range rising sharply on both sides of the road. There's an attractive fieldstone church on your left at the end.

8. Left and just ahead right on Lovers Lane (unmarked). Go 0.8 mile to end (Cemetery Road, unmarked). The restaurant on Route 20 opposite Lovers Lane is a good halfway stop.

9. Right for 1.2 miles to second stop sign (merge head-on onto Route 22). You'll enjoy views of rolling fields with mountains in the background.

10. Straight for less than 0.2 mile to unmarked road on the right (sign says TO ROUTE 20 EAST). Notice the handsome stucco school on the left immediately before the intersection and the graceful stone church on the right just past the intersection.

11. Right for 0.3 mile to end (Route 20). At the end, look to your right for a great view.

12. Left for 0.8 mile to Darrow Road on right. It's a steady climb as you begin the long ascent over the Taconic Range.

13. Turn right for 0.25 mile to Mount Lebanon Shaker Village and then backtrack to Route 20.

    The stone shell of the massive barn, destroyed by fire in 1972, is on the right. The handsome wood and brick buildings of the Darrow School, originally part of the Shaker community, are 0.2 mile beyond the Shaker Village. The Abode of the Message (the Sufi community) is 0.6 mile after the school, at the top of a steep hill.

14. Right for 7.4 miles to McDonald's on right.

You ascend 0.8 mile to the Massachusetts state line and continue uphill another mile to the summit. Just before the top, an overlook on the right provides a panoramic view. Then it's all downhill to the Hancock Shaker Village on your right. From there it's about 3.5 miles to the end.

Directions for the ride: 14 miles—

1. Follow directions for the long ride through number 3.
2. Right for 1.2 miles to crossroad (Dublin Road). You'll pass an old cemetery on the right after 0.25 mile.
3. Left for 1.6 miles to end (Route 20).
4. Right for 3.9 miles to McDonald's on right. The entrance to Hancock Shaker Village is on your right after 0.2 mile.

Lenox Loop
Pittsfield–Lenox–Richmond

Number of miles:	25 (20 without Richmond extension, 16 with shortcut omitting Lenox Dale)
Terrain:	The two shorter rides are rolling; the long ride is hilly.
Facilities:	Grocery and restaurants in Lenox. Store selling apples and cider in Richmond.
Safety concerns:	The long ride goes past Tanglewood, which breeds traffic jams on the narrow nearby roads before and after concerts. The concert season runs from the beginning of July through Labor Day. In general, daytime concerts begin at 10:30 A.M. on Saturday (these are rehearsals) and 2:30 P.M. on Sunday. Concerts last about two hours.
	The two shorter rides have a steep descent with sharp curves where you must take it easy. Be sure your brakes are in good working order.

A few miles south of Pittsfield is the gracious town of Lenox, which, along with neighboring Stockbridge, contains the largest concentration of grand estates in the Berkshires. Most of the estates were built in the late 1800s as summer "cottages" for financial and industrial tycoons. A few were built for artists, writers, and political figures. These buildings live on today as museums, schools, centers for the performing arts, and resorts. Cycling past these noble structures, the lovely town center of Lenox, and rich farmland in the outlying areas is pure pleasure as long as you're not fighting for road space with Tanglewood traffic.

The ride starts about 0.7 mile south of the center of Pittsfield and heads south through an attractive residential area on secondary roads. Shortly before the Lenox town line you'll pass Arrowhead, an eighteenth-century farmhouse where Herman Melville lived from 1850 to 1863. The house, including the studio where he wrote *Moby Dick*, is open to the public. There's a good view of Mount Greylock, about 15 miles to the north, from the meadow next to the house. Continuing south past farms with mountain views in the background, you'll come to the first estate, Eastover (now a resort), after about 3 miles.

Beyond Eastover, the route rolls up and down and then descends gradually to the Housatonic River, which flows from Pittsfield to Long Island Sound near Bridgeport, Connecticut. The graceful former Lenox train station, built in 1902, stands on the riverbank. It is now a railroad museum and the locale of the Berkshire Scenic Railway, which offers short train rides on an old passenger car. You'll follow the river through the quiet village of Lenox Dale, passing a fine wooden church and a handsome stucco school building that has been tastefully converted into apartments.

From Lenox Dale you'll climb gradually away from the river, passing four grand estates within 2 miles. The first one is Blantyre, an exclusive, very private resort built in the style of a Scottish manor. Just ahead is Cranwell, now a resort, conference center, and golf club. The Berkshire Opera Company performs in its round, boldly architectured auditorium. Next you'll come to The Mount, the splendid summer mansion of Edith Wharton, the first woman to win a Pulitzer prize. The theater group Shakespeare and Company performs on the grounds of the estate. Finally you'll pass Canyon Ranch, a health spa that was formerly an estate called Bellefontaine, built in the style of a

French palace. (There are no canyons nearby—the name comes from the original spa in Tucson, Arizona.)

Shortly after the Canyon Ranch, you'll arrive at the classically elegant center of Lenox. It is dominated by the Curtis, a brick, four-story former hotel that has been converted into apartments. Next to it is the graceful Lenox Library, originally built in 1815 as a courthouse. The handsome, pillared town hall stands across the street from the Curtis. Surrounding the center of town are large wooden houses with gabled roofs and wide porches, most of them converted into inns.

From the center of Lenox, a descent leads to the main entrance to Tanglewood, the summer home of the Boston Symphony Orchestra. The entrance is in Lenox, but the actual performance area, called the Shed, is in Stockbridge. You may walk (not ride) through the grounds when there are no concerts scheduled. The toughest hill on the ride comes up shortly after Tanglewood, but you can take a break near the top at an overlook that provides a magnificent view of Stockbridge Bowl, a lake just south of Tanglewood rimmed by mountains. A steep descent leads into a fertile valley. The rest of the ride winds through rolling farmland, and you'll pass an apple and cider store about 5 miles from the end.

The 20-mile ride bypasses the Tanglewood area by following a more direct route from the center of Lenox back to Pittsfield. You'll pass the classically elegant Church on the Hill, built in 1805, a half mile from the center of Lenox. The last 5 miles retrace the way you started in order to avoid Routes 7 and 20, a busy and unattractive road. The 16-mile ride bypasses most of the estates by heading directly into the center of Lenox before reaching the railroad station.

The center of Pittsfield is worth a visit. The Berkshire Athenaeum (the public library), with an outstanding Melville collection, is excellent. Just south of Park Square is the Berkshire Museum, with exhibits of art, local history, artifacts, and natural history.

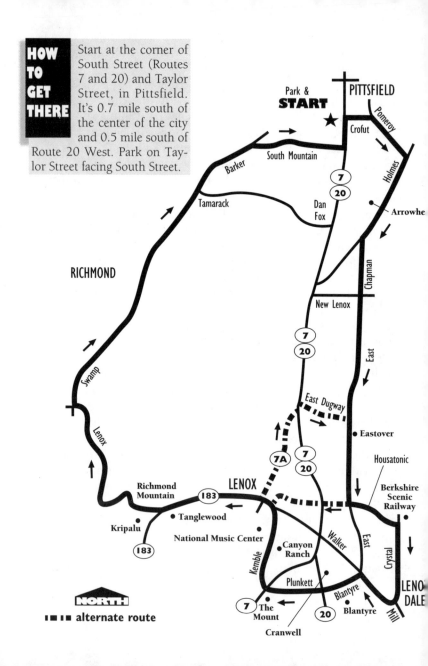

HOW TO GET THERE

Start at the corner of South Street (Routes 7 and 20) and Taylor Street, in Pittsfield. It's 0.7 mile south of the center of the city and 0.5 mile south of Route 20 West. Park on Taylor Street facing South Street.

Park &
START

PITTSFIELD

Crofut

Pomeroy

South Mountain

Barker

7
20

Holmes

Tamarack

Dan Fox

Arrowhe

RICHMOND

Chapman

New Lenox

7
20

East

Swamp

East Dugway

Lenox

Eastover

7A   7
20

Housatonic

Richmond Mountain

183

LENOX

Berkshire Scenic Railway

Kripalu

Tanglewood

National Music Center

Canyon Ranch

Walker

East

183

Kemble

Plunkett

Blantyre

Crystal

LENO DALE

7   The Mount

20   Blantyre

Mill

Cranwell

NORTH

▪■▪■ alternate route

Directions for the ride: 25 miles—

DIRECTIONS
FOR
THE RIDE

1. Jog left on South Street and then immediately right on Crofut Street, at traffic light. Go 0.3 mile to end (Pomeroy Avenue).
2. Right for 0.9 mile to end (Holmes Road).
3. Right for 1.5 miles to Chapman Road on left, opposite Tamie Way on right. You'll pass Arrowhead (Herman Melville's home) on your right after 1 mile, at top of hill.
4. Left for 3.7 miles to crossroads and stop sign (Housatonic Street). Here the 16-mile ride turns right.

    Chapman Road becomes East Street at the Lenox town line. You'll enjoy views of the mountains on your left. The Eastover resort is on the left after 2.7 miles.
5. Left for 0.8 mile to crossroads where the main road turns right and a dirt road goes straight. Here the ride turns right, but if you go left for 50 yards, you'll see the Lenox railroad station and Berkshire Scenic Railway on the right.
6. Right (left if you visited the railroad station) for 1.2 miles to fork where Mill Street turns left across a bridge and the main road curves right. **CAUTION**: Watch for potholes and cracks.

    You'll ride through Lenox Dale, passing the former Crystal Hill School (now apartments) and a graceful brown church on the right.
7. Curve right, passing small brick church on left. Go 0.6 mile to crossroads (East Street on right, Blantyre Road on left), just after top of hill.
8. Left for 0.6 mile to crossroads and stop sign (Route 20).

    You pass Blantyre on your left, hidden behind gatehouses and woods. It is a former grand estate that is now an exclusive inn (the grounds are not open to the public). When you get to Route 20 you'll see Cranwell, another former estate that is worth a look, on the right.

9. Straight for 0.9 mile to traffic light (Route 7). There are sweeping views to the left. You'll pass The Mount (Edith Wharton's home and the locale of Shakespeare and Company) on the left immediately before the light. The mansion is set back 0.3 mile from the road.

10. Straight for 1.4 miles to end, at stop sign (Walker Street, unmarked).

    You'll pass Canyon Ranch (a former estate that is now a health spa) on the right and the National Music Center (formerly a boys' school) on the left. At the end, notice the handsome stone church on the right.

11. Left for 0.2 mile to monument in the center of Lenox. Here the 25-mile ride bears left and the 20-mile ride bears right.

    At the monument the former Curtis Hotel (now apartments) is on your right, and the town hall is on your left. If you bear right for 100 yards you'll see the Lenox Library, built in 1815, on the right.

12. Bear left onto Route 183 for 1.5 miles to fork where Richmond Mountain Road bears right (it's unmarked; a sign points to Route 41, Richmond).

    You'll enjoy a long, steady descent out of Lenox. The main entrance to Tanglewood is on the left just before the fork, and the entrance to the Kripalu Center for Yoga and Health (formerly a Jesuit monastery) is immediately after it.

13. Bear right for 3.2 miles to crossroads and stop sign (Swamp Road).

    You'll climb steeply at the beginning, level off, and then climb steeply once more. As you're making the second ascent, an overlook on the left provides a stunning view of Stockbridge Bowl far below, with Rattlesnake Hill rising behind it. After cresting the summit, you'll descend very steeply on a smooth road.

14. Right for 5.4 miles to South Mountain Road (unmarked), which bears right just after Westview Road on right. You'll pass Bartlett's Orchard, an excellent apple and cider store, on the right after 2.4 miles.

15. Bear right for 1.5 miles to end (South Street, Routes 7 and 20). You'll skirt the base of South Mountain on your right.

16. Left for 0.5 mile to Taylor Street on left, immediately before traffic light.

Directions for the ride: 20 miles—

1. Follow directions for the 25-mile ride through number 11.

2. Bear right on Route 7A for 1.2 miles to end (Routes 7 and 20).

   The Lenox Library, built in 1815, is on the right immediately after the Curtis. The Federal-style Lenox Academy, built in 1805, is on the left just past the library. The picturesque Church on the Hill, also built in 1805, is on the left 0.3 mile beyond the Academy.

3. Left and just ahead right on East Dugway Road (it goes up a short hill). Go 1 mile to end (East Street, unmarked). **CAUTION**: Steep descent with sharp curves—please take it easy.

4. Left for 2.6 miles to crossroads and stop sign at top of hill (Holmes Road, unmarked).

5. Right for 1.5 miles to Pomeroy Avenue on left. The Canoe Meadows Audubon Sanctuary is just past the intersection on the right.

6. Left for 0.9 mile to Crofut Street on left. Pomeroy Avenue bears right at the intersection.

7. Left for 0.3 mile to end (Routes 7 and 20).

8. Jog left and then immediately right on Taylor Street.

Directions for the ride: 16-miles—

1. Follow directions for the 25-mile ride through number 4.

2. Right for 0.5 mile to traffic light (Routes 7 and 20). This is a gradual climb.

3. Straight for 0.8 mile to crossroads (Church Street). A one-way street in the wrong direction is straight ahead. You pass an attractive brick school on your right.

4. Left for 0.1 mile to end (Route 7A, Walker Street). Here the ride turns right, but if you go left for 200 yards you'll see several gracious old mansions, now inns, on your left.

5. Right for 0.1 mile to monument in the center of Lenox (Route 7A bears right). The town hall is on your left at the intersection, and the former Curtis Hotel (now apartments) is on your right.

6. Follow directions for the 20-mile ride from number 2 to the end.

Mansions, Mills, Mountains, Museums, Music, and Meditation

Housatonic–Stockbridge–Lenox

Number of miles:	23 (13 without Lenox extension)
Terrain:	The short ride is gently rolling. The long ride is fairly hilly, with several short, steep climbs and two long, steady ones.
Facilities:	Restaurants and grocery stores in the towns.
Safety concerns:	The long ride goes past Tanglewood, which breeds traffic jams on the narrow nearby roads before and after concerts. See "Safety concerns" for ride 5 for more information.

The neighboring towns of Stockbridge and Lenox, about 5 to 10 miles south of Pittsfield, boast the largest concentration of estates and cultural attractions in the Berkshires. The centers of both towns are elegant—the traditional New England townscape at its finest, graced with handsome churches, inns, libraries, and town halls. In contrast, Housatonic is a mill town with a wonderful example of Victorian industrial architecture. The region's well-maintained secondary roads, winding past mansions and estates with mountain views across their extensive lawns, promise bicycling at its best.

The ride starts from Monument Mountain Reservation, a natural area maintained by the Trustees of Reservations. Two hiking trails lead to the summit of the mountain, a narrow ridge with distinctive rocky cliffs. The view from the top, about 800 feet above the surrounding valleys, is spectacular. At the beginning of the ride you'll descend gradually to the Housatonic River and pass the splendid brick mill of the Rising Paper Company, adorned with graceful towers and built in 1876. About a mile ahead is the center of Housatonic, a small mill town (part of Great Barrington) that has seen better days, but it has begun to rebound as a center for artists and craftspeople who have set up studios in the cavernous brick and stone mills along the river. Three fine churches and a handsome library grace the center of town.

From Housatonic you'll follow the river of the same name into the outskirts of Stockbridge. After about 3 miles, you may detour a short way off the route to visit Chesterwood, the summer home and studio of sculptor Daniel Chester French from 1898 to 1931. French's most famous works are the statue of Abraham Lincoln at the Lincoln Memorial in Washington, D.C., and the statue of the Minute Man in Concord. Just ahead is the wonderful Norman Rockwell Museum, which moved in 1993 from the center of Stockbridge to more spacious quarters on the grounds of a former estate outside of town. Rockwell, loved for his incredibly realistic illustrations of everyday American life, lived in Stockbridge from 1953 until he died in 1978. Shortly beyond the museum is the lovely Berkshire Botanical Garden, with displays of flowers, herbs, and shrubs.

At this point the short ride turns east, heading toward the center of Stockbridge. Stockbridge is the quintessential traditional New England town. It became famous in the 1930s as the locale of the Berkshire Theater Festival and of the Tanglewood Music Festival, and later as the setting for many of Norman Rockwell's illustrations. In 1967 Stockbridge received another boost of fame as the scene of Arlo Guthrie's adventures, described in his narrative ballad (and movie two years later), "Alice's Restaurant." The song became an anthem for the hippie era and the movement against the draft during the Vietnam War. Shortly before the center of town you'll see the tall, brick Congregational Church, a graceful clock tower (called the Children's Chimes) in front of it, and the handsome pillared town hall next door. Just ahead are two historic houses. The Merwin House, dating from around 1825, is a brick, Federal-style gem with period furnishings. The Mission House, built in 1739, is a weathered frame house built by John Sergeant, the first missionary to the local Native Americans.

Just beyond the Mission House is the town's main intersection, dominated by the rambling, four-story Red Lion Inn. A handsome row of ornate Victorian buildings, now mainly shops and boutiques, stands next to the inn, and a dignified stone church guards the opposite corner. Another Stockbridge landmark (0.6 mile off the route, east of town on Route 7) is the Berkshire Theater Festival headquarters, a graceful wooden building designed by Stanford White in 1889. From the Red Lion Inn it's 3 miles back to the starting point. You'll pass the traditional old train station, now vacant, just outside of town.

The long ride continues north at the Berkshire Botanical Garden toward Lenox and loops back into the center of Stockbridge farther along the route. You'll go through the tiny village of Interlaken (part of Stockbridge), passing a graceful brick church. About 2 miles farther on you'll catch glimpses of Stockbridge Bowl (also called Lake Mahkeenac), a beautiful clear lake surrounded by mountains and set back from the road. Just ahead is one of the Berkshires' more unusual landmarks, the Kripalu Center for Yoga and Health. Kripalu (accented on the second syllable) is a center for self-discovery, holistic health, meditation, and spiritual enrichment situated on a broad hillside with a splendid view of Stockbridge Bowl and the mountains beyond. The site originally boasted Shadowbrook, the grandest of the Berkshire estates. After that dwelling burned down in 1956, the surprisingly unattractive current building was constructed as a Jesuit monastery.

Just beyond Kripalu is the main entrance to Tanglewood, the summer home of the Boston Symphony Orchestra since 1936. The performance area (called the Shed) is in Stockbridge, but the entrance is in Lenox. You may walk (not ride) around the beautifully landscaped grounds, with mountain views in the distance, if there is no concert scheduled. From Tanglewood it's about 1.5 miles to the center of Lenox, with the last 0.75 mile going steadily uphill.

Like Stockbridge, Lenox is an archetypal gracious New England town. The center of town is dominated by the Curtis, a four-story, brick former hotel that has been tastefully recycled into apartments. Next to the Curtis is the Lenox Library, framed by tall columns and a graceful cupola. It was built in 1815 as a courthouse. The handsome brick town hall stands across the street from the Curtis. You'll descend steeply out of town past gracious old houses, some of which are now inns. About a mile out of town, just over the Stockbridge line, you'll pass Wheatleigh, a former estate that is now an elegant hotel. (The name is English, but the architecture is Italian Renaissance.) Just ahead the road dips down to the shore of Stockbridge Bowl, a lake rimmed by mountains, and then it climbs onto a hillside past mansions with mountain views.

A steep descent brings you into the center of Stockbridge, but it's worth interrupting it to see two more attractions across the road from each other. Naumkeag is a gracious, gabled mansion designed by Stanford White in 1885 and now maintained by the Trustees of Reservations. It served as the summer estate of Joseph Hodges Choate, a prominent attorney and ambassador to England. Across the road is Eden Hill, a shrine and monastery of the Marians of the Immaculate Conception. The ornate stone chapel (open to visitors), set amidst rolling fields, was built by hand between 1950 and 1960, but it looks like it was transplanted from Central Europe 500 years ago.

When you arrive in the center of town, you'll make a brief out-and-back excursion past the Mission House, the Merwin House, the Congregational Church and clock tower in front of it, and the town hall. From the Red Lion Inn it's a flat, smooth 3 miles back to the starting point.

Directions for the ride: 23 miles—

DIRECTIONS
FOR
THE RIDE

1. Turn right (south) on Route 7 for 0.8 mile to the first right (it's unmarked; a sign says TO ROUTE 183).
2. Right for 0.5 mile to stop sign (merge left on Route 183). You will turn sharply right here.
3. Sharp right for 2.3 miles to crossroads where Route 183 turns right, in Housatonic. It's immediately after you go under a railroad bridge.

   You'll pass the Rising Paper Mill, built in 1876, on the left and then ride along the dammed-up Housatonic River.
4. Straight for 0.1 mile to end (Main Street).
5. Right for 0.3 mile to end (Route 183 again). You'll pass three attractive churches and a stately library on the left.
6. Left for 2.6 miles to crossroads where Glendale Middle Road turns right and Christian Hill Road turns left.

   You'll follow the river on your right. When you get to the crossroads, the ride goes straight, but if you'd like to visit Chesterwood (Daniel Chester French's home and studio), turn left up steep hill for 0.3 mile to end. Turn left again for 0.3 mile to Chesterwood on right. The last 0.2 mile is dirt road.
7. Straight for 1.3 miles to crossroads and stop sign (Route 102). Here the short ride turns right.

   The Norman Rockwell Museum is on your right after 0.5 mile; it's about 0.25 mile off the road. To see the Berkshire Botanical Garden, turn left on Route 102 for 0.1 mile to the garden on left.

HOW TO GET THERE

Start at the Monument Mountain Reservation, Route 7, Great Barrington. It's about halfway between the center of that town and Stockbridge, on the west side of the road.

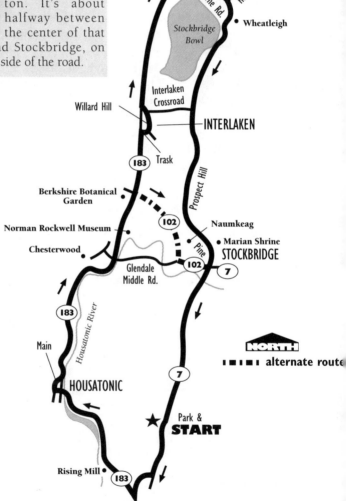

Kripalu

Tanglewood

183

LENOX

Hawthorne Rd.

Hawthorne St.

Old Stockbridge

Stockbridge Bowl

Wheatleigh

Interlaken Crossroad

Willard Hill

INTERLAKEN

183

Trask

Prospect Hill

Berkshire Botanical Garden

Norman Rockwell Museum

102

Naumkeag

Marian Shrine

STOCKBRIDGE

Chesterwood

Pine

102

7

Glendale Middle Rd.

183

Main

Housatonic River

NORTH

▪■▪■▪ alternate route

7

HOUSATONIC

★ Park & **START**

Rising Mill

183

8. Straight for 1 mile to Trask Lane on right, as you come into the village of Interlaken.

9. Right and just ahead left up steep hill on Willard Hill Road (unmarked). Go 0.3 mile to a large, grassy traffic island. The graceful brick Congregational church is on the right at the top of the hill. The Interlaken School of Art, an ornate Victorian mansion with a central tower, is opposite the church.

10. Bear left and just ahead merge right on Route 183. Go 4.1 miles to crossroads in the center of Lenox, at top of hill (Old Stockbridge Road on right).

    After 2.1 miles you'll pass the entrance to the Kripalu Center for Yoga and Health on the left. There's a stunning view of Stockbridge Bowl, with Rattlesnake Hill rising behind it, from in front of the main building. The main entrance to Tanglewood is 0.6 mile past Kripalu. There's a long, steady climb into Lenox. When you arrive in the center of town the Curtis, an attractive brick hotel recycled into apartments, is on the far left corner. The elegant Lenox Library is next to it, and the imposing brick town hall is on the far right corner.

11. Right for 0.3 mile to Hawthorne Street on right, at bottom of steep part of hill.

12. Right for 1.2 miles to end (Hawthorne Road), passing large, gracious homes.

13. Left for 4.7 miles to crossroads and stop sign (Route 102), in the center of Stockbridge.

    After 0.2 mile you'll pass Wheatleigh on the left, tucked out of sight off the road. A half mile ahead you'll ride along Stockbridge Bowl on your right. The large building on the far side of the lake is the Kripalu Center. About 3 miles beyond Stockbridge Bowl you'll pass Naumkeag on the right, opposite the entrance to Eden Hill (the Marian shrine) on the left. The lovely chapel is 0.3 mile off the road.

When you get to Route 102, notice the handsome stone church on your left. The Red Lion Inn is on the far left corner. The ornate brick building two doors to the left of the inn was built in 1884 as the town hall; it now contains shops.

14. Turn right for 0.4 mile to where Route 102 turns right, and backtrack to crossroads.

    This brief out-and-back stretch is too special to omit from the ride. The entire way is lined with elegant houses, estates, and other buildings. You'll pass the Mission House (1739) on the right and the Merwin House (c. 1825) on the left. Just ahead on the left, at the point where you make the U-turn, you'll see the impressive town hall and the brick Congregational Church. The graceful Children's Chimes clock tower stands in front of the church.

15. Turn right onto Route 7 South, passing the Red Lion Inn on your left. Go 3 miles to starting point on right.

    After 0.3 mile you'll pass the old train station, now vacant, on your left. It was designed by Stanford White and built in 1893.

Directions for the ride: 13 miles—

1. Follow directions for the long ride through number 7.
2. Right for 1.4 miles to end (Route 102 turns left).

    The handsome brick Congregational Church is in front of you at the intersection, with the white-pillared town hall next to the church on the left. The graceful Children's Chimes clock tower stands in front of the church.

3. Left (still Route 102) for 0.4 mile to crossroads in the center of Stockbridge where Route 7 South turns right.

    This section is lined with elegant houses and estates. You'll pass the Merwin House (c. 1825) on the right and the Mission House (1739) on the left. When you get to the crossroads, the Red Lion Inn is on the far right corner and a handsome stone church is on the far left corner. Here the ride turns right, but it is worth continuing straight for 1 block to see the wonderful row of Victorian buildings immediately after the Inn. The brick, step-gabled former town hall, built in 1884, is especially striking; it now contains shops.

4. Follow direction number 15 of the long ride.

West Stockbridge–
Great Barrington–Alford

Number of miles: 25
           Terrain: Rolling, with several steep climbs.
        Facilities: Grocery and restaurants in Great
                       Barrington. Country store and
                       restaurant in West Stockbridge, near
                       starting point.

The western edge of Massachusetts, about a third of the way between the state's southern and northern borders, provides spectacular bicycling through a landscape of farms and meadows, with
wooded hills and mountains rising abruptly on the horizon. The
classic New England villages of West Stockbridge and Alford,
along with the handsome commercial town of Great Barrington,
add variety to the serenely rural area.

The beginning of the ride passes through West Stockbridge,
which is not as well known and much less visited than neighboring Stockbridge, 5 miles to the southeast. The center of the village
contains shops and eateries in old wooden buildings and a former
train station that now houses retail establishments. You'll follow
Route 41, a gently rolling secondary road with light traffic, for
nearly 10 miles to the outskirts of Great Barrington. Midway
along this stretch is the hamlet of Williamsville (part of West
Stockbridge), where you'll ride past the Williamsville Inn, a traditional New England hostelry in a rambling wooden building.
Beyond Williamsville the countryside becomes more open, and
you'll enjoy views of hills rising behind dairy farms.

Great Barrington, the largest town in southwestern Massachusetts, seems bigger than a community of 7,500. The bustling

downtown area boasts several impressive churches and a business district with handsome, three-story brick buildings from the late 1800s. The Searles Castle, a 40-room stone mansion built during the 1880s by the widow of railroad tycoon Mark Hopkins, is a downtown landmark. It is now the John Dewey Academy, a school for teenagers with emotional problems. A tough, 0.7-mile-long hill greets you as you leave Great Barrington. About 2 miles out of town is tiny Simon's Rock College, with about 300 students. The college, which enrolls many of its students after their sophomore or junior year of high school, emphasizes seminar-style education and close relationships between students and faculty. The starkly modern campus is set back about 0.3 mile from the road.

The picture-book hamlet of Alford—with a graceful church, elegant town hall, and rustic little schoolhouse, all in traditional New England white—is about 3 miles beyond the college. Most of the return trip from Alford back to West Stockbridge follows a beckoning country road that rolls up and down through farmland, with forested hills and mountains in the distance.

DIRECTIONS
FOR
THE RIDE

1. Turn right (east) on Route 102 and follow it for almost 0.8 mile to Route 41 on right, at top of hill. You'll go through the center of West Stockbridge.

2. Right for 9.5 miles to traffic light (merge right on Route 7), on the outskirts of Great Barrington.

   This long stretch is gently rolling. The first 4.5 miles, to the hamlet of Williamsville, are mostly wooded. Then the landscape opens up, and you'll enjoy views of the hills on your left.

3. Bear right for 0.7 mile to Taconic Avenue on right, at traffic light, just past the business district. **CAUTION**: The downtown area is very busy on summer weekends—watch for parked cars pulling out, car doors opening in front of you, and pedestrians.

43

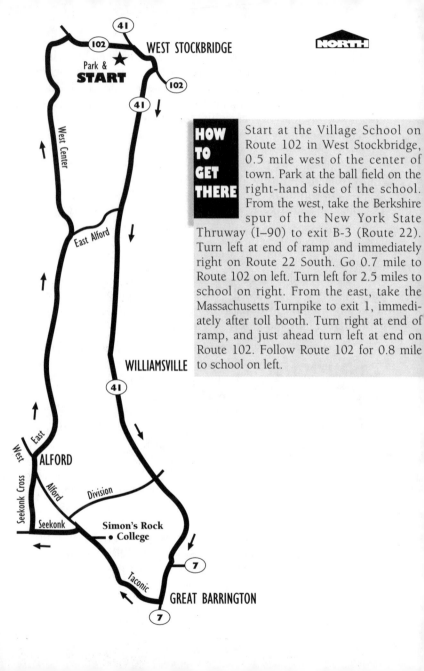

NORTH

WEST STOCKBRIDGE

Park & **START**

West Center

East Alford

WILLIAMSVILLE

East

West

ALFORD

Seekonk Cross

Alford

Division

Seekonk

Simon's Rock
• College

Taconic

GREAT BARRINGTON

HOW TO GET THERE
Start at the Village School on Route 102 in West Stockbridge, 0.5 mile west of the center of town. Park at the ball field on the right-hand side of the school. From the west, take the Berkshire spur of the New York State Thruway (I–90) to exit B-3 (Route 22). Turn left at end of ramp and immediately right on Route 22 South. Go 0.7 mile to Route 102 on left. Turn left for 2.5 miles to school on right. From the east, take the Massachusetts Turnpike to exit 1, immediately after toll booth. Turn right at end of ramp, and just ahead turn left at end on Route 102. Follow Route 102 for 0.8 mile to school on left.

You'll pass two handsome stone churches on your left just before the center of town. Searles Castle, hidden behind a high stone wall, is on your left when you come to Taconic Avenue.

4. Turn right and just ahead bear left on main road. Stay on main road for 2.1 miles to Seekonk Road on left, shortly after Simon's Rock College on right.

    You'll have a steady climb of 0.7 mile at the beginning, with a steep section near the top. Farther on there's another steady hill that's 0.4 mile long.

5. Turn left. **CAUTION**: Metal-plate bridge as soon as you turn; walk across if the road is wet. Go 1.1 miles to Seekonk Cross Road on right, just as you start to climb a steep hill.

6. Right for 1.2 miles to stop sign (merge left at bottom of hill). You'll climb steeply onto a ridge with fine views. Just before the end you'll see the distinctive hump of Tom Ball Mountain in front of you to the right.

7. Bear left for 0.2 mile to fork in the center of Alford (West Road bears left, East Road bears right). A traditional white church and little wooden school stand in the middle of the fork.

8. Bear right for 4.1 miles to fork where East Alford Road bears right and West Center Road bears left.

    In the first mile you'll have two steep climbs, each about 0.2 mile long. After the second hill, the road rolls up and down through rich farmland with glorious views.

9. Bear left for 4 miles to end (Route 102). The superb scenery continues, with the last mile heading mostly downhill.

10. Right for 1.1 miles to school on right, just past bottom of hill.

8 Lee–Otis–Monterey–Tyringham

Number of miles:	29
Terrain:	Hilly.
Facilities:	Country stores in Otis and Monterey. McDonald's on Route 20, 0.3 mile west of starting point.

This ride makes a circuit of a town and three small villages in the southeastern part of Berkshire County. Unlike the elegant, estate-sprinkled towns of Lenox and Stockbridge to the north, the communities on this ride are workaday farming villages that have hardly changed in generations, with traditional white churches, weathered graveyards, and appealing country stores that aren't filled with tourists. The route winds through primarily wooded countryside (with the lovely, open Tyringham Valley for contrast), passing several ponds along the way.

The ride starts from Lee, a small town with a handsome brick business block and a tall white church. (The center of town is about a mile northwest of the starting point on Route 20.) As you head east out of town, you'll climb gradually into the surrounding hills, passing Greenwater Pond, with rustic cottages along its shore, and then Shaw Pond. Shortly before Otis you'll pass a poultry farm with a bit of folk wisdom written on a row of chicken coops. Otis is typical of the smaller Berkshire communities off the tourist path, with a lovely white church and a small general store that serves nearly as much as a community center as a place to shop.

From Otis the route winds up and down to Monterey, another village with some handsome old houses, a white church, and an inviting country store with a bulletin board out front and old wooden benches on the porch. Outside of town, just off the route, you can visit Joyous Springs Pottery, where pottery is crafted using traditional Japanese methods. A little farther off the route on the same road is the Bidwell House, a handsome white farmhouse built around 1750 and filled with period furnishings. The route plunges steeply for 1.5 miles and suddenly you enter the Tyringham Valley, a broad expanse of soft green fields and meadows with wooded hills rising behind them. The tiny hamlet of Tyringham, with only a few lovely wooden houses, a white church with a small cemetery behind it, and an attractive stone library-plus-post office, lies on the edge of the valley.

Just beyond the village you'll pass the architectural highlight of the ride, Santarella (also called the Gingerbread House or the Witch House). It is a cottage that consists primarily of a thick, waving roof, designed to resemble thatch and evoke the spirit of the rolling hills. It was built in 1916 by sculptor Henry Kitson, best known for his statue of the Minute Man in Lexington, and it served as his studio for many years. It is now a museum and art gallery open to the public. From Santarella it's about 3 miles back to the starting point.

DIRECTIONS
FOR
THE RIDE

1. Right (east) on Route 20 for 6.6 miles to fork where Routes 8 North and 20 East bear left, and Route 8 South goes straight.

   For the first 2 miles you'll climb gradually, with one steeper section near the top. After 0.8 mile, notice the handsome Victorian house on your left. You'll ride along Greenwater Pond on the right about 4 miles farther on.

2. Straight (don't bear left) for 5.6 miles to Route 23 West, which turns sharply right as you come into Otis.

   You'll pass the Egg Factory Outlet Store on the left after 2.7 miles; the message "Egg eaters make better lovers" is written on a row of little red sheds. When you get to Route 23 West the ride turns right, but if you continue straight

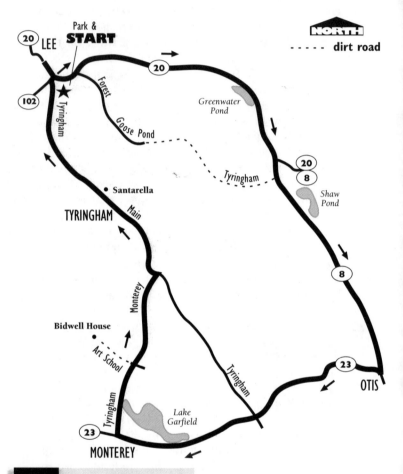

HOW TO GET THERE

Start at the Berkshire Outlet Village, Route 20 in Lee, just east of exit 2 of the Massachusetts Turnpike.

you'll reach the center of Otis just ahead, with a country store on the right.

3. Sharp right for 7.1 miles to Tyringham Road (unmarked) on right, in the center of Monterey. It's immediately before the country store on the left. (Ignore another Tyringham Road on the right after about 3.5 miles.)

   A small, Gothic-style church and hillside cemetery are on your left as you turn onto Route 23. You'll climb steadily out of Otis, with three short, steep pitches. Royal Pond is on the left at the Monterey town line. The ride turns right in Monterey, but Bidwell Park is just past the intersection on the left. Here the Konkapot River flows over a small dam; it's a good spot to enjoy the snack you bought at the country store.

4. Right for 3.8 miles to end.

   You'll pass Lake Garfield on the right after 0.75 mile, and then come to the second of two crossroads 0.7 mile farther on (Mount Hunger Road on right; Art School Road on left). If you turn left here, Joyous Springs Pottery will be on the right after 0.2 mile, and the Bidwell House is 0.8 mile beyond it (it's a steady climb on a dirt road).

   The long, steep descent into the Tyringham Valley begins shortly after the crossroads. **CAUTION**: Keep your speed under control; the road is not completely smooth.

5. Left for 5.5 miles to end (Route 102; sign says TO ROUTE 20).

   The road follows the Tyringham Valley on your left. You'll come into the center of Tyringham after 1.4 miles, and Santarella (the Gingerbread House) will be on the right 0.8 mile farther on.

6. Right for 0.2 mile to outlet mall on right.

Antiques Alley
Great Barrington–Sheffield–Ashley Falls–South Egremont

Number of miles:	29 (17 without Ashley Falls extension)
Terrain:	Gently rolling, with one moderate hill and one steep one. The short ride bypasses the steep hill.
Facilities:	Grocery and snack bar in Sheffield and South Egremont.

The southwestern corner of Massachusetts abounds with elegant villages and fertile farmland, with views of gently rounded Mount Everett, the second-highest mountain in the Berkshires with an elevation of 2,602 feet, in the distance. The valleys near the Connecticut state line are broad and flat, providing some of the easiest bicycling in Berkshire County. If you like antiques, you're in the right place—the villages of Sheffield and South Egremont boast the highest concentration of antiques shops (most of them in handsome wooden, stone, or brick houses about 200 years old) in the state. The long ride goes by Bartholomew's Cobble, a rocky hill overlooking the Housatonic River with wonderful views.

Starting from the southern edge of Great Barrington, the ride follows a back road through the nearly level valley of the Housatonic River, passing dairy farms that extend to the river's edge. After about 6 miles you'll come to Sheffield and pass dozens of antiques shops on Route 7, the only busy road on the ride (fortunately, it has a wide shoulder). From Sheffield, the route continues along the valley past more dairy farms to the crossroads hamlet of Ashley Falls, where you'll see several more antiques shops in fine old houses. About a mile beyond Ashley Falls is the scenic highlight of the ride, Bartholomew's Cobble, which consists of a pair of small rocky outcroppings that rise about 100 feet above the Housatonic River. Foot trails lead about 100 yards to the first hill and a quarter mile to the second one, affording panoramic views of the meandering river below and mountains in the distance. Just beyond Bartholomew's Cobble is the Colonel Ashley House, the oldest house in Berkshire County, built in 1735. Both the Cobble and the Colonel Ashley House have modest admission fees.

Just past the Colonel Ashley House, you'll ascend the only tough hill on the ride and cross into Salisbury, Connecticut, for about 4 miles. Shortly beyond the state line you'll pass the conference center of the Institute of World Affairs, a nonpartisan organization devoted to international understanding and the peaceful resolution of conflict. The hamlet of Taconic, where the main building is the post office, is about a mile farther on. As you reenter Massachusetts, you'll pass the Option Institute and Fellowship, a former estate that is now a facility for personal and emotional growth. It also houses a center for children with special needs, with an emphasis on autism.

The ride now heads north to South Egremont along Route 41, a beautiful secondary road with the rugged Mount Washington Range (of which Mount Everett is the highest peak) on your left, and farms and meadows on your right. You'll pass the handsome brick Stagecoach Hill Inn and then the Berkshire School, a top-quality, coeducational prep school with elegant stone buildings nestled at the foot of Mount Bushnell. South Egremont is a traditional New England village with several antiques shops, the Egremont Inn built in 1780, and a unique little library dating from 1830. The final section back to Great Barrington passes through sweeping expanses of farmland bordered by wooded hills. Shortly before the end you'll see an unusual statue of a newsboy hawking a newspaper; it was cast in 1895 for one of the owners of the *New York Daily News*.

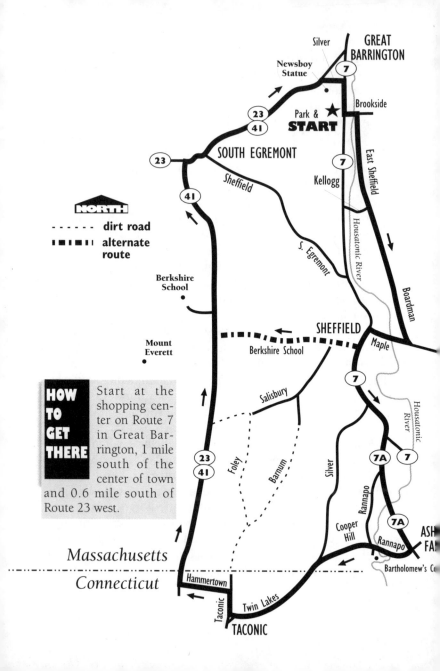

GREAT
BARRINGTON

Silver

Newsboy
Statue

7

Brookside

23

41

Park &
START

7

East Sheffield

SOUTH EGREMONT

23

Sheffield

41

Kellogg

S. Egremont

Housatonic River

Boardman

NORTH

· · · · · dirt road

▪ ▪ ▪ ▪ ▪ alternate
          route

Berkshire
School

SHEFFIELD

Maple

Berkshire School

7

Mount
Everett

Housatonic River

**HOW
TO
GET
THERE**

Start at the
shopping cen-
ter on Route 7
in Great Bar-
rington, 1 mile
south of the
center of town
and 0.6 mile south of
Route 23 west.

Salisbury

7

23
41

Foley

Barnum

Silver

7A   7

Rannapo

Massachusetts

Cooper
Hill

Rannapo

7A

ASH
FA

Bartholomew's C

Connecticut

Hammertown

Twin Lakes

Taconic

TACONIC

The short ride heads west from Sheffield on a flat road with good views of Mount Everett at its far end and rejoins the long ride shortly before the Berkshire School.

DIRECTIONS
FOR
THE RIDE

Directions for the ride: 29 miles—

1. Turn right (south) on Route 7 for 0.3 mile to Brookside Road on left (sign says TO JOSEPH EISNER CAMP INSTITUTE).

2. Left for 0.25 mile to East Sheffield Road on right. The Joseph Eisner Camp Institute, a Jewish summer camp, is on your left at the intersection.

3. Right for 4.9 miles to end (Maple Avenue). **CAUTION**: Watch for potholes for the first mile, up to the Sheffield town line. You'll follow the Housatonic River closely at the beginning. Then you'll ride past prosperous dairy farms lying between the road and the river, with good views of Mount Everett on your right.

4. Right for 0.8 mile to end (Route 7), in Sheffield. You'll pass a graceful white church on your right.

5. Left for 0.4 mile to Berkshire School Road (unmarked) on right, immediately after church on right. Here the short ride turns right.

   You'll go through the center of Sheffield, passing a grocery and snack bar on your right and several antiques shops.

6. Straight for 1.4 miles to fork where Route 7 bears left and Route 7A bears right.

   You'll pedal past numerous antiques shops. Route 7 and the next two roads are nearly as flat as a pancake—enjoy the terrain while it lasts.

7. Bear right for 2.4 miles to crossroads and blinking light (East Main Street on left, Rannapo Road on right). This is Ashley Falls, a village in Sheffield.

8. Right for 1 mile to unmarked fork (Rannapo Road bears right, Cooper Hill Road bears left). You'll see Mount Everett in front of you.

    Just before the fork, a dirt road on the left leads 0.1 mile to the entrance to Bartholomew's Cobble, which is worth a stop. It's only a five-minute walk to the top of the closest hill and back along Eaton Trail. Other trails lead along the Housatonic River and up the next hill.

9. Bear left for 1.2 miles to yield sign (merge left).

    The Colonel Ashley House is on your left near the beginning, and you'll have wonderful views of mountains rising behind farmland. Then you'll climb very steeply for 0.3 mile toward the end—the toughest hill of the ride.

10. Bear left for 2.3 miles to fork at a large triangular traffic island (or a small green—take your pick), in the hamlet of Taconic, which is part of Salisbury, Connecticut. You'll cross into Connecticut after 0.3 mile and pass the conference center of the Institute of World Affairs on your right 0.7 mile farther on.

11. Bear right at fork and immediately turn right at end (Taconic Road, unmarked). Go 0.4 mile to Hammertown Road on left. There's a spectacular view of the Mount Washington Range on your left as you approach the intersection.

12. Left for 0.9 mile to end (Route 41).

13. Right for 8.3 miles to end (Route 23).

    Most of this long stretch, which hugs the base of the Mount Washington Range on the left, is gently rolling. You'll pass the Option Institute and Fellowship after 0.4 mile at the Massachusetts state line. About 2.5 miles farther on you'll see the elegant, redbrick Stagecoach Hill Inn on your left. The Berkshire School is on the left, set back 0.5 mile from the road, about 2 miles beyond the inn. Mill Pond is on your left at the end.

14. Right for 0.5 mile to fork in the center of South Egremont (Routes 23 and 41 bear left). You'll pass a country store and restaurant on the right.
15. Bear left for 3 miles to Silver Street on right, immediately after Newsboy Statue on right.

    Just after you bear left, a small road turns sharply right. If you look down this road, the first building on the left looks like a small church. It is the town library, built in 1830 as a private school.
16. Right for 0.3 mile to end (Route 7).
17. Right for less than 0.4 mile to shopping center on right.

Directions for the ride: 17 miles—
1. Follow directions for the long ride through number 5.
2. Right for 2.7 miles to end (Route 41).

    The road is flat and mostly wooded. You'll pass a little dam and Fawn Lake (a small pond) on your left after 2 miles. Mount Everett looms in front of you at the end.
3. Right for 3.7 miles to end (Route 23). You'll pass the Berkshire School, set back 0.5 mile from the road on your left, after 0.4 mile. Mill Pond is on your left at the end.
4. Follow directions for the long ride from number 14 to the end.

Chapter 2: The Hill Towns

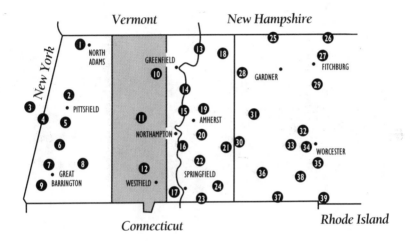

Bridge of Flowers, Shelburne Falls

10 Shelburne Falls–Conway–Ashfield–Buckland

Number of miles:	26
Terrain:	Rolling, with one long, steady climb and a steep, half-mile hill.
Facilities:	Country stores in Conway and Ashfield. Snack bar in Ashfield. Restaurants at end.

This ride makes a circuit of four unspoiled small towns southwest of Greenfield. Far from any metropolitan area, the landscape is very rural, with virtually no traffic except for a brief stretch on Route 2 near the end of the ride. You'll traverse a harmonious mix of woods and farmland, with hills rising in the distance across the fields.

The ride starts from Shelburne Falls, an attractive town with galleries and craft shops gracing the handsome brick buildings in the downtown area. The town spans both sides of the Deerfield River, although most of the activity is on the east bank. Crossing the river is the lovely Bridge of Flowers, a pedestrian bridge lined with plants and flowers on both sides. Built as a trolley bridge in 1908, it carried trolleys until 1928. A small trolley museum stands at the east end of the bridge, across the street from the starting point.

Another attraction in Shelburne Falls is the Glacial Potholes, a cluster of circular holes carved into the rocks along the riverbed by the swirling of water over millions of years. The larger potholes are perfect swimming holes in hot weather and a great spot to cool off after the ride.

When you leave Shelburne Falls you'll head south, following the Deerfield River, which flows far below you through a steep, narrow valley. The road diverges from the river, climbing gradually through hillside farms and then descending into Conway, a small village with a handsome domed library. You'll pass the Conway Covered Bridge, built in 1869, a short distance west of town. It is closed to traffic.

From Conway, it's all uphill to Ashfield—gradually at first as you follow the South River upstream, and then steeply for the last half mile into town. Ashfield is a pristine New England village with two white churches, a fine stone library, and a graceful town hall with a bell tower. A historic landmark in town is the Zachariah Field Tavern (now a house), a long red building dating from 1792. Just past Ashfield you'll ride along Ashfield Lake, where there's a small beach and a snack bar.

From Ashfield it's all downhill to Buckland, a nearly undiscovered village tucked away on a side road off Route 112. Here you'll ride past some handsome old houses, a traditional white church, a small brick library, and a historical museum. From Buckland it's several flat miles back to Shelburne Falls through the valley of the Deerfield River; you'll follow the river closely at the end.

HOW TO GET THERE Start at municipal parking lot on Water Street in Shelburne Falls, which is about 10 miles west of Greenfield and just south of Route 2. From Route 2 West, turn left on Route 2A West for 0.6 mile. Turn right on Water Street immediately before bridge, and the parking lot is just ahead on the right. From Route 2 East, turn right on Route 2A East for 0.7 mile. Turn left across bridge and left on Water Street. Parking lot is just ahead on the right.

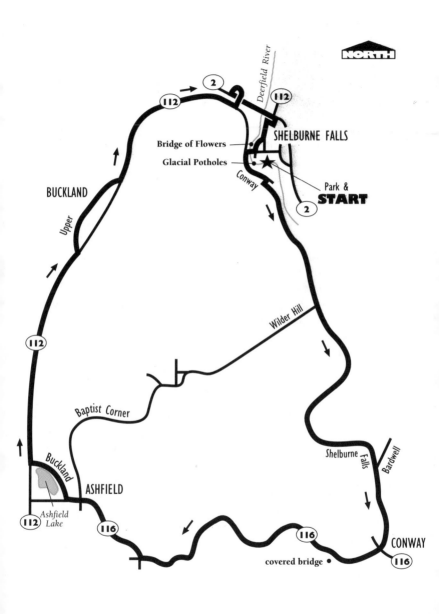

NORTH

Deerfield River

2
112
112
SHELBURNE FALLS
Bridge of Flowers
Glacial Potholes
Conway
Park &
START
2
BUCKLAND
Upper
112
Wilder Hill
Baptist Corner
112
Buckland
Shelburne Falls
Bardwell
ASHFIELD
Ashfield
Lake
112
116
116
CONWAY
covered bridge
116

1. Turn left out of the parking lot on Water Street. You'll immediately come to a crossroads and stop sign (Bridge Street, unmarked). Here the ride turns right across the bridge, but to see the glacial potholes, go straight for 100 yards. Steps lead to the potholes from behind the candle shop. The center of town is to your left at the crossroads.

2. Right across bridge for 100 yards to end. The Bridge of Flowers is on the right, parallel with the automobile bridge you're crossing.

   Opposite the far end of the bridge is McCusker's Market, a wonderful, old-fashioned country store. The Salmon Falls Marketplace, where you can view the works of numerous local artists and craftspeople, is on the hillside to the left of McCusker's Market.

3. Turn left and then immediately bear left at fork on Conway Street, following the river on your left. Stay on main road for 8.6 miles to crossroads and stop sign (Route 116), in Conway. The main road turns 90 degrees right after 0.3 mile. **CAUTION**: Diagonal railroad tracks 0.4 mile beyond this point.

   You'll climb gradually as the road diverges from the river, which flows through the steep, narrow valley on your left. There's a steep descent about 2 miles before Conway. When you come to Route 116, the ride goes straight, but the center of Conway is to your left. The graceful domed library, 0.2 mile from the intersection, is worth a look.

4. Go straight onto Route 116 North and stay on it for 7.1 miles to Buckland Road on right, shortly after the center of Ashfield. You'll pass a country store shortly after you get onto Route 116, and you'll see the covered bridge on your

left after 0.7 mile. There's a steep, 0.5-mile climb into Ashfield.

5. Right for 0.8 mile to end (Route 112). You'll follow Ashfield Lake on your left, passing a beach and a snack bar.

6. Right for 3 miles to Upper Street, which bears left, parallel with the main road (sign may say TO BUCKLAND CENTER). It's 1 mile after the Buckland town line. Most of this section is a steady, relaxing descent—enjoy it!

7. Bear left for 1.4 miles to end (Route 112 again). You'll go through the center of Buckland after about a mile.

8. Left for 3.1 miles to end (Route 2).

9. Left (**CAUTION** here) for 0.6 mile to Route 112 North on right, just after the bridge over the Deerfield River.

10. Right and just ahead right again (still Route 112 North). Go 0.1 mile to end.

11. Left for 0.2 mile to Water Street (unmarked), which bears right. You'll follow the Deerfield River on your right.

12. Bear right for 0.25 mile to parking lot on left. The Bridge of Flowers and trolley museum are on the right, opposite the lot.

William Cullen Bryant Homestead, Cummington

The Heart of the Hill Towns
Cummington–Goshen–Chesterfield–Worthington

Number of miles:	27
Terrain:	Very hilly. This ride is the second toughest in the book.
Facilities:	Country stores in the towns.

The region midway between Pittsfield and the Connecticut River, and halfway between the Connecticut and Vermont borders, is about as rural as you can get in Massachusetts. Bicycling in this area is challenging but exciting, with long climbs balanced by thrilling descents and inspiring mountain scenery. And just when you need a rest or a bite to eat, along comes an unspoiled, traditional New England village. The ride includes a scenic highlight and also a historical one—the rugged Chesterfield Gorge and the William Cullen Bryant Homestead—both administered by the Trustees of Reservations.

The ride starts just outside Cummington, the first of the four villages on the route. You'll go through the center of town at the end of the ride. From Cummington you'll follow the fast-flowing Westfield River for about 2 miles and then endure a long, steady climb to the lovely hilltop village of Goshen. Here you'll see a handsome stone library with columns, a school with a clock tower, and the traditional white church. From Goshen, a secondary road traverses several shorter ups and downs to Chesterfield, another classic New England village with a graceful white church and pillared town hall facing each other across the road, big clapboard houses, and an inviting country store.

From Chesterfield there's a heart-stopping descent to the Westfield River—the road drops nearly 700 feet in 2 miles. You'll follow the river for about a mile to Chesterfield Gorge, a craggy canyon with the river rushing below. A steep climb brings you onto a plateau with prosperous dairy farms and views of hills on the horizon. The route then climbs more gradually to the elegant hilltop villages of Worthington Center and Worthington Corners, which are about a mile apart. Worthington Center contains an attractive white church, a town hall with columns framing the entrance, and rambling wooden houses. Worthington Corners is a classic crossroads village with an appealing country store, an old wooden library, and handsome Federal-era and Greek Revival–style houses.

Another pulse-quickening descent plunges from Worthington Corners into a narrow valley; then it's up and down (but mostly up) to the homestead of William Cullen Bryant, the eminent nineteenth-century poet and newspaper editor. The graceful, twenty-three-room mansion, with a gambrel roof and a broad porch, is set on a hillside with a sweeping view of the valley of the Westfield River and distant hills. From the Bryant Homestead it's all downhill back to the river. Just ahead, at the end of the ride, is the attractive town center of Cummington, with a brick town hall ornamented by white columns and a bell tower.

DIRECTIONS
FOR
THE RIDE

1. Right on Route 9 for 6.8 miles to fork where Route 9 bears left and South Main Street goes straight, shortly after the village of Goshen.

   At the beginning you'll cross the Westfield River and follow it closely on your right for 2 miles. The road then diverges from the river and climbs steadily for 3 miles, with a steep section about 0.5 mile long at the top. There's a country store on your right in Goshen.

2. Straight and then immediately right on West Street. Go 3.3 miles to crossroads and stop sign (Willcutt Road on right,

North Road on left). This stretch is mostly wooded and very rolling, with some steep ups and downs.

3. Left for 0.9 mile to crossroads and stop sign (Route 143), in Chesterfield. You'll climb steeply for about 0.4 mile near the end.

4. Right for 2.2 miles to crossroads at bottom of long, steep hill (Cummington Road on right, Ireland Street on left).

   There's a country store on your right at the beginning as you start to go downhill. The descent is gradual at first and very steep toward the bottom. You'll cross the Westfield River again immediately before the crossroads, in the hamlet of West Chesterfield. A little yellow post office, formerly a library, is on your left immediately before the bridge.

5. Left for 1.7 miles to fork, while ascending a steep hill (Ireland Street bears left, Partridge Road bears right).

   After 0.8 mile you'll see a dirt road on your left just as you start to climb sharply. It leads 100 yards to Chesterfield Gorge, which is worth a stop. Then you'll grind up a steep, steplike hill to the fork.

6. Bear right for almost 1.7 miles to Radiker Road on left, at bottom of hill. You'll climb steadily for 0.4 mile, descend briefly, and climb again steeply for 0.2 mile to an open hilltop with fine views.

7. Left for 0.8 mile to end (Route 112). It's all uphill, with a steep section at the beginning. A graceful, Gothic-style house is on your left at the end.

8. Right for 1.7 miles to traffic light, in Worthington Corners. Most of this section is a very gradual climb, with a short, steep hill at the end. You'll see a small airfield on your right at the beginning and come into Worthington Center after 0.7 mile.

9. Turn right and just ahead curve left (still Route 112), passing the country store on your right. Go 0.9 mile to where Route 143 goes straight and Route 112 turns left, at bottom

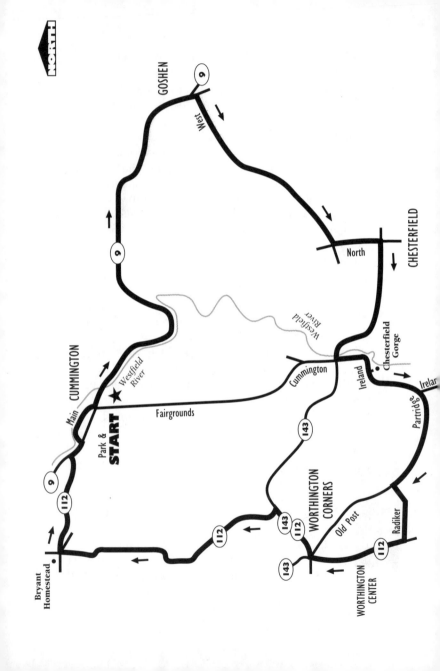

of steep hill. Don't miss the intersection—you'll have to backtrack up a long, steep hill if you do.

10. Left (**CAUTION** here) for 4.1 miles to crossroads where Route 112 turns right and the Bryant Homestead is to your left.

    CAUTION: There's a steep, curving descent at the beginning. Then you'll climb steeply for 0.4 mile, go downhill briefly, and ascend steadily for 0.9 mile with a very steep spot near the top. At the crossroads the ride turns right, but if you turn left you'll come to the Bryant Homestead after 0.2 mile. The view across the field in front of the house is magnificent.

11. Turn 90 degrees right (still Route 112) for 1.5 miles to end (Route 9), at bottom of hill. It's all downhill! There's an excellent country store and snack bar on your right at the end.

12. Right for 0.4 mile to first left (sign says TO ROUTE 116, PLAINFIELD). You'll follow the Westfield River on your left.

13. Left for 0.7 mile to crossroads and stop sign (Route 9 again). The starting point is on the far left side of the intersection. You'll go through the center of Cummington and pass the town hall on your right.

HOW TO GET THERE

Start at the Cummington General Store (the post office is also in the building), at the junction of Route 9, Main Street, and Fairgrounds Road, in Cummington. It's on the south side of Route 9, about 20 miles west of Northampton and 25 miles east of Pittsfield.

I Will Lift Up Mine Eyes Unto the Hills

Westfield–Montgomery–Westhampton– Southampton

Number of miles:	36 (20 without Montgomery-Westhampton extension)
Terrain:	The short ride is gently rolling, with one tough hill. The long ride is the toughest in the book, with two steep climbs more than 1 mile long, and several shorter hills.
Facilities:	Convenience store in Southampton (short ride). Country store in Norwich Bridge. Farm stand in Westhampton. Restaurant in Southampton (long ride). Friendly's Ice Cream and Bickford's Pancakes at end.

Just northwest of Springfield, delightful bicycling abounds in the small valley tucked between the East Mountain–Mount Tom range on the east and rugged, wooded hill country on the west. Lying in the small watershed of the Manhan River, the valley presents a harmonious blend of broad, gently rolling farms and stands of woodland, with views of the surrounding hills across the fields.

The ride starts on the outskirts of Westfield, a small industrial city that for many years was best known as the home of Columbia bicycles. You'll immediately head into farm country as you wind along the western edge of the valley on back roads to the handsome town of Southampton, with its magnificent old white church and a brick turn-of-the-twentieth-century library. From here you'll head through prosperous farmland to Pequot Pond and return to Westfield, skirting the base of East Mountain.

The long ride challenges the cyclist with a taste of the rugged hill country that extends across the western quarter of the state. As you struggle across the steep, nearly unpopulated landscape, you'll understand why the hill towns were the last part of the state to be settled. Leaving the valley, you'll climb nearly 1,000 feet to the tiny, unspoiled hilltop town of Montgomery, complete with a little red schoolhouse, a traditional white church, a wooden town hall, and an inviting little library. From here you'll revel in a screaming descent to the Westfield River, only to face another long climb as you head northeast toward Westhampton. This is another New England gem of a town, with a dignified white church commanding the hillside; a small, well-kept green; and a white, pillared town hall. Beyond Westhampton you'll coast primarily downhill to Southampton, enjoying spectacular views of the Mount Tom range. In Southampton you'll pick up the short ride and follow it past Pequot Pond back to Westfield.

DIRECTIONS
FOR
THE RIDE

Directions for the ride: 36 miles—

1. Right on Routes 10 and 202, and then immediately right at traffic light on Arch Road. Go 1.6 miles to Cabot Road, which bears left just after the Agway plant on right. **CAUTION**: Bad diagonal railroad tracks after 1.1 miles.

2. Bear left for 0.7 mile to end (Russellville Road, unmarked).

3. Left for 0.2 mile to stop sign (merge left on Montgomery Road). You will turn sharply right here.

4. Sharp right for 2 miles to fork (Montgomery Road bears left, North Road bears right). Here the short ride bears right.

5. Bear left for 7 miles to end, at stop sign (merge right on Route 112).

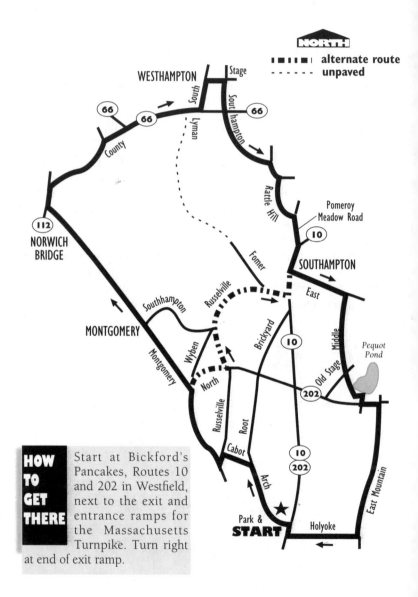

NORTH

▉▉▉▉▉ alternate route
▪ ▪ ▪ ▪ ▪ unpaved

WESTHAMPTON

Stage

66   66   South   Southampton   66

County   Lyman

112   Rattle Hill

NORWICH
BRIDGE   Pomeroy
Meadow Road

10

Fomer   SOUTHAMPTON

Southhampton   Russelville   East

MONTGOMERY   Wyben   Brickyard   10   Middle   Pequot
Pond

Montgomery   North   Old Stage

Russelville   202

Root   202

Cabot   10

Arch   East Mountain

HOW TO GET THERE   Start at Bickford's Pancakes, Routes 10 and 202 in Westfield, next to the exit and entrance ramps for the Massachusetts Turnpike. Turn right at end of exit ramp.

Park &
START   Holyoke

It's a steady climb to Montgomery; you ascend 600 feet in 2 miles. Almost at the top, at the crossroads, is a red, one-room schoolhouse on the left, built in 1868. A mile farther on you'll pass the town hall and library. From here it's a breathtaking downhill plunge to the Westfield River. **CAUTION**: There are some sharp curves toward the bottom—don't let yourself go too fast. At the end the ride bears right, but if you turn left for 0.1 mile there's a country store in the hamlet of Norwich Bridge, which is part of the town of Huntington.

6. Bear right for 0.7 mile to County Road, which bears right up a steep hill.

7. Bear right for 2.4 miles to fork where County Road turns right and Searle Road curves left, just before the church. You climb 600 feet in the first 1.2 miles, an average grade of 10 percent.

8. Right for 0.6 mile to stop sign (merge head-on into Route 66 East).

9. Straight for 3 miles to South Road on left, at bottom of hill (sign says TO WESTHAMPTON, 1 MILE).

10. Left for 1.3 miles to crossroads, at the church (Tob Road on left, Stage Road on right). This is the gracious village center of Westhampton. Notice the pillared town hall on your left at the intersection.

11. Right for 0.5 mile to crossroads almost at bottom of hill (Southampton Road).

12. Right for 1.2 miles to crossroads and stop sign (Route 66, Main Road). There's a farm stand on the far right corner.

13. Straight for 2.3 miles to end (Lead Mine Road). There's a magnificent view on your left at the beginning.

14. Right for 0.25 mile to Rattle Hill Road on right.

15. Right for 0.9 mile to yield sign (main road turns left). Look for fine views of the Mount Tom Range to your left.

16. Left for 0.3 mile to end (Pomeroy Meadow Road).

17. Right for 0.5 mile to end (Route 10). At the end there's a restaurant in the small shopping center on your left, and another one in front of you.
18. Right for 0.5 mile to East Street on left, immediately before traffic light. This is Southampton. There's a stately white church just beyond the intersection on your right.
19. Left for 1.9 miles to Middle Road on right, at top of hill.
20. Right for 2 miles to crossroads and stop sign (Old Stage Road).
21. Straight for 0.5 mile to where the main road turns 90 degrees left along the shore of Pequot Pond. Immediately after the turn, Long Pond Road (unmarked) turns right.
22. Right and just ahead left at crossroads on Route 202 (**CAUTION** here). Go 0.7 mile to traffic light (Old County Road on left, East Mountain Road on right). You'll pass a state-run beach on Pequot Pond on your left.
23. Right for 2.9 miles to Holyoke Road on right, immediately after you go underneath the Massachusetts Turnpike and a railroad bridge.
24. Right for 1.9 miles to end (Routes 202 and 10).
25. Turn right, and Bickford's is just ahead on left.

Directions for the ride: 20 miles—
1. Follow directions for the long ride through number 4.
2. Bear right for 0.3 mile to fork where Wyben Road bears slightly left and North Road bears right.
3. Bear right for 0.8 mile to crossroads and stop sign (Russellville Road).
4. Left for 3.7 miles to end (Route 10). After about 1 mile you'll climb steeply for 0.4 mile—the worst hill of the short ride.
5. Left for 0.7 mile to East Street on right, immediately after traffic light in the center of Southampton. Shortly before the

light a handsome brick library is on your right, and at the intersection a beautiful white church is on your left.

6. Right for 1.9 miles to Middle Road on right, at top of hill.
7. Follow directions for the long ride from number 20 to the end.

Chapter 3: The Pioneer Valley

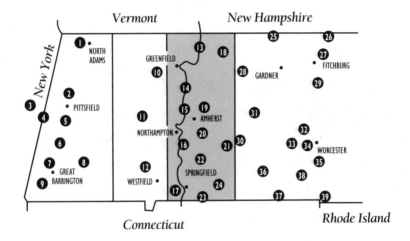

Turners Falls–Gill–Northfield –Millers Falls

Number of miles:	29 (23 without Northfield loop)
Terrain:	Rolling, with several hills. 1.1 miles of hard-packed dirt road, which can be avoided.
Facilities:	Grocery and restaurants in Northfield. Grocery and snack bar in Millers Falls. Stores and restaurants in Turners Falls, at end..

This ride takes you exploring the Pioneer Valley just south of the Vermont and New Hampshire borders. The valley in this region is rugged and narrow, with steep hills rising almost at the water's edge, and thinly populated. Surprisingly, this remote area is home to two magnificently situated preparatory schools only 4 miles apart—Mount Hermon on the west bank of the river and Northfield on the east bank. The two schools are administered together and are collectively called the Northfield–Mount Hermon School.

You start from Turners Falls, a planned industrial community right out of the nineteenth century. A compact business section of ornate brick Victorian buildings lines the unusually wide main street. On the cross streets are brick rowhouses that seem transplanted from an English industrial city. Two magnificent brick churches stand proudly over the town. As you leave the town, you'll cross the Connecticut River above an impressive dam and immediately head into rugged hill country to the tiny valley village of Gill. The village center has a country store, a church, an old cemetery, a few old wooden homes, and not much else. Two miles beyond Gill, you suddenly come upon the Mount Hermon campus, impressive as any in New England, with gracious red-brick buildings spread along a broad hillside overlooking the river, and surrounded by miles of farmland and forest. Shortly after Mount Hermon, you'll cross the river again to the town of Northfield, on the east bank.

When you get to the east bank you'll pass the campus of the Northfield School, another imposing group of handsome stone buildings on a hillside over the river. The town of Northfield is a New England jewel, with gracious old homes, several fine churches, and a couple of former Victorian resort hotels spaced along the main street. The elegant stone library is a New England classic. Below Northfield, you'll bike through large expanses of rich farmland extending to the water's edge. You'll pass near an underground hydroelectric power plant with a fascinating visitors center. The facility offers boat trips on the Connecticut River from June to October. Behind the visitors center is Northfield Mountain, an extensive area with 25 miles of trails and a reservoir on top. It's a popular place for cross-country skiing. Near the end of the ride, you'll go through Millers Falls, a fascinating old mill town whose main industry is paper manufacturing. The town is also the home of Renovators Supply Company, which sells old-fashioned fittings and supplies for renovating old houses.

When you arrive back in Turners Falls at the end of the ride, you'll bike past an attractive riverfront park with a fish ladder, open May and June, next to it. Just ahead you'll follow the power canal, which runs parallel to the river. Long brick mills from the late 1800s line the opposite bank of the canal.

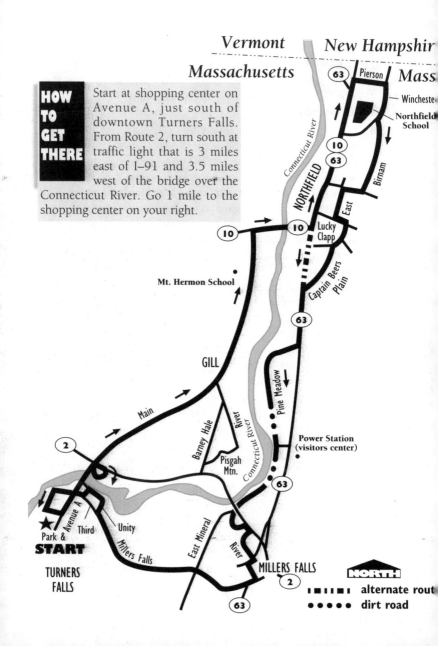

HOW TO GET THERE

Start at shopping center on Avenue A, just south of downtown Turners Falls. From Route 2, turn south at traffic light that is 3 miles east of I–91 and 3.5 miles west of the bridge over the Connecticut River. Go 1 mile to the shopping center on your right.

Vermont

New Hampshir

Massachusetts

Mass

63 Pierson

Wincheste

Northfield School

63

10

63

NORTHFIELD

Connecticut River

Birnam

East

10 Lucky Clapp

Captain Beers Plain

Mt. Hermon School

63

GILL

Pine Meadow

Main

Barney Hale

River

Power Station (visitors center)

Connecticut River

Pisgah Mtn.

2

63

Avenue A

Third

Unity

East Mineral

River

Park & START

Millers Falls

MILLERS FALLS

2

TURNERS FALLS

63

NORTH

▪▪▪▪▪ alternate rout

●●●●● dirt road

Directions for the ride: 29 miles—

DIRECTIONS
FOR
THE RIDE

1. Left (north) on Avenue A for 0.9 mile to traffic light (Route 2), just after the bridge across the Connecticut River.

    Notice the splendid brick church on your left, set back from the road, at the beginning. It was built in 1885.

    The Great Falls Discovery Center, a combined tourist information and environmental education center, is on your left just before the bridge. When you come to Route 2, you'll make a small clockwise loop along the river and return to this same intersection after 0.9 mile.

2. Right for 0.3 mile to second right (Riverview Drive).

3. Right for 0.6 mile to end (Route 2 again).

4. Jog left and immediately right (north) at traffic light. **CAUTION** here; it's safest to walk across Route 2. Go 6.5 miles to a wide crossroads and stop sign (Route 10), shortly after the Mount Hermon campus.

    You'll start off with a long, steady climb, followed by a fast descent into Gill. Beyond Gill is rolling, open farmland with views of the mountains on the east bank of the river.

5. Right for 1.2 miles to end. Route 10 turns left here, and Route 63 South turns right. At this point the short ride turns right.

6. Turn left and follow Route 10 for 2.9 miles to Pierson Road on right. It's 0.4 mile after Route 63 turns left.

7. Right for 0.5 mile to end (Winchester Road).

8. Right for 0.6 mile to Birnam Road (unmarked), which bears left at a traffic island. The gracious campus of the Northfield School, on your right at the intersection, is worth exploring.

9. Left for 1.5 miles to end.

10. Right for less than 0.4 mile to crossroads and stop sign (East Street).

11. Left for 0.4 mile to end.

12. Left and just ahead right on Captain Beers Plain Road. Stay on main road for 0.7 mile to fork (Lucky Clapp Road, unmarked, bears right).

13. Bear left (still Captain Beers Plain Road) for 0.7 mile to end (Route 63).

14. Left for 1.4 miles to Pine Meadow Road on right. Here the ride turns right, but if you want to avoid the dirt road, go straight for about 5.5 miles to Millers Falls. Resume with direction number 19, heading straight uphill where Route 63 bears left onto Federal Street.

15. Right for 3.1 miles to crossroads just after a 0.6-mile stretch of dirt road. **CAUTION**: There are bad diagonal railroad tracks after 0.5 mile; please dismount. Watch for bumpy spots also.

    At the crossroads the ride goes straight, but if you turn right there's a lovely picnic area on the riverbank. If you'd like to visit the fascinating visitors center of the Northeast Utilities hydroelectric plant, turn left at crossroads for 0.2 mile to Route 63. Turn right and immediately left for 0.1 mile to visitors center on right.

16. Straight for 1.9 miles to end (Route 2). There's a 0.5-mile stretch of dirt road near the beginning.

    You'll follow the Connecticut River and go underneath the high French King Bridge, which carries Route 2 across the river. Just after the bridge, a small lane on your right crosses the mouth of the Millers River over a rickety little bridge, currently blocked off to cars. It's a picturesque spot.

17. Right and just ahead right again on River Road (it's unmarked; a sign says TO MILLERS FALLS, AMHERST). Go 0.8 mile to end (Route 63), in Millers Falls.

18. Turn right and stay on Route 63 for 0.4 mile to where it 63 bears left onto Federal Street. (You will go straight uphill here.) Route 63 turns left and then right on this stretch.

If you go straight at the first point where Route 63 turns left, Renovators Supply is just ahead, in an old mill on the riverbank.

19. Straight for 3.9 miles to Unity Street, which goes straight down a steep hill where the main road curves left. The intersection comes up while you're going downhill.

20. Straight for almost 0.4 mile to L Street on left, at stop sign.

    The road follows the river, providing an excellent view of the dam. The fish ladder (open May and June) is on your right just past the intersection.

21. Left for 0.1 mile to crossroads and stop sign (Third Street).

22. Turn right and just ahead go straight at traffic light. Stay on main road for almost 0.4 mile to shopping center on right.

    You'll follow the power canal on your right at the end. After turning into the lot, notice the magnificent church just ahead on your left.

Directions for the ride: 23 miles—

1. Follow directions for the long ride through number 5.

2. Right for 2.4 miles to Pine Meadow Road on right. Here the ride turns right, but see direction number 14 of the long ride if you want to avoid the dirt road.

3. Follow directions for the long ride from number 15 to the end.

14 Turners Falls–Deerfield– Sunderland–Montague Center

Number of miles:	24
Terrain:	Gently rolling, with several short hills. The optional climb to the Poet's Seat is moderately difficult; the optional climb up South Sugarloaf Mountain is very difficult.
Facilities:	Groceries or restaurants in the towns.

This ride has us explore a beautiful segment of the Pioneer Valley, where it is narrowed by hills rising close beside the riverbank. South of the bridge between Deerfield and Sunderland, the valley is generally wide and filled with broad tobacco farms, but as you head north of the bridge, it becomes progressively narrower all the way to the Vermont–New Hampshire line. The ride has a historical highlight: Historic Deerfield (also known as Old Deerfield), a restored community of gracious homes and inns dating from the eighteenth and early nineteenth centuries.

You start from Turners Falls, an attractive mill town right out of the nineteenth century (see the introduction and direction number 1 of ride 13 for a fuller description). Just outside of town you cross the Connecticut River and enter the valley of the Deerfield River, a major tributary. You can detour 1.2 miles to the Poet's Seat, a ledge perched 350 feet above the river. An observation tower offers a fine view of Greenfield, the larger twin city of Turners Falls, and the Connecticut River. A short ride brings you to Historic Deerfield, a wonderful example of how an early community can be restored to its original grandeur. It's not as well known as Old Sturbridge Village, but it is equally fascinating. You can visit the houses singly or in various combinations. In the center of the village is the elegant Deerfield Inn; a handsome brick church; a spacious green; and the large, gracious campus of Deerfield Academy, a prestigious preparatory school. Also in the village is the Memorial Hall Museum, which houses a collection of artifacts and relics spanning the long history of the community.

From Old Deerfield you'll follow the gently rolling valley of the Deerfield River, with soft, green hills in the distance, and then traverse a small ridge back to the Connecticut River. For a real workout you can tackle the steep climb up South Sugarloaf Mountain, where one of the finest views in the state—the entire sweep of the Pioneer Valley all the way down to Springfield—unfolds before you. You cross the river into the graceful rural town of Sunderland, where you'll see the largest sycamore tree in New England. From here you'll head north along the east bank of the river through rich farmland to a splendid waterfall.

The route now heads away from the river to the lovely New England village of Montague Center, where you'll pass an inviting country store, a brick church with white columns, and an attractive brick town hall built in 1858. Just ahead is the Montague Mill, a four-story landmark perched on a steep hillside with another waterfall behind it. Built in 1834, the mill now contains a secondhand bookstore, a cafe, and a crafts shop. From Montague Center you'll descend gradually toward the river and enjoy a fairly flat ride back to Turners Falls.

DIRECTIONS
FOR
THE RIDE

1. Right on Avenue A for 2 miles to the far end of the bridge over the Connecticut River. As you leave the lot, notice the handsome church on your left. The village of Montague City is just before the bridge. At the far end of the bridge you're in Greenfield.

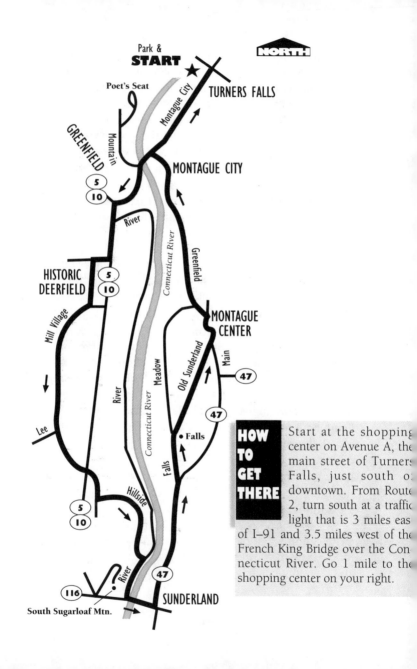

NORTH

Park &
START

Poet's Seat

TURNERS FALLS

Montague City Mountain

GREENFIELD

(5)
(10)

MONTAGUE CITY

River

Connecticut River

Greenfield

HISTORIC
DEERFIELD

(5)
(10)

Mill Village

MONTAGUE
CENTER

Main

(47)

Meadow

Old Sunderland

River

Connecticut River

(47)

Lee

• Falls

Falls

(5)
(10)

Hillside

**HOW
TO
GET
THERE**

Start at the shopping center on Avenue A, the main street of Turners Falls, just south of downtown. From Route 2, turn south at a traffic light that is 3 miles east of I–91 and 3.5 miles west of the French King Bridge over the Connecticut River. Go 1 mile to the shopping center on your right.

River

(116)

(47)

SUNDERLAND

South Sugarloaf Mtn.

Here the ride bears left, but if you'd like to visit the Poet's Seat, which is 1.2 miles uphill off the route, turn right on Mountain Road. Go 0.8 mile to a narrow lane that bears right at top of hill, and bear right for 0.4 mile to lookout tower.

2. Bear left for 1 mile to a large traffic island where Routes 5 and 10 turn left. (Routes 5 and 10 also go straight at this intersection.) The Deerfield River is on your left toward the end.

3. Left (**CAUTION** here) for 1.3 miles to your first right (sign says HISTORIC DEERFIELD).

4. Right and just ahead left on main road. Go 0.9 mile, through Historic Deerfield, to a grassy traffic island where Mill Village Road bears right and another road turns left.

5. Bear right for 3.3 miles to crossroads and stop sign (Routes 5 and 10, Greenfield Road).

    Mill Village Road is a lovely lane through prosperous, broad farms, with a section along the Deerfield River. As you approach Routes 5 and 10, the two hump-shaped mountains in front of you are North Sugarloaf Mountain, elevation 791 feet, and South Sugarloaf Mountain, elevation 652 feet.

6. Straight for 0.7 mile to Hillside Road on left.

7. Left for 1.7 miles to end (River Road, unmarked), at bottom of hill. A moderate climb is followed by a relaxing descent to the valley floor.

8. Right for 1.4 miles to end (Route 116). This is a beautiful ride along the riverbank, with broad farms on the right ending abruptly at the steep side of Sugarloaf Mountain.

    At Route 116 the ride turns left, but if you'd like to tackle South Sugarloaf (1.2 miles off the route), turn right for 0.4 mile to your first right, Sugarloaf Street. Turn right and then immediately turn right again uphill to the summit.

You climb 450 feet in 0.8 mile, for an average grade of 11 percent. **CAUTION**: On the return trip it's essential to take it easy. On one extremely steep pitch, at the hairpin turn, you should walk your bike—some bicycle brakes simply are not designed for these conditions.

9. Left across river for 0.4 mile to traffic light (Route 47) in the center of Sunderland.

10. Left for 1.4 miles to Falls Road, which bears left at bottom of little hill.

     The bell-towered former town hall, now a school, is on your right after 100 yards. An enormous sycamore tree, the largest in New England, is just beyond it on your left.

11. Bear left for 1.8 miles to Old Sunderland Road (unmarked), which bears right uphill just past the Montague town line. A beautiful waterfall is on your right just before the town line.

12. Bear right and stay on main road for 1.4 miles to crossroads and stop sign (East Taylor Hill Road).

13. Straight for 0.6 mile to end, where you merge left at traffic island onto Main Street. (Bear left at island.)

14. Bear left and stay on main road for 0.5 mile to Greenfield Road on left. The main road bears left and then curves sharply right, passing through Montague Center.

15. Left for 4.1 miles to end (Montague City Road). The Montague Mill is on your left at the very beginning, and the village of Montague City is at the end.

16. Right for 1.8 miles to shopping center on left.

Tobacco Road
Northampton–Hatfield–Sunderland–Hadley

Number of miles:	28
Terrain:	Flat. The optional climb up South Sugarloaf Mountain is very difficult.
Facilities:	Grocery and snack bar in Sunderland. Stores and restaurants in Northampton, at end.

The heart of the Pioneer Valley, midway between the Connecticut and Vermont–New Hampshire borders, is the prime tobacco-growing region of Massachusetts. The valley here is broad and flat, with long, weathered tobacco sheds standing guard over the wide, sweeping fields, and with mountains rising in the distance.

Northampton, a city of 30,000, is one of the most attractive communities for its size in New England. In the downtown area (a few blocks off the route), the unusually wide main street is lined with gracious, ornate buildings from the nineteenth century: churches, the county courthouse, city hall, the Forbes Library, old commercial buildings, and many others. It's worth visiting the downtown area on foot after the ride. Adjacent to downtown is Smith College, largest of the "Seven Sisters" schools, with 2,500 students. The tree-shaded campus mixes gracious buildings in many architectural styles. Behind the campus the Mill River flows over a beautiful little dam with a footbridge just below it.

From Northampton you'll head into tobacco country to Hatfield, among the finest of the Pioneer Valley towns, graced by a stately white church built in 1849, a handsome brick library, and old wooden homes. Many of the homes have plaques stating when they were built. Some go back to the 1700s. From Hatfield you'll continue along the Connecticut River to Sunderland, another gracious New England town. For a real challenge, you can climb South Sugarloaf Mountain and gaze in wonder at a spectacular vista with few equals in the state as the broad sweep of the Pioneer Valley unfolds for miles before you.

From Sunderland you'll parallel the river through extensive tobacco farms to the tiny village of North Hadley, with two old churches and a country store. Just ahead is the Porter-Phelps-Huntington House, an outstanding eighteenth-century residence elaborately furnished by six generations of a prominent family. A little farther on you'll ride alongside the river into Hadley, where you'll pass gracious old houses framing a long, slender green. Just beyond Hadley, you'll cross the river back into Northampton on an old railroad trestle that is part of Norwottuck Rail Trail.

DIRECTIONS
FOR
THE RIDE

1. Head west on Route 9 for 1.3 miles to North Elm Street, which bears right at traffic light.
2. Bear right for 0.3 mile to crossroads (Hatfield Street). You'll cross the Northampton Bikeway immediately before the crossroads. To your left, the bikeway (formerly a railway) runs 1.6 miles to Look Memorial Park, an unusually attractive city park. (Turn left at end of bikeway onto Bridge Road, and immediately cross Route 9 into park.). To your right, the bikeway runs 1 mile to State Street, about 0.7 mile north of downtown Northampton.
3. Right for 0.3 mile to end (Bridge Road).
4. Right and then immediately left on Hatfield Street. Go 0.6 mile to end (merge left on Routes 5 and 10).
5. Bear left (**CAUTION** here) for 1.1 miles to a road on your right that crosses I–91 (signs say TO HATFIELD and I–91 NORTH).
6. Right for 9.2 miles to fork where Sugarloaf Extension bears left and River Road bears right.

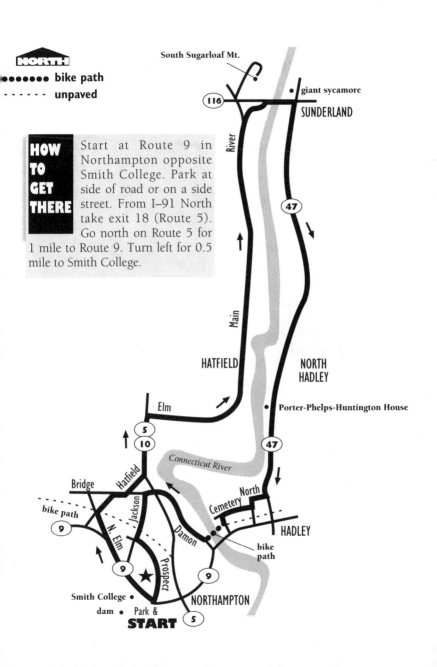

NORTH

•••••• bike path
- - - - - unpaved

South Sugarloaf Mt.

giant sycamore

SUNDERLAND

116

River

47

HOW TO GET THERE
Start at Route 9 in Northampton opposite Smith College. Park at side of road or on a side street. From I–91 North take exit 18 (Route 5). Go north on Route 5 for 1 mile to Route 9. Turn left for 0.5 mile to Smith College.

Main

HATFIELD

NORTH HADLEY

Elm

Porter-Phelps-Huntington House

5
10

47

Connecticut River

Bridge

Hatfield

Jackson

North

Cemetery

bike path

9

HADLEY

N. Elm

Damon

bike path

9

Prospect

9

Smith College •

dam • Park &

NORTHAMPTON

START   5

You'll pass a splendid Victorian house on your left after 1.6 miles. Beyond Hatfield you'll see the distinctive hump of South Sugarloaf Mountain across the tobacco farms. The mountain rises in front of you at the fork.

7. Bear slightly right for 0.4 mile to end (Route 116).

Here the ride turns right, but for a real challenge you can climb South Sugarloaf (1.1 miles off the route). Turn left on Route 116 for 0.3 mile to your first right, Sugarloaf Street. Turn right and immediately turn right again uphill. It's 0.8 mile to the summit, and you climb 450 feet, for an average grade of 11 percent. The view is absolutely worth the climb, even if you walk your bike. **CAUTION**: There is one extremely steep pitch as you're going down, just before the hairpin turn. You should walk your bike on this section, because some brakes may not be able to handle the gradient.

8. Right for 0.5 mile to traffic light (Route 47), in the center of Sunderland. You'll cross the Connecticut River.

9. Right for 9 miles to North Lane on right, just as you come into the built-up section of Hadley. It's shortly after the Hadley Health Center (in the Hadley Professional Building) on right.

After about 6.5 miles you'll go through the tiny village of North Hadley. Here you'll pass a picturesque little dam on your left, just beyond the point where Mount Warner Road bears left. A mile beyond the dam, the Porter-Phelps-Huntington House is on your right. Shortly after, the road hugs the Connecticut River closely.

10. Right for 0.7 mile to Cemetery Road on right. At the beginning, the river is behind the embankment on your right. Then you'll follow a long, slender green framed by fine homes.

11. Turn right on Cemetery Road. After 0.7 mile the main road turns 90 degrees left. Continue 0.25 mile to the Norwottuck Rail Trail, which crosses the road immediately before the end.

12. Right for 0.6 mile to end (Damon Road, unmarked), immediately after the bridge over the Connecticut River.
13. Right for 1.1 miles to second traffic light (Jackson Street on left). **CAUTION**: Busy, narrow road. Most of the traffic behind you will turn right at the first light; get in the middle lane as you approach it.
14. Left for 0.6 mile to crossroads and stop sign (Prospect Street).
15. Left for 0.8 mile to where the main street curves right and a smaller street goes straight downhill.
16. Curve right (still Prospect Street) for 0.2 mile to end (Route 9). Smith College is in front of you, and downtown Northampton is 0.4 mile to your left.

   To see the dam behind the college, turn right on Route 9 and just ahead left on College Lane. Go 0.3 mile to dam on right.

The Dinosaur Ride
Hadley–Granby–South Hadley

Number of miles:	28 (21 omitting Granby, 10 without South Hadley–Granby extension). You can cut 2.5 miles off each ride by following the Norwottuck Rail Trail toward the end.
Terrain:	Gently rolling, with two tough hills. The optional climb up Mount Holyoke is very challenging.
Facilities:	Burger King at end. Groceries and restaurants in South Hadley (long ride).

On this ride you explore the countryside surrounding the Holyoke Range, a prominent feature of the Pioneer Valley. The mountains lie on an east-west axis 6 miles long, averaging 800 to 900 feet high. The highest point, Mount Norwottuck, has an elevation of 1,106 feet. The range is broken in the center by a steep defile known as the Notch. A road leads to the summit of Mount Holyoke, the westernmost peak, which provides a magnificent view of the valley's broad sweep and the silvery ribbon of the Connecticut River curving through it for miles.

The ride starts midway between Hadley and Amherst and immediately heads across broad farms with dramatic views of the Holyoke Range in the background. You'll pass the striking modern campus of Hampshire College. Just ahead, you'll ascend into the Notch, a steady half-mile climb, and enjoy the run down the other side. At the top of the Notch is Holyoke Range State Park, which includes a network of hiking trails and a visitors center.

Shortly after the Notch you'll come to Nash Dinosaur Tracks, a rocky ledge that preserves dinosaur footprints. Just ahead is a true beauty spot of this state: the Aldrich Mill, a weathered wooden building dating from the 1830s, across the road from a picturesque dam.

From here you have a short ride to Granby, a New England gem of a town, with a large green framed by the traditional white church, Victorian town hall, and stately wooden homes. A short climb out of the town brings you onto a plateau with sweeping views. You'll now proceed to South Hadley, another gracious old town. Its centerpiece is the magnificent campus of Mount Holyoke College, the oldest women's college in the country, founded in 1837. The extensive campus, in part designed by Frederick Law Olmsted, has two ponds, a delightful little dam, and a wealth of impressive stone and brick Gothic-style buildings.

From South Hadley you'll parallel the Connecticut River to Hadley, passing Skinner State Park, in which is the summit of Mount Holyoke. The optional climb is grueling, but the view will make it worth your while. The center of Hadley is another New England jewel, with a handsome old town hall, traditional white church, and fine old homes. The Hadley Farm Museum, in the center of town, displays early farm implements and other artifacts. A little farther on you can visit the Porter-Phelps-Huntington House, which is 0.3 mile off the route. Built in 1752, it holds an impressive collection of furnishings owned by six generations of one family.

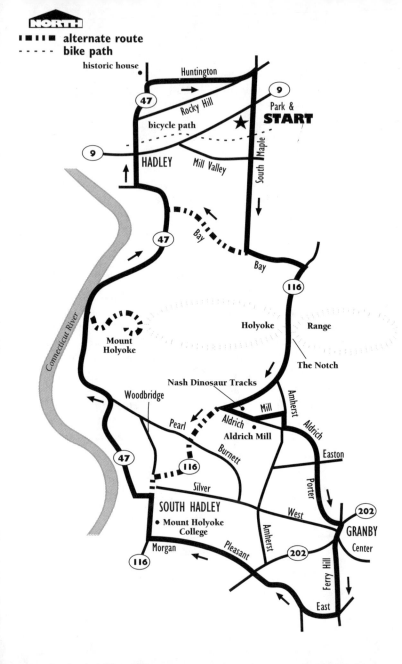

Directions for the ride: 28 or 21 miles—

1. Right on South Maple Street (not Route 9) for 2.4 miles to end (Bay Road), heading toward Holyoke Range.

   You'll cross the Norwottuck Rail Trail at the beginning. The 10-mile ride turns right at the end.

2. Left for 1.1 miles to end (Route 116). Hampshire College, set back out of sight from the road, is on your left just before the end.

3. Right for 2.9 miles to Aldrich Street, which turns sharply left (sign says NASH DINOSAUR TRACKS). It's a steady 0.5-mile climb to the top of the Notch, where you'll pass the Holyoke Range State Park visitors center on your left.

   The 28-mile ride turns sharply left on Aldrich Street. For the 21-mile ride, go straight for 2.5 miles to Route 47 on right, in South Hadley. (Mount Holyoke College is just beyond the intersection on your left.) Resume with direction 13, turning right on Route 47 instead of left.

4. Sharp left for 0.7 mile to fork where one road bears right and the other goes straight. You'll pass Nash Dinosaur Tracks on your left and, just ahead, the Aldrich Mill on your right. Opposite the mill is a fine dam.

5. Straight (don't bear right) for 0.2 mile to end. The millpond is on your left.

HOW TO GET THERE

Start at the Burger King, Mountain Farms Mall, on the south side of Route 9 in Hadley. It's 4 miles east of I–91 and 2 miles west of the center of Amherst.

6. Right for less than 0.2 mile to small crossroads (Aldrich Street).

7. Left for 2 miles to end (Route 202), in the center of Granby. The wooden Victorian town hall is across Route 202 a little to your right.

8. Right for 0.3 mile to the second road that bears left (Ferry Hill Road). Notice the splendid church on your right and the graceful little library on your left.

9. Bear left for 1.8 miles to crossroads and stop sign (East Street). After a short hill, you'll ride along a plateau with sweeping views.

10. Right for 1.6 miles to traffic light (Route 202, West State Street).

11. Straight for 1.8 miles to end (Route 116). Mount Holyoke College is on your right at the end.

12. Right for 0.5 mile to Route 47 (Hadley Street) on left, in the center of South Hadley. You'll ride alongside the campus on your right.

13. Left for 7.1 miles to crossroads and blinking light where Route 47 turns right.

    If you'd like to tackle Mount Holyoke, turn right after 3.5 miles on Mountain Road, at the sign for Skinner State Park. You'll have a steady 2-mile climb with some very steep pitches and gain 700 feet of elevation. You'll see the Connecticut River on your left shortly after Mountain Road.

14. Right for 0.5 mile to traffic light (Route 9, Russell Street), in the center of Hadley. The Hadley Farm Museum is on your right at the intersection behind the town hall.

15. Straight for 1.7 miles to Huntington Road on right.

    You'll cross the Norwottuck Rail Trail after less than 0.2 mile. To shorten the ride by 2.5 miles, turn right on the bikeway for 2.1 miles to South Maple Street (unmarked), and left for 0.2 mile to entrance to shopping center on left.

You'll follow the river on your left about 0.7 mile beyond the rail trail. The ride turns right on Huntington Road, but if you go straight for 0.3 mile you'll come to the Porter-Phelps-Huntington House on your left.

16. Right for 1.7 miles to stop sign (merge left on Rocky Hill Road). After you crest the hill, there's a good view of the University of Massachusetts campus.

17. Bear left and just ahead turn right at traffic light (North Maple Street). Go 1 mile to traffic light (Route 9). Burger King is on the far side of the intersection on your right.

Directions for the ride: 10 miles—

1. Follow direction number 1 for the long ride.
2. Right for 1.7 miles to end (Route 47).
3. Right for 0.6 mile to crossroads and blinking light where Route 47 turns right.
4. Follow directions for the long ride from number 14 to the end.

Agawam–Suffield, Connecticut –Southwick

Number of miles:	30 (20 without Southwick loop, 15 with shortcut)
Terrain:	Gently rolling, with a few short hills.
Facilities:	Snack bars near Riverside Park in Agawam. Stores and restaurants just off the route in Southwick (long ride). McDonald's at end.

This ride takes you exploring the prosperous farm country on the west bank of the Connecticut River, straddling the Massachusetts-Connecticut border just southwest of Springfield. As you head farther west, you proceed into tobacco country, with long, weathered tobacco sheds silhouetted against broad, flat, open fields.

The ride starts in Agawam, a middle-class suburb of Springfield, best known for Riverside Park, the largest amusement park in New England. Near the beginning you'll cruise for nearly 2 miles along the Connecticut River and then pass Riverside Park with its convoluted roller coaster. As you head south and then west, the countryside quickly becomes rural rather than suburban. Suffield, Connecticut, is an affluent town of extensive, gently rolling farms with some fine homes. Although close to both Springfield and Hartford, it is primarily rural rather than suburban. From Suffield you'll cross back into Agawam and ride through pleasant residential neighborhoods as you return to the starting point.

The longer ride heads farther west into tobacco country and to Southwick, which you've probably noticed on maps because the town dips several miles below the otherwise straight border between Massachusetts and Connecticut. The jog stems from a boundary dispute that Massachusetts won in 1642. You'll go across the Congamond Lakes, a chain of three ponds separated by narrow necks of land. In the center of town, just off the route, is a handsome church built in 1824 and the Southwick Inn, an old-fashioned restaurant in an early wooden building.

DIRECTIONS
FOR
THE RIDE

Directions for the ride: 30 or 20 miles

1. Turn right (east) on Silver Street and just ahead cross Route 75 at traffic light. Go 0.9 mile to another light (Route 159). You'll pass an old brick factory on your left.

2. Straight for 0.3 mile to end (Monroe Street, unmarked).

3. Right and just ahead right again at end (School Street, unmarked). Go 1 mile to end (River Road, unmarked). The Connecticut River is in front of you.

4. Right for 2.3 miles to end (Route 159, Main Street).

5. Left for 1.8 miles to fork (Mapleton Avenue, unmarked, bears right). You'll pass Riverside Park on your left and then enter Connecticut 0.5 mile ahead.

6. Bear right for 1.1 miles to crossroads (Barndoor Hills Road on left, Halladay Avenue on right). Here the 15-mile ride turns right. Notice a beautiful Victorian house set back from the road on your right near the beginning.

7. Straight for 1.3 miles to end (Route 75). You'll have good views of the valley on your left.

8. Left for 0.2 mile to Russell Avenue on right.

9. Right for 2.3 miles to yield sign at top of hill (merge right). A graceful white church is on your left at the end.

10. Bear right and then immediately turn left on Spruce Street. Go 0.9 mile to crossroads and stop sign (Route 187).

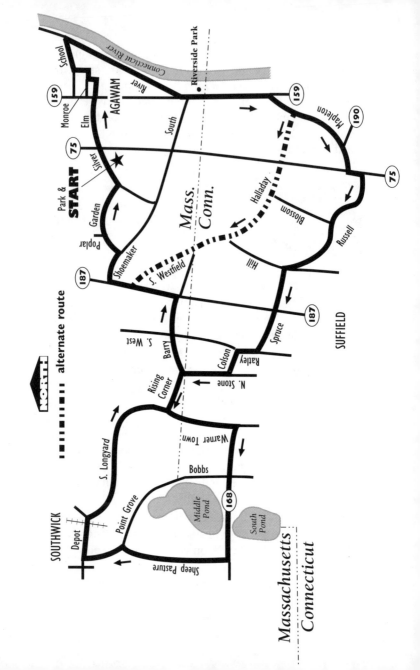

11. Straight for 0.7 mile to end (Ratley Road).
12. Right for less than 0.2 mile to Colson Street (unmarked) on left.
13. Left for 0.5 mile to end (North Stone Street, unmarked).
14. Right for 0.6 mile to fork (Barry Street bears right, Rising Corner Road bears left). Here the 30-mile ride bears left. To shorten the ride to 20 miles, resume with direction 23, bearing right on Barry Street instead of bearing left.
15. Bear left for 0.3 mile to end, at top of little hill.
16. Left for 1.3 miles to a road on your right, just before a stop sign. You'll ride past broad farms and weathered wooden tobacco sheds.
17. Right and just ahead straight at stop sign onto Route 168. Go 2.6 miles to Sheep Pasture Road on right, just as you start to climb a short hill.

    You'll ride between two ponds after 2.1 miles. They are part of the Congamond Lakes chain—South Pond is on your left and Middle Pond is on your right.
18. Right for 1.9 miles to end (Point Grove Road).
19. Left for 0.5 mile to end (Depot Street). Here the ride turns right, but if you turn left for 0.2 mile you'll come to the center of Southwick. The Southwick Inn is a good place for a bite.
20. Right for 0.3 mile to fork (Powdermill Road bears left, South Longyard Road bears right).

HOW TO GET THERE

Start at the McDonald's in Southgate Plaza, on Route 75 in Agawam, 1 mile south of Route 57, at the corner of Silver Street.

21. Bear right and stay on main road for 2.8 miles to fork where Rising Corner Road (unmarked) bears left down a sharp hill at a traffic island. It's 0.8 mile after Foster Road turns sharply left. This is a beautiful stretch through tobacco fields.

22. Bear left for 0.3 mile to another fork (North Stone Street bears right, Barry Street bears left). Yes, you were here before; you've just finished the western loop.

23. Bear left for 1.5 miles to second crossroads and stop sign (Route 187, Pine Street).

24. Left for 1.6 miles to traffic light (Shoemaker Lane), shortly after Route 57 on right.

25. Right for 0.3 mile to Poplar Street on left.

26. Turn left and stay on main road for 1.6 miles to end (Silver Street). The main road bears right onto Garden Street after 0.4 mile.

27. Left for 0.7 mile to shopping center on right, just before traffic light.

Directions for the ride: 15 miles—

1. Follow directions for the long ride through number 6.

2. Right for 0.8 mile to crossroads and stop sign (Route 75, North Street).

3. Go straight and stay on main road for 3.6 miles to end (Route 187).

    The road winds past fine homes and small farms. You'll cross back into Agawam after 2.4 miles and then pass a reformatory (euphemistically called a criminal justice school) on your left.

4. Right for less than 0.7 mile to traffic light (Shoemaker Lane), shortly after Route 57 on right.

5. Follow directions for the long ride from number 25 to the end.

18 Orange–Wendell–Shutesbury –New Salem

Number of miles:	31
Terrain:	Hilly.
Facilities:	Country store in Wendell; it may be closed. Restaurant and country store in New Salem.

This is a tour of the remote, isolated hill country northwest of the Quabbin Reservoir. The region is sparsely populated, with rugged, wooded hills and tiny, perfectly preserved hamlets almost unchanged since the century gone by. As you bike along the narrow, twisting roads, you're nearly as likely to encounter horses and cows in the roads as cars.

The ride starts in Orange, a compact mill town on the Millers River. It is best known for its airport, which is the major center for skydiving in the state. From Orange you'll head through deep woods and small farms to the tiny hilltop hamlet of Wendell. A miniature town hall, library, fire station, church, and school cluster around the green, some in need of a little upkeep.

From Wendell you'll enjoy a relaxing descent to Lake Wyola, where you can take a swim at a state-run beach before proceeding to Shutesbury, another pristine hilltop hamlet consisting of an elegant white church, a tiny post office, several rambling old homes, and not much else. From Shutesbury you'll scream downhill to the watershed of the Quabbin Reservoir and then proceed to New Salem, a marvelous museum piece of a town, set just far enough from the main road that the only way anyone would find it would be by accident. Fronting the large green are a splendid church, an old wooden town hall, and a wonderful old schoolhouse on top of

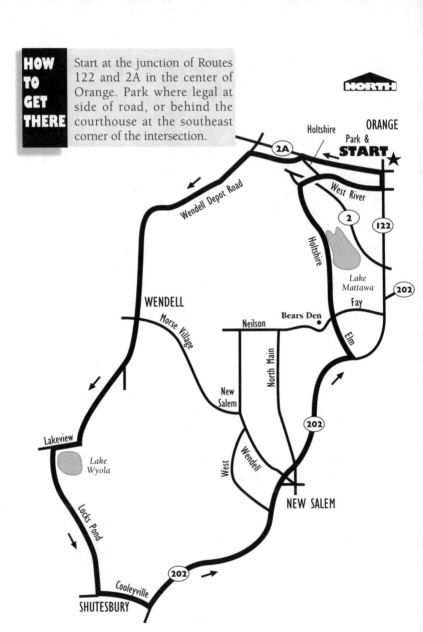

HOW TO GET THERE

Start at the junction of Routes 122 and 2A in the center of Orange. Park where legal at side of road, or behind the courthouse at the southeast corner of the intersection.

NORTH

Holtshire

ORANGE
Park &
START

2A

West River

2

122

Wendell Depot Road

Holtshire

Lake Mattawa

202

WENDELL

Fay

Morse Village

Neilson

Bears Den

Elm

North Main

New Salem

202

Lakeview

Lake Wyola

West

Wendell

NEW SALEM

Locks Pond

202

Cooleyville

SHUTESBURY

the hill. The return leg to Orange brings you along the shore of Lake Mattawa. Just off the route you can visit the Bears Den, a steep gorge with a stream cascading over the rocks.

DIRECTIONS
FOR
THE RIDE

1. Head west on Route 2A for 1.8 miles to Holtshire Road on left, at bottom of hill (sign says TO LAKE MATTAWA).
    Here the ride turns left across a bridge. If the bridge is closed for construction, continue straight for 1 mile to crossroads, turn left for 4.6 miles to crossroads in the center of Wendell, and resume with direction number 4.

2. Turn left and just ahead bear right at fork on far side of bridge. Go 0.9 mile to end (Wendell Depot Road). There's a short, steep hill at the beginning.

3. Left for 4.4 miles to crossroads in the center of Wendell (Montague Road on right, Morse Village Road on left), at top of long, gradual hill.

4. Go straight and stay on main road for 4 miles to Locks Pond Road on left, at far end of Lake Wyola on left.
    A country store is on your left near the beginning. The main road bears right 1.3 miles after you leave Wendell and curves 90 degrees right 2 miles ahead.

5. Left for 4 miles to end, in the center of Shutesbury (Leverett Road on right, Cooleyville Road on left). At first there's a long hill with steep sections.

6. Left for 1.3 miles to end (Route 202). Notice the homey wooden library on your left at the beginning. **CAUTION**: Steep descent. The end comes up while you're going downhill.

7. Left for 5 miles to crossroads and blinking light (sign points right to New Salem Center). After a mile you'll climb

steadily for 1.6 miles. There's another climb of 0.6 mile at the end of this section.

8. Turn right and just ahead bear right uphill at five-way intersection. Go 0.3 mile to the far end of the green in New Salem, then backtrack to Route 202.

9. Right for 2.8 miles to Elm Street, which turns sharply left almost at bottom of long hill (sign says TO NORTH NEW SALEM, LAKE MATTAWA). You'll pass a country store and a restaurant on your left at the beginning. After 0.5 mile, a small dirt turnoff on your right provides a fine view. Most of this stretch is downhill.

10. Sharp left for 4.2 miles to end (West River Street). You'll go along Lake Mattawa on your right after 2 miles.

    To see the Bears Den, turn left after 0.8 mile at crossroads (Fay Road on right, Neilson Road on left). Go 0.4 mile to a small dirt turnoff on the right. A short trail leads to the gorge.

11. Turn right and stay on main road for 1.5 miles to traffic light in center of Orange (Route 122).

12. Left for 0.2 mile to Route 2A.

Amherst–Leverett–Shutesbury

Number of miles:	31 (21 without North Leverett–Shutesbury extension)
Terrain:	Hilly.
Facilities:	None until the end of the ride. Grocery stores and restaurants in Amherst.

The wooded hills between the Connecticut River and the Quabbin Reservoir provide challenging but rewarding cycling. This is a remote, very sparsely populated area, with a few tiny pristine villages and several ponds. From Amherst you'll gain 1,000 feet in elevation as you wind your way through deep valleys up to Shutesbury; then it's all downhill back to Amherst.

Amherst, which sits on top of a gradual rise at the eastern edge of the Connecticut Valley, is the largest community between Worcester and Springfield. With three colleges—University of Massachusetts, Amherst College, and Hampshire College—Amherst is the largest true "college town" in the state. During the school year, the students outnumber the residents. The three institutions are totally different in appearance and character. The massive campus of the University of Massachusetts, with more than 25,000 students, dominates the town with its sprawling, ever-growing expanse of new high-rise buildings, virtually burying the smaller number of older, traditional ones. Amherst College, in contrast, is a perfect example of the gracious, traditional New England campus. Amherst College matches the Ivy League schools in prestige and difficulty of admission requirements. Hampshire College, surrounded by farmland and orchards about

3.5 miles south of town, was founded in 1970 and has a stark, boldly modern campus. Hampshire is the most unstructured and experimental of the three schools and has maintained much of the atmosphere of student activism prevalent during the late 1960s and early 1970s.

Leaving Amherst, you'll bike through a blend of farm country and woodland to the tiny villages of Leverett and North Leverett, where many residents live in harmony with nature in the spirit of the late 1960s. Leverett is the home of Leverett Crafts and Arts, one of the major centers in New England for teaching and working on traditional rural crafts. In North Leverett you can visit the Peace Pagoda, a magnificent Buddhist monument on a hilltop. It is a gleaming white dome with a gold-colored statue of the Buddha in front of it. A temple and residence for Buddhist monks is under construction next to it. A couple of miles ahead, you can see a coke oven dating from the 1800s and a dramatic waterfall just off the route.

Beyond North Leverett you'll climb steadily to the unspoiled hilltop village of Shutesbury, elevation 1,225 feet. It consists of a splendid church, a minuscule post office, a few rambling old homes, and that's about all. From here you finally get paid for all the work you've done up to now—it's a relaxing gradual descent on good roads almost all the way back to Amherst.

The short ride bypasses North Leverett and Shutesbury but comes within a mile of the latter village if you'd like to see it.

DIRECTIONS
FOR
THE RIDE

Directions for the ride: 31 miles

1. Left (west) on Amity Street and just ahead cross University Drive at traffic light. Go almost 0.7 mile to Plainville Road on right.
2. Right for 0.25 mile to end (North Maple Street, unmarked).

3. Right for 2.7 miles to second traffic light (Route 63 on left), in North Amherst. You'll have good views of the University of Massachusetts on your right.

4. Straight for 0.4 mile to State Street, which bears left downhill.

5. Bear left for 1 mile to end.

   If you turn left at crossroads after 0.4 mile and go 50 yards you'll see an attractive dam on your right. Factory Hollow Pond, also called Puffers Pond, a favorite swimming hole for University of Massachusetts students, is just beyond the crossroads on your left.

6. Turn left at end and immediately left again on Leverett Road. (The short ride turns left at end but then continues straight ahead.) Stay on main road for 2.6 miles to fork where Depot Road bears left up a short, steep hill with a church on top. This is the tiny village of Leverett Center. Leverett Pond is on your left just before the fork.

7. Bear left at fork for 2 miles to Cave Hill Road, which bears right. It's just after Rattlesnake Gutter Road, a dirt road on right. You'll pass the crafts center, a long red wooden building, on your right just after you bear left up the hill.

   For a spectacular side trip, turn right on Rattlesnake Gutter Road, which is notched into the steep side of a deep, boulder-strewn ravine. It's a steady 0.9-mile climb to the top of the ravine; use **CAUTION** coming back down.

8. Bear right for 2.3 miles to end (North Leverett Road). There is a long, tough climb at the beginning. After 1.3 miles, at the top, the Peace Pagoda is on the right. It's 0.4 mile off the route on a dirt road. To see it, turn right on the entrance road for 100 yards, curve right into parking lot, continue 0.1 mile, and bear right uphill for 0.2 mile to top. A sign requests that you walk.

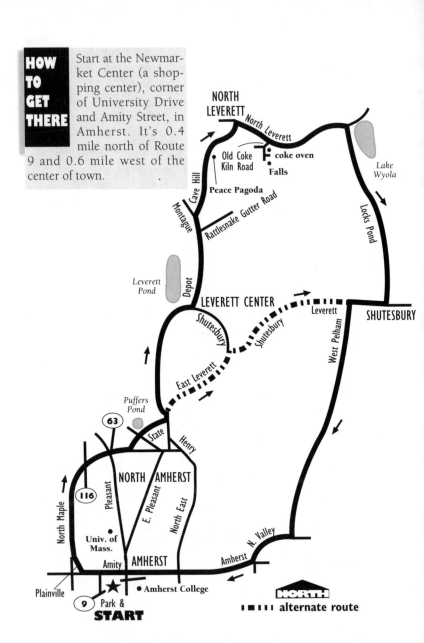

HOW TO GET THERE

Start at the Newmarket Center (a shopping center), corner of University Drive and Amity Street, in Amherst. It's 0.4 mile north of Route 9 and 0.6 mile west of the center of town.

NORTH LEVERETT

North Leverett

Old Coke Kiln Road

coke oven

Falls

Lake Wyola

Peace Pagoda

Cave Hill

Montague

Rattlesnake Gutter Road

Locks Pond

Leverett Pond

Depot

LEVERETT CENTER

Leverett

SHUTESBURY

Shutesbury

Shutesbury

West Pelham

East Leverett

Puffers Pond

63

State

Henry

NORTH AMHERST

Pleasant

E. Pleasant

North East

116

North Maple

Univ. of Mass.

N. Valley

Amity

AMHERST

Amherst

Plainville

9

Park & **START**

★

Amherst College

NORTH

▪▪▪▪▪ **alternate route**

When you get to the end of Cave Hill Road, you're in North Leverett, another tiny community. At the end, there's a small dam and an old sawmill on your left.

9. Turn right and stay on main road for 3.4 miles to Locks Pond Road on right. Lake Wyola is on the far side of the intersection.

   If you'd like to visit the coke oven and waterfall, turn right after 1.1 miles on Old Coke Kiln Road, a dirt road, for 0.1 mile to fork. Bear left on dirt road for 0.2 mile to the white, conical oven on your left. If you bear left just beyond the oven, the waterfall is 100 yards ahead on your right.

10. Right for 4 miles to end, in the center of Shutesbury (Cooleyville Road on left; Leverett Road on right). At the beginning is a long, steady climb with some steep pitches. At the end you're 1,000 feet higher than the starting point. Now the fun begins.

11. Right for 0.9 mile to the second left, West Pelham Road. Notice the one-room schoolhouse on the far left corner.

12. Turn left and stay on main road for 6 miles to crossroads and stop sign (Amherst Road, unmarked). The main road curves sharply right onto North Valley Road after 4.7 miles.

    After a short climb at the beginning, it's a nearly unbroken descent all the way to the end.

13. Right for 2.6 miles to third traffic light (Pleasant Street), at top of hill in the center of Amherst.

    Here the ride goes straight, but if you'd like to see Amherst College, turn left for 0.2 mile to another light (Route 9). The college is on the far side of the intersection on the left.

14. Straight onto Amity Street for 0.6 mile to shopping center on left, just before traffic light.

Directions for the ride: 21 miles—

1. Follow the directions for the long ride through number 6.

2. Left for 2.1 miles to Shutesbury Road on right, at top of short hill.
3. Right for 3.3 miles to West Pelham Road on right. After the initial steep pitch comes a long, gradual climb; you ascend from 400 to 1,100 feet. Notice the one-room schoolhouse at the intersection. Here the ride turns right, but it's worth continuing straight for 0.9 mile to visit the tiny hilltop town of Shutesbury.
4. Follow the directions for the long ride from number 12 to the end, turning right on West Pelham Road instead of left.

Amherst–Belchertown

Number of miles:	27 (18 without Belchertown extension)
Terrain:	Rolling, with several short, steep hills and a long, gradual climb into Belchertown on the longer ride.
Facilities:	Grocery and restaurants in Belchertown. Burger King at end.

On this ride you explore the rolling, rural countryside on the eastern edge of the Pioneer Valley. You'll start by heading east across gently rising farmland with views of the spectacular Holyoke Range rising abruptly from the valley floor. After a few miles you'll come into South Amherst, a still-unspoiled village with a graceful white church and a large green. If you wish, you may ride the first 6 miles on the Norwottuck Rail Trail, a bicycle path built along an abandoned Boston and Maine railroad line. The bikeway is flat and smooth, with no busy road crossings. Personally, I prefer to ride on the roads, which afford better views and are less isolated from human geography.

From South Amherst you'll proceed on narrow back roads to Belchertown, among the most gracious towns in the Pioneer Valley. The magnificent town green, accented by a bandstand in the middle, is a quarter mile long and is framed by several fine churches and large, old wooden homes. Just behind the green is an old cemetery with many gravestones dating back to the 1700s. The town hosts an old-fashioned country fair each June. From Belchertown you'll return to the start on secondary roads through prosperous, rolling farmland with views of the Holyoke Range in the distance.

The short ride bypasses the center of Belchertown by taking a shortcut at Arcadia Lake.

Directions for the ride: 27 miles—

DIRECTIONS
FOR
THE RIDE

1. Right on South Maple Street (not Route 9) for 0.2 mile to the Norwottuck Rail Trail, which crosses South Maple Street. Continue straight on South Maple, but if you wish to use the bikeway, turn left on it for 6 miles to end (Warren Wright Road, unmarked) and resume with direction 8. **CAUTION**: The bikeway is heavily used by both cyclists and noncyclists. Keep alert for walkers, joggers, skaters, children, and dogs. Call out "Passing on your left" or "Coming through" in a clear voice when passing.

2. Straight for 0.9 mile to second crossroads (Moody Bridge Road).

3. Left for 1.5 miles to crossroads and stop sign (Route 116).

4. Straight for 0.8 mile to another crossroads and stop sign (Middle Street). This is South Amherst.

5. Left for 0.1 mile to the third right (the roads come in quick succession), opposite brick school on left.

6. Turn right and then immediately go straight at crossroads onto Station Road. Go 0.9 mile to bicycle path on right immediately before railroad tracks. At the beginning you'll ride through broad farms with views of the Holyoke Range on your right.

7. Right for 1.4 miles to end (Warren Wright Road, unmarked). The bikeway is the eastern end of the Norwottuck Rail Trail.

8. Right for 0.8 mile to crossroads (Orchard Street).

9. Left for 1.3 miles to stop sign (merge right on Federal Street, unmarked). 10. Bear right for 0.5 mile to fork (Metacomet Street bears right). You'll follow Arcadia Lake on your left. At the fork the short ride bears right.

10. Bear right for 0.5 mile to fork (Metacomet Street bears right). You'll follow Arcadia Lake on your left. At the fork the short ride bears right.

11. Bear left for 0.7 mile to end (merge right on Route 9, Amherst Road). **CAUTION**: Bad diagonal railroad tracks after 0.4 mile. Walk your bike across them.

12. Bear right for 1.3 miles to traffic light (Route 202).

13. Bear right for 0.7 mile to Jackson Street on right, just before the center of Belchertown. The green is on your left immediately beyond the intersection.

14. Right for 2 miles to fork where George Hannum Road goes straight and Boardman Road bears left. **CAUTION**: Bad diagonal railroad tracks after 0.5 mile, while you're going downhill. There's a great view of the Holyoke Range just after the tracks.

15. Bear left for 1.5 miles to crossroads and stop sign (Route 202). You'll pass through broad fields bordered by a stately row of trees.

16. Right for 0.7 mile to crossroads (School Street).

17. Right for 3.2 miles to end (Bay Road). Shortly after turning, you'll pass Saint Hyacinth Seminary, run by the Franciscan Fathers, on your left, and Forge Pond on your right.

18. Left for 2.7 miles to South East Street on right. It's 0.5 mile after Hulst Road on right.

19. Right for 1.9 miles to fork at the South Amherst green (Shays Street, unmarked, bears left). Notice the white church, built in 1825.

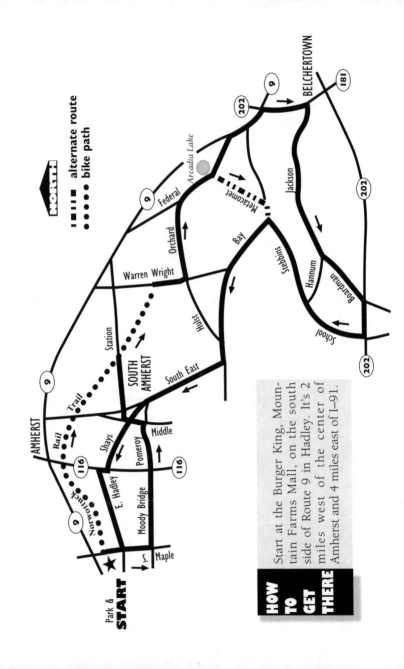

NORTH

I■■■ alternate route
●●●● bike path

BELCHERTOWN

181

202
9

202

9 Federal
Arcadia Lake
Metacomet

Jackson

Orchard

Bay

Stebbins

Hannum

Boardman

202

School

Warren Wright

Hulst

Station

SOUTH AMHERST

South East

AMHERST

Trail

Rail

116

Shays

Pomeroy

Middle

116

E. Hadley

Moody Bridge

Norwood

9

S. Maple

Park &
★ START

HOW TO GET THERE

Start at the Burger King, Mountain Farms Mall, on the south side of Route 9 in Hadley. It's 2 miles west of the center of Amherst and 4 miles east of I-91.

20. Bear left and just ahead go straight at stop sign. Go 1.1 miles to end (Route 116). Look for good views of the Holyoke Range to your left.
21. Right for less than 0.4 mile to East Hadley Road on left. An old gristmill, now an antiques shop, is on your right just before the intersection.
22. Left for 1.8 miles to crossroads and stop sign (South Maple Street).
23. Right for 0.4 mile to shopping center on left. You'll cross the bikeway again after 0.2 mile. If you turn left, it leads 3.9 miles to its western end in Northampton, just beyond the Connecticut River.

Directions for the ride: 18 miles—
1. Follow the directions for the long ride through number 10.
2. Bear right for 0.9 mile to end (Bay Road).
3. Right for 3 miles to South East Street on right. It's 0.5 mile after Hulst Road on right.
4. Follow the directions for the long ride from number 19 to the end.

Quabbin Reservoir

The Quabbin Reservoir Ride
Belchertown–Bondsville–Ware

Number of miles:	27
Terrain:	Hilly.
Facilities:	None on the route. Groceries and restaurants in Belchertown.

This is a tour of the southern shore of the Quabbin Reservoir, by far the largest lake in Massachusetts, with spectacular rides along Goodenough Dike and Winsor Dam, the massive, half-mile-long embankments that hold the water in its place. South of the reservoir is magnificent, rolling farmland.

You'll start from the elegant, classic New England town of Belchertown, among the finest in the Pioneer Valley. The magnificent green, highlighted by a bandstand in the middle, is a quarter of a mile long and is framed by several fine churches and large, old wooden homes. Just behind the green is an old cemetery with many gravestones dating back to the 1700s. Belchertown hosts an old-fashioned country fair in June.

From Belchertown you'll head south through rolling farmland and orchards to the little valley town of Bondsville, which straddles the Belchertown-Palmer line along the Swift River. From here you'll follow the delightful valley of the Ware River, with views of rugged hills on both sides, to the outskirts of Ware, a nineteenth-century mill town straight out of the Industrial Revolution. Ware is one of the great bargain centers for clothing and sportswear in New England; most of the mills have factory outlets. The majority of the mills are clustered in one enormous complex just east of the center of town.

Beyond Ware comes the exciting part of the ride, as you follow the southern shore of the Quabbin Reservoir back to Belchertown. Physically, the reservoir is impressive, 15 miles long and dotted with rugged, mountainous islands rising steeply from the water like dorsal fins. The uninhabited Prescott Peninsula splits the reservoir into two unequal parts, the western arm a long, slender ribbon less than a mile wide. Access to the water is limited, because most of the shoreline consists of cliffs and steep hills rising directly from the water's edge. The Quabbin was created in 1939 and 1940 by damming the Swift River, flooding five small villages. Its waters flow 80 miles through an elaborate system of aqueducts to supply the Boston metropolitan area, passing through the Wachusett Reservoir, the state's second-largest lake, en route.

You first encounter the reservoir at the 2,000-foot-long Goodenough Dike and then climb 400 feet to the handsome stone lookout tower atop Quabbin Hill, elevation 1,025 feet. From the observation deck a spectacular view of the entire reservoir unfolds in front of you. On a clear day you can easily see Mount Monadnock, 40 miles to the north. The watershed is a breeding ground for bald eagles, and if you're very lucky you may see one glide past. From the tower it's all downhill to 125-foot-high Winsor Dam, the second-largest earth dam east of the Mississippi (the largest is Saluda Dam in South Carolina). After the spectacular ride across the top of the dam, it's a short way back to Belchertown.

Directions for the ride

DIRECTIONS
FOR
THE RIDE

1. Head south on Route 202, following the green on your left, and just ahead go straight at traffic light onto Route 181. Go 2.1 miles to Cold Spring Road, a small road that bears left at top of hill.

Notice the handsome stone library on your left just beyond the traffic light. There's a relaxing descent out of Belchertown.

2. Bear left for 0.7 mile to fork (Cold Spring Road bears left, Michael Sears Road bears right). You'll ride past farms and orchards.

3. Bear right for 1.2 miles to end (Route 181). You'll ride along a ridge with panoramic views.

4. Turn left and stay on main road for 1.6 miles to end, in Bondsville. You'll cross the Swift River immediately before the end.

5. Right (still Route 181) for 0.2 mile to crossroads, facing a church (State Street on left). Here the ride turns left, but if your turn right for 50 yards you'll see a fine dam across the Swift River on your right.

6. Left for 1.5 miles to Emery Street on left, at bottom of steep hill after railroad tracks and immediately before bridge.

7. Left for 2.5 miles to Old Belchertown Road, which turns right down a steep hill. It's the first right after the airport. **CAUTION**: Diagonal railroad tracks after 0.6 mile.

8. Turn right and stay on main road for 1.6 miles to end, at T-intersection (Route 32). The main road merges right after 0.7 mile.

   You'll follow the Ware River on your right at the end.

9. Left for 1.1 miles to crossroads (Malboeuf Road on right, Anderson Road on left.) You reach the crossroads while you're going downhill.

10. Left for 1.2 miles to end (Route 9). There's a short, steep hill at the end.

11. Left for 2.4 miles to a road that bears right through a pair of stone pillars about 100 yards ahead. You'll climb steeply for 0.2 mile at the beginning.

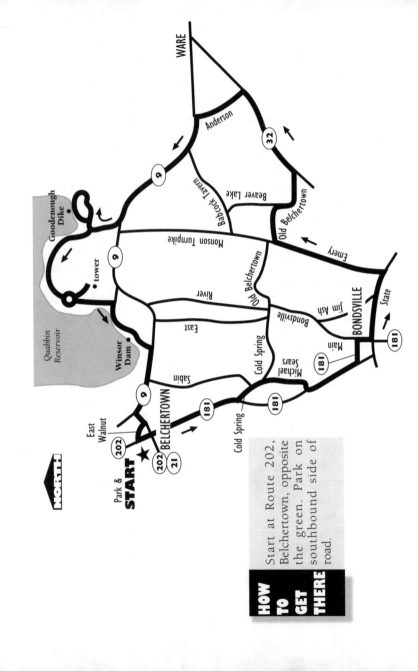

NORTH

WARE

Anderson

32

Beaver Lake

Old Belchertown

Emery

9

Babcock Tavern

Monson Turnpike

Goodenough Dike

Quabbin Reservoir

• tower

9

River

Old Belchertown

Bondsville

Jim Ash

BONDSVILLE

State

181

East

Winsor Dam

Cold Spring

Michael Sears

Main

181

East Walnut

202

9

Sabin

BELCHERTOWN

181

181

181

Cold Spring

Park & START

202 21

★

HOW TO GET THERE

Start at Route 202, Belchertown, opposite the green. Park on southbound side of road.

12. Bear right for 0.8 mile to fork (sign points right to Goodenough Dike).

13. Bear right and just ahead bear slightly right downhill. Go 1.6 miles to a grassy traffic island where the main road curves sharply right and another road turns left.

    You'll pass below the dike, climb steeply to the level of the reservoir, and bike along the top of the dike.

14. Curve right and just ahead bear right at fork (sign points right to Winsor Dam). Go 2.5 miles to rotary.

    There's a steady, mile-long hill at the end. Be sure to stop at Enfield Lookout, shortly before the rotary, for a panoramic view of the entire reservoir.

15. Go two-thirds around the rotary, head uphill for 0.3 mile to summit, and backtrack to rotary. The view from the observation tower is magnificent.

16. Go almost all the way around the rotary, following the sign to Winsor Dam, and go 1.4 miles to end. This is an exhilarating descent.

17. Turn right and then immediately curve right on the main road. Go 1.1 miles to end (Route 9), riding along the top of Winsor Dam.

18. Right for 2 miles to Route 21 (Jabish Street) on left.

19. Left for 0.5 mile to East Walnut Street on right. It's the next street after Eastview Drive on right.

20. Right for 0.3 mile to end (Route 202, North Main Street), at top of hill.

21. Turn left, and the Belchertown green is on your left.

Ludlow–Belchertown–Three Rivers

Number of miles:	25 (17 without Belchertown–Three Rivers extension)
Terrain:	Gently rolling, with two long, tough hills and one moderate hill.
Facilities:	Grocery and restaurant in Belchertown and Three Rivers (25-mile ride). Friendly's at end.

The region northeast of Springfield, consisting of rolling farmland and low, forested hills, provides relaxing bicycling on a network of lightly traveled back roads. Ludlow is an old industrial town with an enormous nineteenth-century mill complex stretching half a mile along the Chicopee River (it's not on the route). The ride starts from the outskirts of town and immediately heads north into rolling farm country with views of the Holyoke Range rising in the background. You'll cut across a wooded ridge and climb sharply into Belchertown, a gracious hilltop town with a long green that has a bandstand in the middle. From Belchertown you'll descend into a beautiful valley with expansive, gently rolling farms and orchards. Suddenly you'll enter the small mill town of Three Rivers (part of Palmer), where the Ware and Quaboag Rivers join to form the Chicopee, which flows into the Connecticut River at Springfield. From here you'll parallel the Chicopee River to a fine old dam with a spillway 40 feet high; behind it the river is backed up into an unspoiled pond.

The short ride bypasses Three Rivers to take a more direct route back to Ludlow. You'll pass the Springfield Reservoir, part of the water supply for Springfield, and then bike through the part of

Ludlow that was its center before the town became industrialized, with a distinctive church and an old cemetery.

Directions for the ride: 25 miles—

1. Left (north) on Route 21 for 0.8 mile to Rood Street on left. It's 0.3 mile after traffic light. There's a great fruit and vegetable stand at the intersection.

2. Left for 0.7 mile to Church Street on right.

3. Right for 0.2 mile to fork where Munsing Street bears left.

4. Bear left for 1 mile to end (merge left on Lyons Street; no stop sign).

5. Bear left for 1.9 miles to end (Carver Street). You pass through inspiring, rolling farmland, with glimpses of the Holyoke Range in the distance. The peak with the distinctive sharp drop-off is Long Mountain.

6. Right for 3.2 miles to Rockrimmon Road (unmarked), which turns left immediately before you start to go downhill on Granby Road. It's just after Maplecrest Drive and house number 176 on left. **CAUTION**: Bumpy spots and potholes on the first half of this stretch.

7. Left for 0.9 mile to end (Route 21). Here the short ride turns right.

8. Left for 1.3 miles to end (Route 202).

9. Right for 1 mile to traffic light in the center of Belchertown (Route 202 on left, Route 181 on right). There's a steep hill at the end. At the intersection the ride turns right, but the town green and business district are to your left.

10. Right for 0.25 mile to North Washington Street (unmarked), which bears right. A sign may say TO THREE RIVERS. Notice the handsome stone library on your left at the beginning.

HOW TO GET THERE

Start at a small shopping center at 477 Center Street (Route 21), next to Friendly's in Ludlow. It's immediately north of the entrance and exit ramps for the Massachusetts Turnpike. Turn right at end of exit ramp.

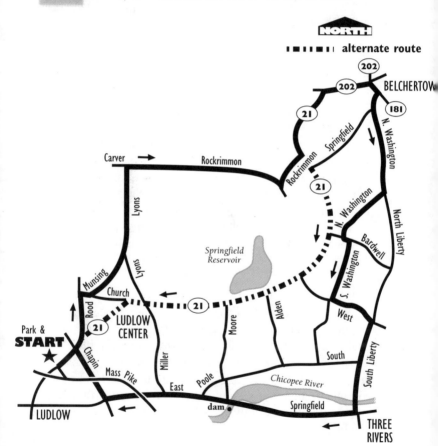

11. Bear right for 2.1 miles to where North Washington Street bears right onto a smaller road and North Liberty Street goes straight. **CAUTION**: Sharp S-curve under a narrow railroad bridge after 1.4 miles; sand often builds up here.
12. Bear right for 1 mile to end, at traffic island.
13. Jog left and then immediately right on South Washington Street. Go 1.3 miles to crossroads (West Street). This is beautiful, open farmland.
14. Left for 0.9 mile to crossroads and stop sign (North Liberty Street on left, South Liberty Street on right).
15. Right for 2.1 miles to crossroads and stop sign just after bridge (Springfield Street, unmarked, on right).

    From the bridge there's a fascinating view on your right of the Chicopee River as it flows between two old mills. At the crossroads the ride turns right, but if you turn left, stores and restaurants are just ahead in the center of Three Rivers.
16. Right for 5 miles to traffic light (Chapin Street).

    You'll see the dammed-up Chicopee River on your right after 2.4 miles, while going downhill. Just ahead you'll pass another dam and an old brick pumping station on your left and then cross the river at the bottom of the hill.
17. Right for 1.1 miles to Route 21 (Center Street), at traffic light.
18. Left for 0.5 mile to shopping center on right.

Directions for the ride: 17 miles—
1. Follow directions for the long ride through number 7.
2. Right for 8.2 miles to shopping center on right. You'll pass the Springfield Reservoir on your right. About 1.5 miles beyond the reservoir you'll go through the old center of Ludlow; Route 21 bears left here at a fork.

23

Longmeadow–East Longmeadow –Somers, Connecticut– Enfield, Connecticut

Number of miles:	29 (18 without eastern hills extension, 14 with shortcut)
Terrain:	Gently rolling, with one moderate hill and one tougher one. The 29-mile ride has an additional steady climb 1.5 miles long.
Facilities:	None until near the end of the ride. Better bring your own.

The gently rolling farmland southeast of Springfield, with views of the rugged hills several miles to the east across broad fields, provides relaxed and very scenic biking on a wealth of lightly traveled secondary roads. The ride starts from the center of Longmeadow, Springfield's most prosperous suburb. The town is well named—the green is so long it's practically a meadow. Its half-mile length makes it the longest green in the state. It is also one of the most gracious, lined on both sides with handsome old homes dating back to the 1800s and earlier; a graceful church; and two old brick schools.

From Longmeadow you'll head along quiet suburban streets to East Longmeadow, another pleasant residential community, best known as the home of Milton Bradley, the games company. As you head east out of town and then south across the Connecticut line, the landscape becomes more and more rural, with broad sweeps of farmland and views of the mountains in the distance. You'll go past a cluster of Connecticut state prisons, incongruously located in the midst of acres of rolling farmland.

The long ride offers a real workout by heading eastward beyond the valley into the wooded hills. You'll climb 500 feet to a plateau dotted with small farms and then enjoy the long, gradual descent back into the valley. The return to Longmeadow leads through gently rolling farmland with inspiring views of the mountains you've just conquered.

The 14-mile ride takes a more direct route from East Longmeadow back to the end and is not quite so rural.

DIRECTIONS
FOR
THE RIDE

Directions for the ride: 29 miles—

1. Head east on Williams Street for 2.6 miles to third traffic light (Dwight Road on left, Benton Drive on right). Shortly before the first light, Route 192 bears right onto Shaker Road, but go straight here on Williams Street.

2. Straight for 1.3 miles to stop sign in the center of East Longmeadow, where seven roads come together. Here the 14-mile ride turns right onto Route 186 (Prospect Street) immediately after the stop sign, and the two longer rides continue straight.

3. Straight across Route 83 onto Pleasant Street. Stay on main road for 1.8 miles to crossroads and blinking light (Parker Street). The main road curves sharply right at bottom of hill after 0.9 mile.

4. Right for 1.9 miles to crossroads and stop sign (Hampden Road).

5. Straight for 0.6 mile to end. Notice the old church to your right at the intersection.

6. Turn left and then immediately bear left on Mill Road. (The 18-mile ride turns left and then curves right on the main road.) Go 1.7 miles to end (Somers Road).

7. Right for 1.1 miles to fork (Somers Road bears right, Isaac Bradway Road bears left).

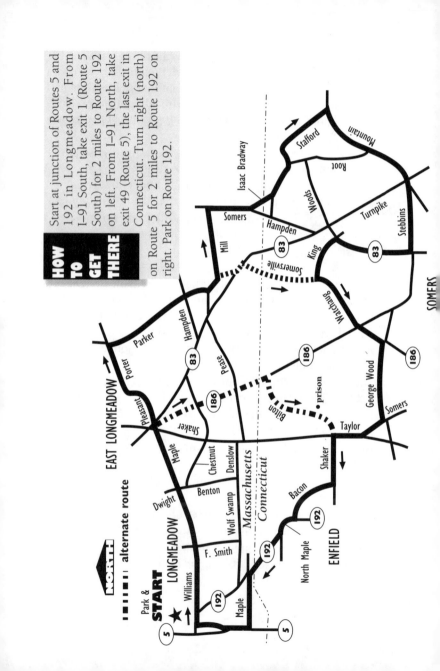

HOW TO GET THERE

Start at junction of Routes 5 and 192 in Longmeadow. From I-91 South, take exit 1 (Route 5 South) for 2 miles to Route 192 on left. From I-91 North, take exit 49 (Route 5), the last exit in Connecticut. Turn right (north) on Route 5 for 2 miles to Route 192 on right. Park on Route 192.

8. Bear left for 0.4 mile to stop sign (merge left on Stafford Road). You are now in Somers, Connecticut.

9. Bear left for 0.6 mile to fork where Root Road bears right and the main road bears slightly left. It's all uphill.

10. Bear left for 1.9 miles to end (Old Springfield Road on left, Mountain Road on right).

    Most of this section is a long, steady climb with some steep pitches. If you turn right after 1.6 miles at the crossroads on Camp Road, a dirt road, you'll find a little pond after 0.1 mile. It's a great spot to rest after the long climb.

11. Turn right onto Mountain Road and go 2.4 miles to crossroads and stop sign (Turnpike Road). This is a steady descent. Notice the castlelike stone house on your left after 1.6 miles.

12. Go straight and just ahead bear right on Stebbins Road. Go 1 mile to crossroads and stop sign (Springfield Road, Route 83).

13. Right for 1.5 miles to a small crossroads (Grist Mill Terrace on right, King Road on left).

14. Left for 1.1 miles to end (Watchaug Road).

15. Left for 1 mile to crossroads and stop sign (Four Bridges Road). You'll ride past broad farms with mountains in the distance.

16. Straight onto Route 186, bearing left as you go through the intersection. Go 0.5 mile to crossroads and blinking light (George Wood Road).

17. Right for 1.3 miles to crossroads and stop sign (Somers Road).

18. Right for 0.2 mile to end (Taylor Road, unmarked).

19. Right for 0.4 mile to unmarked crossroads and stop sign (Cybulski Road on right, Shaker Road on left). The buildings at the top of the hill to your right are a Connecticut state prison.

20. Left for 0.8 mile to Bacon Road on right. You'll pass another prison on the right at the beginning.
21. Right for 0.7 mile to end (Route 192).
22. Right for 0.3 mile to stop sign where North Maple Street (Route 192) bears right.
23. Bear right for 0.9 mile to crossroads and blinking light (Maple Road), immediately after you cross the state line back into Longmeadow.
24. Left for 1.5 miles to end (Route 5).
25. Right for 1.2 miles to Route 192 on right. When you get to the green, there's less traffic if you take the road along the right-hand side of the green.

Directions for the ride: 18 miles—
1. Follow directions for the 29-mile ride through number 5.
2. Turn left and then immediately curve right on main road. Go 0.4 mile to end (Route 83).
3. Left and then immediately right on Somersville Road. Stay on main road for 2.5 miles to crossroads and stop sign (Four Bridges Road). Route 186 goes straight at the intersection. You'll ride past horse pastures and broad farms with views of the distant mountains.
4. Follow the directions for the 29-mile ride from number 16 to the end.

Directions for the ride: 14 miles—
1. Follow directions number 1 and 2 for the 29-mile ride.
2. Right immediately after the stop sign onto Prospect Street, Route 186 (don't turn right directly at the stop sign onto Shaker Road). Go 2.4 miles to Bilton Road, which turns sharply right just beyond the Connecticut line. It's 0.8 mile beyond the second crossroads and stop sign (Pease Road).

You'll climb a long, gradual hill, passing expensive homes; then you'll enjoy a relaxing descent with views of the mountains.

3. Sharp right for 2.1 miles to crossroads and stop sign (Taylor Road, unmarked). You'll pass several Connecticut state prisons.

4. Straight for 0.8 mile to Bacon Road on right. You'll pass another prison on your right at the beginning.

5. Follow directions for the 29-mile ride from number 21 to the end.

Wilbraham–Monson–Hampden

Number of miles:	22 (17 without Monson extension)
Terrain:	Hilly in the first half; gently rolling in the second half.
Facilities:	Grocery and restaurant in Monson and Hampden.

The rounded hills beyond the Pioneer Valley east of Springfield provide challenging but dramatic bicycling on good roads. This is an area of long climbs but equally long descents, with fine views from the tops of the ridges. The ride starts from Wilbraham, a well-to-do suburb of Springfield that lies partly in the valley and partly along the steep hills rising from its eastern edge. The town is more rural than suburban. The center of town is graced by the handsome campus of Wilbraham and Monson Academy, a prestigious preparatory school. The town is also the site of the main office of the Friendly's Ice Cream chain, which has restaurants in every town of any size throughout the state. You may have noticed Friendly's floral "Welcome to Wilbraham" greeting planted on a hillside as you're driving west on the Massachusetts Turnpike.

As you leave Wilbraham you'll immediately climb onto Wilbraham Mountain, the high ridge forming the eastern edge of the Pioneer Valley. It's a long ascent but the view from the top is superb. On a clear day you can see far beyond Springfield to the Berkshires. After enjoying the spectacular ride along the top of the ridge, you'll head mostly downhill through a mixture of woods and rolling farmland to the quiet crossroads town of Hampden. Hampden is best known as the home of Thornton Burgess, one of America's best-known writers of animal stories. His house, built in

1742, stands next to the Laughing Brook Educational Center and Wildlife Sanctuary, run by the Massachusetts Audubon Society. In the center of town stands Academy Hall, a splendid old schoolhouse built in Greek Revival style. Leaving Hampden, you'll enjoy a smooth, fairly flat ride back to Wilbraham, passing small farms and fine older houses.

The longer ride heads farther east to the small mill town of Monson (pronounced Munson). As mill towns go, Monson is one of the most attractive in the state, with a graceful white church, a handsome Victorian stone library, and an ornate granite town hall with a clock tower, built in 1884. Leaving Monson, you wind gradually uphill through rolling, pastoral countryside. You'll be rewarded with some fine views and a smooth descent into Hampden.

Directions for the ride: 22 miles—

DIRECTIONS
FOR
THE RIDE

1. At the end of Burt Lane and Crane Park Drive, turn right on Main Street for 0.1 mile to Mountain Road on right. Notice the beautiful stone church on the far corner. The impressive main building of Wilbraham and Monson Academy is just beyond the church on your right.

2. Right for 1.4 miles to end, at traffic island (Ridge Road). This is a long, steady climb.

3. Right for 1.7 miles to end (Monson Road, unmarked). A dirt road goes straight here. You'll enjoy unsurpassed views of the Pioneer Valley on your right across the lawns of expensive homes.

4. Left for 3.1 miles to stop sign at bottom of hill (merge left). Here the short ride turns sharply right onto Upper Hampden Road (unmarked). There's a steep descent at the beginning.

5. Bear left for 2.3 miles to the second of two stop signs a block apart, where you merge head-on into Route 32 in Monson. Immediately before the intersection there's a handsome

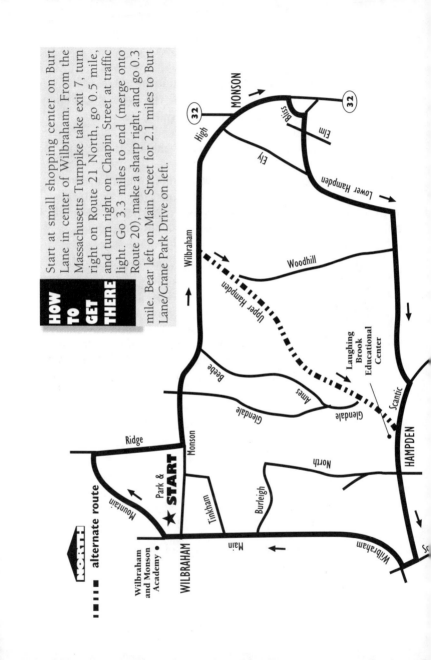

HOW TO GET THERE

Start at small shopping center on Burt Lane in center of Wilbraham. From the Massachusetts Turnpike take exit 7, turn right on Route 21 North, go 0.5 mile, and turn right on Chapin Street at traffic light. Go 3.3 miles to end (merge onto Route 20), make a sharp right, and go 0.3 mile. Bear left on Main Street for 2.1 miles to Burt Lane/Crane Park Drive on left.

NORTH

alternate route

Wilbraham and Monson Academy

Mountain

Ridge

Monson

Park & **START**

Tinkham

Main

WILBRAHAM

Burleigh

North

Wilbraham

Ridge

Glendale

Beebe

Ames

Glendale

Laughing Brook Educational Center

Scantic

HAMPDEN

Woodhill

Upper Hampden

Wilbraham

Ely

Lower Hampden

High

MONSON

Bliss

Elm

32

32

stone church on the left. An ornate Victorian library built in 1881 is on your right at the intersection.

6. Straight for 0.9 mile to Bliss Street (unmarked) on right, just after a redbrick mill on your left. You'll pass the tall Victorian town hall on your left.

7. Turn right. After 0.2 mile the main road bears right between two abandoned mills. Just beyond the mills is a diagonal crossroads (Elm Street).

8. Straight onto Lower Hampden Road for 5.4 miles to end (Scantic Road). **CAUTION**: After 2.4 miles the main road curves 90 degrees right while you're going down a steep hill.
    You'll start off with a long, steady climb; then the road descends through magnificent rolling countryside.

9. Right for 2.5 miles to end (Somers Road). After 0.5 mile you'll pass the Laughing Brook Educational Center on your right just beyond a stop sign. Then you'll go through the center of Hampden 0.5 mile ahead.

10. Right and just ahead right again at unmarked crossroads (East Longmeadow Road on left, Wilbraham Road on right). Go 4.4 miles to Burt Lane and Crane Park Drive on right, back in Wilbraham. Notice the fine old homes as you come into the town.

11. Turn right, and shopping center is just ahead.

Directions for the ride: 17 miles—

1. Follow directions for the long ride through number 4.

2. Turn sharply right and stay on main road for 6.4 miles to end (Somers Road). Most of this section is a relaxing, gentle downgrade. After about 4 miles the road curves sharply to the right, and you'll immediately pass the Laughing Brook Educational Center on your right. Then you'll go through the center of Hampden 0.5 mile ahead.

3. Follow directions for the long ride from number 10 to the end.

Chapter 4: Central Massachusetts

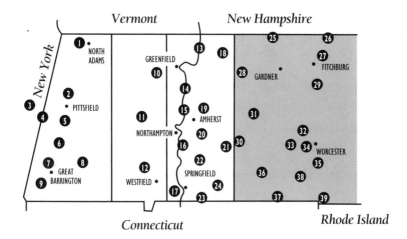

Vermont

New Hampshire

New York

Connecticut

Rhode Island

NORTH ADAMS

GREENFIELD

FITCHBURG

GARDNER

PITTSFIELD

AMHERST

NORTHAMPTON

WORCESTER

GREAT BARRINGTON

WESTFIELD

SPRINGFIELD

Cathedral of the Pines Ride
Winchendon–Rindge, New Hampshire

Number of miles:	20
Terrain:	Rolling, with several moderate hills and one tough one. Six-tenths of a mile of dirt road, which can be avoided.
Facilities:	Convenience store and pizza shop in Rindge. Groceries and Dunkin' Donuts just before end.

On this ride you explore a very rural, primarily wooded area of low hills around Lake Monomonac, the largest lake in the vicinity. You'll head several miles north of the state line through the stately hilltop town of Rindge to the Cathedral of the Pines, one of New England's true beauty spots, and return to Winchendon on back roads by way of the classic New England village of Winchendon Center.

The ride starts in Winchendon, a small, compact mill town that for years was the country's prime producer of wooden toys, especially rocking horses. Most of the original toy factories have been demolished, and the few remaining mills now house diversified industries.

From Winchendon you'll head north across the New Hampshire border along narrow wooded roads to Rindge, a graceful old hilltop town with a traditional New England church and green, along with a fine redbrick Victorian library. From here you're not far from the Cathedral of the Pines, one of New England's most beautiful attractions. It is a nondenominational chapel set in a grove of pines on top of a hill with a magnificent view of Mount

Monadnock and its neighboring peaks. A tall, delicate bell tower stands at the entrance to the grove. The chapel was founded in 1945 by Douglas and Sybil Sloane, who lived in the farmhouse at its entrance, as a memorial to their son, a pilot who was shot down over Germany during World War II.

From the Cathedral of the Pines you'll head back to Winchendon with a ride along Lake Monomonac, passing rustic cottages nestled in the pines along its shore. Just before the end you'll go through the tiny hilltop village of Winchendon Center, with a beautiful old church standing proudly above a little green, and enjoy a fast descent back into town. The road leading to Winchendon Center is dirt, but you can easily bypass the village by following Route 12.

DIRECTIONS
FOR
THE RIDE

1. Turn right (north) on Route 202 for 0.2 mile to where Route 202 turns right on Maple Street and Central Street bears slightly left.

2. Bear left and stay on main road for 1.2 miles to where the main road (Forristall Road, unmarked) turns left and a smaller road goes straight up a steep hill.

3. Left for 2.4 miles to wide crossroads and stop sign (Route 202). You are now in New Hampshire.

4. Straight for 0.6 mile to where Lord Brook Road turns right and Middle Winchendon Road bears left.

5. Bear left for 1 mile to crossroads (Hunt Hill Road on left, Todd Hill Road on right). There's a good view of Mount Monadnock to your left at the intersection.

6. Right for 0.7 mile to end, at the church in the center of Rindge. At the end, notice the fine redbrick library 100 yards down the hill to your right.

7. Left on Payson Hill Road, passing cemetery on right (don't turn sharply left uphill). Go 0.5 mile to crossroads and stop

NORTH

●●●●● **dirt road**

HOW TO GET THERE

Start at the parking lot for the W. P. Clark Memorial Community Center, on Route 202 in the center of Winchendon. It's 0.25 mile north of Route 12.

Cathedral of the Pines ●

Cathedral

Shaw Hill

Payson Hill

Hunt Hill

Todd Hill

Cutter Hill

119

Old New Ipswich

RINDGE

Middle Winchendon

Lord Brook

Danforth

Wellington

202

Main

Lake Monomonac

East Monomonac

11

New Hampshire

- - - - - - - - - - -

Massachusetts

Forristall

202

Lakeview

Elmwood

Park & **START**

202

202

Glenallen

202 ★

WINCHENDON

Ash

12

High

Hall

WINCHENDON CENTER

Teel

sign at bottom of steep hill (Route 119). **CAUTION** here. A combined convenience store and pizza shop is on the far left corner.

8. Straight for 1.7 miles to Shaw Hill on right, at top of hill. The Cathedral of the Pines is on your left just before the intersection. Be sure to go up to the altar at the far end of the chapel to enjoy the view of the Monadnock Range.

9. Right for 1.9 miles to the third left, at traffic island (Old New Ipswich Road). The first left is also Old New Ipswich Road; go straight here.

10. Left for 0.2 mile to end (Route 119).

11. Left for 1 mile to second right (East Monomonac Road).

12. Right for 2.9 miles to end (Lakeview Drive). You cross back into Massachusetts after about 2 miles and then follow the narrow southern end of Lake Monomonac on your right.

13. Left for 0.9 mile to end (Route 202). You'll ride along Whites Mill Pond on your left.

14. Turn left and then immediately bear slightly left at fork (sign says TO FITCHBURG). Go 1.6 miles to Route 12, at large traffic island. (Bear right at island.)

    At this point the ride will soon follow a dirt road for 0.6 mile. If you wish to avoid it (and miss Winchendon Center), bear right on Route 12 for 0.8 mile to Route 202 on right. Turn right for 0.25 mile to parking lot on right.

15. Bear right and immediately cross Route 12 diagonally onto a narrow lane (Hall Road). Go 0.3 mile to crossroads and stop sign. The Winchendon School, a coeducational preparatory school, is on your right on the far side of the golf course.

16. Straight for 0.9 mile to end (Teel Road). The first 0.6 mile is dirt. This is a steady but very gradual hill.

17. Right for 0.2 mile to crossroads at top of hill (Old County Road on left). This is Winchendon Center.

18. Right for 1.5 miles to crossroads and stop sign (Route 12).
    Notice the graceful old church on your left and the fine view to your right at the beginning. Then a fast descent leads to a little millpond on your right and two old mills on your left.
19. Cross Route 12 onto Route 202 (Central Street). Go 0.25 mile to parking lot on right. Notice the old brick industrial building with a tower behind the lot.

Ashby–New Ipswich, New Hampshire–Greenville, New Hampshire

Number of miles:	26 (17 omitting New Ipswich–Greenville loop)
Terrain:	Rolling, with two tough hills.
Facilities:	Grocery in New Ipswich. Grocery and restaurant in Greenville. Grocery at end.

This is a fascinating and very scenic tour of the pristine little towns north of Fitchburg in the region straddling the Massachusetts–New Hampshire border. The terrain is delightfully rolling, with some fine views from the tops of broad, open ridges. The twin towns of New Ipswich and Greenville, only 2 miles apart, contrast dramatically with each other. New Ipswich is a museum-piece rural town with an outstanding Federal-era mansion, and Greenville is a classic, well-maintained mill town.

The ride starts from Ashby, a fine little town with a classic white church and green and a rambling, wooden Victorian town hall. Outside of town you'll go along two undeveloped reservoirs and then head north into New Hampshire, skirting the base of 1,830-foot Mount Watatic, second highest mountain in the state east of the Connecticut River. Just over the border is the elegant, perfectly preserved village of New Ipswich. Gracing the center of town are two stately white churches (one of them recycled into an office building), rambling white wooden homes with dark shutters, a miniature wooden library, and a handsome brick schoolhouse at the head of a large green. And if this isn't enough, the pride of the village is the Barrett House, an elegant Federal-era mansion built in 1800 and stocked with impressive period furnishings. It is administered by the Society for the Preservation of New England Antiquities (SPNEA) and is open afternoons from June 1 to October 15.

From New Ipswich you take a short ride to Greenville, a beautiful and unusually graceful old mill town. You first see it from a hillside spread out beneath you in its entirety. In the center of town is a fine Gothic-style church, gracious brick and wooden homes, an elegant inn, and an impressive high dam. A mile outside of town, in splendid isolation, is a marvelous five-story Victorian mill that's more like a castle. The return to Ashby is a delight, following the dammed-up Souhegan River and then traversing open ridges with fine views.

DIRECTIONS
FOR
THE RIDE

1. Head south on South Road and just ahead bear left at fork (still South Road). Go 1.7 miles to end (Richardson Road), at traffic island with a monument. You'll pass the Ashby Reservoir on your left near the end.

2. Right for 1.2 miles to crossroads and stop sign (Rindge Road). You'll go along the Fitchburg Reservoir on your left.

3. Right for 3.3 miles to end (Route 119), at a T-intersection. You'll pass Ward Pond on the left shortly before the end.

4. Right and just ahead left on Pillsbury Road. Go 1 mile to fork (Bennett Road bears left). You can see Mount Watatic on your left.

5. Right for 0.6 mile to your first left (West Road). West Road also goes straight here.

6. Left for 1.8 miles to crossroads and stop sign (Ashby Road). West Road becomes Route 123A at the New Hampshire line.

   When you reach Ashby Road the ride turns left, but if you wish to shorten the ride to 17 miles, turn right. Resume with direction number 13, turning right on Ashby Road instead of left.

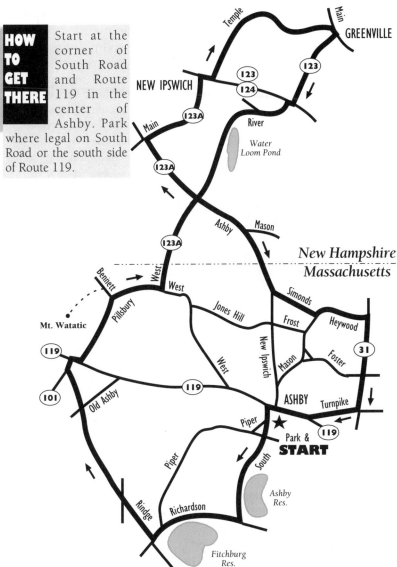

HOW TO GET THERE Start at the corner of South Road and Route 119 in the center of Ashby. Park where legal on South Road or the south side of Route 119.

NORTH

GREENVILLE

Temple

Main

123

124

123

NEW IPSWICH

123A

Main

River

Water
Loom Pond

123A

Ashby

Mason

123A

New Hampshire
Massachusetts

Bennett

West

West

Simonds

Pillsbury

Jones Hill

Frost

Heywood

Mt. Watatic

New Ipswich

Mason

Foster

31

119

West

101

Old Ashby

119

ASHBY

Turnpike

Piper

★

Piper

Park &
START

119

South

Piper

Ashby
Res.

Rindge

Richardson

Fitchburg
Res.

7. Turn left (still Route 123A) and stay on main road for 1.3 miles to another crossroads (Smithville Road on left; Main Street on right). Route 123A turns right here.

8. Right for 1.4 miles to end (Routes 123 and 124, Turnpike Road).

    Toward the end you'll go through New Ipswich, New Hampshire, passing the Barrett House on your left and then a church on your right. If you look to your right immediately after the church, you'll see the stately brick Appleton Academy standing proudly over the green.

9. Turn right and just ahead left at blinking light on Temple Road. Stay on main road for 2.5 miles to end (Main Street), at stop sign, at the bottom of a steep hill.

    This is Greenville. At the brow of the hill, notice the Gothic-style church on your left.

10. Right and just ahead right again on Route 123 North (River Street) immediately after the bridge. There's an impressive dam on your right at the bridge. Go 1.6 miles to end (Route 124, Turnpike Road). The dammed-up Souhegan River is on your right at the beginning, and a splendid Victorian mill is on your right at the end.

11. Jog right and then immediately left uphill on River Road. Go 0.6 mile to fork where the main road bears left and a smaller road (Old Country Road) goes straight.

12. Bear left for 1.7 miles to crossroads and stop sign (Ashby Road). You'll pass Water Loom Pond on your left.

13. Left for 2.4 miles to Simonds Road, which bears left suddenly as you're going down a little hill.

    You are now back in Massachusetts. The first half of this stretch is a gradual climb to a hilltop with a good view; then you'll descend.

14. Bear left and stay on main road for 1.9 miles to end (Greenville Road, Route 31). **CAUTION**: After 1 mile the

main road curves sharply left while going downhill. Also
watch for bumps and sandy spots.

15.   Right for 1.5 miles to third crossroads (Turnpike Road), at
blinking light.

16.   Right for 0.9 mile to end (merge right on Route 119).

17.   Bear right for 0.4 mile to South Road on left, in the center
of Ashby. Notice the graceful brick library on your left just
before the end.

Fitchburg–Ashby

Number of miles:	21 (16 without Trap Falls extension)
Terrain:	Hilly.
Facilities:	Grocery store in Ashby.

The rolling hills north of Fitchburg offer challenging but very scenic biking on narrow, winding roads. Once you get a mile north of Fitchburg, the area is very rural, with only the tiny town of Ashby interrupting the large, sparsely populated expanses of woods and hilltop farms.

Fitchburg, a thriving industrial city of 40,000 lying in the steep valley of the North Nashua River, does not have the shabby appearance of some other mill cities in New England. The downtown area, with many fine nineteenth-century buildings flanking the main street in close formation, has been rehabilitated. A steady supply of local money has provided the city with an impressive library, civic center, planetarium, and art museum.

Fitchburg is also an active bicycling center, with an excellent bike shop and a major race held on Fourth of July weekend. A bicycle race is an exciting event to watch, with the racers traveling around and around a short course in a tight cluster, leaning into the corners at gravity-defying angles, and constantly jockeying for position—all at an average speed of 25 miles per hour.

Hemmed in by steep hills, Fitchburg is compact, with wooded acres within a mile of downtown. You'll start from the northern edge of the city and have a long, steady climb to a broad, rolling plateau to the north. At the top you'll go past the Fitchburg and Ashby Reservoirs to the picture-book New England village of

Ashby, with a pair of graceful old churches framing the small green and a handsome Victorian town hall.

From Ashby you'll wind across rolling hills and small farms to Trap Falls, a picturesque little waterfall where the water cascades around both sides of a large rock. You'll return to Fitchburg along a high, open ridge with spectacular views and then enjoy a long descent back into the city.

The short ride bypasses Trap Falls by taking a shortcut on Routes 119 and 31, which are both good cycling roads without heavy traffic. You'll detour past Damon Pond, which has a small, state-run beach. A stream flowing from the pond beneath a covered footbridge is a picturesque spot.

DIRECTIONS
FOR
THE RIDE

Directions for the ride: 21 miles—

1. Right out of parking lot for 1 mile to crossroads and stop sign (Route 31).
2. Straight for 4.4 miles to crossroads (Crocker Road on left, Piper Road on right). The first half of this section is a long, gradual climb. Just before the crossroads, the Fitchburg Reservoir is on your right, nestled among the pines.
3. Right for 0.4 mile to fork (Piper Road bears left, Richardson Road bears right).
4. Bear right for 0.8 mile to South Road, which turns left at a traffic island with a granite monument. An elegant brick house is on your right at the intersection.
5. Left for 1.8 miles to end (Route 119), in the center of Ashby.

    The Ashby Reservoir is on your right at the beginning. At the end the ride turns right, but the handsome town hall is 200 yards to your left.
6. Right and just ahead left on New Ipswich Road. (The short ride continues straight on Route 119.) Go 0.3 mile to fork at bottom of hill (Mason Road bears right).

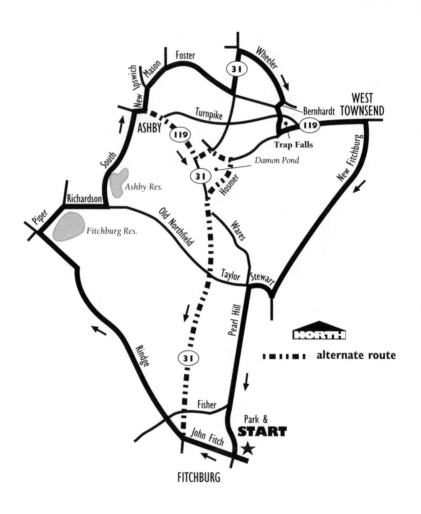

Start at Wallace Civic Center and Planetarium, John Fitch Highway, Fitchburg. From Route 2 West take exit 31B. Head north on Route 12 for 1.6 miles to traffic light (Wanoosnoc Road on left, Bemis Road on right). Turn right for 2.4 miles to civic center on right. Bemis Road becomes John Fitch Highway.

From Route 2 East take exit 28. Turn left (north) on Route 31 for about 4 miles to downtown Fitchburg. Here Route 31 makes a U-turn to the left around a traffic island and then bears right. Continue 1 mile to crossroads (Rindge Road on left, John Fitch Highway on right). Turn right for 1 mile to civic center on left.

7. Bear right for 0.3 mile to unmarked fork (Mason Road bears left, Foster Road bears right). You come to it while you're going downhill.

8. Bear right for 1.2 miles to crossroads and stop sign (Greenville Road, Route 31).

9. Left for 0.8 mile to crossroads (Dump Road on left, Wheeler Road on right).

10. Right for 1.2 miles to unmarked fork at bottom of hill (Wheeler Road bears left; Bernhardt Road bears right).

11. Bear right for 0.1 mile to another fork (Foster Road bears right).

12. Bear left and just ahead go straight at crossroads and stop sign. Go almost 0.2 mile to end (merge right on Route 119). **CAUTION**: Steep descent with bumps and sand. You will turn sharply left at the end.

13. Sharp left for 1.8 miles to New Fitchburg Road on right, opposite church on left in the village of West Townsend. Trap Falls is on your left at the beginning. Notice the circular wooden house on your right shortly before New Fitchburg Road.

14. Right for 3.4 miles to Stewart Road (unmarked), which turns very sharply right. This is a pleasant ride through woods, passing a state recreation area.

15. Sharp right for 0.3 mile to crossroads (Pearl Hill Road on left).
16. Left for 2.1 miles to fork at bottom of long, steady hill (Fisher Road bears right downhill). You'll have a long, steady climb to the top of a ridge with magnificent views.
17. Bear *left* for 0.8 mile to crossroads and blinking light (John Fitch Highway, unmarked). It's all downhill!
18. Left for 0.2 mile to civic center on left.

Directions for the ride: 16 miles—
1. Follow directions for the long ride through number 5.
2. Right for 1.5 miles to where Route 119 turns left and Route 31 South goes straight. It's all downhill!
3. Left and just ahead right (still Route 119). Go 0.3 mile to your first right (sign says DAMON POND). The road may be closed by a gate when it's not beach season.
4. Turn right on this road. Immediately ahead on your right is Damon Pond, a great place for a swim on a hot day. On your left, across from the pond, a stream rushes under a small covered footbridge.
5. Straight past pond for 0.6 mile to end (merge left on Route 31). There's a short, steep hill at the beginning. At the top you'll have to walk your bike around a barrier that keeps out cars. **CAUTION**: Bumps and sand near the barrier.
6. Bear left for 3.7 miles to crossroads (Rindge Road on right, John Fitch Highway on left).
7. Left for 1 mile to civic center on left.

28 Athol–Royalston–Phillipston –Petersham

Number of miles:	34 (21 without Phillipston-Petersham extension)
Terrain:	Hilly.
Facilities:	Country store in South Royalston. Country store in Petersham (long ride).

This is a tour of the wooded hills northeast of the Quabbin Reservoir, passing through a trio of unspoiled, classic New England towns. A highlight of the tour is Doane Falls, a beautiful waterfall maintained by the Trustees of Reservations. The terrain is hilly, but most of the hills are gradual. Only two hills are really steep, and they are fairly short. Numerous small farms and a couple of open ridges with fine views add variety to the landscape.

The ride starts in Athol, an old mill town on the Millers River straight out of the Industrial Revolution; the grim, fortresslike mills form a nearly unbroken wall along the river for several blocks. The main industry is the manufacture of tools. In the compact downtown area, three- and four-story Victorian commercial buildings line both sides of the main street.

From Athol you'll head north, passing Tully Lake and Dam. Just ahead is Doane Falls, one of the state's unspoiled and nearly unknown beauty spots. A spectacular chain of small waterfalls, separated by deep, crystal-clear pools, flows through a wooded gorge from beneath a graceful arched stone bridge. From the falls it's not far to Royalston, one of the most elegant classic towns in the state. Commandingly located atop a hill, the town boasts a large green framed by a stately white church and gracious old wooden homes.

From Royalston you'll have a fast descent into South Royalston, another attractive little town with an old wooden church and schoolhouse. You'll now head along a couple of open ridges to the tiny hamlet of Phillipston, which has an old church, a cemetery, a school, and not much else. Phillipston's main claim to fame is the Baldwin Hill Bakery, a producer of good, old-fashioned stone-ground bread without the additives, preservatives, and re-fined-down-to-nothing flour found in most breads today.

A few miles beyond Phillipston is the dignified hilltop town of Petersham, with a large green accented by a bandstand, traditional white church, ornate stone library, and a rambling wooden building that was formerly a resort hotel. The return run to Athol leads past small farms and along a high ridge, with a fast descent at the end.

The short ride bypasses Phillipston and Petersham, taking a direct route back to Athol along Route 2A past the Phillipston Reservoir. There's an exhilarating descent at the end.

DIRECTIONS
FOR
THE RIDE

Directions for the ride: 34 miles

1. Turn left from back of parking lot onto South Street, which is parallel to Route 2A and 1 block south of it. Just ahead turn left on Exchange Street for 1 block to traffic light (Route 2A).

2. Straight for 0.3 mile to crossroads at base of steep hill (Pequoig Avenue).

3. Left for 1.2 miles to Pinedale Avenue on right.

4. Right for 0.6 mile to end (Route 32). You'll pass a stately row of tall pine trees and see Sportsmans Pond on your right.

5. Left for 2.7 miles to Doane Hill Road on right. It's the first right after you pass Tully Lake and Dam on your right.

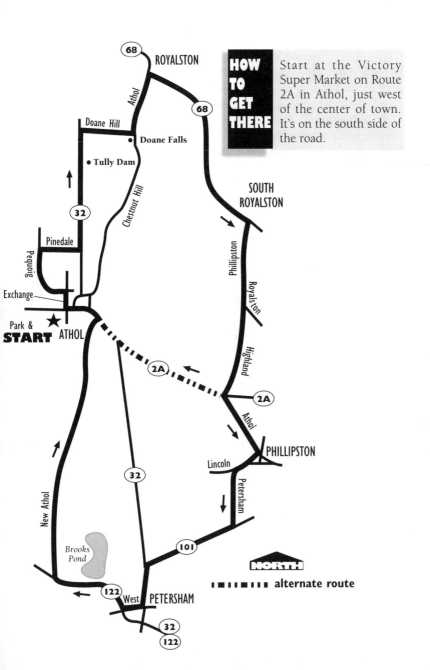

ROYALSTON

68

68

Athol

Doane Hill

Doane Falls

Tully Dam

SOUTH
ROYALSTON

32

Chestnut Hill

Phillipston

Royalston

Pinedale

Pequoig

Exchange

Highland

Park &
START ATHOL

2A

2A

Athol

PHILLIPSTON

Lincoln

32

Petersham

New Athol

101

Brooks
Pond

122 West PETERSHAM

NORTH

■ ■ ■ ■ ■ ■ ■ **alternate route**

32

122

HOW TO GET THERE Start at the Victory Super Market on Route 2A in Athol, just west of the center of town. It's on the south side of the road.

6. Right for 1.2 miles to end (Athol Road, unmarked), at top of steep hill. At the end you'll see an arched stone bridge on your right. Below the bridge is Doane Falls—don't miss it!

7. Left for 1.9 miles to end (merge head-on into Route 68), in Royalston. Here the ride turns sharply right, but it's worth going straight for 100 yards to see the gracious town center.

8. Sharp right for 4.5 miles to Phillipston Road, which bears right uphill just beyond railroad tracks at bottom of long, steep hill. **CAUTION**: These are bad diagonal tracks.

   You'll go through South Royalston and cross the Millers River just before the tracks.

9. Bear right for 2.1 miles to fork (Highland Avenue bears right uphill).

10. Bear right for 2.1 miles to end (Route 2A). Here the short ride turns right. You'll ride along a ridge with fine views.

11. Turn left and then immediately bear right downhill on Athol Road. Go 1.8 miles to end (merge right at stop sign).

12. Bear right and just ahead bear right again on main road (Petersham Road) in the center of Phillipston. Notice the fine church on your left. Go 0.2 mile to fork where Lincoln Road goes straight and the main road bears left.

13. Bear left for 1.8 miles to end (Route 101, Queen Lake Road), at a large, grassy traffic island.

14. Bear right for 3.1 miles to end (Route 32). There's a wonderful descent at the beginning.

15. Left for 1.1 miles to crossroads and blinking light in the center of Petersham (East Street on left, West Street on right). A country store is on the left at the intersection.

16. Right for 0.6 mile to crossroads and stop sign (Route 122). **CAUTION**: It comes up while you're going down a steep hill.

17. Right for 2.2 miles to New Athol Road, which bears right (road sign visible after you make the turn). You'll pass Brooks Pond on your right.

18. Bear right for 6 miles to end (Route 2A, Main Street). **CAUTION**: Route 2A comes up suddenly at bottom of steep hill.
19. Left (**CAUTION** here) for 1.4 miles to supermarket on left, just beyond downtown Athol. It's a fast downhill ride back into town.

Directions for the ride: 21 miles—
1. Follow the directions for the long ride through number 10.
2. Right for 4.7 miles to supermarket on left, just beyond downtown Athol. It's a fast downhill ride into the town.

Mount Wachusett Challenge
West Boylston–Princeton–Sterling

Number of miles:	34 (30 if you don't go to summit)
Terrain:	Guess!
Facilities:	Pizza shop in Princeton. Grocery store and snack bar in Sterling. Because the ride is demanding and there may not be a place to purchase food before the summit, you should carry food with you.

The area between Worcester and Fitchburg is dominated by 2,006-foot Mount Wachusett, the highest point in Massachusetts east of the Connecticut River. The symmetrical, gently rounded mountain, with no other mountains nearby, is a landmark for miles around. The long climb to the summit, a net gain in elevation of 1,600 feet from the starting point, offers a difficult but rewarding challenge to the adventuresome cyclist. The view from the summit, a nearly 360-degree panorama, is among the state's most spectacular. The breathtaking descent drops nearly 600 feet in the first mile, a gradient of more than 10 percent.

The ride starts from the western edge of the Wachusett Reservoir, elevation 390 feet, and follows its slender western arm to Oakdale, a small village in West Boylston. From here you'll climb gradually to Princeton, elevation 1,200 feet, along lightly traveled Route 31. The ascent does not become steep until the last quarter mile, which runs into Princeton.

Princeton is an elegantly classic New England town crowning a hillside, with a proud old church, Victorian town hall, and handsome clock-towered library poised above the large, sloping green. Before the turn of the twentieth century, Princeton was a fashionable summer resort with rambling Victorian hotels, including one on the summit of Mount Wachusett. Unfortunately, none remain.

From Princeton you'll ride along the eastern flank of the mountain, enjoying sweeping views to the east. At the beginning of the summit road is a visitors center with exhibits on the history of the mountain and the native wildlife. The summit road climbs 800 feet in 3 miles, with most of the elevation gain in two steep sections in the first and last half mile. A succession of hotels stood on the summit until 1970, when the last one burned. The only thing up there now is a fire tower, which is not open to the public, along with a couple of radio towers.

The descent is a thriller. When you get to the end of the summit road, there's more coming—the main road drops another 400 feet in the next mile. The main entrance and base lodge of the Mount Wachusett ski area is at the bottom. You'll now pedal along lovely narrow roads, passing prosperous farms and orchards, to the attractive valley town of Sterling, which is best known as the locale of "Mary Had a Little Lamb." A small statue of a lamb on the green commemorates the nursery rhyme. From Sterling you'll return to the start, passing through woods and farmland along lightly traveled secondary roads.

DIRECTIONS
FOR
THE RIDE

1. Head north on Route 140, paralleling the western arm of the reservoir on your left. Go 1.4 miles to Laurel Street on left, shortly after yield sign (sign says TO HOLDEN).

   As soon as you start, notice the Old Stone Church, built in 1890, on your left. Only the stone shell remains. The village of Oakdale (part of West Boylston) is immediately before the intersection.

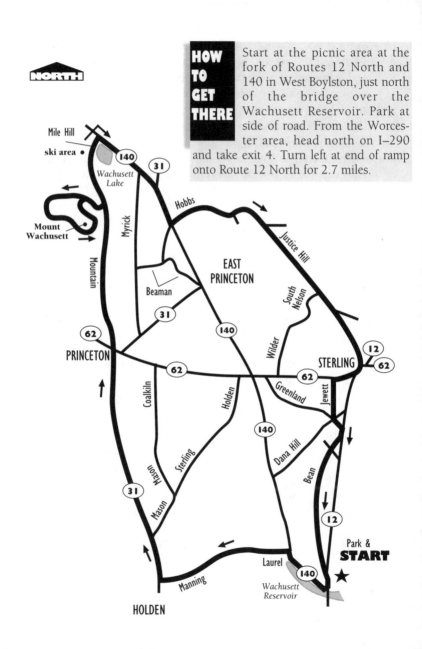

NORTH

Mile Hill
ski area •

HOW TO GET THERE Start at the picnic area at the fork of Routes 12 North and 140 in West Boylston, just north of the bridge over the Wachusett Reservoir. Park at side of road. From the Worcester area, head north on I–290 and take exit 4. Turn left at end of ramp onto Route 12 North for 2.7 miles.

140
31
Wachusett Lake
Myrick
Hobbs
Justice Hill

Mount Wachusett

Mountain
Beaman
EAST PRINCETON
South Nelson

31
140
Wilder

62
PRINCETON
62
62
STERLING
12
62

Coalkiln
Holden
Greenland
Jewett

Sterling
140
Dana Hill
Bean

Mason
31
12

Manning
Laurel
Park & START
140
★
Wachusett Reservoir

HOLDEN

2. Left for 3.3 miles to end (Route 31).

3. Right for 5.5 miles to Route 62, at blinking light in the center of Princeton. Here the ride goes straight, but if you turn left on Route 62 for 0.2 mile there's a pizza shop on your left. This is a good spot to get some food if it's open because the summit road begins in 3 miles.

4. Go straight uphill, following the green on your left. Notice the redbrick, turreted town hall, built in 1884, and the elegant stone library, built in 1883, at the end of the green. Go 3.2 miles to summit road on left, at top of hill (sign says MOUNT WACHUSETT STATE RESERVATION). To bypass the summit, resume with direction number 9, going straight downhill instead of turning left.

5. Turn left on the summit road. The visitors center is just ahead on your left. Be sure to get water here. Continue 2.9 miles to a road on left that climbs steeply (sign says TO SUMMIT).

6. Left for 0.2 mile to summit.

7. From the summit, backtrack 0.2 mile to end. Turn left and descend very steeply for 0.8 mile to end. **CAUTION**: Keep your speed under control.

8. Right for 0.6 mile to end, at the entrance to the state reservation.

9. Left for 1.7 miles to end (Route 140, Worcester Road). **CAUTION**: The first mile is a steep descent on aptly named Mile Hill Road. Keep your speed under control.

   The Mount Wachusett Ski Area is on your left toward the bottom, and Wachusett Lake is on your right just before the end.

10. Right for 2.4 miles to the second crossroads, Hobbs Road (sign on right says SHADY LANE GREENHOUSE).

11. Left for 1.5 miles to an intersection where one road turns right and the other bears left uphill. **CAUTION**: Steep descent with bumps and sandy spots—take it easy.
12. Bear left and stay on main road for 5.1 miles to end, in Sterling (merge right on Routes 12 and 62). The first 0.5 mile climbs steeply—a piece of cake compared to Mount Wachusett. The Sterling town green is on your left at the end.
13. Bear right and just ahead bear right again on Route 62. Go 0.4 mile to Jewett Road (unmarked) on left.
14. Left for 1 mile to a five-way intersection, at stop sign.
15. Turn 90 degrees left immediately after the stop sign, staying on Jewett Road. (Don't turn sharply left directly at the stop sign.) Go 0.25 mile to end (merge right onto Route 12).
16. Bear right and just ahead bear right again on Bean Road (unmarked). Go 2.7 miles to end (merge right on Route 12).
17. Bear right for 0.2 mile to starting point.

Covered-Bridge Ride
Ware–Hardwick–Gilbertville

Number of miles:	28 (16 without northern loop)
Terrain:	Hilly.
Facilities:	Country store in Hardwick. Grocery and snack bar in Gilbertville. Friendly's at end.

The section of Massachusetts between Worcester and the Quabbin Reservoir provides challenging but extremely scenic cycling. This is a very rural area of high, open ridges with spectacular views, dotted with unspoiled, picture-book New England towns. The cycle of tough climb, plateau atop a ridge, and exhilarating descent repeats itself as you wind through the inspiring landscape on untraveled back roads. On this ride you explore the area fairly close to the reservoir, passing through the classic village of Hardwick and then across one of only two covered bridges in the state east of the Connecticut River (the other is in Pepperell).

You start from Ware, a nineteenth-century mill town right out of the Industrial Revolution. Most of the mills have factory outlets selling to the public, making Ware one of the prime bargain centers in New England for clothing, woolen goods, and sportswear. The majority of the mills are clustered in one massive complex on Route 9 just east of downtown.

From Ware you quickly head into ridge country to Hardwick, a beautiful classic town among the many spread across Worcester County. The large, well-kept green is framed by two graceful old churches facing each other and by the handsome, white, pillared town hall. From Hardwick you'll traverse a ridge with inspiring views and enjoy a long descent into Gilbertville, a small, attractive mill town with a magnificent stone church. In Gilbertville you'll cross the Ware River over the covered bridge and return to Ware across yet another ridge along a narrow country lane.

The longer ride makes a loop north of Hardwick through more ridge-and-valley country. As you head north out of Hardwick, you come closer to the Quabbin Reservoir and catch glimpses of it far below. At the northern tip of the ride, you can go a quarter of a mile off the route to the water's edge. From here you'll return to Hardwick along ridges with fine views.

Directions for the ride: 28 miles—

1. Right on Route 9 and right immediately after movie theater on Parker Street. Go 0.1 mile to end (Pleasant Street).

2. Left for 0.5 mile to fork where Crescent Street bears left and Greenwich Road bears right. You'll pass an attractive little dam on your right.

3. Bear right for 2.3 miles to Hardwick Pond Road, which bears right.

4. Bear right for 3.5 miles to end (merge head-on into Route 32A). **CAUTION**: Bumpy and sandy spots, and no stop sign at end. This is a winding narrow road ascending gradually onto a ridge with fine views.

5. Straight for 1.2 miles to Barre Road on right, in the center of Hardwick. Here the short ride turns right.

6. Straight for 0.4 mile to fork (North Road bears right). An ornate brick library with a cupola is on your left at the beginning.

7. Bear left (still Route 32A) for 4.8 miles to a road on the right at the bottom of the second long descent (a rusty sign says TO BARRE). Here the ride turns right, but if you turn left onto a blocked-off road for 0.3 mile you'll come to the

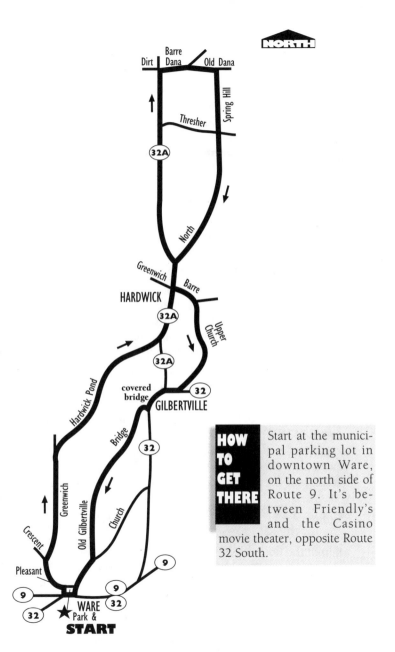

NORTH

Dirt
Barre Dana
Old Dana
Spring Hill
Thresher
32A
North
Greenwich
Barre
HARDWICK
32A
Upper Church
32A
covered bridge
32
GILBERTVILLE
Hardwick Pond
Bridge
32
Greenwich
Old Gilberville
Church
Crescent
9
Pleasant
9
9
32
WARE
Park &
32
START

HOW TO GET THERE Start at the municipal parking lot in downtown Ware, on the north side of Route 9. It's between Friendly's and the Casino movie theater, opposite Route 32 South.

narrow eastern arm of the Quabbin Reservoir. A sign says NO BICYCLING, so walk.

8. Right for 0.9 mile to fork (Old Dana Road, unmarked, bears right uphill). It's a steady climb to the fork.

9. Bear right for 0.5 mile to Spring Hill Road on right, at top of hill.

10. Right for 5 miles to end (merge left onto Route 32A). You'll ride along a ridge with fine views.

11. Bear left for 0.3 mile to fork at the Hardwick town green (Route 32A, unmarked here, bears slightly right).

12. Bear left for 0.1 mile to end (Barre Road, unmarked). Here the ride turns left, but there's a country store 100 yards to your right.

13. Left for 0.4 mile to Upper Church Street, which bears right uphill.

14. Bear right for 2.8 miles to end (merge right on Route 32, Lower Road). This is another narrow road that climbs onto a ridge with great views. After you crest the ridge, a relaxing descent takes you to the Ware River Valley.

15. Bear right for 0.2 mile to stop sign (Route 32 bears left). This is Gilbertville, which is part of the town of Hardwick.

16. Bear left for almost 0.4 mile to Bridge Street on right (sign says COVERED BRIDGE). You can see the bridge from the corner. **CAUTION**: Diagonal railroad tracks after 0.25 mile.

    You'll pass an old brick mill on your right and cross the Ware River. The ride turns right on Bridge Street, but you'll find a magnificent stone church if you go straight for 200 yards.

17. Right for 3.2 miles to end (Church Street, unmarked), at bottom of hill.

18. Right for 0.8 mile to traffic light (Route 9). It's all downhill!

19. Right for less than 0.2 mile to parking lot on right.

Directions for the ride: 16 miles—

1. Follow directions for the long ride through number 5.
2. Right for 0.5 mile to Upper Church Street, which bears right uphill. A country store is on your right at the beginning.
3. Follow directions for the long ride from number 14 to the end.

Central Massachusetts Spectacular

North Brookfield–Oakham–Barre–New Braintree

Number of miles:	30
Terrain:	Hilly.
Facilities:	Grocery and snack bar in Barre. Country store in Old Furnace.

The rolling, open hills, ridges, and valleys midway between Worcester and Springfield provide some of the most inspiring scenery in Massachusetts. The terrain is challenging—a recurrent cycle of steep climbs and exhilarating descents—but the panoramic vistas from atop every hill will more than reward your efforts. Here is rural countryside at its best: rambling old farmhouses, weathered red barns with woodpiles neatly stacked beside them, stone walls zigzagging across broad, sloping fields where cows and horses graze. Dotting this Currier-and-Ives landscape are unspoiled museum-piece towns and hamlets, hardly changed since the 1800s.

The ride starts from one of these towns, North Brookfield, a New England jewel with a stately old church and green, a handsome stone library, and an ornate Victorian town hall built in 1864. When the Rolling Stones needed a place to practice for their 1981 American tour, they chose North Brookfield. From here you'll bike across ridgetops and along two delightful ponds to Oakham, a pristine hilltop hamlet buried off the beaten path among a maze of back roads. No one would ever find it except by accident. A graceful white church, fine stone library, schoolhouse, and old cemetery make up the village center. From Oakham you'll wind your way on deserted country lanes to the larger town of Barre, also a New England classic. The extensive green, ornamented with a bandstand in the center, forms a nucleus from which eight roads radiate like spokes. Adjoining the green are a stately wooden church, an old town hall, and a compact little business block.

From Barre you'll traverse more ridges with sweeping views to the nearly depopulated hamlet of New Braintree. The center of town has a fine white church, an old cemetery, a tiny post office, a handful of weathered farmhouses, and not much else. The training academy for the state police stands on a hilltop a short distance south of the village center (a Seventh-Day Adventist academy formerly stood on the site). From New Braintree, we're soon back to North Brookfield, biking through magnificently rolling, open farmland.

DIRECTIONS
FOR
THE RIDE

1. Head north (uphill) on Route 67 for 0.7 mile to Route 148 North (Oakham Road), which bears right. You'll pass a beautiful church on your right after 0.3 mile.

2. Bear right for 5.3 miles to second crossroads (Spencer Road on right, Ware Corner Road on left). You'll pass Doane Pond on the left after about a mile.

3. Left for 1.1 miles to Maple Street on left, at top of hill. This is the center of Oakham. Notice the fine stone library on your left at the intersection. This stretch is a steady climb.

4. Left and just ahead right at top of hill (still Maple Street). Stay on main road for 1.6 miles to end (Old Turnpike Road, unmarked).

    The main road bears right after 0.8 mile and then descends steeply.

5. Left for 0.2 mile to Hunt Road on right. A country store is on the far right corner.

6. Turn right and stay on main road for 0.8 mile to fork where Happy Hollow Road turns left and the main road bears

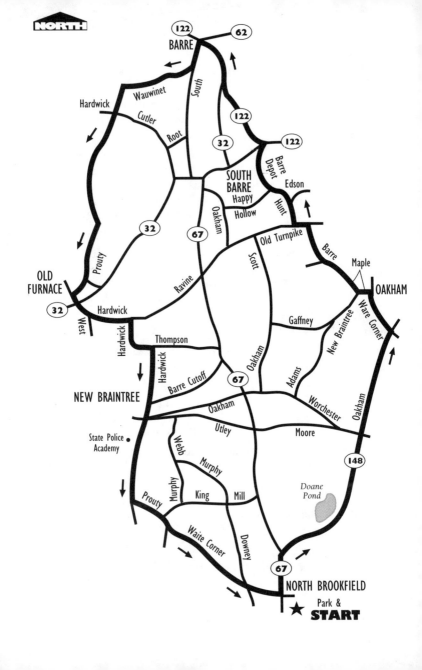

Start at the center of North Brookfield, on Route 67. You can park without time restrictions on School Street, the cross street on the east side of Route 67.

right. Notice the unusual stone tower on your right as you're going down the hill shortly before the fork.

7. Bear right for 1 mile to stop sign at bottom of hill (merge right on Vernon Avenue, unmarked). **CAUTION**: Steep descent with sharp curves, bumps, and sandy spots—take it easy.

   From the top of the hill you can see Mount Wachusett, the highest mountain in central Massachusetts, elevation 2,006 feet, on your right.

8. Bear right for 0.1 mile to end (Route 122). You'll cross the Ware River; notice the dam on your right as you cross the bridge.

9. Left for 2.9 miles to Common Street, which turns sharply left at the far end of the Barre town green. The last mile is a steady climb.

10. Sharp left for 0.6 mile to Wauwinet Road, which bears right while you're going uphill.

    The Barre Historical Society, a white mansion with columns, is on your right at the beginning. Then you'll pass the Cook's Canyon Audubon preserve on the left. The name is an exaggeration—the canyon is a small ravine with a brook trickling through it.

11. Bear right for 2.5 miles to crossroads and stop sign (Cutler Road on left, Hardwick Road on right).

12. Go straight and stay on main road for 4.1 miles to end, at bottom of hill (Barre Road, unmarked). **CAUTION** here—the

175

end comes up suddenly. At the end of this stretch you'll enjoy a long descent with magnificent views. The hamlet of Old Furnace (part of the town of Hardwick) is at the end.

13. Turn left and just ahead cross Route 32 (country store on right). Go 1.2 miles to Hardwick Road (unmarked), which turns right across a small bridge.

14. Turn right. After 0.6 mile the main road curves 90 degrees left uphill. Go 0.5 mile to Hardwick Road (unmarked) on right. A white, pillared mansion is on your left at the intersection.

15. Right for 3.2 miles to Prouty Road on left, at bottom of long hill. You'll go through New Braintree and pass the state police training academy.

16. Turn left and stay on main road for 3.4 miles to Route 67, in the center of North Brookfield. Some smaller roads branch off, but follow the main road. There's a steep, 0.3-mile climb into town.

North of Worcester
Worcester–Paxton–Holden–Rutland

Number of miles:	30 (24 with shortcut, 13 without Paxton-Rutland extension)
Terrain:	The short ride is rolling with one tough hill. The longer rides are hilly.
Facilities:	Grocery stores and snack bars in the towns.

Just northwest of Worcester is a prime area for cycling. It has wooded hills interspersed with ponds and reservoirs, occasional open ridges with fine views, and unspoiled towns that haven't yet become suburban. Worcester is fortunate to be a relatively compact city with almost no suburban sprawl beyond its borders. Within a mile of the start you're in wooded countryside before you even cross the city line.

The ride starts from the Tatnuck section of Worcester, near its western edge, and almost immediately enters forested landscape. The Cascade, a steep, rocky ravine that becomes a dramatic waterfall after heavy rain and a delicate, icy fairyland in the winter, is 0.6 mile off the route at the beginning. Just beyond the city line you'll enjoy a relaxing ride beside the Holden Reservoirs. Soon you'll arrive Holden, an attractive community with two graceful old churches and a Federal-era mansion framing the center of town. From Holden you'll enjoy a gradual descent back into Worcester and return to the start through gracious residential neighborhoods.

The long ride heads farther west and north to the graceful old town of Paxton. Although less than 10 miles from downtown Worcester, Paxton remains an unspoiled New England gem of a

Dairy farm in Rutland

town with a stately white church, an old town hall, fine white wooden homes, and the gracious Paxton Inn, all clustered around the village center. From Paxton you'll head north over hill, dale, and ridge to Rutland, another refreshingly unspoiled town crowning a hilltop. From Rutland you'll thread your way to Holden along a labyrinth of winding, roller-coastering lanes, passing a buffalo farm along the way. In Holden you'll pick up the short ride and follow it back to Worcester.

Directions for the rides: 30 or 24 miles—

1. Turn right (downhill) on Pleasant Street, and immediately bear right at traffic light on Mower Street. Go 0.2 mile to fork (Olean Street bears right).

2. Bear right and stay on main road for 2.9 miles to fork where South Road bears left uphill. This is a beautiful ride along the Holden Reservoirs. The 13-mile ride bears right at the fork.

If you're taking the ride after a heavy rain, be sure to visit the Cascade, which is 0.6 mile off the route. After bearing right on Olean Street, take your first left on Fernside Road. Go to end, turn right and immediately left on Windemere Road, and go to end. Turn right and go almost 0.4 mile to Cascade on left. Backtrack to Olean Street.

3. Bear left on South Road for 1 mile to end (Route 31). This is a steady climb with some steep sections.

4. Turn left and stay on Route 31 for 2.3 miles to second T-intersection (Route 56, Richards Avenue). Route 31 turns left after 1.6 miles and then right 0.2 mile farther on.

When you come to Route 56 you're in Paxton. The center of town is on your left. Notice the fine church to your left at the intersection.

5. Right for 4.7 miles to end (Route 122A, Main Street), in the center of Rutland. Here the 30-mile ride turns left, but you can shorten the route by 6 miles if you turn right for 1.7

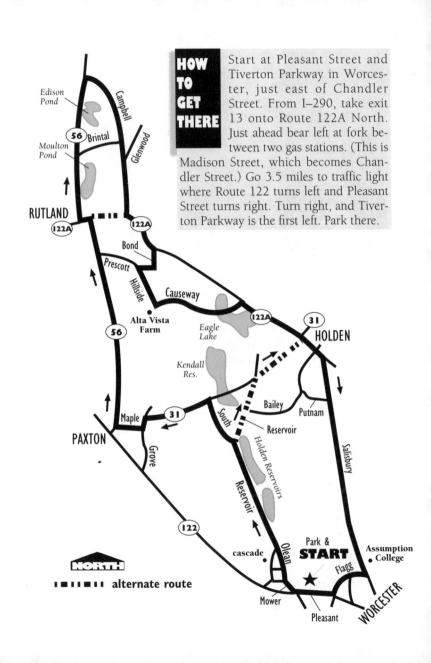

HOW TO GET THERE

Start at Pleasant Street and Tiverton Parkway in Worcester, just east of Chandler Street. From I–290, take exit 13 onto Route 122A North. Just ahead bear left at fork between two gas stations. (This is Madison Street, which becomes Chandler Street.) Go 3.5 miles to traffic light where Route 122 turns left and Pleasant Street turns right. Turn right, and Tiverton Parkway is the first left. Park there.

Edison Pond

Campbell

Glenwood

56 Brintal

Moulton Pond

RUTLAND

122A

122A

Bond

Prescott

Hillside

Causeway

Alta Vista Farm

Eagle Lake

122A

31 HOLDEN

Kendall Res.

Bailey

Putnam

56

Maple 31

South

Reservoir

PAXTON

Grove

Holden Reservoirs

Salisbury

122

Reservoir

cascade

Olean

Park & START

Assumption College

Flagg

NORTH

■ ▪ ■ ■ ▪ ■ ■ alternate route

Mower

Pleasant

WORCESTER

miles to Bond Road on right at the Holden town line. Resume with direction number 10.

6. Left and just ahead right on Pommogussett Road (still
    Route 56). Go 3.3 miles to Campbell Street on right. It's 0.5
    mile after Edison Pond on right. There's a great descent out
    of Rutland, and you'll pass Moulton Pond on your right at
    the bottom.

7. Right for 1.8 miles to yield sign (merge right on Glenwood
    Road).

8. Bear right for 1.5 miles to end (Route 122A).

9. Left for 1 mile to Bond Road on right, at the Holden town
    line.

10. Right for 0.7 mile to end (Hillside Road).

11. Left for 3.1 miles to fork immediately after you pass be-
    tween two ponds (Hilltop Avenue, unmarked, bears right).
    CAUTION: Bumpy and sandy spots.

    After 0.8 mile you'll see a farm with a statue of an Ameri-
    can buffalo on your right. This is Alta Vista Farm, which
    raises the animals. A store at the farm sells buffalo meat,
    hides, and buffalo-themed gifts.

12. Bear left for 0.2 mile to end (Route 122A).

13. Right for 1.5 miles to traffic light (Route 31) in the center of
    Holden. Just before the light you'll pass two graceful
    churches and a Federal-era mansion on your left.

14. Straight for 0.7 mile to Salisbury Street, which bears right at
    traffic light.

15. Bear right for 4.4 miles to Flagg Street on right, shortly
    after Assumption College on left. You'll pass Dawson Pond
    on the right after 0.6 mile. Notice the handsome, domed
    Albanian Orthodox church on the right about 3.5 miles
    farther on.

16. Right for 0.4 mile to fork (Richmond Avenue, unmarked,
    bears left).

17. Bear right for 0.5 mile to crossroads and stop sign (Pleasant Street).
18. Right for 0.7 mile to Tiverton Parkway on right.

Directions for the ride: 13 miles—
1. Follow directions 1 and 2 for the long rides.
2. Bear right for 1.5 miles to crossroads and stop sign (Route 31, South Road). You'll climb steeply for 0.25 mile midway through this section.
3. Right for 1.3 miles to traffic light (Route 122A). This is the center of Holden. At the intersection, notice the two fine churches and the Federal-era mansion to your left on Route 122A.
4. Right for 0.7 mile to Salisbury Street, which bears right at traffic light.
5. Follow directions for the long rides from number 15 to the end.

The Brookfields Ride
East Brookfield–Brookfield–West Brookfield–
North Brookfield

Number of miles:	26 (22 omitting western loop)
Terrain:	Delightfully rolling, with several short hills and one tough one.
Facilities:	Groceries and restaurants in the towns, except Brookfield.

On this ride you explore the four similarly named towns midway between Worcester and Springfield. The surrounding landscape, a harmonious mixture of magnificent rolling farmland, wooded hills, ridges with inspiring views, and several lakes, promises biking at its best along a wide-ranging network of rural lanes and lightly traveled secondary roads. The terrain is not as hilly as the more rugged ridge country surrounding it.

The rides start in East Brookfield, smallest and least distinctive of the quartet, attractively located along the shore of Lake Lashaway. A couple of miles out of town is a beautiful ride along Quaboag Pond, largest lake in the area, followed by another ride beside Quacumquasit Pond (say it three times fast). From here you'll ascend gradually onto a hillside with magnificent views across the well-groomed fields of estates and horse farms. Just ahead you'll cross the Quaboag River and climb a short hill into the classic New England village of Brookfield. The long, slender green is framed by two dignified churches, an ornate brick Victorian library, and fine old homes. Just off the green, the compact business block is a relic from the turn of the twentieth century.

Leaving Brookfield, you'll climb onto another ridge with fine views and descend into West Brookfield, most elegant of the four towns. The long, triangular green, highlighted by a fountain in the middle, is surrounded by a fine church and gracious wooden and brick homes. Just west of town you'll make a circuit around Wickaboag Pond and thread your way between rolling hills to North Brookfield, yet another New England gem of a town, with a traditional white church; a green, graceful stone library; and an ornate Victorian town hall with a bell tower, built in 1864. A statue on the green honors the soldiers killed in the War of the Rebellion, the official Union name for the Civil War.

From North Brookfield you'll enjoy a relaxing descent through orchards back to the shore of Lake Lashaway and East Brookfield.

DIRECTIONS
FOR
THE RIDE

1. Head west on Route 9 for 2.1 miles to Quaboag Street on left. It's your first left after the Brookfield town line.
2. Turn left and stay on main road for 2.1 miles to West Sturbridge Road on right, at top of hill. You'll go along Quaboag Pond on your right.
3. Right for 1.7 miles to fork where West Sturbridge Road bears left and South Pond Road bears right.
4. Bear right for 0.7 mile to Lake Road, which bears right after you pass Quacumquasit Pond on your left.
5. Bear right for 2.1 miles to end, at bottom of hill (merge right on Rice Corner Road). There is no stop sign here.
      You'll ride along a hillside with a good view on your right.
6. Bear right for 0.25 mile to end (merge right on Route 148).
7. Bear right for 1.1 miles to end (Route 9). You'll pass an old wooden mill on your right and then ascend to the Brook-field town green. Notice the Victorian library on the right at beginning of green.
8. Left for 0.6 mile to West Brookfield Road, which bears right uphill.

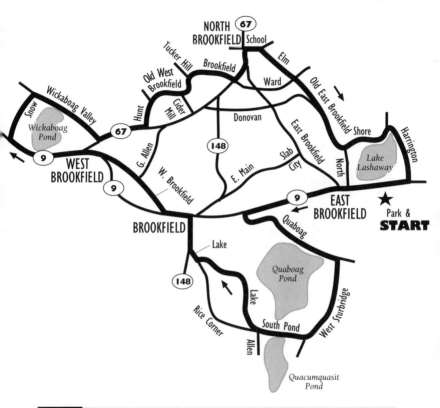

9. Bear right for 1.7 miles to end (merge right on Route 9). The road climbs onto a ridge with fine views, passing fields bordered by graceful rows of shade trees.

10. Bear right for 0.3 mile to far end of green in West Brookfield (Route 67 North turns sharply right). Here the longer ride goes straight, but you can chop off 4 miles by turning sharply right for 1.2 miles to Hunt Road on left and resuming with direction number 15.

11. Straight for 1.8 miles to Snow Road on right. You'll pass Wickaboag Pond on your right. If you come to the Salem Cross Inn (an elegant restaurant), you've gone 0.2 mile too far.

12. Right for 1.2 miles to end (Wickaboag Valley Road, unmarked).

13. Turn right and stay on main road for 1.9 miles to crossroads and stop sign (Route 67). You'll pass Wickaboag Pond again. At the crossroads, the West Brookfield town green is on the far right corner.

14. Left for 1 mile to Hunt Road on left.

15. Left for 0.5 mile to fork (Old West Brookfield Road bears right).

16. Bear right for 0.6 mile to fork at triangular traffic island (Cider Mill Road bears right).

17. Bear left and stay on main road for 1.1 miles to crossroads and stop sign (Route 67). The main road bears right after 0.2 mile.

18. Left for 0.5 mile to stop sign at top of hill (Route 67 turns left).

19. Left for 0.1 mile to crossroads in the center of North Brookfield (Summer Street on left, School Street on right). Notice the marvelous town hall on the far left corner.

20. Right for 0.2 mile to fork (Elm Street bears right).

21. Bear right and stay on main road for 3.5 miles to unmarked road on right that crosses a small bridge. It's shortly after you see Lake Lashaway and pass River Road on your right. Most of this section is downhill.

22. Turn right and stay on main road for 1.2 miles to end (Route 9). You'll follow Lake Lashaway on your right at the beginning.

23. Right for 0.8 mile back to start.

Llama farm in Leicester

West of Worcester
Spencer–Paxton–Leicester

Number of miles:	25 (15 without Paxton extension)
Terrain:	Hilly.
Facilities:	Groceries and restaurants in the towns.

The region just west of Worcester, a harmonious mixture of rolling farmland and woods dotted with ponds, provides very scenic biking on a network of traffic-free rural roads. Although close to the city, the area is pleasantly rural because Worcester is fortunate in not being surrounded by dreary, sprawling suburbs. In addition to the countryside, two landmarks highlight this ride: a Trappist monastery and the fine Moore State Park.

The ride starts from Spencer, an attractive, compact mill town clinging to steep hillsides, located about 12 miles west of Worcester. A magnificent old church, a nineteenth-century brick business block, and fine old Victorian homes give charm to the town. A few miles north of town is one of the state's more unusual places of interest, Saint Joseph's Abbey, a Trappist monastery. The church, which is open to the public, is a large, impressive stone building with an interior shrouded in nearly total darkness. Inside, the silence is overpowering. The monks sing Gregorian chants at their services every couple of hours throughout the day, beginning with vigils at 3:30 in the morning. To listen to these slow, unaccompanied intonations in the darkness is a haunting experience. At the entrance to the grounds is a gift shop selling books, recordings of Gregorian chants, religious articles, and jams and preserves made by the monks. A monk in flowing robes minds the shop.

A few miles beyond the monastery is a brighter spot, Moore State Park. Here a stream cascades in a file of waterfalls past a beautifully restored old mill. Above the mill is a small millpond. From here it's not far to the graceful town of Paxton, another mostly rural community less than 10 miles from downtown Worcester. A traditional wooden church, an old town hall, some fine, white wooden homes, and the elegant Paxton Inn grace the center of town.

From Paxton you have an enjoyable ride to the handsome hilltop town of Leicester along the shores of several ponds. Although its town center is only 7 miles from downtown Worcester, Leicester is a surprisingly unspoiled rural community. The large rectangular green is framed by an impressive stone church and the campus of Becker College. From Leicester you'll head past Cedar Meadow Pond and the Stiles Reservoir back to Spencer.

The short ride bypasses Paxton by heading from Spencer directly toward Leicester. After about 2 miles on Route 9 (which has a wide shoulder), you'll proceed onto back roads that go past a llama farm and weave through fine rolling farmland.

Directions for the ride: 25 miles—

1. Turn left out of parking lot onto Route 31 North. (The short ride starts off by heading east on Route 9.) Go 5.2 miles to crossroads (Browning Pond Road on left, Thompson's Pond Road on right).

   The entrance road to Saint Joseph's Abbey is on the left after 3.9 miles. It's 0.9 mile up a steady hill to the abbey church, with a steep pitch at the end.

2. Right for 1.8 miles to South Street on left. You'll climb steeply, descend to Thompson's Pond, and climb steeply again.

3. Left for 0.7 mile to end (Route 31).

4. Left for 0.5 mile to Black Hill Road, which bears right while you're going downhill. It's the second road that bears right.

5. Bear right for 0.2 mile to bridge. **CAUTION**: Bumps and potholes. Be sure to look to your right at the bridge; there's a fine view of the waterfall and the old mill in Moore State Park.

6. Just after the bridge, make a hairpin right turn onto a narrow lane that passes through a pair of stone pillars uphill into the park. The lane is blocked off to cars. Walk your bike; there's a no vehicles sign at the other end of the lane. Follow the lane for 0.5 mile to end (merge left onto Route 31).

7. Bear left for 1.3 miles to traffic light in the center of Paxton (Route 122).

8. Right for 1.3 miles to crossroads where Route 56 turns right.

9. Right for 1.8 miles to Manville Street (unmarked), which bears left along a reservoir. It's shortly after a crossroads. You pass Kettle Brook Reservoirs Number 4 and 3, both bordered by stately groves of pines, on your right.

10. Bear left for 1.5 miles to end. Kettle Brook Reservoir Number 2 is on your left at the beginning.

11. Turn left and just ahead bear right at fork on Chapel Street. Go 0.5 mile to Waite Street (unmarked) on right, just beyond Waite Pond on right.

12. Right for 0.4 mile to end (merge right on Route 9). Notice the handsome brick church in front of you at the end.

13. Bear right for 0.2 mile to fork (Main Street bears right uphill).

14. Bear right for 0.5 mile to stop sign (merge head-on into Route 9 West). You'll climb steeply at the beginning. Becker College and the Leicester town green are on your right at the top of the hill.

HOW TO GET THERE

Start at the municipal parking lot at the intersection of Routes 9 and 31 North, in Spencer. Entrance is on Route 31 North.

15. Straight for 0.5 mile to small crossroads (Lake Avenue on right, Rawson Street on left). It's just after the Castle Restaurant on the right. Notice the handsome stone library on your right at the beginning.

16. Turn left and stay on main road for 2.2 miles to end (Greenville Road, unmarked. The end is almost a crossroads—Kingsbury Road continues on the far side of the intersection about 20 feet to your right).

    You'll climb steeply for 0.3 mile near the beginning and pass Cedar Meadow Pond on your left toward the end.

17. Left for 0.8 mile to end (Chickering Road). The Stiles Reservoir is in front of you at the end.

18. Right for 0.5 mile to fork (G. H. Wilson Road bears right, Chickering Road bears left).

19. Bear left along water for 0.6 mile to end (Clark Road).

20. Right for 0.3 mile to Marble Road on right.

21. Turn right and stay on main road for 1.3 miles to Ash Street, which bears right shortly after G. H. Wilson Road on right. The main road bears right after 0.8 mile.

22. Bear right for 0.7 mile to a wide fork (R. Jones Road on right).

23. Left (still Ash Street) for 1.4 miles to end (Route 9, Main Street). You go straight at two stop signs near the end. At the end a beautiful old church is to your right on Route 9.

24. Left (**CAUTION** here) for 0.3 mile to second traffic light, at bottom of steep hill (Route 31 North on right). You're back in the center of Spencer. Notice the fine Victorian homes along Route 9.

25. Right and then immediately left into parking lot. Notice the turreted library opposite the entrance to the lot.

Directions for the ride: 15 miles—

1. Right and then immediately left (east) on Route 9. Go 2.3 miles to unmarked road on left immediately after the Leicester town line.
2. Left for 0.2 mile to Watson Street on left.
3. Turn left and stay on main road for 0.5 mile to fork where Moose Hill Road bears left and Bond Street bears right. A llama farm is on your left just after you turn onto Watson Street.
4. Bear right for 0.7 mile to end, at traffic island (Whittemore Street, unmarked).
5. Right for 1.9 miles to end (Route 56), passing through splendid rolling farmland. Here the ride turns right, but if you turn left for 0.3 mile you'll come to Hot Dog Annie's, a marvelously dilapidated, honky-tonk snack bar—1950s roadside kitsch at its best.
6. Right for 0.7 mile to end. The Leicester town green is on your left at the end.
7. Right for 100 yards to stop sign (merge head-on into Route 9 West).
8. Follow directions for the long ride from number 15 to the end.

South of Worcester
Auburn–West Millbury–Sutton–Oxford–Charlton–Rochdale

Number of miles:	29 (21 without Charlton-Rochdale extension, 10 with shortcut)
Terrain:	Hilly.
Facilities:	None on 10-mile ride. McDonald's in Oxford. Grocery in Charlton (29-mile ride).

This is a tour of rolling farm country, dotted with lakes and graceful villages, south and a little west of Worcester. Although close to the city, the region is delightfully rural because, unlike Boston and Springfield, Worcester has no dreary suburbs despoiling the surrounding area. Biking in this part of the state is challenging because the landscape is hilly, but you'll be rewarded with fine views from ridgetops, narrow lanes twisting past old barns and grazing cattle, and several stretches along ponds.

The ride starts from Auburn, Worcester's closest approximation to a bedroom suburb, but quickly heads into sparsely developed countryside. After about 5 miles you'll proceed through West Millbury, a hamlet with a small white church and some sturdy wooden houses, and then descend to Singletary Lake. Two miles ahead you'll arrive in the classic New England village of Sutton, which crowns a hilltop. A small green with a gazebo, an elegant white church, and an old wooden town hall stand at the village crossroads.

Beyond Sutton you'll tackle a short but very steep hill with a glorious view from the top before descending into West Sutton, another hamlet with a little church, a few old houses, and not much else. The road rolls onto a ridge with fine views and descends to Oxford, an attractive town with a handsome brick town hall and a slender green. Oxford is best known as the birthplace of Clara Barton, founder of the American Red Cross. It's 0.8 mile off the route up a tough hill and open during the warmer half of the year. Call (508) 987–5375 for hours. From Oxford the terrain is mostly flat back to Auburn as you follow the valley of the French River to the mill village of North Oxford, but there's a challenging hill shortly before the end. It was necessary to include it so as to avoid an unsafe section of Route 12 at the end of the ride.

The long ride heads farther west into the rolling hills and ridges of Charlton, crossing the Buffumville Reservoir. A small beach here provides a good rest stop before the long, steady ascent just ahead. Near the end of the ride you'll follow Rochdale Pond to the fascinating mill village of Rochdale (which rhymes with Notchdale), which is part of the town of Leicester (pronounced Lester). You pass the Dark Brook Reservoir just before the end.

The 10-mile ride bypasses all the towns and villages except North Oxford, where you can visit Clara Barton's birthplace off the route. There's a challenging hill shortly before the end of the ride; I included it to avoid a dangerously busy stretch of Route 12 at the end.

DIRECTIONS
FOR
THE RIDE

Directions for the ride: 29 miles—

1. Right on Route 12 for 0.2 mile to Faith Avenue (unmarked) on right, at traffic light.

2. Right for 0.5 mile to Route 20, at stop sign.

3. Straight (**CAUTION** here) for 1.2 miles to Cedar Street on left. You'll follow Eddy Pond on your left, on the far side of I–395.

4. Left for 0.6 mile to yield sign (merge right).

5. Bear right across diagonal railroad tracks (**CAUTION** here). Go 0.2 mile to end (Barnes Street on left, South Street on right). **CAUTION**: Bumpy road. Here the 10-mile ride turns right.

6. Left for 2.9 miles to end (merge left at bottom of hill). You'll climb onto a ridge with fine views to your left and descend to West Millbury.

7. Bear left for 0.3 mile to Harris Avenue, a small lane on right. You follow Singletary Lake on your right.

   The ride turns right on Harris Avenue, but for a fascinating side trip continue straight for 1 mile to the mill village of Bramansville (part of Millbury), passing several Industrial Revolution-era mills, a millpond, and a stately white church. Bear right at fork on return trip.

8. Right for 0.8 mile to end (merge right).

9. Bear right for 0.9 mile to crossroads and stop sign (Boston Road, unmarked), in the center of Sutton.

   There's a good view of Singletary Lake on your right at the beginning, and a country store on your right just before the crossroads. Notice the gazebo and church on the far left corner.

10. Right for 1.5 miles to traffic island where the main road bears left.

11. Bear left for 0.2 mile to Town Farm Road, which bears right.

12. Bear right for 0.9 mile to crossroads and stop sign (West Sutton Road, unmarked).

13. Straight up a very steep hill—I won't blame you for walking it—for 1.1 miles to end (Central Turnpike, unmarked). At the top of the hill you'll be rewarded by a panoramic view of rolling green hillsides. The hamlet of West Sutton is at the end.

14. Right for 3.6 miles to traffic light (Route 12) in the center of Oxford. Here the 21-mile ride turns right.

HOW TO GET THERE

Start at Auburn Plaza, Route 12, Auburn. From I–290 West or I–395 North, take exit 6B (Route 20 West). Go 0.7 mile to second traffic light (Prospect Street). Turn right and the shopping center is on your right From the Massachusetts Turnpike, take exit 10 and follow signs to Route 12 South. At end of ramp go 0.3 mile to shopping center on left.

After a short climb, you'll relax on a gradual descent with fine views and pass Robinson Pond on the left. When you come to Route 12, notice the handsome redbrick town hall on the far right side of the intersection.

15. Straight for 2 miles to crossroads and stop sign at top of hill(Conlin Road).

16. Straight for 2 miles to end. You'll cross the Buffumville Reservoir, where there's a swimming area on your right, and then climb steadily for 0.8 mile.

17. Right for 1.5 miles to traffic light (Route 20). There's a grocery on the far left corner.

18. Go straight and just ahead bear left at fork on Hammond Hill Road. Go 1.5 miles to end (merge right at large traffic island). **CAUTION**: The last 0.5 mile is bumpy.

19. Bear right for 0.4 mile to Smith Road (unmarked), which bears left just after bridge over railroad.

20. Bear left and stay on main road for 2.1 miles to end. Notice the dam and millpond on the far side of the intersection. This is Greenville, a small village that is part of Leicester.

21. Right for 0.8 mile to crossroads and stop sign (Stafford Street). You'll follow Rochdale Pond on your right. The mill village of Rochdale, which is also part of Leicester, is at the crossroads.

22. Turn left and just ahead bear right on Mill Street. Go almost 0.7 mile to crossroads and stop sign (Route 56). You pass and old brick mill on your left.

23. Straight for 0.9 mile to West Street on right.

24. Right for 1.2 miles to end (Route 12). The Dark Brook Reservoir is on your left near the end.

25. Left (**CAUTION** here) for 0.3 mile to shopping center on right.

Directions for the ride: 21 miles—

1. Follow the directions for the long ride through number 14.

2. Right for 3.7 miles to Prospect Street (unmarked), which bears right immediately after Route 56 on left.

   Notice the attractive brick library on your left after 0.1 mile. Then you'll pass the Oxford town green on your right.

   You'll go through North Oxford after about 3 miles, passing a distinctive stone mill on your left and then a handsome white church on your right. To visit the Clara Barton Birthplace Museum, turn left after 3.1 miles onto Clara Barton Road. Go 0.8 mile (mostly uphill) to birthplace on right.

3. Bear right on Prospect Street for 2.1 miles to shopping center on right, just past traffic light at Route 20. **CAUTION**: The light is at bottom of steep hill.

   You climb steadily for 0.7 mile, with a steep 0.2-mile section halfway up, and then descend sharply to Route 20.

Directions for the ride: 10 miles—

1. Follow the directions for the 29-mile ride through number 5.

2. Right for 1.8 miles to fork immediately after diagonal railroad tracks. **CAUTION**: Bumpy spots. Walk across tracks.

3. Bear left for 0.9 mile to end (Federal Hill Road, unmarked). **CAUTION**: Dangerous diagonal railroad tracks after 0.2 mile. Walk across them.

4. Right for 0.3 mile to end (Route 12).

5. Right for 2.3 miles to Prospect Street (unmarked), which bears right immediately after Route 56 on left.

   You'll go through North Oxford after about 1.5 miles, passing a distinctive stone mill on your left and then a handsome white church on your right. To visit the Clara Barton Birthplace Museum, turn left after 1.7 miles onto Clara Barton Road. Go 0.8 mile (mostly uphill) to birthplace on right.

6. Follow last direction of the 21-mile ride.

Spring plowing at Old Sturbridge Village

Old Sturbridge Village Ride
Sturbridge–Brimfield–Warren–Brookfield

Number of miles:	30 (15 without Brimfield-Warren extension)
Terrain:	The short ride is rolling, with one long, steady hill. The long ride is hilly. One hundred yards of dirt road.
Facilities:	Grocery and snack bar in Brimfield and Warren. Burger King at end.

The magnificent ridge, valley, and lake country of south-central Massachusetts provides superb bicycling on a network of nearly untraveled country roads, with spectacular vistas spread before you as you crest each ridge. The ride passes through Brimfield and Warren, two of the numerous classic New England towns dotting the middle of the state.

The ride starts across the road from Old Sturbridge Village, an outstanding historical restoration, among the best in the country. If you've never been there, it would be worthwhile to set aside several hours before or after the ride to visit it. With painstaking historical research and attention to detail, Old Sturbridge Village re-creates life in an early nineteenth-century New England community as closely as possible. No power mowers trim the green—sheep do the job just as effectively. Dirt paths become muddy when it rains and dusty in the summer heat just as in 1800, when the luxury of blacktop hadn't diffused to the country towns. In the ramshackle little shops and outbuildings, apprentices dressed in historically accurate garments learn and apply traditional un-mechanized crafts and trades like spinning yarn, making water-tight casks, tanning leather, blacksmithing, and cabinetmaking.

No attempt has been made to artificially glamorize the village or dress it up. As in most post-Revolutionary small towns, it has only one impressive house, which belonged to the community's most prominent family; everyone else lived in simple, sparsely furnished cottages, scratching a living from the soil, a small business, or a trade.

Old Sturbridge Village also has several galleries exhibiting artifacts from everyday life in early New England, a fascinating garden of medicinal and culinary herbs, and a full range of educational programs.

The success of Old Sturbridge Village has spawned several other attractions, including a doll museum, an antique-auto museum, Saint Anne's Shrine with a collection of Russian icons, and too many overpriced antiques and crafts shops.

From Sturbridge you'll head into lake country, going along the Brimfield Reservoir. Just off the route is East Brimfield Dam, holding the waters in place. A couple of miles ahead you'll pass beautiful Holland Pond, where you can take a swim. Next you go through a valley to the elegant old town of Brimfield. The larger-than-average green is framed by a graceful white church, rambling old wooden homes, and an ornate pink-purple Victorian town hall. Brimfield hosts a giant, weeklong antiques fair three times a year: the week before Mother's Day, the week after Independence Day, and the week after Labor Day.

From Brimfield you'll head north on nearly deserted Route 19, detouring for 1.5 miles onto a ridge with sweeping views. Route 19 brings you into Warren, an unspoiled jewel of a small town built around a central square. Framing the square are the brick town hall adorned with a bell tower, an old-fashioned former train station (now used for offices), the handsome stone library, the town green with a bandstand on it, and a white church on top of the hill.

There's a long, tough climb out of Warren. After a couple of miles you'll cross the town line into Brookfield. Here you'll bike past gracious horse farms, with views of Quaboag Pond and distant hills in the background, and then hug the shore of Quacumquasit Pond. The return to Sturbridge leads through woods and small farms along a quiet country road.

The short ride heads directly toward Brookfield on a quiet back road, bypassing Holland Pond, Brimfield, and Warren. You'll rejoin the long ride shortly before Quacumquasit Pond.

Directions for the ride: 30 miles—

1. Right (west) on Route 20 for almost 0.9 mile to Arnold Road on right. It's immediately after an attractive red-brick building (currently a senior citizens center) on the right. Here the short ride turns right.

2. Straight for 0.6 mile to traffic light (Route 148 on right).
   You'll go through Fiskdale, a village in Sturbridge, just before the light. Saint Anne's Shrine is to your right on Church Street (up a short, steep hill) just before the light.

3. Straight for 1.6 miles to Holland–East Brimfield Road on left, at the far end of the East Brimfield Reservoir (sign says TO QUINEBAUG COVE CAMPGROUND).
   To visit East Brimfield Dam, turn left after 0.6 mile onto Riverview Avenue, opposite a motel. The dam is 0.25 mile ahead.

4. Left for 1.9 miles to Morse Road, which turns right downhill. It's just after Long Hill Road turns left up a steep hill.

5. Right for 0.25 mile to Morse Lane, a dirt road that turns sharply left downhill. There's a red, barn-shaped building on the left at the intersection.

6. Turn sharply left and just ahead turn sharply right at bottom of hill, following Holland Pond on your left. **CAUTION**: Walk down the hill, which is rough and rocky, with sand at the bottom. Go 0.5 mile to end (Brimfield Road).

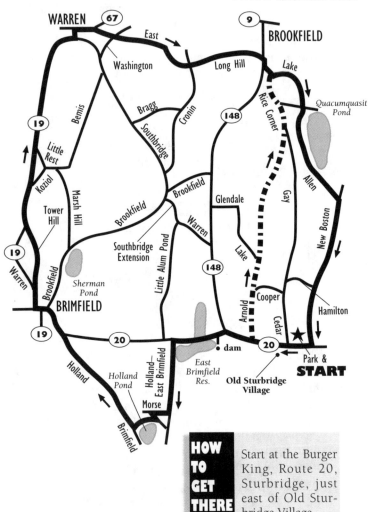

WARREN (67)

East

9

BROOKFIELD

Washington

Long Hill

Lake

Bragg

Cronin

Rice Corner

Quacumquasit Pond

19

Bemis

Southbridge

148

Little Rest

Koziol

Marsh Hill

Brookfield

Brookfield

Glendale

Gay

Allen

New Boston

Tower Hill

19

Warren

Warren

Lake

Southbridge Extension

Little Alum Pond

148

Cooper

Hamilton

Brookfield

Sherman Pond

BRIMFIELD

Arnold

Cedar

★

19

20

dam

20

Holland—East Brimfield

East Brimfield Res.

Old Sturbridge Village

Park & START

Holland

Holland Pond

Morse

Brimfield

HOW TO GET THERE

Start at the Burger King, Route 20, Sturbridge, just east of Old Sturbridge Village.

7. Right for 3.1 miles to end (merge left on Route 20).
8. Bear left (**CAUTION** here) for 0.7 mile to Warren Road on right, immediately after church on right in the center of Brimfield. Notice the attractive stone library on your left at the intersection.
9. Right for 0.9 mile to Tower Hill Road, which bears right.
   Here the ride bears right and climbs steadily for 0.8 mile onto a hillside with fine views. For an easier but less scenic ride, stay on main road for 5.7 miles to Warren, where Routes 19 and 67 turn left at bottom of hill. Resume with direction 12.
10. Bear right for 1.5 miles to yield sign at bottom of hill (merge right on Route 19). **CAUTION** here.
11. Bear right for 4.2 miles to Routes 19 and 67 on left, at bottom of hill in Warren. This road goes under a railroad bridge.
12. Left for 100 yards to a small traffic circle with a monument. This is the center of Warren. The yellow-brick town hall is to your left, the old railroad depot and town green are on your right, and the elegant stone library is in front of you a little to the right.
13. Right on Route 67 North for 0.2 mile to East Road, which bears right uphill.
14. Bear right for 2.8 miles to crossroads and stop sign. **CAUTION**: This stretch has some steep ups and downs; take it easy on the descents. You climb steeply for 0.8 mile at the beginning.
15. Straight for 2.5 miles to end (Route 148). **CAUTION**: Steep, bumpy descent at the beginning.
16. Turn right and just ahead bear left on Lake Road. Go 0.25 mile to fork where Rice Corner Road goes straight and Lake Road bears left.

17. Bear left for 2.1 miles to end. This is an inspiring ride along a hillside past estates and horse farms, with views of Quaboag Pond below.

18. Jog right and immediately left (at the same intersection) on Allen Road. Go 2.1 miles to end (New Boston Road, unmarked). You'll follow Quacumquasit Pond on your left at the beginning.

19. Right for 2.8 miles to end (Route 20).

20. Right for almost 0.4 mile to Burger King on right.

Directions for the ride: 15 miles—

1. Right (west) on Route 20 for almost 0.9 mile to Arnold Road on right. It's immediately after an attractive redbrick building (currently a senior citizens center) on the right.

2. Right for 1.7 miles to fork (Lake Road, a smaller road, bears left).

3. Curve slightly right on main road for 3.3 miles to stop sign (merge left on Rice Corner Road). It's 0.5 mile after Gay Road merges into the main road on your right.

4. Bear left for 1.4 miles to Lake Road on right.

5. Follow the directions for the long ride from number 17 to the end, turning right on Lake Road instead of bearing left.

Southbridge–Woodstock, Connecticut

Number of miles:	25 (14 without Woodstock extension)
Terrain:	Very rolling, with several short, steep hills.
Facilities:	Country store in Woodstock. McDonald's at end.

This ride has us explore the very rural, very rolling, ridge-and-valley country straddling the Massachusetts-Connecticut border roughly midway between Worcester and Springfield. Steep-sided wooded ridges, running north to south, become more open and rounded as you head south into Connecticut. The long ride passes through the magnificent hilltop town of Woodstock, Connecticut.

You start from the small industrial city of Southbridge, one of the most attractive mill towns in Massachusetts. Southbridge became known as a one-industry town—optical products—with factories of the largest company, American Optical, lining the banks of the Quinebaug River in a seemingly endless row. The company's former main building is a massive yet graceful Victorian structure resembling an Elizabethan castle. It is now a business center housing diversified industries and commercial enterprises. In the downtown area, graceful brick buildings line the wide, gently curving main street, which leads up a hill to a large, elegant church standing proudly over the town.

From Southbridge you'll head south through open farmland and along unspoiled Morse Pond into Connecticut. After a few miles on country lanes winding past old farms and broad fields, you cross back into Massachusetts and follow the crest of a high ridge with spectacular views. The descent back into Southbridge is a screamer.

The long ride heads farther south into Connecticut to the unspoiled hilltop town of Woodstock, a classic New England jewel. Framing the large green are the traditional white church, the handsome old wooden main building of Woodstock Academy, and the Bowen House, a marvelous pink Gothic mansion. Also called Roseland Cottage, it was built in 1846 by Henry C. Bowen, a businessman who invited presidents Grant, Hayes, Harrison, and McKinley there for Fourth of July gatherings. Now run by the Society for the Preservation of New England Antiquities and open to the public afternoons from May to October, the mansion has period furnishings and a private bowling alley, one of the earliest in the country.

Beyond Woodstock you'll weave through inspiring, very rolling farmland and rejoin the short ride just in time to enjoy the high ridge and fast descent into Southbridge.

DIRECTIONS
FOR
THE RIDE

Directions for the ride: 25 miles—

1. Left on Route 131 for 0.25 mile to Ashland Avenue on right. Route 131 curves sharply left at the intersection.

2. Right for 0.3 mile to crossroads and stop sign (Route 169). There's a short, steep hill at the beginning.

3. Left for 5.2 miles to English Neighborhood Road, which turns sharply right almost at the bottom of hill, and just before a blinking light (Route 197). Here the short ride makes a sharp right. Morse Pond is on your right after about 2.5 miles, just before you enter Connecticut.

4. Straight for 3.7 miles to Plaine Hill Road, which bears slightly right where Route 169 curves left downhill. It's 0.4 mile after the pink Bowen House on your right.

You go through the hamlet of North Woodstock at the beginning. Notice the graceful church on your left immediately after the stop sign.

The main building of Woodstock Academy, with an ornate belfry, is on your left opposite the Bowen House, on the far side of the Woodstock town green. There's a magnificent view to your left when you reach Plaine Hill Road.

5. Bear right for 0.5 mile to end (Route 171), at bottom of steep hill. **CAUTION** here.

6. Turn right and stay on main road for 4.4 miles to crossroads (Perrin Road on left, Bradford Corner Road on right). This is the hamlet of West Woodstock.

7. Turn right and then immediately curve right (still Bradford Corner Road), passing church on left. Go 1 mile to end (Center Road).

8. Right and just ahead left on Brickyard Road. Go 2 miles to fork (Redhead Hill Road bears right up steep hill).

9. Bear left (still Brickyard Road) for 1.7 miles to English Neighborhood Road on right.

10. Right for 0.5 mile to Lebanon Hill Road on left.

11. Left for 3.8 miles to fork where Everett Street bears right and the main road (Elm Street, unmarked) bears slightly left. It's just after you enter the built-up section of Southbridge.

After 0.9 mile look for a granite marker at the state line dated 1906. A small wooden chapel, built by a nearby resident in 1995, is on your right opposite the marker. Then you'll have a thrilling descent with magnificent views.

12. Bear left for 0.5 mile to end (Route 131), in downtown Southbridge.

Just before the end, notice the castlelike town hall on the right, built in 1888, and the bell-towered fire station on the left. When you come to Route 131, the main business district is on your left.

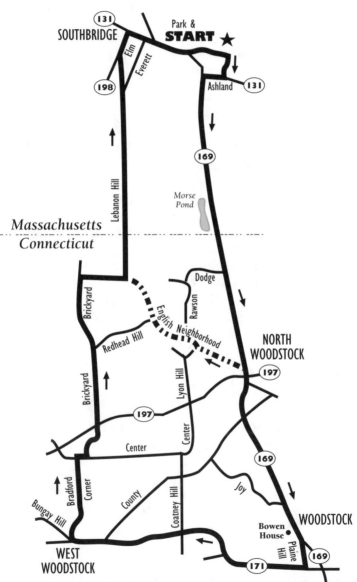

NORTH

NORTH
▪ ▪ ▪ ▪ ▪ alternate route

131 SOUTHBRIDGE

Park &
START ★

198

Ashland

131

Elm

Everett

169

Lebanon Hill

Morse Pond

Massachusetts
Connecticut

Dodge

Brickyard

Rawson

English Neighborhood

Redhead Hill

NORTH
WOODSTOCK

197

Brickyard

Lyon Hill

197

Center

Center

Bradford

Corner

County

Coatney Hill

169

Joy

Bungay Hill

WEST
WOODSTOCK

**Bowen
House** ●

Plaine Hill

WOODSTOCK

169

171

13.   Turn right and stay on Route 131 for 1.4 miles to McDonald's on left.

Route 131 bears right at a rotary after 0.4 mile. Glance to your left at the rotary to see the castlelike former main building of American Optical Company (now a business center). You'll follow the Quinebaug River on your left after the rotary.

Directions for the ride: 14 miles—

1.   Follow directions for the long ride through number 3.
2.   Turn sharply right and stay on main road for 2.9 miles to Lebanon Hill Road on right. The first half of this section is a steady climb.
3.   Follow directions for the long ride from number 11 to the end, turning right on Lebanon Hill Road instead of left.

HOW TO GET THERE

Start at the shopping center behind McDonald's on Route 131 in Southbridge. It's 1.5 miles east of the center of town.

Ridge and Valley Ride
Dudley–Charlton–North Woodstock, Connecticut

Number of miles:	31 (19 with shortcut omitting North Woodstock)
Terrain:	Hilly.
Facilities:	Grocery and luncheonette in Charlton. Restaurant in Quinebaug.

The rolling, rural countryside between Worcester and Springfield consists primarily of high, open ridges that provide some of the most spectacular bicycle riding in the state. This ride tours the southeastern portion of the region, ascending and descending from one ridge to another on smooth, lightly traveled roads with sweeping vistas around every bend. The graceful New England hilltop towns of Charlton and Dudley add to the appeal and variety of the ride.

The ride starts from Dudley, a two-faced town with old, grim mills on the French River that forms the border with Webster, which contrast with a classic town center on a hilltop 3 miles to the west. After 3 miles you'll crest a short hill and enjoy the first of many dramatic views. A mile ahead you'll ride alongside Pierpont Meadow Pond, framed by rustic houses and cottages nestled in the woods. The route proceeds into the ridge country to Charlton, among the most appealing and spectacularly located central Massachusetts towns. The handsome church, turn-of-the-twentieth-century brick schoolhouse, town hall, and an old cemetery crown the top of a hill with superb views to the west. From here you'll head south to Dudley on Route 31, an absolute paradise for biking. Three miles out of town is the Dresser Hill Dairy, with some of the best ice cream in Worcester County. From here you'll climb onto more open ridges with inspiring vistas, dip downhill, climb and dip some more, and finally enjoy a thrilling 2-mile descent into the Quinebaug Valley.

The route continues south through more glorious ridge-and-valley country to the pristine hamlets of East Woodstock and then North Woodstock, Connecticut, which contain only a graceful white church and a few sturdy, well-kept houses. Near the end of the ride you'll climb one more hill to the gracious town center of Dudley. It consists primarily of Nichols College, which is mainly a business school. Adjoining the campus are some handsome old homes and a distinctive brick church with a tall, slender clock tower. From here it's a short downhill ride to the end.

The short ride stays in Massachusetts, bypassing the long descent into the valley of the Quinebaug River (and the climb back out). Shortly after the Dresser Hill Dairy, you'll turn onto a rustic back road for about 1.5 miles to the town center of Dudley, which is a mile from the starting point.

Directions for the rides: Dudley start—

DIRECTIONS
FOR
THE RIDE

1. Turn left from *side* of parking lot onto Alton Drive (unmarked), passing Cumberland Farms on right. (Don't get on Airport Road or Route 197.) Go 0.5 mile to end (Jesse Road).

2. Right for 0.2 mile to end (Mason Road, unmarked).

3. Left for 0.3 mile to Sawmill Road on right.

4. Right for 0.9 mile to end (Charlton Road, unmarked).

5. Left for 1.1 miles to Pierpont Road on left, shortly after a large grassy traffic island with a monument. You'll climb a short hill with a sweeping view and descend to Wallis Pond on your right.

6. Left for 1.9 miles to crossroads and stop sign (Potter Village Road). You'll follow Pierpont Meadow Pond on your right.

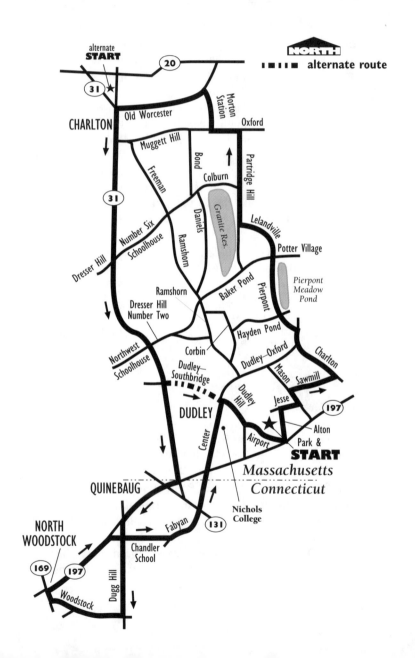

HOW TO GET THERE Start at the Dudley Plaza, a shopping center on Airport Road, Dudley. It's just north of Route 197, 2 miles west of downtown Webster. An alternate starting point, closer to the Worcester area, is Carpenter Plaza, a small shopping center on Route 31 in Charlton, 0.6 mile south of Route 20. This starting point also offers a shortcut that shortens the ride to 19 miles. Directions for the Charlton start are at the end. The Dudley start offers the advantage of being 320 feet lower.

To get to the Dudley start, take exit 2 from I–395 onto Route 16 West. Just ahead, go straight at traffic light onto Route 12 South into Webster. After 1.7 miles go straight onto Route 197. Go 1.1 miles, turn right on Airport Road, and the shopping center is on your right. To get to the Charlton start, take exit 6B (Route 20 West). Go 7.4 miles to traffic light (Center Depot Road on right, North Main Street on left). Turn left for 0.6 mile to Carpenter Plaza on right.

7. Straight for 0.7 mile to end (Partridge Hill Road), at top of hill.

8. Right for 2.1 miles to end (Oxford Road). You'll follow the Granite Reservoir on your left at the beginning.

9. Left for 0.5 mile to Morton Station Road on right. It comes up as you start to go downhill—don't whiz past it.

10. Right for 0.5 mile to end (Old Worcester Road, unmarked).

11. Left for 1.5 miles to crossroads and stop sign (Route 31). You'll pass an orchard on your right as soon as you turn left. When you get to Route 31, a grocery and luncheonette are on the far right side of the intersection.

12. Left on Route 31 for 6 miles to crossroads (Dudley-South-bridge Road, unmarked). A sign points left to Dudley Center. Here the short ride, from either the Dudley or the Charlton start, turns left. (See end of this direction.)

   At the beginning of this stretch you'll go through the center of Charlton. The Dresser Hill Dairy is 3 miles ahead on your right, atop a ridge. Immediately after the dairy, go straight (don't bear right downhill).

To do the short ride, turn left for 1.3 miles to crossroads and stop sign (Center Road). The gracious town center of Dudley is to your right at the intersection. Resume with direction 22, going straight at crossroads instead of turning right.

13. Straight for 2.2 miles to crossroads and stop sign at bottom of long hill (Route 197). **CAUTION**: Keep alert for bumps and cracks.

14. Right for 0.2 mile to traffic light (Route 131). This is the village of Quinebaug, Connecticut (part of the town of Thompson), which is 200 yards south of the Massachusetts border.

15. Go straight (don't bear right on Route 131) for 1.4 miles to diagonal crossroads where Converse Road turns sharply right and Dugg Hill Road bears left. Notice the fine stucco church on your right at the beginning.

16. Bear left for 1.8 miles to crossroads and stop sign at bottom of hill (Hibbard Road on left, Woodstock Road on right).

17. Turn right and stay on main road for 1.7 miles to end (Route 169). Don't bear left on County Road after 1.2 miles. You'll go through the hamlet of East Woodstock, Connecticut, after 0.5 mile.

18. Right and just ahead right again at crossroads and stop sign (Route 197). This is North Woodstock, another tiny village. Go 1.8 miles to Chandler School Road, which bears right.

19. Bear right for 1.2 miles to end (merge left at stop sign). **CAUTION**: You reach the end suddenly at bottom of short hill.

20. Bear left for 0.9 mile to stop sign and blinking light (Route 131). There's a grocery on the far left corner.

You'll cross the Quinebaug River and go through Fabyan, a hamlet that is part of the town of Thompson.

21. Straight for 2.1 miles to second crossroads and stop sign (Dudley Hill Road, unmarked, on right). It's shortly after Nichols College and brick church on left. You'll climb steeply for 0.7 mile to the college.

22. Right for 0.4 mile to fork immediately after stop sign (Dudley Hill Road bears right, Airport Road bears left).

23. Bear left for 0.6 mile to shopping center on left, at bottom of hill.

Directions for the rides: Charlton Start—

(Start at the small shopping center on Route 31.)

1. Follow direction 12 for the ride starting in Dudley, turning left out of the parking lot and then immediately right at crossroads onto Route 31 South. Be sure that you're heading south (away from Route 20) on Route 31.

2. Follow directions number 13 through 23, and then 1 through 11, for the ride starting in Dudley.

Tri-State Tour
Webster–Douglas–Pascoag, Rhode Island–Thompson, Connecticut

Number of miles:	33 (19 without Pascoag-Thompson extension)
Terrain:	Rolling, with one tough hill.
Facilities:	Groceries at two campgrounds in Sutton, open during camping season. Grocery and snack bar in Pascoag. Friendly's Ice Cream at end.

This is a tour of the very rural, mostly wooded, lake-studded countryside surrounding the point where Massachusetts, Rhode Island, and Connecticut meet. The terrain is not as hilly as in the surrounding areas. The lightly traveled back roads, winding through the woods and along several ponds, promise enjoyable and peaceful bicycling.

The ride starts in Webster, a small and rather bleak mill city on the French River just north of the Connecticut line. You'll immediately head into rolling, wooded countryside to the tiny village of West Sutton and pass Sutton Falls, a small dam with a little covered bridge above it. Just ahead are pleasant roads along Manchaug Pond and then Whitins Reservoir, where you'll pass a waterslide (here's your chance to descend a different type of hill). From here it's a short way to the graceful, classic New England village of Douglas, with a stately white church, old cemetery, and triangular green.

From Douglas you'll follow a smooth secondary road to the attractive little mill town of Pascoag, in the northwestern corner of

Rhode Island. Pascoag is typical of the many mill villages hugging the fast-flowing rivers throughout that state. Leaving the town, you'll skirt the Wilson Reservoir and then climb gradually to the top of Buck Hill, one of Rhode Island's highest points.

You now speed down two steep hills into the northeastern corner of Connecticut. After about 3 miles of narrow lanes, you'll cross back into Webster and return into town along the shore of Lake Chargoggagoggmanchaugagoggchaubunagungamaug (usually called Webster Lake), which in the Nipmuc Indian language means, "I fish on my side, you fish on your side, and nobody fishes in the middle." If it hasn't been stolen, a sign spelling out the name of the lake may greet you as you cross the state line.

The short ride heads directly from Douglas back to Webster without leaving Massachusetts. There's a great descent near the end, and you'll ride along Webster Lake at the bottom.

DIRECTIONS
FOR
THE RIDE

Directions for the ride: 33 miles—

1. Left (east) and just ahead straight at traffic light onto Route 16 East. Go 0.3 mile to Sutton Road on left, immediately after the I–395 underpass.

2. Left (**CAUTION** here)for 0.3 mile to where Sutton Road turns right.

3. Right for 3.8 miles to end. You'll pass Nipmuck Pond on your right.

4. Right for 0.2 mile to fork (main road bears left downhill).

5. Bear left for 1 mile to second right (Manchaug Road; sign says TO SUTTON FALLS CAMPING AREA). It's almost at bottom of long hill. The hamlet of West Sutton is just before the intersection.

6. Right for 2.3 miles to fork where Torrey Road goes straight down steep hill. Notice the covered bridge at Sutton Falls Camping Area on your right after 0.8 mile. Then you follow Manchaug Pond on your right.

NORTH

■ ▪ ■ ▪ ■ **alternate route**

WEST SUTTON

Manchaug

Joe Jenny

Douglas

Manchaug Pond

Nipmuck Pond

Sutton

Holt

Northwest Main

Whitins Reservoir

Park & **START** ★

12

WEBSTER

16

16

DOUGLAS

193

Lake Chargoggagoggman-chaugagoggchau-bunagungamaug

Southwest Main

Wallum Lake

96

Connecticut

Sand Dam

THOMPSON

Massachusetts

Rhode Island

Buck Hill

100

100

River

107

PASCOAG

HOW TO GET THERE

Start at shopping center behind Friendly's Ice Cream, Route 12, Webster. From I–395, head west onto Route 16 (take exit 2). Just ahead go straight at traffic light, and you'll immediately see Friendly's on your right.

7. Straight (don't bear left) for 0.3 mile to Holt Road, which bears right.

8. Bear right for 1.3 miles to fork where Wallis Street bears right and Northwest Main Street bears left. You'll see Manchaug Pond and pass a grocery on the right at the beginning.

9. Bear left for 0.7 mile to another fork. You'll follow Whitins Reservoir on your right and pass a waterslide after 0.2 mile.

10. Bear right along water for 0.8 mile to end (merge left; Wallis Street is on right). There is no stop sign here.

11. Bear left for 0.6 mile to fork.

12. Bear left for 0.4 mile to fork (church on right), in the village center of Douglas.

13. Bear right and just ahead merge right on Route 16. Go 50 yards to blinking light where Route 16 turns right. Here the short ride turns right.

14. Go straight and just ahead bear left at fork on Route 96 (South Street) Go 6.6 miles to end, at stop sign. Route 96 turns left here. The second half of this long stretch is in Rhode Island.

15. Left and just ahead right on River Street. Go 0.1 mile to end (Route 107, Chapel Street).

16. Bear right and stay on main road for 1.4 miles to end, opposite a supermarket in the center of Pascoag, Rhode Island. Route 107 twists and turns, but stay on the main road. Notice the small waterfall on your left just before the end.

17. Left for 1 block to end (Route 100 on right).

18. Right and just ahead right on main road (still Route 100). Go 3.2 miles to Buck Hill Road, which bears left (sign says TO CONNECTICUT ROUTE 12).

   After 0.9 mile you'll pass a wonderful schoolhouse on your right. Then you'll go by the Wilson Reservoir on your right.

19. Bear left and just ahead bear left again on main road. Go 3 miles to end, at bottom of second long descent (Quaddick Town Farm Road, unmarked). You are now in Connecticut. **CAUTION**: Watch for sand at the end.
20. Bear right for 1.2 miles to end, at church.
21. Turn right and just ahead bear left on Sand Dam Road. Go 2 miles to end, at stop sign (merge right on Route 193).
22. Bear right for 3 miles to the third traffic light (Routes 16 and 12). You'll pass Webster Lake on the right.
23. Turn left (**CAUTION**: Busy intersection). Friendly's is just ahead on right.

Directions for the ride: 19 miles—
1. Follow directions for the long ride through number 13.
2. Right for 7 miles to Friendly's on right. It's just past the traffic light after the I–395 underpass. You'll enjoy a long descent near the end and then pass Webster lake on your left.

About the Author

Howard Stone grew up in Boston, went to college in Maine and Illinois, and returned to his native New England, where he is now a librarian at Brown University. For many years Howard was the touring director of the Narragansett Bay Wheelmen, the major bicycle club for southeastern Massachusetts and Rhode Island. He is the author of *Short Bike Rides in Eastern Massachusetts* and *Short Bike Rides in Rhode Island*, also published by The Globe Pequot Press, and he has also written bicycling guides for Maine and the Hudson Valley. Howard has done extensive bicycle touring, including a cross-country trip from Newport, Oregon, to Newport, Rhode Island, in 1978.

Overview of the Rides

		Historic Sites	Unique Spots
1	The Northwest Corner	●	●
2	Pittsfield–Cheshire–Adams	●L	●L
3	Chatham, New York	●	●
4	The Shaker Village Ride	●	●
5	Lenox Loop		●
6	Mansions, Mills, Mountains, Museums, Music and Meditation	●	●
7	West Stockbridge–Great Barrington–Alford		●
8	Lee–Otis–Monterey–Tyringham		●
9	Antiques Alley		●
10	Shelburne Falls–Conway–Ashfield–Buckland		●
11	The Heart of the Hill Towns	●	●
12	I Will Lift Mine Eyes Unto the Hills		
13	Turners Falls–Gill–Northfield–Millers Fall		●
14	Turners Falls–Deerfield–Sunderland–Montague Center	●	
15	Tobacco Road	●	
16	The Dinosaur Ride		●
17	Agawam–Suffield, Connecticut–Southwick		●
18	Orange–Wendell–Shutesbury–New Salem		
19	Amherst–Leverett–Shutesbury		●
20	Amherst–Belchertown		
21	The Quabbin Reservoir Ride		●
22	Ludlow–Belchertown–Three Rivers		
23	Longmeadow–East Longmeadow–Somers, CT–Enfield, CT		
24	Wilbraham–Monson–Hampden		
25	Cathedral of the Pines Ride		●
26	Ashby–New Ipswich, NH–Greenville, NH	●	
27	Fitchburg–Ashby		●
28	Athol–Royalston–Phillipston–Petersham		●
29	Mount Wachusett Challenge		
30	Covered-Bridge Ride		●
31	Central Massachusetts Spectacular		
32	North of Worcester		●
33	The Brookfields Ride		
34	West of Worcester		●
35	South of Worcester		
36	Old Sturbridge Village Ride	●	
37	Southbridge–Woodstock, Connecticut	●	
38	Ridge and Valley Ride		
39	Tri-State Tour		

L Long ride only, S Short ride only

Lakes, Ponds	Rivers, Dams	Mill Villages	New England Villages	Open Land, Views	Easy	Hilly	
	•	•	•	•			**1**
•			•	•		•L	**2**
			•	•			**3**
•L					•	•L	**4**
	•		•	•		•L	**5**
•L		•	•L	•		•L	**6**
			•	•		•	**7**
			•	•		•	**8**
•	•		•	•	•S		**9**
	•		•			•	**10**
	•		•	•			**11**
•			•	•		•L	**12**
	•	•	•	•			**13**
	•		•	•			**14**
	•		•	•	•		**15**
	•		•	•			**16**
•L	•						**17**
•		•	•			•	**18**
•			•			•	**19**
•			•	•			**20**
•	•	•	•	•		•	**21**
•S	•		•	•			**22**
			•	•			**23**
		•L	•	•			**24**
•			•				**25**
•	•L	•	•				**26**
•			•	•		•	**27**
•	•		•	•		•	**28**
•			•	•		•	**29**
		•	•	•		•	**30**
•	•		•	•		•	**31**
•			•	•		•	**32**
•			•	•			**33**
•			•			•	**34**
•		•	•	•		•	**35**
•			•L			•L	**36**
	•		•L	•			**37**
•			•	•		•	**38**
•		•L	•				**39**

Appendix
Bicycle Clubs and Organizations

If you would like to bike with a group and meet other people who enjoy cycling, join a bicycle club. Most clubs have weekend rides of comfortable length, with a shortcut if you don't want to go too far. Usually a club will provide maps and mark the route by painting arrows in the road so that nobody gets lost. Joining a club is especially valuable if you don't have a car, because you'll meet people who do and who'll be able to give you a lift to areas beyond biking distance from home. To find out about clubs in your area, ask at any good bike shop. Addresses of clubs riding in western and central Massachusetts (subject to change) are as follows:

Seven Hills Wheelmen
Box 144, Auburn, MA 01501. Worcester area

Cyclonauts Bicycling Club
34 Call Street, Chicopee, MA 01013. Springfield area

Franklin-Hampshire Freewheelers
RFD3, 20 Two Mile Road, Amherst, MA 01002

Berkshire Cycling Association
24 Alba Avenue, Pittsfield, MA 01201

Northeast Sport Cyclists
55 Franklin Street, Westfield, MA 01085.

These clubs are affiliated with the League of American Bicyclists, which is the main national organization of and for bicyclists. It publishes an excellent monthly magazine and has a dynamic legislative-action program. The address of the league is 1612 K Street NW, Suite 401, Washington, DC 20006.

Another organization worth listing is the Massachusetts Bicycle Coalition, or MassBike, 44 Bromfield Street, Suite 207, Boston, MA 02108 (phone 617–542–2453; Web site www.MassBike.org). It is a political action group devoted to improving conditions for bicyclists.

There are certainly other clubs in the state that I'm not aware of. Your local bike shop will know about them.

Bicycle Shops
Area code is 413 unless otherwise specified.

Adams
Berkshire Outfitters, Route 8; 743–5900

Agawam
Axler's Bicycle Corner, 315 Springfield Street; 786–4994

Ski-In, 303 Walnut Street; 789–2800

Amherst
Bicycle World, 63 South Pleasant Street; 253–7722

Levels, 18 North Pleasant Street; 236–3066

Valley Bicycles, 319 Main Street; 256–0880

Athol
Dick's Bike Shop, 516 New Sherborn Road; (978) 249–4325

Barre
Country Bike & Sports, 12 Exchange Street; (978) 355–2219

Canaan, Connecticut
Bike Doctor & Sports Center, 97 Church Terrace; (860) 824–5577

Cheshire
A.T. Bicycle Works, 477 North State Road; 743–2088

Chicopee
Mickey's Bike Shop, 520 East Street; 592–4282

Dudley
Goatwheels Bicycle Shop, 30 Oxford Avenue; (508) 949–2012

East Longmeadow
Bob's Bike Shop, 15 Vreeland Avenue; 734–6843

Competitive Edge, 612 North Main Street; 737–7495

Family Bike & Sports, 217 Shaker Road; 525–2346

Easthampton
Easthampton Bicycle, 95 Main Street; 529–0319

Feeding Hills
Bianco & Sons Bicycle Center, 1110 Springfield Street; 786–8660

Fitchburg
Gamache Cyclery, 65 Laurel Street; (978) 343–3140

Florence
F. J. Rogers, 3 Main Street; 584–1727

Rob's Precision Bicycle Repair, 16C North Maple Street; 585–5930

Gardner
O'Neil's Bicycle Shop, 108 Main Street; (978) 632–7200

Great Barrington
Berkshire Bike & Blade, 326 Stockbridge Road; 528–5555

Harland B. Foster, 15 Bridge Street; 528–0564

Greenfield
Bicycle World, 104 Federal Street; 774–3701

Bicycles Unlimited, 322 High Street; 772–2700

Waltz Ski & Bike, 309 Conway Street; (800) 577–5306

Hadley
Competitive Edge, 374 Russell Street; 585–8833

Valley Bicycles, 8 Railroad Street; 584–4466

Holyoke
Competitive Edge, Route 5; 538–7662

Highland Hardware & Bike Shop, 917 Hampden Street; 539–9314

Peak Performance Bicycle Shop, 1584 Dwight Street; 535–2453

Lenox
Arcadian Shop, 91 Pittsfield Road; 637–3010
Main Street Sports & Leisure, 48 Main Street; 637–4407
Mean Wheels Bike Shop, 57A Housatonic Street; 637–0644

Leominster
Gear Works Cyclery, 510 North Main Street; (978) 534–2453
Joe's Bicycle Shop, 71 North Main Street; (978) 537–5487
O'Neil's Bicycle Shop, 39 Mechanic Street; (978) 537–6464

Longmeadow
State Line Cycles, 1734 Longmeadow Street; 567–1668

Ludlow
Action Sports & Bikes, 390 East Street; 547–2628

New Ipswich, New Hampshire
Absolutely Bicycles, 211 Main Street; (603) 878–4059

North Adams
Sports Corner, 61 Main Street; 664–8654

Northampton
Axler's Bicycle Corner, 16 Armory Street; 585–1188
Bicycle World, 32 Masonic Street; 585–9100
Northampton Bicycle, 319 Pleasant Street; 586–3810

Northfield
The Bicycle Barn, 56 Main Street; (800) 498–7929

Palmer
Pro Bike, 1438 North Main Street; 289–1400

Pittsfield
Mike's Bike Shop, 11 Goodrich Street; 445–5878
Mike's Bike Shop, 547 Tyler Street; 442–9344
Ordinary Cycles, 247 North Street; 442–7225
Plaine's Bike & Ski, 55 West Housatonic Street; 499–0294

Southampton
Southampton Bicycle Center, 247 College Highway; 527–9784

Southbridge
Sotar Bicycles, 100 Central Street; (508) 764–3657

Spencer
Whitco Toy & Bike, 140 Main Street; (508) 885–9343

Springfield
Apollo Bicycle Center, 23 Hamburg Street; 781–3019
Pro Bicycle Shop, 1344 Allen Street; 783–4834

Turners Falls
Basically Bicycles, 88 Third Street; 863–3556

West Boylston
Wachusett Cycle & Multisport, 71 Sterling Street; (508) 835–6100

West Brookfield
Too Wheels & More, 12 East Main Street; (508) 867–7070

West Springfield
Aggressive Thread, 705 Union Street; 734–3678

Westfield
Custom Cycle, 88 Elm Street; 568–6036
New Horizons Sports, 55 Franklin Street; 562–5237

Wilbraham
Ski-In, 2006 Boston Road; 543–4980

Williamstown
Mountain Goat Bicycle Shop, 130 Water Street; 458–8445
The Spoke Bicycles, 620 Main Street; 458–3456

Worcester
Barney's Bicycle, 165 Chandler Street; (508) 757–3754
Bicycle Alley, 1067 Main Street; (508) 752–2230
Fritz's Bicycle Shop, 328 West Boylston Street; (508) 853–1799
O'Neil's Bicycle Shop, 1094 Main Street; (508) 798–0084
Ski Market, 322 Southbridge Avenue; (508) 832–8111

Further Reading and Resources

Massachusetts is covered by other bicycling guides if you'd like to explore new territory:

Short Bike Rides in Eastern Massachusetts, Third Edition, by Howard Stone. Guilford, CT: Globe Pequot Press, 1999.

Bicycling the Pioneer Valley and Beyond, by Marion Gorham. North Amherst, MA: New England Cartographics, 1998.

Touring Jacob's Ladder Trail, by the Pioneer Valley Planning Commission. West Springfield, MA: The Commission, 1994. Covers the general corridor along Route 20 between Westfield and Lee.

Bicycle Touring in the Pioneer Valley, Revised and Expanded Edition, by Nancy Jane. Amherst: University of Massachusetts Press, 1996.

The Best Bike Rides in New England, Fourth Edition, by Paul Thomas, edited by Paul Angiolillo. Guilford, CT: Globe Pequot Press, 1998.

The Bicyclist's Guide to the Southern Berkshires, by Steve Lyons. Lenox, MA: Freewheel Publications, 1993. Out of print.

Bike Rides in the Berkshire Hills, Revised and Updated Edition, by Lewis C. Cuyler. Lee, MA: Berkshire House, 1995.

New England Over the Handlebars, by Michael Farny. Boston: Little, Brown, 1975.

Western Massachusetts Bicycle Map, Cambridge, MA: Rubel BikeMaps, 1997. Available at most bike shops. An excellent resource; keep one in your handlebar bag.

Central Massachusetts Bicycle Map, Cambridge, MA: Rubel BikeMaps, 1998. Another superb resource that you should take with you.

The Best Bike Paths of New England, by Wendy Williams. New York: Simon & Schuster, 1996

Bike Paths of Massachusetts: A Guide to Rail Trails and Other Car-Free Places, by Stuart Johnstone. Carlisle, MA: Active Publications, 1996.

Rails-To-Trails: Maine, New Hampshire, Vermont, Massachusetts, Rhode Island, Connecticut, by Cynthia Mascott. Guilford, CT: The Globe Pequot Press, 2000.

The Ride. A monthly magazine that covers all aspects of bicycling in the Northeast: recreational, racing, off-road, commuting, couriers, organized group rides, and advocacy. Available at many bike shops or by subscription. The address is 1173 Massachusetts Avenue, Arlington, MA 02476.